CW00449932

LONDON
RECOLLECTED

THE VILLAGE LONDON SERIES

Other titles already published in hard back are:

VILLAGE LONDON Volume I
VILLAGE LONDON Volume II
LONDON RECOLLECTED Volume I
LONDON RECOLLECTED Volume II
LONDON RECOLLECTED Volume III
LONDON RECOLLECTED Volume IV
LONDON RECOLLECTED Volume V

VILLAGE LONDON ATLAS

Other titles already published in paperback

VILLAGE LONDON Pt. 1 West and North
VILLAGE LONDON Pt. 2 North and East
VILLAGE LONDON Pt. 3 South-East
VILLAGE LONDON Pt. 4 South-West

OLD FLEET STREET
CHEAPSIDE AND ST. PAUL'S
THE TOWER AND EAST END
SHOREDITCH to SMITHFIELD
CHARTERHOUSE to HOLBORN
STRAND to SOHO
COVENT GARDEN and the THAMES to WHITEHALL

KENNINGTON COMMON AND CHURCH IN 1830.

LONDON RECOLLECTED

ITS HISTORY, LORE AND LEGEND

by

EDWARD WALFORD.

VOLUME VI

THE ALDERMAN PRESS

London

First published in 1872-8 by Cassell, Petter, Galpin & Co.
under the title *Old and New London.*

British Library Cataloguing in Publication Data.

Walford, Edward.
    [Old and new London] London Recollected: its
    history, lore and legend.
    Vol 6.
    1. London (England)_____History
    I. Title
    942.1   DA677

ISBN 0-946619-07-7

Published by The Alderman Press, 1987
1/7 Church Street, London N9 9DR

Printed in Great Britain by
Robert Hartnoll (1985) Ltd,
Bodmin, Cornwall.

CONTENTS.

———◆———

THE SOUTHERN SUBURBS.

CHAPTER I.

INTRODUCTORY.—SOUTHWARK.

Introductory Remarks—Geological Observations—Earliest Mention of Southwark in History—Its Etymology—Southwark as a Roman Settlement—Old London Bridge—Knut's Trench—Reception of William the Conqueror by the Natives of Southwark—The Civic Government of Southwark—Its Annexation to the City—An Icelander's Account of Old London Bridge—The Story of Olaf's Destruction of the Bridge—Hymn sung on the Festival of St. Olave 1

CHAPTER II.

SOUTHWARK (*continued*).—OLD LONDON BRIDGE.

Controversy respecting the Trench from Rotherhithe to Battersea—How London Bridge was "built on Woolpacks"—Religious and Royal Processions at the Bridge-foot—Partial Destruction of Old London Bridge by Fire—Conflict between the Forces of Henry III. and those of the Earl of Leicester—Reception of Henry V. after the Battle of Agincourt—Fall of the Southern Tower of London Bridge—Southwark wholly destitute of Fortifications—Jack Cade's Rendezvous in Southwark—Death of Jack Cade—Heads on London Bridge—Reception of Henry VI. and Henry VII.—Reception of Katharine of Aragon—Cardinal Wolsey—Insurrection of Sir Thomas Wyatt—Rebuilding of the Northern Tower—Standards of the Spanish Armada placed on London Bridge—Southwark Fortified by the Parliamentarians, to oppose King Charles—Reception of Charles II.—Corn Mills on London Bridge—Tradesmen's Tokens—Bridge-foot—The "Bear" Inn—The "Knave of Clubs"—Bridge Street—The Shops on London Bridge—The Bridge House—General Aspect of Southwark in the Middle Ages—Gradual Extension of Southwark—Great Fire in Southwark in 1676—Building of New London Bridge . . . . , ... 8

CHAPTER III.

SOUTHWARK (*continued*).—ST. SAVIOUR'S CHURCH, &c.

The Limits of Southwark as a Borough—The Liberty of the Clink—The Old High Street—The Clock-tower at London Bridge—The Borough Market—Old St. Saviour's Grammar School—The Patent of Foundation granted by Queen Elizabeth—St. Saviour's Church—The Legend of Old Audrey, the Ferryman—Probable Derivation of the Name of Overy, or Overie—Foundation of the Priory of St. Mary Overy—Burning of the Priory in 1212—Building of the Church of St. Mary Magdalen—Historical Events connected with the Church—Religious Ceremonies and Public Processions—Alterations and Restorations of St. Saviour's Church—The Lady Chapel used as a Bakehouse—Bishop Andrewes' Chapel—John Gower, John Fletcher, and other Noted Personages buried here—Hollar's Etchings—Montague Close 16

CHAPTER IV.

SOUTHWARK (*continued*).—WINCHESTER HOUSE, BARCLAY'S BREWERY, &c.

Stow's Description of Winchester House—Park Street Chapel—Marriage Feast of James I. of Scotland at Winchester House—The Palace attacked by the Insurgents under Sir Thomas Wyatt—John, Duke of Finland, lodged here—The Palace sold to the Presbyterians, and turned into a Prison for the Royalists—Its Recovery by the Bishop of Winchester—Remains of the Old Palace—The "Stews" on the Bankside—"Holland's Leaguer"—"Winchester Birds"—Old Almshouses—Messrs. Barclay and Perkins' Brewery—Its Early History—Mr. and Mrs. Thrale—Dr. Johnson's Intimacy with the Thrales—Purchase of the Brewery by Mr. David Barclay—Origin of the Firm of Barclay and Perkins—Mrs. Piozzi, and her Literary Acquaintances—Account of the various Processes of Malting, Brewing, &c.—The Brewery described—Monster Vats—Attack on General Haynau—Richard Baxter—Zoar Street Chapel—Oliver Goldsmith—Holland Street—Falcon Glass Works—The "Falcon" Tavern—Hopton's Almshouses—Messrs. Potts' Vinegar Works—St. Peter's Church—St. Saviour's Grammar School—Improvements in Southwark—Southwark Street—The Hop Exchange 29

CHAPTER V.

SOUTHWARK (*continued*).—BANKSIDE IN THE OLDEN TIME.

Appearance of Bankside in the Seventeenth Century—The Globe Theatre—Its Destruction by Fire—Shakespeare's Early Connection with the Playhouse—James Burbage—Rebuilding of the Globe Theatre—Public and Private Theatres—The Rose Theatre—Ben Jonson—

CONTENTS.

The Hope and Swan Theatres—Paris Garden—Bear-baiting—Prize-fighting—Samuel Pepys' Description of the Sport—John Evelyn's Visit to Bankside—The "Master of the King's Bears"—Bad Repute of Paris Garden—Visit of Queen Elizabeth to Paris Garden—Bear Alley—Public Gardens in Southwark—Bankside at the Time of the Great Fire of London—Dick Tarleton—The "Tumble-down Dick"—Waterside Public-houses 45

CHAPTER VI.

SOUTHWARK (*continued*).—HIGH STREET, &c.

The Southwark Entrance to London Bridge—The Town Hall—Southwark Fair—Union Hall—Dr. Elliotson—Mint Street—Suffolk House—Lant Street—Charles Dickens's Home when a Boy—The Mint—Great Suffolk Street—The "Moon-rakers"—The Last Barber-surgeon—Winchester Hall—Finch's Grotto Gardens—The Old Workhouse of Southwark—King's Bench Prison—Major Hanger, Dr. Syntax, Haydon, and George Moreland, Inmates of the King's Bench—The "Marshal" of the King's Bench—Alsager's Bleaching-ground—Blackman Street—Sir James South—Eliza Cook—Kent Street—A Disreputable Neighbourhood—The Lock Hospital—A Hard-working Philanthropist—St. George's Church—The Burial-place cf Bishop Bonner—Marriage of General Monk and Nan Clarges—The Marshalsea—Anecdotes of Bishop Bonner—Colonel Culpeper—Dickens's Reminiscences of the Marshalsea—The Sign of "The Hand"—Commercial Aspect of Southwark—Sanitary Condition of Southwark—Appearance of Southwark in the Seventeenth Century 57

CHAPTER VII.

SOUTHWARK (*continued*).—FAMOUS INNS OF OLDEN TIMES.

Old Inns mentioned by Stow—The "Tabard"—The Abbot of Hide—The "Tabard" as the Rendezvous for Pilgrims—Henry Bailly, the Hosteller of the "Tabard," and M.P. for Southwark—Description of the old "Tabard"—Change of Name from the "Tabard" to the "Talbot"—Demolition of the old Inn—Chaucer and the Canterbury Pilgrims—Characters mentioned by Chaucer in the "Canterbury Tales"—Stow's Definition of "Tabard"—The "George"—The "White Hart"—Jack Cade's sojourn here—The "Boar's Head"—The "White Lion"—"Henry VIII." a Favourite Sign—The "Three Brushes"—The "Catherine Wheel"—The "Three Widows"—The "Old Pick my Toe"—Tokens of Inn-keepers 76

CHAPTER VIII.

SOUTHWARK (*continued*).—OLD ST. THOMAS'S HOSPITAL, GUY'S HOSPITAL, &c.

Foundation of St. Thomas's Hospital—A Well-timed Sermon of Bishop Ridley—Purchase of the Old Building by the Citizens of London—The Lease of the Hospital in Pawn—The Edifice Rebuilt and Enlarged—Description of the Building—Statue of Sir Robert Clayton—Removal of the Hospital to Lambeth—Value of Land near London Bridge—St. Thomas's Church—Gerard Johnson, the Sculptor of Shakespeare's Bust—Foundation of Guy's Hospital—Anecdotes of Thomas Guy, the Founder—Description of the Hospital—Statue of Guy—Medical Staff of the Hospital—London Bridge Railway Terminus--The Greenwich Railway—The South-Eastern Railway—The London, Brighton, and South Coast Railway—Watson's Telegraph to the Downs—Southwark Waterworks—Waterworks at Old London Bridge 89

CHAPTER IX.

BERMONDSEY.—TOOLEY STREET, &c.

Derivation of the Name of Bermondsey—General Aspect of the Locality—Duke Street—Tooley Street—St. Olave's Church—Abbots' Inn of St. Augustine—Sellinger's Wharf—The Inn of the Abbots of Battle—Maze Pond—The House of the Priors of Lewes—St. Olave's Grammar School—Great Fires at the Wharves in Tooley Street--Death of Braidwood, the Fireman--The "Lion and Key"—The Borough Compter—The "Ship and Shovel"—Carter Lane Meeting House—Dr. Gill and Dr. Rippon—The "Three Tailors of Tooley Street"—The "Isle of Ducks"—Tunnels under London Bridge Railway Station—Snow's Fields—A Colony of Hatters—Horselydown—Fair Street—The Birthplace of Thomas Guy—The Church of St. John the Evangelist—Goat's Yard—Keach's Meeting-house—Absence of Singing in Dissenting Meeting-houses two Centuries ago—Queen Elizabeth's Grammar School—A Description of Horselydown and the adjacent Neighbourhood in Former Times—Dockhead—"Shad Thames"—Jacob's Island 100

CHAPTER X.

BERMONDSEY (*continued*).—THE ABBEY, &c.

The Dissolution of Monasteries by Henry VIII.—Earliest Historical Mention of Bermondsey Abbey—Some Account of the Cluniac Monasteries in England, and Customs of the Cluniac Order—Grant of the Manor of Bermondsey to Bermondsey Abbey—Queen Katherine, Widow of Henry V., retires hither—Elizabeth Woodville, Widow of Edward IV., a Prisoner here—Form of Service for the Repose of the Souls of the Queen of Henry VII. and her Children—Grant of the Monastery to Sir Robert Southwell—Its Sale to Sir Thomas Pope—Demolition of the Abbey Church—Remains of the Abbey at the Close of the Last Century—Neckinger Road—The Church of St. Mary Magdalen—A Curious Matrimonial Ceremony—An Ancient Salver—The Rood of Bermondsey—Grange Walk and Grange Road—The Tanning and Leather Trades in Bermondsey—"Simon the Tanner"—Fellmongery—Bermondsey Hide and Skin Market—Russell Street—St. Olave's Union—Bricklayers' Arms Station—Growth of Modern Bermondsey—Neckinger Mills—The Spa—Baths and Wash-houses—Christ Church—Roman Catholic Church of the Most Holy Trinity, and Convent of the Sisters of Mercy—Jamaica Road—The Old "Jamaica" Tavern—The "Lion and Castle"—Cherry Garden—St. James's Church—Traffic on the Railway near Bermondsey—Messrs. Peek, Frean, and Co.'s Biscuit Factory—Blue Anchor Road—Galley Wall 117

CONTENTS.

CHAPTER XI.

ROTHERHITHE.

PAGE

Derivation of the Name of Rotherhithe—The Place frequently called Redriff—Knut's Trench—History of the Descent of the Manor—Traditional Visit of Charles II. to Rotherhithe—Dreadful Fire in Rotherhithe—Condition of Rotherhithe at the Commencement of the Present Century—Mill Pond—Vineyards in Rotherhithe—Southwark Park—The "Halfpenny Hatch"—China Hall—The "Dog and Duck"—St. Mary's Church—Christ Church—All Saints' Church—St. Barnabas Church—The Skeleton of a Giant—Spread of Education in Rotherhithe and Bermondsey—Noted Residents in Rotherhithe—St. Helena Tea-gardens—The Thames Tunnel—The Commercial Docks, and the Grand Surrey Canal—Cuckold's Point—The King and the Miller's Wife 134

CHAPTER XII.

DEPTFORD.

Derivation of the Name of Deptford—Division of the Parish—The River Ravensbourne—The Royal Dockyard—Sir Francis Drake's Ship, the *Golden Hind*—References to Deptford in the Diaries of Evelyn and Pepys—Peter the Great as a Shipwright—Captain Cook's Ships, the *Resolution* and the *Discovery*—Biography of Samuel Pepys—Closing of the Dockyard—The Foreign Cattle-Market—Saye's Court—John Evelyn, the Author of "Sylva"—Evelyn at Home—Grinling Gibbons—Removal of Evelyn to Wotton—Saye's Court let to Admiral Benbow—Peter the Great as a Tenant—Visit of William Penn, the Quaker—Demolition of Saye's Court—Formation of a Recreation-ground on its Site—The Royal Victoria Victualling Yard—The Corporation of the Trinity House—The Two Hospitals belonging to the Trinity House—St. Nicholas' Church—St. Paul's Church—The Roman Catholic Church of the Assumption—St. Luke's Church—The Grand Surrey Canal—Evelyn's Account of the Capture of a Whale at Deptford—Origin of the Sign of the Black Doll . 143

CHAPTER XIII.

GREENWICH.

Situation and Origin of the Name of Greenwich—Early History of the Place—The Murder of Archbishop Alphege—Encampments of the Danes—The Manor of Greenwich—The Building of Greenwich Palace, or "Placentia"—Jousts and Tournaments performed here in the Reign of Edward IV.—Henry VIII. at Greenwich—Festivities held here during this Reign—Birth of Queen Elizabeth—The Downfall of Anne Boleyn—Marriage of Henry VIII. with Anne of Cleves—Will Sommers, the Court Jester—Queen Elizabeth's Partiality for Greenwich—The Order of the Garter—The Queen and the Countryman—Maundy Thursday Observances—Personal Appearance of Queen Elizabeth—Sir Walter Raleigh—Greenwich Palace settled by James I. on his Queen, Anne of Denmark—Charles I. a Resident here—The Palace during the Commonwealth—Proposals for Rebuilding the Palace—The Foundation of Greenwich Hospital 164

CHAPTER XIV.

GREENWICH (*continued*).—THE HOSPITAL FOR SEAMEN, &c.

Greenwich Hospital as a Monument to Queen Mary, and of the Victory of La Hogue—Appointment of the Commissioners by William III.—Sir Christopher Wren's Share in the Building—John Evelyn as Treasurer—Description of the Building—Memorials of Joseph René Bellot, and the Officers who fell in the Indian Mutiny—The Chapel—The Painted Hall—Nelson's Funeral Car—The Nelson Room—The Hospital—Sources of its Revenue—The Old Pensioners and their Accommodation—The Royal Naval College—The Naval Museum—The Nelson and other Relics—The Infirmary for the Pensioners—The Seamen's Hospital—The *Dreadnought*—The Royal Naval School—Officers connected with Greenwich Hospital since its establishment—Fund for Disabled Seamen 177

CHAPTER XV.

GREENWICH (*continued*).—THE PARISH CHURCH, &c.

Gradual Extension of London—Greenwich as a Parliamentary Borough—The Assizes for Kent formerly held here—The Present Condition and Population of Greenwich—The Church of St. Alphege—Portraits of Queen Elizabeth, Charles I., Queen Anne, and George I., formerly in Greenwich Church—Greenwich one of the Head-quarters of the Huguenot Refugees—The "Spanish Galleon"—Dr. Johnson a Resident in Greenwich—General Withers and Colonel Disney Residents here—Queen Elizabeth's College—The Jubilee Almshouses—Baths and Wash-houses—The Lecture Hall—The Theatre—Croom's Hill—The Roman Catholic Church—The "New Church" of St. Mary—Greenwich Market—Spring Gardens—Lennier's Collection of Pictures—Strange Monsters exhibited here—The Duke of Norfolk's College—A Remarkable High Tide—Sir John Winter's Project for Charring Sea-coal—The Royal Thames Yacht Club—The Tilt-Boat—The Admiralty Barge—The Royal State Barge—River-side Hotels—Whitebait Dinners—The Origin of the Ministerial Fish Dinner—Samuel Rogers and Curran—Charles Dickens at Greenwich—The Touting System—Greenwich Fair . . 190

CHAPTER XVI.

GREENWICH (*continued*).—THE PARK, THE ROYAL OBSERVATORY, &c.

May-day Morning in the Reign of Henry VIII.—Historical Reminiscences—The Planting of the Park by Order of Charles II.—Castle Hill—Description of the Park—One-Tree Hill—Proposed Monumental Trophy in honour of the Battle of Trafalgar on Castle Hill—The View from One-Tree Hill—Greenwich Park at Fair-time—The Wilderness—The Ranger's Lodge—The Princess Sophia of Gloucester a Resident at Montagu House—Chesterfield Walk—The Residence of General Wolfe—Ancient Barrows or Tumuli—Greenwich Observatory—Appointment of John Flamsteed as First Astronomer-Royal—Flamsteed and Sir Isaac Newton—Dr. Halley—Dr. Bradley—Dr. Bliss—Dr. Maskelyne—The "Nautical Almanack"—Mr. John Pond—Sir George Biddell Airey—Description of the Observatory and of the Instruments in Use—The Magnetic Observatory—The Galvanic Clock—Work accomplished at the Observatory . . . 206

CONTENTS.

CHAPTER XVII.

BLACKHEATH, CHARLTON, AND ITS NEIGHBOURHOOD.

PAGE

Situation and Description of Blackheath—Derivation of its Name—Discovery of Numerous Tumuli—Encampment of the Danish Army—Wat Tyler's Rebellion—Reception of Richard II. at Blackheath—The Emperor of Constantinople—Reception of Henry V. on his Return from Agincourt—Other Royal Receptions—Jack Cade and his Followers—Henry VI. and the Duke of York—The Cornish Rebels—The Smith's Forge—Reception of Cardinal Campegio, and of Bonevet, High Admiral of France—Princess Anne of Cleves—Arrival of Charles II., on his Restoration—Blackheath Fair—The "Chocolate House"—Present Condition of Blackheath—East Coombe and West Coombe—Lavinia Fenton ("Polly Peachum"), Duchess of Bolton—Woodlands—Montagu House—The Princess Charlotte—Mrs. Mary Anne Clarke and the Duke of York—Flaxman, the Sculptor—Maize Hill—Vanbrugh Castle—The Mince-pie House—Charlton—St. Luke's Church—Charlton House—Horn Fair—Shooter's Hill—The Herbert Hospital—Severndroog Castle—Morden College—Kidbrook 224

CHAPTER XVIII.

ELTHAM, LEE, AND LEWISHAM.

Situation and Derivation of the Name of Eltham—Descent of the Manor—The Palace—Henry III. keeps his Christmas here—Edward II. and his Court—John, King of France—Richard II. and Anne of Bohemia—Froissart here presents the King with a Copy of his Works—Henry IV. and his Court—Royal Christmas Festivities—Eltham Palace abandoned by the Court—The Palace during the Civil Wars—Dismantling of the Parks—Description of the Palace—Sale of the Middle Park Stud of Racehorses—Eltham Church—Well Hall—Lee—Lewisham—Hither Green, Catford, and Ladywell—Loam Pit Hill—New Cross—Royal Naval Schools—Hatcham' . 236

CHAPTER XIX.

THE OLD KENT ROAD, &c.

The Course of the Old Watling Street—M. Sorbierre's Visit to London in the Reign of Charles II.—Evelyn's Account of the Return of Charles II., on his Restoration—Anecdote of Pitt and Dundas—Mrs. Mapp, the celebrated Bone-setter—Condition of the Old Kent Road in the Last Century—The Licensed Victuallers' Asylum—The South Metropolitan Gas Works—Christ Church—The Canal Bridge—Marlborough Chapel—St. Thomas à Watering—Old Taverns and Roadside Inns—The "World Turned Upside Down"—The Deaf and Dumb Asylum—The New Kent Road—Lock's Fields—Great Dover Street—Trinity Square and Trinity Church—Horsemonger Lane Gaol—Leigh Hunt a Prisoner there—Execution of the Mannings—The Surrey Sessions' House—Newington Causeway . . . 248

CHAPTER XX.

NEWINGTON AND WALWORTH.

Etymology of Newington Butts—The "Elephant and Castle"—Joanna Southcott—Singular Discovery of Human Remains—The Drapers' Almshouses—The Fishmongers' Almshouses—Newington Grammar School—Hospital of Our Lady and St. Catherine—Newington Theatre—The Semaphore Telegraph—The Metropolitan Tabernacle—Mr. C. H. Spurgeon—Mr. Spurgeon's Almshouses and Schools—St. Mary's Church, Newington—The Old Parish Church—The Graveyard laid out as a Public Garden—The Clock Tower—The Old Parsonage House—The "Queen's Head" Tea Gardens—A Great Flood—An Eminent Optician—The Surrey Zoological Gardens—The Music Hall—Walworth Road—Carter Street Lecture Hall—The Walworth Literary and Mechanics' Institution—St. Peter's Church—St. John's Church 255

CHAPTER XXI.

CAMBERWELL.

Antiquity of the Parish—Its Etymology—Its Condition at the Time of the Conquest—Descent of the Manor—Sir Thomas Bond's House—The Bowyer Family—Bowyer Lane, now Wyndham Road—The Royal Flora Gardens—St. Giles's Church—The Burial-place of Mrs. Wesley, and of "Equality" Brown—Camden Chapel—St. George's Church—The Vestry Hall—Camberwell Green—Camberwell Fair—Abolition of the Fair, and the Green converted into a Park—The "Father Redcap"—The Old House on the Green—The Green Coat and National Schools—The Camberwell Free Grammar School—The Aged Pilgrims' Friend Asylum—Rural Character of Camberwell in the Last Century—Myatt's Farm—Cold Harbour Lane—Denmark Hill Grammar School—Grove Hill and Dr. Lettsom's Residence there—The Story of George Barnwell—Grove Hall—The "Fox-under-the-Hill"—Old Families of Camberwell—Tom Hood a Resident here—Camberwell Lunatic Asylum 269

CHAPTER XXII.

PECKHAM AND DULWICH.

Situation of Peckham—Queen's Road—Albert Road—The Manor House of Peckham—Hill Street—Shard Square and the "Shard Arms"—Peckham House—Old Mansions in Peckham—Marlborough House—The "Rosemary Branch"—Peckham Fair—The "Kentish Drovers"—Hanover Street—Hanover Chapel—Basing Manor—Rye Lane—The Railway Station—The Museum of Fire-arms—Peckham Rye—Nunhead Green—The Asylum of the Metropolitan Beer and Wine Trade Association—Nunhead Cemetery—Nunhead Hill—The Reservoirs of the Southwark and Vauxhall Waterworks—Heaton's Folly—Honour Oak—Camberwell Cemetery—Friern Manor Farm—Goose Green—Lordship Lane—The "Plough" Inn—The Scenery round Dulwich—The Haunt of the Gipsies—Visit of the Court of Charles I. to Dulwich, for the Purposes of Sport—Outrages in Dulwich Wood—The Stocks and Cage at Dulwich—The "Green Man" Tavern—Bew's Corner—Dulwich Wells—Dr. Glennie's School—Byron a Scholar there—The "Crown," the "Half Moon," and the "Greyhound" Taverns—The Dulwich Club—Noted Residents of Dulwich—The Old Manor House—Edward Alleyn at Home—Dulwich College—Dulwich Picture-gallery—The New Schools of Dulwich College 286

CONTENTS.

CHAPTER XXIII.

SYDENHAM, NORWOOD, AND STREATHAM.

PAGE

Situation of Sydenham—Its Rapid Growth as a Place of Residence—Sydenham Wells—The Poet Campbell—Death of Thomas Dermody—Thomas Hill—Churches at Sydenham—Rockhill—Sir Joseph Paxton—The Crystal Palace—Anerley—Norwood—The Home of the Gipsies—Knight's Hill—Beulah Spa—North Surrey District Schools—The Catholic Female Orphanage—The Jews' Hospital—Norwood Cemetery—The Royal Normal College and Academy of Music for the Blind—Death of the Earl of Dudley—Streatham—Mineral Springs—Anecdote of Lord Thurlow—The Residence of Mrs. Thrale at Streatham—The Magdalen Hospital 303

CHAPTER XXIV.

BRIXTON AND CLAPHAM.

The Royal Asylum of St. Ann's Society—The Female Convict Prison, Brixton—Clapham Park—Etymology of Clapham—Clapham Common—The Home of Thomas Babington Macaulay—The Old Manor House—The Residence of Sir Dennis Gauden—Pepys a Resident here—Death of Samuel Pepys—The Residence of the Eccentric Henry Cavendish—The Beautiful Mrs. Baldwin—The Home of the Wilberforces—Henry Thornton—The Parish Church—St. Paul's Church—St. John's Church—St. Saviour's Church—The Congregational Chapel, and the Roman Catholic Redemptorist Church and College—Nonconformity at Clapham—The "Clapham Sect"—Lord Teignmouth's House—Nightingale Lane—The Residence of Mr. C. H. Spurgeon—The "Plough" Inn—The "Bedford" Arms—Clapham Rise—Young Ladies' Schools—The British Orphan Asylum—The British Home for Incurables—Clapham Road 319

CHAPTER XXV.

STOCKWELL AND KENNINGTON.

Etymology of Stockwell—Its Rustic Retirement Half a Century ago—The Green—Meeting of the Albion Archers—The Stockwell Ghost—Old House in which Lord Cromwell is said to have lived—St. Andrew's Church—Small-pox and Fever Hospital—Mr. John Angell's Bequest—Trinity Asylum—Stockwell Orphanage—Mr. Alfred Forrester—Kennington Manor—Death of Hardicanute—Kennington a Favourite Residence of the Black Prince—Masques and Pageants—Isabella, the "Little Queen" of Richard II.—The Last of the Old Manor House—Cumberland Row—Caron House—Kennington Oval—Beaufoy's Vinegar Distillery—The Tradescants—Kennington Common—Execution of the Scottish Rebels—"Jemmy" Dawson—Meeting of the Chartists in 1848—Large Multitudes addressed by Whitefield—The Common converted into a Park—St. Mark's Church—"The Horns" Tavern—Lambeth Waterworks—The Licensed Victuallers' School 327

CHAPTER XXVI.

ST. GEORGE'S FIELDS.

St. George's Fields in the Time of the Roman Occupation—Canute's Trench—Charles II. entertained at St. George's Fields on his Restoration—The Populace resort hither during the Great Fire—The Character of St. George's Fields in the Last Century—The Apollo Gardens—The "Dog and Duck" Tavern—St. George's Spa—A Curious Exhibition—The Wilkes' Riots—The Gordon Riots—Death of Lord George Gordon—Gradual Advance of Building in St. George's Fields—The Magdalen Hospital—Peabody Buildings—The Asylum for Female Orphans—The Philanthropic Society—The School for the Indigent Blind—The Obelisk 341

CHAPTER XXVII.

ST. GEORGE'S FIELDS (*continued*).—BETHLEHEM HOSPITAL, &c.

The Priory of the Star of Bethlehem—Its Conversion into a Hospital for Lunatics—"Tom o' Bedlams"—Purchase of the Site for a New Hospital in St. George's Fields—Public Subscription to raise Funds for its Erection—Sign of the Old "Dog and Duck"—The New Hospital described—Cibber's Statues of "Melancholy and Raving Madness"—The Air of Refinement and Taste in the Appearance of the Female Wards—Viscomte d'Arlingcourt's Visit to Bedlam—Gray's Lines on Madness—The Ball-room—The Billiard-room—The Dining-room—The Chapel—The Infirmary Ward—A Picture of the "Good Samaritan," painted by one of the Inmates—The Council Chamber—The Men's Wards—A Sad Love Story—General Particulars of the Hospital, and Mode of Admission of Patients—King Edward's School—Christ Church, Westminster Bridge Road—St. George's Roman Catholic Cathedral—The School for the Indigent Blind—The British and Foreign School Society, Borough Road 351

CHAPTER XXVIII.

BLACKFRIARS ROAD.—THE SURREY THEATRE, SURREY CHAPEL, &c.

Formation of Blackfriars Road—The Surrey Theatre, originally the "Royal Circus and Equestrian Philharmonic Academy"—The Circus burnt down in 1805—The Amphitheatre rebuilt, and under the Management of Elliston—The Manager in a Fix—The Theatre burnt down in 1865, and rebuilt the same year—Lord Camelford and a Drunken Naval Lieutenant—The "Equestrian" Tavern—A Favourite Locality for Actors—An Incident in Charles Dickens's Boyhood—The Temperance Hall—The South London Working Men's College—The South London Tramway Company—The Mission College of St. Alphege—Nelson Square—The "Dog's Head in the Pot"—Surrey Chapel—The Rev. Rowland Hill—Almshouses founded by him—Paris Garden—Christ Church—Stamford Street—The Unitarian Chapel—Messrs. Clowes' Printing Office—Hospital for Diseases of the Skin—The "Haunted Houses" of Stamford Street—Ashton Lever's Museum—The Rotunda—The Albion Mills 368

CONTENTS.

CHAPTER XXIX.

LAMBETH.

Parochial Division of Lambeth—The Early History of the Parish—Descent of the Manor—Appearance of Lambeth in the time of Charles II.—Lambeth in the Last Century, as viewed from the Adelphi—The Romance of Lambeth—Lady Arabella Stuart a Prisoner here—Morland, the famous Mechanist—John Wesley preaches here—Pepys' Visits to Lambeth—Messrs. Searle's Boat-building Establishment—Lambeth Marsh—Narrow Wall and Broad Wall—Pedlar's Acre—The "Duke of Bolton," Governor of Lambeth Marsh—Belvedere Road—Belvedere House and Gardens—Cuper's Gardens—Cumberland Gardens—The "Hercules" Inn and Gardens—The Apollo Gardens—Flora Gardens—Lambeth Fields—Lambeth Wells—Outdoor Diversion in the Olden Time—Taverns and Public-houses—The "Three Merry Boys"—The "Three Squirrels"—The "Chequers"—The "Three Goats' Heads"—The "Axe and Cleaver"—The Halfpenny Hatch 383

CHAPTER XXX.

LAMBETH (*continued*).—THE TRANSPONTINE THEATRES.

The Morality of the Transpontine Theatres—The building of the Coburg Theatre—Its Name changed to the Victoria—Vicissitudes of the Theatre—The Last Night of the Old Victoria—The Theatre altered and re-opened as the Royal Victoria Palace Theatre—A Romantic Story—Origin of Astley's Amphitheatre—Biographical Sketch of Philip Astley—His Riding School near the Halfpenny Hatch—He builds a Riding School near Westminster Bridge—The Edifice altered, and called the Royal Grove—Destruction of the Royal Grove by Fire—The Theatre rebuilt and opened as the Amphitheatre of Arts—The Theatre a second time destroyed by Fire—Again rebuilt, and called the Royal Amphitheatre—Astley and his Musicians—Death of Mr. Astley—The Theatre under the Management of Mr. W. Davis—Ducrow and West—Description of the Theatre—Dickens's Account of "Astley's"—The third Theatre burnt down—Death of Ducrow—The Theatre rebuilt by Batty—Its subsequent History—Its Name altered to Sanger's Grand National Amiphitheatre . 393

CHAPTER XXXI.

LAMBETH (*continued*).—WATERLOO ROAD, &c.

Ecclesiastical Divisions of the Parish of Lambeth—The Lambeth Water-works—The Shot Factory—Belvedere Road—Royal Infirmary for Children and Women—The General Lying-in Hospital—St. John's Church—The Grave of Elliston—The South-Western Railway Terminus—The New Cut—Sunday Trading—The Victoria Palace Theatre—Dominic Serres—St. Thomas's Church—Lambeth Marsh—Bishop Bonner's House—Erasmus King's Museum—The "Spanish Patriot"—All Saints' Church—The Canterbury Hall—The Bower Saloon—Stangate—"Old Grimaldi"—Carlisle House—Norfolk House—Old Mill at Lambeth—The London Necropolis Company—St. Thomas's Hospital—The Albert Embankment—Inundations in Lambeth—Lambeth Potteries and Glass Works—Schools of Art—Manufactures of Lambeth 407

CHAPTER XXXII.

LAMBETH PALACE.

History of the Foundation of Lambeth Palace—Successive Additions and Alterations in the Building—Fate of the Palace during the Time of the Commonwealth—The Great Gateway—The Hall—Hospitality of the Archbishops in Former Times—The Library and Manuscript Room—The Guard Chamber—The Gallery—The Post-room—The Chapel—Desecration of the Chapel—Archbishop Parker's Tomb—The Lollards' Tower—The Gardens—Bishops' Walk—Remarkable Historical Occurrences at Lambeth Palace—The Palace attacked by the Insurgents under Wat Tyler—Queen Mary and Cardinal Pole—Queen Elizabeth and Archbishop Parker—The "Lambeth Articles"—The Archbishop's Dole—The Palace attacked by a London Mob in 1641—Translation of Archbishop Sheldon—The Gordon Riots—The Pan Anglican Synod—The Arches Court of Canterbury—The Annual Visit of the Stationers' Company—Lambeth Degrees—St. Mary's Church—Curious Items in the Parish Registers—The Tomb of the Tradescants 426

CHAPTER XXXIII.

VAUXHALL.

First recorded Notice of the Gardens—The Place originally known as the Spring Gardens—Evelyn's Visit to Sir Samuel Morland's House—Visit of Samuel Pepys to the Spring Gardens—Addison's Account of the Visit of Sir Roger de Coverley to Vauxhall—The Old Mansion of Copped Hall—Description of Sir Samuel Morland's House and Grounds—The Place taken by Jonathan Tyers, and opened for Public Entertainment—Roubiliac's Statue of Handel—Reference to Vauxhall in Boswell's "Life of Johnson"—How Hogarth became connected with Vauxhall Gardens—A *Ridotto al Fresco*—Character of the Entertainments at Vauxhall a Century ago—Character of the Company frequenting the Gardens—A Description of the Gardens as they appeared in the Middle of the Last Century—How Horace Walpole and his Friends visited Vauxhall, and minced Chickens in a China Dish—Byron's Description of a *Ridotto al Fresco*—Fielding's Account of Vauxhall—Sunday Morning Visitors to Vauxhall—Vauxhall in the Height of its Glory—Goldsmith's Description of a Visit—Sir John Dinely and other Aristocratic Visitors—How Jos Sedley drank Rack Punch at Vauxhall—Wellington witnessing the Battle of Waterloo over again—The Gardens in the Last of their Glory—Hayman's Picture of the "Milkmaids on May-day"—Lines on Vauxhall, by Ned Ward the Younger—Balloon Ascents—Narrow Escape of the Gardens from Destruction by Fire—Closing of the Gardens, and Sale of the Property 447

CHAPTER XXXIV.

VAUXHALL (*continued*) AND BATTERSEA.

Boat-racing at Vauxhall—Fortifications erected here in 1642—A Proposed Boulevard—The Marquis of Worcester, Author of the "Century of Inventions"—The Works of the London Gas Company—Nine Elms—Messrs. Price's Candle Factory—Inns and Taverns—Origin of the Name of Battersea—Descent of the Manor of Battersea—Bolingbroke House—A Curious Air-mill—Reminiscences of Henry St. John, Lord Bolingbroke—Sir William Batten—York House—The Parish Church of Battersea—Christ Church—St. Mark's Church—St.

CONTENTS.

George's Church—The National School—St. John's College—The Royal Freemasons' Girls' School—The "Falcon" Tavern—The Victoria Bridge—Albert Bridge—The Old Ferry—Building of Battersea Bridge—Battersea Fields—The "Red House"—Cæsar's Ford —Battersea Park and Gardens—Model Dwellings for Artisans and Labourers—Southwark and Vauxhall Waterworks—Market Gardens —Battersea Enamelled Ware—How Battersea became the Cradle of Bottled Ale 467

CHAPTER XXXV.

WANDSWORTH.

The River Wandle—Manufactories—French Refugees—The Frying-pan Houses—High Street—St. Peter's Hospital—The Union Work-house--The Royal Patriotic Asylum—The Surrey County Prison—The Craig Telescope—The Surrey Lunatic Asylum—The Friendless Boys' Home—The Surrey Industrial School—The Surrey Iron Tramway—Clapham Junction—Wandsworth Bridge—All Saints' Church—St. Anne's Church—St. Mary's, St. John's, and Holy Trinity Churches—Nonconformity at Wandsworth—Francis Grose the Antiquary, Bishop Jebb, and Voltaire Residents here—Mock Elections of the "Mayors of Garratt"—Wandsworth Fair—Horticulture and Floriculture 479

CHAPTER XXXVI.

PUTNEY.

The Fishery which formerly existed here—Putney Ferry—High Street—Fairfax House—Chatfield House—The "Palace"—The Bridge of Boats—Putney House—The Almshouses—The Watermen's School—Cromwell Place—Grove House—D'Israeli Road—Nicholas West Bishop of Ely—Wolsey's Secretary, Cromwell—An Incident in the Life of Wolsey—Bishop Bonner's House—Essex House--Lime Grove—The Residence of Edward Gibbon, the Historian—David Mallet, the Scotch Poet—John Tolland and Theodore Hook Residents here—Mrs. Shelley—Putney School—Douglas Jerrold—Bowling-Green House—Death of William Pitt—The Residence of Mrs. Siddons —James Macpherson—The Fire-proof House, and the Obelisk—The Royal Hospital for Incurables—Putney Heath—Celebrated Duels fought here—Duel between the Duke of Buckingham and the Earl of Shrewsbury at Barn-elms—Reviews on Putney Heath—Putney Park—Wimbledon Common—The Meetings of the Rifle Volunteers—The Oxford and Cambridge Boat-races—Evelyn's Visits to Putney —Putney Church—The Residence of Gibbons' Grandfather—Putney Bridge—The Aqueduct of the Chelsea Waterworks 489

CHAPTER XXXVII.

FULHAM.

Probable Derivation of the Name of Fulham—Boundaries of the Parish—The High Street—Egmont Villa, the Residence of Theodore Hook—Anecdotes of Hook—All Saints' Church—Fulham Bells—Sir William Powell's Almshouses—Bishop's Walk—Fulham Palace— The Gardens—A Bishop's Success in a Competition for Lying—The Manor of Fulham—Bishops Bonner, Aylmer, Bancroft, and Juxon—The Moat—Craven Cottage—Jew King, the Money-lender—The "Crab Tree"—The Earl of Cholmondeley's Villa—Fulham Cemetery—The "Golden Lion"—The Old Workhouse—Fulham at the Commencement of the Last Century—Fulham Road, Past and Present—Holcrofts Hall—Holcrofts Priory—Claybrooke House—The Orphanage Home—Fulham Almshouses—Burlington House—The Reformatory School for Females—Munster House—Fulham Lodge—Percy Cross—Ravensworth House—Walham Lodge —Dungannon House and Albany Lodge—Arundel House—Sad Fate of a Highwayman—Park House—Rosamond's Bower—Parson's Green—Samuel Richardson, the Author of "Pamela," &c.—East-end House—Mrs. Fitzherbert and Madame Piccolomini Residents here—Sir Thomas Bodley—Eelbrook Common—Peterborough House—Ivy Cottage—Fulham Charity Schools—The Pottery—A Tapestry Manufactory—A Veritable Centenarian 504

CHAPTER XXXVIII.

FULHAM (continued).—WALHAM GREEN AND NORTH END.

Vine Cottage—The Pryor's Bank—The "Swan" Tavern—Stourton House—Ranelagh House—Hurlingham—Broom House--Sandy End— Sandford Manor House, the Residence of Nell Gwynne, and of Joseph Addison—St. James's, Moore Park—Walham Green—St. John's Church—The Butchers' Almshouses—A Poetic Gardener—North End—Browne's House—North End Lodge—Jacob Tonson —North End Road—Beaufort House—Lillie Bridge Running-ground—The Residence of Foote, the Dramatist—The Hermitage—The Residence of Bartolozzi—Normand House—Wentworth Cottage—Fulham Fields—Walnut-tree Cottage—St. Saviour's Convalescent Hospital—The Residence of Dr. Crotch—Samuel Richardson's House—Other Noted Residents at Fulham 521

CHAPTER XXXIX.

HAMMERSMITH.

Ecclesiastical Division of Hammersmith from Fulham—The Principal Streets and Thoroughfares—The Railway Stations—The "Bell and Anchor" Tavern—The "Red Cow"—Nazareth House, the Home of "The Little Sisters of the Poor"—The Old Benedictine Convent, now a Training College for the Priesthood—Dr. Bonaventura Giffard—The West London Hospital—The Broadway—Brook Green—The Church of the Holy Trinity—St. Joseph's Almshouses—St. Mary's Normal College—Roman Catholic Reformatories—Blythe House— Market Gardens—Messrs. Lee's Nursery--The Church of St. John the Evangelist, in Dartmouth Road—Godolphin School—Ravens-court Park- The Ancient Manor House of Pallenswick—Starch Green—The Old London Road—A Quaint Old Pump—Queen Street— The Parish Church—The Monument of Sir Nicholas Crispe—The Enshrined Heart of Sir Nicholas Crispe—The Impostor, John Tuck—Latymer Schools—The Convent of the Good Shepherd—Sussex House—Brandenburgh House—George Bubb Dodington— The Margravine of Brandenburgh-Anspach—The Funeral of Queen Caroline—Hammersmith Suspension Bridge—Hammersmith Mall —The High Bridge—The "Dove" Coffee-house, and Thomson the Poet—Sir Samuel Morland—The Upper Mall—Catharine, Queen of Charles II.—Dr. Radcliffe—Arthur Murphy—De Loutherbourg—Other Eminent Residents—Leigh Hunt—St. Peter's Church—A Public-spirited Artist—The Hammersmith Ghost 529

CONTENTS.

CHAPTER XL.

CHISWICK.

PAGE

Earliest Historical Records of Chiswick—Sutton Manor—Chiswick Eyot—The Parish Church—Holland, the Actor—Ugo Foscolo—De Loutherbourg—Kent, the Father of Modern Gardening—Sharp, the Engraver—Lady Thornhill—Hogarth's Monument—A Curious Inscription—Extracts from the Churchwardens' Books—Hogarth's House—Hogarth's Chair—The "Griffin" Brewery—Chiswick Mall—The "Red Lion"—The "White Bear and Whetstone"—The College House—Whittingham's Printing-press—Barbara, Duchess of Cleveland—Dr. Rose and Dr. Ralph—Edward Moore, the Journalist—Alexander Pope's Residence—The Old Manor House—Turnham Green—Encampment of the Parliamentarians during the Civil Wars—The Old "Pack Horse" Inn—The Chiswick Nursery—Chiswick House—Description of the Gardens—The Pictures and Articles of *Vertu*—Royal Visits—Death of Charles James Fox and George Canning—Garden Parties—Corney House—Sir Stephen Fox's House—The Gardens of the Royal Horticultural Society .   . 549

CHAPTER XLI.

GENERAL REMARKS AND CONCLUSION.

A General View of London—Length of its Streets, and Number of Dwellings—Growth of London since the Time of Henry VIII.—The Population at Various Periods since 1687—The Population of London compared with that of other Cities—Recent Alterations and Improvements in the Streets of London—The Food and Water Supply—Removal of Sewage—The Mud and Dust of London—Churches and Hospitals—Places of Amusement—Concluding Observations 567

LIST OF ILLUSTRATIONS.

	PAGE
Kennington Common and Church . . *Frontispiece*	
St. Thomas's Hospital; St. Saviour's, Southwark;	
Lambeth Palace	1
South End of Old London Bridge, with Shot Tower	
and St. Olave's Church, in 1820	6
The Bridge-foot, Southwark, in 1810 . . .	7
Priory of St. Mary Overy, 1700	12
Old Houses formerly at Bankside	13
Interior of St. Saviour's Church . . .	18
Views of St. Saviour's Church	19
Consistory Court, St. Saviour's Church, 1820 .	24
John Gower	25
Tomb of John Gower in St. Saviour's Church .	26
View of St. Mary Overy, 1647	30
Winchester House, 1660	31
Hall of Winchester House, 1647 . . .	33
Mrs. Thrale	36
Barclay's Brewery, 1829	37
Plan of Bankside, early in the Seventeenth Century .	42
The Globe Theatre, temp. Elizabeth . . .	43
Ben Jonson	48
Map of Southwark, 1720	49
The Borough, High Street, in 1825	54
Southwark Fair	55
The Mint, Southwark, in 1825	60
The King's Bench, Southwark, in 1830 . . .	61
The Marshalsea Prison, in the Eighteenth Century .	66
The Marshalsea, in 1800	67
The Old "Tabard" Inn, in the Seventeenth Century	72
The Old "Tabard" Inn, shortly before its demolition	73
Geoffrey Chaucer	78
Old Inns in Southwark	79
Boar's Head Court-yard	84
The Old "White Hart" Inn	85
St. Thomas's Hospital, 1840	90
Guy's Hospital	91
Folly Ditch, Jacob's Island	96
The Great Fire at Cotton's Wharf, Tooley Street, 1861	97
St. Olave's Church, in 1820	102
The Grammar School of St. Olave's, 1810 . .	103
Millpond Bridge, in 1826	109
Hall of the Southwark "Train-Bands," in 1813 .	114
Old Houses in London Street, Dockhead, about 1810	115
Bermondsey Abbey, 1790	120
St. Mary Magdalen's Church, Bermondsey, 1809	121
Bridge and Turnpike in the Grange Road, about 1820 .	126
Garden Front of Jamaica House, 1826 . . .	127
Cherry Garden Street, with Jamaica House, 1826	127
St. James's Church, Bermondsey	132
Rotherhithe Church, 1750	133
Diving Bell used in Constructing the Thames Tunnel	138

	PAGE
Floating Dock, Deptford, 1820	139
The Royal Dock, Deptford, end of Seventeenth	
Century	144
Samuel Pepys	145
Peter the Great's House at Deptford, 1850 . .	150
The Royal Dockyard, Deptford, in 1810 . . .	151
Deptford Creek	156
Deptford and Greenwich, in 1815 . . .	157
St. Nicholas Church, Deptford, in 1790 . . .	162
John Evelyn	163
Placentia, 1560	168
Old Conduit, Greenwich Park, in 1835 . . .	169
Old Palace of Greenwich, in 1630	174
A View of the Ancient Royal Palace, called Placentia	175
Greenwich Hospital, from the River . . .	180
The Painted Hall, Greenwich Hospital . . .	181
Old View of Greenwich Palace	183
Group of Greenwich Pensioners, 1868 . . .	186
The Royal Naval School, Greenwich, 1830 . .	187
The Parish Church, Greenwich	192
The Duke of Norfolk's Almshouses, in 1796 . .	193
"Crown and Sceptre" Inn, Greenwich . . .	198
Easter Monday in Greenwich Park	199
Lane Leading into Ship Street, Greenwich, 1830 .	204
View from One-Tree Hill, Greenwich Park, in 1846 .	205
View in Greenwich Park	210
Houses Round Greenwich Park	211
Flamsteed House	216
Entrance to Greenwich Observatory, in 1840 .	217
The Magnetic Clock, Greenwich Observatory .	222
The Great Equatorial Telescope in the Dome, Green-	
wich Observatory	223
West Coombe, in 1794	228
The "Green Man," Blackheath	229
Vanbrugh Castle	234
Charlton House, in 1845	235
Eltham Palace, in 1790	240
Hall of Eltham Palace, in 1835	241
Lee Church, in 1795	246
The Royal Naval School, New Cross . . .	247
The Licensed Victuallers' Asylum	252
The Telegraph Tower, in 1810	256
Newington Butts, in 1820	258
The Fishmongers' Almshouses, in 1850 . . .	259
Fountain in the Surrey Gardens	262
Old Newington Church, in 1866	264
The Music Hall, Surrey Gardens, 1858 . . .	265
View in the Surrey Gardens, 1850	267
Old Camberwell Church, in 1750	270
Bowyer House	271
Old Camberwell Mill	276

	PAGE
Old House on Camberwell Green	277
Dr. Lettsom's House, Grove Hill	282
Grove Lane, Camberwell	283
The "Rosemary Branch," in 1800	288
"Heaton's Folly," in 1804	289
Dr. Glennie's Academy, Dulwich Grove, in 1820	294
Views in Camberwell and Dulwich	295
Dulwich College, in 1790	300
Dulwich College, in 1750	301
Sydenham Wells, in 1750	306
Site of the Crystal Palace, in 1852	307
The Crystal Palace, from the South	312
Margaret Finch's Cottage, Norwood, in 1808	313
Lord Thurlow's House, Knight's Hill	318
Mrs. Thrale's House, Streatham	319
View of Clapham, in 1790	324
Old Clapham Church, in 1750	325
Views in Old Stockwell	330
Kennington, from the Green, 1780	331
The Chartist Meeting on Kennington Common, 1848	336
Tradescant's House, South Lambeth	337
The "Horns" Tavern, Kennington, in 1820	342
The Freemasons' Charity School, St. George's Fields, in 1800	343
Old Sign of the "Dog and Duck"	344
The Obelisk in St. George's Circus	349
Bethlehem Hospital	354
"Melancholy and Raving Madness"	355
A Ward in Bethlehem Hospital	360
King Edward's School	361
Christ Church, Westminster Road	367
The Surrey Theatre	372
Rowland Hill's Chapel, in 1814	373
Rowland Hill	378
Interior of the Rotunda, Blackfriars Road, in 1820	379
The South Side of the Thames, taken from Adelphi Terrace	384
Searle's Boat-yard, in 1830	385
The Pedlar and his Dog, from Lambeth Church	388
Old Windmills at Lambeth, about 1750	390
Old Views in Lambeth	391
The Old "Coburg" Theatre, in 1820	396
Astley's Riding School, in 1770	397
Entrance to Astley's Theatre, in 1820	402
Interior of Astley's Amphitheatre, in 1843	403
The Houses in Waterloo Bridge Road	408
View in the New Cut	409
Bishop Bonner's House, in 1780	414
Drug Mill of the Apothecaries' Company	415
The Chevalier D'Eon	418
St. Thomas's Hospital	420
The Entrance Hall, St. Thomas's Hospital	421
Lambeth Palace, from Millbank, in 1860	426
Lambeth Palace, from the River, 1709	427
The Lollards' Tower, Lambeth Palace	432
The Chamber in Lambeth Palace in which the Lollards were Confined	433
Interior of the Great Hall, Lambeth Palace, 1800	438
Lambeth Palace	439
Old Whitehall Stairs	444
Lambeth Church, 1825	445
The Old Manor-house at Vauxhall, about 1800	450
Views in Vauxhall Gardens	451
The Old Village of Vauxhall, with Entrance to the Gardens, in 1825	456
The Italian Walk, Vauxhall Gardens	457
Chinese Pavilion in Vauxhall Gardens	462
Balloon Ascent at Vauxhall Gardens, 1849	463
Old Battersea Mill, about 1800	468
York House, 1790	469
Old Battersea Church, 1790	474
The Tropical Gardens, Battersea Park	475
The Lake, Battersea Park	480
Wandsworth, in 1790	481
Lines of Rail at Clapham Junction	483
The Fishmongers' Almshouses, Wandsworth	486
The Garratt Election	487
Putney House, 1810	492
Lime Grove, Putney, in 1810	493
Fairfax House, Putney	495
Bowling-green House	498
In and About Putney	499
Essex House, Putney	502
Old Putney Bridge	504
Fulham Church, in 1825	505
The Moat, Fulham Palace	510
Fulham Palace, in 1798	511
Holcrofts and the Priory, Fulham	516
Richardson's House at Parson's Green, 1799	517
Peterborough House	520
Nell Gwynne's House	522
In and About Fulham	523
Ranelagh House	528
The "Red Cow" Inn, Hammersmith	529
The Convent, Hammersmith, in 1800	534
The River Front of Hammersmith, from the Eyot at Chiswick to the Bridge, 1800	535
Hammersmith Parish Church, in 1820	538
Brandenburgh House, in 1815	540
Hammersmith, in 1746	541
The Old "Pack Horse" Inn, Turnham Green	546
Hammersmith Mall, in 1800	547
Old Cottages on Back Common	552
Hogarth's House	553
Entrance to Chiswick	558
At Chiswick	559
Chiswick House, in 1763	564
Corney House, in 1760	565
Chiswick Mall, in 1820	571

SUB-TROPICAL GARDEN

BATTERSEA PARK

St THOMAS'S HOSPITAL

St SAVIOUR'S SOUTHWARK

LAMBETH PALACE

LONDON.

THE SOUTHERN SUBURBS.

CHAPTER I.

INTRODUCTORY. —SOUTHWARK.

" Superat pars altera curæ."—Virgil.

Introductory Remarks—Geological Observations—Earliest Mention of Southwark in History—Its Etymology—Southwark as a Roman Settlement—Old London Bridge—Knut's Trench—Reception of William the Conqueror by the Natives of Southwark—The Civic Government of Southwark—Its Annexation to the City—An Icelander's Account of Old London Bridge—The Story of Olaf's Destruction of the Bridge—Hymn sung on the Festival of St. Olave.

HAVING now completed our survey of the West End and of the northern suburbs of London, it will be necessary for us again to take in hand our pilgrim staff, and to make a fresh start, with a view of reconnoitring that large and interesting district which, though it lies on the southern bank of the Thames, forms, and has formed for centuries, an integral part of this great metropolis. We will therefore do so without further delay, and only ask our readers to accompany us mentally to

London Bridge, from the south end of which it is our purpose to commence our peregrinations, which in this, the concluding volume of the work, will be mainly confined to the metropolitan and strictly suburban districts in the county of Surrey; for we have not forgotten the promise with which we set out on our wanderings, to confine ourselves to those regions, be they greater or smaller in extent, from which can be seen "the glimmer of the gilded cross of St. Paul's."

The district which we are about to traverse, though not equal in its reminiscences to the City of Westminster, will be found on examination to be full of antiquarian interest. In St. Saviour's Priory Church, in Bermondsey Abbey, in the old "Tabard" Inn, in the Globe and other theatres on Bankside, in the archiepiscopal palace at Lambeth, in the once royal palace at Kennington, in the Mint and the old Marshalsea, we shall find a rich mine of archæological wealth, and one which it will take a long time to exhaust. At Deptford we shall again meet with our old friends, Samuel Pepys and John Evelyn; at Greenwich we shall see our Tudor kings and queens in the midst of a splendid court; on Blackheath we shall meet Wat Tyler and his rebel bands; at Newington Butts we shall witness the cavalcade of the Canterbury Pilgrims, as they wend their way along the old road into Kent; at Kennington we shall find the Black Prince "at home," and perhaps witness the execution of some of the Scottish rebels; at Dulwich and Camberwell we shall drop in and make the acquaintance of Edmund Alleyn, the "player" and friend of a certain "Will Shakespeare;" while a little nearer home, at Stockwell, we shall find a veritable "Ghost," scarcely inferior to its rival of Cock Lane; at Clapham we shall find Mr. Wilberforce and the Evangelicals busy in founding the Bible Society; in St. George's Fields we shall spend a day with the inmates of New Bedlam, and try to cheer them with our presence; and then mentally transport ourselves to the same spot in the days of Lord George Gordon and his riots, to witness their bonfires. We shall "assist" at the founding and opening of the Surrey and Victoria Theatres, and take our stand by the side of Mr. Astley when, supported by Ducrow, he first encloses his riding-school. We shall peep in and hear a sermon from Rowland Hill, in his well-known chapel in the Surrey Road; spend an evening in the Surrey Zoological Gardens; and then look in at Lambeth Palace, to witness the records of the "Lollard" prisoners, and make acquaintance with Archbishops Chicheley, and Cranmer, and Parker, and Laud. Thence, having

glanced in at the Museum of the Tradescants, we shall make our way to Faux or Vaux Hall, and take a view of the old place before it was turned into "Gardens." Thence we shall walk on to Battersea, and shake hands with Lord Bolingbroke before he goes forth into exile, and reconnoitre sundry clusters of old houses, both in that village and in Wandsworth and Putney. There we shall try and arrange our visit so as to come in for the annual contest between Oxford and Cambridge for the blue riband of the London waters; then, crossing the river, we shall make a halt at Fulham in order to investigate at leisure the mansion which for so many centuries has been the residence of successive Bishops of London. Turning then back, in a north-westerly direction, it is our intention to make a perambulation of Hammersmith, so rich in literary and religious associations, and we shall conclude our wanderings with a brief visit to the grave of Hogarth, the painter and moralist, in Chiswick churchyard.

It is just possible, indeed, that we may be led to go even a little farther afield in search of subjects of interest, past and present; but if such should prove to be the case, we shall not forget that it is London and London life with which we have to deal, and that where London has extended its social life into the suburbs we must follow it up. At all events, we shall take good care not to leave any street or any house unexplored which can have an interest for the readers of "Old and New London."

With these few words of preface, we will commence our journey at the point where London Bridge abuts on the east end of the "Ladye" Chapel of St. Saviour's. And here we cannot do better than repeat the words which we employed on first starting from Temple Bar:*—"Southwark, a Roman station and cemetery, is by no means without a history. It was burnt by William the Conqueror, and had been the scene of a battle against the Danes. It possessed palaces, monasteries, a mint, and fortifications. The Bishops of Winchester and Rochester once lived here in splendour, and the locality boasted its four Elizabethan theatres. The 'Globe' was Shakespeare's summer theatre, and here it was that his greatest triumphs were attained. What was acted there is best told by making Shakespeare's share in the management distinctly understood; nor can we leave Southwark without visiting the 'Tabard' inn, from whence Chaucer's nine-and-twenty jovial pilgrims set out for Canterbury—

'The holye blissful martyr for to seek.'"

---

* See Vol. I., p. 9.

Hitherto, as our readers are aware, we have been concerned with those portions of our great metropolis which lie to the north of the Thames, and within the boundaries of the county of Middlesex; but the moment that we cross London Bridge we find ourselves in another county—that of Surrey—so called from South-rey—*i.e.*, the south side of the river.

If we were to travel far into the interior of this county we should come upon scenes very unlike what we have seen in Middlesex; but the limits of our present pilgrimage will scarcely carry us so far afield as to the borders of the chalk formation which fringes the basin of clay and gravel which underlies the whole of London south, as well as London north, of the Thames.

There was a time, some two thousand years ago, when the whole of the district now covered by Southwark and Lambeth, and most of the adjacent district, as far south as the rising grounds of Brixton, Streatham, and Clapham, was little more than a dull and dreary swamp, inhabited by the bittern and the frog, and when painted savages roamed and prowled about the places which are now not only busy thoroughfares, but the marts of foreign commerce. But this change was the work of very many ages.

In the early Saxon times there is no notice of any large town being situated here; but a tradition of Bartholomew Linsted, or Fowle, the last prior of St. Mary Overie, as preserved to us by Stow in his "History of London," tells us that the profits of the ferry—for before a bridge spanned the Thames a ferry had existed here—were devoted by the owner, "a maiden named Mary," to the foundation and endowment of a convent or house of sisters, which was afterwards converted into a college of priests; and that these priests built a bridge of timber, which in the course of time was converted into a bridge of stone.

Maitland, in his "History of London," refuses to believe this tradition, which, if it be true, would carry back the date of the foundation of St. Mary Overie's to a period far anterior to any historic notice of Southwark; but whether we accept it in its entirety or not, at all events the legend must be regarded as fair evidence of the early establishment of a religious house at this spot, and of the bestowal of the proceeds of the ferry for its support.

The earliest mention of Southwark by name in history is in A.D. 1023, when the Saxon chronicle tells us that Knut, and Egelnoth, Archbishop of Canterbury, with some other distinguished persons, carried by ship the body of Alphege, saint and martyr, across the Thames to "Suthgeweorke," on its way to its resting-place at Canterbury. In "Domesday Book" the name appears under the form of "Sudwerche."

It is generally said that Southwark was never fortified till quite a recent period. How, then, did its name, "wark" or "werke," arise? Is it the same word as in bul*wark*? A fortress built by the Earl of Mar, in Scotland, is called "Mar's wark or werke;" and possibly the same word is embodied in the word "Southwark."

Mr. Worsaae, in his "Account of the Danes and Norwegians in England," refers to the possession by those peoples of Southwark, the very name of which, he adds, is unmistakably of Danish or Norwegian origin. "The Sagas relate that, in the time of King Svend Tveskjæg, the Danes fortified this trading place, which, evidently, on account of its situation to the south of the Thames and London, was called Sydvirke (Sudvirke), or the southern fortification. From Sudvirke, which in Anglo-Saxon was called Sud-geweorc, but which in the Middle Ages obtained the name of Suthwerk or Swerk, arose the present form—Southwark. The Northmen had a church in Sudvirke, dedicated to the Norwegian king, Olaf the Saint." It is stated that the name of Southwark has been spelled in no fewer than twenty-seven different ways in old writings.

We shall not attempt to invade too far the domain of learned antiquaries, and waste our readers' time and patience by a long disquisition on the question whether the natives of Southwark, twelve hundred years ago—as a portion of the inhabitants of the county of Surrey—were descendants of the Regni or the Cantii, the Atrebates or the Bibroci. It is enough for us to know that the men of Surrey were among the tribes conquered by the legions of Julius Cæsar, and that having belonged at one time to the kingdom of Mercia, and at another to Kent, Surrey became after the Conquest part and parcel of the territory of the son-in-law of William, the powerful Earl of Warrenne, and that, lying so near to the chief city of the kingdom, in spite of the *fluvius dissociabilis*, the Thames, it was gradually absorbed into the great metropolis, of which it became a suburb in the strictest sense, even before it was formally "annexed" to London.

As already indicated, the low flat tongue of land bounded on three sides by the Thames in the bend which it makes between Greenwich and Vauxhall, was doubtless originally overflowed by the tide, and formed a large marsh extending to the foot of the slight eminences which bound its fourth side upon the south. It is almost certain that this space was banked in artificially by the Romans, so as to secure it against being overflowed; and Roman remains, which have been dug up in St. George's Fields and elsewhere about Southwark and its neighbourhood, are sufficient proofs that the Romans formed there a settlement of some kind or other. Indeed, as Ptolemy tells us that London was in the territory of the Cantii, it has been inferred—though somewhat too hastily—that the original London stood on the south of the river; but this theory is generally rejected as being contrary to evidences of various kinds. It is far more probable that Ptolemy wrote with an imperfect knowledge of the geography of so distant and unimportant a place, and confounded the two sides of a distant river. No doubt, however, from very early times there was on the south side a suburb consisting of dwelling-houses connected with the city by a ferry, where the great Roman road of the Watling crossed the Thames.

The history of Southwark up to the period of the Norman Conquest is obscure and uncertain; but there is no doubt that the place was inhabited by the Romans, for Charles Knight tells us that "clear vestiges of Roman dwelling-houses have been found, not only in Southwark, but here and there along the bank of the river as far east as Deptford."

It has been asserted that there was no bridge between London and Southwark as early as the tenth century, because we are told that in A.D. 993 Anlaf, the King of Norway, sailed up the river as far as Stane (Staines); but this inference is by no means to be accepted as certain, for we learn from William of Malmesbury, and from the "Saxon Chronicle," that in the very next year there was a bridge here which obstructed the flight of Sweyn's forces, when he attacked London and was repulsed by its brave citizens. Again, little more than twenty years later, when Knut attacked London, there certainly was a bridge of one kind or another, which formed an obstacle to the advance of his ships up the river; and in order to avoid this obstacle (according to the Saxon Chronicle), he dug on the south side a trench, through which he conveyed his vessels to a point "above bridge." It is curious that in the accounts of these transactions which have come down to us there is no actual mention of Southwark by name; and yet there must have been some "werke" or defence, at all events, at the entrance of the bridge. Again, in 1052, Godwin, then in rebellion against Edward the Confessor, came with his fleet to Southwark, and passing the bridge without any opposition, proceeded to attack the king's vessels which lay off

Westminster, though further hostilities were averted by an offer of peace.

Perhaps it was the error of Sweyn in getting his fleet foul of London Bridge which made his son Knut go so laboriously to work with the waters of the Thames on his invasion in 1016, the story of which shall be briefly related in the words of the "Saxon Chronicle:"—"Then came the ships to Greenwiche, and, within a short interval, to London, where they sank a deep ditch on the south side, and so dragged their ships to the west side of the bridge. Afterwards they trenched the city without, so that no man could go in or out, and often fought against it; but the citizens bravely withstood them."

There have been several persons who have raised sceptical doubts about this history; but the honest historian, Maitland—who loved to get to the bottom of all such statements, and who set himself to discover proofs of Knut's trench—tells us that this artificial water-course began at the great wet-dock below Rotherhithe, and passing across the Kent Road, continued in a crescent form as far as Vauxhall, and fell again into the Thames at the lower end of Chelsea Reach. As proofs of the historic truth of this hypothesis, he brought forward the great quantities of hazels, willows, and brushwood, pointing northwards, and fastened down by rows of stakes, which were found at the digging and clearing out of Rotherhithe Dock in 1694, as well as numbers of large oaken planks and piles, found also in other parts on the Surrey side of the river.

Southwark, very naturally, figures in the chapter of English history which immediately follows on the Battle of Hastings. As soon as he had won the battle, we read that William marched upon London, where the citizens had declared Edgar Atheling king of England. On reaching Southwark, which then was an inconsiderable suburb—though not wholly unfortified, as may be gathered from its name—the Conqueror was so roughly handled by the sturdy citizens of London, that though he repulsed them by the aid of some five hundred horse, and laid the suburb in ashes, he found it necessary, or at all events prudent, to retire, and accordingly marched off in a westerly direction.

Southwark is mentioned in history as far back as A.D. 1053, and was a distinct corporation governed by its own bailiff until 1327, when Edward III. made a grant of it to the City of London, whose mayor was thenceforth to be its bailiff, and to govern it by his deputy. "Great inconvenience having been found to arise from its affording a refuge to offenders of various kinds," the City was ordered to pay to the royal exchequer the sum of

£10 annually as a fee-farm rent. In this charter Southwark is called a "villa," which may mean anything from a town down to a village ; but if we take the term in the latter sense, it must have been a tolerably large "village," for it had no less than four churches : viz., St. Mary's (a chapel of the great conventual church of St. Mary over the Rie); St. Margaret's (where the Town Hall lately stood); St. Olave's ; and, lastly, St. George's; to say nothing of the hospital of St. Thomas, two prisons (namely, those of the King's Bench and the Marshalsea), and also the houses of several prelates, abbots, and nobles.

Some time after this, however, the inhabitants recovered their former privileges ; but in the reign of Edward VI. the Crown granted the district to the City of London for a money grant of a little less than £650 ; in consideration of a further sum of 500 marks, it was "annexed" to the said City, and by virtue of the same grant it continues subject to its Lord Mayor, who has under him a steward and a bailiff ; and it is governed (or rather represented in the councils of the City) by one of its aldermen, whose ward is styled by the name of "Bridge-without." The property granted to the City on the above occasion is regarded as specially liable to the repairs and maintenance of London Bridge. By this incorporation, however, Southwark did not cease to be part and parcel of the county of Surrey. From this arrangement certain lands were exempted, such as Southwark Mansion and Park, which belonged to the king.

According to the "Penny Cyclopædia" (1842), this ward appears never to have been represented in the Common Council, nor do the inhabitants now elect their aldermen. The senior alderman of London is always alderman of this ward, and on his death the next in seniority succeeds him. He has no ward duties to perform, so that his office is little else than a sinecure. The City of London appoints a high bailiff and steward for Southwark ; but the county magistrates of Surrey exercise jurisdiction in several matters.

"It is curious to observe," says Mr. Robertson, in his "Lecture on Southwark," "that London was first indebted to Southwark for its bridge ; that the first bridge was built by the priests of the monastery in Southwark ; that the Bridge-house was in Southwark, and not in London ; that the revenues for the maintenance of the bridge were not derived from London, but from the southern side of the Thames ; and although land could not have been difficult to obtain close to the bridge, the expensive experiment was resorted to of building houses on the bridge—literally, on the Thames."

The earliest description of London Bridge, singularly enough, is given by an Icelander, who lived in the middle of the thirteenth century, and may be found quoted by the Rev. James Johnstone, in his "Antiquitates Celto-Scandicæ" (Copenhagen, 1786, 4to), in connection with the Battle of Southwark, which was fought in 1008, in the luckless reign of Ethelred II., surnamed the "Unready." It runs as follows :—

"They (i.e., the Danish forces) first came to shore at London, where their ships were to remain, and the city was taken by the Danes. Upon the other side of the river is situate a great market called Southwark—Sudurvirke in the original—which the Danes fortified with many defences ; framing, for instance, a high and broad ditch, having a pile or rampart within it, formed of wood, stone, and turf, with a large garrison placed there to strengthen it. This the king, Ethelred, ... attacked and forcibly fought against ; but by the resistance of the Danes it proved but a vain endeavour. There was at that time a bridge erected over the river between the City and Southwark, so wide that if two carriages met they could pass each other." This structure King Olave and his Norsemen destroyed by rowing their ships up close to the bridge, and making them fast to it by ropes and cables. With these they strained the piles so vigorously, aided by the strong flow of the tide, that the piles gave way, and the whole bridge fell. "And now it was determined to attack Southwark," continues the Icelander ; "but the citizens seeing their river occupied by the enemy's navy so as to cut off all intercourse that way with the interior provinces, were seized with fear, and having surrendered the city, received Ethelred as king." In remembrance of this expedition, thus sang Ottar Suarti, in a sort of rhythmic prose, which reminds one of Macpherson's "Ossian :"—

"And thou hast overthrown their bridges, oh ! thou storm of the sons of Odin ! skilful and foremost in the battle. For thee it was happily reserved to possess the land of London's winding city. Many were the shields which were grasped, sword in hand, to the mighty increase of the conflict ; but by thee were the iron-banded coats of mail broken and destroyed.

"Thou, then, hast come, defender of the land, and hast restored to his kingdom the exiled Ethelred. By thine aid is he advantaged, and made strong by thy valour and prowess ; bitterest was that battle in which thou didst engage. Now, in the presence of thy kindred, the adjacent lands are at rest, where Edmund, the relative of the country and of the people, formerly governed.

"That was truly the sixth fight which the mighty king fought with the men of England, wherein King Olaf, the chief himself, a son of Odin, valiantly attacked the bridge at London. Bravely did the swords of the Volsces defend it ; but through the trench which the sea-kings, the men of

Vikesland, guarded, they were enabled to come, and the plain of Southwark was full of his tents."

The story of the destruction of London Bridge by Olaf is thus told in Southey's "Naval History of England," with all the details of historical narrative :—"Among them (*i.e.* Ethelred and his forces) came a certain king Olaf (perhaps the same who had been baptized in this country) : he brought with him a strong fleet ; and, with the aid

they might hope to destroy the bridge ; and Olaf undertook to make the attempt with some of his ships, if the other leaders would join in the assault. Causing, therefore, some deserted houses to be pulled down, he employed the beams and planks in constructing projections from the sides of the ships, under cover of which, when they were laid alongside the bridge, the assault might be made : a contrivance intended to serve the same purpose

SOUTH END OF OLD LONDON BRIDGE, WITH SHOT TOWER AND ST. OLAVE'S CHURCH, IN 1 20.

of these Scandinavian ships, the King of England resolved upon attempting to re-take London from the Danes. The fleet was of little use unless it could pass the bridge. But this, which was of wood, wide enough for the commodious passage of two carriages, and supported upon trestles, had been strongly fortified with towers, and a parapet breast high ; and at its south end it was defended by a military work, placed on what the Icelandic historian calls the great emporium of Southwark. This fortress was of great strength, built of wood and stone, with a deep and wide ditch and ramparts of earth. A first attack upon the bridge failed ; for the Danes had manned it well, and defended it bravely. Grieved at his repulse, Ethelred held a council of war, to deliberate in what manner

as those machines which, under the names of 'cats' and 'sows,' were used in sieges. He expected that the roofing would be strong enough to resist the weight of any stones which might be thrown upon it ; but in this expectation he had calculated too much upon the solidity of his materials, and too little upon the exertions and activity of the defenders ; and when, with the advantage of the flowing tide, the ships had taken their station, stones of such magnitude were let fall upon them, that the cover was beaten in ; shields and helmets afforded no protection ; the ships themselves were shaken and greatly injured, and many of them sheered off. Olaf, however, persisted in his enterprise. Under cover of such a bulwark, he succeeded in fastening some strong

THE BRIDGE-FOOT, SOUTHWARK, IN 1810.

cables or chains to the trestles which supported the bridge : and, when the tide had turned, his rowers, aided by the returning stream, tore away the middle of it, many of the enemy being precipitated into the river. The others fled into the city, or into Southwark ; and the Thames was thus opened to the fleet. The south work was then attacked and carried; and the Danes were no longer able to prevent the Londoners from opening their gates and joyfully receiving their king."

Such, according to ancient story, were the martial feats of King Olaf, or Olave, upon the water; but for his more pious and peaceful actions on land, which caused the men of Southwark to venerate his memory, it is needful only to turn to the church which bears his name, at the south-eastern corner of the bridge, and of which we shall speak presently.

It was, in reality, one of the two southern landmarks and boundaries of the old bridge, the Church of St. Saviour's, at the south-western corner of the bridge, being the other.

The author of "Chronicles of London Bridge" gives the following version of part of a Latin hymn from the Swedish Missal, sung on St. Olave's festival in his honour :—

"Martyred king ! in triumph shining !
Guardian saint ! whose bliss is shrining !
To thy spirit's sons inclining
From a sinful world confining,
  By thy might O set them free !
Carnal bonds around them twining,
Fiendish arts are undermining,
All with deadly plagues are pining ;
But, thy power and prayers combining,
  Safely shall we rise to thee.   Amen."

CHAPTER II.

SOUTHWARK (*continued*).—OLD LONDON BRIDGE.

" Ablegandæ Tiberim ultra."—*Horace.*

Controversy respecting the Trench from Rotherhithe to Battersea—How London Bridge was "built on Woolpacks"—Religious and Royal Processions at the Bridge-foot—Partial Destruction of Old London Bridge by Fire—Conflict between the Forces of Henry III. and those of the Earl of Leicester—Reception of Henry V. after the Battle of Agincourt—Fall of the Southern Tower of London Bridge—Southwark wholly destitute of Fortifications—Jack Cade's Rendezvous in Southwark—Death of Jack Cade—Heads on London Bridge—Reception of Henry VI. and Henry VII.—Reception of Katharine of Aragon—Cardinal Wolsey—Insurrection of Sir Thomas Wyatt—Rebuilding of the Northern Tower—Standards of the Spanish Armada placed on London Bridge—Southwark fortified by the Parliamentarians, to oppose King Charles—Reception of Charles II.—Corn Mills on London Bridge—Tradesmen's Tokens—Bridge-foot—The "Bear" Inn— The "Knave of Clubs"—Bridge Street—The Shops on London Bridge—The Bridge House—General Aspect of Southwark in the Middle Ages—Gradual Extension of Southwark—Great Fire in Southwark in 1676—Building of New London Bridge.

STOW, in his "Survey of London," advances as highly probable the hypothesis that when the first stone bridge was erected over the Thames the course of the river was temporarily changed, being diverted into a new channel, "a trench being cut for that purpose, beginning, as it is supposed, east, about Rotherhithe, and ending in the west, about Patricksey, now Battersea."

Strype, too, seems to support this view, when he writes: "It is much controverted whether the river Thames was turned when the bridge over it was built. . . . . But from all that hath been seen and written upon the turning of the river, it seems very evident to me that it *was* turned whilst the bridge was building." But Sir Christopher Wren, and after him Maitland, are of the contrary opinion, and think that Stow confused the ditch of the tenth century with that dug in the time of Knut.

Old London Bridge was said to have been "built on woolpacks:" this, however, is, of course, a play upon words, for, in reality, it was built largely out of the produce of a tax on wool. Stow also

states that the bridge-gate at the Southwark end was one of the four chief gates of the City of London, and that it stood there long before the Norman Conquest, when the bridge was only of timber. But this supposition again is strongly denied by Maitland.

Of London Bridge itself, and many of the historical scenes that were enacted upon it, we have already spoken in a previous part of this work ;[*] but Southwark has played too important a part on several occasions, in scenes connected with the bridge, to be altogether lost sight of here. Indeed, the bridge-foot must have seen very fine and gay sights in the old days before the Reformation, in the shape of religious and royal processions. For instance, in 1392, when Richard II. suspended and seized on the Charter of the City of London, and the citizens offered to re-purchase their rights for a sum of money, the king was graciously pleased to travel up to London from Windsor, "to re-assure

---

* See Vol. II., pp. 9--17.

them of his favour." The ceremony of publicly receiving their Majesties, we are told, began at Wandsworth, "with great splendour and a considerable train," when four hundred of the citizens of London, well mounted, and habited in livery of one colour, rode forth to meet the king. "At St. George's Church, in Southwark," says Thomas of Walsingham, "the procession was met by Robert Braybrooke, Bishop of London, and his clergy, followed by five hundred boys in surplices. . . . . When the train arrived at the gate of London Bridge, nearly the whole of the inhabitants, arranged in order according to their rank, age, and sex, advanced to receive it, and presented the king with a fair milk-white steed, harnessed and caparisoned in cloth of gold, brocaded in red and white, and hung about with silver bells; whilst to the queen (Anne of Bohemia) they presented a palfrey, also white, and caparisoned in like manner in white and red."

In 1212, the Priory of Southwark, and other parts adjoining the south end, were destroyed by fire, along with the greater part of the bridge itself, which was then of wood. The flames having caught the beams of the bridge, many of the Londoners lost their lives by fire, and others by water, being drowned in attempting to escape.

In the reign of Henry III. (A.D. 1307), Southwark was the scene of a conflict between the forces of the king and those of Simon de Montfort, the sturdy Earl of Leicester, which were marched, we are told, through the county of Surrey, and being victorious near the foot of the bridge, forced the king to beat a retreat, while De Montfort passed in triumph over the bridge into the City: the citizens of London being, nearly to a man, upon his side.

Splendid pageants were, doubtless, seen frequently here whilst the Court lived at the Tower, and when London Bridge was the only way from the south of England into the City. Of some of these we have already spoken in the chapter above referred to, particularly of those in the reign of Richard II., which was, indeed, a memorable reign for London Bridge.

King Henry V. was received here in great state on his return to London after the victory of Agincourt; an event which was celebrated in verse by John Lydgate or Lidgate, the monk of Bury:—

" To London Brygge then rode our kyng,
    The processions there they met him right;
Ave, rex Anglorum, they 'gan syng,
    Flos mundi, they said, Godde's knight.
To London Brygge when he com right
    Upon the gate he stode on hy—
A gyant that was full grym of myght
    To teche the Frenchmen curtesy.

Wot ye well that thus it was;
    Gloria tibi, Trinitas!"

Fabyan tells us, in his "Chronicles," that in 1437, on Monday, the 14th of January, the great stone gate and the tower standing upon it, next Southwark, fell suddenly down at the river, with two of the fairest arches of the said bridge." To which Stow piously adds, "And yet no man perished in body, which was a great work of Almighty God."

It appears from the narratives which have come down to us concerning the insurrections of Wat Tyler, Jack Cade, and Falconbridge, that in the Middle Ages Southwark was still somewhat destitute of fortifications; and, probably, its first regular defences were those of the circuit of fortifications thrown up by order of the Parliament during the civil war.

Jack Cade seems to have made Southwark his head-quarters all through his rebellion. In Shakespeare's vivid scenes of this rebellion (Henry VI., Part II.), a messenger tells the king:—

" Jack Cade hath gotten London Bridge; the citizens
    Fly and forsake their houses," &c.

Jack Cade, after his skirmish on Blackheath, took up his quarters at the "Hart Inn," both before and after his entry into the City. On the night of Sunday, July 5th, 1450, Cade being then in Southwark, the city captains, the mayor, aldermen, and commonalty of London, mounted guard upon the bridge. "The rebelles," says Hall, in his "Chronicle," "which neuer soundly slepte, for feare of sodayne chaunces, hearing the bridge to be kept and manned, ran with great haste to open the passage, where betwene bothe partes was a ferce and cruell encounter. Matthew Gough, more expert in marciall feates than the other cheuetaynes of the citie, perceiuing the Kentish men better to stand to their tacklyng than his ymagination expected, aduised his company no farther to procede toward Southwarke till the day appered; to the entent that the citizens hearing where the place of the ieopardye rested, might seccurre their enemies and releue their frendes and companions. But this counsail came to smal effect: for the multitude of the rebelles draue the citizens from the stulpes [wooden piles] at the bridge-foote, to the drawe-bridge, and began to set fyre in diuers houses. Alas! what sorow it was to beholde that miserable chaunce: for some desyringe to eschew the fyre lept on hys enemies weapon, and so died; fearfull women, with chyldren in their armes, amased and appalled, lept into the riuer; other, doubtinge how to saue them self betwene fyre, water, and sworud, were in their houses suffocate and smoldered; yet the captayns nothyng regarding these chaunces, fought on this drawe-bridge all the nyghte valeauntly, but in conclusion the rebelles gat the drawe-bridge, and drowned many, and slew John Sutton, alderman, and Robert Heysande, a hardy citizen, with many other, besyde Matthew Gough, a man of greate wit, much experience in feates of chiualrie, the which in continuall warres had valeauntly serued the king, and his father, in the partes beyond the sea. But it is often sene, that he which many tymes hath vanquyshed his enemies in straunge countreys, and returned agayn as a conqueror, hath of his owne nation afterward been shamfully murdered and brought to confusion. This hard and sore conflict endured on the bridge till ix of the clocke in the mornynge in doubtfull chaunce and fortune's balaunce: for some tyme the Londoners were bet back to the stulpes at Sainct Magnus Corner; and sodaynly agayne the rebelles were repulsed and dryuen back to the stulpes in Southwarke; so that both partes beyng faynte, wery, and fatygate, agreed to desist from fight, and to leue battayll till the next day, vpon condition that neyther Londoners should passe into Southwarke, nor the Kentish men into London."

During the truce that followed this defence of London Bridge, a general pardon was procured for Cade and his followers by the Lord High Chancellor, Archbishop Stafford; and all began to withdraw by degrees from Southwark with their spoil. Cade, however, was soon afterwards slain, and his dead body having been brought up to London, his head was placed over the south gate of London Bridge. Mr. Mark A. Lower has been at the trouble of recording the fact that he was slain, not at Hothfield, in Kent, but at Heathfield, near Cuckfield, in Sussex, where a roadside monument is erected in his honour. It bears the following inscription:—

"Near this spot was slain the notorious rebel,
JACK CADE,
By Alexander Iden, Sheriff of Kent, A.D. 1450.
His body was carried to London, and his head fixed on London Bridge.
This is the success of all rebels, and this fortune chanceth ever to traitors."—*Hall's Chronicle.*

By that awful gate which looked towards Southwark, for a period of nearly three hundred years, under Tudor and Stuart sovereigns, it must have been a rare thing for the passenger to walk without seeing one or more human heads stuck upon a pike, looking down upon the flow of the river below, and rotting and blackening in the sun. The head of the noble Sir William Wallace was for many

months exposed on this spot. In 1471 Falconbridge—"the bastard Falconbridge"—made Southwark his head-quarters in his impudent attack on London. He arrived here in May, giving out that he came to free King Henry from his captivity; and by way of proof of his intention, burnt part of the bridge, together with some of the houses in the suburbs of Southwark. After meeting with defeat, his head and those of nine of his comrades were stuck together on ten spears, where they remained visible to all comers, till the elements and the carrion crows had left nothing of them there but the bones. At a later period the head of the pious Fisher, Bishop of Rochester, was stuck up here, along with that of the honest and philosophic Sir Thomas More. The quarters of Sir Thomas Wyatt, the son of the well-known poet of that name, were exhibited here, at the end of the bridge, during the reign of Queen Mary.

One of the most imposing pageants witnessed at London Bridge was that accorded here by the citizens to Henry VI., on his return to London, after having been crowned King of France in the church of Notre Dame at Paris; the "pageant" consisting, if Fabyan may be trusted, of a "mighty gyaunt standyng, with a swoard drawen," and figures of three "emperesses," representing Nature, Grace, and Fortune; with seven maidens, all in white, representing the seven orders of the angelic host, who addressed the king in verses recorded at full length by Lydgate, of which the following stanza may serve as a sample:—

"God the (thee) endue with a crowne of glorie,
    And with a sceptre of clennesse and pité,
    And with a shield of right and victorie,
    And with a mantel of prudence clad thou be:
    A shelde of faith for to defendé the,
    An helme of hettlé wrought to thine encres
    Girt with a girdel of loue and perfect peese (peace)."

Henry VII. was received here in pomp, after defeating the insurgents, in 1497; the heads of the leaders of the outbreak, Flamoke and Joseph, being set over the entrance to the bridge.

In 1501, Prince Arthur, eldest son of Henry VII., with his bride, Katharine of Aragon, was welcomed here on his way from "Lambhithe" to witness the rejoicings prepared for them in the City. Stow tells us, in his "Annals," "that at the entrance of London Bridge they were greeted by a costly pageant of St. Katharine and St. Ursula, with many virgins." How little did she then think of the fate that awaited her!

Cardinal Wolsey rode in great state over the bridge, and through the High Street, Southwark, and along the Kentish Road, when he left the kingdom in 1526, for the purpose of arranging a marriage between Henry VIII. and the Duchess d'Alencon. Two years later, the public entry of Cardinal Campeggio, as legate from the Pope, into London, to deal with the question of Henry's divorce from Queen Katharine, must have been a brave sight. The nobility rode in advance from Blackheath towards London Bridge, "well mounted, and wearing elegant attire;" then came the cardinal himself, in magnificent robes, "glittering with jewels and precious stones;" then his "cross-bearers, the carriers of his pole-axes, his servants in red livery, his secretaries, physicians, and general suite." Next came two hundred horsemen and a "vast concourse of people." The procession is said to have grown to two miles in length before it reached the City gates. From St. George's Church to the foot of the bridge the road was lined on both sides by the monks and the other clergy, dressed in their various habits, with copes of cloth of gold, silver and gold crosses, and banners, who, we are told, as the legate passed, "threw up clouds of incense and sang hymns." At the foot of the bridge two bishops received the cardinal, the people shouted for joy, whilst all the bells of the City were rung, and the roar of artillery from the Tower and the river-forts "rent the air"—to use Wolsey's own words—"as if the very heavens would fall."

In the insurrection of Sir Thomas Wyatt in 1553-4,* Southwark formed the rallying-point for that misguided rebel and his force, some four thousand strong. His soldiers, meeting with but little opposition on the south of the Thames, attacked and sacked the palace of the Bishop of Winchester, whose fine library they destroyed. As the artillery in the Tower began to fire on Southwark next day, in order to dislodge Sir Thomas, the inhabitants urged him to retreat, in order to save them from loss and destruction. His subsequent movements and his ultimate fate we have already recorded.

Stow tells us, in his "Survey" (vol. i., p. 64), that in April, 1577, the tower at the northern end having become decayed, a new one was commenced in its place; and that during the interval the heads of the traitors which had formerly stood upon it were set upon the tower over the gate at Bridge-foot, Southwark, which consequently came to be called the Traitors' Gate. It may be remembered that John Houghton, the Prior of the Charter-house, Sir Thomas More, and Bishop Fisher, were among the "traitors" who were thus treated.

About the time when these heads were removed, several alterations and improvements would seem to have been made in the bridge, especially in the erection of a "beautiful and chargeable piece of wood"—i.e., a magnificent wood mansion, which formed a second Southwark Gate and Tower.

It is worthy of note that after the defeat of the Spanish Armada, eleven of the captured standards were hung upon London Bridge at the end looking towards Southwark, on the day of Southwark Fair, "to the great joy of all the people who repaired thither."

When the Parliamentary cause was in the ascendant, and King Charles was expected to attack the City, Southwark was rapidly fortified, particularly about the foot of London Bridge, like the other outlying portions of the metropolis; † and one of Cromwell's officers, Colonel Rainsborough, with a brigade of horse and foot, was able to hold the whole borough of Southwark almost without opposition.

On Tuesday, the 29th of May, 1660, King Charles II. entered London in triumph, after having been magnificently entertained in St. George's Fields. About three in the afternoon he arrived in Southwark, and thence proceeded over the bridge into the City, attended by all the glory of London and the military forces of the kingdom. Lord Clarendon, who makes this "fair return of banished majesty" the concluding scene of his noble "History of the Great Rebellion," gives us but little information as to the details of the king's reception at London Bridge, though we learn incidentally from his pages that "the crowd was very great."

Bloome, one of the continuators of Stow, expressly says that in the Great Fire some of the old houses at the south end of the bridge—several of them built in the reign of King John—escaped the flames.

Two Gothic towers—not uniform in plan, however—defended the southern end of the original bridge, and also of the second. At this end of the bridge were, likewise, four corn-mills, based on three sterlings, which projected far into the river westward. They were covered with a long shed, formed of shingles or thin boards, and could certainly have been no ornament to the structure to which they were an appendage. We have already spoken of the houses and shops which lined the roadway of old London Bridge,‡ but we may here make mention of the tradesmen's tokens which were once in use here. A full list of those used in

---

Southwark will be found in the appendix to Manning and Bray's "History of Surrey." Several of these tokens relate to London Bridge. The author of "Chronicles of London Bridge" gives illustrations of several, among which is a copper token, farthing size, having on the one side, to speak heraldically, a bear passant, chained; and on the reverse, the words "Abraham Browne, at y° Bridge-foot, Southwark; his half penny." Another copper frequently by name by writers of the seventeenth century.

Thus Pepys writes, under date April 3, 1667 :— "I hear how the king is not so well pleased of this marriage between the Duke of Richmond and Mrs. Stuart, as is talked; and that he, by a wile, did fetch her to the 'Bear' at the Bridge-foot, where a coach was ready, and they are stole away into Kent without the King's leave." Mr. Larwood

PRIORY OF ST. MARY OVERY, 1700.

token shows the same device, with the legend "Cornelius Cook, at the 'Beare' at the Bridge-foot." Another displays a sugar-loaf, with the name, "Henry Phillips, at the Bridj-foot, Southwark."

The end of London Bridge, on the Southwark side, was known as Bridge-foot. The "Bear" here was, for some centuries, one of the most popular of London taverns; indeed, if we may accept Mr. Larwood's statement, it was the resort of aristocratic pleasure-seekers as early as the reign of Richard III. Thus, in March, 1463–4, it was repeatedly visited by the "Jockey of Norfolk," then Sir John Howard, who went thither to drink wine and shoot at the target. Peter Cunningham, in his "London, Past and Present," adds that the "Bear" is mentioned

observes that the wine sold at this establishment did not meet with the approbation of the fastidious searchers after claret in 1691 :—

"Through stinks of all sorts, both the simple and compound,
  Which through narrow alleys our senses do confound,
  We came to the Bear, which we now understood
  Was the first house in Southwark built after the flood;
  And has such a succession of visitors known,
  Not more names were e'er in Welch pedigrees shown;
  But claret with them was so much out of fashion,
  That it has not been known there for a whole generation."
    (*Last Search after Claret in Southwark*, 1691.)

This old tavern was taken down in December, 1761, when a quantity of coins, dating as far back as the reign of Elizabeth, were found, as may be seen by a reference to the *Public Advertiser* of that date. We learn from the Harleian manuscripts that there was here another old inn, known as the "Knave of Clubs," kept by one Edward Butling, whose advertisement states that he "maketh and selleth all sorts of hangings for rooms, &c.," and who, probably, also sold playing-cards, if his sign had any meaning.

Bridge Street, probably, extended itself gradually on to the bridge itself; the houses being distinguished by signs, some of which have come down to our times, in the works of antiquaries and on on London Bridge, facing Tooley Street, sells all sorts (of) leather breeches, leather, and gloves, wholesale and retail, at reasonable rates." It is clear, from these notices, that it was very doubtful where London Bridge ended and Bridge Street actually began.

In the sixteenth century, the street on the bridge ranked with St. Paul's Churchyard, Paternoster Row, and Little Britain, as one of the principal literary emporia of the City. "The Three Bibles," "The

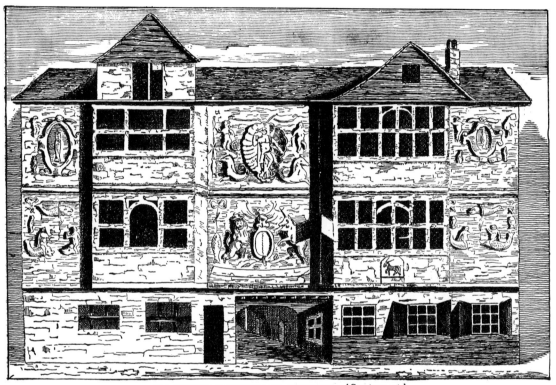

OLD HOUSES FORMERLY AT BANKSIDE. (*See page* 45.)

tradesmen's tokens and bill-heads. For instance : there is extant a small copper-plate tobacco paper, probably of the reign of Queen Anne, with a coarse and rude engraving of a negro smoking, and holding in his hand a roll of tobacco ; above his head is a crown, two ships in full sail are behind, and the sun issues from the right-hand corner above ; in the foreground are four little negroes planting and packing tobacco, and beneath is the name "John Winkley, Tobacconist, near yͤ Bridge, in the Burrough, Southwark." We have also seen another shop bill, of about the same date, displaying, within a rich cartouche frame, a pair of embroidered small-clothes and a glove : beneath is the legend, "Walter Watkins, Breeches-maker, Leather-seller, and Glover, at the sign of the 'Breeches and Glove,'

Angel," and "The Looking-Glass," are some of the signs of the publishers established "on London Bridge," and mentioned on the title-pages of books published at this date.

John Bunyan at one time certainly used to preach in a chapel in Southwark ; but, in all probability, the author of "Wine and Walnuts" is using the vagueness of after-dinner talkers when he says that the converted tinker lived on London Bridge. Perhaps he was led into the error by the fact that one of Bunyan's lesser books was published there.

The Bridge House and Yard in Tooley Street are closely connected with the history of the bridge itself. For Stow tells us, in his "Survey" (vol. ii., p. 24), that they were so called as being "a store-house for stone, timber, or whatsoever pertaineth to the building or repairing of London Bridge." He adds that this Bridge House "seemeth to have taken beginning with the first foundation of the bridge, either of stone or timber;" and that it covers "a large plot of ground on the banks of the river Thames, containing divers large buildings for the stowage of materials" for the bridge. The Bridge House, in fact, was long used as a receptacle of provisions for the navy, and as a store-house for the public in times of dearth; ovens were attached to it, in which the biscuit for the Royal Navy was baked. It was also used on certain occasions as a banqueting-hall, when the Lord Mayor came in his official capacity to the borough. One of these occasions was at the opening of Southwark Fair, of which we shall have more to say presently. We may state here, however, that the fair was instituted in the reign of Edward VI., and was held annually in the month of September. "At the time of this fair, anciently called 'Our Lady's Fair in Southwark,'" observes the author of "Chronicles of London Bridge," "the Lord Mayor and Sheriffs used to ride to St. Magnus' Church after dinner, at two o'clock in the afternoon, the former being vested with his collar of SS., without his hood, and all dressed in the scarlet gowns, lined, without their cloaks. They were attended by the sword-bearer, wearing his embroidered cap, and carrying the 'pearl' sword; and at church were met by the aldermen, all of whom, after evening prayer, rode over the bridge in procession, and passed through the fair, and continued either to St. George's Church, Newington Bridge, or the stones pointing out the City Liberties at St. Thomas of Waterings. They then returned over the bridge, or to the Bridge House, where a banquet was provided, and the aldermen took leave of the Lord Mayor; all parties being returned home, the Bridge Masters gave a supper to the Lord Mayor's officers."

"The two governors of the bridge," writes the author of the work above quoted, "have an excellent house in the suburb of Southwark, as well as a store-house, containing everything belonging to their occupation." From the same work we learn that a cross, charged with a small saltire, is supposed to have been the old heraldic device for Southwark or the estate of London Bridge; and we know that the arms used for those places are still Azure, an amulet, ensigned with a cross patée, Or, interlaced with a saltire, conjoined in base of the second.

The following just remarks on the general aspect of Southwark in the Middle Ages are taken from Dr. R. Paule's " Pictures of Old London : "—" On the other side of the river lay many points, isolated and unconnected with one another, which are now joined together into a district of the town that numbers its hundreds of thousands of inhabitants. It was only at the outlet of the bridge at Southwark that, from different causes, there had arisen in ancient times a town-like settlement. Two great priories—the monastery of St. Mary Overies and the convent of Bermondsey—had early given rise to the active and busy intercommunication which naturally resulted from the vicinity of such ecclesiastical institutions as these were. Near to St. Mary's, and not far from the bridge, there stood till the time of the Reformation the magnificent palace of the Bishop of Winchester, one of the wealthiest and most powerful prelates in the land, and whose extensive spiritual jurisdiction included the county of Surrey. The most important agent in this great intercommunication was the high road which ran from the bridge, and extended through the southern counties to the ports of Kent, Sussex, and Hampshire. Here heavily-laden wagons were constantly moving to and fro; and here, too, assembled, at the appointed seasons of the year, the motley crowd of pilgrims who were bound for the shrine of the holy Thomas à Becket at Canterbury. The 'Tabard' inn had been known far and near for many ages, from the vivid descriptions given by Chaucer of the busy life and stir which blended there with devotion and adventure. All remains of it are not yet (1861) effaced, although there has been erected in its immediate neighbourhood the railway terminus of that great overland route which connects England with India. . . . . The greater part of the land lying on the opposite (i.e., the Surrey) bank of the river consisted of fields and gardens, with a few larger hamlets, and some places of amusement, where bear-baiting and cock-fighting were practised. Immediately opposite to Westminster rose the chapel and castellated towers and walls of the princely residence which the Archbishops of Canterbury had chosen before the close of the twelfth century for their town residence, in the immediate neighbourhood of the chief offices of state and the tribunals of justice." Such must have been, speaking generally, the appearance of Southwark five centuries ago.

In the time of Elizabeth, if we may rely on the statements of the "Penny Cyclopædia," Southwark appears to have consisted of a line of street extending from the bridge nearly to where now is the Borough Road, formerly called "Long Southwark;" Kent Street, then the high road to Canterbury and Dover, and of which only the part near St. George's Church was lined with houses; a line of street, including Tooley or St. Olave's Street, extending from the "Bridge-foot" to Rotherhithe Church; another line of street running westward by Bankside to where is now the Blackfriars Road; and, lastly, Bermondsey Street, branching off from Tooley Street to Bermondsey Church. Excepting near St. Saviour's Church, there were at that time scarcely any back or cross streets. Near Bankside were the Bishop of Winchester's palace, the Globe Theatre, the "Stews," and two "Bear Gardens" for baiting bulls and bears. The "villages" of Lambeth, Kennington, Newington, and Walworth were then separated from Southwark, and from each other also, by open fields.

Towards the end of the seventeenth century Southwark had extended itself considerably. The houses on the east side of Blackman Street now stretched to Newington and Walworth, which thus became joined on to the metropolis, though St. George's Fields, on the western side, still remained open country. Back streets, also, and alleys had been formed on either side of High Street, as far as St. George's Church. In the early part of the eighteenth century the buildings of Southwark extended along the river-side as far as Lambeth; and in the opposite direction Rotherhithe Street was continued to and even beyond Cuckold's Point, where the river bends to the southward. Later still, in the middle of the eighteenth century, the opening of Blackfriars Bridge led to the formation of Great Surrey Street; and towards the close of the century, St. George's Fields were enclosed and laid out in new streets. Since the commencement of the present century, Lambeth Marsh—which formerly separated Southwark from Lambeth—has been covered with new streets and buildings; and in every direction Southwark has spread itself till it has united itself with all the surrounding villages, from Greenwich in the far east to Battersea in the far west, and combined them into one large town, having a population of about 300,000, of which Southwark proper may be regarded as the nucleus.

In a little less than ten years after the Great Fire of London—namely, in May, 1676—Southwark was visited by a fire which did, in proportion, almost equal damage with the conflagration which has become historical. "It broke out," writes Mr. C. Walford, in the "Insurance Cyclopædia," "at an oilman's, between the 'George' and 'Tabard' inns, opposite St. Margaret's Hill. The front of the 'Tabard' was consumed, but was immediately rebuilt, presumably in *fac-simile* of the original, with its court-yard, galleries, pilgrim's hall, and quaint old sleeping-rooms. It is doubtful," he adds, "how far any part of the hotel then burnt may have been part of the actual inn described by Chaucer: where, on the eve of a pilgrimage, the pretty prioress, the 'Wife of Bath,' the 'Knight,' the 'Squire,' the 'Sumpnour,' and the 'Pardoner,' met, chatted, laughed, and flirted. The 'White Hart,' whose name was connected with that of Jack Cade, was also burnt in this fire. The fire-engines were first worked with hose-pipes on this occasion, and did good service. It was probably owing to these that the conflagration was stayed at St. Thomas's Hospital."

The king (Charles II.) was so much touched by the sight, which recalled vividly the scenes which he had witnessed ten years before, that he went down the river in his state-barge to London Bridge, in order "to give such orders as His Majesty found fit for putting a stop to it." It is difficult, however, to see how a king could be of more use in such an emergency than a good chief-fireman, or even of as much service. The buildings being as yet, like those of Old London, chiefly of timber, lath, and plaster, the fire spread extensively; and its farther progress was stayed only "after that about 600 houses had been burnt or blown up."

Old London Bridge, and the street winding southward from it, were situated about a hundred feet eastward of the present bridge and its approach from the High Street. The building of New London Bridge was actually commenced on the 15th of May, 1824, when the first coffer-dam for the southern pier was driven into the bed of the river; the first stone was laid in June, 1825; and the bridge was publicly opened by William IV. and Queen Adelaide on the 1st of August, 1831. "I was present, a few days ago," writes Lucy Aikin, in September of that year, "at the splendid spectacle of the opening of new London Bridge. It was covered half-way over with a grand canopy, formed of the flags of all nations, near which His Majesty dined with about two thousand of his loyal subjects. The river was thronged with gilded barges and boats, covered with streamers, and crowded with gaily-dressed people; the shores were alive with the multitude. In the midst of the gay show I looked down the stream upon the old, deserted, half-demolished bridge, the silent remembrancer of seven centuries. I thought of it fortified, with a lofty gate at either end, and encumbered with a row of houses on each side. I beheld it the scene of tournaments; I saw its barrier closed against the rebel Wyatt; and I wished myself a poet for its sake."

CHAPTER III.

SOUTHWARK (*continued*).—ST. SAVIOUR'S CHURCH, &c.

> " How many an antique monument is found
> Illegible, and faithless to its charge !
> That deep insculp'd once held in measured phrase
> The mighty deeds of those who sleep below :
> Of hero, sage, or saint, whose pious hands
> Those ponderous masses raised—forgotten now,
> They and their monuments alike repose."

The Limits of Southwark as a Borough—The Liberty of the Clink—The Old High Street—The Clock-tower at London Bridge—The Borough Market—Old St. Saviour's Grammar School—The Patent of Foundation granted by Queen Elizabeth—St. Saviour's Church—The Legend of Old Audrey, the Ferryman—Probable Derivation of the Name of Overy, or Overie—Foundation of the Priory of St. Mary Overy—Burning of the Priory in 1212—Building of the Church of St. Mary Magdalen—Historical Events connected with the Church—Religious Ceremonies and Public Processions—Alterations and Restorations of St. Saviour's Church—The Lady Chapel used as a Bakehouse—Bishop Andrewes' Chapel—John Gower, John Fletcher, and other Noted Personages buried here—Hollar's Etchings—Montague Close.

BEFORE proceeding with an examination of the various objects of antiquarian interest abounding in the locality, it may be as well to state that Southwark is a general name, sometimes taken and understood as including, and sometimes as excluding Rotherhithe, Bermondsey, and Lambeth. We shall use it, at present, in the latter sense.

Black's "Guide to London," published in 1863, divides the district south of the Thames into two principal portions :—" 1. Southwark, known also as 'the Borough,' including Bermondsey and Rotherhithe, with a population of about 194,000. 2. Lambeth, with the adjacent but outlying districts of Kennington, Walworth, Newington, Wandsworth, and Camberwell, with a population of 386,000." Southwark is always called "the Borough" by Londoners; and very naturally so, for it has been a "borough" literally, having returned two members to Parliament since the twenty-third year of Edward I., and it was for several centuries the only "borough" adjacent to the "cities" of London and Westminster. Under the first Reform Bill (1832) its limits as a borough were extended by the addition of the parishes of Christ Church, Bermondsey, and Rotherhithe, and also of the "Liberty of the Clink."

The Liberty of the Clink, as we learn from the "Penny Cyclopædia" (1842), belongs to the Bishop of Winchester, whose palace, of which we shall presently speak, stood near the western end of St. Saviour's Church, and who appoints for it—or, at all events, till very lately appointed—a steward and a bailiff. This part of Southwark appears not to have been included in the grant to the City.

In the "New View of London" (1708) we read, "The Manor of Southwark, by some called the Clink Liberty, is, in extent, about a quarter of the parish of St. Saviour's. The civil government of it is under the Bishop of Winchester, who keeps court by his steward and bailiff, who hold pleas as at the Burrough (*sic*) for debt, damage, &c., for which manor there is a prison."

There is nothing romantic, to say the least, in the situation of Southwark. At the best it is a dead flat, unmixed by a single acre of rising ground. "What a contrast," exclaims Charles Mackay, in "The Thames and its Tributaries," "is there now, and always has been, in both the character and the appearance of the two sides of the river ! The London side, high and well built, thickly studded with spires and public edifices, and resounding with all the noise of the operations of a various industry ; the Southwark and Lambeth side, low and flat, and meanly built, with scarcely an edifice higher than a wool-shed or timber-yard, and a population with a squalid, dejected, and debauched look, offering a remarkable contrast to the cheerfulness and activity visible on the very faces of the Londoners. The situation of Southwark upon the low swamp is, no doubt, one cause of the unhealthy appearance of the dwellers on the south side of the Thames ; but the dissolute and rakish appearance of the lower orders among them must be otherwise accounted for. From a very early age, if the truth must be told, Southwark and Lambeth, and especially the former, were the great sinks and receptacles of all the vice and immorality of London. Down to the year 1328 Southwark had been independent of the jurisdiction of London—a sort of neutral ground which the law could not reach—and, in consequence, the abode of thieves and abandoned characters of every kind. They used to sally forth in bands of a hundred or two hundred at a time to rob in the City ; and the Lord Mayor and aldermen for the time being had not unfrequently to keep watch upon the bridge for nights together, at the head of a troop of armed men, to prevent their inroads. The thieves, however, on these occasions took to their boats at midnight, and rowing up the river landed at Westminster, where they drove all before them with as much valour and as great impunity as a border chieftain upon a foray into Cumberland. These things induced the magistrates of London to apply to Edward III. for a grant of Southwark. The request was complied with, and the vicious place was brought under the rule of the City. Driven, in some measure, from their nest, the thieves took refuge in Lambeth, and still set the authorities at defiance. From that day to this the two boroughs have had pretty much the same character, and have been known as the favourite resort of thieves and vagabonds of every description." It is to be hoped that in this description of the character of the "Londoners over the water," Dr. Mackay has written with a little of poetical licence, not to say exaggeration, as he certainly has over-stated the squalidity of their buildings. The huge palaces of commerce erected on either side of Southwark Street in 1875 give the most palpable contradiction to his statements, which perhaps were a little in excess of the truth in 1840, when he wrote.

Down to the time of the demolition of Old London Bridge, and the consequent formation of the present broad approach to the new bridge, Southwark retained much of its antique character. The old High Street, then rich with its pointed gables, and half-timbered over-hanging storeys, with florid plaster-work and diamond casements, such as characterised the street architecture of ancient London—is now quite altered in appearance. All the picturesque features here mentioned have long been swept away, and their place was for a time supplied by the unbroken parapets and the monotonous brick front of lines of shops; but even these in turn have in part been superseded by buildings altogether of another age and style; we refer to the Grecian and Italianised façade of the western side of the present High Street, immediately on our right as we leave the bridge.

"The street of Old Southwark," writes John Timbs, in his "Autobiography," "was in a line shelving down from the bridge, and crowded with traffic from morn till night. We remember, about 1809, watching from our nursery window the demolition of a long range of wood-and-plaster and gabled houses on the west side of High Street; and in 1830 were removed two houses of the time of Henry VII., with bay windows and picturesque plaster decorations, reported, though we know not with how much truth, to have been the abode of Queen Anne Boleyn."

Brayley, in his "History of Surrey," remarks: "The principal street [of Southwark] is the High Street, forming a portion of the great road from London through Surrey, and running in a south westerly direction from London Bridge to St. Margaret's Hill, and thence to St. George's Church. The part between the bridge and St. Margaret's Hill was formerly called *Long* Southwark, but is now called Wellington Street, from which the way is called High Street as far as St. George's Church."

Near the foot of the bridge, and at the point where the high level of the bridge begins to slope down to the original level of the ground, the road is crossed by the railway bridge over which are carried the lines connecting London Bridge station with the stations at Cannon Street and Charing Cross. Here, too, in the centre of the roadway, stood for some few years a clock-tower of Gothic design, surmounted by a spire, and originally intended, we believe, to have contained a statue of the Duke of Wellington. The tower itself was erected about the year 1854, but the statue was never placed in it; and having been found to be a continual block to the traffic over the bridge, the tower itself was in the end demolished.

At the time of the alterations made here, in consequence of the rebuilding of London Bridge, advantage was taken to carry out another improvement for the benefit of the locality, namely, the erection of a new market-place. Inconvenience having arisen from the situation of the old market, which used to be held in the High Street, between London Bridge and St. Margaret's Hill, two Acts of Parliament were obtained in the middle of the last century, in pursuance of which a market-house was erected on a piece of ground westward of the High Street, called Rochester Yard, from having been formerly the site of a mansion belonging to the see of Rochester, which was taken down in the year 1604, and the site of which is still marked by Rochester Street. The market-place now consists of a large open paved space on the south side of St. Saviour's churchyard; in one corner of it a neat granite drinking-fountain has been erected. Several buildings, of a light and airy character, to serve the purposes of the dealers and others in the market—which, by the way, is devoted to the sale of vegetables, &c.—occupy the south side of the open space; the principal feature in these buildings is the large central dome. A considerable addition of space was made to the market-place in 1839 by the demolition of the old St. Saviour's Grammar School, which had existed on that spot since the time of Queen Elizabeth. "The old school," as we learn from the *Mirror*, vol. xxxv. (1840), "was a handsome structure, with very spacious school-room, having the master's seat, with sounding-board over. The exterior was a brick fabric, consisting of three casement windows on each side of a large doorway, ascended by three semi-circular stone steps, with a handsome carved dome, representing two children supporting the Bible. The second storey had seven lofty case-

wark, having been purchased by the inhabitants as a parish church, the desire of instilling useful knowledge among youth induced Thomas Cure, the queen's saddler, and several other benevolent persons, to found the grammar-school we are now describing for the instruction of thirty boys of the

INTERIOR OF ST. SAVIOUR'S CHURCH.

ment windows ; the rooms panelled. The school was screened from the churchyard by an iron railing."

When Queen Elizabeth came to the throne, following the example of her brother, Edward VI., she considered the importance of diffusing knowledge among the people, to forward which she not only re-founded the grammar-school of Westminster, but encouraged her subjects to other like acts of benevolence.

The priory church of St. Mary Overy, South-

same parish ; and for this purpose they obtained letters patent from Queen Elizabeth, in the fourth year of her reign. In these it is recited of the said grammar-school :—

"That Thomas Cure, William Browker, Christopher Campbell, and other discret and *more sad* inhabitants of St. Saviour's, had, at their own great costs and pains, devised, erected, and set up a grammar-school, wherein the children of the poor, as well as the rich inhabitants, were freely brought up ; that they had applied for a charter to establish

VIEWS OF ST. SAVIOUR'S CHURCH.

1. Interior of Chapel, East End of St. Saviour's.   2. Lady Chapel.   3. Part of Priory of St. Saviour's.   4. St. Saviour's Church.
5. Montague Close.   6. Chapel at End of St. Saviour's.

a succession ; she therefore wills that it shall be one grammar-school for Education of the Children of the Parishioners and Inhabitants of St. Saviour, to be called 'A Free Grammar-school of the Parishioners of St. Saviour in Southwark,' to have one master and one under-master ; six of the more discreet and *sad* inhabitants to be governors, by the name of 'Governors of the Possessions and Revenues and Goods of the Free Grammar-school of the Parishioners of the Parish of St. Saviour, Southwark, in the county of Surrey, incorporate and erected ;' and they are thereby incorporated, to have perpetual succession, with power to purchase lands, &c., and that on death or other causes the remaining governors, and twelve others of the more discreet and godliest inhabitants, by the governors to be named, should elect a meet person or governor . . . having power, with advice of the Bishop of Winchester, or he being absent, with advice of any good or learned man, to appoint a schoolmaster and usher from time to time, &c., ... and also power to purchase lands not exceeding £40 a year.

"All that the parishioners obtained by this patent of Queen Elizabeth was to be made a corporate body with succession ; the queen gave them nothing to endow their school. It seems to have been some time before they proceeded any farther, for the first patent of Elizabeth granted a lease of the rectory for sixty years, in order that a school should be erected ; but by a subsequent patent it appears that it had not been built till after 1585. "In 1676 the school was burnt in the great fire which then destroyed a large part of Southwark, but it was soon rebuilt."

The new building having become sadly dilapidated in 1830, the governors resolved on erecting a new school near St. Peter's Church, in Sumner Street, the ground being given for the purpose by Dr. Sumner, Bishop of Winchester, and accordingly the ancient grammar-school was taken down. We shall have more to say about St. Saviour's Grammar School when we reach Sumner Street.

St. Saviour's Church—one of the finest parochial churches in the kingdom—in spite of the barbarous mutilation which it underwent when its nave was pulled down, is now almost the sole remaining object of "Old Southwark." In spite of the loss of its original nave, it is deservedly styled by Mr. A. Wood, in his "Ecclesiastical Antiquities of London," "the second church in the metropolis, and the first in the county of Surrey." It is one of the few parish churches in the kingdom possessing a "lady chapel" still perfect.

Before the Reformation it was styled the priory church of St. Mary Overy, and its early history is almost lost in the mists of ancient tradition. There is a curious legend connecting the building of the original London Bridge with the church of St. Mary Overy, but it has been much discredited. The story is related on the authority of Stow, who chronicled it as the report of the last prior, Bartholomew Linsted :—

"A ferry being kept in the place where now the bridge is builded, at length the ferryman and his wife deceasing, left the same ferry to their only daughter, a maiden named Mary, who, with the goods left her by her parents, as also with the profits of the said ferry, built an house of Sisters on the place where now standeth the east part of St. Mary Overy's Church, above the quire, where she was buried, unto which house she gave the oversight and profits of the ferry. But afterwards the said house of Sisters being converted into a college of priests, the priests builded the bridge of timber, as all the other great bridges of this land were, and from time to time kept the same in good reparation ; till at length, considering the great charges which were bestowed in the same, there was, by aid of the citizens and others, a bridge builded with stone."

The story of the miserly old ferryman, Audrey, Mary's father—how he counterfeited death in order that his household might forego a day's victuals, as he never supposed but that their sorrow would make them fast at least so long ; and how strangely he was deceived—has already been told by us.* As the story, however—regardless of its improbability —is as closely connected with this venerable fabric as it is with London Bridge itself, we may be pardoned for recapitulating some of the main incidents of the tradition. No sooner had the old man—so runs the story—been decently laid out, than those about him fell to feasting and making merry, rejoicing at the death of the old sinner, who, stretched in apparent death, bore their rioting for a short time, but at length sprang from his bed, and, seizing the first weapon at hand, attacked his apprentice. The encounter was fatal to him ; and his daughter, the gentle, fair-haired Mary, the heiress of his wealth, devoted it to the establishment of a House of Sisters as above mentioned. The house bore her name of Mary Audrey, with the saintly prefix ; but in the lapse of time, Audrey became corrupted into "Overie." Some old writers, however, suggest that the religious house was originally founded in honour of the popular Saxon saint Audrey, or Etheldreda, of Ely. But a more pro-

---

* See Vol. II., p. 9.

bable derivation of the name than either of the foregoing is from " over the rie," that is " over the water." Even in these days Londoners north of the Thames invariably designate the whole of the southern suburbs as " over the water ; " and the phrase may perhaps be as old as the time of the building of St. Mary's " over the rie."

Long after the good Mary Audrey (or Overie) died—if, indeed, she ever lived—a noble lady named Swithen changed the House of Sisters into a college for priests ; and in 1106 two Norman knights, William Pont de l'Arche and William Dauncey, re-founded it as a house for canons of the Augustine order. Giffard, then Bishop of Winchester, built the conventual church and the palace in Winchester Yard close by. It was in this priory that the fire broke out in 1212, when the greater part of Southwark was destroyed, and another fire breaking out simultaneously at the northern end of London Bridge an immense crowd was enclosed between the two fires, and 3,000 persons were burned or drowned. The canons thus burnt out established a temporary place of worship on the opposite side of the main road, which they dedicated to St. Thomas, and occupied for about three years until their own church was repaired.

The church was then dedicated to St. Mary Magdalen. In 1273, Walter, Archbishop of York, granted an indulgence of thirty days to all who should contribute to the rebuilding of the sacred edifice, and towards the end of the following century the church was entirely rebuilt. Gower, the poet, it is stated, contributed a considerable portion of the funds.

In 1404 Cardinal Beaufort was consecrated to the see of Winchester, and two years later was celebrated in this church the marriage of Edmund Holland, Earl of Kent, with Lucia, eldest daughter of Barnaby, Lord of Milan. Henry IV. himself gave away the bride " at the church door," and afterwards conducted her to the marriage banquet at Winchester Palace. It was in this church, too, a few years subsequently (1424), that James I. of Scotland wedded the daughter of the Earl of Somerset, and niece of the great Cardinal, the golden-haired beauty, Jane Beaufort, of whom, during his imprisonment at Windsor, the royal poet had become enamoured, doubting, when he first saw her from his window, whether she was

> " A worldly creature,
> Or heavenly thing in likeness of nature."

At all events, the king describes her in his verses as

> " The fairest and the freshest yonge flower
> That ever I saw, methought, before that hour."

The marriage feast on this occasion, too, was kept in the great hall of Winchester Palace, and in a style befitting the munificence of the cardinal. The marriage, as we are told, was a happy one, and the bards of Scotland vied with each other in singing the praises of the queen, and in extolling her beauty and her conjugal affection. In 1437 James was murdered by his subjects, his brave queen being twice wounded in endeavouring to save his life.

At the dissolution of religious houses, in 1539, the priory of black canons—for such was that of St. Mary Overy's—of course shared the general fate of monastic establishments ; but the last prior, Bartholomew Linsted, had the good fortune of obtaining from Henry VIII. a yearly pension of £100. The inhabitants of the parishes of St. Mary Magdalen and St. Margaret-at-Hill—which latter church stood on the west side of the High Street, on the spot till recently occupied by the Town Hall—purchased, with the assistance of Stephen Gardiner, Bishop of Winchester, the stately church of St. Mary. The priory church was also at the same time purchased from the king, and the two parishes were united under the title of St. Saviour's, the priory church having been recognised by the name of St. Saviour's for nearly thirty years before. At the same time the churchwardens and vestry were constituted a " corporation sole." Six years before that period a dole had been given at the door of the church, and so great was the crowd and pressure on that occasion that several persons were killed. In pre-Reformation times this church was the scene of many religious ceremonies and public processions. One of these, conducted with great pomp and ceremony, is described by Fosbroke in his economy of monastic life, as follows :—

> " Then two and two they march'd, and loud bells toll'd :
>   One from a sprinkle holy water flung ;
>   This bore the relics from a chest of gold,
>   On arm of that the swinging censor hung ;
>   Another loud a tinkling hand-bell rung.
>   Four fathers went that singing monk behind,
>   Who suited Psalms of Holy David sung ;
>   Then o'er the cross a stalking sire inclined,
>   And banners of the church went waving in the wind."

Various alterations and restorations have at different times been made in the fabric of the church. The Lady Chapel, at the eastern end, is a relic of the older edifice. The tower of the church was repaired in 1689 ; and in 1822 a complete restoration of the fine Gothic edifice was commenced. The brick casings with which generations of " Goths " had hidden the beautiful architecture were removed ; groined roof and transepts were restored, and a circular window of rare beauty added. But even in this great work the taste of the age, as represented by the vestry and church-wardens, interfered; the noble vista of the " long-drawn aisle" was broken, and a new and sorry modern nave constructed in its place.

The edifice is very spacious, and is built on the plan of a cathedral. In its style of architecture, excepting its tower, it somewhat resembles Salisbury Cathedral. It comprises a nave and aisles, transepts, a choir with its aisles, and at the eastern end, as above stated, the chapel of the Blessed Virgin, or, as it is more commonly called, the Lady Chapel. Contiguous, but extending farther eastward, was added a small chapel, which in time came to be called the Bishop's Chapel, from the tomb of Bishop Andrewes having been placed in its centre. This latter chapel was entered from the Lady Chapel under a large pointed arch. The chapel itself was rather over thirty feet in length, and had a stone seat on each side, and at the east end. However, as it was thought to injure the effect of the eastern elevation of the church, as seen from the new bridge road, it was taken down in the year 1830. A view of the Bishop's Chapel, from the last sketch that was taken of it, is given in Taylor's " Annals of St. Mary Overy."

At the intersection of the nave, transepts, and choir, rises a noble tower, 35 feet square and 150 feet in height, resting on four massive pillars adorned with clustered columns. The sharp-pointed arches are very lofty. The interior of the tower is in four storeys, in the uppermost of which is a fine peal of twelve bells. Externally, the tower, which is not older than the sixteenth century, somewhat resembles that of St. Sepulchre's Church, close by Newgate. It is divided into two parts, with handsome pointed windows, in two storeys, on each front; it has tall pinnacles at each corner, and the battlements are of flint, in squares or chequer work.

This tower has been in great jeopardy on more than one occasion, once through the vibration caused by the ringing of the bells, when damage was done to the extent of several thousand pounds; and more recently, when the south-eastern pinnacle was struck down by lightning, and fell upon the roof of the south transept, doing considerable damage.

We are told that, during and after the progress of the Great Fire of London, Hollar busied himself from his old and favourite point of view, the summit of this tower, in delineating the appearance of the city as it lay in ruins, which is so well known to us by the help of the engraver's art.

The western front of the church, as well as its southern side, has been restored with rubble-stone within the last half century in a style that reflects but little credit on the architect. In each corner rises a slight octagonal tower. In the buttresses, on each side of the large window, flintwork is ornamentally inserted. Over the door, which is in three compartments, in pointed arches, is a plain sunken entablature, occupying the space formerly devoted to a range of small pillars, forming niches, the centre having a bracket, on which is supposed to have stood the figure of the Virgin. From the repairs and alterations that have from time to time taken place in the fabric, the beauty of the interior, especially in the nave, has been much impaired. But it is still a noble structure; indeed, it has been proposed to restore the nave and make the church into a cathedral, as a memorial to the late Bishop Wilberforce.

The nave, as it at present exists, is awkwardly reached from the transept by a flight of several steps, a huge screen blocking up the view from east to west. The roof of the nave originally was supported by twenty-six columns, thirteen on each side, of which the four nearest the western end were of the massy round Norman character. The other columns were octangular, with small cluster-columns added at the four cardinal points. Corresponding with these columns are semi-columns in the walls, from which spring the arches of the aisles. There is a gallery in the window storey of the nave, which was formerly continued over the arches of the transept and choir. The altar-piece, or screen, at the east end of the nave forms a complete separation between this part of the structure and the choir. In fact, the transepts and chancel, under the existing arrangements, are utterly useless.

From the great supporting columns of the tower to the altar-screen at the east end of the choir run five lofty pointed arches, enriched with mouldings, and the groined roof, of stone, is exceedingly fine. The screen dividing the choir from the Lady Chapel is rich in its carving and decoration. On the east side of the south transept formerly stood the chapel of St. Mary Magdalen, founded and built by Peter de Rupibus, Bishop of Winchester. This chapel was thus described by Mr. Nightingale in 1818:—" The chapel itself is a very plain erection. It is entered on the south, through a large pair of folding doors leading down a small flight of steps. The ceiling has nothing peculiar in its character; nor are the four pillars supporting the roof, and the unequal arches leading into the south aisle, in the least calculated to convey any idea of grandeur or feeling of veneration. These arches have been cut through in a very clumsy manner, so that scarcely any vestige of the ancient church of St. Mary Magdalen now remains. A small doorway and windows, however, are still visible at the east end of this chapel; the west end formerly opened into the south transept; but that also is now walled up, except a part, which leads to the gallery there. There are in different parts niches which once held the holy water, by which the pious devotees of former ages sprinkled their foreheads on their entrance before the altar. I am not aware that any other remains of the old church are now visible in this chapel. Passing through the eastern end of the south aisle, a pair of gates leads into the Virgin Mary's Chapel." A correspondent of the *Mirror*, writing in 1832, says that it was this chapel, and not the Lady Chapel as had been previously stated, that contained the gravestone of one Bishop Wickham, who, however, was not the famous builder of Windsor Castle in the time of Edward III., but who died in 1595, the same year in which he was translated from the see of Lincoln to that of Winchester. "His gravestone," he adds, "now lying exposed in the churchyard, marks the south-east corner of the site of the aforesaid Magdalen Chapel." This chapel was pulled down in 1822. Amongst the alterations and additions consequent on its removal are the present windows and doorway of the transept. The angle formed by the north transept and the choir was formerly the Chapel of St. John, now appropriated as the vestry. Beyond the choir-screen, as already mentioned, is the Lady Chapel, which was restored by Mr. Gwilt in 1832; its four gables and groined roof are very fine. In Queen Mary's time it was used as a consistorial court by Bishop Gardiner, and here Bishop Hooper and John Rogers were tried as heretics, and condemned to the stake.

After the parish had obtained the grant of the church, the Lady Chapel was let to one Wyat, a baker, who converted it into a bakehouse. He stopped up the two doors which communicated with the aisles of the church, and the two which opened into the chancel, and which, though visible, long remained masoned up. In 1607 Mr. Henry Wilson, tenant of the Chapel of the Holy Virgin, found himself inconvenienced by a tomb "of a certain cade," and applied to the vestry for its removal, which, as recorded in the parish books, was very "friendly" consented to, "making the place up again in any reasonable sort."

The following curious particulars of the Lady Chapel appear in Strype's edition of Stow's Survey :—"It is now called the *New* Chapel; and indeed, though very old, it now may be called a new one; because newly redeemed from such use and employment as, in respect of that it was built to (divine and religious duties), may very well be branded with the style of wretched, base, and unworthy. For that which, before this abuse, was, and is now, a fair and beautiful chapel, was, by those that were then the corporation, &c., leased and let out, and this house of God made a bakehouse.

"Two very fair doors, that from the two sideaisles of the chancel of the church, and two, that through the head of the chancel went into it, were lathed, daubed, and dammed up: the fair pillars were ordinary posts, against which they piled billets and bavins. In this place they had their ovens; in that, a bolting-place; in that, their kneading-trough; in another, I have heard, a hog's trough. For the words that were given me were these :—' *This place have I known a hog-sty; in another, a store-house, to store up their hoarded-meal; and, in all of it, something of this sordid kind and condition.*' "

The writer then goes on to mention the four persons, all bakers, to whom in succession it was let by the corporation; and adds, that one part was turned into a starch-house.

In this state it continued till the year 1624, when the vestry restored it to its original condition, at an expense of two hundred pounds. In the course of two centuries it again became ruinous ; and in 1832 a public subscription was commenced, and the beautiful chapel was thoroughly restored. The roof is divided into nine groined arches, supported by six octangular pillars in two rows, having small circular columns at the four points. In the east end, on the north side, are three lancet-shaped windows, forming one great window, divided by slender pillars, and having mouldings with zigzag ornaments. At the north-east corner of the chapel, a portion had been divided off from the rest by a wooden enclosure, in which were a table, desk, and elevated seat. This part was the Bishop's court; but it was usual to give this name to the whole chapel, in which the Bishop of Winchester, even almost down to the time of the above-mentioned restoration, held his court, and in which were also held the visitations of the deanery of Southwark.

At the east end of the Lady Chapel, as stated above, was Bishop Andrewes' Chapel, which was ascended by two steps, and was so called from the tomb of Dr. Lancelot Andrewes, Bishop of Winchester, standing in the centre of it. The Bishop's Chapel having been wholly taken down, this fine monument has been removed into the Lady Chapel. The Bishop is represented the size of life, in a recumbent posture, and dressed in his robes, as prelate of the Order of the Garter. Originally this tomb had a handsome canopy, supported by four black marble pillars; but the roof of the Bishop's Chapel falling in, and the chapel itself being much defaced by fire, in 1676, the canopy was broken, and not repaired. In

the Bible. He was born in London in 1555, and received the rudiments of his education first at the free school of the Coopers' Company, in Ratcliff Highway, and afterwards at the Merchant Taylors' School. He afterwards graduated at Pembroke College, Cambridge. He soon became widely

CONSISTORY COURT, ST. SAVIOUR'S CHURCH, 1820.

taking down the monument, at the time of the demolition of the Bishop's Chapel, a heavy leaden coffin, containing the remains of the deceased prelate, and marked with his initials " L. A.," was found built up within the tomb; and on the re-erection of the monument against the west wall of the Lady Chapel, the coffin was carefully replaced in its original cell.

Dr. Andrewes, a prelate distinguished by his learning and piety, was one of the translators of

known for his great learning; and, in due course, found a patron in the Earl of Huntingdon, whose chaplain he became. After holding for a short time the living of Cheam, near Epsom, in Surrey, he was appointed Vicar of St. Giles's, Cripplegate, and in a short time after, prebendary and residentiary of St. Paul's, and also prebendary of the collegiate church of Southwell. In these several capacities he distinguished himself as a diligent and excellent preacher, and he read divinity lectures three days in the week at St. Paul's during term time. Upon the death of Dr. Fulke, he was chosen master of Pembroke Hall, to which college he afterwards became a considerable benefactor. He was next appointed one of the chaplains in ordinary to Queen Elizabeth, who took great delight in his preaching, and promoted him to the deanery of Westminster, in 1601. He refused a bishopric in this reign, because he would not submit to the interest, or solicitations on the part of himself or his friends: it is likewise observed, that though he was a privy councillor in the reigns of James I. and Charles I., he interfered very little in temporal concerns; but in all affairs relative to the Church, and the duties of his office, he was remarkably diligent and active. After a long life of honour and tranquillity, in which he enjoyed the esteem of three successive sovereigns, the friendship of

JOHN GOWER.

spoliation of the ecclesiastical revenues. In the next, however, he had no cause for such scruple, and having published a work in defence of King James's book on the "Rights of Sovereigns," against Cardinal Bellarmine, he was advanced to the bishopric of Chichester, and at the same time appointed lord-almoner. He was translated to the see of Ely in 1609; and in the same year he was sworn of the king's privy council in England, as he was afterwards of Scotland, upon attending his majesty to that kingdom.

When he had sat nine years in the see of Ely, he was translated to that of Winchester, and also appointed dean of the royal chapel; and to his honour it is recorded of him, that these preferments were conferred upon him without any court all men of letters, his contemporaries, and the veneration of all who knew him, Bishop Andrewes died at Winchester House, in Southwark, in September, 1626, at the age of seventy-one.

One of the most ancient memorials preserved in the church is the oaken cross-legged effigy of one of the Norman knights who founded the priory; it is in a low recess in the north wall of the choir. But better known is the monument on the east side of the south transept, to John Gower, the poet, and his wife. "This tomb," says Cunningham, "was originally erected on the north side of the church, where Gower founded a chantry. It was removed to its present site, and repaired and coloured, in 1832, at the expense of the Duke of Sutherland, whose family claimed relationship or

descent from the poet Gower. But, according to
the *Athenæum* (No. 1,537, p. 68), Sir H. Nicolas
and Dr. Pauli have shown that the family of the
Duke of Sutherland and Lord Ellesmere must
relinquish all pretension to being related to, or

TOMB OF JOHN GOWER IN ST. SAVIOUR'S CHURCH.

even descended from, John Gower. They have
hitherto depended solely upon the possession of
the MS. of the 'Confessio Amantis,' which was
supposed to have been presented to an ancestor
by the poet; but it turns out, on the authority of
Sir Charles Young, that it was the very copy of
the work which the author laid at the feet of
King Henry IV. while he was yet Harry of
Hereford, Lancaster, and Derby!"

Gower, as we have stated above, contributed
largely towards the rebuilding of the church at the
close of the fourteenth century. He was certainly
a rich man for a poet, and he gave, doubtless,
large sums during the progress of the work; but it
is absurd to suppose, as some have imagined, that
the sacred edifice was wholly built by his money.
Lest any such foolish idea should be entertained,
Dr. Mackay, in his "Thames and its Tributaries,"
places on record the following witty epigram:—

"This church was rebuilt by John Gower, the rhymer,
　Who in Richard's gay court was a fortunate climber;
　Should any one start, 'tis but right he should know it,
　Our wight was a lawyer as well as a poet."

The fact is that Gower was a "fortunate
climber," not only in the court of Richard, but in
that of the Lancastrian king who succeeded him.
Like many other poets, he "worshipped the rising
sun," and his reward was that, to use his own
words, "the king laid a charge upon him," namely,
to write a poem. It is commonly supposed that he
was poet laureate to both of the above-mentioned
kings; but if this was the case, the post was its
own reward—at all events, no salary is known to
have been attached to it.

Gower is, perhaps, the earliest poet who has
sung the praises of the Thames by name. He
relates in one of his quaint poems how that being
on the river in his boat, he met the royal barge
containing King Henry IV.:—

"As I came nighe,
Out of my bote, when he me syghe (saw),
He bade me come into his barge,
And when I was with him at large,

Amongst other thynges said,
He had a charge upon me laid."

The Chapel of St. John, in the north transept of
this church, having been burnt and nearly destroyed
in the thirteenth century, was sumptuously rebuilt
by Gower almost at his sole cost; he founded also
a chantry there, endowing it with money for a
mass to be said daily for the repose of his soul,
and an "obit" to be performed on the morrow
after the feast of St. Gregory. In this chapel, we
are quaintly told, "he prepared for his bones a
resting, and there, somewhat after the old fashion,
he lieth right sumptuously buried, with a garland
on his head, in token that he in his life-daies
flourished freshly in literature and science." The
stone effigy on his tomb represented the poet with
long auburn hair reaching down to his shoulders
and curling up gracefully, a small curled beard,
and on his head a chaplet of red roses (Leland
says that there was a "wreath of joy" interspersed
with the roses); the robe was of green damask
reaching down to the feet; a collar of SS. in gold
worn round the neck, and under his head effigies of
the three chief books which he had compiled, viz.,
the "Speculum Meditantis," the "Vox Clamantis,"
and the "Confessio Amantis." On the wall hard
by were painted effigies of three virtues—Charity,
Mercy, and Pity—with crowns on their heads, and
each bearing her own device in her hand. That of
Charity ran thus :-

"En toy qui es fils de Dieu le Pere,
Sauve soit qui gist soubs cest piere."

That of Mercy thus :—

"O bone Jesu, fais la mercie
A l'ame dont le corps gist icy."

Whilst that of Pity ran as follows :—

"Par ta Pitie, Jesu, regarde
Et met cest aime en sauve garde."

Not far off was also a tablet with this inscription:—
"Whoso prayeth for the soul of John Gower, as
oft as he does it, shall have M.D. days of pardon.'
Gower's wife, we may add, was buried near him.

We know little enough of Gower—the "moral
Gower," as Chaucer calls him—except that he came
of a knightly family connected with Yorkshire, and
that he owned property not far from London, to
the south of the Thames, and probably in Kent.
Though no lover of abuses, he was a firm and
zealous supporter of the ancient Church, and
opposed to the fanaticism of those sectaries who
from time to time endeavoured to uphold the
standard of reform in matters of faith. Henry IV.
before he came to the throne, conferred on him
the Lancastrian badge of the Silver Swan.

" Of the rest of his life," writes Dr. R. Pauli, in his " Pictures of Old England," " we know, in truth, very little. It was not till his old age, when his hair was grey, that, wearying of his solitary state, he took a wife in the person of one Agnes Groundolf, to whom he was married on the 25th of January, 1397. His very comprehensive will does not mention any children, but it makes ample provision for the faithful companion and nurse of his latter years. After prolonged debility and sickness, he lost his eye-sight in the year 1401, and was then compelled to lay aside his pen for ever. He died in the autumn of 1408, when upwards of eighty years of age. He lies buried in St. Saviour's Church, near the southern side of London Bridge; and we find from his last will that he had been connected in several ways with London, through his estates, which were all in the neighbourhood of the City. St. John's Chapel, in the church already referred to, still contains the monument which he had himself designed, and which, notwithstanding the many subsequent renovations which it has undergone, is tolerably well preserved. He lies clothed in the long closely-buttoned habit of his day, with his order on his breast, and his coat of arms by his side; but whether the face, with its long locks, and the wreath around the head, is intended as a portrait, it is difficult to say. Greater significance attaches . . . to the three volumes on which his head is resting, and which may be said to symbolise his life—the 'Speculum Meditantis,' the 'Vox Clamantis,' and 'Confessio Amantis.' "

Gower's works maintained their popularity long beyond the age in which his lot was cast, as may be gathered from the fact that his was the mine from which Shakespeare drew the materials for his *Pericles, Prince of Tyre*. In 1402, when blind and full of years, he followed his old friend Chaucer to the tomb. Prosaic and unpoetical as is now the aspect of Southwark, there is no spot in this great metropolis more worthy of being called the Poet's Corner. Chaucer, as we shall presently see, has conferred upon the Tabard Inn a literary immortality. Shakespeare himself dwelt for many years in a narrow street close by the church of St. Mary Overy; there he wrote many of his great dramas, while the neighbouring Bankside witnessed their performance. Edmund Shakespeare was, as the register-book of the parish tells us, a " player," no doubt through the connection of his brother with the Globe Theatre hard by. He was the immortal poet's youngest brother. The register at Stratford-on-Avon tells us that he was baptised there on the 3rd of May, 1580; that of

St. Saviour's records the fact that he was buried here on the last day of the year 1607. So probably William Shakespeare stood by his grave. Such is the brief summary of all that is known to history of Edmund Shakespeare; " and," as Mr. Dyce remarks, " since his connection with the stage is ascertained from no other source, he probably was not distinguished in his profession."

Fletcher, the friend and fellow play-writer with Shakespeare, died of the plague of London, in August, 1625, at the age of forty-six, and was buried in this church. He had survived his friend and literary partner, Beaumont—with whom he lived at Bankside—just nine years. John Fletcher was a son of the Rev. Dr. Richard Fletcher, who was successively Bishop of Bristol, of Worcester, and of London under Queen Bess. The names of Beaumont and Fletcher appear as jointly responsible for upwards of fifty dramas, but there are reasons for thinking that Fletcher had not much to do with more than half that number. The circumstances of his death are thus described by Sir John Aubrey:—" In the great plague of 1625, a knight of Norfolk or Suffolk invited him into the country. He stayed in London but to make himself a suit of clothes, and when it was making, fell sick and died. This I heard from the tailor, who is now a very old man, and clerk of St. Marie Overie."

" From the proximity of this church to the Globe Theatre and others on Bankside," writes Dr. Mackay, in his " Thames and its Tributaries," " many of the players of Shakespeare's time who resided in the neighbouring alleys found a final resting-place here when their career was over. Among others, unhappily, Philip Massinger, steeped in poverty to the very lips, died in some hovel adjacent, and was buried like a pauper at the expense of the parish." Born at Salisbury, in the year 1584, and having been educated at Alban Hall, Oxford, Philip Massinger, the playwright and poet, and the friend and immediate successor of Shakespeare, came to London to seek his bread by his pen, which furnished nearly forty plays for the stage. But in spite of their great celebrity at the time when they were written and performed, few of them are known to the present race of play-goers. *A New Way to Pay Old Debts* is occasionally performed; and the *Fatal Dowry* and *Riches* (altered from *The City Madam*) have been found amongst modern revivals. Massinger's last days were probably spent in Southwark, though accounts differ as to the latter portion of his career. He died in 1639, for the register in that year records, " buried, Philip Massinger, a stranger "—

that is, a non-parishioner. It is probable, therefore, that he wished in death to be joined with some of those who had been his fellow-craftsmen. His grave is unmarked by any stone or other memorial.

Among the remaining monuments in St. Saviour's Church is one bearing the following epitaph on a member of the Grocers' Company :—

> "Garrett some call him, but that was too high ;
> His name is Garrard who now here doth lie.
> Weep not for him, for he is gone before
> To heaven, where there are grocers many more."

Another epitaph to a girl ten years of age contains this quaint thought, borrowed from an earthly court :—

> "Such grace the King of kings bestowed upon her
> That now she lives with Him a maid of honour."

Near the tomb of the poet Gower is another which exhibits a diminutive effigy of a man, an emaciated figure, in a winding-sheet, lying on a marble sarcophagus. At the back is a black tablet with the following inscription in letters of gold :—

> "Here vnder lyeth the body of WILLIAM EMERSON, who lived and died an honest man. He departed ovt of this life the 27th of June, 1575, in the year of his age 92. VT SVM SIC ERIS."

A curious effigy is that lying on the floor, on the east side of the north transept, which has been supposed by some persons to be that of the old "ferryman" above spoken of. Grose has inserted a representation of this figure in his "Antiquities of England and Wales," observing that it is a skeleton-like figure, of which the usual story is told that the person thereby represented attempted to fast for forty days in imitation of Christ, but died in the attempt, having first reduced himself to that appearance. There is also an engraving of this effigy in J. T. Smith's "Antiquities of London and its Environs," 1791, 4to. Be this figure, however, who or what it may, at all events its monument has long survived him ; whether he carried passengers over the river Thames, or was occupied in teaching others how to cross that last fatal river which, as John Bunyan so quaintly says, "hath no bridge," can matter but little to us now.

St. Saviour's parish church differs in point of clerical administration from almost every other church in the kingdom, for it has neither rector nor vicar, nor what is popularly called a "curate," but under a peculiar grant the tithes are secured to the churchwardens for the maintenance of two "chaplains" or "preachers." The parishioners here elect their own preachers, and the parish election vies in scandals with borough elections. In consequence, it has been proposed by the more respectable portion to cede the right to the Bishop.

There is an interesting view of St. Mary Overy's Church among the etchings of Hollar ; it was worked at Antwerp in 1647. The view is taken from the north, and shows a porch leading into the north aisle of the chancel ; there is also an ugly side aisle of Jacobean architecture running on the north side parallel to the nave. Another etching by the same artist, of which we give a copy on page 30, taken from the other side of the church, shows a glimpse of St. Paul's and the City across the river. Hollar's studies of buildings, his little landscape and water-side etchings, are always charming. He is an excellent delineator of architecture, his drawing and perspective being admirably executed. He can render landscape also with great subtilty, giving, for instance, in a small sketch of a few inches square the knolls and hollows of a piece of hilly river-bank with marvellous truth and naturalness. Some one has written of Hollar that, "whether dealing with brick and stone, or fields and streams, he is always dexterous and exact ; and if we were asked to name the principal characteristic of his work, we should say it was a perfectly simple and earnest striving after truth. To some modern etchers, who have all sorts of marvellous methods of their own, who cover the paper with an incomprehensible chance-medley of black lines and call it 'green moonlight sleeping on a bank,' or something of the sort, Hollar's art may appear but homely, for it is only the art of transferring what was before him to paper, so that others may see it as he saw it."

The antiquarian author of "Chronicles of London Bridge" tells us that in his day, when the church-wardens and vestrymen of St. Mary Overy's met for convivial purposes, one of their earliest toasts was that of their church's patron saint, under the irreverent name of "Old Moll." It is to be hoped that such gross irreverence is now at an end.

St. Saviour's and its neighbourhood have, however, much historic interest on quite another score; for adjoining the northern side of St. Saviour's Church, and on the site of the Cloisters, Sir Anthony Browne, Viscount Montague, built after the Dissolution a handsome mansion, which gave name to the still existing Montague Close. In the memorable year 1605, Lord Monteagle was residing there when he received the anonymous letter advising him "as you tender your life, to devise you some excuse to shift off your attendance at this Parliament, for God and man have concurred to punish the wickedness of this time." The suspicions excited by this mysterious warning led to the discovery of the Gunpowder Plot. Monteagle was rewarded by a grant of £200 per annum in land and a pension of £500 in hard cash; and in remembrance of the great event, persons then and afterwards residing in Montague Close were exempted from actions for debt or trespass. The place became, in fact, a sort of minor Sanctuary, the privileges of which grew ultimately to be such a public nuisance that they were suppressed by the strong arm of the law.

CHAPTER IV.

SOUTHWARK (*continued*).—WINCHESTER HOUSE, BARCLAY'S BREWERY, &c.

"Kings and heroes here were guests,
In stately hall at solemn feasts;
But now no dais, nor halls remain,
Nor fretted window's gorgeous pane.
*   *   *   *   *   *
No fragment of a roof remains
To echo back their wassail strains."—*Sir W. Scott, "Kenilworth."*

Stow's Description of Winchester House—Park Street Chapel—Marriage Feast of James I. of Scotland at Winchester House—The Palace attacked by the Insurgents under Sir Thomas Wyatt—John, Duke of Finland, lodged here—The Palace sold to the Presbyterians, and turned into a Prison for the Royalists—Its Recovery by the Bishop of Winchester—Remains of the Old Palace—The "Stews" on the Bankside—"Holland's Leaguer"—"Winchester Birds"—Old Almshouses--Messrs. Barclay and Perkins' Brewery—Its Early History—Mr. and Mrs. Thrale—Dr. Johnson's Intimacy with the Thrales—Purchase of the Brewery by Mr. David Barclay—Origin of the Firm of Barclay and Perkins—Mrs. Piozzi, and her Literary Acquaintances—Account of the various Processes of Malting, Brewing, &c.—The Brewery described—Monster Vats—Attack on General Haynau—Richard Baxter—Zoar Street Chapel—Oliver Goldsmith—Holland Street—Falcon Glass Works—The "Falcon" Tavern—Hopton's Almshouses—Messrs. Potts' Vinegar Works—St. Peter's Church—St. Saviour's Grammar School—Improvements in Southwark—Southwark Street—The Hop Exchange.

THE site of the Priory of St. Mary Overy, and of Winchester House, the palace of the Bishops of Winchester, adjoins the north-west corner of the nave of St. Saviour's Church, and extends towards Southwark Bridge; it is now occupied by various wharves, warehouses, manufactories, and other buildings, among them being the new Bridge House Hotel, which opens on the main street, close by the foot of London Bridge. Of the priory we have already spoken in the preceding chapter. Winchester House was built early in the twelfth century, by Walter Giffard, Bishop of Winchester, on land held of the prior of Bermondsey. Stow, in his "Chronicles," mentions it as being in his time "a very fair house, well repaired, with a large wharf and landing-place, called the Bishop of Winchester's Stairs." It was, in fact, a stately palace, with gardens, fountains, fish-ponds, and an extensive park—long known as Southwark Park—which reached back nearly as far, in the direction of Lambeth, as Gravel Lane, and which is still kept in remembrance by "Park" Street. In New Park Street is—or rather was—the chapel in which Mr. C. H. Spurgeon first became known as a popular preacher. The congregation formerly assembling in the Baptist meeting-house in Carter Lane, Tooley Street, migrated to New Park Street Chapel in 1833, on the demolition of their old chapel to make room for the approaches to new London Bridge; and here they continued till, under the pastorate of Mr. Spurgeon, they migrated to the music-hall in the Surrey Gardens, Newington,

and finally to the Metropolitan Tabernacle. The chapel in Park Street has since become converted to business purposes, and has been made to serve as a store-room or goods depôt.

Winchester Yard, between St. Saviour's Church and Messrs. Barclay and Co.'s brewery, in Park Street, occupies the place of the court-yard of the old palace; and Messrs. Pott's extensive vinegar works, on part of the site of the park, are, we believe, still held under lease direct from the see of Winchester.

Cardinal Beaufort lived here in the early part of the fifteenth century, whilst holding the important see of Winchester. In his time the great hall of the palace, which ran east and west parallel with the river, was the scene of a splendid banquet; for here took place the marriage-feast on the occasion of the matrimonial alliance of James I. of Scotland with the Lady Joan Somerset, daughter of the Earl of Somerset, as stated in the previous chapter. But the palace witnessed at times other scenes besides those of festivity; for we read of great "brawls" taking place between the cardinal's servants and the citizens at the Bridge Gate. Old Stow describes a disgraceful scene which took place in Winchester House, when the insurgents against the government of Queen Mary, under Sir Thomas Wyatt, had entered Southwark, on the 3rd of February, 1554. Wyatt's intention was to have entered the City by way of London Bridge, as we have already seen; but notwithstanding that the citizens of London had cut down the drawbridge, the inhabitants of the borough received him well. Sir Thomas issued a proclamation that no soldier of his should take anything without paying for it; notwithstanding which, some of them attacked the Bishop of Winchester's house, made havoc of his goods, and cut to pieces all his books, "so that men might have gone up to their knees in the leaves so torn out." Wyatt stayed here only two or three days, when the inhabitants, finding that

turned the episcopal palace into a prison for the royalists; and in 1649 it was sold for £4,380 to one Thomas Walker, of Camberwell. It was recovered by the Bishop of Winchester, at the Restoration, but was not again used as a residence. Until the time of the civil wars, the Bishops of Winchester resided here during the sitting of Parliament; but afterwards they removed to Chelsea, where, as we have seen,* they had another house

VIEW OF ST. MARY OVERY   *From an Etching by Hollar, 1647.*   (*See page* 18.)

the Governor of the Tower of London had planted several pieces of ordnance against the foot of the bridge and on the steeples of St. Olave and St. Mary Overy, became alarmed, and desired Sir Thomas to leave them, which he did.

The Swedish envoy, John, Duke of Finland, was lodged in the Bishop of Winchester's palace when he came to solicit the hand of Queen Elizabeth for his elder brother, Eric, the son and heir of the King of Sweden. He went in state to visit the Queen at Greenwich; but his father's death recalled him to Sweden.

Bishop Lancelot Andrewes, as we have already stated, died at Winchester House in 1626, and was carried hence to his last resting-place in St. Saviour's Church. Twenty years later, the Presbyterians

provided for them under the sanction of an Act of Parliament in 1661. A part of the palace was standing, occupied as tenements and warehouses, till within the last few years, a fire which occurred in August, 1814, having destroyed some of the surrounding buildings, and brought to view a portion of the old hall, with a magnificent circular window.

Allen, in his "History of Surrey," published in 1829, says, "Vain would be the attempt to determine the extent and arrangement of this palace from its present remains. The site was probably divided into two or more grand courts, the principal of which appears to have had its range of state apartments fronting the river; and part of this

---

* See Vol. V., p. 53.

WINCHESTER HOUSE. (*From a View by Hollar, 1660.*)

range is now almost the only elevation that can be traced. Though its external decorations on the north or river front have been either destroyed or bricked up, yet in the other, facing the south, are many curious doorways and windows in various styles, from that of the Early Pointed down to the era of Henry VIII., but wofully mutilated, and concealed by sheds, stables, and warehouses." What little remained of the palace after the fire above mentioned was very soon considerably diminished. The great wall, which divided the hall from the other apartments, with the large circular window, some fourteen feet in diameter, was built against in the early part of 1828. There was likewise remaining a doorway, in the spandrils of which appeared the arms of Bishop Gardiner, and the same impaling those of the see of Winchester. A correspondent of the *Gentleman's Magazine*, writing at the above period, observes that "this doorway is connected with, and, in fact, led into, a range of buildings shown in Hollar's 'View of London,' *circa* 1660, branching southward of the hall to a considerable distance, much of which is still standing."

The antiquary Pennant, whilst pretending to do nothing of the kind, insinuates that the Bishops of Winchester and Rochester, and the Abbots of St. Augustine's, Canterbury, Lewes, Hyde, Waverley, and Battel, had their town residences here on account of their adjoining the Bordello or "Stews" on the Bankside. These "stews" comprised nearly twenty houses along the river-side, and were licensed under certain regulations confirmed by Act of Parliament.

The houses, which were indeed a most unsavoury adjunct to Southwark, were nothing more nor less than a collection of public brothels, leased from the Bishops of Winchester by various persons, one of whom was no other than Sir William Walworth, who struck down Wat Tyler, and thus gave the dagger to the City arms. We read that, "on Thursday the Feast of Corpus Christi, June 13th, 1381, in the morning the Commons of Kent brake down the stew-houses near to London Bridge, at that time in the hands of the power of Flanders, who had farmed them of the Mayor of London. After which they went to London Bridge, in the hopes to have entered the City; but the mayor (the famous Sir William Walworth) coming thither before, fortified the place, caused the bridge to be drawn up, and fastened a great chaine of yron acrosse to restraine their entry." Thus wrote Stow, and the same story is told in other words by the old chronicler, Thomas of Walsingham.

As far back as 1162, some Parliamentary "Ordinances" were issued, "touching the government of the Stewholders in Southwark, under the direction of the Lord Bishop of Winchester;" the purpose of which seems to have been to restore the state of things there, "according to the ovlde customes that hath been vsed and accustomed tyme out of mynde." These regulations were numerous; no single woman was to be kept against her will, and all were "to be voyded out of the lordship" on Sundays and other holidays. When the ordinances were first enjoined, the number of stewhouses was eighteen; but in the reign of Henry VII., when some fresh regulations were made, it was reduced to twelve. One of the houses, says Pennant, but he gives no authority for the statement, bore the sign of the "Cardinal's Hat." Cardinal's Cap Alley is, however—or, at all events, was till lately—to be found in the neighbourhood. If the holders of the houses broke certain wholesome rules which were issued respecting them, they were committed to the episcopal prison of the Clink, at the corner of Maid Lane. This prison was removed in 1745 to Deadman's Place, Bankside (so named from the number buried there during the great plague), but was burnt down in the riots of 1780, and no other prison has since taken its place. The poor women living in these houses, though licensed by the bishops, were not allowed Christian burial, but were thrown when dead into unconsecrated graves at a spot called the Cross Bones, at the corner of Redcross Street. Henry VII. closed these dens of infamy, but they were soon opened again, though his son and successor finally cleared them out, having issued a proclamation enjoining his subjects "to avoide the abominable place called the Stewes." *

In Holland Street, at the end of Bankside, near Blackfriars Bridge, was another notorious "stew" frequented by King James I. and his court; amongst others by the royal favourite, George Villiers, as we learn from a little tract entitled "Holland's Leaguer." It is recorded that "many of the inhabitants of the Bankside, especially those who lived in the stews adjoining the palace of the Bishops of Winchester, were known throughout London by the court term of the 'Winchester Birds.' Low players also, then ranking (not, perhaps, quite undeservingly) with these and other similar characters, under the common designation of vagabonds, flocked together to the same spot, together with fraudulent bankrupts, swindlers, debtors, and all sorts of persons who had misunderstandings with the law. Here in former

---

* See "Stews in Bankside," in the *Antiquarian Magazine*, Vol. II., p. 70.

years stood the 'Mint' and the 'Clink;' and here in the present day (1840) stands the privileged King's Bench, within whose 'Rules' are congregated the same vicious and demoralised class of people that always inhabited it. 'Stews' also still abound, and penny theatres, where the performers are indeed 'vagabonds,' and the audience thieves." Thus wrote Charles Mackay, in his agreeable work, "The Thames and its Tributaries," as lately as 1840. Things, however, have much improved since that day; at all events, we may hope that such has been the case.

HALL OF WINCHESTER HOUSE.
(*From an Etching by Hollar,* 1647.)

In Deadman's Place, on the south-west side of the Borough market, were almshouses for sixteen poor persons, which were founded in 1584, by Thomas Cure, and called Cure's College. Thomas Cure was saddler to Edward VI., Mary, and Elizabeth, and was also M.P. for Southwark, and jointfounder of the Grammar School.

Another cluster of almshouses close by, in Soap Yard, were built and endowed by the retired actor, Edward Alleyn, of whom we shall have more to say when we come to Dulwich College. Alleyn's almshouses have been rebuilt at Norwood. Alleyn directed by his will (1626) that his executors should within two years of his death erect ten almshouses in this parish for five poor men and five poor women, who should be drafted hence, as vacancies occurred, into his college at Dulwich. The almshouses were accordingly "built on part of an enclosure called the Soap Yard belonging to the College of the Poor." The College of the Poor was founded by letters patent of Queen Elizabeth in 1584, and was largely endowed. It provided a home and sustenance for sixteen poor persons, one of whom was to act as warden and read prayers

daily. In 1685 Henry Jackson founded almshouses in Southwark for two women, with twenty pence a week each; and sundry others of a like nature were founded in different parts of the parish. St. Saviour's is, in fact, particularly rich in benefactions. According to the "Account of Public Charities in England and Wales," published in 1828, it would appear that the annual income of the various charities of this parish amounted to nearly £2,700.

Between St. Saviour's Church and Southwark Bridge Road, with its principal entrance in Park Street, is the renowned brewery of Messrs. Barclay and Perkins. Southwark held a reputation for strong ale from very early times. We have met somewhere with an old couplet—

"The nappy strong ale of Southwirke
Keeps many a gossip from the kirke."

Chaucer's host at the Old Tabard drank it, doubtless; and so did the Knight and the Franklin, and perhaps the mincing "Nonne" herself. That there were breweries here as far back as the fourteenth century we have reason to know, for Chaucer speaks of "the ale of Southwark" in his time; and readers of that poet will not have forgotten, among the inhabitants of this part—

"The miller that for dronken was all pale,
So that unethes upon his hors he sat."

"Foreigners are not a little amazed," writes Boswell, in his "Life of Johnson," "when they hear of brewers, distillers, and men in similar departments of trade, held forth as persons of considerable consequence. In this great commercial country it is natural that a situation which produces much wealth should be considered as very respectable; and no doubt honesty is entitled to esteem." Brewing is one of the oldest objects of industry among us; and in early ages the quantity of ale consumed was somewhat larger than is the case now in proportion to the population and wealth of the nation. Little is known of the trading practices of the early brewers; but the process, so far as the malting and brewing is concerned, is, doubtless, essentially the same now as it was three centuries ago, when hops were imported into this country from Flanders. By a liberal attention to the improvements of the age, Messrs. Barclay and Perkins have placed their large establishment in its present eminence among the breweries of the world. "Formerly," writes Mr. Brayley, in his "History of Surrey," "our great porter brewers left ale to minor establishments: this is now partially but not entirely changed; two coppers at Barclay and Perkins' are therefore applied, as the occasion requires, to ale-brewing. On the other hand, some of the less extensive establishments, in former times only occupied with ale, now produce porter also. The difference of the two consists of modifications in the process, and of certain additions for the purpose of flavouring or colouring. The malt and hops are the same, but a very small portion of malt, when burnt black, suffices to colour porter and stout. These liquors are more luscious than ale, and less vinous from undergoing a less perfect fermentation, that process being considerably shortened, usually to one-third of the time allowed for ale."

Before proceeding to describe the brewery in its various details, it will be as well, perhaps, to speak of the firm to which it belongs. As early as the middle of the last century, or a hundred years or so after the "Globe" Theatre had passed away, there stood upon this site a small brewery, owned by a certain Mr. Edmund Halsey, whose daughter had married the Lord Cobham of that time. Having made a fortune out of the establishment, Mr. Halsey sold the brewery to the elder Mr. Thrale, who eventually became member of Parliament for Southwark, and being a landowner at Streatham, served as high sheriff of Surrey. Dr. Johnson used to give the following account of the rise of this gentleman :—" He worked at six shillings a week for twenty years in the great brewery, which afterwards was his own. The proprietor of it had an only daughter, who was married to a nobleman. It was not fit that a peer should continue the business. On the old man's death, therefore, the brewery was to be sold. To find a purchaser for so large a property was a difficult matter ; and after some time it was suggested that it would be advisable to treat with Thrale, a sensible, active, honest man, who had been employed in the house, and to transfer the whole to him for thirty thousand pounds, security being taken upon the property. This was accordingly settled. In eleven years Thrale paid the purchase-money." On his death, in 1758, his son, Mr. Henry Thrale, succeeded him, and found the brewery so profitable a concern, that, although he had been educated to other tastes and habits, he determined not to part with it. This Mr. Thrale was a handsome man of fashion, and was wedded to a pretty and clever girl, Miss Hester Lynch Salusbury, of good Welsh extraction, and, as Boswell informs us, " a lady of lively talents, improved by education." The lady, we may add, was short, plump, and brisk. She has herself given us a lively view of the idea which Dr. Johnson had of her person, on her appearing before him in a dark-coloured gown : " You little

creatures should never wear those sort of clothes ; . . . . they are unsuitable in every way. What ! have not all insects gay colours?" Mrs. Thrale was destined, nevertheless, as the mistress of Streatham Villa, the friend of Johnson, and the wife of Piozzi, to become a shining light in English literature. Boswell tells us, in his "Life of Johnson," that the great doctor's introduction into Mr. Thrale's family, which contributed so much to the happiness of his life, was owing to her desire for his conversation, is very probable and the general supposition ; " but," he adds, " it is not the truth. Mr. Murphy," Boswell continues, " who was intimate with Mr. Thrale, having spoken very highly of Dr. Johnson, he was requested to make them acquainted. This being mentioned to Johnson, he accepted of an invitation to dinner at Thrale's, and was so much pleased with his reception, both by Mr. and Mrs. Thrale, and they so much pleased with him, that his invitations to their house were more and more frequent, till at last he became one of the family, and an apartment was appropriated to him, both in their house at Southwark, and in their villa at Streatham."

" The first time," says Mrs. Piozzi, " I ever saw this extraordinary man was in the year 1764, when Mr. Murphy, who had long been the friend and confidential intimate of Mr. Thrale, persuaded him to wish for Johnson's conversation, extolling it in terms which that of no other person could have deserved, till we were only in doubt how to obtain his company, and find an excuse for the invitation."

Dr. Johnson had a very sincere esteem for Mr. Thrale, as a man of excellent principles, a good scholar, well skilled in trade, of a sound understanding, and of manners such as presented the character of a plain independent English squire. " I know no man," said he, " who is more master of his wife and family than Thrale. If he but holds up a finger, he is obeyed. It is a great mistake to suppose that she is above him in literary attainments. She is more flippant, but he has ten times her learning : he is a regular scholar, but her learning is that of a schoolboy in one of the lower forms."

Thrale, it has been stated, but falsely, married Miss Salusbury " because she was the only pretty girl of his acquaintance who would live in Southwark ; and having married her, proceeded to enjoy himself with ladies of doubtful reputation at the theatres, leaving his gay wife to do the honours at Streatham to old Sam, Fanny Burney, and others of the set, not forgetting charming, learned Sophy Streatfield, the mysterious S. S., who won not only

Thrale's heart, but those of right reverend bishops and grave schoolmasters, by her beauty, ready tears, soft caresses, and fluent Greek and Hebrew. But the time came when Thrale's gay career was suddenly stopped. The bailiffs and the auctioneer invaded the Southwark brewery; but his clever wife begged and borrowed till she bought it in."

Mr. Thrale resided in a house adjoining the brewery, and here he entertained his friends as well as at his country seat at Streatham. For some reason or other he appears to have been unpopular with the mob, for Boswell tells us that in the Gordon Riots his house and stock were in great danger : "The mob was pacified at their first invasion with about £50 in drink and meat; at the second they were driven away by the soldiers." It will be remembered that Dr. Johnson helped Mr. Thrale in his contests for the representation of Southwark, writing for him advertisements, letters, and addresses ; one of these, dated September 5, 1780, is preserved by Boswell.

After Mr. Thrale's death, in 1781, the brewery was put up for sale by auction, and Johnson, of course, was present as one of the executors. Lord Lucan (writes Boswell) tells a very good story, which, if not precisely exact, is at least characteristic—that while the sale was going on, Johnson appeared bustling about, with an ink-horn and a pen in his button-hole, like an exciseman ; and on being asked what he considered to be the value of the property which was to be disposed of, answered, " Sir, we are not here to sell a parcel of boilers and vats, but the potentiality of growing rich beyond the dreams of avarice."

The brewery was bought by Mr. David Barclay, junior, then the head of the banking firm of Barclay and Co., for the sum of £135,000. This gentleman placed in the brewing firm his nephew, from America, Mr. Robert Barclay, who afterwards settled at Bury Hill, and Mr. Perkins, who had been in Thrale's establishment as manager or superintendent ; so that while Mr. Barclay brought the money to carry on the business, Mr. Perkins may be said to have contributed the "brains"— hence the firm of " Barclay and Perkins."

So far and so wide are the joint names of Barclay and Perkins known upon the sign-boards of way-side inns, in London and the country, that Mr. G. A. Sala, in his " Gaslight and Daylight," suggests that " a future generation may be in danger of assuming that Messrs. Barclay and Perkins were names possessed in an astonishing degree by London citizens, who, proud of belonging to such respectable families, were in the habit of blazoning the declaration of their lineage in blue and gold on oblong boards, and affixing the same to the fronts of their houses !"

But we have not yet quite done with the beautiful Mrs. Thrale. After the death of her first husband, as we have already intimated, she became—contrary to the wishes and advice of Dr. Johnson—the wife of a Mr. Piozzi, and spent much of her time in her charming abode at Streatham, in the enjoyment of a select circle of literary acquaintances. Rogers was very intimate with the Piozzis, and often visited them at Streatham. He says, " The world" (in which Dr. Johnson was, of course, included) "was most unjust in blaming Mrs. Thrale for marrying Piozzi ; he was a very handsome, gentlemanly, and amiable person, and made her a very good husband. In the evening he used to play to us most beautifully on the piano. Mrs. Piozzi's daughters would never see her after that marriage ; and, poor woman, when she was of a very great age, I have heard her say that she would go down on her knees to them if they only would be reconciled to her."

Tom Moore, who breakfasted with her after she was turned eighty, speaks of her as still a " wonderful old lady," with all the quickness and intelligence of a gay young woman : " faces of other times seemed to crowd over her as she sat—the Johnsons, Reynoldses, &c." Madame D'Arblay speaks of her as " a wonderful character for talents and eccentricity, for wit, genius, generosity, spirit, and powers of entertainment." Miss Seward said that " her conversation was that bright wine of the intellect which has no lees ; " and even Dr. Johnson, who did not think very highly of the female sex, owned that "her colloquial wit was a fountain of perpetual flow." Indeed, he used to dwell on her praises with a peculiar delight and a paternal fondness, which showed that he was quite proud and vain of being so intimately acquainted with her. Macaulay commends her as " one of those clever, kind-hearted, engaging, vain, pert young women, who are perpetually saying or doing something that is not exactly right ; but who, do or say what they may, are always agreeable." Add to this the words of Sir Nathaniel Wraxall : " She was the provider and conductor of Dr. Johnson, who lived almost constantly under her roof, or more properly under that of Mr. Thrale both in London and at Streatham. He did not, however, spare her any more than other women in his attacks if she courted and provoked his animadversions. She was also a butt of the satirists ; thus Gifford writes :—

" See Thrale's gay widow with a satchel roam,
And bring in pomp laborious nothing home."

And Dr. Wolcot (Peter Pindar), even more maliciously :—

> "For that Piozzi's wife, Sir John, exhort her
> To draw her immortality from porter;
> Give up her anecdotical inditing,
> And study housewif'ry instead of writing."

year burnt to the ground, with the exception of a very small portion of the walls. As it is one of the "sights" of the metropolis, and indeed of Europe, our readers may be interested with a somewhat detailed account of the establishment, and of the various processes of malting, brewing, &c., as here

MRS. THRALE.

Mrs. Thrale left three daughters. One of them was Lady Keith, another a Mrs. Mostyn; her collection of relics of Mr. Thrale and Dr. Johnson was sold at Silwood Lodge, Brighton, in the autumn of 1857, soon after Mrs. Mostyn's death.

The brewery of Messrs. Barclay and Perkins, one of the greatest establishments of the kind in the world, occupies some thirteen or fourteen acres of ground; the present building dates its erection from 1832, the old brewery having been in that

carried on. To begin at the beginning, then, we will commence with a description of the process of malting, the object of which is—by forced vegetation of the grain, and then checking that tendency, by gradually and slowly increasing heat from 130 to 160 degrees—to separate the particles of starch, and render the saccharine matter formed easily soluble in hot water. For this purpose, the barley is steeped for about two days, in which time it imbibes nearly half its weight of water. It next lies, a few inches deep, on a floor for a fortnight, during which time it is repeatedly stirred to prevent its heating. When the grain is sprouted, its roots extending about half an inch in length, it is kiln-dried on an iron floor heated by coke, gradually and slowly, commencing at 90 degrees, and not exceeding at last 160 degrees, an operation of two or three days ; after this the sprouts are separated by sifting from the malt, which is then fit for the from the copper duly boiled, the hop dregs are strained off, and the wort must be cooled as fast as possible, otherwise the disposition of the beer to turn sour will be much greater ; even a larger proportion of hop will hardly save it. When the wort is quite cool it is to be fermented. Wine from grapes will ferment of itself, but beer requires yeast, or barm, from a previous brewing. This is usually added gradually as the wort appears to require it,

BARCLAY'S BREWERY, 1829.

brewer or distiller. In describing the process of brewing, the author above quoted says : "The brewer, having first ground the malt, mixes it with as much hot water as it will imbibe, stirring the mixture until it is perfectly and equally soaked ; the heat of the water must be some degrees below the boiling-point, or it will cake the meal. When well stirred, or mashed, it is covered up from external air for about three hours ; then the liquor is drawn off, and boiled for an hour or more with a due proportion of hops (hop blossom), say a pound to the bushel. As all the saccharine matter is not by this first mashing extracted, a second, and even a third, is had recourse to, requiring, however, less time, and allowing hotter water than the first. When the liquor, or wort, as it is called, is drawn and in various proportions, according to the intention of the brewer, whether he wishes to save time in the operations, and to produce a full luscious beverage for early use, or a more vinous and clear liquor of great strength for long preservation. Such are the simple objects of brewing ; but a variety of circumstances in the practice requires great care and experience, and not a little acuteness of perception. Even with all these qualifications, the effects of weather used often to be highly injurious, and are so still to persons who brew in a small way without the improvements lately acquired from science. These are so great that with them brewing is carried on indifferently in hot or cold weather, throughout the year, and not as formerly, in March and October chiefly. The principal improvements are in the formation of mashing-tuns or rakes, whereby the malt is mashed in an exceedingly small space of time, and without exposure to the atmosphere, so that all is equally soaked; boilers that afford the most speedy and controllable supply of hot water at the least expense of fuel, an arrangement for drawing off the wort and passing it through iron pipes laid in cold water many hundreds or thousands of yards in continuity, so that the wort is cooled in an incredible short time, and other modes of effecting the same purpose by quick evaporation in metallic shallow vessels. The fermentation is, on the contrary, carried on in wooden vessels of very great depth, perhaps of thirty feet; whilst a perfect control is maintained that enables the superintendent to promote the generation of carbonic acid gas, or to draw it off, as the case may require."

At the brewery of Messrs. Barclay and Perkins all these operations are to be seen in the utmost perfection, and on the most magnificent scale. The brewhouse, or mashing stage, is 225 feet long, by 60 feet in width, and very lofty, with an ingenious and elaborate iron roof. Within this large space are five complete sets of brewing apparatus, perfectly distinct in themselves, but directly connected with the great supply of malt from the floor above, of water-cisterns from below, and of motive force from the steam-engine behind, as well as the vast coolers, fermenting vats, &c. Each of the copper boilers cost nearly £5,000 (about £24,000 altogether); each consists of a furnace, a globular copper that holds 350 barrels, a pan or covering boiler that contains 280 barrels, and a cylindrical cistern that will contain 120 barrels, on arrangements equally beautiful and useful, from its compactness and the economy of heat. The hot water is drawn from one of these copper boilers to the corresponding mash-tun underneath, which measures about twenty feet in diameter, and holds 150 quarters of malt. It is supplied with machinery that works from a centre on a cog-rail which extends over the circumference of the tun, and stirs the malt. The mash-tun has a false bottom, which in due time lets off the " wort " through small holes to an under-back, whence it is pumped back to the emptied copper, from which it received the hot water, and there mixed with hops, to be boiled, and again run off into a cistern thirty feet each way, where, passing through a perforated bottom, it leaves the hops, and is pumped through the cooling tubes, or refrigerator, into an open cooler, and thence to the fermenting squares, which are coffers about twenty-five or thirty feet deep, and fifteen feet square, in which the fermentation by

yeast is carried on for some days; from these it is drawn off into pontoons, where the fermentation acquires a fresh activity for a few days longer, when it gradually ceases, and the liquor becomes clearer: it is then put into the large vat, where it remains till required for use. The vats at Barclay and Perkins' establishment are nearly 200 in number, the smallest containing 600 barrels of beer, and the largest 3,300 barrels, measuring 36 feet in diameter at top, 40 feet at the bottom (or 125 feet in circumference), and 40 feet in height. Altogether, they must hold more than 150,000 barrels; and the number of casks (butts or barrels), many of them filled, amount to something over 64,000.

We have stated that the brewery contains five magnificent boilers with corresponding mash-tuns, and every adjunct. So far the arrangement and explanation are simple enough, and so is, to the eye of an experienced engineer, the machinery that connects and keeps in motion every part of these stupendous operations. It is otherwise to persons unaccustomed to the variety and multiplicity of cog-wheels working at different angles, which communicate action in different and opposite directions from one end of the premises to the other, in what may be denominated a maze of systematic order. The malt is conveyed from one building to another, even across a street, entirely by machinery, and again to the crushing rollers and mash-tun; the cold and the hot water, and the wort and the beer, are pumped in various directions, almost to the exclusion of human exertions, nearly every portion of the heavy toil being accomplished by the steam-engine. Of all the combinations, none is more complete than what is called the " Jacob's ladder:" this consists of an endless chain working on two rollers at a considerable distance from each other. Along this chain buckets are fastened close to each other; these buckets dipping into a heap of malt near one extremity of the chain, carry it on to the other end, where, revolving on the other roller, they are capsized, and thus emptied; they, of course, return to the first roller, where a second inversion places them again in the position required for filling by their own progress through the heap of malt to be removed. There are no less than twenty-four lofts, each capable of containing 1,000 quarters of malt. The " Jacob's ladders " and the refrigerators are among the greatest improvements achieved: the one saves immense labour, simplifies and perfects the work, and, of course, reduces the expenses, and concentrates the operations; the other economises time, and improves the beverage. More space and more hands can be applied to those portions of the business that require them ; and hence a remarkable degree of method, neatness, cleanliness, and quiet are observable throughout the establishment.

The portions of the brewery which we have described above lie on either side of Park Street, being connected by a bridge, which is reached from the upper storeys. On leaving these parts of the establishment, we pass through the engine-room, on the ground-floor, and emerging into the yard, notice the well from which the great supply of water is drawn for consumption in the brewery. In connection with this well, we may state a curious geological fact. This brewery, as we have shown above, is situated near the south bank of the Thames ; that of the City of London Brewery Company is in Thames Street, on the opposite side of the river. It is not a little singular that when the pump of the well at Messrs. Barclay's is worked, the level of the water in the well of the City brewery is visibly affected, thus proving that the watery stratum passes clean under the Thames, just as it would under dry land, without being in any way connected with the water of the river.

The long ranges of building on the north side of the brewery are used as the carpenters' shops, the cooperage, &c. In the former a very large amount of work is done in connection with fittings for the various public-houses belonging to the firm, besides other work which may be required in the brewery. On the south side of the yard is another range of buildings, separated from the other by an avenue, over which a large pipe crosses to convey the beer from the "rounds"—as the huge tanks which contained it are called—to the store-vats. These vats are contained in a series of store-rooms, apparently almost interminable. Long galleries, branching off north, south, east, and west, are crammed as full of vats as the circular form of the vessels will permit, some larger than others, but all, nevertheless, of gigantic proportions. Some idea may be formed of the extent of the vat-galleries when we state that there are nearly 200 vats, the average capacity of which, large and small together, is upwards of 30,000 gallons. Two of the vats are each capable of containing 3,500 barrels of thirty-six gallons each, and the weight, when full of porter, is stated to be about 500 tons. By the aid of a guide we ascend one of the steep ladders, and mounting to the top, obtain a kind of bird's-eye view of these mighty monsters, and then emerging through a small doorway in the roof, obtain a good view not only of the whole range of buildings forming the brewery, but also of St. Saviour's Church and other places round about. The store-rooms in front of us, as we look

down on the north side, we were informed, had gradually and completely enclosed a small grave-yard, which has at last been partially built upon, and all traces of its previous uses swept away. As this grave-yard does not appear to have been parochial, or attached to any church, it was, in all probability, the same as that which we have mentioned above as having been formerly used as the burial-place of the unfortunate victims of the plague in Bankside. On the south side of the brewery is an extensive range of stabling, spacious enough to afford proper accommodation for 200 dray-horses.

Messrs. Barclay and Perkins, down to a comparatively recent period, stood quite at the head of the principal porter and ale brewers of London ; but latterly Messrs. Hanbury and Co. seem to have taken the lead. Nevertheless, a very large business is done annually by Messrs. Barclay and Perkins, not only in the way of home consumption, but also for shipment abroad, and the average quantity of malt consumed by them amounts to about 130,000 quarters annually, or about 650 quarters every working day throughout the year, besides a proportionably large quantity of hops. The brewery is a great attraction for visitors to London, and more especially foreigners, and the "visitors' book" will be found to contain the names of many eminent personages. One of the best-remembered visitors, perhaps, is Marshal Haynau, who was speedily and unceremoniously ejected by the draymen some years ago, in consequence of his alleged ill-treatment of Polish or Hungarian women, which had come to the knowledge of Messrs. Barclay and Perkins' draymen.

Marshal Haynau, during the sanguinary war in 1849 against the Hungarians, had gained considerable notoriety from his excessive cruelty towards the Magyars, particularly the women. The following year, having fallen into disgrace with the Imperial Court of Vienna, and losing his military command, he occupied himself in a tour through Europe, visiting London in due course. On the 4th of September, 1850, he paid a visit to Barclay's brewhouse, and complied with the customary practice of signing the visitors' book on entering the brewery. In less than two minutes the word was passed throughout the establishment that the notorious Hungarian woman-flogger was then in the building. A number of the men quickly gathered round him as he was viewing the large vat, and commenced showing signs of hostility. Finding that his presence was so decidedly objectionable, the marshal was about to retire, but this he was not permitted to do without receiving some marks of violence from the draymen and workmen employed in the brewery. A truss of straw was dropped on his head as he was passing through the stables, his hat was then beaten over his eyes, his clothes torn off his back, and he was almost dragged along by his beard and moustaches, which were of enormous length. Some of the carters employed in the brewery and labourers from the Borough Market commenced lashing him with their whips, accompanied with the cry, "Down with the Austrian butcher!" "Give it him!" Both himself and his two companions endeavoured to defend themselves against the mob of workmen, now swelled to upwards of 500. In his attempts to escape from his pursuers he rushed along Bank-side, and entered the "George" public-house, close by followed by the throng. Several rooms were entered by the mob, but in vain. At last the marshal was discovered crouching in a dust-bin attached to the house. In the meantime the police having been sent for, appeared on the scene, and with some difficulty the crowd was dispersed and the marshal conveyed through a back-door to a police galley which happened to be near at hand. He was then rowed to Waterloo Bridge, and conveyed to Morley's Hotel.

"We have often," writes Charles Knight, "had occasion to sigh over the poverty of London in the article of genuine popular legends; one brewhouse is among the exception. The names of Henry Thrale and Dr. Samuel Johnson must go down to posterity together. The workmen at Barclay and Perkins's will show you a little apartment in which, according to the tradition of the place, Johnson wrote his dictionary. Now this story," he adds, "has one feature of a genuine legend—it sets chronology at defiance." He might have added that it sets at defiance topography also; for it is well known that the dictionary was compiled, as shown by us in our first volume,* in the neighbourhood of Fleet Street.

The site of the Globe Theatre, of which we shall speak in the following chapter, is believed to be covered by part of the premises of Messrs. Barclay and Perkins' brewery, at a short distance from the spot on which once stood the town-house of Mr. Thrale.

Deadman's Place, according to tradition, took its name from the number of dead interred there in the great plague, soon after the Restoration. Elmes, in his "Topographical Dictionary," says it is the second turning on the left in Park Street, going from the Borough Market; as shown above,

it has now become partly absorbed in Messrs. Barclay and Perkins' brewery. Pike tells us that little more than fifty years ago there existed in Southwark Park a burial-ground in which many of the Nonconformist worthies were interred. This cemetery was called Deadman's Place, and was situated not far from New Park Street Chapel.

Not far from the brewery, in Park Street, there stood formerly a timber edifice, where Mr. Wadsworth's congregation was accustomed to assemble, and where Richard Baxter was wont occasionally to preach. "Just when I was kept out of Swallow Street," says Baxter, "his [Mr. Wadsworth's] flock invited me to Southwark, where, though I refused to be their pastor, I preached many months in peace, there being no justice willing to disturb us." Baxter died in the Charterhouse in 1691.

At a short distance westward, in Zoar Street, an obscure part of the Borough, close by Gravel Lane, which forms the western boundary of Southwark, there is, or, at all events, there was till very lately, an old Dissenting meeting-house, but now converted into a carpenter's shop, which tradition affirms to have been used by John Bunyan for religious worship. "It is known," says Mr. R. Chambers, in his "Book of Days" (vol. ii., p. 290), "to have been erected a short while before the Revolution, by a few earnest Protestants, as a means of counteracting a Catholic school which had been established in the neighbourhood under the auspices of James II. But Bunyan may have preached in it once or twice, or even occasionally during the year preceding his death in 1688." One of its ministers was John Chester, the ejected minister of Wetherby, in Leicestershire. When Bunyan preached in this chapel, thousands of people were attracted by the charm of his magic eloquence. It mattered not whether the service was held on the Sunday, or "a morning lecture by seven o'clock on a working-day in the dark winter-time." In 1740 this congregation removed to Deadman's Place, and about fifty years later they migrated to Union Street. The old chapel in Zoar Street was subsequently used by the Wesleyans, and at last became a brewery and a factory. A view of the chapel, as it appeared in 1812, has been engraved for the standard edition of Bunyan's works; and another view of the edifice, as it was in 1864, will be found in the "Book of Days," at the page quoted above.

It was in Bankside at one time that poor Oliver Goldsmith was practising medicine on his own account, though without much success. This was in the interval after he had been engaged as an assistant in a chemist's shop near Fish Street Hill,

---

* See Vol. I., p. 112.

and before he became a schoolmaster at Peckham. Goldsmith's strong passion for dress, at this period of his checkered career, we are told, exhibited itself in a second-hand suit of green and gold, which made him a rather conspicuous personage in the thoroughfares of the Borough ; while a want of neatness, and of money to pay the washerwoman, was clearly betrayed in his shirt and neckcloth, often of a fortnight's wear. But contentment or pride provided a covering for his poverty, and he told a friend that " he was practising physic, and doing very well." The green suit was afterwards changed for a black one, with a patch on the left breast, which he ingeniously concealed by holding up his cocked hat when he was conversing with his patients. A polite person once endeavoured to relieve him from this apparent incumbrance, " which only made him press it more devoutly to his heart."

Bankside is described in the " New View of London," published in 1708, as lying " between Upper Ground Street and St. Saviour's Dock." The thoroughfare now bearing the name extends from St. Saviour's Church westward nearly to Black-friars Bridge. Not far from Bankside there was a Crucifix Lane, near Barnaby (now Bermondsey) Street and Parish Street, which, with Cardinal's Hat Court, seem to have been so named as belonging at some distant period to the old religious house of St. Mary Overy.

A little to the west of St. Saviour's Church is Stoney Street, which ran down to the water-side, nearly opposite to Dowgate, and probably was the continuation of the Watling Street road. " This," says Pennant, " is supposed to have been a Roman *trajectus*, and the ferry from Londinum into the province of Cantium." Marks of the ancient cause-way have been discovered on the London side. Of this the name evinces the origin. The Saxons always gave the name of Street to the Roman roads, and here they gave it the addition of Stoney, from the pavement they found beneath it.

Between Southwark Bridge Road and the southern end of Blackfriars Bridge is Holland Street, which marks the site of the ancient moated manor-house, called Holland's Leaguer, of which we have spoken above. All vestiges of the house have long been swept away. In Holland Street, on the spot where once stood the tide-mill of the old manor of Paris Garden, are the Falcon Glass Works, one of the most important manufactories in Southwark. It may be mentioned here, in passing, that old Southwark was noted for its artists in glass, who are known to have glazed the windows of King's College Chapel, Cambridge, in the reign of Henry VIII. The Falcon Works have existed here for more than a century. " Their present importance and excellence," as we learn from Brayley's " History of Surrey " (1843), " are mainly due to the taste and exertions of the present proprietor [Mr. Apsley Pellatt], and the employment of skilful hands on materials that science and experience approve. By these means the most elegant productions of the Continent are advantageously rivalled, and in some respects surpassed. The number of persons employed is from one hundred to one hundred and twenty in the glasshouse, and about thirty elsewhere. The weight of glass manufactured in the course of a year, into chandeliers, illuminators for ships or cellars, toilet or smelling-bottles, ornamental glasses of every description for the table, and various objects for medical and philosophical purposes, has been 20,000 lbs." Since the repeal of the excise duty on glass the quantity worked has been very largely increased, and the quality improved. Mr. Apsley Pellatt, who was for some years M.P. for Lambeth, died in 1864.

Close by the glass works, on the site of the Falcon drawing-dock, was situated the " Falcon Tavern," famous for its connection with the name of William Shakespeare. Here the great " poet of all time " and his companions would refresh themselves after the fatigue of the afternoon performances at the Globe hard by. " It long continued," says Mr. Larwood, " to be celebrated as a coaching inn for all parts of Kent, Surrey, and Sussex, till it was taken down in 1808." The name, as shown above, is still preserved in the Falcon Glass Works, and also in the Falcon Stairs. A house is still standing, or was till lately, which is considered to have been part of the original tavern, and, at all events, occupies its site and immortalises his name.

In the rear of the Falcon Glass Works, opening upon Holland Street—or that part of it which was till lately called the " Green Walk "—is a small cluster of almshouses, founded in 1730, by a Mr. Hopton, for the purpose of affording shelter for " poor decayed householders of the parish of Christchurch," together with a yearly pension of £12 to each inmate.

Previous to the erection of Southwark Bridge, in 1814, Bankside, from London to Blackfriars Bridges, presented a comparatively uninteresting succession of wharves and warehouses, together with irregular-built dwelling-houses ; but upon the formation of the viaduct to the new bridge, extensive improvements were planned on each side, the most important of which was the erection of a huge pile of building westward, by the Messrs. Pott, upon a tract of ground which, for upwards of two centuries, has been used for manufacturing purposes. These premises were occupied as vinegar-works by a Mr. Rush, so long ago as 1641, and continued in his family till 1790, when they came into the possession of the Messrs. Pott, whose family had carried on a manufactory of the same kind for seventy years in Mansel Street, Whitechapel. The ground here, as we have already shown, originally formed a portion of the park of the ancient palace of the Bishops of Winchester. The property, as we have stated, is still held of the

wish of a certain Miss Hyndman, to the erection of churches in populous districts. A further sum of about £1,700 was raised by subscription among the parishioners, for the enclosure, decoration, and furniture of the edifice.

Since the annexation of Southwark to London, as stated in a previous chapter, its ecclesiastical districts have gradually been increased by sub-divisions. The two parishes of St. Mary's and St. Margaret's, indeed, as we have already shown, have been united, the old church of St. Saviour's being made to do duty for both; but the parish of Christ Church, as nearly as possible co extensive

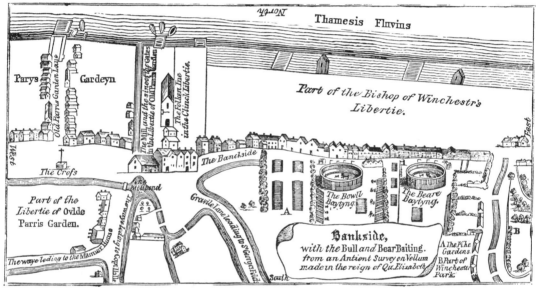

PLAN OF BANKSIDE, EARLY IN THE SEVENTEENTH CENTURY.

see of Winchester, by Messrs. Pott, who, conjointly with the Bishop of Winchester, in 1838-9, gave a portion of the grounds for the site of the new parish church of St. Peter's, and of the new grammar-school of St. Saviour's.

The church and school stand on the north side of Sumner Street—so named after Dr. Sumner, late Bishop of Winchester—which connects South-wark Bridge Road with Park Street. The church is a poor building, in imitation of the Pointed style, and is constructed of fine light brick, with stone dressings. At the western end rises an embattled tower, with square turrets at the angles; the eastern gable is surmounted with an enriched cross, turrets, &c.; the principal entrances are at the west end, and at the south side, under an enriched stone headway, beneath the central window. The cost of building was contributed by the trustees of "Hyndman's Bounty;" being a portion of the donation of £100,000 devoted, in fulfilment of the

with the Manor of Paris Garden, has been formed out of St. Saviour's, as also has the still more modern parish of St. Peter's, of which we have spoken above. The parish of St. John's, Horsely-down, has in like manner been taken out of St. Olave's; and the hospital church of St. Thomas has been made parochial. Of the churches belonging to the two last-named parishes, and also of Christ Church, Blackfriars Road, we shall speak in due course.

St. Saviour's Grammar School, as we have already had occasion to state, stood originally on the south side of St. Saviour's Church; it was founded by Queen Elizabeth in 1562, for the use of the parishioners, "poor as well as rich." It was burnt down a few years after its establishment, but was rebuilt. In 1839 the school was removed to a more convenient site in Sumner Street, where the present school and schoolhouse were built about the year 1838. At the same time the statutes were revised by the Court of Chancery, and the education now given is that of a public school, while the endowment is sufficient to allow of the charges being reduced to a most moderate scale. The school was reformed in 1850 under a scheme approved by the Court of Chancery, the usual classical and commercial course being prescribed. The visitor is the Bishop of Rochester, though formerly that office was held by the successive Bishops of Winchester. By the statutes it is provided that the the Bishop of Winchester, " or any other good and learned man." Immediately after the charter, the governors ordered that the schoolmaster's wages should be £20 yearly ; that children of the parish should be taught free, paying 2s. 6d. entrance, and 8d. per annum towards brooms and *rods*. The whole number of scholars was not to exceed 100; the head-master taking forty for his own advantage ; in 1614 he was allowed a dwelling-house in the parish, rent-free ; and the governors

THE GLOBE THEATRE, TEMP. ELIZABETH. (*See page* 45.)

master shall be " a man of a wise, sociable, loving disposition, not hasty or furious, or of any ill example, but wise and of good experience to discern the nature of every several child ; to work upon the disposition for the greatest advantage, benefit, and comfort of the child, and to learn with the love of his book, if such an one can be got."

The school and master's house, &c., which nearly adjoin the western end of St. Peter's Church, are built of brick, with stone dressings, in the Elizabethan Domestic style, from the designs of Mr. Christopher Edmonds, architect. By the charter of incorporation, the original endowment amounted to £40 per annum ; six governors were appointed, who were to be advised in the appointment and government of the master and usher by had the discretion of increasing his stipend, and taking children of other parishes and places. In the above year also, John Bingham, one of the governors of the school, founded an endowment for two poor scholars at Cambridge or Oxford— " none but poor and such as were forward in learning, and might be fit for the University." According to the Parliamentary Report, in 1818, the annual income of this school amounted to £387 15s. 1d. At that time there were sixty-eight boys upon the foundation ; each paid £1 entrance, and 5s. a quarter to the writing-school, and the like to the classical school. The above report states, " With the exception of writing and arithmetic, the education given at the school is, according to the provisions of the charter, entirely classical. It appears that this has operated to deter poor persons who might be entitled to send their children there from so doing; but we are assured that no poor child, whose parents have applied for his admission, has been refused." The average number of children is now about 120, and the school is thrown entirely open. There are several valuable scholarships; and the pupils are prepared for the Universities, Civil Service, and other public examinations, combined with a thorough commercial education.

To the south of Sumner Street, and connecting the two great thoroughfares of the Borough and Blackfriars Road, is a broad roadway, called Southwark Street. It was formed about the year 1860, and its sides are lined with some lofty and handsome warehouses, offices, and other places of business, which present a marked improvement on the ordinary street architecture of old Southwark. In the formation of this street a large number of courts and alleys were swept away, and a great alteration was made in the west side of the High Street, by the removal of the Town Hall, of which we shall presently speak. The preparations for the erection of Southwark Bridge had cleared away several narrow streets on the Surrey side of the river, and materially altered the appearance of the neighbourhood. Bandyleg Walk, a dirty lane between Maid Lane (now New Park Street) and Queen Street (now Union Street), are on the spot where formerly was a waste piece of ground. The Dyers' Field, with a filthy pond in the centre, became Great Guildford Street; and the name of Union Street was conferred upon the thoroughfare between the end of Charlotte Street and the Borough. The district between the Blackfriars Road and Bandyleg Walk had an unsavoury reputation in the last century. Gravel Lane, Ewer Street, and the adjacent courts and alleys, were the St. Giles's of Southwark, inhabited by a dense colony of Irish, whose frequent drunken bouts and faction fights were, in those days of the old "Charlies," sufficiently desperate to warn off steady-going people from the locality. On the north side of the street, westward of Southwark Bridge Road, are some extensive blocks of model lodging-houses, erected by the Peabody trustees. The range of buildings covers a large extent of ground; and the houses themselves, which are constructed of brick, and upon the most improved principles, are several storeys in height.

At the eastern end of Southwark Street, near its junction with the High Street, and close by the Borough Market, stands the Hop Exchange, which was built about 1865, from the designs of Mr. Moore. This is a large and magnificent range of buildings, several storeys in height, in which are offices, &c., used by hop merchants and others, and enclosing a lofty hall, in which the business of the exchange is carried on. The hall, which is approached from the street by a short flight of steps, and a vestibule, in which are some handsome iron gates, is surrounded by three galleries, which serve as means of communication to the various offices. In the rear are some extensive warehouses and stowage for hops, &c. The railings of the galleries are appropriately decorated, and the hall itself is covered in with a glass roof.

It has been said of St. Petersburg that more labour is expended in the foundations of the houses than on the houses themselves; and so it is with Southwark Street. The subway which runs along its centre, as stated in a previous part of this work,* is a piece of building which will last for many generations. Underneath that subway, which is seven feet high in the centre, is the sewer; the gas and water pipes are laid in the subway. There is a communication from it for gas and water to every house, the repair of the pipes will not necessitate the opening of the streets, and passengers are saved the disagreeable intelligence of " No thoroughfare," when driving in a cab to catch a train. This subway, indeed, is a most excellent piece of building, and has been finished in a masterly manner; and the same degree of excellent workmanship may be said to have been bestowed upon the fronts of the houses on either side of the street. Altogether, Southwark Street is more like an old Roman street, especially in its subway, than anything of modern times. In architecture it may be called Parisian, for the style of the houses is borrowed from that which dominates in Paris, and is identified with the period of Louis XIV. Near the eastern end of the street the roadway is crossed by a railway arch, over which passes the lines connecting London Bridge and Cannon Street Stations with Waterloo and Charing Cross; whilst the other end of the street passes under the London, Chatham, and Dover Railway, close by Blackfriars Bridge Station. In the middle of the roadway, at either end of the street, are ornamental shafts, surrounded by lamps, for the ventilation of the subway.

Altogether, the Bankside of to-day is a notably different place from the Bankside of theatres and pleasure-gardens as it appeared two centuries ago, and which we shall now proceed to describe.

* See Vol. V., p. 239.

CHAPTER V.

SOUTHWARK (*continued*).—BANKSIDE IN THE OLDEN TIME.

" Totus orbis agit histrionem."

Appearance of Bankside in the Seventeenth Century—The Globe Theatre—Its Destruction by Fire—Shakespeare's Early Connection with the Playhouse—James Burbage—Rebuilding of the Globe Theatre—Public and Private Theatres—The Rose Theatre—Ben Jonson—The Hope and Swan Theatres—Paris Garden—Bear-baiting—Prize-fighting—Samuel Pepys' Description of the Sport—John Evelyn's Visit to Bankside—The " Master of the King's Bears "—Bad Repute of Paris Garden—Visit of Queen Elizabeth to Paris Garden—Bear Alley— Public Gardens in Southwark—Bankside at the Time of the Great Fire of London — Dick Tarleton—The " Tumble-down Dick "—Waterside Public-houses.

In the present chapter we must ask our readers to transport themselves along with us, mentally, some 250 or 300 years, to the Bankside with which Shakespeare and Burbage, and Ben Jonson, and Beaumont and Fletcher were familiar. They will see no rows of densely-crowded courts and alleys, with their idle and dissolute, gin-drinking inhabitants; but before their eyes there will rise at least three large round structures of singular appearance, not unlike small martello towers, open to the sky above, together with one or two plots of enclosed ground scaffolded about for the use of spectators. These are the Paris Gardens, and the Globe, the Hope, and the Swan Theatres. And besides these, there are the stately palaces of the Bishops of Winchester and Rochester, as we have already shown; and all to the south are green fields and hedgerows.

"On the southern bank of the Thames," writes Mr. J. H. Jesse, in his "London," between Black-friars Bridge and Southwark Bridge, is Bankside. Here was the Globe Theatre, immortalised as the spot where Shakespeare trod the stage; here was the celebrated 'Paris Garden;' here stood the circuses for 'bowll-baytyng' and 'beare-baytyng,' where Queen Elizabeth entertained the French ambassadors with the baiting of wild beasts. Here stood the Falcon Tavern—the 'Folken Inne' as it is styled in the ancient plans of Bankside—the daily resort of Shakespeare and his dramatic companions; here, between Southwark Bridge and London Bridge, the site still pointed out by 'Pike Gardens,' were the pike-ponds, which once supplied our monarchs with fresh-water fish; and, lastly, here were the park and the palace of the Bishop of Winchester."

It will be seen at once, from the above quotation, that the ancient topography of the southern bank of the Thames (or Bankside) between London and Blackfriars Bridges, is peculiarly interesting to the lover of dramatic lore, as well as to the student of the sports and pastimes of our ancestors. Down to the middle of the seventeenth century, and probably much later, with the exception of a few houses extending westward along the bank of the river, and sundry places of amusement, the greater part of the land hereabouts would seem to have been waste and unenclosed.

The Globe Theatre, as already mentioned by us, occupied part of the site now covered by Messrs. Barclay and Perkins' Brewery.

In the "History of St. Saviour's, Southwark," published in 1795, we read that "the passage which led to the Globe Tavern, of which the playhouse formed a part, was, till within these few years, known by the name of Globe Alley, and upon its site now stands a large storehouse for porter." It was called the Globe from its sign, which was a figure of Hercules, or Atlas, supporting a globe, under which was written, " *Totus mundus agit histrionem* " ("All the world acts a play"); and not, as many have conjectured, from its circular shape; for the Globe, though a rotunda within, was to the outward view a hexagon.

We have no description of the interior of the Globe, but that it was somewhat similar to our modern theatres, with an open space in the roof; or perhaps it more resembled an inn-yard, where, in the beginning of Queen Elizabeth's reign, many of our ancient dramatic pieces were performed. The galleries in both were arranged on three sides of the building; the small rooms under the lowest, answered to our present boxes, and were called rooms; the yard bears a sufficient resemblance to the pit, as at present in use, and where the common people stood to see the exhibition; from which circumstance they are called by Shakespeare " the *groundlings*," and by Ben Jonson " the *understanding* gentlemen of the *ground*." The stage was erected in the area, with its back to the gateway, where the admission money was generally taken. The price of admission into the best *rooms*, or boxes, was in Shakespeare's time a shilling, though afterwards it appears to have risen to two shillings and half-a-crown. The galleries, or scaffolds, as they were sometimes called, and that part of the house which in private theatres was named the pit, seem to have been the same in price, which was sixpence, while in some meaner playhouses it was only a penny, and in others twopence.

The Globe Theatre, according to Mr. Dyce, in his " Life of Shakespeare," was first opened late in 1594, or early in the following year; at all events, within twenty years of the opening of the first theatre in London. During the summer, the Lord Chamberlain's " servants,"—of whom Shakespeare was one—acted at the Globe, returning in the winter to the theatre at Blackfriars, which was more effectually sheltered from the weather. They also occasionally changed their *venue* by playing at the " Curtain," in Shoreditch, and at the theatre in Newington Butts.

No sooner did James I. ascend the throne, than he issued from Greenwich a royal proclamation, authorising, by name, " Our servants, Lawrence Fletcher, William Shakspeare, Richard Burbage," &c. &c., " freely to use and exercise the art and faculty of plays, comedies, tragedies, histories, interludes, morals, pastorals, stage-plays, &c. &c., as well within their now usual house, called the Globe, within our County of Surrey, as also within any town halls . . . or other convenient places within the liberties . . . of any other city, university, town, or borough whatever within our realms."

Shakespeare and his associates at this time were at the head of the Lord Chamberlain's company, performing at the Globe in the summer; but by virtue of it they ceased to be the Lord Chamberlain's servants, and became " the king's players." It may be added that " Mr. Shakespeare, of the Globe," is mentioned in a letter from Mrs. Alleyn to her husband, the founder of Dulwich College.

If any doubt exist as to the extent of Shakespeare's connection with the theatres in Bankside, it will be removed by the lines of Ben Jonson, in allusion to the fondness for dramatic performances which marked our last Tudor and our first Stuart sovereign :—

> " Sweet Swan of Avon, what a sight it were
> To see thee in our waters yet appear,
> And make those flights upon the banks of Thames
> That so did take Eliza and our James."

" It was here," writes Charles Mackay, in his " Thames and its Tributaries," " near the spot still called the Bankside, that the Globe Theatre stood at the commencement of the seventeenth century; the theatre of which Shakespeare himself was in part proprietor, where some of his plays were first produced, and where he himself performed in them. It was of an octagonal form, partly covered with thatch, as we learn from the account in Stow, who tells us that in 1613, ten years after it was first licensed to Shakespeare and Burbage, and the rest, the thatch took fire by the negligent

discharge of a piece of ordnance, and in a very short time the whole building was consumed. The house was filled with people to witness the representation of *King Henry the Eighth;* but they all escaped unhurt. This was the end of Shakespeare's theatre ; it was rebuilt, however, apparently in a similar style, in the following year."

Theatres in those times were very different structures from what they are in the present day; they were unroofed, circular or hexagonal edifices, shielded from the rain by a canvas covering, and without scenery or decorations, as well as innocent of " stalls " or " boxes," for the more aristocratic part of the audience sat upon the stage, among the performers, drinking beer and enjoying a friendly pipe. The central area in the public theatres was termed " the yard," the word " pit " being restricted to private theatres ; the pits were furnished with seats, which was not the case with the " yards." " Cressets, or large open lanterns," writes Mr. Dyce, " served to illuminate the body of the house ; and two ample branches, of a form similar to those now hung in churches, gave light to the stage. The band of musicians, which was far from numerous, sat, it is supposed, in an upper balcony, over what is now called the stage-box ; the instruments chiefly used were trumpets, cornets, hautboys, lutes, recorders, viols, and organs. Nearly all these theatres were of wood ; and the public theatres were open to the sky, the luxury of a roof being confined to 'private' theatres—whatever these may have been. On the outside of each was a sign indicative of its name ; and on the roof a flag was hoisted during the time of performance."

The peculiar construction of the theatre in Shakespeare's time is referred to by the poet himself, for he thus speaks of the Globe Theatre in the play of *Henry V. :—*

> " Can this vast cockpit hold
> The field of vasty France ? or can we cram
> Into this wooden O the very casques
> That did affright the air at Agincourt ? "

In these early days of the drama, a curtain occupied the place of scenery, while the scene supposed to be represented was inscribed on a board, and hung up at the back of the stage, such, for instance, as " This is a house," or " This is a garden."

> " Piece out our imperfections with your thoughts "

is the bidding of the poet ; and he spoke to an audience who could do even better than that, who could forget them altogether, in their apprehension of the spiritual grandeur and magnificence that was then with them in the cockpit. " There is something, it must be owned," observes Charles Knight, in his " London," " occasionally amusing, as well as delightful, in the simplicity of the old stage : in Greene's *Pinner of Wakefield*, two parties are quarrelling, and one of them says, ' Come, sir, will you come to the town's end, now ? ' in order to fight. ' Aye, sir, come,' answers the other ; and both then, we presume, move a few feet across the stage, to another part; but evidently that is all, for in the next line the speaker continues, ' Now we are at the town's end—what shall we say now ? ' " And yet it was here, and with such accessories as those mentioned above, that were first produced nearly all the wonderful plays of the mighty poet.

An account of the accident mentioned above is given by Sir Henry Wotton, in a letter dated July 2, 1613 : " Now to let matters of state sleepe, I will entertain you at the present with what happened this week at the Banks side. The King's players had a new play, called *All is True*, representing some principal pieces of the reign of Henry VIII., which set forth with many extraordinary circumstances of pomp and majesty even to the matting of the stage ; the knights of the order with their Georges and Garter, the guards with their embroidered coats, and the like ; sufficient in truth within awhile to make greatness very familiar, if not ridiculous. Now King Henry making a masque at the Cardinal Wolsey's house, and certain cannons being shot off at his entry, some of the paper or other stuff, wherewith one of them was stopped, did light on the thatch, where, being thought at first but idle smoak, and their eyes more attentive to the show, it kindled inwardly, and ran round like a train, consuming within less than an hour the whole house to the very ground. This was the fatal period of that virtuous fabrick, wherein yet nothing did perish but *wood* and *straw*, and a few forsaken cloaks ; only one man had his breeches set on fire, that would perhaps have broyled him, if he had not, by the benefit of a provident wit, put it out with a bottle of ale."

From a letter of Mr. John Chamberlaine to Sir Ralph Winwood, dated July 8, 1613, in which this accident is likewise mentioned, we learn that the theatre had only two doors. " The burning of the Globe or playhouse on the Bankside on St. Peter's day cannot escape you ; which fell out by a peal of chambers (that I know not upon what occasion were to be used in the play), the tampin or stopple of one of them lighting in the thatch that covered the house, burn'd it down to

the ground in less than two hours, with a dwelling-house adjoyning ; and it was a great marvaile and a fair grace of God that the people had so little harm, having but *two narrow doors* to get out."

In 1613 was entered in the Stationers' books, " A doleful Ballad of the General Conflagration of the famous Theatre called the Globe."

Taylor, the water poet, commemorates the event in the following lines :—

" As gold is better that in fire's tried,
　　So is the Bankside Globe, that late was burn'd ;
For where before it had a thatched hide,
　　Now to a stately theatre 'tis turn'd ;
Which is an emblem that great things are won
　　By those that dare through greatest dangers run."

It is also alluded to in some verses by Ben Jonson, entitled " An Execration upon Vulcan," from which it appears that Ben Jonson was in the theatre when it was burnt.

The exhibitions given at the Globe appear to have been calculated for the lower class of people, and to have been more frequent than those at the Blackfriars, till early in the seventeenth century, when it became less fashionable and frequented. The Globe was immediately contiguous to the Bear Garden ; and it is probable, therefore, that those who resorted thither went to the theatre when the bear-baiting sports were over, and such persons were not likely to form a very refined audience.

It has often been said that Shakespeare, on his first arrival in London from Stratford-on-Avon, was received into the playhouse in a subordinate position, and associated with company of a mean and low rank ; but Mr. Dyce sees reason for believing that " he never was attached to any other company (of players) than that which owned the Blackfriars and the Globe." Among Shakespeare's fellows at this time were Marlowe, Greene, Lodge, Beaumont, Fletcher, Peele, Chettle, Burbage, and a few others.

We have already made some mention of Burbage in our account of Blackfriars Theatre,* but as there is a certain sense in which " Master " James Burbage, carpenter, &c., of the parish of St. Leonard's, Shoreditch, may be regarded as the father of the English stage, some additional notice of him here, in connection with the Globe, may not be altogether out of place. Although the drama had flourished in the shape, at all events, of miracle-plays and such-like performances in the ages before the Reformation, yet under our Tudor sovereigns the drama was not held in high

---

* See Vol. I., p 201.

honour, nor was the profession of a dramatist regarded as worthy of respect. Royal and court authority had all along set its face against plays and interludes as dangerous to the morals of the young, and, therefore, things to be forbidden to the citizens of London and their apprentices. Indeed, all plays were strictly interdicted within the City; and on one occasion, when it became

Lord Mayor's jurisdiction. Two circumstances favoured his idea: firstly, his father-in-law was a man of substance, owning a few houses at Shoreditch; and secondly, in the previous year, just prior to the revels at Kenilworth, Queen Elizabeth had permitted her favourite, the Earl of Leicester, to collect a body of actors, and to enrol them under a patent from the crown. At the head of

BEN JONSON.

known that a play was to be performed at the "Boar's Head," in Aldgate, the Lord Mayor received an order from Queen Mary to stop the performance. In the early part of Elizabeth's reign it was found that the dramatic element was too strongly mixed up with human nature to be quite suppressed, and that it was better to bear with and hold in check what could not be utterly forbidden. Accordingly, in the year 1575, when the Lord Mayor had issued an edict altogether inhibiting plays within the circuit of the City, one James Burbage, a carpenter, bethought himself that he would erect a structure of wood, which would serve for a theatre, on a site just beyond the

this body was placed James Burbage. Aided by the help of his father-in-law, he obtained from a neighbour a lease of some land in Shoreditch, with permission from the landlord to build on it a theatre of wood. He did so forthwith; the play-house was opened; crowds flocked to it, and it was soon known over London as "The Theatre." Its success was so great that some opposition was soon threatened; but Burbage saw his chance, and built hard by a rival theatre, which he called "The Curtain." These two buildings became the nursery of the English stage. In the one Ben Jonson obtained his first engagement as a writer and vamper of plays, and took to the stage for a living. Encouraged by his double success at Shoreditch, James Burbage grew bolder, and soon afterwards erected a third theatre at Blackfriars, under the nose of the Lord Mayor and of the lords and ladies who lived around the Bridewell Palace; and in spite of their remonstrances, he held his own, supported, no doubt, by Leicester's influence. In the year 1576 he opened the Black-friars Theatre, which soon became the leading play-

some sense, manager too, there was no combined effort at producing a genuine English drama. But from the moment that James Burbage, like a second Thespis, erected his wooden theatre in Shoreditch, the calling of the player began to assume a definite character, and acting grew into the dignity of an art and a profession. Shake-speare found all these theatres, and others too, in existence when he came to London from Stratford

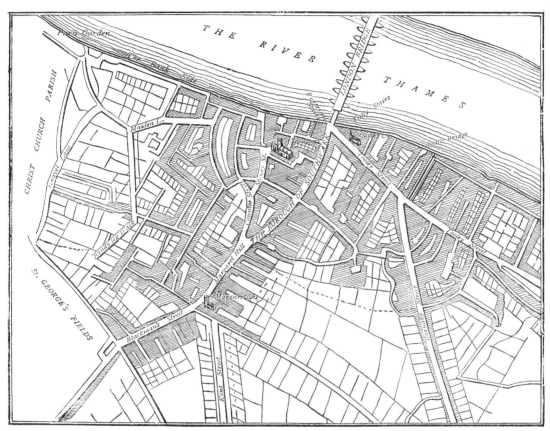

MAP OF SOUTHWARK, 1720.

house of the metropolis, and which is connected with the name of William Shakespeare.

Several other playhouses now sprung up in quick succession—viz., the "Red Bull" and the "Fortune," in the north of London; and on the south of the river, in Southwark, the "Rose," the "Hope," the "Swan," and the "Globe," near the "Bear Garden." Driven out of the City, and put to their wits' end for an honest livelihood, the poor players, who now began to style themselves "Her Majesty's Servants," began to build theatres in all the suburbs; and to James Burbage is due the credit of having enabled them to do so. In fact, until he came forward to assist the poor dramatists by his skill as a carpenter, and, in

in 1585 or the following year; and it is quite possible that, if it had not been for James Burbage, he would never have come to the metropolis, or written for us and for all time either *Hamlet* or *Macbeth*, as he would have had no stage on which to perform them. At all events, when he came to town, and joined the company at the Black-friars, he became a fast friend of James Burbage and of his son Richard, who became the Roscius of his age, and the original actor of most of Shakespeare's principal characters. The elder Burbage did not live to see the lease of his first theatre expire, and the building demolished and carried across the river into Southwark by his son Cuthbert. But he saw the Earl of Leicester's actors formally established as members of a recognised profession, and able to influence the age in which they lived. James Burbage died about the year 1594; his son Richard survived him for twenty years, dying two years before his friend Will Shakespeare. It may be of interest to add that the whole Burbage family lived and died in Holywell (now High) Street, Shoreditch, and were buried, along with several other "poor players," in St. Leonard's churchyard.

In 1596 Shakespeare appears to have lived near the Bear Garden, in Southwark. "I have yet to learn," writes Mr. Dyce, "that the fancy of Shakespeare could not luxuriate in rural images, even amid the fogs of Southwark and Blackfriars."

Shakespeare does not appear to have sustained any loss by the burning of the Globe Theatre, for he had parted with his interest in theatrical property on retiring to Stratford-on-Avon. His late partners, however, were sufferers to a very considerable extent, and Shakespeare, in all probability, contributed—along with King James and many of the nobility and gentry of the day—to the rebuilding of the theatre in the course of the following year.

As is well known, the line quoted as a motto to this chapter was the motto of the Globe Theatre; but it may not be known that this motto was the cause of two couplets of verse, by Ben Jonson and Shakespeare respectively, quoted by Mr. Dyce from "Poetical Characteristics," a manuscript formerly in the Harleian collection. Ben asks—

"If but stage-actors all the world displays,
    Where shall we find spectators of their plays?"

To this "Gentle Will" replies, with pleasant repartee:—

"Little or much of what we see we do;
    We're all both actors and spectators too."

Besides the Globe, there were, as stated above, three other theatres on the Bankside, called the "Rose," the "Hope," and the "Swan." These appear, for some undiscovered reason, to have been called "private" theatres. "There was this difference between these and the Globe and other public theatres, that the latter were open to the sky, except over the stage and galleries; but the private theatres were completely covered in from the weather. On the roof of all of them, whether public or private, a flag was always hoisted to mark the time of the performances.

The Rose Theatre had the honour of numbering Ben Jonson, in his early days, as one of its play-writers. In Henslowe's "Diary," the manager, under date July 28, 1597, acknowledges the receipt

of 3s. 9d. as part of "Bengemmens Johnsone's share;" and, from another entry, it would appear that on the same day Henslowe lent him four pounds. Early in the December of the same year, there is an entry of twenty shillings lent to Jonson upon a book which he was to write for the company before Christmas, the plot having been already shown to its members. These facts show that he had then gained some standing, though not, perhaps, a very high one, as a dramatic writer.

From the Rose we follow him to the Globe, where we find him for the first time associated with Shakespeare, on whose recommendation the company of that theatre accepted his first very successful hit, *Every Man in his Humour*, which drew on him the notice of Queen Elizabeth.

Whilst writing for the theatres, Ben Jonson lived on the Bankside, whence he afterwards removed to the house of a wool-comber, just outside Temple Bar, and close to the "Devil Tavern," where we have already made his acquaintance.*

The Rose Theatre stood at the north end of what was formerly called Rose Alley; it is mentioned by Taylor the "water-poet," in his "True Cause of the Waterman's Suit concerning Players," 1615. The Hope Theatre was near at hand, though we cannot identify its site precisely.

The Swan Theatre, near the Globe, was standing previous to 1598, and was so named from a house and tenement called the "Swan," mentioned in a charter of Edward VI., by which the manor of Southwark is granted to the City of London. It fell into decay in the reign of James I., was closed in 1613, and was subsequently used only for gladiatorial exhibitions. Yet in its time it had been well frequented; for a contemporary author says, "It was the continent of the world, because half the year a world of beauties and brave spirits resorted to it."

It may be mentioned here, in passing, that on this side of the Thames there was also another theatre at Newington Butts, of which, however, we know little except the fact that it was "frequented by the citizens in summer." In the days of the late Tudors and early Stuarts, the performances usually commenced at 3 p.m., and the prices of admission ranged from "a shilling for the best boxes or rooms," down to sixpence, twopence, and even a penny for the pit and galleries; and it is worthy of note that in the reign of the Protestant Elizabeth plays were acted both publicly and at Court on Sundays as well as on other days of the week, and under her successor at Court.

---

* See Vol. I., p. 39.

But the theatres were not, as already hinted, the only places of public amusement along the Bankside. A sort of circus, called at the time the Paris Garden, was erected and opened here about the middle of the sixteenth century, as a place for bear-baiting. The public were admitted by the payment of a penny at the gate, a penny at the "entry of the scaffold" or raised seats, and a third penny for "quiet standing." So popular indeed did the sport become that it even trenched on the theatres proper, and reduced their receipts. In 1591, as Mr. Chambers tells us in his "Book of Days," an order was issued from the Privy Council forbidding plays to be acted on Thursdays, because that day had been long set apart for "bear-baiting and such pastimes." The Lord Mayor of London appears to have followed with a public notice complaining that "in some places the players do use to recite their plays to the great hurt and destruction of the game of bear-baiting and such like pastimes, which are maintained for her Majesty's pleasure." It may be remarked that Elizabeth had been right royally entertained by Lord Leicester at Kenilworth with combats of dogs and bears, and no doubt often amused herself by witnessing the same scenes nearer home; so that in all probability she was occasionally present at Bankside, when, as we are told, "the baiting of bulls and of bears was the favourite holiday pastime of her Londoner subjects."

In Aggas's plan of London, taken in 1574, and in the plan taken by Braun about the same time, the bear-gardens are represented as plots of ground with scaffolding for the spectators, bearing the names of the "Bowlle Baytyng," and the "Beare Baytynge." "In both plans," says Thomas Allen, in his "History of Surrey," "the buildings appear to be circular, and to have been evidently intended as humble imitations of the ancient Roman amphitheatre. They stood in two adjoining fields, separated only by a small strip of land; but some differences are observable in the spots on which they are built. In Aggas's plan, which is the earlier of the two, the strip of land which lies between them contains only one large pond, common to the two places of exhibition; but in Braun's this appears divided into three ponds, besides a similar conveniency near each theatre. The use of these pieces of water is very well explained in 'Brown's Travels' (1685), where we find a plate of the 'Elector of Saxony his beare garden at Dresden,' in which is a large pond, with several bears amusing themselves in it, the account of which is highly curious:—' In the hunting-house in the old town are fifteen bears, very well provided

for, and looked unto. They have fountains and ponds to wash themselves in, wherein they much delight; and near to the pond are high ragged posts or trees set up for the bears to climb up, and scaffolds made at the top to sun and dry themselves; where they will also sleep, and come and go as the keeper calls them.' The ponds and dog-kennels for the bears on the Bankside are clearly marked in the plans alluded to; and the construction of the amphitheatres themselves may be tolerably well conceived, notwithstanding the smallness of the scale on which they are drawn. They evidently consisted, withinside, of a lower tier of circular seats for the spectators, at the back of which a sort of screen ran all round, in part open, so as to admit a view from without, evident in Braun's delineation by the figures who are looking through on the outside. The buildings are unroofed, and in both plans are shown during the time of performance, which in Aggas's view is announced by the display of little flags or streamers on the top. The dogs are tied up in slips near each place of 'baytyng,' ready for the sport, and the combatants are actually engaged in Braun's plan. Two little houses for retirement are at the head of each theatre."

The "Bear Garden," as this place came in process of time to be called, was still a place of frequent and favourite resort among the cavaliers of the reign of Charles I.; but the sport of bear-baiting went against the consciences, or, at all events, the stomachs, of the "Roundheads," who did their very best to suppress it. At the Restoration, however, it was revived (with some of the least good points of the Royalist faith and practice), and the Paris Garden again looked up, though only for a time.

As a specimen of the sort of amusements which went on here under the Stuart kings, let us take the following out of Samuel Pepys's "Diary" for 1666. He writes, under date of August 14, a few days before the Great Fire of London :—"After dinner, I went with my wife and Mercer to the Bear-Garden, where I have not been, I think, of many years, and saw some good sport of the bulls tossing the dogs—one into the very boxes; but it is a very rude and nasty pleasure. We had a great many Hectors in the same box with us (and one very fine went into the pit and played his dog for a wager, which was a strange sport for a gentleman), where they drank wine, and drank Mercer's health first, which I pledge with my hat off."

On the 28th of May in the following year, Pepys was again here; for under that date we find him writing :—"Abroad, and stopped at Bear-garden Stairs, there to see a prize fought. But the house so full there was no getting in there, so forced to go through an ale-house into the pit, where the bears are baited; and upon a stool did see them fight, which they did very furiously, a butcher and a waterman. The former had the better all along, till by-and-by the latter dropped his sword out of his hand, and the butcher, whether or not seeing his sword dropped I know not, but did give him a cut over the wrist, so as he was disabled to fight any longer. But Lord! to see in a minute how the whole stage was full of watermen to revenge the foul play, and the butchers to defend their fellow, though most blamed him: and there they all fell to it, knocking and cutting down many on each side. It was pleasant to see; but that I stood in the pit and feared that in the tumult I might get some hurt. At last the battle broke up, and so I away."

Again he writes, under date September 9th of the same year: "To the Bear Garden, where now the yard was full of people, and those most of them seamen, striving by force to get in. I got into the common pit, and there, with my cloak about my face, I stood and saw the prize fought, till one of them, a shoemaker, was so cut in both his wrists, that he could not fight any longer; and then they broke off. His enemy was a butcher. The sport very good; and various humours to be seen among the rabble that is there."

The inimitable secretary would seem to have been rather partial to this rough kind of sport, for we again find him here on the 12th of April, 1669, as shown by the following entry, under that date in his "Diary:"—"By water to the Bear Garden, and there happened to sit by Sir Fretchville Hollis, who is still full of his vain-glorious and prophane talk. Here we saw a prize fought between a soldier and a country fellow, one Warrel, who promised the least in his looks, and performed the most of valour in his boldness and evenness of mind, and smiles in all he did, that ever I saw; and we were all both deceived and infinitely taken with him. He did soundly beat the soldier, and cut him over the head. Thence back to White Hall, mightily pleased all of us with the sight, and particularly this fellow, as a most extraordinary man for his temper and evenness in fighting."

John Evelyn went on one occasion to witness the "sports" at Bankside, but apparently he was too disgusted to go there again. Here is the record of his visit, as told in his "Diary" under date of 16th of June, 1670 :—"I went with some friends to the Bear Garden, where was cock-fighting, dog-fighting, beare and bull baiting, it being a famous day for all these butcherly sports, or rather bar-

barous cruelties. The bulls did exceeding well, but the Irish wolfe-dog exceeded, which was a tall greyhound, a stately creature indeede, who beate a cruell mastiff. One of the bulls toss'd a dog full into a *lady's lap*, as she sat in one of the boxes at a considerable height from the arena. Two poore dogs were kill'd, and so all ended with the ape on horseback, and I most heartily weary of the rude and dirty pastime."

Chambers, in his "Book of Days," quotes a statement from the learned Erasmus, who visited England in the reign of Henry VIII., to the effect that the royal establishment included a "Master of the King's Bears," and that even the great noble-men had their bear-wards; and that "many 'herds of bears' were regularly trained for the arena." He also extracts from Laneham's account of the festivities at Kenilworth Castle the following pic-turesque description of a bear-baiting held on July 14, 1575, the sixth day of her Majesty's stay, when thirteen bears and a number of ban-dogs (a kind of mastiff) were tied up ready in the inner court. Laneham quaintly writes, comparing the baiting to a scene in Westminster Hall :—"The bears were brought forth into the court, the dogs set to them, to argue the points, even face to face. They had learned counsel also of both parts (*i.e.*, on both sides) . . . . Very fierce, both th' one and tother, and eager in argument. If the dog in pleading would pluck the bear by the throat, the bear, with traverse, would claw him again by the scalp; confess an he list but avoid he could not that was bound to the bar: and his counsel told him that it could do him no policy in pleading. Therefore, thus with fending and fearing, with plucking and tugging, scratching and biting, by plain tooth and nail to (the one) side and tother, such expense of blood and of leather was there between them as a month's licking, I ween, will not recover; and yet they remain as far out as ever they were. It was a sport very pleasant of these beasts to see the bear with his pink eyes leering after his enemy's approach, the nimbleness and weight of the dog to take his advantage, and the force and experience of the bear again to avoid the assault: if he were bitten in one place, he would pinch in another to get free: if he were taken once, then what shift with biting, with clawing, with roaring, tossing, and tumbling, he would work to wind himself from them, and when he was loose, to shake his ears twice or thrice, with the blood and the slaver about his phisnomy (*sic*) was a matter of goodly relief."

Ben Jonson is reproached by Dekker with having been so degraded as to have performed at Paris

Garden. These places seem always to have been in bad repute even when they flourished most. Crowley, a versifier of the reign of Henry VIII., thus speaks of the Paris Garden :—

> "What folly is this to keep with danger
> A great mastiff dog and foul ugly bear,
> And to this anent, to see them two fight
> With terrible tearings, a full ugly sight :
> And methinks these men are most fools of all
> Whose store of money is but very small.
> And yet every Sunday they will surely spend
> One penny or two, the bearward's living to mend.

> "At Paris Garden, each Sunday, a man shall not fail
> To find two or three hundred for the bearward's vale :
> One half-penny apiece they use for to give,
> When some have not more in their purses, I believe.
> Well, at the last day their consciences will declare
> That the poor ought to have all that they may spare.
> If you, therefore, go to witness a bear-fight,
> Be sure God His curse will upon you light."

Pennant, who quotes these verses, seems to consider the last two lines as a prophecy of the calamity that happened at the Garden in the year 1582. An accident, "heaven-directed," as he says, befell the spectators ; the scaffolding, crowded with people, suddenly fell, and more than a hundred persons were killed or severely wounded. The Bear Garden, it may be added, in spite of its name, would appear to have been chiefly used, during the latter period of its existence, for bull-baiting. Randolph, in his "Muse's Looking-glass," makes the following reference to this particular species of amusement :—

> "　——Lastly, he wished
> The bull might cross the Thames to the Bear Garden,
> And there be sorely baited."

It was to the Globe Theatre and the Bear Garden probably that Hentzner alludes in his "Travels in England," published in the reign of Elizabeth, when he writes :—"Without the city are some theatres, where actors do represent almost every day some tragedy or comedy to numerous audiences : these are concluded with excellent music, a variety of dances, amid the excessive applause of those that are present. There is also another place, built in the form of a theatre, which serves for the baiting of bulls and of bears ; they are fastened behind, and then worried by great English bull-dogs, but not without great risque to the dogs, from the horns of the one, and the teeth of the other ; and it sometimes happens they are killed on the spot ; fresh ones are immediately supplied in the places of those that are wounded or tired. To this entertainment there often follows that of whipping a blinded bear, which is performed by five or six men, standing circularly with whips, which they exercise upon him without any mercy,

as he cannot escape from them because of his chain ; he defends himself with all his force and skill, throwing down all who come within his reach, and are not active enough to get out of it ; on which occasions he frequently tears the whips out of their hands, and breaks them. At these spectacles, and everywhere else, the English are constantly smoking tobacco. In the theatres, fruits, such as apples, pears, and nuts, according to the season, are carried about to be sold, as well as ale and wine."

The theatres and gardens at Bankside, however, in spite of their bad reputation, were occasionally patronised by royalty ; for we read that Queen Elizabeth, on the 26th of May, 1599, went by water with the French ambassadors to Paris Gardens, where they saw a baiting of bulls and bears. Indeed, Southwark seems to have long been of sporting notoriety, for, in the *Humorous Lovers*, printed in 1617, one of the characters says, "I'll set up my bills, that the gamesters of London, Horsley-down, *Southwark*, and New-market may come in and bait him [the bear] here before the ladies," &c. It may here be added, as a scrap of antiquarian information, that the first exhibition of bear-baiting in England of which we read, was in the reign of King John, at Ashby-de-la-Zouch, where "thyss straynge passtyme was introduced by some Italyans for his highness' amusement, wherewith he and his court were highly delighted."

It is clear that the "sport" to be witnessed in the Bear Garden was still under the patronage and countenance of royalty some century or so later than the reign of Elizabeth, for in 1675 we read of a warrant signed by Lord Arlington, ordering ten pounds to be paid to Mr. James Davies, the "master of his Majesty's bears, bulls, and dogs," for "making ready the rooms at the Bear Garden, and baiting the bears before the Spanish ambassadors."

The celebrated actor, Alleyn—the founder of Dulwich College, of whom we shall have more to say anon—enjoyed this lucrative post as "keeper of the king's wild beasts, or master of the Royal Bear Garden, situated on the Bankside in Southwark." The profits of this place are said by his biographer to have been "immense," sometimes amounting to £500 a year ; and will account for the great fortune of which he died possessed. A little before his death, he sold his share and patent to his wife's father, a Mr. Hinchtoe, for £580.

Isaac D'Israeli, in his "Life of Charles I.," mentions the fact that the Sabbatarian view of Sunday was much advanced in London by the accident mentioned above which occurred here in 1582 :—

"At Paris Garden, where public amusements were performed on Sundays, a crowded scaffold gave way; and by this accident, some were killed, and many were wounded." The Lord Mayor (who was a leading Puritan) made religious capital out of the fact by sending a formal notice of it to Lord Burleigh, as a "judgment of heaven for the violation of the Sabbath," thereby confusing the seventh with the first day of the week.

reasons alleged for this royal grant are stated by Anderson, in the quaint language of the time, to have been for "the honest and reasonable recreation of good and civil people, who for their quality and ability may lawfully use the games of bowling, tennis, dice, cards, tables, nine-holes, or any other game hereafter to be invented."

The Puritans' aversion to the sport, however, as Macaulay remarks, arose not so much from pity for

THE BOROUGH, HIGH STREET, IN 1825.

We find that, in spite of his Puritan education, King James I. had the good sense to legalise those rational amusements without which life in a crowded metropolis would be past endurance. It is well known that he published the "Book of Sports," but it is not equally well known that in 1620 he issued his royal licence to Clement Cottrell, the groom-porter of his household, to license certain houses for bowling-alleys and tennis-courts, and even for cards and dice. Twenty-four bowling-alleys were licensed under this authority in London and Westminster, four more in Southwark, one in St. Catherine's, one in Shoreditch, and two in Lambeth. Within these same limits, fourteen tennis-courts were allowed, and also forty "taverns or ordinaries for playing at cards and dice." The

the bull or the bear, as from envy at the pleasure felt by the spectators. Verily, an amiable and saint-like trait! On the Restoration of Charles II., and the downfall of the Puritan faction, it can hardly be a matter of surprise to find that the legislation which had so long been applied to the suppression of even rational amusements should have taken a swing in the opposite direction.

It may be added, that although bear-baiting and bull-baiting never flourished under our later Stuart or our earlier Hanoverian sovereigns, it was not until 1835 that the practice was actually put down by Act of Parliament, which forbade the keeping of any house, pit, or other place for baiting or fighting any bull, bear, dog, or other animal. "And thus," observes Mr. Chambers, "after an existence

SOUTHWARK FAIR.   *After Hogarth's Picture.*   *See page* 58.)

of at least seven centuries, this ceased to rank among the amusements of the English people."

Strype, in his first edition of "Stow," published in 1720, speaking of Bear Alley, on this spot, says, "Here is a glass-house, and about the middle a new-built court, well inhabited, called Bear Garden Square, so called, as being built in the place where the Bear Garden formerly stood, until removed to the other side of the water; which is more convenient for the butchers and such like, who are taken with such rustic sports as the baiting of bears and bulls."

In the early part of the last century it would seem that another Bear Garden at Hockley-in-the-Hole, near Clerkenwell, had superseded this place of amusement in the public favour, probably on account of the absence of bridges across the Thames; and consequently, when it is suggested in the *Spectator* of August 11th, 1711, that those who go to theatres merely for a laugh had better "seek their diversion at the Bear Garden," in all probability the reference is *not* to Bankside.

The name of the Bear Garden, however, still exists in this neighbourhood, being painted up at the corner of a court between the Bankside and Sumner Street.

The old Paris Garden—the name of which, too, still survives in this locality—was circular, open to the sky, surrounded with a high wall, without external windows; the scaffolds, or boxes, were in a wooden structure in the interior, surmounted by a high-pitched roof and a cupola.

The names of these and of many other such places of amusement bear testimony to the spirit of national jollity on the part of Londoners during the eighteenth century. But pleasure-gardens are almost as transitory as pleasure itself; of all these not one now remains "the sad historian of the pensive tale" of bygone mirth and merriment. The jests have passed away, and so are the trees beneath which, and the walls within which, those jests were uttered, and those who pealed back echoes of the loudest laughter are silent in their graves.

In the neighbourhood of the theatres were several public gardens near the Thames, then a pellucid and beautiful stream. There were the Queen's Pike Gardens (now Pye Gardens), where pike were bred in ponds; the Asparagus Garden, and Pimlico Garden. The last-named was a very fashionable resort, and famous for the handsome dresses of the promenaders. Indeed, to "walk in Pimlico" was a proverbial phrase for an introduction to the very *élite* of society.

In Chambers' "Book of Days" is given a view of London during the Great Fire in 1666, as seen from the rear of Bankside, from a print of the period by Visscher. The foreground is poetically raised, so as to represent a fairly high hill, though there is no high ground all the way down to Clapham; on it are sitting well-dressed citizens coolly surveying the disaster, while their dogs are lying asleep by their side. Evelyn writes in his "Diary:"—"2 Sept. This fatal night, about ten, began that deplorable fire neere Fish Streete in London.—3. I had public prayers at home. The fire continuing, after dinner I took coach with my wife and sonn, and went to the Bankside in Southwark, where we beheld the dismal spectacle, the whole City in dreadfull flames neare the water side; all the houses from the Bridge, all Thames Street, and upwards towards Cheapside, downe to the Three Cranes, were now consum'd. . . . . The poore inhabitants were dispers'd about St. George's Fields, and Moorefields as far as Highgate, and several miles in circle, some under tents, some under miserable hutts and hovells, many without a rag or any necessary utensils, bed or board, who from delicatenesse, riches, and easy accommodations in stately and well furnish'd houses, were now reduced to extreamest misery and poverty."

Chambers tells us, in his work above quoted, that there was an ale-house in Southwark, which had on its walls an authentic portrait of Dick Tarleton, the eccentric comic actor of Elizabeth's time. No doubt this "ale-house" was in the neighbourhood of Bankside; but though Dick's name was kept up by tradition for upwards of a century, and though his jests were collected and published, with notes and illustrations, by the Shakespeare Society, it is impossible now to identify the house in which many of Shakespeare's players no doubt used to congregate.

Another old tavern, formerly standing in the neighbourhood, bore the sign of "The Tumble-down Dick," which afforded, as the "Adventurer" says, a fine moral on the instability of human greatness, and the consequences of ambition. It refers, of course, to Richard Cromwell, and his fall from the power bequeathed to him by his father Oliver. An allusion to this tumbling propensity occurs in Butler's "Remains," in the tale of the "Cobbler and the Vicar of Bray:"—

> "What's worse, old Noll is marching off;
>   And Dick, his heir apparent,
> Succeeds him in the Government,
>   A very lame Vice-Gerent.
> He'll reign but little time, poor tool!
>   But sink beneath the state,
> That will not fail to ride the fool
>   'Bove common horseman's weight."

Of several of the old inns and taverns of Southwark we shall have occasion to speak when dealing with the High Street; but we may remark here that those in Bankside, and along by the river generally, had a peculiar characteristic of their own, which has been well described by Charles Dickens in "Our Mutual Friend" and some other of his works. George Augustus Sala, too, in his "Gaslight and Daylight," tells us, with a certain amount of drollery, how that "the Surrey shore of the Thames, at London, is dotted with damp houses of entertainment;" and then he goes on to describe the typical waterside public-house, the "Tom Tug's Head," as "surrounded on three sides by mud, and standing on rotten piles of timber, and with its front always unwashed."

CHAPTER VI.

SOUTHWARK (continued).—HIGH STREET, &c.

"Brevis est via."—Virgil, "Eclogues."

The Southwark Entrance to London Bridge—The Town Hall—Southwark Fair—Union Hall—Dr. Elliotson—Mint Street—Suffolk House—Lant Street—Charles Dickens's Home when a Boy—The Mint—Great Suffolk Street—The "Moon-rakers"—The Last Barber-surgeon—Winchester Hall—Finch's Grotto Gardens—The Old Workhouse of Southwark—King's Bench Prison—Major Hanger, Dr. Syntax, Haydon, and George Moreland, Inmates of the King's Bench—The "Marshal" of the King's Bench—Alsager's Bleaching-ground—Blackman Street—Sir James South—Eliza Cook—Kent Street—A Disreputable Neighbourhood—The Lock Hospital—A Hard-working Philanthropist—St. George's Church—The Burial-place of Bishop Bonner—Marriage of General Monk and Nan Clarges—The Marshalsea—Anecdotes of Bishop Bonner—Colonel Culpeper—Dickens's Reminiscences of the Marshalsea—The Sign of "The Hand"—Commercial Aspect of Southwark—Sanitary Condition of Southwark—Appearance of Southwark in the Seventeenth Century.

THE Borough, High Street, as we have already shown, serving for many centuries as the entrance into London from Surrey and Kent, and, indeed, from the Continent, has always been a very important thoroughfare of the metropolis; but, as a pleasant, gossiping writer of modern times, Mr. Miller, has truthfully observed in his "Picturesque Sketches"—"What a different feature does the Southwark entrance to London Bridge present to what it did only a few brief years ago! Every few minutes omnibuses are now thundering to and from the railway terminus; while passengers think no more of journeying to Brighton and back, and remaining eight or ten hours there, on a long summer's day, than they formerly did of travelling to Greenwich; for it took the old, slow stage-wagons as long to traverse the five miles to the latter as our iron-footed steed to drag the five hundred passengers at his heels, and land them within sight of the wide, refreshing sea."

Starting from St. Saviour's Church, and passing under the railway bridge which spans the road, we now make our way southward. The alterations made in the High Street, when Southwark Street was planned and formed, involved the demolition of the Town Hall. This building stood at the angle formed by the High Street and Compter Street, and dated its erection from the close of the last century, when it was built in place of an older edifice, which had become ruinous. The old Town Hall, in its turn, too, occupied the place of a still older hall, having been rebuilt in the reign of Charles II. After the union of the parish of St. Margaret-at-Hill with that of St. Saviour's, the old church of the former parish was desecrated, being used partly as a prison, and partly as a court of justice. The building was destroyed in the fire of 1676. A statue of the king was placed in front of the building by which it was succeeded; and on the base of the pediment was an inscription notifying the "re-edification," with the date 1686. On one side of the statue were the arms of London; and on the other, those of Southwark. On the occasion of the rebuilding of the hall in 1793, the statue of the king, instead of being replaced in its original situation, was sold, and set up in a neighbouring court called Three Crown Court, upon a pedestal of brickwork, the inside of which, strange to say, was made to serve as a watch-box for a "Charley." At the same time, a figure of Justice, which had formerly, in conjunction with one of Wisdom, supported the Lord Mayor's seat in the Town Hall, was placed near the bar of a neighbouring coffee-house. On this event, the following *jeu d'esprit* is preserved in Concanen and Morgan's "History of the Parish of St. Mary Overy:"—

"Justice and Charles have left the hill,
    The City claimed their place;
Justice resides at Dick West's still;
    But mark poor Charles's case:
Justice, safe from wind and weather,
    Keeps the tavern score;
But Charley, turned out altogether,
    Keeps the watch-house door."

After remaining for some time in Three Crown Court, the poor unfortunate monarch, we believe, found a resting-place in the shady nook of a garden in the New Kent Road. The prison, or compter, as it was called, was removed to Mill Lane, Tooley Street, but has since been demolished.

The new Town Hall was a very plain and unpretending structure. It consisted of a rusticated basement, from which rose four Ionic pilasters. The windows were arched, and the interior was fitted up as a police-office. The police-court was eventually removed further southward, to Blackman Street. In front of the Town Hall, facing Blackman Street, the hustings for the election of representatives for the borough were usually erected.

The Town Hall has been occasionally used for criminal trials. Thus we read that on the 23rd of June, 1746, eight of the judges went in procession from Serjeants' Inn to the Town Hall on St. Margaret's Hill, and opened the special commission for the trial of the prisoners concerned in the rebellion in Scotland. Those prisoners who were found guilty and received sentence of death were soon afterwards hung, drawn, and quartered on Kennington Common. Between their trial and execution the prisoners were confined in the new gaol, Southwark.

On St. Margaret's Hill, in the immediate neighbourhood of the Town Hall, Southwark Fair was formerly held. This fair, afterwards so famous, was established by virtue of a charter from King Edward VI., dated 1550. The charter cost the good citizens of London nearly £650—a large sum at that period—and the fair itself was to be held on the 7th, 8th, and 9th of September. It was one of the three great fairs of special importance, described in a proclamation of Charles I., "unto which there is usually extraordinary resort out of all parts of the kingdom." The fairs here referred to, according to Rymer, were "Bartholomew Fair, in Smithfield; Sturbridge Fair, in Cambridge; and Our Lady Fair, in the borough of Southwark." It was opened in great state by the Lord Mayor and Sheriffs, who rode over London Bridge, and so on to Newington, thence back to the Bridge House, where, of course, was a banquet. "The 'hood-bearer' on this occasion," writes John Timbs, "wore a fine embroidered cap, said to have been presented to the City by a monastery in 1473."

Allusions to the fair are frequent enough in the old writers; but it is most familiar to us through Hogarth's picture of "Southwark Fair." In his time the fair lasted fourteen days, and extended from St. Margaret's Hill, the spot where it was originally held (near the Town Hall), to the Mint; and of course the visitors comprised a considerable portion of the inhabitants of that favoured locality. In Hogarth's plate—a copy of which we reproduce on page 55—we see Figg, the prize-fighter, with plastered head, riding on a miserable nag; Cadman, a celebrated rope-dancer, is represented flying by a rope from the tower of St. George's Church to that part of the Mint which lies in the rear of the houses opposite. The portrait of another famous rope-dancer, Violante, is introduced by Hogarth. From the steeple of the church of St. Martin's-in-the-Fields, soon after its completion, this slack-rope performer descended, head foremost, on a rope stretched across St. Martin's Lane to the Royal Mews, in the presence of the princesses and a host of noble personages. Besides these characters, Hogarth shows us a beautiful woman beating a drum, attended by a black boy with a trumpet; a booth tumbling down, and the name of the piece to be performed, the *Fall of Bagdad*, is inscribed on the tottering paper lantern. Tamerlane, in full armour, is being taken into custody by a bum-bailiff; and in the background are shows with enormous placards announcing the Royal Wax-work, the horse of Troy, and the wonderful performances of Bankes and his horse. If the company frequenting the fair was of a strange sort, the entertainments offered appear to have been of a suitable character. From old advertisements of the fair, of dates between 1730 and 1740, we learn that at Lee and Harper's great booth was performed a thrilling tragedy called *Bateman, or the Unhappy Marriage;* but, lest the audience should be too much affected, it was lightened by the *Comical Humours of Sparrow, Pumpkin, and Sheer going to the Wars.* There appears to have been as great a taste for burlesque as that which now exists; but the subjects were curiously chosen. We have the rudiments of a modern pantomime in *The Fall of Phaëton*, interspersed with comic scenes between Punch, Harlequin, Scaramouch, Pierrot and Columbine, "which," we are told, "the town has lately been in expectation to see performed." The performers, it should be remembered, were not wretched show-folk, but the regular actors of the large theatres, who regularly established booths at Bartholomew's and Southwark Fairs, in which the most charming actresses and accomplished actors thought it no disgrace to appear in the miserable trash mentioned above. In the biography of "Jo Miller," we read that the sound of Smithfield revelry had but just died away, to be caught up, as if in echo, by Southwark, when the *Daily Post*, having shed a tearful paragraph upon the opening sepulchre of " Matt Prior," proceedeth to tell how that " Mr. Doggett, the famous player, is likewise dead, having made a standing provision annually for a coat and badge, to be rowed for by six watermen on the 1st of August, being the day of His Majesty's happy accession to the Throne." This was on the 23rd of September, 1721. Two days afterwards we read, "Yesterday the remains of Mr. Dogget were interred at Eltham, in Kent." So far the humble player—now for the courtier poet. "The same evening the remains of Matthew Prior, Esquire, were carried to the Jerusalem Chamber, and splendidly interred in Westminster Abbey." When "Jo" received the news of Doggett's death, we have not the smallest doubt that he was too much overcome to go on with the part he was playing at Southwark Fair; and having that day divided the profits of the Smithfield speculation with Pinkey and Jubilee Dickey, he assiduously mourned his departed master at the "Angel Tavern," which then stood next door to the King's Bench.

Besides the theatrical entertainments, Faux's sleight of hand and the mechanical tricks and dexterity of Dr. Pinchbeck were for many years favourite adjuncts of Southwark Fair.

John Evelyn in his "Diary," under date 13th September, 1660, says, "I saw in Southwark, at St. Margaret's Faire, monkies and asses dance and do other feates of activity on ye tight rope; they were gallantly clad *à la mode*, went upright, saluted the company, bowing and pulling off their hatts; they saluted one another with as good a grace as if instructed by a dancing-master. They turned heels over head with a basket having eggs in it, without breaking any; also with lighted candles in their hands and on their heads, without extinguishing them, and with vessells of water, without spilling a drop. I also saw an Italian wench daunce and performe all the tricks on ye tight rope to admiration; all the Court went to see her. Likewise here was a man who tooke up a piece of iron cannon of about 400 lb. weight, with the haire of his head onely."

From Pepys's own quaint and amusing description, too, we glean some further particulars of the entertainments provided here. On the 21st of September, 1668, he writes: " To Southwark Fair, very dirty, and there saw the puppet-show of Whittington, which is pretty to see; and how that idle thing do work upon people that see it, and even myself too! And thence to Jacob Hall's dancing on the ropes, where I saw such action as I never saw before, and mightily worth seeing; and here took acquaintance with a fellow who carried me to a

tavern, whither came the music of this booth, and by-and-by Jacob Hall himself, with whom I had a mind to speak, whether he ever had any mischief by falls in his time. He told me, 'Yes, many, but never to the breaking of a limb.' He seems a mighty strong man. So giving them a bottle or two of wine, I away."

In the reign of George II. the fairs of London were in the zenith of their fame. Mr. Frost observes in his "Old Showmen:"—" During the second quarter of the eighteenth century they were resorted to by all classes of the people, even by royalty; and the theatrical booths which formed part of them boasted of the best talent in the profession. Not only were they regarded as the nurseries of histrionic ability, as the provincial theatres came afterwards to be regarded; but they witnessed the efforts to please of the best actors of the London theatres when in the noon of their success and popularity. Cibber, Quin, Macklin, Woodward, Shuter, did not disdain to appear before a Bartholomew Fair audience, nor Fielding to furnish them with the early gushings of his humour. The inimitable Hogarth made the light of his peculiar genius shine upon them, and the memories of the 'Old Showman' are preserved in more than one of his pictures." Southwark Fair was not finally suppressed till 1763. The booth-keepers used to collect money for the relief of the prisoners in the Marshalsea hard by.

In the registers of the parish of St. Margaret's occurs the following curious entry, under date 1451-2: "Rec^d in dawnsing [dancing] money of the Maydens, iii$s.$ viij$d.$" To what this may refer, whether to any religious ceremony or public procession, it is at this distant period difficult to tell.

At the east end of Union Street, close by St. Margaret's Hill, formerly stood Union Hall. On the opening of this street to the Borough by taking down the "Greyhound Inn," in 1781, Union Hall was built by subscription, for the use of the magistrates, previous to which time they sat at the "Swan Inn," which was afterwards converted into a private house. On the passing of the Police Act in 1830 Union Hall was made one of the Metropolitan police offices. On the destruction of the old Town Hall, as above mentioned, the sessions for the county were held there, though it was not adequate to the business till the county gaol and a sessions house were built nearer to Newington Butts.

At No. 104 in the High Street was born Dr. Elliotson, F.R.S., the celebrated physician. He was the son of a chemist and druggist, whose house bore the sign of the " Golden Key," of which a token exists. Dr. Elliotson was a devoted student of mesmerism and mesmeric influences, upon which he wrote largely. Thackeray, it may be added, was taken ill when writing "Pendennis," and was saved from death by Dr. Elliotson, to whom, in gratitude, he dedicated the novel when he lived to finish it. Dr. Elliotson died in 1868.

Mint Street, opposite St. George's Church, keeps in remembrance a mint for the coinage of money, which was established here by Henry VIII. at Suffolk House, the residence of his brother-in-law,

Edward VI., in the second year of his reign, came from Hampton Court and dined at this house, where he knighted John Yorke, one of the Sheriffs of London. He afterwards returned through the City to Westminster. Queen Mary gave the mansion to Nicholas Heath, Archbishop of York, "and to his successors for ever, to be their inn or lodging for their repair to London," as a recompense for York House, Westminster, which was taken from Wolsey and the see of York by her royal father.

THE MINT, SOUTHWARK, IN 1825.

Charles Brandon, Duke of Suffolk. The mansion was a large and stately edifice, fronting upon the High Street. It was ornamented with turrets and cupolas, and enriched with carved work; at the back, the range of outbuildings formed an enclosed court. The house was sometimes called the "Duke's Palace," as well as Suffolk House; and it is likewise mentioned as "Brandonne's Place, in Southwarke," in Sir John Howard's expenses, under the year 1465. It was exchanged by the Duke of Suffolk with Henry VIII., the king giving him in return the house of the Bishop of Norwich in St. Martin's-in-the-Fields. On this exchange the mansion took the name of Southwark Place, and a mint was established here for the king's use.

Archbishop Heath sold the premises, which were partly pulled down, many small cottages being built on the site. Some portion of the house which was left became the residence of Edward Bromfield, who was Lord Mayor in 1637. He was owner of the premises in 1650. His son John was created a baronet in 1661, and in 1679 he was described as "of Suffolk Place, Bart.," in the marriage settlement with Joyce, only child of Thomas Lant, son and heir of William Lant, a merchant of London. This estate devolving to the Lant family, we find that in the reign of Queen Anne an Act was passed for the improvement of Suffolk Place, empowering Thomas Lant to let leases for fifty-one years. In 1773 it was advertised to be let as seventeen acres, on which were 400 houses, with a rental of £1,000 per annum. The entire estate was sold early in the present century, in ninety-eight lots, the rental of the estate having been just doubled. The family of Lant are still kept in remembrance by Lant Street, which runs from Blackman Street parallel with Mint Street.

A back attic at the house of an "Insolvent-court agent" belonging to the Marshalsea, in Lant late Duke of Suffolk, in the reign of Henry VIII., coming into the king's hands, was called Southwork (*sic*) Place, and a mint of coinage was there kept for the king. The inhabitants of late—like those of the White Fryars, Savoy, &c.—have assumed to themselves a protection from arrests for debts, against whom a severe though just statute was made in the 8 and 9 William and Mary, whereby any person having moneys owing from any in these

THE KING'S BENCH, SOUTHWARK, IN 1830.

Street, was one of the temporary homes of Charles Dickens when a boy; it was the same in which he described Mr. Bob Sawyer as living many years afterwards. "A bed and bedding," he writes, "were sent over for me and made up on the floor. The little window had a pleasant prospect of a timber-yard; and when I took possession of my new abode, I thought it was a Paradise." The various members of the family of the Insolvent-Court Agent are immortalised as the "Garlands" in the "Old Curiosity Shop."

The Mint is thus curiously described in the "New View of London," published in 1708:—"It is on the west side of Blackman Street, near against St. George's Church, and was so called for that a sumptuous house, built by Charles Brandon,

pretended privileged places, may, upon a legal process taken out, require the Sheriffs of London and Middlesex, the head Bailiff of the Dutchy Liberty, or the High Sheriff of Surrey, or Bailiff of Southwork, or their deputies, to take out a *posse comitatus*, and arrest such persons, or take their goods upon execution." And then follows a long list of penalties, including the pillory, to which all persons resisting their authority are exposed. It is added, "Yet notwithstanding this place pretends as much to Privilege as before, though this Act has supprest all other (such-like) places. And these streets are reckoned within the compass of this Mint—viz., Mint Street, Crooked Lane, and Bell's Rents; also Cannon Street, Suffolk Street, St. George Street, Queen Street, King Street, Peter Street, Harrow

Alley, Anchor Alley, and Duke Street, all in the parish of St. George's, Southwork." The Mint, as the district was called, consisted, therefore, of several streets, whose inhabitants claimed the privilege of protection from arrest for debt—a privilege which, says the "Ambulator" (1774), "has since been suppressed by the legislature, who have lately passed an Act for establishing a Court of Conscience here for the better recovery of small debts."

The place had become a refuge for the worst characters—in fact, another Alsatia, into which few bailiffs or officers of justice dared to venture. Felons and outlaws, debtors and vagabonds, herded there ; and to this day it is one of the plague-spots of the metropolis. Marriages, not à la mode, like those of Mayfair and the Fleet, were performed here constantly, and highwaymen and burglars found a secure retreat in its mazy courts. " Mat o' the Mint " is one of Macheath's companions, and Jonathan Wild was a frequent visitor. To poor authors it was a more secure Grub Street ; but though duns could not enter, starvation and death could. Here, in 1716, died Nahum Tate, once poet laureate, and, in conjunction with Brady, the author of that metrical version of the Psalms which superseded Sternhold and Hopkins's psalmody in prayer-books. Allusion is often made to the precincts of the Mint by the poets and comic writers. The reader of Pope's satires will not forget the lines—

> " No place is sacred, not the church is free,
> E'en Sunday shines no ' Sabbath Day ' to me ;
> Then from the Mint walks forth the man of rhyme,
> Happy to catch me just at dinner-time."

Nathaniel Lee, the dramatist, lived often in the Mint ; he had frequent attacks of insanity, and at one period of his life spent four years in Bedlam. He wrote eleven plays, and possessed genius (as Addison admitted) well adapted for tragedy, though clouded by occasional rant, obscurity, and bombast. Latterly, this ill-starred poet depended for subsistence on a small weekly allowance from the theatre. He died in 1691 or 1692. Pope often alludes to the Mint with scorn, and he makes mention of Lee's existence here in the following couplet :—

> " In durance, exile, Bedlam, or the Mint,
> Like Lee or Budgell, I will rhyme and print."

There are numerous allusions in old gossiping books and pamphlets of the seventeenth century to the customs of the Mint, the vagabond population of which maintained their privileges with a high hand. If a bailiff ventured to cross the boundary of the sanctuary, he was seized and searched for proofs of his calling ; then, when the perilous documents were found, dragged by the mob from pump to pump, and thoroughly soused. A ducking in one of the open sewer ditches followed, and then he was made to swear, kissing a brickbat debaubed with filth from the *cloaca*, that he would never again attempt to serve a process in the Mint. The next step was the payment of certain fees for the purchase of gin. If he had no money in his pockets, he was handed over to the tender mercy of the women and boys, who gave him a few more duckings and shampooings with filthy brickbats, and then kicked him out of the precincts.

An attempt was made to curtail the privilege of protection afforded by the Mint in the reign of William III., but it was not finally suppressed till the Georgian era.

Thomas Miller, in his " Picturesque Sketches of London," published in 1852, gives the following description of the old Mint, which he had written seven years previously, after visiting the remains of this dilapidated neighbourhood :—" Stretching from St. George's Church, in the Borough, into the high road which leads to the cast-iron bridge of Southwark, are no end of narrow courts, winding alleys, and ruined houses, which a bold-hearted man would hesitate to thread after dusk. Here stand numbers of houses which are unroofed and uninhabited. Years ago they were doomed to be pulled down, and it was resolved that a wide open street should be built upon the space they now occupy. Years may still roll on before they are removed. There is no place like this in the suburbs of London, no spot that looks so murderous, so melancholy, and so miserable. Many of these houses, besides being old, are very large and lofty. Many of these courts stand just as they did when Cromwell sent out his spies to hunt up and slay the Cavaliers, just as they again were hunted in return, after the Restoration, by the Royalists, who threaded their intricacies, with sword and pistol in hand, in search of the fallen Roundheads. There is a smell of past ages about these ancient courts, like that which arises from decay—a murky closeness—as if the old winds which blew through them in the time of the Civil Wars had become stagnant, and all old things had fallen and died just as they were blown together, and left to perish. So it is now. The timber of these old houses looks bleached and dead ; and the very brickwork seems never to have been new. In them you find wide, hollow-sounding, decayed staircases, that lead into great ruinous rooms, whose echoes are only awakened by the shrieking and running of large black-eyed rats, which eat through the solid floors, through the wainscot, and live and die without being startled by a human voice. From the Southwark Bridge Road you may see the roofs of many of these great desolate houses; they are broken and open; and the massy oaken rafters are exposed to the summer sun and the snow of winter. Some of the lower floors are still inhabited; and at the ends of these courts you will see standing, on a fine day, such characters as you will meet with nowhere besides in the neighbourhood of London. Their very dress is peculiar; and they frequent the dark and hidden public-houses which abound in these close alleys—placed where the gas is burning all day long. Excepting the courts behind Long Lane, in Smithfield, we know no spot about London like this, which yet fronts St. George's Church, in the Borough."

"The Mint," says Charles Knight, in his "London," "was the scene of 'the life, character, and behaviour' of Jack Sheppard; and within the same precincts, at the 'Duke's Head,' still standing in Redcross Street, his companion in villainy, Jonathan Wild, kept his horses. The Mint and its vicinity has been an asylum for debtors, coiners, and vagabonds of every kind, ever since the middle of the sixteenth century. It is districts like these which will always furnish the population of the prisons, in spite of the best attempts to reform and improve offenders by a wise, beneficent, and enlightened system of discipline, until moral efforts of a similar nature be directed to the fountain-head of corruption. There are districts in London whose vicious population, if changed to-day for one of a higher and more moral class, would inevitably be deteriorated by the physical agencies by which they would be surrounded, and the following generation might rival the inhabitants of Kent Street or the Mint."

The Mint is awfully memorable in modern annals; for amid the squalor of its narrow streets appeared, in 1832, the first case of Asiatic cholera in the metropolis. Again, Thomas Miller, in his work above quoted, refers to this miserable locality when he says, "The 'Land of Death,' in which we dwelt, was Newington, hemmed in by Lambeth, Southwark, Walworth, Bermondsey, and other gloomy parishes, through which the pestilence* stalked like a destroying angel in the deep shadows of the night and the open noon of day."

In the autobiographical reminiscences of his childhood, which are embodied in his "Life," by Mr. John Forster, Charles Dickens describes the quaint old streets of "low-browed" shops which lay between Rowland Hill's chapel in the Blackfriars Road, and his humble lodgings in Lant Street, mentioned above, along which he had to

pass night by night, in returning from his drudgery at Hungerford Stairs. He tells us of the boot-lace and hat and cap shops which he patronised, and of another shop conspicuous for its sign of "a golden dog licking a golden pot," over the door, and which may still be seen at the corner of Charlotte Street, Blackfriars Road. He tells us also how on Saturday nights he would be seduced into the inside of show-vans containing the "Fat Pig," the "Wild Indian," and the "Little Dwarf Lady," in this immediate neighbourhood.

In 1877 steps were taken by the Metropolitan Board of Works with the view of levelling with the ground a large part of the disreputable neighbourhood now under notice, and comprising Mint Street, King Street, and Elizabeth Place. A great improvement has since been effected. In Southwark Bridge Road are now the headquarters of the Metropolitan Fire Brigade, moved hither from Watling Street. Here also is the Evelina Hospital for Sick Children, founded in 1869, by Baron Ferdinand de Rothschild, in memory of his deceased wife. This hospital affords relief in the course of a year to nearly 6,000 poor children.

Great Suffolk Street, nearer "Stones' End," is named from Charles Brandon, Duke of Suffolk, who, as stated above, lived here, in Suffolk House. This street was formerly known by the name of "Dirty Lane," an appellation which it very well deserved. The "Moon-rakers" is the sign of a public-house in this street, where it has stood for upwards of half a century. "The original of this," says Mr. Larwood, in his "History of Sign-boards," "may have been one of the stories of the 'Wise Men of Gotham.' A party of them going out one bright night, saw the reflection of the moon in the water; and, after due deliberation, decided that it was a green cheese, and so raked for it. Another version is, that some Gothamites, passing in the night over a bridge, saw from the parapet the moon's reflection in the river below, and took it for a green cheese. They held a consultation as to the best means of securing it, when it was resolved that one should hold fast to the parapet whilst the others hung from him hand-in-hand, so as to form a chain to the water below, the last man to seize the prize. When they were all in this position, the uppermost, feeling the load heavy, and his hold giving away, called out, 'Hallo! you below, hold tight while I take off my hand to spit on it!' The wise men below replied, 'All right!' upon which he let go his hold, and they all dropped into the water, and were drowned."

In this street lived the last barber who let blood and drew teeth in London, the last of the barber-

---

* The cholera, during the visitation of 1849.

surgeons; he died there about 1821, as Mr. Cunningham was told by an old and intelligent hairdresser in the Strand; "To which," adds Mr. John Timbs, in his "Autobiography," "I may add my remembrance of his shop-window, with its heap of drawn teeth, and the barber's pole at the door. His name was Middleditch, and, *renovare dolorem*, I have a vivid recollection of his dentistry."

At the corner of Great Suffolk Street and Southwark Bridge Road stands Winchester Hall. This is neither more nor less than a concert-room, of the ordinary music-hall type, and is attached to a public-house which originally bore the sign of "The Grapes." Close by this spot, in former times, were some well-known pleasure-grounds. They bore the name of Finch's Grotto Gardens, and were situated on the west side of Southwark Bridge Road. They were first opened as a place of public resort about the first year of the reign of George III. Here Suett and Nan Cuttley acted and sang, if we may trust the statement of John Timbs, who adds that the old Grotto House was burnt down in 1796, but soon afterwards rebuilt, a stone being inserted in its wall with the following inscription:—

> " Here herbs did grow
> And flowers sweet ;
> But now 'tis called
> St. George's Street."

"Within my remembrance," writes Mr. John Reynolds in his agreeable work, "Records of My Life," "there was a place called Finch's Grotto Gardens, a sort of minor Vauxhall, situated near the King's Bench Prison. There was a grotto in the middle of the garden, and an orchestra and rotunda. The price of admission was sixpence, and the place was much frequented by the humbler classes." He goes on to say, as a proof of the estimate in which the place was held, that "Tommy Lowe, after having once been proprietor of Marylebone Gardens, and having kept his carriage, "was absolutely reduced to the necessity of accepting an engagement at these Grotto Gardens."

Finch's Grotto Gardens, doubtless, was one of those suburban tea-gardens which were at one time pretty plentiful in the outskirts of London. The Prussian writer, D'Archenholz, in his account of England, published towards the close of the last century, is represented by Chambers as observing that, "The English take a great delight in the public gardens near the metropolis, where they assemble and take tea together in the open air. The number of these in the neighbourhood of the capital is amazing, and the order, regularity, neatness, and even elegance of them are truly admirable. They are, however," he adds, "very rarely frequented by

people of fashion; but the middle and lower ranks go there often, and seem much delighted with the music of an organ which is usually played in an adjoining building."

A large building, occupying three sides of a quadrangle, adjoining Finch's Grotto Gardens, was at one time the workhouse of St. Saviour's parish. It was built at an expense of about £5,000, and was opened in 1777. Under the new Poor Law Act, the parish of St. Saviour's forms a union with that of Christchurch; St. Saviour's is the larger parish of the two.

At the south-west corner of Blackman Street, and at the entrance to the Borough Road, stood a large building, surrounded by a high brick wall, formerly known as the King's (or Queen's) Bench Prison. It was pulled down in 1880. The original King's Bench Prison was on the east side of the High Street, near the Marshalsea, and was certainly as old as the time of Richard II. Thither Prince Hal (afterwards Henry V.) was sent by Judge Gascoigne for endeavouring to rescue a convicted prisoner, one of his personal attendants— that is, if we may believe the genial old gossiper, Stow—but some historians have repudiated the story altogether. It is, however, mentioned by Hall, Grafton, and Sir Thomas Elyot in his book called " The Governour."

In a play called *Henry V.*, written in the time of Elizabeth, before 1592, in the scene in which the historical account of the violence of the prince against the chief justice is introduced, Richard Tarlton, a famous comedian and mimic, acts both judge and clown. One Knell, another droll comedian of the time, acted the prince, and gave the chief justice such a blow as felled him to the ground, to the great diversion of the audience. Tarlton, the judge, goes off the stage, and returns as Tarlton, the clown: he demands the cause of the laughter. "Oh," says one, "hadst thou been here to have seen what a terrible blow the prince gave the judge." "What! strike a judge!" says the clown: "terrible indeed must it be to the judge, when the very report of it makes my cheek burn."

Readers of the " Uncommercial Traveller " of Charles Dickens will not forget the glimpse that we catch from him of the interior of the old King's Bench Prison, and of its many inmates suffering and dying of the " dry-rot." The prison was removed to this neighbourhood towards the close of the last century. Wilkes was confined here in 1768, and the mob endeavoured to rescue him. A riot ensued, the military were called out, and fired on the people in St. George's Fields, which at that time extended as far as this spot. A spectator, William Allen, was killed, and the jury returned a verdict of "wilful murder" against the soldier who fired the shot. The soldier was a Scotchman, a countryman of "Jack Boot," and in those days that was enough to condemn him. The tomb of Allen might be seen in the old church at Newington Butts. The King's Bench Prison was burnt down by Lord George Gordon's rioters in 1780. It was, however, speedily rebuilt, and is thus described by Mr. Allen, in his "History of Surrey," 1829 :—"The prison occupies an extensive area of ground; it consists of one large pile of building, about 120 yards long. The south, or principal front, has a pediment, under which is a chapel. There are four pumps of spring and river water. Here are 224 rooms, or apartments, eight of which are called state-rooms, which are much larger than the others. Within the walls are a coffee-house and two public-houses; and the shops and stalls for meat, vegetables, and necessaries of almost every description, give the place the appearance of a public market; while the numbers of people walking about, or engaged in various amusements, are little calculated to impress the stranger with an idea of distress, or even of confinement. The walls surrounding the prison are about thirty feet high, and are surmounted by *cheveaux de frise;* but the liberties, or 'rules,' as they are called, comprehend all St. George's Fields, one side of Blackman Street, and part of the Borough High Street, forming an area of about three miles in circumference. These rules are usually purchasable after the following rate, by the prisoners : five guineas for small debts; eight guineas for the first hundred pounds of debt, and about half that sum for every subsequent hundred pounds. Day-rules, of which three may be obtained in every term, may also be purchased for 4s. 2d. for the first day, and 3s. 10d. for the others. Every description of purchasers must give good security to the governor, or, as he is called, marshal. Those who buy the first-mentioned may take up their residence anywhere within the precincts described; but the day-rules only authorised the prisoner to go out on those days for which they are bought. These privileges," adds the writer, "render the King's Bench the most desirable (if such a word may be thus applied) place of incarceration for debtors in England; hence persons so situated frequently remove themselves to it by *habeas corpus* from the most distant prisons in the kingdom." A strict attention to the "rules," it may be added, was very seldom enforced—a fact so notorious, that when Lord Ellenborough, as

chief justice of the King's Bench, was once applied to for an extension of the "rules," his lordship gravely replied that he really could perceive no grounds for the application, since to his certain knowledge the rules already extended to the East Indies ! In cases of this kind, however, when discovery took place, the marshal became answerable for the escape of the debtor. This prison was properly a place of confinement for all cases that could be tried in the Court of King's Bench.

"The discipline of the prison," writes Mr. Richardson, in his "Recollections of the Last Half-Century," "was tyrannical, yet lax, capricious and undefined. The regulations were either enforced with violence and suddenness, or suffered to become a dead letter. Nobody cared much about them; and at one time or other they were broken by every prisoner within the walls. Occasionally an example was made of a more than usually refractory inmate; but the example was despised as a warning, and operated as an incentive to infraction. The law by which the prisoners were kept in some sort of moral subordination emanated from themselves, and from the necessity which is recognised in all communities of combinations of the weak to resist the oppressions of the strong, a very mild administration of justice was acknowledged and enforced. The exigencies of the system demanded dispatch and vigour. A sort of 'lynch-law' superseded the orders of the marshal. It was the duty of that functionary to reside in a house in the court-yard, within the outward boundary of the prison. It was meant by the legislature that he should be at hand to administer justice, to attend to applications for redress, to enforce obedience by his presence, prevent disturbance among the unruly host of his subjects, and to carry into effect the orders which, as a servant of the Court of King's Bench, he was bound to see respected. It is notorious that Mr. Jones, for many years the marshal of the prison, did not reside. He was only in attendance on certain days at his office, and held a sort of court of inquiry into the state of his trust, the turnkeys and the deputy-marshal acting as *amici curiæ*, and instructing him in his duties. He made, at stated times, inspections of the prison; and in his periodical progress was attended by his subordinates in great state. He was a fat, jolly man, rather slow in his movements, not very capable of detecting abuses by his own observation, and not much assisted in his explorations by others. It was a mere farce to see him waddle round the prison. His visits produced no beneficial effect : the place, somewhat more orderly during the time of his stay, on the moment of his departure relapsed into its normal state of irregularity and disorder. In the halcyon days of his authority there was no such institution as the Court for the Relief of Insolvent Debtors. The legislature from time to time cleared out the over-gorged prisons by passing Acts to discharge ranks, callings, professions and mysteries—nobles and ignobles, parsons, lawyers, farmers, tradesmen, shopmen, colonels, captains, gamblers, horse-dealers, publicans, butchers, &c. The wives of many of these shared the fortunes and misfortunes of their husbands; and scores of widows and

THE MARSHALSEA PRISON, IN THE EIGHTEENTH CENTURY.

unfortunate insolvents, and what was called the 'Lords' Act' helped to prevent the enormous conflux of such people. But this inefficient kind of legislation was not what was wanted; it acted as a temporary alleviation of the miseries and abominations of the system, but it failed to abate the nuisance, which may be said to have flourished with renewed vigour from the prunings which removed its effects. The consequence was that the prison was crowded with persons of all classes, spinsters were amongst the majority who could not pass the gates. It may be calculated that the numerical strength of this strange colony amounted to an average of eight hundred or a thousand individuals."

The state of this gaol is thus described by Smollett, about the time of its establishment in the Borough Road; it was much in the same state down till late in the present century :—" The King's Bench Prison . . . appears like a neat little

THE MARSHALSEA IN 1800.

1. The Racquet Court of the Marshalsea.   2. Interior of the Palace Court of the Marshalsea.

regular town, consisting of one street, surrounded by a very high wall, including an open piece of ground, which may be termed a garden, where the prisoners take the air, and amuse themselves with a variety of diversions. Except the entrance, where the turnkeys keep watch and ward, there is nothing in the place that looks like a gaol, or bears the least colour of restraint. The street is crowded with passengers; tradesmen of all kinds here exercise their different professions; hawkers of all sorts are admitted to call and vend their wares, as in any open street in London. There are butchers' stands, chandlers' shops, a surgery, a tap-house, well frequented, and a public kitchen, in which provisions are dressed for all the prisoners gratis, at the expense of the publican. Here the voice of misery never complains, and, indeed, little else is to be heard but the sound of mirth and jollity. At the further end of the street, on the right hand, is a little paved court leading to a separate building, consisting of twelve large apartments, called state-rooms, well furnished, and fitted up for the reception of the better sort of Crown prisoners; and on the other side of the street, facing a separate direction of ground, called the common side, is a range of rooms occupied by prisoners of the lowest order, who share the profits of a begging-box, and are maintained by this practice and some established funds of charity. We ought also to observe that the gaol is provided with a neat chapel, in which a clergyman, in consideration of a certain salary, performs divine service every Sunday."

John Howard, the philanthropist, found in the King's Bench Prison a subject for deserved complaint. He describes the Gatehouse at Westminster as empty, but this as full to overflowing. Indeed, it was so crowded in the summer of 1776, that a prisoner paid five shillings for a separate bed, and many who had no crown-pieces to spare for such a luxury, lay all night in the chapel. The debtors, with their families, amounted to a thousand, two-thirds of whom were lodged within the prison walls, the rest "living within the rules."

Here, at the close of the last century, the notorious George Hanger, Lord Coleraine, was an inmate for nearly a twelvemonth. We have already had occasion to speak of this eccentric and unfortunate nobleman.* At one time he tried to "make both ends meet" by recruiting for the East India Company, and at another by starting as a coal merchant. With respect to the former occupation, he tells us that he spent £500—"costs

out of pocket," as the lawyers say—in establishing and organising agencies for recruits in all the large towns of England, but that an end was put to this work by various disputes among the directors in Leadenhall Street as to the best place for recruiting barracks. The decision, wherever it placed the depôt, threw him out of employ, robbed him of his £500 and six years' labour, and lost him an income of £600 a year. The result was that he was sent to the King's Bench, and had to start afresh with a capital of £40 in hand! No wonder that next year he thought of trade in earnest as much better than such precarious work. Not long before this, Major Hanger—as he was more frequently called—had become one of the jovial associates of the then Prince of Wales, who made him one of his equerries, with a salary of £300 a year, an appointment which, together with the employment which he undertook of raising recruits for the East India Company, afforded him the means of living for a time like a gentleman. His good fortune did not, however, last long, and the major was soon on the high road to the King's Bench, which he entered in June, 1798. He spent about ten months in "those blessed regions of rural retirement," as he jokingly styles his prison, possibly remembering the lines of Lovelace—

"Stone walls do not a prison make,
　Nor iron bars a cage;
Minds innocent and peaceful take
　That for a hermitage;"

and he declares that he "lived there as a gentleman on three shillings a day." Released from prison, he now applied for employment on active service, but in vain; so he formed the resolution of taking to trade, and set up at one time as a coal merchant, and at another as dealer in a powder for the special purpose of setting razors. Specimens of this powder he carried about in his pocket to show to "persons of quality," whom he canvassed for their patronage! How far he flourished in the coal business we do not hear; but, as he mentions a kind friend who gave him a salary sufficient to keep the wolf from the door, in all probability he did not make one of those gigantic fortunes which the coal owners and coal merchants are in the habit of realising now-a-days at the cost of the long-suffering British householder.

In this prison were confined many of the objects of Government prosecutions during the ministries of Pitt, Addington, Perceval, and Lord Liverpool.

John Timbs tells us, in his "Autobiography," that amongst those who were living here in lodgings, "within the rules of the King's Bench," in 1822, was the indefatigable and eccentric William

* See Vol. V., p. 294.

Coombe, better known as "Dr. Syntax," the author of "A Tour in Search of the Picturesque." He wrote this to fit in with some drawings by Rowlandson; and the two combined, published by Ackerman, in the Strand, became one of the luckiest of literary ventures. Besides the above work, Coombe was also the author of "The Letters of a Nobleman to his Son" (generally ascribed to Lord Lyttelton), the "German Gil Blas," &c. He had travelled, when young, as a man of fortune, on the Continent, and had made "the grand tour," and had been a companion of Lawrence Sterne. In middle life, however, he ran through his fortune, and took to literature as a profession, and among other connections he had formed one with Mr. Walter, of the *Times*. Mr. Crabb Robinson tells us in his "Diary" that "at this time, and indeed till his death, he was an inhabitant of the King's Bench Prison," and that "when he came to Printing House Square it was only by virtue of a day-rule. I believe," adds Mr. Robinson, "that Mr. Walter offered to release him from prison by paying his debts; but this he would not permit, as he did not acknowledge the justice of the claim for which he suffered imprisonment. He preferred to live upon an allowance from Mr. Walter, and was, he said, perfectly happy." Coombe is said to have been the author of nearly seventy various publications, none, however, published with his own name. He ran through more than one fortune, and died at an advanced age.

Poor Haydon,* about 1828, was an inmate of this prison, where he painted a "Mock Election" that was held within its walls. The picture was purchased by George IV. for £500. Another painter of note who was consigned to the King's Bench was George Morland. In 1799 he was arrested, and being allowed to live "within the rules," instead of within the gaol itself, he took a house in the neighbourhood, in St. George's Fields, which soon became the haunt of all the profligates of the prison. "In this cavern of indolence, dissipation, and misery," writes the author of "Great Painters and their Works," "Morland reigned and revelled. But the inevitable end was approaching. He was struck with palsy; and when the Insolvent Act of 1802 brought release, it was to the poor miserable wreck—physical, intellectual, and moral —of what had once been George Morland."

In the early part of the present century, the emoluments of the "marshal" of the King's Bench amounted to about £3,590 a year; of which £872 arose from the sale of beer, and £2,823 from the

"rules." About the year 1840 an Act was passed for the better regulation of this prison, by which the practice of granting "day-rules" was abolished; and the prison thenceforth, till its abolition as a debtor's prison about the year 1861, was governed according to regulations provided by one of the secretaries of state. After the abolition of imprisonment for debt, this prison remained unoccupied for a short period. It was afterwards used as a military prison, and about 1870 it passed into the hands of the Convict Department.

Near the King's Bench Prison was the manufactory and bleaching-ground of Mr. Alsager, who gave up his prosperous business in order to write the "City Articles" for the *Times*, in which he ultimately came to own a share.

Again making our way towards London Bridge, we pass by "Stones' End" into Blackman Street, a thoroughfare mentioned in "The Merry Man's Resolution" published in the "Roxburgh Ballads:"

> "Farewel to the Bankside,
> 　Farewel to Blackman's Street,
> Where with my bouncing lasses
> 　I oftentimes did meet;
> Farewel to Kent Street garrison,
> 　Farewel to Horsly-down,
> And all the smirking wenches
> 　That dwell in Redriff town:
> 　　And come, love,
> 　　　Stay, love,
> Go along with me;
> For all the world I'll forsake for thee."

In a large house, on the east side of this street, resided for many years Mr. (afterwards Sir James) South, the son of a chemist and druggist. While practising medicine, South gave special attention to astronomy. Between 1821 and 1823, from the roof of his house, which was nearly opposite Lant Street, he, in conjunction with Mr. (afterwards Sir) J. F. Herschel, made some valuable observations on 380 double and triple stars, both astronomers being armed with what in that day were considered powerful telescopes of five inches aperture, constructed by Tulley. A few years later South removed to Campden Hill, Kensington, where he fitted up a telescope of larger dimensions. Of the sale of his instruments at the last-named place we have given an account in a former chapter.* He was one of the founders of the Royal Astronomical Society, and was knighted by William IV. in 1830. He died in 1867.

George IV., in his last hours, expressed a desire that Sir James should receive from the Civil List a pension of £300 per annum, which was con-

---

* See Vol. V., p. 209.　　　　　　　　　　* See Vol. V., p. 131.

ferred by King William IV. Many years ago, when it was thought desirable by some persons to have a second national observatory, Sir James South offered to build it at his own expense, and endow it with his own magnificent instruments; but the offer was declined by the Government. A scientific account of Sir James South's astronomical observations in Blackman Street, and of their results, accompanied by an elaborate description of the five-feet and seven-feet telescopes with which they were made, will be found in the "Philosophical Transactions" for 1825.

Another distinguished native of the same part of Southwark is the gifted poetess, Eliza Cook, who was born here in December, 1818, and who from early womanhood has stirred the hearts of the middle classes of Englishmen and Englishwomen by her spirited and hearty songs as few other poets have done. Joseph Lancaster, the educationist, was born in Kent Street in 1778.

Until the formation of the Dover Road early in the present century, Kent Street, commencing eastward of St. George's Church, at the north end of Blackman Street, was part of the great way from Dover and the Continent to the metropolis. This narrow thoroughfare, originally called Kentish Street, was a wretched and profligate place. As far back as 1633 it was described as "very long and ill-built, chiefly inhabited by broom-men and mumpers," and to the last it was noted for its turners' and brush-makers' shops, and broom and heath yards; yet some of these men rose to wealth and position. John Evelyn tells us of one Burton, a broom-man, who sold kitchen-stuff in Kent Street, "whom God so blessed that he became a very rich and a very honest man, and in the end Sheriff of Surrey." During the plague in 1665, Evelyn, under date of 7th September, writes: "Came home, there perishing neere 10,000 poor creatures weekly; however, I went all along the City and suburbs from Kent Street to St. James's, a dismal passage, and dangerous to see so many coffins expos'd in the streetes, now thin of people; the shops shut up, and all in mournful silence, as not knowing whose turn might be next. I went to the Duke of Albemarle for a pest-ship, to wait on our infected men, who were not a few."

Kent—now Tabard—Street was the route taken by Chaucer's pilgrims, of whom we shall have more to say when dealing with the "Tabard" Inn; by the Black Prince, when he rode a modest conqueror with the French king by his side; and by which Jack Cade's rabble rout poured into the metropolis, quite as intent, we may fairly suppose, upon plunder as upon political reform. In this

street, as early as the fourteenth century, stood the Loke, an hospital for lepers, afterwards known as the Lock, a name still retained by the well-known hospital in the Harrow Road, Paddington.* An open stream, or rather ditch, dividing the parishes of St. George and St. Mary, Newington, was also called the Lock; but whether it derived its name from the hospital, or the hospital from the stream, is uncertain. It rose in Newington (the open ground on its banks being called Lock's Fields, a name which it still retains), was crossed from early times by a bridge at the end of Kent Street, and flowed through Bermondsey into the river.

Tabard Street has borne its evil reputation to the present day; and it is immortalised in Charles Dickens's "Uncommercial Traveller" as "the worst kept part of London—in a police sense, of course—excepting the Haymarket." Smollett says, "It would be for the honour of the kingdom to improve the avenue to London by way of Kent Street, which is a most disgraceful entrance to such an opulent city. A foreigner, in passing this beggarly and ruinous suburb, conceives such an idea of misery and meanness, as all the wealth and magnificence of London and Westminster are afterwards unable to destroy. A friend of mine who brought a Parisian from Dover in his own post-chaise, contrived to enter Southwark when it was dark, that his friend might not perceive the nakedness of this quarter." Since the formation of the Dover Road, this street has been no longer the great highway to Kent, a fearful necessity to timid travellers; but it still retains much of its old character, as the chosen resort of broom and brush makers. Towards the close of the last century this street, although the only thoroughfare from the City to the Old Kent Road, presented a scene of squalor and destitution unequalled even in St. Giles's. Gipsies, thieves, and such-like characters, were to be met with in almost every house; and men, women, children, asses, pigs, and dogs were often found living together in the same room. Filled with a noble desire to do something to instruct and improve the condition of the rising generation in this crowded neighbourhood, Thomas Cranfield, a hard-working tailor, then residing in Hoxton, and formerly a corporal at the siege of Gibraltar in 1782, resolved, if possible, to establish a Sunday-school in Kent Street. For this purpose, in 1798, he hired a room, and at once undertook, with no other help than that given by his wife, the education of the "wild Arabs" who came to receive instruction in this novel manner. The

---

* See Vol. V., p. 215.

reputation borne by the neighbourhood for vice and profligacy was in itself quite sufficient to deter many persons with any benevolent intentions from venturing into the street. Undaunted by the magnitude of the undertaking, for some months this philanthropic individual and his wife, travelling every Sunday all the way from Hoxton with three of their children, occupied themselves with the task they had set themselves, and with so much success, that in a short time the fruits of their self-denying exertions became conspicuously apparent to others, and at last other voluntary teachers summoned up courage to undertake the same work. Finding his labours in Kent Street rewarded with success, and being now reinforced by additional volunteers, Cranfield determined to open a similar school in the Mint, close by, a locality even worse than Kent Street. This school also succeeded, and soon after their establishment these schools were incorporated with the Sunday-school carried on in Surrey Chapel, under the title of the "Southwark Sunday-school Society," the Rev. Rowland Hill becoming the first president. Nine of these schools still exist, and many of the children born in Southwark within the last seventy years owed their education and their position in after life to the voluntary instruction given in these Sunday-schools. A nobleman on one occasion being present at one of these Sunday-school anniversaries at Surrey Chapel, and being struck not only with the cleanly appearance of the children, but with the respectability of the teachers, asked Rowland Hill what salary the latter received for their arduous duties. Mr. Hill gave the following reply: "It is very little of this world's goods that they get, unless it is now and then a flea, or another insect not quite so nimble in its movements."

St. George's Church, at the corner of the High Street, Borough, and of Blackman Street, is dedicated to St. George the Martyr, the patron saint of England. The original church, which stood here, belonged to the Priory of Bermondsey; it was a very ancient edifice, and was dedicated to St. George of Cappadocia. It is described in the "New View of London," published in 1708, as "a handsome building, the pillars, arches, and windows being of Gothic design, and having a handsome window about the middle of the north side of the church, whereon were painted the arms of the twenty-one companies of London who contributed to the repair of this church in 1629, with the names of the donors; the sums respectively given by them amounting in all to £156 16s. 8d. This edifice was sixty-nine feet long to the altar-rails, sixty feet wide, and thirty-five feet high. The tower, in which were eight bells, was ninety-eight feet high."

We hear of the old church as having been given in 1122, by Thomas Arderne, on whose ancestor the parish had been bestowed by the Conqueror, to the abbot and monks of Bermondsey. It is stated in the work above mentioned that among the distinguished persons who lie buried in St. George's Church, are Bishop Bonner,* who is said to have died in 1557, in the Marshalsea Prison (a place, as Dr. Fuller observes, the safest to secure him from the people's fury); and the famous Mr. Edward Cocker, a person so well skilled in all parts of arithmetic as to have given rise to the classic phrase, "according to Cocker." The tradition in Queen Anne's time was that Bonner's grave was under the east window of the church, and that Cocker, "the most eminent composer and engraver of letters, knots, and flourishes of his time," lay "in the passage at the west end, within the church, near the school." Such, at all events, was the statement of the then sexton; and, as he died about the year 1677, in all probability the tradition may be accepted. Cocker's fame was chiefly made by his "Vulgar Arithmetic," published after his death by his friend, John Hawkins, who possibly wrote the following epigram upon him :—

"Ingenious Cocker! now to rest thou'st gone,
No art can show thee fully but thine own.
Thy vast arithmetic alone can show
The sums of thanks we for thy labours owe."

Here also was interred John Rushworth, the author of "Historical Collections" relating to proceedings in Parliament from 1618 to 1640. Rushworth died in the King's Bench. In the grave-yard of this church it was the custom to bury prisoners who died in the King's Bench and the Marshalsea.

In this church General George Monk, afterwards Duke of Albemarle, was married in 1652, to Nan Clarges,† the daughter of a farrier in the Strand, and widow of another farrier named Radford or Ratford, who had been his sempstress, and "used to carry him linen." Mr. Henry Jessey, who subsequently became an Anti-Pædobaptist, and was immersed by Hanserd Knollys, was, during the Commonwealth, the minister of this church.

The old church having undergone many repairs, and being ruinous, the parishioners applied to Parliament, and obtained an Act to have another church erected in its place; in consequence of which the present edifice was begun in 1734, and

---

* Others, however, hold that he lies buried at Copford, in Essex.
† See Vol. III., p. 122.

finished in about two years. The architect was a Mr. John Price, and the expense of the building was defrayed by a grant of £6,000 out of the funds appropriated for building fifty new churches in the metropolis and its vicinity. It was repaired in 1808, at a cost of £9,000. The plan of the building is a parallelogram, with a square tower at the west end, surmounted by a second storey of an octagon form, and crowned by an octangular spire,

that the large bell of this church is tolled nightly, and is probably a relic of the curfew custom.

About midway between St. George's Church and London Bridge, stood in very remote times the Marshalsea, or prison of the Court of the Knight Marshal, in which all disputes arising between servants of the royal household, and offences committed within the King's Court, were adjudicated upon. Its jurisdiction extended for twelve miles

THE OLD "TABARD" INN, IN THE SEVENTEENTH CENTURY.

finished with a ball and vane. The church throughout is very plain. It is built of dark red brick, with stone dressings, in a heavy Dutch style, and has altogether a tasteless aspect. In looking at such a building as this, well may we exclaim in the words of a divine of the nineteenth century, "Ichabod! the glory of the Church has departed. I never observe the new churches on the Surrey side of the river without imagining that their long bodies and short steeples look, from a distance, like the rudders of so many sailing-barges. Where is the grand oriel? where is the old square tower? What have we in their stead? A common granary casement and a shapeless spire." Pennant describes the steeple of St. George's Church as "most awkwardly standing upon stilts." It may be added

round Whitehall, the City of London excepted. It was once of high dignity, and coeval with the Courts of Common Law. This Marshal's, or Palace Court, as it was afterwards called, was removed from Southwark to Scotland Yard in 1801; it was abolished by Act of Parliament in 1849, and ceased to exist from the end of that year. For very many years no legal business was transacted in the Marshalsea Court, though it continued to be opened and closed with the same legal formalities as the Palace Court, the judges and other officers being the same in both.

In the "New View of London" we read: "The Marshal's Court, situate or kept in the Marshalsea Prison on the eastern side of the Burrough (sic) of Southwark, was first intended for determining causes or differences among the king's menial servants, held under the Knight Marshal, whose steward is judge of this court, and whereunto also belong four council (*sic*) and six attorneys." Here follow the names of these ten privileged gentlemen, with a note to the effect that "none except members of Clifford's Inn may practise in this court." In 1774 we find the Marshalsea described as "the county gaol for felons and the Admiralty gaol for pirates."

stated above) a prisoner in the Marshalsea, where he had been ordered to be confined. He had been previously imprisoned there during the reign of Edward VI. He was buried, as we have already seen, in St. George's Church, hard by.

"Another anecdote is told of Bishop Bonner," says Charles Knight, in his "London," "at the period of his committal to the Marshalsea, which is worth repeating here, as it shows his temper

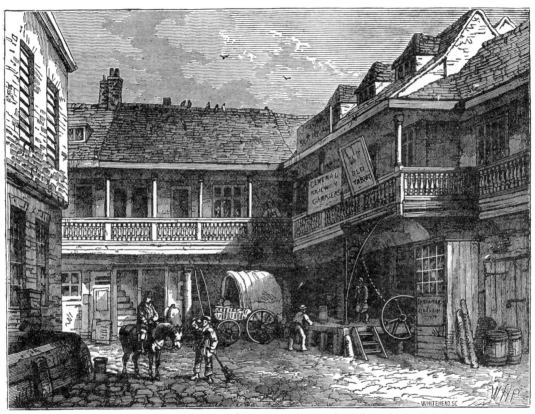

THE OLD "TABARD" INN. (*From a Sketch taken shortly before its demolition.*)

We have no exact record of the first establishment of the Marshalsea prison, but we find it casually mentioned in an account of a mob riot in 1377. A sailor belonging to the fleet commanded by the Duke of Lancaster, Lord High Admiral, was killed by a man of gentle blood, who was imprisoned in the Marshalsea; but it being supposed by the sailors that powerful friends were at work to obtain his pardon, a number of sailors broke into the prison, murdered the offender, and then hanged his body on the gallows, returning afterwards to their ships with trumpets sounding. Four years afterwards, Wat Tyler's followers seized and murdered the marshal of the prison. Bishop Bonner, the last Roman Catholic Bishop of London, having been deposed by Queen Elizabeth, died (as

in a more favourable light than that which the voice of the public ascribes to him. On his way to the prison, one called out, 'The Lord confound or else turn thy heart!' Bonner coolly replied, 'The Lord send thee to keep thy breath to cool thy porridge.' To another, who insulted him on his deprivation from the episcopal rank, he could even be witty. 'Good morrow, Bishop *quondam*,' was the remark. 'Farewell, knave *semper*,' was the reply." Bonner died on the 5th of September, 1569, having been a prisoner here for about ten years. In Queen Elizabeth's time, the Marshalsea was the second in importance among the prisons in London. Political satirists, George Wither among them, were confined there; and, in conjunction with the other Southwark prisons, it was the place of durance of Udal and other Puritan martyrs. Among other notorious inmates was George Barnwell, who killed his uncle at Camberwell, if we may believe the mock heroic lines on that hero of the shop and counter in the "Rejected Addresses."

In 1685 Colonel Culpeper was consigned to the Marshalsea as a prisoner. John Evelyn tells the story of his seizure, in his "Diary," under date July 9th of the above year :—"Just as I was coming into the lodgings at Whitehall, a little before dinner, my Lord of Devonshire standing very neere his Majesty's bed-chamber doore in the lobby, came Colonel Culpeper, and in a rude manner looking my lord in the face, asked whether this was a time and place for excluders to appear. My lord at first tooke little notice of what he said, knowing him to be a hot-headed fellow, but he reiterated it, my lord asked Culpeper whether he meant him ; he said, yes, he meant his lordship. My lord told him he was no excluder ; the other affirming it againe, my lord told him he lied, on which Culpeper struck him a box on the eare, which my lord return'd, and fell'd him. They were soone parted ; Culpeper was seiz'd, and his majesty order'd him to be carried to the Greene Cloth officer, who sent him to the Marshalsea as he deserved."

The Marshalsea escaped Lord George Gordon's rioters, in June, 1780, when the King's Bench, the Borough, and Clink prisons were demolished ; but shortly afterwards it was removed nearer to St. George's Church, where it remained until its abolition in 1849. At that time it contained sixty rooms and a chapel.

For a description of this prison as it was half a century ago, the reader may as well be referred to the "Little Dorrit" of Charles Dickens, who lays within its precincts most of the scenes of the first part, and several in the latter part of the second. These scenes were drawn from life, as the elder Dickens passed here a considerable part of his days while his son was a lad ; and here the future "Boz," coming to visit his selfish and indolent father, picked up much of his practical acquaintance with the lower grades of society and London life, which he afterwards turned to account. "The family," he writes, "lived more comfortably in prison than they had done for a long time out of it. They were waited on still by the maid-of-all-work from Bayham Street, the orphan girl from Chatham workhouse, from whose sharp little worldly, yet also kindly, ways I took my first impressions of the Marchioness in 'The Old Curiosity Shop.'"

Most readers of Dickens's works will remember old Mr. William Dorrit, the "father of the Marshalsea," and Amy, the "Little Mother"—the "child of the Marshalsea."

In 1856, whilst engaged in the purchase of Gad's Hill, Charles Dickens paid a visit to the Marshalsea, then in the course of demolition, to see what traces were left of the prison, of which he had received such early and vivid impressions as a boy, and which he had been able to rebuild almost brick by brick in "Little Dorrit," by the aid of his wonderfully retentive memory. He writes to his friend, John Forster, "Went to the Borough yesterday morning before going to Gad's Hill, to see if I could find any ruins of the Marshalsea. Found a great part of the original building, now 'Marshalsea Place.' I found the rooms that had been in my mind's eye in the story. . . . There is a room there, still standing, that I think of taking. It is the room through which the ever-memorable signers of Captain Porter's petition filed off in my boyhood. The spikes are gone, and the wall is lowered ; and any body can go out now who likes to go, and is not bed-ridden."

Some considerable portion of the Marshalsea is still standing, in Angel Court, on the north side of St. George's Church ; it is now used for business purposes.

In 1663 was published a book entitled "The Ancient Legal Course and Fundamental Constitution of the Palace-Court or Marshalsea ; with the Charges of all Proceedings there, and its present Establishment explained, whereby it will appear of what great authority this Court hath been in all Times." This is a very scarce little volume, known to few, and unmentioned by the bibliographers. At the time of publication the Court, whose authority was held by Fleta to be next to the High Court of Parliament, was kept every Friday in the Court House on St. Margaret's Hill, and might be held in any other fit place within twelve miles of Whitehall.

In the neighbourhood of the Marshalsea prison there was formerly an inn with a sign-board called the "Hand." If we may trust a statement in Tom Brown's "Amusements for the Meridian of London," this board, whether it represented the hand of a man or of a woman, was always regarded as an evil sign.

Southwark, it is almost needless to remark, embraces an important manufacturing and commercial district. Along the water-side, from Bermondsey to Lambeth, there is a long succession of wharves and warehouses, which all seem to ply a busy trade. A considerable hat manufacture is carried on in and around St. Saviour's parish.

Bermondsey abounds with tanners and curriers. Southwark is also the chief place of business for persons connected with the hop trade; and within its limits are probably the largest vinegar-works, and certainly one of the largest breweries in the world. Apparently, some of the tradesmen of "the Borough" were persons of substance in the Middle Ages. At all events, a writer in *Notes and Queries*, on the authority of Mr. W. D. Cooper, says "that a certain Harry Baily, or Bailly, a 'hostelry keeper' of Southwark, represented that borough in Parliament in the reigns of Edward III. and Richard II." Mr. Timbs confirms his identity by an extract which he quotes from the Subsidy Roll of 4 Richard II., A.D. 1380, in which Henry Bayliff, "Ostyler," and Christian, his wife, are assessed at two shillings. He adds, "We cannot read Chaucer's description of the Host without acknowledging the likelihood of his being a popular man among his fellow-townsmen, and one likely to be selected for his fitness to represent them in Parliament." As we have shown in a previous chapter, too, coming down to more recent times, the elder Mr. Thrale, the founder of Barclay and Perkins's brewery, was for some time a representative of Southwark in the House of Commons, as also was Mr. Apsley Pellatt, of the Falcon Glass Works.

The tradesmen of Southwark—even if some of them have attained to opulence—are, however, we fear, like those of most other places; and there are, or have been, "black sheep" among them, for in the "History of Quack Doctors" we read that in the reign of Edward VI. one Grig, a poulterer in Surrey, was set in the pillory at Croydon, and again in the Borough, for "cheating people out of their money, by pretending to cure them by charms, or by only looking at the patient."

The principles of free trade would seem to have been almost unknown in the reign of Edward I., if, as stated by Maitland in his "History of London," it was ordained that "no person should go out of the City into Southwark to buy cattle," and the bakers of Southwark in like manner were forbidden to trade in the City.

The Surrey side of the Thames being generally so low and flat, and extremely monotonous, was in past ages regarded more as a pleasure resort than as a centre of commercial activity. Added to this, its rents were low, on account of the tolls upon the bridges, and hence a sufficient number of acres to constitute a public garden were easily obtainable, even by somewhat impecunious speculators, and the very great success of Vauxhall Gardens had somehow or other familiarised the public mind with the idea that it was the "right thing" to go across the water for pleasure, leaving the cares of home for the north side of the river.

The sanitary arrangements of Southwark certainly were not good in the early part of the reign of George III. Pigs and sheep were killed for the London markets in many parts of the Borough. "The kennels of Southwark," writes Dr. Johnson, during his Scottish Tour, with reference to this circumstance, "run blood two days in every week."

We can form a tolerably accurate notion of the extent and appearance of Southwark at the beginning of the seventeenth century. Southward of St. George's Church and the Mint spread St. George's Fields, reaching nearly to the archiepiscopal palace at Lambeth, and the village of Newington. The Kent Road was a lane between hedgerows; and there were bishops' palaces and parks, mansions, theatres, and pleasure-gardens near the green banks of the river. There were forts for the defence of the borough at the end of Blackman Street, near the Lock Hospital, and in St. George's Fields, where afterwards stood the "Dog and Duck," at the eastern end of the present Bethlehem Hospital. The old High Street of Southwark had gabled houses and large quadrangular inns, dating from the early Norman times; and between them and the Abbey of Bermondsey were open spaces and streams flowing gently towards the river. Pasture-lands, farms, and water-mills were farther east towards Redriff (now Rotherhithe), and Horselydown was indeed a grazing place for horses. Now all that is changed; but it is pleasant to think of the old days, even amid the constant bustle and crowding at the entrance of the busiest of London railway stations.

The journal of a London alderman, at the close of the last century, under date of Sunday, 25th June, 1797, thus describes the Southwark of his day:—"I dined in the Boro' with my friend Parkinson *en famille*, and in the evening walked thro' some gardens near the Kentish Road, at the expense of one halfpenny each. We went and saw a variety of people who had heads on their shoulders, and eyes and legs and arms like ourselves, but in every other respect as different from the race of mortals we meet at the West-end of the town as a native of Bengal from a Laplander. This observation may be applied with great truth in a general way to the whole of the Borough and all that therein is. Their meat is not so good, their fish is not so good, their persons are not so cleanly, their dress is not equal to what we meet in the City or in Westminster; indeed, upon the whole, they are one hundred years behindhand in civilisation."

CHAPTER VII.

SOUTHWARK (*continued*).—FAMOUS INNS OF OLDEN TIMES.

"Chaucer, the Druid-priest of poetry,
First taught our muse to speak the mystic lore,
And woke the soul to heavenly minstrelsy,
Which Echo on the wind delightful bore."

Old Inns mentioned by Stow—The "Tabard"—The Abbot of Hide—The "Tabard" as the Rendezvous for Pilgrims—Henry Bailly, the Hosteller of the "Tabard," and M.P. for Southwark—Description of the old "Tabard"—Change of Name from the "Tabard" to the "Talbot"—Demolition of the old Inn—Chaucer and the Canterbury Pilgrims—Characters mentioned by Chaucer in the "Canterbury Tales"—Stow's Definition of "Tabard"—The "George"—The "White Hart"—Jack Cade's sojourn here—The "Boar's Head"—The "White Lion"—"Henry VIII." a Favourite Sign—The "Three Brushes"—The "Catherine Wheel"—The "Three Widows"—The "Old Pick my Toe"—Tokens of Inn-keepers.

IT was probably on account of its proximity to one of our earliest theatres (the Globe), as well as on account of its being on the great southern thoroughfare, that the High Street of Southwark came to abound to such an extent with inns and hostelries. In bygone days it is probable that these inns were still more numerous, as all traffic from the south and south-west of England must have entered London by that route at a time when old London Bridge was the only entrance into the City for traffic and travellers from the south of the Thames.

We have historic proof that the borough of Southwark—and more especially the High Street—has been for ages celebrated for its inns. Stow, in his "Survey," published at the close of the sixteenth century, says :—"From thence [the Marshalsea] towards London Bridge, on the same side, be many fair inns for receipt of travellers, by these signs : the Spurre, Christopher, Bull, Queen's Head, Tabard, George, Hart, King's Head," &c. Of these inns mentioned by the old chronicler, some few remain to this day ; whilst most of the buildings surrounding the old-fashioned yards have been converted into warehouses or booking-offices for the goods department of different railway companies, &c.

First and foremost of these ancient hostelries, and one which retained most of its ancient features down to a comparatively recent date, was the "Tabard Inn," renowned by Chaucer as the rendezvous of the Canterbury Pilgrims, five hundred years ago. Its name, however, had become changed for that of the "Talbot." It stood on the east side of the street, about midway between St. George's Church and London Bridge, and nearly opposite the site of the old Town Hall. The first foundation of this inn would appear to be due to the Abbots of Hyde, or Hide, near Winchester, who, at a time when the Bishops of Winchester had a palace near St. Saviour's Church, fixed their residence in this immediate neighbourhood. The land on which the old "Tabarde" stood was pur-

chased by the Abbot of Hyde in the year 1307, and he built on it not only a hostel for himself and his brethren, but also an inn for the accommodation of the numerous pilgrims resorting to the shrine of "St. Thomas of Canterbury" from the south and west of England, just at the point where the roads from Sussex, Surrey, and Hampshire met that which was known as the "Pilgrims' Way." There can be no doubt that by the end of the fourteenth century the "Tabard" was already one of the inns most frequented by "Canterbury Pilgrims," or else Chaucer would scarcely have introduced it to us in that character.

The Abbey of Hide was founded by Alfred the Great, and the monks were Saxon to the backbone. When the Conqueror landed at Pevensey, the abbot and twelve stout monks buckled on their armour, and with twenty armed men hurried to join Harold. Not one returned from the fatal field of Hastings. Abbot, monks, and men-at-arms all lay dead upon the field ; and Norman William never forgave their patriotic valour, but avenged it by taking from the abbey twelve knights' fees and a captain's portion—that is, twelve times the amount of land necessary to support a man-at-arms and a baron's fief. Chaucer must have known this history, and his honest English heart must have glowed with the remembrance as he sat in the old hall of the town residence of the successors of the brave Abbot of Hide. Here it was that the genial poet and the nine-and-twenty pilgrims met, and agreed to enliven their pilgrimage to the shrine of St. Thomas à Becket, at Canterbury, by reciting tales to shorten the way. Macaulay says, "It was a national as well as religious feeling that drew multitudes to the shrine of à Becket, the first Englishman who, since the Conquest, had been terrible to the foreign tyrants." The date of the Canterbury Pilgrimage is generally supposed to have been the year 1383; and Chaucer, after describing the season of spring, writes :—

"Befelle that in that season, on a day,
In Southwerk, at the Tabard as I lay,

Redy to wenden on my pilgrimage
To Canterbury, with devoute couràge,
At night was come into that hostelrie
Well nine-and-twenty in a compagnie
Of sondry folk, by aventure yfalle
In felawship ; and pilgrimes were they alle,
That toward Canterbury wolden ride,
The chambres and the stables weren wyde,
And wel we weren esed atte beste,
And shortly, when the sonne was gone to reste,
So hadde I spoken with hem everich on
That I was of hir felawship anon,
And I made forword erly for to rise,
And take oure way ther as I you devise."

The "Tabard" is again mentioned in the following lines :—

"In Southwerk at this gentil hostelrie,
That highte the Tabard, faste by the Belle."

John Timbs, in an account of this inn, in the *City Press*, says :—"Henry Bailly, the host of the 'Tabard,' was not improbably a descendant of Henry Tite or Martin, of the borough of Southwark, to whom King Henry III., in the fifteenth year of his reign, at the instance of William de la Zouch, granted the customs of the town of Southwark during the king's pleasure, he paying to the Exchequer the annual fee and farm rent of £10 for the same. By that grant Henry Tite or Martin was constituted bailiff of Southwark, and he would, therefore, acquire the name of Henry the bailiff, or Le Bailly. But be this as it may, it is a fact on record, that Henry Bailly, the hosteller of the 'Tabard,' was one of the burgesses who represented the borough of Southwark in the Parliament held at Westminster, in the fiftieth Edward III., A.D. 1376; and he was again returned to the Parliament held at Gloucester in the second of Richard II., A.D. 1378." We have already mentioned him in the previous chapter. After the dissolution of the monasteries, the "Tabard" and the abbot's house were sold by Henry VIII. to John Master and Thomas Master ; and the particulars of the grant in the Augmentation Office afford description of the hostelry called "the Tabard of the Monastery of Hyde, and the Abbots' place, with the stables, and garden thereunto belonging."

The original "Tabard" was in existence as late as the year 1602 ; it was an ancient timber house, accounted to be as old as Chaucer's time. No part of it, however, as it appeared at the time of its demolition in 1874, was of the age of Chaucer ; but a good deal dated from the time of Queen Elizabeth, when Master J. Preston newly repaired it. "The most interesting portion was a stone-coloured wooden gallery, in front of which was a picture of the Canterbury Pilgrimage, said to have been painted by Blake. The figures of the pilgrims were copied from the celebrated print by Stothard. Immediately behind was the chamber known as the pilgrims' room, but only a portion of the ancient hall. The gallery formerly extended throughout the inn-buildings. The inn facing the street was burnt in the great fire of 1676." Dryden says, "I see all the pilgrims in the Canterbury tales, their humour, with their features and their very dress, as distinctly as if I had supper with them at the 'Tabard,' in Southwark." A company of gentlemen assembled at the inn, in 1833, to commemorate the natal day of Chaucer, and it was proposed annually to meet in honour of the venerable poet, whose works Spenser characterises as

"The well of English undefiled,
On Fame's eternal beadroll worthy to be filed."

But the idea, if ever seriously entertained, was soon abandoned.

The house was repaired in the reign of Queen Elizabeth, and from that period probably dated the fireplace, carved oak panels, and other portions spared by the fire of 1676, which were still to be seen in the beginning of the present century. In this fire, of which we have already had occasion to speak, some six hundred houses had to be destroyed in order to arrest the progress of the flames ; and as the "Tabard" stood nearly in the centre of this area, and was mostly built of wood, there can be little doubt that the old inn perished. It was, however, soon rebuilt, and as nearly as possible on the same spot; and although, through the ignorance of the landlord or tenant, or both, it was for a time called, not the "Tabard," but the "Talbot," there can be no doubt that the inn, as it remained down till recently, with its quaint old timber galleries, and not less quaint old chambers, was the immediate successor of the inn and hostelry commemorated by our great poet.

In Urry's edition of Chaucer, published in 1721, there is a view of the "Tabard" as it then stood, the yard apparently opening upon the street. Down to about the close of the year 1873 the entrance to the inn-yard was under an old and picturesque gateway ; this, however, has been removed altogether, and in its place, on our left hand, a new public-house, approaching the gin-palace in its flaunting appearance, has been erected, and, as if in mockery, it has assumed the name of the "Old Tabard." The buildings in the inn-yard, as they remained down to the period above mentioned, consisted of a large and spacious wooden structure, with a high tiled roof, the ground floor of which had been for many years occupied as a luggage office, and a place of call for carmen and railway vans. This was all that remained of the structure erected in the reign of Charles II., out of the old materials after the fire. The upper part of it once was one large apartment, but it had been so much cut up and subdivided from time to time

hall, the room of public entertainment of the hostelry, or, as it was popularly called, "The Pilgrims' Room;" and here it is conjectured Chaucer's pilgrims—if that particular Canterbury pilgrimage was a reality, and not a creation of the poet's brain—spent the evening before wending

GEOFFREY CHAUCER.

to adapt it to the purpose of modern bed-rooms that it presented in the end but few features of interest.

There was an exterior gallery, also of wood, on the left, which, with the rooms behind it, have been levelled with the ground, in order to make room for a new pile of warehouses. The rooms, dull, heavy, dingy apartments as they were, are said by tradition to have occupied the actual site, or rather to have been carved out of the ancient

their way along the Old Kent Road towards the shrine of St. Thomas à Becket—

"The ho'y blissful martyr for to seeke."

From the old court-yard, however, actually rode forth the company that lives and moves for ever in Chaucer's poetry, or, at any rate, many a company of which the "Canterbury Tales" present a life-like copy. In that room lay the seemly prioress and her nuns; here the knight, with the

OLD INNS IN SOUTHWARK.

" yong Squier" sharing his chamber, and waiting dutifully upon his needs ; that staircase the burly monk made re-echo and quake with his heavy tread ; and here, leaning upon the balustrade-work, the friar and the sompour (summoner or attorney) had many a sharp passage of arms.

Mr. Corner, who has left the best account* of the old Southwark inn, was of opinion, from personal examination, that there was nothing at all in the remains of the "Tabard," as they existed at the time of its demolition, earlier than the Southwark fire of 1676, after which was built the "Pilgrims' Hall," the fireplaces of which were of this date. The Rev. John Ward, in his "Diary," remarks that "the fire began at one Mr. Welsh's, an oilman, near St. Margaret's Hill, betwixt the 'George' and 'Talbot' inns, as Bedloe (the Jesuit) in his narrative relates."

The sign was ignorantly changed from the "Tabard" to the "Talbot"—an old name for a dog—about the year 1676, and Betterton describes it under its new name in his modernised version of Geoffrey Chaucer's prologue. On the beam of the gateway facing the street was formerly inscribed, "This is the inn where Sir Jeffry Chaucer and the nine-and-twenty pilgrims lay in their journey to Canterbury, anno 1383." This was painted out in 1831 ; it was originally inscribed upon a beam across the road, whence swung the sign ; but the beam was removed in 1763, as interfering with the traffic.

In Urry's view the several wooden buildings are shown. The writing of the inscription over the sign seemed ancient; yet Tyrwhitt is of opinion that it was not older than the seventeenth century, since Speght, who describes the "Tabard" in his edition of Chaucer, published in 1602, does not mention it. Probably it was put up after the fire of 1676, when the "Tabard" had changed its name into the "Talbot."

The sign in reality was changed in 1673, when the signs of London were taken down, "and when," says Aubrey, "the ignorant landlord or tenant, instead of the ancient sign of the Tabard, put up the Talbot, or dog." Aubrey tells us further that before the fire it was an old timber house, "probably coeval with Chaucer's time." It was probably this old part, facing the street, that was burnt.

"Chaucer has often been named as 'the well of English undefiled ;' but from a general review of all his works," writes Dr. Johnson, in his "Lives of the Poets," "it will appear that he entertained a

very mean opinion of his native language, and of the poets who employed it, and that, during a great part of his life, he was incessantly occupied in translating the works of the French, Italian, and Latin poets. His 'Romaunt of the Rose' is a professed translation from William de Lorris and Jean de Meun ; the long and beautiful romance of 'Troilus and Cressida' is principally translated from Boccaccio's Filostrato ; the 'Legend of Good Women' is a free translation from Ovid's Epistles, combined with the histories of his heroines, derived from various chronicles. The 'House of Fame' is a similar compilation ; and 'Palamon and Arcite' is known to be an imitation of the 'Theseide' of Boccaccio. On the whole, it may be doubted whether he thought himself sufficiently qualified to undertake an original work till he was past sixty years of age, at which time . . . . he formed and began to execute the plan of his 'Canterbury Tales.'"

This elaborate work—the scene of which is laid in the guest-chamber and in the court-yard of the "Tabard"—was intended to contain a sketch of all the characters of society in his time. These were to be sketched out in an introductory prologue, to be contrasted by characteristic dialogues, and probably to be engaged in incidents which should further develop their characters and dispositions ; and as stories were absolutely necessary in every popular work, an appropriate tale was to be put into the mouth of each of the pilgrims. It is not extraordinary that the remainder of Chaucer's life should not have been sufficient for the completion of so ambitious a plan. What he has actually executed can be regarded only as a fragment of a larger whole ; but, imperfect as it is, it contains more information respecting the manners and customs of the fourteenth century than could be gleaned from the whole mass of contemporary writers, English and foreign. "Chaucer's vein of humour," remarks Warton, "although conspicuous in the 'Canterbury Tales,' is chiefly displayed in the characters, described in the Prologue, with which they are introduced. In these his knowledge of the world availed him in a peculiar degree, and enabled him to give such an accurate picture of ancient manners as no contemporary nation has transmitted to posterity. It is here that we view the pursuits and employments, the customs and diversions, of our ancestors, copied from the life, and represented with equal truth and spirit by a judge of mankind whose penetration qualified him to discern their foibles and discriminating peculiarities, and by an artist who understood that proper selection of circumstances and those pre-

---

* See "Collections of the Surrey Archæological Society," vol. ii,, part 2.

dominant characteristics which form a finished portrait. We are surprised to find, in an age so gross and ignorant, such talent for satire and for observation on life—qualities which usually exert themselves in more civilised periods, when the improved state of society, by . . . . establishing uniform modes of behaviour, disposes mankind to study themselves, and renders deviations of conduct and singularities of character more immediately and more necessarily the objects of censure and ridicule. These curious and valuable remains are specimens of Chaucer's native genius, unassisted and unalloyed. The figures are all British, and bear no suspicious signatures of classical, Italian, or French imitation." In fact, in his " Canterbury Tales " Chaucer is at his best, and those Canterbury tales belong especially to the street and house of which we are now treating.

It may not be out of place here to give a brief outline of the plan of the immortal work which, as long as the English language lasts, will stand connected with the hostelry of the "Tabard." The framework of the "Canterbury Tales," it need hardly be said, embraces a rich collection of legends and narratives of various characters. The plot may have been suggested by the "Decameron" of Boccaccio, but that is all; for, instead of adopting the tame and frigid device of assembling a bevy of Florentine youths and maidens, who tell and listen to amorous tales, with no coherence or connection, Chaucer has sketched in bold and sharp outlines life-like pictures of the manners and social condition of his age, and has made his figures stand picturesquely forth, as types of the several classes which they represent.

"Who has not heard," asks Dr. Pauli, in his " Pictures of Old England," " of the far-famed sanctuary of Canterbury, where rested the bones of the archbishop, Thomas Becket, who bravely met his death to uphold the cause of the Roman Church, and who, venerated as the national saint of England, became renowned as a martyr and worker of miracles? To that sanctuary, year by year, and especially in the spring months, crowds of devout pilgrims flocked from every part of the Christian world; and although such pilgrimages were no doubt often undertaken from the most laudable motives, it is certain that even in the fourteenth century they had become, among the great masses of the people, too often a pretext for diversion . . . . It was such a pilgrimage as this that Chaucer took for the framework of his great poem; and, as a Kentish man, he was probably able to describe from experience and personal observation all that occurred on an occasion of this kind. The prologue, which is of extraordinary length, begins with a short description of spring, when nature begins to rejoice, and men from every part of the land seek the ' blissful martyr's ' tomb at Canterbury. At such a season—and some writers have calculated that Chaucer refers to the 27th of April, 1383—the poet was staying, with this purpose in view, at the ' Tabard,' where pilgrims were wont to assemble, and where they found good accommodation for themselves and their horses before they set forth on their way, travelling together, no doubt, at once for companionship and for mutual protection. Towards evening, when the host's room was filled, Chaucer had already made acquaintance with most of the guests, who were of all conditions and ranks. The twenty-nine persons who composed the party are each introduced to us with the most individual and life-like colouring. A knight most appropriately heads the list. For years his life has been spent either in the field or in the Crusades; for he was present when Alexandria was taken, and helped the Teutonic knights in Prussia against the Russians, fought with the Moors in Granada, with the Arabs in Africa, and with the Turks in Asia. One may see by his dress that he seldom doffs his armour; but, however little attention he pays to externals, his careful mode of speech, and his meek and Christian-like deportment, betray the true and gentle knight. He is accompanied by his son, a slim, light-haired, curly-headed youth of twenty, the perfect young squire of his day, who is elegantly and even foppishly dressed. He has already made a campaign against the French, and on that occasion, as well as in the tourney, he has borne him well, in the hopes of gaining his lady's grace. Love deprives him of his sleep; and, like the nightingale, he is overflowing with songs to his beloved; yet he does not fail, with lowly service, to carve before his father at table. In attendance on him is a yeoman, probably one of his father's many tenants, who, clad in green, with sword and buckler, his bow in his hand, and his arrows and dagger in his belt, represents, with his sunburnt face, that has grown brown among woods and fields, the stalwart race who won for the Plantagenets the victories of Crecy, of Poitiers, and Agincourt.

"In contrast with this group appears a daughter of the Church, Madame Eglantine,* a prioress of noble birth, as her delicate physiognomy, and the nicety with which she eats and drinks, testify plainly. With a sweet but somewhat nasal tone, she chants the Liturgy, or parts of it; she speaks

---

* See Vol. V., p. 571.

French, too, by preference, but it is the French, not of Paris, but of 'Stratford atte Bow.' She would weep if they showed her a mouse in a trap, or if they smote her little dog with a rod. A gold brooch, ornamented with the letter A, encircled with a crown, bearing the inscription *Amor vincit omnia*, hangs from her string of coral beads. Next to her comes a portly monk of the Benedictine order, whose crown and cheeks are as smooth as ,lass, and whose eyes shine like burning coals. He, too, is elegantly dressed, for the sleeves of his robe are trimmed with the finest fur, while a golden love-knot pin holds his hood together. Clear is the sound of the bells on his bridle, for he knows well how to sit his horse; whilst hare-hunting and a feast on a fat swan are more to him than the rule of St. Benedict and the holy books in his cell. A worthy pendant to this stately figure is the Mendicant Friar, whose ready familiarity and good humour make him the friend of the country-folks, and the favourite Father Confessor. No one understands better than he how to collect alms for his cloister; for he knows how to please the women with timely gifts of needles and knives, whilst he treats the men in the taverns, in which he always knows where to find the best cheer. He lisps his English with affected sweetness; and when he sings to his harp his eyes twinkle like the stars on a frosty night.

"The next in order is a merchant, with his forked beard, his Flemish beaver, and his well-clasped boots. He knows the money-exchange on both sides of the Channel, and best of all does he understand how to secure his own interest. Then follow a couple of learned men. First comes the Clerk of Oxenford (Oxford), hollowed-cheeked, and lean as the horse on which he rides, and with threadbare coat, for he has not yet secured a benefice; but his books are his whole joy, and chief among them is his Aristotle. He knows no greater joy than learning and teaching; yet he shrinks back modestly and timidly, and nowhere pushes himself forward. The other is a widely-known Serjeant of the Law, who has at his fingers' ends the whole confused mass of all the laws and statutes from the days of William the Conqueror to his own times, and knows admirably also how to apply his learning practically. Although his heavy fees and rich perquisites make him a rich man, he goes forth on his pilgrimage dressed in a plain and homely fashion. Next follows a Franklyn, who is described as the owner of a freehold estate, and as a man of note in his country, as having already served as knight of the shire, and also as sheriff. There is no stint of good eating and drinking in his house; for the dishes on his board come as thick and close as flakes of snow, each in its turn, according to the season of the year.

"The working classes are represented by a haberdasher, a carpenter, a weaver, a dyer, and a tap'ster, honest industrious folk, each clad in the dress that appertains to his order, and wearing the badge of his guild. They have all interest and money enough to make aldermen at some future time; and their wives would gladly hear themselves greeted as 'madame,' and would fain go to church in long and flowing mantles. With these are associated a cook, who is master of all the delicacies of his art, but who is not the less able on that account to relish a cup of London ale. The 'shipman,' of course, could not be absent from such a gathering; and here we see him as he comes from the west country, sunburnt, and clad in the dress of his class, equally prepared to quaff a draught of the fine Burgundy that he is bringing home while the master of the ship slumbers in his cabin, or to join in a sea-fight against the foes of his native land. He has visited every shore, from Gothland to Cape Finisterre, and he knows every harbour and bay in his course. The doctor of physic, too, is well versed in all the branches of his art; for, in addition to the skilful practice of his profession, he has systematically studied both astronomy and the science of the horoscope, and is familiar with all the learned writers of Greece and Arabia. He dresses carefully, and smartly; but he knows how to keep the treasures which he amassed during the prevalence of the 'black death.'

"Next follows a Wife of Bath, rich and comely, who especially attracts the poet's attention, and who is more communicative in regard to her own affairs than any one else in the company. She wears clothing of the finest stuffs, a broad hat with a new-fashioned head-attire, red and tight-fitting stockings, and a pair of sharp spurs on her heels. She is already well advanced in years, has been three times to Jerusalem, and has seen Rome and Bologna, Compostella, and Cologne. Her round, fair, reddish face looks a little bold, and shows that after her many experiences of life it would not be easy to put her out of countenance. She relates to her fellow-travellers, with the most edifying frankness, that she has been married five times, and that, therefore, independently of other considerations, she is entitled to say a word or two about love. She tells them how in her young and giddy days she beguiled and deluded her first three husbands, who were old but rich; and she does not even withhold from them the narration of some sharp 'curtain-lectures.' Her fourth marriage terminated, she tells them, in both parties taking their own way; but her last husband, although he is only twenty years old, has studied at Oxford, and is not to be drawn away from the perusal of a ponderous tome, in which are collected the injunctions of the Fathers of the Church to men to lead a life of celibacy, enriched by examples culled from ancient and modern times, of the manner in which wives are wont to circumvent their husbands. Once, when in her spite she tore some leaves out of this book, she says that he beat her so hard that ever since she has been deaf in one ear, but that since they have got on admirably together. In opposition to this dame, who forms one of the most important links of connection between the different members of the miscellaneous circle, we have another admirably-drawn character, a poor Parson, the son of humble but honest parents, who, notwithstanding his scanty benefice, is ever contented, even when his tithes fall short, and who never fails, even in the worst of weather, to sally forth, staff in hand, in order to visit the sick members of his flock. He is always ready to comfort and aid the needy; and undismayed by the pride of the rich and great, faithfully and honestly proclaims the word of the Lord in his teaching. The Parson is accompanied by his brother, a hard-working, honest, and pious ploughman; and thus the two are brought forward as belonging to that class which was bound to the soil which it tilled.

"Before the poet leaves this rank of the social scale, he brings before us also several other prominent characters belonging to the people of his day. There is the miller, a stout churl, bony and strong, with a hard head, a fox-red beard, and a wide mouth. He was not over-scrupulous in appropriating to himself some of the corn which his customers brought to his mill. Over his white coat and blue hood he carried a bag-pipe, and we fear it must be added, that his talk was of a wanton kind. Next comes the Manciple of a religious house, who is connected with at least thirty lawyers, and knows how to make his own profits whilst he is buying for his masters. The Reeve of a Norfolk lord, a man as lean as a rake, shaven and choleric, appears dressed in a blue coat, riding a grey horse. In his youth he had been a carpenter; but no one knows better than he how to judge of the yielding of the seed, or of the promise of the cattle. Nobody could well call him to account, for his books are always in the best order, and he and his master are in good accord. The Summoner of an archdeacon, with a fiery-red face, which no apothecary's art can cool down, is appropriately described as

one of the lowest and least reputable of the company. Lustful and gluttonous, he cares most of all for his wine; and when he is 'half seas over,' he speaks nothing but bad Latin, having picked up some scraps of that tongue in attendance in the Courts. His rival in viciousness is a Pardoner, who has come straight from the Court of Rome. His hair is as yellow as flax, and he carries in his wallet a handful of relics, by the sale of which he gets more money in a day than the Parson can make in two months."

Such are the troop of worthy, and some perhaps rather unworthy, guests who assembled in the ancient hostelry a little less than five hundred years ago, and whom the host, Harry Baily, right gladly welcomes in his guesten-room, with the best cheer that the "Tabard" can supply. Whilst the wine is passing round among the company, he proposes, with a boldness often to be seen in men of his craft, to join them on the morrow in their pilgrimage; but takes the liberty of suggesting first that it would be a good means of shortening the way between London and Canterbury, if each pilgrim were to tell one tale going and returning also, and that the one who should tell the best tale should have a supper at the inn at the expense of the rest upon their safe return. Next, without more ado, he offers himself to act as judge of the performances; and his proposition meets with general approval. The company then retire to rest, and the next morning, when the sun is up and the day is fine, they mount their horses at the door of the "Tabard," and, turning their backs on London, take the road into Kent. The plan of our work will not allow us to follow them beyond St. George's Church, where they branch to the left along the Old Kent Road, towards Blackheath and Rochester, and so on to Becket's shrine. It only remains to add that the poet did not live to complete even half of his projected poem, which breaks off somewhat abruptly before the pilgrims actually enter Canterbury, and hence, to our lasting regret, we lose the expected pleasure of a graphic description of their sayings and doings in that city, and of their promised feast upon returning to Southwark. With the tale, or rather discourse, of the Parson, Chaucer brings his pilgrims to Canterbury; "but," observes Mr. T. Wright, "his original plan evidently included the journey back to London. Some writer, within a few years after Chaucer's death, undertook to continue the work, and produced a ludicrous account of the proceedings of the pilgrims at Canterbury, and the story of Beryn, which was to be the first of the stories told on their return. These are printed by Urry, from a manuscript, to which, however, he is anything but faithful."

As regards the name of the inn now under notice, Stow says of the "Tabard" that "it was so called of a jacket, or sleeveless coat, whole before, open on

Tabarders, as certain scholars or exhibitioners are termed at Queen's College, Oxford. It may be added that the name of the author of the "Canterbury Tales" will still be kept in remembrance in Southwark by the "Chaucer" lodge of Freemasons

BOAR'S HEAD COURT-YARD.

both sides, with a square collar, winged at the shoulders. A stately garment of old time, commonly worn of noblemen and others, both at home and abroad in the wars; but then (to wit, in the wars) with their arms embroidered depicted upon them, that every man by his coat of arms might be known from others. But now these tabards are only worn by the heralds, and be called their coats of arms in service." The name of the dress is, or was till very lately, kept in remembrance by the

which has been instituted at the "Bridge House Tavern."

In the middle of the last century, the "Tabard" (or Talbot) appears to have become a great inn for carriers and for posting, and a well-known place of accommodation for visitors to London from distant parts of the country. Mr. Thomas Wright, F.S.A., remarks, "When my grandfather visited London towards the close of the reign of George II., or early in that of George III., he tells me in his

'Autobiography' that he and his companions took up their quarters as guests at the 'Talbot,' in Southwark."

Not far from the "Tabard" was another old inn called the "Bell," for Chaucer mentions "the gentil hostelrie that heighte the 'Tabard'" as being "faste by the 'Bell.'"

following lines from the *Musarum Deliciæ*, upon a surfeit by drinking bad sack at the 'George Tavern,' in Southwark :—

' Oh, would I might turn poet for an hour,
To satirise with a vindictive power
Against the drawer ; or could I desire
Old Johnson's head had scalded in the fire ;

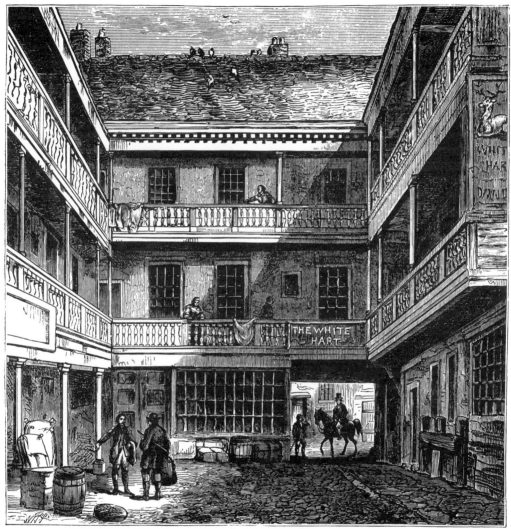

THE OLD "WHITE HART" INN.

Among the historic inns of Southwark to which we are introduced by Mr. John Timbs in his "London and Westminster," is one called the "George," which also stood near the "Tabard." "This inn," says Mr. Timbs, "is mentioned by Stow, and even earlier, in 1554, the thirty-fifth year of King Henry VIII. Its name was then the 'St. George.' There is no further trace of it till the seventeenth century, when there are two tokens issued from this inn. Mr. Burn quotes the

How would he rage, and bring Apollo down
To scold with Bacchus, and depose the clown
For his ill government, and so confute
Our poets, apes, that do so much impute
Unto the grape inspirement.' "

In the year 1670 the "George" was in great part burnt down and demolished by a fire which broke out in this neighbourhood, and it was totally consumed by the great fire of Southwark some six years later ; the owner was at that time one John

Sayer, and the tenant Mark Weyland. "The present 'George Inn,'" continues Mr. Timbs, "although built only in the seventeenth century, seems to have been rebuilt on the old plan, having open wooden galleries leading to the chambers on each side of the inn-yard. After the fire, the host, Mark Weyland, was succeeded by his widow, Mary Weyland; and she by William Golding, who was followed by Thomas Green, whose niece, Mrs. Frances Scholefield, and her then husband, became landlord and landlady in 1809. Mrs. Scholefield died at a great age in 1859. The property has since been purchased by the governors of Guy's Hospital.

"The 'George' is mentioned in the records relating to the 'Tabard,' to which it adjoins, in the reign of King Henry VIII., as the 'St. George Inn.' Two tokens of the seventeenth century, in the Beaufoy Collection at Guildhall Library, admirably catalogued and annotated by Mr. Burn, give the names of two landlords of the 'George' at that period—viz., 'Anthony Blake, tapster,' and 'James Gunter.'"

The "White Hart," on the same side of the High Street, was, according to Hatton, the inn which had the largest sign in London, save and except the "Castle" in Fleet Street. This also is one of the inns mentioned by Stow in his "Survey;" but, as John Timbs tells us, it possesses a still earlier celebrity, having been the head-quarters of Jack Cade and his rebel rout during their brief possession of London in 1450. Shakespeare, in the Second Part of *King Henry VI.*, makes a messenger enter in haste, and announce to the king—

" The rebels are in Southwark. Fly, my lord !
Jack Cade proclaims himself Lord Mortimer,
Descended from the Duke of Clarence' house,
And calls your grace usurper openly,
And vows to crown himself in Westminster."

And again, another messenger enters, and says—

"Jack Cade hath gotten London Bridge ;
The citizens fly and forsake their houses."

Afterwards, Cade thus addresses his followers :— "Will you needs be hanged with your pardons about your necks? Hath my sword therefore broke through London gates, that you should leave me at the 'White Hart,' in Southwark ?"

Fabyan, in his "Chronicles," has this entry :— "On July 1, 1450, Jack Cade arrived in Southwark, where he lodged at the 'Hart;' for he might not be suffered to enter the City." The following deed of violence committed by Cade's followers at this place is recorded in the "Chronicle of the Grey Friars :"—"At the Whyt Harte, in Southwarke, one Hawaydyne, of Sent Martyns, was beheddyd."

It is quite possible, however, that Shakespeare, and the historians who have been content to follow in his wake, have done injustice to the character of Cade, exaggerating his faults, and suppressing all notice of his virtues. As Mr. J. T. Smith remarks, in his work on "The Streets of London :"—"In an unhappy time, when the fields of England were strewed with dead, in the quarrels of contending factions, when the people had scarcely the shadow of a right, and were never thought of by the rulers of the land, except when they wanted folks to fight their battles, or when they needed money that could by any possibility be wrung or squeezed out of the population, this man, the despised Jack Cade, stood forward to plead the cause of the million. He made himself the voice of the people : he understood their grievances, and made a bold effort to redress them; and if that effort was a violent one, it was the fault of the age, rather than of the man. A list of the grievances complained of by Cade, preserved in Stow's 'Annals', gives a high opinion of his shrewdness and moderation, and makes him appear anything but the ignorant man it has been the fashion to represent him. The City of London was long in his favour, and its merchants supplied him, without murmur, with sufficient rations for his large army encamped on Blackheath." This fact would seem by itself sufficient to prove that he was not a vile republican and communist of the Parisian type.

Neither the house now bearing the sign of the "White Hart," nor its immediate predecessor, which was pulled down a few years ago, can lay claim to being the same building that afforded shelter to Jack Cade ; for in 1669 the back part of the old inn was accidentally burnt down, and the tavern was wholly destroyed by the great fire of Southwark, in 1676. "It appears, however," says Mr. John Timbs, "to have been rebuilt upon the model of the older edifice, and realised the descriptions which we read of the ancient inns, consisting of one or more open courts or yards, surrounded with open galleries, and which were frequently used as temporary theatres for acting plays and dramatic performances in the olden time."

"There are in London," writes Charles Dickens, in his inimitable "Pickwick Papers," "several old inns, once the head-quarters of celebrated coaches in the days when coaches performed their journeys in a graver and more solemn manner than they do in these times ; but which have now degenerated into little more than the abiding and booking places of country wagons. The reader would look in vain for any of these ancient hostelries among the 'Golden Crosses' and 'Bull and Mouths,' which rear their stately fronts in the improved streets of London. If he would light upon any of these old places, he must direct his steps to the obscurer quarters of the town; and there in some secluded nooks he will find several, still standing with a kind of gloomy sturdiness amidst the modern innovations which surround them. In the Borough especially there still remain some half-dozen old inns, which have preserved their external features unchanged, and which have escaped alike the rage for public improvement and the encroachments of private speculation. Great, rambling, queer old places they are, with galleries, and passages, and staircases wide enough and antiquated enough to furnish materials for a hundred ghost stories, supposing we should ever be reduced to the lamentable necessity of inventing any, and that the world should exist long enough to exhaust the innumerable veracious legends connected with old London Bridge and its adjacent neighbourhood on the Surrey side." It is in the yard of one of these inns—of one no less celebrated than the "White Hart"—that our author first introduces to the reader's notice Sam Weller, in the character of "boots." "The yard," proceeds the novelist, "presented none of that bustle and activity which are the usual characteristics of a large coach inn. Three or four lumbering wagons, each with a pile of goods beneath its ample canopy, about the height of the second-floor window of an ordinary house, were stowed away beneath a lofty roof which extended over one end of the yard; and another, which was probably to commence its journey that morning, was drawn out into the open space. A double tier of bedroom galleries, with old clumsy balustrades, ran round two sides of the straggling area, and a double row of bells to correspond, sheltered from the weather by a little sloping roof, hung over the door leading to the bar and coffee-room. Two or three gigs and chaise-carts were wheeled up under different little sheds and penthouses; and the occasional heavy tread of a cart-horse, or rattling of a chain at the further end of the yard, announced to anybody who cared about the matter that the stable lay in that direction. When we add that a few boys in smock-frocks were lying asleep on heavy packages, woolpacks, and other articles that were scattered about on heaps of straw, we have described as fully as need be the general appearance of the yard of the 'White Hart Inn,' High Street, Borough, on the particular morning in question."

Another celebrated inn in the High Street was the "Boar's Head," which formed a part of Sir John Fastolf's benefactions to Magdalen College

at Oxford. Sir John Fastolf* was one of the bravest of English generals in the French wars, under Henry IV. and his successors. The premises are said to have comprised a narrow court of ten or twelve houses, but they were removed in 1830 to make the approach to New London Bridge. We learn from Mr. C. J. Palmer's "Perlustration of Great Yarmouth," that the Fastolf family had their town residence in Southwark, nearly opposite to the Tower of London, and that the "Boar's Head Inn" was the property of Sir John Fastolf. Henry Windesone, in a letter to John Paston, dated August, 1459, says, "An it please you to remember my master (Sir John Fastolf) at your best leisure, whether his old promise shall stand as touching my preferring to the 'Boar's Head,' in Southwark. Sir, I would have been at another place, and of my master's own motion he said that I should set up in the 'Boar's Head.'" In the churchwardens' account for St. Olave's, Southwark, in 1614 and 1615, the house is thus mentioned:—"Received of John Barlowe, that dwelleth at yᵉ 'Boar's Head' in Southwark, for suffering the encroachment at the corner of the wall in yᵉ Flemish Church-yard for one yeare, iiijs."

There is in existence a rare small brass token of the "Boar's Head;" on one side is a boar's head, with a lemon in its mouth, surrounded by the words, "AT THE 'BOAR'S HEAD;'" and on the other side, "IN SOUTHWARK, 1649."

Mr. John Timbs, in his "Autobiography," says: "Of a modern-built house, nearly opposite the east end of St. Saviour's Church, my father and brother had a long tenancy, though the place has better claim to mention as being one of the ancient inns, the 'Boar's Head,' Southwark, and the property of Sir John Fastolf, of Caistor, Norfolk, and of Southwark, and who had a large house in Stoney Lane, St. Olave's. Sir John was a man of military renown, having been in the French wars of Henry VI., and was Governor of Normandy; he was also a man of letters and learning, and at the instance of his friend, William Waynflete, Bishop of Winchester, the founder of Magdalen College, Oxford, Sir John Fastolf gave the 'Boar's Head' and other possessions towards the foundation. In the 'Reliquiæ Hearnianæ,' edited by Dr. Bliss, is the following entry relative to this bequest: '1721, June 2.—The reason why they cannot give so good an account of the benefaction of Sir John Fastolf to Magd. Coll. is, because he gave it to the founder, and left it to his management, so that 'tis

---

* This Sir John Fastolf is not to be confounded—though often confounded—with Shakespeare's Falstaff.

suppos'd 'twas swallow'd up in his own estate that he settled upon the college. However, the college knows this, that the " Boar's Head," in Southwark, which was then an inn, and still retains the name, tho' divided into several tenements (which brings the college £150 per annum), was part of Sir John's gift.' The property above mentioned was for many years leased to the father of the writer, and was by him principally sub-let to weekly tenants. The premises were named ' Boar's Head Court,' and consisted of two rows of tenements, vis-à-vis, and two houses at the east end, with a gallery outside the first floor of the latter. The tenements were fronted with strong weatherboard, and the balusters of the staircases were of great age. The court entrance was between the houses Nos. 25 and 26 east side of High Street, and that number of houses from old London Bridge; and beneath the whole extent of the court was a finely-vaulted cellar, doubtless the wine-cellar of the ' Boar's Head.' The property was cleared away in making the approaches to new London Bridge; and on this site was subsequently built part of the new front of St. Thomas's Hospital."

The " White Lion," which formerly stood at the south end of St. Margaret's Hill, nearly opposite the " Tabard Inn," was in its latter days, as we have already seen, a prison " for felons and other notorious malefactors." Stow, writing in 1598, says, " The ' White Lion ' is a gaol, so called for that the same was a common hostelrie for the receipt of travellers by that sign. This house was first used as a gaol within these forty years last past." In 1640, as Laud tells us in his " History of his Troubles," the rabble apprentices released the whole of the prisoners in the " White Lion." The place is mentioned in records of the reign of Henry VIII. as having belonged to the Priory of St. Mary Overy.

Henry VIII., as we all know, in spite of his cruelty, lust, and tyranny, was a favourite sign among hostelries both in London and up and down the country. " Only fifty or sixty years ago," writes Mr. J. Larwood, in 1866, " there still remained a well-painted half-length portrait of Bluff Harry as the sign of the ' King's Head ' before a public-house in Southwark. His personal appearance doubtless, more than his character as a king, was at the bottom of this popular favour. He looked the personification of jollity and good cheer; and when the evil passions expressed by his face were lost under the clumsy brush of the sign-painter, there remained nothing but a merry ' beery-looking ' Bacchus, well adapted for a public-house sign."

Another ancient inn bore the sign of the " Three Tuns;" all that is known of it, however, is that it formed one of the favourite resorts of the Philanthropic Harmonists.

Apropos of these old inns in the Borough, we may add that Mr. Larwood tells us that in 1866 the " Sun and Hare," a carved stone sign, still existed, walled up in the façade of a house here.

Many of these inns had a religious, or quasi-religious character. Such was the hostelry which bore the sign of the " Three Brushes," or " Holy-water Sprinklers," in allusion to the brushes used at the " Asperges," in the commencement of high mass in the Catholic Church. This house stood near the White Lion Prison. It had in it a room with a richly-panelled wainscot, and a ceiling ornamented with the arms of Queen Elizabeth. Probably it had been a court-room for the " justices " at the time when the " White Lion " was used as a prison. Its existence is proved by tokens of one " Robert Thornton, haberdasher, next the ' Three Brushes,' in Southwark, 1667."

Between Union Street and Mint Street, opposite St. George's Church, and on the site where now stands the booking-office of the Midland Railway Goods Depôt, stood, till about the year 1870, an old and well-known inn, called " The Catherine Wheel." It was a famous inn for carriers during the seventeenth and eighteenth centuries. " The ' Catherine Wheel,' " writes Mr. Larwood, " was formerly a very common sign, most likely adopted from its being the badge of the order of the knights of St. Catherine of Mount Sinai, formed in the year 1063, for the protection of pilgrims on their way to and from the Holy Sepulchre. Hence it was a suggestive, if not an eloquent, sign for an inn, as it intimated that the host was of the brotherhood, although in a humble way, and would protect the traveller from robbery in his inn—in the shape of high charges and exactions—just as the knights of St. Catherine protected them on the high road from robbery by brigands. These knights wore a white habit embroidered with a Catherine-wheel (i.e., a wheel armed with spikes), and traversed with a sword, stained with blood. There were also mysteries in which St. Catherine played a favourite part, one of which was acted by young ladies on the entry of Queen Catherine of Aragon (queen to our Henry VIII.) in London in 1501. In honour of this queen the sign may occasionally have been put up. The Catherine-wheel was also a charge in the Turners' arms. Flecknoe tells us in his ' Enigmatical Characters ' (1658), that the Puritans changed it into the Cat and Wheel, under which it is still to be seen on a public-house at Castle Green, Bristol."

Another inn, called the "Three Widows," was probably a perversion of the "Three Nuns"—the ignorant people after the Reformation confounding the white head-dresses of the religious sisterhood with those of disconsolate relicts. Here, "at the 'Three Widows,' in Southwark," a foreigner, Peter Treviris, in the early part of the sixteenth century, set up a printing-press, which he kept constantly at work for several years, as we learn from the title-pages of his books.

Among the quaint old signs which prevailed along this road, Mr. Larwood mentions one not generally known, "The Old Pick my Toe," which he suggests was "a vulgar representation of the Roman slave who, being sent on a message of importance, would not stop to pick even a thorn out of his foot by the way." This curious sign, Mr. Larwood further tells us, is represented on a trade-token issued by one Samuel Bovery in George Lane.

From the fact of Southwark being the chief seat of our early theatres, its houses of entertainment were very numerous, in addition to the old historic inns which abounded in the High Street. "In the Beaufoy collection," writes Mr. John Timbs, "are several tokens of Southwark taverns: among them those of the 'Bore's (Boar's) Head,' 1649; the 'Dogg and Ducke,' St. George's Fields, 1651; the 'Green Man,' still remaining in Blackman Street; the 'Bull Head' Tavern, 1667 (mentioned by Edmund Alleyne, the founder of Dulwich College, as one of his resorts); the 'Duke of Suffolk's Head,' 1669; and the 'Swan with Two Necks'—properly 'Nicks.'"

CHAPTER VIII.

SOUTHWARK (*continued*).—OLD ST. THOMAS'S HOSPITAL, GUY'S HOSPITAL, &c.

"I cannot walk through Southwark without thinking of Chaucer and Shakespeare."—*Leigh Hunt.*

Foundation of St. Thomas's Hospital—A Well-timed Sermon of Bishop Ridley—Purchase of the Old Building by the Citizens of London—The Lease of the Hospital in Pawn—The Edifice Rebuilt and Enlarged—Description of the Building—Statue of Sir Robert Clayton—Removal of the Hospital to Lambeth—Value of Land near London Bridge—St. Thomas's Church—Gerard Johnson, the Sculptor of Shakespeare's Bust—Foundation of Guy's Hospital—Anecdotes of Thomas Guy, the Founder—Description of the Hospital—Statue of Guy—Medical Staff of the Hospital—London Bridge Railway Terminus—The Greenwich Railway—The South-Eastern Railway—The London, Brighton, and South Coast Railway—Watson's Telegraph to the Downs—Southwark Waterworks—Waterworks at Old London Bridge.

WE have already mentioned, in a previous chapter,[*] the temporary church dedicated to St. Thomas by the canons of St. Mary Overy's, whose priory had been partly or entirely burnt down in the reign of King John. About the same time—or to give the exact date, in 1213—Richard, Prior of Bermondsey, with the consent of the convent, founded close by it, in the land appropriated to the cellarer, an "almery," or hospital, for converts and boys, which was dedicated to St. Thomas the Martyr (à Becket). For this ground, which adjoined the wall of the monastery, we read that the prior appointed a payment by the almoner to the cellarer, of 10s. 4d. annually, on the feast of St. Michael; and this almery, like the parent monastery, was exempt from all episcopal jurisdiction. After the priory church of St. Mary Overy had been repaired, and the canons had returned thither, the temporary building above mentioned, which stood within the precincts of the Priory of Bermondsey, was assigned for the use of the poor, and the support of certain brethren and sisters. In 1228 this hospital of St. Mary Overy was transferred from the land belonging to the priory to that of Amicius, Archdeacon of Surrey, who was custos, or warden, of the hospital founded by the monks of Bermondsey, which had the advantage of a better supply of spring water, and pure air; and the two institutions being united, the hospital was dedicated anew to the celebrated Archbishop of Canterbury, under the title of the "Hospital of St. Thomas the Martyr." The new arrangement took place under the auspices of Peter de Rupibus, Bishop of Winchester, who granted an indulgence for twenty days to all such as should contribute to the expenses of the hospital, the bishop himself becoming a benefactor to it; hence it was always accounted as a foundation of the bishops of Winchester, and the prelates of that see had the patronage of it.

At the Dissolution, this hospital, or almery, was surrendered to the king. At this time its members were a master and six brethren, and three lay sisters. They made forty beds for poor infirm people, who also had victuals and firing supplied to them. The institution, however, was suffered to go to decay; but in 1552, Ridley, Bishop of London,

* See *ante*, p. 21.

by a well-timed sermon preached before King Edward VI., awakened the benevolence of his disposition. The young king consulted with him how he should commence some great charitable institutions, and by his advice, addressed a letter to the mayor and corporation of London, announcing his opened it for the reception of the sick poor, under the patronage of the young king. In the course of four months after the purchase of the hospital, the institution had received no less than 260 poor infirm people. In the following year a charter of incorporation was granted for this foundation; but

ST. THOMAS'S HOSPITAL, 1840.

intention, and requiring their advice. After some consultation, at which the bishop assisted, three different institutions were suggested, which at length produced Christ's Hospital, for the education of youth; Bridewell, for the poor, and correcting the profligate; and this of St. Thomas, for the relief of the lame and sick.

The citizens of London purchased the old building, and after having repaired and enlarged it, seven years afterwards the hospital was so poor that the lease was pawned for £50. Funds, however, were obtained for its support, and the establishment subsequently throve.

In 1664, part of St. Thomas's Hospital was used as a military hospital, as we learn from the following entry in John Evelyn's "Diary," under date of 2nd of December of that year:—"We deliver'd the Privy Council letters to the Governors of St.

Thomas's Hospital, in Southwark, that a moiety of the house should be reserv'd for such sick and wounded as should from time to time be sent from the Fleete during the war."

Much injury was done to the property belonging to this establishment by the fires which, as already stated, took place in Southwark in the Stuart times, although the hospital itself received no damage on either occasion. However, towards the close of

Prince of exemplary piety, and wisdom above his years, the glory and ornament of his age, and most munificent Founder of this Hospital, was erected at the expense of Charles Joyce, Esq., in the year MDCCXXXVII.'

"Through the first court is the entrance to the second, by a descent of steps. This court has a Doric colonnade with a cornice, on which is the basement to nine pilasters. On the north side is the chapel for the use of the patients, in which

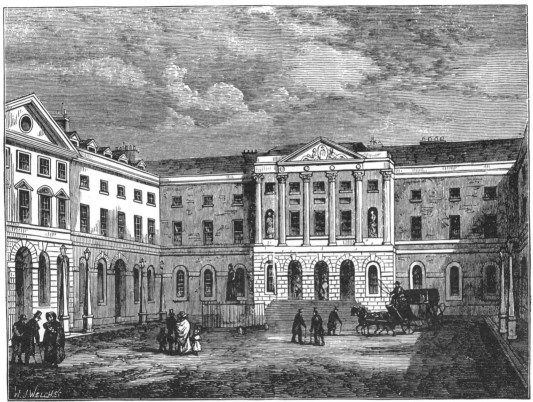

GUY'S HOSPITAL.

the seventeenth century the building had become so much decayed that a public subscription was made in order to re-edify and enlarge it, and the first stone of the new edifice was laid by Sir John Fleet, who was Lord Mayor of London in 1692. The whole was executed at different times, and the work was not completed till the year 1732.

The following description of the edifice is given in Brayley's "History of Surrey," published in 1843 :—"The hospital buildings now consist of several quadrangles; in the centre of the first of which, facing Wellington Street, is a brazen statue of Edward VI., by Scheemakers, bearing this inscription, on one side in Latin, on the other in English :—

' This Statue of King Edward the Sixth, a most excellent

service is performed daily ; on the south, the parish church ; on the east, the hall, elevated on Tuscan columns, with compartments for the chaplain, treasurer, steward, &c. ; in the north-east corner is the kitchen. The court-room is over the colonnade.

"The third court is surrounded by a colonnade of the Tuscan order, with an entablature, from which ascends a long range of pilasters of the Ionic order. In the centre is a statue of Sir Robert Clayton, in his robes as Lord Mayor, with the following inscription, in Latin and in English :—

' To Sir ROBERT CLAYTON, Knt., born in Northampton-shire, Citizen and Lord Mayor of London, President of this Hospital, and Vice President of the new Workhouse, and a bountiful benefactor to it ; a just Magistrate, and brave Defender of the Liberty and Religion of his Country ; who (besides many other instances of his charity to the poor) built the Girls' Ward in Christ's Hospital; gave first toward the rebuilding of this house £600; and left by his last Will £2,300 to the poor of it. This statue was erected in his life-time by the Governors an. Dom. MDCCI. as a monument of their esteem of so much worth; and, to preserve his memory after death, was by them beautified anno Dom. MDCCXIV.'

"In a small court, farther to the east, are two wards for salivation (now little used), and what is called the cutting-ward. Here also are the surgery, bathing-rooms, theatre, and dead-house, in which corpses are deposited until the time of interment. In the court-room are portraits of Edward VI., William III., and Queen Mary; Sir Robert Clayton, by Richardson; Sir Gilbert Heathcote; Sir Gerard Conyers; Sir John Eyles, by Vanloo; Sir James Campbell, &c. The gentlemen here named were presidents, and most of them patrons also, of the foundation." A tablet over the entrance to the court-room in the old building, in allusion to the great fire of Southwark, May, 1676, bore this inscription: "In the midst of judgment God remembered mercy, and by His goodness in remembering the poor and the distressed, put a stop to the fire at this house, after it had been touched several times therewith; by which, in all probability, all this side of the Borough was preserved."

Northouck tells us that the reason why this fire was so wide in its devastation was the fact that the houses there were chiefly built of timber, lath, and plaster; he adds that afterwards commissioners were appointed for rebuilding them regularly and substantially with brick, "as now (1773) appears from the Bridge-foot up to St. Margaret's Hill beyond it."

There were at the above period twenty wards for the reception of patients, each under the care of a sister or female superintendent, and two or three nurses. The number of beds was 485. The grand entrance, with its gates, lodges, &c., was from Wellington Street, between the north and south wings. In front was a dwarf stone wall, surmounted by lofty and massive iron railings, which were carried on and flanked the north side of the north wing, running along Duke Street, up to the offices of the South-Eastern Railway.

Imposing as the building was, it seems to have had its drawbacks; for we read in a topographical account of it published many years ago, that "The magnitude of St. Thomas's Hospital, with the relief of its many colonnades, will not permit us wholly to exclude the character of the edifice from a species of grandeur. But it is time to rebuild this hospital in a better style; and with this improvement might commence a system of decorating the borough of Southwark and its vicinity, which

at present are more than a century behind the northern bank of the river in the progress of refinement; and to this it may be added, that if the practice of wholly surrounding a space with buildings, so as to stagnate the air within the quadrangle, is as unhealthy as we deem it to be, no plan can be so unfit for an hospital as an accumulation of courts behind each other."

Of the "inner life" of St. Thomas's Hospital we shall have more to say when we reach Lambeth, where the institution is now located. But we may add here that it is one of the oldest hospitals in the kingdom as an asylum where all sick poor could be relieved. Its charter dates from the time of Edward VI., who gave it some of its lands, which were then of such little value that—as we have shown above—the whole freehold was pawned to the City for £50, for the hospital was then in debt, as it had been ever since it was first founded, in 1213, by "ye Priore of Bermondseye." How the value of land has increased at that spot near London Bridge since then need not be told, beyond saying that some was sold by the hospital about the year 1865 at the rate of £55,000 per acre, and some a little later at the rate of £70,000 an acre. St. Thomas's, too, was made in the olden time into a distinct parish, and had peculiar rights of its own. Still, ancient possession and modern usefulness proved no adequate bar to the march of that universal leveller—the railway. The site was wanted, and the site was taken; certainly at a very heavy price—nearly £300,000. When thus "disestablished," the choice of the hospital authorities for a new site was rather limited. It was felt necessary that the new building should be on the south side of the water; that it should be in the midst of a poor neighbourhood, to the wants of which it could administer; and that, above all, it should have a certain amount of open space around it. This latter was a difficult desideratum, and while waiting a choice, St. Thomas's Hospital, its patients, and its staff were located in the music-hall which stood in the midst of what was once the Surrey Zoological Gardens at Kennington. Fortunately, at this time the southern Thames Embankment was being made, and the necessities of its construction compelled a considerable reclamation from the slimy foreshore of the river opposite the Houses of Parliament. The advantages of this site were instantly seen, and about eight and a half acres were bought by the hospital from the Board of Works for about £100,000. On this land the new hospital has been built. The south wing of the old hospital has been left standing, and has been converted into a chapel.

On the north side of St. Thomas's Street—the first turning from the High Street southward of the London Bridge Station—stands St. Thomas's Church. It is a donative, in the gift of the governors of St. Thomas's Hospital, the church having been originally part of the hospital—as, indeed, it continued down to the time of the removal of the hospital as above mentioned—forming a part of the south side of it. The old church having become ruinous and dilapidated, it was rebuilt early in the last century, at an expense of £3,000 granted out of the coal duty, with the further assistance of the governors and others. The present edifice is a plain and unsightly building of red brick, with stone dressings, of a nondescript character, having a square tower in three storeys attached to the south side. In the south side of the church, which is open to the street, are four lofty circular arched windows, the key-stones of which are carved with cherubim; its elevation is finished with an attic over a cornice; in the centre is a pediment. The ground-floor of the tower forms a porch to the church. The interior of the church is exceedingly plain. The altar-screen is composed of oak, and encircled with Corinthian pilasters, surmounted by their entablature and a segmental pediment. This is crowned by "the royal arms of George I., and over them a crest; on the side pilaster is the lion and unicorn; the whole executed in dark oak."

Gerard Johnson, a Hollander, who made the monumental bust and tomb of Shakespeare in Stratford-on-Avon Church, lived in the parish of St. Thomas, as ascertained by Mr. Peter Cunningham and Mr. J. O. Halliwell. Dugdale assures us that Gerard Johnson must often have *seen* Shakespeare.

On the south side of St. Thomas's Street, and covering a large space of ground, stands Guy's Hospital—perhaps the noblest institution in London founded by one man. It was founded, along with other charities, by an eccentric but philanthropic individual, Thomas Guy, a bookseller of London, of whom we have spoken in a previous volume, in our account of the Stock Exchange.* The son of a lighterman and coaldealer, he was born in Horselydown, Southwark, in 1645. He was apprenticed to a bookseller in Cheapside, and having been admitted a freeman of the Stationers' Company in 1668, was received into their livery in 1673. He began business with a stock of about £200, in the house which, till about the year 1834, formed the angle between Cornhill and Lombard Street, but which was pulled down for the improvements then made in that neighbourhood. His first success was owing to the great demand for English Bibles printed in Holland, in which he dealt largely; but on the importation of these being stopped by law, he contracted with the University of Oxford for the privilege of printing Bibles; and having furnished himself with types from Holland, carried on this branch of business for many years, with great profit.

It has been stated by other writers, and also in the previous volume of this work, referred to above, that whatever foundation he might have laid for his future wealth, in the usual course of trade, no small portion of his property arose from his purchase of seamen's tickets. These, it is asserted, he bought at a large discount, and afterwards subscribed in the South Sea Company, which was established in 1710, for the purpose of discharging those tickets, and giving a large interest. Here, it is added, Mr. Guy was so extensively, as well as cautiously, concerned that in 1720 he was possessed of £45,500 stock, by disposing of which when it bore an extremely advanced price, he realised a considerable sum. But Charles Knight, in his "Shadows of the Old Booksellers," has shown good reasons for believing that seamen's tickets were not in use after Thomas Guy was out of his apprenticeship, and that therefore we must look to his sale of Bibles as the real basis of his wealth.

"With regard to the South Sea Stock," observes a writer in the *Saturday Magazine* in 1834, "Mr. Guy had no hand in framing or conducting that scandalous fraud; he obtained the stock when low, and had the good sense to sell it at the time it was at its height. Never, indeed, can we approve of that speculative spirit which leads men to step out of the line of a particular calling, and to '*make haste* to be rich;' nor, while we admire the *mode* in which a fortune has been spent, and contemplate some splendid endowment that has derived its origin from the 'bad success' of gambling or avarice, can we be so far misled as to allow that the end justifies the means. Gay, who, under the form of a fable, often couched just and biting satire, alluding to the large fortunes suddenly made by means of the 'South Sea Bubble,' remarks—

> ' How many saucy airs we meet,
>   From Temple Bar to Aldgate Street !
>   Proud rogues who shared the South Sea prey,
>   And sprung, like mushrooms, in a day.' "

Being a single man, Mr. Guy is reported to have spent but a very small portion of his profits as a

* See Vol. I., p. 474.

bookseller. He dined on his counter, with no other tablecloth than a newspaper, and was not more nice about his wearing apparel. "For the application of this fortune to charitable uses," says Highmore, in his "History of the Public Charities of London," "the public are indebted to a trifling circumstance. He employed a female servant, whom he had agreed to marry. Some days previous to the intended ceremony, he had ordered the pavement before his door to be mended up to a particular stone which he had marked, and then left his house on business. The servant, in his absence, looking at the workmen, saw a broken stone beyond this mark which they had not repaired, and on pointing to it with that design, they acquainted her that Mr. Guy had not ordered them to go so far. She, however, directed it to be done, adding, with the security incidental to her expectation of soon becoming his wife, 'Tell him I bade you, and he will not be angry.' But she too soon learnt how fatal it is for any one in a dependent situation to exceed the limits of his or her authority; for her master, on his return, was enraged at finding that they had gone beyond his orders, renounced his engagement to his servant, and devoted his ample fortune to public charity." Another anecdote has been related of Guy, which exhibits him in another light. He was so complete a pattern of economy, that the celebrated Vulture Hopkins once called upon him to have a lesson in the art of saving. Being introduced into the parlour, Guy, not knowing his visitor, lighted a candle; but when Hopkins said, "Sir, I always thought myself perfect in the art of getting and husbanding money, but being informed that you far exceed me, I have taken the liberty of waiting upon you to be satisfied on this subject." Guy replied, "If that is all your business, we can as well talk it over in the dark," and immediately put out the candle. This was evidence sufficient for Hopkins, who acknowledged Guy to be his master, and took his leave.

The following anecdote which has been told concerning Mr. Guy will bear repetition:—"The munificent founder of Guy's Hospital was a man of very humble appearance, and of a melancholy cast of countenance. One day, while pensively leaning over one of the bridges, he attracted the attention and commiseration of a by-stander, who, apprehensive that he meditated self-destruction, could not refrain from addressing him with an earnest entreaty, 'not to let his misfortunes tempt him to commit any rash act;' then, placing in his hand a guinea, with the delicacy of genuine benevolence, he hastily withdrew. Guy, roused from his reverie, followed the stranger, and warmly expressed his gratitude, but assured him he was mistaken in supposing him to be either in distress of mind or of circumstances, making an earnest request to be favoured with the name of the good man, his intended benefactor. The address was given, and they parted. Some years after, Guy, observing the name of his friend in the bankrupt list, hastened to his house; brought to his recollection their former interview; found, upon investigation, that no blame could be attached to him under his misfortunes; intimated his ability and also his full intention to serve him; entered into immediate arrangements with his creditors; and, finally, re-established him in a business which ever after prospered in his hands, and in the hands of his children's children, for many years in Newgate Street."

Thomas Guy served in several Parliaments as member for Tamworth, in Staffordshire, where his mother was born, and where he founded almshouses for poor persons, besides bestowing considerable benefactions. To Christ's Hospital he gave a perpetual annuity of £400, to receive, on the nomination of his trustees, four children yearly, who must be his connections; and there are always applicants. He left £1,000 to discharge poor prisoners in London, Middlesex, and Surrey, at £5 each, and another £1,000 to be distributed among poor housekeepers at the discretion of his executors. The erection of the hospital now under notice, the earliest part of which was built by Dance, is said to have cost nearly £19,000, the amount of the residue of Guy's personal property being stated at upwards of £219,000. His death happened on December 27, 1724, in the eightieth year of his age, before which he saw his hospital covered with the roof. Besides his public expenses he gave during life to many of his poor relations £10 or £20 a year, and to others money to advance them in life; to his aged relations £870 in annuities; and to his younger relations and executors the sum of £75,589.

Before Guy had founded the hospital to which he gave his name, he had contributed £100 annually to St. Thomas's Hospital for eleven years, and had erected the stately iron gate with the large houses on each side.

It is now time to speak more of the hospital which bears his name. At the age of seventy-six Mr. Guy procured from the governors of St. Thomas's Hospital the lease of a large piece of ground for a term of 999 years, at a rent of £30 a year. Having cleared the space, which was then occupied by a number of poor dwelling-houses, he laid the first stone of his new building in the spring of 1722. He lived to see it covered in; but before the excellent institution was in full work the benevolent founder was laid in the grave; for the hospital received within its walls the first sixty patients on the 6th of January, 1725. His trustees faithfully effected the completion of his great and good design, and shortly after procured an Act of Parliament for establishing the foundation, according to the directions of his will. Large and profitable estates were afterwards purchased in Herefordshire and Essex, for the benefit of the institution; the lease of an additional piece of ground was also obtained, for which, with the former, the governors still pay an annual sum to St. Thomas's. On this were erected two handsome wings, connected by an iron railing and gates. These gates open into a square court, in the centre of which is a bronze statue of the founder, by Scheemakers. In front of the pedestal is this inscription:—"Thomas Guy, sole Founder of this Hospital in his life-time, A.D. MDCCXXII." On the west side of the pedestal is represented, in basso relievo, the parable of the Good Samaritan; on the south side are Mr. Guy's armorial bearings; and on the west, a representation of our Saviour healing the impotent man.

The centre of the principal front of the hospital is of stone, and consists of a rusticated basement, in which are three arched entrances to the quadrangle, and two windows. This supports two pilasters and four Ionic columns, the intercolumniation containing three windows and two niches, in which are two emblematic figures, Æsculapius, the heathen god of medicine, and Hygieia, the goddess of health, daughter of Æsculapius. The tympanum is ornamented with an emblematic relief. This front was new faced about the year 1778, and is, with the statues, the work of Bacon, who was a native of Southwark. Passing through the arches, the visitor enters a long corridor, on each side of which are several of the wards for the patients. The court-room, with its painted ceiling, is a handsome apartment; over the president's chair is a portrait of the founder, by Dahl.

The chapel, in the west wing, is plainly fitted up. At the end opposite the entrance is a marble statue of Guy. It was executed by Bacon, in 1779, and is said to have cost £1,000. Mr. Guy is represented in his livery gown, holding out one hand to raise a poor invalid lying on the earth, and pointing with the other to a distressed object, carried on a litter into one of the wards, the hospital being in the background. On the pedestal is this inscription:—

Underneath are deposited the remains of
THOMAS GUY,
Citizen of London, Member of Parliament, and the sole founder of this hospital in his life-time.
It is peculiar to this beneficent man to have preserved, during a long course of prosperity and industry, in pouring forth to the wants of others, all that he had earned by labour, or withheld from self-indulgence.
Warm with philanthropy, and exalted by charity, his mind expanded to those noble affections which grow but too rarely from the most elevated pursuits.
After administering with extensive bounty to the claims of consanguinity, he established this asylum for that stage of languor and disease, to which the charity of others had not reached: he provided a retreat for hopeless insanity, and rivalled the endowments of kings.
He died the 27th of December, 1724, in the 80th year of his age.

The hospital was founded for the reception of 400 patients, but having been enlarged through the aid of a munificent bequest in 1829, from Mr. William Hunt, of Petersham, it now contains 720 beds; an additional wing having been constructed accommodating 320 more patients. The hospital buildings form an extensive and handsome range, and, with the large airing-grounds attached, occupy an area of about six acres. The administration of its affairs is under the care of sixty governors; the treasurer being the general acting manager, and having the especial direction of the Medical School. The annual income of the institution is about £40,000, of which nearly £30,000 are available for hospital purposes.

The ordinary medical staff consists of three physicians and three assistant-physicians for general medical cases; two obstetric physicians; four surgeons, and three assistant-surgeons for general surgical cases; also ophthalmic, dental, and aural surgeons; besides other professors not engaged in the care of patients, who assist as lecturers and demonstrators in the school.

The school department comprises anatomical, pathological, and comparative anatomy museums, materia medica museum, model-room, dissecting-room, electrifying-room, chemical laboratories, library, besides every appurtenance that modern science has devised for medical institutions of the first magnitude. Close by, a commodious theatre was erected by Dr. Edward Grainger, whose early death, in 1823, was a loss to the medical world. At the age of twenty-two, he commenced here a course of lectures on anatomy and physiology; but his pupils increasing beyond the capacities of his theatre, he built a larger room, and turned the former into a museum.

Passing to the rear of the hospital buildings, amidst trees which flourish well and give a look of cheerfulness, so delightful to many a languid sufferer when permitted to walk forth into the air,

and as one of the first schools of medicine in Europe. Some idea of the magnitude of its benevolent work may be gathered from the fact that in the course of a year it receives into its wards upwards of 5,000 in-patients, and affords medical relief to upwards of 70,000 out-patients, including

FOLLY DITCH, JACOB'S ISLAND (*see next Chapter*).

the visitor reaches the museum. This is a neat edifice, comprising a valuable surgical collection, the principal feature of which is a vast variety of wax models, illustrative of the wonders of the human frame, and of remarkable cases of disease.

Guy's Hospital, we need scarcely add, has long held a prominent position among the philanthropic institutions in this country, both in respect to the great scope of the charity it dispenses as a hospital,

a large number of minor accidents and urgent surgery cases, and upwards of 2,000 lying-in women, who are attended to at their own homes.

It should also be stated that a fund has been established for relieving the families of deserving and very poor patients in Guy's Hospital, by gifts of coal and other provisions, and in some instances by money. The chief distress of mothers and children must be during the absence of their

THE GREAT FIRE AT COTTON'S WHARF, TOOLEY STREET, 1861. (See pages 105, 106.)

"bread-winner" in hospital, and few—except those who have undergone the trial—can conceive what this is, or what the anxiety which a patient suffers while powerless to help his family.

Between St. Thomas's Street East and Tooley Street, and covering some considerable part of the ground formerly occupied by St. Thomas's Hospital, is the cluster of stations, irregularly combined, and without any unity of plan or architectural beauty, forming the terminus of the following railways :— The Crystal Palace; the London, Brighton, and South Coast; the South-Eastern; the North Kent; the South London, &c. From London Bridge the approach is by an inclined road, which passes under an iron bridge, over which is carried the Cannon Street and Charing Cross extension of the South-Eastern Railway, which originally had its terminus here. The approach, previous to the above-mentioned extension, was bounded on the south-west by St. Thomas's Hospital and grounds, and on the north-east by a range of shops, communicating with Tooley Street. The south-western portion of the station comprises the booking-offices of the Brighton and South-Coast line, and also the offices of the Crystal Palace and of the South London lines. On the extreme south is the Railway Hotel, one of those monster establishments of which we have already had occasion to speak in our notices of the Midland and other railway stations.

The London and Greenwich Railway was the first line opened here, and, indeed, in the neighbourhood of London. It is remarkable as standing upon one continuous series of 878 brick arches, and is interesting to engineers from the experiment tried upon it as regards the respective value of stone sleepers (or square slabs) at intervals, or continuous bearers of wood, for the support of the rail. Stones were first used, but with such unsatisfactory result, that they were taken up and replaced with timber. The improvement, it is said, has been most decisive. With reference to its formation, we read that in 1834 the substructions of this work were advancing rapidly, and so great was the quantity of bricks required for them, that the price of brick-work in and about London had been "materially affected by this extraordinary consumption of that material." At first, the third-class carriages on this line were simply common trucks, with no seats, and no covering overhead. The author of the "Wonders of Nature and Art" writes, "We have anticipated this line to be a failure, unless it be extended to Dover, in which case an immense advantage would be secured to the public. Colonel Landmann, the engineer, estimated the cost at £400,000, but the expenditure thus far has exceeded £600,000, and a considerable sum is still required in order to complete it."

The original Act of the South-Eastern Railway Company was obtained in 1836, for the express purpose of constructing a railway from London to Dover, the expenses of which were calculated at £1,400,000, to be raised in £50 shares ; but by subsequent Acts the company was authorised to form branch lines, and for that purpose to make loans and issue new shares, involving for the Maidstone and Isle of Thanet branches an expenditure of £3,564,170 ; besides which there has been a further outlay of about £1,800,000, to complete the Hastings branch and that from Reigate, through Dorking and Guildford, to Reading.

The Greenwich Line, as stated above, had been previously constructed ; and the Croydon Company had obtained the sanction of Parliament to pass over three miles thereof to New Cross, whence they continued their line seven miles and a half to Croydon. The next ten miles and a quarter, as far as Red Hill, or the Reigate Junction, belonged originally to the South-Eastern and Brighton Companies in joint shares ; but the whole has subsequently, as sanctioned by Act of Parliament, been purchased by the South-Eastern Company ; so that the whole line, together with the Greenwich Line, which it holds on a lease of 999 years, belongs to this company. More recently, also, besides constructing several branch lines, the South-Eastern Company has purchased the North Kent Line, thus becoming master of the whole railway communication for Kent, East Surrey, and a part of Sussex.

The railway was opened as far as Tunbridge, forty miles from London, in May, 1842 ; from thence to Ashford in the following December ; as far as Folkestone in June, 1843 ; and to Dover in February, 1844. The branch line to Maidstone was opened in September of the same year ; that to Hastings, in February, 1852 ; and the junction line to Reading in 1849. This railway has seven tunnels on its main line to Dover, and four on its branch lines, some of them of a stupendous nature, involving not only very great engineering skill, but a vast outlay of capital ; besides which, there are numerous embankments, deep cuttings, viaducts, and bridges, which bespeak no ordinary skill. Since 1868, however, the greater number of the main-line trains to Hastings, Dover, Margate, &c., pass over a part of the North Kent Line by a more direct route to Tunbridge ; the original main line to Red Hill being used for the Dorking and Reading trains, as well as by the Brighton Company.

The construction of the London and Brighton Railway seems to have been a somewhat slow and laborious undertaking; at all events, we read in "Wonders of Nature and Art," 1839, that—"After the immense bustle in Parliament, and the shameless stock-jobbing of some of the directors and managers of this line of road, we are unable to report the progress of it. That it has been commenced and is proceeding is quite true; but it is proceeding slowly, and as yet the public is quite in the dark as to its present expenditure and its anticipated cost." This railway, however, we need hardly state, was at length completed, and opened in September, 1841, or in about three years from the time of its commencement.

On either side of the booking-office of the Brighton and South-Coast Railway, when it was first erected, was a screen, one masking the gateway of the carriage-road arrival side of this railway, and the other giving access to the carriage-road of the Dover line. The South-Eastern booking-office faces the approach road, and forms the main portion of the façade. Beyond it are the North Kent and Greenwich booking-offices. On the first-floors of these several buildings are the offices, board-rooms, and other accommodations for the chief officials. There are spare lines for the reception of empty carriages under the same roofs as the respective arrival and departure lines. The roofs themselves are somewhat remarkable; and there are particular details connected with the roadway of a nature to merit prolonged examination. Immediately in the rear of the station are several elevated signal-boxes, furnished with the latest and most approved appliances for signalling the arrival and departure of the several trains; so that, notwithstanding the large number of the lines of rail entering the station there is scarcely any room for accidents—indeed, an accident here is very rarely heard of.

A few words concerning the various lines of railway from London Bridge Station may not be out of place here. By the *Brighton* line, fifty-one miles in length, that favourite watering-place has been made a "suburb of London:" it has many branch lines; and from Brighton, railways run east and west along the coast. The *South-Eastern* originally branched off from the Brighton line at the station of Red Hill, near Reigate, and reached Dover by a roundabout course, with a branch from Tunbridge through Tunbridge Wells to Hastings; but passengers are now generally conveyed to Dover, Hastings, &c., by the new line *viâ* Sevenoaks. The metropolitan extension of this line crosses the river by an iron bridge to Cannon Street, and also to the Charing Cross Station, built on the site of Hungerford Market. The *Croydon* passes by Forest Hill, Sydenham, and Norwood, with a short branch line through Mitcham to the South-Western Railway at Wimbledon, and another branch through Epsom to Horsham, on the London and Portsmouth line. The *Crystal Palace* line branches off from the Sydenham station, and after passing close to Lower Norwood, Streatham, and Balham, reaches its terminus at the Victoria Station, Pimlico. The *North Kent* line passes by a tunnel under Shooter's Hill to Woolwich, Gravesend, and Rochester, and thence to Maidstone. The *South London* line runs parallel with the Greenwich Railway as far as South Bermondsey, then passes southward to Clapham, and unites with western London at Victoria Station, Pimlico.

At the entrance to Duke Street—which leads from London Bridge down to Tooley Street, by the side of the railway approach—might have been seen during 1842-3, a lofty building bearing this inscription, "Watson's Telegraph to the Downs." This telegraph station, which occupied the summit of a building once used as a shot tower, and erected in 1808, was established by a Mr. Watson, of Cornhill, about the year 1842, with the object of connecting London with Deal by means of the old semaphore telegraph. The first station near St. Olave's Church was placed in communication with a similar station near Forest Hill, and with others on elevated spots between the metropolis and Deal. At the summit of the tower were two masts about twenty feet apart, and fifty feet high. On each side of these masts were the semaphore arms, which were to be seen in various positions, and were worked by levers in the tower below. This telegraph station, which was a conspicuous object to foot-passengers proceeding over London Bridge, was entirely consumed in the great fire in which St. Olave's Church was destroyed, with the surrounding buildings, on the 19th of August, 1843. This system of telegraphy was in its turn superseded by the electric telegraph, which very soon afterwards came into operation on all the railway lines in Great Britain, and thus rendered unnecessary the old cumbrous system of semaphore telegraphy, the success of which depended so much on clear weather for the accurate interpretation of the signals. The shot-tower, close by St. Olave's Church, is shown in pages 6, 102, and 103 of the present volume.

Before closing this chapter, and making our way into Bermondsey, we may be pardoned for saying a word or two concerning the water-supply of Southwark about half a century ago. In the *Mirror* for 1828, we read that "the Southwark Water Works (the property of an individual) are supplied from the middle of the Thames, below Southwark and London Bridges ; and the water thus taken is sent out to the tenants without standing to settle or any filtration, further than that it receives from passing through wire grates and small holes in metallic plates. The number of houses supplied by these works is about 7,000, and the average daily supply about 720,000 gallons." *Apropos* of these water works, we may state that in 1581 Peter Morris, a Dutchman, established a wheel worked by the tide at London Bridge to lift water from the river, and propel it into the houses of the citizens, whose

admiration he captivated by forcing a jet over the steeple of St. Magnus' Church, close by. These water-works, a cumbrous-looking structure of wood, stood on the Middlesex side of the Thames, adjoining the bridge, and near the site of Fishmongers' Hall steam-boat pier. The works subsequently passed into the possession of the New River Company, and lasted for 240 years, until demolished by Act of Parliament in 1822. On the Surrey side of the old bridge formerly stood the water-works for supplying the inhabitants of Southwark, which we have already mentioned, but these were removed long before the bridge was demolished.

CHAPTER IX.

BERMONDSEY.—TOOLEY STREET, &c.

" Trans Tiberim longè cubat hic."—*Horace, " Satires."*

Derivation of the Name of Bermondsey—General Aspect of the Locality—Duke Street—Tooley Street—St. Olave's Church—Abbots' Inn of St. Augustine—Sellinger's Wharf—The Inn of the Abbots of Battle—Maze Pond—The House of the Priors of Lewes—St. Olave's Grammar School—Great Fires at the Wharves in Tooley Street—Death of Braidwood, the Fireman—The " Lion and Key "—The Borough Compter—The " Ship and Shovel "—Carter Lane Meeting House—Dr. Gill and Dr. Rippon—The " Three Tailors of Tooley Street "—The " Isle of Ducks "—Tunnels under London Bridge Railway Station—Snow's Fields—A Colony of Hatters—Horselydown—Fair Street—The Birthplace of Thomas Guy—The Church of St. John the Evangelist—Goat's Yard—Keach's Meeting-house—Absence of Singing in Dissenting Meeting-houses two Centuries ago—Queen Elizabeth's Grammar School—A Description of Horselydown and the adjacent Neighbourhood in Former Times—Dockhead—" Shad Thames "—Jacob's Island.

IN a previous chapter of this volume we have considered the Borough High Street as the line of demarcation between the eastern and western portions of the southern suburbs of Bermondsey and Southwark; here, then, we may fittingly separate their respective histories. The name Bermondsey—the " land of leather," as it has been called in our own day—is generally supposed to be derived from Beormund, the Saxon lord of the district, and *ea*, or *eye*, an " island," descriptive of the locality, near the river-side, and intersected by numerous small streams and ditches ; though one antiquary has suggested, with more than ordinary rashness, that *beorm* is Saxon for prince, and that *mund* signified security or peace, so that Bermondsey may be interpreted as " the prince's security by the water's side." Wilkinson, in his account of Bermondsey Abbey in " Londina Illustrata," states that the words *ea*, or *eye*, " are frequent in the names of places whose situation on the banks of rivers renders them insular and marshy ; " and the word still exists in the longer form of " eyot."

" Looking, then," writes Charles Knight, " upon the original Bermondsey as a kind of marshy island when the tide was out, and a wide expanse of water when it was in, till gradually reclaimed and made useful, one cannot help being struck with the many indications of the old state of things yet remaining, although the *present* Bermondsey is densely covered

with habitations and houses. The descent down the street leading from London Bridge tells you how low lie the territories you are about to explore ; the numerous wharves, the docks, the water-courses, the ditches, which bound and intersect so considerable a portion of it, seem but so many memorials of the once potent element ; the very streets have a damp *feel* about them ; and in the part known as Jacob's Island the overhanging houses, and the little wooden bridges that span the stream, have, notwithstanding their forlorn look, something of a Dutch expression. In short, persons familiar with the history of the place may everywhere see that Beormund's Ea still exists, but that it has been embanked and drained—that it has grown populous, busy, commercial. Its manufacturing prosperity, however, strikingly contrasts with the general aspect of Bermondsey. Its streets generally are but dreary-looking places, where, with the exception of a picturesque old tenement, projecting its storey beyond storey regularly upwards, and fast ' nodding to its fall,' or the name of a street suggestive of some agreeable reflections, there is little to gratify the delicate eye. . . . Noble arches here and there bestride the streets of Bermondsey, bearing up a railway, with its engines puffing like so many overworked giants, and its rapid trains of passengers; an elegant free school enriches one part, and a picturesque church another ; but they all serve by contrast to show more vividly the unpleasant features of the neighbourhood, and, whilst they cannot but command the spectator's admiration, make him at the same time wonder how they got there. The answer is at hand. There is great industry in Bermondsey, and the wretchedness is more on the surface than in the depth of this quarter of the town." Both here, and also in the adjoining parish of Rotherhithe, extensive manufactures are carried on : in Bermondsey the tanners and rope-makers abound ; at Rotherhithe, timber merchants, sawyers, and boat-builders. It would not, perhaps, be far from the truth to say that Bermondsey may be regarded not only as a region of manufactures, but as a region of market gardens, as a region of wholesale dealers, or as a maritime region, according to the quarter where we take our stand.

Running east and west through the parish, parallel with the river Thames, and by Dockhead, winding its way towards Rotherhithe and Greenwich, is Tooley Street, a narrow and winding thoroughfare, which in some parts still bears many traces of its antiquity. One would have liked out of sheer malice to have been here to see the little gossiping Secretary of the Admiralty, Samuel Pepys, and his friend and patron, Lord Sandwich, floundering about in these parts in January, 1665-6, when, owing to the bad weather, they could not find a boat to convey them by water, and in consequence they were forced to walk. "Lord ! what a dirty walk we had, and so strong the wind, that in the fields we many times could not carry our bodies against it, but were driven backwards. It was dangerous to walk the streets, the bricks and tiles falling from the houses, so that the whole streets were covered with them. . . . . We could see no boats in the Thames afloat but what were broke loose and carried through the bridge, it being ebbing water. And the greatest sight of all was among other parcels of ships driven hither and thither in clusters together, one was quite overset, and lay with her masts all along in the water, and her keel above water." The desolation and wintry chilliness of this picture is enough to make us shiver even in the dog-days.

Passing onward on our journey from the foot of London Bridge, down the steep incline of Duke Street, which bounds the north side of the approach to the railway station, we find ourselves in Tooley Street, whose name, we are told, is a strange corruption of the former appellation, St. Olave's Street, and whose shops exhibit a singular mixture of the features which are found separate in other parts of the district—wharfingers, merchants, salesmen, factors, and agents ; outfitters, biscuit-bakers, store-shippers, ship-chandlers, slop-sellers, block-makers, and rope-makers ; engineers, and others, together with the usual varieties of retail tradesmen—all point to the diversified, and no less busy than diversified, traffic of this street. "Here," it has been said truly, "the crane and the pulley seem never to be idle."

The parish of St. Olave is bounded on the north by the river Thames, whence it extends in an irregular line towards the Dover Road, separating Bermondsey from Rotherhithe and Deptford parishes ; it enters Bermondsey Street by Snow's Fields, and proceeds thence to St. Saviour's (once called Savory) Dock. St. Olave's, like many other parishes in the suburbs of London, having been greatly increased in the number of its inhabitants, in 1732 one of the fifty new churches provided by the Act of Queen Anne was built for the district of Horselydown, which was made a separate parish by an Act of Parliament passed in the following year, and to which was given the name of St. John.

The parish church of St. Olave stands on the north side of Tooley Street, near its western end ; and with the exception of the south side, is concealed from public observation. St. Olave, or Olaf, in whose honour it is dedicated, was the son of Herald, Prince of Westford, in Norway, in which country he was celebrated for having expelled the Swedes, and for recovering Gothland. After performing these exploits he came to England, and remaining here for three years as the ally of Ethelred, he expelled the Danes from several English cities, towns, and fortresses, and returned home laden with great spoils. He was recalled to England by Emma of Normandy, the surviving queen of his friend, in order to assist her against Knute ; but finding that a treaty had been made between that king and the English, he withdrew, and was created king of Norway by the voice of the nation. To strengthen his throne, he married the daughter of the king of Sweden ; but his zeal for the Christian faith caused him to be much troubled by domestic wars, as well as by the Danes abroad ; yet these he regarded not, as he plainly declared that he would rather lose his life and his kingdom than his faith in Christ. Upon this, the men of Norway complained to Knute, king of Denmark, and afterwards of England, charging Olaf with altering their laws and customs ; and he was murdered by a body of traitors and rebels near Drontheim, about A.D. 1029. The Bishop of Drontheim, whom he had taken with him across the sea from England in order to assist him in establishing the Christian faith in Norway, commanded that he should be honoured as a martyr, and invoked as a saint. He was buried at Drontheim, where his body was found uncorrupted in 1541, when the Lutherans plundered his shrine of its gold and jewels, for it was reckoned the greatest treasure of the Church in the north. His feast is commemorated on the 29th of July. Such was St. Olaf, to whose memory no less than four churches were built in London, and rightly so, for, says Newcourt, "he had well

Southwark, standing upon the river Thames between the Bregge house (Bridge-house) and the Church of St. Olave." A still fuller account of St. Olave will be found in the "Acta Sanctorum" of the Bollandists.

In 1736, part of the old church having fallen down, and the rest being in an unsafe condition, owing to the graves having been dug too near the foundation, the parishioners applied to Parliament

ST. OLAVE'S CHURCH, IN 1820.

deserved, and was well beloved by our English nation, as well for his friendship in assisting them against the Danes, as for his holy and Christian life."

In Alban Butler's "Lives of the Saints" will be found several interesting particulars of the life of this heroic and saintly prince. We meet with him under a variety of names, as Anlaf, Unlaf, Olaf Haraldson, Olaus, and Olaf Helge, or Olaf the Holy. The antiquity of his church in Southwark is proved by William Horn's "Chronicle of the Acts of the Abbots of St. Austin's, Canterbury" (printed in Roger Twisden's "Historiæ Anglicanæ Scriptores Decem"), who tells us that John, Earl of Warren, granted, about the year 1281, to Nicholas, the then abbot, "all the estate which it held in

for power to rebuild it; which being granted, they were enabled to raise £5,000 by granting annuities for lives, not exceeding £400 on the whole; for payment of which a rate was to be made, not exceeding 6d. in the pound, two-thirds to be paid by the landlord, and one by the tenant, to cease on the determination of the annuities. The new church, constructed chiefly of Portland stone, was completed in 1740. It has a nave, with side aisles, and a square tower, which was originally designed to be surmounted by a spire. In 1843 this church had a narrow escape from total destruction by fire. On the 19th of August in that year, a conflagration broke out on the premises of an oilman, near the entrance of Topping's wharf (which is close by the church), which was totally destroyed,

THE GRAMMAR SCHOOL OF ST. OLAVE'S, 1810. (*From a Contemporary Print.*)

with a sacrifice of property to the amount of £10,000. The fire consumed the shot tower, then lately used as Watson's Telegraph, as stated at the close of the last chapter, and afterwards caught the roof of St. Olave's Church. The flames spread rapidly, and the interior of the structure, with all the bells, was destroyed, little more than the tower and the bare walls remaining. Fortunately, the church was insured, and was speedily rebuilt.

The plan of the body of this church is a parallelogram, divided into nave and aisles. The columns, which separate these three compartments from each other, are fluted, of the Ionic order, with sculptured capitals, in each range four in number. Against the eastern and western walls are also four pilasters, corresponding with the columns. The nave is prolonged eastwardly by a semi-circular apse, containing the altar. Over the entire nave extends a beautiful and highly-finished groined ceiling of five divisions; in the perpendicular side of each compartment of the groining is a semi-circular headed window. The ceiling of the altar-apse is a semi-dome, forming a rich piece of gilt coffered work. The east window is of stained glass, with a central representation, in an oval, of the Lord's Supper, after Carlo Dolce. At the west end of the church is a large and handsome organ, remarkable for the richness of its tone. This instrument, designed by Dr. Gauntlett, organist of St. Olave's, was erected at an expense of £800; it was commenced in 1844, by Mr. Lincoln, and completed in 1846, by Messrs. Hill and Co., the builders of the great organs in York Minster, Worcester Cathedral, &c.

Eastward from the church is—or was till lately—a quay, which in the year 1330, by the licence of Simon Swanland, mayor of London, was built by Isabel, widow of Hammond Goodchepe. Adjoining this quay was "a great house of stone and timber, belonging to the Abbot of St. Augustine, Canterbury, which was an ancient piece of work, seeming to be one of the first builded houses on that side of the river over against the city. It was called the Abbot's Inn of St. Augustine, in Southwark, and was held of the Earls of Warren and Surrey, as appears by a deed made in 1281. The house afterwards belonged to Sir Anthony St. Leger, then to Warnham St. Leger, and is now," says Stow, "called St. Leger House, and divided into many apartments." A wharf on the site keeps in remembrance the name of this knightly family, although by the process of time it has become corrupted into Sellinger's Wharf.

The Abbot of Battle, an important personage as the superior of the monastery erected on the spot where the fate of Saxon England was decided, and especially patronised by the Conqueror, had a fine residence near the same spot, with well laid-out gardens, as an agreeable change from the natural beauties of hilly, leafy Sussex, adorned with parterres in Norman fashion, with a fish-pond and a curiously-contrived maze. The abbot has gone, and the palace and gardens are gone too; and Londoners of the nineteenth century hurry through Maze Pond, at the back of Guy's Hospital, little thinking whence the dirty street derived its name. The "Maze"—now an assemblage of small streets on the south side of the London Bridge Railway Station—is stated by Mr. Charles Knight in his "London," to have "once been the garden attached to the manor-house, or 'inn,' of the abbots of Battle, the house itself having stood on the north side of Tooley Street, in what is now called Mill Lane, which leads down to Battlebridge Stairs." Aubrey, in his "Anecdotes and Traditions," says, "At Southwark was a maze, which is now converted into buildings bearing that name;" but Peter Cunningham in his "Handbook of London," says that Maze Pond is so called from the "Manor of Maze," which formerly existed here.

Opposite St. Olave's Church, in Tooley Street, and adjoining Church Alley, which has become absorbed in the Brighton and South-Eastern Railway terminus, says Allen in his "History of Surrey," "formerly stood a spacious stone building, the city residence of the Priors of Lewes, in Sussex, whenever occasion led them to visit London or its vicinity on parliamentary or ecclesiastical duty." Strype, noticing St. Olave's Church, says, "On the south side of the street was sometime one great house, builded of stone, with arched gates, which pertained to the Prior of Lewes, in Sussex, and was his residence when he came to London; it is now a common hostelry for travellers, and hath a sign of the 'Walnut-Tree.'" In Maitland's time it became converted into a cider-cellar, and is described as follows:—"Opposite St. Olave's Church recently stood a spacious stone building, the city mansion of the Prior of Lewes, in Sussex; the chapel of which, consisting of two aisles, being still remaining at the upper end of Walnut-tree Alley; it is converted into a cider-cellar or warehouse, and by the earth's being greatly raised in this neighbourhood it is at present underground; and the Gothic building, a little westward of the same (at present a wine-vault belonging to the 'King's Head' Tavern), under the school-house, a small chapel, I take to have been part of the said mansion-house. There are," continues Allen, " two entrances to the crypt in White Horse Court, leading from Tooley House to Southwark House, formerly the 'King's Head' Tavern, and prior to that the sign of the 'Walnut-Tree.' Entering by the north entrance, it is seven feet six inches long by six feet wide, which leads to a large semicircular arched vault, thirty-nine feet three inches long, by eighteen feet wide; on one side is a well from which water is at present conveyed to the houses above. Towards the farther end is a doorway, leading to another semi-circular vaulted arch, thirty-one feet long, by thirteen feet ten inches wide; from this is a passage seven feet by six feet, which leads to the principal apartment of this ancient building, the whole length of which is forty feet six inches by sixteen feet six inches in width. At the farther end are two windows. This ancient apartment consists of four groined arches, supported on dwarf columns. From this is an entrance to another vault of various dimensions, but the length is twenty-seven feet four inches. Part of this vault is arched as the former, and part groined, over which the stairs leading to the grammar-school are erected." All this, however, has now been removed, but is recorded here for the benefit of future antiquaries.

The school here referred to was originally styled the "Free Grammar School of Queen Elizabeth, in the parish of St. Olave's," that queen having incorporated sixteen of the parishioners to be the governors. The school was founded in 1561 for "instructing the boys of the parish in English grammar and writing." In 1674, Charles II., "for the better education of the rich as well as of the poor," granted a further charter, enabling them (the governors) to hold revenues to the amount of £500 a year, which were to be applied "in maintenance of the schoolmaster, ushers, the house and possessions, the maintenance and education of two scholars at the university (not confining it to either Oxford or Cambridge), for setting forth poor scholars apprentices, for the relief of poor impotent persons of the parish, maintaining a workhouse, and to other purposes." By order of the vestry of St. Olave's parish, the vestry-hall was fitted up for the purposes of the school, which was kept there until the year 1829, soon after which period the building was pulled down for forming the approaches to new London Bridge. After a succession of changes, the London and Greenwich Railway Company provided a piece of ground in Bermondsey Street on which a new school-house was erected. This building, which was completed in 1835, was in the Tudor style of architecture; it was constructed of red brick with stone dressings, and formed two sides of

a quadrangle, which was cut diagonally by the roadway. In the centre of the building was an octagonal tower, containing, on the ground-floor, a porch open on three sides, and leading to a corridor of general communication. On one side of this octagonal tower were the school-rooms, large and well-lighted apartments, and on the other side were the head-master's house, and also the court-room in which the governors met to transact business, and which also served as the school library. The building is said to have been highly creditable to all concerned in its erection; but it was unfortunate with regard to its situation. It could be seen, and then to great disadvantage, only from the school-yard, or from the railway, which intersected the school-yard diagonally, at a height of about twenty feet above the level of the ground. The entrance to the school was from Bermondsey Street, through one of the arches of the railway. The location of the school in this spot was not destined to be of long duration; for on the widening of the railway, in consequence of the formation of the South-Eastern and London and Brighton Railways, its site was wanted, and the school was once more transferred farther eastward, at the end of Tooley Street, where we shall have more to say of it when speaking of the new building.

We have already, in our notice of the High Street, Southwark, spoken of the Mint which was established there by Henry VIII.; but it appears that there was a Mint on this side of the river as far back as the Saxon times. It is supposed to have occupied the spot where afterwards was the house of the Prior of Lewes, and under the Norman kings there was a Mint nearly on the same spot.

The wharves and buildings near St. Olave's Church have been the scene of some extensive conflagrations. One of these took place in 1836, in which Fenning's Wharf was consumed. Another fire broke out on the same spot on the 19th of August, 1843, and during the time it raged several of the buildings in its vicinity were almost totally destroyed. Among these, as we have previously stated, were St. Olave's Church, Topping's Wharf, Watson's telegraph, and other adjacent buildings. It was stated at the time that the church might have been saved, but Mr. Braidwood, the superintendent of the London Fire Brigade, considered it advisable to direct his attention to preventing the fire reaching the valuable surrounding property, amounting to upwards of £500,000 in value. A few years later, on the 22nd of June, 1861, a most destructive fire, said to have been caused by spontaneous combustion, broke out at Cotton's Wharf, Tooley

Street, a little to the east of St. Olave's Church, and continued smouldering for several days. In his endeavours to check the ravages of this fire, Mr. Braidwood lost his life. He was buried, as we have already seen, at Abney Park Cemetery, and a tablet has been inserted in the wall near the entrance to the wharf to mark the spot where he fell. The damage caused by this fire amounted to £2,000,000. In some of these conflagrations, considerable damage has been done to the shipping on the river, by the burning oil and pitch overspreading the surface of the river. In the "Cyclopædia of Insurance," we read that in July, 1731, a large number of vessels were burnt on the Thames through the overturning of a pot of boiling pitch! Verily there is, after all, some truth in the old saying about "setting the Thames on fire."

To return to Mill Lane, we may add that there is—or, at all events, was in 1866—an inn here called the "Lion and Key," no doubt a corruption of the "Lion on the Quay."

The Borough Compter, formerly situated in this lane, was one of the prisons visited and described by John Howard. He pictures it as in a deplorable condition, "out of repair and ruinous, without an infirmary and even without bedding; while most of the inmates were poor creatures from the 'Court of Conscience,' who lay there till their debts were paid." The Compter was removed hither from St. Margaret's Hill, as stated in a previous chapter.* Till a comparatively recent period (1806), prisoners accused of felonies were here detained, and debtors were imprisoned here. If they could pay sixpence a day, they could have the luxury of a room eight feet square. They were allowed a twopenny loaf a day, but neither straw for bedding, fire, medical or religious attention; and a man might be imprisoned on this regimen for a debt of a guinea for forty days without being able to change his clothes or wash his face or hands during the period of his imprisonment. This miserable state of things was strongly represented to the Lord Mayor in 1804, but no answer was received to the expostulation.

In a narrow turning out of Tooley Street, near the back of Guy's Hospital, is a small inn, much frequented by seafaring persons, called the "Ship and Shovel." The sign may allude to the shovels used in taking out ballast, or cargoes in bulk, or it may refer to the gallant but unfortunate Sir Cloudesley Shovel, whose wreck and death at the Scilly Islands we mentioned in our account of the monuments in Westminster Abbey.†

In Carter Lane, a turning out of Tooley Street,

* See *ante*, p. 58.
† See Vol. III., p. 420.

near St. Olave's Church, stood, till 1830, when it was pulled down to make room for the approaches of the new London Bridge, the meeting-house of the Anabaptist congregation, under the pastorate successively of Dr. Gill and Dr. Rippon. This chapel, an ugly structure, erected in 1757, deserves mention here from the fact that the congregations assembling successively within its walls during several generations, after migrating to New Park Street, are now located at Newington, in the Metropolitan Tabernacle, under Mr. Spurgeon. The connection of this body with Carter Lane dates back to the time of the Commonwealth. Benjamin Keach, author of some controversial works, was the minister from 1668 to 1704. In his time the congregation met in a small chapel in Goat's Yard Passage, Horselydown. It must not be overlooked that two centuries back Dissenting congregations did not aim at attracting notice either in the architectural details of their chapels, or in placing them in conspicuous places, as we see in modern times. This fact will explain the circumstance that Dissenting meeting-houses were formerly to be met with in back streets and courts. Dr. Gill's ministry extended from 1720 to 1771; and he in turn was succeeded in 1773 by Dr. Rippon, whose pastorate extended to 1836, so that in the long period of 116 years, the congregation and their successors had but two ministers. Dr. Gill was one of the most learned men whom his denomination ever produced, and some account of him may be given here. He was born at Kettering, in Northamptonshire, in 1697. He was educated at the grammar-school of his native town, and at an early age was famed for his acquaintance with the classic writers. His zeal for knowledge was so great that he was accustomed to spend a few hours every week in the shop of a bookseller in Kettering on market days, when only it was opened, and there he first saw the learned works of various writers in Biblical lore, in which he afterwards became so greatly distinguished. So constant was his attendance at this shop, that the market people, speaking proverbially, were wont to say, "As surely as Gill is in the bookseller's shop." An attempt on the part of the schoolmaster to enforce on Gill a regular attendance at the parish church led to his withdrawal from the school. With a view to enable him to enter the Nonconformist ministry, application was made for his admission into the Mile End Academy, but his precocity in learning seemed to the principals of that institution a sufficient bar to his reception by them. He was now compelled to work at the loom, but found time to study the Greek Testament, and to obtain a little insight into Hebrew. Becoming a preacher of his own denomination in his native county, his fame as a scholar in due time led to an invitation to come to London to supply the pulpit at Goat's Yard, then vacant by the death of Mr. Benjamin Stinton, the son-in-law of Keach. Soon after his arrival in London, Gill became acquainted with Mr. John Skepp, a Hebrew scholar, and minister of a congregation in Cripplegate. At Skepp's death, many of his books in divinity and Rabbinical literature were purchased by Gill, to whom they proved a valuable acquisition. He was soon able to read the Talmud and the Targums in the original, as well as the ancient commentators thereon. Even amidst these severe studies, he still found time to study the Fathers of the Church; and the fruits of these labours soon began to appear in the learned works he subsequently published. In 1745 he issued proposals for printing an "Exposition of the Whole New Testament," in three folio volumes, which was completed in 1748. For this undertaking Gill received the degree of Doctor of Divinity, from Marischal College, Aberdeen. When his friends congratulated him on this token of respect, he remarked, "I neither thought it, nor bought, nor sought it." Between 1746 and 1760 he published "An Exposition of the Old and New Testament," in nine volumes, which Robert Hall considered to be "a continent of mud," while John Ryland characterised it as "an ocean of divinity." He also published "A Body of Divinity," "The Cause of God and Truth," and other learned works.

He was at times keenly engaged in controversy, and contended in turn with Whitby, Wesley, and other opponents of the Calvinistic school of theology. How he managed to prepare for publication such an array of learned literary matter surprised many of his friends. He was accustomed to rise as soon as it was light in the winter, and usually before six in the summer; and by this disposal of his time, to say nothing of the duties of his pastorate, and the frequent demands on the preaching services of such an eminent scholar, he was able to send forth to the world some ponderous tomes, the preparation of which, and its subsequent correction for the press, must have been no ordinary undertaking. It is stated that although his folio volumes would be sufficient to fill 10,000 printed quarto pages, he never employed an amanuensis in preparing his copy for the press. He died at Camberwell on the 4th of October, 1771. As a proof that "relics" are still held in honour among Protestants, it may be added that the pulpit in which Dr. Gill preached is now used by the students in the college attached to the Metro-

politan Tabernacle; and the chair once used by the doctor in his study has been transferred to the vestry of the Tabernacle of Mr. Spurgeon.

Among the anecdotes related of Dr. Gill, one may be given, as it throws some light upon the "service of song" a century or more back. In his days the psalmody in many of the Dissenting Chapels was at the lowest possible ebb, and the stock of hymn-tunes possessed by Dr. Gill's clerk must have been very small; for on one occasion an aged dame waited on the doctor to complain that the clerk, in about three years, had introduced two new tunes. Not that he was a famous singer, or able to conduct a great variety of song, but he did his best. The young people of the congregation, naturally enough, were pleased with the new tunes; but the good woman could not bear the innovation. The doctor, after patiently listening, asked her whether she understood singing. "No," she replied. "What! can't you sing?" She confessed that she was no singer, nor her aged father before her; and though they had had about a hundred years between them to learn the Old Hundreth Psalm, they could not sing it nor any other tune. The doctor did not hurt her feelings by telling her that people who did not understand singing were the last who ought to complain; but he meekly said, "Sister, what tunes should you like us to sing?" "Why, sir," she replied, "I should very much like David's tunes." "Well," said he, "if you will get David's tunes for us, we can then try to sing them." It need scarcely be added that in Dr. Gill's meeting-house at Horselydown the duty of leading the psalmody devolved on the clerk, whose salary, it appears, was half the sum paid to the pew-opener, or only forty shillings per annum!

Whiston, the translator of "Josephus," intended to hear Dr. Gill preach, and would have done so had he not learned the fact that the doctor had written a volume on the Song of Solomon, which, in Whiston's opinion, did not form any part of the canonical Scriptures. For this reason Whiston declined to enter Gill's chapel.

Dr. Rippon, who succeeded Dr. Gill at Carter Lane in 1773, and continued the minister of the congregation after their removal to New Park Street, died in 1836, in the eighty-fifth year of his age, his pastorate having extended through the long period of sixty-three years. His name does not shine in the literary world with such splendour as his predecessor, neither was he to be compared with Dr. Gill in theological and Oriental attainments. He compiled a selection of hymns for the use of Dissenting congregations, by whom it was extensively used as a supplement to Dr. Watts's hymn-book. Besides editing "The Baptist Annual Register," he projected, in 1803, a "History of Bunhill Fields," in six volumes, which did not meet with sufficient encouragement to enable him to carry out the intention, although ten years had been occupied in the preparation of the materials for the undertaking. In his time the singing had improved considerably, for a tune-book once used in many Dissenting congregations bears his name.

An anecdote, which gives us an insight into the character of Dr. Rippon, has been related of him. On a special occasion he was deputed to read an address from the Dissenters to George III., congratulating him on his recovery from sickness. The doctor read on with his usual clear utterance till he came to a passage in which there was a special reference to the goodness of God, when he paused and said, "Please your majesty, we will read that again," and then proceeded with his usual cool dignity to repeat the sentence with emphasis. No other man in the denomination would have thought of doing such a thing; but from Rippon it came so naturally that no one censured him, or if they did, it would have had no effect upon him.

"Tooley Street," says Peter Cunningham, "will long continue to be famous from the well-known story related by Canning of 'The Three Tailors of Tooley Street,' who formed a meeting for redress of popular grievances, and though no more than three in number, began their petition to the House of Commons with the somewhat grand opening of '*We*, the people of England!'"

The name of Tooley Street has not always been spelt in the same way. For instance, to a notice put forth in Cromwell's time by Thomas Garway, the founder of Garraway's Coffee-house, in the City, are appended the following words:*—"Advertisement. That Nicholas Brook, living at the sign of the 'Frying-pan,' in St. Tulie's Street, against the Church, is the only known man for making of Mills for grinding of Coffee powder, which Mills are by him sold from 40 to 45 shillings the Mill."

On the south side, near the middle of the street, according to the "New View of London," published in the reign of Queen Anne, was a place called the "Isle of Ducks;" but little or nothing is now known either of its history, or of its exact situation.

The streets branching off on the south side of Tooley Street, especially those near the western end, such as Joiners' Street, Weston Street, Dean

Street, and Bermondsey Street (which, Northouck says, is corruptly called Barnaby Street), pass immediately under the railway station, and therefore appear like so many underground tunnels, in which long rows of gas-lamps are continually burning. In spite of this light, however, they are unknown to history.

John Street, Webbe Street, and Weston Street, all modern thoroughfares in the neighbourhood of the Maze Pond, keep in remembrance the names of the late Mr. John Webbe Weston, who owned much of the land hereabouts. Winding south-westwards across some of these streets from the eastern end of St. Thomas's Street, are Snow's Fields, which have now anything but a verdant aspect. "Moor Fields are fields no more!" It is true that from this thoroughfare—for it is nothing more nor less than a narrow street—a glimpse is caught of some green and flourishing foliage in the rear of Guy's Hospital; but all traces of garden grounds are fast disappearing. John Timbs has a word or two to say about this spot in his "Autobiography." Speaking of his boyhood, he observes: "The love of gardening and raising flowers has ever been with me a favourite pursuit. Even in that sooty suburb in Southwark, Snow's Fields, at a very early age, I had the range of a large garden, and a plot set apart for my special culture. But I had fancied failures:

'Oh! ever thus from childhood's hour
    I've seen my fondest hopes decay;
I never loved a tree or flower,
    But 'twas the first to fade away.'

Still, what I attributed to fate was, in most cases, traceable to the poisonous atmosphere of the manufacturing suburb."

"There was a time," says Mr. Charles Knight, in his "London," "when the manufacture of hats formed one of the characteristics of this neighbourhood; but this branch of manufacture, from some cause with which we are not well acquainted, has suffered a curious migration. At about the end of the last century and the beginning of the present, the 'Maze' (a district between Bermondsey Street and the Borough High Street), Tooley Street, the northern end of Bermondsey Street, and other streets in the immediate vicinity, formed the grand centre of the hat manufacture of London; but since then some commercial motive-power has exerted a leverage which has transferred nearly the whole assemblage farther westward. If we wish to find the centre of this manufacture, with its subordinate branches of hat-block makers, hat-dyers, hat-lining and leather cutters, hat shag-makers, hat-tip makers, hat-bowstring makers, hat-furriers,

---

* See "Ellis's Letters" (Second Series), vol. iv.

hat-trimming makers, &c., we must visit the district included between the Borough High Street and Blackfriars Road. A glance at that curious record of statistical facts, a 'London Directory,' will show to what an extent this manufacture is carried on in the district just marked out. It is true that Bermondsey still contains one hat-factory, which has been characterised as the largest in the world, and that Tooley Street still exhibits a

and, agreeably to an Act of the 6th Geo. II., 1733, "the district of Horsey-down, Horsa-down or Horsley-down (so called from its having been used by the inhabitants as a grazing-field for their horses and cattle), was appointed for the new parish." Elmes observes, very absurdly: "Popular legends derive its name from a belief that the horse of King John lay down with that monarch upon his back, and hence *horse-lye-down;* but as

MILL POND BRIDGE, IN 1826.

sprinking of smaller firms; but the manufacture is no longer a feature to be numbered among the peculiarities of Bermondsey."

Passing from Snow's Fields, under the railway arches, by way of Crucifix Lane, a name which savours of "the olden time," we enter Artillery Street, Horselydown, or, as it was formerly called, Horsey Down. The parish of St. Olave's having greatly increased both in houses and population, the commissioners for erecting fifty new churches within the "bills of mortality" purchased a site for a church and cemetery, consisting of a field, which was walled in and called the "Artillery Ground," from the fact that the train-bands of Southwark used to practise therein. The church was accordingly built, and dedicated to St. John,

the entire tract so called was, according to Stow, a grazing-ground, called Horse-down, it is more probably a corruption of that title." In speaking of the derivation of the name of Horselydown, the author of "A New View of London" (1708), remarks: "This street, as I was told by a sober counsellor at law, who said he had it from an old record, was so called for that the water, formerly overflowing it, was so effectually drawn off that the place became a green field, where horses and other cattle used to pasture and lye down before the street was built." Near it, as we further learn from the same work, was Horselydown Fair Street, described as a considerable street, between Paris Street, Tooley Street, and Five Foot Lane, Southwark.

Thomas Guy, the founder of the famous hospital bearing his name, was born in this street. His birthplace is thus accurately fixed by Maitland:— "He (Guy) was born in the north-east corner house of Pritchard's Alley (two doors east of St. John's Churchyard), in Fair Street, Horsleydown." "Amidst the changes of old London," says Charles Knight, in his "Shadows of the Old Booksellers," "Fair Street still exists, and has a due place in the Post Office Guide to principal streets and places. It is at the eastern extremity of Tooley Street, where Horselydown begins, and at a short distance from the Thames. The Down, where horses once grazed, and where probably the child Thomas Guy once played, is now built over. The father of this boy was a lighterman and coal-dealer, and it is most likely that the young son of a man so occupied would be familiar with the locality between Horselydown and London Bridge. One building seems to have lived in his memory in connection with early associations. St. Thomas's Hospital, an old almonry, had been bought by the citizens of London, at the dissolution of the religious houses, as a place of reception for diseased people. It was fast falling into decay when Thomas Guy looked upon it in his boyhood."

The church, dedicated to St. John the Evangelist, was finished in 1732; it is a plain stone building, lighted by two ranges of windows, and has an apsidal termination at the eastern end. The square tower, containing ten bells, is surmounted with a spire in the form of a fluted Ionic pillar. The church is seen to the northward from the London and Greenwich Railway.

In Goat's Yard, Horselydown, was the meeting-house of the celebrated Benjamin Keach, who, from 1668 to 1704, was the minister of a Non-conformist congregation assembling there, one of the oldest of such congregations in Southwark and Bermondsey, and the precursor of the congregation now assembling in the Metropolitan Tabernacle. For very excellent reasons, the Dissenters of those stirring times in English history were not anxious to attract notice in the style of architecture of their meeting-houses, nor did they erect them in conspicuous situations, for during the reign of Charles II. they almost met by stealth, much in the same way as the Roman Catholics were wont to do a century or so later. When Charles II. issued his declaration of indulgence in 1672, Keach, among others, took advantage of it, and his congregation erected their first meeting-house in Goat's Yard. This chapel no longer exists, for a century later, the lease having run out, it became a cooperage, and afterwards a blacksmith's forge. In front of the chapel was a court, bounded by a brick wall, and a peep through the iron gates would have shown an avenue of limes leading to the principal entrance. It must have been thought a building of some magnitude at that epoch, seeing that it accommodated as many as 1,000 persons. One curious fact connected with Keach's chapel may here be mentioned, as it throws some light upon the manners and customs of two centuries ago. In many of the Dissenting chapels of the times of the later Stuarts there was no singing—not, as some persons have erroneously supposed, lest their sounds might be heard by their enemies; but from the idea that only the really spiritual persons ought to sing, and not the unconverted. There was a great controversy about this question among the Nonconformists, and many pamphlets were written on both sides of the question. Keach contended that all the congregation ought to sing, and he fought zealously for this practice for many years, and lived to see his ideas make way. At one time there was a sort of drawn battle between Keach and some of his people, and an understanding was at length come to that at one period of the service, during the psalmody, those who objected to the singing should leave the chapel and walk about the chapel-yard, among the graves of the *silent* dead, and then come in again after what they objected to was over! Keach was the author of "An Exposition of the Parables," "A Key to open Scripture Metaphors," and some controversial pamphlets. At one time he found it necessary to reply to some persons who had contrived to unsettle the minds of the young people and apprentices of the congregation, by arguing that Saturday was the true Sabbath. For the publication of a series of discourses on this subject, under the title of "The Jewish Sabbath Abrogated," in which he treated the subject controversially, Keach was complimented by the Archbishop of Canterbury. The death of Keach was thus celebrated by one of his congregation in the following lines:—

"Is he no more? has Heaven withdrawn his light,
    And left us to lament, in sable shades of night,
        Our loss?
    Death boasts his triumph; for the rumour's spread
    Through Salem's plains, that Keach, dear Keach, is
        dead."

Southwark, as is generally known, was a famous rendezvous of the Nonconformists two centuries ago, and such it has continued to be down to our own day. In the time of Charles II., and even earlier, the Anabaptists were accustomed to practise immersion in the river, and at that date several quiet spots existed on the banks of the Thames, not far eastward from London Bridge, suitable for that purpose. But the increase of dwellings in the neighbourhood of the river soon rendered this practice impossible. A building for this particular object, Mr. Pike tells us, existed in Horselydown in the seventeenth century. It was called the Baptisterion, and attached to it were dressing-rooms. It was the common place of adult immersion for southern London. A conference, which assembled in 1717, provided funds for the rebuilding of the structure. The chapel never appears to have had any regular congregation associated with it, but elderly persons were living at the commencement of the present century who remembered the place being used as a preaching station. The passage leading to the meeting-house was called "Dipping Alley."

Near the north-east corner of St. John's churchyard, and at the eastern end of Tooley Street, stands the new Free Grammar School of the united parishes of St. Olave's and St. John's, of which we have spoken above. The building, like its predecessor in Bermondsey Street, is in the Tudor style of architecture, and is altogether an ornament to the neighbourhood. It comprises a residence for the master and the usual school buildings; but the chief architectural feature is the central tower, over the doorway of which is a statue of the founder, Queen Elizabeth.

"Early in the reign of Elizabeth," writes Mr. Corner, in his account of the above seminary, in the *Gentleman's Magazine*, January, 1836, "when the foundation of public schools was promoted throughout the country, under the authority of the legislature and the patronage of the crown, the parishioners of St. Saviour's, Southwark, set a noble example to their neighbours in the establishment of their admirable Free Grammar School; and the inhabitants of the parish of St. Olave were not slow to follow so enlightened and benevolent a policy. St. Olave's School was set on foot in the year 1560, and constituted 'The Free Grammar School of Queen Elizabeth of the Parishioners of the parish of St. Olave, by letters patent issued in 1571.'"

In this institution provision is made for a commercial as well as a classical education. The ancient seal of the school bears the date of 1576. It represents the master seated in the school-room, with five boys standing near him. The rod is a prominent object, as in other school seals, which may be seen in Carlisle's "Grammar Schools," some of which are also inscribed with the well-known maxim of King Solomon, then strictly maintained, but now nearly exploded, "Qui parcit virgam odit filium" ("He who spares the rod spoils the child"). A fac-simile of the seal, in cast iron or carved in stone, is placed in front of most of the houses belonging to the school. Robert Browne, a Puritan minister, and founder of the sect of Brownists, was master of St. Olave's Grammar School from 1586 till 1591.

The following particulars of this locality, of which but scant notices are found in any local history or topographical work, were given by the late Mr. G. R. Corner, F.S.A., at a special general meeting of the Surrey Archæological Society, held at St. Olave's Branch School-house, in 1856. "It is difficult," he said, "to imagine that a neighbourhood now so crowded with wharves and warehouses, granaries and factories, mills, breweries, and places of business of all kinds, and where the busy hum of men at work like bees in a hive is incessant, can have been, not many centuries since, a region of fields and meadows, pastures for sheep and cattle, with pleasant houses and gardens, shady lanes where lovers might wander (not unseen), clear streams with stately swans, and cool walks by the river-side. Yet such was the case; and the way from London Bridge to Horselydown was occupied by the mansions of men of mark and consequence, dignitaries of the Church, men of military renown, and wealthy citizens. First, in St. Olave's Street, opposite to the church, was the London residence of the Priors of Lewes. Adjoining to the church, on the east side, where Chamberlain's wharf now stands, was the house of the Priors of St. Augustine at Canterbury; next to which was the Bridge House; and a little further eastward was the house of the Abbots of Battle, in Sussex, with pleasant gardens and a clear stream (now a black and fœtid sewer), flowing down Mill Lane, and turning the abbot's mill at Battle Bridge Stairs. On this stream were swans, and it flowed under a bridge (over which the road was continued to Bermondsey and Horselydown), from the Manor of the Maze, the seat of Sir William Burcestre or Bourchier, who died there in 1407, and Sir John Burcestre, who died there in 1466, and was buried at St. Olave's; and afterwards of Sir Roger Copley. The site is now known by the not very pleasant name of Maze Pond. From the corner of Bermondsey Street to Horselydown was formerly called Horselydown Lane; and here, on the west side of Stoney Lane, which was once a Roman road leading to the *trajectus*, or ferry over the river to the Tower (as Stoney Street, in St. Saviour's, was a similar Roman road leading to the ferry to Dowgate), was the mansion of Sir John Fastolf, who fought at Agincourt, and was Governor of Normandy. He died at his castle of Caistor, in Norfolk, in 1460, at the age of eighty-one years.

"During the insurrection of Jack Cade in 1450, Sir John Fastolf furnished his place in Southwark with the old soldiers of Normandy, and habiliments of war, to defend himself against the rebels ; but having sent an emissary to them at Blackheath, the man was taken prisoner, and narrowly escaped execution as a spy. They brought him, however, with them into Southwark, and sent him to Sir John, whom he advised to put away all his habiliments of war and the old soldiers ; and so he did, and went himself to the Tower, with all his household. He was, however, in danger from both parties, for Jack Cade would have burned his house, and he was likely to be impeached for treason for retiring to the Tower, instead of resisting and attacking the rebels, which probably he had not force enough to attempt, as they had entire possession of the Borough.

"Further east, and nearly opposite to the Tower of London, was 'The Rosary.' This belonged to the family of Dunlegh, who appears to have been of some consequence in Southwark at an early period. Richard Dunlegh was returned to the Parliament held at York, 26th Edward I., as one of the representatives of the borough of Southwark, and so was Henry le Dunlegh to the Parliament held at Lincoln, in the 28th of Edward I.

"Still further eastward on the bank of the river was the Liberty of St. John. The Prior of the Hospital of St. John of Jerusalem held in the reign of Edward I. three water-mills, three acres of land, one acre of meadow, and twenty acres of pasture, at Horsedowne (sic) in Southwark, which in the reign of Edward III. Francis de Bachenie held for the term of his life, on the demise of brother Thomas le Archer, late Prior. Courts were held for this manor down to a period comparatively recent. Messrs. Courage's brewery stands on the site of the mill and manor-house ; and in a lease from Sir William Abdy to Mr. Donaldson, dated in 1803, there was an exception of the hall of the mill-house, court-house, or manor-house, to hold a Court once or oftener in every year.

"At the time of the dissolution of the monasteries, St. John's mill was in the tenure of Hugh Eglesfield, by virtue of a lease granted by the Prior of St. John to Christopher Craven, for sixty years, from Midsummer, 23rd Henry VIII., at the yearly rent of £8. It was sold by the king, in his thirty-sixth year, to John Eyre. The estate has for many years belonged to the family of Sir William Abdy, Bart., having come to them from the families of Gainsford and Thomas, whose names are commemorated in Gainsford Street and Thomas Street. Shad Thames is a narrow street, running along the water-side, through the ancient Liberty of St. John, from Pickle Herring to Dockhead.

"Horselydown was a large field anciently used by the neighbouring inhabitants for pasturing their horses and cattle, and was called Horsedown or Horseydown. It was part of the possessions of the Abbey of Bermondsey, and is within the lordship of the manor of Southwark, surrendered to King Henry VIII. with the other possessions of the abbey in 1537. This manor is now called the Great Liberty Manor, and is one of the three manors of Southwark belonging to the Corporation of London, King Edward VI. having granted this manor, with the manor or lordship of Southwark (now called the King's Manor, and formerly belonging to the see of Canterbury), to the City of London, by charter of 1st Edward VI. Horseydown was probably the common of the Great Liberty Manor.

"After the surrender to Henry VIII., Horseydown became the property of Sir Roger Copley, of Galton, Surrey, and the Maze, in Southwark, of whom it was purchased by Adam Beeston, Henry Goodyere, and Hugh Eglisfeilde, three inhabitants of the parish of St. Olave, and was assured to them by a fine levied to them by Sir Roger Copley and Dame Elizabeth his wife, in the reign of Henry VIII. The parish of St. Olave came into possession of Horseydown in 1552, under a lease which the same Hugh Eglisfeilde had purchased of one Robert Warren, and which the parish purchased of him for £20 and twelve pence (the sum he had paid to Warren for it), and the grazing of two kine in Horsedown for his life. (Minutes of Vestry, 5 March, 1552.) . . . .

"The freehold of Horseydown having become vested solely in Hugh Eglisfeild as the surviving joint-tenant, it descended to his son Christopher Eglisfeild, of Gray's Inn, gentleman, who by deed dated 29th December, 1581, conveyed Horseydown to the governors of St. Olave's Grammar School, to whom it still belongs ; and it is one of the remarkable instances of the enormous increase in the value of property in the metropolis, that this piece of land, which was then let to farm to one Alderton, who collected the weekly payments for pasturage, and paid for it a rental of £6 per annum, now produces to the governors for the use of the school an annual income exceeding £3,000."

It is not known whether Southwark Fair was

ever held on "Horseydown;" but it is worthy of remark that when the down came to be built over, about the middle of the seventeenth century, the principal street across it, from west to east, was, and is to the present day, called Fair Street; and a street of houses, running from north to south, near to Dockhead, is called Three Oak Lane, traditionally from three oaks formerly standing there. In Evelyn's time, however ("Diary," 13th September, 1660), the fair appears to have been held at St. Margaret's Hill, in the Borough, as we have already seen.*

The old Artillery Hall of the Southwark "Train-bands" stood on the site of the present workhouse in Parish Street, a little to the west of St. John's Church. It was erected in the year 1639, when the governors of the school granted a lease to Cornelius Cooke and others, of a piece of ground forming part of Horseydown, and enclosed with a brick wall, to be employed for a Martial Yard, in which the Artillery Hall was built. In 1665 the governors granted the churchwardens a lease of part of the Martial Yard for 500 years for a burial-ground; but they reserved all the ground whereon the Artillery House then stood, and "all the herbage of the ground, and also liberty for the militia or trained bands of the borough of South-wark, and also his Majesty's military forces, to muster and exercise arms upon the said ground." The election for Southwark was held at the Artillery Hall in 1680; and at the following sessions—then held at the Bridge House—Slingsby Bethell, Esq., sheriff of London, who had been a losing candidate at the election, was indicted for and convicted of an assault on Robert Mason, a waterman, from Lambeth, who was standing on the steps of the hall with others, and obstructing Mr. Bethell's friends. Mr. Bethell was fined five marks.

In the year 1725 the Artillery Hall was converted by the governors into a workhouse for the parish, and in 1736 the parish church of St. John, Horselydown, as stated above, was built on part of the martial ground. The hall was entirely demolished about the year 1836. Messrs. Courage and Donaldson's brewery, at the corner of Shad Thames, stands, as we have already stated, on the site of the manor-house of St. John of Jerusalem, which formerly belonged to St. John's Hospital, in Clerkenwell. This estate, and that of the governors of the Grammar School, and another estate belonging to Magdalen College, Oxford, called the Isle of Ducks, mentioned above, comprehend almost the whole of this parish. It has been conjectured that the name of the street running along the river-side, and from St. Saviour's Dock to Dockhead, and called Shad Thames, may be an abbreviation of "St. John-at-Thames." Shad Thames, and, indeed, the whole river-side, contain extensive granaries and storehouses for the supply of the metropolis. Indeed, from Morgan's Lane—a turning about the middle of Tooley Street, on the north side, to St. Saviour's (once called Savory) Dock, the whole line of street—called in one part Pickle Herring Street, and in another Shad Thames—exhibits an uninterrupted series of wharves, warehouses, mills, and factories, on both sides of the narrow and crowded roadway. The buildings on the northern side are contiguous to the river, and through gateways and openings in these we witness the busy scenes and the mazes of shipping which pertain to such a spot. The part of Bermondsey upon which we are now entering is as remarkable for its appearance as for its importance, in past times at least, seeing that it was connected with the manufactures of Bermondsey.

The waterside division of Bermondsey, or that part of the parish situate east of St. Saviour's Dock, and adjoining the parish of Rotherhithe, is intersected by several streams or watercourses. Upon the south bank of one of these, between Mill Street and George Row, stand—or stood till very recently—a number of very ancient houses, called London Street. All Londoners have heard of the "Rookery"—or, as it was more universally called, the "Holy Land"—which formerly existed in St. Giles's; and of the "shy neighbourhood" of Somers Town, which we have already described.† Charles Dickens, in his "Uncommercial Traveller," speaks of another "shy neighbourhood" over the Surrey side of London Bridge, "among the fastnesses of Jacob's Island and Dockhead." Little, perhaps, was known of Jacob's Island, in Bermondsey, until it was rendered familiar to the public in the pages of one of Dickens's most popular works, "Oliver Twist," where the features which this spot presented a few years ago—and in part exhibit at the present time—are described so vividly, and with such close accuracy, that we cannot do better than quote the passage. He first speaks of the ditch itself and the houses exterior to the island. "A stranger, standing on one of the wooden bridges thrown across this ditch in Mill Street, will see the inhabitants of the houses on either side lowering, from their back doors and windows, buckets, pails, and domestic utensils in

---

which to haul the water up; and when his eye is turned from these operations to the houses themselves, his utmost astonishment will be excited by the scene before him. Crazy wooden galleries, common to the backs of half-a-dozen houses, with holes from whence to look on the slime beneath; windows, broken and patched, with poles thrust out on which to dry the linen that is never there; rooms so small, so filthy, so confined, that the air

Rough and wild as the spot appears when the ditch is filled at high tide, yet, if we visit it six hours afterwards, when mud usurps the place of water, more than one organ of sense is strongly and unpleasantly appealed to. Wilkinson gave a view of this spot in the "Londina Illustrata" in the early part of the present century, and the interval of time does not seem to have produced much change in the appearance of the scene. In the

HALL OF THE SOUTHWARK "TRAIN-BANDS," IN 1813.

would seem too tainted even for the dirt and squalor which they shelter; wooden chambers thrusting themselves out above the mud, and threatening to fall into it, as some of them have done; dirt-besmeared walls and decaying foundations—all these ornament the banks of Folly Ditch." This is the scene in the narrow passages near the Island, two of which are known by the humble names of Halfpenny Alley and Farthing Alley. In Jacob's Island itself the "warehouses are roofless and empty, the walls are crumbling down, the windows are now no windows, the doors are falling into the street, the chimneys are blackened, but they yield no smoke; and, through losses and Chancery suits, it is made quite a desolate island indeed."

plate here alluded to, the spectator is supposed to be standing on Jacob's Island, and looking across the Folly Ditch, to the crazy, ancient houses of London Street.

"The history of this ditch or tide-stream," says Charles Knight in his "London," "is connected, in a remarkable way, with the manufacturing features of Bermondsey. When the abbey was at the height of its glory, and formed a nucleus to which all else in the neighbourhood was subordinate, the supply of water for its inmates was obtained from the Thames through the medium of this tide. Bermondsey was probably at one time very little better than a morass, the whole being low and level: indeed, at the present time, manufacturers in that locality find the utmost difficulty

OLD HOUSES IN LONDON STREET, DOCKHEAD, ABOUT 1810.

in obtaining a firm foundation for their buildings, such is the spongy nature of the ground. In the early period just alluded to, the spot, besides being low, was almost entirely unencumbered with buildings; and thus a channel from the Thames, although not many feet in depth, was filled throughout the entire district at every high tide. There was a mill at the river-side, at which the corn for the granary of the abbey was ground; and this mill was turned by the flux and reflux of the water along the channel. When the abbey was destroyed, and the ground passed into the possession of others, the houses which were built on the site still received a supply of water from this watercourse. In process of time tanneries were established on the spot, most probably on account of the valuable supply of fresh water obtainable every twelve hours from the river. This seems to be an opinion entertained by many of the principal manufacturers of the place."

A writer in the *Morning Chronicle*, some years ago, alluding to this particular locality, remarks: "The striking peculiarity of Jacob's Island consists in the wooden galleries and sleeping-rooms at the back of the houses, which overhang the dark flood, and are built upon piles, so that the place has positively the air of a Flemish street, flanking a sewer instead of a canal; while the little rickety bridges that span the ditches and connect court with court, give it the appearance of the Venice of drains." The same writer observes that "in the reign of Henry II. the foul stagnant ditch, which now makes an island of this pestilential spot, was a running stream, supplied with the waters which poured down from the hills about Sydenham and Nunhead, and was used for the working of the mills which then stood on its banks. These had been granted to the monks of St. Mary and St. John to grind their flour, and were dependencies upon the Priory of Bermondsey; and what is now a straw-yard skirting the river was once the City Ranelagh, called Cupid's Gardens, and the trees, now black with mud, were the bowers under which the citizens loved, on the summer evenings, to sit beside the stream drinking their sack and ale."

Dickens's graphic picture of the filth, wretchedness, and misery of Jacob's Island, at the time it was written—some thirty years ago—was by no means overdrawn. A vast deal has been done, however, towards removing its worst evils, although more remains to be done. One of the missionaries of the London City Mission, in 1876, furnished a report on the district as it was when he entered it twenty-one years ago, and as it now exists. Many of the horrors, he admits, have passed away:—

"The foul ditch no longer pollutes the air. It has long been filled up; and along Mill Street, where 'the crazy wooden galleries' once hung over it, stands Messrs. Peek, Frean, and Co.'s splendid biscuit bakery. The ditch which intersected the district along London Street served as a fine bathing-place for the resident juveniles in summer-time. I have seen," continues the writer, "many of the boys rolling joyously in the thick liquid, undeterred by the close proximity of the decomposing carcases of cats and dogs. Where this repulsive sight was often witnessed there is now a good solid road. Many of the houses, too, in London Street have been pulled down, and the vacant space added to the houses in Hickman's Folly, thus affording them a little yard or garden. In Dickens's sketch of the district he states that 'the houses have no owners, and they are broken open and entered upon by those who have the courage.' This, in many cases, I know to be literally true. Much of the property of the district has no rightful owners, and many of the houses no claimants. In not a few cases persons have got possession of them and have never been asked for rent. I recollect a young unmarried man occupying one of these unclaimed houses. He remained in it as long as he pleased, and then sold it to a bricklayer for £5. The structure of many of the old houses shows that they have been adapted to the concealment of crime. Subterranean connection between houses, and windows opening on to the roofs of other dwellings, bear witness to its being a place where desperate characters found a sure hiding-place, and where pursuit and detection were rendered next to impossible. Most of these dens have been pulled down since I have been on the district. Part of London Street, the whole of Little London Street, part of Mill Street, beside houses in Jacob Street and Hickman's Folly, have been demolished. In most of these places warehouses have taken the place of dwelling-houses. The revolting fact of many of the inhabitants of the district having no other water to drink than that which they procured from the filthy ditches is also a thing of the past. Most of the houses are now supplied with good water, and the streets are very well paved. Indeed, so great is the change for the better in the external appearance of the district generally, that a person who had not seen it since the improvements would now scarcely recognise it. Such a place as Jacob's Island, especially before improvements were made, cannot excite surprise that during the prevalence of any epidemic it should come in for a very severe scourge and heavy death-rate. During the cholera visitations of 1849 and 1854 the victims were alarmingly numerous. In one fever visitation the number of cases in Jacob's Island were frightfully numerous, reaching to upwards of two hundred, many of which were fatal. I remember that in one house in London Street there were nineteen cases. During the present visitation of small-pox the district has also suffered somewhat severely. The occupations of the people are various, including more largely watermen and waterside labourers, costermongers, and wood-choppers. The wood-choppers form a rather numerous class in the district. In the centre of the district is a large wood-yard, containing immense stacks of wood imported from Norway. Round the yards are sheds in which about 200 persons, including men, women, boys, and girls, work. These people are generally of the lowest class, and being congregated together, young and old, they corrupt one another. It has been for a long time a thriving nursery for immorality. But I am glad to say that lately an improvement has taken place. The great majority never saw the interior of a church, except on the occasion of a christening, or when they wanted the clergyman to sign a paper. They looked upon public worship as something 'out of their line altogether.' I found persons who had not entered a place of worship for forty or fifty years. Drunkenness was a predominant vice in the district, not only with men, but equally with women."

For some considerable time past an agitation has been going on as to the desirability of having a high-level bridge near this spot, as a means of affording more direct communication between the two sides of the river than at present exist. In December, 1876, a meeting of the Court of Common Council was held, when the question was discussed, and the plans and estimates which had been prepared were carefully examined and considered. The site for a bridge which appeared to be most eligible to the court was that approached from Little Tower Hill and Irongate Stairs on the north side, and from Horselydown Stairs on the south side of the river. Since the above date several meetings have been held, and petitions drawn up, with the view of facilitating the construction of a bridge, but up to 1884 nothing definite had been decided upon. One great and much-needed improvement, however, has been effected in the neighbourhood by the widening of the eastern end of Tooley Street, towards Dockhead.

CHAPTER X.

BERMONDSEY (continued).—THE ABBEY, &c.

"'The sacred tapers lights are gone,
Grey moss has clad the altar-stone,
The holy image is o'erthrown,
        The bell has ceased to toll;
The long-ribb'd aisles are burst and shrunk,
The holy shrine to ruin sunk,
Departed is the pious monk;
        God's blessing on his soul!"—*Scott.*

The Dissolution of Monasteries by Henry VIII.—Earliest Historical Mention of Bermondsey Abbey—Some Account of the Cluniac Monasteries in England, and Customs of the Cluniac Order—Grant of the Manor of Bermondsey to Bermondsey Abbey—Queen Katherine, Widow of Henry V., retires hither—Elizabeth Woodville, Widow of Edward IV., a Prisoner here—Form of Service for the Repose of the Souls of the Queen of Henry VII. and her Children—Grant of the Monastery to Sir Robert Southwell—Its Sale to Sir Thomas Pope—Demolition of the Abbey Church—Remains of the Abbey at the Close of the Last Century—Neckinger Road—The Church of St. Mary Magdalen—A Curious Matrimonial Ceremony—An Ancient Salver—The Rood of Bermondsey—Grange Walk and Grange Road—The Tanning and Leather Trades in Bermondsey—"Simon the Tanner"—Fellmongery—Bermondsey Hide and Skin Market—Russell Street—St. Olave's Union—Bricklayers' Arms Station—Growth of Modern Bermondsey—Neckinger Mills—The Spa—Baths and Wash-houses—Christ Church—Roman Catholic Church of the Most Holy Trinity, and Convent of the Sisters of Mercy—Jamaica Road—The Old "Jamaica" Tavern—The "Lion and Castle"—Cherry Garden—St. James's Church—Traffic on the Railway near Bermondsey—Messrs. Peek, Frean, and Co.'s Biscuit Factory—Blue Anchor Road—Galley Wall.

READERS of English history need scarcely be told how that King Henry VIII., in his selfish zeal for novelties in religion, laid violent hands on all the abbeys and other religious houses in the kingdom, except a very few, which were spared at the earnest petition of the people, or given up to the representatives of the original founders. Before proceeding to the final suppression, under the pretext of checking the superstitious worshipping of images, he had laid bare their altars and stripped their shrines of everything that was valuable; nor did he spare the rich coffins and crumbling bones of the dead. Although four hundred years had passed away since the murder of Thomas Becket in Canterbury Cathedral, the venerated tomb was broken open, and a sort of criminal information was filed against the dead saint, as "Thomas Becket, sometime Archbishop of Canterbury," who was formally cited to appear in court and answer to the charges. As the saint did not appear at the bar of this earthly court, which was held in Westminster Hall in 1539, it was deemed proper to declare that "he was no saint whatever, but a rebel and traitor to his prince, and that therefore he, the king, strictly commanded that he should not be any longer esteemed or called a saint; that all images and pictures of him should be destroyed; and that his name and remembrance should be erased out of all books, under pain of his majesty's indignation, and imprisonment at his grace's pleasure." Other shrines had been plundered before, and certain images and relics of saints had been broken to pieces publicly at St. Paul's Cross; but now every shrine was laid bare, or, if any escaped, it was owing to the poverty of their decorations and offerings. "In the final seizure of the abbeys and monasteries," writes the author of the "Comprehensive History of England," "the richest fell first. After Canterbury, Battle Abbey; Merton, in Surrey; Stratford, in Essex; Lewes, in Sussex; the Charterhouse, the Blackfriars, the Greyfriars, and the Whitefriars, in London, felt the fury of the same whirlwind, which gradually blew over the whole land, until, in the spring of the year 1540, all the monastic establishments of the kingdom were suppressed, and the mass of their landed property was divided among courtiers and parasites. . . . All the abbeys were totally dismantled, except in the cases where they happened to be the parish churches also; as was the case at St. Albans, Tewkesbury, Malvern, and elsewhere, where they were rescued, in part by the petitions and pecuniary contributions of the pious inhabitants, who were averse to the worshipping of God in a stable." Of the "lesser monasteries" which were thus ruthlessly swept away was the Abbey of Bermondsey, which is now kept in remembrance mainly by the names given to a few streets which cover its site, and through which we are about to pass.

The earliest mention of this abbey occurs in the account of Bermondsey in "Domesday," from which may be gathered some idea of the solitude and seclusion which the place then enjoyed; when it is stated that there was "woodland" round about for the "pannage" of a certain number of hogs; and that there was also "a new and fair church, with twenty acres of meadow." Soon after the Norman conquest, a number of Cluniac monks settled in this country; and in 1082 a wealthy citizen of London, Aylwin Childe, founded a monastery at Bermondsey, which some of the ecclesiastics from the Monastery of La Charité, on the Loire, made their new home in the land of their adoption.

"The Cluniacs," writes Mr. A. Wood in his "Ecclesiastical Antiquities," "derived their name from Clugni, in Burgundy, where Odo, an abbot in the tenth century, reformed the Benedictine rule. Their habit was the same as the Benedictine. The order was introduced into England in 1077, when a Cluniac house was established at Lewes, in Sussex, under the protection of Earl Warenne, the Conqueror's son-in-law. In the twelfth century the Abbey of Clugni was at the height of its reputation under Peter the Venerable (1122–1156). From the 13th of September till Lent, the Cluniacs had one meal only a day, except during the octaves of Christmas and the Epiphany, when they had an extra meal. Still eighteen poor were fed at their table. There were never more than twenty Cluniac houses in England, nearly all of them founded before the reign of Henry II. Until the fourteenth century, all the Cluniac houses were priories dependent on the parent house. The Prior of St. Pancras, Lewes, was the high-chamberlain, and frequently the vicar-general of the Abbey of Cluny, and exercised the functions of a Provincial in England. The English houses were all governed by foreigners, and the monks were oftener of foreign than of English extraction. In the fourteenth century, however, there was a change; many of the houses became denizen, and Bermondsey was made an abbey."

The following interesting particulars of the customs of the Cluniac order are gathered from Stevens's translation of the French history of the monastic orders, given in his continuation of Dugdale, and transcribed in the great edition of the "Monasticon:"—"They every day sung two solemn masses, at each of which a monk of one of the choirs offered two hosts. If any one would celebrate mass on Holy Thursday, before the solemn mass was sung, he made no use of light, because the new fire was not yet blessed. The preparation they used for making the bread which was to serve for the sacrifice of the altar is worthy to be observed. They first chose the wheat, grain by grain, and washed it very carefully. Being put into a bag, appointed only for that use, a servant, known to be a just man, carried it to the mill, washed the grindstones, covered them with curtains above and below, and having put on himself an alb, covered his face with a veil, nothing but his eyes appearing. The same precaution was used with the meal. It was not boulted till it had been well washed; and the warden of the church, if he were either priest or deacon, finished the rest, being assisted by two other religious men, who were in the same orders, and by a lay brother particularly appointed for that business. These four monks, when matins were ended, washed their faces and hands; the three first of them did put on albs; one of them washed the meal with pure clean water, and the other two baked the hosts in the iron moulds; so great was the veneration and respect the monks of Cluni paid to the Holy Eucharist." The sites of the mill and the bakehouse of Bermondsey Abbey were both traceable as late as the year 1876.

William Rufus enriched the abbey by the grant of the manor of Bermondsey; and the establishment soon became one of the most important in England. In 1213, Prior Richard erected an almonry or hospital adjoining the monastery; but no traces of that now exist. The parish church of St. Mary Magdalen, rebuilt in 1680, at the junction of Bermondsey Street and Abbey Street, occupies nearly the site of the conventual church. The monastic buildings were, doubtless, very extensive and magnificent; and the monks maintained a splendid hospitality and state. Katherine of France, widow of Henry V., retired hither to mourn, perhaps the victor of Agincourt, to whose memory she had erected, in Westminster Abbey, a life-sized silver-gilt statue; or it may have been her second husband, Owen Tudor, who perhaps little thought he would ever become the progenitor of two of the greatest monarchs who ever sat on the English throne—bluff King Henry and Queen Bess, not to mention Henry's father, the conqueror of crook-backed Richard, and Elizabeth's boy-brother and her sister Mary. Katherine died at Bermondsey, a double widow, in January, 1437. In the convent here Elizabeth Woodville, the widow of Edward IV., was shut up as a sort of prisoner by Henry VII., shortly after the marriage of the latter with her daughter Elizabeth. The Queen Dowager died in 1492. A few days before her death she made her will, and a pathetic document it is. Her son-in-law, Henry VII., cruelly neglected her; and when in after years he ordered an anniversary service to be sung on the 6th of February, by the monks of Bermondsey, for the repose of the souls of his late queen and children, his father and his mother, he forgot to include poor Elizabeth, the mother of his wife, once queen of England, but who ended her days almost a pauper in the very abbey where the stately service was performed.

As a glimpse of what was sometimes doing in the old church, as well as of the old custom itself the following extract will be found interesting:—
"The abbot and convent of St. Saviour of Bermondsey shall provide at every such anniversary a hearse, to be set in the midst of the high chancel of the same monastery before the high altar, covered and apparelled with the best and most honourable stuff in the same monastery convenient for the same. And also four tapers of wax, each of them weighing eight pounds, to be set about the same hearse, that is to say, on either side thereof one taper, and at either end of the same hearse another taper, and all the same four tapers to be lighted and burning continually during all the time of every such *Placebo, Dirige*, with nine lessons, lauds and mass of *Requiem*, with the prayers and obeisances above rehearsed."

At the dissolution of the monasteries, Bermondsey Abbey, with its rich manor, was seized—as was the case with other similar places—by Henry VIII. At that time the Abbot of Bermondsey had no very tender scruples about conscience or principle, like so many of his brethren, but arranged everything in the pleasantest possible manner for the king; and he had his reward. While the poor monks had pensions varying from £5 6s. 8d. to £10 a year each allowed them, the good Lord Abbot's pension amounted to £336 6s. 8d. The monastery itself, with the manor, demesnes, &c., were granted by the Crown to Sir Robert Southwell, Master of the Rolls, who sold them to Sir Thomas Pope, the founder of Trinity College, Oxford. In 1545 Sir Thomas pulled down the old priory church, and built Bermondsey House upon the site and with the materials. Here died, in 1583, Thomas Radcliffe, Earl of Sussex, Lord Chamberlain to Queen Elizabeth. This was the Earl of Sussex who, according to Sir Walter Scott in his interesting romance of "Kenilworth," was visited by "Master" Tressilian at Sayes Court, Deptford, and restored from a dangerous illness by the skill of Wayland Smith, to the great wonder of Walter Raleigh and Sir Thomas Blount. About 1760, the east gate of the monastery was removed; and early in the present century nearly all that was left of the old buildings shared the same fate, and Abbey Street was built upon the site. The Neckinger Road—at a short distance southward of Jacob's Island, Dockhead, and the other waterside places mentioned towards the close of the preceding chapter—marks the ancient water-course, formerly navigable as far as the precincts of the abbey. This road, which is at the junction of Parker's Row with Jamaica Road, leads westward.

by Abbey Street and Long Lane, into the Borough High Street, close by St. George's Church. This, then, is the spot on which the ancient monastery once flourished; there are, however, scarcely any remains of the conventual building left standing, and a walk over the site of the great abbey of the Cluniacs can now afford but little gratification. The entire site is now pretty well covered over with modern houses and dirty streets and courts.

"The Long Walk," as Charles Knight pleasantly

felt themselves a part of the old abbey, and had no business to survive its destruction. They will not have much longer to wait; little remains to be destroyed. In the Grange Walk is a part of the gate-house of the east gateway, with a portion of the rusted hinge of the monastic doors. In Long Walk, on the right, is a small and filthy quadrangle (once called, from some tradition connected with the visits of the early English monarchs to Bermondsey, King John's Court, now Bear Yard) in which are a few

BERMONDSEY ABBEY, 1790.

suggests in his "London," "was once perhaps a fine shady avenue, where the abbot or his monks were accustomed to while away the summer after-noon, but is about one of the last places that would now tempt the wandering footstep of the stranger; the 'Grange Walk' no longer leads to the pleasant farm or park of the abbey, and is in itself but a painful mockery of the associations roused by the name; the 'Court,' or Base Court-yard, is changed into Bermondsey Square, flanked on all sides by small tenements, the handiwork of the builders who completed a few years ago what Sir Thomas Pope began; and though some trees are yet there, of so ancient appearance that, for aught we know, they may have witnessed the destruction of the very conventual church, yet they are dwindling and dwindling away, as though they

dilapidated houses, where the stonework, and form and antiquity of the windows, afford abundant evidence of their connection with the monastery. Lastly, in the churchyard of the present church of St. Mary Magdalen are some pieces of the wall that surrounded the gardens and church of the Cluniacs."

Although Bermondsey is, perhaps, not the most civilised and scholastic part of London now, it is no small credit to the churchmen of the early Norman times, that, according to Fitzstephen, as interpreted to us by honest John Stow, the three earliest schools for youth in London and its neigh-bourhood were founded under the shadows respec-tively of Old St. Paul's, of St. Peter's Abbey, West-minster, and of the Abbey of Bermondsey.

In Faithorne's map of London and Southwark

(1643-8) the abbey is shown as standing in its entire condition in its own enclosed grounds.

The church of St. Mary Magdalen, at the corner of Abbey Street and Bermondsey Street, stands on the site of the ancient conventual church. It is a brick-built structure, consisting of a chancel, nave, two aisles, and a transept; and at the western end is a low square tower with a turret. The church contains no monuments worthy of note. In 1830 the tower was repaired and "beautified"

THE MAN'S SPEECH.

Elizabeth, my beloved wife, I am righte sorie that I have so long absented myself from thee, whereby thou shouldest be occasioned to take another man to be thy husband. Therefore I do now vowe and promise, in the sight of God and this company, to take thee again as my owne, and will not onlie forgive thee but live with thee, and do all other duties to thee, as I promised at our marriage.

THE WOMAN'S SPEECH.

Raphe, my beloved husband, I am righte sorie that I have in thy absence taken another man to be my husband; but

ST. MARY MAGDALEN'S CHURCH, BERMONDSEY, 1809.

after the usual "churchwarden" fashion of the period, and at the same time the Gothic windows were restored, and since that date the church has been re-seated, and otherwise greatly improved. The registers commence in 1538, and have been continued with very few interruptions up to the present time. Some of the entries are very singular and curious. Here, for instance, is one which we give *in extenso*, since it may serve as a model for such transactions in these days of judicial separations. It is headed, "The forme of a solemn vowe made betwixt a man and his wife, having been long absent, through which occasion the woman being married to another man, (the husband) took her again as followeth:"—

here, before God and this companie, I do renounce and forsake him; I do promise to keep myself only to thee duringe life, and to perform all the duties which I first promised to thee in our marriage.

Then follows a short prayer, suited to the occasion, and the entry thus concludes:

The 1st day of August, 1604, Raphe Goodchild, of the parish of Barkinge, in Thames Street, and Elizabeth his wife were agreed to live together, and thereupon gave their hands one to another, making either of them solemn vow so to do in the presence of us, William Steres, *Parson;* Edward Coker; and Richard Eyres, *Clerk.*

Another entry in the register also is remarkable. "James Herriott, Esq., and Elizabeth Josey, Gent., were married Jan. 4., 1624-5. N.B. This James Herriott was one of the forty children of his father, a Scotchman." It is to be hoped, for the sake of the family, that the history of the parent did not repeat itself in that of the son.

In this church is a very curious ancient salver of silver, now used for the collection of the alms at the offertory. On the centre is a beautifully-chased representation of the gate of a castle or town, with two figures, a knight kneeling before a lady, who is about to place his helmet on his head. The long-pointed solleretts of the feet, the ornaments of the armpits, and the form of the helmet, are supposed to mark the date of the salver as that of Edward II. The other memorial to which we have referred is of a much more interesting character; it is thus recorded in the "Chronicle of Bermondsey:"—"Anno Domini 1117. The cross of St. Saviour is found near the Thames." And again, under the date of 1118:—"William Earl of Morton was miraculously liberated from the Tower of London through the power of the holy cross." This Lord Morton was a son of the Earl of Morton mentioned in Domesday Book as possessing "a hide of land" in this parish, on which, it appears from another part of the record, he had a mansion-house. The above-mentioned nobleman seems to have had a perfect faith in the truth of the miracle; for the chronicle subsequently states: "In the year 1140 William Earl of Morton came to Bermondsey, and assumed the monastic habit." In our account of old St. Paul's Cathedral * we have spoken of the scene which was witnessed at Paul's Cross on the breaking up of the "Rood of Grace," which had been brought from Boxley Abbey, in Kent; and we may mention here that the degradation of the "Rood of Bermondsey" formed, as it were, an appendix to that day's proceedings. A reference to this transaction is to be found in an ancient diary of a citizen, preserved among the Cottonian MSS., under the date of 1558, in the following passage :—" M. Gresham, Mayor. On Saint Matthew's day, the Apostle, the 24th day of February, Sunday, did the Bishop of Rochester preach at Paul's Cross, and had standing afore him all his sermon time the picture of Rood of Grace in Kent, and was [i.e. which had been] greatly sought with pilgrims; and when he had made an end of his sermon, was torn all in pieces; then was the picture of Saint Saviour, that had stood in Barmsey Abbey many years, in Southwark, taken down." The word "picture," it may be stated, was often used in the widest sense to express an image or statue; and it may be remarked, with reference

to the Rood in Bermondsey Abbey, that the words are "taken down," not that it was actually destroyed. In front of the building attached to the chief or north gate of the abbey was a rude representation of a small cross, with some zigzag ornamentation; the whole had the appearance of being something placed upon or let into the wall, and not a part of the original building; and there it remained till the comparatively recent destruction of this last remnant of the monastic pile. In a drawing made of the remains of the Abbey in 1679, which was afterwards engraved by Wilkinson, in his "Londinia Illustrata," the same cross appears in the same situation; from this it has been conjectured, apart from the corroborative evidence of tradition, that this was the old Saxon cross found near the Thames, or that it was a part of the "picture" before which pilgrims used to congregate in the old conventual church.

In Wilkinson's work above mentioned is engraved a ground-plan of the site and precincts of Bermondsey Abbey, copied from a survey made in 1679. It exhibits a ground-plot of the old conventual church, with gardens enclosed by stone walls, and bounded on the north by the churchyard of St. Mary Magdalen; the west and north gates, leading into the "base court-yard," the site of the mansion, with its long gallery, built by Sir Thomas Pope; and the east gate, leading into "Grange" Walk. In the same work is a general view of the remains of the monastic and other old buildings, with the adjacent country, taken in 1805, from the steeple of the adjoining church, and also an east view of the ancient gateway, with several other engravings relating to the abbey and its attached buildings. The east gate of the monastery, in Grange Walk, was pulled down about the middle of the last century. We learn from Brayley's "History of Surrey," that "the great gate-house, or principal entrance, the front of which was composed of squared flints and dark-red tiles, ranged alternately, was nearly entire in the year 1806; but shortly afterwards it was completely demolished, together with nearly all the adjacent ancient buildings, and Abbey Street was erected on their site. The north gate led into the great close of the abbey, now Bermondsey Square, and surrounded by modern houses. Grange Road, which was built on the pasture-ground belonging to the monastery, commences near the south-west corner of the square, and extends to what was till lately the Grange Farm, and continues onward to the ancient water-course called the Neckinger, over which is a bridge, leading to the water-side division of the parish. In 1810 the present churchyard

---

* See Vol. I., p. 243.

(which had been previously extended in 1783) was enlarged by annexing to it a strip of land sixteen feet in width, that formed a part of the conventual burial-ground; in doing which many vestiges of sculpture were found, together with a stone coffin."

We may add that King Stephen was a great benefactor to the abbey, on which he bestowed broad lands in Writtle, near Chelmsford, in Essex, and in other places.

In the previous chapter we have stated that Bermondsey, in a certain sense, may be regarded as a "region of manufacturers." Indeed, for several centuries this locality has been the centre of the tanning and leather trades. But even this un-savoury trade has its advantages. When the Great Plague raged in the City of London, many of the terror-stricken creatures fled to the Bermondsey tan-pits, and found strong medicinal virtues in the nauseous smell. The great leather market has been established on this spot for above 200 years. Hat-making, too, is most extensively carried on; and it is said that in no place in the kingdom of equal area is there such a great variety of important manufactures. The intersection of the district by innumerable tidal ditches gave unusual facilities for the leather manufacture, but at the same time it also entailed frightful misery on the crowded inhabitants. If we draw a line from St. James's Church, in the Jamaica Road, to the intersection of the Grange Road with the Old Kent Road, we shall find to the west, or rather to the north-west, of that line, nearly the whole of the factories con-nected with the leather and wool trade of London. "A circle one mile in diameter, having its centre at the spot where the abbey once stood," says Charles Knight, in his "London," "will include within its limits most of the tanners, the curriers, the fellmongers, the woolstaplers, the leather-factors, the leather-dressers, the leather-dyers, the parchment-makers, and the glue-makers, for which this district is so remarkable. There is scarcely a street, a road, a lane, into which we can turn with-out seeing evidences of one or other of these occu-pations. One narrow road—leading from the Grange Road to the Kent Road—is particularly distinguishable for the number of leather-factories which it exhibits on either side; some time-worn and mean, others newly and skilfully erected. Another street, known as Long Lane, and lying westward of the church, exhibits nearly twenty dis-tinct establishments where skins or hides undergo some of the many processes to which they are subjected. In Snow's Fields; in Bermondsey New Road; in Russell Street, Upper and Lower; in Willow Walk, and Page's Walk, and Grange Walk,

and others whose names we cannot now remember —in all of these, leather, skins, and wool seem to be the commodities out of which the wealth of the inhabitants has been created. Even the public-houses give note of these peculiarities by the signs chosen for them, such as the 'Woolpack,' the 'Fellmongers' Arms,' 'Simon the Tanner,' and others of like import. If there is any district in London whose inhabitants might be excused for supporting the proposition that 'There is nothing like leather,' surely Bermondsey is that place!"

The old-established house, known as "Simon the Tanner," is situated in Long Lane. The sign makes allusion, of course, to the tanner of Joppa, of whom we read in the Acts of the Apostles, as having St. Peter as his lodger. "The sign," says Mr. Larwood, "is supposed to be unique."

From the following enumeration of some of the manufacturers in Bermondsey Street alone, it will be seen how many branches of industry are carried on here in connection with the leather trade: hide-sellers, tanners, leather-dressers, morocco leather dressers, leather sellers and cutters, curriers, parch-ment-makers, wool-staplers, horsehair manufac-turers, hair and flock manufacturers, patent hair-felt manufacturers. There are besides these skin and hide salesmen, fellmongers, leather-dyers, and glue-makers, in other parts of the vicinity.

Bermondsey Market, the great emporium for hides and skins, is in Weston Street, on the north side of Long Lane. It was established on this spot about the year 1833; and the building, together with the ground whereon it stands, cost nearly £50,000. It is a long series of brick ware-houses, lighted by a range of windows, and having an arched entrance gateway at either end. These entrances open into a quadrangle or court, covered for the most part with grass and surrounded by warehouses, and enclosing others for the stowage of hops. In the warehouses is transacted the business of a class of persons who are termed "leather factors," who sell to the curriers or leather-sellers leather belonging to the tanners; or sell London-tanned leather to country purchasers, or country-tanned leather to London purchasers; in short, they are middle-men in the traffic in leather, as skin-salesmen are in the traffic in skins. Beyond this first quadrangle is a second, called the "Skin Depository," and having four entrances, two from the larger quadrangle, and two from a street leading into Bermondsey Street. This depository is an oblong plot of ground terminated by semi-circular ends; it is pitched with common road-stones along the middle, and flagged round with a broad foot-pavement. Over the pavement, through its whole extent, is an arcade supported by pillars; and the portion of pavement included between every two contiguous pillars is called a "bay." There are about fifty of these "bays," which are let out to skin-salesmen at about £15 per annum each; and on the pavement of his bay the salesman exposes the skins which he is commissioned to sell. Here on market-days may be seen a busy scene of traffic between the salesmen on the one hand and the fellmongers on the other. The carts, laden with sheepskins, come rattling into the place, and draw up in the roadway of the depository; the loads are taken out, and ranged on the pavement of the bays; the sellers and buyers make their bargains; the purchase-money is paid into the hands of the salesman, and by him transmitted to the butcher; and the hides or skins are removed to the yards of the buyers.

As was supposed, when the New Skin Market was built, the trade in hides, as well as that in skins, has come to be carried on here. A large quantity of ox-hides, however, from which the thicker kinds of leather are made, are still sold at Leadenhall Market, which was long the centre of this trade; and nearly all the leather manufacturers in Bermondsey are still proprietors in that market.

The whole of the fellmongers belonging to the metropolis are congregated within a small circle around the Skin Market in Weston Street. It forms no part of the occupation of these persons to convert the sheepskins into leather. The skins pass into their hands with the wool on, just as they are taken from the sheep; and the fellmonger then proceeds to remove the wool from the pelt, and to cleanse the latter from some of the impurities with which it is coated.

"The produce of the fellmongers' labours," writes Charles Knight, "passes into the hands of two or three other classes of manufacturers, such as the wool-stapler, the leather-dresser, and the parchment-maker. The wool-staplers, thirty or forty in number, are, like the fellmongers, located almost without a single exception in Bermondsey. They are wool dealers, who purchase the commodity as taken from the skins, and sell it to the hatters, the woollen and worsted manufacturers, and others. They are scarcely to be denominated manufacturers, since the wool passes through their hands without undergoing any particular change or preparation; it is sorted into various qualities, and, like the foreign wool, packed in bags for the market. In a street called Russell Street, intersecting Bermondsey Street, the large warehouses of these wool-staplers may be seen in great number; tiers of ware or store-rooms, with cranes over them;

wagons in the yard beneath; huge bags filled with wool, some arriving and others departing— these are the appearances which a wool-warehouse presents. It may, perhaps, not be wholly unnecessary to observe that the sheep's wool here spoken of is only that portion which is taken from the pelt or skin of the slaughtered animal, and which is known by the name of skin-wool. The portion which is taken from the animal during life, and which is called 'shear wool,' possesses qualities in some respects different from the former, and passes through various hands. As very few sheep are sheared near London, the shear-wool is not, generally speaking, brought into the London market, except that which comes from abroad."

Russell Street, in which we have now found ourselves, perpetuates the name of a somewhat eccentric individual who lived in Bermondsey in the latter part of the last century—Mr. Richard Russell, who died at his house in this parish, in September, 1784. In Manning and Bray's "History of Surrey" we read that he was a bachelor, that he desired to be buried in the church of St. John, Horselydown, and that "he left, amongst other legacies, to the Magdalen Hospital, £3,000; to the Small-pox Hospital, £3,000; to the Lying-in Hospital, near Westminster Bridge, £3,000; to the Surrey Dispensary, £500; for a monument in St. John's Church, £2,000; to each of six young women to attend as pall-bearers at his funeral, £50; to four other young women to precede his corpse and strew flowers whilst the 'Dead March' in *Saul* was played by the organist of St. John's, each £20; to the Rev. Mr. Grose, for writing his epitaph, £100 (originally to Dr. Johnson, but by a codicil altered to Mr. Grose); all the residue to the Asylum for Young Girls, in Lambeth (supposed to be about £15,000); eight acting magistrates of Surrey to attend the funeral. The executors were Sir Joseph Mawbey, Samuel Gillam, Thomas Bell, and William Leavis, Esquires. There had not been anything apparent in the life of this person to entitle him to any particular respect, and the pompous funeral prepared for him produced no small disorder." As regards the monument to the memory of the deceased in St. John's Church, it may be stated that the provisions of his will were not complied with, but that his executors are said to have considered a payment which they made to the Rev. Mr. Peters, for a painting of the patron saint of the church over the altar, as an equivalent compensation.

In Russell Street is St. Olave's Union, which consists of some extensive ranges of buildings, forming a large square court, and covering a considerable space of ground. It affords a home for a large number of poor persons, worn out with age, or otherwise incapacitated from earning their livelihood.

Retracing our steps through Bermondsey Street, and by Star Corner, we make our way to the south side of the Grange Road, mentioned above. Here we again encounter evidences of the manufacturing industry of Bermondsey, in the shape of its tan-yards—another of the numerous branches of trade arising out of the leather manufacture, which gives to Bermondsey so many of its characteristics. In Willow Walk, and one or two other places in the vicinity, may be seen instances of one of the purposes to which tan is appropriated. A large plot of ground contains, in addition to heaps of tan, skeleton frames about five or six feet in height, consisting of a range of shelves one above another ; and on these shelves are placed the oblong, rectangular pieces of " tan-turf," with which the middle classes have not much to do, but which are extensively purchased for fuel, at " ten or twelve for a penny," by the humbler classes.

" All the tanneries in London, with, we believe, one exception," says Charles Knight, " are situated in Bermondsey, and all present nearly the same features. Whoever has resolution enough to brave the appeals to his organ of smell, and visit one of these places, will see a large area of ground— sometimes open above, and in other cases covered by a roof—intersected by pits or oblong cisterns, whose upper edges are level with the ground. These cisterns are the tan-pits, in which hides are exposed to the action of liquid containing oak-bark. He will see, perhaps, in one corner of the premises, a heap of ox and cow-horns, just removed from the hide, and about to be sold to the comb-makers, the knife-handle makers, and other manufacturers. He will see in another corner a heap of refuse matter about to be consigned to the glue-manufacturer. In a covered building he will find a heap of hides exposed to the action of lime, for loosening the hair with which the pelt is covered ; and in an adjoining building he will probably see a number of men scraping the surfaces of the hides to prepare them for the tan-pits. In many of the tanneries, though not all, he will see stacks of spent tan, no longer useful in the tannery, but destined for fuel or manure, or gardeners' hot-beds. In airy buildings he will see the tanned leather hanging up to dry, disposed in long ranges of rooms or galleries. Such are the features which all the tanneries, with some minor differences, exhibit."

Between Willow Walk and the Old Kent Road, and stretching away from Page's Walk on the north-west to Upper Grange Road on the south-east, is the Bricklayers' Arms Station, the principal luggage and goods depôt of the South-Eastern Railway. In the station itself, from an architectural point of view, there is nothing requiring special mention. The arrangements for the reception and delivery of the goods at this station are in nowise remarkable, nor are there any warehouses or stores worthy of particular notice. The site was purchased by the South-Eastern Railway Company in 1843, and the lines of railway laid across the market-gardens of Bermondsey, in order to form a junction with the main line near New Cross. Besides being used as a heavy goods depôt, the Bricklayers' Arms Station was for many years—in fact, until the erection of the station at Charing Cross—used as the terminus for the arrival and departure of foreign potentates visiting this country, and also for members of our own Royal Family going abroad. Hither the body of the Duke of Wellington was brought by rail from Walmer Castle, in 1852, in order to be conveyed to Chelsea Hospital, preparatory to its interment in St. Paul's Cathedral.

It is mentioned in the histories of England that shortly after the battle of Edgehill the Common Council of London passed an act for fortifying the City, which was done with such dispatch, that a rampart, with bastions, redoubts, and other bulwarks, was shortly erected round the cities of London and Westminster and the borough of Southwark. It has been suggested that Fort Road —the thoroughfare running parallel with Blue Anchor Road, on the south side, from Upper Grange Road to St. James's Road—may mark the site of some of the fortifications here referred to.

A glance at a map of London of half a century ago—or, indeed, much more recently—will show that nearly the whole of the land hereabouts consisted of market-gardens and open fields. At a short distance eastward of the Upper Grange Road, and south of the Blue Anchor Road, stood a windmill, the site of which is now covered by part of Lynton Road. On the east side of the abbey enclosures was the farm known as " The Grange," after which the Grange Road and Grange Walk are named ; and near the Grange wound the narrow tide-stream or ditch called the Neckinger, which was here spanned by a bridge. The Neckinger was formerly navigable, for small craft, from the Thames to the abbey precincts, and gives name to the Neckinger Road. When the abbey was destroyed, and the ground passed into the possession of others, the houses which were built on the site still received a supply of water from this water-course. In process of time tanneries were established on the spot, most probably on account of the valuable supply of fresh water obtainable every twelve hours from the river. "There appears reason to believe," says Charles Knight, "that the Neckinger was by degrees made to supply other ditches, or small water-courses, cut in different directions, and placed in communication with it; for, provided they were all nearly on a of water from the river, at every high tide, was confirmed to the discomfiture of the mill-owner. Since that period there were occasional disagreements between the manufacturers and the owners of the mill respecting the closing of sluice-gates, the repair and cleansing of the ditch, and the construction of wooden bridges across it; but the tide, with few exceptions, still continued to flow daily to and fro from the Thames to the neighbour-

BRIDGE AND TURNPIKE IN THE GRANGE ROAD, ABOUT 1820.

level, each high tide would as easily fill half a dozen as a single one. Had there been no mill at the mouth of the channel, the supply might have gone on continuously; but the mill continued to be moved by the stream, and to be held by parties who neither had nor felt any interest in the affairs of the Neckinger manufacturers. Disagreements thence arose; and we find that, towards the end of the last century, the tanners of the central parts of Bermondsey instituted a suit against the owner of the mill for shutting off the tide when it suited his own purpose so to do to the detriment of the leather manufacturers. The ancient usages of the district were brought forward in evidence, and the result was that the right of the inhabitants to a supply hood of the Grange and Neckinger Roads. Many of the largest establishments in Bermondsey were for years dependent on the tide-stream for the water—very abundant in quantity—required in the manufacture of leather. Other manufacturers, however, constructed artesian wells on their premises, while the mill at the mouth of the stream was worked by steam power, so that the channel itself became much less important than in former times. Latterly this ditch, or 'tide-stream,' as it was sometimes called, was under the management of commissioners, consisting of the principal manufacturers, who were empowered to levy a small rate for its maintenance and repair."

The Neckinger Mills, which cover a large space of ground between the Neckinger Road and the

GARDEN FRONT OF JAMAICA HOUSE.   CHERRY GARDEN STREET, WITH JAMAICA HOUSE.
(*From Original Drawings*, 1826.)

South-Eastern Railway, were erected a century or more ago by a company who attempted the manufacture of paper from straw; but this failing, the premises passed into the hands of others who established the leather manufacture.

An attempt was made in the latter part of the last century to raise Bermondsey to the dignity of a fashionable watering-place. Although that portion of the district near the river was so close and filthy, there were, as stated above, pleasant fields stretching away towards the Kent Road. The abbot's fat meadows were still green; and, indeed, a singular characteristic of the eastern parts of Bermondsey to this day (especially notice-able from the railway) is the strange mingling of factories, in which the most offensive trades are vigorously carried on, with market-gardens and green fields. In 1770 a chalybeate spring was discovered in some grounds adjoining the Grange Road, of which advantage was taken by the proprietor with the view of inducing the water-drinkers and the lovers of a fashionable lounge and promenade to resort thither, and in that manner caused this district to become for a brief interval what Hampstead* had just ceased to be—a favourite suburban watering-place. In the *Era Almanac*, for 1870, it is stated that a public-house called the "Waterman's Arms" having become vacant, an artist, Mr. Thomas Keyse, purchased it, in 1766, along with some adjoining grounds, and formed it for the amusements of a "tea-garden." He ornamented it with his own paintings, and the discovery in the grounds of a mineral spring, which was found to be an excellent chaly-beate, so increased the attractions of the gardens that Bermondsey found the word "Spa" added to its name. On application to the Surrey magis-trates in 1784, Mr. Keyse obtained a licence for music at his gardens, and this, with an ex-penditure of £4,000 on their decorations, gave them a considerable popularity. The space before the orchestra, which was about a quarter of the size of that at Vauxhall, was totally destitute of trees, the few that the gardens could then boast being planted merely as a screen to prevent the outside public from overlooking the interior of the place. The paintings executed by Keyse himself long existed, and were exhibited in an oblong room known as the "Picture Gallery;" they were chiefly representations of a butcher's shop, a green-grocer's shop, and so forth, all the details being worked out with Dutch minuteness.

Mr. J. T. Smith, in his "Book for a Rainy Day,"

tells us how, on one occasion, he was induced to pay a visit to this place, and how, when he reached the "Picture Gallery," he at first considered him-self the only spectator. When he had gone the round of the gallery he voluntarily re-commenced his view, but what followed will be best told in Mr. Smith's own words:—"Stepping back to study the picture of the 'Green-stall,' 'I ask your pardon,' said I, for I had trodden upon some one's toes. 'Sir, it is granted,' replied a little thick-set man, with a round face, arch look, and closely-curled wig, surmounted by a small three-cornered hat put very knowingly on one side, not unlike Hogarth's head in his print of the 'Gates of Calais.' 'You are an artist, I presume; I noticed you from the end of the gallery, when you first stepped back to look at my best picture. I painted all the objects in this room from nature and still life.' 'Your "Green-grocer's Shop,"' said I, 'is inimitable; the drops of water on that savoy appear as if they had just fallen from the element. Van Huysum could not have pencilled them with greater delicacy.' 'What do you think,' said he, 'of my "Butcher's Shop?"' 'Your pluck is bleeding fresh, and your sweetbread is in a clean plate.' 'How do you like my bull's eye?' 'Why, it would be a most excellent one for Adams or Dollond to lecture upon. Your knuckle of veal is the finest I ever saw.' 'It's young meat,' replied he; 'any one who is a judge of meat can tell that from the blueness of its bone.' 'What a beautiful white you have used on the fat of that Southdown leg! or is it Bagshot?' 'Yes,' said he, 'my solitary visitor, it is Bagshot; and as for my white, that is the best Nottingham, which you or any artist can procure at Stone and Puncheon's, in Bishopsgate Street Within. Sir Joshua Reynolds,' continued Mr. Keyse, 'paid me two visits. On the second, he asked me what white I had used; and when I told him, he observed, "It's very extra-ordinary, sir, how it keeps so bright; I use the same." "Not at all, sir," I rejoined: "the doors of this gallery are open day and night; and the admission of fresh air, together with the great ex-pansion of light from the sashes above, will never suffer the white to turn yellow. Have you not observed, Sir Joshua, how white the posts and rails on the public roads are, though they have not been re-painted for years?—that arises from con-stant air and bleaching." Come,' said Mr. Keyse, putting his hand upon my shoulder, 'the bell rings, not for prayers, nor for dinner, but for the song.' As soon as we had reached the orchestra the singer curtsied to us, for we were the only persons in the gardens. 'This is sad work,' said he, 'but the woman must sing, according to our

---

contract.' I recollect that the singer was handsome, most dashingly dressed, immensely plumea, and villanously rouged; she smiled as she sang, but it was not the bewitching smile of Mrs. Wrighten, then applauded by thousands at Vauxhall Gardens. As soon as the Spa lady had ended her song, Keyse, after joining me in applause, apologised for doing so, by observing that as he never suffered his servants to applaud, and as the people in the road (whose ears were close to the cracks in the paling to hear the song) would make a bad report if they had not heard more than the clapping of one pair of hands, he had in this instance expressed his reluctant feelings. As the lady retired from the front of the orchestra, she, to keep herself in practice, curtsied to me with as much respect as she would had Colonel Topham been the patron of a gala-night. 'This is too bad,' again observed Mr. Keyse, 'and I am sure you cannot expect fireworks!' However, he politely asked me to partake of a bottle of Lisbon, which upon my refusing, he pressed me to accept of a catalogue of his pictures. Blewitt, the scholar of Jonathan Battishill, was the composer for the Spa establishment. The following verse is perhaps the first of his most admired composition:—

     " ' In lonely cot, by Humber's side.' "

A large picture model of the "Siege of Gibraltar," painted by Keyse, and occupying about four acres, was exhibited here in the year 1784. Keyse died about sixteen years later, and their popularity having waned away, the gardens were shut up in 1804, leaving the modern Spa Road to perpetuate their name. There are a few "tokens" of the place extant; and the locality is also kept in remembrance by the "Spa Road" Station on the Greenwich Railway.

"What was once the suburbs of London," says the author of " Walks round London " (1832), " but which now forms an integral part of the town itself, was, in days long gone by, famous for its wells, of real or imaginary virtues. Springs, or holy wells, generally had their existence near some abbey, monastery, or religious house, and often formed no trifling addition to the revenues of the pious dwellers in those edifices. These wells have, with few exceptions, sunk into total disuse. In the south there was the long famous Bermondsey Spa. In the east was Holy Well, which has given its name to a neighbourhood. Not far distant was St. Agnes-le-Clair, still resorted to as a bath. On the northern side of the metropolis is Chad's Well, in Gray's Inn Road; Islington Spa, still of some account, and where in 1733 the Princesses Caroline and Amelia are said to have drank the waters; Bagnigge Wells, and Clerk's, or Clerkenwell—all famous in their day. A second Holy Well was near the Strand, and many others have sunk into oblivion."

At the corner of Neckinger and Spa Roads are some public baths and wash-houses. These institutions, which are now to be met with in almost every part of London, as well as in the country, originated in a public meeting held at the Mansion House in 1844, when a large subscription was raised to build an establishment to serve as a model for others, which it was anticipated would be erected, when it had been proved that the receipts, at the very low rate of charge contemplated, would be sufficient to cover the expenses, and gradually to repay the capital invested. The great need which existed for such means of cleanliness among the industrial classes is testified by the numbers who have used them.

Close by stands the new Town Hall, built in 1881-2. It is in the Renaissance style, freely adapted to modern requirements.

At the junction of Neckinger Road with the Jamaica Road is Parker's Row, at the southern end of which stands Christ Church, a brick-built edifice, of Romanesque architecture, erected in 1848. It was built chiefly out of the Southwark Church and School Fund. At the north-western corner of Parker's Row is a large Roman Catholic church and convent. "It is a curious circumstance," writes Charles Knight, in his work quoted above, "and one in which the history of many changes of opinion may be read, that within forty years after what remained of the magnificent ecclesiastical foundation of the abbey of Bermondsey had been swept away, a new conventual establishment rose up, amidst the surrounding desecration of factories and warehouses, in a large and picturesque pile, with its stately church, fitted in every way for the residence and accommodation of thirty or forty inmates—the Convent of the Sisters of Mercy." This edifice, then, which was founded in 1839, was the first convent of the Sisters of Mercy established in the metropolis. The convent adjoins the Roman Catholic Church of the Most Holy Trinity, which was built from the designs of Mr. A. W. Pugin. The first stone of the church was laid in 1834, by Dr. Bramston, the then Vicar-Apostolic of the London district, and it was formally opened in the following year. The church is a fine brick-built structure, in the Early Pointed style of Gothic architecture. The plot of ground on which it stands was purchased at the expense of a benevolent lady, the Baroness

Montesquieu, who also bought and furnished a well-built house adjoining.

The convent of the Sisters of Mercy is also in the Gothic style of architecture, in keeping with the church. Lady Barbara Eyre contributed no less than £1,000 towards its erection. Considerable additions were made to the edifice in 1876-7. In addition to a large school conducted by the "religious" of Our Lady of Mercy, there are four other numerously-attended Roman Catholic schools in this district.

The edifice mentioned above was erected on a site which had previously served as a tan-yard, supplied with water from the tide-stream, which at one time passed close to the convent in its progress from the "Folly" to the neighbourhood of the Neckinger Mills, of which we have already spoken.

Jamaica Road, which winds eastward in the direction of Rotherhithe and Deptford, is so named from an inn called the "Jamaica," which stood in this immediate neighbourhood, in what is now Cherry Garden Street, down till a comparatively recent date. The house itself, which was named, in compliment, no doubt, to the island which was the birthplace of rum, is traditionally said to have been one of the many residences of Oliver Cromwell, but we cannot guarantee the tradition. It is thus mentioned, in a work published in 1854:—"The building, of which only a moiety now remains, and that very ruinous, the other having been removed years ago to make room for modern erections, presents almost the same features as when tenanted by the Protector. The carved quatrefoils and flowers upon the staircase beams, the old-fashioned fastenings of the doors—bolts, locks, and bars—the huge single gable (which in a modern house would be double), even the divided section, like a monstrous amputated stump, imperfectly plastered over, patched here and there with planks, slates, and tiles, to keep out the wind and weather, though it be very poorly, all are in keeping; and the glimmer of the gas, by which the old and ruinous kitchen is dimly lighted, seems to 'pale its ineffectual fire,' in striving to illuminate the old black settles and still older wainscot." Mr. J. Larwood, in his "History of Sign-boards," tells us that after the Restoration this house became a tavern; and he reminds us how, after the homely, kindhearted custom of the times, Sam Pepys, on Sunday, April 14, 1667, took his wife and her maids there to give them a day's pleasure. "Over the water," writes the Secretary to the Admiralty in his "Diary," "to the Jamaica house, where I never was before, and then the girls did run wagers on the bowling-green, and

there with much pleasure spent but little, and so home." It is added that Pepys appears in after times to have frequently resorted to this place—possibly without madame—and it has been considered by some writers to be the same which he elsewhere terms the "Halfway House," probably in allusion to the dockyard at Deptford. From a reference to modern maps, however, it would appear that the "Halfway House" was about a mile nearer Deptford. A tavern called the "New Jamaica" has been built on the west side of Jamaica Level, near the Jamaica Road and Mill Pond Bridge. At Cherry Garden Stairs, Bermondsey Wall—as that part of the river-side north of the Jamaica Road is called—was an inn bearing the sign of the "Lion and Castle." This sign is often thought to be derived from some of the marriages between our own royal House of Stuart and that of Spain; though, as Mr. Larwood says, we need not accept this version, but may simply refer to "the brand of Spanish arms on the sherry casks, and have been put up by the landlord to indicate the sale of genuine Spanish wines, such as sack, canary, and mountain."

The Cherry Garden itself, the site of which is now covered by a street bearing that name, was a place of public resort in the days of the Stuarts. It is mentioned by Pepys in his "Diary," under date 15th June, 1664: "To Greenwich, and so to the Cherry Garden, and thence by water, singing finely, to the bridge, and there landed." Charles Dickens, too, speaks of the place in one of his inimitable works.

On the south side of Jamaica Road, and at the northern end of Spa Road, stands the parish church of St. James. It is a spacious building of brick and stone. The edifice, which is in the Grecian style, was built in 1829, and consists of a nave and side aisles, with a chancel and vestibules. The west front has a portico in the centre, composed of four Ionic columns, surmounted by an entablature and pediment. The steeple, which rises from the centre of this front, is square in plan, and of four stages or divisions. The spire is crowned with a vane in the form of a dragon. In the tower is a fine peal of ten bells.

Among the recently-built churches of Bermondsey are St. Ann's, Thorburn Square; St. Augustine's, Lynton Road; and St. Crispin's, Southwark Park Road.

Near St. James's Church is the Spa Road Station, on the Deptford and Greenwich Railway. We have already spoken of the formation of this line of railway; but it may not be out of place to add here that few persons are aware of the enormous traffic passing daily in each direction between London Bridge Station and Spa Road, where the railway assumes its greatest width. The accompanying diagram, which represents the number of lines of

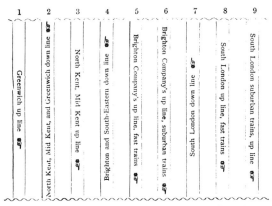

1   2   3   4   5   6   7   8   9

Greenwich up line

North Kent, Mid Kent, and Greenwich down line

North Kent, Mid Kent up line

Brighton and South-Eastern down line

Brighton Company's up line, fast trains

Brighton Company's up line, suburban trains

South London down line

South London up line, fast trains

South London suburban trains, up line

RAILWAY LINES THROUGH BERMONDSEY, LOOKING EASTWARD.*

railway seen at a point about a mile east of the London Bridge Station, will give some idea of what this traffic really is. A passenger travelling over this particular spot will see eight lines of rails, besides the one on which he is travelling, and over nearly all these lines trains are constantly passing. This is more than double the width of any other railway in England, the utmost number of pairs of rails seen elsewhere being four. The line numbered No. 1 is the up line from Greenwich, which, to avoid crossing from side to side at a point more distant, is on the left hand instead of the right; the down line to Greenwich being the same as that used for the North Kent, Mid Kent, &c. (No. 2). No. 3 is the North Kent and Mid Kent up line. Over No. 4 run the main line and many of the suburban down trains of the Brighton Company, as well as a few trains of the South-Eastern Company. No. 7 is the South London down line to Victoria, Sutton, &c. Till about the year 1868, when the South London line was opened, there were six lines of rails running side by side for the first mile and a half from London Bridge. The South London first branches off on the right, and at some distance lower down Nos. 4, 5, and 6 diverge from Nos, 1, 2, 3; and a short distance farther, the North Kent line parts company with the Greenwich, which for the rest of the distance pursues its course alone to Deptford and Greenwich. Between 6.0 a.m. and 12.0 midnight, over line No. 2 pass daily about 48 trains to Greenwich, about 20 for the Mid Kent Branch,

---

* The ☞ indicates the direction in which each train is proceeding.

about 82 for the North Kent line, and about 40 of the South-Eastern main line trains : total, with engines and empties, 227. Over No. 4, during the same period, the South-Eastern and Brighton and South-Coast Companies run 119 trains and 59 engines and empties. Over No. 7 also about 100 trains pass to Victoria, *via* Peckham, and also to Wimbledon, Sutton, Croydon, and Clapham Junction, &c. Thus, without reckoning the extra trains on Saturdays, we have the astonishing number of 500 trains running daily, in one direction, over three lines of railway for comparatively short distances ; and if to this number we add the return trains running over lines Nos. 1, 3, 5, 6, 8, 9, we have more than 1,000 trains running for the accommodation of persons residing principally in the southern suburbs of London.

In Drummond Road, close by St. James's Church, is the biscuit factory of Messrs. Peek, Frean, and Co. The manufactory covers a large space of ground immediately on the north side of the railway, near the Spa Road Station. It comprises several high blocks of buildings, for the most part connected with each other, and gives employment to a very large number of hands. In the centre of the building is a lofty clock-tower.

The Blue Anchor Road—so named from a tavern bearing that sign, at the corner of Blue Anchor Lane—commences at the Grange Road, and winding in a north-easterly direction under the railway, and so on to the end of the Jamaica Road, forms the boundary between the parishes of Bermondsey and Rotherhithe. In a map of London and its environs, published in 1828, and also in Coghlan's map (1834), the whole of this thoroughfare, which in those times had but few houses built along it, is marked as "Blue Anchor Road ;" but in the Post Office Directory of the present day, that part of the road lying northward of the railway is called "Jamaica Level," the west side being entered as belonging to the parish of Bermondsey, and the east side to that of Rotherhithe. In the maps above mentioned a narrow roadway running eastward across the market-gardens is marked as the "Galley Wall." This thoroughfare, which diverges from the Blue Anchor Road at the point where the latter passes under the railway, is now almost entirely built upon on both sides, and has been for many years known as the Manor Road. In the early part of the year 1877, however, the Commissioners of the Board of Works caused it to resume its original name of "Galley Wall." What may have been the origin of that name it is now somewhat difficult to decide. Close by the eastern end of this roadway there was till within the last few years a narrow canal or ditch winding its sluggish course from the Thames, across the Deptford Road, and through the fields and market-gardens, in a south-westerly direction. This ditch, although for the most part now filled up and obliterated, is the boundary line separating the counties of Kent and Surrey.

was employed in making the 'great wet dock at Rotherhithe' in the year 1694, and who remembered that in the course of that work a considerable body of fagots and stakes were discovered," which Maitland considers as "part of the works intended to strengthen the banks of the canal." Allen adds, in his "History of London," a remark to the effect that "it is allowed by many eminent antiquaries that there might have been such a

ST. JAMES'S CHURCH, BERMONDSEY.

It is said by historians that in order to reduce London, Knute cut a trench or canal through the marshes on the south of the Thames ; and Maitland considered that he had discovered its course, from its "influx into the Thames at the lower end of Chelsea Reach" through the Spring Garden at Vauxhall, by the Black Prince at Kennington, and the south of Newington Butts, and across the Deptford Road, to its "outflux where the great wet dock below Rotherhithe is situated."

It is quite possible that Maitland was rather credulous, like many other antiquaries and topographers ; though certainly it ought to be added that he does not "speak without book," but honestly gives his authority ; for he says that he "inquired of a carpenter named Webster, who

water-course as Maitland describes from the wet dock at Deptford round by St. Thomas à Watering and Newington Butts, quite up to Vauxhall, and into the Thames at Chelsea Reach." It has been suggested that the ditch here referred to may have been the same which we have mentioned above as passing by the end of Galley Wall ; and that there may have been near this spot, in very remote times, a "wall" or landing-stage for the shipment of merchandise from the ancient "galleys." The trade of the Venetians in the spices and other merchandise which they brought overland from India and sent to London in their "galleys" has passed away ; and few are reminded by the name of "Galley Quay," in Thames Street, that their proud argosies were once accustomed to ride at anchor there. It is just possible that there may have been a similar quay—or galley wall—at this spot for the use of the inhabitants of the south side of the Thames.

It may be here remarked that in the early part in a summer evening indulge in an hour or two of delightful musing and wholesome promenade." The locality here referred to lies about midway between Long Lane and Kent Street, near the junction of Baalzephon and Hunter Streets.

ROTHERHITHE CHURCH, 1750. (*See page* 136.)

of the present century there were pleasant walks about the Kent Road and Bermondsey where we should now look in vain for rural enjoyments. The favourite route from Southwark to the Old Kent Road was by way of the Halfpenny Hatch, the name of which is still retained, though the poplars and willows, and airy walks by the side of the small canals, are no more. "It is," writes an enthusiastic cockney of our grandfathers' times, "a delightful spot, where the pensive mind may

We may remark here, by way of a conclusion to this chapter, that Bermondsey and Rotherhithe are both well matched in point of filth, dirt, and unsavoury smells with their neighbour across the river—Wapping. But squalid as is their general appearance, they abound in wealth, the fruits of industry and labour, no inconsiderable portion of it their own, while the remainder is stored up and warehoused within their boundaries for the convenience of their richer neighbours.

CHAPTER XI.

ROTHERHITHE.

" Farewell to Kent-street garrison,
Farewell to Horsly-down,
And all the smirking wenches
That dwell in Redriff town."
Roxburgh Ballads—" The Merry Man's Resolutions."

Derivation of the Name of Rotherhithe—The Place frequently called Redriff—Knut's Trench—History of the Descent of the Manor—Traditional Visit of Charles II. to Rotherhithe—Dreadful Fire in Rotherhithe—Condition of Rotherhithe at the Commencement of the Present Century Mill Pond—Vineyards in Rotherhithe—Southwark Park—The "Halfpenny Hatch"—China Hall—The "Dog and Duck"—St. Mary's Church—Christ Church—All Saints' Church—St. Barnabas Church—The Skeleton of a Giant—Spread of Education in Rotherhithe and Bermondsey—Noted Residents in Rotherhithe—St. Helena Tea-gardens—The Thames Tunnel—The Commercial Docks, and the Grand Surrey Canal—Cuckold's Point—The King and the Miller's Wife.

ROTHERHITHE, or, as it is occasionally called, "Redriff," is worthy of note as the first place where docks were constructed for the convenience of London. The parish adjoins Bermondsey on the east, and extends along the southern shore of the Thames as far as Deptford. The compiler of the "New View of London," published in 1708, considers Rotherhithe as "equivalent to 'Red Rose Haven,' probably from some such sign being there, as 'Rother' Lane (now called Pudding Lane) had that name from the sign of a red rose there." Northouck, too, supports this view, telling us that the name of the place was formerly Red Rose Hithe, "from the sign of the Red Rose." Maitland, however, with greater reason, supposes the name to be of Saxon origin, and that it was derived from the two words, *redhra*, a mariner, and *hyth*, a haven. *Hithe*, or *hythe*, as is well known, is a common name for the lower port or haven of maritime towns, such as Colchester, Southampton, &c. Rotherhithe, we may remark, was chiefly inhabited a hundred years ago, as now, by seafaring persons and tradesmen whose business depended on seamen and shipping. The place is summarily dispatched in the "Ambulator" for 1774, in the following terms :—" Rotherhith (*sic*), vulgarly called Rederiff, was anciently a village on the south-east of London, though it is now joined on to Southwark, and as it is situated along the south bank of the Thames, is chiefly inhabited by masters of ships and other seafaring people." It will be remembered that Gay, in the *Beggar's Opera*, makes mention of the place in the following lines :—

Filch. These seven handkerchiefs, madam.

Mrs. Peachum. Coloured ones, I see. They are of sure sale, from our warehouse at Redriff among the seamen.

The place appears to have gone by the name of Redriff as long ago as the reign of Edward I. It is frequently mentioned by Pepys in his "Diary," and always by the appellation of Redriff.

It was at Rotherhithe that King Knut is said to have begun his famous trench to Vauxhall, for the purpose of laying siege to London, as stated in a previous chapter.* The channel through which the tide of the Thames was turned in the year when London Bridge was first built of stone, is supposed by Stow and by several antiquaries to have followed the same course, though many writers have dissented from this view.

In a grant of the time of Edward III., by which Constance, then Prior of Bermondsey, assigned certain messuages to the king, the name is spelt "Rethereth." At the time of the Domesday survey the place was included in the royal manor of Bermondsey; but Henry I. granted part of it to his natural son Robert, Earl of Gloucester. In the reign of Edward III. one of the two manors into which Rotherhithe was divided belonged to the Abbey of St. Mary of Grace, on Tower Hill; but in the following year it was devised to the convent of St. Mary Magdalen, at Bermondsey, whose sisterhood already possessed that portion of the other manor which had not been given to the Earl of Gloucester. About the middle of the fifteenth century the manor appears to have come into possession of the Lovel family. It was at this time a place of some note. In the reign of Edward III. a fleet had been fitted out there by order of the Black Prince and John of Gaunt. Afterwards Henry IV. resided there in an old stone house, when afflicted with leprosy; he is said to have dated two charters thence. The Lovel family highly distinguished themselves during the wars of the Roses, on the Lancastrian side. When Richard of Gloucester ascended the throne, Francis Lord Lovel was made Lord Chamberlain, and so great was his influence with his royal master that he was joined with Catesby and Ratcliffe in the familiar couplet—

" The Cat, the Rat, and Lovel the Dog
Rule all England under a Hog;"

* See *ante*, pp. 4 and 132.

Richard's emblem, the boar, being of course intended by the last-named animal. Lovel fought well at Bosworth, and was fortunate enough to escape to Burgundy after the defeat. He returned in the following year, and, in conjunction with Lord Stafford, raised forces in Worcestershire, which the king's troops, commanded by the Duke of Bedford, soon dispersed. Lovel re-appeared on the scene in May, 1487, with the Germans, under command of the Earl of Lincoln and Martin Swartz, who came over to support the claims of Lambert Simnel. They were defeated at Stoke-upon-Trent, and the Earl of Lincoln, with 4,000 of his men, was killed. Lovel escaped, but his fate is uncertain. Holinshed says he was slain, but many years afterwards a skeleton was discovered hidden away in the old manor-house of Minster Lovel, which, from the remains of the dress and other circumstances, was supposed to be that of the great Lord Lovel, who had hidden from pursuit, and was starved to death.

In 1516, Lovel being dead and gone, the Bermondsey monks claimed the manor of Rotherhithe, and gained it; but they did not long enjoy their possession, for in the year 1538 it was surrendered to the king, and remained royal property till Charles I. granted it to Sir Allen Apsley.

We hear and read but little of Rotherhithe during the next century or so. It is true that there is a dim and misty tradition of Charles II. on one occasion having made a frolicsome excursion to this neighbourhood; but probably that was a very exceptional case, his Majesty's frolics being mostly restricted to the Court quarter of the town; or, if he crossed the river, it was mostly in the direction of Lambeth and Vauxhall. Evelyn records in his "Diary," under date June 11, 1699, a dreadful fire near the Thames side here, which destroyed nearly 300 houses, and burnt also "divers ships." On the 1st of June, 1765, another terrible fire, caused by a pitch-kettle boiling over, broke out in Princes Street, Rotherhithe, and before it could be extinguished more than 200 houses, besides warehouses and other buildings, were entirely consumed, reducing at least 250 families to the most terrible distress. This conflagration was doubtless of some service in clearing the close mass of ill-built houses, and causing the erection of a better class of edifices.

At the beginning of the present century Rotherhithe consisted of a few streets, with good gardens to the houses, extending from the Blue Anchor Road (the boundary between Bermondsey and Rotherhithe) to Hanover Street, beyond which were marshes intersected by sluggish, dirty streams.

The southern limit of the houses followed the line of Paradise Street and Adam Street, leading from Blue Anchor Road to the end of the Deptford Lower Road. Blue Anchor Road (the river end of which was called West Lane) ran southwards, skirting the dirty streams and stagnant pools of Milford, to the end of Rogue's Lane, which ran through marshy fields to the "Halfway House," past the "St. Helena" tavern and tea-gardens. Near the "Halfway House"—which, by the way, was a neighbourhood noted as a resort of footpads—at the top of Trundley's Lane stood a few houses, still existing, and named Mildmay Houses. There were a few plots of market-garden ground here and there to be seen, near the spot now occupied by the Grand Surrey Docks, and adjoining Globe Stairs Alley, in the Blue Anchor Road; but the greater portion of the entire district between Rotherhithe and the Kent Road consisted of marshy fields. Mill Pond was the name given to a number of tidal ditches—not unlike those of Jacob's Island—which intersected the space between Blue Anchor Road and the Deptford Lower Road. A larger stream discharged itself into the Thames at King's Mill; but that disappeared when the Grand Surrey Docks were constructed. Within the last half century the inhabitants of the streets around Mill Pond were dependent upon these dirty tidal ditches for their supply of water, which was fetched in pails. Of late years, however, Mill Pond has been drained away, and rows of houses, some known as Jamaica Level, occupy the site.

Few Londoners, at first sight, would suspect Rotherhithe of having a soil or situation well suited to the growth of vines; but such would appear to have been once the case, if we may believe Hughson, who tells us, in his "History and Survey of London and its Suburbs," that an attempt was made in 1725, in East Lane, within this parish, to restore the cultivation of the vine, which, whether from the inauspicious climate of our island, or from want of skill in the cultivation, was at that time nearly lost, though there are authentic documents to prove that vineyards* did flourish in this country in ancient times. It appears that about the time indicated a gentleman named Warner, observing that the Burgundy grapes ripened early, and conceiving that they might be grown in England, obtained some cuttings, which he planted here as standards; and Hughson records the fact that though the soil was not particularly suited, yet, by care and skill, he was rewarded by success, and

---

* See Vol. IV., p. 4.

that his crop was so ample that it afforded him upwards of one hundred gallons annually, and that he was enabled to supply cuttings of his vines for cultivation in many other parts of this island.

At about the middle of that part of the Blue Anchor Road which is now called Jamaica Level, are the gates and lodge-house of Southwark Park, which stretches away eastward to Rotherhithe New Road, and northward to the Union Road and Deptford Lower Road, in each of which thoroughfares there are entrances. The park, which covers about seventy acres of ground, was laid out and opened in 1869, under the auspices of the Metropolitan Board of Works. It comprises a good open level piece of turf available for cricket—not, perhaps, to be compared with "Lord's"—and also several plots of ground laid out as ornamental flower-gardens, interspersed with shrubs and trees. In one part of the grounds, near the entrance from Jamaica Level, are two mounds formed by the earth which was excavated from under the bed of the river during the construction of the Thames Tunnel.

Before the formation of this park all the land hereabout consisted of fields and market-gardens, some considerable portion of which still exist in the neighbourhood of Rotherhithe and Deptford, in all their freshness. We may remark here that the market-gardening—not only in these parts, but also in the districts near Battersea, Fulham, Hammersmith, and more remote parts—has attained a perfection which renders it a beautiful as well as interesting sight to examine the regularity and richness of the crops, the rapid system of clearing and fresh-cropping, and the mode of preparing and packing the produce for market. Perhaps in no one department has English gardening arrived at more excellence, or is managed with more method and skill, than is to be witnessed in the market-gardens which supply the metropolis.

In former times a narrow pathway, called the "Halfpenny Hatch," extended through the meadows and market-gardens from Blue Anchor Road to the Deptford Lower Road, where it emerged close by an old and much-frequented public-house called the "China Hall." The ancient tavern, which was a picturesque building partly surrounded by an external gallery, was pulled down within the last few years, and in its place has been erected a more modern-looking tavern, bearing the same sign. Our old friend Pepys mentions going to China Hall, but gives us no further particulars. "It is not unlikely," says Mr. Larwood in his "History of Sign-boards," "that this was the same place which, in the summer of 1777, was opened

as a theatre. Whatever its use in former times, it was at that time the warehouse of a paper manufacturer. In those days the West End often visited the entertainments of the East, and the new theatre was sufficiently patronised to enable the proprietors to venture upon some embellishments. The prices were—boxes, 3s.; pit, 2s.; gallery 1s.; and the time of commencing varied from half-past six to seven o'clock, according to the season. *The Wonder, Love in a Village*, the *Comical Courtship*, and the *Lying Valet* were among the plays performed. The famous Cooke was one of the actors in the season of 1778. In that same year the building suffered the usual fate of all theatres, and was utterly destroyed by fire."

The Halfpenny Hatch was continued beyond the "China Hall," across the fields in the rear, to the "Dog and Duck" tavern, near the entrance to the Commercial Docks. Any one patronising the "China Hall," and partaking of refreshment, had the privilege of passing through the "Halfpenny Hatch" without payment of the halfpenny toll.

With respect to the sign of the "Dog and Duck," we need hardly remark that it refers to a barbarous pastime of our ancestors, when ducks were hunted in a pond by spaniels.* The pleasure consisted in seeing the duck make her escape from the dog's mouth by diving. It was much practised in the neighbourhood of London, and particularly in these southern suburbs, till the beginning of this century, when it went out of fashion, as most of the ponds were gradually built over.

The parish church of Rotherhithe is dedicated to St. Mary, and stands not far from the river-side. It is built of brick, with stone quoins, and consists of a nave, chancel, and two aisles, supported with pillars of the Ionic order. At the west end is a square tower, upon which is a stone spire, supported by Corinthian columns. The church was built in the early part of the last century, on the site of an older edifice, which had stood for four hundred years, but which had at length become so ruinous that Parliament was applied to for permission to pull it down. The present church has lately been thoroughly "restored," and the old unsightly pews of our grandfathers' time have been superseded by open benches. In the churchyard lies buried an individual with whose name and affecting history the youth of this country must still be familiar—we refer to Lee Boo, Prince of the Pelew Islands, who died in London from the

---

* See Vol. IV., p. 352.

effects of the small-pox in 1784, when only twenty years of age, after he had learned the manners and studied the civilisation of Europe, with the view of introducing them into his native country. He was the son of Abba Thulle, rupack or king of the island of Coo-roo-raa, one of the Pelew group in the Indian Ocean. In August, 1783, the *Antelope* frigate was wrecked off the island, and so great was the kindness of the king to Captain Wilson and the crew, that the captain offered to take his son to England to be educated. Young Lee Boo, an amiable young man, accordingly visited this country, but died in the following year, as stated above. The epitaph on his tomb concludes with the following couplet:—

> " Stop, reader, stop ! Let Nature claim a tear,
> A Prince of *mine*, Lee Boo, lies buried here."

There are no monuments of any interest within the walls of the church, but in the vestry is preserved a portrait of Charles I. in his robes, kneeling at a table and holding a crown of thorns. This portrait, if we may trust Aubrey's " Antiquities of Surrey," formerly hung in the south aisle of the church. How it came into the possession of the parish is not stated.

The church of Rotherhithe is in the diocese of Rochester, having been transferred to it from that of Winchester. The advowson formerly belonged to the priory of Bermondsey, but after the suppression of that monastery it passed through various hands. In 1721 it was sold to James, Duke of Chandos, of whom it was purchased a few years later by the master and fellows of Clare Hall, Cambridge. There is in the Tower a record of sundry grants to the rector of Rotherhithe. It was " presented " to the commissioners appointed to inquire into the state of ecclesiastical benefices, in 1658, that the rectory of " Redereth " was worth about £92 per annum.

The increase of population, partly owing to the opening of the extensive docks, was accompanied by an addition to the number of churches. In the year 1835 the Commissioners for Building New Churches gave £2,000 towards the erection of two churches, and the trustees of Hyndman's Bounty, a local charity, offered to build a third.

Christ Church, in Union Road, opposite the gates on the north side of Southwark Park, is a plain and unpretending structure, of " debased Gothic " architecture, and dates its erection from about the year 1840. Here was buried in 1875 one of the most distinguished of our veteran generals, Field Marshal Sir William Gomm, Constable of the Tower.

All Saints', in Deptford Lower Road, a Gothic edifice with a tower, surmounted by a lofty spire, was built from the designs of Mr. Kempthorne about the same time as the above, and at a cost of upwards of £3,000. Holy Trinity Church, in the eastern part of the parish, is a spacious edifice, in the Pointed style, capable of accommodating 1,000 persons. This church was consecrated in 1839.

St. Barnabas' Church, a Gothic brick-built edifice, in Plough Road, near the Commercial Docks, was erected mainly through the instrumentality of Sir William Gomm. It was built in 1872, from the designs of Mr. Butterfield.

In the *Weekly Packet*, December 21–28, 1717, we read : " Last week, near the new church at Rotherhithe, a stone coffin of a prodigious size was taken out of the ground, and in it the skeleton of a man ten feet long ; " but this we do not expect our readers to accept as literally true.

A free school was founded in the parish of Rotherhithe about the beginning of the last century, by Peter Hills and Robert Bell, and endowed with a small annual income " for the education of eight sons of seamen, with a salary of three pounds per annum for the master." The school-house, which is situated near St. Mary's Church, was rebuilt by subscription in 1745. Various benefactions have since been made to the school, so that the number of scholars has been considerably increased.

A notice of Bermondsey and Rotherhithe would scarcely be complete without some reference to the educational movement which has of late years sprung up in these parishes, as, indeed, is the case with most other parishes in the metropolis. In the Manor Road, Jamaica Level, Rotherhithe New Road, and other parts, School-Board schools have been erected, which are altogether architectural adornments of the neighbourhood. Before the opening of the " board-schools," it appears that there were in the Southwark district upwards of 42,000 children for whom provision ought to have been made in elementary schools, but that the existing accommodation was wholly inadequate, only about 13,000 children having so much as their names inscribed on the rolls of the inspected schools. But since the erection of the schools above-mentioned large numbers of children have been added to the rolls, and attempts have been made to secure uniformity of fee within each of the schools. The policy of the regulation seems doubtful, since every neighbourhood contains a variety of classes among those depending upon the elementary schools for education, and the schools lie at considerable distances from one another.

"In fixing the uniform fee," as we learn from the report of Her Majesty's Inspector of Schools for this district, "if regard is paid to the best class of the neighbourhood, wrong is done to all with lower incomes who require schooling; but if to the worst, the equitable interests of ratepayers are overlooked. In one of the large School-Board schools the weekly fee is 4d.; in four it is 3d. (including one temporary school); in six it is 2d. (likewise

Jonathan Swift, was born at Rotherhithe, or, as he styles it, "Redriff"—a fact of which Gulliver doubtless boasted to his courtly friends at Lilliput and Brobdingnag. George Lillo, the dramatist, whose play of *George Barnwell* was for many years the stock piece performed at our theatres before the pantomime on Boxing-night, is said to have kept a jeweller's shop at Rotherhithe.

The St. Helena Tea-gardens, in Deptford Road,

DIVING-BELL USED IN THE CONSTRUCTION OF THE THAMES TUNNEL.

including one temporary school); and in two of the new permanent schools, besides several temporary schools, it is 1d."

Between the years 1740 and 1750 the manor of Rotherhithe was held by Admiral Sir Charles Wager. Another renowned admiral, Sir John Leake, was born in this parish in 1656, and was buried here sixty-four years afterwards. "Redriff" also long laid claim to brave old Admiral Benbow as a son of the soil. Allen, in his "History of Surrey," says he "was born in Wintershull Street, now called Hanover Street;" curious biographers, however, have discovered that the stout old sailor first saw the light at Shrewsbury. Another well-known hero, but in a different line of life, Lemuel Gulliver, according to his veracious biographer,

were opened in 1770, and, after undergoing sundry vicissitudes, ceased to exist in 1881, and their site has since been built upon. A newspaper advertisement in May, 1776, announces that there are "tea, coffee, and rolls every day, with music and dancing in the evening." The place was chiefly supported by the lower classes of the neighbourhood, the families of men who worked in the docks. In the summer there were brass bands and dancing platforms, singing, tumbling, and fireworks, for the delectation of the merry souls of "Redriff;" but the place never attained more than a local celebrity, or affected to be a rival of Ranelagh or Vauxhall.

A notice of Rotherhithe would be incomplete without at least some reference to that grand triumph of engineering skill, the Thames Tunnel, connecting Rotherhithe and Wapping. We have already spoken at some length of this great work ;* but, nevertheless, a few more words concerning it may not be out of place here. In 1805 a company was incorporated as the Thames Archway Com-

yet George Stephenson achieved that feat ; and another great engineering genius, Isambard Brunel, happening, about the year 1814, to observe in the dockyard at Chatham the little passages bored through timber by a marine insect, took from it a hint as to the construction of tunnels. In

FLOATING DOCK, DEPTFORD (1820).

pany. A shaft was sunk at Rotherhithe, and a driftway pushed to within 200 feet of the Limehouse shore. Then the water broke in, and the project was given up. More than fifty engineers of eminence declared it to be impracticable to construct a tunnel of any useful size beneath the bed of the Thames. But as much was said afterwards against carrying a railroad across Chat Moss, and

course of time he matured the idea. In 1824 a company was formed, and Brunel set to work, and with his celebrated "shield," an adaptation and imitation of the "teredo," or marine worm, began the great tunnel. There were many mishaps. Twice the water broke in. Then came want of funds, and the work was suspended for seven years. Public subscriptions raised £5,000, and once more Brunel set to work. On the 25th of March, 1843, the tunnel was opened as a public

* See Vol. II., p. 128, *et seq.*

thoroughfare, and the successful engineer was knighted by Queen Victoria. Of the diving-bell used in the construction of the Thames Tunnel we give an illustration on page 138. During the suspension of the work, great doubt was often expressed as to whether the tunnel would ever be completed. Tom Hood wrote an "Ode to M. Brunel," in which occur these lines :—

> "Other great speculations have been nursed,
> Till want of proceeds laid them on the shelf :
> But thy concern, Brunel, was at the worst,
> When it began to *liquidate* itself."

And again—

> "Well ! Monsieur Brunel,
> How prospers now thy mighty undertaking,
> To join by a hollow way the Bankside friends
> Of Rotherhithe and Wapping ?
> Never be stopping ;
> But poking, groping, in the dark keep making
> An archway, underneath the dabs and gudgeons,
> For colliermen and pitchy old curmudgeons,
> To cross the water in inverse proportion,
> Walk under steam-boats, under the keel's ridge,
> To keep down all extortion,
> And with sculls to diddle London Bridge !
> In a fresh hunt a new great bore to worry,
> Thou didst to earth thy human terriers follow,
> Hopeful at last, from Middlesex to Surrey,
> To give us the 'view hollow.'"

We need scarce add that for many years the great work was numbered with the splendid failures connected with the name of Brunel ; and the tunnel, which had cost nearly half a million of money, became converted into little more than a penny show. The roadway, which would have made it available for vehicular traffic, it is stated, would have required nearly £200,000 more, and the money was not forthcoming. As this kind of approach has now been formed, the tunnel may be said to have realised its original purpose, though not in the way designed by Sir M. I. Brunel. In 1871 the tunnel was closed for pedestrians, and converted into a railway in connection with the East London line. This railway passes, by a gradual incline from the station of the Brighton and South-Coast line at New Cross, through the market gardens on the south side of Deptford Lower Road. Near the St. Helena Estate there is a station for the convenience of this rapidly-increasing district. Thence, passing under the roadway, the line skirts the south-west side of the Commercial Docks, and then shortly afterwards finds its level at the mouth of the tunnel, where there is another station, between sixty and seventy feet below the surface of the ground.

Rotherhithe has been for a considerable period celebrated for its docks. The great dry dock here has existed for nearly two centuries, having been opened in 1696 ; the great wet dock was finished in the year 1700. After the bursting of the South Sea Bubble in 1720, the directors took a lease of this dock, where their ships, then engaged in the whale-fisheries of Greenland, landed their cargoes of unfragrant blubber. The docks, known as the Commercial, are still used for the same purposes. Adjoining to them are the Great East Country Dock, and several smaller ones. From the situation of these very extensive docks, which include within their boundaries nearly a hundred acres, of which about eighty are water, they might doubtless be made, now that the trade of the port of London has so wonderfully increased, to rank among the most prosperous establishments of the metropolitan harbour.

The Commercial Docks and Timber Ponds, and also the East Country Dock, are now incorporated with the Grand Surrey Canal Dock, the opening of which into the Thames is about two miles below London Bridge. In the Timber Ponds and East Country Docks, timber, corn, hemp, flax, tallow, and other articles, which pay a small duty, and are of a bulky nature, remain in bond, and the surrounding warehouses are chiefly used as granaries, the timber remaining afloat in the dock until it is conveyed to the yards of the wholesale dealer and the builder. The Surrey Dock is merely an entrance basin to a canal, and can accommodate 300 vessels ; whilst the warehouses, chiefly granaries, will contain about 4,000 tons of goods. The Commercial Docks, a little lower down the river, occupy an area of about forty-nine acres, of which four-fifths are water, and there is accommodation for 350 ships, and in the warehouses for 50,000 tons of merchandise. They were used originally, as stated above, for the shipping employed in the Greenland fishery, and provided with the necessary apparatus for boiling down the blubber of whales ; but the whale fishery being given up, the docks were, about the year 1807, appropriated to vessels engaged in the European timber and corn trade, and ranges of granaries were built. The East Country Dock, which adjoins the Commercial Docks on the south, is capable of receiving twenty-eight timber ships, and was constructed about the same period for like purposes. It has an area of about six acres and a half, and warehouse-room for nearly 4,000 tons.

The various docks and basins embraced in the elaborate system belonging to the Surrey Commercial Dock Company are no less than thirteen in number, and are named respectively the Main Dock, the Stave Dock, the Russia Dock, Quebec Pond, Canada Pond, Albion Pond, Centre Pond,

Lady Dock, Acorn Pond, Island Dock, Norway Dock, Greenland Dock, and South Dock.

In all that concerns the bustle of trade and industry, no capital in the world can compare with London. Foreign travellers, like the Viscount D'Arlingcourt, own that the Neva is in this respect as far below the Thames as it is above it in splendid buildings and scenery. "What can be more wonderful," he asks, "than its docks? Those vast basins, in the midst of which are barracked whole legions of vessels, which the sovereign of maritime cities receives daily? These vessels enter thither from the Thames by a small canal, which opens for their admittance and closes after them. The docks are surrounded by immense warehouses, where all the products of the universe are collected together, and where each ship unloads its wealth. It would be impossible, without seeing it, to fancy the picture presented by these little separate harbours in the midst of an enormous city, where an innumerable population of sailors, shopkeepers, and artisans are incessantly and tumultuously hurrying to and fro."

"In 1558," writes Mr. Charles Knight in his "London," "certain wharfs, afterwards known as the "Legal Quays," were appointed to be the sole landing-places for goods in the port of London. They were situated between Billingsgate and the Tower, and had a frontage of 1,464 feet by 40 wide, and of this space 300 feet were taken up by landing-stairs and by the coasting-trade, leaving, in the year 1796, only 1,164 for the use of the foreign trade. Other wharfs had, it is true, been added from time to time, five of these 'sufferance wharfs,' as they were called, being on the northern side of the river, and sixteen on the opposite side, comprising altogether a frontage of 3,676 feet. The warehouses belonging to the 'sufferance wharfs' were capable of containing 125,000 tons of merchandise, and 78,800 tons could be stowed in the yards. The want of warehouse room was so great that sugars were deposited in warehouses on Snow Hill, and even in Oxford Street. Wine, spirits, and the great majority of articles of foreign produce, especially those on which the higher rates of duties were charged, could be landed only at the Legal Quays. In 1793 sugars were allowed to be landed at the sufferance wharfs, but the charges were higher than at the Legal Quays; extra fees had to be paid to the revenue officers for attendance at them, though at the same time they were inconveniently situated, and at too great a distance from the centre of business. The above concession to the sufferance wharfs was demanded by common

sense and necessity, for the ships entered with sugar increased from 203 in 1756, to 433, of larger dimensions, in 1794. Generally speaking, the sufferance wharfs were used chiefly by vessels in the coasting trade, and for such departments of the foreign trade as could not by any possibility be accommodated at the Legal Quays. Even in 1765 commissions appointed by the Court of Exchequer had reported that the latter were 'not of sufficient extent, from which delays and many extraordinary expenses occur, and obstructions to the due collection of the revenue.' But the commerce of London had wonderfully increased since that time, its progress in the twenty-five years, from 1770 to 1795 having been as great as in the first seventy years of the century." Among the various plans for docks, quays, and warehouses, which were drawn up at the end of the last century, with the view of remedying the evils spoken of above, was one which displayed considerable ingenuity, and consisted, in fact, of four distinct projects: —1. To form a new channel for the river in a straight line from Limehouse to Blackwall; the Long Reach round the Isle of Dogs thus constituting a dock with flood-gates at each entrance. 2. To continue the new channel below Blackwall towards Woolwich Reach, so as to convert another bend of the old channel into a dock. 3. To make a new channel from Wapping, and to form three docks out of the three bends, to be called Ratcliffe Dock, Blackwall Dock, and Greenwich Dock. The Trinity House objected that the King's Dock at Deptford would be injured by the latter plan, on which it was proposed—4. To make a new channel from Wapping to the old channel between Greenland Dock (now the Commercial Docks) and Deptford, thence inclining to the northward until it opened into Woolwich Reach, thus forming two spacious docks out of the bends of the river (above and below) at Blackwall.

The Commercial Docks have an entrance from the Thames, between Randall's Rents and Dog-and-Duck Stairs, nearly opposite the King's Arms Stairs in the Isle of Dogs. They are the property of the Surrey Commercial Dock Company. A considerable extension of their area has been made within the last few years, with a view to meeting the increased requirements of the timber trade in the port of London, by the addition of a new dock which has been named the Canada Dock. It is 1,500 feet in length, 500 feet in width, and has a water area of sixteen acres and a half. It communicates with the Albion Dock by an entrance fifty feet in width, and the quay space around is upwards of twenty-one acres in extent.

On the river side of the Commercial Docks, just below Rotherhithe Church, at the bend in the river forming the commencement of Limehouse Reach, is "Cuckold's Point," which was formerly distinguished by a tall pole with a pair of horns on the top, and concerning which a singular story is told. From this point of the river, lying away to the right above Greenwich, is seen the village of Charlton, with which the tradition is connected. The manor-house there, of which we shall have more to say presently, although built only in the reign of James I., was long called King John's Palace by the country people, who doubtless confounded it with the old palace at Eltham in the vicinity, which, however, was not itself in existence in King John's day. "The Charlton people, however," writes Dr. Mackay in his "Thames and its Tributaries," "cling to King John, and insist that their celebrated Horn Fair, held annually on the 18th of October, was established by that monarch. Lysons, in his 'Environs of London,' mentions it as a vague and idle tradition; and such, perhaps, it is; but, as we are of opinion that the traditions of the people are always worth preserving, we will repeat the legend, and let the reader value it at its proper worth. King John, says the old story, being wearied with hunting on Shooter's Hill and Blackheath, entered the house of a miller at Charlton to repose himself. He found no one at home but the mistress, who was young and beautiful; and being himself a strapping fellow, handsome withal, and with a glosing tongue, he, in a very short time—or as we would say in the present day, in no time—made an impression upon her too susceptible heart. He had just ventured to give the first kiss upon her lips when the miller opportunely came home and caught them. Being a violent man, and feeling himself wounded in the sorest part, he drew his dagger, and rushing at the king, swore he would kill them both. The poet of all time hath said, 'that a divinity doth hedge a king;' but the miller of Charlton thought such proceedings anything but divine, and would no doubt have sent him unannealed into the other world if John had not disclosed his rank. His divinity then became apparent, and the miller, putting up his weapon, begged that at least he would make him some amends for the wrong he had done him. The king consented, upon condition also that he would forgive his wife, and bestowed upon him all the land visible from Charlton to that bend of the river beyond Rotherhithe where the pair of horns are now (1840) fixed upon the pole. He also gave him, as lord of the manor, the privilege of an annual fair on the 18th of

October, the day when this occurrence took place. His envious compeers, unwilling that the fame of this event should die, gave the awkward name of Cuckold's Point to the river boundary of his property, and called the fair 'Horn Fair,' which it has borne ever since." Peter Cunningham, in his "Handbook of London," thus gives his version of the story :—" King John, wearied with hunting on Shooter's Hill and Blackheath, entered the house of a miller at Charlton to refresh and rest himself. He found no one at home but the miller's wife, young, it is said, and beautiful. The miller, it so happened, was earlier in coming home than was usual when he went to Greenwich with his meal; and red and raging at what he saw on his return, he drew his knife. The king being unarmed, thought it prudent to make himself known, and the miller, only too happy to think it was no baser individual, asked a boon of the king. The king consented, and the miller was told to clear his eyes, and claim the long strip of land he could see before him on the Charlton side of the river Thames. The miller cleared his eyes, and saw as far as the point near Rotherhithe.
The king admitted the distance, and the miller was put into possession of the property on one condition—that he should walk annually on that day, the 18th of October, to the farthest bounds of the estate with a pair of buck's horns upon his head." Of this tradition our readers may believe as much, or as little, as they please. "Horn Fair," adds Mr. Cunningham, "is still kept every 18th of October, at the pretty little village of Charlton, in Kent; and the watermen on the Thames at Cuckold's Point still tell the story (with many variations and additions) of the jolly miller and his light and lovely wife." The horns, we need scarcely add, have long disappeared from Cuckold's Point, and the disreputable fair formerly held at Charlton has, fortunately, now become a thing of the past.

Taylor, the "water-poet," makes mention of the above tradition in the following lines :—

"And passing further, I at first observed
That Cuckold's Haven was but badly served :
For there old Time hath such confusion wrought,
That of that ancient place remained nought.
No monumental memorable Horn,
Or tree, or post, which hath those trophies borne,
Was left, whereby posterity may know
Where their forefathers' crests did grow, or show.
Why, then, for shame this worthy port maintain?
Let's have our Tree and Horns set up again,
That passengers may show obedience to it,
In putting off their hats, and homage do it.
But holla, Muse, no longer be offended ;
'Tis worthily repaired and bravely mended."

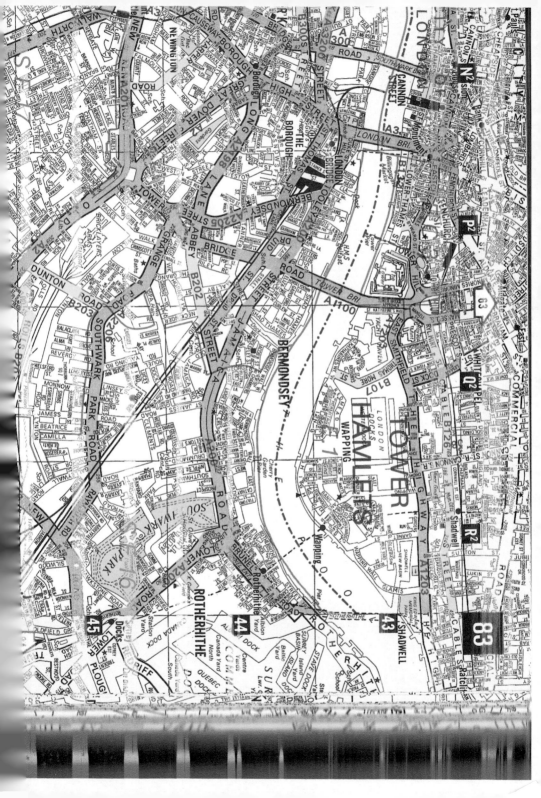

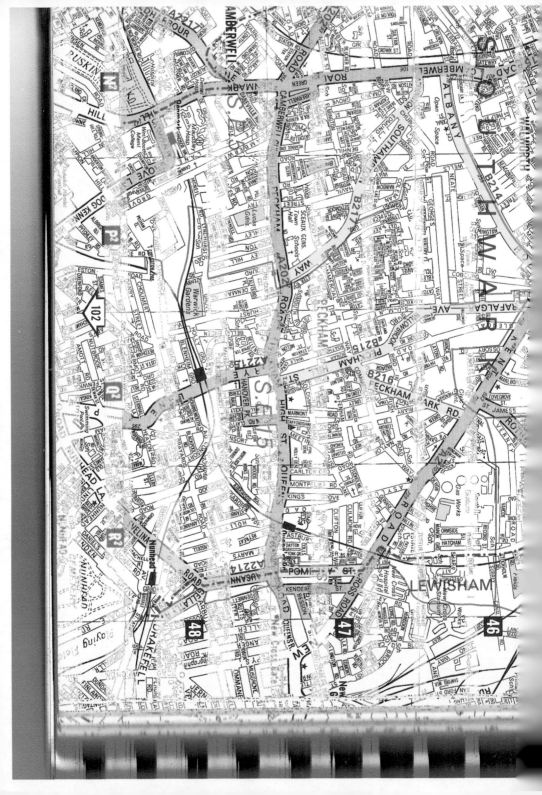

CHAPTER XII.

DEPTFORD.

" Such place hàth Deptford, navy-building town."—*Pope.*

Derivation of the Name of Deptford—Division of the Parish—The River Ravensbourne—The Royal Dockyard—Sir Francis Drake's Ship, the *Golden Hind*—References to Deptford in the Diaries of Evelyn and Pepys—Peter the Great as a Shipwright—Captain Cook's Ships, the *Resolution* and the *Discovery*—Biography of Samuel Pepys—Closing of the Dockyard—The Foreign Cattle-Market—Saye's Court—John Evelyn, the Author of "Sylva"—Evelyn at Home—Grinling Gibbons—Removal of Evelyn to Wotton—Saye's Court let to Admiral Benbow—Peter the Great as a Tenant—Visit of William Penn, the Quaker—Demolition of Saye's Court—Formation of a Recreation-ground on its Site—The Royal Victoria Victualling Yard—The Corporation of the Trinity House—The Two Hospitals belonging to the Trinity House—St. Nicholas' Church—St. Paul's Church—The Roman Catholic Church of the Assumption—St. Luke's Church—The Grand Surrey Canal—Evelyn's Account of the Capture of a Whale at Deptford—Origin of the Sign of the Black Doll.

THE town of Deptford—anciently written Depeford—which lies on the east side of Rotherhithe, and stretches away to Lewisham on the south, and to Greenwich on the east, was, at a very remote period, known as West Greenwich. It derived its present name from being the place of a "deep ford" over the little river, the Ravensbourne, near its influx into the Thames, where a bridge was many years ago built over it, just before it widens into Deptford Creek.

It is described in the "Ambulator," in 1774, as "a large and populous town, divided into Upper and Lower Deptford, and containing two churches." The place was of old famous for its naval shipbuilding yard, a fact which is thus noticed in the work above quoted : "Deptford is most remarkable for its noble dock, where the royal navy was formerly built and repaired, till it was found more convenient to build the larger ships at Woolwich, and at other places, where there is a greater depth of water." Notwithstanding this, the yard is enlarged to more than double its former dimensions, and a vast number of hands are constantly employed. It has a wet dock of two acres for ships, and another with an acre and a half, with vast quantities of timber and other stores, and extensive buildings as storehouses and offices for the use of the place, besides dwelling-houses for the use of those officers who are obliged to live upon the spot in order to superintend the works. Here the royal yachts of our Tudor and Stuart sovereigns were generally kept.

By an Act of Parliament passed in 1730, Deptford was divided into two parishes, distinguished by the names of St. Nicholas and St. Paul. The parish of St. Nicholas, which includes the old town, lies mainly along the river Thames, and the combined parishes have now a population of about 60,000 souls.

According to the author of "Le Guide de l'Etranger à Londres," published in 1827, it is the last *relais* of the traveller by the posting road from Dover to London. He states that it is divided into an upper and lower town, and draws attention to its two churches of St. Nicholas and St. Paul, and to its Royal Marine Arsenal, the creation of Henry VIII., where cables, masts, anchors, &c., are manufactured, and the royal state yachts are kept. He mentions also the Red House to the north of Deptford, the "grand depôt of provisions for the fleet," burnt down in 1639, and again in 1761. The town at that time numbered 17,000 inhabitants.

The change of the name of this place from West Greenwich to that which it now bears, and has borne for some hundreds of years, must, as we have intimated above, have been owing to the "deep ford" by which the inhabitants had to cross the river Ravensbourne here, just above its meeting with the Thames. The ford, however, has long since been superseded by a bridge. This bridge, according to Charles Mackay, in his "Thames and its Tributaries," is memorable in history for the total defeat of Lord Audley and his Cornish rebels in the year 1497. Headed by that nobleman and by a lawyer named Flammock and Joseph, a blacksmith of Bodmin, they had advanced from Taunton with the design of taking possession of London. The Kentish men flocked to their standard, and on their arrival at Blackheath they amounted altogether to about 16,000 men. Lord Daubeny, who had been sent against them by King Henry VII., made a furious attack upon them at Deptford Bridge, and after great slaughter put them to flight. Lord Audley, Flammock, and Joseph were all taken prisoners, and shortly afterwards were executed on Tower Hill, the latter boasting in his hour of death that he died in a just cause, and that he would make a figure in history. Such are the vain and foolish hopes with which low-bred rebels and impostors, from his day to that of the Orton and Tichborne trial, have too often buoyed themselves up.

The little stream of the Ravensbourne, which is here called Deptford Creek, rises upon Keston Heath, near Hayes Common, in Kent, and runs a course of about twelve miles in all, passing Bromley and Lewisham and the southern borders of Blackheath. It was formerly sometimes called the Brome, from Bromley. An old legend is told to account for its romantic name :—" It is said that Julius Cæsar, on his invasion of Britain, was encamped with all his force a few miles distant from its source. The army was suffering a good deal from want of water, and detachments had been sent out in all directions to find a supply, but without any success. Cæsar, however, fortunately observed that a raven frequently alighted near the

account for the name which he found already established by immemorial custom. In some legends we can trace an element of truth ; but in this we fail to discover even "the shadow of a shade" of anything except romance.

The Ravensbourne, it may be here stated, is still, as it is described by some poet quoted in Hone's "Table Book,"

" A crystal rillet, scarce a palm in width,
  Till creeping to a bed, outspread by art,
  It shoots itself across, reposing there ;
  Thence through a thicket sinuous it flows,

THE ROYAL DOCK, DEPTFORD ; END OF SEVENTEENTH CENTURY.

camp, and conjecturing that it came to drink, he ordered its arrival to be carefully noted. This command was obeyed, and the visits of the raven were found to be to a small clear spring on Keston Heath. The wants of the army were supplied, and the spring, says the legend, and the rivulet of which it is the parent, have ever since been called the "Raven's Well" and the "Ravensbourne." This legend, however, it is to be feared, is more pretty than true. For even if the facts occurred as stated, it is scarcely likely that the Roman legions would have communicated them to the wild and savage tribes whom they were so bent on subduing to the iron rule of Imperial Rome ; and if they did teach the Britons so pretty a story, they would not have been likely to use the British or the Saxon tongue in communicating it to them. We may, therefore, safely dismiss it as a mere fable, invented by some poetically-minded individual, in order to

  And crossing meads and footpaths, gathering tribute
  Due to its elder birth from younger branches,
  Wanders, by Hayes and Bromley, Beckenham Vale,
  And straggling Lewisham, to where Deptford Bridge
  Uprises in obeisance to its flood."

But small and insignificant as the stream may now appear, the Ravensbourne is a river which has a name in history. We have recorded above how it witnessed the rout and capture of Lord Audley's rebel forces ; but this is not all. "More than one tumultuous multitude," writes Charles Mackay, "has encamped upon its banks, shouting loud defiance to their lawful rulers. Blackheath, its near neighbour, was overrun by Wat Tyler and the angry thousands that followed in his train ; and in the Ravensbourne, perchance, many of those worthy artisans stooped down to drink its then limpid waters, when, inflamed by revenge and by the hope of plunder and of absolute power, they prepared to march upon London. Jack Cade and his multitudes in their turn encamped about the self-same spot; and the Ravensbourne, after an interval of eighty years, saw its quiet shores disturbed by men who met there for the same purposes, and threatening bloodshed against the peaceful citizens of London, because, feeling the scourge

King George III., was born there on the 28th of May, 1759.

There are, and have been for many centuries, corn and other mills situated on the Ravensbourne in its picturesque windings through Deptford and Brockley, and so on to its source. To one of these John Evelyn refers in his "Diary," where,

SAMUEL PEPYS.

of oppression, they knew no wiser means of obtaining relief, and were unable to distinguish between law and tyranny on the one hand, and freedom and licentiousness on the other." The same author reminds us that as Perkin Warbeck met his adherents near about the same spot, the same scene must have occurred here again during the reign of Henry VII. It may not be out of place to record here the fact that at Hayes, not far from the sources of the Ravensbourne, was the favourite seat of the great Lord Chatham, whose illustrious son, William Pitt, the "heaven-born" minister of

under date of April 28, 1668, he writes : "To London, about the purchase of the Ravensbourne Mills and land round it (*sic*) in Upper Deptford."

As shown in the line quoted as a motto at the head of this chapter, Deptford is styled by Pope, in his well-known lines on the Thames, a "navy-building town," and right well in former years did it deserve its name ; for the Trinity House here, and also the docks and the once extensive yards for ship-building, all date from the reign of Henry VIII., and were here established by that sovereign, to whom belongs, at all events, the credit of having been the founder of the British navy.

It is a matter of history that Deptford, notwithstanding its contiguity to the main road through Kent, and its nearness to the metropolis, continued little more than a mean fishing village till Henry VIII. first erected a store and made the royal dock there, from which time the town has continued to increase both in size and population.

The Royal Dock, or "King's Yard," as it was locally called in former times, was esteemed one of the most complete repositories for naval stores in Europe. It covered not less than thirty acres of ground, and contained every convenience for building, repairing, and fitting out ships-of-the-line—those veritable "wooden walls of Old England" with which we were familiar before the introduction of armour-plated vessels. Artificers in wood and in iron had here large ranges of workshops and storehouses; and here the hammer and the axe were scarcely ever idle, even in times of peace; but where, during the prevalence of war, they were plied incessantly "in the construction of those floating bulwarks for which England is, or rather was, renowned, and which carry a hundred and twenty guns and a thousand men to guard her shores from the invader, or to bear her fame with her victories to the remotest seas of the ocean."

The yard was occupied by various buildings, such as two wet docks (one double and the other single), three "slips" for men-of-war, a basin, two mast ponds, a model loft, mast houses, a large smith's shop, together with numerous forges for anchors, sheds for timber, &c., besides houses for the officers who superintended the works. The finest machinery in the world is said to have been employed in Deptford Dockyard for spinning hemp and manufacturing ropes and cables for the service of the navy. The large storehouse on the north side of the quadrangle was erected in the year 1513. This may be said to have been the commencement of the works at Deptford, which under successive sovereigns gradually grew up and extended.

The old storehouse, which was a quadrangular pile, appears to have consisted originally only of a range on the north side, where, on what was formerly the front of the building, is the date 1513, together with the initials H R in a cipher, and the letters A X for Anno Christi. The buildings on the east, west, and south sides of the quadrangle were erected at different times; and a double front, towards the north, was added in 1721. Another storehouse, parallel to the above, and of the same length, having sail and rigging lofts, was completed towards the close of the last century; and a long range of smaller storehouses was built under the direction of Sir Charles Middleton, afterwards Lord Barham, about the year 1780.

In Charnock's "History of Marine Architecture" is given "A note how many ships the King's Majesty (Henry VIII.) hath in harbour, on the 18th day of September, in the 13th year of his reign (1521); what portage they be of; what estate they be in the same day; also where they ride and be bestowed." From this we are enabled to see what use was made of Deptford as a naval station at that time:—"The *Mary Rose*, being of the portage of 600 tons, lying in the pond at Deptford beside the storehouse there, &c. The *John Baptist*, and *Barbara*, every of them being of the portage of 400 tons, do ryde together in a creke of Deptford Parish, &c. The *Great Nicholas*, being of portage 400 tons, lyeth in the east end of Deptford Strond, &c. . . . The Great Barke, being of portage 250 tons, lyeth in the pond at Deptford, &c. The Less Barke, being of the portage of 180 tons, lyeth in the same pond, &c. The twayne Row Barges, every of them of the portage of 60 tons, lye in the said pond, &c. The Great Galley, being of portage 800 tons, lyeth in the said pond, &c."

Deptford dockyard, in its time, received many royal and distinguished visitors; the earliest of whom we have any record was Edward VI., who thus tells us of the provision made for his reception:—"June 19th, 1549. I went to Deptford, being bedden to supper by the Lord Clinton, where before souper i saw certaine [men] stand upon a bote without hold of anything, and rane one at another til one was cast into the water. At supper Mons. Vieedam and Henadey supped with me. After supper was ober a fort [was] made upon a great lighter on the Temps [Thames] which had three walles and a Watch Towre, in the meddes of wich Mr. Winter was Captain with forty or fifty other soldiours in yellow and blake. To the fort also apperteined a galery of yelow color with men and municion in it for defence of the castel; wherfor ther cam 4 pinesses [pinnaces] with other men in wight ansomely dressed, wich extending to give assault to the castil, first droue away the yelow piness and aftir with clods, scuibs, canes of fire, darts made for the nonce, and bombardes assaunted the castill, beating them of the castel into the second ward, who after issued out and droue away the pinesses, sinking one of them, out of wich al the men in it being more than twenty leaped out and swamme in the Temps.

Then came th' Admiral of the nauy with three other pinesses, and wanne the castel by assault, and burst the top of it doune, and toke the captain and under captain. Then the Admiral went forth to take the yelow ship, and at length clasped with her, toke her, and assaulted also her toppe and wane it by compulcion, and so returned home." This royal record of a mimic naval engagement on the Thames appears in the Cotton MSS. in the British Museum, and is quoted by Cruden in his " History of Gravesend."

"On the 4th of April, 1581," writes Lysons in his " Environs of London," " Queen Elizabeth visited Captain Drake's ship, called the *Golden Hind.* Her Majesty dined on board, and after dinner conferred the honour of knighthood on the captain. A prodigious concourse of people assembled on the occasion, and a wooden bridge, on which were a hundred persons, broke down, but no lives were lost. Sir Francis Drake's ship, when it became unfit for service, was laid up in this yard, where it remained many years, the cabin being, as it seems, turned into a banqueting-house : ' We'll have our supper,' says Sir Petronel Flash, in a comedy called *Eastward-hoe,* written by Ben Jonson and others, ' on board Sir Francis Drake's ship, that hath compassed the world !' It was at length broken up, and a chair made out of it for John Davis, Esq., who presented it to the University of Oxford." It is recorded that Queen Elizabeth not only partook of a collation on board Drake's ship, and afterwards knighted him, but that she also consented to share the golden fruits of his succeeding adventures. Miss Strickland observes, with reference to this record, that "as some of Drake's enterprises were of a decidedly piratical character, and attended with circumstances of plunder and cruelty to the infant colonies of Spain, the policy of Elizabeth, in sanctioning his deeds, is doubtful." She gave orders that his ship, the *Golden Hind,* should be preserved here as a memorial of the national glory and of her great captain's enterprise. For long years, accordingly, in obedience to her royal command, the vessel was kept in Deptford dockyard until it fell into decay, when all that remained sound of her was converted into a chair, which was presented to the University of Oxford, and is still kept in the Bodleian library. The chair was thus characteristically apostrophised by Cowley :—

" To this great ship, which round the world has run,
  And match'd, in race, the chariot of the sun,
  This Pythagorean ship (for it may claim,
  Without presumption, so deserved a name,
  By knowledge once, and transformation now),

In her new shape this sacred port allow.
  Drake and his ship could not have wished from fate
  A happier station, or more bless'd estate !
  For lo ! a seat of endless rest is given
  To her in Oxford, and to him in heaven."

As might be expected, Deptford dockyard is frequently mentioned in the diaries of Evelyn and Pepys ; by the former on account of its nearness to Saye's Court, and by the latter on account of his official connection with the navy.

It was in 1651 that Evelyn first settled in Deptford, as we find from the following entry in his "Diary : "—" I went to Deptford, where I made preparation for my settlement, either in this or some other place, there being now so little appearance of any change for the better, all being entirely in the Rebells' hands, and this particular habitation and the estate contiguous to it (belonging to my father-in-law) very much suffering for want of some friend to rescue it out of the power of the usurpers ; so as to preserve our interest I was advis'd to reside in it, and compound with the souldiers. I had also addresses and cyfers to correspond with his majesty and ministers abroad : upon all which I was persuaded to settle in England, having now run about the world neere ten yeares. I likewise meditated sending over for my wife from Paris." A few days later Evelyn thus writes : " I saw the *Diamond* and *Ruby* launch'd in the dock at Deptford, carrying forty-eight brasse cannon each. Cromwell present."

Experiments would appear to have been made from time to time ; at all events, here is the record of one of which Evelyn was an eye-witness. On July 19, 1661, he writes : " We tried our Diving-Bell or Engine in the water-dock at Deptford, in which our Curator continu'd half an hour under water ; it was made of cast lead, let down with a strong cable."

At or about this time Samuel Pepys was a frequent visitor here, in his official capacity, as " one of the principal officers of the navy " (Clerk of the Acts). Under dates of January 11–12, 1660–1, he thus records in his " Diary " an account of a visit on the occasion of a reported " rising of Fanatiques : "—" This morning we had order to see guards set in all the King's yards : and so Sir William Batten goes to Chatham, Colonel Slingsby and I to Deptford and Woolwich. . . We fell to choosing four captains to command the guards, and choosing the place where to keep them, and other things in order thereunto. Never till now did I see the great authority of my place, all the captains of the fleete coming cap in hand to us." On the next day, the 13th, he writes : " After sermon to Deptford again; where, at the Commissioner's and the 'Globe,' we staid long. But no sooner in bed, but we had an alarme, and so we rose; and the Comptroller comes into the yard to us; and seamen of all the ships present repair to us, and there we armed every one with a handspike, with which they were as fierce as could be. At last we hear that it was five or six men that did ride through the guard in the towne, without stopping to the guard that was there: and, some say, shot at them. But all being quiet there, we caused the seamen to go on board again."

On January 15, 1660–1, he makes this entry: "The King [Charles II.] hath been this afternoon to Deptford, to see the yacht that Commissioner Pett is building, which will be very pretty; as also that his brother at Woolwich is making."

Pepys, in his "Diary," January, 1662, mentions a certain project of Sir Nicholas Crisp to make a great "sasse," or sluice, in "the king's lands about Deptford," "to be a wett-dock to hold 200 sail of ships." This project is also mentioned by Evelyn and by Lysons.

Pepys writes under date April 28th, 1667:— "To Deptford, and there I walked down the yard, . . . and discovered about clearing of the wet docke, and heard (which I had before) how, when the docke was made, a ship of nearly 500 tons was there found; a ship supposed of Queen Elizabeth's time, and well wrought, with a great deal of stone-shot in her, of eighteen inches diameter, which was shot then in use; and afterwards meeting with Captain Perryman and Mr. Castle at Half-way Tree, they tell me of stone-shot of thirty-six inches in diameter, which they shot out of mortar pieces."

Again, in the following May:—"By water to Deptford, it being Trinity Monday, when the Master is chosen. And so I down with them; and we had a good dinner of plain meat, and good company at our table; among others my good Mr. Evelyn, with whom, after dinner, I stepped aside and talked upon the present posture of our affairs." Again, when in June, 1667, the alarm was raised that the Dutch fleet was already off the Nore and in the Medway, Samuel Pepys relates another official visit: "So we all down to Deptford, and pitched upon ships, and set men at work; but Lord! to see how backwardly things move at this pinch."

In this same year, as we are told by John Evelyn, a large fire, breaking out in Deptford dockyard, "made such a blaze and caused such an uproar in London, that everybody believed the Dutch fleet had sailed up the river and fired the Tower."

Here were launched many of the "wooden walls of old England," especially during the reigns of the later Stuarts. For example, Evelyn tells us that he stood near the king here in March, 1668, at the launch of "that goodly vessel, *The Charles.*" Pepys, too, was here on this occasion, for under date of March 3, 1668, he writes:—"Down by water to Deptford; where the King, Queene, and Court are to see launched the new ship built by Mr. Shish, called *The Charles.* God send her better luck than the former!"

Evelyn tells us that many of the dockyard *employés* rose to independence, and even affluence. Among others he mentions the funeral here of the above-mentioned old Mr. Shish, master shipwright, whose death he styles a public loss, for his excellent success in building ships, though altogether illiterate. "I held the pall," he writes, "with three knights, who did him that honour, and he was worthy of it. . . . It was the custom of this good man to rise in the night, and to pray kneeling in his own coffin, which he had by him many years."

At the close of the seventeenth century Peter the Great visited the dockyard for the purpose of studying naval architecture, residing during his stay at Evelyn's house, Saye's Court, where we shall again meet with him presently. In the dockyard, it is on record that he did the work of an ordinary shipwright, and that he also paid close attention to the principles of ship-designing. His evenings were mostly spent in a public-house in smoking and drinking with his attendants and one or two chosen companions.

It may be worthy of a note that in the "Life of Captain Cook" we are told that the two ships, the *Resolution* and the *Discovery*, in which he made his last voyage to the Pacific, lay here whilst being equipped by the shipwrights for their distant voyage. The *Queen Charlotte* (120 guns) was launched from this yard in July, 1810.

Samuel Pepys, the author of the "Diary" from which we have culled so many interesting pieces of intelligence during the progress of this work, and whose portrait we present to our readers on page 145, was descended from a family originally seated at Diss, in Norfolk, and who settled at Cottingham, in Cambridgeshire, early in the sixteenth century. His father, John Pepys, at one time followed the trade of a tailor; he had a numerous family. Samuel Pepys was born in 1632, and was educated at St. Paul's School,* London, and afterwards at the University of Cambridge. At the age of about

---

* See Vol. I., p. 274.

twenty-three he took to himself a wife in the person of one Elizabeth St. Michael, then a beautiful girl fifteen years old. At this time, Pepys' relation, Sir Edward Montagu, afterwards first Earl of Sandwich, proved his friend, and prevented the ill consequences which such an early marriage might have entailed upon him. Sir Edward took young Pepys with him on his expedition to the Sound, in 1658, and upon his return obtained for him a clerkship in the Exchequer. Through the interest of Lord Sandwich, Pepys was nominated "Clerk of the Acts," and this was the commencement of his connection with a great national establishment, to which in the sequel his diligence and acuteness were of the highest service. "From his papers, still extant," writes Lord Braybrooke, "we gather that he never lost sight of the public good; that he spared no pains to check the rapacity of contractors, by whom the naval stores were then supplied; that he studied order and economy in the dockyards, advocated the promotion of the old-established officers in the navy; and resisted to the utmost the infamous system of selling places then most unblushingly practised. . . . He continued in this office till 1673; and during those great events, the plague, the fire of London, and the Dutch war, the care of the navy in a great measure rested upon Pepys alone." He afterwards rose to be Secretary of the Admiralty, an office which he retained till the Revolution. On the accession of William and Mary he retired into private life. He sat in Parliament for Castle Rising, and subsequently represented the borough of Harwich, eventually rising to wealth and eminence as Clerk of the Treasurer to the Commissioners of the affairs of Tangier, and Surveyor-General of the Victualling Department, "proving himself to be," it is stated, "a very useful and energetic public servant." He suffered imprisonment for a short time in 1679–80, in the Tower, on a charge of aiding the Popish Plot. In 1684 he was elected President of the Royal Society, and held that honourable office for two years in succession. Pepys had an extensive knowledge of naval affairs; and in 1690 he published some "Memoirs relating to the State of the Royal Navy in England for ten years, determined December, 1688." He died in London in 1703.

In the early part of the present century the dockyard was closed for some years. It was re-opened, however, with renewed vigour in 1844, from which time down to the period of its final closing in 1869, several first-rate vessels were built and launched there, including the *Hannibal*, the *Emerald*, the *Termagant*, the *Terrible*, the *Spitfire*, the *Leopard*, the *Imperieuse*, and many others. But when iron began to supersede wood, and a heavier class of vessels was required for the purposes of war, the shallow water in the river opposite the slips, and other inconveniences of the site, caused the yard to be pretty much restricted to the building of gunboats, and it was finally decided to abandon the dockyard and to transfer the workmen to other establishments. The last vessel launched here was the screw corvette *Druid*, which took place in the presence of Princess Louise and Prince Arthur, on the 13th of March, 1869. At the end of the same month the yard was finally closed.

Shortly afterwards it became necessary, under the Contagious Diseases (Animals) Act, 1869, to provide a place for the sale and slaughter of foreign animals brought into the port of London, and the Corporation of the City of London having undertaken the duty, purchased the greater part of the old dockyard for about £95,000, for the site of the new market. The works necessary for converting the place into a cattle-market amounted to about £140,000; and in December, 1871, it was opened under the title of the Foreign Cattle Market. This market covers an area of about twenty-three acres, and is provided with covered pens, each pen having its water-trough and food-rack, sufficient for sheltering 4,000 cattle and 12,000 sheep; besides this, there is sufficient available open space for accommodating several thousands more. The ship-building slips of the old dockyard, with their immense roofs, were adapted as pen-sheds, and connected by ranges of substantial and well-ventilated buildings. The old workshops were converted into slaughter-houses for oxen, the boat-houses for sheep, and fitted with travelling pulleys, cranes, and various mechanical appliances for saving labour and facilitating the slaughter of the animals. The market has a river frontage of about 360 yards; and three jetties, with a connected low-water platform, provide ample means for landing animals at all states of the tide.

In 1872, by order of the City officials, a board was put up in the Foreign Cattle Market, bearing the following inscription:—"Here worked as a ship-carpenter Peter, Czar of all the Russias, afterwards Peter the Great, 1698." The Czar's sojourn here is likewise commemorated by his name being given to a street in Deptford—a very wretched and woe-begone street, by the way, and quite unworthy of so illustrious a name.

The Dockyard, though so important, was small, when compared with the others, as we learn from the following statement which appeared in a Kentish newspaper in 1839:—"The English dockyards extend over nearly 500 acres. Deptford covers 30 acres; Woolwich, 36; Chatham, 90; Sheerness, 50; Portsmouth, 100; Plymouth, 96; and Pembroke, 60."

Near the docks was the seat of John Evelyn, called Say's or Saye's Court, where, as stated above, Peter the Great, Czar of Muscovy, resided

Saye's Court was not based on a very secure footing, for he tells us in 1660–1 that he had repeated visits from his Majesty's surveyor "to take an account of what grounds I challeng'd at Saye's Court." In 1663 Charles II. granted a new lease at a reserved annual rental of 22s.

The property, it appears, had been leased by the Crown to the family of the Brownes, one of whom, Sir Richard Browne, in 1613, purchased the greater

PETER THE GREAT'S HOUSE AT DEPTFORD (1850).

for some time whilst completing in the dockyard his knowledge and skill in the practical part of naval architecture. The mansion was originally the manor-house of the manor of West Greenwich, which had been presented by the Conqueror to Gilbert de Magnimot, who made it the head of his barony, and erected, it is said, a castle on the site, every vestige of which has long been swept away. After passing through the hands of numerous possessors, the manor was resumed by the Crown at the Restoration. The manor-house with its surrounding estate, which had obtained the name of Saye's Court from its having been long held by the family of Says or Sayes, became in 1651 the property of John Evelyn, the celebrated author of "Sylva." It would appear that Evelyn's claim to

portion of the manor. "A 'representative of that ancient house,'" writes Mr. James Thorne, in his "Environs of London," "Sir Richard Browne, a follower of the Earl of Leicester, was a privy councillor and clerk of the Green Cloth, under Elizabeth and James I., and died at Saye's Court in 1604. He it must have been, and not an Evelyn, as Sir Walter Scott wrote, by a not unnatural slip of the pen, who, taking a 'deep interest in the Earl of Sussex, willingly accommodated both him and his numerous retinue in his hospitable mansion,' the 'ancient house, called Saye's Court, near Deptford;' and which hospitable service led to the events recorded in chapters xiii.—xv. of 'Kenilworth,' among others the luckless visit which Queen Elizabeth paid her sick servant at Saye's

THE ROYAL DOCKYARD, DEPTFORD, IN 1810.

Court; 'having brought confusion thither along with her, and leaving doubt and apprehension behind.'" Here, as we have already stated, "Master Tresillian" visited the Earl of Sussex. The last Sir Richard Browne, who died in 1683, was Clerk of the Council to Charles I., and his ambassador to the Court of France from 1641. His death is thus recorded by Evelyn in his "Diary," under date, February, 1683:—

"This morning I received the newes of the death of my father-in-law, Sir Richard Browne, Knt. and Bart., who died at my house at Saye's Court this day at ten in the morning, after he had labour'd under the gowt and dropsie for neere six moneths, in the 78th yeare of his age. His grandfather, Sir Richard Browne, was the greate instrument under the greate Earl of Leicester (favourite to Queene Eliz.) in his government of the Netherlands. He was Master of the Household to King James, and Cofferer; I think was the first who regulated the compositions thro' England for the King's household provisions, progresses, &c."

John Evelyn, whom Southey styles a "perfect model of an English gentleman," and "whose 'Sylva,'" as Scott writes, "is still the manual of British planters," married in 1647 the only daughter and heir of the above-mentioned Sir Richard Browne; and Sir Richard being resident in Paris, gave up Saye's Court to his son-in-law. That Evelyn was located here soon after his marriage seems pretty certain, for in 1648 we find an entry in his "Diary" to the effect that he "went through a course of chemistrie at Saye's Court."

The estate had been seized by the Parliamentary commissioners; but Evelyn succeeded in buying out, towards the close of 1652, those who had purchased it of the Trustees of Forfeited Estates. Thenceforth he made Saye's Court his permanent residence, and at once set about the accomplishment of those works which helped so much to make the place classic ground. Under date 17th of January, 1653, he writes: "I began to set out the ovall Garden at Saye's Court, which was before a rude orchard, and all the rest one intire field of 100 acres, without any hedge, except the hither holly hedge joyning to the bank of the mount walk. This was the beginning of all the succeeding gardens, walks, groves, enclosures, and plantations there."

The chatty old diarist tells us all the secrets of his domestic life: how he " set apart in preparation for the B. Sacrament, which Mr. Owen administered " to him and all his family in Saye's Court; how he entertained royalty and some of

the highest of the nobility; how he planted the orchard, "the moon being new, and the wind westerly;" and how he kept bees in his garden in a "transparent apiary," &c. &c.

Evelyn resided chiefly at Saye's Court for the next forty years of his life, carrying out there, as far as the site allowed, the views of gardening set forth in his "Sylva," to the "great admiration" of his contemporaries. Occasionally royalty would "drop in" to pay him a visit, or to see how his work was progressing—facts which we find duly recorded in his "Diary." For instance, Henrietta Maria, the widow of Charles I.—the "Queen Mother," as she was called—landed at Deptford, on her return to England, July 28th, 1662, and was waited upon by John Evelyn, who entertained her, the Earl of St. Alban's, and the rest of her retinue, at Saye's Court.

On the 30th of April, in the following year, "came his Majesty to honour my poore villa with his presence, viewing the gardens and even every roome of the house, and was pleas'd to take a small refreshment."

Evelyn had, of course, many other visitors, Clarendon and the Duke of York among them. One entry in his "Diary" about this time is as follows:—"Came my Lord Chancellor (the Earle of Clarendon) and his lady, his purse and mace borne before him, to visit me. They had all ben our old acquaintance in exile, and indeed this greate person had ever ben my friend. His sonn, Lord Cornbury, was here too."

But it was not only royal and political celebrities who visited Evelyn here; there was a welcome also for men of letters and science. His "Diary" for 1673 bears testimony to this fact. "June 27. Mr. Dryden, the famous poet, and now laureate, came to give me a visite. It was the anniversary of my marriage," he adds, "and the first day that I went into my new little cell and cabinet, which I built below, towards the South Court, at the east end of the parlor."

All this while his garden, we may be sure, was not neglected. "I planted," he writes in his "Diary," "all the out-limites of the garden and long walks with holly." In 1663, on the 4th of March, occurs this entry: "This Spring I planted the Home and West-field at Saye's Court with elmes, the same yeare they were planted in Greenewich Park."

Two years later our genial friend Pepys takes a quiet stroll through the grounds of Saye's Court, as he informs us in *his* "Diary," under date of 5th of May, 1665: "After dinner to Mr. Evelyn's; he being abroad, we walked in his garden, and a lovely noble ground he hath indeed. And among other rarities, a hive of bees, so as being hived in glass, you may see the bees making their honey and combs mighty pleasantly." This was the transparent apiary already mentioned. It was not merely in gardening that Evelyn was so proficient, for he appears to have been something of a poet, and to have cultivated a taste for the fine arts, if we may form any conclusion from the following entry in Pepys' "Diary:"—"5 Nov., 1665. By water to Deptford, and there made a visit to Mr. Evelyn, who, among other things, showed me most excellent paintings in little, in distemper, Indian-incke, water-colours, graveing, and, above all, the whole secret of mezzo-tinto, and the manner of it, which is very pretty, and good things done with it. He read to me very much also of his discourse, he hath been many years and now is about, about Gardenage; which will be a most noble and pleasant piece. He read me part of a play or two of his making, very good, but not as he conceits them, I think, to be. He showed me his Hortus Hyemalis : leaves laid up in a book of several plants kept dry, which preserve colour, however, and look very finely, better than an herball. In fine, a most excellent person he is, and must be allowed a little for a little conceitedness ; but he may well be so, being a man so much above others. He read me, though with too much gusto, some little poems of his own, that were not transcendant, yet one or two very pretty epigrams ; among others, of a lady looking in at a grate, and being pecked at by an eagle that was there." It is amusing to see one of the two rival diarists of Charles II.'s reign portrayed by the other, and that must be our excuse for quoting the above sketch.

Evelyn was, moreover, apparently a collector of "autographs," or, at all events, he seems to have possessed a few treasures in this way ; for a few days later we find Pepys paying him another visit, the entry of which records the fact that "among other things he showed me a lieger [ledger] of a treasurer of the navy, his great grandfather, just one hundred years old, which I seemed mighty fond of ; and he did present me with it, which I take as a great rarity, and he hopes to find me more older than it. He also showed me several letters of the old Lord of Leicester's, in Queen Elizabeth's time, under the very hand-writing of Queen Elizabeth, and Queen Mary, Queen of Scots, and others, very venerable names. But, Lord ! how poorly, methinks, they wrote in those days, and in what plain uncut paper."

Evelyn stayed at Saye's Court during the plague, for he writes in 1665 : "There died in our parish this year 406 of the pestilence," and he afterwards tells us that his wife and family returned to him from Wotton, the ancient family seat near Dorking, in Surrey, when it was at an end. In the MSS. preserved at Wotton, and quoted in the appendix to his "Memoirs," Evelyn has left a pretty full account of what he did at Saye's Court : "The hithermost grove I planted about 1656 ; the other beyond it, 1660 ; the lower grove, 1662 ; the holly hedge, even with the mount hedge below, 1670. I planted every hedge and tree not onely in the garden, groves, &c., but about all the fields and house since 1653, except those large, old, and hollow Elms in the Stable Court, and next the Sewer ; for it was before all one pasture field to the very garden of the house, which was but small ; from which time also I repaired the ruined house, and built the whole end of the kitchen, the chapel, buttry, my study (above and below), cellars, and all the outhouses and walls, still-house, Orangerie, and made the gardens, &c., to my great cost, and better I had don to have pulled all down at first ; but it was don at several times."

It was in the neighbourhood of Saye's Court, in 1671, that Evelyn first met with the celebrated sculptor, Grinling Gibbons, whom he afterwards befriended. On the 18th of January in that year he writes : "This day I first acquainted his Majesty with that incomparable young man Gibbons, whom I had lately met with in an obscure place by meere accident as I was walking neere a poore solitary thatched house in a field in our parish, neere Saye's Court. I found him shut in ; but looking in at the window I perceiv'd him carving that large cartoon or crucifix of Tintoret, a copy of which I had myselfe brought from Venice. I asked if I might enter ; he open'd the door civilly to me, and I saw him about such a work as for the curiosity of handling, drawing, and studious exactnesse, I never had before seene in all my travells. I questioned him why he worked in such an obscure place ; he told me it was that he might apply himselfe to his profession without interruption. I asked if he was unwilling to be made knowne to some greate man, for that I believed it might turn to his profit ; he answer'd he was yet but a beginner, but would not be sorry to sell off that piece ; the price he said £100. The very frame was worth the money, there being nothing in nature so tender and delicate as the flowers and festoons about it, and yet the work was very strong ; in the piece were more than 100 figures of men. I found he was likewise musical, and very civil, sober, and discreete in his discourse."

The lease of the pastures adjacent to Saye's Court, as Evelyn tells us, was renewed to him by the king in January, 1672, though, "according to his solemn promise, it ought to have passed to us in fee farm." The king's engagement to this effect, under his own hand, is among the treasures of the Evelyns still preserved at Wotton.

In the summer of 1693, Evelyn transferred himself, after so many years, from his old home at Saye's Court to Wotton. On the 4th of May of that year he writes :—"I went this day with my wife and four servants from Saye's Court, removing much furniture of all sorts, books, pictures, hangings, bedding, &c., to furnish the apartment my brother assign'd me, and now, after more than forty years, to spend the rest of my dayes with him at Wotton, where I was born; leaving my house at Deptford full furnish'd, and three servants, to my *son-in-law* Draper, to pass the summer in, and such longer time as he should think fit to make use of it."

Two or three years afterwards, having succeeded to Wotton by his brother's death, he let Saye's Court, for a term of years, to the gallant Admiral Benbow, "with condition to keep up the garden;" and afterwards, as we learn from Evelyn's "Diary," April, 1698, "The Czar of Muscovy, being come to England, and having a mind to see the building of ships, hir'd my house at Saye's Court, and made it his Court and Palace, new furnished for him by the king."

John Evelyn was one of the most excellent persons in public and private life. His career was one of usefulness and benevolence. Horace Walpole bears a high testimony to his personal worth when, on account of having designed with his own hand some illustrations of his tour in Italy, he reckons him among those English artists whose lives afford materials for his "Anecdotes of Painting."

The following account of the life led by Peter the Great* at Saye's Court we extract from a Memoir of his Life, in the "Family Library:"— "One month's residence having satisfied Peter as to what was to be seen in London, and the monarch having expressed a strong desire to be near some of the king's dock-yards, it was arranged that a suitable residence should be found near one of the river establishments; and the house of the celebrated Mr. Evelyn, close to Deptford Dockyard, being about to become vacant by the removal of Admiral Benbow, who was then its tenant, it was immediately taken for the residence of the czar and his suite; and a doorway was broken

through the boundary wall of the dockyard, to afford a direct communication between it and the dwelling-house. This place had then the name of Saye's Court; it was the delight of Evelyn, and the wonder and admiration of all men of taste at that time. The grounds are described, in the 'Life of the Lord Keeper Guildford,' as 'most boscaresque,' being, as it were, an exemplary of his (Evelyn's) 'Book of Forest Trees.' Admiral Benbow had given great dissatisfaction to the proprietor as a tenant, for the latter observes in his 'Diary:' 'I have the mortification of seeing every day much of my labour and expense there impairing for want of a more polite tenant.' It appears, however, that the princely occupier was not a more 'polite tenant' than the rough sailor had been, for Mr. Evelyn's servant thus writes to him :—'There is a house full of people, and right nasty. The czar lies next your library, and dines in the parlour next your study. He dines at ten o'clock, and six at night, is very seldom at home a whole day, very often in the King's Yard, or by water, dressed in several dresses. The king is expected here this day; the best parlour is pretty clean for him to be entertained in. The king pays for all he has.' But this was not all: Mr. Evelyn had a favourite holly hedge, through which, it is said, the czar, by way of exercise, used to be in the habit of trundling a wheel-barrow every morning with his own royal hands. Mr. Evelyn probably alludes to this in the following passage in his 'Sylva,' wherein he asks, 'Is there under the heavens a more glorious and refreshing object, of the kind, than an impregnable hedge, of about four hundred feet in length, nine feet high, and five in diameter, which I can still show in my ruined garden at Saye's Court (thanks to the Czar of Muscovy) at any time of the year, glittering with its armed and variegated leaves; the taller standards, at orderly distances, blushing with their natural coral? It mocks the rudest assaults of the weather, *beasts*, or *hedge-breakers et illum nemo impune lacessit !*'"

"While at Saye's Court," writes Dr. Mackay, in his "Thames and its Tributaries," "the czar received a visit from the great William Penn, who came over from Stoke Pogis to see him, accompanied by several other members of the Quaker body. Penn and he conversed together in the Dutch language; and the czar conceived from his manners and conversation such favourable notions of that peaceful sect, that during his residence at Deptford he very often attended Quaker meetings, conducting himself—if we may trust his biographers—'with great decorum and condescension, changing seats, and sitting down, and standing up, as he could best accommodate others, although he could not understand a word of what was said.'" If this be true, the czar was not so uncivilised a being after all.

We have but little evidence, except tradition, that the czar, during his residence here, ever actually worked with his hands as a shipwright; it would seem he was employed rather in acquiring information on matters connected with naval architecture from the commissioner and surveyor of the navy, Sir Anthony Deane, who, next after the Marquis of Carmarthen, was his most intimate English acquaintance. His fondness for sailing and managing boats, however, was as eager here as in Holland, where he had studied some time before coming to England; and these gentlemen were almost daily with him on the Thames, sometimes in a sailing-yacht, and at other times rowing in boats—an exercise in which both the czar and the marquis are said to have excelled. The Navy Board received directions from the Admiralty to hire two vessels, to be at the command of the czar whenever he should think proper to sail on the Thames, in order to improve himself in seamanship. In addition to these, the king made him a present of the *Royal Transport*, with orders to have such alterations made in her as his majesty might desire, and also to change her masts, riggings, sails, &c., in any such way as he might think proper for improving her sailing qualities. But his great delight was to get into a small decked boat belonging to the dockyard, and, taking only Menzikoff and three or four others of his suite, to work the vessel with them, he being the helmsman; by this practice he said he should be able to teach them how to command ships when they got home. Having finished their day's work (as stated by us previously*), they used to resort to a public-house in Great Tower Street, close to Tower Hill, to smoke their pipes, and drink their beer and brandy. The landlord had the Czar of Muscovy's head painted and put up for his sign, which continued till the year 1808, when a person of the name of Waxel took a fancy to the old sign, and offered the then occupier of the house to paint him a new one for it. A copy was accordingly made from the original, which remained in its position till the house was rebuilt, when the sign was not replaced, and the name only remains; it is now called the "Czar's Head."

The czar, in passing up and down the river,

was much struck with the magnificent building of Greenwich Hospital, which, until he had visited it and seen the old pensioners, he had thought to be a royal palace; but one day when King William asked how he liked his hospital for decayed seamen, the czar answered, "If I were the adviser of your majesty, I should counsel you to remove your court to Greenwich, and convert St. James's into a hospital." He little knew that St. James's also was a hospital† in its origin.

While residing at Deptford, the czar frequently invited Flamsteed from the Royal Observatory at Greenwich to come over and dine with him, in order that he might obtain his opinion and advice, especially upon his plan of building a fleet. It is stated in Chambers's "Book of Days," that the king promised Peter that there should be no impediment to his engaging and taking back with him to Russia a number of English artificers and scientific men; accordingly, when he returned to Holland, there went with him captains of ships, pilots, surgeons, gunners, mast-makers, boat-builders, sail-makers, compass-makers, carvers, anchor-smiths, and copper-smiths; in all nearly 500 persons. At his departure he presented to the king a ruby valued at £10,000, which he brought in his waistcoat pocket, and placed in William's hand wrapped up in a piece of brown paper.

Evelyn seems to have sustained a considerable loss by Peter's tenancy; for he writes in his "Diary" under date 5th of June, 1698: "I went to Deptford to see how miserably the czar had left my house after three months' making it his court. I got Sir Christopher Wren, the king's surveyor, and Mr. Loudon, his gardener, to go and estimate the repairs, for which they allowed £150 in their report to the Lords of the Treasury." It appears, however, that in spite of having had such bad tenants in admirals and in royalty, Evelyn again let his house at Deptford to Lord Carmarthen, Peter's boon companion.

Alas! for the glory of the glittering hollies, trimmed hedges, and long avenues of Saye's Court. Time, that great innovator, has demolished them all, and Evelyn's favourite haunts and enchanting grounds became in the end transformed into cabbage gardens and overrun with weeds.

After Evelyn's death Saye's Court was neglected, and at the end of the last century Lysons writes, "There is not the least trace now either of the house or the gardens at Saye's Court; a part of the garden walls only with some brick piers are [is]

---

remaining. The house was pulled down in 1728 or 1729, and the workhouse built on its site." That portion of the victualling yard where till recently oxen and hogs were slaughtered and salted for the use of the navy, now occupies the place of the shady walks and trimmed hedges in which the good old Evelyn so much delighted. On another part rows of mean cottages were built; and the only portion unappropriated was that

the latter purpose, was no doubt the scene of many a jovial night spent by the admiral and his successor, the czar. What remains of Evelyn's garden is now a wilderness of weeds and rank grass, hemmed in by a dingy wall which shuts out some of the filthiest dwellings imaginable. The avenue of hovels through which we passed from the abode of former greatness bore the name of Czar Street, a last lingering memento of the

DEPTFORD CREEK.

left for the workhouse garden; this still remains. The private entrance through which Peter the Great passed into the dockyard from Saye's Court was in the wall close by, but is now bricked up.

When Mr. Serjeant Burke was preparing for the press his " Celebrated Naval and Military Trials," he visited Deptford. " But," he writes, " to look at Saye's Court now! The free-and-easy way of living, common to the rough seaman and the rude northern potentate, could not, in wildest mood, have contemplated such a condition. It has gradually sunk from bad to worse; it has been a workhouse, and has become too decayed and confined even for that. It is now attached to the dockyard, as a kind of police-station and place for paying off the men. The large hall, used for

imperial sojourn. The illustrious czar was so great a man that he could nowhere set his foot without leaving an imprint behind. A monument to him is not needed; but it would be pleasing to have found in Deptford some memorial carved in brass or stone of our gallant Benbow. Yet, after all, it matters not much while the British public, ever mindful of greatness in the British navy, permits no oblivion to rest on his personal worth, his achievements, and his fame."

The workhouse mentioned above is still standing, though it has long since ceased to be used as such. It is a large brick-built house of two storeys, oblong in shape, and with a tiled roof. The rooms are low-pitched, and about a dozen in number; some of them are about thirty feet long, and those on

DEPTFORD AND GREENWICH IN 1815.

the ground floor are paved with brick. There is nothing in the building to show that it was ever occupied by persons of affluence; but, in spite of this fact, there is in Deptford and its neighbourhood a general and fondly-cherished impression that it is Saye's Court, and the identical house in which the Czar lived. Mr. Thorne, in his "Environs of London," considers that the house "looks more like an adaptation of a part of the old house than a building of the year 1729." It may, perhaps, have been one of the offices or outbuildings of the original mansion.

In 1869, on the closing of the dockyard, Mr. W. J. Evelyn, of Wotton—the present representative of the family of the author of "Sylva," and the owner of some considerable part of the parish of Deptford—determined to purchase back from the Government as much of the site of Saye's Court as was available, to restore it to something like its original condition, and to throw it open to the inhabitants as a recreation-ground. The transformation was effected in 1876–7. There were originally about fourteen acres of open ground; but some of these have since been covered with rows of houses or enclosed for private purposes; and two acres remain attached to the old house above mentioned, which has been converted by Mr. Evelyn into almshouses for about twenty poor persons. In 1881 about three acres more were absorbed into the Foreign Cattle Market, so that the recreation-ground is now about seven acres in extent. The grounds were laid out with grass plats, hedged with flowers and shrubs, and intersected with broad and level walks, and in one corner a large building was erected, to serve as a museum and library. The public, however, do not appear to have appreciated the boon, and the gardens have given place to a piece of level turf for athletic sports, whilst the museum building is now made to serve the purposes of a ball-room.

We are told that in former times the king's household used to be supplied with corn and cattle from the different counties; and oxen being sent up to London, pasture grounds in the various suburbs were assigned for their maintenance. Among these were lands near Tottenham Court, and others at Deptford, which were under the direction of the Lord Steward and the Board of Green Cloth. A certain Sir Richard Browne had the superintendence of those at Deptford; and this fact may explain the entry in Evelyn's "Diary" already mentioned, where he records the visit of the Comptroller of that Board "to survey the land at Saye's Court, to which I had pretence, and to make his report."

To the north-west of Deptford was the "Red House," "so called as being a collection of warehouses and storehouses built of red bricks." This place was burnt down in July, 1639, it being then filled with hemp, flax, pitch, tar, and other commodities. The Victualling Office, in former times called the "Red House," from its occupying the site of the above-mentioned storehouses, is now an immense pile, erected at different times, and consisting of many ranges of buildings, appropriated to the various establishments necessary in the important concern of victualling the navy. The full official title of the place is now the "Royal Victoria Victualling Yard." On the old "Red House" being rebuilt, it was included in the grant of Saye's Court to Sir John Evelyn, in 1726, and was then described as 870 feet in length, thirty-five feet wide, and containing 100 warehouses. The whole of the land comprised in the present yard has been purchased from time to time from the Evelyn family, the last addition being made to it in 1869, when some portion of the gardens formerly attached to old Saye's Court was purchased from Mr. W. J. Evelyn. The premises were for some time rented by the East India Company; but on their being re-purchased of the Evelyns by the Crown, a new victualling house was built on the spot in 1745, to replace the old victualling office on Tower Hill. This new building was also accidentally burnt down in 1749, with great quantities of stores and provisions. It was, however, subsequently rebuilt, and now comprises extensive ranges of stores, workshops, and sheds, with river-side wharf, and all the necessary machinery and appliances for loading and unloading vessels and carrying on the requisite work in the yard. This place is the depôt from which the two other victualling yards—those at Devonport and Gosport—are furnished, and is considerably the largest of the three. From it the navy is supplied with provisions, clothing, bedding, medicines, and medical comforts, &c. In former times, and down to a comparatively recent date, cattle were slaughtered here; but this has been abandoned. At the proper season, however, beef and pork are received in very large quantities, and salted and packed in barrels; meat boiled and preserved in tin canisters, on Hogarth's system of preserving; wheat ground; biscuits made; and the barrels in which all are stored manufactured in a large steam cooperage. The stock of medicine constantly kept in store is sufficient for 5,000 men for six months; but the demand for it is so great and regular that supplies arrive and leave almost daily. The general direction of the yard rests with a resident superintending storekeeper, and in all about 500 persons are employed on the establishment.

On the west side of the Royal Victualling Yard is a goods depôt of the Brighton and South-Coast Railway. It occupies the site of what was formerly Dudman's Dock, and comprises a basin and quay for the landing of goods from vessels coming up the Thames, and also extensive ranges of storehouses, &c. It is connected with the above-mentioned railway by a branch line from New Cross, which passes over the Deptford Lower Road.

"Besides its dock and victualling yard," writes Dr. Mackay, in his "Thames and its Tributaries," "Deptford is noted for two hospitals, belonging to the Corporation of the Trinity House, or the pilots of London. A grand procession comes (1840) from London to these hospitals annually on Trinity Monday, accompanied by music and banners, and is welcomed by the firing of cannon." Trinity Monday, we need scarcely say, was a "red-letter day" in Deptford down to the time when these visits of the Corporation of the Trinity House ceased, which was in 1852, on the death of the Duke of Wellington, who had for many years held the office of Master. We have in a previous volume* given an account of the foundation of the above-mentioned corporation, and also of the duties appertaining to the society; we may, however, remark here that Lambarde, in his "Perambulations of Kent" (1570), writes concerning Deptford—or, as he spells it, Depeforde—"This towne, being a frontier betweene Kent and Surrey, was of none estimation at all, untill that King Henry the VIII. advised (for the better preservation of the royall fleete) to erect a storehouse, and to create certaine officers there; these he incorporated by the name of the Maister and Wardeins of the Holie Trinitie, for the building, keeping, and conducting of the Navie Royall." It would appear from this that Henry VIII. established the Trinity House about the same time that he constituted the Admiralty and the Navy Office. Charles Knight, in his "London," however, says that "some expressions in the earliest charters of the corporation that have been preserved, and the general analogy of the history of English corporations, lead us to believe that Henry merely gave a new charter, and entrusted the discharge of important duties to a guild or incorporation of seamen which had existed long before. When there was no permanent royal navy, and even after one had been

created, so long as vessels continued to be pressed in war time as well as men, the King of England had to repose much more confidence in the wealthier masters of the merchant-service than now. They were at sea what his feudal chiefs were on shore. Their guild, or brotherhood, of the Holy Trinity of Deptford Strond was probably tolerated at first in the assumption of a power to regulate the entry and training of apprentices, the licensing of journeymen, and the promotion to the rank of master in their craft, in the same way as learned and mechanical corporations did on shore. To a body which counted among its members the best mariners of Britain, came not unusually to be entrusted the ballastage and pilotage of the river. By degrees its jurisdiction came to be extended to such other English ports as had not, like the Cinque Ports, privileges and charters of their own; and in course of time the jurisdiction of the Trinity House became permanent in these matters, with the exception of the harbours we have named, over the whole coast of England from a little way north of Yarmouth on the east to the frontiers of Scotland on the west. Elizabeth, always ready to avail herself of the costless service of her citizens, confided to this corporation the charge of English sea-marks. When lighthouses were introduced, the judges pronounced them comprehended in the terms of Elizabeth's charter, although a right of chartering private lighthouses was reserved to the Crown. When the navigation laws were introduced by Cromwell, and re-enacted by the government at the Restoration, the Trinity House presented itself as an already organised machinery for enforcing the regulations respecting the number of aliens admissible as mariners on board a British vessel. James II., when he ascended the throne, was well aware of the use that could be made of the Trinity House, and he gave it a new charter, and the constitution it still retains, nominating as the first master of the reconstructed corporation his invaluable Pepys."

The establishment of the Corporation of the Trinity House here is a proof that Deptford was already a rendezvous for shipping and the resort of seamen. The ancient hall in Deptford, at which the meetings of this society were formerly held, was taken down about the beginning of the present century, and the building erected on Tower Hill, which we have already noticed in the volume above referred to. Evelyn, in his "Diary," under date of 1662, writes: "I dined with the Trinity Company at their house, that corporation being by charter fixed at Deptford." Evelyn's wife, as it appears from his "Diary," gave to the Trinity House

---

* See Vol. II., p. 115.

Corporation the site for their college, or alms-houses.

Notwithstanding that the Corporation of the Trinity House ceased to hold their meetings here after the building of their new hall, their connection with Deptford was till very recently marked by their two hospitals for decayed master mariners and pilots and their widows. In the "Ambulator" (1774) we thus read: "In this town are two hospitals, of which one was incorporated by King Henry VIII., in the form of a college for the use of the seamen, and is commonly called 'Trinity House of Deptford Strond.' This contains twenty-one houses, and is situated near the church. The other, called Trinity Hospital, has thirty-eight houses fronting the street. This is a very handsome edifice, and has large gardens, well kept, belonging to it. Though this last-named is the finer structure of the two, yet the other has the preference, on account of its antiquity; and as the Brethren of the Trinity hold their corporation by that house, they are obliged at certain times to meet there for business. Both these houses are for decayed pilots, or masters of ships, or their widows, the men being allowed twenty and the women sixteen shillings a month."

Both these buildings have within the last few years been "disestablished," so far as their use as almshouses is concerned. One of them, a triangular block of houses, comprising about twenty dwellings standing on the green at the back of St. Nicholas' Church, a short distance eastward from the Foreign Cattle Market, is at present let out in weekly tenements; the other, known as the "Trinity House, Deptford," was a large and noteworthy old red-brick quadrangular pile, fronting Church Street, and overlooking the burial-ground of St. Paul's Church. It was rebuilt in 1664–5, and was demolished, with the exception of the hall, in the early part of the year 1877, to make room for a new street, and a row of private houses in Church Street. In the great hall at the back of the building, which has been left standing, the Master and Elder Brethren of the Trinity House used, down to the period above mentioned, to assemble on Trinity Monday, and, after transacting the formal business, walk in state to the parish church of St. Nicholas, where there was a special service and sermon. On the conclusion of the ceremony in Deptford the company returned to London in their state barges, the shipping and wharves on the Thames being gaily decked with bunting in honour of the occasion, and the proceedings of the day closed with a grand banquet at the Trinity House. Both the meeting and the banquet are now held at the new Trinity House on Tower Hill, and the sermon is preached in Pepys' favourite church of St. Olave, Hart Street, near the Custom House and Corn Exchange.

The town of Deptford contains, as we have stated above, two parish churches, dedicated respectively to St. Nicholas and St. Paul, besides which there are the churches of four recently-formed ecclesiastical districts, together with several chapels of all denominations. The old church of St. Nicholas, the patron saint of seafaring men, occupies the site of a much older edifice, and, with the exception of the tower, dates from the end of the seventeenth century. John Evelyn, in his "Diary" for 1699, records the building of "a pretty new church" here. The ancient church, it appears, was pulled down in 1697, in consequence of its being found inadequate to the wants of the increasing population. Whatever beauty the new church may have possessed in Evelyn's eyes, it does not seem to have been very substantially built, for it underwent a "thorough restoration" before twenty years had passed away. The body of the church is a plain dull red-brick structure, consisting of nave, aisles, and chancel. At the western end is an embattled tower of stone and flint, somewhat patched; this tower is of the Perpendicular period, or early part of the fifteenth century, and the only relic of the old church. The interior contains a few monuments of some former Deptford worthies, among them one of Captain Edward Fenton, who accompanied Sir Martin Frobisher in his second and third voyages, and had himself the command of an expedition for the discovery of a north-west passage; another of Captain George Shelvocke, who was bred to the sea-service under Admiral Benbow, and who, "in the years of Our Lord 1719, '20, '21, and '22, performed a voyage round the globe of the world, which he most wonderfully, and to the great loss of the Spaniards, compleated, though in the midst of it he had the misfortune to suffer shipwreck upon the Island of Juan Fernandez, on the coast of the kingdom of Chili." He died in 1742. Another monument records the death, in 1652, of Peter Pett, a "master shipwright in the King's Yard," whose family were long distinguished for their superior talents in ship-building, and who was himself the inventor of that once useful ship of war, the frigate. The register of this church records also the burial here of Christopher Marlowe, or Marlow, the dramatist. He was born in 1563–4. The son of a shoemaker at Canterbury, and having been educated in the King's School of that city, he took his degree in due course at Cambridge.

On quitting college he became connected with the stage, and was one of the most celebrated of Shakespeare's immediate predecessors. He is styled by Heywood the " best of poets ; " and this may possibly have been true, for no great dramatist preceded him, whilst his fiery imagination and strokes of passion communicated a peculiar impulse to those who came after him. He was the author of six tragedies, and joined with Nash and Day in the production of two others. The plots of his pieces assumed a more regular character than those of previous dramatists, and no doubt he would have become even more celebrated if he had not been cut off in a strange affray. The entry in the parish register runs simply thus :— " 1st June, 1593. Christopher Marlow, slaine by Francis Archer."

In this church lie the two sons of John Evelyn, whose early deaths he records in his " Diary " for 1658, in the most touching phrases. Sir Richard Browne, Evelyn's father-in-law, the owner of Saye's Court, died there in 1683, and was buried at his own desire outside this church, under the south-east window—not in the interior, considering that interments in churches were unwholesome. He was evidently in advance of his age.

Before passing on to St. Paul's Church, we may remark that Dr. Lloyd, curate of Deptford in Evelyn's day, was promoted to the see of Llandaff, and that the register of the old church contains records of the following instances of longevity :— Maudlin Augur, buried in December, 1672, aged 106 ; Catherine Perry, buried in December, 1676, " by her own report, 110 years old ; " Sarah Mayo, buried in August, 1705, aged 102 ; and Elizabeth Wiborn, buried in December, 1714, in her 101st year.

The church of St. Paul, a good example of the Romanesque style, is situated between the High Street and Church Street, near the railway station. It was built in 1730, on the division of Deptford into two parishes, as above stated ; and was one of the churches " erected under the provisions of certain acts passed in the reign of Queen Anne, for the building of fifty new churches in and near London." It is a solid-looking stone building, with a semi-circular flight of steps and a portico of Corinthian columns at the western end, above which rises a tapering spire ; the body of the fabric consists of nave, aisles, and a shallow chancel, the roof being supported by two rows of Corinthian columns. The heavy galleries, old-fashioned pews, carved pulpit, and dark oak fittings of the chancel, impart to the interior a somewhat sombre effect. Among the monuments in this church is one by

Nollekens, in memory of Admiral Sayer, who " first planted the British flag in the island of Tobago," and who died in 1760. In the churchyard is the tomb of Margaret Hawtree, who died in 1734 ; it is inscribed as follows :—

" She was an indulgent mother, and the best of wives ;
   She brought into this world more than three thousand
      lives ! "

The explanation of this, as Lysons informs us, is, that she was an " eminent midwife," and that she evinced the interest she took in her calling by giving a silver basin for christenings to this parish, and another to that of St. Nicholas. Dr. Charles Burney, the Greek scholar and critic, whose large classical library was purchased after his death, in 1817, for the British Museum, was for some time rector of St. Paul's. The old rectory-house, on the south side of the churchyard, a singular-looking red-brick structure, said to have been designed by Vanbrugh, was pulled down in 1883.

Close by the station on the London and Greenwich Railway, which here crosses the High Street, is the Roman Catholic Church of the Assumption. It is a plain brick-built structure, with lancet windows and an open roof, and was commenced in 1844. A temporary chapel, which had been provided in the previous year, was, on the opening of the church, made to do duty as a school. Adjoining the church is a presbytery, which was built in 1855. The Roman Catholics are somewhat numerous in Deptford, a fact which may perhaps be attributed to the large number of Irish formerly employed in the dockyard and on the wharves in the neighbourhood. Close by, are St. Vincent's Industrial School (Roman Catholic) and the Deptford Industrial Home and Refuge for Destitute Boys.

In Evelyn Street, as the thoroughfare connecting the High Street with the Deptford Lower Road is called, stands St. Luke's Church, a substantial and well-built Gothic edifice, erected in 1872, mainly at the cost of the present head of the Evelyn family, Mr. William J. Evelyn, of Wotton.

Near St. Luke's Church the Grand Surrey Canal passes under the roadway at the end of Evelyn Street, on its way towards Camberwell and Peckham. *Apropos* of canals, we may state that in the *Monthly Register* for 1803, it is announced, with becoming gravity, that " Another canal of great national importance is about to be constructed from Deptford to Portsmouth and Southampton, passing by Guildford, Godalming, and Winchester." After giving the estimate, the editor remarks in a manner which, with our subsequent experience of half a century and more, will cause a smile : " A canal, in this instance, is to be preferred to an iron railway road, because the expense of carriage by a canal is much cheaper than that of carriage by a railway. It has been found, for instance, that sixty tons of corn could not be carried from Portsmouth to London for less than £125 10s.; but that by a canal the same quantity of grain may be conveyed the same distance for an expense not exceeding £49 5s." We need scarcely add that this canal was never carried out.

the place, culled from his "Diary." Under date June 3, 1658, he writes:—"A large whale was taken betwixt my land butting on the Thames and Greenwich, which drew an infinite concourse to see it, by water, coach, and on foote, from London and all parts. It appeared first below Greenwich at low water, for at high water it would have destroyed all the boats; but lying now in shallow water, incompassed with boats, after a long conflict it was killed with a harping yron, struck in the

ST. NICHOLAS' CHURCH, DEPTFORD, IN 1790.

Among the most famous residents of Deptford, besides the Czar Peter and John Evelyn, Dr. Mackay enumerates Cowley, the poet, and the Earl of Nottingham, Lord High Admiral of England, who played so leading a part in the defeat of the Spanish Armada. "The house which he inhabited," writes Dr. Mackay, "was afterwards converted into a tavern and named the 'Gun;' and his armorial bearings, sculptured over the chimney-piece of the principal apartment, were long shown to curious visitors."

The name of John Evelyn is so closely associated with the past history of Deptford, that we may be pardoned for closing this chapter with one or two amusing scraps of information concerning

head, out of which it spouted blood and water by two tunnells, and after a horrid grone it ran quite on shore and died. Its length was fifty-eight foote, height sixteen, black skin'd like coach-leather, very small eyes, greate taile, and onely two small finns, a picked snout, and a mouth so wide that divers men might have stood upright in it; no teeth, but suck'd the slime onely as thro' a grate of that bone which we call whale-bone; the throate yet so narrow as would not have admitted the least of fishes. The extremes of the cetaceous bones hang downwards from the upper jaw; and was hairy towards the ends and bottom within-side; all of it prodigious; but in nothing more wonderful than that an animal of so greate a bulk should be nourished onely by slime through those grates." Again, under date March 26, 1699: "After an extraordinary storm there came up the Thames a whale fifty-six feet long. Such, and a larger one of the spout kind, was killed there forty years ago, June, 1658; that year died Cromwell." Whether

trade in this great metropolis; and, as might be expected, the side streets of the town swarm with second-hand shops, some of which, it is to be feared, are made repositories for stolen goods. One of these shops, with its sign of a huge black doll, is graphically described by M. Alphonse

JOHN EVELYN.

Evelyn regarded the appearance of a whale in the Thames as an omen it would be difficult to say.

At another time Evelyn gravely tells us how he dined with the Archbishop of Canterbury, at Lambeth, and stayed late, "and *yet* returned to Deptford at night." What would he have said now, in these days of tram-cars and railways?

Deptford has the honour of having been the birthplace of the rag and bottle, or "marine store,"

Esquiros, in the second series of his "English at Home." He enters into the traditional origin of the black doll as a sign, as first adopted by a woman who, travelling abroad, brought back with her a black baby as a speculation, but finding that such an article had no value in England, wrapped it up in a bundle of rags and sold it to one of the founders of the trade. The little nigger was reared at the expense of the parish—so goes the story—

grew up and married, opened a shop in this same line of business, made a fortune, and is said to have been the ancestress of all the dealers from that day to this. In order to account for this fact, it is said that she and her children started fifty shops, at each of which a black doll was hung out as a sign. Some of these dolls have three heads, and, if we may believe M. Esquiros, this is a symbol of the trade extending through the three kingdoms. It is only fair, however, to add that he remarks, "I am afraid that the explanation given by the owners of these shops will not satisfy antiquaries, who have adopted a far more probable opinion, namely, that these repositories are the successors of the old shops where Indian and Chinese curiosities were sold, and which had a 'joss'—a sort of Chinese idol—for their sign."

The rag and bottle shops are the places whence rags are supplied to the wholesale dealer, who sells them to the owners of the paper-mills which abound near Dartford. It is not a little singular, however, that many of the rags have crossed the seas, and have found their way to England from Germany and even from India and Australia. Charles Dickens, in his "Sketches by Boz," mentions the marine store shops of Lambeth, and also those of the neighbourhood of the King's Bench prison. Is it possible that he could have been ignorant of their connection with Deptford, or of the romantic story above mentioned?

CHAPTER XIII.

GREENWICH.

"On Thames's bank, in silent thought we stood
Where Greenwich smiles upon the silver flood ;
Struck with the seat that gave Eliza birth,
We kneel, and kiss the consecrated earth,
In pleasing dreams the blissful age renew,
And call Britannia's glories back to view,
Behold her cross triumphant on the main,
The guard of commerce and the dread of Spain."—*Dr. Johnson's "London."*

Situation and Origin of the Name of Greenwich—Early History of the Place—The Murder of Archbishop Alphege—Encampments of the Danes—The Manor of Greenwich—The Building of Greenwich Palace, or " Placentia "—Jousts and Tournaments performed here in the Reign of Edward IV.—Henry VIII. at Greenwich—Festivities held here during this Reign—Birth of Queen Elizabeth—The Downfall of Anne Boleyn—Marriage of Henry VIII. with Anne of Cleves—Will Sommers, the Court Jester—Queen Elizabeth's Partiality for Greenwich—The Order of the Garter—The Queen and the Countryman—Maundy Thursday Observances—Personal Appearance of Queen Elizabeth—Sir Walter Raleigh—Greenwich Palace settled by James I. on his Queen, Anne of Denmark—Charles I. a Resident here—The Palace during the Commonwealth—Proposals for Rebuilding the Palace—The Foundation of Greenwich Hospital.

THE town and parliamentary borough of Greenwich, which we now enter, lies immediately eastward of Deptford, from which parish it is separated by the river Ravensbourne. As to the origin of the name, Lambarde, in his "Perambulations of Kent," says that in Saxon times it was styled *Grenevic*— that is, the "green town ;" and the transition from *vic* to *wich* in the termination is easy. Lambarde adds that in "ancient evidences" it was written "East Greenewiche," to distinguish it from Deptford, which, as we have already stated, is called "West Greenewiche" in old documents. Under the name of West Greenwich it returned two members to Parliament, in the reign of Elizabeth ; but no fresh instance of such an honour is recorded in its subsequent history. Down to about the time of Henry V. the place was known chiefly as a fishing-village, being adapted to that use by the secure road or anchorage which the river afforded at this spot. It was a favourite station with the old Northmen, whose "host" was frequently encamped on the high ground southward and eastward of the town, now called Blackheath. In the reign of King Ethelred, when the Danes made an attack on London Bridge, a portion of their fleet lay in the river off Greenwich, whilst the remainder was quartered in the Ravensbourne Creek at Deptford. It was to Greenwich that, after their raid upon Canterbury in 1011, the Danes brought Archbishop Alphege to their camp, where he was kept a prisoner for several months ; and the foundation of the old parish church of Greenwich, which we shall presently notice, was probably intended to mark the public feeling as to the memorable event that closed his personal history. A native of England, St. Alphege was first abbot of Bath, then Bishop of Winchester, in A.D. 984, and twelve years later translated to the see of Canterbury. On the storming of that city by the Danes under Thurkill, in the year above mentioned, he distinguished himself by the courage with which he defended the place for twenty days against their assaults. Treachery, however, then opened the gates, and Alphege, having been made prisoner, was loaded with chains, and treated with the greatest severity, in order to make him follow the example of his worthless sovereign Ethelred, and purchase an ignominious liberty with gold. Greenwich, as we have stated, at that time formed the Danish head-quarters, and hither the archbishop was conveyed. Here he was tempted by the offer of a lower rate of ransom; again and again he was urged to yield by every kind of threat and solicitation. "You press me in vain," was the noble Saxon's answer; "I am not the man to provide Christian flesh for Pagan teeth by robbing my poor countrymen to enrich their enemies." At last the patience of the heathen Danes was worn out; so one day, after an imprisonment of seven months' duration (the 19th of April, 1012—on which day his festival is still kept in the Roman Catholic Church), they sent for the archbishop to a banquet, when their blood was inflamed by wine, and on his appearance saluted him with tumultuous cries of "Gold! gold! Bishop, give us gold, or thou shalt to-day become a public spectacle." Calm and unmoved, Alphege gazed on the circle of infuriated men who hemmed him in, and who presently began to strike him with the flat sides of their battle-axes, and to fling at him the bones and horns of the oxen that had been slain for the feast. And thus he would have been slowly murdered, but for one Thrum, or Guthrum, a Danish soldier, who had been converted by Alphege, and who now in mercy smote him with the edge of his weapon, when he fell dead. "It is storied," writes Hone, in his "Every-day Book," quoting from the "Golden Legend," "that when St. Alphege was imprisoned at Greenwich, the devil appeared to him in the likeness of an angel, and tempted him to follow him into a dark valley, over which he wearily walked through hedges and ditches, till at last, when he was stuck in a most foul mire, the devil vanished, and a real angel appeared, and told St. Alphege to go back to prison and be a martyr; and so he gained a martyr's crown. Then after his death, an old rotten stake was driven into his body, and those who drove it said, that if on the morrow the stake was green, and bore leaves, they would believe; whereupon the stake flourished, and the drivers thereof repented, as they said they would, and the body being buried at St. Paul's Church, in London, worked miracles."

From the encampments of the Danes in this place may possibly be traced the names of East Coombe and West Coombe, two estates on the borders of Blackheath—*coomb*, as well as *comp*, signifying a *camp*.

The manor of Greenwich, called in the early records East Greenwich, as we have already seen, belonged formerly to the abbey of St. Peter at Ghent. It remained in the possession of the monks, however, but for a very short time, being seized by the Crown upon the disgrace of Odo, Bishop of Bayeux. At the dissolution of the alien priories it was granted by King Henry V. to the monastery of Sheen, or Richmond. Henry VI. granted it to his uncle, Humphrey, Duke of Gloucester, who was so pleased with the spot that he built on it a palace, extending, with its various courts and gardens, from the river to the foot of the hill on which the Observatory now stands. Upon his death it became again the property of the Crown. The royal manors of East and West Greenwich and of Deptford-le-Strond still belong to the sovereign, whose chief steward has his official residence at Macartney House, on Blackheath.

According to Lysons, in his "Environs of London," however, there appears to have been a royal residence here as early as the reign of Edward I., when that monarch "made an offering of seven shillings at each of the holy crosses in the chapel of the Virgin Mary, at Greenwicke, and the prince an offering of half that sum;" though by whom the palace was erected is not known. Henry IV. dated his will from his "Manor of Greenwich, January 22nd, 1408," and the place appears to have been his favourite residence. The grant of 200 acres of land in Greenwich, made by Henry VI. to Duke Humphrey, in 1433, was for the purpose of enclosing it as a park. Four years later the duke and Eleanor, his wife, obtained a similar grant, and in it licence was given to its owners to "embattle and build with stone" their manor of Greenwich, as well as "to enclose and make a tower and ditch within the same, and a certain tower within the park to build and edify." Accordingly, soon after this, Duke Humphrey commenced building the tower within the park, now the site of the Royal Observatory, which was then called Greenwich Castle; and he likewise rebuilt the palace on the spot where the west wing of the Royal Hospital—or, more properly speaking, Royal Naval College—now stands, which he named from its agreeable situation, Pleazaunce, or Placentia; but this name was not commonly used until the reign of Henry VIII. Edward IV. enlarged the park, and stocked it with deer, and then bestowed the palace as a residence upon his queen, Elizabeth Woodville. In this reign a royal joust or tournament was performed at Greenwich, on the occasion of the marriage of Richard, Duke of York, with Anne Mowbray. In 1482 the Lady Mary, the king's daughter, died here; she was betrothed to the King of Denmark, but died before the solemnisation of the marriage. Henry VII. having—as shown in a previous page *—committed Elizabeth, queen of Edward IV., on some frivolous pretence, to close confinement in the Abbey at Bermondsey, where some years afterwards she ended her days amidst poverty and solitude, the manor and appurtenances of Greenwich came into his possession. He then enlarged the palace, adding a brick front towards the riverside; finished the tower in the park, which had been commenced by Duke Humphrey; and built a convent adjoining the palace for the Order of the Grey Friars, who came to Greenwich about the latter end of the reign of Edward IV., "from whom," says Lambarde, "they obtained, in 1480, by means of Sir William Corbidge, a chauntrie, with a little Chapel of the Holy Cross." The convent above mentioned, after its dissolution in the reign of Henry VIII., was re-founded by Queen Mary, but finally suppressed by Elizabeth soon after her accession.

Henry VIII. was born at Greenwich in June, 1491, and baptised in the parish church by the Bishop of Exeter, Lord Privy Seal. This monarch spared no expense to render Greenwich Palace magnificent; and, perhaps from partiality to the place of his birth, he resided chiefly in it, neglecting for it the palace at Eltham, which had been the favourite residence of his ancestors. Many sumptuous banquets, revels, and solemn jousts, for which his reign was celebrated, were held at his "Manor of Pleazaunce." On the 3rd of June, 1509, Henry's marriage with Catherine of Arragon was solemnised here. Holinshed, in his "Chronicles," informs us how that on May-day, in 1511, "the king lying at Grenewich, rode to the wodde to fetch May; and after, on the same day, and the two dayes next ensuing, the King, Sir Edward Howard, Charles Brandon, and Sir Edward Nevill, as challengers, held jousts against all comers. On the other parte the Marquis Dorset, the Earls of Essex and Devonshire, with other, as defendauntes, ranne againste them, so that many a sore stripe was given, and many a staffe broken." On May 15th other jousts were held here, as also in 1516, 1517, and 1526. In 1512 the king kept his Christmas at Greenwich "with great and plentiful cheer," and in the following year " with great

solemnity, dancing, disguisings, mummeries, in a most princely manner." In an account of Greenwich and Hampton Court Palaces, in *Chambers' Journal*, the writer observes :—"Henry VIII., up to middle age, always kept Christmas with great festivity at one or other of these palaces. Artificial gardens, tents, &c., were devised in the hall, out of which came dancers, or knights, who fought. After a few years Henry contented himself with a duller Christmas, and generally gambled a good deal on the occasion. In the brief reign of Edward VI. a gentleman named Ferrers was made the 'Lord of Misrule,' and was very clever in inventing plays and interludes. The money lavished on these entertainments was enormous; one of his lordship's dresses cost fifty-two pounds, and he had besides a train of counsellors, gentlemen ushers, pages, footmen, &c. Mary and Elizabeth both kept Christmas at Hampton Court; but the entertainments of the latter were far gayer than those of her sister."

The following amusing account of these Christmas festivities may be appropriately quoted here from Hall's "Chronicles :"—"The king, after Parliament was ended, kept a solemne Christemas at Grenewicke to chere his nobles, and on the twelfe daie at night, came into the hall a mount, called the riche mount. The mount was sett ful of riche flowers of silke, and especially full of brome slippes full of coddes; the braunches wer grene sattin, and the flowers flat gold of damaske, whiche signified Plantagenet. On the top stode a goodly bekon, gevyng light; rounde about the bekon sat the Kyng and five other, al in coates and cappes of right crimosin velvet, embroudered with flat golde of damaske; the coates set full of spangelles of gold. And four woodhouses drewe the mount till it came before the Quene, and then the Kyng and his compaignie descended and daunced; then sodainly the mount opened, and out came six ladies, all in crimosin satin and plunket embroudered with gold and perle, and French hoddes on their heddes, and thei daunced alone. Then the lordes of the mount took the ladies, and daunced together; and the ladies re-entred, and the mount closed, and so was conveighed out of the hall. Then the Kyng shifted hym and came to the Quene, and sat at the banqute, which was very sumpteous." At the Christmas festivities in 1515 was introduced the first masquerade ever seen in England. The following account of it and the other ceremonies on the occasion, given in the work above quoted, may not prove uninteresting, as it affords some insight into the amusements of the period :—

* See *ante*, p 119.

" The Kyng this yere kept the feast of Christmas at Grenewich, wher was such abundance of viandes served to all comers of any honest behaviors, as hath been few times seen ; and against New-yere's night was made, in the hall, a castle, gates, towers, and dungeon, garnished with artilerie and weapon after the most warlike fashion ; and on the frount of the castle was written, *Le Fortresse dangerus ;* and within the castle wer six ladies clothed in russet satin laid all over with leves of golde, and every owde knit with laces of blewe silke and golde, on ther heddes coyfes and cappes all of gold. After this castle had been carried about the hal [hall], and the Quene had behelde it, in came the Kyng with five other appareled in coates, the one halfe of russet satyn spangled with spangels of fine gold, and the other halfe rich clothe of gold ; on ther heddes caps of russet satin, embroudered with workes of fine gold bullion. These six assaulted the castle, the ladies seyng them so lustie and coragious wer content to solace with them, and upon further communicacion to yeld the castle, and so thei came down and daunced a long space. And after the ladies led the knightes into the castle, and then the castle sodainly vanished out of ther sightes. On the daie of the Epiphanie, at nighte, the Kyng with xi other wer disguished after the manner of Italie, called a maske, a thing not seen afore in Englande ; thei wer appareled in garmentes long and brode, wrought all with gold, with visers and cappes of gold ; and, after the banket doen, those maskers came in with six gentlemen disguised in silke, bearing staffe torches, and desired the ladies to daunce ; some wer content, and some that knewe the fashion of it refused, because it was not a thing commonly seen. And after thei daunced and commoned together, as the fashion of the maske is, thei tooke ther leave and departed, and so did the Quene and all the ladies."

At the palace here both of the daughters of Henry VIII., Mary and Elizabeth, first saw the light. On the 13th of May, 1515, the marriage of Mary, Queen Dowager of France (Henry's sister), with Charles Brandon, Duke of Suffolk, was publicly solemnised in the parish church of Greenwich.

Of the many splendid receptions and sumptuous entertainments of foreign princes and ministers, that which was given here in 1527 to the French ambassadors appears to have been particularly striking ; so much so, in fact, that honest old John Stow is obliged to confess that he " lacked head of fine wit, and also cunning in his bowels," to describe it with sufficient eloquence. This embassy, we are told, that it might correspond with the English Court in magnificence, consisted of eight persons of high quality, attended by six hundred horse ; they were received with the greatest honours, " and entertained after a more sumptuous manner than had ever been seen before." The great tilt-yard was covered over, and converted into a banqueting-room. The Hampton Court banquet given by Wolsey to the same personages just before was, says the annalist, a marvellously sumptuous affair ; yet this at Greenwich excelled it " as much as gold excels silver," and no beholder had ever seen the like. " In the midst of the banquet there was tourneying at the barriers, with lusty gentlemen in complete harness, very gorgeous, on foot ; then there was tilting on horseback with knights in armour, still more magnificent ; and after this was an interlude or disguising, made in Latin, the players being in the richest costumes, ornamented with the most strange and grotesque devices. This done," Stow further tells us, " there came such a number of the fairest ladies and gentlewomen that had any renown of beauty throughout the realm, in the most rich apparel that could be devised, with whom the gentlemen of France danced, until a gorgeous mask of gentlemen came in, who danced and masked with these ladies. This done, came in another mask of ladies, who took each of them one of the Frenchmen by the hand to dance and to mask. These women maskers every one spoke good French to the Frenchmen, which delighted them very much to hear their mother tongue. Thus was the night consumed, from five of the clock until three of the clock after midnight."

" After the king's marriage to Anne Boleyn," writes Charles Mackay, in his " Thames and its Tributaries," " he took her to reside at Greenwich ; and when it pleased him to declare the marriage publicly, and have her crowned, he ordered the Lord Mayor to come to Greenwich in state, and escort her up the river to London. It was on the 19th of May, 1533, and Father Thames had never before borne on his bosom so gallant an array. First of all the mayor and aldermen, with their scarlet robes and golden chains, followed by the common councilmen in their robes, and by all the officers of the City in their costume, with triumphant music swelling upon the ear, and their gay banners floating upon the breeze, walked down to the water-side, where they found their own barges ready to receive them, and fifty other barges filled with the various City companies, awaiting the signal of departure. Then, amid the firing of cannon, and the braying of trumpets, the procession started. A foist, or large flat-bottomed boat, took the lead, impelled by several fellows dressed out to represent devils, who at intervals spouted out blue and red flames from their mouths, and threw balls of fire into the water. 'Terrible and monstrous wild men they were,' says Stow, 'and made a hideous noise. In the midst of them sat a great red dragon, moving itself continually about, and discharging fire-balls of various colours into the air, whence they fell into the water with a gold. When they arrived at Greenwich, they cast anchor, 'making all the while great melody.' They waited thus until three o'clock, when the queen appeared, attended by the Duke of Suffolk, the Marquis of Dorset, the Earl of Wiltshire, her father, the Earls of Arundel, Derby, Rutland, Worcester, Huntingdon, Sussex, Oxford, and many other noblemen and bishops, each one in his barge. In this order they rowed up the Thames to the

PLACENTIA, 1560.

hissing sound. Next came the Lord Mayor's barge, attended by a small barge on the right side filled with musicians. It was richly hung with cloth of gold and silver, and bore the two embroidered banners of the king and queen, besides escutcheons splendidly wrought in every part of the vessel. On the left side was another foist, in the which was a mount, and on the mount stood a white falcon, crowned, upon a root of gold, environed with white and red roses, which was the Queen's device, and about the mount sat virgins, singing and playing melodiously.' Then came the sheriffs and the aldermen, and the common councilmen and the City companies, in regular procession, each barge having its own banners and devices, and most of them being hung with arras and cloth of

Tower stairs, where the king was waiting to receive his bride, whom he kissed 'affectionately and with a loving countenance,' in sight of all the people that lined the shores of the river, and covered all the housetops in such multitudes that Stow was afraid to mention the number, lest posterity should accuse him of exaggeration."

Here, on the 7th of September following, was born, writes Miss Lucy Aikin, "under circumstances as peculiar as her after life proved eventful and illustrious," Elizabeth, daughter of King Henry VIII. by his second consort, Anne Boleyn. Her birth is thus quaintly but prettily recorded by the contemporary historian Hall :—"On the 7th day of September, being Sunday, between three and four o'clock in the afternoon, the queen was delivered of a faire ladye, on which day the Duke of Norfolk came home to the christening." The Princess was baptised on the Wednesday following, in the midst of great pomp and ceremony, at the neighbouring church of the Grey Friars, but of which ancient edifice not a single vestige is now remaining.

in his work on the "Thames and its Tributaries," "had continued to reside alternately at the palaces of Placentia and Hampton Court until the year 1536, when poor Anne Boleyn became no longer pleasing in the eyes of her lord. On May-day in that year Henry instituted a grand tournament

OLD CONDUIT, GREENWICH PARK, IN 1835.

In 1536, on May-day, after a tournament, Anne Boleyn, the mother of the Princess Elizabeth, was arrested here by order of the king, who saw her drop her handkerchief, and fancied that it was meant as a signal to one of her admirers. She was beheaded on the 19th of the same month, on Tower Hill, as every reader of English history knows.

"The royal couple," observes Charles Mackay,

in Greenwich Park, at which the queen and her brother, Lord Rochford, were present. The sports were at their height, when the king, without uttering a word to his queen or anybody else, suddenly took his departure, apparently in an ill-humour, and proceeded to London, accompanied by six domestics. All the tilters were surprised and chagrined; but their surprise and chagrin were light in comparison to those of Anne Boleyn. The very same night her brother and his friends, Norris, Brereton, Weston, and Smeton, were arrested and conveyed up the river to the Tower, bound like felons. On the following morning the queen herself was arrested, and a few hours afterwards conveyed to the same prison, where, on the fifth day of her captivity, she indited that elegant and feeling epistle to her tyrant, dated from her 'dolefull prison in yᵉ Tower,' which every one has read and hundreds have wept over. The king had long suspected her truth; and the offence he took at the tilting match was that she had dropped her handkerchief, accidentally it would appear, but which he conceived to be a signal to a paramour. On the 19th, the anniversary of her coronation and triumphal procession from Greenwich three years before, her young head was smitten from her body by the axe of the executioner, within the precincts of that building where she had received the public kiss, in sight of the multitudes of London! Alas! poor Anne Boleyn!"

Here, in January, 1540, Henry VIII., "magnanimously resolving to sacrifice his own feelings for the good of his country—for once in his life," as Miss Lucy Aikin remarks with dry humour, was married "with great magnificence, and with every outward show of satisfaction," to his fat and ungainly consort, Anne of Cleves. Three years later the king here entertained twenty-one of the Scottish nobility, whom he had taken prisoners at Salem Moss, and gave them their liberty without ransom.

It was here that Will Sommers, the Court fool to Henry VIII., was chiefly domesticated. He used his influence with the king in a way that few Court favourites—not being "fools"—have done before or since. He tamed the royal tyrant's ferocity, and occasionally, at least, urged him on to good and kind actions, himself giving the example by his kindness to those who came within the humble sphere of his influence and act. Armin, in his "Nest of Ninnies," published in 1608, thus describes this laughing philosopher: "A comely fool indeed, passing more stately; who was this forsooth? Will Sommers, and not meanly esteemed by the king for his merriment; his melody was of a higher straine, and he lookt as the noone broad waking. His description was writ on his forehead, and yee might read it thus:—

'Will Sommers, born in Shropshire, as some say,
Was brought to Greenwich on a holy day;
Presented to the king, which foole disdayn'd
To shake him by the hand, or else ashamed;
Howe're it was, as ancient people say,
With much adoe was wonne to it that day.
Leane he was, hollow-ey'd, as all report,
And stoope he did, too: yet in all the Court

Few men were more belov'd than was this foole,
Whose merry prate kept with the king much rule.
When he was sad the king and he would rime,
Thus Will he exil'd sadness many a time.
I could describe him, as I did the rest;
But in my mind I doe not think it best.
My reason this, howe'er I do descry him,
So many know him that I may belye him;
Therefore to please all people one by one,
I hold it best to let that paines alone.
Only thus much: he was the poore man's friend,
And help'd the widdows often in the end;
The king would ever grant what he did crave,
For well he knew Will no exacting knave;
But wisht the king to do good deeds great store,
Which caus'd the Court to love him more and more.'"

It is a comfort to think that Henry VIII. had at least one honest and kind-hearted counsellor, even though he was a—Court fool.

Henry VIII. at one period of his reign was so much attached to Greenwich Palace, that he passed more of his time there than at any of his other royal abodes. He adorned and enlarged it at considerable expense, and made it so magnificent as to cause Leland, the antiquary, to exclaim with rapture, as he gazed upon it—

"How bright the lofty seat appears,
Like Jove's great palace, paved with stars!
What roofs! what windows charm the eye!
What turrets, rivals of the sky!"

Such, at least, is Hasted's translation of Leland's Latin verses. During the reign of the two succeeding sovereigns, Greenwich lost that renown for gaiety which it had acquired from the festivals and constant hospitality of Henry VIII. Here his son, the boy-king, Edward VI., died on the 6th of July, 1553, not without some suspicion of poison; and here Dudley sent for the Lord Mayor, and aldermen and merchants of London, and showed them a forged will, or letters patent, giving the crown to the Lady Jane Grey, who had married his son.

Mary, too, during her brief reign, was an occasional resident at the Palace of Placentia. It is recorded that on one occasion of her sojourn here a very singular accident occurred. The captain of a vessel proceeding down the Thames, observing the banner of England floating from the walls, fired the customary salute in honour of royalty. By some oversight the gun was loaded, and the ball was driven through the wall into the queen's apartments, to the great terror of herself and her ladies. None of them, however, received any hurt.

With the reign of Elizabeth the glories of Greenwich revived. It was her birthplace, and the favourite residence of her unfortunate mother; and during the summer months it became, for the greater part of her reign, the principal seat of her Court. In the year of her accession she here reviewed a large force of companies, raised by the citizens of London in consequence of the Duke of Norfolk's conspiracy. The number of men present on this occasion was 1,400, and the proceedings included a mock fight in the park, which, we are told, "presented all the appearances of a regular battle, except the spilling of blood." The following is the account of the "entertainment," as told by Miss Agnes Strickland, in her "Lives of the Queens of England:"—"The Londoners were so lovingly disposed to their maiden sovereign, that, when she withdrew to her summer bowers at Greenwich, they were fain to devise all sorts of gallant shows to furnish excuses for following her there, to enjoy from time to time the sunshine of her presence. They prepared a sort of civic tournament in honour of her Majesty, July 2nd, each company supplying a certain number of men at arms, 1,400 in all, all clad in velvet and chains of gold, with guns, morris pikes, halberds, and flags, and so marched they over London Bridge, into the Duke of Suffolk's park, at Southwark, where they mustered before the Lord Mayor; and, in order to initiate themselves into the hardships of a campaign, they lay abroad in St. George's Fields all that night. The next morning they set forward in goodly array, and entered Greenwich Park at an early hour, where they reposed themselves till eight o'clock, and then marched down into the lawn, and mustered in their arms, all the gunners being in shirts of mail. It was not, however, till eventide that her Majesty deigned to make herself visible to the doughty bands of Cockaine—chivalry they cannot properly be called, for they had discreetly avoided exposing civic horsemanship to the mockery of the gallant equestrians of the Court, and trusted no other legs than their own with the weight of their valour and warlike accoutrements, in addition to their velvet gaberdines and chains of gold, in which this midsummer bevy had bivouacked in St. George's Fields on the preceding night. At five o'clock the queen came into the gallery of Greenwich Park gate, with the ambassadors, lords, and ladies—a fair and numerous company—to witness a tilting match, in which some of the citizens, and several of her grace's courtiers took part."

While Elizabeth kept Court at her natal palace of Greenwich, she regularly celebrated the national festival on St. George's Day, with great pomp, as the Sovereign of the Order of the Garter, combining, according to the custom of the good old times, a religious service with the picturesque ordinances of this chivalric institution. "All her Majesty's chapel came through the hall in copes, to the number of thirty, singing, 'O God the Father of heaven,' &c., the outward court to the gate being strewed with green rushes."

Elizabeth's first chapter of the Order of the Garter was certainly held in St. George's Hall, at Greenwich; for we find that the same afternoon she went to Baynard's Castle, the Earl of Pembroke's place, and supped with him, and after supper she took boat, and was rowed up and down on the river Thames, hundreds of boats and barges rowing about her, and thousands of people thronging the banks of the river to look upon her Majesty, all rejoicing at her presence, and partaking of the music and sights on the Thames. It seems there was an aquatic festival, in honour of the welcome appearance of their new and comely liege lady on the river; for the trumpets blew, drums beat, flutes played, guns were discharged, and fireworks played off, as she moved from place to place. This continued till ten o'clock, when the queen departed home.

Great hospitality was exercised in the palace at Greenwich, which no stranger who had ostensible business there, from the noble to the peasant, ever visited, it is said, without being invited to either one table or the other, according to his degree. No wonder that Elizabeth was a popular sovereign, and her days were called "golden;" for the way to an Englishman's heart is a good dinner.

The royal park was the scene of a good story, thus told by Miss Agnes Strickland:—"One of her majesty's purveyors having been guilty of some abuses in the county of Kent, on her removal to Greenwich, a sturdy countryman, watching the time when she took her morning walk with the lords and ladies of her household, placed himself conveniently for catching the royal eye and ear, and when he saw her attention perfectly disengaged, began to cry, in a loud voice, 'Which is the queen?' Whereupon, as her manner was, she turned herself towards him, but he continuing his clamorous question, she herself answered, 'I am your queen; what wouldst thou have with me?' 'You,' rejoined the farmer, archly gazing upon her with a look of incredulity, not unmixed with admiration—'you are one of the rarest women I ever saw, and can eat no more than my daughter Madge, who is thought the properest lass in our parish, though short of you; but that Queen Elizabeth I look for devours so many of my hens, ducks, and capons, that I am not able to live.' The queen, who was exceedingly indulgent to all suits, offered through the medium of a compliment, took this homely admonition in good part, inquired the purveyor's name, and finding that he had acted with great dishonesty and injustice, caused condign punishment to be inflicted upon him;" indeed, our author adds that "she ordered him to be hanged, his offence being in violation of a statute-law against such abuses."

Holinshed relates in his "Chronicle," that in 1562, at the reception of the Danish ambassadors here, there was a bull-bait, at the end of which the people were delighted with the sight of a horse with an ape on his back—a sight which, no doubt, gave birth to the sign named among those of London two centuries ago, in the *Spectator*,* the "Jackanapes on Horseback."

The old annalists make constant mention of other proceedings of Elizabeth at Greenwich. One interesting ceremony which has been described was that enacted on Maundy Thursday, on March 19, 1572. The Court being then located here, the queen, according to ancient custom, washed the feet of the poor on that festival, in remembrance of our Saviour washing the feet of the apostles. "Elizabeth will scarcely be blamed in modern times," writes Agnes Strickland, "because she performed the office daintily. The palace hall," she continues, "was prepared with a long table on each side, with benches, carpets, and cushions, and a cross-table at the upper end, where the chaplain stood. Thirty-nine poor women, being the same number as the years of her Majesty's age at that time, entered, and were seated on the forms; then the yeoman of the laundry, armed with a fair towel, took a silver basin filled with warm water and sweet flowers, and washed all their feet, one after the other; he likewise made a cross a little above the toes, and kissed each foot after drying it; the sub-almoner performed the same ceremony, and the queen's almoner also. Then her Majesty entered the hall, and went to a priedieu and cushion, placed in the space between the two tables, and remained during prayers and singing, and while the gospel was read, how Christ washed His apostle's feet. Then came in a procession of thirty-nine of the queen's maids of honour and gentlewomen, each carrying a silver basin with warm water, spring flowers, and sweet herbs, having aprons and towels withal. Then her Majesty, kneeling down on the cushion placed for the purpose, proceeded to wash, in turn, one of the feet of each of the poor women, and wiped them with the assistance of the fair bason-bearers; moreover, she crossed and kissed them, as the others had done. Then, beginning with the first, she gave each a sufficient broad cloth for a gown, and a pair of shoes, a wooden platter, wherein was half a side of salmon, as much ling, six red herrings, two manchetts, and a mazer, or wooden cup, full of claret. All these things she gave separately. Then each of her ladies delivered to her Majesty the towel and the apron used in the ablution, and she gave each of the poor women one a-piece. This was the conclusion of the ladies' official duty of the maundy. The treasurer of the royal chamber, Mr. Heneage, brought her Majesty thirty-nine small white leather purses, each with thirty-nine pence, which she gave separately to every poor woman. Mr. Heneage then supplied her with thirty-nine red purses, each containing twenty shillings; this she distributed to redeem the gown she wore, which by ancient custom was given to one chosen among the number." Our readers will remember that part, but part only, of the same ceremony is still annually performed by some representative of the sovereign on each Maunday Thursday, at Whitehall.†

In Hentzner's "Itinerarium" ("A Journey into England"), written at the close of the sixteenth century, will be found a graphic account of the court of Queen Elizabeth, at Greenwich Palace, in the latter years of her reign. The writer tells us how he was admitted to the Presence Chamber, which he found hung with rich tapestry, and the floor, "after the English fashion, strewed with hay" [rushes]. It was a Sunday, when the attendance of visitors was greatest; and there were waiting in the hall the Archbishop of Canterbury, the Bishop of London, a great number of councillors of state, officers of the court, foreign ministers, noblemen, gentlemen, and ladies. At the door stood a gentleman dressed in velvet, with a gold chain, ready to introduce to the queen any person of distinction who came to wait upon her. The queen passed through the hall on her way to prayers, preceded in regular order by gentlemen, barons, earls, knights of the Garter, all richly dressed and bareheaded. Immediately before the queen came the Lord Chancellor, with the seals in a red silk purse, between two officers bearing the royal sceptre and the sword of state. The queen wore a dress of white silk, bordered with pearls of the size of beans, her train borne by a marchioness. As she turned on either side, all fell on their knees. She "spoke graciously first to one, then to another, whether foreign ministers, or those who attended for different reasons, in English, French, and Italian." The ladies of the court,

---

"very handsome and well-shaped, and for the most part dressed in white, followed next to her, and fifty gentlemen pensioners, with gilt battle-axes, formed her guard." In the ante-chamber, next the hall, she received petitions most graciously; and to the acclamation, "Long live Queen Elizabeth!" she answered, "I thank you, my good people." After the service in the chapel, which lasted only half an hour, the queen returned in the same state as she had entered. The table had been set "with great solemnity" in the banqueting-room, but the queen dined in her inner and private chamber. "The queen dines and sups alone, with very few attendants; and it is very seldom that anybody, foreign or native, is admitted at that time, and then only at the intercession of somebody in power." The German traveller is particular in describing with exact minuteness the personal appearance of the queen, who was then in her sixty-fifth year, and "very majestic:" "her face," he says, "was oblong, fair but wrinkled; her eyes small, yet black and pleasant; her nose a little hooked; her lips narrow, and her teeth black (a defect the English seem subject to, from their too great use of sugar). She had in her ears two pearls with very rich drops; she wore false hair, and that red. Upon her head she had a small crown. Her bosom was uncovered, as all the English ladies have it till they marry; and she had a necklace of exceeding fine jewels." We may add here that in Walpole's "Catalogue of Royal and Noble Authors" there is a curious head of Queen Elizabeth when old and haggard, done with great exactness from a coin, the die of which was broken. A striking feature in the queen's face was her high nose, which is not justly represented in many pictures and prints of her. She was notoriously vain of her personal charms, and, affirming that shadows were unnatural in painting, she ordered one artist, Isaac Oliver, to paint her without any. There are three engravings of her Majesty after this artist, two by Vertue, and one, a whole length, by Crispin de Pass, who published portraits of illustrious personages of this kingdom during the sixteenth century.

Greenwich Palace was, as we have just seen, much mixed up with the domestic life of Queen Elizabeth; but it was not all sunshine with her, as the following episode, told by Miss Agnes Strickland, will show:—"The terror of the plague was always uppermost in the minds of all persons in the sixteenth century, at every instance of sudden death. One day, in November, 1573, Queen Elizabeth was conversing with her ladies in her privy chamber, at Greenwich Palace, when, on a sudden, the 'mother of the maids' was seized with illness, and expired directly in her presence. Queen Elizabeth was so much alarmed at this circumstance, that in less than an hour she left her palace at Greenwich, and went to Westminster, where she remained."

On the return of Sir Walter Raleigh to England, with a high reputation for courage and discretion, after successfully quelling the disturbances of the Desmonds, in Munster, he was introduced to Queen Elizabeth at Greenwich Palace, and soon obtained a prominent position in the Court. His advancement is said to have been greatly promoted by an almost fantastic display of gallantry, which he made on one occasion before the queen. He was, it is stated by some historians, "attending her Majesty in a walk, when she came to a place where her progress was obstructed by a mire. Without a moment's hesitation he took off his rich plush cloak, and spread it on the ground for her foot-cloth. She was highly pleased with this practical flattery, and it was afterwards remarked that this sacrifice of a cloak gained him many a *good suit.*" The grounds of Saye's Court have been fixed upon by some writers as the scene of this little episode; others, however, state that Raleigh placed his cloak on the landing-stage opposite the palace at Greenwich on one occasion when her Majesty alighted from her barge, the customary floor-cloth having by some oversight been forgotten.

The antiquarian reader will not have forgotten the fact that ladies, when as yet coaches had not been invented and introduced into England, were accustomed to make their journeys on horseback, seated on pillions behind some relative or serving-man. In this way Queen Elizabeth, when she went up to London from her palace at Greenwich, used to seat herself behind her Lord Chancellor or Chamberlain.

In 1605 James I. settled Greenwich Palace and Park on his queen, Anne of Denmark, who forthwith rebuilt with brick the garden front of the palace, and laid the foundation of a building near the park, called the "House of Delight," in which the governor of Greenwich Hospital afterwards resided, and which now forms the central building of the Royal Naval Schools. In the following year the Princess Mary, daughter of James I., was christened at Greenwich with great solemnity.

Charles I. resided much at Greenwich previous to the breaking out of the civil war; and Henrietta Maria so "finished and furnished" the house which Anne of Denmark had begun, that, as Philipott, the Kentish historian, wrote, "it far surpasseth all other houses of the kind in England." Inigo

Jones was employed as the architect to superintend the work carried on in the building, and it was completed in 1635. Rubens was frequently in attendance on the Court of Charles at Greenwich; and it is stated that Queen Henrietta was anxious to form a cabinet of pictures here, and to have the ceilings and walls of her oratory and other rooms painted by Jordaens or Rubens, and that negotiations were entered into with those painters for the

and in the distance we see the parish church, and the shipping on the river. The palace, by the river-side, appears as an irregular Gothic structure with two towers. In the middle distance stands a more modern mansion, apparently in the middle of a corn-field. As already mentioned by us,* over the buttery there formerly stood two rude wooden figures, known as "Beer" and "Gin;" they are now in the Tower of London.

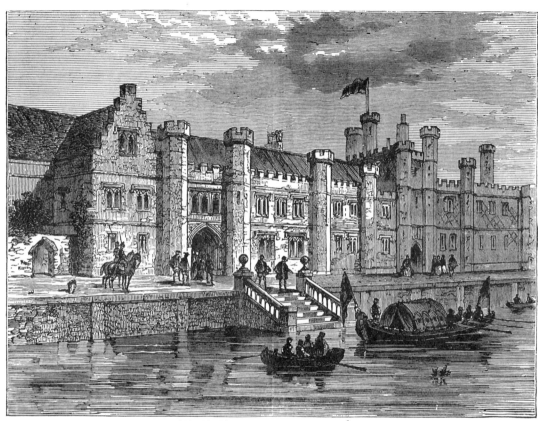

OLD PALACE OF GREENWICH, IN 1630.

purpose, but pecuniary or political difficulties intervened. Most of the ceilings in the palace were subsequently painted for Charles I. by Gentileschi. Some idea of the general external appearance of the palace at this time may be obtained from what is called "The Long View of Greenwich," printed in 1637; it is to be seen among the etchings of Hollar, in a few choice collections. It was originally dedicated to Queen Henrietta Maria; and it is said that Hollar worked this plate for a publisher for thirty shillings! The latter, finding the queen's unpopularity to interfere with the sale of the plate, induced Hollar to erase the dedication, and to substitute in its place a copy of verses which are found in some impressions. In the foreground is the observatory hill and park, with ladies promenading,

King Charles left Greenwich palace with the fatal resolution of taking his journey northward, and the turbulent state of the times prevented him from again visiting it. In the night of the 3rd of November, 1642, three companies of foot and a troop of horse were sent by the Parliament to search the town and palace of Greenwich for concealed arms; but, says Lysons, "they found only a few two-handed swords without scabbards." On the king's death, in 1648, the palace passed out of the royal keeping. In 1652, the Commonwealth requiring funds for their navy, the House of Commons resolved "that Greenwich House, park, and lands should be immediately sold for ready money."

---

* See Vol. II., p. 87.

A VIEW OF THE ANCIENT ROYAL PALACE CALLED PLACENTIA.
(From a Print published by the Society of Antiquaries in 1767, after an Early Drawing.)

A survey and valuation of them was ordered to be made, just as had been done in the case of Hyde Park,* and finally an ordinance was passed for carrying the sale into execution. Particulars were accordingly made out of the "Hoby stables" and other smaller premises belonging to the palace, which were sold, but no further proceedings as to the rest of the estate were taken at this time. John Evelyn, in his "Diary," under date of April 29, 1652, writes: "We went this afternoone to see the Queene's House at Greenwich, now given by the rebells to Bulstrode Whitlock, one of their unhappy counsellors and keepers of pretended liberties." In 1654, when the Crown lands were sold, Greenwich was reserved, and eventually it was appropriated to the Lord Protector as a residence. On the restoration of Charles II., in 1660, it reverted to the Crown, with the other royal demesnes. The king, finding the old palace greatly decayed by time, and the want of necessary repairs during the Commonwealth, ordered it to be taken down, and a new palace was commenced in its place. One wing of this new palace was completed at a cost of £36,000, and now forms, with additions, the west wing of the present edifice. Sir John Denham, the poet, was at that time the royal surveyor, or official architect; but as he knew little of building practically, he employed Webb, the son-in-law of Inigo Jones, from whose papers his designs are said to have been made. Evelyn evidently did not think much of Sir John's qualifications as an architect, for he writes in his "Diary," under date of October 19, 1661: "I went to London to visite my Lord of Bristoll, having first been (*sic*) with Sir John Denham (his Majesty's surveyor), to consult with him about the placing of his palace at Greenwhich, which I would have had built between the river and the Queenes house, so as a large square cutt should have let in the Thames like a bay; but Sir John was for setting it on piles at the very brink of the water, which I did not assent to, and so came away, knowing Sir John to be a better poet than architect."

"His Majesty," writes Evelyn, under date of January 24, 1662, "entertained me with his intentions of building his Palace of Greenwich, and quite demolishing the old one; on which I declared my thoughts." What his "thoughts" were, he does not tell us; but probably they were in accordance with those of his brother "diarist," Samuel Pepys,

who, on March 4th, 1663-4, writes: "At Greenwich I observed the foundation laying of a very great house for the king, which will cost a great deal of money." On the 26th of July of the following year, Pepys writes: "To Greenwich, where I heard the king and duke are come by water this morn from Hampton Court. They asked me several questions. The king mightily pleased with his new buildings there." A few years later—viz., in March, 1669—Pepys, after recording a visit paid to him by "Mr. Evelyn, of Deptford, a worthy good man," and his own visit subsequently to Woolwich, goes on to tell us how that he returned "thence to Greenwich by water, and there landed at the king's house, which goes on slow, but is very pretty."

The widowed Queen of Charles I., Henrietta Maria, spent several months at Greenwich after the restoration of her son; bonfires were lit to greet her on her arrival here. She continued to keep her Court in England till July, 1665, when she finally embarked for France. She died at Colombe, near Paris, in 1669; and her son, James II., says of her that "she excelled in all the good qualities of a good wife, a good mother, and a good Christian."

Notwithstanding the apparent eagerness of King Charles II., at first, for the construction of the palace and the improvements of the grounds, he seems to have given up the idea of continuing the work after the completion of the wing mentioned above, and nothing further was done to the building either by him or his successor to the crown. As William III. divided his time between Kensington and Hampton Court, Greenwich was no longer thought of as a royal residence; but Queen Mary conceived even a nobler use for the then unfinished building. Charles II. had, in 1682, laid the foundation of the hospital at Chelsea for disabled soldiers; but this was only completed by William and Mary in 1690. Mary, we are told, thought there should be a similar hospital for disabled seamen. "Amid the rejoicings called forth by the great victory of La Hogue, in May, 1692, the feelings of the queen were harrowed by the large number of maimed and wounded soldiers landed at our naval ports. William was in Holland, and Mary, as his vicegerent, after making every possible provision for the wounded, now publicly declared in her husband's name that the building commenced by Charles should be completed, and should be a retreat for seamen disabled in the service of their country." As such we shall deal with it in the following chapter.

* See Vol. IV., p. 380.

CHAPTER XIV.

GREENWICH (*continued*).—THE HOSPITAL FOR SEAMEN, &c.

" Go, with old Thames, view Chelsea's glorious pile,
And ask the shattered hero whence his smile?
Go view the splendid domes of Greenwich—go,
And own what raptures from reflection flow."
S. Rogers, " *Pleasures of Memory.*"

Greenwich Hospital as a Monument to Queen Mary, and of the Victory of La Hogue—Appointment of the Commissioners by William III.—Sir Christopher Wren's Share in the Building—John Evelyn as Treasurer—Description of the Building—Memorials of Joseph René Bellot, and the Officers who fell in the Indian Mutiny—The Chapel—The Painted Hall—Nelson's Funeral Car—The Nelson Room—The Hospital—Sources of its Revenue—The Old Pensioners and their Accommodation—The Royal Naval College—The Naval Museum—The Nelson and other Relics—The Infirmary for the Pensioners—The Seamen's Hospital—The *Dreadnought*—The Royal Naval School—Officers connected with Greenwich Hospital since its establishment—Fund for Disabled Seamen.

THE reader will not have forgotten the account which Macaulay gives of the causes which led to the foundation of Greenwich Hospital, immediately after the death of Queen Mary, the Consort of William III. " The affection with which her husband cherished her memory," he writes, " was soon attested by a monument, the most superb that was ever erected to any sovereign. No scheme had been so much her own, none had been so near her heart, as that of converting the palace into a retreat for seamen. It had occurred to her when she had found it difficult to provide good shelter and good attendance for the thousands of brave men who had come back to England wounded after the battle of La Hogue. Whilst she lived, scarcely any step was taken towards the accomplishment of her favourite design; but it should seem that, as soon as her husband had lost her, he began to reproach himself for having neglected her wishes. No time was now lost. A plan was furnished by Wren, and soon an edifice, surpassing that asylum which the magnificent Louis had provided for his soldiers, rose on the margin of the Thames. Whoever reads the inscription which runs round the frieze of the hall will observe that King William claims no part of the merit of the design, and that the praise is ascribed to Mary alone. Had the king's life been prolonged, a statue of her who was the real foundress of the institution would have had a conspicuous place in that court which presents two lofty domes and two graceful colonnades to the multitudes who are perpetually passing up and down the imperial river. But that part of the plan was never carried into effect; a few of those who now gaze on the noblest of European hospitals are aware that it is a memorial of the virtues of the good Queen Mary, of the love and sorrow of William, and of the great victory of La Hogue."

This magnificent structure, which is considered tne finest specimen of classical architecture in this or almost any other country, occupies the site of the old royal palace, on the southern bank of the Thames, between that river and Greenwich Park. It was established, as before stated, in the reign of William and Mary, who, " for the encouragement of seamen and the improvement of navigation," by their letters patent, dated October 25th, 1694, granted to Sir John Somers, Knight, Keeper of the Great Seal; Thomas, Duke of Leeds; Thomas, Earl of Pembroke and Montgomery; Charles, Duke of Shrewsbury; Sidney, Lord Godolphin; and others—" all that piece or parcell of ground situate, lying, and being within the Parish of East Greenwich, and being parcell or reputed parcell of our Mannor of East Greenwich aforesaid, containing in the whole, by admeasurement, eight acres, two roods, and thirty-two square perches; and all that capital messuage lately built, or in building, by our royall uncle, King Charles II., and still remaining unfinished, commonly called by the name of our Palace at Greenwich, standing upon the piece or parcell of ground aforesaid; and those edifices and tofts called the chapel and vestry there;" and other tenements, to erect and found a hospital " for the reliefe and support of seamen serving on board the shipps or vessells belonging to the Navy Royall of us, our heires, or successors; or imploy'd in our or their service at sea; who, by reason of age, wounds, or other disabilities, shall be incapable of further service at sea, and be unable to maintain themselves; and also for the sustentation of the widows, and maintenance and education of the children of seamen happening to be slaine or disabled in such sea service.' Queen Mary, who, as we have shown, was the first projector of this charitable institution, died on the 28th of December, 1694, two months after the grant was made for carrying her wishes into effect.

In March of the following year, the king appointed nearly two hundred commissioners; including George, Prince of Denmark; the principal

Officers of State ; the Archbishops, Bishops, Judges, the Lord Mayor and Aldermen of London ; and the Masters, Wardens, &c., of the Trinity House. John Evelyn gives us, in his " Diary," an accurate account of the successive steps taken by himself and his brother commissioners in establishing the hospital, of which he was appointed treasurer. The first meeting of the commissioners was held at the Guildhall, May 5th, 1695, the Archbishop of Canterbury, Lord Godolphin, the Duke of Shrewsbury, and Sir Christopher Wren, and others being present. In the course of that month several other meetings were held, at which Evelyn, Wren, and two other commissioners, having gone to Greenwich to survey the place, made a report to the effect that "the standing part (of the palace) might be made serviceable at present for £6,000," and what extent of ground would be requisite in order to complete the design. The draft of the hospital was settled in the following April, and the first stone of the new edifice laid on the 30th of June, by Evelyn himself, supported by Wren and Flamsteed, "the king's astronomical professor." Evelyn records even the exact hour at which the ceremony took place : " Precisely at five o'clock in the evening, after we had dined together ; Mr. Flamsteed observing the punctual time by instruments." Evelyn's salary, as treasurer, was £200, much of the work being done by his son-in-law Draper, as his deputy, though the works as they progressed kept him at Saye's Court, away from his beloved Wotton, during the entire summer. Draper, we may add, succeeded Evelyn in the treasurership. The subscriptions received during the first twelve months towards the hospital amounted, according to Evelyn, to upwards of £9,000, including £2,000 from the king, and £500 apiece from nearly all the leading statesmen. According to a note by the treasurer, four months after the foundation, the work done amounted to upwards of £5,000, towards which the treasurer had received only £800, there being among the defaulters the king's £2,000, paid by exchequer tallies on the Post Office, "which," says he, "nobody will take at 30 per cent. discount," a statement which, if true, does not redound to King Charles's credit. Part of the expense of the erection of the structure was raised by state lotteries. Evelyn writes, in his " Diary " for May, 1699: " All lotteries, till now cheating the people, to be no longer permitted than to Christmas, except that for the benefit of Greenwich Hospital." From an entry which he makes in his " Diary " in January, 1705, it appears that the building was so far advanced that the committee had already admitted some

pensioners : " I went to Greenwich Hospital, where they now begin to take in wounded and worn-out seamen, who are exceedingly well provided for." He adds, *more suo*, "The buildings now going on are very magnificent." In a note in Evelyn's " Diary " is published his debtor and creditor account for the erection of the hospital. The total of subscriptions, &c., seems to have been £69,320, exclusive of the produce of lottery tickets, £11,434, and malt tickets, £1,000; but the exact meaning of this last item is not very clear.

The hospital is elevated on a terrace upwards of 280 yards in length, and in its completed form consists of four distinct blocks of building. The two blocks nearest the river, known respectively as King Charles's and Queen Anne's Buildings, stand on either side of the " Great Square," 570 feet in width. The two blocks south of them, King William's and Queen Mary's Buildings, are brought nearer to each other by the width of the colonnades ; and the cupolas at the inner angles form a fine central feature, and impart unity to the general composition. The view from the north gate, in the centre of the terrace, is very striking. Beyond the square are seen the hall and chapel, with their finely-proportioned cupolas and gilt vanes, and the two colonnades, which form a kind of avenue terminated by the Royal Naval School, above which, on an eminence in the park, appears the Royal Observatory.

In the centre of the great square is a statue of George III. It was the gift of Admiral Sir John Jennings, who was governor of the hospital in the reign of that king. It was sculptured by Rysbrach, out of a single block of white marble, which weighed eleven tons, and had been captured from the French by Sir George Rooke.

At each extremity of the terrace in front of the hospital is a small pavilion ; their use, however, is not very apparent, they were erected in 1778, and named respectively after King George III. and Queen Charlotte, but it is not on record that their majesties ever used them for tea-parties or other purposes. On the terrace, in front of the gates, is a granite obelisk, erected as " a memorial of the gallant young Frenchman, Joseph René Bellot, who perished in the search for Sir John Franklin, August, 1853." In the north-west corner of the grounds, in front of the " Ship " hotel, is another obelisk, put up in memory of several officers who fell during the Indian Mutiny.

King Charles's Building is on the west side of the great square. The eastern portion formed the unfinished palace of Charles II. ; it is built about an inner quadrangle, and is constructed of Portland stone. In the centre is a portico of the Corinthian order, crowned with an entablature and pediment; and in the pediment is a piece of sculpture, consisting of two figures, one representing Fortitude, and the other the Dominion of the Sea. At each end is a pavilion formed by four pilasters of the Corinthian order, and surmounted by an attic. The four fronts of this block of buildings nearly correspond with each other. In the pediment on the eastern side is a piece of sculpture representing Mars and Fame. Some part of this block having become very much decayed, it was rebuilt in 1814. Richardson, in his "History of Greenwich," states that Admiral George Byng was "confined in that quarter of Greenwich Hospital known as King Charles's Building, in the year 1756, previous to his execution at Portsmouth in 1757." He also adds, "The individual to whom the author is indebted for his information waited on the admiral in the capacity of servant to the Marshal of the Admiralty, in whose custody the admiral then was, and, accompanying his master and the prisoner to Portsmouth, it eventually fell to his lot to place the cushion for the admiral to kneel upon when he was shot."

Queen Anne's Building, the corresponding block facing the river, was commenced in 1698, and was so named on the accession of Anne to the throne. It resembles King Charles's Building, except that the pediments are without sculpture. This building now serves as the Naval Museum, of which we shall have more to say presently.

To the south of Queen Anne's Building is another block, named after Queen Mary, the north side of which forms the chapel. The lofty cupola at the western extremity of the chapel serves as the vestibule, in which are statues of Faith, Hope, Meekness, and Charity, from designs by Benjamin West. From this vestibule a flight of steps leads into the chapel, through folding doors of mahogany, highly enriched and carved. The original chapel being destroyed by fire in January, 1779, the present structure was erected in its place, from the designs of James Stuart ("Athenian Stuart"), and was opened for service in 1789. The chapel is upwards of 100 feet long, and more than 50 feet wide. The nave, and space round the communion-table and organ-gallery, is paved with black and white marble, and in the centre of the nave is the representation of an anchor and a seaman's compass. The ceiling is divided into compartments, ornamented with foliage and other designs in the antique style. The whole interior of the chapel is richly decorated with coloured marbles, scagliola, and fancy woods, sculpture, carving, and painting.

Entrance to the chapel is gained through an elaborately-sculptured marble screen with a frieze, by Bacon; and at each end of the chapel are four marble columns of the Corinthian order, supporting the roof. In recesses above the gallery door, &c., are figures of prophets and evangelists, by Benjamin West; whilst over the communion-table is a large painting, also by West, representing the "Preservation of St. Paul from Shipwreck on the Island of Melita."

King William's Building, at the south-west side, like the corresponding block, has massive Doric columns, and comprises the great, or Painted Hall, the dining-hall of the original institution, with its vestibule and cupola. This part of the hospital was so far completed by the commencement of the year 1705, as to be capable of receiving forty-two seamen. Three years later there were 300 pensioners within the walls. The colonnades to King William's and Queen Mary's Buildings are each 347 feet long, with returns of seventy feet. Each contains 300 coupled Doric columns twenty feet high.

That portion of the structure of which Evelyn laid the foundation was completed in two years, the architect being Sir Christopher Wren, who, it is said, generously undertook the work of that post without any emolument, his labours being equivalent to a large subscription. In 1698, Sir Christopher Wren submitted to the committee a plan for a large dining-hall (now the Painted Hall), which being approved of by them, the necessary portion of ground was immediately laid out, and the work prosecuted with such diligence, that the whole was roofed in and the dome erected by August, 1703, forming what is now called "King William's Building." The hall, originally intended as the hospital refectory, now serves as the gallery of naval pictures. It is upwards of 100 feet in length, by fifty feet in width, and about the same in height. It is sufficiently well lighted for the purpose for which it was originally designed, but hardly so for a picture-gallery. It is entered by a noble vestibule, open to one of the lofty cupolas, from which it receives a very dim and shadowy light. A short flight of steps leads up into the hall, the ceiling of which at once rivets the attention of the visitor. This was painted by Sir James Thornhill, and is divided into compartments. Its praises were first sounded by Sir Richard Steele, who, in his play of *The Lover*, has given an admirable description of it. In the central compartment appear King William and Queen Mary, surrounded by allegorical personages, intended to typify national prosperity, and the compartments are filled with figures representing the Seasons, the Elements, the Zodiac, with portraits of Copernicus, Newton, &c. ; emblems of science and naval trophies. Every one remembers the marvellous story of Sir James Thornhill stepping back to see the effect of his painting upon the ceiling, and being prevented from falling to the floor by some person defacing a portion of his work, thus causing the painter to rush forward and save himself from death.

number of its inmates, the space proved inadequate to their accommodation ; the table of the officers was discontinued, and other dining-halls for the men were provided on the basement storey. The noble apartment had been thus unoccupied nearly a century, when, in 1794, the Lieutenant-Governor, Mr. Locker, suggested its appropriation to the service of a National Gallery of Marine Paintings, to commemorate the eminent services of the Royal

GREENWICH HOSPITAL, FROM THE RIVER.

The painting of this hall occupied Sir James Thornhill nineteen years, from 1708 to 1727 ; and he was paid at the rate of £3 a square yard for the ceiling, and £1 a yard for the walls. On the latter are fluted Corinthian pilasters, trophies, &c. Beyond the great hall is a raised apartment, called the "upper hall."

The great hall, as we have said, was at first intended to be used as the common refectory of the institution, the upper chamber being appropriated to the table of the officers, and the lower to those of the pensioners. But when the growing revenue of the Hospital gradually led to an increase of the

Navy of England. This tasteful design was not then executed ; but in 1823 it was again proposed by Governor Locker's son, who, with the consent of the then commissioners and governor, began the collection of the various paintings. The plan was warmly patronised by George IV., who promptly and liberally gave directions that the extensive and valuable series of portraits of the celebrated admirals of the reigns of Charles II. and William III. at Windsor Castle and Hampton Court should be transferred hither ; and the king subsequently presented several other valuable and appropriate paintings from his private collection at

St. James's Palace and Carlton House. Thus was formed the nucleus of "The Naval Gallery." The example thus set by royalty was promptly followed by gifts of pictures from many noble and other liberal benefactors; and thus, in the course of a few years, the walls of the Painted Hall were naval heroes who have arisen in our isle since we became "super-eminent as a sea-faring and a sea-conquering people," beginning with Raleigh, Willoughby, Hawkins, and Drake, there are here large numbers of naval pictures of great interest, such as the Defeat of the Spanish Armada, the

THE PAINTED HALL, GREENWICH HOSPITAL.

adorned with portraits of our celebrated naval commanders, and representations of their actions. To these, five other valuable pictures were added by King William IV., in the year 1835. The collection removed hither from Hampton Court included Sir Godfrey Kneller's series of portraits known as "Queen Anne's Admirals," a series of some little value to the student of costume, as showing all the modifications of the flowing wig which marked the era of the later Stuarts. Besides the portraits of most of the celebrated Battle of Barfleur, Duncan's Victory at Camperdown, Nelson's Victory of the Nile, the Battle of Trafalgar, &c. The "upper hall" is painted in a style to correspond with the great hall, but here the walls, as well as the ceiling, are covered. The ceiling exhibits Queen Anne and her consort, Prince George of Denmark; other figures personify the four quarters of the globe; and on the walls below are represented, on one side, the landing of William III. at Torbay in 1688, on the other the arrival of George I. at Greenwich. The central wall, facing the entrance, presents a group of portraits of King George I. and two generations of his family. The dome of St. Paul's, then newly erected, appears in the background, amidst a cloud of tutelary virtues; and in front is to be seen Sir James Thornhill, the painter. The models of old men-of-war, the Franklin relics, and other objects formerly exhibited here, are now removed to the Naval Museum, which we shall presently notice. One object, however, which was formerly shown here, has altogether disappeared. This was the funeral car in which the body of Nelson was conveyed, "with all the pomp befitting the gratitude of a great nation to the illustrious dead," to St. Paul's Cathedral. "Of all the pageantry that Greenwich has witnessed since it became a town," writes Charles Mackay, in his "Thames and its Tributaries," "this was, if not the most magnificent, the most grand and impressive. The body, after lying in state for three days in the hospital, during which it was visited by immense multitudes, was conveyed, on the 8th of January, 1806, up the river to Whitehall, followed in procession by the City Companies in their state barges. The flags of all the vessels in the river were lowered half-mast high, in token of mourning, and solemn minute-guns were fired during the whole time of the procession. The body lay all that night at the Admiralty, and on the following morning was removed on a magnificent car, surmounted by plumes of feathers and decorated with heraldic insignia, to its final resting-place in St. Paul's Cathedral. From the Admiralty to St. Paul's the streets were all lined with the military. The procession was headed by detachments of the Dragoon Guards, the Scots Greys, and the 92nd Highlanders, with the Duke of York and his staff, the band playing that sublime funeral strain, the 'Dead March in Saul.' Then followed the pensioners of Greenwich Hospital and the seamen of Lord Nelson's ship, the *Victory*, a deputation from the Common Council of London, and a long train of mourning coaches, including those of the royal family, the chief officers of state, and all the principal nobility of the kingdom. When the coffin, covered with the flag of the *Victory*, was about to be lowered into the grave, an affecting incident occurred: the attendant sailors who had borne the pall rushed forward, and seizing upon the flag, before a voice could be raised to prevent them, rent it into shreds, in the intensity of their feelings, that each might preserve a shred as a memento of the departed." The car and its trappings gradually decayed, and becoming worm-eaten and past repair, were broken up.

A small apartment adjoining the upper hall, called the Nelson Room, contains an admirable portrait of Nelson, painted by Abbot, and also some half-dozen pictures illustrative of events in the great admiral's life, together with Benjamin West's strange admixture of realism and allegory, called the Apotheosis of Nelson.

"When we consider the entire dependence of every great work of this class on the caprice of successive rulers," writes the author of "Bohn's Pictorial Handbook of London," "we shall think it much more remarkable that every royal family, except that of England, should have been able to begin and finish a palace (and in some cases more than one), than that English sovereigns should have not yet achieved such a work. Greenwich is the attempt that most nearly reached realisation; and, as when it is seen from the river the patchwork is mostly out of sight, the group becomes the most complete architectural scene we possess. The two northern masses of building are from a design of Jones; though the first was not erected till after his death, by his pupil and son-in-law Webb; and the other not till Queen Anne's reign, after whom it is named. The older (or King Charles's) building was partly rebuilt in 1811–14, and distinguished by sculpture of artificial stone in the pediment. The southern masses are chiefly from a design of Sir Christopher Wren, and were commenced by William and Mary, whose names they bear; but their construction proceeding slowly, successive periods have left the melancholy marks of steadily declining taste and increasing parsimony; that which begins in Portland stone and Corinthian splendour sinking at length into mean brickwork, or unable to afford in inferior stone the most ordinary degree of finish. The design of the brick portions is in the most corrupt taste of Vanbrugh, but whatever is visible from the centre of the group is by Jones or Wren. The inferiority of the latter is obvious in the comparative want of repose, and greater crowding and flutter of small and multiplied parts. The two pyramidising masses crowned by domes are finely placed, and quite characteristic of his style, as is also the coupling of columns in the colonnades. There is nothing so majestic as either the inward or river elevations of Jones's work, but more picturesqueness and variety. The two not only show the distinction between the tastes of these masters, but also exemplify, in some measure, that between the Roman and Venetian schools of modern architecture; the northern buildings having some resemblance to the former, though, in general, both our great architects were followers of the latter."

Such, then, is the general appearance of Greenwich Hospital, an edifice which, as stated in an earlier chapter, was considered by Peter the Great more fitted to be the abode of royalty than that of worn-out seamen. Samuel Rogers, in his poem, the " Pleasures of Memory, thus speaks of the institution :

> " Hail ! noblest structure, imaged in the wave,
> A nation's grateful tribute to the brave ;
> Hail ! blest retreat from war and shipwreck, hail !
> That oft arrest the wondering stranger's sail.
> Long have ye heard the narratives of age,
> The battle's havoc, and the tempest's rage ;
> Long have ye known Reflection's genial ray,
> Gild the calm close of Valour's various day.
> Time's sombrous touches soon correct the piece,
> Mellow each tint, and bid each discord cease ;
> A softer tone of light pervades the whole,
> And steals a pensive languor o'er the soul."

blue clothes, a hat, three pairs of stockings, two pairs of shoes, five neck-cloths, three shirts, and two nightcaps.

According to Richardson's work on Greenwich, quoted above, the funds, by means of which this institution has been raised and maintained, were derived from the following sources :—" The sum of £2,000 per annum granted by the king in 1695, and other subscriptions ; a duty of sixpence per month from every mariner, granted by Act of Parliament in 1696 ; the gift of some land by King William in 1698 ; the grant of £19,500 in 1699, being the amount of fines paid by various merchants for smuggling ; £600, the produce of a lottery, in 1699 ; the profits of the markets at Greenwich, granted by Henry, Earl of Romney, in 1700 ; the grant by the Crown, in 1701, of the ground where

OLD VIEW OF GREENWICH PALACE. (*After Hollar.*)

The idea here shadowed forth may be a little exaggerated, and " discord " may, perhaps, not have wholly " ceased " within the walls of the hospital to the extent pictured by the poet—at all events, whilst the old pensioners occupied its apartments ; but still these lines give expression to a truth which has been felt and acknowledged by hundreds and thousands of visitors both before and since they were penned.

The hospital, as we have seen, was first opened as an asylum in 1705, when forty-two disabled seamen were admitted. In 1738 the number of pensioners had increased to 1,000, which had become doubled in the course of the next forty years. The number was subsequently increased to about 3,000, independently of about 32,000 out-pensioners. Each of the pensioners had a weekly allowance of seven loaves, weighing 1 lb. each, 3 lbs. of beef, 2 lbs. of mutton, a pint of pease, 1¼ lb. of cheese, 2 oz. of butter, 14 qrts. of beer, and one shilling a week tobacco money ; besides which he received, once in two years, a suit of

the market was formerly kept, and some edifices adjoining, in perpetuity ; £6,472 1s., the amount of the effects of Kid, the pirate, given by Queen Anne in 1705 ; the moiety (valued at £20,000) of an estate bequeathed by Robert Osbolston, Esq., in 1707 ; and the profits of the unexpired lease of the North and South Foreland Lighthouses (since renewed for ninety-nine years to the hospital) ; a grant of land in 1707 ; forfeited and unclaimed shares of prize-money, granted by Act of Parliament in 1708, and several subsequent acts ; £6,000 per annum, granted by Queen Anne in 1710, out of a duty on coal, and continued for a long term by George I. ; the wages of the chaplains of the hospital, and the value of their provisions, &c., as chaplains of Deptford and Woolwich Dockyards— an increase of salary having been given them in lieu thereof ; the amount of the half-pay of all the officers of the hospital—salaries being allowed in lieu thereof ; £10,000, grant in 1728, and several subsequent years, by Parliament ; the grant by the king, in 1730, of a small piece of land, with the crane, adjoining the river; an estate given by Mr. Clapham at Eltham, in 1730, consisting of several houses and warehouses near London Bridge; and the forfeited estates of the Earl of Derwentwater, given by Act of Parliament in 1735, deducting an annual rent-charge of £2,500 to the Earl of Newburgh and his heirs male. Several contributions have also been made by private individuals, among which may be noticed £10,000 Three per Cent. Consols, and £2,600, both anonymous benefactions; £1,110 by Captain J. Turroyman; £500 by Captain J. Matthews; and £210, being part of a sum subscribed at Lloyd's Coffee-house, on account of an action fought October 11th, 1797."

By Queen Anne's Commission, dated July 21st, 1703, there were appointed seven commissioners, who were to form a general court; the Lord High Admiral, the Lord Treasurer, or any two privy councillors, to form a quorum; the governor and treasurer were appointed by the Crown, and all the other necessary officers by the Lord High Admiral, on the recommendation of the general court. The same commission appointed twenty-five directors, called the "standing committee," who met once every fortnight, and vested the internal government in the governor and a council of officers who were appointed by the Lord High Admiral. By a charter, granted by George III., the commissioners became a body corporate, with full power to finish the building, to provide for seamen either within or without the hospital, to make bye-laws, &c.; and this charter was followed by an Act of Parliament, which vested in the commissioners, thus incorporated, all the estates held in trust for the benefit of the hospital. By an Act passed in 1829, "for the better management of the affairs of Greenwich Hospital," this corporation of commissioners and governors was dissolved, and five commissioners appointed in their stead, and in them the estates and property of the hospital — amounting, from the various sources mentioned above, to nearly £170,000 annually—was vested. These commissioners were generally members of Parliament who had served in the inferior offices of the ministry, ex-lords of the Treasury, Admiralty, &c. Complaints of great want of economy in the employment of this large revenue, the evidently increasing disinclination of seamen to enter the hospital as in patients, and a doubt whether the institution was adapted to the existing social condition of the class which it was intended to benefit, led, ultimately, to a Commission of Enquiry, on whose recommendation, in 1865, an Act of Parliament was passed, by which improved arrangements were made as to

the out-pensioners, and advantageous terms were offered to such inmates of the hospital as were willing to retire from it, with a view of closing it as an almshouse.

Out of 1,400 in-pensioners then in the hospital, nearly a thousand at once elected to leave. A second act, passed in 1869, effected a final clearance; and in the following year Greenwich Hospital ceased to be an asylum for seamen, though the last-mentioned act provides that in case of war the building shall be at all times available for its original purpose. On the departure of the old veteran seamen, for whom this great work was erected, Greenwich lost many of its distinctive and most glorious associations. The change was a severe one for many of the old men, and it is said that more than half the number died within a very short time of vacating their old quarters. It seems, however, to have been the opinion of many who knew the old pensioners and the present race of "salts," that the new arrangement—by which they receive their pensions in money, and live where and as they please with their relatives or friends— is better for them mentally as well as physically, and is more acceptable to the present generation of sailors.

It was a pleasing sight, on a fine day, to see the old pensioners standing about in groups, or taking a solitary walk in the courts of the Hospital, or intent upon some newspaper, or perchance a book of adventures by sea, which recalled to them the experiences of early life. In the beautiful park hard by they appeared to find much gratification in rambling; and many of them would establish themselves on some green knoll, provided with a telescope, the wonders of which they would exhibit to strangers, and point out, with all the talkativeness of age, the remarkable objects which might be seen on every side. The appearance of these veterans—some without a leg or arm, others hobbling from the infirmities of wounds, or of years, and all clothed in old-fashioned blue coats and breeches, with cocked hats—would oddly contrast with the splendour of the building which they inhabited, did not the recollection that these men were amongst the noblest defenders of their country give a dignity to the objects which everywhere presented themselves, and make the crutch of the veteran to harmonise with the grandeur of the fabric in which he found his final port after the storms of a life of enterprise and danger.

The habitations of the pensioners were divided into wards, each bearing a name which had been, or might be, appropriated to a ship. These wards consisted of large and airy rooms, on either side of which there were little cabins, in which each man had his bed. Every cabin had some convenience or ornament, the exclusive possession of its tenant; and these little appendages might have led one to speculate upon the character of the man to whom they belonged. In one might be seen a ballad and a ludicrous print; in another a Christmas carol and a Bible. In large communities, and particularly in a collegiate life, men must greatly subdue their personal habits and feelings into harmony with the general character of their society; but the individuality of the human mind will still predominate, displaying itself in a thousand little particulars, each of which would furnish to the accurate inquirer an increased knowledge of the human heart. The pensioners messed in common, and they assembled on Sundays for their devotions in the chapel of the Hospital. Now that the aged veterans have departed, we may well exclaim in the words of the poet:—

"——The race of yore
Who danced our infancy upon their knee,
And told our marvelling boyhood legends store
Of their strange 'ventures happ'd by land or sea,
How are they blotted from the things that be!"

After the pensioners left their old home, the Hospital remained closed and unoccupied for some short time, but it was eventually decided to make it the seat of a Royal Naval College. With this view, the interior of King Charles's Building was remodelled and converted into class-rooms for the naval students; the rooms in Queen Mary's Building were renovated and fitted up as dormitories and as general and mess rooms for the engineer officers and students, whilst the Hospital Chapel in this block became the College Chapel. It was also proposed that the Painted Hall should become the college dining-hall, but this intention was ultimately abandoned. The rest of the building was remodelled so as to provide a lecture theatre and comfortable mess-rooms.

The college was opened in February, 1873, having been organised, to use the words of the Order in Council which sanctioned its foundation, "for the purpose of providing for the education of naval officers of all ranks above that of midshipmen in all branches of theoretical and scientific study bearing upon their profession." The money necessary for the establishment of the new college upon an adequate scale was willingly voted by Parliament, and the votes for its subsequent maintenance, although amounting to a comparatively large sum, have been likewise passed, year by year, without a question, so that nothing has hindered the Admiralty from carrying out its intentions of giving to the executive officers of the Navy generally every possible advantage in respect of scientific education. The college receives as students naval officers of all grades, from captains and commanders, to sub-lieutenants, as also officers of the Royal Marine Artillery, Royal Marine Light Infantry, and Naval Engineers, and also a limited number of apprentices selected annually by competitive examinations from the Royal Dockyards. By special permission, officers of the mercantile marine, and private students of naval architecture and marine engineering, are admitted to the college classes; but they must reside outside the precincts of the Hospital. At the head of the college is a flag officer as president, who is assisted by a naval captain in matters affecting discipline; and by a Director of Studies, who is charged with the organisation and superintendence of the whole system of instruction and the various courses of study. For the carrying out of a complete system of scientific and practical instruction, there is a large staff of professors, lecturers, and teachers. In the first annual report on the Royal Naval College which was presented to both Houses of Parliament, the president stated that "the results of the year show that the standard of examination is so adjusted as to enable officers of good abilities, who on entering the navy dilligently apply themselves to studying their profession, to obtain their lieutenant's commission; while, on the other hand, it affords to those who are backward and ignorant on joining the college an opportunity of retrieving lost time and of maintaining their place in the navy if they earnestly avail themselves throughout the whole period of study of the means afforded them at the college."

Queen Anne's Building, as we have stated above, has been fitted up as a naval museum, primarily for the use of the college, but open also to the inspection of the public, except on Fridays and Sundays. It contains the models of ancient and modern ships formerly exhibited at South Kensington, and a great variety of other objects of maritime interest brought from that institution, from the Painted Hall, from Woolwich, Portsmouth, and different naval stations both at home and abroad. It presents, in fact, a complete epitome of naval history, and a most instructive and valuable series of illustrations of the progress and development of naval architecture and engineering. The museum occupies seventeen rooms, and they still retain the respective names which were bestowed upon them after the ships in which their pugnacious old occupants had won their victories—such, for instance, as the "Howe," the "Windsor

Castle," the " Victory," the " Vanguard," and so on. Space will not admit of our giving more than a hurried glance at the very interesting collection of objects here brought together. In the east wing are placed models showing the construction of dockyards, docks, plans for hauling up and dock-carrying 122 guns, thirteen of which were nine-pounders !—the models present various intermediate stages of development until we arrive at the modern iron-clad and turret-ship. The complete revolution which has taken place in all fighting-ships, and the rapidity with which it has been

GROUP OF GREENWICH PENSIONERS, 1868.

ing ships, classification of masts, yards, &c. ; life-boats, rafts, lowering apparatus for saving life at sea, models of engines and machinery, &c. In the west wing, the models of line-of-battle ships are very interesting, even to those who cannot boast of any knowledge of naval matters. The series begins with the well-known *Great Harry*, which was built in 1513 to replace one destroyed by the French a year or two previously ; and from this comparatively primitive craft—which, however, could boast of brought about, are very strikingly shown here. Models which only a few years ago represented the utmost achievements of our naval architects and engineers, look now to be a very trivial advance upon the *Great Harry*. In an adjoining room are models of ships' ventilating arrangements, screws, paddles, windlasses, anchors, and so forth ; besides which there is an imposing array of missiles and explosives of various kinds. The shells of various sizes and forms, exhibited in longitudinal sections, afford at a glance a great deal of information on the internal nature of these deadly messengers; then there are some diabolical-looking machines in the form of torpedoes and submarine mines. In a small room dividing the "Victory" from the "Vanguard" are deposited the interesting collection of relics of Sir John Franklin and his party, which the Lords of the Admiralty presented to Greenwich Hospital many years ago, and which

At a short distance westward of King William's Building is a large, substantial brick structure of two storeys, forming a closed square, which served as the infirmary for the old pensioners. It was built in the early part of the reign of George III., but was partly destroyed in the fire of 1811. When the buildings above described were appropriated for the purposes of a Naval College, this infirmary was assigned by the Government to that

THE ROYAL NAVAL SCHOOL, GREENWICH. (*From a Drawing made in* 1830.)

had hitherto remained in the Painted Hall with the "Nelson relics," which likewise have been removed here. The coat which Nelson wore at the battle of the Nile, when placed here with other relics by King William IV., was an object of attraction to thousands of modern relic-worshippers. It was given to the king by the Hon. Mrs. Damer, the well-known sculptress, to whom it was given by Nelson, when he sat to her for his bust. The walls of this room are adorned with a valuable collection of sketches by Benjamin West, representing the rough designs for paintings and sculptures in the hospital chapel. The same apartment contains, on a pedestal, the famous old "astrolabe," constructed for Sir Francis Drake's expedition to the West Indies, and presented to the hospital by the same king.

excellent institution, the Seamen's Hospital Society, whose hospital ship, the *Dreadnought*, moored off Greenwich, was for years so familiar to all passengers on the Thames. The infirmary was opened in 1870, as a "Free Hospital for Seamen of All Nations." It contains in all upwards of sixty rooms, together with a chapel, library, museum, surgery, dispensary, and apartments for the medical staff and their assistants. The building, which appears to be well adapted to its purpose, can provide space for 300 beds; between 2,000 and 3,000 patients are received here annually. The Seamen's Hospital Society dates from the year 1821, when their floating asylum was originally established on board the *Grampus*, a 50-gun ship, which had been granted for the purpose by the Board of Admiralty

It claims particular attention on account of its great usefulness, being exclusively appropriated to the relief of a class of men who had till that time been entirely destitute of a hospital suited to their peculiar habits, being the only establishment for the reception of sick seamen arriving from abroad, or to whom accidents may happen in the river. In 1831, the *Grampus* being found incapable of furnishing sufficient accommodation, the *Dreadnought*, a 98-gun ship, which had once captured a Spanish three-decker in Trafalgar Bay, was granted by the Government, and to her the patients were transferred; but in 1870 it was decided, on sanitary and other grounds, to discontinue the hospital afloat, and the *Dreadnought* was abandoned, the occupants being removed on shore to the infirmary. Here are received the sick and disabled seamen of every nation, on presenting themselves, no recommendation being necessary; and here they are maintained, and, when necessary, clothed, until entirely convalescent. It is worthy of note that this excellent institution is supported mainly by voluntary contributions, and that no money is received from the Government towards the annual expenditure. The Duke of Northumberland, in a letter to the *Times* in February, 1877, thus presses the claim of the Seamen's Hospital on the support of the public: "The seaman, for whose benefit this institution was founded, has ever been recognised as having a special title to the succour and sympathy of this nation, which owes its grandeur, nay, its existence, to his labour and sufferings in her cause. To him no other introduction is needed than sickness, disease, or accident, without distinction of colour, creed, or nation. This society affords a refuge, not only during actual illness, but until the sufferer has gained strength to resume his occupation; 170,000 patients have already received relief at its hands, and the annual admissions have increased with the increased accommodation consequent on the transfer to the society of the infirmary of Greenwich Hospital, a noble grant from the Imperial Government, conveying with it, as it were, a national recognition of its services. To maintain it in full efficiency a more liberal support on the part of the public is required, not only on account of the additional number of patients received, but of the extra expense which the general rise in prices has brought on the funds of the establishment. An increase of the annual subscription-list from its present amount of £2,500 to £6,000 is the only sound method of ensuring this object, donations only affording a casual and uncertain resource. I feel assured that the attention of the benevolent has only to be drawn to these facts to secure for the Seaman's Hospital Society all the help it requires to develop to the full the capabilities of an institution, national in its origin and cosmopolitan in the scope and range of the benefits it confers." It may not be out of place to state here that Her Majesty the Queen contributes 100 guineas annually to the funds of this institution, annually expressing "her anxiety for the maintenance of so excellent a charity, which grants relief when most needed to seamen of all nations."

Close by this building are the western gates, the piers of which are crowned by two large stone globes—one the celestial and the other the terrestrial—each six feet in diameter; on the former the meridians and circles, and on the latter the parallels of latitude and longitude are said to have been laid down, and the globes adjusted with great accuracy, by the authorities of the Observatory.

The Queen's House, as the building on the south side of Greenwich Hospital was once called, now serves as the Royal Naval School, and thither we will now proceed. The building, which was commenced by Anne of Denmark, and finished by Henrietta Maria, forms the centre of the present range of buildings devoted to the purposes of the school, and immediately faces the central avenue of the hospital. It bears on the front the date 1635, but it has been much altered since then. The wings are united to the central building by a colonnade 180 feet long. The Queen's House, after being long used as the ranger's lodge, when it was known as Pelham House, was, in 1807, appropriated to the use of the Royal Naval Asylum, which had been originally established at Paddington. The Royal Naval Schools, although cut off from the actual precincts of Greenwich Hospital, in spite of many internal changes, are among the earliest foundations in connection with it. In the original charter it was provided that out of the funds provision was to be made for "the maintenance and education of the children of seamen happening to be slain or disabled in the service of the royal navy." In pursuance of this provision a school was founded at Greenwich in 1712, for boys and girls, the qualification being that they were the children of "pensioners or other poor seamen." At first the number of boys was only ten; but, with a gradual increase in the revenue of the hospital, this number was increased to 200 in the year 1803. In 1821 the Royal Naval Asylum, which at that time educated 680 boys and 200 girls, was incorporated with these schools. After some other changes, the Greenwich schools were open to receive the sons of officers, and they supplied an education by no means contemplated either in character or cost by the original act. An investigation made by a committee in 1871 discovered not only that the schools were being improperly administered, but that boys were entered who were totally unfit for sea life; and in nearly every conceivable respect they found the intentions of the founders of these schools had been compromised. They recommended, therefore, a radical alteration in their organisation, they re-imposed the old conditions of entry, and insisted on a preparation for sea life being considered an indispensable condition of entry. Under this revision, which was speedily carried out, the schools became, as was intended, a sort of nursery for the navy. The boys, under this system, are now entered at ten years of age; and if, at the age of thirteen, they are unwilling or unable to enter the navy, they are compelled to leave the school, and make way for boys who are fit for naval service. The number of boys under instruction is nearly 1,000, and besides the ordinary rudiments of education they are taught seamanship as well as it possibly can be taught on shore, and they are also trained to all kinds of industrial occupations, such as cooking, bread-making, tailoring, washing (the heavy work being done by labour-saving machinery), ironing, carpentering, and other like work—the whole of the clothes for the school being made on the spot, the repairs of the building done by the inmates, and the food cooked, the boys doing the greater part of the labour.

In connection with the Royal Naval School there is a spacious swimming-bath, where all the boys are taught to swim; there is also a capacious gymnasium; and last, not least, a full-rigged model ship, a corvette, on the lawn in front of the principal building, in which the juvenile crew are taught the "duties of men of the sea." In the year 1877 it was announced that the Admiralty proposed to make an important alteration in the school, requiring henceforth that the boys who entered it should give a guarantee that, if judged to be physically fit, they would enter Her Majesty's navy at the conclusion of their training.

The administration of the affairs of Greenwich Hospital, down to the time of its "disestablishment" as such, were, as we have stated above, in the hands of a Board of Commissioners, appointed under royal charter. The principal officers were a governor, lieutenant-governor, four captains, eight lieutenants, a treasurer, a secretary, an auditor, a surveyor, a clerk of the works, a clerk of the cheque, two chaplains, a physician, a surgeon, a steward, and various other assistants.

It would, of course, be impossible for us in these pages to speak of all the distinguished men who have taken part in these different offices; but we may be pardoned for mentioning two or three. Among the former chaplains, then, was the Rev. Nicholas Tindal, the fellow-worker with Morant in the "History of Essex," and also in the translation of Rapin's "History of England." He died at an advanced age, and was buried in the new cemetery. Of Evelyn and his son-in-law, Draper, we have already spoken as acting as treasurers; another person who occupied that position was Mr. Swynfen Jervis, a solicitor, the father of a great naval commander, Lord St. Vincent, whose after-life, too, in a manner became interested in the affairs of Greenwich Hospital. How Lord St. Vincent's early difficulties were overcome by native hardihood and determination, we learn from his own words. " My father," he says, " had a very large family, with very limited means. He gave me at starting in life £20, and that was all he ever gave me. After I had been a considerable time at the station [Jamaica] I drew for twenty more, but the bill came back protested. I was mortified at this rebuke, and made a promise, which I have ever kept, that I would never draw another bill without a certainty of its being paid. I immediately changed my mode of living; quitted my mess, lived alone, and took up the ship's allowance, which I found quite sufficient; washed and mended my old clothes; and made a pair of trousers out of the ticking of my bed; and having by these means saved as much money as redeemed my honour, I took up my bill, and from that time to this I have lived within my means."

Edward, first Earl of Sandwich—the " My lord " of Pepys's " Diary "—in his official capacity as Lord High Admiral of England, took an active part in the administration of the affairs of Greenwich Hospital. As Sir Edward Montagu he had been distinguished as a military commander under the Parliamentarian banner in the civil war, and was subsequently joint High Admiral of England, in which capacity, having had sufficient influence to induce the whole fleet to acknowledge the restored monarchy, he was elevated to the peerage by Charles II. After the Restoration, he obtained the highest renown as a naval officer, and fell in the great sea-fight with the Dutch, off Southwold Bay, in 1672. His great-grandson, John, the fourth Earl of Sandwich, was likewise officially, and perhaps not very creditably, connected with Greenwich Hospital. This nobleman, an eminent diplomatist and statesman, assisted at the congress of Aix-la-Chapelle, in the year 1748; he was subsequently Secretary of State, and first Lord of the Admiralty.

The appointment of Sir Hugh Palliser, in 1778, to the governorship of Greenwich Hospital, was the subject of a vote of censure on the ministry, proposed by no less a person than Charles James Fox. The motion was negatived, and Palliser held the post till his death in 1796 ; but no First Lord of the Admiralty ever ventured again to give him active employ at sea.

It will be remembered by the readers of history that the affairs of this hospital gave Lord Erskine his first start in that profession of which he rose to be so great a luminary. Having left the navy, and been called to the Bar, he was engaged in a prosecution for libel, which was in fact instituted by the First Lord of the Admiralty, Lord Sandwich, who had abused the munificent institution which was under his official control by appointing landsmen as pensioners, in order to serve the electioneering purposes of his party. Such was the effect of Mr. Erskine's indignant speech in this case that the hitherto unknown advocate had thirty retaining fees offered him on the spot, and he may be said to have left the court with his fortune made. He ultimately became, as is well known, Lord Chancellor, in the ministry of "All the Talents," and a peer of the realm.

When the Act of Parliament above referred to came into operation, the offices of commissioners, governor, and lieutenant-governor were abolished, and the Admiralty had conferred upon them the power to dismiss any other officials they thought proper ; but every such official would be allowed to receive an annuity for life equal in amount to the salaries and emoluments he then enjoyed, and he would also continue to receive any superannuation allowance he might at the time be in receipt of. The governor and lieutenant-governor were allowed to retain their titles and their residences in the hospital.

The entire control of the hospital and institutions attached to it is now in the Admiralty, subject to the *veto* of the council, and the expenses are, in the first instance, paid out of money provided by Parliament for that purpose. All the property belonging to the hospital is vested in the Admiralty under the same provisions as lands vested in the Board under the Admiralty Lands and Works Act of 1864, together with the £20,000 paid annually out of the Consolidated Fund.

In concluding this chapter, we may remark that before the "chest," or fund for disabled seamen, was removed to Greenwich, in order to be better regulated, the pensioners, who resided at a distance from the spot, and whose appearance before the commissioners was only occasionally required, were accustomed to barter away their stipends to certain usurers, who made large fortunes at their expense. These were the speculators in "seamen's tickets," of whom it is generally, though erroneously, supposed that Thomas Guy was a specimen.*

CHAPTER XV.

GREENWICH (*continued*).—THE PARISH CHURCH, &c.

" To Greenwiche, that many a shrew is in."—*Chaucer's " Canterbury Tales."*

Gradual Extension of London—Greenwich as a Parliamentary Borough—The Assizes for Kent formerly held here—The Present Condition and Population of Greenwich—The Church of St. Alphege—Portraits of Queen Elizabeth, Charles I., Queen Anne, and George I., formerly in Greenwich Church—Greenwich one of the Head-quarters of the Huguenot Refugees—The " Spanish Galleon "—Dr. Johnson a Resident in Greenwich—General Withers and Colonel Disney Residents here—Queen Elizabeth's College—The Jubilee Almshouses—Baths and Wash-houses—The Lecture Hall—The Theatre—Croom's Hill—The Roman Catholic Church—The " New Church " of St. Mary—Greenwich Market—Spring Gardens—Lennier's Collection of Pictures—Strange Monsters exhibited here—The Duke of Norfolk's College—A Remarkable High Tide—Sir John Winter's Project for Charring Sea-coal—The Royal Thames Yacht Club—The Tilt-Boat —The Admiralty Barge — The Royal State Barge—River-side Hotels—Whitebait Dinners—The Origin of the Ministerial Fish Dinner—Samuel Rogers and Curran— Charles Dickens at Greenwich—The Touting System—Greenwich Fair.

ALTHOUGH Greenwich is four miles distant from London either by road or rail, and five miles from London Bridge by the river, it has, nevertheless, for these many years lost its separate existence, and been absorbed into the great metropolis, just as many larger places around London have been swallowed up before and since ; and Greenwich at the present moment is almost as much a part of the great metropolis as St. John's Wood and Islington.

Of the early history of the manor of Greenwich we have already spoken ; the present local importance of the town, however, must be attributed to the establishment, firstly of the royal residence here, and ultimately of the Royal Hospital. It sent members to Parliament in the fifth and sixth years of Philip and Mary's reign, but discontinued to do so afterwards. This was the more strange on account of the affection with which the royal town of Greenwich was regarded by Queen Elizabeth. Two centuries later, however, that honour was restored to it; for under the Reform Bill of 1832 Greenwich, conjointly with Deptford, Woolwich, Charlton, and Plumstead, was created a Parliamentary borough, returning two members to Parliament. Among the distinguished men who have been returned as its representatives, we may mention Sir David Salomons, the first member of the Jewish community who ever took his seat in the House of Commons; Admiral Sir Houston Stewart, some time Governor of Greenwich Hospital; General Sir William Codrington, Governor of Gibraltar, and head of the army in the Crimea; and last, not least, Mr. W. E. Gladstone, who took refuge here on his rejection by South Lancashire, in 1868.

In the reign of Queen Elizabeth, the assizes for the county of Kent were held here on three occasions. The town in itself has not much in the way of public buildings to be described in these pages. Originally a small fishing village—like its neighbour, Deptford—the place has gone on increasing gradually to its present size; the streets, consequently, are somewhat irregular in plan and diversified in character, but possess no features either imposing or picturesque. At the commencement of the present century the number of inhabitants was 14,000, which had swelled to 46,000 at the taking of the census in 1881.

Numerous improvements were made in the town during the first decade of the present century; these considerably altered its appearance. Mr. Richardson, in his work already referred to, published in 1834, says that, "To show the rural character of the place to a very recent period, it may be mentioned that within the last twenty years there were posts and rails to divide the footpath from the road on Croom's Hill, and that till the year 1813 there were trees standing in the very centre of the town, nearly opposite the church. London Street, the leading thoroughfare on entering the town from the metropolis, has also, within the last thirty years, assumed a much altered appearance in its change of character from a street of private residences to one of commerce, almost every house within it now presenting a shop frontage; whereas, at the period alluded to, the shops were very few in number, and almost wholly confined to that end nearest the centre of the town."

The parish church, dedicated to St. Alphege, stands in the centre of the town, at the junction of London Street, Church Street, and Stockwell Street. It is one of the "fifty new churches" provided for by Act of Parliament in the reign of Queen Anne; and it occupies the site of the old parish church, the roof of which fell in and seriously damaged the rest of the fabric in November, 1710. A writer in the *Gentleman's Magazine*, for May, 1805, p. 422, after alluding to the pernicious consequences arising from the old practice of burying in churches, by which the pavement was defaced, and the windows filled up with monuments, remarks, "But, what is worse, I have known the whole building demolished, and thrown into a heap of rubbish, by the digging of a grave too near the foundation of a pillar, so that, being undermined, great hath been the fall thereof. Thus fell the ancient church of Greenwich a few years since, but, by the providence of Heaven, no person was therein." In this church was a portrait, on glass, of Humphrey, Duke of Gloucester; there were also several monuments and brasses to the distinguished worthies who were buried there, among whom were Thomas Tallis, the great composer of church music, and musician in the royal chapels in the reigns of Henry VIII., Edward VI., and Queens Mary and Elizabeth; he died in 1585, and a brass plate recording his burial here has been affixed in the present church; there also rest Robert Adams, architect (1595); William Lambarde, the antiquary, and author of the "Perambulation of Kent" (1601); and Thomas Philipott, writer of the "Villare Cantianum" (1682). The monuments in the old church perished with the building, with the exception of that of Lambarde, which was rescued from the wreck and removed to Sevenoaks Church. In commemoration of St. Alphege was put up in the old church the following inscription—"This church was erected and dedicated to the glory of God, and the memory of Saint Alphege, Archbishop of Canterbury, here slain by the Danes." Mention is made of the old parish church by our gossiping friends Evelyn and Pepys. The former, under date of April 24, 1687, writes: "At Greenwich, at the conclusion of the church service, there was a French sermon preach'd after the use of the English Liturgy translated into French, to a congregation of about 100 French refugees, of whom Monsieur Ruvigny was the chiefe, and had obtain'd the use of the church after the parish service was ended." Unlike the excellent John Evelyn, Pepys occasionally notes in his "Diary" facts which do not raise our estimate of his morals or his religion; for instance, he writes: "By coach to Greenwich church, where a good sermon, a fine church, and a great company of handsome women."

The present church of St. Alphege was completed in 1718, and consecrated by Bishop Atterbury. It is a thoroughly solid-looking edifice of Portland stone, and was built from the designs of John James, a local architect. The building is cruciform in plan, with a tower of three stages, tapering to a spire, at the western end. In 1813,

new church are Admiral Lord Aylmer, Governor of Greenwich Hospital and Ranger of the Park, who died in 1720; General Wolfe, the victor of Quebec (1759); and Lavinia, Duchess of Bolton (famous as an actress for her impersonation of "Polly Peachum"), who was interred here in 1760.

There were formerly hung upon the walls of this church portraits of Queen Elizabeth, Charles I., Queen Anne, and George I.; but becoming, by

THE PARISH CHURCH, GREENWICH.

during a violent thunderstorm, the spire of this church was struck by the electric fluid and shivered to pieces, but it has been replaced. The style of architecture is the Roman Doric of the period. The interior is spacious: it has a broad nave with aisles, shallow transepts, and a coved recess for the chancel. Deep galleries extend along the two sides, and across the western end, the latter containing the organ. In 1870 the old-fashioned square pews were converted into open sittings, and various other alterations were made. The galleries, pulpit, and fittings generally are of dark oak, highly carved and polished. The columns are of the Corinthian order; and the decorations of the altar-recess are ascribed to Sir James Thornhill.

Among the notable personages buried in the

lapse of time, dingy and faded, they were stowed away as lumber in the organ-loft of the church, and ultimately sold by the churchwardens. The portrait of Queen Anne went to the Painted Hall, in Greenwich Hospital, for the sum of £10, the permission of the Lords Commissioners of the Admiralty having been obtained to pay that sum for it. The portraits of Queen Elizabeth, Charles I., and George I. were sold to a general dealer living in New Cross for £20 15s., and were subsequently sold by him at a profit of 50s. to a picture-dealer in New Bond Street, by whom they were restored. The portrait of King George represents the king in full coronation dress, the heavy ermine cloak being thrown back in front, revealing a rich close-fitting dress, while round the shoulders is a massive chain, from which is suspended the prancing horse of Hanover. On the table beside his Majesty are the crown and sceptre, the king's hand grasping the ball and cross. In the background is a view of Westminster Abbey. The value of this picture is stated to be over £500. The portrait of Charles I., ten feet square, is supposed to be the work of Sir Peter Lely. The painting represents the king in a prayerful attitude, and is believed to be even more

the roof of the former structure fell in at midnight, 28th November, 1710, and when the present church was erected, several monuments and all the stained glass in the windows containing armorial bearings, were missing; and upon inspecting the parish chest some years ago, the whole of the ancient charters and papal bulls relative to this church, known to have been there in 1816, were not to be found."

Queen Elizabeth, as we have already remarked,

THE DUKE OF NORFOLK'S ALMSHOUSES, IN 1796.

valuable than that of George I. All the monarchs mentioned were associated with Greenwich, but their portraits are now scattered.

With reference to the manner in which these portraits came into the possession of the parish, a correspondent of the *Times* in 1876 wrote:—
"According to a list, taken in 1706, 'the picture of Queen Elizabeth in a handsome black frame, with ornaments of gilding about it, was painted at the parish charge.' 'The picture of King Charles the Martyr, with a fair frame, fillited with gold, was the gift of Mrs. Mary Squib' probably about 1671). The remaining portraits were doubtless bestowed on the parish by the Crown (the lord of the manor), or loyal parishioners. The antiquities of the church of St. Alphege have been very unfortunate. After

made the palace her favourite summer residence. Charles I. passed much of his time at the "House of Delight." Queen Anne, as we have seen, built one of the wings of the Hospital, which still bears her name; while George I. landed at Greenwich on his arrival from Hanover.

Greenwich became one of the head-quarters of the Huguenot refugees, after the revocation of the Edict of Nantes; and in London Street was, in the reigns of James II. and William III., a chapel for their use. It was erected by one of their most distinguished members, the aged Marquis de Ruvigny, a person of learning, who had been ambassador at St. James's and at other courts, as well as Deputy of the Protestants of France in the Parliament at Paris, and who formed the centre of a large circle of his countrymen. Before their chapel was ready for use the Huguenots were allowed to use the parish church, at the end of the afternoon service, on Sundays. John Evelyn, in his " Diary," as we have seen above, records the fact of his being present at this service, in 1687. The little foreign colony is extinct, and the chapel is now occupied as a Nonconformist meeting-house.

In Church Street is an inn bearing the very singular title of the " Spanish Galleon." The sign owes its existence, in all probability, to the fact of its standing so near to the pictures of our naval victories in the Royal Hospital, in which captured Spanish galleons figure somewhat frequently.

It may possibly be remembered by readers of Boswell that, when Dr. Johnson first wrote to Edmund Cave, the proprietor and editor of the newly-founded *Gentleman's Magazine*, it was from "Greenwich, next door to the 'Golden Heart,' in Church Street," where he had taken apartments when he first came from his native Lichfield to town, in order to write the parliamentary articles for the above-mentioned publication.

The following list of Dr. Johnson's places of residence after he had entered the metropolis as an author is based on Boswell's Life :—Exeter Street, Strand ; Greenwich ; Woodstock Street, Hanover Square ; No. 6, Castle Street, Cavendish Square ; Strand ; Boswell Court ; Strand again ; Bow Street ; Staple's Inn ; Gray's Inn ; No. 1, Inner Temple Lane ; No. 7, Johnson's Court ; and No. 8, Bolt Court.

Greenwich appears to have been a favourite place with the old lexicographer ; much of his tragedy of *Irene* was written whilst he was living here ; and, as Boswell tells us, it was partly composed beneath the spreading elms in Greenwich Park. Railways being at that time a mode of conveyance undreamed of, the river was Johnson's favourite highway between Greenwich and London. The following anecdote, told concerning an incident which took place on one occasion when Boswell and Johnson were proceeding thither in a boat from the Temple, may bear repeating :— " Boswell asked Johnson if he really thought a knowledge of the Greek and Latin languages an essential requisite to a good education. *Johnson :* ' Most certainly, sir ; for those who know them have a very great advantage over those who do not. Nay, sir, it is wonderful what a difference learning makes upon people even in the common intercourse of life, which does not appear to be much connected with it.' *Boswell :* ' And yet people go through the world very well, and carry on the business of life to good advantage, without

learning.' *Johnson :* ' Why, sir, that may be true in cases where learning cannot possibly be of any use ; for instance, this boy rows us as well without learning, as if he could sing the song of Orpheus to the Argonauts, who were the first sailors.' He then called to the boy, ' What would you give, my lad, to know about the Argonauts ? ' ' Sir,' said the boy, ' I would give what I have.' Johnson was much pleased with his answer, and we gave him a double fare."

Other noted residents of Greenwich about this time were General Withers and Colonel Disney, convivial friends of Pope ; the latter is mentioned in Lady Mary Wortley Montagu's letters as " Duke Disney." They are thus jointly commemorated by Pope in his Panegyrics :—

" Now pass we Gravesend with a friendly wind,
    And Tilbury's white fort, and long Blackwall ;
Greenwich, where dwells the friend of human kind ;
    More visited than either park or hall,
Withers the good, and with him ever joined
    Facetious Disney, greet thee first of all ;
I see his chimney smoke, and hear him say,
' Duke ! that's the room for Pope, and that for Gay.

" ' Come in, my friends, here ye shall dine and lie,
    And here shall breakfast, and shall dine again ;
And sup and breakfast on, if ye comply ;
    For I have still some dozens of champagne.'
His voice still lessens as the ship sails by,
    He waves his hand to bring us back in vain ;
For now I see, I see proud London's spires,
Greenwich is lost, and Deptford Dock retires."

In the Greenwich Road, nearly opposite the railway station, stands Queen Elizabeth's College, founded by William Lambarde, the historian of Kent, in 1576, for twenty poor men and their wives. It is said, and perhaps truly, to have been the first public charity of the kind founded after the Reformation. The almshouses were rebuilt early in the present century ; each of the inmates has a separate tenement and garden, and £20 a year in hard cash. The endowment, which has been greatly augmented in value since Lambarde's time, is under the control of the Drapers' Company, who have of late built some additional houses, and made other improvements. The founder, with the consent of the Bishop of Rochester, composed a form of morning and evening prayer, to be used in the college ; and he made his endowment void, if it should ever become unlawful, by the statutes of the realm, to use it.

The Jubilee Almshouses, in this road, were founded by a subscription raised among the townspeople in 1809, in commemoration of King George III. having, on the 25th of October of that year, entered upon the fiftieth year of his reign

Additional almshouses have since been added on several public occasions; and there are now twenty houses in all, and each of the occupants receives a small annuity.

At the corner of Royal Hill are some commodious baths and wash-houses, near to which is a large lecture-hall and also a theatre; but with regard to these buildings nothing need be said further than that they meet their several requirements. There was formerly a theatre in London Street, but it was destroyed by fire in 1831. A few years later the proprietor, a Mr. Savill, constructed, on a novel principle, another theatre of iron, all the parts of which were put together with screws, so as to be capable of being taken to pieces, and conveyed to different towns.

Eastward of Royal Hill, and skirting the western side of Greenwich Park, is Croom's Hill, a steep and winding thoroughfare leading from the town up to Blackheath. A conspicuous object here is the lofty tower and spire of St. Mary's Roman Catholic Church, which, with its external statue of St. Mary, "star of the sea," is built so as to strike the eye of mariners as they sail up the river.

Near the bottom of Croom's Hill, close by the principal entrance to the park, stands the "new church" of St. Mary. It is a neat edifice of a semi-classic style of architecture, constructed of Suffolk brick and Bath stone, and the chief feature of the exterior is an Ionic portico at the western end, above which rises a tower of two stages. The "first stone" of the structure was laid by the Princess Sophia in 1823, and the church was consecrated in 1825. Over the altar is a picture of "Christ giving Sight to the Blind," painted by Richter, and presented by the British Institution.

From this church a broad thoroughfare called King Street leads direct to the pier, close by the Ship Hotel; and on the west side of this street, is the Market-place, which has its principal entrance in Clarence Street, and another entrance in Nelson Street, a broad well-built street so called after England's great naval hero. The market was erected by the Commissioners of the Royal Hospital near the site of a former market, and was opened in 1831. It contains spacious accommodation for vendors of meat, fish, vegetables, &c., and the whole is surrounded by a block of good substantial houses, with shops. The profits of the market being vested in Henry, Earl of Romney—whose name is still perpetuated in Romney Place—were given by him, in 1700, to the Royal Hospital, as stated in the preceding chapter.

Like St. James's Park and Hampstead, Greenwich in former times could boast of its "Spring Gardens." In the *General Advertiser* for May 25, 1771, occurs the following announcement :—

"SPRING GARDENS, GREENWICH.—The Evening Entertainments at this place will begin this day, the 25th inst., with a good Band of Vocal and Instrumental Musick. To be continued on Saturday and Monday Evenings during the Summer Season. N.B.—The Grand Room in the garden is upwards of fifty feet long."

These gardens, as a correspondent of *Notes and Queries* tells us, were situate near Christ Church, in East Greenwich, and, for many years after they were closed as a place of amusement, were turned into garden ground, but, as is the fate of many such places in the vicinity of London, the site is now nearly built over.

On account of the contiguity of this town to Deptford, it is frequently mentioned by Evelyn and likewise by Pepys in their amusing diaries. The former, writing in 1652, makes this entry :— "Came old Jerome Lennier, of Greenwich, a man skill'd in painting and musiq, and another rare musitian, called Mell. I went to see his collection of pictures, especially those of Julio Romano, which surely had been the king's, and an Egyptian figure, &c. There were also excellent things of Polydore, Guido, Raphael, Tintoret, &c. Lennier had been a domestic of Qu. Elizabeth's, and show'd me her head, an intaglia in a rare sardonyx, cut by a famous Italian, which he assur'd me was exceedingly like her."

For the same reason, too, naturally enough, Greenwich became a depôt for strange and foreign *curiosa;* at all events, Evelyn informs us in his " Diary " that he came hither in 1657 to see "a sort of catt, brought from the East Indies, shap'd and snouted much like the Egyptian racoon, in the body like a monkey, and so footed; the eares and taile like a catt, onely the taile much longer and the skin variously ringed with black and white; with the taile it wound up its body like a serpent, and so got up into trees, and with it would wrap its whole body round. Its haire," he adds, " was woolly, like a lamb's; it was exceedingly nimble and gentle, and purr'd as does the catt."

If we may believe the paragraph writers of the London journals in 1683, this place has been often haunted by other strange monsters; as witness the following item extracted from their columns :—" A perfect mermaid was, by the last great wind, driven ashore near Greenwich, with her comb in one hand and her looking-glass in the other. She seemed to be of the countenance of a most fair and beautiful woman, with her arms crossed, weeping out many pearly drops of salt tears ; and afterwards she, gently turning herself upon her back, swam away without being seen any more." Probably the writer believed the substance of this paragraph, and only exercised his journalistic talent in decorating his fact with tender and romantic incidents.

In or about 1749 there was exhibited at the " Rose and Crown," near the gates of the park, a strange collection of wild beasts, from the catalogue of which we take the following items :—" 1. A large and beautiful young camel, from Grand Cairo, in Egypt, near eight feet high, though not two years old, and drinks water but once in sixteen days. 2. A surprising hyæna, from the Coast of Guinea. 3. A beautiful he panther, from Buenos Ayres, in the Spanish West Indies. 4. A young riobiscay, from Russia ; and several other creatures too tedious to mention. Likewise a travelling post-chaise, from Switzerland, which, without horses, keeps its stage for upwards of fifty miles a day, without danger to the rider. Attendance from eight in the morning till eight at night." This list we take from Mr. Frost's " Old Showmen ;" but what the " riobiscay " can have been is beyond our power to discover.

At the eastern end of the town, fronting the Thames, is a college for the maintenance of twenty old and decayed housekeepers, twelve of whom are to be chosen from Greenwich, and the rest alternately from two parishes in Norfolk. It is called the Duke of Norfolk's College, though it was founded not by one of the Dukes of Norfolk, but by his brother Henry, Earl of Northampton, who committed it to the care of the Mercers' Company. The earl's body rests in the chapel of the college, having been brought there from Dover Castle about the year 1770. The edifice, which is commonly styled Trinity Hospital, is situated at a short distance eastward of Greenwich Hospital. It is a large quadrangular pile of brick buildings, with a tower.

A stone let into the wall of the wharf, opposite the entrance to the college, bears upon it a line denoting a " remarkable high tide, March 20, 1874 ;" the line is two feet four inches above the pavement, and consequently several feet above the ordinary high-water mark. *Apropos* of this mention of the tide, we may state that the whole valley of the Thames was once a gulf or bay of the sea, being, in fact, but a breach or cleft in the ordinary mass of deposit which once rose for 200 or 300 feet above what is now the bed of the river.

There was a ferry here more than two centuries ago, for Evelyn records in his " Diary," July, 1656, how he returned by it out of Essex to Saye's Court.

" Here," Evelyn writes, " I saw Sir John Winter's new project of charring sea-coale to burn out the sulphur, and render it sweete. He did it by burning the coals in such earthen pots as (those in which) the glasse-men mealt (*sic*) their mettall, so firing them without consuming them ; using a barr of yron in each crucible or pot, which bar has a hook at one end, so that the coales, being melted in a furnace with other crude sea-coales under them, may be drawn out of the potts sticking to the yron, whence they are beaten off in greate half-exhausted cinders, which, being rekindled, make a cleare, pleasant chamber fire, deprived of their sulphur and arsenic malignity. What success it may have time will discover." Unfortunately, Evelyn does not tell us whether ultimately Sir John Winter found his project remunerative ; but it may be added that within the present century the late Lord Dundonald tried to revive the plan, with the projected improvement of extracting and saving the tar. His lordship, however, failed to make it answer ; but the coal thus charred is now sold by almost every gas company under the name of coke.

It may not be out of place to record here that the Royal Thames Yacht Club close their annual season by an excursion down the river. The yachts rendezvous in the afternoon at Greenwich, and come to an anchor for the night at Erith. The commodore takes the chair in the evening at the " Crown Inn." On the following morning the members and their friends proceed on various cruises, many of these trips extending to several days. It may interest some of the members to know that their excursions have had a forerunner in times long gone by ; for Evelyn tells us how, in the summer of 1661, he sailed with " the merry monarch " in one of his " yachts or pleasure boats," and raced another yacht all the way to Gravesend and back, the king himself sometimes steering. " The king," he adds, " lost it in going, the wind being contrary ; but sav'd stakes in returning." It was by joining with his subjects in these amusements that King Charles gained that personal popularity which, in spite of his many vices, never forsook him.

Not only with Dr. Johnson, of whom we have spoken above, but with the public at large the river Thames has always been the favourite way of reaching Greenwich from London, both before and since the introduction of steamboats. In former times the chief mode of conveyance on the river was by small boats rowed by watermen ; but the " tilt boat " is often mentioned, in the reign of George III., as one of the regular conveyances which carried passengers down the river—to Greenwich, Woolwich, Gravesend, &c. These boats started from the Dark House, at Billingsgate; they took twelve hours on the journey to Gravesend if the weather was fair, and the wind not utterly adverse; but more, of course, if that was the case, and if they had not reached their destination when the tide turned. These boats were superseded by steamers, after the model of those already in use upon the Clyde, about the year 1816. The name of the "Tilt Boat" is still preserved on the signboards of one or two river-side inns.

The Admiralty barge was constantly employed on the silent highway of the Thames, down to a comparatively recent date, in showing the "lions" of the metropolis to distinguished foreigners. Thus Lady Lepel Hervey, in the reign of George II., relates how one of the lords of the Admiralty, Mr. Stanley, did the honours on behalf of his country to the Spanish Ambassador, his family, and several people of fashion, "the greatest part of whom he carried in barges down to Greenwich, nothing being wanting of water equipage; salutes upon the river, in the greatest pomp and order; and a reception at the landing at the hospital by the admiral, the governor, and all the officers."

Greenwich has been the place of debarkation of many illustrious visitors, and several royal personages, among whom may be noticed the Princess Augusta of Saxe Gotha, afterwards married to Frederick, Prince of Wales; and the Princess Caroline of Brunswick, who landed here in order to become the much-injured and unhappy wife of George, Prince of Wales (afterwards George IV.). From this place the latter passed on to London, in the midst of universal shouts of popular joy, her progress being almost a triumphal procession. Alas! in how short a time was she destined to rue the day! After her separation she lived for many years at Charlton, on the edge of Blackheath.

One of the last state visits of the sovereign to Greenwich was made in October, 1797, when King George III. proceeded in the royal yacht to Greenwich, and thence to Sheerness to review the fleet at the Nore, and to see the Dutch ships which had been lately captured by Lord Duncan at the battle of Camperdown.

The royal state barge was used as late as 1843, when the Prince Consort made a progress in it from Whitehall to the Brunswick Pier, at Blackwall, for the purpose of inspecting the *Victoria and Albert* steam-yacht, then in process of construction in the East India Docks. The barge, which had just been re-fitted and re-gilt at Woolwich Dockyard, was sixty-four feet in length, and about seven feet in width; the head and stern were elaborately carved, and gilt, and, with her highly-varnished timbers, had a right royal splendour. The vessel was rowed by twenty-two watermen in scarlet liveries, and the Admiralty barge, which accompanied it, by ten men in scarlet coats. The state barge, we are told, "in its progress to and from Blackwall, attracted many spectators on the river and its banks, and, with the Admiralty barge, formed a splendid piece of water pageantry, such as is but rarely witnessed on London's majestic river." It has long been disused, and is now laid up, destined never, probably, to be launched again. In 1883 it was on view at the Fisheries Exhibition at Kensington.

Overlooking the Thames, and in the immediate vicinity of the Royal Hospital, are those noted water-side hotels which have become celebrated for public dinners, and particularly for whitebait. The chief of these taverns are the "Ship," a little to the westward of the Hospital, and the "Crown and Sceptre," and the "Trafalgar," the latter of which has become celebrated for its "Ministerial fish dinners."

"At what period the lovers of good living first went to eat whitebait at 'the taverns contiguous to the places where the fish is taken,' is not very clear. At all events," writes John Timbs, in his "Club Life of London," "the houses did not resemble the 'Brunswick,' the 'West India Dock,' the 'Ship,' or the 'Trafalgar' of the present day, these having much of the architectural pretension of a modern club-house. Whitebait have long been numbered among the delicacies of our table; for we find 'six dishes of whitebait' in the funeral feast of the munificent founder of the Charterhouse, given in the Hall of the Stationers' Company, on May 28, 1612—the year before the Globe Theatre was burnt down, and the New River completed. For aught we know, these delicious fish may have been served up to Henry VIII. and Queen Elizabeth in their palace at Greenwich, off which place, and Blackwall opposite, whitebait have been for ages taken in the Thames at flood-tide. To the river-side taverns we must go to enjoy a 'whitebait dinner,' for one of the conditions of success is that the fish should be directly netted out of the river into the cook's caldron.

"About the end of March, or early in April, whitebait make their appearance in the Thames, and are then small, apparently but just changed from the albuminous state of the young fry. During June, July, and August, immense quantities are consumed by visitors to the different taverns at Greenwich and Blackwall. Pennant says: 'Whitebait are esteemed very delicious when fried with fine flour, and occasion, during the season, a vast resort of the *lower order of epicures* to the taverns contiguous to the places where they are taken.' If this account be correct," adds Mr. Timbs, " there must have been a strange change in the grade of epicures frequenting Greenwich and Blackwall since Pennant's days ; for at present the fashion of eating whitebait is sanctioned by the highest authorities, from the Court of St. James's in the

rather be regarded as a sort of prandial wind-up of the Parliamentary session than as a specimen of refined epicurism.

" We remember many changes in matters concerning whitebait at Greenwich and Blackwall. Formerly, the taverns were mostly built with weather-board fronts, with bow-windows, so as to command a view of the river. The old 'Ship,' and the 'Crown and Sceptre' taverns at Greenwich

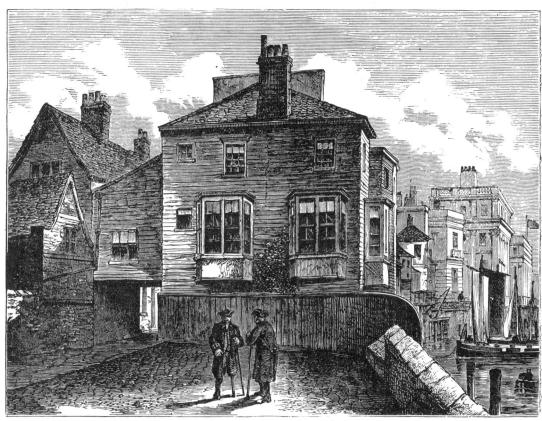

CROWN AND SCEPTRE INN, GREENWICH.

West, to the Lord Mayor and *his* Court in the East ; besides the philosophers of the Royal Society, and Her Majesty's Cabinet Ministers. Who, for example, does not recollect such a paragraph as the following, which appeared in the *Morning Post* of the day on which Mr. Yarrell wrote his account of whitebait, September 10, 1835 : ' Yesterday, the Cabinet Ministers went down the river in the Ordnance barges to Lovegrove's "West India Dock Tavern," Blackwall, to partake of their annual fish dinner. Covers were laid for thirty-five gentlemen.' For our own part, we consider that the Ministers did not evince their usual good policy in choosing so late a period as September, the whitebait being finer eating in July or August ; so their ' annual fish dinner ' must

were built in this manner ; and some of the Blackwall houses were of humble pretensions ; these have disappeared, and handsome architectural piles have been erected in their places. Meanwhile, whitebait have been sent to the metropolis, by railway or steamer, where they figure in fishmongers' shops, and tavern *cartes* of almost every degree.

" Perhaps the famed delicacy of whitebait rests as much upon its skilful cookery as upon the freshness of the fish. Dr. Pereira has published a mode of cooking in one of Lovegrove's ' bait kitchens ' at Blackwall. The fish should be dressed within an hour after being caught, or they are apt to cling together. They are kept in water, from which they are taken by a skimmer as required ; they are then thrown upon a layer of flour, contained in a large

FEASTING AT GREENWICH.

EASTER MONDAY IN GREENWICH PARK. (*From an Engraving by Rawle, in the "European Magazine" of 1802.*)

napkin, in which they are shaken until completely enveloped in flour; they are then put into a colander, and all the superfluous flour is removed by sifting. The fish are next thrown into hot lard contained in a copper caldron or stew-pan placed over a charcoal fire. In about two minutes they are removed by a tin skimmer, thrown into a colander to drain, and served up instantly, by placing them on a fish-drainer in a dish. The rapidity of the cooking process is of the utmost importance, and if it be not attended to, the fish will lose their crispness, and be worthless. At table, lemon-juice is squeezed over them, and they are seasoned with cayenne pepper, brown bread-and butter is substituted for plain bread; and they are eaten with iced champagne or punch."

Every year the approach of the close of the Parliamentary session is indicated by what is termed the "Ministerial Fish Dinner," in which whitebait forms a prominent dish, and Cabinet Ministers are the company. The dinner takes place at one of the principal taverns, usually at Greenwich, but sometimes at Blackwall. The dining-room is decorated for the occasion, which is of the nature of a State entertainment. Formerly, it was customary for the Ministers to go down the river from Whitehall in an Ordnance barge, ornamented with gold and other colours, and with streamers; now, however, a more prosaic steamer is employed. The origin of the annual festivity is told by Mr. Timbs in his work quoted above:—"On the banks of Dagenham Lake or Reach, in Essex, many years since, there stood a cottage occupied by a princely merchant, named Preston, a baronet of Scotland and Nova Scotia, and sometime M.P. for Dover. He called it his 'fishing-cottage,' and often in the spring he went thither, with a friend or two, as a relief to the toils of his Parliamentary and mercantile duties. His most frequent guest was the Right Hon. George Rose, Secretary of the Treasury, and an Elder Brother of the Trinity House. Many a day did these two worthies enjoy at Dagenham Reach; and Mr. Rose once intimated to Sir Robert that Mr. Pitt, of whose friendship they were both justly proud, would no doubt delight in the comfort of such a retreat. A day was named, and the Premier was invited; and he was so well pleased with his reception at the 'fishing-cottage'—they were all two if not three-bottle men—that, on taking leave, Mr. Pitt readily accepted an invitation for the following year.

"For a few years, the Premier continued a visitor to Dagenham, and was always accompanied by Mr. George Rose. But the distance was considerable; the going and coming were somewhat inconvenient for the First Minister of the Crown. Sir Robert Preston, however, had his remedy, and he proposed that they should in future dine nearer London. Greenwich was suggested: we do not hear of whitebait in the Dagenham dinners, and its introduction probably dates from the removal to Greenwich. The party of three was now increased to four, Mr. Pitt being permitted to bring Lord Camden. Soon after, a fifth guest was invited—Mr. Charles Long, afterwards Lord Farnborough. All were still the guests of Sir Robert Preston; and, one by one, other notables were invited—all Tories—and, at last, Lord Camden considerately remarked that, as they were all dining at a tavern, it was but fair that Sir Robert Preston should be relieved from the expense. It was then arranged that the dinner should be given as usual by Sir Robert Preston—that is to say, at his invitation—and he insisted on still contributing a buck and champagne; the rest of the charges were thenceforth defrayed by the several guests; and on this plan, the meeting continued to take place annually, till the death of Mr. Pitt.

"Sir Robert was requested, next year, to summon the several guests, the list of whom, by this time, included most of the Cabinet Ministers. The time for meeting was usually after Trinity Monday —a short period before the end of the session. By degrees, the meeting, which was originally purely gastronomic, appears to have assumed, in consequence of the long reign of the Tories, a political or semi-political character. Sir Robert Preston died; but Mr. Long (now Lord Farnborough) undertook to summon the several guests, the list of whom was furnished by Sir Robert Preston's private secretary. Hitherto, the invitations had been sent privately; now they were dispatched in Cabinet boxes, and the party was, certainly, for some time, limited to the members of the Cabinet. A dinner lubricates Ministerial as well as other business; so that the 'Ministerial Fish Dinner' may 'contribute to the grandeur and prosperity of our beloved country.'"

From that day to the present the Ministerial dinner has been an annual festival, except when some sudden death has lately carried off a member of the existing Cabinet. The dinner is usually held a day or two before the prorogation of the Houses of Parliament.

But some other statesmen, who have not been Ministers of the Crown, have regaled themselves here on whitebait. Samuel Rogers, for instance, tells us that he once dined with Curran in the public room of the chief inn at Greenwich, when the Irish orator, as usual, began to indulge in his favourite exaggerations. "I had rather be hanged on twenty gallows"—he began, when a stranger sitting at the next table quietly asked, "Do you not think, sir, that one would be enough?" Curran was, for once, fairly taken aback and struck dumb at the witty retort.

But few dinners at Greenwich, perhaps, were more jovial and pleasant than that which, in 1842, celebrated the return of Charles Dickens from his first visit to America. Talfourd, Milnes, Procter, Maclise, Stanfield, Marryat, Barham, Hood, John Forster, and George Cruikshank were there; and a home tour into Cornwall was then and there arranged between "Boz," Maclise, Stanfield, and his future biographer—all now, alas! no more. It was at a dinner here—preceded by a drive over Blackheath—that Dickens and Douglas Jerrold met for the last time, just previous to the sudden death of the latter, in 1856.

A great change has come over the inns and taverns of half a century ago; they are now "hotels," and grand ones too; the "Trafalgar" still has its bow-windows fronting the river; but of the old "Ship" and the "Crown and Sceptre," their earlier and more attractive features have now disappeared, giving way to architectural piles of greater pretensions, and in which, therefore, the cost of a dinner must be largely increased, in order to pay the builder.

It is remarked by more than one writer, that Greenwich is about the last place where the practice of "touting" for customers is kept up at the doors of small coffee-houses; but, perhaps, the well-known cry of the butchers in the lesser streets on Saturday evenings, "Come, buy! buy! what will you buy?" may be regarded as the last remnant of a custom once nearly universal. Here you cannot walk along the streets which lie between the town and the park without being solicited by ten or a dozen rival houses to step in and regale yourself. If you take every card that is offered you, you will have a good store in your pocket on returning home at night. "Tea, eightpence, with a pleasant view of the river." "Tea made, with shrimps, ninepence," and so forth. The inhabitants of Greenwich would seem to be the most accommodating and hospitable people in the world. You can walk straight into almost every other house along the route and order tea, and can depart again only a few pence the poorer. Numbers of cockneys, however, come to the park already well provided; and you may see pater and materfamilias and half a dozen of their hopeful progeny all munching bread-and-butter, and drinking cold tea, in one group beneath the chestnuts.

For very many years, and down to a comparatively recent date (1857), there were two fairs held annually in Greenwich—namely, on the Monday, Tuesday, and Wednesday in Easter and Whitsun weeks. They were formerly held in the road now occupied partly by St. Mary's Church, and the remainder by the Hospital Burial-ground; latterly, the fairs were held in the public thoroughfares, principally in Bridge Street, which extends from near the church of St. Alphege to the bridge over the Ravensbourne at Deptford Creek. In an account of Greenwich Fair, the "Kalendar of Amusements" (1840) somewhat bombastically observes: "This great national event, which neither desires nor deserves any colouring at our hands, is one of those gaudy and glittering occasions which, like powerful magnets, attract all the base ore of the metropolis. The objects of commiseration, who have groaned through a long winter with afflictions (stated in coloured chalks on the portion of pavement they diurnally occupy), who, in the Van Amburgh spirit, have taught a little dog to implore and to accept contributions for them—the absence of arms, tongues, eyes, legs, &c., in a great measure preventing them officiating *personally* —now, vigorous and volatile, spring nimbly on the apex of the metropolitan mail, articulating 'Greenwich, ho!' Now, the fervid children of Erin, with a 'Horroo! Faugh a ballagh!' ('Clear the road!') enlarge themselves from the liberties of little Hibernia, and turn their frontispieces towards Greenwich. (Their less energetic brethren have preceded them a *week*, that being the time they annually consume in *drinking* their way down.)

"Now, from the cigar-divans in the Strand and the Quadrant, fair count(er)esses may be observed stepping into private carriages driven by private gentlemen, who, dispensing with their slaves in livery, and hoping the populace will mistake them for 'those blackguard lords,' whirl through the streets, as a Bristol Byron says, 'in all the majesty of mud.' Now, upon the road may be seen stages-and-four, coaches-and-two, and cabs-and-one with *cram* licences—a term well known to the *whipsters*, who upon this day, by superhuman exertions, prove their right to the title. Here, like Atlas struggling under a giddy world, a wretched donkey wags (we use the next word advisedly) *under* a wagon, which must have been erected to mock the efforts of a troop of horse. Countless hands, armed with countless missiles, stimulate the martyr in the rear, whilst a child precedes him holding a wisp of hay to his mouth. The bait has its effect: of the posterior applications he appears happily unconscious. But who and what are they that occupy that vehicle? Alas! none but themselves know who they are, or what they would be. The police reports, it is true, afford some information, and that of a nature perhaps to satisfy a *moral* curiosity.

"How shall we describe Greenwich? Confusion and consternation! hilarity and horror! Children not visible, pocket-handkerchiefs not forthcoming (distress for each equally evident). People here full of frenzy, exclaiming, 'What imposition!' Others there, full of frolic, lisping out, 'What fun!' Sirens insinuating, 'Tea and coffee! tea and coffee!' and slaughterers shouting, 'One shilling a head, sump-tu-ous dinners!' At night, the 'fair and free' assemble in the 'Crown and Anchor,' 'The Palladium of British Freedom,' 'The Thunderdox,' and 'The Roaring-Rattling-Rioters'' booths, where the waltz is done strict justice to, and the orchestra, assisted by the united exertions of all present, absolutely intoxicates the ear. Outside, they revel also, the 'shilling considerers,' preferring a penny privilege, are swung up into the face of heaven, and *vice versâ*, in a machine very like a gallows, which is put in motion by a fellow very like an executioner. Others speculate in porter and pudding, and laugh at the vanity of human nature."

There was not, however, a goodlier day of merry-making, for the regular traditional Monday-keepers, passed in the neighbourhood of London, than at Greenwich Fair. The Pool and the Port of London are always objects of astonishment to a foreigner; but to see them on Whit Monday, or at the commencement of a fine Easter-week, was the most extraordinary sight he could meet with. "The river below bridge," writes Mr. Albert Smith, "presented a singularly animated scene. Nearly all the vessels in the Pool hoisted their flags, in compliment to the holiday—bands of music, that only appeared competent to play 'Love not' and 'Jeannette and Jeannot,' were stationed at some of the wharfs, or on board the boats; and almost every minute a steamer passed, deep in the water, by reason of her crowded freight of human beings. It was only by extreme look-out that numberless accidents were avoided; for the highway was covered with small boats as well, together with ships being towed into dock, and heavy barges always getting directly across the way, so that sometimes a perfect stoppage of several minutes was necessary. Every available corner of the decks, cabins, and paddle-boxes of the steamers was occupied; and more than two-thirds of the voyagers were obliged to be content with standing-room during the journey—which, under these circumstances, was not made very rapidly. In-

deed, we were but little under the hour going from Swan Stairs to Greenwich Pier; but everybody was in thorough good temper with themselves and everybody else, so that there was no grumbling at the want of accommodation. They appeared only too happy to get there at all, albeit all the way the boats rolled and swayed until the water nearly washed in at the cabin windows.

"The fair began directly you landed. From the 'Ship Torbay Tavern' up to the park gates, the road was bordered on either side with stalls, games, and hand-wagons, containing goods or refreshments of every description. Mr. Punch, too, set up the temple of his illegitimate drama at three or four points of the thoroughfare, at each of which (in our belief that there is but one Punch, and that he is ubiquitous) he was pursuing that reckless career of vice and dissipation with which his audience are always so delighted. Snuff-boxes to throw at—refreshments of singularly untempting appearance, which nevertheless found eager purchasers—vendors of spring rattles, who ensured 'the whole fun o' the fair for a penny'—speculators in heavy stocks of Waterloo crackers and detonating balls—proprietors of small percussion guns, to shoot with at targets for nuts—kept increasing, together with the visitors, as we neared the park; until the diminished breadth of the street brought them all together in one struggle to get through the gates, like the grains of sand in an egg-glass. . . . The 'fair,' properly so called, was a long narrow thoroughfare of stalls, booths, and shows, in a lane leading from the town to the bridge at Deptford Creek. Perhaps this was the least attractive part of the day's amusement. The crowd was so dense and disorderly as to threaten each minute the erection of barricades of 'brandy-snaps,' and the overthrow and deposition of the gilt gingerbread kings ranged on each side. More refreshment stalls bordered the way—wonderfully uninviting shell-fish, of shapes you had never before encountered—mysterious effervescing drinks, like dirty soapsuds and carbonic acid mixed together—eels in different states of cookery, pickled, stewed, and in pies—strangely indigestible lumps of pudding, studded at uncertain intervals with black lumps, presumed to be plums—masses of cold fried fish, liberally peppered with dust; and dreadful oysters as large as soup-plates—oysters in June! But all were doing good business, and rapidly disposing of their stock.

"The shows, possibly, were our greatest delight, for we love to be harmlessly imposed upon at these wandering exhibitions. The last time we were at Greenwich Fair we saw one held in a dismantled dwelling-house, where various forms in wax-work, of the true Mrs. Jarley breed, were set up for inspection. In the recess of a window were placed two figures, evidently intended, originally, for Amy Robsart and the Earl of Leicester, but which represented, we were now told, Queen Victoria and Prince Albert, enjoying the retirement of private life, apart from the pomp of royalty. Why they should have chosen to enjoy retirement in fancy dresses of the Elizabethan period, those best acquainted with the habits of those august personages can possibly inform us. All the characters of the exhibition were, however, old friends. We fancied that we once knew them in High Holborn, where the organ turned at the door, and the monkey sat on the hot gas-pipe. At all events, if they were not the identical ones, the artist had cast two in the same mould whilst he was about it. We do not think he had been happy in the likenesses. Sir Robert Peel was, unmistakably, Mr. Buckstone grown a foot taller, and wearing a light flaxen wig. Lady Sale we once knew as Queen Adelaide; and Oxford had transmigrated into Wicks, the eyes having been manifestly wrenched violently round to form the squint of the latter miserable culprit. In one point the artist had excelled nature. He had preserved the apparent dryness and coolness of the skin, whilst the folks looking on were melting with the heat.

" In another show were some learned birds. This was also held in an unfinished house. A curtain nailed to the rafters divided the rude interior into two parts; by pushing it aside we saw a flock-bed upon the ground, a mouldering fire, and a tin saucepan: a thin, unhappy dog was persuading himself that he was asleep on the bed. In front of the *penetralia* was a dirty breeding-cage, in which five or six poor little ragged canaries were sitting on a perch, huddled up together as if for better self-defence. A man came to the front and said, 'Stand back, gents, and then all can see—the canaries, the performing canaries, brought from the Canary Islands for the Queen.' The birds were then taken out, and had to pull carts and draw water, sit on the end of a trumpet whilst it was played, and fire cannon; the explosion of the gunpowder throwing them into a state of tumbling, chuffing, and sneezing, from which they did not recover by the conclusion of the entertainment.

" As soon as it was dusk, the crowd in the fair thickened; and its sole object appeared to be to push a way violently through everything to the extreme end, and then return again in the same manner. In the town every tavern and public-house was filled to overflowing with hungry, or rather thirsty, occupants; the clouds of tobacco-smoke from the open windows proving the crowded state of the apartments. The steamboats had now ceased to ply, but the trains on the railway continued until a late hour. If you returned to town by the latter method of conveyance, you met hundreds more proceeding to Greenwich, even at very advanced periods of the evening. Where they got to when they arrived, how they contrived to return home again when the fair closed, is beyond conjecture. Those, however, who went simply to look on were not sorry, by this time, to get clear of the increasing riot and confusion, to which, on arriving once more in London, the bustle of Cheapside appeared almost seclusion and tranquillity."

The fag-end, as we may call it, of the fair was almost always noisy and disreputable. It is thus described by Mr. J. R. Planché, in his " Recollections," as it appeared to him and a French friend, his fellow-traveller, on his return from Paris in 1820:—" It was broad daylight by the time we reached the junction of the Greenwich and Old Kent Roads, and a sight suddenly presented itself to the eyes of our visitor which astonished, interested, and amused him to the greatest extent. On each side of the road, four or five deep, a line of human beings extended as far as the eye could reach: men and women, boys and girls, the majority of the adults of both sexes in every possible stage of intoxication, yelling, screaming, dancing, fighting, playing every conceivable antic, and making every inconceivable noise. For the instant I was almost as much surprised as my companion, and as little able to account for the extraordinary and unexpected scene; but after a few minutes I recollected it was the morning of the Wednesday in Easter week, and the end of Greenwich Fair, and these dregs of the London populace, which had for three days made the pretty Kentish borough a bear-garden, and its fine old park a pandemonium, were now flowing in a turbid flood of filth, rags, debauchery, and drunkenness, back to their sources in the slums of the metropolis. There was no picturesque costume to fascinate the eye of the artist, no towering *cauchoise* with its frills and streamers, no snow-white caps, short scarlet petticoats, and blue stockings, no embroidered velvet bodices, no quaint gold or silver head-gear, no jacket gay with countless buttons, no hat bedecked with ribbons, no coquettish Montero; all was dirt and squalor, draggled dresses, broken bonnets, hats without crowns, coats and trousers in tatters. Such was the British public as it first appeared to 'the great French comedian.'"

A writer in the *Somerset House Gazette and Literary Museum*, in 1824, could complain, and apparently with some show of truth, that even in his time Greenwich merry-making was but the ghost of what it had been. He bewails the utter attired in suits of gold leaf; to swallow one of the doughty heroes would have been to realise the fate of Crassus. Next succeeded the legerdemain and 'rowly-powly' gentry; the mermaids and mountebanks, and wonders of every class, from a penny to

LANE LEADING INTO SHIP STREET, GREENWICH (1830).

absence of that "joyous vulgarity, that freedom, fun, and variety," which had been its boast and attraction; but "still," he adds, by way of compensation, "there was a tolerable display, a sickly smile of gaiety about the place. I passed through a formidable array of gingerbread soldiers, drawn up in front of a booth, as if for the protection of the watches, horses, turkey-cocks, old ladies, and gridirons, which were ranged behind. The uniform of the military was very imposing; they were sixpence, which showed that the fair had not altogether declined from its ancient character. To quote the old ballad about another fair—

' In houses of boards men walk upon cords
    As easie as squirrels crack filberds;
And the cut-purses they do bite and away,
    But these we suppose to be ill-birds.

' For a penny you may see a fine puppet-play,
    And for two pence a rare piece of art;
And a penny a cann, I dare swear a man
    May put six of them into a quart.

' Their sights are so rich they are able to bewitch
   The heart of a very fine man-a ;
Here's patient Grizel here, fair Rosamunda there,
   And the history of Susannah.'

The literary part of the amusements," he continues, " was sadly neglected. In vain did learned dogs boast of their erudition, or dandy-pigs shuffle the cards and play dominoes. . . . The showman of one of these establishments, sadly mortified, paraded in front of his booth ; by turns he listened

and Foker dine at Greenwich, and Blanche cries out, "I adore Richmond, that I do ; and I adore Greenwich, and I say I should like to go there." It will be remembered that the major, being an old soldier, allowed the young men to pay for the dinner between them.

Charles Dickens devotes one of his "Sketches by Boz" to a description of the cockneys making a holiday on Easter Monday at Greenwich Fair, describing, in his usual graphic style, the frolics

VIEW FROM ONE-TREE HILL, GREENWICH PARK, IN 1846 (*p.* 207).

to the chattering of his monkey and the grunting of the youthful porkers." He then records a row and its issue, a general *mêlée ;* and adds, in conclusion, " I had seen quite enough of the fair, and was soon on my way back from Greenwich."

Reference is made to the fair in Thackeray's "Sketches and Travels in London," where Mr. Brown says threateningly to his nephew, " If ever I hear of you as a casino-hunter, or as a frequenter of races and Greenwich fairs, and such amusements in questionable company, I give you my honour you shall benefit by no legacy of mine, and I will divide the portion that was (and is, I hope) to be yours among your sisters." The fair figures also in his " Pendennis," where the major, Sir Francis,

and dangers of the road thither, the jostling of the crowds of fathers, mothers, apprentices and their sweethearts playing at " Kiss in the ring" or " Thread the needle," and dining and supping, and smoking *al fresco*, and crowding into Richardson's show, the dancing-booths, and the wild beast caravans, from noon-day till long past the hour of midnight. He writes, " If the parks be the lungs of London, we wonder what Greenwich Fair is—a periodical breaking-out, we suppose ; a sort of spring rash ; a three days' fever, which cools the blood for six months afterwards, and at the expiration of which London is restored to its old habit of plodding industry as suddenly and as completely as if nothing had ever occurred to disturb them."

CHAPTER XVI.

GREENWICH (*continued*).—THE PARK, THE ROYAL OBSERVATORY, &c.

" Heavens ! what a goodly prospect spreads around
Of hills, and dales, and woods, and lawns, and spires,
And glittering towns, and gilded streams, till all
The stretching landscape into smoke decays."—*Thomson.*

May-day Morning in the Reign of Henry VIII.—Historical Reminiscences—The Planting of the Park by Order of Charles II.—Castle Hill—
Description of the Park—One-Tree Hill—Proposed Monumental Trophy in honour of the Battle of Trafalgar on Castle Hill—The View from
One-Tree Hill—Greenwich Park at Fair-time—The Wilderness—The Ranger's Lodge—The Princess Sophia of Gloucester a Resident at
Montagu House—Chesterfield Walk—The Residence of General Wolfe—Ancient Barrows or Tumuli—Greenwich Observatory—Appointment
of John Flamsteed as First Astronomer-Royal—Flamsteed and Sir Isaac Newton—Dr. Halley—Dr. Bradley—Dr. Bliss—Dr. Maskelyne—
The " Nautical Almanack "—Mr. John Pond—Sir George Biddell Airy—Description of the Observatory and of the Instruments in Use—
The Magnetic Observatory—The Galvanic Clock—Work accomplished at the Observatory.

IT was, no doubt, the peculiar charm of this unrivalled prospect that made Greenwich for so many
ages the favourite seat of our Tudor monarchs, to
whose purposes it was excellently adapted, both
for its vicinity to the metropolis and its commanding situation. But far different must have been
the scene when (we are told) Henry VIII., in the
seventh year of his reign, on a fine May-day morning, with Queen Katharine his wife, accompanied
also by many lords and ladies, rode a-Maying from
Greenwich to the high ground of Shooter's Hill,
where, as they passed by the way, they espied a
company of tall yeomen all in green, with hoods,
and with bows and arrows, to the number of two
hundred. Since that day, alterations have taken
place which must astonish even the last generation,
large tracts of land, which then were either market-
gardens or pastures for cattle, being now converted
into docks or built over as streets.

"Let us pause," writes Mr. T. Miller, in his
" Picturesque Sketches of London," " on the brow
of this hill, and recall a few of the scenes which
these aged hawthorns have looked upon. They
are the ancient foresters of the chase, and many of
them have stood here through the wintry storms of
past centuries, and were gnarled, and knotted, and
stricken with age, long before Evelyn planned and
planted those noble rows of chestnuts and elms.
Below, between the plain at the foot of the hill
and the river, stood the old palace of Greenwich,
in which Henry VIII. held his revels, and where
Edward VI., the boy-king, breathed his last. That
ancient palace was, no doubt, rich with the spoils
of many a plundered abbey and ruined monastery
—in vessels of gold and silver which had once been
dedicated to holy purposes, but were then red with
the dregs of the wine shed at many a midnight
revel by the ' Defender of the Faith '—the woman-
murdering monarch. Perhaps," he suggests, with a
vein of dry humour, " the walls of that old palace
were hung with the portraits of the wives whom he
had caused to be beheaded, whilst his own likeness

in the centre gazed, like a tiger, out of the frame
upon his prey. On this hill, again, Cardinal
Wolsey may have meditated, ' with all his blushing
honours thick upon him.' Katharine, the broken-
hearted queen, may here have reined-in her palfrey,
or from this aged hawthorn have torn off a sprig,
when fragrant and white with may-blossom, as now,
and have presented it with a smile to the royal
savage who rode beside her. On yonder plain,
where so many happy faces are now seen, in former
days the tournament was held. There gaudy galleries were erected, over which youth and beauty
leant as they waved their embroidered scarves.
We can almost fancy that we can see the crowned
tiger smile as he closes the visor of his helmet,
bowing his plume while he recognises some fair
face which was soon to fall on the scaffold, with
its long tresses dabbled in blood. . . . . In
this park the crafty Cecil mused, doubtless, for
many an hour, as he plotted the return of the
Princess Mary, while the ink was scarcely dry in
which he had recorded his allegiance to the Lady
Jane Grey. In fact, the whole scenery of the park
teems with the remembrance of old stirring events
and grave historical associations. Hal, the royal
murderer, comes straddling and blowing up the
hill ; the pale and sickly boy-king rides gently by,
and breathes heavily as he inhales the sweet air on
the summit ; the titter and merry laugh of the ill-
starred queens seems to fall upon the ear from
behind the trees that conceal them. And then
we have voices of mourning and loud lament from
fair attendants, who refuse to be comforted, for
those whom they loved and served are there no
more." This, we may add, is a very pretty and
poetical picture, but none the less true for all that.

This park is the same as that previously men-
tioned* as having been enclosed by Humphrey,
Duke of Gloucester, in 1433, by licence of King
Henry VI. It contains nearly 200 acres, and was

---

* See *ante*, p. 165.

walled round by James I. Here, as in Kensington Gardens, we find the umbrageous trees that were planted by Gilpin and Le Notre, and the gardeners of William III. It was chiefly laid out by Le Notre, about the same time as St. James's Park, by order of Charles II., who, it is recorded, watched with great eagerness the work of laying out this park. As early as the spring of 1662, Pepys records that, "The king hath planted trees and made steps in the hill up to the castle, which is very magnificent." The "castle" here referred to was a tower erected by Duke Humphrey, on the site now occupied by the Observatory. Traces of Le Notre's "steps" or terraces are still observable in the hill-side leading to it. Castle Hill, it would seem, was at one time used as a "butt" or target for military practice; at all events, Evelyn, in his "Diary," under date of June 1, 1667, writes: "I went to Greenewich, where his Majesty was trying divers granados shot out of cannon at the Castle Hill from the house in the park; they brake not till they hit the mark; the forg'd ones brake not at all, but the cast ones very well. The inventor was a German." Of the time when the chief avenues were planted we get the exact date from the following entry in Evelyn's "Diary," where, under date of March 4, 1664, he writes: "This Spring I planted the Home-field and West-field about Saye's Court with elmes, being the same yeare that the elmes were planted by his Majesty in Greenewich Park." Now, however, except in the remains of some of the avenues, there are not very strong traces of the stiff and formal style of Le Notre left, as it is not on a beautifully-varied surface like this that straight walks and regular lines of trees are at all tolerable. The natural advantages of this park are certainly superior to those of any in the immediate vicinity of the metropolis. "The ground itself," says the author of "Bohn's Pictorial Handbook of London," "is undulated with great variety, sometimes being thrown up into the softest swells, and in other places assuming a bolder and more sudden elevation. Around the site of the Observatory it is particularly steep, and attains a considerable height. Everywhere, too, it is studded with noble specimens of ancient trees; and in this respect there are none of the other London parks at all equal to it. Some of the best trees are Spanish chestnuts, and the largest are on the south side. Many of these are truly fine and venerable, and would command admiration even if found in the heart of a purely rural district. The elms, which are abundant, are likewise large and noble; and there are some picturesque Scotch firs in the neighbourhood of the Observatory. These last are old enough to show the peculiar warm reddish colouring of the stems, and the characteristic horizontal or tufted heads. In this state, the Scotch fir is certainly one of the most picturesque trees we possess, and is the more valuable because each individual plant commonly takes a shape and character of its own. The avenues still remaining in Greenwich Park are composed chiefly of elm and Spanish chestnut, the latter being mostly confined to the upper part of the park. They are of different widths, and take various directions, many of them not appearing to have any definite object, and some being formed of two single rows, others of two double rows of trees. But there is one avenue—perhaps the finest—which, widening out at the base to correspond with the width of the hospital, is there composed of elms, but as it ascends the hill is made up wholly of Scotch firs, which are exceedingly good. In a general way, the trees in the avenues have been planted much too thickly, and have greatly injured or spoiled each other. In many instances, too, where plants have died out, they have been replaced by a most unhappy mixture of sorts, which, being also very poor specimens, detract much from the effect. At the upper part of the park are some aged and fine thorns, which have become very picturesque." The chestnuts in Blackheath Avenue have passed maturity, and every year seems to be telling on their strength. Many of them have magnificent trunks, and a few of them exceed eighteen feet in girth; some of the chestnuts, too, have attained a noble growth. The oaks are comparatively few, but among them are some of the largest trees in the park. The whole extent of the park is greatly varied in surface, and hence its great charm. As Mr. James Thorne, in his "Environs of London," remarks, "Everywhere the scenery is different, and everywhere beautiful; while from the high and broken ground by the Observatory and One-Tree Hill the distant views of London and the Thames, with its shipping, are matchless of beauty and interest. The park," he continues, "is the most popular of our open-air places of resort, and on a fine holiday is really a remarkable spectacle. It says something for the conduct of the crowds who resort hither, that the deer, of which there is a large number in the park, are so tame and fearless, that they will not only feed from visitors' hands, but even steal cakes from unwary children."

"One Tree Hill"—that particular spot rendered famous by George Cruikshank, in his "Comic Almanack," in the familiar lines—

> "Then won't I have a precious lark
> Down One Tree Hill in Greenwich Park!"

is so called from there having been but one tree on its summit; this tree, however, has long been greatly decayed, and six others were, some years ago, planted near it. It was in former times called " Five-tree Hill."

About the year 1816 it was proposed to raise a monumental trophy, in honour of the battle of Trafalgar, on the summit of Castle Hill, near the Observatory, but the project was relinquished for want of sufficient funds. This trophy was intended to have been elevated to a height of about 200 feet, and, had it been carried into effect, would have been a landmark to vessels on the river, and a conspicuous object to the country for miles around. On the brow of the hill, in the park, and about the front of the Observatory, you would see, till very recently, the old pensioners with their telescopes and glasses of every colour. Some of these heroes, who had served under Jervis and Nelson, had lost a leg or an arm, or possibly both; and yet they went about the park with their " baccy " as happy, to all appearance at least, as the credulous cockneys whom they delighted to cram with all sorts of improbable yarns about battles fought by " flood or field," in which they shot their cannon-balls to the very longest of all possible ranges. This hill was a favourite place, not only for the Greenwich pensioners, but for gipsies and fortune-tellers.

" The park," writes the ingenious Arthur Young, in a somewhat poetic strain, " is well stocked with deer, and affords as much variety in proportion to its size as any in the kingdom; but the views from the Observatory and One-Tree Hill are beautiful beyond imagination. . . . The projection of these hills is so bold that you do not look down upon a gradually falling slope, but at once upon the tops of branching trees, which grow in knots and clumps out of dead hollows and embrowning dells. The cattle which feed on the lawns, and appear in the breaks among them, seem to move in a region of fairy-land. A thousand natural openings among the branches of the trees break upon little picturesque views of the swelling turf, which, when lit up by the sun, have an effect pleasing beyond the power of fancy to exhibit. This is the foreground of the landscape; a little further the eye falls upon that noble structure, the hospital, in the midst of an amphitheatre of wood; then the two reaches in the river make that beautiful serpentine which forms the Isle of Dogs. . . . To the left appears a fine (?) tract of country, leading up to the capital itself, which there finishes the prospect."

The same view is thus described by Thomas Miller, in his work above quoted :—" Beautiful as is Greenwich Park within itself, with its long aisles of overhanging chestnuts, through whose branches the sunlight streams, and throws upon the velvet turf rich chequered rays of green and gold, yet it is the vast view which stretches out on every hand that gives its chief charm to the spot. What a glorious prospect opens out from the summit of ' One-Tree Hill!' London, mighty and magnificent, piercing the sky with its high-piled towers, spires, and columns; while St Paul's, like a mighty giant, heaves up his rounded shoulders as if keeping guard over the outstretched city. Far away the broad bright river Thames rolls along till lost in the dim green of the fading distance, whilst its course is still pointed out by the spreading sail. Along this ancient road of the swans vessels approach from every corner of the habitable globe to empty their riches into the great reservoir of London, whence they are again sent through a thousand channels to the remotest homes in her islands and her colonies."

We have already mentioned that this park was a favourite lounge for Dr. Johnson during the time he was lodging in Greenwich. " We walked in the evening in Greenwich Park," writes Boswell. " He asked me, I suppose by way of trying my disposition, ' Is not this very fine?' Having no exquisite relish of the beauties of nature, and being more delighted with ' the busy hum of men,' I answered, ' Yes, sir; but not equal to Fleet Street.' *Johnson*: ' You are right, sir.' "

Greenwich Park, particularly at fair time, was the scene of every variety of joyous hilarity, from " Kiss in the ring," " Drop the handkerchief," and other games, to the exciting rush and tumble down the hill. The frolic and mirth everywhere visible here on these occasions is well described in the following " Ballad Singer's Apology for Greenwich Fair," in " Merrie England in the Olden Time :"—

" Up hill and down hill, 'tis always the same;
    Mankind ever grumbling, and fortune to blame!
    To fortune, 'tis uphill, ambition, and strife;
    And fortune obtain'd, then the downhill of life!

" We toil up the hill till we reach to the top;
    But are not permitted one moment to stop!
    Oh, how much more quick we descend than we climb!
    There's no locking fast the swift wheels of Old Time!

" Gay Greenwich! thy happy young holiday train
    Here roll down the hill and then mount it again.
    The ups and downs life has bring sorrow and care;
    But frolic and mirth attend those at the fair.

" My Lord May'r of London of high City lineage
    His show makes us glad, with, and why shouldn't Greenwich?
    His gingerbread coach a crack figure it cuts!
    And why shouldn't we crack our gingerbread nuts?

"· Of fashion and fame, ye grandiloquent powers,
    Pray take your full swing, only let us take *our's!*
    If you have grown graver and wiser, messieurs,
    The grinning be our's and the gravity your's!"

"' To keep one bright spark of good humour alive,
    Old holiday pastimes and sports we revive.
    Be merry, my masters, for now is your time—
    Come, who'll buy my ballads? they're reason and rhyme."

Groups of nurserymaids and children are familiar features in the modern aspect of Greenwich Park. The latter flit, climb, and leap over every broken hillock, slide into every green dell, swing, toss, and tumble round and upon each sinewy tree, as if they were the legitimate possessors of the park, and lived entirely upon gingerbread, oranges, nuts, and lemonade—viands which, it seems proper to believe, are indispensable to the real enjoyment of these shady avenues.

In Albert Smith's description of Greenwich Fair, from which we have quoted largely in the preceding chapter, part of the scene is laid in the park. "It was a great relief to exchange the dust and jostling of the streets," he writes, "for the greensward and wide area of the park, albeit the grass was, in some places, perfectly shuffled away by the countless feet that passed over it in the course of the day. Observatory Hill was the chief point of attraction, and here the great mass of the people was collected. Nothing could be more animated or mirth-inspiring than the *coup d'œil* from the summit of this rise. The myriads of visitors all in their gayest dresses, for the humblest amongst them had mounted something new, be [were] it only a ribbon, in compliment to the holiday—the perpetual motion of the different groups and their various occupations—the continuation of the bustle to the river, seen beyond the hospital, covered with ships and steamboats as far as the eye could reach —and above all, the clear bright light shed over the entire panorama, except where the cloudy smoke of London hung on the horizon—altogether formed a moving picture of life and festivity only to be witnessed at Greenwich. The maimed and weather-beaten forms of the old pensioners offered odd contrasts to the lively active groups on every side. But even they were keeping holiday. Some of them, it is true, would have found it a task of no small difficulty to climb up the hill, or run down it, with the alacrity or headlong velocity of the younger visitors; so they contented themselves with sitting down upon the smooth turf to watch the others, or entertaining attentive listeners with their accounts of former engagements, in descriptions which depended more or less upon the fertility of their imaginations, but so ingeniously framed that they usually were contrived to end in

an eleemosynary appeal to the generosity of the 'noble captain' or other complimentary officer who listened to them. The other chief entertainments on the Observatory Hill consisted in running down with helter-skelter rapidity, or scrambling oranges and apples amongst the boys on its declivity, which fruits were liberally showered forth by the more wealthy visitors on the summit. Frequently, an unwary damsel, crossing the slope, was entrapped by a handkerchief extended between two swift-footed swains, and compelled to finish her journey down the hill in much quicker time than she intended. And then what struggling there was—what exclamations of 'Ha' done, then!' and 'Be quiet, now!' until there was no breath left to give utterance to these remonstrances, and the victim was hurried to the foot of the steep between her two reckless persecutors, fortunate if she arrived at the foot without any downfall. For such accidents were of common occurrence, and roars of laughter arose from the crowds on either side when any luckless wight overran himself, and saluted the turf in consequence."

"If Easter Monday draws up the curtain of our popular merriments," writes the author of "Merrie England in the Olden Time," "Whit Monday, not a whit less merry, trumpets their continuation. We hail the return of these festive seasons when the busy inhabitants of Lud's town and its suburbs, in spite of hard times, tithes, and taxes, repair to the royal park of Queen Bess to divert their melancholy. We delight to contemplate the mirthful mourners in their endless variety of character and costume; to behold the festive holiday-makers hurrying to the jocund scenes, in order to share in those pleasures which the Genius of wakes, so kind and bounteous, prepares for her votaries. The gods themselves assembled on Olympus presented not a more glorious sight than the laughing divinities of 'One-Tree Hill.' What an animated scene! Hark to the loud laugh of some youngsters that have had their roll and tumble. Yonder is a wedding party from the neighbouring village of Charlton or Eltham. See the jolly tar with his true-blue jacket and trousers, checked shirt, radiant with a gilt brooch as big as a crown-piece, yellow straw hat, striped stockings, and pumps, and his pretty bride, with her rosy cheeks and white favours. How light are their heels and their hearts too! And the blithesome couples that follow in their train, novices in the Temple of Hymen, but who will, ere long, be called upon to act as principals! All is congratulation, good wishes, and good humour. Scandal is dumb; envy dies for the day; disappointment gathers hope; and one wedding—like a fool, or an Irish wake—shall make many."

About June the park may be seen in all its bloom and beauty—the fine old hawthorns are then still in full blossom, and the hundreds of gigantic elms and chestnuts are hung in their richest array of summer green, whilst here and there the deer cross and re-cross the shady avenues, or, crouching amid what is called the "wilderness,"

Chesterfield House, and his connection with it is still kept in remembrance by the name of "Chesterfield Walk," which has been given to the shady pathway running along under the park wall from the top of Croom's Hill. In 1807 the house became the residence of the Duchess of Brunswick, sister of George III., and was thereupon called Brunswick House. The duchess came hither in consequence of her daughter, Caroline, Princess of

VIEW IN GREENWICH PARK.

lie half buried in the fan-like fern. The hill and the plain below, and, in fact, the whole greensward round, are clothed in their holiday attire, the female part of the community lighting up the scene by the varied hues of their dress. At every few yards you meet with a new group of pleasure-seekers, whilst the long avenue which leads up to Blackheath is one continuous stream of merry-looking people.

On the south-west side of the park, and facing Blackheath, stands the Ranger's Lodge, a brick-built mansion, formerly the residence of Philip, Earl of Chesterfield, who purchased it about the middle of the last century, and considerably enlarged and improved it. In his "Letters" the earl calls it "Babiole" and afterwards "La Petite Chartreuse;" but it was commonly known as

Wales, having had the adjoining mansion, Montagu House, assigned her as a residence when appointed Ranger of Greenwich Park, in the year 1806. On her death the house was purchased by the Crown, and appropriated as the residence of the Ranger. Here the Princess Sophia resided from 1816 till her death. In more recent times it was the residence of Prince Arthur, now Duke of Connaught, whilst studying for the Engineers.

Montagu House, which stood immediately to the south of the Ranger's Lodge, owed its name to having belonged to the Duke of Montagu, who bought it in 1714. Whilst it was the residence of the Princess of Wales, the grounds attached to it were enlarged by enclosing a portion of the park, called the "Little Wilderness." This now forms

HOUSES ROUND GREENWICH PARK.

1. Ranger's House.   2. Woodlands, 1804.   3. Lady Hamilton's House.   4 Old Tree in Greenwich Park.

a part of the Ranger's Lodge. Montagu House was pulled down in 1815, but the name is preserved in Montagu Corner, at the end of Chesterfield Walk. At the junction of Chesterfield Walk and Croom's Hill is a large mansion, once the seat of General Wolfe, and the occasional residence of his son, the hero of Quebec, whose remains were brought hither before they were buried in Greenwich Church. The house was afterwards the residence of Lord Lyttelton.

On the south-west side of the park, above the summit of the hill, and in the rear of the house above mentioned, are several barrows, or tumuli, which, it has been conjectured, may have been the burial-places of the Danes during their encampment on Blackheath. Some of them were opened towards the end of the last century, when there were discovered in them spear-heads, human bones and hair, knives, fragments of woollen cloth, and other articles.

It is time now that we made our way once more to the summit of the hill whereon stands the Observatory, a spot which Tickell calls—

" That fair hill where hoary sages boast
To name the stars and count the heavenly host."

The Observatory, as we have mentioned above,* occupies the site of the tower, commonly called "Greenwich Castle," which was built by Duke Humphrey. This tower was repaired, in 1526, by Henry VIII., and was used sometimes as a habitation for the younger branches of the royal family, sometimes as a prison, occasionally as a place of defence, and at other times as a residence for a favourite mistress. "The king" (Henry VIII.), writes Puttenham, in his "Art of English Poesy," "having Flamock with him in his barge, going from Westminster to Greenwich, to visit a fayre lady whom the king loved, who was lodged in the tower in the park ; the king coming within sight of the tower, and being disposed to be merrie, said, ' Flamock, let us run.' " We do not know what was the result of the king's running, or what was its immediate object. In 1482, Mary of York, fifth daughter of Edward IV., died in this tower. In the reign of Queen Elizabeth it was called " Mirefleur," and the Earl of Leicester was confined in it, when he had incurred the Queen's displeasure by marrying the Countess of Essex. Henry Howard, Earl of Northampton, Lord Privy Seal, and the founder of Norfolk College,† in East Greenwich, had a grant of this tower from James I. ; he is said to have enlarged and beautified the building, and to have made it his principal residence. In 1633,

Elizabeth, Countess of Suffolk, died here. Ten years later, being then called "Greenwich Castle," it was considered of so much importance as a place of defence, that the Parliament took immediate measures to secure it against the King.

After the Restoration, M. de St. Pierre, a Frenchman, who came to London about the year 1675, having applied to King Charles II. to be rewarded for his discovery of a method of finding the longitude by the moon's distance from a star, a commission was appointed to investigate his pretensions. Lord Brouncker, President of the then young Royal Society, Sir Christopher Wren, the Surveyor-General, and City architect—for nearly half London was then in ruins—Sir Jonas Moore, Master of Ordnance, and many other "ingenious gentlemen" about the town and court, composed the board, " with power to add to their number," which power they exercised by the addition of a certain Mr. John Flamsteed, who was introduced by Sir Jonas Moore, and whose name, from that day to this, has been associated with this hill.

Flamsteed, who was born at Denby, Derbyshire, in 1646, had already distinguished himself as an astronomer ; for, previous to the erection of this Observatory, he had made sundry observations of the heavenly bodies in a turret of the building called the "White Tower," in the Tower of London, which turret is still called the "Observatory." On hearing the Frenchman's proposals, Flamsteed at once pointed out their impracticability, in consequence of the imperfect state of the tables representing the motions of the moon, and the inaccuracies of the existing catalogues of the fixed stars. He likewise set to work on some observations of his own, which at once frustrated the schemes of St. Pierre, who was no more heard of. The commissioners thereupon communicated the results of Flamsteed's observations to the king ; " his Majesty is startled by the assertion that the stars' places are erroneously known, and exclaims, with his childish vehemence, that ' he must have them anew observed, examined, and corrected for the use of his seamen.' The king is then told how necessary it is to have a good stock of observations of the moon and planets, and he exclaims that ' he must have it done ; ' and when he is asked who could or who should do it, he replies, ' The person who informs you of them.' " Sir Jonas Moore accordingly conveys to the young astronomer the royal warrant appointing him " Our Astronomical Observator," and enjoining him " forthwith to apply himself with the utmost care and diligence to the rectifying the tables of the motions of the heavens and the places of the fixed stars, so as to find out

---

* See *ante*, p. 165.   † See *ante*, p. 196.

the so-much-desired longitude of places, for the perfecting the art of navigation." For this important service he was to receive the munificent stipend of £100 per annum !

The next thing to be settled was the site of the Observatory, and, upon the advice of Sir Christopher Wren, Greenwich Hill was chosen. The old tower was accordingly ordered to be demolished; and the first stone of the new building was laid in August, 1675. In exactly a year from that date the edifice was handed over to Flamsteed, and from him it acquired the name of Flamsteed House. In the following month he began his observations, with a sextant of six feet radius, contrived by himself, and such other instruments as were then known. Notwithstanding his scanty income, and the difficulty he experienced in obtaining such instruments as he required, Flamsteed's zeal overcame all obstacles, and during his lifetime the Observatory rose to that first rank which it has ever since maintained among similar institutions.

It may be worth while to consider here what was the state of practical astronomy at the time when Flamsteed commenced his labours. Neither telescopes nor clocks had yet been introduced into observatories; the star catalogue of Tycho Brahe was derived from observations made with instruments furnished with plain sights; and this, together with the Rudolphine tables of the sun, moon, and planets then known (which were constructed from elements quite as rough), were the only materials existing for the use of the theoretical astronomer. Flamsteed, who knew what was needed, and who had a much better idea than any man of his time of the means necessary for producing comparatively good observations, set about his task with vigour. He was totally unprovided with instruments at the public expense, but he brought with him to the Observatory an iron sextant of six feet radius, and two clocks, given him by Sir Jonas Moore, together with a quadrant of three feet radius, and two telescopes, which he had brought with him from Denby. With these instruments he worked till the year 1678, when he borrowed from the Royal Society a quadrant of fifty inches, which, however, he was allowed to retain only a short time. It must be borne in mind that the advantages of the system of meridian observations were unknown, or nearly so, at this time. The sextant was employed to measure the distances of an object to be observed from some standard stars, or stars whose places were supposed to be better known, and a laborious calculation was necessary to deduce the resulting place of the body in every instance. This gave, however, no

means of fixing the place of the body with respect to the equinox; and Flamsteed, finding the absolute necessity for an instrument fixed in the plane of the meridian, applied to the Government. He was not denied; but being wearied with repeated promises which were never kept, he at length resolved to make a "mural arc" at his own expense, and this instrument was finally erected, and divided with his own hands in 1683. It was, however, a failure; and his observations were continued for several years longer with the sextant. The minor obstructions and vexations to which Flamsteed was subjected we have not space to mention. It is sufficient to say that, during the whole time that he officiated as Astronomer-Royal (nearly half a century from his first appointment), he was not supplied by the Government with a single instrument. The only assistance he was furnished with was that of "a silly, surly labourer" to assist him with the sextant; the other assistants and computers he provided at his own expense.

In 1684 Flamsteed was presented to the living of Burstow, in Surrey; having been from his early life desirous of devoting himself to the duties of the ministry. "My desires," he says, in his "Autobiography," "have always been to learning and divinity; and though I have been accidentally put from it by God's providence, yet I had always thought myself more qualified for it than for any other employment, because my bodily weakness will not permit me action, and my mind has always been fitted for the contemplation of God and his works." His father died a few years afterwards; and these two circumstances improving his estate, he determined to construct a new "mural arc," stronger than the former; and this instrument, famous as really commencing a new era in observing, was constructed by Mr. Abraham Sharp, his friend and assistant, at an expense of £120, no portion of which was reimbursed to him by the Government. All Flamsteed's former observations were of little value; no fundamental point of astronomy was settled by them; and they merely served for forming a preliminary or observing catalogue of objects to be well observed with his new instrument. From the date of the use of this instrument, 1689, the useful labours of Flamsteed commenced; every observation made after this was permanently useful, and could be applied to determine some important point. With this instrument, after verifying its position and determining its adjustment, he set about the determination of those cardinal points in astronomy, the position of the equinox, the obliquity of the ecliptic, and other fundamentals, without which the correct positions of the fixed stars and the planetary bodies could never be ascertained. His methods and processes are explained by himself in the "Historia Cœlestis," a work in three folio volumes, the third of which contains his catalogue of 2,935 stars, carried down to the year 1689. His work still holds a high place in the history of astronomy.

What instruments Flamsteed had to work with, then, we are assured he had to provide and pay for himself; and in order to do this, he was compelled to turn "teacher." Government had already imposed upon him the education, monthly, of two boys from Christ's Hospital, as if his tedious watches by night, and his laborious calculations by day, were not sufficient return for his paltry pittance, which was reduced by a tax to £90 a year. He thereupon, as we have said, gave lessons in his favourite science, and obtained for pupils sundry dukes and lords, with many captains of vessels and East India servants, thus augmenting his pecuniary means.

Flamsteed appears soon to have made many friends, among whom was the venerable John Evelyn, who, under date of September 10th, 1676, makes this entry in his "Diary:"—"Din'd with me Mr. Flamsted, the learned astrologer (sic) and mathematician, whom his Majesty had established in the new Observatory in Greenwich Park, with the choicest instruments. An honest, sincere man." Evelyn, we need scarcely state, should have written "astronomer," instead of "astrologer." But he is not the only person who has made this confusion. For it is a fact worthy of being placed on record that seldom a week passes without ladies driving from London in their carriages to the doors of the Observatory, and inquiring if they can have their "horoscopes" cast, evidently showing that they do not know the difference between astrology and astronomy. It is to be feared that on this subject great superstition prevails, even among the "educated" classes; and that whilst fortune-tellers, who practise on poor servant-girls, are pounced upon by the police, some of the professors of the secret science, called "spiritualism," are making fortunes, by charging a guinea for every consultation, or *séance!* But we must now return to our subject. On the 14th of June, 1680, John Evelyn writes:—"Came to dine Dr. Burnet, author of the 'History of the Reformation.' After dinner we all went to see the Observatory and Mr. Flamsteed, who show'd us divers rare instruments, especially the greate quadrant. My old friend Henshaw was with me." Again, some three years later, namely, on the 1st of August, 1683, we meet with this entry:—"Came to see me Mr. Flamsted, the

astronomer, from his Observatorie at Greenwich, to draw the meridian for my pendule," &c.

About this time, or shortly after, Flamsteed became friendly with Sir Isaac Newton, who was engaged in investigating the irregularities of the moon's motions, for the confirmation of his theory of universal gravitation, and who required accurate observations of the moon for comparison of fact with fancy. No one but Flamsteed could supply these, and from time to time Newton visited him in order to obtain them. But this friendship was not of long duration. A difference arose between them, on account of an innocent statement by Flamsteed, to the effect that he had furnished Newton with a mass of lunar observations to assist him in his investigations, getting into print. Some angry correspondence ensued, and the dispute, after slumbering for a few years, broke out into a lamentable quarrel. In course of time, Flamsteed's valuable store of observations, extending over the period of thirty years which he had then passed as Astronomer-Royal, were prepared for publication. Prince George of Denmark, consort of Queen Anne, undertook to bear the expense of printing; and a committee, with Sir C. Wren and Newton among the number, was appointed to examine the manuscript, and see the work through the press. During its progress, the latent quarrel between Flamsteed and Newton broke out afresh, and arrived at its culmination, turning upon the difference that existed between Flamsteed and the referees concerning the plan of publication of his work. The book, "mangled and garbled," was at length published, and so much did it annoy its author, that when, a few years after, the undistributed copies, about three-fourths of the entire impression, were placed in his hands, he at once committed the whole of them to the flames, "as a sacrifice to heavenly truth," and "that none may exist to show the ingratitude of two of his countrymen, who had used him worse than ever the noble Tycho was used in Denmark." He then resolved to publish a complete edition of his observations on his own plan, and at his own expense. It was to appear in three volumes; but on the completion of the second volume, his life's weary toil was brought to a close, on the last day of the year 1719.

Flamsteed was succeeded by Dr. Halley, an astronomer also of great eminence, who, finding upon his appointment that the Observatory was destitute both of furniture and instruments (Flamsteed's having been removed by his executors as his personal property), furnished it anew, and fixed a transit instrument. Its introduction is stated to have been the most important step that had been made. It is the most simple and effective of all astronomical instruments; and up to the present time, the only changes that have been made in the means for observing the right ascensions of the heavenly bodies, are those which secure to it the utmost possible stability and accuracy of workmanship and adjustment. With it alone Halley continued to make observations of the moon till the year 1725, when an eight-foot mural quadrant, made by Graham, was set up at the public expense. Of the small salary received by Dr. Halley for his important duties the following anecdote has been related :—On the accession of George II., the queen consort, Caroline, made a visit to the Royal Observatory. Being pleased with everything she saw, and understanding the smallness of the astronomer's salary (£100 per annum), her Majesty very graciously said she would speak to the king to have it augmented, to which Dr. Halley replied in alarm, " Pray, your Majesty, do no such thing; for should the salary be increased, it might become an object of emolument to place there some unqualified needy dependant, to the ruin of the institution." However, understanding that the doctor had formerly served the Crown as a captain in the navy, the queen soon after was able to obtain a grant of his half-pay for that commission, which he accordingly enjoyed from that time up to the end of his life.

Halley died in 1742, and his successor was Dr. Bradley. This eminent astronomer made a noble series of observations, extending over the twenty years during which he held the post. In 1750 many valuable additions were made to the stock of instruments. Bradley died in the year 1762, and was succeeded by Dr. Bliss, who lived only till March, 1764. The office next devolved upon Dr. Maskelyne, who for nearly fifty years performed the duties with wonderful assiduity; scarcely ever leaving the Observatory, except on some important scientific business, and making all the laborious and delicate observations himself, although he had the co-operation of a skilful assistant. He first suggested the publication of the *Nautical Almanack*, a work of indispensable use to seamen, of which he edited no less than forty-nine volumes. At his death he left four large folio volumes of printed observations as the result of the patient labour of his life. In 1767 an order was issued by George III. that the observations made at Greenwich should be published, under the superintendence of the Royal Society; they have, accordingly, since been published annually by that learned body. The principal addition made to

the Observatory during Maskelyne's directorship was the building of the "circle" room, contiguous to and east of the transit-room. Maskelyne died in 1811, leaving behind him an enviable reputation. The observations made by this astronomer during his forty-seven years' residence at Greenwich were so valuable, that it has been remarked of him by his biographer, that if the whole materials of science should be lost except the volume of observations left by him, they would suffice to reconstruct the edifice of modern astronomy. He was succeeded by Mr. John Pond, who held office till the year 1835, when ill health compelled him to resign; he died in the following year, and was buried at Lee, in the same tomb with his predecessor, Dr. Halley. During Mr. Pond's directorship the Observatory acquired that organisation which it has since retained, and which was necessary to enable it to meet the demand made upon it by the requirements of modern science. On his entrance upon his duties he began, like his predecessors, with one assistant; but on his representations and urgent entreaties for increase of the establishment, he finally obtained six assistants; and this amount of force for the astronomical department of the Observatory has been continued with some modifications to the present time. Pond was peculiarly skilful in the theory of astronomical instruments, and in the interpretation of the results afforded by them. Sir George Airy, in one of his official reports, states that he regards him as the "principal improver of modern practical astronomy."

On the resignation of Mr. Pond, Mr. George Biddell Airy, then Director of the Observatory at Cambridge, was appointed to the vacant office. " Under his presidency," writes Mr. Carpenter, in the *Gentleman's Magazine* (February, 1866), " the Observatory has been gradually augmented and brought to its present complete and perfect condition. Old instruments, very perfect in their way, but still behind modern requirements, have been laid aside, and new systems introduced. Every improvement and appliance that science could suggest has been made subservient to the utilitarian principles of the Observatory under its present organisation." Sir George Airy resigned in 1881, and Mr. William Christie, M.A., was nominated in his place.

The Observatory was never intended for show, but for work. It was constructed in haste, chiefly with the materials of the old tower, and some spare bricks that lay available at Tilbury Fort. The admissions to the building are strictly limited to such individuals as are most likely to be benefited by visiting it, and idling sightseers are carefully excluded. A card is kept in the porter's lodge, which explains that the privilege of visiting the Observatory is of necessity very limited, those officially privileged being officers of the Royal Navy and gentlemen officially connected with the Admiralty; other visitors are required to be furnished with an introduction from some person of scientific distinction.

A few objects arrest attention outside the walls of the edifice. For instance, the twenty-four hour and time is the only natural standard this earth possesses; it is the only thing that is invariable. Now the British imperial standard yard, by law established, is a measure of length, bearing a certain definite proportion to the length of a pendulum which, at a given temperature and under other specified conditions, beats accurately *seconds of mean solar time*. This is the connection between astronomy and yard-measures. Any one who desires to secure an accurate yard-measure may do

FLAMSTEED HOUSE. (*From Hollar's " Long View."*)

electric clock, supposed by the uninitiated to be kept going by the sun; the public barometer, with its indices, showing the highest and lowest readings during the past few hours; the little windmill like a child's toy on the roof; and the high pole with a light at the top, conjectured to be a beacon to show the longitude at sea. One other external object must not be overlooked: this is an iron plate fixed against the wall, with a number of brass plugs and pins projecting from it, with the inscriptions, " British Yard," " Two Feet," &c., over them. " It will probably be asked," says Mr. Carpenter, in an article in the *Gentleman's Magazine*, from which we have already quoted, " what has a yard-measure to do with astronomy? It has a great deal. One important branch of practical astronomy is the measurement of time, so by carrying to Greenwich a rod about a yard long, and truly adjusting it by means of the appliance there exposed for the public benefit. He will find two plugs, the distance between which is exactly a yard when the temperature of the air is about 60°, and two pins for the support of the rod to be adjusted. The plugs are bevelled off a little on their insides, and the points that are exactly a yard apart are marked upon their upper surfaces by arrow-heads. If the rod will not go in as far as the arrow-heads, it is too long; if it passes them loosely, it is too short. Similar plugs are provided for shorter measures, down to three inches."

On passing inside the gate, the first object that presents itself is a range of low buildings immediately to the left, railed off from the more common portions of the court. The old-fashioned yet rather picturesque gables and roughly-tiled roofs of these buildings, and their general humble aspect, give no evidence of their use, except what may be gathered from the slits, closed by shutters, which in two places intersect them, and the domes that flank them at their eastern and south-western extremities; yet in these unpretending rooms not only are all the observations made which give its fame to the establishment, but the reduction of

A doorway near the eastern end of the range of buildings leads into the transit-circle room, one of the principal observing-rooms of the establishment. To the reader not familiar with the instruments and processes of astronomy it may be desirable to explain that the transit-instrument is a telescope which is supposed theoretically to describe the plane of the meridian. For this special purpose it is furnished with two axes, terminating in two well-

ENTRANCE TO GREENWICH OBSERVATORY, IN 1840.

them is also performed there, and they are rendered fit for the immediate use of the astronomer. The door immediately opposite, as we cross the court, is that of the Astronomer-Royal's residence, all the apartments of which are on the ground-floor, and situated on either side of a long gallery running nearly east and west. On the wall of the building, near this doorway, is a slab containing the original inscription set up at the erection of the Observatory; it is as follows :—

CAROLUS II., Rex Optimus,
Astronomiæ et Nauticæ Artis
Patronus Maximus,
Speculum hanc in utriusque commodum
Fecit,
Anno Dni. MDCLXXVI., Regni Sui xxviii.,
Curante JONA MOORE, milite.

polished equal cylindrical pivots; and these pivots being placed in bearings sunk in the stone piers shaped like the letter Y (technically called "Y's"), the instrument is capable of revolving freely.

We may here remark that the principal duty of the practical astronomer is the determination of right ascensions and polar distances. "Right ascension," says Mr. Carpenter, "is the distance of a heavenly body from an imaginary point—or, more properly, a great circle passing through a point —in the heavens, called the first point of Aries. It is a well-known fact that the earth completes one revolution upon its axis in the course of twenty-four hours; and this rotation affords a ready means of measuring right ascension. We have only to ascertain how much the earth turns between the time that the first point of Aries crosses the meridian, and the time that the star to be measured crosses it. To measure this two things are requisite—a clock, and something like a line to see the stars pass over. . . A telescope is firmly fixed to a horizontal axis, and mounted upon two stone pillars, just as a gun is mounted upon its trunnions, free to move vertically, but incapable of moving horizontally. The telescope is so adjusted, that upon spinning it round, it sweeps out an imaginary plane which lies exactly due north or south of the Observatory. In its focus is placed an extremely fine vertical line—in reality, a fragment of spider's web. Now, to whatever point of the heavens we direct this telescope, bearing in mind that it can only move in a vertical direction, that spider-line represents the astronomical meridian at that point. The virtual meridian of Greenwich is therefore really no more than half an inch of cobweb. If, then, we take a clock, and set it at oh. om. os. when the first point of Aries crosses the meridian, it will be obvious that the time by that clock, when any object passes the spider-line in the telescope, will be its distance from that point expressed in time; for instance, if we direct the telescope to a star that we see approaching the meridian, and observe that it crosses the cobweb at 5h. 21m. 45s., we know, assuming the clock to be correct, and the instrument in proper adjustment, that the right ascension of the star is 5h. 21m. 45s. From the circumstance of all objects crossing or transiting the field of this telescope, it bears the very appropriate title of the 'Transit Instrument.' It was invented by Römer, a Danish astronomer, about the year 1690, and was first used at the Greenwich Observatory by Halley some thirty years after."

Upon the same wall on which hangs Halley's primitive instrument, are suspended two or three other transit instruments, which in their time have doubtless rendered good service to astronomical science. These are the instruments introduced by Dr. Bradley, and also Troughton's noble instrument, used by Maskelyne and Pond, and by Sir George Airy up to the year 1850, when it was dismounted to give place to the gigantic "transit-circle" now in use. This last-mentioned instrument is, in fact, a combination of two instruments, seeing that it has also superseded the "mural quadrant," by means of which a star or planet's polar distance was formerly ascertained. This instrument is twelve feet in length, and its largest glass is eight inches in diameter. Attached to the telescope is the circle which answers to the "mural circle;" around its circumference is a narrow band of silver, upon which are engraved those divisions representing degrees of angular measurement, of which the whole circle contains 360. These degrees are further subdivided into smaller intervals of five minutes, and the intermediate minutes and seconds, and decimals of a second, are what is technically termed "read off" by means of micrometers, six of which are used, and their mean taken, to eliminate errors of observation, &c. These micrometers are affixed to one of the piers supporting the instrument, the pier itself being perforated to allow the divisions to be seen through it. Another circle attached to the telescope is a clamping circle, for the purpose of fixing the instrument rigidly during an observation. Counterpoises in various parts, apparatus for raising the instrument, and other appliances necessary for purposes of adjustment, make up the other details of the "transit circle," in front of which stands the "transit clock," which is its indispensable accessory.

We have arrived, let us suppose, a little before noon; the sun is about to cross the meridian, and an observation is to be made. Shutters in the roof are thrown open, the great telescope is swung up and fixed in position, and an observer seats himself at the lower end of it. Peeping through the instrument, all that could be seen by an "outside" observer would be a number of vertical lines, technically called "wires," but in reality so many pieces of cobweb, as mentioned above, stretched across the field of observation at irregular distances. The centre one is the celebrated meridian of Greenwich, or, at all events, it represents it, and it is curious to reflect that from this centre line ships of all civilised nations, and in all parts of the known world, are reckoning their distances. What the regular observer has to do is to record the precise instant at which the sun's edge, or "limb," as astronomers call it, passes that central "wire." In any single observation, however, he may be a little at fault, and for the sake of greater accuracy, therefore, he notes the instant at which it passes over all the "wires," and then strikes an average between them. Slowly the sun creeps up to the first line, and the observer lightly taps a little spring attached to the telescope. The second "wire" is reached, and again the spring is tapped, and so on throughout the whole seven or nine webs employed in the observation. This spring is connected with a telegraphic wire extending to a "chronograph" in a distant part of the building, which consists of a cylinder, around which a sheet of white paper has been strained. The cylinder itself is revolved by the pendulum of an electric clock, which, instead of oscillating backwards and forwards, swings round in a circle, thus producing a motion perfectly uniform and unbroken. A little steel point, which is travelling over the surface of the paper, is in electric communication with the spring attached to the great telescope ; " and," observes a writer in *Cassell's Family Magazine*, " every time the observer taps the spring, this little travelling point pricks into the paper, thus recording that the sun has just crossed a ' wire.' This in itself, however, would not be a record of the time of transit if it were not that another little steel point, which is in connection with a galvanic clock in another part of the building, has previously marked the sheet of paper into spaces representing precise seconds of time. On the completion of the observation the paper may be removed from the cylinder, and affords a permanent record of it."

One other object in the apartment containing the " transit-circle" should not be passed unnoticed ; it is the identical instrument with which Bradley made his important discovery of the aberration of light.

The next important instrument is the altitude and azimuth, or, as it is termed, for shortness, the " altazimuth," which is located in the south dome of the Observatory buildings. This instrument was erected in 1847, for the sole purpose of observing the moon. Next to the sun, the most important of the heavenly bodies is the moon, for, independently of her use in regulating the division of the year into months, and creating the tides of the ocean, she is indispensable to nautical science, as her motions afford the only means of accurately determining the longitude at sea. The Observatory was originally founded for observations necessary to bring to perfection the lunar tables, and for the improvement of nautical astronomy. The observation of the moon in every part of her orbit has always been, therefore, an object of first-rate importance. To effect this, meridian observations have been regularly made in fixed observatories, as alone giving results of the requisite excellence. But, since the moon is invisible at her meridian passage for nearly one-third of her orbit —viz., for about four days, on the average, before conjunction, and for four days after it—and since also a great many observations in each lunation are necessarily lost by cloudy weather, it became a great desideratum to supply, if possible, by extra-meridional observations, these defects. The altitude and azimuthal instrument was evidently the kind of instrument that must be employed for this purpose, because, its axes being one horizontal and 'he other vertical, the parts of the instrument are

equally affected by gravity in every position, and the only thing wanted to produce observations which should rival those made with the transit-instrument and mural-circle, would be sufficient firmness. To secure this the Astronomer-Royal adopted as his principles of construction, " to form as many parts as possible in one cast of metal, to use no small screws in the union of parts, and to have no power of adjustment in any." The instrument is, therefore, as the visitor would at once see, of unusual weight and solidity. One of the two vertical cheeks that are on each side of the telescope carries, in one cast of metal, the four microscopes for reading the vertical circle, and the supports of the levels parallel to the plane of that circle. The lower piece connecting these cheeks, or the base plate, carries in one cast the four microscopes for reading the horizontal or azimuthal circle, and supports two levels parallel to the horizontal axis; and the upper connecting piece carries two other levels similarly situated on the upper pivot. These pieces are most firmly connected with the side vertical cheeks by means of planed surfaces and screw bolts. The vertical circle was made in two casts of metal—viz., the cylindrical part, the spokes and pivots on one side, the object-end and the eye-end of the telescope were made in one cast ; and in the other cast are included the spokes and pivot on the other side. Thus the whole of the essential parts of the instrument, with regard to firmness, were made in six casts of metal. The weight of these six parts is about sixteen hundredweight.

Some idea of the importance of the Greenwich lunar observations may be inferred from the circumstance that, during the century ending with the year 1851, Greenwich contributed nearly 12,000 observations of the moon towards the improvement and perfection of the vexatious lunar theory ; all reduced under the direction of Sir G. B. Airy, and rendered immediately available for the investigations of the physical astronomer, the lunar tables now in use being chiefly based upon these observations. Since the introduction of the " altazimuth," the number of observations of the moon formerly made here in the course of each year has been about doubled, and, as a natural consequence, the value of the Greenwich lunar observations has been largely increased.

It may be asked by some of our readers, how are the Greenwich observations of the moon connected with navigation ? A few lines by the author quoted above may be given as a reply. " The observing astronomer," he writes, " observes accurately the position of the moon in the heavens at all times and under all circumstances. He turns his observations over to the physical astronomer. The physical astronomer deduces from them the laws that govern the moon's motions, and represents those motions by numerical tables. These tables are put into the hands of the computer of the *Nautical Almanac*, who, by their aid, predicts the place the moon will occupy, with reference to proximate stars and otherwise, at every hour of the day and night throughout the year, and publishes these 'lunar distances' in that work, three or four years in advance, for the benefit of seamen starting on long voyages. The mariner observes the moon and stars near her with his sextant, and from comparison of his observations with the positions given in the *Nautical Almanac* computes his longitude, and ascertains the place of his vessel on the trackless ocean."

We will now pass on to the interior of the very large dome, or rather drum, that caps the south-eastern extremity of the Observatory. In it is a magnificent specimen of the class of instrument known as the "equatorial." The dome itself, which has an opening closed by curved shutters, sliding upwards and downwards, moves round with sufficient ease by means of a toothed wheel and rack, the manual power being applied at the ends of long radial bars. The great equatorial telescope was mounted about the year 1860, under the direction and from the plans of Sir George Airy. The author whom we have already quoted remarks that, "It is the largest instrument in the Observatory, and of its kind is one of the finest in the world. Its object-glass, which is thirteen inches in diameter, and has a focal distance of eighteen feet, alone cost £1,200. The most curious feature in this telescope is the clockwork arrangement by which it follows any object under examination. It is used chiefly for what may be called gazing purposes—such, for instance, as the scrutiny of the marvellous eruptions on the surface of the sun, or the mountains of the moon, and it is often necessary to continue such observations for hours together. It is plain, however, that if an observer is examining the face of the sun, the motion of the earth will gradually bear him and his telescope eastward until the great luminary is lost to view. He will steadily creep out at the western side of the field. This is obviated by the operation of a clock driven by falling water. This powerful piece of mechanism is connected with the great iron framework supporting the telescope, and just as the earth creeps round from west to east, the telescope and all that pertains to it is borne round from east to west.

Thus, so far as the motion of the earth is concerned, the sun, moon, or stars, as seen through the great equatorial, will appear to be perfectly stationary."

We have now seen all the more prominent features of the astronomical department of Greenwich Observatory, though there yet remain many other objects of the utmost scientific interest— such as rain-gauges, hygrometers, anemometers, and thermometers, placed in all kinds of positions, and under all kinds of conditions. In one room is a very large number of Government chronometers, required for the use of ships; while in a building apart from the Astronomical Observatory, is a Magnetic Observatory, established about the year 1840, for the purpose of ascertaining and recording the various phenomena of the magnetic currents of the earth. "The principal instruments in the Magnetic Observatory," writes Mr. J. Carpenter, "are three magnets about two feet long, one suspended by a skein of silk fibres, in the plane of the magnetic meridian, for indicating the variation in declination of the needle; another, suspended by two silk skeins, at right angles to the meridian, for indicating the earth's horizontal magnetic force; and a third, poised upon knife edges, like a scale-beam, for showing the vertical magnetic force. In order to secure as uniform a temperature as possible, these instruments are mounted in a subterranean apartment. Until the year 1847 it was customary to observe the positions of these magnets every two hours throughout the day and night, but it afterwards became evident that some mode of perpetual registration of their movements was absolutely necessary, and a reward of £500 was offered for some system by which this could be effected. The reward was gained by Mr. Brooke, a medical gentleman of London, who so completely solved the problem by the skilful application of photography that his method has ever since been used with perfect success in this and other magnetic observatories, entirely superseding the old system of eye-observation. The simple process is as follows:—Each magnet has a concave mirror affixed to it in such a manner that every deflection of the magnet deflects the mirror also. A gas-burner is so placed that a beam of light from it is always shining upon the mirror. At some distance from the magnet is a cylinder, around which is wrapped a sheet of photographic paper. The beam of gaslight falling on the mirror is reflected, as a little spot of light, on to the paper, and as the magnet moves the spot of light changes its position on the sheet, leaving its trail wherever it goes. The cylinder is made to revolve once in twenty-four hours, and the magnet thus records, night and day, its minute changes of position. Two magnets trace their movements upon the same sheet of paper, which is changed every morning, and the latent image brought out, or 'developed,' in the usual way. Across the centre of the sheet runs a fine straight line, called the *base line*, its place relative to the traces of the magnets serving as a zero from which the various positions of the magnet during the day are measured, the time being ascertained by a time-scale laid down on each sheet. In a similar manner the movements of delicate galvano-meters, placed in the circuits of long lines of telegraph wires with 'earth-plates' (masses of metal buried in the earth) at their extremities, register the fluctuations of those mysterious galvanic currents that are constantly circulating through the earth, and to which the name of 'earth-currents' has been given. The height of the barometer and the changes of temperature during the day and night are simply recorded by photography. In the case of the barometer, this is effected by means of a float on the surface of the mercury in a syphon tube, which, as it rises and falls, raises or lowers a diaphragm with a small hole pierced through it, allowing the light from an adjacent gas-flame to fall upon the sensitive paper, which is, in this case, wrapped around a vertical revolving cylinder. In the case of thermometers, the gas-light is allowed to shine through the glass tube upon the passing paper, and the mercury, rising and falling, serves as a shutter that cuts off the light at various heights corresponding to the various temperatures.

"Here we see the use of the high pole with a light at the summit, that so mystifies the outer world. It is for the purpose of supporting a wire that is suspended from its top to the summit of the Astronomical Observatory. This wire collects electricity from the atmosphere, and conducts it down another wire to the room beneath, where, by means of appropriate electrometers, its quantity is measured and its quality ascertained. The light at the mast-head is for the purpose of preserving the apparatus in a degree of warmth and dryness essential to produce insulation, and prevent the escape of the atmospheric electricity. . . . In connection with this department we must visit the anemometers, or wind-gauges. For this purpose it is necessary to mount to the highest point of the Observatory. One of these anemometers is, to all outward appearance, nothing more than a simple vane; but if we enter the turret upon which it is mounted we shall see that its motions are communicated, through a little simple machinery, to a

pencil which is tracing upon a sheet of paper, moved by clockwork, every motion of the vane above; and thus recording to all futurity every change of wind throughout the day and night. Another pencil is marking the force of the wind, or its pressure in pounds upon the square foot; while a third, only called into use in rainy weather, shows the quantity of rain that falls and the rate of its falling. On another part of the roof is the little windmill to which we have before alluded. This is also an anemometer; its use is to determine the *velocity* of the wind, or, in other words, the length in miles of the current of air that passes over Greenwich in a given time. It consists of four cups, mounted upon horizontal arms attached to a vertical spindle; the rotation of the cups, which are spun round by the wind, is communicated through the spindle to a train of wheels and dials, which latter indicate the exact number of hundreds or thousands of revolutions performed by the cups, and from this the velocity of the wind is deduced.

"Here, too, we are brought into closer contact with the time-signal ball; a wood and leather sphere, five feet in diameter, that is raised every day at five minutes before one o'clock, and dropped at one precisely by the galvanic motor clock, the clock giving a signal that, by means of magnetism, pulls a trigger, and disengages the ball."

Nothing, perhaps, throughout the Observatory is calculated to strike the visitor with greater astonishment than the motor clock above referred to. There is nothing very remarkable in its appearance, but the work it accomplishes renders it, perhaps, the most wonderful clock in the world, and certainly the most important one in England. The writer above quoted continues—"It regulates several clocks within the Observatory, as well as the large one already referred to outside the gates; one at Greenwich Hospital Schools, another at the London Bridge Station of the South-Eastern Railway, another at the Post Office, St. Martin's-le-Grand, and another in Lombard Street. Once every day it telegraphs correct time to the great clock tower at Westminster; it drops the signal-ball over the Observatory, another near Charing Cross, and one at Deal; it fires time-guns at Shields and Newcastle, and every hour throughout the day it flashes out correct time to each of the railway companies. All this is accomplished, as it were, by the mere volition of the clock, and without any human interference whatever. Every morning it is corrected by an actual observation of a star; and thus, without being aware of it, do we every day start our trains, and make our appointments, and take our meals by the motions of the heavenly bodies as observed and recorded during the preceding night."

It is no longer, therefore, "the Horse Guards' clock," but Greenwich Observatory, which regulates the time of all the clocks and watches in London. The Post Office authorities have granted the special use of a system of electric wires to the inventors of a method for synchronising clocks. The arrangements recently completed bring the

is given in the annual report of the Astronomer-Royal, and the results are issued from time to time in a more substantial form in the shape of such works as the Astronomer-Royal's "Corrections of the Elements of the Lunar Theory" (1859); the "Greenwich Catalogue of 2,022 Stars" (1864); and "Catalogue of 2,760 Stars" (1870). More recently the subjects of solar photography and spectroscopy have been added to the routine investigations of the Observatory. From the annual

THE MAGNETIC CLOCK, GREENWICH OBSERVATORY.

Greenwich Observatory into direct communication with the establishment at Cornhill of Messrs. Barraud and Lund, the inventors of an apparatus by means of which existing clocks can be automatically "set to time." The mechanism is of the simplest kind; it interferes in no way with the works of a clock, and can be applied to any timepiece in or out of doors. Any number of clocks, varying in size and calibre, can, upon receipt of one time-signal, be simultaneously set to accord with each other in accurately denoting Greenwich time. A very small outlay, it is said, will secure true Greenwich time to every City establishment.

An account of what has been done at the Greenwich Observatory, as well as of what is in progress,

report published in 1884, we learn that the sun, moon, planets, and fundamental stars had been regularly observed throughout the year, together with other stars from a working catalogue of 2,600, comprising all stars down to the sixth magnitude, inclusive, which had not been observed since 1860. The annual catalogue of stars observed in 1883 contains about 1,550 stars. In the twelve months ending May 20, 1884, photographs of the sun had been taken on 219 days; there were four days on which the sun's disk was observed to be free from spots.

Sir George Airy, in his report for 1875, remarked that the Observatory was expressly built for the aid of astronomy and navigation, for promoting methods of determining longitude at sea, and, as the circumstances that led to its formation show, more especially for determination of the moon's motions. All these imply as their first step the formation of accurate catalogues of stars, and the determination of the fundamental elements of

to maintain the principles of the long-established system in perfect integrity, varying the instruments, the modes of employing them, and the modes of utilising the observations by calculation and publication, as the progress of science might require.

Viewing the instruments, however, then in use,

THE GREAT EQUATORIAL TELESCOPE IN THE DOME, GREENWICH OBSERVATORY.

the solar system. These objects have been steadily pursued from the foundation of the observatory—in one way by Flamsteed, in another way by Halley, and by Bradley in the early part of his career ; in a third form by Bradley in his later years, by Maskelyne (who contributed most powerfully to lunar and chronometric nautical astronomy), and for a time by Pond ; then, with improved instruments, by Pond, and by himself (Sir G. B. Airy) for some years, and subsequently with the instruments now in use. It had been his own intention

and the increase of expenses, which were lower than the work done, the Astronomer-Royal expressed a hope that the National Observatory would always remain on the site where it was first planted, and which early acquired the name of " Flamsteed Hill."

The Observatory is annually inspected by a body of scientific persons of high standing, who are commissioned by the Government of the day to see that the institution is maintained in a state of efficiency.

CHAPTER XVII.

BLACKHEATH, CHARLTON, AND ITS NEIGHBOURHOOD.

" And eastward straight from wild Blackheath the warlike errand went,
And roused in many an ancient hall the gallant squires of Kent."
Macaulay's Ballad of " The Armada."

Situation and Description of Blackheath—Derivation of its Name—Discovery of Numerous Tumuli—Encampment of the Danish Army—Wat Tyler's Rebellion—Reception of Richard II. at Blackheath—The Emperor of Constantinople—Reception of Henry V. on his Return from Agincourt —Other Royal Receptions—Jack Cade and his Followers—Henry VI. and the Duke of York—The Cornish Rebels—The Smith's Forge— Reception of Cardinal Campegio, and of Bonevet, High Admiral of France—Princess Anne of Cleves—Arrival of Charles II., on his Restoration—Blackheath Fair—The " Chocolate House "—Present Condition of Blackheath—East Coombe and West Coombe—Lavinia Fenton (" Polly Peachum "), Duchess of Bolton—Woodlands—Montagu House—The Princess Charlotte—Mrs. Mary Anne Clarke and the Duke of York—Flaxman, the Sculptor—Maize Hill—Vanbrugh Castle—The Mince-pie House—Charlton—St. Luke's Church—Charlton House—Horn Fair—Shooter's Hill—The Herbert Hospital—Severndroog Castle—Morden College—Kidbrook.

BLACKHEATH, which is divided from its aristocratic neighbour only by a wall, pleasantly overlooks a portion of the counties of Kent and Surrey, and affords such extensive views of the distant scenery as can be exceeded only by climbing Shooter's Hill, or some of the neighbouring heights on the left of the heath. In past times it was planted with gibbets, on which the bleaching bones of men who had dared to ask for some extension of liberty, or who doubted the infallibility of kings, were left year after year to dangle in the wind. In the distance the ancient palace of Eltham may just be seen between the trees, heaving up like a large barn against the sky.

Blackheath—which furnishes the name to the hundred to which it belongs—lies chiefly in the parishes of Greenwich and Lewisham, a portion, however, being in the parish, or " liberty," of Kidbrook, while a part of Blackheath Park is in Charlton parish. The name is variously derived from its bleak situation, and from its black appearance. The heath is a broad expanse of open greensward, intersected by several cross-roads. Nearly in the line of the present Dover Road, which traverses the centre of the heath from the top of Blackheath Hill eastward towards Shooter's Hill, ran the ancient Watling Street or Roman Road ; and along this road were numerous tumuli. Many of them, including those within Greenwich Park, near Croom's Hill Gate, of which we have spoken in the previous chapter, were opened towards the end of the last century. They were found to be mostly small conical mounds, with a circular trench at the base, and are presumed to have been Romano-British. No skeletons were discovered in them, but there were " some locks of hair, and one fine braid of an auburn hue was 'tenacious and very distinct,' and 'contained its natural phlogiston.' The *spolia* were chiefly iron spear-heads (one fifteen inches long and two inches broad was found 'in the native gravel'), knives, and nails, glass beads, and woollen and linen cloth. At the south-west

corner of the heath, by Blackheath Hill, urns (some of which are in the British Museum) and other Roman remains have been found." Near the summit of the hill, at a spot called "The Point," a remarkable cavern, extending several hundred feet under ground, was discovered about the year 1780, in laying the foundation of a house. "The entrance," writes Richardson in his "History of Greenwich," "was then through a narrow aperture, but a flight of steps have since been made. It consists of four irregular apartments, in the furthest of which is a well of pure water, twenty-seven feet in depth. They are cut out of a stratum of chalk and flint, and communicate by small avenues ; the bottom of the cavern is sand. From the well at the extremity of this singular excavation, it seems probable that it has, at some distant period, been used as a place of concealment, and the general supposition is that it was used for that purpose during the Saxon and Danish contests, but nothing has been discovered to assist inquiry."

Previous to the erection of the several villa residences with which the heath is now nearly surrounded on three sides, this place was the scene of many important historical and political events.

Here, as we have already had occasion to remark, the main body of the Danish army lay encamped in the reign of Ethelred, while their ships held possession of the river for three or four years in succession. Several places in the neighbourhood are still called "Coombs" and "Comps." East Coombe and West Coombe, two estates on the borders of the heath, are presumed to trace their names from the encampments of the Danes at this place—*coomb* as well as *comp* signifying camp; *coomb* being probably the Saxon term, and *comp* the Danish or corrupt Saxon, both of which tongues were then in use. The manors of East and West Coombe are situated at the north-east corner of the heath ; and there was formerly one called Middle Coombe, otherwise Spittle Coombe, which in all probability, was attached to that of West Coombe. Vestiges of intrenchments were, some years ago, distinctly traced in different parts of the heath, some formed doubtless by the Danes, and others by the various bodies of insurgents who have encamped here at different times. Of these, the most formidable was that in 1381, raised by Wat Tyler, a blacksmith of Dartford, on account of the imposition of a "poll tax" of three groats on all persons above fifteen. When the insurgents of Essex arose, they were joined by those of Kent, and began to assemble on Blackheath; whence, having in a few days increased to 100,000 men, they marched on to London under the command of their principal leaders, Wat Tyler and Jack Straw, and afterwards separated into three parties; one of these proceeded to the Temple, which they burnt to the ground, with all the books and papers deposited there; another party burnt the monastery of St. John of Jerusalem, at Clerkenwell; while the third took up its position at the Tower. Wat Tyler, as all readers of English history know, was soon afterwards slain in Smithfield by William Walworth, Lord Mayor of London; and Jack Straw, with many others, was beheaded.

Again, when Richard II. took for his second wife Isabel, the "little" daughter of the King of France, the royal train, on approaching London, was met on Blackheath by the lord mayor and aldermen, habited in scarlet, who attended the king to Newington (Surrey), where he dismissed them, as he and his youthful bride were to "rest at Kennyngtoun."

In 1400, Manuel Palæologus, Emperor of Constantinople, who had come to England to entreat the assistance of King Henry IV. against Bajazet, Emperor of the Turks, was met on Blackheath by the king, who conducted him to the City with great state and magnificence. In 1415, Henry V. was met here by the lord mayor and aldermen, and a large number of citizens, on his return from the battle of Agincourt; and in the following year this spot was the scene of the reception of the Emperor Sigismund, on his arrival in this country to treat for peace between the crowns of England and France.

On the 21st of February, 1431, Henry VI., who, twelve months after his coronation in England, had gone to France to be crowned in the church of Notre Dame in Paris, was received with great pomp on Blackheath, upon his return, by the lord mayor and aldermen of London.

The following is an extract from a curious poem (transcribed by Sir Harris Nicolas from the Harleian and Cottonian MSS. in the British Museum) written by John Lydgate, the "Monk of Bury," and entitled, "The Comynge of the Kyng out of France to London," when the citizens of every craft—

> "Statly horsyd, after the Mair ridyng,
> Passyd the subbarbes to mete with the Kyng,"

attended by all their officers and servants.

> "To the Blakeheth whanne they dyd atteyne,
> The Mair of prudence in especialle
> Made them hove in renges tweyne,
> A strete betwen, ech party lik a walle,
> Alle clad in whit, and the most principalle,
> Afore in red, with the Mair ridyng,
> Till tyme that he saw the Kyng comyng ;
> Thanne, with his sporys, he toke his hors anone,
> That to beholde it was a noble sight,
> How lyk a man he to the Kyng is gone,
> Right well cheryd of herte, glad, and light,
> Obeienge to hym, as hym ought of right." *

During Jack Cade's noted rebellion in 1449 and 1450, his followers—

> "Rebellious hinds, the filth and scum of Kent"—

were twice encamped "on the plaine of Blackheath between Eltham and Greenwiche," as we learn from Holinshed's "Chronicle." Of Cade's subsequent capture and death we have already spoken in our account of the "White Hart" Inn in the Borough.† On the 23rd of February, 1451, his followers came "in their shirts," and with "halters on their necks," to the king on Blackheath, and begged his pardon on their knees, professing themselves ready to receive from him their "doom of life or death."

In 1452, Henry VI. pitched his tent on Blackheath, when opposing the forces of his cousin, the Duke of York, father of King Edward IV. In 1471 the "bastard" Falconbridge‡ encamped here with his army against Edward IV.; and three years later the lord mayor and aldermen of London, with four hundred citizens, here met the king on his return from France, where he had been with an army of 30,000 to conclude a treaty of peace with Louis, the French monarch.

In 1497, the Cornish rebels,§ amounting to 6,000, headed by Lord Audley, Michael Joseph, a farrier, and Thomas Flammock, a lawyer, were defeated on this heath by the forces under King Henry VII. Two thousand of the insurgents were slain, and the rest forced to surrender. Lord Audley was beheaded on Tower Hill, and Joseph and Flammock were hanged at Tyburn. Lambarde, the Kentish historian, who at the beginning of the seventeenth century lived at West Coombe, and was therefore familiar with the locality, writes in his

---

* "Chronicles of London, from 1089 to 1483."
† See *ante*, p. 86.   ‡ See *ante*, p. 9.
§ See *ante*, p. 10.

"Perambulation of Kent," "There remaineth yet to be seen upon the heath the place of the smith's tent, commonly called his forge, and the grave-hills of such as were buried after the overthrow." The Smith's Forge is a mound of earth partly surrounded by fir-trees, to the south-west of Montagu Corner, which is at the end of Chesterfield Walk. Down to a comparatively recent date, this mound was frequently called "Whitefield's Mount," from the circumstance of that celebrated preacher having delivered from it some of what are termed his "field discourses." The spot seems also to have been used in former times as a butt for artillery practice; for Evelyn in his "Diary," under date of March 16, 1687, writes, "I saw a trial of those develish, murdering, mischief-doing engines called bombs, shot out of a mortar-piece on Blackheath. The distance that they are cast, the destruction [which] they make where they fall, is prodigious."

In 1519, Cardinal Campegio, the Pope's Legate, was received on Blackheath with great state by the Duke of Norfolk, and a large retinue of bishops, knights, and gentlemen, "all richly apparelled." His Eminence was conducted to a tent of cloth of gold, "where," as Hall's "Chronicles" relate, "he shifted himself into a robe of a cardinal, edged with ermines, and so took his moyle [mule], riding towards London. Soon afterwards, another pretty sight was witnessed here, when Bonevet, High Admiral of France, attended by a splendid caval-cade of twelve hundred noblemen and gentlemen, was met by the Earl of Surrey, as High Admiral of England, with a still more gorgeous retinue. Hall tells us how that "the young gallants of France had coats guarded with one colour, cut in ten or twelve parts, very richly to behold; and so all the Englishmen coupled themselves with the French-men lovingly together, and so rode to London."

On the public entry of the Princess Anne of Cleves, Henry VIII.'s new bride, she was met on Blackheath on the 3rd of January, 1540, by the king, accompanied by the lord mayor, aldermen, and citizens of London, with all the foreign mer-chants resident in the City, and escorted in grand state to the royal palace at Greenwich. The old chroniclers record how that on the eastern side of the heath "was pitched a rich cloth of gold, and divers other tents and pavilions, in the which were made fires and perfumes for her and such ladies as should receive her grace;" and "from the tents to the park gate . . . . a large and ample way was made for the show of all persons." Along this way were ranged the mayor and aldermen, citizens, and foreign merchants, all in their richest liveries, esquires, gentlemen, pensioners, and serving-men,

"well horsed and apparelled, that whosoever had well viewed them might say that they, for tall and comely personages, and clean of limb and body, were able to give the greatest prince in Christendom a mortal breakfast if he were the king's enemy." About mid-day Anne came down Shooter's Hill, accompanied by the Dukes of Norfolk and Suffolk, and a large number of other noblemen and bishops, besides her own attendants, and was met and con-ducted to her tent by the lord chamberlain and other officials. Magnificent as was the suite of Anne, it seems to have been outshone in splendour by that of the king, while Henry himself, if we may trust the description given in Hall's "Chronicles," was all ablaze with gold and jewellery. Here is his portrait as sketched by the old chronicler:—"The king's highness was mounted on a goodly courser, trapped in rich cloth of gold, traversed lattice-wise square, all over embroidered with gold of damask, pearled on every side of the embroidery; the buckles and pendants were all of fine gold. His person was apparelled in a coat of purple velvet, somewhat made like a frock, all over em-broidered with flat gold of damask with small lace mixed between of the same gold, and other laces of the same so going traverse-wise, that the ground little appeared: about which garment was a rich guard very curiously embroidered; the sleeves and breast were cut, lined with cloth of gold, and tyed together with great buttons of diamonds, rubies, and orient pearl; his sword and sword-girdle adorned with stones and especial emerodes; his night-cap garnished with stone, but his bonnet was so rich with jewels that few men could value them. Beside all this, he wore in baudrick-wise a collar of such balystes and pearl that few men ever saw the like . . . . And notwithstanding that this rich apparel and precious jewels were pleasant to the nobles and all other being present to behold, yet his princely countenance, his goodly personage, and royal gesture so far exceeded all other crea-tures being present, that in comparison of his person, all his rich apparel was little esteemed." The royal pair were conducted from Blackheath to the palace at Greenwich by a procession of the chief nobles, and afterwards conveyed in the grand City barges, with the lord mayor and chief citizens, to Westminster, where they were married; a few months after, they were divorced; and on the 8th of August of the same year, Catherine Howard, to whom the king had been some time privately married, was publicly declared Queen of England.

On May-day, in the year 1645, Colonel Blunt, in order to gratify the Kentish people, who were partial to old customs, drew up two regiments of foot, and exercised them on the heath, representing a mock fight between the Cavaliers and the Roundheads.

One of the most memorable scenes witnessed on Blackheath, however, was the arrival here of Charles II., on his Restoration, on the 29th of May, 1660, whilst on his way from Rochester to London, "all the ways thither," says Clarendon, "being so full of people, as if the whole kingdom had been gathered there." Macaulay, in his "History of England," gives us the following striking description of the king's reception here :—"Everywhere flags were flying, bells and music sounding, wine and ale flowing in rivers to the health of him whose return was the return of peace, of law, and of freedom. But in the midst of the general joy, one spot presented a dark and threatening aspect. On Blackheath the army was drawn up to welcome the sovereign. He smiled, bowed, and extended his hand graciously to the lips of the colonels and majors. But all his courtesy was vain. The countenances of the soldiers were sad and lowering; and, had they given way to their feelings, the festive pageant of which they reluctantly made a part would have had a mournful and bloody end."

Numerous reviews, &c., of militia and other troops have, at various times, been held on Blackheath. Under date of June 10, 1673, Evelyn writes in his "Diary :"—"We went after dinner to see the formal and formidable camp on Blackheath, raised to invade Holland, or, as others suspected, for another designe."

Blackheath Fair was a celebrated place of resort every year in the months of May and October; and, like its neighbours at Greenwich, Peckham, and Camberwell, was always well supplied with startling monsters, with some of which we have since been familiarised by our Zoological Gardens. These fairs were first established by Lord Dartmouth, as we learn from the following entry in Evelyn's "Diary :"—"May 1, 1683. I went to Blackheath to see the new faire, being the first, procured by Lord Dartmouth. This was the first day, pretended for the sale of cattle, but I think, in truth, to enrich the new tavern at the bowling-greene, erected by Snape, his Majesty's farrier, a man full of projects. There appeared nothing but an innumerable assembly of drinking people from London, pedlars, &c.; and I suppose it is too neere London to be of any greate use to the country."

In "Merrie England in the Olden Time" is printed the following announcement of the exhibition of one of the "strange monsters" above referred to :—

GEO. II. R.

This is to give notice to all gentlemen, ladies, and others, That there is to be seen from eight in the morning till nine at night, at the end of the great booth on Blackheath, a West of England woman 38 years of age, alive, with two heads, one above the other ; having no hands, fingers, nor toes ; yet can she dress or undress, knit, sew, read, sing [Query—a duet with her two mouths ?]. She has had the honour to be seen by Sir Hans Sloane, and several of the Royal Society.

N.B.—Gentlemen and ladies may see her at their own houses if they please. This great wonder never was shown in England before this, the 13th day of May, 1741. Vivat Rex !

The author of the above-mentioned work adds, as a foot-note, "That the caricaturist has been out-caricatured by Nature no one will deny. Wilkes was so abominably ugly that he said it always took him half an hour to talk away his face ; and Mirabeau, speaking of his own countenance, said, 'Fancy a tiger marked with the small-pox !' We have seen an Adonis contemplate one of Cruikshank's whimsical figures, of which his particular shanks were the *bow*-ideal, and rail at the artist for libelling Dame Nature ! How ill-favoured were Lord Lovat, Magliabecchi, Scarron, and the wall-eyed, bottle-nosed Buckhorse the Bruiser ! how deformed and frightful Sir Harry Dimsdale and Sir Jeffry Dunstan ! What would have been said of the painter of imaginary Siamese twins ? Yet we have 'The true description of two Monstrous Children, born in the parish of Swanburne, in Buckinghamshyre, the 4th of Aprill, Anno Domini 1566 ; the two Children having both their belies fast joyned together, and imbracing one another with their armes ; which Children were both alyve by the space of half an hower, and were baptised, and named the one John, and the other Joan.' A similar wonder was exhibited in Queen Anne's reign, viz., 'Two monstrous girls, born in the kingdom of Hungary,' which were to be seen 'from 8 o'clock in the morning till 8 at night, up one pair of stairs, at Mr. William Suttcliff's, a Drugster's Shop, at the sign of the Golden Anchor, in the Strand, near Charing Cross.' The Siamese twins of our own time are fresh in every one's memory. Shakespeare throws out a pleasant sarcasm at the characteristic curiosity of the English nation. Trinculo, upon first beholding Caliban, exclaims, 'A strange fish ! were I in England now (as I once was), and had but this fish painted, not a holiday fool there but would give a piece of silver ; there would this monster make a man : when they will not give a doit to relieve a lame beggar, they will lay out ten to see a dead Indian.'"

Blackheath Fair lasted, till a very recent date, as a "hog and pleasure " fair—being held on the

12th of May and 11th of October—till the year 1872, when it was suppressed by order of the Government; and the swings, roundabouts, spiced gingerbread, penny trumpets, and halfpenny rattles have now become things of the past.

From the early part of the present century, down to the year 1865, a considerable part of the surface of Blackheath has been greatly disturbed and cut up, owing to the Crown having let, for a rental of

resort of highwaymen. Under the Reform Bill of 1832, it was made one of the polling places for members of Parliament for the western division of Kent. Of late the heath has been built up to, wherever land was available. On the south side, near Tranquil Vale, stands All Saints' Church, a neat Gothic edifice, erected in the year 1859, from the designs of Mr. B. Ferrey. The village, or—as it is beginning to call itself—town of Black-

WEST COOMBE, IN 1794.

£56, the right to excavate an unlimited quantity of gravel. All these, and other such encroachments, however, were brought to an end by the Metropolitan Commons Act of 1866, when Blackheath was secured to the public as a place of healthful recreation. During the summer months the heath is largely resorted to by holiday-makers, and, like Hampstead Heath, it is much infested with donkeys; but owing to the stringent bye-laws that have been passed of late years, the donkey-drivers are not the nuisance that once they were. Cricket matches take place here in the summer; the Royal Blackheath Golf Club also use the heath as their play-ground, and in winter a well-contested match at foot-ball may often be witnessed here.

In the last century Blackheath was a notorious

heath, is built chiefly about Tranquil Vale; it has its churches and chapels, assembly-rooms, railway station, skating rink, banks, besides several good shops. At the end of the heath, near Blackheath Hill, is another collection of shops and dwellings, with a church and schools; here, too, is the principal inn, the "Green Man," well known to holiday-makers. In former times there was a house of entertainment here, called the "Chocolate House;" it is mentioned by the Duke of Richmond, Master-General of the Ordnance, in a private letter; and it would seem to have been largely patronised by the heads of Woolwich Dockyard and the college hard by, and by their friends. The name of this house was long kept in memory by "Chocolate Row." Lord Wrottesley had an observatory on Blackheath for some time, previous to his accession to the title, when he removed the astronomical apparatus to his seat in Staffordshire.

The Manor of East Combe, which lies near the Charlton Road, on the north-eastern side of the heath, was appended for several centuries to that of Greenwich, and was settled, in 1613, on Queen Anne of Denmark for life. It was afterwards leased out by the Crown, and has since been held

resided here for several years with Lavinia Fenton (the original "Polly Peachum" in the burletta of the *Beggar's Opera*), whom he married after the death of his duchess, in 1751—twenty-three years after he had taken her from the stage. Of this lady, Lysons, in his "Environs of London," gives the following particulars :—"The year 1728 is famous in theatrical annals, for having produced the favourite burletta of the *Beggar's Opera*. Its

THE "GREEN MAN," BLACKHEATH.

by several private families ; in the early part of the present century it was the seat of the Countess of Buckinghamshire. A little to the west, and near the north-east corner of Blackheath, is West Coombe, the manor-house of which was at one time the residence of William Lambarde, the learned antiquary, and author of the "Perambulation of Kent," who died there in 1601. Early in the last century the estate was purchased by Sir Gregory Page, who soon afterwards granted a lease of the house to Captain Galfridus Walpole. This gentleman pulled down the old manor-house, and erected the present mansion at a short distance from the original site, from, it is said, the designs of the Earl of Pembroke. The lease came afterwards into the possession of Charles, Duke of Bolton, who

success surpassed all precedent : it was acted more than sixty nights during the first season. The part of 'Polly' was performed by Lavinia Fenton, a young actress, whose real name, in some of the publications of that day, is said to have been Beswick. Her performance of this character raised her very high in the opinion of the public ; and it is uncertain whether the opera itself, or 'Polly Peachum,' had the greater share of popularity. Her lovers, of course, were very numerous : she decided in favour of the Duke of Bolton, who, to the great loss of the public, took her from the stage, to which she never returned ; and on the sixty-second night of the performance, a new 'Polly' was, to the great surprise of the audience, who expected to see their old favourite, introduced on the boards. After the death of his first wife, from whom he had been long separated, the duke, in 1751, married Miss Fenton, who, surviving him a few years, resided at West Coombe Park, in this parish, and died Duchess-dowager of Bolton, in the month of January, 1760." We have already spoken of her interment in Greenwich Church in a previous chapter.

Between East and West Coombe, in the Charlton Road, is Woodlands, long the residence of the Angersteins. The mansion was erected and the grounds laid out about the year 1770; they command a beautiful view of the valley of the Thames and the opposite coast of Essex. Here, in 1823, died Mr. John J. Angerstein, whose splendid collection of pictures—of which Waagen gives an account in his "Art and Artists" in England—formed the nucleus of our National Gallery.* Caroline, Princess of Wales, resided here for a short time. In a letter from Geneva, dated May 20, 1820, she tells Miss Berry that she shall go to "the Maison Angerstein à Blackheath" on her return to England. St. John's Church, in Charlton Lane, was built at the cost of the late Mr. W. Angerstein.

In former times, apparently, Blackheath was not considered an aristocratic neighbourhood; at all events, Horace Walpole contrasts the genealogies of illustrious families with those of the denizens of "Paddington and Blackheath," whom he classes epigrammatically together. Nevertheless, the place seems to have improved as time wore on, for from about 1797 to 1814, the Princess Caroline, the much-injured but foolish and frivolous Consort of George IV., was living here at Montagu House. This was after the birth of her child, the Princess Charlotte, whom she saw once every week at the house of the Duchess of Brunswick, close by. "The princess's villa at Blackheath," wrote Miss Aikin, "is an incongruous piece of patchwork; it may dazzle for a moment when lighted up at night, but it is all glitter, and glare, and trick; everything is tinsel and trumpery about it; it is altogether like a bad dream. One day the princess showed me a large book in which she had written characters of a great many of the leading persons in England; she read me some of them; they were drawn with spirit, but I could not form any opinion of their justice."

"About this time" (1811), writes the Hon. Miss Amelia Murray in her "Recollections," "there was an extravagant *furore* in the cause of the Princess of Wales. She was considered an

ill-treated woman, and that was enough to rouse popular feeling. My brother was among the young men who helped to give her an ovation at the opera. A few days afterwards he went to breakfast at a place near Woolwich. There he saw the princess in a gorgeous dress, which was looped up to show her petticoat covered with stars, and with silver wings on her shoulders, sitting under a tree with a pot of porter on her knee; and as a *finale* to the gaiety, she had the doors opened of every room in the house, and selecting a partner, she galloped through them, desiring all the guests to copy her example. It may be guessed," adds the writer, "whether the gentlemen were anxious to clap her at the opera again."

The pious Robert Nelson was living here in 1702. Here, too, was living the celebrated Mrs. Mary Anne Clarke when she first made the acquaintance of the Duke of York. She was the daughter of a journeyman-printer, named Farquhar, who lived in a court north of Fetter Lane, though Cyrus Redding affirms that she was the daughter of a Colonel Frederick, and granddaughter of Theodore, King of Corsica. A parliamentary inquiry in 1809 brought to light the extent to which she and the duke had trafficked in the sale of commissions in the army; although nominally acquitted of that offence, the duke had to retire from the post of Commander-in-chief.

Flaxman, the sculptor, when tired of his town rooms near Buckingham Gate, would take country lodgings in Blackheath; Crabb Robinson tells us in his "Diary" that he visited him here in 1812.

From the north-eastern corner of Blackheath, a somewhat steep and winding road, called Maze Hill, leads down to East Greenwich. On this hill, nearly opposite the eastern gate of Greenwich Park, which opens upon the pathway leading to One-Tree Hill, stands an irregular castellated brick-built structure, called "Vanbrugh Castle." It stands on the Page-Turner estate, and was erected, about the year 1717, by Sir John Vanbrugh. It is entered by an embattled gateway, profusely overgrown with ivy; the "castle" itself is a large red-brick building, resembling a fortification, with battlements and towers. The edifice, which has for some years been used as a ladies' boarding-school, was in former times called the "Bastille," from a fancied resemblance to its prototype at Paris. At a short distance from this building are the Vanbrugh Fields, in which is another singular-looking house, also built by Vanbrugh, and still called after his name. It was at one time called the "Mince-pie House," doubtless having been used as a place of public entertainment. An arched

---

gateway, with a lodge on each side, now standing some distance within the principal field, appears to have formed the original entrance from the heath. Vanbrugh House is a brick building, ornamented with raised bands : it has a round tower at either end, and a central porch.

Passing along Charlton Road, which runs eastward from Vanbrugh Park, a short walk brings us to the pretty little village of that name, which stands on the high ground between Greenwich and Woolwich, and has a charming look-out over the valley of the Thames. Here we find ourselves upon the chalky soil of Kent; and although the place has within the last few years lost much of its rural character, through the gradual extension of buildings, it is still green and pleasant. In this neighbourhood, if we may believe the *Gentleman's Magazine*, in 1734, a large eagle was captured, and, strange to say, by a tailor. Its wings, when expanded, were three yards eight inches in length. It was claimed by the lord of the manor, but was afterwards demanded by the king's falconer as a royal bird, and carried off to Court. Its subsequent fate is not recorded.

In Philipott's " Survey of Kent " (1659) we find that Charlton was " anciently written *Ceorlton*, that is, the town inhabited with honest, good, stout, and usefull men, for tillage and countrye business ; " the Saxon word *ceorl* signifying a husbandman, or *churl*, as it is termed in old English, whence Churlestown or Charlestown was easily derived, and so by abridgment Charlton.

The church, a red brick-built edifice, dedicated to St. Luke, has a lofty embattled tower, which serves as a landmark for those who sail up or down the river. It has a double roof, supported by pillars, forming arches down the centre of the building. The edifice was erected by the trustees of Sir Adam Newton, in 1630–40. The chancel was added by the rector in 1840; in it is a handsome stained-glass window. Among the monuments in this church is one for the Hon. Brigadier Michael Richards, Surveyor-General of the Ordnance, who died in 1721; he is represented by a life-size figure of a man in armour, holding a truncheon in his right hand, with military trophies, &c. A marble statue, by the younger Westmacott, commemorates Sir Thomas Hislop, G.C.B., who died in 1834; and there is also a monument to Sir William Congreve, the inventor of the rockets which bear his name : he died in 1814. A neat tablet by Chantrey records the interment in the vaults below of the Right Hon. Spencer Perceval, the Prime Minister, who was assassinated by John Bellingham, in the lobby of the House of Com-

mons,* on the 11th of May, 1812. In the churchyard, close by the porch, lies buried Mr. Edward Drummond, who was shot in the neighbourhood of the Houses of Parliament, in January, 1843, in mistake for Sir Robert Peel, the then Prime Minister, whose private secretary he was. Here, too, is buried James Craggs, Postmaster-General, and father of Pope's friend, Mr. Secretary Craggs, who, in consequence of the scandal occasioned by their connection with the South Sea Bubble, destroyed himself by poison in March, 1721; there is a monument to his memory in Westminster Abbey.†

Immediately to the south of the church stands Charlton House, the seat of the lord of the manor, Sir Spencer Maryon-Wilson. The manor of Charlton was given by William the Conqueror to his half-brother Odo, Bishop of Bayeux, from whom it passed to Robert Bloet, Bishop of Lincoln, who, about the end of the eleventh century, gave it to the priory of St. Saviour's, Bermondsey. Having reverted to the Crown at the Dissolution, it was given by James I. to one of his Northern followers, John, Earl of Mar, by whom it was sold in 1606 to Sir James Erskine, who, in turn, disposed of it in the following year to Sir Adam Newton, Dean of Durham, tutor to Henry, Prince of Wales. In 1659 it passed to Sir William Ducie, afterwards Viscount Downe, and subsequently it was owned successively by the Langhornes, Games, and Maryons, and also by Lady Spencer Wilson, from whom it has descended to the present owner. The mansion, which Evelyn describes as " a faire house built for Prince Henry," is pleasantly situated in extensive park-like grounds; it was commenced by Sir Adam Newton in 1607, and completed in about five years. The house is very pleasantly situated on rising ground overlooking the Thames and the opposite shores of Essex, and commands a most delightful prospect, which has been described by Evelyn as " one of the most noble in the world for city, river, ships, meadows, hill, woods, and all other amenities "—a prospect, by the way, which has been considerably abridged of late years by the growth of the surrounding trees. Its situation might indeed well recall to memory those charming lines by Mrs. Hemans, descriptive of the halls of our old nobility :—

" The stately homes of England,
    How beautiful they stand !
Amid their tall ancestral trees,
    All o'er the pleasant land."

The mansion is certainly one of the finest specimens extant of the domestic architecture of the time of James I., having been erected when the architecture then in vogue was about to be supplemented by what was then thought to be a purer style. When first erected, its appearance must have formed a striking contrast to the more sombre structures of a preceding age. Red brick—so popular in that era—is the material used in its construction; this, however, is relieved with white stone quoins and dressings, and mullioned windows. Its form is an oblong, with slightly projecting wings at each end. The centre of the principal front also projects, but to a less extent than the wings; this compartment has a richly decorated porch, and is entirely of stone. The principal ornamentation of the exterior appears to have been bestowed on this central projection; the arched doorway has plain double columns of the Corinthian order on each side, whilst above it there is a niche containing the bust of a female figure. The first storey has quaintly-carved columns on either side of its mullioned window, and over it a series of grotesquely sculptured brackets. To this succeeds another storey, with another row of similar brackets. Along the entire front is carried an open stone balustrade of somewhat peculiar character, and at each end of the building there is a small square turret, surmounted by a cupola, one of which contains a clock.

The entrance-hall is spacious and oak-panelled, with a gallery at the western end of a comparatively recent date; whilst a deep central pendant hanging from the ceiling adds considerably to the general ornamentation. At the bottom of the grand staircase is the dining-room, a very handsome apartment, the side of which overlooks the garden and forms a kind of arcade, separated from the room by a row of elegant marble columns with semicircular arches. Adjoining the dining-room, and occupying the north-east angle of the building, is a small chapel, dedicated to St. James. The apartment—for it can hardly be called by any other name—is furnished in accordance with the rest of the building; each side is occupied by a row of pews, and in the recess formed by the bay-window at the eastern end is the communion-table, enclosed by a wooden railing. In the centre of the chapel is a curious font, the circumference of which is almost equal to that of a quart basin. The ancient doors of both the chapel and the dining-room are elaborately carved in oak, and ornamented with bright steel hinges and fastenings.

The upper floors are reached by a spacious and richly-ornamented staircase of chestnut, its arabesque balusters being surmounted by capitals of the Tuscan, Ionic, and Corinthian orders, and also the armorial bearings of the Wilson family, supported by a wolf, whilst the walls are enriched with arabesque mouldings, intermixed with fruit and flowers. The principal or "state" apartments are situated upon the second floor. The first of these, which is entered from the grand staircase, is the gallery (seventy-six feet in length), extending the whole depth of the house. The walls of this room are wainscoted with oak, the ceiling is elaborately moulded with arabesque ornamentation; and in the bay-windows at either end are stained-glass armorial bearings of the Ducies (former owners of Charlton) and their alliances. In the room adjoining the gallery, called the north sitting-room, the ceiling of which is also very rich, is a most elaborately carved chimney-piece, representing the mythological story of Medusa, beneath which are two allegorical basso-relievos. From this room we enter the saloon, a lofty and well-proportioned apartment, lighted at either end by large mullioned windows; in the ceiling of one of the recesses are the royal arms of James I., the ostrich feathers—the cognisance of the Prince of Wales—occupying a similar position opposite. This room has some highly-wrought marble chimney-pieces, and its ceiling is likewise enriched with arabesque ornamentation, intermixed with fruit and flowers, and decorated with elaborate pendants. In the room next entered, called the south sitting-room, it is traditionally related, on the authority of Dr. Plot, that the marble chimney-piece—a very handsome piece of workmanship in black marble—was so exquisitely polished, that Lord Downe, one of the former owners of the mansion, "did see in it the reflection of a robbery committed on Blackheath, whereupon, sending out his servants, the thieves were taken."

Interspersed throughout the various rooms are some choice works of art, and also a very fair collection of family portraits; and one of the outbuildings, at a short distance from the house, has been converted into a museum, in which are several interesting objects of natural history, chiefly brought together by Lady Wilson, but greatly augmented by the late Sir Thomas Maryon-Wilson during his travels in the north and south of Europe.

The park, although containing but about one hundred acres, is well timbered with trees of magnificent growth, among which are several venerable yews; whilst the gardens are laid out with considerable taste, and abound in shrubs and plants, both native and foreign. In the grounds in front of the mansion is a picturesque building of red brick, said to have been originally erected as a "drinking house," but now made use of as an orangery. Until very recently, this structure had been for several years overshadowed by a solitary cypress-tree, the only one at that time remaining of a long row mentioned by Evelyn as having adorned the front of the mansion, and which Hasted refers to as seeming "to be of great age, and perhaps the oldest in England." The ancient gateway, immediately in front of the principal entrance, has long been disused. The mansion is presumed to have been erected from the designs of Inigo Jones, who resided for some time in a house, said to be still standing, in the immediate neighbourhood; and from the fact of the principal apartments being situated on the second floor, it is inferred that it was built shortly after the return of that celebrated architect from Italy, where the state apartments are usually placed upon the uppermost storey.

Henry III. granted to Charlton a market and also a fair, both of which appear to have been given up prior to the middle of the seventeenth century. Notwithstanding the discontinuance of the fair, the village had been for ages, until late in the last century, famous for a "disorderly fair" held there on St. Luke's day, October 18. It was called "Horn Fair," according to Philipott, "by reason of the great plentie of all sorts of winding hornes and cups and other vessels of horne there brought to be sold." Concerning the origin of this fair there are several wild traditions, but that most usually accepted is that it was held to keep in remembrance the little episode between King John and the miller's wife, of which we have already given the details in dealing with Cuckold's Point.* Mr. S. C. Hall, however, in his "Baronial Halls," observes that the more probable origin of the term "horn fair" is that it was symbolic of the ox of St. Luke, by which he is usually distinguished in ancient paintings. The fair was formerly held upon a green opposite the church, and facing Charlton House; but this piece of ground having some years ago been enclosed so as to form part of the gardens belonging to the mansion, the fair was subsequently held in a private field at the other end of the village, under the auspices of a few speculative publicans. During the reign of Charles II. it was a carnival of the most unrestrained kind, and those frequenting it from London used to proceed thither in boats, "disguised as kings, queens, millers, &c., with horns on their heads; and men dressed as females, who formed in procession and marched round the church and

fair." Nicholas Breton, in a poem published in 1612, entitled "Pasquil's Nightcap, or Antidote for the Headache," gives an amusing account of these annual gatherings, which shows that they were held in great pomp, and with an immense concourse of people, all of whom

> "In comely sort their foreheads did adorne
> With goodly coronets of hardy horne;"

but the decadence of this ancient custom was at that time evidently anticipated, for Breton ends his poem by indignantly telling us that—

> "Long time this solemne custome was observ'd,
> And Kentish-men with others met to feast;
> But latter times are from old fashions swerv'd,
> And grown repugnant to this good behest.
> For now ungratefull men these meetings scorn,
> And thanklesse prove to Fortune and the horn;
> For onely now is kept a poor goose fair,
> Where none but meaner people doe repaire."

The reader, of course, will not have forgotten the mysteries attached to "swearing in" on the horns at Highgate, of which we have already spoken at some length.†

In "Merrie England in the Olden Time" we read that "at Horn Fair, a party of humorists of both sexes (query, of either sex) cornuted in all the variety of bull-feather fashion, after perambulating round Cuckold's Point, startled the little quiet village of Charlton on St. Luke's Day, shouting their emulation, and blowing voluntaries on rams' horns, in honour of their patron saint." Ned Ward gives a curious picture of this odd ceremony, and the press of Stonecutter Street (the worthy successor of Aldermary churchyard) has consigned it to immortality in two broadsides—"A New Summons to all the Merry (Wagtail) Jades to attend at Horn Fair," and "A New Summons to Horn Fair," both without a date, inspired by the Helicon of the Fleet—

> "Around whose brink
> Bards rush in droves like cart-horses to drink,
> Dip their dark beards among its streams so clear,
> And while they gulp it, wish it ale or beer."

Leaving Charlton House behind us, and pursuing a south-western course, we make our way to the southern side of the Great Dover Road after it crosses Blackheath. Here we pass, at a short distance on our left, the steep ascent of Shooter's Hill, which, as Philipott writes, was "so called for the thievery there practised, where travellers in early times were so much infested with depredations and bloody mischiefs, that order was taken in the sixth year of Richard II., for the enlarging the highway, according to the statute made in the time

---

of King Edward I., so that they venture still to rob here by prescription." The road continued a steep and narrow thoroughfare, closed in by thick woods—a convenient harbour for highwaymen—down till about the year 1733, when, as Hasted informs us, "a road of easier ascent and of great width was laid out at some distance from the old one;" but still the highwaymen lingered about the neighbourhood, and consequently the hill main-

rather abruptly—if there be any truth in the poet's words which follow—by the sudden attack of a highwayman.

For the discouragement of these knights of the road the usual methods were adopted here; and in former times Shooter's Hill was seldom without the ornament of a gibbet. Pepys tells us in his "Diary," under date of April 11, 1661, how that of all the journeys he ever made, "this [from Dartford

VANBRUGH CASTLE.

tained its reputation long after the new road was made. Byron has rendered the spot familiar to his readers by his description of the prospect from the summit of the hill looking towards London—

> " A mighty mass of brick, and smoke, and shipping,
>   Dirty and dusky, but as wide as eye
> Could reach, with here and there a sail just skipping
>   In sight, then lost amidst the forestry
> Of masts; a wilderness of steeples peeping
>   On tip-toe through their sea-coal canopy;
> A huge dim cupola, like a foolscap crown
>   On a fool's head—and there is London town."

Here, too, probably, was the scene of Don Juan's musings on the morality, or immorality, of "the great city"—"Here are pure wives, safe lives;" a reverie which was destined to be broken off

to London] was the merriest. . . . Amongst other things," he adds, "I got my lady to let her maid, Mrs. Anne, ride all the way on horseback. . . . Mrs. Anne and I rode under the man that hangs upon Shooter's Hill, and a filthy sight it was to see how his flesh is shrunk to his bones." With the improved condition of the times in which we live, however, an end came some years ago to the practice of the highwaymen; but a somewhat ludicrous attempt at its revival was made in the year 1877, and in this very neighbourhood, with some little success; but the young ruffians having been brought to justice, it is to be hoped that henceforth the midnight wayfarer may proceed on his way over Blackheath or Shooter's Hill in security.

CHARLTON HOUSE IN 1845.

On the western slope of the hill, close by the road leading to Eltham, stands the hospital for the Woolwich garrison, called the Herbert Hospital, after Mr. Sidney Herbert, afterwards Lord Herbert of Lea. The building was erected in 1866, from the designs of Captain Galton, R.E., during the period when Lord Herbert was Secretary of State for War. It is constructed on the pavilion system, and comprises six parallel blocks, in which are the hospital wards, providing accommodation for between 600 and 700 patients. On the summit of the hill beyond we just catch a glimpse of Severn-droog Castle, which was erected by Lady James, in 1784, in commemoration of the gallantry of her husband, Sir William James, who died in the preceding year, "and in a peculiar manner to record the conquest of the Castle of Severn Droog, on the coast of Malabar, which fell to his superior valour and able conduct on the 2nd day of April, 1755." The castle is a triangular brick edifice, of three floors, with turrets at the angles, and contains a few specimens of armour, weapons, &c., captured at Severndroog.

Since the close of the last century considerable progress has been made in the erection of villas in the immediate neighbourhood of Blackheath, particularly in that part lying to the south-east, known as Blackheath Park. This park forms an estate anciently called Witenemers, or Wricklesmarsh, which during the reign of William the Conqueror formed part of the possessions of Odo, Bishop of Bayeux. At the close of the seventeenth century it came into the possession of Sir John Morden, the founder of Morden College, who, dying in 1708, bequeathed the estate to his widow. Soon after Lady Morden's death, in 1721, it was sold to Sir Gregory Page, who pulled down the old house and erected a large edifice of stone, consisting of a centre and two wings, united by a colonnade; and

this mansion is described in the "Ambulator" for 1774 as "very magnificent, and one of the finest seats in England belonging to a private gentleman." The writer enters into almost as many details about it, and the picture-gallery which it contained, as he does in describing Lord Burlington's mansion at Chiswick; and the catalogue of the paintings alone occupies three pages. On the death of Sir Gregory Page, the mansion and estate passed to a great-nephew, who sold the estate, and the house was soon after pulled down.

At the south-east extremity of Blackheath, but in Charlton parish, is Morden College, so named from its founder, Sir John Morden, a wealthy Turkey merchant, mentioned above. He erected this structure in Great Stone Field, near his own residence, in 1695, and placed in it, during his lifetime, twelve decayed merchants; and by his will (dated October 15, 1702) devised all his real and copyhold estates, after the decease of Lady Morden, to the Turkey Company, in trust, for the support of this college, and for the maintenance of poor, aged, and decayed merchants of England, "whose fortunes had been ruined by the perils of the sea, or other unavoidable accidents." The premises occupy a spacious quadrangle, and are built of brick, with stone quoins and cornices. There is a lofty entrance gateway, and the lodgings of the inmates, dining-hall, and chapel form a quadrangle. Over the entrance are statues of the founder and his wife. The college provides a comfortable home, including lodging, maintenance, and attendance, for about forty pensioners, who have each an annual stipend of £72.

From the grounds attached to Morden College a walk of a mile and a half by the footpath by Kidbrook Church, and across some pleasant fields, brings us to Eltham, which will be the limit of our perambulation in this direction.

CHAPTER XVIII.

ELTHAM, LEE, AND LEWISHAM.

"Stant ibi regifico constructa palatia luxu."—*Ovid.*

Situation and Derivation of the Name of Eltham—Descent of the Manor—The Palace—Henry III. keeps his Christmas here—Edward II. and his Court—John, King of France—Richard II. and Anne of Bohemia—Froissart here presents the King with a Copy of his Works—Henry IV. and his Court—Royal Christmas Festivities—Eltham Palace abandoned by the Court—The Palace during the Civil Wars—Dismantling of the Parks—Description of the Palace—Sale of the Middle Park Stud of Racehorses—Eltham Church—Well Hall—Lee—Lewisham—Hither Green, Catford, and Ladywell—Loam Pit Hill—New Cross—Royal Naval Schools—Hatcham.

ELTHAM is situated on the high road leading from London to the Crays, and thence to Maidstone, at a distance of about two miles south-eastward from Greenwich. The place was anciently called

Eald-ham (the old home or dwelling-place), and was formerly a market town of considerable importance; the markets, however, were discontinued *temp.* James I., shortly after the palace ceased to be used as a royal residence. The manor, in the time of Edward the Confessor, belonged to the Crown, of whom it was held by one Alwold. William the Conqueror granted it, together with many other estates in the county of Kent, to his half-brother, Odo, Bishop of Bayeux, Earl of Kent; and at the time of the Domesday survey it was held of him by Hamo, Sheriff of Kent. On the confiscation of Odo's estates, however, some four years later, this manor reverted to the Crown, and, becoming divided, one part of it was retained by the sovereign, and the other part was given to the family of De Mandeville, whence the place obtained the name of Eltham Mandeville. The part held by the Crown was afterwards granted by Edward I. to John de Vesci, Lord of Eltham, who subsequently obtained the whole by exchange with Walter de Mandeville.

The manor was afterwards granted to Anthony Bec, Bishop of Durham and Patriarch of Jerusalem, to hold in trust for his natural son, who was called William de Vesci, of Kildare. Through a betrayal of the trust reposed in him, however, the bishop, on the death of the last Lord de Vesci, appears to have obtained possession of the estates, and to have bestowed great cost on the buildings at Eltham. He died here in the year 1311, having bestowed the estate on Queen Eleanor, the consort of Edward I. The manor was next granted to Sir Gilbert de Aton, and afterwards to Geoffrey le Scrope, to hold by the accustomed services. It subsequently again reverted to the Crown, having, it is said, been given to Queen Isabella, consort of Edward II. It has remained in the possession of the Crown since that period, having been occasionally granted for terms of years on lease to various persons. It may be mentioned that the title of Lord Eltham has been more than once refused to individuals who were anxious to assume it on being raised to the peerage, on the express ground that the Barony of Eltham belongs to the sovereign. The precise date of the erection of a palace here is quite a matter of uncertainty; the earliest mention of it by our old historians as a royal residence is in the continuation of the "Historia Major" of Matthew of Paris, ascribed to William Rishanger, a monk of St. Albans, who brought it from the year 1259 down to the close of the reign of Henry III. Lambarde's allusion to this work runs as follows:—"King Henrie the Third (saith Mat. Parise), toward the latter ende of his reigne (1270), kept a Royall Christmas (as the manner then was) at Eltham, being accompanied with his Queene and Nobilitie: and this (belike) was the first warming of the house (as I may call

it) after that the Bishop had finished his worke. For I doe not hereby gather that hitherto the king had any propertie in it, for as much as the Princes in those daies used commonly both to soiourne for their pleasures, and to passe their set solemnities also, in Abbaies and in Bishops' houses."

In 1315, the queen having taken up her residence at Eltham Palace, there gave birth to a son, who was called, from the place of his nativity, John of Eltham, and who was afterwards created Earl of Cornwall. Edward II. frequently resided at Eltham, and in 1329 and 1375 Edward III. held his parliament here; and it was at the last-mentioned period that a petition was presented by the Commons, requesting the king to make his grandson, Richard, Prince of Wales. In 1347 the Duke of Clarence, the king's son, in the absence of his father, kept a public Christmas here.

In 1364, John, King of France, Edward III.'s prisoner by conquest, came as an unwilling guest to England, and was entertained by the king and queen at Eltham. Froissart mentions how that on a Sunday afternoon King Edward and Queen Philippa waited at the gates of the palace to receive the fallen monarch, and how, " between that time and supper, in his honour were many grand dances and carols, at which the young Lord de Courcy distinguished himself by singing and dancing." This entertainment must have appeared strange indeed to the feelings of the captive prince, who, when asked to join in the conviviality, pathetically replied, "How can I sing in a strange land?" Captive as he was, he seems to have had but little cause for regret on his own account, for, becoming enamoured of the Princess Royal, he urged his suit, and was fortunate enough to succeed in obtaining her as his bride.

Eltham Palace was one of the favourite residences of Richard II. and Anne of Bohemia. In Holinshed's " Chronicles," under date of 1386, it is recorded that " King Richard II. holding his Christmasse at Eltham, thither came to him Leo, King of Armenia, whose countrie and realme being in danger to be conquered of the Turks, he was come into these west parts of Christendome for aid and succour at the hands of the Christian princes here. The king honourablie received him, and after he had taken counsell touching his request, he gave him great summes of money and other rich gifts, with a stipend, as some write, of a thousand pounds yearly, to be paid to him during his life."

Froissart, the famous poet and historian, in his " Chronicles," makes several allusions to the royal palace of Eltham; in 1395 he came to England for the purpose of presenting to Richard II. a volume of his writings. The details of this visit are thus given by Froissart himself :—"The king arrived at Eltham on a Tuesday ; on the Wednesday the lords came from all parts. There were the Duke of Gloucester, the Earls of Derby, Arundel, Northumberland, Kent, Rutland, the Earl Marshal, the Archbishops of Canterbury and York, the Bishops of London and Winchester, in short, all who had been summoned arrived at Eltham on the Thursday by eight o'clock in the morning.

"The Parliament was holden in the king's apartment, in the presence of the king, his uncles, and the council. The matter in deliberation was the solicitation of the chieftains in Aquitaine that they might remain attached to the crown of England. Thomas of Woodstock, Duke of Gloucester, the king's brother, opposed their petition, with a view to keep his brother, the Duke of Lancaster, abroad ; and to show that he was the man who governed the king, and was the greatest in the council, as soon as he had delivered his opinion, and saw that many were murmuring at it, and that the prelates and lords were discussing it in small parties, he quitted the king's chamber, followed by the Earl of Derby, and entered the Hall at Eltham, where he ordered a table to be spread, and they both sat down to dinner, while others were debating the business.

"On the Sunday the whole council were gone to London, excepting the king and Sir Richard Sturry ; these two, in conjunction with Sir Thomas Percy, mentioned me [Froissart] again to the king, who desired to see the book I had brought for him. I presented it to him in his chamber, for I had it with me, and laid it on his bed. He opened it and looked into it with much pleasure. He ought to have been pleased, for it was handsomely written and illuminated, and bound in crimson velvet, with ten silver-gilt studs, and roses of the same in the middle, with two large clasps of silver-gilt, richly worked with roses in the centre. The king asked me what the book treated of ; I replied, 'Of Love !' He was pleased with the answer, and dipped into several places, reading aloud, for he read and spoke French perfectly well, and then gave it to one of his knights, Sir Richard Credon, to carry it to his oratory, and made me acknowledgments for it."

Parliament met here to arrange King Richard's second marriage with Isabella of Valois ; she was brought hither after her bridal, and from the gates of Eltham Palace she departed in state to her coronation. Henry IV. was frequently at Eltham with his Court. Here he was espoused to Joan of Navarre, in the presence of the primate and the chief officers of state, Antonio Riezi acting as the lady's proxy, and actually having the ring placed upon his finger. In 1409, according to Stow, Henry kept his Christmas here with his queen, and Lambarde tells us that in 1412 he kept his last Christmas at Eltham. His son and successor, Henry V., also resided here, and in 1414, "the king keeping his Christmasse at the manor of Eltham, was advertised that Sir Roger Acton, a man of great wit and possessions, John Browne, Esquire, John Beverlie, priest, and a great number of others, were assembled in armour against the king." This report, it seems, had some effect on the king, for, as Lambarde states, "he was faine to depart suddenly, for feare of some that had conspired to murder him." The meeting, which took place in St. Giles's Fields, under the instigation of Sir John Oldcastle, notwithstanding the treasonable character that was given it by most writers of the period, appears to have been nothing more than a convention of the inoffensive people styled Lollards, to hear the preaching of one of their pastors.

Henry VI. once kept his Christmas festivities at Eltham ; and here, unconscious of his critical position, this unhappy prince forsook his studies to hunt and join in the sports of the field under the watchful eye of his keeper, the Earl of March, while his wife and son, for whom he had restored the palace, were sheltering in Harlech Castle.

Edward IV. resided much at Eltham Palace, and on the 9th of November, 1480, his third daughter, Bridget, was born here. She was christened in the chapel in the palace, by the Bishop of Chichester, and subsequently assumed the garb of a nun at Dartford. Following in the footsteps of his predecessors, Edward IV. kept his Christmas here in great state in the year 1482–3, on which occasion, it is stated, more than two thousand persons were there daily entertained. This king is recorded to have laid out large sums on the buildings here, and, as will be presently shown, is supposed to have entirely rebuilt the great hall as it now stands.

Lambarde, in his "Perambulation of Kent," published in 1576, states that "it is not yet fully out of memorie that King Henry VII. set up the faire front over the mote there ; since whose reigne, this house, by reason of the neerenesse to Greenewiche (which also was much amended by him, and is, through the benefite of the river, a seate of more commoditie), hath not beene so greatly esteemed : the rather also that for the pleasures of the emparked groundes here, may be in manner as well enjoyed, the Court lying at Greenewiche, as if it were at this house it selfe."

Henry VII., like his predecessors, generally resided here, and was wont to dine every day in the hall surrounded by his barons. The "faire front," alluded to by Lambarde, was, no doubt, the north face of the moated square, approached by the Gothic bridge of three arches.

Although Henry VIII. preferred the palace at Greenwich, he appears sometimes to have resided at Eltham, and in 1515 he kept his Christmas here. Holinshed thus records the entertainment on this occasion :—"In the year 1515 the king kept a solemn Christmas at his manor of Eltham, and on the Twelfe Night, in the hall, was made a goodlie castle, wonderouslie set out, and in it certaine ladies and knights, and when the kinge and queene were set, in came other knights, and assailed the castle, where many a good stripe was given, and at last the assailants were beaten away, and then issued knights and ladies out of the castle, which ladies were strangelie disguised, for all their apparel was in braids of gold, fret with moving spangles of silver-gilt set on crimson satin, loose and not fastened ; the men's apparell of the same suite made like julis [*sic*] of Hungary, and the ladies' heads and bodies were after the fashion of Amsterdam ; and when the dancing was done the banket [banquet] was served in of two hundred dishes."

Towards the close of the year 1526 the plague raged so fiercely in London that the king and his Court removed to Eltham. Henry VIII. again kept his Christmas here in that year, and in 1556 Queen Mary paid a visit to the palace, attended by Cardinal Pole and the Lord Montagu. In the first year of Queen Elizabeth's reign Eltham Palace was for a few days the royal abode ; but an idea having arisen that the stagnant waters of the moat rendered the palace unhealthy, it was thenceforth but little frequented by royalty. Sir Christopher Hatton was keeper of Eltham Palace in the reign of Queen Elizabeth. In 1606 James I. was visited at Greenwich by his brother-in-law, the King of Denmark, and the two kings went together to Eltham, where they hunted with "greate pleasure, and killed three buckes on horsebacke."

During the Civil Wars, Eltham Palace was occupied by the Parliamentary General, Robert, Earl of Essex, who died there in September, 1646.

After the death of Charles I. the royal residence was seized by the Parliament, and in a survey made by the commissioners in the above year it is stated that the palace was built of brick, wood, stone, and timber, and consisted of one fair chapel, one great hall, thirty-six rooms and offices below stairs, two large cellars, seventeen lodging-rooms

on the king's side, twelve on the queen's, nine on the princes', seventy-eight rooms in the offices round the court-yard, which contained one acre of ground.

There were three parks attached to this mansion, covering a very extensive tract of ground. The Great Park contained 596 acres ; the Little, or Middle Park, 333 acres ; and Home, or Lee Park, 336 acres ; the whole of which were well stocked with deer. The deer, as may easily be imagined, were well hunted and destroyed by the soldiery and others during the time of the Commonwealth ; besides which most of the trees were cut down.

In 1648, the parks having already been partly broken up and the deer destroyed, Nathaniel Rich purchased the house and a great part of the lands attached to it. Evelyn describes its condition a few years later ; under date of April 22, 1656, he writes in his "Diary," "Went to see his Majesty's house at Eltham ; both the palace and chapel in miserable ruins, the noble wood and park destroyed by Rich the rebel."

After the Restoration, the manor of Eltham was bestowed by Charles II. on Sir John Shaw, in recognition of his friendship to him when in exile at Brussels and Antwerp ; and, with the exception of certain portions of land originally in the royal park which are still vested in the Crown, it continues in the possession of his descendants.

Like most of the moated manor-houses of the Middle Ages, the palace of Eltham was nearly square in plan, and embraced four courts or quadrangles enclosed by a high wall. The moat which surrounded it was of great width ; the principal entry was over a stone bridge and through a gateway in the north wall. There was also another gateway and bridge on the opposite side of the enclosure. The most important part of the buildings consisted of a high range which crossed the court from east to west, and included the hall, the chapel, and the state apartments. The principal courts were spacious and befitting the abode of royalty, and lodging-rooms and offices, as notified in the above survey, were very numerous ; of these, however, not a vestige now remains, save the foundations, some of which are traceable round the sides of the area enclosed by the moat. Of the chapel, not even the site can now be ascertained. In fact, the only parts now remaining are the banqueting-hall ; an ivy-covered bridge of three ribbed arches which spans the moat on the north side, and still forms the entrance to the building ; part of the embattled wall, flanked with loopholed turrets ; some curious drains, supposed formerly to have been used as sallyports on occasions of emergency; and a building at the east end of the hall, with fine corbelled attics and ancient gables, formerly the buttery, but now a private residence, called the Court House. This latter building was thoroughly restored, and a new wing added to it in 1859, at which time the great hall, which had been for many years used as a barn, was cleared out, and the eastern end of it considerably altered, being made to serve as the entrance to the house.

periods, laid the palace low. Desolation has reached its very walls, and the hand of wanton mischief has dared to injure where it could not destroy; but still the hall of Eltham Palace has not, with the exception of the louvre, been entirely deprived of its smallest constituent feature.

"Its north and south sides were both open to quadrangles. Their architecture corresponded precisely, excepting that the south parapet was plain,

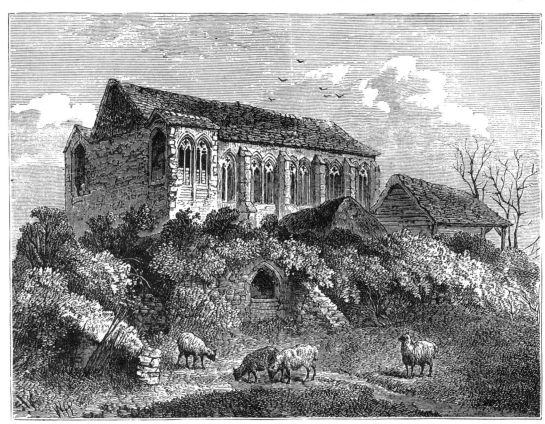

ELTHAM PALACE IN 1790.

By far the most interesting of these remains is the magnificent banqueting-hall, with its beautiful high-pitched roof, entirely constructed of oak, in tolerable preservation, with hammer-beams, carved pendants, and braces supported on corbels of hewn stone. Its dimensions are 100 feet in length, 55 in height, and 36 in breadth.

"The hall," writes Mr. Buckler, in his "Historical and Descriptive Account of the Royal Palace at Eltham" (1828), "was the master feature of the palace. With a suite of rooms at either extremity, it rose in the centre of the surrounding buildings, as superior in the grandeur of its architecture, as in the magnificence of its proportions and the amplitude of its dimensions. This fair edifice has survived the shocks which, at different

while that on the other side, facing the principal gate of entrance, was embattled, and the cornice enriched with sculptured corbels.

"In this majestic structure the architect scrupulously avoided the frequent use of carvings, which, it is evident, would have destroyed the elegant simplicity of his design; and, besides its intrinsic excellence, this specimen of the palace will abundantly prove how well the ancients could apply the style to domestic purposes, how far removed from gloom were their habitations where defensive precautions could be dispensed with, and how skilfully they prosecuted whatever they undertook in architecture.

"The proportions of Eltham Hall, and the harmony of its design, attest the care and skill which were exerted in its production. Other halls may surpass it in extent, but this is perfect in every useful and elegant feature belonging to a banqueting-room. It was splendidly lighted, and perhaps required painted glass to subdue the glare admitted by two-and-twenty windows. There are no windows which in some instances the thick trails of ivy impart a highly picturesque effect, which is heightened by the broad streams of cheerful sunlight that fall through the empty panels; and every space is divided by a buttress, which terminates below the cornice, and at the foot of the windows has twice

HALL OF ELTHAM PALACE IN 1835.

over the high pace or the screen, and there were none in the majority of examples, though, from unavoidable circumstances, Westminster and Guildhall receive their light in these directions."

The windows of the hall are ranged in couples, in five spaces on both sides, occupying the length of the building, from the east wall to the angle of the bays; every window is cinquefoil-headed and divided by a mullion without a transom, around the projection of the upper half. Altogether, however, these supports are slender, and partake of the same light and elegant proportions which characterise the whole building. The walls alone are adequate to the weight which presses on them, but their strength is increased by the buttresses —features which are almost inseparable from the ancient style of architecture, and were frequently used for ornament even when their strength was superfluous. The buttresses at Eltham are, however, both useful and ornamental; and, as if to determine for which purpose they were most required, several of those facing the south are mangled or destroyed.

At the eastern end of the hall were three doorways communicating with the buttery above mentioned, and also other arched doorways leading into the court-yards. These entrances were concealed by a wooden screen ornamented with carved work, over which was the minstrels' gallery, the framework of which remains to this day. At the western or upper end, where the *daïs* was placed, is on either side a bay, or recess, the ceilings of which are composed of very elegant groining and minute tracery, and which were illuminated by two windows of the lightest order of Gothic. In these recesses it was customary, on state occasions, to display the rich and costly vessels then in use. The recesses are now in a sadly mutilated condition, but the main body of the hall was rescued from speedy decay by order of Government in 1828, when £700 were expended on it. When it was first used as a barn, now more than a century ago, most of the windows were bricked up, and three pairs on the north side remain in that condition at the present time. The holes for the timber supports of the elevated platform, or *daïs*, are still visible in the western wall; and above the same spot, at a considerable elevation, was a window whence the king might look from his own private apartments on the revellers in the hall, an arrangement commonly in use in old houses of this description.

The date of the erection of the banqueting-hall unquestionably corresponds with the time of King Edward IV. Not only is this opinion borne out by the depressed Gothic arch of the roof and the double ranges of windows, which much resemble those in the hall at Crosby Place, Bishopsgate, and in a building at Nettlested, now used as a malt-house, both known to have been erected *temp.* Edward IV., but there is also in the northeast doorway the device or badge of Edward IV., in very good preservation, namely, the *rose en soleil*, or blazing sun in conjunction with the rose. This doorway, headed by a label moulding (characteristic of the architecture of the latter end of the fifteenth century), was formerly for many years protected from the weather by a shed, to which is to be attributed its excellent preservation. The badge appears on one of the spandrils, between the label and the arch. Besides this, the falcon and fetterlock, another device of Edward IV., may be observed among the carvings of the oriel windows.

The great hall has for ages gone by the name of "King John's Barn," probably from some confusion between King John and a son of Edward II., who was born here, and who, as already stated, was called "John of Eltham."

Subterranean passages have been traced for some distance in a south-easterly direction, but these are now converted into drains. It appears to have been about the year 1836 that the discovery of these passages was made; and from a pamphlet published a few years ago we learn that a trap-door under the ground-floor of one of the apartments led into a room below, ten feet by five in dimensions, from which a narrow passage about ten feet in length led to a series of passages, with decoys, stairs, and shafts, some of which were vertical and others on an inclined plane: these were once used for admitting air, and for hurling down missiles and pitch-balls upon the heads of those below. These passages were explored to a distance of nearly 500 feet, 200 of which lay under the moat. In a field between Eltham and Mottingham the arch had been broken into, but still the passage could be traced farther, proceeding in the same direction. In that part immediately under the moat two iron gates were found, completely carbonised, whilst large stalactites, formed of super-carbonate of lime, which hung down from the roof of the arch, sufficiently indicated the lapse of time since these passages had been previously entered. The passages now serve as drains in connection with the dwelling-house which now stands upon the site of the ancient buttery at the eastern end of the great hall.

The moat, which still surrounds the entire building, has been partially drained and turfed, and that part lying on the north side, which is spanned by the ancient bridge, is exceedingly picturesque, the effect being heightened by the herons and other species of water-fowl that adorn its banks. The old tilt-yard or tilting-court in the palace "pleasaunce" was for many years converted—alas! for this prosaic age—into a market garden; its high wall and archway of ruddy brick, which alone remain to mark its site, are well worthy of notice.

We have already spoken of the three parks which formerly belonged to Eltham Palace, and of the havoc made in them by the Parliament during the Civil Wars. The Middle Park, however, has remained to this day, and has gained some notoriety —at least, in the racing world—as the home of the famous stud of racehorses belonging to the late Mr. William Blenkiron. After the death of this gentleman, the "stud," which included the celebrated horses Gladiateur and Blair Athol, was sold by auction in 1872, realising a sum of £107,100. The Middle Park establishment is kept in remembrance by the "Middle Park Plate," founded in 1866, and which is one of the chief races at the Newmarket Second October Meeting. The memory of the Horn Park is still preserved in Horn Park Farm, at some little distance to the west of the palace.

On the east side of Eltham Palace a broad thoroughfare, called the Court Road, in which are numerous neat-built villas, leads to the Eltham Station of the South-Eastern Railway (North Kent line), which is situated at Mottingham, about a mile from the village. The latter lies at a short distance northward of the palace, and has a quiet, old-fashioned air. The church, dedicated to St. John the Baptist, is a large Gothic edifice of stone, comprising nave, aisles, transepts, and chancel. It was erected in 1876-7, to supersede an old parish church which stood on the same spot. The latter building was a singular brick-built structure, which had been patched up at different times and in so many ways that in the end it had a somewhat unsightly appearance. On a tablet over the doorway on the north side was the date 1667. The wooden tower and shingle spire of the old church have been left standing at the south-west corner of the new church. In the churchyard is the monument, surmounted by an urn, of George Horne, Bishop of Norwich, author of the "Commentary on the Book of Psalms." He was a native of Kent, and died in 1792. He was buried in the vault of the Burtons, into whose family he had married. Thomas Dogget, the comedian, and founder of the "coat and silver badge" which bears his name, and which is rowed for on the Thames by London watermen's apprentices annually on the 1st of August, was buried here September 25th, 1721. We have already in a previous volume[*] spoken at some length of Tom Dogget as an actor, and also of the aquatic contest which he instituted. We may add here that the only portrait of him that is known to exist is a small print representing him in the act of dancing "The Cheshire Round," with the motto "Ne sutor ultra crepidam." Here, likewise, lies buried, among many others, Sir William James, the captor of Severndroog, on the coast of Malabar, in 1755, of whom we have spoken in the preceding chapter.[†]

In the hollow, on the north side of the church, by the side of the road leading to Woolwich, and near the footpath across the fields of Kidbrook, stands a long red-brick farmhouse, of Elizabethan architecture; it is known as Well Hall, and is said at one time to have been the residence of Sir Thomas More's favourite daughter, Margaret Roper. "Among other notables who have dwelt in Eltham," writes Mr. James Thorne, in his "Environs of London," "was Vandyck, the painter, who lived here in the summer, tempted, it may be, by the residence in the Park Lodge of his friend, Sir Theodore de Mayerne, the king's physician, who was chief ranger of the park before it was seized by the Parliament." According to a statement of Walpole, in his "Anecdotes of Painting in England," "in an old house at Eltham, said to have been Vandyck's, Vertue saw several sketches of stories from Ovid in two colours, ascribed to that great painter; but if they were his, all trace of them has long been lost, and of the house also. The quarrelsome Commonwealth major, John Lilburne—'Freeborn John,' as he was styled—Cromwell's opponent in the army and in the House of Commons, here spent his last years 'in perfect tranquillity.' Having joined the Quakers, 'he preached among that sect in and about Eltham till his death' there, August 29th, 1657." Here Dr. James Sherard formed his famous botanic gardens, of which he published an account under the title of "Hortus Elthamensis." In the preparation of this work he was assisted by Dillenius, who came to England in 1721 specially to superintend Dr. Sherard's garden, an event which, Dr. Lindley says, "forms an important point in the history of botany in this country." Lysons speaks of Dr. James Sherard as the founder of the botanical professorship at Oxford; and in this he is followed by most subsequent writers on Eltham. "The founder of the professorship," writes Mr. Thorne, "was William Sherard, the Oriental traveller, the brother of James, who, however, was a zealous promoter of the science and patron of botanists."

Passing on our way along the high road towards London, a short walk brings us to the rapidly-increasing village of Lee, the principal part of which is built on the rising ground sloping up towards Blackheath. Since the formation of the branch line of the North Kent Railway through the parish, a considerable increase has been made in the number of dwellings, which are now springing up in every direction, in consequence of the easy facility of reaching town afforded by the railway. A small rivulet takes its rise in this parish, and, after watering the village, flows into the river Ravensbourne, in the adjoining parish of Lewisham. The church, dedicated to St. Margaret, dates its erection from the year 1841, and stands on an eminence near Blackheath, on the opposite side of the road to the old church, which has been demolished, with the exception of a small portion of the tower. The new church is a florid Gothic structure, consisting of nave, chancel, side aisles, with tower and spire; it is built of brick, and cemented, and ornamented with stone facings. The graveyard is crowded with monuments and tombs, among which is a plain tomb for Dr. Halley, the celebrated astronomer, who lies buried under it. Nathaniel Bliss, who succeeded Dr. Bradley in the post of Astronomer-Royal, also lies buried here.

At Lee lived Mr. Bohun (or Boone), the friend of John Evelyn and tutor to his sons; and here he was often visited by the genial old gossip. His house was a cabinet of curiosities, mostly Indian, Japanese, and Chinese, and adorned with carving by Grinling Gibbons. Mr. Bohun must have been more fortunate than most tutors, if he was able, as recorded by Evelyn, to build here and endow a hospital for eight poor persons, with a chapel attached. The almshouses, which are situated at the west end of the village, by the side of the high road, were rebuilt in 1874. At the back of these are thirty comfortable-looking houses, erected by the Merchant Taylors' Company, in which a number of widows of freemen belonging to that company are supported. At the south end of the parish, down to a comparatively recent date, were the remains of an ancient moated mansion, said to have been contemporary with the palace at Eltham; a fine avenue of lime-trees, some of which still remain, formed the approach to the entrance, and over the moat a strong brick arch is thrown. Dacre House is described in Hasted's "Kent" as "an elegant modern-built seat, late belonging to Sir Thomas Fludyer;" it was long the seat of the Dacre family, whose name is perpetuated by one of the streets in the village being named after them. John Timbs, in his "Autobiography," in describing a visit he once paid in his younger days to the then rural village of Lee, says:—"Here I often saw the devout Lady Dacre crossing Lee Green in her daily pilgrimage to her dear lord's tomb in Lee churchyard. She usually rode there from Lee Place on a favourite pony, and wore a large drab beaver hat, and a woollen habit nearly trailing on the ground. At the foot of her lord's grave she was accustomed to kneel and pour forth a fervent prayer, beseeching the Creator again to join her in blissful union with her beloved husband in the realms above. At home she cherished her affection by placing his chair at the dinner-table as during his lifetime. After fourteen years' widow-hood, Lady Dacre died, in 1808, and was buried with her husband."

"During our stay at Lee," adds Mr. Timbs, "the Green was my favourite resort: here the village stocks excited my curiosity, and I soon understood the wooden machine to be used for the punishment of disorderly persons by securing their legs." Mr. Timbs tells how that he remembered the stocks in many an English village, and also in many parts of London, that in Duke Street, Lincoln's Inn, being the last to disappear. He then reminds us how that "the rustic beauty of Lee has been sacrificed to the railway, and its rural sounds and songs to the noisy steam-horse; though the village possesses attractions for riper years, in its beautiful pointed church, rebuilt upon much older foundations; it is famed, too, for its brasses, and tombs of marble and alabaster; and for the resting-place of Halley, the Astronomer-Royal, who wrote a treatise on comets when he was nineteen years old."

From its proximity to Blackheath, and its easy distance from London, Lee has of late years become a favourite place of residence for City merchants and men of business, and every available plot of ground has been covered with terraces of detached and semi-detached villas and genteel cottages for their accommodation; and such names as Belmont Park, Manor Park, Dacre Park, Grove Park, &c., in which the more respectable class of houses are built, imparts a somewhat pretentious air to the locality. New churches, too, have also sprung up, consequent upon the increased growth of the place. One of these is Christ Church, in Lee Park, a building in the Early English style of architecture, erected in 1855; another, and still more handsome edifice of similar architecture, is the Church of the Holy Trinity; this was built in 1864.

At Burnt Ash, near Lee, in 1837, a Mr. Cocking made an unsuccessful attempt to descend from a balloon in a parachute, and was dashed to pieces. His body was carried into the Tiger's Head Inn, at Lee.

Continuing our course westward along the main road, we soon arrive at Lewisham, a parish and pleasant village situated on the Ravensbourne, a stream which, as we have already seen, flows through Deptford into the Thames. With regard to this stream, the "Kentish Traveller's Companion" (1789) says: "The river Ravensbourne directs its course through this parish; at the hamlet of Southend it moves the engine by which the late Mr. How made those knife-blades now so famous throughout England." The name of this place is supposed to be derived from the Saxon *leswe*, a meadow, and *ham*, a dwelling.

Lying along the valley of the Ravensbourne, with the land rising gently on either side, Lewisham, down to a very recent date, was a pleasant rural district; but, like all the other outlying districts of London, the green fields which hemmed it in are fast giving place to bricks and mortar. Granville Park occupies the sloping ground on the north, between Lewisham and Blackheath.

The old parish church, dedicated to St. Mary, was taken down in 1774, when the present edifice was erected on its site. The church is a plain oblong structure of stone, with a shallow, semicircular recess instead of a chancel at the east end, a square tower at the west end (the lower part of which is ancient), and a portico on the south side supported by four Corinthian columns. This church, which was heated by means of a large stove and flues, having been opened for divine service on Christmas Day, 1830, it is supposed that the flues becoming overheated, set fire to some portion of the woodwork of the interior, as at a very early hour on the following morning the building was discovered to be in flames, and notwithstanding every exertion, the conflagration continued till the interior of the church was almost entirely destroyed, leaving only the walls and roof standing. The inhabitants of the parish shortly after raised a handsome subscription to repair the injury thus occasioned. The church contains a few interesting monuments, particularly one by Banks and another by Flaxman; the former, which has a poetical epitaph by Hayley, is in memory of a daughter of Mr. William Lushington; it represents an angel directing the mourning mother to the text inscribed above the tablet, " Blessed are they that mourn," &c. In the churchyard is a monument, inscribed with some verses from his own " Fate of Genius," to the unfortunate young poet, Thomas Dermody, who was buried in 1802, at the age of twenty-eight. Dermody, whose early death reminds us, in a certain sense, of the fate of Chatterton and Keats, was a native of Ennis, in Ireland, and was born in 1775. He displayed poetical powers at an early age. In 1792 he published a volume of poems written in his thirteenth year. In the following year appeared " The Rights of Justice," a political pamphlet. In 1801 and 1802 he published " Peace," " The Battle of the Bards," and other poems. Soon afterwards he became a soldier, but disgraced himself by intemperance, and died in poverty in the adjoining parish of Sydenham. In 1806 Mr. G. Raymond published his life, &c., in two volumes, and subsequently his poetical works, under the title of " The Harp of Erin."

The parish of Lewisham contains several other churches, but only two of these come under our notice here, namely, St. Stephen's and St. Mark's. The former was built and endowed in 1865 by the Rev. S. Russell Davis; it was erected from the designs of Sir Gilbert Scott, and is in the Early English style of architecture. The church of St. Mark the Evangelist, in College Park, a rapidly rising district on the east side of the Bromley Road, is a handsome Decorated edifice, built in 1870, from the designs of Mr. W. C. Banks.

Down to a very recent date Lewisham consisted chiefly of one principal street, and the road for the most part was bordered with lofty elms, many of which still remain in all their freshness. The salubrity of the air made the locality, at one time, a favourite place of abode for London merchants and wealthy families, and it still retains a few good old houses. We learn from Hasted and other historians that the manor of Lewisham, with its appendages of Greenwich and Coombe, was given by Elthruda, King Alfred's niece, to the Abbey of St. Peter, at Ghent, to which Lewisham then became a cell, or " alien " priory; this grant is said to have been confirmed by King Edgar, and by Edward the Confessor. Kilburne tells us that Lewisham Priory was founded during the reign of Henry III., by Sir John Merbury; but it is more probable that he added to its endowments, and thus became its second founder. Priory Farm, at the south end of Rushey Green, on the Bromley Road —now, in effect, a southern extension of Lewisham village—marks the site of the Benedictine priory.

On the suppression of alien priories by Henry V., this priory was transferred, together with the manor of Lewisham, to the monastery of Sheen, or Richmond. In 1538 it reverted to the Crown, with the other conventual property throughout the country; and ten years later it was granted for life to Thomas, Lord Seymour. John, Earl of Warwick, eldest son of the Duke of Northumberland, next possessed the manor, but on his attainder, in the year 1553, it again reverted to the Crown. Queen Elizabeth, however, re-granted it to the earl's brother, Sir Ambrose Dudley, who had been restored in blood, and created Baron L'Isle and Earl of Warwick. James I. granted the manor to John Ramsay, Earl of Holderness. In 1664 it was sold to Reginald Grahame, who in turn conveyed it to Admiral George Legge, who was shortly afterwards created Lord Dartmouth. His son William was, in 1711, created Viscount Lewisham and Earl of Dartmouth, and with his descendants the property has since continued. Lord Dartmouth resided at his seat on Blackheath, in this parish, for which place, as we have already seen,* he procured the grant of a market.

Two charity-schools in Lewisham, one of which is a free grammar-school, were founded by the Rev. Abraham Colfe, vicar of this parish, in the latter part of the seventeenth century, and are under the patronage of the Leathersellers' Company. The intentions of the founder were extended by a scheme settled by the Court of Chancery in 1857.

veneration by the "faithful." Here there is a station on the Mid-Kent Railway. Close by is Brockley Hill, across which are pleasant walks to Dulwich, Peckham, and other outlying places which we shall presently visit. Between Ladywell Station and Brockley Lane is the cemetery belonging to the parishes of Deptford and Lewisham; it covers a large space of ground, and is tastefully laid out.

Retracing our steps through the village, and

LEE CHURCH IN 1795.

There are also almshouses for six poor women that owe their foundation to the same benevolent individual. Other almshouses have lately been erected in the village, under the will of Mr. John Thackeray, for six poor females.

Half a mile to the south-east of the village is Hither Green, which, together with Catford and Catford Bridge, on the Ravensbourne, and also Rushey Green (mentioned above), are hamlets belonging to Lewisham.

A narrow lane turning out of the main road by the side of the parish church, leads our steps to Ladywell, a spot doubtless so called from a well or spring whose waters were at one time held in

leaving on our right the station on the North Kent Railway, we make our way up Loam Pit Hill, passing the church of St. John's, lately built, and soon find ourselves at New Cross, an outlying district belonging to the parish of Deptford. This noted locality, which takes its name from the old coaching-house and hostelry bearing the sign of the "Golden Cross," has been famous for at least a couple of centuries; for John Evelyn tells us in his "Diary," under date of 10th November, 1675, how he went to "New Crosse" from Saye's Court, in his coach, to accompany his friend, Lord Berkeley, as far as Dover, on his way to Paris as ambassador. It may amuse the reader to learn that his lordship's retinue consisted of three coaches (exclusive of Evelyn's), as many wagons, and "about forty

* See *ante*, p. 227.

horses." Our diplomatists move about now-a-days with less state and less incumbrance.

On Counter Hill, Upper Lewisham Road, the rising ground in the rear of the tavern, stands the Royal Naval School, a good substantial-looking brick building, with white stone dressings, the "first stone" of which was laid by Prince Albert, in 1843, on the "Glorious First of June," the anniversary of Lord Howe's victory. To the opening of the school, in 1833, upwards of 3,000 boys have partaken of its advantages, many of whom had distinguished themselves, and several had lost their lives in the service of their country. During the twenty years previous to 1877 more than 300 pupils had become naval officers, many of them distinguished men. During the same period eighty pupils had entered as officers in the Royal Marines, one-third of that number having

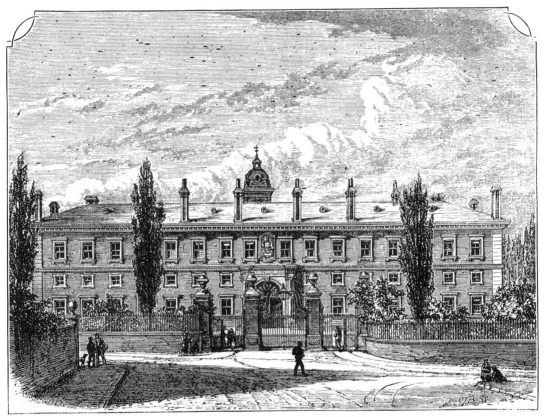

THE ROYAL NAVAL SCHOOL, NEW CROSS.

traveller who steps from the New Cross station to the main road, it presents an imposing appearance, with its long line of red-brick frontage, its numerous windows, its sweep of green turf before the house, its iron outer gates, and its great gates of oak, which, when open, disclose the quadrangle and the arcades under which the boys wander after school-hours when not disposed for play in the spacious grounds beyond. The school, which was founded and provisionally opened at Camberwell in 1833, has an average of 200 pupils, mostly the sons of naval and military officers in necessitous circumstances; and the object of the school is to qualify them, at the least possible expense, for any pursuit, giving a preference to the orphans of those who may have fallen in their country's service. Since the gained the Artillery, and eleven having passed first in their entrance examinations. Captain Sir George Nares, the commander of the Arctic Expedition, won his way into the Royal Navy by gaining in this school the Admiralty Prize Naval Cadetship in 1845. Colonel Sir F. W. Festing, who so gallantly distinguished himself in the Ashantee campaign, also passed direct from this school into the Royal Marine Artillery. These are but two out of the many pupils who have distinguished themselves in the service of their country.

At New Cross are important stations and works on the South-Eastern, and also on the London, Brighton, and South-coast Railways.

The manor of Hatcham, in the immediate neighbourhood of the above-mentioned station, was at one time part and parcel of the parish of St. Paul, Deptford; but, pursuant to an Act of Parliament, it has been created a distinct parish, called Hatcham New Town. The church, dedicated to St. James, is a large and lofty Gothic edifice; it

was consecrated in 1850, but was only recently completed. In 1877 this church acquired considerable notoriety from the ritualistic practices of its incumbent, who was suspended on that account from his spiritual functions by order of the Arches Court of Canterbury, under Lord Penzance.

CHAPTER XIX.

THE OLD KENT ROAD, &c.

"*Inde iter in Cantium.*"—*Cæsar.*

The Course of the Old Watling Street—M. Sorbierre's Visit to London in the Reign of Charles II.—Evelyn's Account of the Return of Charles II., on his Restoration—Anecdote of Pitt and Dundas—Mrs. Mapp, the celebrated Bone-setter—Condition of the Old Kent Road in the Last Century—The Licensed Victuallers' Asylum—The South Metropolitan Gas Works—Christ Church—The Canal Bridge—Marlborough Chapel —St. Thomas à Watering—Old Taverns and Roadside Inns—The "World Turned Upside Down"—The Deaf and Dumb Asylum—The New Kent Road—Lock's Fields—Great Dover Street—Trinity Square and Trinity Church—Horsemonger Lane Gaol—Leigh Hunt a Prisoner there—Execution of the Mannings—The Surrey Sessions' House—Newington Causeway.

FOLLOWING the course of the old Watling Street, we now make our way back to the southern extremity of the Borough, by the broad thoroughfare of the Old Kent Road. All trace of Watling Street at this point, we need hardly remark, has long since disappeared. The branch of the ancient Watling Street, which extended from Dover to Canterbury, and thence through Faversham and Rochester to London, was the road followed by nearly all travellers from the days of the Romans, the days of pilgrimages and crusades, and thence again until the formation of railways diverted their steps into another track. M. Sorbierre, a French gentleman of letters, who visited London in the reign of Charles II., thus writes:—"That I might not take post, or be obliged to use the stage-coach, I went from Dover to London in a wagon; I was drawn by six horses, one before another, and driven by a wagoner, who walked by the side of it. He was clothed in black, and appointed in all things like another St. George: he had a brave 'mounteror' on his head, and was a merry fellow, fancied he made a fine figure, and seemed highly pleased with himself."

Along this road travelled Charles II. and a gay train of cavaliers, on his Restoration and return, by way of Dover to London, in May, 1660. Evelyn draws the following picture of the happy event:— "This day his Majesty Charles II. came to London after a sad and long exile, and calamitous suffering both of the king and Church. This was also his birthday, and with a triumph of about 20,000 horse and foote, brandishing their swords and shouting with inexpressible joy; the wayes strew'd with flowers, the bells ringing, the streets hung with tapestrie, fountaines running with wine:

the Maior, Aldermen, and all the Companies in their liveries, chaines of gold, and banners; lords and nobles clad in cloth of silver, gold, and velvet; the windows and balconies well set with ladies; trumpets, music, and myriads of people flocking even so far as from Rochester, so as they were seven hours in passing into the Citty, even from two in the afternoon till nine at night."

In the days nearer to our own, when there were no railroads, even this unfashionable thoroughfare was used by the most distinguished travellers. Stothard, the painter, for instance, tells us that, happening to be one evening at an inn on this road, he met Pitt and Dundas (afterwards Lord Melville), who had been obliged to rest there for the night on their way from Walmer to London. Next morning, as they were stepping into their carriage, the waiter said to Stothard, "Sir, do you observe those two gentlemen?" "Yes," was the reply; "I see they are Mr. Pitt and Mr. Dundas." "And how much wine do you think they drank last night, for the good of the house?" Stothard could not guess. "Seven bottles," was the waiter's answer.

We find in Jeaffreson's "Book about Doctors," the following ludicrous story relative to this part of the metropolis:—"One of the sights of the Old Kent Road at the beginning of the eighteenth century was the cavalcade of Mrs. Mapp, the celebrated bone-setter, on her way to the City. On one occasion, we are told, as the lady was proceeding along the Old Kent Road towards the Borough in her carriage-and-four, and manifesting by her manner that she had partaken too freely of Geneva water, she found herself in a very trying position. Her fat frame, eccentric dress, and dazzling equipage, were, in the eyes of the mob, sure signs of royalty, so that she was immediately taken for a court lady of German origin and unpopular repute, whose word was omnipotent at St. James's. Soon a crowd gathered round the carriage, and, with the proper amount of yelling and hooting, were about to break the windows with stones, when, acting very much as Nell Gwynne did on a similar occasion, she exclaimed, in a manner more emphatic than polite, 'What! don't you know me? I'm Mrs. Mapp, the bone-setter!'" The tale is familiar to all readers of the "Eccentric Biography."

The Old Kent Road, known as Kent Street Road until the end of the last century, was a continuation of Kent (now Tabard) Street, of which we have already spoken,* and was the highway from Kent to the metropolis. There were but few houses in the Kent Road a century ago. Rocque's Map, published in 1750, shows the thoroughfare lined with hedgerows, bespeaking its rural character in the days of George II.

In 1827 the Licensed Victuallers' Asylum was founded, on six acres of freehold land lying just off the Old Kent Road. It consists of a group of one-storeyed houses, chapel, chaplain's residence, board and court rooms, library, &c., set round two green lawns. The Duke of Sussex was its first patron in 1827, and he was succeeded by the Prince Consort, on whose death the Prince of Wales assumed the office. The idea of establishing an institution wherein the distressed members of the licensed victuallers' trade, and their wives or widows, might be enabled to spend the latter part of their days in peace and quietness, was conceived by the late Mr. Joseph Proud Hodgson, in the year 1826, when he called a meeting of several influential gentlemen in the trade, and ventilated his views; and, after serious consideration, it was determined that a society should be formed under the title of the Licensed Victuallers' Asylum.

Subscriptions were solicited, and the hearty response that was accorded to the scheme by those most deeply interested in its success enabled the committee to purchase the land above mentioned, upon which it was resolved to erect an asylum, to consist of one hundred and one separate houses, containing three rooms each, besides the requisite conveniences. In May, 1828, the foundation-stone was laid, with full Masonic honours, by the Duke of Sussex, in the presence of a distinguished company, many of whom in after years exhibited a sincere attachment to the institution.

At this time it was determined by the promoters of the institution to erect the central portion of the building, to consist of forty-three houses, which were perfected, and speedily became the abode of as many deserving individuals.

The applicants for admission being numerous, it was deemed advisable to perfect the asylum as early as circumstances would permit, and consequently, in the year 1831, the south wing was erected, and in 1833 the north wing, thus completing the original design of the institution. The friends of the society, being relieved of the anxiety of erecting additional houses, in the year 1835 turned their attention to the advisability of granting weekly allowances of money to the inmates of the asylum, in order to provide them with the necessaries of life, and, as might be imagined, the proposal met with cordial approval, and allowances were then commenced, since which period they have been increased from time to time, until they have reached the sum of twelve shillings per week for married couples and eight shillings for single persons—members of the Incorporated Society of Licensed Victuallers receiving one shilling per week extra. In addition to the allowances, a weekly supply of coal is granted to each inmate, besides being supplied with medical attendance, medicine, and wine, when recommended by the medical officer. In 1842 a charter of incorporation was granted to the institution, and in the following year, on the death of the Duke of Sussex, Prince Albert became patron.

In 1849 was commenced the "ladies' wing," comprising twenty-three habitations, the foundation-stone being laid by H.R.H. the Prince Consort: this wing was completed in the following year. Several years having elapsed since an addition was made to the asylum, this important subject was considered, and so readily approved of by those who had the management of the institution, that in the year 1858 a new wing was commenced, the asylum being again honoured by its royal patron condescending to lay the foundation-stone. These buildings were designated the Albert Wing, in compliment to his Royal Highness, and consist of thirty-four houses.

A donation of one thousand guineas having been made to the institution in 1866, by a Mr. William Smalley, it was resolved that the only remaining space on the asylum grounds available for building purposes should be utilised. This was accordingly carried out, and ten additional houses built, which were named the Smalley Wing, the foundation-stone being laid by the Duke of Edinburgh. This addition completed the asylum as a building, and it

---

* See *ante*, p. 70.

now consists of one hundred and seventy separate and distinct houses.

The beautiful little chapel is enriched with stained-glass memorial windows, and also several handsome marble tablets, in memory of donors to the institution; whilst upon the grounds in front of the building, and facing the Asylum Road, is erected a marble statue of the late Prince Consort, which was unveiled in 1864 by the Prince of Wales.

The expenses attending the institution are about £7,000 annually, which is met by the subscriptions among the members of the trade, by bequests, by the proceeds of a ball given annually at Willis's Rooms or the Freemasons' Tavern, and also by the proceeds of the anniversary festival.

Close by the canal bridge, at a short distance westward of the Asylum Road, are the works belonging to the South Metropolitan Gas Company, whose operations extend over thirteen square miles, from the New Kent Road southwards as far as Croydon parish, taking in considerable portions of Newington, St. George the Martyr, a small part of Bermondsey, nearly all Camberwell, a large portion of Lambeth, and all Streatham. The company has altogether about 170 miles of main-pipes; it consumes annually about 84,000 tons of coal, and supplies about 800,000,000 feet of gas in a year. The number of retorts is about 500, and the seven gas-holders are capable of storing nearly 4,000,000 feet of gas; while the greatest quantity made in a day somewhat exceeds that amount. This gas company was founded in 1833, for the supply of cannel gas, and incorporated in 1842, with an authorised capital of £200,000. In 1853 the south side of the Thames was divided into districts, which arrangements were sanctioned by Parliament in the Metropolis Gas Act, 1860. The company first supplied gas in 1834; and after four years' trial it was convincingly proved that to supply cannel gas made from the common coal was a financial mistake, and therefore cannel gas was abandoned in 1838. In consequence of the gradual extension of these works, the district church of Christ Church, Camberwell, which was built in 1838, on the north side of the Old Kent Road, has been demolished, and a new church built on the opposite side of the road. The new edifice, a brick building of Gothic architecture, was erected in 1868.

Beyond mentioning the canal bridge, which spans the Grand Surrey Canal close by the above-mentioned gas-works, and making a passing reference to Marlborough (Congregational) Chapel, and also to the new Nonconformist chapel at the corner of Albany Road—built for the congregation formerly assembling at the old Maze Pond Chapel, —there is little or nothing in this thoroughfare calling for special remark till we arrive near the junction of the Old and New Kent Roads with Great Dover Street.

St. Thomas à Watering was once the boundary of the City liberties, and in the "olden time," when the lord mayor and sheriffs " in great state " crossed the water to open Southwark Fair and to inspect the City boundaries, the City magistrates continued either to St. George's Church, Newington Bridge, or " to the stones pointing out the City liberties at St. Thomas à Watering." The precise situation was as near as possible that part of the Old Kent Road which is intersected by the Albany Road, and the memory of the place is still kept alive by St. Thomas's Road, close by, and by the tavern-signs in the neighbourhood. " At the commencement of the present century," writes Mr. Blanch, in his history of " Ye Parishe of Camerwell," " there was a stream here which served as a common sewer, across which a bridge was built; and in going from Camberwell into Newington or Southwark, it was not unusual for people to say they were going over the water. The current from the Peckham hills was at times so strong as to overflow at least two acres of ground."

St. Thomas à Waterings was situated close to the second milestone on the Old Kent Road, and was so called from a brook or spring, dedicated to St. Thomas à Becket. Chaucer's pilgrims, as we have seen in a previous chapter,* passed it on their way to the shrine of St. Thomas à Becket at Canterbury :—

> " And forth we riden a litel more than pas,
> Unto the watering of Seint Thomàs,
> And then our host began his hors arrest."

Ben Jonson, in *The New Inn*, makes mention of the spot in the following lines :—

> " These are the arts
> Or seven liberal deadly sciences,
> Of pagery, or rather paganism,
> As the tides run ! to which if he apply him,
> He may perhaps take a degree at Tyburn
> A year the earlier ; come to read a lecture
> Upon Aquinas at St. Thomas à Waterings."

This spot was in the old Tudor days the place of execution for the northern parts of Surrey ; and here the Vicar of Wandsworth, his chaplain, and two other persons of his household, were hung, drawn, and quartered in 1539 for denying the supremacy of Henry VIII. in matters of faith.

In 1553 (January 3rd) " was caried from the

* See *ante*, p. 83.

Marshalleshe unto Saynt Thomas of Wateryng a talman, and went thedur with the rope a-bowt ys neke, and so he hanggd a whylle, and the rope burst, and a whylle after and then they went for a-nodur rope, and so lyke-wyss he burst ytt and fell to the ground, and so he skapyd with his lyffe."

On the 3rd of October, 1559, a "nuw payre of galows was sett up at Sant Thomas of Watering;" and on the 12th of February, 1650-1, "was reynyd [arraigned] in Westmynster Hall v men, iij was for burglare, and ij were cutpurses, and cast to be hanged at Sant Thomas of Watering: one was a gentyllman."

One of the quarters of Sir Thomas Wyatt, who was beheaded for rebellion in April, 1554, was exposed at this place; and on the 18th of June, 1556, a younger son of Lord Sandys was executed here for robbing a cart, coming from a fair, at Beverley. The booty was estimated at about four thousand pounds.

In 1559 five men were executed here. Macbyn, in his Diary, thus records the event:—"The ix day of Feybruary at after-none a-bowt iij of the cloke, v men wher hangyd at Sant Thomas of watherynges; one was captyn Jenkes, and (blank) Warde, and (blank) Walles, and (blank) Beymont, and a-nodur man, and they were browth [brought] up in ware [war] all their lyffes,—for a grett robere done."

John Henry, the author of some of the "Martin Mar-Prelate Tracts," was hung here in 1593; and Franklin, one of the agents implicated in the murder of Sir Thomas Overbury, was executed at the same place in 1615.

The last persons executed at St. Thomas à Watering were a father and son, who suffered the penalty of the law for murder about the year 1740.

The most noticeable feature in the Old Kent Road is the number of public-houses, each with its swinging sign and drinking-trough for horses. Among these houses of "entertainment for man and beast" is the "Kentish Drovers," which has existed here for about a couple of centuries, and was a well-known halting-place on the road to Kent, at a time (not very far distant) when the thoroughfare was bordered on either side by green fields and market gardens. The "Thomas à Becket," at the corner of Albany Road, commemorates the spot where the pilgrims first halted on their way from London to Canterbury (as mentioned above); the "Shard Arms" perpetuates the cognisance of the once powerful and wealthy Shard family, who were large landowners in the neighbourhood. Among the oldest inns in the Old Kent Road, perhaps, is one near the Bricklayers'

Arms Station, which rejoices in the somewhat singular sign of "The World Turned Upside Down." The house is supposed to have commemorated the discovery of Australia and Van Diemen's Land, and down to about 1840 its sign-board represented a man walking at the South Pole. Mr. Larwood, in his work on "Sign-boards," interprets this sign as "meaning a state of things the opposite of what is natural and usual: a conceit in which," he adds, "the artists of former ages took great delight, and which they represented by animals chasing men, horses riding in carriages, and similar conceits and pleasantries." The old sign-board was blown down many years ago; and in 1868 the house itself was in great part rebuilt and wholly new-fronted.

The Bricklayers' Arms Inn, at the corner of the Old Kent Road and Bermondsey New Road, was a famous house of call for all journeys from the south-eastern parts of London for several centuries. There can be no doubt that at an early date an inn stood on the spot now occupied by the Bricklayers' Arms, the descent from which to the present house, which was built in 1880, is unbroken. In the time of Edward III. the Burgundian lords who came over after the battle of Cressy to issue a general challenge to English knights in a tournament to be held in Smithfield, lodged, we are told by Philip de Comines, "in a vaste hostel on the olde rode from Kent into Southwarke, about two thirdes of a league from the bridge across the Thames"; a description which evidently applies to a house occupying this site. Among the illustrious personages who have since been known to make this inn their halting-place may be mentioned Sir Francis Drake, Sir Cloudesley Shovel, Admiral Duncan (afterwards Lord Camperdown), Lord Hood, and the gallant Nelson.

Nearly opposite this old hostelry stood for many years the Deaf and Dumb Asylum, a large but plain and unpretending edifice, separated from the roadway by a grove of trees. Miss Priscilla Wakefield, in her "Perambulations," published in 1809, commences one of her "letters" as follows: —"We continued our excursions into the county of Kent, stopping on the Kent Road to view a handsome building now erecting for the Asylum for poor Deaf and Dumb Children, an unfortunate class of persons, too long overlooked, or ineffect-ually commiserated among us." The applicants becoming so numerous that not one-half of them could be admitted, it was resolved to extend the plan. A new subscription was set on foot for the purpose, and the present building was raised, with-out encroaching on the former funds of the institu-

the Rev. C. Crowther preaching the sermon. A memorial bust of the Rev. Mr. Townsend has been placed in the committee-room. The pupils, male and female, are such children only as are deaf and dumb, not being deficient in intellect. Other children are admitted on payment of £20 annually for board; and private pupils are also received. The term of each pupil's stay is five years; they are taught to read, write, draw, and

From the report for 1876 we learn that during that year seventy-six children were admitted and sent to the branch asylum at Margate. Eighty-one children left the London asylum during the year, and thirty-five were apprenticed to various trades. As many as 4,170 children had been admitted since the foundation of the Asylum, and 1,550 apprenticed since the year 1812. The ordinary receipts in 1876, including a balance from the pre-

THE LICENSED VICTUALLERS' ASYLUM.

cipher, to speak by signs, and in many instances to articulate so as to be clearly understood. They are wholly clothed and maintained by the charity, are instructed in working trades, and in some cases apprentice-fees are given. The Asylum is amply supported by the wealthy; and besides its annual receipts from subscriptions, donations, and legacies, &c., it has some funded stock. The pupils are elected half-yearly, without reference to locality, sect, or persuasion. The importance of this Asylum is attested by the fact that in 1833, in twenty families of 159 children, ninety were deaf and dumb."

In connection with the above-mentioned institution, there is a branch establishment at Margate, which was used for the first time in August, 1876.

vious year of £1,296, amounted to upwards of £9,354, and the general expenses to £12,055, the deficit having to be met by absorbing the sum of £3,334 bequeathed as legacies instead of being funded.

Close by the Deaf and Dumb Asylum the Old Kent Road terminates in the branch thoroughfares of New Kent Road, which trends south-westwardly to the "Elephant and Castle," and of Great Dover Street, which unites with the Borough, close by St. George's Church. The former of these thoroughfares—formerly called the Greenwich Road—is a broad and open roadway; it has been lately planted on either side with trees, so that in course of time it will doubtless form a splendid boulevard, of the Parisian type, and one worthy of being copied in many other parts of London. Great Dover Street is of comparatively recent growth, having been formed since the commencement of the present century to supersede the old, narrow, and disreputable Kent Street, which runs parallel with it on the north side, and to which we have referred above.

Among the residents of this street was Mr. T. C. Noble, the author of "Memorials of Temple Bar," and of other antiquarian works. It may be recorded that in 1869, when a bill was introduced into the House of Commons to divest some of the great City companies of the estates in the north of Ireland which they had purchased from James I., Mr. Noble published a series of letters, which had an important effect in causing the abandonment of the bill. For his successful opposition to the scheme, Mr. Noble received two special votes of thanks from the Court of the Irish Society, likewise the thanks of the London Livery Companies, being also presented with the freedom of the City and of the Company of Ironmongers.

"At the east end of Kent Street, in 1847," writes Mr. Blanch, in his "History of Camberwell," "was unearthed a pointed arched bridge of the fifteenth century, probably erected by the monks of Bermondsey Abbey, lords of the manor. In Rocque's Map, this arch, called Lock's Bridge, from being near the Lock Hospital,* carries the road over a stream which runs from Newington Fields to Bermondsey!" Lock's Fields, which are still in existence—at all events in name—on the south side of the New Kent Road, were doubtless so named for the same reason.

In Trinity Street—which diverges from Great Dover Street, and terminates at the junction of Blackman Street with Newington Causeway—is Trinity Square, and also Trinity Church, a modern edifice of the Grecian style of architecture. This church is situated on the south side of Trinity Square, at a short distance from Blackman Street, and nearly on the verge of the parish of St. Mary, Newington. It is enclosed in a small square of respectable-looking houses, with a plantation in the centre, in which is erected a statue of King Alfred. The portico and principal front of the church, with the steeple, is placed on the north side of the body of the edifice ; the portico consisting of six fluted Corinthian columns supporting a plain entablature and pediment. The body of the church is a parallelogram, and is divided into two storeys by a plain course. The interior presents a vast unbroken area, roofed in one span,

and the ceiling is panelled. The galleries, resting on Doric pillars, extend round three sides of the church, and the altar-screen, situated below the eastern window, consists of a pediment surmounting four slabs, inscribed with the Decalogue, &c. The first stone of the edifice was laid by the Archbishop of Canterbury in June, 1823, and the building was consecrated in December of the following year. The ground on which the church is built was given by the corporation of the Trinity House, which possesses considerable property in the vicinity.

On the south side of Trinity Square, with its principal entrance in Union Road (formerly Horsemonger Lane), stood the prison and place of execution for the county of Surrey, commonly known as Horsemonger Lane Gaol. It was a substantially-built structure, chiefly of brick, arranged upon the approved plan of John Howard, the prison philanthropist. It was of a quadrangular form, with three storeys above the basement, and was completed for the reception of prisoners in 1798, and had accommodation for 300 prisoners. On the passing of the Prisons' Regulation Act in 1878, this gaol was abolished, and shortly afterwards the buildings, with the exception of the outer wall and the entrance lodge-house, were pulled down. A portion of the site has since been let to the Metropolitan Playground Association, at a nominal rent of 5s. a year, and in May, 1884, it was opened as a recreation-ground for the children of the neighbourhood, who resort to it in large numbers.

In 1802, Colonel Despard, and about thirty of his accomplices, were arrested at the "Oakley Arms" public-house in Lambeth, on a charge of treasonable conspiracy, tending to dethrone the king and subvert the Government. In the following February they were tried by a special commission, held in the Sessions' House adjoining the prison, and the colonel and six of his colleagues were hung and beheaded here. It may be added that the "hurdle" on which the colonel was drawn from the cell in which he was last confined to the place of execution—in conformity with the sentence formerly passed upon criminals convicted of high treason—remained in the gaol till very recently, and was regarded as an object of curiosity.

This spot has its romance, for Leigh Hunt was for two years (1812–1814) imprisoned here for libellously styling the Prince Regent, afterwards George IV., an "Adonis of fifty ;" and here it was that Moore and Lord Byron paid that memorable visit to "the wit in the dungeon," when the noble poet saw him for the first time in his life. Mr.

---

* See Vol. V., pp. 14, 215, and 528 ; and also *ante*, p. 70.

Cyrus Redding, in his "Recollections," says :—"I remember paying Leigh Hunt a visit in Horsemonger Lane Jail, a miserable low site. I missed Byron and Moore by only about half an hour, on the same errand. Horace Smith and Shelley used to be visitors there, and many others of Hunt's friends. He was composing 'Rimini,' a copy of which he gave me, and which I still possess. His apartment, on the ground floor, was cheerful for such a place, but that only means a sort of lacquered gloom after all. I thought of his health, which seemed by no means strong. I am certain, if the place was not unwholesome, it lay close upon the verge of insalubrity. Hunt bore his confinement cheerfully, but he must have had unpleasant moments. He was naturally lively, and in those days I never knew a more entertaining companion. For such an one to be alone for weary, dreary hours, must have been punishment enough even to satisfy an Ellenborough or a Jeffries."

"Times and rules are changed since then," writes Mr. Hepworth Dixon, in his "London Prisons :" "the 'luxurious comforts—the trellised flower-garden without, the books, busts, pictures, and pianoforte within'—which Moore describes on the occasion when Byron dined with him in the prison—would be looked for in vain now." Here is a picture of the interior of the prison at the time Mr. Dixon's book was published, only a quarter of a century ago (1850):—"There are for criminals," he writes, "ten classes, or wards, each ward having its yard and day-room. On entering one of these, the visitor is painfully impressed with the absence of all rule and system in the management. He finds himself in a low, long room, dungeon-like, chilly, not very clean, and altogether as uncomfortable as it can conveniently be made. This room is crowded with thirty or forty persons, of all ages and shades of ignorance and guilt—left to themselves, with no officer in sight. Here there is no attempt to enforce discipline. Neither silence nor separation is maintained in the largest prison in the metropolitan county of Surrey ! In this room we see thirty or forty persons with nothing to do —many of them know not how to read, and those who do are little encouraged so to improve their time. Some of them clearly prefer their present state of listless idleness : with hands in their pockets, they saunter about their dungeon, or loll upon the floor, listening to the highly-spiced stories of their companions, well content to be fed at the expense of the county—upon a better diet, better cooked, than they are accustomed to at home— without any trouble or exertion on their own part.

Conversing with them, we find that a few of these pariahs of civilisation hate the listless, apathetic bondage in which they are kept ; that they would be glad to have work to do—to get instruction if they could. But the majority prefer the state of vegetation as more congenial to their cherished habits of inaction. Here they are gratified to their wish." This state of things, we need scarcely inform our readers, ceased to exist on the passing of the Prisons' Discipline Act in 1865, when the silent system was adopted here, and the regulations of the prison were carried out on much the same principle as those at Holloway.* The abolition of this gaol may be regarded as an unconscious attempt to realise in modern London the boast of Rome under its kings, that it was content with a single prison !

Down to the passing of the Act by which executions ceased to take place in public, the scaffold for the execution of criminals at this gaol was erected upon the roof of the gateway ; and the roadway in front, during these "exhibitions," became the scene of the wildest depravity. Charles Dickens, who was present at the execution of the Mannings on the 13th of November, 1849, gives us the following description of what he saw :—"I was a witness," he writes, "of the execution at Horsemonger Lane this morning. I went there with the intention of observing the crowd gathered to behold it, and I had excellent opportunities of doing so at intervals all through the night, and continuously from daybreak until after the spectacle was over. I believe that a sight so inconceivably awful as the wickedness and levity of the immense crowd collected at that execution could be imagined by no man, and could be presented in no heathen land under the sun. The horrors of the gibbet and of the crime which brought the wretched murderers to it faded in my mind before the atrocious bearing, looks, and language of the assembled spectators. When I came upon the scene at midnight, the shrillness of the cries and howls that were raised from time to time, denoting that they came from a concourse of boys and girls already assembled in the best places, made my blood run cold. As the night went on, screeching, and laughing, and yelling in strong chorus of parodies on negro melodies, with substitutions of 'Mrs. Manning' for 'Susannah,' and the like, were added to these. When the day dawned, thieves, low prostitutes, ruffians, and vagabonds of every kind, flocked on to the ground, with every variety of offensive and foul behaviour. Fightings, faintings, whistlings, imitations of Punch,

* See Vol. III., p. 380.

brutal jokes, tumultuous demonstrations of indecent delight when swooning women were dragged out of the crowd by the police with their dresses disordered, gave a new zest to the general entertainment. When the sun rose brightly—as it did—it gilded thousands upon thousands of upturned faces, so inexpressibly odious in their brutal mirth or callousness, that a man had cause to feel ashamed of the shape he wore, and to shrink from himself, as fashioned in the image of the devil. When the two miserable creatures who attracted all this ghastly sight about them were turned quivering into the air, there was no more emotion, no more pity, no more thought that two immortal souls had gone to judgment, no more restraint in any of the previous obscenities, than if the name of Christ had never been heard in this world, and there were no belief among men but that they perished like the beasts. I have seen, habitually, some of the worst sources of general contamination and corruption in this country, and I think there are not many phases of London life that could surprise me. I am solemnly convinced that nothing that ingenuity could devise to be done in this city, in the same compass of time, could work such ruin as one public execution; and I stand astounded and appalled by the wickedness it exhibits. I do not believe that any community can prosper where such a scene of horror and demoralisation as was enacted this morning outside Horsemonger Lane Gaol is presented at the very doors of good citizens, and is passed by, unknown or forgotten."

The Sessions' House, for the meetings of the magistrates of the county of Surrey, adjoins the western side of the prison, and has its front towards Newington Causeway. This building, together with the gaol, was completed in 1799, having been built in conformity with an Act of Parliament, passed in the year 1791, entitled "An Act for building a new common gaol and sessions' house, with accommodations thereto, for the county of Surrey." In pursuance of this Act, three acres and a half of land, used by a market gardener, were purchased; and the two buildings were erected under the direction of the late Mr. George Gwilt, the county surveyor, the total cost having amounted to nearly £40,000. The Sessions' House has been recently rebuilt; and since 1875 the whole of the interior has been reconstructed upon improved principles, and the building new fronted, under the direction of the county surveyor, Mr. Howell.

CHAPTER XX.

NEWINGTON AND WALWORTH.

" Utrum rus an urbem appellem, prorsus hæreo."—*Plautus.*

Etymology of Newington Butts—The " Elephant and Castle "—Joanna Southcott—Singular Discovery of Human Remains—The Drapers' Almshouses—The Fishmongers' Almshouses—Newington Grammar School—Hospital of Our Lady and St. Catherine—Newington Theatre—The Semaphore Telegraph—The Metropolitan Tabernacle—Mr. C. H. Spurgeon—Mr. Spurgeon's Almshouses and Schools—St. Mary's Church, Newington—The Old Parish Church—The Graveyard laid out as a Public Garden—The Clock Tower—The Old Parsonage House—The " Queen's Head " Tea Gardens—A Great Flood—An Eminent Optician—The Surrey Zoological Gardens—The Music Hall—Walworth Road—Carter Street Lecture Hall—The Walworth Literary and Mechanics' Institution—St. Peter's Church—St. John's Church.

NEWINGTON is within the limits of the parliamentary borough of Lambeth; it is a parish of itself, and adjoins Southwark on the south. It was anciently called Neweton, or New Town. Lysons considers that in early times the church of this parish stood at Walworth, and that on its removal further westward, the buildings erected around it gradually acquired the name of " the New Town."

A small portion of the main road through the parish, running southward from the " Elephant and Castle," is called Newington Butts, which, writes Northouck, is thought to have been so designated, " from the exercise of shooting at the butts which was practised there, as in other parts of the kingdom, to train the young men in archery." Other writers, however, are of opinion that the derivation is from the family of Butts, or Buts, who owned an estate here.

The " Elephant and Castle " public-house, now a mere central starting-point for omnibuses, was formerly a well-known coaching house; its sign was the crest of the Cutlers' Company, into whose trade ivory enters largely.

This celebrated tavern is situated about one mile and a half from Westminster, Waterloo, and Blackfriars Bridges, and on a spot where several cross roads meet, leading from these bridges to important places in Kent and Surrey. Before railways drove our old stage-coaches from the road, the " Elephant and Castle " was a well-known locality to every traveller going anywhere south of London. Its character, however, has become to a certain extent changed, and it is now chiefly known to the inhabitants of Camberwell, Dulwich, Herne Hill, Kennington, Stockwell, and Clapham.

In the Middle Ages, as we are reminded by Mr. Larwood, in his "History of Signs," the elephant was nearly always represented with a castle on his

had an additional renown. Within a few doors of the old inn, Joanna Southcott, of whom we have spoken in our notice of St. John's Wood,* set up a meeting-house for her deluded followers. Her disciple, Mr. Carpenter, covered the walls with strange pictures representing, as he said, visions

THE TELEGRAPH TOWER, IN 1810.

back. Early manuscripts represent the noble brute with a tower strapped on his back, in which are seen five knights in chain armour, with swords, battle-axes, cross-bows, and emblazoned shields, thus realising the words of the Roman satirist, Juvenal—

"Partem aliquam belli et euntem in prælia turrim."

The "castle," in elaborate and costly sets of chessmen, is often set on the back of an "elephant."

In the early part of the present century this spot

he had received; "thousands of delusionists," observes a writer in the *Dispatch*, "visited the chapel, and prayed that old Joanna might speedily be delivered of the expected Shiloh. But though a silver cradle was subscribed for and presented, Nature refused to work a miracle, and no Shiloh came. After a time, Joanna and her friend Carpenter quarrelled. The old woman retired with

* See Vol. V., p. 253.

another disciple, Mr. Tozer, to Duke Street, Lambeth, and there built another chapel, leaving Carpenter in possession of the Newington house. What he preached there we know not; but in fulness of time Joanna died, and then numbers awoke to the delusion, and wondered how they could have believed in the divine mission of the ignorant, quarrelsome old woman."

In 1875, whilst some workmen were engaged in laying down pipes for the water company, a portion of the roadway in front of the "Elephant and Castle," and within a few feet of the kerb, was opened, when one of the men came upon what he thought at first was a box, but what in the end proved to be a coffin containing human remains. These were found to be those of a person, it was believed, of some sixteen years of age. All the parts were nearly complete, but, singular to state, there was an absence of either hands or feet. The skull was in a wonderful state of preservation, but on one side there was an indentation, as though a blow had been given causing a fracture. In the coffin was found a clasp-knife, somewhat resembling that carried by sailors. There was also a piece of woollen fabric, upon which were marks believed to be those of blood. The discovery was considered as very singular, considering the frequent alterations that had been made in the roadway for years past. It was believed that the coffin and contents must have been under ground for quite 150 years.

In Cross Street, near the "Elephant and Castle," are the Drapers' Almshouses, founded by Mr. John Walter, in 1651. The houses are of brick, and were rebuilt in 1778. To these almshouses the parish has the privilege of nominating six of its own parishioners; the remainder are appointed by the Drapers' Company.

On the west side of the Kennington Road, and on the site now occupied by the horse repository, the Metropolitan Tabernacle, and the colossal block of buildings at the corner of St. George's Road, stood for many years, down till the year 1851, a picturesque cluster of almshouses belonging to the Fishmongers' Company. There were two separate buildings. One, St. Peter's Hospital, was built by the company in 1615–18; the other, due to the munificence of Mr. James Hulbert, a liveryman, dated its erection from 1719. These almshouses were quaint, old-fashioned, quadrangular piles of building, of Gothic architecture, with mullioned windows; they were enclosed by low walls, and in part surrounded by patches of garden-ground, sunk below the roadway. They appear to have been, from the first, in part supported by a voluntary appropriation, by the Company of Fishmongers,

of a portion of the revenues of Sir Thomas Kneseworth's estate; but the earliest benefaction which can be considered as a specific endowment, and which seems to have given occasion to the erection of the hospital, was that by Sir Thomas Hunt, who, " by will [April 26, 1615], gave out of his land in Kent (or Kentish) Street, Southwark, £20 a year to the poor of the Company of Fishmongers, on condition that the company should build an hospital, containing houses for six poor freemen, and to have the houses rent free, and a yearly sum of 40s. a-piece, to be paid quarterly; and every of them, on St. Thomas's Day, to have a gown of three yards of good cloth, of 8s. a yard, and also 6s. in money to make it up; that if any alms-man should die, and leave a wife, so long as she should continue a widow, she should have her dwelling free, but if she should marry, she should not tarry there; and 40s. and a yearly gown should go to some honest brother of the company, who should wear the gown at times convenient, with the donor's arms on it, and the dolphin at its top."

William Hunt, Esq., son of the above-mentioned Sir Thomas, in accomplishment of his father's will, executed two several grants of annuities of £20 each, dated 16th of November, 1618, issuing from cottages and lands in Kent Street, which annuities were granted "To the governors of St. Peter's Hospital, founded by the wardens and commonalty of the Mystery of Fishmongers."

In 1616 Mr. Robert Spencer gave £50 towards erecting twelve or more almshouses for the company's poor; and in the following year, on mention of Hunt's legacy and Spencer's donation, and an estimate by the wardens that twelve dwellings could be erected for £400, the court of the company consented to the erecting thereof, " with all convenient speed;" and they obtained, on petition, from James I., dated October 2, 1618, permission to erect and establish the said almshouses, to be called "St. Peter's Hospital," and the court of the company to be incorporated by the name of " the Governors of St. Peter's Hospital, founded by the wardens and company of the Mystery of Fishmongers of the City of London," &c., with a common seal, power to hold lands, &c., and to make statutes for the government of the said hospital. The court ordered (November 23rd, 1618) that thirteen poor men and women should be placed in the hospital at the next Christmas, six of them being pursuant to Hunt's will. Each of them were to receive so much money weekly as, with the company's alms and Hunt's legacy, should make their pensions two shillings weekly.

By degrees more houses were added to those

originally built, and the whole building as it stood, down to the time of its demolition, consisting of twenty-two dwellings, a chapel, and a hall, was finished in 1636, as appeared by an inscription on the east front of the hall. The windows of the hall were enriched with painted glass, and over the chimney-piece were the arms, supporters, crest, and motto of the Fishmongers' Company. St. Peter's Hospital is now located at Wandsworth.

At the beginning of the seventeenth century there was in this parish a theatre, in which the Lord Admiral's and Lord Chamberlain's "servants" performed. This theatre was occasionally used by the players from the "Globe" at Bankside, in Shakespeare's time.* The exact site of the above-mentioned theatre is not known, but it was probably very near to the spot where now stands the "Elephant and Castle" Theatre, on the south

NEWINGTON BUTTS IN 1820.

Hulbert's Almshouses were erected on a piece of ground belonging to the Fishmongers' Company, lying on the south side of St. Peter's Hospital. It was a neat and imposing little pile, consisting of three courts with gardens behind, together with a dining-hall and chapel, and a statue of the founder on a pedestal in the centre of the enclosure.

In the high road between the "Elephant and Castle" and Kennington Park stood the old Newington Grammar School, with the date 1666 over the door, but is now removed.

There was formerly a hospital of Our Lady and St. Catherine at Newington, which continued till the year 1551, when their proctor, William Cley-brooke, being dispossessed of his home, was fortunate enough to obtain a licence to beg!

side of the New Kent Road, near the railway station.

At a short distance westward of the Fishmongers' Almshouses, near to West Square, on the south side of St. George's Road, formerly stood the tall boarded structure represented in our illustration on page 256. It served for some time the purposes of a semaphore telegraph tower.

Nearly opposite the "Elephant and Castle," and on part of the ground formerly occupied by the Fishmongers' Almshouses, stands the Metropolitan Tabernacle—better known as "Spurgeon's Chapel,"—the first stone of which was laid by Sir Samuel Morton Peto in August, 1859. The edifice, which

* See *ante*, p. 50.

ALCOVE IN GARDEN.

THE FISHMONGERS' ALMSHOUSES IN 1850.

is upwards of 140 feet long, 80 feet broad, and 60 feet high, is approached at the eastern end by a flight of steps which extend the whole width of the building. The principal entrances are beneath a noble portico, the entablature and pediment of which are supported by six lofty Corinthian columns. The chapel contains some 5,500 sittings of all kinds. There is room for 6,000 persons without excessive crowding; and there are also a lecture-hall capable of holding about 900, a school-room for 1,000 children, six class-rooms, "kitchen, lavatory, and retiring-rooms below stairs." Besides these the building contains "a ladies' room for working meetings, a young men's class-room, and a secretary's room on the ground floor; three vestries, for pastor, deacons, and elders on the first floor; and three store-rooms on the second floor."

As we have already had occasion to state,* the congregation for whom this edifice was erected, met originally in New Park Street Chapel, South-wark. In the month of December, 1853, Mr. Charles Haddon Spurgeon, being then nineteen years of age, preached there for the first time. It may not be out of place here to say a few words about the career of so eminent a preacher as Mr. Spurgeon. Born at Kelvedon, in Essex, in June, 1834, he was educated at Colchester, and as youth advanced he became usher in a school at New-market. "Some of his relatives who were Inde-pendents," as we gather from "Men of the Time," "proposed that he should enter one of their colleges, and undergo a training for the ministry. But his own convictions were in favour of other views; and accordingly he joined the church formerly presided over by the late Robert Hall, at Cambridge. From this period he became almost entirely a village preacher and tract distributor. At Teversham, a village near Cambridge, Mr. Spurgeon, under the designation of 'the Boy Preacher,' delivered his first sermon; and shortly afterwards he was invited to become pastor at a small Baptist chapel at Waterbeach. The invitation was accepted. The lad of seventeen soon became a celebrated character; the barn at Waterbeach was filled with auditors, while listening crowds contented themselves with the sound of his voice from the outside. Invitations to preach were sent to him from the surrounding places. His fame reached London; and the church at New Park Street, in Southwark, whose pulpit had in former days been occupied by Dr. Rippon, now courted his favours. This call being accepted, Mr. Spurgeon made his first appearance before a London congre-

gation in 1853, with so much success, that ere two years had passed away it was considered necessary to enlarge the building, pending which alteration he officiated for four months at Exeter Hall; and that edifice was always so crowded, that hundreds were turned away from the doors. The enlarge-ment of Park Street Chapel, however, proved to be insufficient. His hearers multiplied so rapidly that it became expedient to engage the Surrey Music Hall. A lamentable accident, however, having occurred within its walls in October, 1856, his followers erected for him a handsome new chapel in the Kennington Road, which was publicly opened in 1861." During the first seven years of Mr. Spurgeon's ministry in London, and in con-sequence of his untiring perseverance, upwards of £31,000 had been subscribed for the building, and the structure was accordingly opened free of debt.

During the short time that Mr. Spurgeon occupied the platform at Exeter Hall, paragraphs appeared in the newspapers announcing that "the Strand was blocked up by crowds who gathered to hear a young man in Exeter Hall." Remarks of no very flattering character appeared in various journals, and the multitude was thereby increased. Carica-tures adorned the printsellers' windows; among them one entitled "Catch-'em-alive-O!" wherein the popular preacher was depicted with his head surmounted by one of those peculiarly-prepared sheets of fly-paper known by that name, to which were adhering or fluttering all sorts of winged characters—from the Lord Chancellor down to Mrs. Gamp—and in the most ridiculous attitudes; Mr. Spurgeon's name, too, continued to be made more and more known by pamphlets and letters in the papers, which all tended to swell the crowd. As we shall have more to say of Mr. Spurgeon and his preaching presently, when dealing with the music-hall in the Surrey Gardens, we will only add here that in treating of the hostility which the Puritans and Nonconformists have always shown to the stage, M. Alphonse Esquiros remarks in his "English at Home," that "one of the fiercest diatribes against the dramatic art was lately (1862) uttered by Mr. Spurgeon;" and he adds, "As Mr. Spurgeon is an eloquent preacher, but borrows several of his best effects from theatrical action, it has been asked whether a little professional jealousy has not been mixed up with his attacks." It would seem, however, as if there were no limits to Mr. Spurgeon's popularity, as was shown on the occasion of his 50th birthday, in 1884.

In connection with the Metropolitan Tabernacle are some almshouses and schools; a college

* See *ante*, p. 29.

for training young men for the Nonconformist ministry; and an orphanage at Stockwell.

At a short distance beyond the Metropolitan Tabernacle, down to the close of the year 1875, the roadway running southward was considerably narrowed, and formed an awkward bend, by the inconvenient position of the old parish church of St. Mary, Newington, the eastern end of which closely abutted on the roadway. The extent of St. Mary's parish is thus set forth in the "New View of London" (1708):—"Beginning at the windmill near Mr. Bowyer's by Camberwell, and two fields thence westward and to Kennington Common, it extends northward from thence to Newington Church, and thence both sides of the road to the Fishmongers' Almshouses exclusive: and then on the easterly side of the way to the turning to Kent Street, with all the western side of that street to the Lock; then they pass, in walking the bounds, through Walworth Field and Common, and thence to the said windmill again: in which circuit is contained the number of 620 dwelling houses."

Not only Lysons, as we have already mentioned, but also other writers on the churches of Surrey, have stated that St. Mary's Church stood at some distance farther eastward, or have at all events expressed some difference of opinion upon the subject. Dr. H. C. Barlow, in an article in the *Builder* in May, 1874, endeavours to prove that the original site of the church—that, at least, of the Domesday Record—was where the fabric stood down to the time of its recent removal. Dr. Barlow writes:—"By means of an old document, found some years ago among my grandfather's papers—a copy of a *terrier* of the glebe lands, houses, &c., made in 1729, and of which he took a copy in 1799, when Rector's Warden—I am enabled to demonstrate that the church, since the Norman Conquest, has never changed its situation. In that portion of Domesday Book which relates to Surrey, there is a description of the manor of Waleorde (Walworth), where it is said there is a church with eight acres of meadow-land. The first mention of Neweton (Newington) occurs in the Testa de Nevil (*sive Liber Feodorum in Curia Saccarii*), of the time of Henry III., or the first half of the thirteenth century; it is there stated that the queen's goldsmith holds of the king, *in capite*, one acre of land in Neweton, by the service of rendering a gallon of honey. In the taxation of spiritualities made by Pope Nicholas IV., in 1292, the church is spoken of as being at Newington; and in the Archbishop of Canterbury's Register, 1313, the parish is called Newington *juxta* London.

"The living was a rectory, then in the archbishop's gift, and of increasing value. In the time of King Edward the Confessor it was worth only xxx. *solidi*, but when the Domesday Survey was made it was worth double that sum. The manor, on the contrary, was becoming of less importance. The first notice we have of it is that Edmund Ironside gave it to Hitard, his jester, who, on going to Rome, gave it to Christ Church, Canterbury. In King Edward's time it was taxed for five hides (500 acres), but at the time of the survey, for three hides and a half only, nearly one-third less. After the thirteenth century we hear no more of the church at Walworde; from that time the church is said to be at Newington. The question, therefore, is, did the original church stand at Walworth, and was subsequently moved to Newington, or did it only change its name with the new name given to the parish? Lysons, who wrote, in 1791, 'Environs of London,' suggests that the church might have been rebuilt on a new site, and becoming surrounded by houses, the locality received the name of Neweton, or Newtown, subsequently Newington. But this suggestion is a mere hypothesis. Where churches have been first built there is a general disposition on the part of ecclesiastics to retain them; the pious commonly desire to worship God where their forefathers knelt before them, and it is the duty of the clergy to encourage this sentiment. In those days there were no London improvements required at Newington to endanger the sacred fabric and change its hallowed locality. When churches need rebuilding, it has been the rule in England to rebuild them where they stood before, and I shall be able to show that the church at Walworde, otherwise Newington, was no exception to this laudable practice.

"The words of Domesday record are—'*Ibi Ecclesia et* viii. *acræ prati.*' These eight acres of meadow-land were attached to the church, and formed the church field. They were also contiguous to the manor, which was of large extent, and in King Edward's time, consisting of 500 acres, occupied nearly the whole of the present parish, which contains only 630 acres, including Walworth Common. Even the 350 acres, the extent of the manor at the time of the Conquest, supposing the present manor-house to stand near the site of the original one, and to indicate the probable centre of the manor, would bring the situation of Newington Church within the full meaning of the words '*Ibi Ecclesia et* viii. *acræ prati.*' The old church at Newington had a low square tower of flint and rag-stone, similar to other church towers in Surrey that date from the fourteenth century, or somewhat earlier, and its becoming surrounded with houses was comparatively a recent event.

"Manning and Bray, in their great history of Surrey, have no hesitation in considering Waleorde (Walworth), still the name of the manor, to be the same as Newington; and the Rev. Mr. Hussey, in his account of the churches in Surrey, remarks, if this be so, then the Domesday church was at Newington, not at Walworth. The Domesday church was where the eight acres of meadow-land were, and these were at Newington.

"Among the items contained in the *terrier* of the glebe lands, &c., made in 1729, when the Rev. Wm. Taswell was rector, is one which begins as follows:—'*Item.* On the south side of the churchyard there lies a parcel of pasture and meadow ground, called the church-field, in the occupation of the Widow Harwood, containing about seven and a-half acres. This church-field formerly contained eight acres, but in the year 1648, part of it, containing in length about two hundred yards, and in breadth about four yards, was taken out of it to make a footway leading from Newington to the east end of Kinnington Lane; and in the year 1718, the trustees for mending and repairing the road from Newington to Vauxhall took about fourteen feet in breadth, and about forty-eight feet in length, from the church-field aforesaid, to widen the road turning from Newington to Kinnington, which road was before so narrow, that two waggons could not meet there. . . . .'

"The *terrier* also states that two small pieces of the church-field were taken, one about 1637, and the other in 1665, to enlarge the churchyard. There can be no manner of doubt, therefore, but

that the church, with its eight acres of meadow-land, recorded in 'Domesday Book,' was one and the same with the church at Newington, and that we may say of the latter, as the record says of the former, '*Ibi Ecclesia et* viii. *acræ prati*,' though it would now be impossible to find any portion of the latter which has not been brought into subjection under the despotic law of the spread of bricks and mortar."

The old parish church of Newington appears to have been, in earlier days, a very small and insignificant structure; Sir Hugh Brawne added a north aisle about the year 1600. In the early part of the last century several hundred pounds were expended in repairing and "ornamenting" the fabric; but this was all to very little purpose, for in a few years it was found necessary that the whole building, except the tower, should be taken down. The new church, on the same inconvenient spot, by the side of a great road, was opened in March,

FOUNTAIN IN THE SURREY GARDENS.

1721. Being found inadequate to the increased number of inhabitants, an Act of Parliament was obtained in 1790 for rebuilding the church upon a larger scale. The work of reconstruction was commenced in the following year, and completed in about two years. The unsightly structure was constructed of brick, with a portico in the west front, and on the roof was a small bell-turret.

In this church, according to Manning and Bray's "History of Surrey," was buried a certain facetious individual, Mr. Serjeant Davy, who died in 1780, and of whom a good story is told. He was originally a chemist at Exeter; and a sheriff's officer coming to serve on him a process from the Court of Common Pleas, he civilly asked him if he would not take something to drink. While the man was leisurely quenching his thirst Davy contrived to heat the poker, and then told the bailiff that if he did not eat the writ, which was of sheepskin, he should be made to swallow the poker. The officer very naturally preferred the parchment; but the Court of Common Pleas, not being then accustomed to Davy's jokes, sent him an order to appear at Westminster Hall, and committed him to the Fleet Prison for contempt. From this strange circumstance he acquired his first taste for the law. On his discharge from prison he applied himself to the study of it in earnest, was called to the bar, obtained the coif, and enjoyed a good practice for many years.

Here, too, was buried Thomas Middleton, author of the *Mask of Cupid; A Mad World, my Masters;* the *Spanish Gipsy; Anything for a Quiet Life*, and very many other comedies, besides sundry less well-known tragedies. He died in July, 1627; and his widow, who followed him to the grave next year, was buried at the expense of the Corporation of London, who had employed her husband to write the *Mask of Cupid*, performed with other "solemnities" at Merchant Taylors' Hall, to commemorate the marriage of the infamous Earl and Countess of Somerset.

On the floor of the old church was, among others, the grave-stone of George Powell, who is said, by the editor of "Aubrey's Perambulations of Surrey," to have been styled "King of the Gipsies," and to have died in the year 1704, in very flourishing circumstances—in fact, as rich, or rather as poor, as a king.

The churchyard, which was enlarged by Act of Parliament in the reign of George II., contains among its numerous monuments one to the memory of William Allen, a young man who was killed by the firing of the soldiers in the riots which took place in St. George's Fields, in 1768, on the occasion of the confinement of John Wilkes in the King's Bench Prison; around the monument are several inscriptions expressing strong political feelings.

"The most eminent ecclesiastic who ever held this rectory," writes Thomas Allen, in his "History of Surrey," "was Dr. Samuel Horsley, who was presented to it in 1759. This eminent character was born in the parish of St. Martin-in-the-Fields, in October, 1733. He was educated at Westminster School, and Trinity Hall, Cambridge, where he took the degree of LL.B. In 1767 he was chosen a Fellow of the Royal Society, and he soon after published some elaborate treatises. In 1768 he took the degree of LL.D., and in 1773 he was elected secretary to the Royal Society, and not long after the Earl of Aylesford presented him to the rectory of Aldbury, in this county. About 1784 Dr. Horsley withdrew from the Royal Society, and about the same period commenced a literary conference with the great champion of Unitarianism, Dr. Priestley. The talent and energy with which he exerted himself called forth the approbation of Lord Chancellor Thurlow, who characteristically remarked that 'those who defended the Church ought to be supported by the Church,' and accordingly presented him to a prebendal stall in Gloucester Cathedral, and shortly after he was made Bishop of St. David's. In his episcopal character he supported the reputation for learning and ability which he had previously acquired. In Parliament he was the strenuous advocate for the existing state of things in religion and politics; and the merit of his conduct will accordingly be differently appreciated with reference to the various opinions of different persons. His zeal did not go unrewarded, for he was presented to the see of Rochester in 1793, and made Dean of Westminster; and in 1802 he was translated to St. Asaph. He died at Brighton, October 4, 1806, and was interred in St. Mary's Church, Newington."

In this church was baptised, about the year 1810, George Alexander Gratton, a spotted negro boy, who was shown about London and the provinces as a curiosity by Richardson. He died when only five years old, in February, 1813, and was buried at Great Marlow, where there is a monument to his memory.

In 1871, it was proposed by the Board of Works, under the Metropolitan Improvements Act, to have the church removed, with the view of widening the roadway at that point, and an offer of £5,000 was made by the Board for that special purpose. In 1875 a grant of £4,000 was obtained from the London Churches Fund, and a subscription, headed by the rector with £1,000, was opened among the parishioners for the remainder of the money required, about £9,000. A site for a new church was obtained from the Ecclesiastical Commissioners, in a more central part of the parish, on the east side of the Kennington Park Road. This church, a large and lofty Gothic edifice of stone, having been completed, with the exception of the tower, the demolition of the old church was forthwith commenced. In 1876 the materials of the old edifice were disposed of by public auction, and realised a sum of £538. The remains of some five hundred persons were carefully removed from the churchyard, and re-interred in a vault built for the purpose. In one instance two bodies were taken from under the altar, and the inscriptions on the coffins showed that they were the remains of Dr. Horsley and his wife, the latter of whom died in 1805. The remains were in a state of preservation, having been buried some fifteen feet below the surface. They were removed to Thorley, in Herts, by the family of the deceased bishop. Among the other remains which were disinterred there was the skeleton of a man who had been buried in a complete suit of black, the coat and boots being perfect.

Besides the old church several houses in the High Street close by were demolished at the same time, and the graveyard, thus curtailed by the widening of the road, was set in order and opened to the public as a garden. The whole is enclosed by some neat iron railings and gates; and a hand-

of a position in which it can be well seen, cost the donor £5,000.

The old parsonage-house, which stood in the rear of the church and of Mr. Spurgeon's "Tabernacle," and which was reputed to date from the sixteenth century, was built of wood, and surrounded at one time by a moat, over which were several bridges. The land in the immediate neighbourhood was formerly intersected by numerous ditches, some of

OLD NEWINGTON CHURCH IN 1866.

some Gothic clock-tower has been erected on the site of the church. This tower is fourteen feet square at the base, and carried up in five stages with buttresses to a height of about a hundred feet. The clock-face is placed at the height of seventy feet. In the lower part of the building the material is Portland stone, the remainder being of Bath stone, and the front to Newington Butts, as well as the two sides, is enriched with carvings in florid Gothic. There is a doorway in the centre of the front, with windows in the upper part. On the left side of the doorway is the following inscription: —"This tower was built at the expense of Robert Faulconer, Esq., Anno Domini 1877, on the site of the old parish church of St. Mary's, Newington." This handsome gift, which has the great advantage

which existed till quite recent times. They ran in various directions, completely surrounding the rectory grounds. To reach the "Queen's Head" tea-gardens, which occupied the site of the present National Schoolroom, it was necessary to cross some of these ditches by a small wooden bridge. The tea-gardens were in a line with Temple Street, at the western end of the Metropolitan Tabernacle. Indeed, so well watered was the neighbourhood of Newington Butts, that, if we may believe tradition, in 1571 occurred a great flood, so that the people were obliged to be conveyed in boats from the church "to the pinfolds, near St. George's, in Southwark."

Among the residents of Newington in the middle of the last century, was James Short, an eminent optician, and a native of Edinburgh. He enjoyed a high reputation in his day for the excellence of his reflecting telescopes, of the Gregorian kind, by the sale of which he amassed a large fortune. He died at Newington in 1768.

On the east side of Kennington Park Road, and soon after obtained possession of the grounds formerly attached to the 'Manor House' at Walworth. The grounds comprised in all about fifteen acres, which were utilised to their fullest extent, exclusive of a sheet of water covering nearly three acres more. The gardens were approached from

THE MUSIC HALL, SURREY GARDENS, 1858.

near the junction of that thoroughfare with Kennington Lane and Newington Butts, is Penton Place, through which is one of the approaches to the Surrey Gardens, formerly known as the Surrey Zoological Gardens. This place of entertainment, which has undergone many vicissitudes, is thus described by a writer in the *Era* Almanack for 1871 :—

"When Exeter Change ceased to exist, the then proprietor, Mr. Edward Cross, removed his menagerie to the King's Mews at Charing Cross,

Manor Place, Walworth, and there was a second entrance from Penton Place, Kennington Road. The large conservatory, three hundred feet in circumference, and containing upwards of 6,000 feet of glass, was at that time the largest building of its kind in England. This was afterwards used to enclose the cages of the lions, tigers, and other carnivora. In the year 1834 was exhibited here a one-horned Indian rhinoceros, for which Cross paid £800; two years later three giraffes were added to his collection. The first picture was 'Mount Vesuvius,' painted by Danson, in 1837, the lake representing the Bay of Naples, and a display of fireworks serving vividly to illustrate the eruption, which was nightly repeated in the presence of admiring crowds, and served as the chief attraction of the place for upwards of two years. Then followed, in 1839, a representation of 'Iceland and Mount Hecla;' in 1841, the 'City of Rome,' which occupied five acres, and was painted on a surface upwards of 250,000 feet square; in 1843, the 'Temple of Ellora;' in 1844, 'London during the Great Fire of 1666;' in 1845, the 'City of Edinburgh.' In 1846 'Vesuvius' was reproduced; in 1848 there was a revival of 'Rome;' in 1849 there was the 'Storming of Badajoz,' with 'new effects of real ordnance.' In this same year M. Jullien organised a series of promenade concerts on four evenings in each week, the admission remaining fixed, as before, at a shilling. The fireworks were always a great attraction of the gardens. In 1850 was exhibited 'Napoleon's Passage over the Alps;' in this picture were represented some fifty thousand men in motion, who, in the front, appeared of life-size, and who, in fact, were living men, but who were made, by an optical illusion, to dwindle gradually at different distances to the veriest specks which the eye could track along the zigzag line of ascent towards the summit of the Alpine Pass, where stood the monastery of St. Bernard, ready to receive the weary and half-frozen troops and their imperial master. On the death of Mr. Cross the proprietorship and management of the gardens devolved on his secretary and assistant, a man named Tyler, who conducted them for some years, when the property became vested in a Limited Liability Company. In 1856 the gardens were put up to auction, and the Surrey Music Hall was erected upon a portion of the grounds. The gardens were used in 1856 for the purpose of entertaining the Guards with a public dinner after their return from the Crimea; and again, in 1862, they were re-opened with a picture of the 'City and Bay of Naples,' showing Vesuvius in the distance. But the fitful taste of the public did not care for the revival; and though a variety of fresh amusements in succession was announced and provided, yet it was found that the place had lost its popularity to a degree which was irretrievable, and accordingly the gardens were closed. The grounds were afterwards more advantageously occupied, as the temporary Hospital of St. Thomas, before its removal to Lambeth Walk."

The principal walks and avenues were planted with every description of native and exotic forest trees that would endure the climate; whilst the beautiful sheet of water, mentioned above, was spotted with islands, shrubberies, and plantations of great richness. Numerous rustic-looking buildings, with thatched roofs, were to be seen in different parts, each of them adding to the picturesqueness of the grounds. Mr. Loudon, the editor of the *Gardeners' Magazine*, thus speaks of the buildings these gardens at the time of their opening:—

"The London Zoological Society has certainly the merit of taking the lead in this description of garden; but Mr. Cross has not only proceeded more rapidly than they have done, but has erected more suitable and more imposing structures than are yet to be found in the gardens in the Regent's Park. What is there, for example, in the latter garden which can be at all compared with the circular glass building 300 feet in diameter, combining a series of examples of tropical quadrupeds and birds, and of exotic plants? In the plan of this building the animals (lions, tigers, leopards, &c.) are kept in separate cages or compartments towards the centre; exterior to them is a colonnade, supporting the glazed roof, and also for cages of birds; within this colonnade will be placed hot-water pipes for heating the whole, and beyond it is an open paved area for spectators; next, there is a channel for a stream of water, intended for gold, silver, and other exotic fishes; and, beyond, a border, under the front wall, for climbing plants, to be trained on wires under the roof."

The grounds were laid out under the superintendence of Mr. Henry Phillips, the author of "Sylva Florifera," and it is almost impossible to give the reader an idea of their beauty and variety. Besides the large glass building mentioned above, there were several movable aviaries and cages for the feathered tribes; whilst one of the prettiest spots was the "beaver-dam," a small pond partly enclosed by rockwork. Altogether, at one time these gardens offered a great rival attraction to those at the Regent's Park, which we have already described.* In 1834 a live female gorilla was added to this menagerie, and proved a great favourite of the visitors. The collection here was not so extensive as that in the Regent's Park, but some of the animals were much finer, particularly one of the lions.

A story—we fear rather apocryphal—is told of one of the lions here in the early part of their existence. A small black spaniel being thrown into his cage, instead of killing and eating it, the king of beasts took it under his protection, fondled it, and played with it; and when it died, the lion was so deeply grieved that he survived the loss of his companion only a few days!

The volcanic exhibitions at the Surrey Zoological Gardens probably had their origin in the Ranelagh spectacles of the last century; for in 1792 was shown in the latter gardens a beautiful representation of Mount Etna, with the flowing of the lava

---

* See Vol. V., p. 282.

down its sides. The height of the boarded work which represented the mountain was about eighty feet, and the whole exhibited a curious specimen of machinery and pyrotechnics. Of the Surrey Gardens, as they existed in the year of grace 1850, Mr. H. Mayhew wrote, " Mount Etna, the fashionable volcano of the season, just now is vomiting here its sky-rockets and Roman candles."

During the last few years of their existence, these gardens added the attractions of music. A large covered orchestra, capable of accommodating a large number of performers, was fitted up on the margin of the lake, for the purpose of giving open-

his first sudden rush into popularity in London; and on the first occasion of holding these services, —the evening of October 19, 1856—it was the scene of a serious and fatal accident, seven persons being killed by a false alarm of fire raised by some reckless and wanton jesters. We have already spoken of Mr. Spurgeon in our account of the Metropolitan Tabernacle, but we may further remark here that, notwithstanding the above-mentioned occurrence, large numbers continued for the space of three years to hear Mr. Spurgeon on Sunday mornings. A letter, signed " *Habitans in Sicco*," and dated from " Broad Phylactery, West-

VIEW IN THE SURREY GARDENS, 1850.

air concerts on a gigantic scale; and this was retained during the summer months by Jullien's band. Jullien led the orchestra at the concerts here in 1851, the year of the Great Exhibition.

The Surrey Music Hall, mentioned above—a large oblong building—is admirably adapted for the purposes for which it was built. At each corner are octagonal towers containing staircases, originally crowned by ornamental turrets. An arcade surrounds the ground-floor, whilst to the first and second floors are external galleries covered by verandas. The great hall, which holds 12,000 persons, exclusive of the orchestra, cost upwards of £18,000. It is twenty feet longer and thirty feet wider than the Great Room at Exeter Hall.

On Sundays it was used temporarily for the religious services held by Mr. C. H. Spurgeon, on

minster," appeared at this period in the *Times;* part of it ran as follows :—" ' I want to hear Spurgeon; let us go.' Now, I am supposed to be a High Churchman, so I answered, ' What! go and hear a Calvinist—a Baptist !—a man who ought to be ashamed of himself for being so near the Church, and yet not within its pale ?' ' Never mind; come and hear him.' Well, we went yesterday morning to the Music Hall, in the Surrey Gardens. . . . . Fancy a congregation consisting of 10,000 souls, streaming into the hall, mounting the galleries, humming, buzzing, and swarming—a mighty hive of bees—eager to secure at first the best places, and, at last, any place at all. After waiting more than half an hour—for if you wish to have a seat you must be there at least that space of time in advance—Mr.

Spurgeon ascended his tribune. To the hum, and rush, and trampling of men, succeeded a low, concentrated thrill and murmur of devotion, which seemed to run at once, like an electric current, through the breast of every one present, and by this magnetic chain the preacher held us fast bound for about two hours. It is not my purpose to give a summary of his discourse. It is enough to say of his voice, that its power and volume are sufficient to reach every one in that vast assembly; of his language, that it is neither high-flown nor homely; of his style, that it is at times familiar, at times declamatory, but always happy, and often eloquent; of his doctrine, that neither the 'Calvinist' nor the 'Baptist' appears in the forefront of the battle which is waged by Mr. Spurgeon with relentless animosity, and with Gospel weapons, against irreligion, cant, hypocrisy, pride, and those secret bosom-sins which so easily beset a man in daily life; and to sum up all in a word, it is enough to say of the man himself, that he impresses you with a perfect conviction of his sincerity. But I have not written so much about my children's want of spiritual food when they listened to the mumbling of the Archbishop of ——, and my own banquet at the Surrey Gardens, without a desire to draw a practical conclusion from these two stories, and to point them by a moral. Here is a man not more Calvinistic than many an incumbent of the Established Church who 'humbles and mumbles,' as old Latimer says, over his liturgy and text—here is a man who says the complete immersion, or something of the kind, of adults, is necessary to baptism. These are his faults of doctrine; but if I were the examining chaplain of the Archbishop of ——, I would say, ' May it please your grace, here is a man able to preach eloquently, able to fill the largest church in England with his voice, and, what is more to the purpose, with people. And may it please your grace, here are two churches in the metropolis, St. Paul's and Westminster Abbey. What does your grace think of inviting Mr. Spurgeon, this heretical Calvinist and Baptist, who is able to draw 10,000 souls after him, just to try his voice, some Sunday morning, in the nave of either of those churches?'"

In June, 1861, shortly after being vacated by Mr. Spurgeon, the Music Hall was destroyed by fire. It was, however, rebuilt, and for a time was occupied as a temporary hospital during the demolition of St. Thomas's Hospital at London Bridge and the erection of the new building near Westminster Bridge.

The old Manor House of Walworth is kept in remembrance by Manor Road and Manor Place, the last-named thoroughfare uniting Penton Place with Walworth Road. Close by, in Penrose Street, is a commodious lecture-hall, built in 1862, under the auspices of the Walworth Mechanics' Institute. This institution was founded in 1845, in Manor Place, and is the only literary and scientific institution on a large scale on the south side of the Thames; the library contains some 5,000 volumes, and it has a reading-room in the Walworth Road.

Since the commencement of the present century a considerable advance has been made in the way of buildings in this neighbourhood, particularly on the east side of the Walworth Road. Lock's Fields, formerly a dreary swamp, and Walworth Common, which was at one time an open field, have been covered with houses. In Paragon Row the Fishmongers' Company have erected several model dwellings, with the aim of benefiting a very poor locality. The dwellings have been built on the "flat" system, realising as nearly as possible the idea of the cottage character, and replacing old and dilapidated houses of an inferior class.

Whatever this locality may be in the present day, it has not been without its places of amusement in former times, for we learn from Colburn's "Kalendar of Amusements" for 1840, that the Marylebone and Oxford cricket clubs played a match in that year at the "Beehive" grounds, Walworth.

In 1823 the first stone of St. Peter's Church, Walworth, was laid by the Archbishop of Canterbury, immediately after the performance of the like ceremony at Trinity Church, in this parish.* The church, which is situated at a short distance on the eastern side of the Walworth Road, is built of brick, with the exception of the steeple and architectural ornaments, which are constructed of stone. The basement is occupied by spacious catacombs.

St. John's Church, which stands a short distance backward on the eastern side of the Walworth Road, near York Street, is a lofty and handsome Gothic building, in the Decorated style, and was erected in 1865, at a cost of upwards of £5,000. It was endowed by the Dean and Chapter of Canterbury, who are the patrons.

Walworth is not entirely devoid of historical memorabilia, if tradition is to be trusted; a native of this village—for such it must have been in his day—was William Walworth, the celebrated Lord Mayor of London, who slew Wat Tyler with his own hand, and who, in memory of the deed, caused a dagger to be added to the arms of the City.

---

* See ante, p. 253.

CHAPTER XXI.

CAMBERWELL.

" Hæ latebræ dulces, et jam, si credis, amœnæ."—Horace.

Antiquity of the Parish—Its Etymology—Its Condition at the Time of the Conquest—Descent of the Manor—Sir Thomas Bond's House—The Bowyer Family—Bowyer Lane, now Wyndham Road—The Royal Flora Gardens—St. Giles's Church—The Burial-place of Mrs. Wesley, and of " Equality " Brown—Camden Chapel—St. George's Church—The Vestry Hall—Camberwell Green—Camberwell Fair—Abolition of the Fair, and the Green converted into a Park—The " Father Redcap"—The Old House on the Green—The Green Coat and National Schools—The Camberwell Free Grammar School—The Aged Pilgrims' Friend Asylum—Rural Character of Camberwell in the Last Century —Myatt's Farm—Cold Harbour Lane—Denmark Hill Grammar School—Grove Hill and Dr. Lettsom's Residence there—The Story of George Barnwell—Grove Hall—The " Fox-under-the-Hill "—Old Families of Camberwell—Tom Hood a Resident here—Camberwell Lunatic Asylum.

CAMBERWELL is now so truly part and parcel of the metropolis that it would be impossible to write an account of London south of the Thames without some notice of its past and present history. No one, we are told, can assert at what period the parish became an inhabited spot. Local antiquaries find pleasure in tracking the path of the Roman conquerors of Britain across the hills and valleys which surround the metropolis. Their legions, as we know, had various camps in the neighbourhood of Londinium, and it is not improbable that they formed one on the pretty hill, known in later days as Ladlands, or Primrose Hill, best reached from Camberwell by way of Dog-kennel Lane, in the southern part of the parish. It must have been a commanding position in those days, when the Thames at high tide expanded into a vast lake, reaching to the base of the rounded Surrey hills, near which were marshes inhabited by bitterns, herons, and other waterfowl. Herne Hill, in this neighbourhood, by the way, is thought by some to have been originally Heron Hill, "heron" being the old orthography.

Coming down to times the history of which is more defined and authentic, we find Camberwell mentioned in Domesday Book as a manor of some value. The name is written "Ca'brewelle," and the adjoining manor, Peckham, is described as " Pecheha." In subsequent records we meet with " Camerwell," " Cambwell," and " Kamwell." Some etymologists trace the first portion of the name to the British *owm hir*, long valley ; and suppose that the last syllable has reference to some springs of water, at one time famous. This may be the case, for there are, or were, mineral springs at Dulwich, Norwood (the Beulah Spa is memorable), and other places in the neighbourhood. It may be added that, as the parish church has been dedicated from Saxon times to St. Giles, the especial patron of cripples, it has been suggested that there were certain springs in the neighbourhood possessing salutary virtues for persons so afflicted ; and that as the old British word *cam* signifies " crooked," Camberwell may simply mean

"the well of the crooked." Within the last century or so three ancient wells were discovered in a field in the parish, but they were covered in again by the owner of the land.

At the time of the Conquest, Camberwell is described as being " large and well inhabited." Its inhabitants were cottars and men of a lower grade, ceorls or churls. There was so much wood and waste ground in the neighbourhood that the lord of the manor had paid to him a rent of sixty fat hogs, which were fed on the beech-masts and acorns which abounded in the neighbourhood. There were, besides, sixty-three acres of meadow-land, and, as we have said, a church. In the Saxon times there was but one manor here, which was held of Edward the Confessor by Haims, " Viscount," or Count Depute, of Brixton Hundred, or, as some writers have it, Sheriff of Surrey. Somewhat later we hear of the manor of Pecheha, or Peckham, being granted to William's half-brother, Odo, Bishop of Bayeux, who sub-let to the Bishop of Lisieux. There were also other manors of Bretynghurst, Dovedale (D'Ovedale, or Dowdale), Camberwell, Frierne, Basyng, Hatcham, Cold Herbergh, and Milkwell. William, Earl of Gloucester, natural son of Henry I., who possessed a portion of the original Camberwell manor, including Peckham, gave the church to the monks of Bermondsey, but the manor remained in the family until the year 1350. Margaret, daughter and heiress of Hugh, the then earl, married Ralph, the first Earl of Stafford, whose descendant became Duke of Buckingham. The manor was then named Camberwell-Buckingham, and remained the property of the family until Edward, Duke of Buckingham, was attainted and beheaded in 1521. After passing through various hands, it was purchased in 1583 by one Edmund Bowyer, whose descendants yet retain a considerable portion of it. The manors of Bretynghurst, Basyng, and Dovedale were so named from their original possessors, and the brethren of the hospital of St. Thomas, Southwark, held the manor of Milkwell, and subsequently granted it to the church of St. Mary Overie.

After the suppression of religious houses it was granted to Sir Thomas Wyatt, who, as we know, was beheaded for his attempted rebellion, in the first year of Queen Mary's reign.

The main road from Kent, intersecting the eastern portion of the parish, was known in the fourteenth century as Bretynghurst or Dredynghurst Road; and afterwards as Kinges Street, because along that thoroughfare the royal and state pro-

Camberwell, as it is now written, was officially and locally recognised. Lysons, in his "Environs of London," writes, "I can find nothing satisfactory with respect to its etymology; the termination seems to point out some remarkable spring; a part of the parish is called Milkwell, and a mineral water was discovered some years ago [1739] near Dulwich." There was formerly a fine brick well on the De Crespigny estate, on Denmark Hill;

OLD CAMBERWELL CHURCH IN 1750.

cessions passed on their way from Kent to London and Westminster.

Camberwell is described by Priscilla Wakefield, in her "Perambulations," published in 1809, as a "pleasant retreat for those citizens who have a taste for the country whilst their avocations daily call them to town."

In the Domesday Book this parish is called "Ca'berwelle." Subsequently the letter *b* was changed, and from the eleventh to the sixteenth century the name of the parish is generally written in official documents as Camwell, Cammerwell, or Camerwell. In the seventeenth century, as Mr. Blanch informs us in his "History of the Parish," the *b* found its way back again; but it was not until the middle of the eighteenth century that

but Dr. Lettsom, whose villa on Grove Hill we shall have occasion to notice presently, laid claim to the honour of possessing in his grounds the identical well from which this parish derived its appellation. Salmon, the Surrey historian, says, "It seems to be named from some mineral water which was anciently in it;" and Bray adopts the same idea. The author of "A Short Historical and Topographical Account of St. Giles's Church"— the parish church of Camberwell—writes, "It has been conjectured that, as the name of St. Giles conveys an idea of cripples, the well which gave part of the name to the village might have been famous for some medicinal virtues, and might have occasioned the dedication of the church to this patron saint of cripples and mendicants." "This interpretation," adds Mr. Blanch, "is not by any means an improbable one, and it assists us somewhat in the solution of the first part of the name. Given the well, it does not call for a violent exercise of our imaginative faculties to suppose it to be 'cambered' over for protection. Again,

Other solutions of the etymology of Camberwell have been advanced. Here is one by the author of "London: How it Grew:"—"All honour to St. Giles, whose miraculous springs gave a name to the spot; unless, indeed, our friends in the parish will accept a theory of our own—that, as Camber

BOWYER HOUSE.

'cam' is a very crooked word, and is applied to anything out of square, or out of condition. Having regard, therefore, to the fact already noticed, that the church is dedicated to the patron saint of cripples, we are certainly justified in assuming the word 'cam' to be in this instance descriptive of individual condition; and the well would then become the well of the 'crooked' or crippled."

was the name of a son of the Trojan Brute who is said to have conquered this tight little island about 4,000 years ago, perhaps that prince discovered the wells, as Prince Bladud did the waters of Bath, and so unwittingly handed his name down to posterity and the panels of omnibuses."

The name of the place is often pronounced as "Camerwell," and is so written by Evelyn. Under date of September 1, 1657, the diarist writes, "I visited Sir Edmund Bowyer at his melancholie seate at *Camerwell*."

Evelyn mentions in his "Diary," in 1685, an urn full of bones, which had been dug up at Camberwell in repairing a highway, being exhibited at a meeting of the Royal Society, for at that date the Society of Antiquaries did not exist; "it was found," he tells us, "entire with its cover, amongst many others believed to be truly Roman and ancient." No doubt, in the present day a more exact account would have been placed on record.

The most ancient part of the village is that which surrounds what till lately was the Green; but the more pleasant and favourite spot is the Grove, which stands high, and commands pleasant views over Dulwich, as we shall presently see. Of the old sites of Camberwell very few now remain. In the sixteenth and seventeenth centuries there were many good houses in the parish. The Scotts, who held the manor of Camberwell, had a noble mansion and fine grounds at the foot of the Grove. The Muschamps, who possessed the Peckham estate, lived in the manor-house near the High Street. The house was pulled down in the reign of Charles II. by Sir Thomas Bond, who, in 1672, built on the site a very fine mansion, surrounded by a tastefully laid-out garden, famed for the number of its foreign fruit-trees, which attracted the notice of John Evelyn, who, it may be presumed, frequently walked over, being a friend of the family, from his residence at Saye's Court.

He speaks of it as "a new and fine house by Peckham." "It stands," he adds, "on a flat; but has a fine garden and prospect through the meadows to London." The house had a north frontage, and was approached under a canopy of stately elms, "at the end of which was a beautiful prospect, terminated by a view of St. Paul's and the Tower of London. The beauties of this prospect were greatly increased by the masts of the ships being seen over the trees as far as Greenwich." The centre of the garden was, it is stated, like "a wilderness"—a name by which the place was known down till the early part of the present century. Bond was a devoted adherent of the Stuarts, and, at the abdication of James II., followed his master to France. His house was plundered by the Whig mob, and his beautiful gardens laid waste. In 1797 the house was pulled down. Many houses built on the site of Sir Thomas Bond's gardens are now known as Hill Street.

The Bowyer family, who occupy a distinguished place in the annals of Camberwell, settled there in the time of Henry VIII. The family mansion, the manor-house of Camberwell-Buckingham, which

stood on the right-hand side of the road from London to Camberwell Green, was built apparently about the reign of Queen Elizabeth. Evelyn, as stated above, in recording a visit paid to Sir Edmund Bowyer, speaks of his mansion as a "melancholie seate." "He has," says the author of "Sylva," "a very pretty grove of oakes, and hedges of yew in his garden, and a handsome row of tall elms before his court." These trees were specially noticeable from the high road. "No vestige of the elms or oaks," says Mr. Blanch, "have been seen by the 'oldest inhabitant,' but a ring of yew-trees stood round the front lawn very recently. It will be noticed," he adds, "that Evelyn says nothing of the fine cedar which, at the beginning of the present century, formed a conspicuous feature to the left of the grand entrance."

There is a tradition that Sir Christopher Wren resided here during the rebuilding of St. Paul's Cathedral, and that some of the frescoes with which the rooms were adorned were painted by Sir James Thornhill. It is also asserted that James II. was concealed here for some time previous to his escape.

Early in the present century much of the beauty of the interior of Bowyer House was destroyed, the owner removing several choice carvings and ornaments. A substantial wall and iron railings were erected about the same time. Later on, the old mansion became tenanted by the Camberwell Literary and Scientific Institution; and it was subsequently converted into a school for young ladies. The house was pulled down in 1861, on its being purchased by the London, Chatham, and Dover Railway Company. Bowyer Lane, now Wyndham Road, long preserved the memory of the old family. This thoroughfare forms a connecting link between the Old and New Camberwell Roads, and is near the boundary line between the parishes of Camberwell and Newington. Freeman's Mill (see page 276), close by Bowyer Lane, was a picturesque old wooden building, and was formerly a conspicuous parochial boundary-mark. Early in the present century Bowyer Lane was the abode of questionable characters of all sorts. Greenacre lived here in 1836—the year of the murder now associated with his name; and it is stated that the body of a man who was executed for horse-stealing was for some time exhibited by the family living in Bowyer Lane at a shilling a head.

The Royal Flora Gardens, in the Wyndham Road, formed for some time a favourite resort for the pleasure-seekers of South London during the summer months. Their most prosperous period was about the year 1849, when the gardens were well laid out and brilliantly illuminated; but the reputation of the place speedily declined, and it met the fate of all such speculations.

The old church, dedicated to St. Giles, was an antique and rude structure, the body large and shapeless, with a square tower surmounted by a turret. It is described by Priscilla Wakefield, in the year 1809, as "an ancient structure, though its appearance has been much modernised by coats of plaster and rough-cast. The south aisle," she adds, "was greatly enlarged lately by an additional brick building, and the whole has been repaired and ornamented."

The first church of Camberwell is one of the very few of which we have authentic mention in "Domesday Book," and is considered by some to have dated its erection from within sixty years of the first landing of St. Augustine, or about the middle of the seventh century. In the reign of King Stephen, 1152, the original structure underwent extensive changes, and two years afterwards became subject to the abbey of St. Saviour, Bermondsey, by gift of William de Mellent. It has been conjectured by some topographers that portions of this church existed down to the time of its destruction by fire in 1841. Lysons, however, fixes the date of the old building towards the beginning of the reign of Henry VIII., at which period the entire edifice was either so completely altered as to lose its original character, or rebuilt on the site of the former church, which had been granted to the monks of Bermondsey. In confirmation of this view Mr. Blanch states that, in preparing the foundation of the new church, the foundations of two former structures were distinctly visible.

The old church was a large edifice, with a "lady chapel," and contained many interesting monuments, brasses, and painted windows. It would be difficult to estimate the amount spent at different times in altering, enlarging, beautifying, and repairing St. Giles's Church, from the time when the first entry occurs in the vestry minutes in 1675; for from that date down to the time of its destruction by fire in 1841, the condition of the church appears to have been the principal theme discussed by the parishioners "in vestry assembled." Under date of September 14, 1675, the following entry appears on the vestry records:—"Upon examination of the charges for the repairing the parish church, it was consented to and ordered, that the sum of Fifty pounds be raysed forthwith by way of tax for that purpose, and the payment of some arreares due for former reparations which was allowed, and to be included in this tax of £50, and to be paid

accordingly, and to be brought on account in the churchwardens' accounts, as also that the present churchwardens shall give an account how the sum of £50 hath been expended." This sum, it appears, was found insufficient for the repairs, and so in 1679 an order was made for an additional £40, "for mending the seats, bells, and windows, and for buying prayer-books and a surplice;" and soon after another sum of £40 was voted for a new church clock "and other expenses." There is mention also in 1675 of an agreement entered into between Antony Bowyer, Esq., and Richard Kettlethorpe, whereby the latter undertook to keep St. Giles's clock "going and in good order" for the sum of twenty shillings yearly; but Richard Kettlethorpe apparently found it a more difficult undertaking than he imagined, for, as stated above, a new clock was ordered about four years later.

In 1688 a gallery was built; in 1708 the church was "new pewed, paved, and glazed; three new galleries were erected, and a vault was sunk." In 1786 further additions were made; and in 1799 the building was "beautified," after the usual fashion so dear to vestries and churchwardens; and as parish officers in those days were wholly ignorant of ecclesiastical art, the effect was not brilliant. In 1825 the church was greatly enlarged.

Notwithstanding these various repairs and alterations, the old church retained much of its antiquarian character to the last. The massive clustered columns and pointed arches separating the nave from the side aisles, the venerable sedilia in the south wall of the chancel—which, by the way, had been for many years concealed behind some wainscoting put up in 1715 by the Bowyers—and the fragments of ancient stained glass in its windows, were all vestiges of the olden time.

A fire broke out on the night of Sunday, the 7th of February, 1841, by which the building was completely destroyed. Funds were at once raised for its re-erection. The first stone of the new church was laid in September, 1842, and in November, 1844, the new building was consecrated by the Bishop of Winchester. It was erected from the designs of Messrs. George Gilbert Scott and W. B. Moffatt, at an expense, including furniture, &c., of about £24,000. It is one of the finest and largest of the new parish churches in the kingdom. The style of architecture is the transition between the Early English and the Decorated, which prevailed at the close of the thirteenth century. The building is of a cruciform plan, with a central tower and spire, the latter rising to the height of about 210 feet. The walls of the church, which are of considerable thickness, are constructed chiefly of Kentish rag, with dressings of Caen stone. Several of the windows are enriched with stained glass.

In the old church there was a handsome effigy in brass of Edward Scott, who died in 1537. It is engraved in Hone's "Year-Book," page 913. There was also a monument to Agnes Skinner, or Skuner, who died in 1515, at the age of 119, having survived her husband, it is said, no less than ninety-two years!

The churchwardens' accounts contain several very curious entries. Thus, in 1809, Mr. Churchwarden Baker paid "John Wilkins, for a vagabond, 3s. 10d.;" "for carrying a vagabond to church, 3s.;" "paid for a coffin and shroud for him, 6s. 6d." The bishop, it seems, was usually regaled with "biscuits and wine" when he came to preach at Camberwell; but in the above-mentioned year, Mr. Churchwarden Davis makes the following entry: "Paid for meat and drink for the bishop, 2s. 6d."

Among the notabilities buried here is Mrs. Wesley, the somewhat shrewish wife of the Rev. John Wesley, who died in 1781. A stone in the churchyard asserts her to have been "a woman of exemplary virtue, a tender parent, and a sincere friend." The monument says nothing of her excellence as a wife; for it is on record that, after making her husband thoroughly miserable, and having been a "thorn in his flesh" for twenty years, she left his house, carrying off her husband's papers and journals, which she never returned. John Wesley never saw her, nor sought to see her, again. "By her outrageous jealousy and abominable temper," writes Southey, in his "Life of Wesley," "she deserves to be classed in a triad with Xanthippe and the wife of Job, as one of the three bad wives." Her death must have been a happy release for the great John. It appears that more than one separation took place between them. On different occasions she laid hands upon his person and tore his hair. When in the north of Ireland, a friend of Wesley's caught her in the act of trailing him on the floor by the hair of his head. "I felt," continues Hampson, in his account of the incident, "that I could have knocked the very soul out of her."

In the churchyard, too, lies Miss Lucy Warner, better known as the "Little Woman of Peckham." Her height was exactly thirty-two inches, her growth having been stunted at the early age of three. She kept a school. In the newer part of the churchyard a handsome tomb covers the remains of the notorious democrat, well known as "Equality Brown," of Peckham; and a gravestone also commemorates James Blake, who sailed round the world with Captain Cook.

Camden Chapel, situated on the northern side of Peckham Road, was built in 1797, and duly licensed as an Episcopal Chapel in 1829. Under the ministry of the late Rev. Henry Melvill, who occupied the pulpit for many years, it became one of the most famous places of worship in the metropolis for pulpit oratory of a high order. So great was Mr. Melvill's popularity, that very soon after his appointment, it was found necessary to make a considerable enlargement in the building, and transepts were made at the north end, thus giving to the edifice the ground-plan of the letter T. A writer in a critique on Camden Chapel and its pastor, in the "Metropolitan Pulpit" (1839), remarks: "The Rev. Henry Melvill, of Camden Chapel, is the most popular preacher in London. I am doing no injustice to other ministers, whether in the Church or out of it, in saying this. The fact is not only susceptible of proof, but is often proved in a manner which all must admit to be conclusive. When a sermon is advertised to be preached by Mr. Melvill, the number of strangers attracted to the particular place is invariably greater than is ever drawn together in the same church or chapel when any of the other popular ministers in London are appointed to preach on a precisely similar occasion." Mr. Melvill, who was subsequently rector of Barnes, died in 1871, and was buried in St. Paul's Cathedral, of which he had been for some years a canon residentiary.

A new district church, dedicated to St. George, on the south bank of the Surrey Canal, after the model of one of the churches in Rome, was built about 1830. There are few churches in or near London which have witnessed more extraordinary changes in their immediate neighbourhood than this. Originally built among green fields, with a windmill close at hand, it now stands in the midst of a teeming population. The edifice, which is in the Grecian style of architecture, was built from the designs of Mr. Bedford. A new bridge over the Surrey Canal, close by the church, was erected in the year 1862.

Previous to 1827, the parochial business was carried on either at the workhouse or the vestry-room of St. Giles's Church. In that year was erected a vestry-hall, which was in use for a little over forty years. The building, however, seems to have been ill adapted for the transaction of parochial business, and in 1873 it was superseded by a new hall, a large and imposing edifice on the north side of old Church Street, at the corner of Havil Street, and occupying the site of old Havil House. The style of architecture is that known as Renaissance, and the general arrangement of the design is a centre with two wings. The principal front is constructed entirely of Bath stone, and the side front of white Suffolk bricks, with cornices, string-courses, &c. The principal front is divided into two storeys, the lowermost of which has considerable dignity imparted to it by reason of its being raised some four feet above the level of the roadway. On the ground storey, the centre has rusticated piers, with Doric granite columns and a recessed portico, leading up to which is a flight of stone steps, with ornamental pillar-lamps on each side. The upper storey consists of coupled Ionic pilasters, with a central composition comprising a circular-headed window, flanked by two narrow recessed openings, and an elliptical projecting balcony; the whole is surmounted by an attic having a pedimented clock-storey, on either side of which are groups of statuary representing "Law" and "Prudence," while a figure of "Justice" crowns the summit of the pediment. On the pedestals of the balustrades, over each group of coupled pilasters, are also emblematical figures of "Science" and "Industry." The roof of this central portion of the building is of ornamental design, with a balustrade. Each of the wings of the main front is divided into three openings on both sides.

At the western end of Church Street and the southern end of Camberwell Road is an oblong plot of ground, rather over an acre in extent—laid out in grass-plats, planted with trees, shrubs, and flowers, and enclosed with iron railings—rejoicing in the name of Camberwell Park. This spot, formerly known as Camberwell Green, was in bygone times the scene of an annual fair, almost rivalling in riotousness that at Greenwich, which we have already described.*

How, or at what time, Camberwell Fair became established is a matter of uncertainty. Bray, in his "History of Surrey," says that it was appointed to be held on the 9th of August, and to terminate on the 1st of September—the feast of St. Giles, the patron saint; thus it must have lasted for twenty-three days. In recent times, however, it was held on the 18th, 19th, and 20th of August. The fair appears to have been held in the High Street, "opposite 'The Cock' public-house," before the Green was fixed upon as its head-quarters.

The following account of these saturnalia is taken from the "Annual Register," 1807:—"The sports of Camberwell Fair began, and were continued till Thursday, the 20th, with more animation than

usual. An unlucky accident happened on Wednesday to a black magician, who professed to be acquainted with the secrets of nature, to be descended from the magi of Persia, and to profess the highest veneration for the Greubes or worshippers of fire. In addition to his legerdemain, he exhibited a puppet-show, in the last scene of which a battle was introduced between Lucifer and Buonaparte. As the infernal king was conveying the effigy of the Corsican to the region of fire, an unlucky boy blew up a sausage-pan in the rear of the magician's booth, and Buonaparte's catastrophe was attended by real fire, for the flames, in consequence of the explosion, caught the hangings of the booth, and the disciple of Zoroaster found himself inclosed by the element he so much admired. In vain he summoned water to his aid; none could be obtained, and he was compelled to bury the devil, &c., in the ruins. Fortunately, the flames did not communicate to the adjoining shows, but the magician was necessitated to begin his incantations *de novo*."

The *Observer* of August 19th, 1832, thus describes the fair:—"Camberwell Fair.—The revels of this fair commenced yesterday with much spirit, notwithstanding the weather was so unfavourable. Richardson's theatre occupies a large space of ground in the centre of the Green, and is fitted up with a degree of splendour we could not have anticipated. Alger's 'Crown and Anchor' tavern, as usual, eclipses all others of its contemporaries; it ranges from one end of the Green to the other, and its interior is ornamented with chandeliers, variegated lamps, flags, banners, &c., which present a very splendid effect. There are numerous other sources of amusement to satiate the appetites of the public, and the Bonifaces anticipate a plentiful harvest should the weather but prove congenial."

The following curious particulars of Camberwell Fair are taken from Colburn's "Kalendar of Amusements" (1840):—"Camberwell Fair is one of the most amusing and orderly occurring near the metropolis. It continues in vogue three days, during which, precisely till the departure of daylight, it is attended by nursery-maids and their incipient masters and mistresses; and regularly till the return of the same, by all sorts and sizes of animated nature. The green is filled with booths, displaying articles of *virtu* and *taste* (corn-craiks and gingerbread); with theatres which preserve the legitimate drama with a commendable fidelity, admitting no other change of performances than from *Douglas* to *Hamlet*, and from *Hamlet* to *Douglas*; and with shows of wonderful objects,

* See *ante*, p. 202.

which Nature continues to produce in order, most probably, to keep alive that spirit of curiosity in man which works so beneficially for that portion of society called the *Hamaxobii*, or cart-dwellers. These latter are said to be capable of only one occupation, viz., expatiating ; and a profane proverb says that ' they are of no other use either to God or to man.' A story is told of one of them, who, observing a man fall into a river, continued to

tude beneath them, whom they incite by every possible inducement to pay their pence and judge for themselves. One of them, elevated so as to become the ' observed of all observers,' is revealing that, ' There is here, and only here, to be seen what you can see nowhere else, the lately-caught, and highly-accomplished young mermaid, about whom the Continental journals have written so ably. She combs her hair in the manner practised in China,

OLD CAMBERWELL MILL. (*Copied, by permission, from Mr. Blanch's History of Camberwell.*)

watch his struggles with a placid and unmoved countenance, exclaiming repeatedly in a low voice, ' If there *was* anybody *could* fling him this here rope, he might be saved !' It is, moreover, a common saying that they never undress, from their perfect ignorance of the manner in which their garments should be resumed. The reply of Dr. Johnson to the political turncoat, who, in endeavouring to extenuate his knavery, exclaimed, ' You know I must live, doctor.' ' I see no necessity for that, sir !' might very judiciously be applied to them.

"At Camberwell fair a multitude of these creatures may be inspected ; they are generally stationed in very prominent positions, making strange statements and assurances to the open-mouthed multi-

and admires herself in a glass in the manner practised—everywhere. She has had the best instructors in every peculiarity of education, and can argue on any given subject, from the most popular way of preserving plums, down to the necessity of a change of Ministers. She plays the harp in the *new effect*-ual style prescribed by Mr. Bochsa, of whom we wished her to take lessons, but, having some mermaiden scruples, she begged to be provided with a less popular master. Being so clever and accomplished, she can't bear to be contradicted, and lately leaped out of her tub and floored a distinguished fellow of the Royal Zoological Society, who was pleased to be more curious and cunning than she was pleased to think agreeable. She has composed various poems for the periodicals, and airs with variations for the harp and piano, all very popular and pleasing. That gentleman (pointing to an organ-grinder, who appears to be watching for his cue) will favour you with one of his latest *mélanges*.' The organist strikes up 'God save the Queen,' which appears to make the people

Regina!' Before the curtain of one of the great national preservers of the two legitimate stock plays we have mentioned, chieftains in plaid, lawyers in symbolical black, kings in rabbit ermine, ladies in glazed satin, and gentlemen in disguise—

'Like Banquo's ghost, nine farrow of one sow,'

OLD HOUSE ON CAMBERWELL GREEN.

thoughtful, as if they had heard something similar to it before. The showman, observing this effect, orders the note to be changed. 'Jim Crow,' accompanied by a roar of laughter, is the result, at the subsiding of which, the sonorous voice of the showman is heard bellowing, 'Walk up, walk up, ladies and gentlemen ; the entertainment is now a-going for to go to commence, and the charge has been *medicated*, according to the prudence of the times, to the sum of only one penny. *Vivat*

strut, shuffle, stamp, sweep, paddle, and *lavolt* across the stage to the time and tune of one solitary fiddler, the strings of whose *fidicula* might easily be mistaken for the *fidiculæ*, or little cords, formerly used to stretch people on the rack. This person is provokingly broken in upon by 'Johnny Black,' of a rival house, who is propounding to a motley mob, whom he obligingly mistakes for ladies and gentlemen, a series of extemporaneous conundrums."

"Much pain," we read in the *Tourist*, for 1832, has been taken of late to do away with the annual fair held on the Green, which some of the inhabitants deem a nuisance; but, being at once a manorial right, and a source of emolument, it still remains." A petty session was held at Union Hall, in Southwark, in 1823, in order to put down Camberwell fair; but it was held to no purpose. The complaints of the inhabitants against the continuance of the fair were both loud and numerous; but it nevertheless survived, and was allowed to bring annual annoyance to the district till August, 1855, in which month the Green was encumbered for the last time with these disreputable gatherings. In that year the manorial rights in the Green were purchased by a subscription raised among the principal inhabitants of the district, and the place was transformed into a park, as above stated.

At the end of Camberwell Road, close by the park, is an inn called the "Father Redcap;" this hostelry, however, has no connection with the "Mother Redcap" of Camden Town,* or other places, but was probably only a flight of some publican's fancy.

There formerly stood on the south side of the Green a curious old mansion, which in its time had, doubtless, been the subject of many an idle tale. It was for many years known as the "old house on the Green." "The house itself," as Mr. Blanch tells us in his work before referred to, " was a fine specimen of a country mansion, and stood alone in its grandeur, as though it had found its way to Camberwell by mistake, so different was it from the surrounding buildings. Its magnificent hall was adorned with frescoes on walls and ceilings by the famous artist, Sir James Thornhill, and the noble oak staircase was of great width, and beautifully carved. The dining and drawing rooms were of unusual proportions, and elaborately worked medallion and other decorations were profusely arrayed. Tradition fixes this spot as the residence of Sir Christopher Wren, apparently without any authority, although local nomenclature has come to the rescue of tradition by naming the road which now occupies the site of this ancient structure as Wren Road."

The north side of the park is occupied chiefly by the Green-coat and National Schools. The building, which was erected in 1871, stands on the site of a former school, founded in 1721, by Mr. Henry Cornelisen, "for the Christian instruction of poor children."

The Camberwell Free Grammar School, which dated its foundation from the reign of James I., has become a thing of the past. It was instituted by the Rev. Edward Wilson, Vicar of Camberwell, and the rules and regulations drawn up by him are quaint and peculiar. The master, we are told, was to be "chosen out of the founder's kindred before any others;" he was to be "sound in religion, body, and mind; gentle, sober, honest, virtuous, discreet, and approved for a good facility in teaching—if such a one may be gotten!" The master was enjoined "to be careful of the behaviour of the scholars in coming in, going out, and sitting; and especially in repetition for good grace, countenance, pronunciation, and carriage, &c.; reverence abroad of scholars to their betters, elders, &c.; behaviour, courteous speech, and fair condition required, and reformation of such as do amiss." For all these varied duties and accomplishments the master was to receive "for his stipend, ten pounds yearly," and the best scholar was to "welcome him with a Latin oration." Whatever the school may have been in its early days, it does not appear to have been in a very flourishing condition at the commencement of the present century. In 1824 the governors sold and conveyed to the Charity Commissioners a portion of the charity-land as an addition to the churchyard of the parish; and in 1842 an information was filed in the Court of Chancery against the governors and the then master of the school, with respect to its past and future management. In consequence of these proceedings, in 1845 the school buildings were razed to the ground, and for nearly eighteen years the land on which they stood was let out for grazing and the school has not been revived. Its absence, however, is now supplied by the Mary Datchelor Charity Schools, for the education of girls of the middle classes, at the foot of Camberwell Grove. These schools were erected in 1880 at the cost of £12,000. The buildings are of red brick with facings of Portland stone.

In Westmoreland Place, contiguous to the main road, is the Aged Pilgrims' Friend Asylum. Of the many valuable institutions with which London abounds, few deserve a higher place in the estimation of the philanthropist than the Aged Pilgrims' Friend Society, of which we have already had occasion to speak in our account of Upper Holloway.† It was established in the year 1807, for the purpose of giving life-pensions of ten guineas and five guineas per annum to poor, aged, and infirm Protestants of either sex. The almshouses here were commenced in 1834. The edifice is of brick, with stucco mouldings and ornaments, having an embattled centre, flanked by two towers. A low pointed gateway leads through this part of the structure to a quadrangle with a lawn in the centre, and surrounded by buildings in the same style.

The rural character of Camberwell at the latter part of the eighteenth century may be gathered from the fact that the trees and hedges of the village are alluded to in the vestry minutes; and in 1782 caterpillars so abounded in the parish, that the overseers spent £10 in "apprehending them," at the rate of sixpence per bushel. The caterpillars were described as being dangerous to the public in general. "The Camberwell Beauty," the delight of entomologists, is still one of the finest butterflies of the summer; but it is now rarely seen. It was most abundant when Camberwell was a straggling suburban parish of about 4,000 inhabitants. But Camberwell is now a congeries of streets, and forms part of the great metropolis itself.

Close by the Camberwell Station of the London, Chatham, and Dover Railway, stood Myatt's Farm, a picturesque building in the midst of gardens, celebrated for their strawberries as lately as the present reign. Camberwell, in fact, was, down to a comparatively recent date, famous for its flowers and fruit. In Cold Harbour Lane, which leads from the southern end of the High Street towards Brixton, are still located one or two well-known florists. In this lane was Strawberry Hall, now pulled down to form a site for Loughborough Park Chapel; beyond this was the "river" Effra, which, having been diverted from its original channel, or otherwise effaced, is now kept in remembrance by a modern thoroughfare called Effra Road. Cold Harbour—a name by no means rare in the rural districts—is supposed to have originally signified a place of entertainment for travellers and drovers, but the derivation is uncertain.

At the foot of Denmark Hill, or rather at the fork made by the junction of that road with Cold Harbour Lane, stood Denmark Hill Grammar School, "a handsome and imposing structure," with its extensive grounds skirting the parish boundary, and which "was reckoned among the *maisons grandes* of Camberwell." The grounds were enclosed by a high brick wall; and the house itself, which faced Denmark Hill, stood only a few yards from the road. It was a lofty structure, built of red and white bricks, with dressings of Portland stone, and the interior contained some curious and quaint carvings and frescoes.

At the beginning of the present century there lived at Grove Hill Dr. John Lettsom, one of the most extraordinary men of his day. As a Quaker physician he was most successful, realising sometimes as much as £12,000 a year. He was as liberal and philanthropic as he was wealthy. At Grove Hill he entertained some of the most eminent *literati* of his time. He used to sign his prescriptions "I. Lettsom." This signature occasioned the following epigram—

> "When any patients call in haste,
> I physics, bleeds, and sweats 'em;
> If after that they choose to die,
> Why, what cares I?
> I let's 'em."

Dr. John Coakley Lettsom was the son of a West Indian planter, and was born in the year 1744. Having completed his education in England, he was apprenticed to a Yorkshire apothecary. He afterwards returned to the West Indies, and settled as a medical practitioner at Tortola. After about five or six months, he again found his way into Europe. In 1769, he was admitted a licentiate of the Royal College of Physicians of London, and in the following year elected a Fellow of the Society of Antiquaries. Dr. Lettsom's rise in his profession was rapid; but whilst realising a handsome fortune, he was not forgetful of the wants of his needy brethren, and the poorer order of clergy and struggling literary men received from him not only gratuitous advice, but substantial aid; whilst his contributions to charitable institutions placed him in the front rank of earnest and practical philanthropists. Dr. Lettsom deserves also to be remembered as the original proprietor of the sea-bathing Infirmary at Margate, which dates from 1792 or thereabouts. Numerous anecdotes have been published about the celebrated physician, but the following will sufficiently illustrate his proverbial generosity, which we tell on the authority of Mr. Blanch:—"As he was travelling on one occasion in the neighbourhood of London, a highwayman stopped his carriage; but from the awkward and constrained manner of the intruder, the doctor correctly imagined the young man was somewhat of a novice in his new vocation, and that he was an outlaw more from necessity than from choice; and so it turned out. The doctor interested himself in his behalf, and eventually obtained him a commission in the army. On one of his benevolent excursions, the doctor found his way into the squalid garret of a poor woman who had seen better days. With the language and deportment of a lady, she begged the physician to give her a prescription. After inquiring carefully into her case, he wrote on a slip of paper to the overseers of the parish: 'A shilling per diem for

Mrs. Moreton. Money, not physic, will cure her.'"
Unhappily, though Dr. Lettsom had been successful in his profession, his latter years were darkened
with adversity.

Dr. Lettsom's house is called by Priscilla Wakefield, in 1809, "an elegant villa." She is at the
pains of describing it as follows:—"The front is
adorned with emblematical figures of Flora and the
Seasons. One of the chief ornaments of the house
is a noble library, in which are tastefully disposed
the busts of many distinguished literary characters.
The gardens and pleasure-grounds are laid out in
a pleasing manner, and display a variety of statues
and models of ancient temples. That of the
Sibyls is on the model of one at Tivoli, and is
supported on the trunks of eighteen oak-trees,
around which are entwined ivy, virgin's bower,
honeysuckle, and other climbing shrubs."

The author of "The British Traveller," in describing the parish in 1819, makes no mention of
anybody or anything in Camberwell further than
this, that it contained the residence of the "late
famous Dr. Lettsom." The house is described in
Manning and Bray's "History of Surrey" as "standing on a considerable eminence, rising gradually
for about three-quarters of a mile from the village
of Camberwell, and passing through an avenue of
elms retaining the name of Camberwell Grove,
part of the plantations which belonged to the house
that was Sir Thomas Bond's, and afterwards Lord
Trevor's." This, however, is more than doubtful,
as Sir Thomas Bond's house was situated in Peckham, at least one mile distant.

Scott, the "bard of Amwell," inscribed one of
his lesser poems to his hospitable friend, Dr. Lettsom; and Boswell, who was a frequent visitor at
Grove Hill, in an ode to Charles Dilly, celebrated
at once the beauties of the physician's country seat
and its owner's humane disposition:—

"My cordial friend, still prompt to lend
　　Your cash when I have need on't;
　We both must bear our load of care—
　　At least we talk and read on't—

"Yet are we gay in every way,
　　Not minding where the joke lie;
　On Saturday at bowls we play,
　　At Camberwell, with Coakley.

"Methinks you laugh to hear but half
　　The name of Dr. Lettsom;
　From him of good—talk, liquors, food—
　　His guests will always get some.

"And guests has he, in every degree
　　Of decent estimation;
　His liberal mind holds all mankind
　　As an exalted nation.

"O'er Lettsom's cheer we've met a peer—
　　A peer, no less than Lansdowne!
　Of whom each dull and envious skull
　　Absurdly cries—'The man's down!

"Lettsom we view a Quaker true:
　　'Tis clear he's so in one sense;
　His spirit strong and ever young
　　Refutes pest Priestley's nonsense.

"In fossils he is deep, we see,
　　Nor knows beasts, fishes, birds ill!
　With plants not few, some from Pelew,
　　And wondrous mangel-wurzel!

"West Indian bred, warm heart, cold head,
　　The City's first physician;
　By schemes humane, want, sickness, pain,
　　To aid is his ambition.

"From terrace high, he feasts his eye,
　　When practice grants a furlough,
　And while it roves o'er Dulwich groves,
　　Looks down—even upon Thurlow."

Dr. Lettsom's house was subsequently occupied
by Mr. Charles Baldwin, the proprietor of the *St.
James's Chronicle*, and afterwards of the *Standard*
newspaper.

Camberwell Grove is said to be the spot on
which George Barnwell murdered his uncle: an
event which furnished Lillo with the plot of his
tragedy. Fountain Cottage—which was till very
recently commemorated by Fountain Terrace, a
name which the Metropolitan Board of Works
have thought fit to abolish—was fixed upon as the
residence of the unfortunate uncle. A writer, at
the commencement of the present century, informs
his readers that "in the Grove (at Camberwell)
was committed that tragic act, recorded by Lillo,
in the drama of *George Barnwell*." And, again, in
the *European Magazine* for June, 1803, it is recorded that "at the fatal spot where this murder
was committed rises a stream of limpid water,
which falls into the canal (at Fountain Cottage)
through a vase on which a naiad, in ornamental
stone, reclines. It is this spring," the writer
further tells us, with an amount of simplicity and
ignorance which is charming, "which gives the
name of Camberwell to the village so called!" In
the "Memoirs of George Barnwell, by a descendant
of the family," published in 1810, the author, in
purporting to give "a full, true, and particular
account" of the whole affair, fixes upon Camberwell Grove as the residence of the uncle and the
scene of the murder. Maurice, the historian of
Hindostan, in his poem entitled "Grove Hill," thus
apostrophises this touching and romantic story:—

"Ye towering elms, on whose majestic brows
A hundred rolling years have shed their snows,
Admit me to your dark, sequester'd reign,
To roam with contemplation's studious train!

Your haunts I seek, nor glow with other fires
Than those which friendship's ardent warmth inspires ;
No savage murderer with a gleaming blade—
No *Barnwell* to pollute your sacred shade !"

In the prologue to Lillo's tragedy, "as acted at the Theatre Royal, Drury Lane, by his Majesty's servants, in 1731," it is openly stated that the tragedy is based upon the original ballad of "George Barnwell : "—

"Forgive us, then, if we attempt to show,
In artless strains, a tale of private woe.
A London 'prentice ruined is my theme,
Drawn from the famed old song that bears his name."

According to Bishop Percy, the original ballad was printed at least as early as the seventeenth century. In that production Barnwell's uncle is described as a wealthy grazier, dwelling in Ludlow :—

"I an uncle have,
Who doth in Ludlow dwell ;
He is a grazier, which in wealth
Doth all the rest excel."

The ballad also describes the murder as having been committed in a wood near that town ; and the Ludlow Guide-book notices the circumstance as traditional there, and the very barn and homestead, a short distance on the left before entering Ludlow from the Hereford Road, are still pointed out as having been the residence of the victim. The ballad, however, lays the scene of Barnwell's dissipation in the metropolis. In Shoreditch lived Mrs. Millwood, who led him astray :—

"George Barnwell, then, quoth she,
Do thou to Shoreditch come,
And ask for Mrs. Millwood's house,
Next door unto the 'Gun.'"

Readers of James Smith's "Rejected Addresses" will not forget how the wretched woman Millwood suggests to the profligate apprentice the murder of his wealthy but hard-hearted relative. The poet tells us :—

"A pistol he got from his love,
'Twas loaded with powder and bullet ;
He trudged off to Camberwell Grove,
But wanted the courage to pull it.
'There's Nunkey as fat as a hog,
While I am as lean as a lizard ;
Here's at you, you stingy old dog !'
And he whips a big knife in his gizzard.

"All you who attend to my song,
A terrible end of the farce shall see,
If you join the inquisitive throng
That followed poor George to the Marshalsea.
'If Millwood were here, dash my wigs,'
Quoth he, 'I would pummel and lam her well ;
Had I stuck to my prunes and my figs,
I ne'er had stuck Nunkey at Cam'erwell.'"

"Lillo's drama," writes the author of the History

of Camberwell, "shows us the culprit, in companionship with his heartless seducer, led from a London prison to the scaffold ; and Dr. Rimbault, writing in 1858, tells us that some few years since an old parochial parchment was said to have come to light, showing that George Barnwell had been the last criminal hanged at St. Martin's-in-the-Fields, before the Middlesex executions were, more generally than before, ordered at Tyburn ; yet the ballad, of much older date than the play, says that Barnwell was not gibbeted there, but sent 'beyond seas,' where he subsequently suffered capital punishment for some fresh crime. In any case," he adds, somewhat sceptically, "we must disclaim, on behalf of Camberwell, the *honour* of the *Barnwell* connection. If such a person ever did commit such a crime as that stated, no reliable evidence whatever has been produced to connect Camberwell with it."

A writer in Hone's "Every-day Book" remarks : —"When Mr. Ross performed the character of George Barnwell, in 1752, the son of an eminent merchant was so struck with certain resemblances to his own perilous position (arising from the arts of a real Millwood), that his agitation brought on a dangerous illness, in the course of which he confessed his error, was forgiven by his father, and was furnished with the means of repairing the pecuniary wrongs he had privately done to his employer. Mr. Ross says : 'Though I never knew his name, nor saw him to my knowledge, I had, for nine or ten years, at my benefit, a note sealed up with ten guineas, with these words :— "A tribute of gratitude from one who was highly obliged, and saved from ruin, by witnessing Mr. Ross's performance of George Barnwell."'" Few persons, on reading this fact, will censure the stage, as such, as being necessarily immoral in its tendency.

In the last century, the Camberwell Tea Gardens, attached to a place of public entertainment called the Grove House, were largely patronised by the lads and lasses of the metropolis. The assembly-room—which is now known as Camberwell Hall—has been the scene of many local balls, which can scarcely, however, be styled fashionable. Charles Dickens, in his "Sketches by Boz," gives an amusing account of a ball held here by certain "aspiring" local residents. *Fêtes* of all kinds were held within the spacious grounds of Grove House. With the Grove House Tavern is associated the history of the Camberwell Club, which, like all similar associations of the past century, was exclusively social. The club—which numbered among its members clergymen, lawyers, and merchants—held its meetings at this famous house of entertainment; and, as Mr. Blanch informs us, "snug dinners, stray balls, and quarterly feasts were the principal *duties* which the members were called upon to perform; and right well did they acquit themselves, if report be true." Political meetings were sometimes held here; and the march of "Citizen" Tierney's supporters thither in 1802 forms the subject of a spirited engraving

Roberts, the architect of the Fishmongers' Hall; it was somewhat in the Tudor style, constructed of white brick, with stone dressings, the principal feature being the cloister which faced the entrance. The school was opened in 1835, as a proprietary establishment, and for some time was moderately successful; but the proximity of Dulwich College and other educational establishments seriously impeded the progress of the college, and in 1867

DR. LETTSOM'S HOUSE, GROVE HILL.

published at the time, beneath which is inscribed—

"The glorious triumph shouting mobs proclaim,
And the thronged Grove House echoes back my fame."

Mr. Tierney, the great friend of Charles James Fox, was elected M.P. for Southwark in 1802, and sat for that place in two or three Parliaments. In a broad-sheet published by Gilray, in 1797, he is represented as the "Friend of Humanity"—the same who was satirised by Canning, a short time previously, in the "Anti-Jacobin."

On the lower Spring-field, on the west side of the Grove, formerly stood the Camberwell Collegiate School, an establishment formed on the principles of King's College. The building was erected in 1834, from the designs of Mr. Henry

it was closed, and the land sold for building purposes.

The dwellers in Camberwell, and especially in that region where it passes into the Grove, ought to feel grateful to Mr. William Black for the dignity and interest which he has conferred upon it in his romance of "Madcap Violet." What Leigh Hunt, Thackeray, and other writers have done for the "Old Court Suburb" of Kensington, Mr. Black has done for this charming part of suburban London. The broad, tree-bordered slope of the Grove, where fine houses to the right and left are embowered among leaves, has been chosen by the author of "Madcap Violet" as the scene of some of the incidents narrated in that romance of modern life.

Camberwell Grove, the sylvan glades of Dulwich

GROVE LANE, CAMBERWELL.

and Norwood, and hilly Sydenham, were favourite resorts of the great painter, William Blake, in his early years.

In Champion Hill, which extends from Camberwell to Lordship Lane, the nightingale is sometimes heard; and Hone, in his "Year-Book," mentions that this bird was in full song here in 1832.

Hone's "Year-Book" also mentions the "Fox-under-the-Hill," at the foot of Denmark Hill—then the Sunday resort of many town-immured beings—as being gradually surrounded by spruce villas, &c. He styles Herne Hill "the elysium of many of our merchants and traders. On the left," he adds, "is a quiet lane, such as Byron would have loved, leading to Dulwich."

The "Fox-under-the-Hill" still remains a well-known Camberwell sign, although the old tavern has been demolished to give place to one more in accord with modern ideas. That the neighbourhood was at one time the haunt of "Reynard" may be inferred from the fact that a thoroughfare close by is called Dog Kennel Lane. The tavern was formerly called "Little Denmark Hall," there being at that time another house of entertainment known as "Great Denmark Hall," which was subsequently converted into one or more private houses. The "Fox-under-the-Hill" was formerly the starting-point of the Dulwich patrol.

Of the "old families" of Camberwell not yet mentioned by us, we have the Cherrys, descended from the De Cheries of Picardy and Normandy—the first of the family who settled in Camberwell being Sir Francis Cherry, Queen Elizabeth's Ambassador to Russia in 1598, of whose proceedings an amusing account is given in the "Egerton Papers" as published by the Camden Society. We have again the De Crespignys, who came from France, as Protestant refugees, in the reign of William III., though they did not settle in Camberwell until early in the eighteenth century. Champion Lodge, at the foot of Denmark Hill, was built in 1717, by Mr. Claude de Crespigny. In 1804, the Prince of Wales visited Champion Lodge, and of course a great *fête* was made on the occasion, and the owner of the house was soon afterwards made a baronet. The park had originally an area of about thirty acres. The house, noticeable for the fine iron gates and the stately cedars in front, was pulled down in 1841, and the site is now occupied by rows of houses. Sir Claude de Crespigny was a Fellow of Trinity Hall, Cambridge, and married the gifted, as well as accomplished, daughter of Mr. J. Clarke, of Rigton, Derbyshire. It was this Lady de Crespigny who wrote the admirable lines which were placed over a grotto standing in the grounds of Champion Lodge, and dedicated to Contemplation.

There were also the Drapers, who came from Nottinghamshire—Robert Draper, of Camberwell, being page of the Jewel Office to Henry VIII.; and his nephew, Sir Christopher Draper, being Lord Mayor of London in 1566—his three daughters marrying respectively, Sir W. Webbe, Sir Wolstan Dixie, and Sir H. Billingsley, all subsequently Lord Mayors in their turn.

Of the "local worthies" of Camberwell not already referred to by us, we may mention the Rev. Dr. Richard Parr, who was rector of this parish for thirty-eight years, commencing with 1653, and who was the chaplain and biographer of Archbishop Usher; Dr. Chandler, a famous Nonconformist divine in the early part of the eighteenth century, whose theological writings excited great attention, and evoked the high commendations of Archbishop Wake; and Dr. William B. Collyer, who attained great fame as a preacher in the earlier part of the present century.

Towards the close of the year 1840, Thomas Hood—the author of "The Song of the Shirt"—took up his residence in Camberwell; the house to which he first brought this family was No. 8, South Place, now 181, Camberwell New Road. He afterwards removed to No. 2, Union Row (now 266, High Street), where he occupied the drawing-room floor. Hood, who was a real wit and humourist in the best sense of the word, was born in London in 1798. His father was a native of Scotland, and for many years acting partner in the firm of Vernor, Hood, and Sharpe, extensive booksellers and publishers. "There was a dash of ink in my blood," he writes; "my father wrote two novels, and my brother was decidedly of a literary turn, to the great disquietude, for a time, of an anxious parent." Young Hood finished his education at Wanostrocht's Academy, at Camberwell; and removed thence to a merchant's counting-house in the City, where he realised his own inimitable sketch of the boy "Just set up in Business :"—

"Time was I sat upon a lofty stool,
   At lofty desk, and with a clerkly pen,
   Began each morning at the stroke of ten
To write in Bell and Co.'s commercial school,
In Warnford Court, a shady nook and cool,
   The favourite retreat of merchant men ;
Yet would my quill turn vagrant even then,
   And take stray dips in the Castalian pool.
Now double entry—now a flowery trope—
   Mingling poetic honey with trade wax:
Blogg, Brothers—Milton—Grote and Prescott—Pope—
   Bristles and Hogg—Glyn, Mills, and Halifax—
Rogers and Towgood—Hemp—the Bard of Hope—
   Barilla—Byron—Tallow—Burns, and Flax."

Mr. Hood's first work was anonymous—his "Odes and Addresses to Great People"—a little, thin, mean-looking sort of a foolscap sub-octavo of poems, with nothing but wit and humour to recommend it. Coleridge was delighted with the work, and taxed Charles Lamb by letter with the authorship. His next work was "A Plea for the Midsummer Fairies," a serious poem of infinite beauty, full of fine passages and of promise. The "Plea" was followed by "Whims and Oddities"—the forerunner of the *Comic Annual*. Then came the "Epping Hunt" and the "Dream of Eugene Aram;" "Tylney Hall," a novel; and "Hood's Own; or, Laughter from Year to Year," a volume of comic lucubrations, "with an infusion of New Blood for General Circulation." His "Song of the Shirt" has been sung through the whole length and breadth of the three kingdoms. During the first year of his residence at Camberwell, he was much amused at witnessing "all the fun of the fair," which then annually ran riot at the latter end of August. In a letter, written from "2, Union Row, High Street, Camberwell," about this time, Hood says: "We have much more comfortable lodgings, and the 'busses pass the door constantly, being in the high road, fifty or a hundred yards townwards of the 'Red Cap,' at the Green. I have a room to myself, which will be worth £20 a year to me—for a little disconcerts my nerves." In another letter from this place, dated April 13th, 1841, Hood writes:—"Camberwell is the best air I could have." At the close of this year he removed to St. John's Wood, where he died about four years later, at the early age of forty-seven.

The loyalty and military spirit of Camberwell, as a constituent portion of the county of Surrey, appear to have been maintained, without interruption, since the days of "good Queen Bess," Camberwell having then furnished a valiant quota to the forces collected to oppose the attempted Spanish invasion; and having again, after the lapse of more than two centuries—namely, in 1798—distinguished itself by forming a "Military Association," under the presidency and command of Claude Champion de Crespigny—the lineal representative of one of the "old families" mentioned above; which Association, in 1804—when the country unanimously resented the menaces of Buonaparte—developed itself into a formal volunteer corps.

In point of population, Camberwell offers, perhaps, the most striking example of increase which can be found throughout the metropolitan suburban area—the number of its inhabitants having grown from 7,059, in 1801, to the astonishing amount of 186,555 in 1881. It seems, indeed, that, with the dawn of this century, Camberwell suddenly broke through the trammels which had been imposed upon suburban buildings during the sixteenth and seventeenth centuries, and had made their prescriptive influence felt throughout the eighteenth. Happy would it have been, both for the citizens and the city of London, had those laws been maintained and enforced in a salutary, judicious, and moderate manner. Then, it has been remarked, we should not have seen, as we do now, so many square miles of fertile agricultural ground covered with useless bricks and mortar, the crowded habitations of a seething population; then, indeed, we should not have had miles of beggarly two-storeyed tenements swallowing up all the open spaces about the metropolis, but should have adopted a system of building more consonant with the principles of sanitary laws, as well as with those of social and political economy.

In few matters, during the first half of the present century, has there been a greater change than in the mode and pace of travelling; and abundant illustration of this fact is shown by a retrospect of the character of the communication between London and Camberwell as existing in the years 1796 and 1877. In the former year, one Camberwell coach was advertised to leave the "Anchor and Vine," Charing Cross, twice daily, and another to leave the "Kings and Key," Fleet Street, three times daily. Now, besides omnibuses, whose name is legion, there are several railway-stations in Camberwell, and, likewise, a line of tramway from Westminster to Camberwell Green and New Cross, besides other tramway lines from Camberwell to Blackfriars and the City. By means of its railway and tramway communication, in addition to the ordinary omnibus service, Camberwell is now placed within easy reach of the centre of the metropolis, of which indeed it forms a part.

In the Peckham Road, by which we now proceed, we pass, on our left, one of the two asylums licensed for the reception of lunatics in Camberwell. This asylum, known as Camberwell House, with its surrounding pleasure and garden grounds, occupies a space of some twenty acres, part of which is laid out in a park-like manner, the remainder being kept for the use of the patients who take an interest in garden pursuits. The principal building, formerly known as Alfred House, was erected by Mr. Wanostrocht for a school, which he conducted for many years with eminent success. The house was afterwards used by the Royal Naval School, which, as we have already seen, was subsequently removed to New

Cross.* The Royal Naval School was projected by Captain Dickson; was started by voluntary contributions, headed by the handsome donation of £10,000 from the late Dr. Bell; and had for its object the education of the sons of those naval and marine officers whose scanty incomes did not allow them to provide a first-rate education for their boys. Its office was represented, from 1831 to 1833, by a second-floor room in Jermyn Street, St. James's; and here its founders and projectors regularly met on board days, and worked for the advancement of the interests of the Royal Naval School. They were famous men who went up those stairs to the humble committee-room in Jermyn Street—men whose names are household words amongst us now,

and whom history will remember. William IV., "the Sailor King," was interested in this school, and met there Yorke, Blackwood, Keats, Hardy, Codrington, and Cockburn—brave admirals and famous "old salts," some of whom could recollect, mayhap, what a struggle it was to live like a gentleman once, and bring up their boys as gentlemen's sons, on officer's pay. Alfred House was for a time the institution which uprose from the committee's first deliberations, from voluntary contributions, and unaided by that Government grant which it deserved as an impetus in the first instance, and which to this day, and for reasons inexplicable to all connected with the service and the school, it has been unable to obtain.

CHAPTER XXII.

PECKHAM AND DULWICH.

Situation of Peckham—Queen's Road—Albert Road—The Manor House of Peckham—Hill Street—Shard Square and the "Shard Arms"—Peckham House—Old Mansions in Peckham—Marlborough House—The "Rosemary Branch"—Peckham Fair—The "Kentish Drovers"—Hanover Street—Hanover Chapel—Basing Manor—Rye Lane—The Railway Station—The Museum of Fire-arms—Peckham Rye—Nunhead Green—The Asylum of the Metropolitan Beer and Wine Trade Association—Nunhead Cemetery—Nunhead Hill—The Reservoirs of the Southwark and Vauxhall Waterworks—Heaton's Folly—Honour Oak—Camberwell Cemetery—Friern Manor Farm—Goose Green—Lordship Lane—The "Plough" Inn—The Scenery round Dulwich—The Haunt of the Gipsies—Visit of the Court of Charles I. to Dulwich, for the Purposes of Sport—Outrages in Dulwich Wood—The Stocks and Cage at Dulwich—The "Green Man" Tavern—Bew's Corner—Dulwich Wells—Dr. Glennie's School—Byron a Scholar there—The "Crown," the "Half Moon," and the "Greyhound" Taverns—The Dulwich Club—Noted Residents of Dulwich—The Old Manor House—Edward Alleyn at Home—Dulwich College—Dulwich Picture-gallery—The New Schools of Dulwich College.

PECKHAM, as a metropolitan suburb, has a history completely of its own, made up of King John, Nell Gwynne, the great Duke of Marlborough, Hannah Lightfoot, Dr. Collyer, and other celebrities; yet it is nevertheless curtly described by Priscilla Wakefield, in her "Perambulations of London," as "a hamlet in the parish of Camberwell, on the road proceeding to Greenwich." The only scrap of information which she adds is that "a large fair is held at Peckham annually, affording a holiday to a vast number of the lower classes of Londoners." Of this fair we shall have more to say presently. The road above referred to leads from the Green at Camberwell, passes the parish church, and, continuing on through the village of Peckham, terminates in Queen's Road, which winds in a north-easterly direction, and ultimately unites with the Old Kent Road, near New Cross. Queen's Road, now a broad and well-built thoroughfare, was formerly known as Deptford Lane, and was re-named in honour of Her Majesty Queen Victoria, who often passed through it on her way to the Royal Naval School at New Cross. It is not so very long ago that Albert Road, a turning

out of the Queen's Road, was known by the not very euphonious appellation of Cow Walk. Within the present century Peckham rejoiced in a park of considerable extent, extending at one time from the High Street as far northward as the Old Kent Road; but its existence is now merely kept in remembrance by Peckham Park Road, which, with Hill Street, unites the two thoroughfares, and has long been built upon. The Manor House of Peckham, which occupied a central position, was standing in 1809, when Priscilla Wakefield wrote her work above quoted. It is said to have been built by Sir Thomas Bond,† one of the confidential friends of James II., and who loyally accompanied that monarch into exile.

Sir Thomas Trevor, Chief Justice of the Court of Common Pleas, created Lord Trevor by Queen Anne in 1711, and one of the twelve individuals who were made peers at once during the struggle for power, purchased the Peckham estate from Sir Henry Bond. The judge resided here occasionally, and after his decease, in 1731, the estate was purchased by a Mrs. Hill, from whom it descended to her nephew, Isaac P. Shard, Esq.; in 1812 it

---

belonged to his second son, Mr. Charles Shard, of Lovel's Hill, near Windsor, who inherited the property from his elder brother. "In 1797," writes Mr. Blanch, in his History of Camberwell, "this ancient mansion was levelled to the ground for the then commencing great metropolitan improvements, and the present Hill Street forms the site of the once magnificent and stately mansion." The Shards are kept in remembrance by Shard Square and the "Shard Arms."

Branching out of the Peckham Road, a number of new thoroughfares have sprung up within the last quarter of a century, the names of which impart quite a legal tone to the district, the roads being dedicated to Lords Lyndhurst, Denman, and Selborne, and to Mr. Justice Talfourd. A few steps out of the High Street is Peckham House, formerly an old private mansion, but for the last half century a lunatic asylum, kept by Dr. Stocker, whose predecessor was a Dr. Armstrong. Its interior has been more than once graphically described by newspaper writers. The fine old mansion and surrounding acres have not always been connected with the sad side of humanity, for prior to 1826 the noble building resounded with the merry laughter of freedom. The wealthy family of Spitta lived here in grand style, giving *fêtes*, or what would now be termed garden-parties, to their neighbours, and dispensing charity with no niggard hand amongst the poor of the locality.

The High Street still boasts of many quaint houses, some of which can date back more than two centuries. The police-station forms part of what was once a fine mansion, formerly occupied by a wealthy family of the name of Dalton, and subsequently used as a convent. The police-station occupies the site of one of its outbuildings. Another house, now a draper's shop, was formerly the head-quarters of the Royal Asylum of St. Ann's Society, which was founded in 1702; whilst Avenue House, since the central office of Miss Rye's establishment for aiding the cause of female emigration, was, in days of old, a family mansion of some note.

Near the High Street, on the ground now covered by Marlborough Road, formerly stood Marlborough House, a fine old mansion, supposed at one time to have been the residence of some members of the Churchill family. The building contained a noble entrance-hall and a fine oak staircase, and frescoes adorned the walls and ceilings. For some years prior to its demolition, the building was used as a workhouse, where the city paupers were farmed. Blenheim House, still standing in the High Street, is thought to have been a minor building attached to the mansion.

The "Rosemary Branch" tavern, in Southampton Street, which stands at the junction of the Commercial Road, although possessing but a local reputation at the present time, was a well-known metropolitan hostelry at the commencement of the century. The old house, which was pulled down many years ago, was a picturesque structure, with rustic surroundings. Its original sign, if we may trust an entry in the churchwardens' accounts for 1707, appears to have been the "Rosemary Bush;" at all events, the entry referred to runs thus: "Received of Mr. Travers, for a stranger dying at yᵉ Rosemary Bush, oo. oo. o4d." Tradition has it, that whenever the landlord of the old house tapped a barrel of beer, the inhabitants for some distance round were apprised of the fact by bell and proclamation! When the new house was erected it was described, in a print of the time, as an "establishment which has no suburban rival." The grounds surrounding it were most extensive, and horse-racing, cricketing, pigeon-shooting, and all kinds of out-door sports and pastimes were carried on within them; just as at Belsize a century ago.* The grounds have now been almost entirely covered with houses.

The "Rosemary Branch" is by no means a common sign for a public-house; but this house at Peckham is perhaps one of the best known in the metropolis. Rosemary was formerly an emblem of remembrance, much as the forget-me-not is now. "There's rosemary, that's for remembrance," says Ophelia, in the play of *Hamlet;* and, in the *Winter's Tale*, Perdita says:

"For you, there's rosemary and rue; these keep
    Seeming and savour all the winter long;
    Grace and remembrance be unto you both."

A local tradition says that King John, hunting at Peckham, killed a stag, and was so pleased with the sport, that he granted its inhabitants an annual fair of three weeks' continuance; but no charter to that effect has been found. Another account says that it was granted, at the instance of Nell Gwynne, by our "merry monarch," on his return from a day's sport in the neighbourhood to the residence of Sir Thomas Bond, already mentioned as one of his favourites. The fair is stated, by the author of "Merrie England in the Olden Time," to have been held in the immediate vicinity of the "Kentish Drovers," an old-established tavern in the Peckham Road, which is said to have existed here for about two centuries. When Peckham was

---

* See Vol. V., p. 496.

a village, surrounded by green fields, the "Kentish Drovers," as the sign implies, was a well-known halting-place for cattle-dealers, &c., on the road to Kent. Peckham Fair, with its wild beast and other shows, was of venerable antiquity at the date of its suppression. It was a famous place of resort with holiday-makers in the last century, and always had more than its share of curious monsters exhibited in its booths. Here, for instance, is one

5. The he-Panther, from Turkey, allowed by the curious to be one of the greatest rarities ever seen in England, on which are thousands of spots, and no two of a likeness.

6 & 7. The two fierce and surprising Hyænas, Male and Female, from the river Gambia. These creatures imitate the human voice, and so decoy negroes out of their huts and plantations to devour them. They have a mane like a horse, and two joints in their hinder legs more than any other creature. It is remarkable that all other beasts are to be tamed, but Hyænas they are not.

8. An Ethiopian Tobo Savage, having all the actions of

THE "ROSEMARY BRANCH" IN 1800.

of its programmes, at the top of which stands the name of "George I. R." :—

TO THE LOVERS OF CURIOSITIES.—To be seen, during the time of Peckham Fair, a grand Collection of Living Wild Beasts and Birds, lately arrived from the remotest parts of the world.

1. The Pelican, that suckles her young with her Heart's blood, from Egypt.

2. The noble Vulture Cock, brought from Archangell, having the finest tallons (sic) of any bird that seeks his prey. The fore part of his head is covered with hair; the second part resembles the wool of a Black; below that is a white Ring, having a Ruff that he cloaks his head with at night.

3. An Eagle of the Sun, that takes the loftiest flight of any Bird that flies. There is no bird but this that can fly to the face of the sun with a naked eye.

4. A curious beast, bred from a Lioness, like a foreign Wild Cat.

the human species, which, when it is at its full growth, will be upwards of five feet high.

9. Also several other surprising Creatures of different sorts. To be seen from 9 in the morning till 9 at night till they are sold. Also all manner of curiosities of different sorts are bought and sold at the above place by John Bennett.

In August, 1787, were to be seen at the fair such examples of the four-footed race as bears, monkeys, dancing-dogs, learned pigs, &c. Mr. Flockton, "in his theatrical booth opposite the 'Kentish Drovers,'" exhibited the Italian fantocini, the farce of the *Conjuror*, and his "inimitable musical clock." Mr. Lane, "first performer to the king," played off his "snip-snap, rip-rap, crick-crack, and thunder tricks, that the grown babies stared like worried cats." This extraordinary genius "will drive about forty twelve-penny nails into any gentleman's breech, place him in a load-stone chair, and draw them out without the least pain! He is, in short, the most wonderful of all wonderful creatures the world ever wondered at." At this fair Sir Jeffrey Dunstan sported his hand-some figure within his booth, outside of which was displayed a likeness of the elegant original in his pink satin smalls. " His dress, address, and

ments. Dramatic performances occasionally took place here as late as the beginning of this century. In 1822, however, the Lancasterian school for boys took possession of the premises.

In the High Street, at the corner of Clayton Road, there formerly stood a very quaint old house, with a thatched roof; it had once been a farm-house. It was pulled down in 1850.

The house at Peckham, where Goldsmith was

"HEATON'S FOLLY," IN 1804.

oratory fascinated the audience; in fact, 'Jeffy was quite tonish.'" Peckham Fair was held on the 21st, 22nd, and 23rd of August. It grew, however, to be a nuisance, as fairs generally do, and was abolished in 1827.

At Peckham—though the statement is very doubtful at best—George III. is said to have been married to the fair Quakeress, Hannah Lightfoot, on the 27th of May, 1759. We have already introduced this lady to our readers in our account of St. James's Market.*

There was in the High Street a theatre, at which, says tradition, Nell Gwynne sometimes performed, and her royal paramour attended the entertain-

employed as tutor in a school under a Dr. Milner, and where he wrote the best part of his " Vicar of Wakefield," was pulled down in 1876. In the Life of Goldsmith prefixed to his " Works " we read: " Tired of practice, or disappointed of suc-cess, he soon exchanged the phial for the ferule, and prescriptions for spelling-books. Goldsmith came out in the character of a schoolmaster's assistant at Peckham, a kind of employment to which he had been used before; and at the table of Dr. Milner—for so the master of the school was named—he became acquainted with Smollett, who first directed him to literature as a means of subsistence, by employing him as a contributor to the *Monthly Review.* Subsequently, physic and literature were combined to eke out a maintenance,

* See Vol. IV., p. 207.

and, in the double capacity of doctor and author, he presents himself to our notice in a wretched lodging by Salisbury Square, Fleet Street. Here we have a peep into the life of a poor literary man of the eighteenth century, to which parallels are numerous enough in the nineteenth. Leaving his lodgings, he kept his appointments at some house of call; the Temple Exchange Coffee-house, Temple Bar, was his most favoured resort. There, indeed, was his ostensible abode; and the people who saw him by day had little idea of the forlorn lodging where he spent his nights." The school was afterwards called in his honour Goldsmith's House. An avenue of trees in the grounds was once known as "Goldsmith's Walk," but it has long since passed away.

Hanover Street, in Rye Lane (formerly South Street), was doubtless intended as a compliment to the House of Hanover, some members of that family having been great patrons of Dr. Collyer, whose chapel, at the entrance to Rye Lane, is also known as Hanover Chapel. Basing Yard, in the rear of Hanover Street, serves as a memorial of Basing Manor, a well-known residence here during the time of the first and second Charles. Among the former residents of Peckham, there was Sir T. Gardyner, of Basing Manor, who, when writing to Lord Dorchester, in 1630, concerning the Papal machinations in Spain, eccentrically remarks that he would write a book on the subject if his time "were not so much occupied with growing melons and other fruits."

In Rye Lane is a large and well-built station, on the South London and the London, Chatham, and Dover Railways. Close by the station, a large building was erected in 1867, as a Museum of Fire-Arms, and for the exhibition of everything connected with gunnery. After standing a few years, it was burnt down, but was subsequently rebuilt. A rifle-range was also connected with the building, which, in process of time, was made to serve the purposes of a pleasure resort; but this in the end was converted into a manufactory of fire-arms.

Peckham Rye—a tract of common said to be upwards of fifty acres in extent—has from "time immemorial" been used as a recreation-ground by the inhabitants, not only of this district, but by thousands upon thousands whose life is principally spent amidst City smoke or over-built suburbs. Peckham Rye formed part of two manors, known as Camberwell Buckingham and Camberwell Friern; but in the year 1868 the manorial rights were purchased by the vestry of the parish. Previous to this acquisition of "the Rye"—as the common is

popularly called—by the vestry, the lord of the manor, Sir William Bowyer Smyth, had granted to a few of the inhabitants in its vicinity leases for twenty-one years, all of which expired in December, 1866. The lessees usually expended about £100 per annum (partly contributed by the inhabitants of the neighbourhood) in keeping the common in good condition.

The lord of the manor formerly held considerable property in the vicinity of Peckham Rye; indeed, as Mr. Blanch tells us, at one time the Bowyer family were the principal landowners in this parish. As far back as 1766, and again in 1789, protests were made by the parishioners against encroachments on the Rye, facts which are duly recorded in the Vestry Minutes. In 1865, a meeting of the inhabitants was held, to consider the best means to be adopted to prevent the erection of buildings on the Rye; and the matter was taken up by Parliament. In his evidence before the Committee of the House of Commons, in 1865, the deputy-steward of the lord of the manor claimed for Sir Bowyer Smyth the absolute ownership of the Rye, and asserted that he was entitled to the full building value of the land, there being at that time, in his opinion, no copy-holder having rights over it. In the end, however, as we have stated above, the manorial rights, whatever they may have been, were purchased by the vestry; and thus the Rye has become the common property of the parish, and made available for the free use of the South Londoner.*

In former times, the people's claims to the commons were stoutly defended—even to the sacrifice of life—not so much for the right of recreation as for the right of grazing or of gathering fuel. An old ditty, embodying the feeling of the people, runs thus :—

"'Tis very bad, in man or woman,
  To steal a goose from off the common ;
  But who shall plead that man's excuse
  Who steals the common from the goose ?"

In some old documents the Rye is spelled "Rey ;" and the old word "ree," a water-course, river, or expanse of water, is considered as probably the origin of the term. On the Rye is a quaint old farm-house, known as Homestead Farm, which takes us back to the time when such holdings abounded throughout the district.

On the north-east side of Peckham Rye is Nunhead, which is rapidly becoming a place of some importance, with a large population, and the head-

---

* This case is as nearly as possible identical with that of Hampstead Heath. See Vol. V., p. 452.

quarters of various centres of industry. Nunhead Green, an open space about one acre in extent, still remains; but its surroundings are now very different to what they were half a century ago, when village lads and lasses were wont to dance and romp there, and when the ancient "Nun's Head," which has been an institution in the locality for above two hundred years, was an object of attraction, through its tea-gardens, to worn-out citizens.

Here is the Asylum of the Metropolitan Beer and Wine Trade Association, which dates from 1851, when, at a general meeting of the beer-trade as a protection society, the idea assumed a substantial form, and a subscription was opened. The beer-sellers actively bestirred themselves to imitate the good example set by the licensed victuallers, by seeking to provide an asylum for their aged and decayed members. Indeed, one of the original objects contemplated by the promoters of the society was, "To raise a fund from which to allow temporary or permanent assistance to members of the trade." It was considered that the most useful permanent assistance that could be rendered would be by the erection of almshouses. The present plot of freehold ground, situate at Nunhead Green, was consequently purchased with the funds in hand for £550. An appeal was then made to the trade for further funds to erect the building, the result of which enabled the committee to commence the work. The first stone was laid by Lord Monteagle (the patron of the society) in June, 1852, and the building was completed and opened for the reception of inmates in September, 1853, the total cost being about £3,000. It comprises seven houses, each containing four rooms and a kitchen, accommodating in all thirteen inmates, and a piece of garden-ground in the rear for the use of the inmates is attached to each holding. In 1872 a new wing was completed, by the erection of eight six-roomed houses, thus providing accommodation for sixteen more inmates. There is an allowance of 6s. per week to single inmates, and 9s. per week to married couples.

Nunhead Cemetery, covering an area of about fifty acres, occupies the summit of some rising ground, whence a good view is obtained of the surrounding neighbourhood. The cemetery was consecrated by the Bishop of Winchester in 1840, and is beautifully laid out with gravel walks, and thickly planted with trees, shrubs, and flowers. The chapels in the grounds are conspicuous objects for miles round.

Nunhead Hill is mentioned by Hone in his "Every-day Book" (1827), as being "the favourite resort of smoke-dried London artisans." A narrow path by the side of the cemetery is all that remains for their Sunday promenade.

On the north side of Nunhead Cemetery are the reservoirs of the Southwark and Vauxhall Water Company, covering several acres of land. The works include four reservoirs—two high-level and two low-level; the former holding 6,000,000 gallons, and the latter double that number. The water is drawn from the Thames, about six miles above Teddington Locks. The water having been pumped up by an engine at Hampton Court, is forced on to Battersea, whence powerful engines again send it on to the reservoirs at Nunhead. The engine-house here, which stands between the upper and lower reservoirs, is a handsome brick structure, with a square tower seventy feet high, and built in the Venetian style of architecture.

Within the grounds now occupied by St. Mary's College, stood a building of some note in the early part of the present century, and known as "Heaton's Folly." This building was capped with a tower, giving it the appearance of a religious edifice. Lysons gives the following account of the structure:—"On the right side of the path leading from Peckham to Nunhead, appears this building, environed with wood. It has a singular appearance, and certainly was the effect of a whim. Various tales are related of its founder; but the most feasible appears his desire of giving employment to a number of artificers during a severe dearth. It is related that he employed five hundred persons in this building, and adding to the grounds; which is by no means improbable, as, on entering the premises, a very extensive piece of water appears, embanked by the properties taken from its bosom. In the centre of it is an island, well cultivated; indeed, the whole ground is now (1796) so luxuriantly spread, that I much doubt if such another spot, within a considerable distance from the metropolis, can boast such a variety and significance. The whole is within a fence; and, time having assisted the maturity of the coppice, you are, to appearance, enjoying the effects of a small lake in the centre of a wood. Motives the most laudable, as before observed, induced the founder of this sequestered spot to give bread to many half-starved and wretched families; and, to use the phrase of our immortal Shakespeare, 'It is like the dew from heaven, and doubly blesses.' If from appearance we are to judge of the phrase, it thrives indeed; and what was meant as assistance to a neighbouring poor, and stragglers, wretched and forlorn, is now, with all propriety, the Paradise of Peckham."

In the neighbourhood of Peckham Rye, on the

road to Forest Hill and Sydenham, is a hill with an oak upon its summit, called the "Oak of Honour:" at present shortened into "Honour Oak." It is said to have been so called because Queen Elizabeth, in one of her excursions on horseback from Greenwich, dined beneath its shade. The original tree has long since perished, having been struck by lightning, but it has been replaced by a successor. Mr. James Thorne, in his "Environs," writes :— "In the Chamberlain's papers for 1602 is this entry : 'On May-day the Queen [Elizabeth] went a-Maying to Sir Richard Buckley's, at Lewisham, some three or four miles off Greenwich.' Bulkeley's house was probably on the Sydenham side of Lewisham, where is Oak of Honour Hill, so named, according to the local tradition, from Queen Elizabeth having sat beneath the oak on its summit when she went hither a-maying."

Honour Oak, which is one of the boundaries of the parish, has witnessed many interesting gatherings, not the least impressive being that performed there, in former times, on the occasion of "beating the bounds," when it was customary for those assembled to join in singing the 104th Psalm, "under the shadow of the Oak of Honour Hill." From the advantages offered by its elevated position, the place formerly served as a beacon-hill, and a semaphore telegraph at one time was raised upon its summit.

On the south side of Forest Hill Road, and within a short distance of Oak of Honour Hill, is Camberwell Cemetery.

Friern Place, on the south-west side of Peckham Rye, keeps in remembrance the name of Friern Manor, the farm of which was known in recent times as a dairy-farm on a large scale. The Manor Farm-house and all its sheds and out-buildings were sold at the end of 1873. The house, which was not the original manor-house, was built by Lord St. John, in 1725; and there is a tradition that Alexander Pope resided there for a season, writing a portion of the "Essay on Man" beneath its roof, but it is merely a tradition. Lordship Lane, which lies on the west side of Friern Manor—uniting Goose Green and East Dulwich with Court Lane and the village of Dulwich—is supposed to have taken its name from the lordship of Friern Manor.

In Lordship Lane, there was, in the time of William Hone, an inn called the "Plough"—an old-fashioned wooden structure—on one of the windows of which was the following inscription, cut with a diamond :—"March 16, 1810. Thomas Jones dined here, eat six pounds of bacon and drank nineteen pots of beer." This record of dis-

gusting gluttony was, no doubt, swept away when the "Plough" was rebuilt some few years ago.

A writer in Hone's "Every-day Book" (1827) thus describes the scenery in this neighbourhood :— " Below me, yet wearing its sober livery of brown, lies the wood, the shadowy haunt of the gipsy tribe ere magisterial authority drove them away. Many a pleasant hour have I spent in my younger days with its Cassandras, listening to their prophetic voices and looking at their dark eyes. I proceed : Sydenham lies before me ; beyond it, in softened distance, Beckenham and Bromley meet the eye, with Dulwich below ; and in the foreground lies a rich variety of upland and dale, studded with snow-white dwellings."

Dulwich, which we now enter, is described in Hone's "Table-Book," with some little exaggeration, as "the prettiest of all the village entrances in the environs of London ;" and Priscilla Wakefield, in her "Perambulations" (1809), says it is "a hamlet to Camberwell, and is pleasantly retired, having no high road passing through it. It was formerly," she adds, "the resort of much company, on account of a medicinal spring, which has now lost its reputation. The house which has the sign of the 'Green Man' was for some time the residence of Lord Thurlow. A fine avenue through the wood faces this house, and leads to a charming prospect. The manor of Dulwich belongs to the college founded there, in 1614, by Master Edward Alleyn, the proprietor of the Fortune playhouse, in Whitecross Street, and also a favourite actor. The foundation was for a master and warden of the lineage and surname of Alleyn (but the impossibility of finding them has obliged the name of Allen to be of late years accepted), also four fellows, six poor brethren, and six poor sisters ; twelve scholars, six assistants, and thirty out-members or pensioners. It was originally built after a design by Inigo Jones, and formed three sides of a square. The picture-gallery, which is on the first floor, contains some scarce and valuable paintings. The chapel is a plain building, which serves as a chapel of ease to the inhabitants of the hamlet. The founder, his wife, and her mother, are buried in it ; and a clause in the statutes permits that privilege to the master, warden, and fellows, but excludes all others."

Notwithstanding the active building operations that of late years have fenced in London and its suburbs with miles of bricks and mortar, the village of Dulwich still presents a rural aspect, and large tracts of meadow-land are yet to be found within its borders. From the high grounds of Champion Hill, Denmark Hill, and Herne Hill, of which we have spoken in the preceding chapter, through the whole length of the intervening valley, and up the opposite slopes to the summit of Sydenham and Forest Hills, may still be heard the song of birds; whilst the beauties of the place are spread out in groves and pleasure-grounds, green lanes, and flowery meadows. The southern portion of the hamlet was formerly an immense wood, intersected with devious paths. It was the sacred home of the gipsy tribe, and the rendezvous of summer parties. At the beginning of the present century, before what may be termed modern Dulwich sprang into existence, Byron, then a schoolboy here, made Dulwich Wood one of his favourite haunts, and, we are told, would there "daily hold converse with motley groups of the vagabond class." But little is left of the wood beyond a memory, which local nomenclature has done something to preserve, in the names of Dulwich Wood Park, Kingswood Road, and Crescent Wood Road. We are told how that, in the days of Charles I., the Court paid frequent visits to Dulwich and its woods for the purposes of sport; and how authority was given by warrant to one Anthony Holland, one of the yeomen-huntsmen in ordinary to his Majesty, to make known his Majesty's commands to the inhabitants of Dulwich "that they forbeare to hunt, chace, molest, or hurt the king's stagges with greyhounds, hounds, gunnes, or any other means whatsoever;" and also how the said Anthony Holland was further authorised "to take from any person or persons offending therein their dogges, hounds, gunnes, crossbowes, or other engynes."

Dulwich Wood has been the scene of several outrages, notably those which occurred in 1738, when a man named Samuel Bentyman was murdered, and in 1803, when Samuel Matthews, known as the Dulwich Hermit, met with a similar fate. Mr. Blanch informs us that the wood has been gradually disappearing from the time when Edward Alleyn issued his statutes and ordinances for the foundation of the college in the early part of the seventeenth century, for by the 106th item it is ordered "that twentye acres of woode be felled and sold yearly, such wood-falls to be made at seasonable times, and in accordance with the laws and statutes of England, for the preservation of timber-trees, such trees to be of the growth of ten yeares;" and by the 110th item it is enacted "that no timber-trees shall be sold to any pson. or psons. whatsoever, but to the tenants of the lands belonging to the said college in Dulwich, for the building or repayring of their tenements."

The same writer justly remarks, in his "History of Camberwell," that "the Dulwich College Building

Act of 1808, the Metropolis Local Management Act of 1855, the Charity Commissioners' scheme of 1857, the formation of the iron roads, and the craving of merchants for suburban residences, have done much to alter the aspect of the place;" but that, "compared with neighbouring suburbs, it has died hard, and not until Cowper's 'opulent, enlarged, and still-increasing London,' by sheer force of circumstances, has laid its hands upon it, will Dulwich surrender its individuality."

The village "stocks" and "cage," with the motto, "It is a sport for a fool to do mischief; thine own wickedness shall correct thee," formerly stood at the corner of the pathway across the fields leading to Camberwell, opposite the burial-ground; and the college "pound," which formerly stood near the toll-gate in the Penge Road, was, in 1862, ordered to be removed to the end of Croxted Lane. One of the most interesting spots within the hamlet is that formerly known as Bew's Corner, Lordship Lane. The "Green Man," a tavern of some note in the middle of the last century, formerly occupied the site, after which time Dr. Glennie's school was built; and that in its turn having disappeared, a beer-house was opened there, by a man named Bew, formerly employed at the college, who made use of some out-buildings of the once famous school, and converted the grounds into a tea-garden.

The famous Dulwich Wells were in close proximity to the "Green Man," and the Dulwich waters were cried about the streets of London as far back as 1678; and for many years, through the high repute of the waters, much custom was drawn to the adjoining tavern, which, in 1748, was described as a "noted house of good entertainment." The proprietor flourished so well, that a publication of the time tells us that "he has lately built a handsome room on one end of his bowling-green for breakfasts, dancing, and entertainment; a part of the fashionable luxury of the present age, which every village for ten miles round London has something of." A full account of the Dulwich mineral waters was communicated to the public through the "Philosophical Transactions," by Professor Martyn, F.R.S. Mr. Bray, in his account of this parish in his "History of Surrey," writes:—"In the autumn of 1739, Mr. Cox, master of the "Green Man," about a mile south of the village of Dulwich, having occasion to sink a well for his family, dug down about sixty feet without finding water. Discouraged at this, he covered it up, and so left it. In the following spring, however, he opened it again; when, the Botanical Professor in the University of Cambridge being present, it was found to contain about twenty-five feet of water, of a sulphureous taste and smell." It was found by experiment to be possessed of purgative qualities, and was for some time used medicinally, but was afterwards neglected.

Dr. Webster, who has been considered a high authority on the subject, writes as follows with reference to these waters :—"The saline spring was, and is, situated on Sydenham Common, in Wells Lane, on the slope of the hill between Dulwich and Sydenham. The little old cottage and garden where the 'Sydenham Wells' are, belongs to two

pupil for two years. The old house was taken down about ten years after, when Dr. Glennie had left, but I remember then seeing a well within the premises, which had been long shut up or disused, and I tasted the water, which was decidedly chalybeate. On the site of the old 'Green Man' now stands the 'Grove Tavern,' of no celebrity in any way unless from the circumstances now stated, and which very few knew besides myself. I knew the supposed localities of both these places many years ago, but it is only recently that Evelyn's "Diary" fell in my way, and it is remarkable that

DR. GLENNIE'S ACADEMY, DULWICH GROVE, IN 1820.

elderly women of the name of Evans, and on my expressing surprise that they had not been 'bought out' for building, as the spot is surrounded by modern mansions and good houses, they replied, they kept possession, as the little property would be beneficial to their deceased brother's children. It is not at all resorted to now for medicinal purposes ; but the water is strongly saline, similar to that at the quondam 'Beulah Spa,' at Streatham Common, and at Epsom. It is situated in the parish of Lewisham, Kent. The Dulwich Spa was a chalybeate spring, situated about a mile S.E. of Dulwich College, close to, or rather, I believe, *in* the premises of the 'Green Man,' then a place of resort on the verge of Dulwich Common. This was as far back as the seventeenth century ; but this house of entertainment was, when I first knew it (1815), a house of instruction, as Dr. Glennie's well-known academy, at which Lord Byron was a

he incidentally mentions them so as to identify the *two* springs. Under date September 2nd, 1675, he notes : 'I went to see Dulwich Colledge, being the pious foundation of one Allen, a famous comedian in King James's time. The chapell is pretty ; the rest of the hospital very ill contriv'd ; it yet maintaines divers poore of both sexes. 'Tis in a melancholy part of Camerwell parish. I came back by certaine medicinal Spa waters at a place called Sydnam Wells, in Lewisham parish, much frequented in summer.' And further on : ' 1677, August 5th, I went to visit my Lord Brounker, now taking the waters at Dulwich.' So you see," adds Dr. Webster, "there were two distinct spas within a mile, but in different parishes and counties, as Dulwich is in Surrey." So, as our readers will observe, fashionable persons resorted to Dulwich for the purpose of "taking the waters," just as they did at Hampstead a century later.

VIEWS IN CAMBERWELL AND DULWICH.

1. St. Mary-le Strand House, Old Kent Road.   2. Goldsmith's House.   3. Bew's Corner, Dulwich.   4. Old Camberwell.

5. Old Crown Inn, Dulwich.   6. Plough Inn, Lordship Lane.

Among the pupils at Dr. Glennie's academy in Dulwich Grove, were several who in after years rose to fame and fortune—Lord Byron, General Le Marchant, Sir Donald M'Leod, Captain Barclay, the celebrated pedestrian, and others. "Once a week did the little party meet together in the spacious entrance-hall for a little rational amusement, and the Saturday evening concerts at Dulwich attracted visitors from outside the family circle. 'Tom' Campbell the poet, Howard and Wilkie, artists and academicians, and Barker the well-known painter of panoramas, and many others, often found themselves at Dulwich. Campbell had not far to come, for he resided at Sydenham for seventeen years before that retired little village became an 'endless pile of brick.' Here the happiest of the poet's days were spent in genial and congenial society, and much concerning 'evenings' there may be found in the memoirs of Moore, Hook, Hunt, the brothers Smith, and others.

"The narrow lane, lined with hedgerows, and passing through a little dell watered by a rivulet—the extensive prospect of undulating hills, park-like enclosures, the shady walks," where the poet was "safe from all intrusion but that of the Muses," as he himself describes them—

"Spring green lanes,
With all the dazzling field-flowers in their prime,
And gardens haunted by the nightingale's
Long trills and gushing ecstasies of song."

With respect to Byron's school-days at Dulwich, there is nothing remarkable for us to record. In a letter to Tom Moore, Dr. Glennie speaks of Byron's ambition to excel in all athletic exercises, notwithstanding his lameness; "an ambition," writes Dr. Glennie, "which I have found to prevail in general in young persons labouring under similar defects of nature." It is said that Byron and his schoolfellows kept up a mimicry of brigandage, and that the stern demand of "Stand and deliver" was often made, to the amusement of the boys, and the fright of the passing stranger. "It must not be imagined," adds Mr. Blanch, in writing of this epoch, "that brigandage in Dulwich was all play, for at the commencement of the present century Sydenham Hill had then a reputation somewhat akin to Hounslow Heath. Dulwich Wood was the halting-place for gipsies; and highwaymen and footpads abounded in the locality."

Dulwich has long been a favourite resort for the working men of London, for the purpose of holding their annual gatherings at one or other of its taverns, the chief of which are the "Greyhound," the "Half Moon," and the "Crown." The "Crown" has been an "institution" in Dulwich for upwards of a century and a half; the greater part of the present house was rebuilt in 1833, and it was further modernised about twenty years later. In the garden of the "Half Moon," at the northern extremity of the village, for many years was to be seen the old tombstone of Edward Alleyn, the founder of Dulwich College, and it doubtless proved advantageous to the landlord in drawing visitors to his house. It has, however, been superseded by a new tombstone in the college chapel. The "Greyhound" is a well-known hostelry here, and has been held by the same family for upwards of a century. Here the Dulwich Club holds its meetings. This association was established in 1772, for the purposes of friendly converse and social cheer among a large body of literary gentlemen; and the club has entertained at its table during its career many distinguished men, such as Dr. Glennie, Thomas Campbell, Dr. Babington, Dickens, Thackeray, Mark Lemon, and others.

Among the residents at Dulwich in recent times have been several whose names have become famous. Of these we may mention Mr. Howard Staunton, who lived at Ivy Cottage, while engaged in his Shakespearean researches at the college. Mr. and Mrs. S. C. Hall, the well-known authors, at one time lived here. Another noted name in connection with Dulwich is that of Henry Bessemer, the inventor of a new process in the manufacture of steel, and whose numerous patents connected with improvements in machinery have been such as to have established his reputation as a scientific and practical engineer of the highest order.

Numerous mansions and seats are scattered about in the neighbourhood of Dulwich, notably Casino, on Dulwich Hill; Mr. Bessemer's house on Denmark Hill; Woodhall, formerly the residence of the late Mr. George Grote, the historian of Greece; the Hoo, on Sydenham Hill; and lastly, the Manor House. This last-mentioned edifice is a building of more than ordinary interest, from the fact that it was once the residence of Edward Alleyn, the Lord Mayor of London, and perhaps, at an earlier period, the summer retreat of the Abbots of Bermondsey. It was formerly called Hall Court. "The house, since Alleyn's time," writes Mr. Blanch, "has undergone sundry additions and alterations, and at the present time is in a marvellous condition for so old a building—a fact which seems to confirm the belief that it was built before Alleyn's time, as the erection of the old college, which was closely watched by the founder, began to tumble to pieces soon after his death. The Manor House had been designed and built in a very different style. The magnificent oak staircase, and spacious entrance-hall, and lofty rooms, are worthy of the majestic actor; and, as one looks around, the form of its dignified host is conjured up; now receiving the poor brethren and sisters, holding consultations with the master, warden, and fellows, and anon holding converse and correspondence with the great men of the land, Alleyn's life at Dulwich must have been delightful. Possessing ample means—much given to home comforts and duties, to which he was so attached that within three months of losing 'his good sweete harte and loving mouse,' he took unto himself another partner—regarded by his neighbours as a man of considerable substance, and treated in a manner befitting the squire of the place—having great worldly knowledge, serene temper, and considerable tact—he made many friends and few enemies; and as his journal teems with payments for sundry bottles of wine when he went to London to see his friends, it is fair to assume that his cellar at the Manor House was well filled, and at the service of his visitors.

"And what more delightful walks could any mortal have had than those surrounding the fine old mansion in Alleyn's time?—when the meadows were yellow with the crowfoot, flushed with the sorrel, or purple with clover; the thornbushes, white or pink with their blossoms; the commons, golden with mellowing fern or glowing with purple heather; and deciduous trees contributing their varied tints to the scene—all this was then a reality! Would that it were so now—and to the same extent!—and the shade of wood and grove, and the ramble

"'O'er many a heath, through many a woodland dun,
     Through buried paths, where sleepy twilight dreams
     The summer-time away;'

and the feast of satisfaction as the founder viewed the progress of his college, at the end of a summer's stroll—all this must have made life more than endurable at the Manor House.

"That Alleyn received at his board many distinguished men of his day is beyond doubt; but, strange to relate, no scrap of evidence has yet been produced in support of the supposition that Shakespeare ever made pilgrimage to Dulwich. It is, to say the least of it, an extraordinary circumstance, that two such prominent characters in the same profession should not have been brought together —or rather, that no evidence should be forth-

coming in support of such a natural supposition. Garrick, Malone, Collier, Ingleby, Staunton, and other able and industrious workers have toiled diligently, and hoped unfalteringly, but without success. And yet Ben Jonson and Michael Drayton were intimate associates both of Shakespeare and Alleyn. They were not divided by disparity of age, for Alleyn was Shakespeare's junior by only two years, four months, and a week, and both relinquished the stage, and invested their earnings in houses and lands, at about the same time."

From the old Manor House, the home of Edward Alleyn, it is but an easy transition to pass to the College, of which he was the founder— or, to give it its full title, to "Alleyn's College of God's Gift." Born in the parish of St. Botolph, Bishopsgate, in September, 1566, Alleyn lived to attain extraordinary celebrity as an actor in an age prolific beyond all others in dramatic talent. Fuller, in his "Worthies," describes him as "the Roscius of our age, so acting to the life that he made any part (especially a majestick one) to become him." The following epigram, addressed by Ben Jonson to Edward Allen, will serve to show the reputation in which the latter was held among the poets and men of letters of his time:—

"If Rome, so great, and in her wisest age,
     Feared not to boast the glories of her stage,
     As skilful Roscius and grave Æsop, men
     Yet crowned with honours as with riches then,
     Who had no less a trumpet of their name
     Than Cicero, whose every breath was fame:
     How can so great example die in me
     That, Allen, I should pause to publish thee?
     Who both their graces in thyself hast more
     Outstript, than they did all that went before;
     And present worth in all dost so contract,
     As others speak, but only thou dost act.
     Wear this renown. 'Tis just, that who did give
     So many poets life, by one should live."

"The connection of the name of Allen (usually spelt Alleyn, but now printed Allen) with the munificent endowment of Dulwich College," writes Mr. Robert Bell, "has eclipsed his reputation as an actor; but, independently of this high encomium of Jonson, ample evidence has been traced, not only of the influential position he held in relation to the stage, but of his great skill as a player. He appears to have been the chief manager of the business of the company for Henslowe, with whom he was part-proprietor of the Fortune, and to whose stepdaughter he was married. He negotiated with authors, and made engagements with actors, for which he was better qualified, in some respects, than Henslowe, who, although an excellent man of business, was illiterate. There is reason to believe, also, from certain entries in Henslowe's diary, that he sometimes helped to reconstruct, or adapt, pieces for the stage. As an actor he certainly stood in the first rank, and his special merits in particular parts are testified by Nash, Dekker, and Heywood. All the particulars of his life that are now likely to be recovered have been collected by Mr. Collier, in the 'Memoir' of him, and in the 'Alleyn Papers,' published by the Shakespeare Society."

In 1606 Alleyn had already commenced the acquisition of property at Dulwich. The most important of the valuable estates which now collectively form the endowment of the college were the lands and lordship of the manor, purchased in the above-mentioned year from Sir Francis Calton, to whose ancestor, Thomas Calton, they had been granted by Henry VIII. upon the dissolution of the Monastery of Bermondsey. The college land stretches southwards from the high ground, known in its several parts as Champion Hill, Denmark Hill, and Herne Hill, through the whole length of the intervening valley, and up the opposite slopes to the summit of Sydenham and Forest Hills, a length of more than three miles as the crow flies. The breadth of the estate from east to west is quite a mile and a half in its widest part. The village of Dulwich occupies a central position on the college lands. It lies, as we have stated above, in the bottom of the valley between the ridge on which rests the Crystal Palace and the less lofty ridge midway between Sydenham Hill and the Thames. It is so shut in by near hills, or by lofty trees, in all directions, that its horizon is nowhere more distant than a mile or two. Visitors constantly remark that when in Dulwich they are as much in the country as if they were fifty miles from London; and yet the village milestone in front of the college, bearing the hospital invitation to wayfarers, "*Siste, Viator*," records the distance of that spot from the Treasury, Whitehall, or from the Standard at Cornhill, to be only five miles.

In 1613 Alleyn contracted with a certain John Benson, of Westminster, for the erection of "a Chappell, a Schoole-house, and twelve Almeshouses," and in the course of the years 1616 and 1617 the first members of his foundation were admitted into the college. But Alleyn's great work was still far from completed. For some years he was engaged in harassing and apparently futile negotiations to obtain a royal patent for the permanent establishment of his foundation. It is interesting to observe that the impediments

which Alleyn experienced seem to have proceeded chiefly from no less eminent a man than the great Lord Bacon, then Lord Chancellor. In a letter to the Marquis of Buckingham, dated August 18th, 1618, Bacon, while he says, with characteristic point and quaintness, "I like well that Allen playeth the last act of his life so well," yet pleads with the king, through Buckingham, for the curtailment of Alleyn's eleemosynary foundation, and the promotion in preference of endowments for the encouragement of learning. In spite, however, of all difficulties, Alleyn's unflinching perseverance at last prevailed, and on the 21st of June, 1619, the great seal of England was affixed to letters patent from James I., giving licence to Edward Alleyn "to found and establish a college in Dulwich, to endure and remain for ever, and to be called 'The College of God's Gift in Dulwich, in the county of Surrey.'"

Aubrey has recorded an amusing story, which the reader may believe or not as he thinks best, that Alleyn was frightened into his generous and charitable scheme by an apparition of the Prince of Darkness, *in propria persona*, among six theatrical demons in a certain piece in which he was playing. In the fright thus occasioned he was said to have made a vow, which he redeemed by the founding of the College of God's Gift.

The college was formally opened with great ceremony on the 13th of September, 1619; and Alleyn had the satisfaction of recording in his diary: "This day was the fowndacion of the Colledge finisht;" and so, in the quaint words of old Fuller, "He who out-acted others in his life, out-did himself before his death." Amongst the distinguished guests on this occasion, of whom Alleyn gives a list, we find "the Lord Chancellor (Lord Bacon), the Lord of Arondell, Lord Ciecell (Cecil), Sir John Howland, High Shreve (Sheriff), and Inigo Jones, the king's surveyor." He adds, "They first herd a Sermond, and after the instrument of creacion was by me read, and after an anthem, they went to dinner."

Alleyn survived the opening of his college seven years, but there is some difficulty in determining the exact day of his death. On the present tombstone (which is, however, of recent erection) it is stated to have been November 21st; but documentary evidence seems to point to Saturday, November 25th, as the correct date. At all events, be this as it may, he affixed his signature to the draft of his Ordinances and Statutes on November 20th, and was buried in the chapel of his college on November 27th, 1626.

"God's Gift College," thus founded and endowed by Edward Alleyn, "to the honour and glory of Almighty God, and in a thankful remembrance of His guiftes and blessings bestowed upon me," consisted of a master and a warden (both to be of the name of Alleyn), four fellows, six poor brethren, six poor sisters, and twelve poor scholars. The almspeople and scholars were chosen in equal proportions from the four parishes severally of St. Botolph without Bishopsgate; St. Saviour's, Southwark; St. Luke's, Middlesex; and St. Giles's, Camberwell. In the letters patent a right was reserved to the founder to frame statutes for the government of the college. Alleyn seems, however, to have overrated the powers thus vested in him, and consequently several of his provisions, after long disputes and litigation, were set aside by the courts of law.

The most important of the modifications introduced by Alleyn's maturer judgment into his original scheme, it appears, were those designed to extend the basis of his educational foundation. He now ordained that his school should be for the instruction of eighty boys, consisting of three distinct classes :—(1) Twelve poor scholars; (2) children of inhabitants of Dulwich (who were to be taught freely); and (3) "Towne or Forreign Schollers," who were to pay "such allowance as the master and warden should appoint."

Though to some extent the issue and production of the stage, Dulwich College never greatly benefited the members of the dramatic profession. Alleyn had resolved to found and endow in his own lifetime an institution of a semi-monastic character, like the Charterhouse, for the reception of aged pensioners, and for the nurture and education of orphan boys. The original statutes and ordinances define the qualifications and duties of the several members of the college, and regulate the distribution of the income. They embrace provisions which have many times proved a fruitful source of costly litigation. Thus, the second statute provides for a large addition, under the designation of six "chanters," six assistants in the government of the college, and thirty out-members, beyond the *personnel* authorised by the letters patent.

In the dietary for the boys is included "a cup of beere" at breakfast and "beere without stint" at dinner, "with such increase of diett in Lent and gawdy days as the surveyor of diett may think fitt." The beef and mutton for the boys were to be "sweet and good, their beere well brewed, and their bread well baked, and made of clean and sweete wheatten meal." Their coats were to be of "good cloth, of sad cullor, the boddys

lined with canvass." A statute fixed twenty-one years as the maximum term of a lease of any part of the college property. This restriction hampered more than any other the development of the college property, and it was eventually rescinded by the Dulwich Building Act of 1808.

Vacancies on the foundation, whether of scholars or old pensioners, or in the superior offices of fellow or warden, were to be filled up by the "drawing of lots" by two selected candidates. Even the mastership was to be filled up in the same way, if at the time of a vacancy there was no warden to succeed. The manner of drawing the lots is minutely described in one of the statutes, and the process continued in force till the re-organisation of the college in 1857. "God's Gift" was written on one of two equal small rolls of paper; the other roll was left blank. Both were placed in a box and shaken thrice up and down. The elder of the two selected candidates then took up one roll, the younger took the other. The fortunate drawer of the God's Gift roll carried the prize. The founder's preference for the four parishes from which the poor scholars and brethren and sisters should be selected was based on his perception of the doctrine that property has its duties as well as its rights. As we have already seen, he owned theatres and houses in St. Saviour's and St. Luke's; his patrimonial estate was in St. Botolph's; and he had acquired by purchase the whole lordship of Dulwich, in the parish of Camberwell.

In spite of Fuller's declaration that "no hospital is tyed with better or stricter laws, that it may not sagg (swerve) from the intention of the founder," there can be little doubt that the want of elasticity in its original constitution prevented, for more than two centuries, any healthy development of the college, and thus effectually frustrated the true "intentions" of Edward Alleyn. Some partial attempts were made under injunctions of several Archbishops of Canterbury, as visitors of Dulwich College, to extend the educational benefits of the foundation; but little was really effected until the passing of the Act of Parliament in 1857, under the provisions of which the college is now administered.

"The founder's scheme," observes a writer in *Macmillan's Magazine*, "too rigid and inelastic to sustain the shock of modern notions, had long ceased to be seriously defended, even by those who dispensed its gifts and luxuriated in its most substantial rewards. Hampered by the fixity of inflexible statutes, embarrassed by riches which it could not spend without shame, and which invited incessant onslaught from the four interested parishes, Alleyn's College succumbed on the last day of 1857 to public opinion, released its members from monastic rule, sent them forth well pensioned into the outer world, and opened its gates next day to its new rulers."

By the Act of Parliament, passed in 1857, Alleyn's foundation was completely re-constituted. The government of the college is now vested in nineteen governors, of whom eleven are nominated into four portions, of which three are assigned to the educational and one to the eleemosynary branch. The educational foundation comprises two distinct schools—the "upper school" and the "lower school." In the "upper school" liberal provision is made for the endowment of exhibitions, tenable either at one of the English Universities, or by a student of any learned or scientific profession or of the fine arts. Sundry scholarships of £20 a

DULWICH COLLEGE IN 1790.

by the Court of Chancery, the rest being elected by the four parishes to which special privileges were attached by the terms of the original foundation. The officers of administration are a "Master of the College" (whose office, however, is no longer restricted to a person of the founder's name), a Chaplain, an Under-Master of the Upper School, a Master of the Lower School, a Receiver, and a Clerk, together with such Assistant-Masters, Professors, and Lecturers as may be required to ensure thorough efficiency to the educational department.

The revenue of the college, which at the time of the founder's death was £800 a year, now amounts to more than £17,000. The surplus revenue (after provision has been made for the maintenance of the fabric, and of the chapel and library) is divided year, tenable in the school, were likewise established in 1870, under authority of the Charity Commissioners. The "lower school" is described as being for the instruction and benefit of the children of the industrial and poorer classes resident in any of the four parishes. It is a separate school, and is entirely distinct in its conduct and arrangements from the "upper school." Provision is made for the establishment in the "lower school" of scholarships and "gratuities" to be awarded to deserving boys, for the purpose of advancing them in the world.

The old college, though the central attraction of the village, has but limited pretensions to architectural merit. It has been thought by some topographers that it was built by the famous Inigo

Jones, but it is scarcely probable that so good an architect could have been employed upon it, as we find that the tower fell down in 1638; moreover, the specification for Benson's erection is still preserved, with memoranda showing payments made to him as the work progressed. The fall of the tower so injured the revenues of the college, as to occasion its being suspended for six months, during which time the master and fellows received no

the short power of his son Richard, the lands and goods of the college were taken away, and its rights set aside; but at the Restoration these were recovered, and have since remained secure.

The old college buildings are spacious, having regard to the limited numbers for whom they were built, and comprise a chapel, dining-hall, parlour, library, school-room, kitchen, and appurtenances. They occupy three sides of a square. The entrance-

DULWICH COLLEGE IN 1750.

salary, but the poor people and scholars had two shillings a week each. Not long after this another portion of the building fell down; and, in 1703, the porch and other parts followed. Frequent repairs were accordingly made, which were marked by dates in different parts of the old building.

Dulwich College suffered its full share of the havoc committed by fanatics in the Civil Wars. It was turned into quarters for a company of soldiers of Fairfax's army, who, it is said, took up the leaden coffins in the chapel, and melted them into bullets. The fellows of the college were in arms for the king; in consequence of which they were deprived of their fellowships, and a schoolmaster and usher were appointed in their stead. During the government of Oliver Cromwell, and

gates are of curiously wrought iron, surmounted with the founder's arms, crest, and the motto, "God's Gift." These lead into an outer court or green. The old chapel, a very plain structure, has long served as a chapel of ease, for this village, to the church of Camberwell. Although built for the college, it is frequented by the inhabitants also, and was long ago enlarged for their accommodation. The font is inscribed with a palindrome, in which the sequence of the letters is the same backwards as forwards—

νίψον ἀνόμημα μὴ μόναν ὄψιν.
(Wash sin, not the face only.)

In the chancel is a marble slab, marking the tomb of Edward Alleyn, the founder.

A curious collection of pictures and portraits

more remarkable, however, with a few exceptions, for their historical associations than for any artistic excellence, was bequeathed sixty years after the founder's time by the grandson of his *confrère*, Cartwright. In this collection (including a few left by Alleyn) are striking and characteristic portraits of the founder himself; one of Frobisher, the scourge of the Spaniards in the old Armada days; Michael Drayton, the poet, who, with Ben Jonson, was a guest at Shakespeare's table at that last "merry meeting," a few days before his death; and also of many players who trod the same stage and shared the same social gatherings with Shakespeare and Alleyn, such as Burbage, Nathaniel Field, Sly, Bond, Perkins, and Cartwright. These pictures were formerly hung in the corridors and staircases of the old college, but are now transferred to the new buildings. In 1840 Mr. J. O. Halliwell exhibited before the Society of Antiquaries a copy of a pen-and-ink drawing from the back of a letter in Dulwich College, and supposed to be a portrait of Shakespeare, by Henslowe, to whom the letter is addressed. The college, as might have been expected, was particularly rich in old plays; these were collected by Henslowe, Alleyn, and Cartwright, and were treasured here until Garrick acquired them from the then master, garden, and fellows, for the inadequate recompense of a parcel of new books. The collection passed, on Garrick's decease, to the British Museum.

The pictures mentioned above are in no way connected with those belonging to the Dulwich College Picture Gallery, which is situated at the south-west corner of the old buildings. The gallery was built from the designs and under the direction of Sir John Soane, and was first opened to the public in the year 1817. The history of the collection is, in many ways, a remarkable one. It owes its foundation to "a noble trio of benefactors." Towards the close of the last century there was living in London, and plying there an active trade in pictures of the highest class, one Noel Joseph Desenfans, who is considered to have been a keen critic of art, and a no less shrewd judge of a bargain. He was a native of Douai, in France, but had settled in London first of all as a teacher of languages. His taste for art, however, and the advantageous sale of a "Claude" in his possession to George III. for 1,000 guineas, induced him to devote himself entirely to the more lucrative employment of a picture-dealer. In course of time he was commissioned by the unhappy Stanislaus—then almost in the dying throes of the fated kingdom of Poland—to purchase pictures to form a National Gallery for Poland. In his negotiations,

Desenfans had been constantly aided by his friend Sir Francis Bourgeois, R.A. On the overthrow of the Polish kingdom, Desenfans offered his pictures to the Czar, Paul I. of Russia, but without success; and in the end it became the nucleus of the Dulwich Gallery. Desenfans spent the last few years of his life at the house of Sir Francis Bourgeois, in Charlotte Street, Portland Place, and on his death, in 1807, bequeathed to him the whole of his large and valuable collection of pictures. Bourgeois, like Desenfans, had no children to claim inheritance in it, and he resolved to carry out what appears to have been the desire also of his friend, and to place their joint collection of pictures in the custody of some public body for the encouragement of the study of fine arts. An accidental acquaintance with one of the fellows of the foundation, we are told, directed his attention to Dulwich College. Accordingly, in 1811, he bequeathed his pictures "to the master, wardens, and fellows of Dulwich College in trust for the public use, under the direction of the Royal Academy." The bequest was accompanied by a condition that a mausoleum should be contained in the gallery, where his own remains and those of his two friends, Monsieur and Madame Desenfans, should be placed. A separate building attached to the rooms where the pictures hang was therefore erected for the purpose. The collection (including four or five pictures which have been presented subsequently by other donors, and a few unfinished sketches) consists of upwards of 370 pictures. It is particularly rich in works of the Dutch and Flemish schools, and contains examples of the Spanish schools which, it is said, are not surpassed by any in this country. The pictures are fully described by Dr. Waagen.* One of the chief ornaments in the gallery is the celebrated "Madonna" of Murillo. At first the gallery was opened to the public on Tuesdays only, and some little difficulty was thrown in the way of free access to the collection : all intending visitors were obliged to obtain tickets previously from one or other of the great London printsellers, who were authorised to supply them *gratis*, and notice was given both at the gallery and in the catalogue that "without a ticket no person can be admitted, and no tickets are given at Dulwich." The limitation to a single day in the week was not long retained, and since 1858 visitors have been admitted without tickets or introduction, on the sole condition of entering their name in the visitors' book.

The new school buildings, now popularly known as "Dulwich College," are situated about a quarter

* "Art and Artists in England," vol. ii., pp. 378—389.

of a mile south of the old building. They are in the "Northern Italian style of the thirteenth century," and were built from the designs of Mr. Charles Barry. The first stone of the new building was laid in June, 1866, and in June, 1870, the edifice was formally opened by the Prince of Wales. The schools comprise three distinct blocks : viz., a central building, containing the public and official rooms, the great hall, the lecture-theatre, library, &c. ; and two wings, connected with the centre building by corridors or cloisters—the south wing being appropriated to the senior section of the upper school, with the residence of the master of the college ; and the north wing to the junior section, with the residence of the under-master of the upper school. The buildings are constructed of red brick with terra-cotta ornamentation, the front of the centre building being the most profusely ornamented ; the decoration is carried entirely round the building. For the most part, the ornamentation is architectural, but a distinctive and characteristic feature is a series of heads, in very high relief, from concave shields, of the principal poets, historians, orators, philosophers, &c., of Greece, Rome, Italy, Germany, and England—the names of each being legibly inscribed in the hollow of the shield. The cost of the new schools was about £100,000 ; the building provides accommodation for between 600 and 700 boys. The college stands in an area of forty-five acres, of which about thirty acres have been appropriated to the schools and playground. The lower school is at present located in the old buildings of the college.

There can be no doubt that the art-schools of the college owe much of their remarkable success to their association with the splendid collection of pictures forming the Dulwich Gallery. It is at least certain that the study of art has been carried much farther and to higher perfection at Dulwich than at any other public school in the kingdom. On the annual "speech day," when the distribution of prizes takes place, dramatic performances are given by the boys in the great hall ; and from 700 to 800 visitors can be readily accommodated on these occasions. Since its new birth, Dulwich College has started on an era of educational advancement ; and the extraordinary increase in the number of boys, and the numerous honours obtained by them in almost every competition open to our public schools—for this college holds its own both at Oxford and Cambridge—speaks eloquently, not only of the appreciation of the school throughout the districts south of the Thames, but of the great need which formerly existed there of increased educational facilities.

In a small *brochure*, entitled "Alleyn's College of God's Gift at Dulwich," issued at the opening of the new schools in 1870, the writer concludes : "Thus, after many struggles and difficulties, and a long period of lethargy more fruitless still, Dulwich College has started at length into fresh and vigorous life, with powers of influence and means of usefulness which few foundations can rival, and with well-founded hopes for the future which far surpass the utmost expectations of its pious and munificent founder."

CHAPTER XXIII.

SYDENHAM, NORWOOD, AND STREATHAM.

"Hinc . . . dominos videre colles
Et totam licet æstimare Romam."—*Martial.*

Situation of Sydenham—Its Rapid Growth as a Place of Residence—Sydenham Wells—The Poet Campbell—Death of Thomas Dermody—Thomas Hill—Churches at Sydenham—Rockhill—Sir Joseph Paxton—The Crystal Palace—Anerley—Norwood—The Home of the Gipsies—Knight's Hill—Beulah Spa—North Surrey District Schools—The Catholic Female Orphanage—The Jews' Hospital—Norwood Cemetery—The Royal Normal College and Academy of Music for the Blind—Death of the Earl of Dudley—Streatham—Mineral Springs—Anecdote of Lord Thurlow—The Residence of Mrs. Thrale at Streatham—The Magdalen Hospital.

"NOTHING," writes Mr. Laman Blanchard, in "A Guide to the Country round London," "can be more charmingly sylvan, or less suggestive of the approximate City, than the walk across the hill to Sydenham, which reveals a varied and expansive prospect over Kent as we approach its precincts. The town lies in a hollow, and has a number of opulent residents, whose elegant mansions contribute to diversify the scene. On the common has recently been built a handsome church, and

along by the railway several stately villas have been called into being by the increased facilities of transit thus afforded, and the acknowledged salubrity of the air." Since this was written, the air remains acknowledged as salubrious as ever ; but bricks and mortar have increased, and there are now two or more lines of railway running through the district, and Sydenham has become a place of great resort.

Of old Sydenham was known only as a "genteel

hamlet of Lewisham "—to which parish the greater part of it belongs—famed for its sylvan retreats, charming prospects, and, as we have stated in the preceding chapter, for its medicinal springs; but after the opening of the Croydon Railway, about the year 1836, it grew rapidly in favour as a place of residence, and still more rapidly after the opening of the Crystal Palace, on the summit of the hill, in 1854. There have now sprung into existence long lines of villas, detached and semi-detached cottages, terraces, so-called parks, and streets.

It was about the middle of the seventeenth century that the mineral waters were discovered on Sydenham Common; and they were occasionally resorted to down to comparatively recent times. Evelyn, after visiting Dulwich College, September 2nd, 1675, "came back [to Deptford] by certain medicinal spa waters, at a place called Sydnam Wells, in Lewisham parish, much frequented in summer." The waters, according to one authority, were "of a mild cathartic quality, nearly resembling those of Epsom;" another writes, that they formed "a purging spring, which has performed great cures in scrofulous, scorbutic, paralytic, and other stubborn diseases;" whilst a third asserts that the waters are "a certain cure for every ill to which humanity is heir." Their popularity waned with that of the other English medicinal waters, but the Wells House continued to attract as a place of summer entertainment, and it served for some time as the head-quarters of the St. George's Bowmen, till the enclosure of Sydenham Common put an end to their archery practice. The Church of St. Philip, in Wells Road, built in 1865-6, covers the site of the wells; it is a neat cruciform structure, with apsidal chancel, and was built from the designs of Mr. Edwin Nash. Mr. James Thorne, in his "Handbook of the Environs of London," tells us there is still standing a cottage in which, according to local tradition, George III. once stayed the best part of a day, whilst he drank of the waters—an escort of the Life Guards forming a cordon around the cottage.

Sydenham is of too modern a growth to have a history; but there are literary associations connected with the place, for "Gertrude of Wyoming" was written there, and its author, the poet Campbell, is almost the only "eminent resident" of the place. His house is on Peak Hill, near Sydenham Station, and, it is said, remains unaltered; but the gardens upon which it looked are gone. Of Campbell, Cyrus Redding writes:— "His mode of life was mostly uniform with that which he afterwards followed in London when he

made it his constant residence. He rose not very early, breakfasted, studied for an hour or two, dined a couple or three hours after noon, and then made calls in the village, oftentimes remaining for an hour or more at the house of a maiden lady, of whose conversation he was remarkably fond. He would return home to tea, and then retire again to his study, often until a late hour, sometimes even to an early one." Here, as he wrote after leaving it, the poet spent his happiest years. He came to live here in 1804, shortly after the publication of the "Pleasures of Hope." The following letter, which Campbell wrote to his publisher, Archibald Constable, November 10, 1804, may be of interest here:—"I find myself obliged to remove a few months sooner than I expected to a new house, of which I have taken a lease for twenty-one years. The trouble of this migration is very serious. . . . I have ventured, on the faith of your support, to purchase the fixtures of a very excellent house, and about £100 worth of furniture, which, being sold along with the fixtures, I get at the broker's appraisement, i.e., half the prime cost. . . . If you come to London, and drink to the health of Auld Reekie over my new mahogany table—if you take a walk round my garden and see my braw house, my court-yard, hens, geese, and turkeys, or view the lovely country in my neighbourhood—you will think this fixture and furniture money well bestowed. I shall, indeed, be nobly settled, and the devil is in it if I don't work as nobly for it."

Soon after, in 1805, Horner wrote as follows:— "This morning I returned from a visit to our poet Campbell. He has fixed himself in a small house upon Sydenham Common, where he labours hard, and is perfectly happy with his wife and child. I have seldom seen so strong an argument from experiment in favour of matrimony, as the change has operated on the general tone of his temper and morals." Doubtless the poet was perfectly happy when he got away from the excitement of the City, and settled at Sydenham.

The annual rental of Campbell's house was forty guineas. It consists of six rooms, two on each floor, the attic or upper storey of which was converted into a private study. From this elevation Campbell, however, was often compelled to descend during the summer months for change of air to the parlour; for in the upper study he felt, to use his own words, as if enclosed within a hotly seasoned pie. A small garden behind the house, with the usual domestic offices at one end, completed the habitation, and furnished all the conveniences to which either the poet or his amiable wife aspired. "Externally, the new situation had much," writes

Dr. Beattie, "to soothe and interest a poetical mind. From the south a narrow lane, lined with hedgerows and passing through a little dell watered by a rivulet, leads to the house, from the windows of which the eye wanders over an extensive prospect of undulating villas, park-like enclosures, hamlets, and picturesque villas shaded with fine ornamental timber, with here and there some village spire shooting up through the forest, reflecting the light on its vane, or breaking the stillness with the chime of its merry bells. Ramifying in all directions he had shady walks where he was safe from all intrusion but that of the Muses, enabling him to combine healthful exercise with profitable meditation. During his leisure hours in summer, as he has sweetly sung, he had a charming variety of—

" ' Spring green lanes,
With all the dazzling field-flowers in their prime,
And gardens haunted by the nightingale's
Long trills, and gushing ecstacies of song.' "

It was while at Sydenham that the idea was started of a poets' club. Let us give Campbell's account of the affair. "One day," he writes— "and how can it fail to be memorable to me when Moore has commemorated it?—Rogers and Moore came down to Sydenham pretty early in the forenoon, and stopped to dine with me. We talked of founding a poets' club, and set about electing the members—not by ballot, but *vivâ voce*. The scheme failed, I scarcely know how; but this I know, that a week or two afterwards I met with Mr. Perry, of the *Morning Chronicle*, who asked me how our poets' club was going on. I said, 'I don't know. We have some difficulty in giving it a name. We thought of calling ourselves "The Bees."' 'Oh!' said Perry, 'that is a little different from the common report, for they say you are to be called "The Wasps."' I was so stung with this waspish retort, that I thought no more of the poets' club."

At Campbell's house there were pleasant dinners, the guests including Byron, Rogers, Moore, Cyrus Redding, and the lesser wits of the day, including Thomas Hill, the original "Paul Pry," who lived close by. Lady Charlotte Campbell, daughter of the Duke of Argyll, a poetess, and lover of learning, became the poet's neighbour at Sydenham. She introduced her clansman to that literary *coterie* which frequented the *salons* of the Princess of Wales at Blackheath.* Another lady who was living at Sydenham at the time Campbell was there, was Mrs. Allsop, a daughter of Mrs. Jordan, whom

Campbell was the means of bringing out on the stage.

Campbell resided here about sixteen years, and during this period wrote "Gertrude of Wyoming," "O'Connor's Child," and "The Battle of the Baltic;" but in course of time he gave up his "noble" work for magazine management, editing, and hack writing, which perhaps redounded but little to his credit. When he undertook the editorship of the *New Monthly Magazine* he gave up his Sydenham house, and removed to London.

Campbell's convivialities, it seems, were not confined to his house. Sir Charles Bell, in one of his "letters," describes a visit he paid to the poet here, and how, after spending the evening in-doors, he and Campbell "rambled down the village, and walked under the delightful trees in the moonlight;" then "adjourned to the inn, and took an egg and plotty. Tom got glorious in pleasing gradation, &c. . . . His wife received him at home, not drunk, but in excellent spirits. After breakfast, we wandered over the forest; not a soul to be seen in all Norwood."

Two years before Campbell settled at Sydenham, a more unfortunate poet, Thomas Dermody, died there (July 15, 1802), as we have already stated in our account of Lewisham Church,† in abject misery, in a brickmaker's hut, at Perry Slough, now called Perry Vale, on the opposite side of the railway. The house has long since been removed.

Thomas Hill, whom we have mentioned above, was a well-known man in his day and generation. He was an eccentric drysalter in the City, who, gathering around him Horace and James Smith, John and Leigh Hunt, George Colman, Campbell, Theodore Hook, Barnes, Mathews, Redding, and a knot of literary acquaintances, set up in the days of the Regency as a sort of City Mæcenas. He was something of an antiquary; knew everybody, and apparently everything about everybody; and was always bustling about the offices of the newspapers and magazines. Poole, the author of "Paul Pry," is said to have drawn that character from him. He was a sort of walking chronicle, especially where literary men and newspapers were concerned. It was once said of him that if he stood at Charing Cross at noonday, he would tell the name and business of everybody that passed Northumberland House. Mathews always declared "Tom Hill," as he was called by all who loved him, one of the oldest men he knew; and a writer in the "Railway Anecdote Book" thus speaks of him:—"Mr. Hill was the *Hull* of his friend Mr.

Theodore Hook's clever novel of 'Gilbert Gurney,' beyond comparison the best book of its class produced in our time. It is also related that Hill furnished Mr. Poole with the original of his humorous character of 'Paul Pry;' but this statement is very doubtful, for 'Paul Pry,' if we mistake not, is of French extraction. It is, however, more certain that 'Pooh, pooh!' and other habitual expressions of Mr. Hill's, may have been introduced

Hill established the *Monthly Mirror*, which brought him much into connection with dramatic poets, actors, and managers. To this periodical Kirke White became a contributor; and this encouragement induced him, about the close of the year 1802, to commit a little volume of poetry to the press. Southey, in his "Life of Kirke White," refers to Mr. Hill as possessing one of the most copious collections of English poetry in existence.

SYDENHAM WELLS IN 1750.

by Mr. Poole into the character. Mr. Hill, it may here be added, had the *entrée* to both Houses of Parliament, the theatres, and almost all places of public resort. He was to be met with at the private view of the Royal Academy, and every kind of exhibition. So especially was he favoured, that it was recorded by a wag that, when asked whether he had seen the new comet, he replied, 'Pooh, pooh! I was present at the private view! Mr. Hill, to borrow from Mr. Hook's portrait, 'happened to know everything that was going forward in all circles—mercantile, political, fashionable, literary, or theatrical; in addition to all matters connected with military and naval affairs, agriculture, finance, art, and science—everything came alike to him.'"

While living at Sydenham, Mr. Hill received his numerous visitors in magnificent style. On one occasion some of the party had to walk to Dulwich to get a conveyance to town. Campbell accompanied his friends. When they separated it was with hats off and three boisterous cheers, "Campbell snatching off his hat," says Cyrus Redding, "not wisely, but too well, pulled off his wig with it, and then, to enhance the merriment upon the occasion, flung both up in the air amidst unbridled laughter." Mr. Adolphus was intimate with Hill for upwards of forty years, and spoke of him as looking fresh and youthful to the last. With reference to his cottage at Sydenham, Mr. Adolphus remarks: "I have dined there with Campbell, James Smith, Jack Johnstone, Mathews, and other celebrities. But gundy and champagne were given in abundance, and at that time, owing to the state of the war, they were of enormous price—I believe a guinea a bottle." As was to be expected, Hill's affairs soon became deranged, and he was made a bankrupt. His fine library was not sold by auction, but by private contract to Messrs. Longman and Co., and formed the ground-work of that collection of which they published a catalogue, under the title of

But news grew scant; what should he do,
But die for want of something new,
Who'd lived to eighty-one the chorus
Of others businesses and stories?
Yet truth to tell they 're many worse,
Whose histories I might rehearse.
The worst of him I can recite,
I've told—so Thomas Hill, good night !

In the early part of the present century, in Sydenham and its environs, eight hundred acres

SITE OF THE CRYSTAL PALACE IN 1852.

"Bibliotheca Poetica Anglicana." He died in chambers in the Adelphi, at the age of eighty-one, in the year 1840, leaving a fortune of £15,000 to a stray friend who used to dine with him on Sundays at Hampstead. The following burlesque epitaph on him is from the pen of Cyrus Redding :—

THOMAS HILL ; Obiit 1840.

Here at last, taciturn and still,
Lies babbling, prying Thomas Hill.
Marvellous his power in explanations
Of others' business or vocations ;
Retailing all he ever knew,
Or knew not—whether false or true,
Happy to give it an addition
That beat Munchausen competition.
With ruddy cheek, and spring-tide eye,
Few thought that he could ever die ;

of common-land were enclosed; and now nearly the whole has been formed into streets, so that this once beautiful rural district is rapidly becoming an integral part of the great metropolis, Sydenham chapelry alone having a population of more than 25,000, and the place altogether comprises some half-dozen ecclesiastical districts. The Church of St. Bartholomew, on what was once Sydenham Common, is a roomy and commodious Gothic edifice, and was erected in 1830. Christ Church, near the Forest Hill railway station, was consecrated in 1855, but was only recently completed by the erection of a tower and chancel; it is in the Early Decorated style of architecture. Holy Trinity Church, Sydenham Park, is of similar architecture, and was built in 1865. St. Saviour's, on Brockley

Hill, at the north extremity of Sydenham, is a large Decorated building, and was consecrated in 1866. St. Michael and All Angels', Lower Sydenham, serves as a chapel of ease to St. Bartholomew's. Of St. Philip's, in Wells Road, we have already spoken. Besides these places of worship, there are Free, Presbyterian, Wesleyan, and other chapels; many schools, both public and private; public halls, library and working men's institutes, local societies, and two weekly newspapers.

The most important feature in connection with Sydenham is the Crystal Palace; we say in connection with, for, though not actually in Sydenham—the greater part being said to be in Lambeth parish—it is always considered to belong to it. It occupies the high ground to the south-west of Sydenham. The land over which the palace grounds—nearly three hundred acres in extent—stretch, falls rapidly away to the east, and from the terrace in front of the palace a prospect is obtained of surpassing beauty, over richly-wooded and undulating plains to the distant hills of Kent and Surrey. A little to the north of the palace, and overlooking the grounds, stands Rockhill, from 1852 the residence of Sir Joseph Paxton, the designer of the Crystal Palace, the Great Exhibition building of 1851, of Chatsworth conservatory and gardens, &c.

Sir Joseph Paxton, who was originally introduced to the Duke of Devonshire by his Grace's secretary, Mr. Ridgway, of May Fair, came into his service as a gardener's lad at fourteen shillings a week. He soon showed, however, talents which led to his advancement, and laid out the gardens at Chatsworth in a manner worthy of " Capability" Brown* himself. As Mr. Mark Boyd tells us in his " Social Gleanings," " Great was Mr. Ridgway's astonishment when, some years afterwards, he sat down to dinner at Chiswick with the duke and the other members of the family, and found himself seated by the side of the former gardener's lad, they being the only guests who were not Cavendishes or Leveson-Gowers." Sir Joseph Paxton designed the Crystal Palace on the plan of a large conservatory which he had erected at Chatsworth, and had the satisfaction of seeing his principles of construction adopted extensively in railway stations and other large structures before his death. He sat for some years as M.P. for Coventry, through the duke's interest, and died at his house at Sydenham in 1865.

As we have already stated,† it was in 1852 that the idea of erecting the Crystal Palace near Sydenham first originated. When the Government declined to purchase the Great Exhibition building in Hyde Park, a few enterprising gentlemen came forward and rescued it from destruction. They purchased it, and the materials were removed to Sydenham, where it was re-erected, but with many modifications of form and detail. The original projectors had no difficulty in securing the aid of Sir Joseph Paxton as director of the park and gardens, which it was intended to unite with the palace; of Mr. Owen Jones and Mr. Digby Wyatt, as directors of the fine art department and of the decorations; and of Mr. Charles Wild, the engineer of the old building, as the engineer for the new one. Sir Charles Fox and Mr. Henderson also were engaged as contractors, and they undertook to take down, remove, and re-erect the structure for £120,000. The " Crystal Palace Company " was then announced, with a capital of £500,000, in 100,000 shares of £5 each. The capital, however, was subsequently increased to £1,000,000, and before the works in the building and grounds were concluded this amount was considerably increased. Two years were spent in extensive and expensive preparations. The first column of the main structure was raised on the 5th of August, 1852. Messrs. Owen Jones and Digby Wyatt were charged with a mission to the Continent, in order to procure examples of the principal works of art in Europe. England was also searched for copies of artistic antiquities; and Sir Joseph Paxton commenced his own operations by securing for the company the extensive and celebrated collection of palms and other plants which it had taken the Messrs. Loddige, of Hackney,‡ a century to collect. The building was formally opened on the 10th of June, 1854, the Queen, the Prince Consort, the King of Portugal, and other distinguished personages, being present at the ceremony.

In several points the Crystal Palace at Sydenham differs from its predecessor in Hyde Park. There are three transepts instead of one, and the roof of the nave is arched instead of flat, being thus raised forty-four feet higher than the old nave. There are many other differences between the appearance of the old and new Crystal Palaces, but these are among the chief. As before, iron and glass are almost the only materials used in the building. The larger portion of the northern wing, including the tropical department and the Assyrian Court, was destroyed by fire on the 30th of December, 1866, and has been only partially rebuilt since.

Originally the main building was 1,608 feet long, while its prototype was 1,851 feet; but there are

* See Vol. V., p. 154.   † See Vol. V., p. 38.   ‡ See Vol. V., p. 514.

wings and a colonnade in the new building, which make a considerable addition in the total length. These wings extend into, and, as it were, enclose the Italian garden. The nave and north and south transepts are 72 feet wide and 104 feet high—just the height of the transept in the Hyde Park building. The central transept is *the* feature of the new building. It is 384 feet long (the north and south transepts being 336), 120 feet wide, and 168 feet from the floor to the top of the ventilator—its total height, from the garden front, being 208 feet, or six feet higher than the Monument. Another difference in the construction of this building is that there is a basement storey, which was long known by the appellation of "Sir Joseph Paxton's Tunnel." This basement storey, or tunnel, contains apparatus for warming the building by rows of furnaces and boilers, and an iron network forming fifty miles of steam-pipes. There are about thirty boilers, arranged in pairs along the tunnel at regular distances. At each extremity of the building are lofty towers. The west front of the palace abuts upon a broad roadway, formed out of Dulwich Wood; it is a light and airy façade, resembling that of the north side of the Crystal Palace in Hyde Park, except that it presents three arched transepts to the eye instead of only one. Attractive as this front of the palace is, that to the east, as seen from the gardens, is much more so. Grace and elegance are certainly combined in the outline; and when the vast edifice reflects the rays of the sun, it sends forth millions of coruscations, and forms an object of surpassing brilliance. The following lines, by a popular poet, appeared shortly after the completion of the building :—

> "But yesterday a naked sod,
>   And see—'tis done !
> As though 'twere by a wizard's rod,
>   A blazing arch of lucid glass
>   Leaps like a fountain from the grass,
>   To meet the sun.
>
> "A quiet green, but few days since,
>   With cattle browsing in the shade,
>   And lo ! long lines of bright arcade
>   In order raised;
> A palace, as for fairy prince,
>   A rare pavilion, such as man
>   Saw never since mankind began,
>   Is built and glazed !"

Thackeray has celebrated the building in a more comic fashion :—

> "With ganial foire,
>   Thransfuse me loyre,
> Ye sacred nympths of Pindus ;
>   The whoile I sing
>   That wondthrous thing,
> The Palace made o' windows.
>
> " Say, Paxton, truth,
>   Thou wondthrous youth,
> What stroke of art celestial,
>   What power was lint
>   You to invint
> This combination cristial ?" *

In the interior there is a long and lofty nave, intersected at regular distances and at right angles by three transepts, and with aisles on each side, occupied by various fine art, industrial, and architectural courts, surrounded by galleries supported on light, airy, and apparently fragile columns, with an arched roof of glass, extending from north to south upwards of 1,000 feet. There are two galleries—in the central transept three; the first is gained from the ground by eight flights of steps, one at each end of the north and south transepts, and two at each end of the centre transept; they are about twenty-three feet high. This gallery is twenty-four feet wide; and the landing-places, in the two end transepts, seventy-two feet long and twenty-four feet wide, form platforms from which excellent views of the nave are obtained. The gallery of the central transept crosses the nave at an elevation of 100 feet; and is gained by spiral staircases at each end of the transept. This gallery, as well as the second, is used only as a promenade. The passage along the latter is carried through a series of ring or "bull's-eye" girders, seven feet in diameter, resting upon the columns which project into the nave. There is a very fine view of the country from this gallery; and looking forward through the long vista of circular girders, diminishing gradually in the distant perspective, produces a very singular but fine effect. The view of the park and grounds from the third gallery will well repay the visitor for the trouble of ascent. "Round the upper gallery," Mr. Phillips informs us in his "Guide," "at the very summit of the nave and transepts, as well as round the ground-floor of the building, are placed louvres, or ventilators, made of galvanised iron. By opening or closing these louvres, a service readily performed, the temperature of the Crystal Palace is so regulated, that, on the hottest day of summer, the dry parching heat mounts to the roof to be dismissed, whilst a pure and invigorating supply is introduced at the floor in its place, giving new life to the thirsty plant, and fresh vigour to man. The coolness thus obtained within the palace will be sought in vain, on such a summer's day, outside the edifice." At night the building is very effectively lighted up from above by the aid of a row of jets

---

* See "Thackeray's Works," vol. xi.

which run round it, just below the spring of the arching roof.

It would be impossible to give within the limits of this work a detailed account of all the varied attractions of the interior of the building; and, indeed, such a task is rendered needless by the "Guide to the Palace and Park," and the Handbooks to the various Courts, which are published by the Crystal Palace Company, and obtainable in the building. A rough glance at the contents, therefore, is all that we can here pretend to take. Commencing at the southern extremity of the nave, immediately in front of the refreshment counters, is a Gothic screen, consisting of a centre and two wings, in which are placed, in niches, statues of the kings and queens of England, from casts of those statues in the new Houses of Parliament; this screen was designed by Mr. Digby Wyatt. From this spot a view of the whole extent of the nave is obtained, and a beautiful view it is. Immediately in front of the spectator is a large ornamental basin, in which is displayed the Victoria Regia and other tropical aquatic plants; in the centre of the basin stands what has been not inaptly termed "the world-famed crystal fountain,"* which on the break-up of the Great Exhibition of 1851 became the property of the directors of the new Crystal Palace. Beyond this, the eye rests upon a long vista, varied on each side with statues, handsome glass cases, displaying various works of modern art and industry, and trees, flowers, and plants, of the tropical regions, blooming in all the brilliance of their native climes; whilst suspended from the galleries are ornamental baskets containing plants.

The Handel Festival Orchestra, which occupies the western portion of the great central transept, was originally erected for the first festival in 1857, and has been since gradually enlarged, until it reached its present pitch of size and completeness. Its diameter is double that of the dome of St. Paul's. At the festival concerts more than 4,000 instrumental and vocal performers are accommodated within its spacious area. The arch which forms the ceiling of the vast structure—one of the largest timber arches yet erected—is of the latest improvement. The organ was built by Messrs. Gray and Davison, expressly for the palace; it has four rows of keys, and contains seventy-four stops and 4,598 pipes.

At the eastern end of the transept, facing the great orchestra, is the theatre, in which are given dramatic performances, pantomimes, &c. Close by is a concert-room capable of containing a large number of performers and listeners, and generally filled on the occasion of the popular concerts given here on Saturday afternoons.

On either side of the nave, on the floor of the palace, are the various courts above referred to, the mere mention of the names of which is sufficient to indicate their nature and character; they are the Egyptian, Greek, Roman, Mediæval, Renaissance, Italian, French, Ceramic, Pompeian, Bohemian, &c. A large portion of the galleries is devoted to the exhibition and sale of pictures, forming one of the main centres of attraction in the building.

Leaving the palace by the flight of granite steps from the central transept, we reach the "upper terrace," which extends along the whole base of the building; it is 1,500 feet long and 50 feet wide. Fifteen feet lower lies the terrace garden, reached by six flights of steps, and bounded on the southern side by a stone balustrade, with numerous recesses. Besides the magnificent central circular basin, throwing out a lofty *jet d'eau*, there are numerous others of an elliptic shape, profusely intermingled with statues, vases, richly-coloured flower-beds, shrubs, and trees, on which the long shadows of the projecting transepts fall. From the terrace gardens three flights of stone steps, their side balustrades adorned in like manner with statuary, conduct the visitor to a garden fifteen feet lower.

A central walk, nearly 100 feet in breadth, leads from the centre of the terrace garden through the lower garden, where it divides, and, re-uniting on the other side of a basin, 200 feet in diameter, continues on through parterres, laid out in a graceful admixture of the Italian and English styles of ornamental gardening.

The extent of the ground in which these fountains are displayed is ingeniously made to appear greater than it really is, by the skilful mode in which it has been treated. Broken ground, mounds, artificially constructed, crowned with forest trees, and groves of rich evergreen shrubs, forming tortuous alleys of perpetual verdure, and intersecting each other in the most natural manner, impart the effect of size and distance to a space that is comprised in about two hundred acres. Two "water temples" and a "rosary" are amongst the most attractive objects in the gardens; but unquestionably the most prominent attraction of the grounds, irrespective of their natural beauty, is formed by the system of waterworks, which, it is said, far surpass, in their completeness and design, any other display in the world, including even those of

---

* See Vol. V., p. 38.

Versailles. The whole system is divided into two series—the upper and lower. The former comprises the six basins in the Italian garden, the large central basin in the broad walk, and the two smaller ones on each side of it; in all, nine fountains. These constitute the display on ordinary occasions. Beyond and below them is the lower series, which consist of the two water temples, the cascades, and the numerous groups of fountains arranged in the large lower basins. These are usually known as the "great fountains," and are played on special and grand occasions only. The two "grand" fountains in the lower grounds are by far the largest in the world, and impart the grandest effect to the whole series. The outlines of their two greatest basins are similar in design, each being 784 feet long, with a diameter of 468 feet. The central jet in each is $2\frac{1}{4}$ inches diameter, and reaches the extraordinary height of more than 250 feet. Around each central jet is a column, composed of fifty 2-inch jets. The force of water which presses on the mouth of these pipes is equivalent to 262 pounds to the square inch. When the whole is in operation, 120,000 gallons of water per minute are poured forth by 11,788 jets; and in one single complete display, lasting half an hour, nearly 4,000,000 gallons are consumed. The artesian well, from which the fountains are supplied with water, is well worthy of notice. It is a brick shaft, $8\frac{1}{2}$ feet in diameter and 247 feet deep. From this depth an artesian bore descends still further for 328 feet, making the entire distance from the surface 578 feet. A supply of water having been thus obtained, the next operation is to raise it from the bottom of the hill, where the well is situate, to a sufficient height to play the fountains. The pressure required to force the respective jets of water to heights ranging from 5 to nearly 300 feet is obtained in the following simple manner. Reservoirs were formed at different levels in the grounds, the highest of all being situated at the top of the hill adjoining the north end of the building; the second, or intermediate reservoir, was on a level with the basin of the great central fountain; and the lower lake, at the extreme end of the grounds, formed the lower reservoir. Three pairs of powerful engines were then erected; one contiguous to the artesian well; the second at the intermediate reservoir; and a third adjoining the north end of the building, close to the highest reservoir. By this system water is pumped by the lower engine to the intermediate reservoir, and from thence by another engine to the upper level, where a third raises it to two enormous tanks, erected on columns, and to the tanks on the top

of the two high towers, which play the main jets of the lower fountains. By this arrangement the water, instead of being wasted, is economised, and passing backwards and forwards from one reservoir to the other, is used again and again; the intermediate reservoir collecting it after a display of the upper series, and the lowest one forming a similar receptacle when a display of the large fountains takes place.

Passing round the margin of the great fountain basin, and crossing the broad central walk, which divides the two lower basins, the visitor, by ascending a flight of steps, reaches the grand plateau, which is an embankment fifty feet wide, and commands a general view of the lake, containing three islands, the two largest wholly occupied by life-sized models of the gigantic animals of the ancient world. It is here that one of the most original features of the Crystal Palace Company's grand plan of instruction has been carried out. There all the leading features of geology are found displayed, in so practical and popular a manner, that a child may discern the characteristic points of that useful branch of the history of nature.

The spectator, standing on the upper terrace of the plateau, has before him the largest educational model ever attempted in any part of the world. It covers several acres, and consists of a display of nearly all the rocks that constitute the known portion of the earth's crust, from the old red sandstone to the latest tertiary beds of drift and gravel. Descending by the path, a few paces to the right, we have a nearer view of the older rocks, immediately facing the rustic bridge, the lowest of which, the old red sandstone, is seen just above the water, forming a foundation upon which is superposed the whole mass of cliff on the right, consisting of mountain limestone, mill-stone grit, bands of ironstone, and beds or seams of coal, capped by the new red sandstone. The coal-measures are thus exhibited between their most evident boundaries, the old red sandstone below, and the new red sandstone above; the whole being re-constructed of several thousand tons of the actual materials, in exact imitation of the Clay Cross coal-beds. The series was carefully tabulated by Professor Ansted, to ensure its geological accuracy, according to Sir Joseph Paxton's designs for the picturesque arrangement of this interesting portion of the grounds.

On the margin of a lake close by are to be seen life-like models of the former gigantic inhabitants of the earth, whose race has long since become extinct, such as the Iguanodon, the Palæotherium, the Anoplotherium, and other antediluvian animals,

THE CRYSTAL PALACE, FROM THE SOUTH.

with names equally interesting, and in all their pristine ugliness.

On gala or *fête* days, or the occasion of any great festival—as when the Odd Fellows, or the Foresters, or the Licensed Victuallers, attend *en masse*—the number of visitors to the palace is prodigious, reaching to seventy or eighty thousand; but, nevertheless, commercially, the place has not proved so successful as was at first anticipated.

fine air and fun. What Londoners want is 'an outing.' It is for this that people go to Sydenham; and for this, it must be admitted on all sides, the most complete provision has now been made. If one really requires a wonder, there is the building itself."

We have alluded above to the accidental fire by which a portion of the building was destroyed. This occurred on the 30th of December, 1866;

MARGARET FINCH'S COTTAGE, NORWOOD, IN 1808.

The undertaking was carried out on too grand a scale. It was at first assumed that what people wanted was scientific amusement; the blunder, however, was a costly one, for it reduced the worth of the five-pound shares to a fifth of their nominal value, and created a great deal of unpleasant feeling in the bosoms of a large class of people who believed, in promoting this scheme of popular amusement and instruction, they had made a good investment for themselves. It has been said, and perhaps truthfully, that "if there is sufficient amusement in the way of fireworks or fountains, of concerts and drama, of exhibitions and flower-shows, of painting and statuary, of machinery in motion—so much the better. But the main objects are the eating and drinking, and

and the larger portion of the northern wing, including the tropical department and the Assyrian Court, was burnt down. An unfortunate chimpanzee, which had been one of the "lions" of the palace, perished in the flames. This wing has only been partially rebuilt, much to the injury of the symmetry of the edifice. Whatever may have been the cause of this disastrous fire, it was, at all events, a curious fact that it occurred on the very day after a lecture on combustion had been given in the palace.

Of late years a large library and reading-room have been added, and lectures on cookery and other branches of useful education, as well as on art and science, have been delivered to numerous classes of students of either sex. A large aquarium also, stocked with salt-water as well as fresh-water fish, now forms one of the attractions of the place; and it is intended by the managers and directors of the company still further to increase the educational appliances of the Crystal Palace.

Anerley, which adjoins Sydenham on the south-east, was at one time noted for its tea-gardens, which for some years served as an attraction to the South Londoners. They were opened in or about the year 1841 by a Mr. Coulson, but do not appear to have attained to a tithe of the popularity of old Ranelagh or of Vauxhall, notwithstanding its swings and "roundabouts," its fireworks, and its *al fresco* dancing platforms. After passing through various hands, they were finally closed in 1868. A corner of the gardens was taken off on the formation of the Croydon Railway. The Croydon Canal, which formerly ran through the grounds in its course from the Thames at Dept-ford, has been drained and filled up.

Stretching away from Anerley, towards Mitcham, Tooting, and Streatham, and lying partly in Croy-don parish, and partly in the parishes of Battersea, Lambeth, Streatham, and Camberwell, is Norwood, which, at no very remote period, was described as "a village scattered round a large wild common."

In a "History of the Gypsies," published in the first part of the present century, it is said that Norwood had long been a favourite haunt of that brotherhood, on account of its remote and rural character, though lying so handy for both London and Croydon. Hither the Londoners of the last century resorted to have their future lot in life foretold by the palmistry of the "Zingari" folk.

A writer in the *Gentleman's Magazine* for 1808 observes that "the post they (the gipsies) have held longest is Norwood, and it is probably the one they chose for head-quarters when they first appeared in Britain. Being on a visit in the year 1790 to a friend at Dulwich, curiosity induced me to visit Norwood; but I did not find so many gipsies there as I expected. . . . However, I saw an aged sybil named Sarah Skemp, who from age and infirmity was unable to go otherwise than upon all-fours. Her prominent and large sinews, bones, and muscles, were all perceptible beneath her rigid hide, which resembled in hue the smoke-dried blanket that partly covered her. If she had occupied a mummy-case in a museum she might have passed for a mummy, and as it was, I could almost have imagined her one, if I had not seen her crawl, and heard her jabber."

Gipsy Hill, and an inn still called the "Queen of the Gipsies," commemorate the inmate of a small outhouse who lived on this hill, and who died here in 1760—it is said at the age of 109 years. Her name was Margaret Finch, and for half a century she had lived by telling fortunes in that rural and credulous neighbourhood. She was buried in a large square box, as, from her constant habit of sitting with her chin resting on her knees, her muscles had become so contracted that at last she could not alter her position. "This woman," observes Mr. Larwood, in his "History of Sign-boards," "when a girl of seventeen, may have been one of the dusky gang that pretty Mrs. Samuel Pepys and her companions went to consult in August, 1668, as her lord records in his 'Diary' the same evening, the 11th: 'This afternoon my wife, and Mercer, and Deb went with Pelling to see the gypsies at Lambeth and have their fortunes told; but what they did I did not enquire.'" "A granddaughter of Margaret Finch," Mr. Larwood adds, "was living in a cottage close by in the year 1800."

Norwood must really have derived its name from being the "wood" that lay to the "north" of the large ecclesiastical town of Croydon; for it lies to the south of London. Two centuries ago Norwood was really a wood and nothing more. Aubrey, giving an account of Croydon at that period, in his "Perambulation of Surrey," writes: "In this parish lies the great wood, called *Norwood*, belonging to the see of Canterbury, wherein was an ancient remarkable tree, called Vicar's Oak, where four parishes meet in a point." These parishes, doubtless, were Lambeth, Camberwell, Lewisham, and Croydon.

The wood and the gipsies too have long since been swept away, and are now known only by tradition. Among the few mansions of note that once existed in this neighbourhood, the most con-spicuous was Knight's Hill, which was built for Lord Chancellor Thurlow by Henry Holland, the architect of Carlton House and of old Drury Lane Theatre, which was burnt down in 1809. Notwithstanding the splendid views said to be obtained from the upper windows of the mansion, it appears that Lord Thurlow never resided in it, but contented himself with a smaller house, called Knight's Hill Farm. In Twiss's "Life of Lord Eldon," it is stated that "Lord Thurlow built a house in the neighbourhood of London. Now," adds the author, "he was first cheated by his architect, and then he cheated himself; for the house cost more than he expected, so he never would go into it. Very foolish, but so it was. As he was coming out of the Queen's Drawing-room, a lady, whom I knew very well, stopped him, and asked him when he was going into his new house.

'Madam,' said he, 'the queen has just asked me that impudent question; and as I would not tell her, I will not tell you.'" Mr. Thorne, in his "Environs of London," states that the house and grounds were reported to have cost £30,000. Both have now disappeared, having, with his lordship's adjoining manor of Leigham, been appropriated for building purposes.

Another noted place in Upper Norwood, during the second quarter of the present century, was Beulah Spa, which was founded on an extensive scale in 1831, for the purpose of rendering available the medicinal properties of a spring strongly impregnated with sulphate of magnesia. The Spa had been known to the inhabitants of Norwood from time immemorial; but it existed only as a bubbling spring, to which the rustics resorted for the cure of trifling maladies, until about the year 1828, when the then proprietor of the surrounding grounds, some thirty acres in extent, expended large sums in converting them into a place of recreation, with charming walks, terraces, and rustic lodges, a " pump," orchestra, reading-room, &c., the whole being carried out from the designs of Mr. Decimus Burton. In its altered state it was opened for public use in August, 1831; and so popular did it become that no less than three separate "Guides" to the place were published between the years 1832 and 1838. It is now forgotten as a place of resort, and even its chalybeate spring has passed comparatively out of memory. The water was a saline purgative, much resembling the Cheltenham water, and, like that of Epsom, owed its medicinal qualities chiefly to the sulphate of magnesia which was dissolved in it.

In 1839 a *fête* for the Freemasons' Girls' School was given here, under the special patronage of the Queen Dowager. The vocal and instrumental concert provided for the occasion was of first-rate order; Grisi, Persiani, Rubini, Ivanhoff, &c., lending their assistance on the occasion.

The readers of Thackeray will not have forgotten the charity *fête* at Beulah Spa, devised by Lady de Sudley, on behalf of the " British Washerwoman's Orphans' Home," which figures in Cox's " Diary."

The Spa is thus described by a writer in the *Mirror* for April, 1832:—" We entered the grounds at an elegant rustic lodge, where commences a new carriage-road to Croydon, which winds round the flank of the hill, and is protected by hanging woods. The lodge is in the best taste of ornate rusticity, with the characteristic varieties of gable, dripstone, portico, bay-window, and embellished chimney: of the latter there are some specimens

in the best style of our older architects. Passing the lodge, we descended by a winding path through the wood to a small lawn or glade, at the highest point of which is a circular rustic building, used as a confectionery and reading-room, near which is the Spa, within a thatched apartment. The spring rises about fourteen feet, within a circular rock-work enclosure; the water is drawn by a contrivance at once ingenious and novel; a glass urn-shaped pail, terminating with a cock of the same material, and having a stout rim and cross-handle of silver, is attached to a thick worsted rope, and let down into the spring by a pulley, when the vessel being taken up full, the water is drawn off by the cock." Notwithstanding that the grounds were furnished with all the appliances for well-to-do water-drinkers, Beulah Spa enjoyed but a brief run of popularity. In the end it collapsed, and the site was handed over to the builders. Some portion of the grounds, however, have been preserved; and there is (or was recently) within them a hydropathic establishment, where the curative qualities of the water may be tested.

On the hill overlooking what was once Beulah Spa, Mr. Sims Reeves has lived for many years.

Norwood is situated on a series of beautiful valleys and hills, the latter rising, it is said, to the height of 300 feet above the level of the sea at low water; but, like Sydenham, is being rapidly converted into a region of bricks and mortar. It possesses seven or eight churches, a large number of dissenting chapels and mission-houses, capacious and comfortable hotels, together with hydropathic and homœopathic establishments. The Queen's Hotel at Norwood, close to the Crystal Palace, is said to be the largest private hotel in the kingdom.

Among the institutions of various kinds which abound in this locality, a prominent place is held by the North Surrey District School, in the Anerley Road. It is a very large and complete establishment, covering an area of about fifty acres. It provides accommodation and the means of industrial training for nearly 1,000 children from the surrounding district unions.

The Roman Catholic Orphanage of Our Lady, founded in 1848, is under the charge of a religious community of ladies, and contains about 320 orphan and poor children, who are lodged, fed, and clothed, until they are fit to be placed in situations as domestic servants, for which they are specially trained. The children, when placed in service, are watched over by the community, who give prizes annually to those who keep their situations longest, and can supply the best characters. There is also a home attached, into which the orphans are received when out of situation and in sickness, provided they have conducted themselves satisfactorily. The institution is a branch from the Monastery de la Notre Dame des Orphelines, at La Delwrande, in Normandy, celebrated for its treatment of orthopœdic diseases, from which many English families are said to have derived great benefit. The building here was commenced in 1855, and was erected from the designs of Mr. Wardell. It is of Gothic design, with a tower in the centre, and covers a large extent of ground. A part of the edifice, entirely distinct from the orphanage, is used as a boarding-school for young ladies of the higher classes.

Noticeable for its architectural as well as philanthropic character is the Jews' Hospital, Lower Norwood, which was erected in 1863, from the designs of Mr. Tillot, " for the maintenance of the aged poor, and the industrial training of friendless children." The Jews' Hospital, one of the oldest charitable institutions of the Jews in England, was originally established in Mile End, in the year 1806. Large sums were collected by its founders, Messrs. B. and A. Goldsmid ; considerable legacies have been bequeathed to it ; the benevolent family of Rothschild have greatly benefited it ; and the members of the Jewish body generally have at all times given it their support. The change from so crowded a locality as Mile End to the present eligible site of the hospital has, doubtless, proved advantageous to the institution, and to the Jewish community generally. The edifice, which is constructed of brick with stone dressings, is a good specimen of the Jacobean style of architecture. Over the hall, &c., is a synagogue, with a gallery, having an open timber roof.

The schools of the Westmoreland Society, for children of parents residing within seventy-five miles of London, are at Lower Norwood. Close by, on the slopes of a gentle hill, and occupying some forty acres of ground, is Norwood South Metropolitan Cemetery. It was one of the earliest of our great metropolitan cemeteries, having been founded in 1839. The grounds are well laid out, and command good views across Sydenham, Penge, and Beckenham. The cemetery is becoming rapidly filled with monuments. Many men of mark have their last resting-place here : among them Justice Talfourd, Douglas Jerrold, Angus Reach, Laman Blanchard, Sir Wm. Cubitt (the celebrated engineer) ; Sharon Turner, the historian ; Sir Wm. Napier, the historian of the Peninsular War ; James Wm. Gilbart, the founder of the London and Westminster Bank ; and Frederick Robson, the comedian.

In Upper Norwood is the Royal Normal College and Academy of Music for the Blind, which was established in 1874, to afford a thorough general and musical education to the youthful blind of both sexes, who possess the requisite talent so as to qualify them for self-maintenance. The founders of the college, recognising that all of the different kinds of handicraft suitable for the blind were thoroughly taught in various establishments throughout the country, have confined themselves to the special work of preparing the blind as teachers, organists, and pianoforte tuners. The college is designed to form a supplement to the other institutions, and in no sense is it expected that it will take the place of the older establishments, or in any way interfere with their work. The college embraces three distinct departments — that of general education, of music, and pianoforte tuning. Each has been carefully planned, furnished with the most modern appliances, and provided with experienced teachers especially adapted to their part of the work.

At Norwood, in 1833, died the Earl of Dudley, having been insane for the last few months of his life. He had always been eccentric ; but in the early part of 1832 he was declared by Sir Henry Halford to be insane, having committed a variety of harmless extravagances ; and his last days were passed in retirement.

On the southern side of Norwood, and extending about a mile and a half along the Brighton road from Brixton Hill towards Croydon, is the village of Streatham, about which we must write somewhat briefly, as we must not travel too far afield from the metropolis. It is a rambling district, occupying for the most part high ground, with a good deal of open heath. It abounds in mansions encompassed by well-wooded grounds.

At the time of the Domesday survey Streatham was divided into several manors, the chief of which, called Totinges, which included the hamlet of Tooting, was held by the Abbot of St. Mary de Bec, and hence came to be known as Tooting-Bec. From that period till the time of the " dissolution " of religious houses, it changed ownership several times. A portion of the ancient priory of Tooting Bec still remains at Bedford Hill. In 1553 the property was sold to Dudley, Earl of Warwick, and half a century later it was purchased by Sir Giles Howland. Elizabeth, daughter and heiress of John Howland, conveyed it, by marriage, in 1695, to Wriothesley, Marquis of Tavistock, afterwards third Duke of Bedford, and Baron Howland of Streatham. The marriage ceremony was performed by Bishop Burnet, at Streatham House,

Lord Wriothesley being only fifteen years old. Francis, fifth Duke of Bedford, conveyed the mansion to his brother, Lord William Russell, who was murdered by his Swiss valet, Courvoisier.* Lord William made the old house his residence, but about the close of the last century conveyed it to the Earl of Coventry, by whom it was rebuilt. The late Duke of Portland had a residence at Streatham. Among other noted residents here were Mr. Dyce, R.A., and Mr. D. Roberts, the well-known artist.

Eastwards from Streatham Green there are mineral springs which, as Aubrey informs us, were discovered about fourteen years before he wrote (A.D. 1659). Persons employed in weeding in dry weather, it appears, drank some of the water, and found it purgative. The owner of the field at first forbade people to take the water ; but before the end of the reign of Charles II. it came into common use. Lysons says that in his time (1810) the Streatham water was sent in large quantities to some of the London hospitals. The well still exists, but its fame has departed.

On the high road between the villages of Streatham and Tooting, somewhat less than a century ago, stood a turnpike gate, which was the scene of an amusing escapade, arising out of the convivial habits of Lord Thurlow. The Lord Chancellor had been dining with Mr. Jenkinson (afterwards Lord Liverpool) at Addiscombe, his seat near Croydon, together with Dundas, and the younger Pitt, then Chancellor of the Exchequer. On their return late in the evening on horseback, they found the gate open, and as they had no servant with them, and were all more or less "merry" with wine, they rode through without staying to pay the toll. The gatekeeper, aroused by the sound of their horse-hoofs as they galloped through, sprang up, rushed out into the road, and fired a blunderbuss after them, but fortunately without effect. He took them, no doubt, for a gang of highwaymen who had been committing robberies along the road. The story got about, much to the amusement of the *quidnuncs* of "Brooks's" and "White's" clubs ; and it was afterwards celebrated in the "Rolliad," the author of which poem writes, alluding to Pitt—

> " How, as he wandered darkling o'er the plain,
> His reason drowned in Jenkinson's champagne,
> A rustic's hand, but righteous fate withstood,
> Had shed a Premier's for a robber's blood."

But Streatham, perhaps, has chiefly derived its celebrity from Dr. Johnson's connection with it.

Streatham Place was the residence of Henry Thrale, the opulent brewer of Southwark, to whom we have already introduced the reader,† when Johnson was first presented to him by his friend Murphy, in 1764 ; and during Thrale's life Streatham Place was to Johnson a second home. Johnson did not become an inmate or constant guest at Mr. Thrale's house here till about 1766, when his constitution seemed to be giving way, and he was visited by fits of deep and gloomy melancholy, which Mrs. Thrale (afterwards Mrs. Piozzi), with her wonted vivacity and cheerfulness, did her best to dispel. An apartment was fitted up for him ; a knife and fork were constantly laid for him ; companions and friends were invited from London without stint, to entertain him and to be entertained by him. His favourite strolling-place in the grounds was known as Dr. Johnson's Walk. The summer-house in the garden was one of the doctor's favourite resorts, when on a visit to his kind and hospitable friends. Here he made many pious meditations and resolutions ; among the latter may be mentioned one which still exists in his own handwriting, dated as late as 1781, " To pass eight hours every day in some serious employment."

As Mrs. Piozzi herself tells us, in her "Johnsoniana," " Dr. Johnson would here spend the middle days of the week, returning to his household near Fleet Street every Saturday, to give them three good dinners and his company, before he came back to us on the Monday night," thus reversing the process of our own day, which usually takes hard-working people into the suburbs from Saturday till Monday. In the drawing-room at Streatham he revelled in the freedom of his discourse, released, as he doubtless felt himself, from the restraints of the clubs and coffee-houses of Covent Garden. It was here, for instance, that, when asked somewhat abruptly by a silly young fellow, whether he would recommend him to marry, he set him down with the quick reply, " Sir, I would advise no man to marry who is not likely to propagate understanding."

Of Mrs. Piozzi (Mrs. Thrale), whose name is destined always to shine in the world of literature as a " queen of society," we have already spoken at some length in the chapter above referred to ; but a few words more about her may not be out of place here. " Mrs. Thrale always appeared to me," writes Sir N. W. Wraxall, in his " Historical Memoirs," " to possess at least as much information and a mind as cultivated as Mrs. Montagu, and even more wit ; but she did not descend among men from such an eminence, and she talked much more, as well as more unguardedly, upon every subject. She was the provider and conductress of Dr. Johnson, who lived almost entirely under her roof, ... both in town and at Streatham. He did not, however, spare her more than other women in his attacks, if she courted or provoked his animadversion." " I cannot withhold from Mrs. Thrale," says Dr. Johnson, " the praise of being the author of that admirable poem, ' The Three

of Garrick, Goldsmith, Dr. C. Burney, Edmund Burke, Lord Lyttelton, Mrs. Piozzi herself and her daughter, and, of course, Dr. Johnson. This gallery of portraits was sold in 1816, when they fetched various prices, ranging from £80 up to £378, at which price the burly doctor himself was knocked down. They would easily fetch four times that price now-a-days. An odd volume of " Saurin on the Bible," with a memorandum by

LORD THURLOW'S HOUSE, KNIGHT'S HILL.

Warnings.'" The long and constant hospitality of Mr. and Mrs. Thrale, at their house at Streatham, to Dr. Johnson, extended over almost the last twenty years of his life.

Miss Thrale, Johnson's "Queeny," was among those who sat by the learned doctor's death-bed, in spite of the differences which had arisen between him and her mother, on account of her second marriage. Baretti, who acted for about ten years as teacher of Italian to the daughters of Mrs. Thrale, on the recommendation of Dr. Johnson, afterwards assailed that lady's memory most ungratefully.

Hung up in the library at Mrs. Piozzi's house was a series of portraits of literary characters, painted by Sir Joshua Reynolds, including those

Dr. Johnson on the title page, and some manuscript notes by Mrs. Piozzi, fetched no less than £42 in a sale of Mrs. Piozzi's effects at Brighton, in 1857. The china teapot which stood on Mrs. Piozzi's table, and from which Dr. Johnson drank never-ending cups of the cheering liquid, was bought at the same time by Mrs. Marryatt. Mrs. Thrale's house was pulled down about 1868. The memory of Mrs. Thrale, however, is still preserved by the name of Thrale Hall, now a boarding-house.

About the year 1870 the Magdalen Hospital was removed hither from Blackfriars Road, where it had existed as one of the best-known charitable institutions in London for upwards of a century, We shall have more to say about it when we reach Blackfriars Road on our return journey.

MRS. THRALE'S HOUSE, STREATHAM.

CHAPTER XXIV.

BRIXTON AND CLAPHAM.

The Royal Asylum of St. Ann's Society—The Female Convict Prison, Brixton—Clapham Park—Etymology of Clapham—Clapham Common—The Home of Thomas Babington Macaulay—The Old Manor House—The Residence of Sir Dennis Gauden—Pepys a Resident here—Death of Samuel Pepys—The Residence of the Eccentric Henry Cavendish—The Beautiful Mrs. Baldwin—The Home of the Wilberforces—Henry Thornton—The Parish Church—St. Paul's Church—St. John's Church—St. Saviour's Church—The Congregational Chapel, and the Roman Catholic Redemptorist Church and College—Nonconformity at Clapham—The "Clapham Sect"—Lord Teignmouth's House—Nightingale Lane—The Residence of Mr. C. H. Spurgeon—The "Plough" Inn—The "Bedford" Arms—Clapham Rise—Young Ladies' Schools—The British Orphan Asylum—The British Home for Incurables—Clapham Road.

LEAVING Streatham Park on our left, we now make our way northward, by way of Streatham Hill and Tulse Hill, to Brixton. The Royal Asylum of St. Ann's Society, which we pass on our right, was founded in 1702, "for the education and support of the daughters of persons once in prosperity, whether orphans or not." The institution is pleasantly situated upon Streatham Hill, and flourishes under royal patronage. The schools, in which are taught, on an average, about 400 children, are examined by the Syndicate of Cambridge, and the pupils are prepared for the Oxford and Cambridge local examinations. The asylum, erected in 1829, is a handsome building of three storeys, having an Ionic portico and pediment, ornamented by a sculpture of the royal arms.

Almost on the summit of Brixton Hill, in one of the most open and salubrious spots in the southern suburbs of London, stands what was till recently one of the metropolitan houses of correction for the county of Surrey; the other, Horsemonger Lane Gaol, we have already described.* Like nearly all the prisons constructed at the close of the last or beginning of the present century, this is planned in the form of a rude crescent, the governor's house being in the common centre. The prison was built in 1820, being calculated for 185 prisoners, and no more: that is, there are (or were) 149 separate cells, and twelve double cells, in each of which, however, three bed-racks were

---

* See *ante*, p. 253.

fitted up, making altogether bed-racks for 185. This number of inmates, however, was often considerably more than doubled; and hence it became unhealthy, in spite of its admirable situation, and long enjoyed the reputation of being very disorderly. Mr. Hepworth Dixon, in his work on the "London Prisons," published in 1850, writes: "Any person who knows aught of the working of a gaol system will at once understand why the Brixton House of Correction is disorderly, why it is dirty, and why it is unhealthy, when we say that, instead of 185 prisoners—its full complement—there are within its walls not less than 431. The daily average for 1848 was not less than 382, more than double the number for which there is any accommodation."

Here the tread-wheel was first employed, about the year 1824; and from that period, down to the time when it ceased to be used as a house of correction, this prison was, *par excellence*, one for hard labour; in fact, it was all tread-wheel, except for the females, who were employed in picking oakum and sewing.

In former times the external appearance of this prison had anything but a show of security against the escape of prisoners, the boundary-wall being much too low. "More than one person," writes Mr. Dixon, at the date above mentioned, "has been known to leap from the top without being at all hurt; it is, in fact, so low as to offer a pressing temptation to escape; and attempts are, therefore, not unfrequent, sometimes," he adds, "as in a recent case, with most disastrous consequences. A man had got on the wall with the design of regaining his freedom: he was observed, and chased by the officers and governor. A quantity of bricks (loose) are placed on the wall to increase its height, and these furnished the man with defensive weapons, by which he was enabled to keep his pursuers at bay. Seeing no other means of capturing him, one of the officers (not the governor, as was stated in the newspapers at the time) fired at him and seriously wounded him. It was thought at first, and so reported, that the wretched man was killed, but, fortunately, it proved otherwise."

As may be inferred from what we have stated above, this prison was one of the worst, in point of management, of any in the kingdom, and the result was that it became a perfect scandal. Access to its precincts was very rarely, if ever, afforded to the outside world; and it is on record that members of Parliament, and even the Duke of Wellington, had been refused admission. Some idea of its character, however, was afforded to the public in a pamphlet, entitled "A Month at Brixton Treadmill," which was published a few years ago. But a change was in store, for the old prison was sold in 1862 to Her Majesty's Government, by whom it has been converted into a convict establishment for females.

Westward of the prison, and stretching away to Balham Hill Road, a large tract of land, some 250 acres in extent, known as Bleak Hill, was, in 1824, taken by Mr. Thomas Cubitt, the builder of Belgravia, and converted into a series of broad roads and open spaces, planted, and built over with capacious detached villas, and named Clapham Park. This was long the "Belgravia of Clapham;" but a newer and perhaps more attractive quarter has since sprung up in "The Cedars," which lies on the opposite side of Clapham Common.

Clapham is supposed to have received its appellation from one of its ancient proprietors, Osgod Clapa, being the name of the Danish lord at whose daughter's marriage-feast Hardicanute died. Mr. Brayley, in his "History of Surrey," however, observes that there is an objection to this supposition, inasmuch as in the Chertsey Register the place is named "Clappenham" as far back as the reign of Alfred. In the Domesday Survey it is entered as "Clopeham." Hughson, in his "History of London" (1808), describes Clapham as a village about four miles from Westminster Bridge, and consisting of "many handsome houses, surrounding a common that commands many pleasing views. This common," he adds, "about the commencement of the present reign, was little better than a morass, and the roads were almost impassable. The latter are now in an excellent state, and the common so beautifully planted with trees, that it has the appearance of a park. These improvements were effected by a subscription of the inhabitants, who, on this occasion, have been much indebted to the taste and exertions of Mr. Christopher Baldwin, for many years an inhabitant, and an active magistrate; and as a proof of the consequent increased value of property on this spot, Mr. Baldwin has sold fourteen acres of land near his own house for £5,000. . . . A reservoir near the Wandsworth Road supplies the village with water." The Common, still about 220 acres in extent, is bounded on the eastern side by Balham Hill Road, which is a continuation of the road through Newington which we have already described; on the north-west by Battersea Rise; and on the south-west by a roadway, dotted at intervals with private residences standing within their own grounds, and "embosomed high in tufted trees." Like Peckham Rye, and such other open spaces of the kind as are left in the suburbs of London, Clapham Common in its time has had its fair share of patronage, either of those who delight in the healthful and invigorating game of cricket, or of those who desire a quiet stroll over its velvet-like turf. Pleasure-fairs, too, were held here on Good Friday, Easter and Whit Mondays, and on "Derby Day;" but these were abolished in 1873. The Common is ornamented with a few large ponds, which add not a little to the charm of the place.

In the year 1874 the Enclosure Commissioners for England and Wales, under the Metropolitan Commons' Act, 1866, and Metropolitan Commons' Amendment Act, 1869, certified a scheme for placing the Common under the control of the Local Board. The Common was purchased for the sum of £17,000, and it was proposed that it should be dedicated to the use and recreation of the public for ever. By the above-mentioned scheme the Board were to drain, plant, and ornament the Common as necessary, but no houses were to be built thereon, except lodges necessary for its maintenance. The Metropolitan Board of Works having thus taken the Common under their protection, at once set to work in order to effect an improvement in its appearance, by the planting of an avenue of young trees, and the formation of new footpaths in an ornamental style. The Board also issued its mandate that no more gravel was to be dug, or turf or furze cut off the Common, and that nothing should be done to disturb its rural aspect. To this day, consequently, "the Common" is, perhaps, one of the least changed of all spots round London, that is, so far as encroachment goes.

In a house a few doors from the "Plough" Inn, and facing the Common (now occupied by a fishmonger), Thomas Babington Macaulay spent the greater portion of his childhood, caring less for his toys than for books, which he read well at three years old! Here Hannah More visited the Macaulays, and, the parents being absent, was horrified at being offered a glass of spirits by the precocious child, who had learned the existence of spirits from the pages of Robinson Crusoe! The Common, at that time, had something poetic about it, at all events, to the imaginative mind of the future historian. "That delightful wilderness of gorse-bushes, and poplar-groves and gravel-pits, and ponds great and small, was to little Tom Macaulay a region of inexhaustible romance and mystery. He explored all its recesses; he composed, and almost believed, its legends;" and his biographer, Mr. G. O. Trevelyan, records the fact

that he would trace out in the hillocks of the Common an imaginary set of Alps, and an equally fanciful range of Mount Sinai. The house formerly stood back from the road, but of late years it has thrown out a shop-front, and, externally, has lost all traces of having been a private gentleman's residence. Lady Trevelyan, a sister of Lord Macaulay, lived for a time at Clapham, after breaking up her *ménage* in Great George Street.

The "Clapham Sect," on whose merits a brilliant panegyric was penned by Sir James Stephen, had its head-quarters at this house, and at that of Lord Teignmouth, close by. The virtues of the "Claphamites," as they were sneeringly called, have been acknowledged even by their most strenuous opponents.

The old Manor House, which was standing at the corner of Manor Street when Priscilla Wakefield wrote her "Perambulations," in 1809, and was then occupied as a ladies' school, was distinguished by a singular tower, octagonal in form.

Skirting the Common, particularly on the eastern side, are still standing several of the spacious old red-brick mansions, the abode of wealthy London merchants, which once nearly surrounded its entire area. Many have fine elms growing in the grounds before them. The place must have been well inhabited, even so far back as John Evelyn's time, for he mentions dining here, at the house of Sir Dennis Gauden, whom he accompanied thence to Windsor on business with the king. Perhaps he was a City magnate, willing to lend money to his ever impecunious sovereign. The house, which was a large roomy edifice, with a noble gallery occupying the whole length of the building, was built by Sir Dennis for his brother, Dr. John Gauden, Bishop of Exeter, the presumed author of "Eikon Basilikè;" and after his death, in 1662, it became the residence of Sir Dennis himself, who sold it to one "Will" Hewer, who rose from being Pepys' clerk to a high position in the civil service, but found his occupation gone at the Revolution. Sir Dennis still, however, lived here, "very handsomely, and friendly to everybody," writes Evelyn, who was often a guest at his table; and he died here a few months after the fall of the Stuarts.

Pepys used often to visit here his friend Gauden, "Victualler of the Navy, afterwards Sheriff of London, and a knight." Under date July 25, 1663, he writes, in his "Diary:"—"Having intended this day to go to Banstead Downes to see a famous race, I sent Will to get himself ready to go with me; but I hear it is put off, because the Lords do sit in Parliament to-day. After some debate, Creed and I resolved to go to Clapham, to Mr. Gauden's.

When I come there, the first thing was to show me his house, which is almost built. I find it very regular and finely contrived, and the gardens and offices about it as convenient and as full of good variety as ever I saw in my life. It is true he hath been censured for laying out so much money; but he tells me he built it for his brother, who is since dead (the bishop), who, when he should come to be Bishop of Winchester, which he was promised (to which bishopricke, at present, there is no house), he did intend to dwell here. By and by to dinner, and in comes Mr. Creed; I saluted his lady and the young ladies, and his sister, the bishop's widow, who was, it seems, Sir W. Russell's daughter, the Treasurer of the Navy, whom I find to be very well bred, and a woman of excellent discourse. Towards the evening we bade them adieu, and took horse, being resolved that, instead of the race which fails us, we would go to Epsom."

Later on, it seems, Pepys took up his residence here with his friend Hewer. John Evelyn writes again in his "Diary," under date Sept. 23rd, 1700: "I went to visit Mr. Pepys, at Clapham, where he has a very noble and wonderfully well-furnished house, especially with Indian and Chinese curiosities: the offices and gardens well accommodated for pleasure and retirement." Three years later, namely, on the 26th of May, 1703, Evelyn made the following entry in his "Diary:"—"This day died Mr. Sam. Pepys, a very worthy, industrious, and curious person, none in England exceeding him in knowledge of the Navy, in which he had passed thro' all the most considerable offices, Clerk of the Acts and Secretary of the Admiralty, all of which he performed with greate integrity. When K. James II. went out of England, he laid down his office and would serve no more, but withdrawing himselfe from all public affaires, he liv'd at Clapham with his partner, Mr. Hewer, formerly his clerk, in a very noble house and sweete place, where he enjoy'd the fruite of his labours in greate prosperity. He was universally belov'd, hospitable, generous, learned in many things, skill'd in music, a very greate cherisher of learned men of whom he had the conversation. His library and collection of other curiosities were of the most considerable, the models of ships especially." He was buried, as already stated, in St. Olave's Church, Hart Street.*

Lord Braybrooke, in his "Memoir of Samuel Pepys," tells us that when he removed to Mr. Hewer's house at Clapham, he left a large portion of his correspondence behind him in York Build-ings, in the custody of a friend. This correspondence eventually found its way into the Bodleian Library, at Oxford. It only remains to add that Hewer's house was pulled down about the middle of the last century.

In a large house on the east side of the Common, at the corner of what is now known as Cavendish Road, lived Mr. Henry Cavendish, the eccentric chemist, of whom we have already had occasion to speak, in our notice of Gower Street.† He died in 1810, leaving more than a million to be divided among his relatives. One of his eccentricities was his utter disregard of money. The bankers with whom he kept his account finding that his balance had accumulated to upwards of £80,000, commissioned one of the partners to wait on him, and to ask him what he wished done with it. On reaching Clapham, and finding Mr. Cavendish's house, he rang the bell, but had the greatest difficulty in obtaining admission. "You must wait," said the servant, "till my master rings his bell, and then I will let him know that you are here." In about a quarter of an hour the bell rang, and the fact of the banker's arrival was duly communicated to the abstracted chemist. Mr. Cavendish, in great agitation, desired that the banker might be shown up, and as he entered the room, saluted him with a few words, asking him the object of his visit. "Sir, I thought proper to wait upon you, as we have in hand a very large balance of yours, and we wish for your orders respecting it." "Oh, if it is any trouble to you, I will take it out of your hands. Do not come here to plague me about money." "It is not the least trouble to us, sir; but we thought you might like some of it turned to account, and invested." "Well, well; what do you want to do?" "Perhaps you would like to have forty thousand pounds invested?" "Yes; do so, if you like; but don't come here to trouble me any more, or I will remove my balance."

Cavendish lived a very retired existence, and to strangers he was most reserved. To such an extent did he carry his solitary habits, that he would never even see or allow himself to be seen by a female servant; and, as Lord Brougham relates, "he used to order his dinner daily by a note, which he left at a certain hour on the hall table, whence the housekeeper was to take it."

His shyness was, not unnaturally, mistaken by strangers for pride. In Bruhn's "Life of Von Humboldt" it is related that, "While travelling in England, in 1790, with George Forster, Humboldt obtained permission to make use of the library of the eminent chemist and philosopher, Henry Cavendish, second son of the Duke of Devonshire, on condition, however, that he was on no account to presume so far as to speak to or even greet the shy and aristocratic owner, should he happen to encounter him. Humboldt states this in a letter to Bunsen, adding, sarcastically, 'Cavendish little suspected, at that time, that it was I who, in 1810, was to be his successor at the Academy of Sciences.'"

Cavendish, who has been styled "the Newton of Chemistry," was distinguished as the founder of pneumatic chemistry, and for his successful researches on the composition of water, and his famous experiment, made at Clapham, for the determination of the earth's density. "The man who weighed the world," wrote his cousin, the late Duke of Devonshire, in his "Handbook for Chatsworth," "buried his science and his wealth in solitude and insignificance at Clapham."

Almost the whole of his house here was occupied as workshops and laboratory. "It was stuck about with thermometers, rain-gauges, &c. A registering thermometer of Cavendish's own construction served as a sort of landmark to his house. It is now in Professor Brande's possession." A small portion only of the villa was set apart for personal comfort. The upper rooms constituted an astronomical observatory. What is now the drawing-room was the laboratory. In an adjoining room a forge was placed. The lawn was invaded by a wooden stage, from which access could be had to a large tree, to the top of which Cavendish, in the course of his astronomical, meteorological, electrical, or other researches, occasionally ascended. His library was immense, and he fixed it at a distance from his house, in order that he might not be disturbed by those who came to consult it. His own particular friends were allowed to borrow books, but neither they nor even Mr. Cavendish himself ever withdrew a book without giving a receipt for it. The mansion of Henry Cavendish, since re-fronted and considerably altered, was in 1877 the residence of Mr. H. S. Bicknell, and is known as Cavendish House.

Here and at Balham, towards the close of the last century, were many residents who belonged to the Wesleyan connexion; and it was at a friend's house at Balham that John Wesley dined and slept less than a week before his death, in March, 1791.

The famous beauty, Mrs. Baldwin—who, when young, turned the head of the Prince of Wales, had her portrait painted and her bust sculptured for foreign emperors and kings, and was kissed publicly by Dr. Johnson, whom she used to meet at

Mrs. Thrale's house at Streatham—lived for many years at Clapham, and died here in July, 1839.

The house known as Broomfield, on the south-west side of the Common, was occupied for some years by Mr. William Wilberforce, M.P., the distinguished philanthropist; and there his no less distinguished son, Samuel Wilberforce, Bishop successively of Oxford and of Winchester, was born, on the 7th of September, 1805.

Close by stood the house once occupied by Henry Thornton, the author and prime mover of the agitation for the "reformation of manners and the suppression of slavery," in which William Wilberforce took such a distinguished part. The conclave, we are told, held their meetings, for the most part, in an oval saloon which William Pitt planned to be added to Thornton's residence. "It arose at his bidding," writes Sir J. Stephen, in his "Essays," "and yet remains, perhaps a solitary monument of the architectural skill of that imperial mind. Lofty and symmetrical, it was curiously wainscoted with books on every side, except where it opened on a far extended lawn, reposing beneath the giant arms of aged elms and massive tulip-trees." *

In Mr. J. T. Smith's "Book for a Rainy Day," we are introduced to one of these old-fashioned mansions:—"On arriving at Mr. Esdaile's gate," he tells us, "Mr. Smedley remarked that this (Clapham) was one of the few commons near London which had not been enclosed. The house had one of those plain fronts which indicated little, but upon ascending the steps I was struck with a similar sensation to those of the previous season, when first I entered this hospitable mansion. If I were to suffer myself to utter anything like an ungrateful remark, it would be that the visitor, immediately he enters the hall, is presented with too much at once, for he knows not which to admire first, the choice display of pictures which decorate the hall, or the equally artful and delightful manner in which the park-like grounds so luxuriantly burst upon his sight."

The parish church, built on the north-western corner of the Common, is a dull, heavy building, a sort of cross between the London parish church of Queen Anne's time and the "chapel of ease" of the last century. It dates from the year 1776. Yet Macaulay was fond of it to the last. He writes, under date Clapham, February, 1849: "To church this morning. I love the church, for the sake of old times; I love even that absurd painted window, with the dove, the lamb, the urn, the two cornucopias, and the profusion of sun-flowers, passion-

---

* Quoted by Mr. J. Thorn in his "Environs of London."

flowers, and peonies." He adds, "I heard a Puseyite sermon, very different from the oratory which I formerly used to hear from the same pulpit." The edifice is an ugly brick structure, with a singular dome-crowned tower at the west end. It contains a mural tablet to the memory of Dr. John Jebb, "the good, great, and pious Bishop of Limerick," who died in 1833; also a monument, by Sir Richard Westmacott, to John

with the instructions of Queen Elizabeth. The old church, however, stood at some little distance from the present parish church, on the high ground between Larkhall Lane and Wandsworth Road. St. Paul's Church, which occupies its site, is a plain brick-built structure, and was erected in 1814. On the south wall is a monument, with bust, of William Hewer, which was saved on the demolition of the old church.

VIEW OF CLAPHAM IN 1790.

Thornton. The remains of the bishop are deposited in the tomb of the Thorntons.

Priscilla Wakefield, in her "Perambulations of London," published in 1809, writes as follows:— "There are now no remains of the old church, except the south aisle, which does not bear the marks of any remote antiquity. It is now out of use, unless for the funeral service, there being no other burying-ground but that which belongs to it. The new church stands on the north side of the Common; it is a plain modern edifice, without aisles or chancel."

Mr. J. T. Smith, the antiquary, states that the walls of the little old parish church, which was demolished to make way for its successor, were adorned with Scripture texts, painted in accordance

St. John's Church, built in 1842, stands on the western side of the Clapham Road, between Stockwell and the Common; it is after the model of a Greek temple, with an Ionic portico and no steeple, but a cross on the top of the pediment. Dr. Bickersteth, the second Bishop of Ripon, was for some years the minister here.

St. Saviour's Church, in Cedars' Road, is a large and handsome cruciform structure, with a central tower in three stages, with pinnacles. It is in the Decorated style of architecture, and was built, in 1864, from the designs of Mr. J. Knowles, at the cost of the Rev. W. Bowyer. The windows are filled with painted glass, by Clayton and Bell. This church remained unconsecrated for several years, in consequence of the bishop of the diocese objecting to the position of a monument of Mrs. Bowyer, which had been placed under the tower, immediately in front of the altar-rails. The monument—an altar-tomb, with a recumbent effigy of Mrs. Bowyer—was removed, in 1873, to the north transept.

By far the finest ecclesiastical-looking structures at Clapham do not belong to the Established Church. These are the Congregational Chapel, in

before one of the courts of law, to silence the bells of St. Mary's as a nuisance. He was successful in his suit; and the case of "Soltau v. De Weld" must be regarded as settling the question as to the right of any clergyman, except one of the Established Church, to ring bells to the annoyance of his neighbours.

The pulpit of Clapham Church, in Macaulay's childhood, it is almost needless to add, rang with

OLD CLAPHAM CHURCH IN 1750.

Grafton Square, built in 1852, one of the most commodious and elegant edifices of which London Nonconformists can boast; and the Roman Catholic Redemptorist Church of St. Mary, built in 1849. These, with their lofty spires, quite dwarf the plain and unpretending parish structures.

Mr. G. O. Trevelyan writes thus, in his "Life of Lord Macaulay:"—"At Clapham, as elsewhere, the old order is changing. What was once the home of Zachary stands almost within the swing of the bells of a stately and elegant Roman Catholic chapel; and the pleasant mansion of Lord Teignmouth, the cradle of the Bible Society, is now turned into a convent of monks;"—he should have said, of "regular clergy." A gentleman who lived close by, in 1851, brought an action

"Evangelical" doctrines. Indeed, Clapham has long been regarded as a suburb whose residents are chiefly distinguished by social prosperity and ardent attachment to "Evangelical opinions;" and hence it is sneeringly spoken of by "Tom Ingoldsby" as "that sanctified ville;" and Thackeray has introduced a picture of the religious life of the place into the opening chapters of "The Newcomes." But he has, perhaps, overdrawn the Nonconformist element in it, and "Hobson" and "Brian Newcome" are scarcely fair specimens of the outcome of the religious influences of "the Clapham Sect" in its palmy days, when it numbered Wilberforce, and James Stephen, the Thorntons, and Charles and Robert Grant. Still, it was the chosen home of the Low-Church party during its golden age, and Churchmen and Nonconformists met there on common ground.

The meetings of Henry Drummond, the elder Macaulay, and the little coterie that gathered round them, and who were designated the "Clapham Sect," first made the ancient home of Osgod Clapa a synonym for devout respectability, and doubtless it will be long before this distinctive description will die out. As Horace writes—

" The cask will long
Retain the sweet scents of its earliest days."

When the "Clapham Sect" first became famous, even along the high road the houses had not crept along in an unbroken line to the Common; the place was literally a village, prim, select, and exclusive. For several generations Nonconformity had had a foothold therein. It is said that between the years 1640 and 1650 Mr. William Bridge, M.A., one of the five divines who, under the leadership of Philip Nye, made a stand for liberty of conscience in the Westminster Assembly of Divines, preached at Clapham, and founded therein an Independent congregation. Be that as it may, it is certain that when Charles II. published, in 1671–72, a declaration of Indulgence, licenses to conduct Nonconformist worship were granted to Dr. Wilkinson, of Clapham, for his own house and school-room, and to Mr. Thomas Lye, of the same place, for his own house. Mr. Lye had been minister of Allhallows, and one of Cromwell's "Triers." He formed a congregation, which continued to assemble in a private house in the time of his successor, Philip Lamb. Subsequently it met in a temporary wooden building, and in 1762 a more substantial edifice was erected, in which for some years laboured Dr. Furneaux, a learned and voluminous writer, with a strong leaning towards Arianism. In this chapel they continued to meet until, in 1852, was erected Grafton Square Chapel. The congregation is large and comparatively wealthy. A commodious lecture-hall, used also as a Sunday-school, is erected in the immediate vicinity of the church, and a mission-hall and schools in the Wandsworth Road.

The "Clapham Sect"—which comprised the leaders of the Evangelical party, mostly Churchmen, but with a sprinkling of Nonconformists, and numbered among them such men as Wilberforce, Zachary Macaulay, Thornton, Stephen, &c.—met, as we have stated before, at Lord Teignmouth's house, at the corner of Clapham Common, now the Redemptorists' College and Monastery; and in this house the Bible Society was founded. One of the "sect," Mr. Henry Thornton, of Clapham,

was said to have spent £2,000 annually in the distribution of Bibles and other religious books.

The practical influence of the " Clapham Sect" was great, though they had no posts or offices with which to bribe followers; they doubtless, also, did much to awaken society to a sense of the great importance of personal religion; but surely Macaulay is guilty of an exaggeration when he writes of them as follows :—"The truth is that from that little knot of men emanated all the Bible societies and almost all the missionary societies in the world. The share which they had," he continues, " in providing means for the education of the people was great. They were the real destroyers of the slave-trade and of slavery. Many of those whom Stephen describes, in his article on the ' Clapham Sect,' were public men of the greatest weight. Lord Teignmouth governed India at Calcutta. Grant governed India in Leadenhall Street. Stephen's father was Perceval's right-hand man in the House of Commons. It is needless to speak of Wilberforce. As to Simeon, if you knew what his authority and influence were, you would allow that his real sway in the Church was far greater than that of any primate." And such was really the case. At the beginning of this century, and for the first thirty years, the men who met at Lord Teignmouth's table here were really the life and soul of the Established Church, and the spring of its active energy.

On the western side of the Common, in Nightingale Lane, a thoroughfare leading from Clapham to Wandsworth Common, lives the Rev. C. H. Spurgeon, of whom we have already spoken in our accounts of the Metropolitan Tabernacle and the Surrey Music Hall.* One of Mr. Spurgeon's first undertakings, on settling in London, was the Pastors' College. The work of the college was for many years carried on in the dark subterranean rooms under the Tabernacle; but in 1874 it was transferred to a more convenient, suitable, and commodious building at the rear of the Tabernacle, which had been erected and furnished at a cost of about £15,000. Here there is a fine hall, large class-rooms, a spacious library, and other conveniences. Of the work that has been done at the Pastors' College some idea may be formed from the following quotation of Mr. Spurgeon's account of the college, written in 1876 :—" There are now 330 men proclaiming the Gospel in connection with the Baptist denomination who have been trained in the college, of whom two are in India, one in China, two in Spain, one in Rio Janeiro, one in St. Helena,

* See *ante*, pp. 29, 260, 267.

one in Turk's Island, one in South Africa, six in Australia, twenty-three in the United States, and ten in the Canadian Dominion."

We now make our way northward from the Common by the Clapham Road, leaving the "Plough" Inn on our left. This sign, we need scarcely remark, leads the mind back to days when the village of Clapham, far removed from the busy hum of London life, was surrounded by green fields and homesteads. "Among agricultural signs," Mr. Larwood tells us, in his "History of Signboards," "the 'Plough' leads the van, sometimes accompanied by the legend, 'Speed the Plough.'" In some cases the sign bears an inscription in verse, such as—

> " He who by the Plough would thrive,
> Himself must either hold or drive."

But if these lines were ever inscribed here, they have long since been obliterated.

Nearer to London is the "Bedford Arms," a tavern doubtless so named in honour of the ducal house of Bedford, whose lands at Streatham, as we have seen, can be reached by this road. From the "Bedford Arms" up to the "Plough" there is a somewhat steep ascent, and the roadway at that point is known as Clapham Rise. This spot has long been noted for its seminaries for young ladies, a fact which is wittily referred to by Tom Ingoldsby, in his amusing mock-heroic poem, "The Babes in the Wood"—

> " And Jane, since, when girls have 'the dumps,'
> Fortune-hunters in scores to entrap 'em rise,
> We'll send to those worthy old frumps,
> The two Misses Tickler of Clapham Rise !"

This locality is also a favourite spot for charitable institutions. At Clapham Rise was founded, in 1827, the British Orphan Asylum, now located at Slough, near Windsor. The design of this institution is "to board, clothe, and educate destitute children of either sex who are really or virtually orphans, and are descended from parents who have moved in the middle classes of society, such as, for example, children of clergymen, and of members of the legal and medical professions, naval and military officers, merchants, and of other persons who in their lifetime were in a position to provide a liberal education for their children."

The British Home for Incurables, now flourishing at Clapham Rise, was established in 1861, with two objects—to provide a home for life, with good nursing, skilled medical attendance, and all necessary mechanical contrivances for the alleviation of the sufferings and afflictions of the patients ; and to grant pensions of £20 per annum for life to those who may have relatives or friends partially able to provide for them, but who are not able wholly to maintain them. All who are afflicted with incurable disease are eligible, without regard to nationality or creed, except the insane, the idiotic, and the pauper class, and those under twenty years of age. The institution extends its operations to all parts of the United Kingdom.

The Clapham Road, a broad and well-built thoroughfare, descends gradually towards Stockwell and Kennington. On every recurring "Derby Day" its appearance, from the vehicular and other traffic which passes along it, is lively and animated in the extreme. The scenes to be witnessed here on these occasions have been graphically and amusingly described by Mr. G. A. Sala, in his "Daylight and Gaslight," to the pages of which we would refer the reader.

CHAPTER XXV.

STOCKWELL AND KENNINGTON.

"Here the Black Prince once lived and held his court."—*Philips.*

Etymology of Stockwell—Its Rustic Retirement Half a Century ago—The Green—Meeting of the Albion Archers—The Stockwell Ghost—Old House in which Lord Cromwell is said to have lived—St. Andrew's Church—Small-pox and Fever Hospital—Mr. John Angell's Bequest—Trinity Asylum—Stockwell Orphanage—Mr. Alfred Forrester—Kennington Manor—Death of Hardicanute—Kennington a Favourite Residence of the Black Prince—Masques and Pageants—Isabella, the "Little Queen" of Richard II.—The Last of the Old Manor House—Cumberland Row—Caron House—Kennington Oval—Beaufoy's Vinegar Distillery—The Tradescants—Kennington Common—Execution of the Scottish Rebels—"Jemmy" Dawson—Meeting of the Chartists in 1848—Large Multitudes addressed by Whitefield—The Common converted into a Park—St Mark's Church—"The Horns" Tavern—Lambeth Waterworks—The Licensed Victuallers' School.

STOCKWELL lies to our right as we journey along the Clapham Road on our way back towards the metropolis. "The etymology of the place," writes Allen, in his "History of Surrey," "is probably derived from 'stoke' (the Saxon *stoc,* a wood), and 'well,' from some spring in the neighbourhood." It is called a "small rural village" by Priscilla Wakefield, in her "Perambulations of London," published in 1809. The place, indeed, retained its characteristics of rustic retirement down to a comparatively recent date. In the "Chimney Corner Companion" is an amusing account of a cockney's "outing" with a gun on the 1st of September, 1825, in which we are told how that he and his friend breakfasted at the "Swan" at Stockwell, and pushed on Kent-wards by way of Brixton to Blackheath, but "without meeting anything beyond yellow-hammers and sparrows !"

Like Lee and other places in the immediate vicinity of London which we have visited in our perambulations, Stockwell once boasted of its "green;" but this, excepting in name, has already become a thing of the past, and bricks and mortar are fast usurping what little is left of its once shady lanes and hedgerows. It was a triangular space on the western side of the high road, nearly opposite the "Swan."

In 1840, as we learn from Colburn's "Kalendar of Amusements," the society of Albion archers held their first grand field-day, to contend for the captaincy and lieutenancy for the month, and Stockwell Park was the place of rendezvous. We are naïvely told that "shooting commences at one, eating and drinking at seven, and the light fantastic toes are agitating at ten o'clock."

In 1778 this place was alarmed by an apparition, known to this day as "the Stockwell Ghost," which spread such terror through the then retired village and neighbourhood that it became suddenly invested with almost as much notoriety as Cock Lane* some years previously.

The story is thus told by Charles Mackay, in his "Extraordinary Popular Delusions:"—"Mrs. Golding, an elderly lady, who resided alone with her servant, Anne Robinson, was sorely surprised, on the evening of Twelfth Day, 1772, to observe an extraordinary commotion among her crockery. Cups and saucers rattled down the chimney; pots and pans were whirled downwards or through the windows; and hams, cheeses, and loaves of bread disported themselves upon the floor just as if the devil were in them. This, at least, was the conclusion to which Mrs. Golding came; and, being greatly alarmed, she invited some of her neighbours to stay with her, and protect her from the evil one. Their presence, however, did not put a stop to the insurrection of china, and every room in the house was in a short time strewed with fragments. The chairs and tables at last joined in the tumult; and things looked altogether so serious and inexplicable that the neighbours, dreading that the house itself would next be seized with a fit of motion and

tumble about their ears, left poor Mrs. Golding to bear the brunt of it by herself. The ghost in this case was solemnly remonstrated with, and urged to take its departure; but the destruction continuing as great as before, Mrs. Golding finally made up her mind to quit the house altogether. With Anne Robinson, she took refuge in the house of a neighbour; but his glass and crockery being immediately subjected to the same persecution, he was reluctantly compelled to give her notice to quit. The old lady, thus forced back to her own house, endured the disturbance for some days longer, when suspecting that Anne Robinson was the cause of all the mischief, she dismissed her from her service. The extraordinary appearances immediately ceased, and were never afterwards renewed — a fact which is of itself sufficient to point out the real disturber. A long time afterwards Anne Robinson confessed the whole matter to the Rev. Mr. Brayfield. This gentleman confided the story to Mr. Hone, who published an explanation of the mystery. It appears that Anne was anxious to have a clear house to carry on an intrigue with her lover, and she resorted to this trick in order to effect her purpose. She placed the china on the shelves in such a manner that it fell on the slightest motion; and she attached horse-hair to other articles, so that she could jerk them down from an adjoining room without being perceived by any one. She was exceedingly dexterous at this sort of work, and would have proved a formidable rival to many a juggler by profession. A full explanation of the whole affair may be found in 'Hone's Every-day Book.'" The pranks of the "ghost" are also described so fully by Sir Walter Scott, in his book on "Demonology and Witchcraft," that there is scarcely any necessity of repeating them more minutely here.

The "little fairy green" before the "Swan," at Stockwell, writes Mr. Thomas Miller, with poetic exaggeration, in 1852, "is now no more." It was a dead, flat, triangular space, with no fairies.

"On the west side of Stockwell Green," writes Allen, in his work above quoted, "is an old house, now (1829) in the occupation of a butcher, in which Mr. Nichols says that Thomas, Lord Cromwell, lived. There is no proof, however," he adds, "that the above individual resided here or at the adjacent manor-house."

At the eastern end of London Road—or what was formerly called Bedford Private Road—and near the triangular space of ground which was once the "Green," stands St. Andrew's Church. This edifice, originally known as Stockwell Chapel,

---

* See Vol II., p. 436.

was in 1829 described as "a plain edifice of brick, with a small turret and bell." The chapel was built about the year 1767, on a piece of ground granted by the Duke of Bedford. In 1810, and again in 1868, it was enlarged and greatly altered, at a cost of £3,400; and on St. Barnabas Day in that year it was consecrated, under the title of St. Andrew. Soon afterwards a consolidated chapelry district, taken out of the new parishes of St. Mark, Kennington, and St. Matthew, Brixton, was assigned to the church.

In the London Road is a small-pox and fever hospital, which was established here in 1870 by the Metropolitan District Asylums Board.

On the east side of Stockwell Road are the Stockwell Training and Kindergarten Colleges and Practising Schools, in connection with the British and Foreign School Society, whose head-quarters are in the Borough Road. The schools here, which are for girls, were erected about the year 1864, and have since been enlarged by the addition of a new wing. Accommodation is afforded here for 135 girls and 125 students. The Kindergarten institution, as we learn from the Report presented to the Society in 1877, had grown rapidly during the preceding year. "It is meant to be self-supporting, and, judging from present experience, the receipts from students and children will pay all the expenses."

In 1784 died Mr. John Angell, who left £6,000 for the purpose of building at Stockwell a college "for seven decayed gentlemen, two clergymen, an organist, six singing-men, twelve choristers, a verger, chapel clerk, and three domestic servants," which he endowed with rent-charges to the amount of £800 a year, besides making a provision for the daily food of the members. The good intentions of the testator, however, were for many years frustrated by a suit in Chancery respecting his will. The residence of Mr. Angell, at Stockwell, a large brick mansion, was for some time occupied as a boarding-school. His name is now kept in remembrance by the Angell Town Estate, on the east side of the Brixton Road. Early in the present century a Mr. Bailey, a merchant in St. Paul's Churchyard, founded here an asylum for twelve aged females. The building, a neat brick edifice, called Trinity Asylum, was erected in Acre Lane in 1822.

Another charitable institution here, and one with more than a local reputation, is the Stockwell Orphanage for boys, founded under the auspices of Mr. Spurgeon, the pastor of the Metropolitan Tabernacle, of whom we have already spoken. The institution, which covers a large space of ground on the Bedford estate, and forms a handsome quadrangle, is approached by a broad avenue from the Clapham Road. At the end of this avenue, which is planted on either side with plane-trees, is the entrance arch, an ornamental structure, surmounted by a bell-turret. On the piers of the archway are appropriate inscriptions, such as—"A Father of the fatherless and a Judge of the widow is God in his holy habitation;" "Solomon in all his glory was not arrayed like one of these;" and, "Your heavenly Father feedeth them."

The following description of the edifice is from the pen of Mr. Spurgeon himself:—"On looking from under the arch the visitor is struck with the size and beauty of the buildings, and the delightfully airy and open character of the whole institution. It is a place of sweetness and light, where merry voices ring out, and happy children play. The stranger will be pleased with the dining-hall, hung round with engravings given by Mr. Graves, of Pall Mall; he will be shown into the board-room, where the trustees transact the business; and he will be specially pleased with the great play-hall, in which our public meetings are held and the boys' sports are carried on. There is the swimming-bath, which enables us to say that nearly every boy can swim. Up at the very top of the buildings, after ascending two flights of stairs, the visitor will find the school-rooms, which from their very position are airy and wholesome. The floors, scrubbed by the boys themselves, the beds made, and the domestic arrangements all kept in order by their own labour, are usually spoken of with approbation." At the further end of the Orphanage grounds stands the infirmary. It is spacious enough to accommodate a large number of children, should an epidemic break out in the institution.

The Orphanage, which was commenced in 1868, and finished by the end of the following year, contains accommodation for 250 children, who are here fed, clothed, and taught; and the expenses of the institution are about £5,000 per annum. It is largely, if not mainly, dependent on voluntary contributions for its support. The Orphanage, it should be stated, receives destitute fatherless boys, without respect to the religion of the parents. Children are eligible for entrance between the ages of six and ten, and they are received without putting the mothers to the trouble and expense of canvassing for votes, the trustees themselves selecting the most needy cases. The family system is carried out, the boys living in separate houses, under the care of matrons.

Not far from the Orphanage, in Portland Place North, Clapham Road, lived Mr. Alfred Forrester,

VIEWS IN OLD STOCKWELL.

1. Old Mansion on Stockwell Common, 1792.   2. Old Inn, Stockwell Common, 1794.   3 Stockwell Chapel, 1800.
4. Stockwell Manor House, 1750.

better known by his *nom de plume* of "Alfred Crowquill," the author of "The Wanderings of a Pen and Pencil," "Railway Raillery," &c. Born in London in 1805, Alfred Forrester was educated at a private institution at Islington, where he was a schoolfellow of Captain Marryatt. In due course he became a notary in the Royal Exchange, but retired from business about 1839. He commenced his literary career, at the age of sixteen, as a con-

was probably derived originally from the Saxon Kyning-tun, "the town or place of the king." "In the parish of Lambeth," writes Hughson, in his "History of London," "is the manor of Kennington, which, in the Conqueror's Survey, is called Chenintun. At that time it was in the possession of Theodoric, a goldsmith, who held it of Edward the Confessor. There is no record to show how it reverted to the Crown; but during the time of

KENNINGTON, FROM THE GREEN, 1780.

tributor to periodical publications. Later in life he devoted himself to drawing, modelling, and engraving both on steel and wood, with the design of illustrating the works of his pen. His first publication was "Leaves from my Memorandum Book," a book of comic prose and verse, illustrated by himself, which was followed by his "Eccentric Tales." In 1828 he joined Mr. B. Disraeli, Theodore Hook, and other writers, in the magazine, edited by Hook, called *The Humorist*, and subsequently contributed to *Bentley's Miscellany*, *Punch*, the *Illustrated London News*, &c.

On the north side of Stockwell, and hemmed in by Walworth, Newington, and South Lambeth, is the once royal manor of Kennington. The name of Kennington, it is said by some topographers,

Edward III. it was made part of the Duchy of Cornwall, to which it still continues annexed. Here was a royal palace, which was the residence of the Black Prince: it stood near the spot now called Kennington Cross. This palace was occasionally a residence of royalty down to the reign of Henry VII. After his time the manor appears to have been let out to various persons. Charles I., however, when Prince of Wales, inhabited a house built on part of the site of the old palace, the stables of which, built of flint and stone, remained *in situ* until the year 1795, when they were known as 'The Long Barn.'"

Kennington is described in the "Tour round London," in 1774, as "a village near Lambeth, in Surrey, and one of the precincts of that parish."

It was formerly a lordship belonging to the ancient Earls of Warren, one of whom, in the reign of Edward II., being childless, gave the manor to the king. It had been already alienated, however, before the sixteenth year of Edward III., and was part of the estate of Roger d'Amory, who was attainted in the same reign for joining with sundry other lords in a seditious movement. Coming once more into the hands of the king, it was made a royal seat, and became shortly afterwards the principal residence of the Black Prince. The author above quoted states of this once abode of royalty, that "there is nothing now remaining of this ancient seat but a building called The Long Barn, which in the year 1709 was one of the receptacles of the poor persecuted Palatines."

It is generally accepted as a certainty that there was a royal residence near the spot now known as Kennington Cross as far back as the Saxon times; and here, says tradition, Hardicanute died in the year 1041. This amiable King of Denmark, third son of Canute, succeeded to the English crown on the death of his brother, Harold Harefoot, whose body, it is related, he caused to be dug up from its tomb at Winchester, and afterwards to be beheaded and thrown into the Thames. "Some good fishermen," so runs the story, "found the mangled trunk of the dead king, and decently interred it in the church of St. Clement Danes. The peculiarly clement Dane who ruled over them, however, directly he heard of their pious act, again ordered his brother's body to be flung into the Thames." Two years afterwards Hardicanute went to Kennington (or, according to another account, to Lambeth), in order to honour the nuptial feast of a Danish lord; and there, within sight of the river on the banks of which Harold's corse had been washed by the stream, he fell dead, amidst the shouting and drinking of the guests assembled at the marriage banquet.

In 1189, Richard of the Lion Heart granted the manor to Sir Robert Percy; and it was afterwards the subject of frequent royal grants. As stated above, it seems to have been rather a favourite residence of Edward the Black Prince; and the road by which he reached the palace from the landing-place at the water-side, following the direction of Upper Kennington Lane, still retains the name of Prince's Road. Here died that powerful vassal of Edward I., John, Earl of Warren and Surrey, in September, 1304.

Again, the kings of Scotland, France, and Cyprus being in England in the year 1363, on a visit to Edward III., Henry Picard, who had been lord mayor, had the honour of entertaining here those monarchs, with the Prince of Wales and other illustrious persons. At another time, the citizens gave a grand masquerade on horseback for the amusement of the Black Prince's son, Richard (then in his tenth year), and his mother, Joan of Kent. The procession set out from Newgate, and proceeded to Kennington, and was composed of stately pageants, in masques, one of which represented the pope and twenty-four cardinals. This "great mummery" consisted of 130 citizens in fancy dresses, with trumpets, sackbuts, and minstrels; and they danced and "mummed" to their hearts' content in the great hall of the palace; after which, having been right royally feasted, they returned again to the City by way of London Bridge.

Nineteen years afterwards, when the young king wanted money, and to that end made up his mind to take a second wife, he married Isabel, daughter of Charles VI. of France—the "little queen," as she was pettily styled, for she was but a child, under eight years of age. The royal train, on approaching London, was met on Blackheath[*] by the lord mayor and aldermen, habited in scarlet, who attended the king to Newington (Surrey), where he dismissed them, as he and his youthful bride were to "rest at Kenyngtoun." When the poor child was taken from Kennington to her lodgings in the Tower, the press to see her was so great that several persons were crushed to death on London Bridge—among them the Prior of Tiptree, in Essex.

At Kennington, John of Gaunt sought refuge from the citizens, after he had quarrelled with the Bishop of London. The proud Lancaster was one of the protectors of Wyclif, who was, of course, particularly unpopular with the prelates, and had bearded the bishop in a very irreverent manner. The good churchmen of London, who had small respect for royalty when royalty chanced to offend them, chased the ducal offender in the very same year in which they danced before his nephew, and he was glad to be quiet for some time in the old palace. His son, the fiery Bolingbroke, after he became king, sometimes resided here, as did his grandson, the unfortunate Henry VI., and Henry VII., and Katharine of Arragon. James I. settled the manor of Kennington on the Prince of Wales, and it has ever since formed part of the princely possessions. The manor had been purchased in November, 1604, by Alleyn, the player, and founder of Dulwich College, for £1,065, and sold five years afterwards by the astute actor—who

---

knew how to turn a penny, and made good use of his savings—for £2,000. It was of him, probably, that it was purchased by James I., who rebuilt the manor-house. The last fragment of the old palace—the "Old Barn," or "Long Barn"—remained till near the close of the last century; and the old manor-house itself, having served for some years as a Female Philanthropic School, finally disappeared in 1875. From an account of the building, published at the time of its demolition, we gather the following interesting particulars:— The first object which struck the visitor was the canopied head to the outer doorway, supported by finely carved trusses. The entrance door was very massive, and the large lock and unwieldy bar were suggestive of the times when every precaution was necessary for the safe custody of property. The rooms were square and lofty, with old-fashioned chimney-openings. The finest specimen of decorative art was, without doubt, the modelled plaster ceiling in the back room. The enrichments were finely undercut and in alto-relief, the mouldings and border being in true character with the other portions. The staircase was of massive oak, and the mouldings cut in the solid. The doors and the wainscot dado were also solid oak, the latter being a particularly fine specimen of wainscoting. The substantial timbers, door, and window-frames and heads to the last were in an excellent state of preservation. The estate having been leased to a speculative builder, the old house was demolished in order to make room for modern residences.

Here, on a waste piece of land belonging to the Prince of Wales, as part of the old royal palace and demesne, lay for some years a quantity of the marble statues which had been removed from Arundel House, in the Strand, and which afterwards decorated "Kuper's Gardens," the site of which we shall presently visit. Here they were discovered by connoisseurs, and were purchased, some by Lord Burlington for his villa at Chiswick, and others by Mr. Freeman, of Fawley Court, near Henley-on-Thames, and by Mr. Edmund Waller, of Beaconsfield. Others were cut up and used to make mantel-pieces for private houses in Lambeth.

It would appear that Kennington is still regarded as an appanage of royalty; at all events, it gave the title of earl to the hero of Culloden, William the "butcher," Duke of Cumberland, the younger son of George II. The duke's name was till lately kept in remembrance here by Cumberland Row, close by the Vestry Hall, Kennington Green: it was a low row of cottages, bearing date 1666. Their unfinished carcases had been used as a lazar-house during the great plague of the previous year.

The Prince of Wales, it may be added, is still the ground landlord of several streets in Kennington.

The manor of Kennington subsequently reverted to the Crown, and was granted by Charles I., when Prince of Wales, to Sir Noel Caron and Sir Francis Cottington. Sir Noel Caron was Dutch Ambassador to the English Court during the early part of the seventeenth century. He erected here a handsome mansion, with two wings. On the front was the inscription, "Omne solum forti patria." He built also on the roadside the almshouses near the third mile-stone for seven poor women. His name is inscribed on their front, with the date, 1618, and a Latin inscription to the effect that "He that hath pity on the poor lendeth to the Lord." Caron House, and the gardens attached to it, are memorable as having been granted by Charles II. to Lord Chancellor Clarendon, who sold them to Sir Jeremias Whichcote. The *London Gazette* tells us that the prisoners from the Fleet were removed hither after the Fire of London; it was pulled down soon after, and the last remains of the house were removed early in the present century. What remained of it in 1806, when Hughson wrote his "History of London and its Suburbs," was used as an academy, and still retained its former name of Caron House. Not far from it was—and perhaps still is—a spring of clear water called Vauxhall Well, which is said not to freeze in the very coldest winters.

A portion of the site of Sir Noel Caron's park is absorbed in the well-known cricket-ground called Kennington Oval, which shares with "Lord's"* the honour of being the scene of many of those doughty encounters between the heroes of the bat and ball which have made the "elevens" of the north and south, of Surrey and Nottingham, Kent and Sussex, United and All England, all but immortal. The Oval, which, within the memory of living persons, was a cabbage-garden, covers about nine acres of ground, and is set apart entirely for cricket-matches. It was first opened as a cricket-ground on the 16th of April, 1846, as the speculation of a man named Houghton. The Surrey Club have held it for many years on a lease from the Duchy of Cornwall, to which the land hereabouts still belongs; a fact which is kept in remembrance by the "Duchy Arms" inn, "Cornwall" Cottages, &c.

In Meadow Street, which testifies to the once rural character of this locality, stands, in grounds of its own, St. Joseph's Convent belonging to the Little Sisters of the Poor, a community about whom we shall have more to say when we pay a visit to their other house at Hammersmith.

In South Lambeth, on the south of Fentiman Road, which crosses the Oval Road, is the extensive vinegar distillery of the Messrs. Beaufoy, which was removed here many years ago from Cuper's Gardens. The works, which cover a space of about five acres, occupy the site of Caron House.

Nearly adjoining to the distillery, southward, is, or was till a recent date, the residence of John Tradescant, the botanist. The house, a plain brick building, with a court-yard in front and large iron gates, had attached to it the physic-garden of the Tradescants, one of the first established in this country. Tradescant's museum was frequently visited by persons of rank, who became benefactors thereto; among these were Charles I. (to whom he was gardener), Queen Henrietta Maria, Archbishop Laud, George, Duke of Buckingham, Robert and William Cecil, Earls of Salisbury, and many other persons of distinction. Among them also appears the philosophic John Evelyn, who, in his "Diary," under date of September 17, 1657, has the following entry:—"I went to see Sir Robert Needham, at Lambeth, a relation of mine, and thence to John Tradescant's museum." Evelyn also speaks of supping at John Tradescant's house, in company with Dr. (subsequently Archbishop) Tenison, the Bishop of St. Asaph, and Lady Clarendon.

"I know," writes Izaak Walton, in his "Complete Angler," "we islanders are averse to the belief of wonders; but there be so many strange creatures to be now seen, many collected by John Tradescant, and others added by my friend Elias Ashmole, Esq., who now keeps them carefully and methodically at his house near to Lambeth, near London, as may yet get belief of some of the other wonders I mentioned. I will tell you some of the wonders that you may now see, and not till then believe, unless you think fit. You may see there the hog-fish, the dog-fish, the dolphin, the coney-fish, the parrot-fish, the shark, the poison-fish, the sword-fish; and not only other incredible fish, but you may there see the salamander, several sorts of barnacles, of Solan geese, and the bird of paradise; such sorts of snakes, and such birds'-nests, and of so various forms and so wonderfully made, as may beget wonder and amazement in any beholder; and so many hundreds of other rarities in that collection, as will make the other wonders I spake of the less incredible."

The Tradescants were the first well-known collectors of natural curiosities in this kingdom; they were followed by Ashmole and Sir Hans Sloane, from whom their spirit was afterwards transfused

into Sir Ashton Lever, whose collection we mentioned in our account of Leicester Square.* It was a great misfortune that the collection, instead of being sold in lots by auction, was not secured for the British Museum.

There are portraits of the Tradescants to be seen in the Ashmolean Museum at Oxford. It is usually said that it was the elder Tradescant who first introduced apricots into England, by entering himself on board of a privateer armed against Morocco, whence he stole that fruit which it was forbidden to export.

In Allen's "History of Surrey" we read:—"On the death of John Tradescant, Dr. Ducarel says his son sold the curiosities to the celebrated Elias Ashmole; but Mr. Nichols, in a note, observes that the doctor must be in error, for, according to the diary of Ashmole, it appears that on December 15, 1659, Mr. Tradescant and his wife signed a deed of gift to Ashmole. The house was purchased, about 1760, of some of Ashmole's descendants, by John Small, Esq. Dr. Ducarel's house, once a part of Tradescant's, adjoins."

Kennington Park, which stretches for some distance along the Kennington Road, and lies to the east of the Oval, was known as Kennington Common till only a few years ago, when it was a dreary piece of waste land, covered partly with short grass, and frequented only by boys flying their kites or playing at marbles. It was encircled with some tumble-down wooden rails, which were not sufficient to keep donkeys from straying there. Field preachers also made it one of the chief scenes of oratorical display. It consisted of about twenty acres. It was suddenly seized with a fit of respectability, and clothed itself around with elegant iron railings, its area being, at the same time, cut up by gravel walks, and flower-beds, and shrubberies. It also engaged a beadle to look after it. And so it became a park, and—it must be owned—an ornament to the neighbourhood.

The Common is described in the "Tour round London," in 1774, as "a small spot of ground on the road to Camberwell, and about a mile and a half from London. Upon this spot is erected the gallows for the county of Surrey; but few have suffered here of late years. Such of the (Scottish) rebels as were tried by the Special Commission, in 1746, and ordered for execution, suffered at this place; amongst whom were those who commanded the regiment raised at Manchester for the use (service) of the Pretender." In fact, very many of those who had "been out" in the Scottish rising of

---

the previous year here suffered the last penalty of the law. Among them were Sir John Wedderburn, John Hamilton, Andrew Wood, and Alexander Leith, and also two English gentlemen of good family, named Towneley and Fletcher, who had joined the standard of "Bonny Prince Charlie" at Manchester.* Wood, it is said, bravely drank a glass to the "Pretender's" health on the scaffold. Others engaged in the same cause also suffered here; among them Captain James (or, as he is still called, "Jemmy") Dawson, over whose body, as soon as the headsman's axe had done its terrible work, a young lady, who was attached to him tenderly, threw herself in a swoon, and died literally of a broken heart. The event forms the subject of one of Shenstone's ballads:—

> "Young Dawson was a gallant boy,
>   A brighter never trod the plain;
> And well he loved one charming maid,
>   And dearly was he loved again. . . .
>
> "The dismal scene was o'er and past,
>   The lover's mournful hearse retired;
> The maid drew back her languid head,
>   And, sighing forth his name, expired."

Dawson and eight others were dragged on hurdles from the new gaol in Southwark to Kennington Common, and there hanged. After being suspended for three minutes from the gallows, their bodies were stripped naked and cut down, in order to undergo the operation of beheading and embowelling. Colonel Towneley was the first that was laid upon the block, but the executioner observing the body to retain some signs of life, he struck it violently on the breast, for the humane purpose of rendering it quite insensible for the remaining portion of the punishment. This not having the desired effect, he cut the unfortunate gentleman's throat. The shocking ceremony of taking out the heart and throwing the bowels into the fire was then gone through, after which the head was separated from the body with a cleaver, and both were put into a coffin. The rest of the bodies were thus treated in succession; and on throwing the last heart into the fire, which was that of young Dawson, the executioner cried, "God save King George!" and the spectators responded with a shout. Although the rabble had hooted the unhappy gentlemen on the passage to and from their trials, it was remarked that at the execution their fate excited considerable pity, mingled with admiration of their courage. Two circumstances contributed to increase the public sympathy on this occasion, and caused it to be more generally expressed. The first was, the appearance at the place of execution of a youthful brother of one of the culprits, of the name of Deacon, himself a culprit, and under sentence of death for the same crime, but who had been permitted to attend the last scene of his brother's life in a coach along with a guard. The other was the fact of a young and beautiful woman, to whom Dawson had been betrothed, actually attending to witness his execution, as stated above.

Most of the rebel lords, and of the others who had borne a share in the Scottish rising of 1745, and who were found guilty of treason, were executed on Tower Hill, as already stated.† Their heads, as well as the heads of those executed here, were afterwards set up on poles on the top of Temple Bar,‡ where we have already seen them bleaching in the sun and rain. Here also was hung the notorious highwayman, "Jerry Abershaw;" his body being afterwards hung in chains on a gibbet on Wimbledon Common.

In the spring of 1848, just after the Revolution which drove Louis Philippe from Paris, Kennington Common obtained a temporary celebrity as the intended rallying-point of the Chartists of London, who, it was said, were half a million in number; but of this number only about 15,000 actually assembled; had the half a million met, it would have required nearly ten times the space of Kennington Common! On the 10th of April the great meeting came off; they were to march thence in procession to Westminster, in order to present a monster petition in favour of the six points of the charter, signed by six millions. But measures were prudently taken by the Government; the Bank and other public buildings were strictly guarded; the military were called out, and posted in concealed positions near the bridges; and 170,000 special constables were enrolled, among whom was Louis Napoleon, the future Emperor of France. On the eventful day the working men who answered to the call of their leaders—Feargus O'Connor and Ernest Jones—were found to be scarcely 50,000, and these gentlemen shrank from a contest with the soldiery. So the crowd broke up, and the petition was presented peaceably.

"Modern times," writes Mr. W. Johnston, in his "England as it Is," "have afforded no such important illustration of the prevailing tone and temper of the British nation, in regard to public affairs, as was presented to the world by the circumstances of the metropolis during the eventful 10th of April, 1848. That day was, in the

---

THE CHARTIST MEETING ON KENNINGTON COMMON, 1848. (*From a Contemporary Print.*)

British Island, the culminating point of the revolutionary progress which, within a period of little more than two months, had shaken almost every throne of Continental Europe. In England nothing was shaken but the hopes of the disaffected. From one end of Europe to the other, the 10th of April was looked forward to by the partisans of revolution as the day which was to add London to the list of capitals submitting to Continental Europe, was frozen into fear by the calm, complete, and stern preparation which was made to encounter and to crush it. The spirit of Wellington was equal to the occasion, and seemed to pervade the might and the energy of the vast metropolis of England while that veteran was at the head of the resisting power. . . . . The 10th of April seemed, as if by mutual consent, to be the day of trial between the rival forces of

TRADESCANT'S HOUSE, SOUTH LAMBETH. (*From Pennant.*)

the dictation of the mob. The spirit of revolt had run like wildfire from kingdom to kingdom, and capital to capital. Paris, Vienna, Naples, Berlin, Dresden, Milan, Venice, Palermo, Frankfort, and Carlsruhe, had all experienced the revolutionary shock, and none had been able completely to withstand it. Now came the turn of London, the greatest capital of all—the greatest prize that the world could afford to revolutionary adventure—the most magnificent prey to the bands of the plunderers who moved about from one point of Europe to another, committing robberies under the name of revolution. London withstood the shock, and escaped without the slightest injury. Even the wild spirit of revolt, made drunk by the extraordinary success it had achieved throughout revolution and of authority, and it then plainly appeared, without any actual collision, that the revolutionists had no chance. All their points of attack had been anticipated. Everywhere there was preparation to receive them, and yet nothing was so openly done as to produce a sense of public alarm. London was armed to the teeth: and yet, in outward appearance, it was not changed. The force that had been prepared lay hushed in grim repose, and was kept out of sight. The revolutionary leaders were, however, made aware of the consequences that would ensue if they went one step beyond that which the authorities deemed to be consistent with the public safety. Foolish and frantic though they were in their political talk, they were not so mad as to rush upon certain destruction. They gave up the conflict; and from that day the spirit of revolution in England drooped and died away. The political conspirators against existing authority failed utterly, not because they were destitute of the enthusiasm meet for such an occasion, or that there were no real grievances in the condition of the people which called for redress, but because the nation had common sense enough to perceive that the ascendancy of such desperate adventurers would make matters worse than better. It was not that the Londoners had no taste for political improvement, but it was that they had a very decided distaste for being robbed. Not only was all the intelligence, the organisation, and the resource of the country arrayed in opposition to the mode of political action which the revolutionists of Europe had adopted, but the familiar instincts of the hundreds of thousands who had property to guard and hearths to preserve inviolate arrayed them in determined resistance to mob violence, whatever might be the avowed object to which that violence should be directed." Thus, in the words of the *Times*, "The great demonstration was brought to a ridiculous issue by the unity and resolution of the metropolis, backed by the judicious measures of the Government, and the masterly military precautions of the Duke of Wellington, though no military display was anywhere to be seen."

During the holiday season, Kennington Common in the last century was an epitome of "Bartlemy Fair," with booths, tents, caravans, and scaffolds, surmounted by flags. It also had one peculiarity, for, as we learn from "Merrie England in the Olden Time," it was a favourite spot for merry-andrews, and other buffooneries in open rivalry, and competition with field-preachers and ranters. It was here that Mr. Maw-worm encountered the brickbats of his congregation, and had his "pious tail" illuminated with the squibs and crackers of the unregenerate.

During the year 1739, when the south of London was a pleasant country suburb, George Whitefield preached frequently on this common, his audience being generally reckoned by tens of thousands. In his "Journal," under date May 6th in that year, he thus remarks: "Preached this morning in Moorfields to about 20,000 people, who were very quiet and attentive, and much affected. Went to public worship morning and evening, and at six preached at Kennington. But such a sight never were my eyes blessed with before. I believe there were no less than 50,000 people, near fourscore coaches, besides great numbers of horses; and what is most remarkable, there was such an awful

silence amongst them, and the word of God came with such power, that all, I believe, were pleasingly surprised. God gave me great enlargement of heart. I continued my discourse for an hour and a half; and when I returned home, I was filled with such love, peace, and joy, that I cannot express it." On subsequent occasions Mr. Whitefield mentions having addressed audiences of 30,000, 20,000, and 10,000 on this same spot. The example thus set by Whitefield was soon afterwards followed by Charles Wesley, with an equal amount of fervour. In June, 1739, Charles Wesley being summoned before the Archbishop of Canterbury to give an account of his "irregularity," he was for a time greatly troubled; but Whitefield, whom he had consulted for advice in this emergency, told him, "Preach in the fields next Sunday; by this step you will break down the bridge, render your retreat difficult, or impossible, and be forced to fight your way forward." This counsel was followed, for in Charles Wesley's diary, June 24th, 1739, occurs this passage:—"I walked to Kennington Common, and cried to multitudes upon multitudes, 'Repent ye, and believe the Gospel.' The Lord was my strength, and my mouth, and my wisdom."

"Kennington Common," wrote Thomas Miller, in his "Picturesque Sketches in London," published in 1852, "is but a name for a small grassless square, surrounded with houses, and poisoned by the stench of vitriol works, and by black, open, sluggish ditches; what it will be when the promised alterations are completed, we have yet to see." That the place, however, has since become completely changed in appearance we need scarcely state, for it was converted into a public pleasure-ground, under the Act 15 and 16 Vict., in June of the above-mentioned year. It now affords a very pretty promenade. What was once but a dismal waste, some twenty acres in extent, is now laid out in grass-plats, intersected by broad and well-kept gravelled walks bordered with flower-beds. A pair of the model farm-cottages of the late Prince Consort were erected in the middle of the western side, near the entrance, about the year 1850. More recently, in addition to the improvements effected by the change of the Common to an ornamental promenade, a church, dedicated to St. Agnes, was built on the site of the vitriol works.

On the first formation of the "park," the sum of £1,800 annually was voted by the Government; but this sum was subsequently reduced, until, in the year 1877, it was only £1,370; and these reductions had been made although there had been an increase in the total sum devoted to public parks.

On the eastern side of the Common, in the middle of the last century, stood a mansion, once the residence of Sir Richard Manley. Near the site of this mansion, occupying the site of the vitriol works just mentioned, and directly facing the central paths of the ornamental garden, now stands the church of St. Agnes. The edifice, which was erected from the designs of Sir G. Gilbert Scott, is in the English Middle Pointed style of architecture of the fourteenth century; and it depends mainly for its effect upon its loftiness, the height being sixty-five feet from the floor to the nave ceiling, and seventy-five feet to the external ridge, and the chancel roof of the same height. The most important feature in the decorative work of the church is the east window of six lights, illustrating the doctrines of the Incarnation and the Atonement, the stained glass of which, costing £1,000, was executed by Mr. C. E. Kempe, and forms a memorial to the lady who was the chief benefactress of the church. The illustration of the Incarnation was "A Tree of Jesse," or genealogical tree of Christ's progenitors, of which the Virgin Mary, holding the Divine Child in her arms, formed the principal figure, the Virgin's head being crowned. When, in accordance with customary usage, the building was inspected by the bishop's representative, the archdeacon, the existence of this design was mentioned, and before the ceremony of consecration was performed, the figure of the Blessed Virgin was removed by the bishop's desire.

On the southern portion of the Common, on the upper part of a small triangular plot of ground, separated from the larger portion of the Common by the road to Brixton and the Camberwell New Road, stands St. Mark's Church, the second of the district churches erected in this parish. What is now the site of the church was formerly the spot where the gallows were erected for the execution of criminals; and it is rendered more interesting by its being the actual spot where many of the unfortunate adherents to the expatriated family of the Stuarts fell a sacrifice to their principles, as we have stated above. In preparing the foundation of the church, the site of a gibbet was discovered; and a curious piece of iron, which it is supposed was the swivel attached to the head of a criminal, was turned up a foot or two below the surface.

St. Mark's Church, which was finished in 1824, from the designs of Mr. D. Roper, consists of two distinct portions. The body of the edifice is a long octagon—a parallelogram, with the corners cut off. The eastern end is brought out to form a recess for the communion-table, and to the western end is attached the tower, sided by lobbies, containing staircases to the galleries; and the whole is fronted by a portico, formed of four columns, supporting an entablature of the Greek Doric order, finished with a pediment. The tower, which is square and massive, is surmounted by a circular structure, composed of fluted Ionic columns, and finished with a plain spherical cupola, on the apex of which is a stone cross of elegant design. The main portion of the church is constructed of brick, and has stone pilasters attached to the piers between the windows, which are singularly plain and uninteresting. The interior of the church, beyond its elliptically-coved ceiling, ornamented at intervals with groups of foliage, contains nothing to call for special remark.

Along the south side of the churchyard once ran a small stream, which was crossed by a bridge, called Merton Bridge, from its formerly having been repaired by the canons of Merton Abbey, who had lands bequeathed to them for that purpose.

Opposite the western gates of the park, and at the entrance to Kennington Road, is the "Horns Tavern." It stands at the junction of the roads leading to London and Westminster Bridges; and the assembly-rooms adjoining have for many years been a great place for public meetings. There is nothing, so far as we are aware, to connect this inn with such ceremonies as those formerly enacted at Highgate[*] and at Charlton,[†] in which, as we have shown, the "horns" played such a conspicuous part; it may have been that a former landlord was desirous of emulating the reputation enjoyed by his professional brethren at Highgate.

Pursuing our course along Kennington Road, we leave on our left the water-works belonging to the South London Company. In 1805 an Act of Parliament was passed for establishing the above-mentioned company, who were "to form reservoirs near Kennington Green, to be supplied from the Thames along Vauxhall Creek, or at a creek on the other side of Cumberland Gardens, between that and Marble Hall, all in this parish." The work was undertaken; a field of five acres, between Kennington Lane and the Oval, was procured, on which two reservoirs were formed, with steam-engines and the requisite offices and buildings. In 1807 the proprietor celebrated the completion of the undertaking by giving a public breakfast. The reservoirs were intended to bring the water into a state of purity before it was distributed; but it was found that it did not answer thoroughly, and

---

a change of site had to be made for the engine-house.

At the point where the road turns off from Kennington Lane to the Oval, was in former times a noted place of entertainment, known as Spring Garden." *   Bray, in his "History of Surrey," says that Moncony mentions a Spring Garden at Lambeth as much frequented in 1663. The gardens were at one time held by Mrs. Cornelys, of whom we have already had occasion to speak in our account of Soho Square.†   Mrs. Cornelys, we are told, had "a large white house for entertainment;" but being frequented by loose and dissolute persons, it was suppressed by the magistracy.

In Upper Kennington Lane, which runs from Kennington Cross to Vauxhall Bridge, is the Licensed Victuallers' School, an establishment more to be regarded for the benevolent views of its patrons than for the architectural beauty of the building which contains the objects of their protection. The society was established in the year 1803, and is supported by the respectable body of licensed victuallers of the metropolis as an asylum and school for the orphans and children of the destitute part of their brethren.   A portion of the profits of their trade journal, the *Morning Advertiser*, is also added to its funds.   The building is a series of dwelling-houses, added together at various times, as the funds and objects of the institution increased, and is therefore little else than a substantial commodious difice, with a spacious playground and gardens, located in an airy situation.   Its original design has been somewhat improved by a central tablet of stucco over the pedimented door as a sort of centre.   The building was constructed with the view of accommodating two hundred children. Great exertions have been made to realise this design, and by the admission of all the approved candidates for three successive years, it was all but accomplished.

At various times, Kennington has been the residence of many eminent persons, among whom we may mention John, seventh Earl of Warrenne and Surrey, father-in-law of John Balliol, who died here in 1304; David Ricardo, the celebrated political economist; the Duke of Brunswick; William Hogarth; and Eliza Cook, who lived here for many years.   It has also been the home of many persons connected with the theatres.   Here died, in 1877, Mr. E. T. Smith, of Cremorne, the Alhambra, and Drury Lane celebrity.

Kennington in its day has seen its deeds of violence; for it appears that in 1323 Elizabeth,

the wife of Sir Richard Talbot, of Goderich Castle, in Herefordshire, was forcibly seized at her house in this parish by Hugh Despencer, Earl of Gloucester, in conjunction with his father, Hugh, Earl of Winchester, and carried off.   It is satisfactory to know that for this act the Despencers suffered the extreme penalty of the law; the head of the younger one being set up on London Bridge. Their estate, of course, became confiscated and pounced upon by royalty; and the king very naturally bestowed it on the Prince of Wales, to whom it still belongs.

Before closing this chapter, we may remark that the maypole nearest to the metropolis that stood longest within the memory of the editor of the "Beauties of England and Wales," was near Kennington Green, at the back of the houses at the south-west corner of the Workhouse Lane, leading from the Vauxhall Road to Elizabeth Place.   The site was then nearly vacant, and the maypole stood in the field on the south side of the Workhouse Lane, nearly opposite to the "Black Prince" public-house.   It remained there till about the year 1795, and was much frequented, particularly by the milkmaids, on May-day.   The maypoles in the country were the scenes of much simplicity of rural manners and innocent mirth and enjoyment; but those set up near London, it is to be feared, were provocative of far more boisterous rudeness.   In 1517 the unfortunate shaft, or maypole, gave rise to the insurrection of that turbulent body, the London apprentices, and the plundering of the foreigners in the City, whence it got the name of Evil May-day.   "From that time," writes the author of "Merrie England in the Olden Time," "the offending pole was hung on a range of hooks over the doors of a long row of neighbouring houses.   In the third year of Edward VI., an over-zealous fanatic, called Sir Stephen, began to preach against this maypole, which inflamed the audience so greatly that the owner of every house over which it hung sawed off as much as depended over his premises, and committed piecemeal to the flames this terrible idol!"   Like the morris-dancers, and the hobby-horse, and other much-applauded merriments of Old England, the maypole in the end has become a thing of the past, for they were put down or allowed to pass into oblivion.

The old Roman road, or Watling Street, for a short distance, intersected the north-eastern corner of Surrey in its progress from *Vagniacis* (supposed by antiquaries to be near Southfleet in Kent) to London, skirting the eastern side of Kennington. This road is presumed to have passed through Old Croydon or Woodcote, Streatham, and Newington,

---

* See Vol. IV., p. 77.   † See Vol. III., p. 188.

to Stone Street in Southwark. If, as some writers have supposed, the ancient *Noviomagus* was at Old Croydon, the Ermyn Street must have followed nearly the present line of roads through Streatham, Kennington, and Newington, into Southwark ; and thence it was continued in a northward direction by way of Stoke Newington, as we have already mentioned in a former volume.*

CHAPTER XXVI.

ST. GEORGE'S FIELDS.

" Saint George's Fields are fields no more,
    The trowel supersedes the plough ;
Huge inundated swamps of yore
    Are changed to civic villas now."

St. George's Fields in the Time of the Roman Occupation—Canute's Trench—Charles II. entertained at St. George's Fields on his Restoration—The Populace resort hither during the Great Fire—The Character of St. George's Fields in the Last Century—The Apollo Gardens—The "Dog and Duck" Tavern—St. George's Spa—A Curious Exhibition—The Wilkes' Riots—The Gordon Riots—Death of Lord George Gordon—Gradual Advance of Building in St. George's Fields—The Magdalen Hospital—Peabody Buildings—The Asylum for Female Orphans—The Philanthropic Society—The School for the Indigent Blind—The Obelisk.

IN the above lines, the Brothers Smith, the authors of the " Rejected Addresses," in 1812, lamented the decline alike of sports and of rural beauty, which were once the chief characteristics of this locality ; but even this description has long ceased to be applicable. Perhaps the following stanza, though less poetic, quoted from Tallis's " Illustrated London," would present the reader of to-day with a more faithful character of St. George's Fields :—

" Thy ' civic villas,' witty Smith,
    Have fled, as well as woodland copse ;
Where erst the water-lily bloomed
    Are planted rows of brokers' shops."

St. George's Fields were named after the adjacent church of St. George the Martyr, and appear once to have been marked by all the floral beauty of meadows, uninvaded by London smoke. We learn from Mr. Cunningham that Gerard came here to collect specimens of his " Herbal." " Of water-violets," he says, " I have not found such plenty in any one place as the water ditches adjoining St. George his fielde near London." And yet these " fields," together with Lambeth Marsh—which lies between them and the Thames —were at one time almost covered with water at every high tide, and across which the Romans threw embanked roads, and on which they reared villas, after the Dutch summer-house fashion, on piles. Indeed, St. George's Fields were certainly occupied by the Romans, for large quantities of Roman remains, coins, tesselated pavements, urns, and bones have been found there. They formed probably one of the *æstiva*, or summer camps ; for in the winter a great part of them, now known as Lambeth Marsh and Marsh Gate, were under water. It is not stated when all this ground was first drained, but various ancient commissions are remaining for persons to survey the banks of the river, here and in the adjoining parishes, and to take measures for repairing them, and to impress such workmen as they should find necessary for that employment ; notwithstanding which, these periodical overflows continued to do considerable mischief ; and Strype, in his edition of Stow's " Survey," informs us that, so late as 1555, owing to this cause and some great rains which had then fallen, all St. George's Fields were covered with water. Inundations, therefore, are no novelty to the lands on the south of the Thames near London.

In 1016, as we have already had occasion to observe,† Canute laid siege to London ; but finding that the bridge was so strongly fortified by the citizens that he could not come up with his vessels to make any impression on the Thames side of the place, he projected the design of making a canal through St. George's Fields, then marshes, wide and deep enough to convey his ships to the west of the bridge, and to enable him by that means to invest the town on all sides. The line of this canal, called " Canute's Trench," ran from the great wet dock, below Rotherhithe, through Newington, to the river Thames again at Chelsea Reach ; but its exact course cannot now be traced.

Dr. Wallis, in a letter to Samuel Pepys, dated in 1699, speaks of having walked, fifty years before, from Stangate, close by Westminster Bridge, to Redriff [Rotherhithe], " across the fields " to Lambeth, meaning there to cross the Thames to Westminster. On this occasion, he writes, a friend " showed me in the passage diverse remains of the

---

old channel which had been heretofore made from Redriff to Lambeth for diverting the Thames whilst London Bridge was a-building, all in a straight line or near it, but with great intervals which had long since been filled up; those remains which then appeared so visible, are now, I suspect, all or most of them filled up, for . . . people in those marshes would be more fond of so much meadow grounds than to let those lakes remain unfilled."

1666, that many of the poor people, who had lost their homes in the City, were dispersed about St. George's Fields; "some under miserable huts and hovels, many without a rag or any necessary utensils, bed or board, who from delicatenesse, riches, and easy accommodation in stately and well-furnished houses, were now reduced to extreamest misery and poverty."

St. George's Fields, down to the commencement

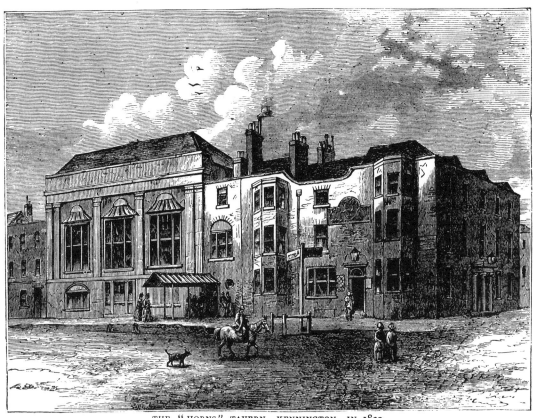

THE "HORNS" TAVERN, KENNINGTON, IN 1820.

In the same letter he speaks of the southern shore of the river as "full of flags and reeds."

St. George's Fields have not been unvisited by royalty, for we are told that at the happy Restoration, on the 29th of May, 1660, the Lord Mayor and Aldermen of London met Charles II., in his journey from Dover to London, in St. George's Fields, where a magnificent tent was erected, and the king was provided with a sumptuous banquet before entering the City.

These fields, according to Pepys and Evelyn, were one of the places of refuge to which the poorer citizens retreated with such of their goods and chattels as they could save from the fire of London.

We read in Evelyn's "Diary," in September,

of the present century, comprised broad open meadows, and stretched from Blackman Street, Borough, to the Kennington Road. Dirty ditches intersected it, travelling show-vans and wooden huts on wheels were squatted there, and some rusty boilers and pipes rotted by the roadside. They were places, as we read in Malcolm, much resorted to by field-preachers, who, during the reign of the Stuart sovereigns, were not allowed to hold forth in London.

Several of the names of the particular plots of land, during the unbuilt state of St. George's Fields, are transmitted to us in old writings, as well as some amusing notices of certain places here, or in the neighbourhood, in scarce books. Among other documents, the parish records of St.

Saviour's mention Checquer Mead, Lamb Acre, and an estate denominated the Chimney Sweepers, as situated in these fields and belonging to that parish ; as also a large laystall, or common dung-hill, used by the parishioners, called St. George's Dunghill. The open part, at the commencement of the last and end of the preceding century, like Moorfields, and some other void places near the metropolis, was appropriated to the practice of archery, as we learn from a scarce tract published

after an ineffectual struggle, lasting through two or three seasons, they were finally closed, and the site was built over." The old orchestra of the gardens, when taken down, was removed to Sydney Gardens, at Bath, to be re-erected there.

The "Dog and Duck" grounds were far more obstinate and also far more unworthy of patronage. At this place there was a long room, with tables and benches, and an organ at the upper end, so that in all probability the place was used for

THE FREEMASONS' CHARITY SCHOOL, ST. GEORGE'S FIELDS.   (*From an Engraving by Rawle, in* 1800.)

near the time, called "An Aim for those that shoot in St. George's Fields."

Here were the "Apollo Gardens" and the "Dog and Duck," both standing till the Regency of George IV. In point of fashion they were a direct contrast to Ranelagh, and even to Vauxhall, to which "the quality" repaired. The former stood opposite the Asylum in the Westminster Road, and they were fitted up on the plan of Vauxhall, though on a smaller scale, by a Mr. Clayett. In the centre of the gardens was an orchestra, very large and beautiful. "A want of the rural accompaniment of fine trees, their small extent, their situation, and other causes, soon made them the resort of only low and vicious characters ; and

"popular concerts." The audience was composed of the riff-raff and scum of the town. Becoming a public nuisance, the gardens were at length put down by the magistrates, and Bethlehem Hospital now occupies the spot which once they covered. The spot was a noted place of amusement for the lower middle classes ; and as the name indicates, it was one of the chief scenes of the brutal diversion of duck-hunting, which was carried on here, less than two centuries ago, in a pond or ponds in the grounds attached to the house. The fun of the sport consisted in seeing the duck make its escape from the dog's mouth by diving. It was much practised in the neighbourhood of London till it was out of fashion, being superseded by pigeon-shooting, and other pastimes equally cruel. In the seventeenth century the place was celebrated for its springs. The "Dog and Duck," in its later days, bore but a bad repute as a regular haunt of thieves and of other low characters. After a long existence, during which it frequently figured in connection with trials for highway robbery and other crimes, it was suppressed by the order of the magistrates. Garrick thus alludes to the tavern and its tea-gardens in his Prologue to the *Maid of the Oaks*, 1774:—

> "St. George's Fields, with taste of fashion struck,
> Display Arcadia at the 'Dog and Duck;'
> And Drury misses here, in tawdry pride,
> Are there 'Pastoras' by the fountain side."

It will be remembered that one of the best scenes in Hannah More's "Cheapside Apprentice" is laid in the infamous Dog and Duck Fields.

The following interesting extract from a MS. by Hone, the author of the "Year-Book," is printed *in extenso* by Mr. Larwood, in his "History of Signboards:"—

"It (the 'Dog and Duck') was a very small public-house till Hedger's mother took it; she had been a barmaid to a tavern-keeper in London, who at his death left her his house. Her son Hedger was then a postboy to a yard at Epsom, I believe, and came to be master there. After making a good deal of money, he left the house to his nephew, one Miles, who, though it still went in Hedger's name, was to allow him £1,000 a year out of the profits; and it was he that allowed the house to acquire so bad a character that the licence was taken away. I have this from one William Nelson, who was servant to old Mrs. Hedger, and remembers the house before he had it. He is now (1826) in the employ of the Lamb Street Water-Works Company, and has been for thirty years. In particular, there never was any duck-hunting since he knew the gardens; therefore, if ever, it must have been in a very early time indeed. Hedger, I am told, was the first person who sold the water (whence the St. George's Spa). In 1787, when Hedger applied for a renewal of his licence, the magistrates of Surrey refused; and the Lord Mayor came into Southwark and held a court, and granted his licence, in despite of the magistrates, which occasioned a great disturbance and litigation in the law courts."

A fort, with four half-bulwarks, at the "Dog and Duck," in St. George's Fields, is mentioned among the defences of London, set up by order of the Parliament in 1642.

The old stone sign of the "Dog and Duck" tea-gardens is still preserved, embedded in the brick wall of the garden of Bethlehem Hospital, visible from the road, and representing a dog squatting on its haunches with a duck in its mouth, and bearing the date 1617.

OLD SIGN OF THE "DOG AND DUCK."

A well of water, celebrated for its purgative qualities, formerly existed near the "Dog and Duck" grounds. Dr. Fothergill tells us that this water had gained a reputation for the cure of most cutaneous disorders, in scrofulous cases, and that it was useful for keeping the body cool, and preventing cancerous diseases; but the exact site of this well is no longer known.

"St. George's Fields," as Malcolm informs us, "abounded with gardens, where the lower classes met to drink and smoke tobacco. But those were not their only amusements. A Mr. Shanks, near Lambeth Marsh, contrived to assemble his customers in 1711 with a grinning match. The prize was a gold-laced hat; the competitors were exhilarated by music and dancing; the hour of exhibition was twelve at noon; the admission sixpence. The same was repeated at six o'clock."

A century ago St. George's Fields became the scene of very fierce gatherings of the "Wilkes and Liberty" mobs; and the populace were very riotous, clamouring for the release of their dissolute and witty favourite from the King's Bench. During the riot which ensued, a young man named William Allen was killed by one of the soldiers. Allen was pursued to the "Horse-shoe Inn," Stones End, and shot in the inn-yard. He was buried, as we have seen, in the churchyard at Newington,[*] where a monument was erected to his memory.

It is not a little strange that the pains-taking and conscientious antiquary, Pennant, though he wrote in 1790, when their memory must have been still fresh, makes no mention of these fields having been the head-quarters of the rioters under Lord George Gordon, who ten years before had well-nigh set fire to all London. He simply speaks of these fields as "now the wonder of foreigners approaching our capital by this road, through avenues of lamps of magnificent breadth and goodness." Whether the "breadth and the goodness" was predicated by Pennant of the "road" or the "lamps" is a little doubtful, more particularly since he refers, in a foot-note, to some new process of adulteration of the oil, and tells the following story almost in the same breath :—"I have heard that a foreign ambassador, who happened to make his entry at night, imagined that these illuminations were in honour of his arrival, and, as he modestly expressed himself, more than he could have expected !"

In previous volumes of this work we have already spoken of the effects of the Gordon Riots in different parts of the metropolis, particularly in the burning of Newgate * and the destruction of Lord Mansfield's house in Bloomsbury Square ;† but as St. George's Fields formed the rallying-point, whence the excited mob was to be led on the House of Commons, some further particulars of the proceedings of the rioters may not be out of place here.

A so-called Protestant Association had been formed in 1779, for the purpose of opposing Sir George Savile's bill for the abolition of Roman Catholic disabilities ; and a fanatical Scotch nobleman, Lord George Gordon, third son of William, Duke of Gordon, then in his thirtieth year, consented to become president of the association, which was fast gaining an influence over the lower classes. Various meetings to arrange for the presentation of a petition to Parliament against the repeal of these disabilities had been held in April and May, 1780, in the "Crown and Rolls Tavern," Chancery Lane, and in the Coachmakers' Hall, and the presentation was finally agreed upon at Coachmakers' Hall, on the 29th of May. At this meeting, which was attended by upwards of 2,000 excited people, under Lord George Gordon's presidency, a petition was then proposed and carried to the following effect :—

"Whereas no hall in London can contain 40,000 persons : resolved, that the Association do meet on Friday next, in St. George's Fields, at ten o'clock in the morning, to consider the most prudent and respectful manner of attending their petition, which will be presented the same day in the House of Commons.

"Resolved, for the sake of good order and regularity, that this Association, in coming to the ground, do separate themselves into four distinct divisions : viz., the London division, the Westminster division, the Southwark division, and the Scotch division.

"Resolved, that the London division do take place upon the right of the ground towards Southwark, the Westminster division second, the Southwark division third, and the Scotch division upon the left, all wearing blue cockades, to distinguish themselves from the Papists and those who approve of the late set in favour of Popery.

"Resolved, that the magistrates of London, Westminster, and Southwark be requested to attend, that their presence may overawe and control any riotous or evil-minded persons who may wish to disturb the legal and peaceable deportment of His Majesty's Protestant subjects.

"By order of the Association,
"Signed, G. GORDON, President.
"Dated, London, May 29."

The enthusiastic and eccentric president then addressed the billowy meeting, informing them that the system of different divisions would be useful, as he could then go from one to the other, and learn the general opinion as to the mode of taking up the petition. As it was very easy for one person to sign 400 or 500 names to a petition, he thought it was better that every one who signed should appear in person to prove that the names were all genuine. He begged that they would dress decently and behave orderly, and, to prevent riots and to distinguish themselves, they should wear blue cockades in their hats. Some one had suggested that, meeting so early, people might get drinking ; but he held that the Protestant Association were not drunken people, and apprehended no danger on that account. Some one had also hinted that so great a number of people being assembled might lead to the military being drawn out ; but he did not doubt all the association would be peaceable and orderly ; and he desired them not to take even sticks in their hands, and begged that if there was any riotous person the rest should give him up.

"If any one was struck, he was not to return the blow, but seek for a constable. Even if he himself should be at all riotous, he would wish to be given up, for he thought it a proper spirit for Protestants, remembering the text, 'If they smite you on one cheek, turn the other also.' He concluded by saying that he hoped no one who had signed would be afraid or ashamed to show himself in the cause ; and he begged leave to decline to present the petition unless he was met in St. George's Fields by 20,000 people, with some mark of distinction on, such as a blue ribbon in their hats, so that he might be able to distinguish their friends from their foes. He would not present the petition of a lukewarm people. They must be firm, like

---

* See Vol. II., p. 442.   † See Vol. IV., p. 539.

the Scotch, to carry their point. He himself would be there to meet them, and would be answerable for any that were indicted for meeting there; indeed, he wished so well to the cause that he would go to the gallows for it (deafening cheers)."

The " true Protestant" rabble, estimated variously at from 40,000 to 100,000 men, all wearing blue ribbons, some of which had the words " No Popery" upon them, met at the appointed day and hour in St. George's Fields—on the very spot, singularly enough, as tradition says, where the high altar of the present Roman Catholic Cathedral is raised : such is the irony of history. Blue banners were flying; and it is said that in the Scotch division bagpipes were playing. In each of the four divisions the " true Protestants" marched, singing hymns, eight or nine abreast, the enormous tree-trunk of a petition being carried on men's heads in a conspicuous part of the procession. They began to advance towards Westminster soon after twelve, one division marching by Blackfriars Bridge, the others by London Bridge and West-minster Bridge. The march was orderly and decorous ; hitherto the passions of these fanatics had been restrained ; it was only when the rabble joined, and a sense of new-felt power came over them, that they turned to wild beasts. When they reached the Houses of Parliament, about half-past two, the " true Protestants" gave such a shout as that before which fell the walls of the fated Jericho. Gibbon, the historian, then a member of the House of Commons, describes the scene " as if 40,000 Puritans of the days of Cromwell had started from their graves."

In Boswell's " Life of Johnson" we read that just when the great doctor was engaged in preparing a delightful literary entertainment for the world, " the tranquillity of the metropolis of Great Britain was unexpectedly disturbed by the most horrid series of outrages that ever disgraced a civilised country. A relaxation of some of the severe penal provisions against our fellow-subjects of the Catholic communion had been granted by the legislature, with an opposition so inconsiderable, that the genuine mildness of Christianity, united with liberal policy, seemed to have become general in this island. But a dark and malignant spirit of persecution soon showed itself in an unworthy peti-tion for the repeal of the wise and humane statute. That petition was brought forward by a mob, with the evident purpose of intimidation, and was justly rejected. But the attempt was accompanied and followed by such daring violence as is unexampled in history." Of this extraordinary tumult, Dr. John-son has given the following concise, lively, and

just account in his " Letters to Mrs. Thrale :"—"On Friday the good Protestants met in Saint George's Fields, at the summons of Lord George Gordon, and, marching to Westminster, insulted the Lords and Commons, who all bore it with great tameness. At night the outrages began by the demolition of the mass-house by Lincoln's Inn. An exact journal of a week's defiance of government I cannot give you. On Monday, Mr. Strahan, who had been insulted, spoke to Lord Mansfield (who had, I think, been insulted too) of the licentiousness of the populace ; and his lordship treated it as a very slight irregularity. On Tuesday night they pulled down Fielding's house, and burnt his goods in the street. They had gutted, on Monday, Sir George Savile's house, but the building was saved. On Tuesday evening, leaving Fielding's ruins, they went to Newgate to demand their companions who had been seized demolishing the chapel. The keeper could not release them but by the Mayor's permission, which he went to ask; at his return he found all the prisoners released and Newgate in a blaze. They then went to Blooms-bury, and fastened upon Lord Mansfield's house, which they pulled down, and as for his goods they totally burnt them. They have since gone to Caen Wood, but a guard was there before them. They plundered some Papists, and burnt a mass-house in Moorfields the same night." Boswell speaks of these riots as " a miserable sedition, from which London was delivered by the magnanimity of the sovereign himself."

Miss Priscilla Wakefield, in her " Perambulations in London," writes as follows concerning these riotous proceedings :—" The metropolis was thrown into a dreadful consternation, in 1780, by a lawless mob, which caused the most alarming scenes of riot and confusion. On the 2nd of June an immense multitude assembled in St. George's Fields, in consequence of an advertisement from the Protestant Association, in order to proceed to the House of Commons with a petition for the repeal of the law passed the last session in favour of the Roman Catholics. Lord George Gordon condescended to be their leader. They preserved tolerable order till they approached the Houses of Parliament, when they showed their hostile dis-position by ill-treating many of the members as they passed along. Lord George encouraged these proceedings by haranguing this tumultuous assembly from the gallery-stairs of the House of Commons, and telling them that they were not likely to succeed in their request, to which he added the imprudence of naming the members who opposed it. Some of them, ripe for active mischief, filed off, and demolished the chapels belonging to the Sardinian and Bavarian ambassadors. The guards being called out, thirteen of the rioters were taken into custody. All remained quiet till Sunday, the 4th, when riotous parties collected in the neighbourhood of Moorfields, and satiated their vengeance on the chapels and dwelling-houses of the Catholics. The next day different parts of the town presented a repetition of the same disgraceful scenes; and in the evening an attempt was made to rescue the rioters confined in Newgate, which, from the firmness of Mr. Akerman, the keeper, they were unable to execute, till, by breaking the windows, battering the entrances of the cells with pick-axes and sledge-hammers, and climbing the walls with ladders, they found means to fire Mr. Akerman's house, which communicated to the prison, and liberated three hundred prisoners. This success increased their fury. They divided into different quarters, with the most mischievous designs. Many were great sufferers from their attacks; but none in whose loss the public was so much interested as Lord Mansfield, in whose house they not only destroyed a great deal of property, and a valuable collection of pictures, but likewise some very scarce manuscripts, besides his lordship's notes on the constitution of England and on important law cases, which, from his advanced age, could never be replaced. The occurrences of Wednesday were still more dreadful. The city was in a state of anarchy; and the evening presented a most awful scene. Flames issued on all sides. The insurgents had set fire to the King's Bench and Fleet prisons, New Bridewell, the toll-gates on Blackfriars Bridge, and private houses in all directions. The civil magistrate had no longer any power. The military were obliged to act to preserve the metropolis from destruction. All parts of the town, particularly those near the Bank and the Court, were guarded by soldiery. Multitudes perished by intoxication, &c." It might be added that the Marshalsea was broken open by the mob on this occasion.

Mr. H. Angelo, in his "Reminiscences," thus writes:—"I soon hurried away, and arrived near the obelisk in St. George's Fields, the space before the King's Bench being then quite open, with no houses. On seeing the flames and smoke from the windows along the high wall, it appeared to me like the huge hulk of a man-of-war, dismasted, on fire. Here, with amazement, I stood for some time, gazing on the spot, when, looking behind me, I beheld a number of horse and foot soldiers approach, with a quick step. Off I went, in an instant, in a contrary direction; nor did I look back till I was on Blackfriars Bridge. That night, if my recollection be correct, must have been the time when the dreadful conflagrations in different parts of the metropolis took place. I recollect it was said that six-and-thirty fires might be seen blazing from London Bridge. When the bridge was assailed by the mob, the latter were repulsed by Alderman Wilkes and his party, and many were thrown clean into the Thames."

Horace Walpole sarcastically calls these riotous proceedings "the second conflagration of London, by Lord George Gordon." The number of persons who perished in these riots could not be accurately gathered. According to the military returns, 210 persons died by shot or sword in the streets, and 75 in the hospitals; and 173 were wounded and captured. How many died of injuries, unknown and unseen, cannot be computed. Many more perished in the flames, or died from excesses of one kind or other. Justice came in at the close, to demand her due. At the Old Bailey, eighty-five persons were tried for taking part in the riots, and finally out of these eighteen were executed, one woman, a negress, being of the number. By a Special Commission for the County of Surrey forty-five prisoners were tried, and twenty-six of them capitally convicted, though two or three were reprieved.

But what, it has been asked, did Lord George Gordon all this while? "Filled with consternation at the riots," as his counsel on trial said, "he, on the 7th of June, the terrible Wednesday, sought an audience of the king, professing that it would be of service in checking the riots. No doubt the poor young nobleman would have asked the king to proclaim the intention of repealing the Relief Bill, as if such a step would have had the slightest effect. But the king told him first to go and prove his loyalty by checking the riots, if he could. Lord George did really go into the City; but the 'President of the Protestant Association' was now powerless, and does not seem even to have spoken to the mobs." Every reader of "Barnaby Rudge" knows the fearful state of London during the continuance of these riots; and one act of Lord George, in his presumed attempt to quell the tumult, is particularly referred to by the author of that work. A young man came to the door of his coach, and besought his lordship to sign a paper drawn up for the purpose, which ran thus:—"All true friends to the Protestants, I hope, will be particular, and do no injury to the property of any true Protestant, as I am well assured the proprietor of this house is a staunch and worthy friend to the cause." It has been insinuated that Lord

George Gordon wrote for friends many protection-papers like this, the language of which certainly implies a knowledge and approval of the intent to attack those who were considered enemies. But the young man proved that it was written by himself, and that Lord George signed it hurriedly in compassion. When shown to the mob, it saved the man's house.

Lord George was arrested on the 9th of June, and conveyed to the Tower under a strong guard. The Government thought it prudent to allow eight months to elapse before trying him, and he was then acquitted; though it seems strange that the ringleader should have been absolved from blame, when a score of his poor dupes were executed for their subordinate share in this bloody work.

Some time after this event a person begging alms from him in the street remarked, "God bless you, my lord! you and I have been in all the prisons in London." "What do you mean, fellow?" cried Lord George; "I never was in any prison but the Tower." "That's true, my lord," replied the sturdy beggar; "and I've been in all the rest."

In 1781 Lord George Gordon coolly wished to offer himself as a candidate for the representation of London, but he withdrew, on finding that the City did not choose to be burnt down once a year for his amusement.

The after-life of this nobleman was marked by vagaries which confirmed the probability of his being really afflicted with insanity. In 1786 he openly embraced the Jewish faith, and soon after was convicted of a libel on the Queen of France. He fled to escape the sentence, but was re-taken in a few months and confined in Newgate, where he lived until fever cut short his career on the 1st of November, 1793, at the age of forty-two. He was much beloved by the prisoners, and with good reason, being generous and humane. Two Jewish maid-servants, partly through enthusiasm, waited on him daily up to his death. The last words of Lord George Gordon were characteristic. The French Revolution had attracted him as a glorious event, and he died crazily chanting its watchword, "Ça ira!"

Northouck, writing in 1773, anticipates the early arrival of a day when St. George's Fields will no more resemble fields, but be covered with buildings, as an ultimate consequence of the erection of Westminster and Blackfriars Bridges. He was right. In the course of the next two decades of years, the hand of the builder had been at work, and streets and terraces were fast rendering the name of St. George's Fields but a meaningless title.

The pleasant and open aspect of St. George's Fields, and indeed the whole neighbourhood of the Kent Road, at the above-mentioned date, and it may, perhaps, be added the moderate price of the land, induced the locality to be selected as the site of several charitable institutions. Foremost among them was the Magdalen Hospital, which for just a century stood near the southern end of Blackfriars Road. It was originally opened, under the name of Magdalen House, by the founders, Robert Dingley and Jonas Hanway, in a large building, formerly the London Infirmary, in Prescott Street, Goodman's Fields, in 1758. The good founders were readily assisted by others, and the fame of the institution even reached to Calcutta; and Omichund, the rich native merchant, who figures conspicuously in the history of Warren Hastings, left more than 18,000 rupees to the funds of the hospital, though, we are sorry to add, his executors contrived to seize and appropriate to themselves the greater portion of the sum.

Jonas Hanway's larger schemes of benevolence have connected his name not only with the Marine Society and the Foundling, but also with the Magdalen; and to his courage and perseverance in smaller fields of usefulness (his determined contention with extravagant veils to servants not the least), the men of Goldsmith's day, as we have seen in our account of Hanway Street,* were indebted for liberty to use an umbrella.

At home no one was more zealous in support of the Magdalen than Dr. Dodd, the fashionable preacher, who was its chaplain, and whose unlucky exit from this world of trouble at Tyburn we have already mentioned.† The doctor, we are informed, was unrivalled in his power of extracting tears and loose cash from his fair hearers, and appealed so effectually in two sermons, that the fashionable ladies, sympathising, perhaps, with female frailty, contributed liberally. The charity was incorporated in 1769, and six and a half acres in St. George's Fields purchased, on which a new hospital was erected. Accordingly, the hospital is called "The New Magdalen" in the "Ambulator," in 1774.

The character of this excellent institution is well described in the will of Mr. Charles Wray, who was for many years a governor of the hospital. "I bequeath to the Magdalen Hospital £500 as a farewell token of my affection, and of my sincere good wishes for the everlasting success and prosperity of that humane and truly Christian institution, which, from my own knowledge, founded on many years' experience, and beyond my most

---

* See Vol. IV., p. 471.   † See Vol. V., p. 193.

sanguine expectations, hath restored a great number of unfortunate young women to their afflicted parents and friends, to honest industry, to virtue, and to happiness."

Thousands of young women who have strayed from the paths of virtue have been admitted, restored to their friends, or placed in service; and it is an invariable rule that no female shall be discharged, unless at her own desire or for mis-

persons admitted, the inferior wards consisting of meaner persons and of those degraded for their behaviour. Each person is employed in such kind of work as is suitable to her abilities, and has such part of the benefits arising from her industry as the committee think proper. Allen, in his "History of Surrey," in dealing with the Magdalen Hospital (and the description so far is applicable to it in its new situation, as well as when it stood in St.

THE OBELISK IN ST. GEORGE'S CIRCUS.

conduct, until means have been provided by which she may obtain an honest livelihood. No recommendation is necessary to entitle the unfortunate to the benefits of this hospital more than that of repentant guilt.

The hospital consisted of four brick buildings, forming a quadrangle. The chapel belonging to the institution was an octangular building, erected at one of the back corners. In the year 1869 the institution was removed to Streatham, as we have already seen.* The unhappy women, for whose benefit this hospital was erected, are received by petition; and there is a distinction in the wards, according to the education or the behaviour of the

George's Fields), writes :—" A probationary ward is instituted for the young women on their admission, and a separation of those of different descriptions and qualifications is established. Each class is entrusted to its particular assistant, and the whole is under the inspection of a matron. This separation, useful on many accounts, is particularly so to a numerous class of women, who are much to be pitied, and to whom this charity has been very beneficial, namely, ' young women who have been seduced from their friends under promise of marriage, and have been deserted by their seducers.' Their relations, in the first moments of resentment, refuse to receive, protect, or acknowledge them; they are abandoned by the world, without character, without friends, without money, without resource;

* See *ante*, p. 318.

and wretched indeed is their situation ! To such especially this house of refuge opens wide its doors; and instead of being driven by despair to lay violent hands on themselves, and to superadd the crime of self-murder to that guilt which is the cause of their distress, they find a safe and quiet retreat in this abode of peace and reflection."

A large block of Peabody Buildings now covers the site of the old Magdalen. The trees which stood in front of the latter are still made to do duty by screening the windows which front the street.

Shortly after the foundation of the Magdalen, another valuable institution, the Asylum for Female Orphans, was established, principally through the exertions of Sir John Fielding, the active magistrate, and St. George's Fields was chosen for its site. Like the Magdalen, this institution has migrated farther into the country, having within the last few years taken up its quarters at Bedington —the fine old Elizabethan dwelling-house of the Carews—near Croydon. While the Foundling Hospital is limited to the reception of infants, the Asylum for Female Orphans has been founded for the reception of destitute children, who are admitted at a more advanced age. The children are educated and industriously employed until sufficiently old to be apprenticed out, when the utmost care is taken that they are provided with suitable situations. The Asylum stood originally at the junction of Kennington Road and Westminster Bridge Road, on the spot now covered by Christ Church. The old building formed three sides of a square, but its dimensions appeared contracted, and not of that commanding character expected from the celebrity of this charity.

The Royal Freemasons' Charity School for Girls, in Elizabeth Place, Westminster Bridge Road, of which we give an illustration on page 343, was founded about the commencement of the present century, for the maintenance and education of the daughters and orphans of decayed members of the Masonic body. The schools were removed a few years ago, to make room for improvements in the neighbourhood.

In 1788 the Philanthropic Society established an industrial school in St. George's Fields, for the rescue of young children from a career of crime. The first place of reception of the Philanthropic Society was at a small house on Cambridge Heath, but the prosperous encouragement it received induced the directors to contract with the Corporation of London for a piece of ground in the London Road, at the corner of Garden Row, not far from the Obelisk; and on this site it remained till about

the year 1850, when the operations of the society were transferred to a more convenient building near the Red Hill station of the Brighton Railway. St. Jude's Church, in St. George's Road, was till 1850 the Philanthropic Society's chapel.

The School for the Indigent Blind, occupying considerable space on the southern side of the Lambeth Road, and shown in our illustration of the Obelisk on page 349, was originated at the premises of the old "Dog and Duck." When new Bethlehem Hospital was erected, in 1812, the site was required, and the Blind School was removed to its present site. Of institutions like this, Dr. Lettsom observed, that "he who enables a blind person, without excess of labour, to earn his own livelihood, does him more real service than if he had pensioned him to a greater amount." While the poor blind were thus cared for in St. George's Fields, those deprived of speech and hearing found a home in the Old Kent Road, where we have already paid them a visit.*

The London Road, which forms a continuation of the Blackfriars Road to the "Elephant and Castle" tavern, may be dismissed with one remark. The South London Palace of Amusement, on the eastern side of the road, was, from 1793 to 1848, in which last-named year St. George's Cathedral was completed, the principal chapel for the Roman Catholics of this part of the metropolis.

Besides witnessing the events mentioned above as having occurred here, St. George's Fields have borne their share of celebrity in the annals of England. They were very often the scenes of royal pomp and knightly cavalcades, as well as the rendezvous of rebellion and discord. It was to this place that Wat Tyler's and Jack Cade's rebels resorted, in order to raise the standard of opposition to the royal authority; and it was hither that the former retired, after the arrest of their leader in Smithfield, and were compelled to yield to the allegiance which they had violated.

From Westminster, Waterloo, and Blackfriars Bridges, broad thoroughfares converge to a point, called St. George's Circus, whence six roads diverge in various directions. It was proposed at one time to erect a large crescent at this spot† in honour of John Howard, the great philanthropist.

In the centre of the circus is an obelisk, erected in 1771, during the mayoralty and in honour of Brass Crosby, Esq., who is stated by Allen, in his "History of Surrey," to have been imprisoned in the Tower "for the conscientious discharge of his

---

* See _ante_, p. 252.　† See _Gentleman's Magazine_, Sept., 1716.

magisterial duty," and to commemorate the independent and patriotic spirit with which he released a printer who had been seized, contrary to law, by the House of Commons. Full particulars of the proceedings which led to the committal of Brass Crosby to the Tower will be found in the pages of the *Gentleman's Magazine* for March, 1771, from which it appears that the printers of several London newspapers had been apprehended on warrants issued against them by order of the House of Commons. On being taken before the Lord Mayor and Alderman Wilkes, the printers were at once discharged, his lordship saying that " so long as he was in that high office he looked upon himself as a guardian of the liberties of his fellow-citizens, and that no power had a right to seize a citizen of London without an authority from him or some some other magistrate." In consequence of this Wilkes and Crosby became martyrs ; but while the name of the former has been handed down to posterity from his connection with the *North Briton*, that of the latter is now almost forgotten. On the north side of the obelisk is inscribed, " One mile 350 feet from Fleet Street ;" on the south side, " Erected in XIth year of the reign of King George the Third, MDCCLXXI., the Right Hon. Brass Crosby, Lord Mayor ;" on the east side, " One mile 40 feet from London Bridge ;" and on the west side, " One mile from Palace Yard, Westminster Hall."

Several Acts of Parliament were passed, at the close of the last and beginning of the present centuries, for the improvement of this part of the metropolis. In 1812 an Act was passed which enabled the City to sell some detached pieces of land, mentioned in a schedule annexed to the Act, and to invest the purchase-money, and a further sum of £20,000, in the purchase of other land there, so as to make their estate in St. George's Fields more compact.

CHAPTER XXVII.

ST. GEORGE'S FIELDS (*continued*).—BETHLEHEM HOSPITAL, ETC.

" Insanire juvat."—Horace, " Odes," III. xix. 18.

The Priory of the Star of Bethlehem—Its Conversion into a Hospital for Lunatics—" Tom o' Bedlams "—Purchase of the Site for a New Hospital in St. George's Fields—Public Subscription to raise Funds for its Erection—Sign of the Old " Dog and Duck "—The New Hospital described—Cibber's Statues of " Melancholy and Raving Madness "—The Air of Refinement and Taste in the Appearance of the Female Wards —Viscomte d'Arlingcourt's Visit to Bedlam—Gray's Lines on Madness—The Ball-room—The Billiard-room—The Dining-room—The Chapel—The Infirmary Ward—A Picture of the " Good Samaritan," painted by one of the Inmates—The Council Chamber—The Men's Wards—A Sad Love Story—General Particulars of the Hospital, and Mode of Admission of Patients—King Edward's School—Christ Church, Westminster Bridge Road—St. George's Roman Catholic Cathedral—The School for the Indigent Blind—The British and Foreign School Society, Borough Road.

MODERN " Bedlam", to which we now come in our progress over St. George's Fields, is a very different place from the " Hospital of the Star of Bethlehem " to which it claims to have succeeded, and of which we will proceed to give a history. It is vulgarly styled " Bedlam," by a corruption of " Bethlem," which again is an abbreviation of " Bethlehem."

It was in the year 1246, and therefore in the reign of Henry III., that Simon Fitz-Mary, then Sheriff of London, made a pious determination to establish the " Priory of the Star of Bethlehem ;" and in order to endow it with sufficient maintenance, gave up those lands of his which were in the parish of St. Botolph Without, Bishopsgate, in the spot now known as Liverpool Street; the priory itself standing on the east side of " Morefield," afterwards called " Old Bethlem." In the year 1330 the religious house became known as a public hospital ; the City of London took it under their protection (an advantage to the establishment which, in those days of disorder, was not the least desirable object to attain), and in 1546 they purchased all the patronage, lands, and tenements belonging to the establishment ; upon which Henry VIII., who perhaps happened to be short of money at the time, wished to make them pay for the house itself ; but finding that they would not become purchasers of what really belonged to themselves, if to anybody at all, the magnanimous monarch took a liberal alternative, and made them a present of the house. The common story is that the king generously gave it to the " citizens of London," as a hospital for lunatics, whom he did not like to have so near to him as Charing Cross ; just as the conscience of the king led him to build the church of St. Martin's in the Fields, because he did not like to see so many funerals pass on the way to Westminster.

The old priory had already been a hospital for lunatics, amongst whom there were certain out-pensioners known as " Tom o' Bedlams," who were relieved and then sent away to beg, being known by a metal badge fastened on the arm : a distinction, of course, often simulated by other mendicants. In 1675 the building had become so dilapidated that it became necessary to erect a new one, and this was done upon a new site on the south side of Moorfields, at a cost of £1,700, raised by subscription. Of the appearance of this building at the commencement of the present century, or down to the time of the removal of this institution to St. George's Fields about the year 1815, we have spoken in a previous part of this work;* it only remains, therefore, to state that the edifice which was erected in Moorfields in 1675 having in its turn fallen into a bad condition, and becoming gradually surrounded by narrow streets, and crowded houses, its site was exchanged for a much larger piece of open ground in St. George's Fields. In the *Monthly Register* for 1802 we read that, "according to a new City plan for building on Moorfields, Bethlehem Hospital is to be pulled down, and re-erected on a more convenient site near Islington." This plan, however, was not carried out.

The present edifice was erected in 1812–15, but various additions have since been made. The building is three storeys high, and has a frontage of about 900 feet in length. It covers, with the offices and gardens, about fifteen acres of ground.

The "first stone" of the new building was laid by the Lord Mayor in April, 1812, and it was erected from the designs and under the direction of James Lewis, architect. The hospital was in 1815 sufficiently advanced for the reception of patients. The cupola, or dome, a comparatively recent addition, which crowns the centre of the roof, and serves as the chapel, was designed by the late Mr. Sydney Smirke.

The cost of the erection was about £122,500, of which £72,819 was granted by Parliament at different times, and £10,229 subscribed by public bodies and private individuals. The Corporation of the City gave £3,000, and the Bank of England £500 towards this sum. The following anecdote, with reference to the above-mentioned subscription, is told in the *Youth's Magazine* for 1812:—"When the collection was making to build Bethlehem Hospital, those who were employed to gather donations for that purpose went to a small house, the door of which being half open, they overheard an old man, the master, scolding his servant-maid for having thrown away a brimstone-match without using both ends. After diverting themselves some time with the dispute, they presented themselves before the old man, and explained the cause of their coming, though, from what had just passed, they entertained very little, if any, hopes of success. The supposed miser, however, no sooner under-

stood the business, than he stepped into a closet, whence he brought a bag, and counted out four hundred guineas, which he gave to them. No astonishment could exceed that of the collectors at this unexpected reverse of their expectations; they loudly testified their surprise, and scrupled not to inform their benefactor that they had overheard his quarrel with the servant-girl. 'Gentlemen,' said he, 'your surprise is occasioned by a thing of very little consequence. I keep house, and save and spend money my own way; the first furnishes me with the means of doing the other. With regard to benefactions and donations, you may always expect most from prudent people who keep their own accounts.' When he had thus spoken he requested them to withdraw without the smallest ceremony, to prevent which he shut the door, not thinking half so much of the four hundred guineas which he had just given away as of the match which had been carelessly thrown in the fire."

The first hospital in Moorfields could accommodate only fifty or sixty patients; and the second only 150, the number immured there in Strype's time. The present building was originally constructed for 198 patients; but this being found too limited for the purposes and resources of the hospital, a new wing was commenced for 166 additional patients, of which the first stone was laid in July, 1838. Since then other portions of the premises have been considerably enlarged.

Light iron railings, together with an entrance-gateway and lodge-house, separate the grounds from the main road. Let into a brick wall, which cuts off from observation the private grounds in front of the hospital, is the old sign-stone of the "Dog and Duck" tavern (shown in page 344), which, as we have stated in the preceding chapter, formerly occupied this site. The sign, which is about a yard square, is cut in high relief, and represents a dog with a duck in its mouth.

It must be owned that the long line of brick frontage of the hospital is somewhat sombre and gloomy in appearance. It consists of a centre and two wings. The former has a handsome and lofty portico, raised on a flight of steps, and composed of six columns of the Ionic order, surmounted by their entablature and a pediment, in the tympanum of which is a relief of the royal arms, and underneath the motto:—HENRICO VIII. REGE FVNDATVM CIVIVM LARGITAS PERFECIT. (Founded by King Henry VIII.; completed by the bounty of the people.) The remainder of the central portion of the building is occupied by the apartments of the officers of the establishment, the council-chamber, &c. On either

---

* See Vol. II., p. 200.

side of the entrance-hall are the houses assigned to the two resident physicians, who, of course, are men who have studied lunacy in all its bearings, both in theory and in practice. If surgical aid of a special nature is required, a surgeon is summoned from St. Thomas's Hospital or Guy's. The hospital has also accommodation for two medical students who wish to qualify themselves for practice in lunacy; and these two studentships, which give each of their holders free maintenance and instruction for six months, are eagerly sought after.

The wings are in three storeys, in addition to a rusticated basement, which show uniformly grated windows. Behind the principal front are two other wings, with the culinary departments between them. In the vestibule were for years preserved the two statues of "Melancholy and Raving Madness," which were sculptured by the elder Cibber, and formerly surmounted the gates of the old hospital in Moorfields. They are of Portland stone, and have been long since removed to the Museum at South Kensington. These statues were repaired by Bacon in 1820. In Lambert's "History of London" there is an engraving of Cibber's "Brainless Brothers," as these statues have been called: a fine piece of design, though the idea is borrowed from Michael Angelo. Virtue has preserved an anecdote that one of them was copied from Oliver Cromwell's gigantic porter, who became insane.

On entering the grand hall, the eye of the visitor is immediately attracted by the spacious staircase, which ascends from the ground-floor to the council-chamber above. On either side passages run laterally through the building, the one to the right leading to the male, the other to the female wards. The basement and three floors are each divided into galleries. The basement gallery is paved with stone, and its ceiling arched with brickwork; the upper galleries are floored with wood, and the ceiling plated with iron. One is struck on entering the female wards, not so much with the exquisite cleanliness of everything as with the air of taste and refinement which may be met with on either hand. The wards are long galleries, lighted on one side by large windows, in each of which stand globes of fish, fern-cases, or green-house plants; while the spaces between are occupied by pictures, busts, or cages containing birds. The whole air of the place is light and cheerful; and although there is, of course, sad evidence of the purposes of the institution in some of the faces, as they sit brooding over the guarded fires which warm the corridors at intervals of about fifty yards, there is a large per-centage of inmates who look for the most part cheerful, and are either working at some business, reading, writing, or playing with the cats or parrots, which seem wisely to be allowed to them as pets.

"I visited Bethlehem Hospital, or, as it is called, 'Bedlam,' which inspired me," writes the Viscomte D'Arlingcourt, in 1844, "with melancholy thoughts. I beheld this noble establishment with mingled admiration and grief. Its galleries, seemingly of interminable extent, are magnificent, but peopled with lunatics, whose sadness or gaiety appear equally fearful. Confined in a double prison, mentally as well as bodily, without light, without hope, and without end, the unfortunate inmates struggle at the same time under a twofold condemnation. It is true that the prisoners in Bedlam have not, like those in Newgate, to endure the tortures of memory and remorse; but even those in Newgate might have, if they would, an advantage over those in Bedlam—namely, the power of fixing their thoughts on heaven. These last would thus have still a hope left; the captive lunatic has none; he is not even on a level with dumb animals, for instinct likewise has forsaken him. He no longer ranks among men, and he is separated by nature from the brute creation. In one of the apartments in Bedlam is a portrait of Henry VIII., painted by Holbein; his disagreeable countenance consists of a screwed-up mouth, a bushy beard, a short nose, small eyes, and a puffy face. This Blue-beard of the English throne, this royal slayer of women, appeared to me in his proper place at Bedlam. But, alas! he himself was not confined there."

Turning again to the unfortunate objects of this institution, their case is thus powerfully depicted, or rather prophesied, by Gray, in his "Ode to Eton College:"—

> " These shall the fury passions tear,
> 　　The vultures of the mind,
> Disdainful anger, pallid fear,
> 　　And shame that skulks behind;
> Or pining love shall waste their youth,
> Or jealousy, with rankling tooth,
> 　　That only gnaws the secret heart;
> And envy wan, and faded care,
> Grim-visaged, comfortless despair,
> 　　And sorrow's piercing dart.

> "Ambition this shall tempt to rise,
> 　　Then whirl the wretch from high,
> To bitter scorn a sacrifice,
> 　　And grinning infamy.
> The stings of falsehood those shall try,
> And hard unkindness' alter'd eye,
> 　　That mocks the tear it forced to flow;
> And keen remorse, with blood defiled,
> And moody madness laughing wild
> 　　Amid severest woe."

Threading our way along the corridor which leads to the female wards, and descending a stone staircase, we were led by our guide to the kitchen and culinary offices in the basement, and in the rear of the central portion of the building. The kitchen is a large octagonal building, admirably furnished, and fitted up with huge boilers, a large steam apparatus, and all the requisite appliances for cooking. The water used by the establishment is

enough to require more rigid measures. Thanks to Dr. Elliotson,* the great modern reformer of the system on which lunatics are treated in this country, all severity—such as the use of chains, manacles, and strait-waistcoats—has now entirely disappeared here; indeed, if a patient on being brought to the hospital should happen to be wearing one, it is stripped off in the hall, and handed back to the patient's friends, often much to their surprise.

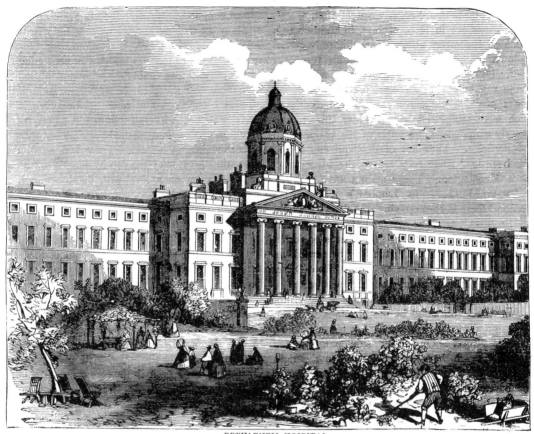

BETHLEHEM HOSPITAL.

drawn from an Artesian well, which is bored down into the chalk underlying the clay soil. Hence probably arises the well-known freedom from diarrhœa and cholera among the inmates of Bethlehem when those terrible diseases have raged all around the walls of the institution.

Near at hand, and in other parts of the grounds, are the workshops, where those patients who, from their previous employment, are qualified for the task, may be seen labouring, with more or less industry, at their respective trades. Those who can work at any sedentary employment are encouraged to do so: not the slightest restriction, however, is placed upon the inmates on this score; and there are but few whose demeanour is violent

Kindness is the only charm by which the attendants exert a mastery over the patients, and the influence thus possessed is most remarkable.

The ground-floor of the main building receives the patients on their admission, and this and the succeeding storey are appropriated for dangerous cases. Here, too, are the bath-rooms, lavatories, and sundry rooms, padded with cork and india-rubber, for the reception of refractory and violent patients.

One of the inmates of the first ward which we visited talked as rationally and sensibly as possible on the subject of her former pupils when she kept

* See Vol. IV., p 326.

a ladies' school ; and nobody could have suspected her of being a "patient" here, had we not known that there was one subject on which it was forbidden to speak.   Another poor woman, though cheerful and even smiling, lived—we were told—under the constant delusion that she hears the workmen erecting the scaffold for her execution on the morrow.   A third, a handsome woman of about fifty, on seeing us enter, came forward to see if we were part of the nuptial party whom she was daily expecting in attendance on her heavenly

Passing up the stone staircases, we made our way through the various rooms on each floor of the southern wing.   Each we found to be furnished with plain couches and lounges, and almost every other comfort which could in any way conduce to the comfort of the wretched inmates.   In several of the wards were pianos.   At the end of the uppermost floor, in this part of the building, is a ball-room, the sight of which would have gratified Lord Lanesborough ; * in it a ball is given every month, and a practice-night also is held fortnightly.

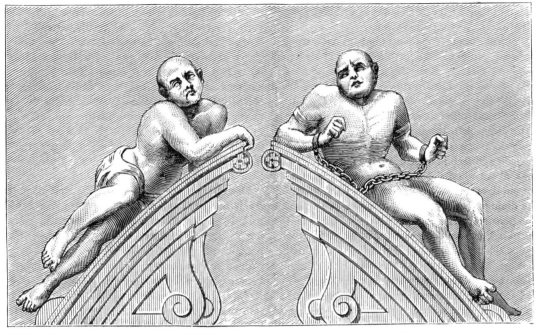

"MELANCHOLY AND RAVING MADNESS." (*Sculptured by Cibber.*)
(*Formerly over the gateway of Bethlehem Hospital, Moorfields.*)

spouse, the Lord himself, and his companion, the prophet Isaiah !   Her disappointment on perceiving her mistake we cannot pretend to describe. "Well, I know he will come before the end of the year.   He is very kind and good to me ; and I am not worthy of him."   Such were her musings. Poor, good, simple soul !   how we felt for the pain which we had unintentionally caused her, as she retired into a corner to sit down and weep ; while an aged crone near her gave vent to a torrent of abuse of the institution !   Another girl was pointed out to us, who sat, and sits day by day, in a dark corner, watching a favourite plant, which she is persuaded will bring her a blessing as soon as it comes into flower.   Poor girl !   how true, again, are the words of Gray—

" —— Where ignorance is bliss
'Tis folly to be wise."

The dancers are those of the patients who are fit to be trusted.

A writer in the *Illustrated Times* most appositely remarks :—"An empty ball-room, whether at Bethlehem or elsewhere, can be but a spacious, well-ventilated, well-boarded, and handsome saloon. But the ball !   Ah, those periodical balls at Bethlehem Hospital !—who can describe, who imagine them—their strange, pervading characteristics ; their underlying peculiarities ; their effects ; the longing anticipations of the relief they must afford by recalling old memories half-submerged in the darker broodings which sometimes flood the recollections of a brighter life ?   Oh !   may they help those poor souls to grope their way back to life and light."

* See Vol. V., p. 4.

In the corresponding wing on the men's side is a billiard-room, to which the most hopeful cases among the male patients have access under certain restrictions. This is a large apartment, which, but for its furniture, would look like an immense and lofty green-house, since it is almost entirely glazed above the height of about six feet—a plan which ensures a capital light upon the table. Around the room are raised cushioned seats for those who desire to watch the play; while nearer the fire a large study-table is filled with magazines, journals, and general literature, in neat, lettered covers, and all uninjured by the stains which ordinarily mark these adjuncts to a public room.

Each of the sleeping-rooms contains a low truckle bedstead, with chair and table, light and air being admitted through a small barred window at the top. Some of them, particularly on the women's side of the hospital, are profusely adorned with pictures and other objects of interest, which may have been left by friends visiting the patient. Each door opens to the gallery, affording a promenade 250 feet in length, where the patients can walk about when the weather proves unfavourable for out-door exercise. To the left of the gallery is the dining-room, capable of accommodating about 100 persons. The diet, which is plain, but of the best kind, is served on wooden bowls and platters, and is seldom unaccompanied by a good appetite. The patients are allowed the use of knives, but these, we remarked, were very blunt.

These long corridors or wards are preserved to an equable temperature through every change of season by the introduction of warm-air pipes and stoves beneath the flooring, so constructed that the warmth of every patient's room can be regulated.

The wards of the women, as already stated, are much more gay and cheerful than those in the men's wing. Their windows are nearly all decked out with evergreens or other plants and flowers, and the prints on the walls have flowers or needlework hung upon them—the latter the work of the patients. Some of these ply the needle as deftly as their saner sisters. One in particular, a girl of about seventeen, who has the reputation of being an excellent darner, showed us her handy-work with great pride, and was evidently delighted by our praise.

Each storey has connected with it one of these galleries, from the last of which a stone staircase conducts to the chapel, a large octagonal apartment covered with a cupola, but of no architectural pretensions, which stands over the central hall. Such of the patients as can be trusted to behave themselves attend service in it twice on a Sunday, the men sitting on one side and the women on the other, each attended by their keepers and attendants. The chaplain generally addresses them in a conversational and homely manner, instead of inflicting on them a written sermon; and the patients themselves form a very fair choir. They have a good organ to aid them in their psalmody.

Beyond the gallery a door opens into a light, airy, and cheerful room, the beds in which, and the air of calm quiet pervading it, prepare you to hear that it is the infirmary ward. Here, once more, we meet with exquisite cleanliness, but still something beyond cleanliness—comfort, elegance, even luxury. The high and neatly-curtained windows admit the light in one pleasant tone, without either glare or shadow, and show flowers, plants, busts, and even the neat white-draped beds, all as pleasant objects. Seated here and there are the partially convalescent, accommodated with easy seats, leg-rests, or pillows, by the aid of which they can lounge over the new number of some favourite periodical, with which a large table is liberally supplied, or plunge more deeply into some book selected from the library.

Descending the staircase to the first floor, we reach the corridor which passes over the central hall, by the head of the grand staircase. Here our attention was drawn to a large painting of the parable of the "Good Samaritan," which was painted some years ago by one of the unfortunate inmates of the hospital—Dadd, a student of the Royal Academy. The wall at the head of the staircase is covered with the names of benefactors to the institution inscribed in letters of gold; and close by is the board-room. This is a fine apartment, adorned with the arms and bequests of every donor to the hospital, together with an excellent portrait of its founder, King Henry VIII., by Holbein, said to be an original. In the "visitors' book," which lies upon one of the tables in the room, are inscribed the signatures of many royal and noble personages, such as the Emperor of Brazil, the Empress of Austria, the King of Spain, &c.; but apparently more valued than all these put together is an autograph signature of Queen Victoria, written when she visited the hospital in 1860: this is preserved under a glass, upon a table by itself in one of the recesses between the windows.

Turning to the right after leaving the board-room, we pass at once to the men's wards. In plan and general arrangement these rooms are the same as on the women's side of the hospital; but, although the male patients are provided with musical instruments, books, and writing materials, there is an absence of that neatness and taste in the decoration of the wards and galleries which is such a striking feature in that portion of the hospital set apart for females.

A ward on the ground floor, on the men's side, contains a small plunging bath, which is constantly in use in the summer months. It was formerly the custom to plunge patients unawares into this bath, by letting them fall into it suddenly through a trap-door, in the hope that the shock to their nervous system might help to work a cure. But such forcible remedies as these have long since been given up, along with strait-waistcoats and other restraints. Mild and gentle treatment, coupled with firmness, is now found to be the best of remedies. The history of the treatment of the patients in Bethlehem, even to a date so late as the beginning of the present century, would be a terrible and sickening recital. In early days the only system adopted in providing for lunatics was one of constant repression and severity, while the common comforts and necessities of life were almost entirely denied to the poor creatures, who, hopeless, chained, and neglected, wore out their fevered lives in the filthy pesthouse, which, in 1598, was reported to be " loathsome."

In 1770, when two wings appropriated to incurables had been added to the main building in Moorfields, the public were admitted to the hospital as one of the regular London sights ; and it may readily be imagined that the promiscuous crowd, who were admitted at a penny each, produced a degree of excitement and confusion which caused incalculable mischief. This state of things lasted, with only partial improvements, till 1815, when the present edifice (or at least the main building) was completed.

Now, instead of chains and loathsome cells, we find light and handsomely-furnished apartments, as shown above, in which the exquisite cleanliness of everything is mingled with an air of taste and refinement, which goes far to diminish the horrors even of lunacy. One room upon the uppermost floor on the men's side of the building is fitted up as a library, magazines and periodicals lying upon the table, for the use of the patients in their saner moments. This apartment is in every respect as quiet, as comfortable, as orderly, and as much adapted to the comfort of the readers as that of most clubs, and more than that of many private houses.

Amongst the men there seems but little conversation, and not much fellowship. Smoking is indulged in by such as care for it, and the general aspect of the patients is that of contentment ; ex-

cepting, of course, those labouring under particular delusions. Kindness, as we have stated, is the only charm by which the attendants exert a mastery over the patients, and the influence thus possessed is most remarkable. Whilst the impression left on the mind of the visitor is that of a mournful gratification, it is yet blended with a feeling of intense satisfaction, arising from a knowledge that the comforts of his afflicted fellow-creatures are so industriously sought after and so assiduously promoted.

The system of employment carried out seems to be that of providing means for such occupation as can consistently be given to the patients according to their several tastes. The decoration, painting, graining, and so on, for the institution, was mostly executed, a few years ago, by two patients, who, having plenty of time before them, and not being hurried (for no work is *exacted*, and no profit by sale is ever made of work done in the hospital), the graining, bird's-eye mapling, and general ornamentation in wood-work, is a sight to see.

In the rear of the building is the " play-ground," a large open space, set apart for the recreation and exercise of the patients, where they may be seen pursuing, with considerable eagerness, the different pastimes in which their fancy leads them to indulge. There are four of these open spaces appropriated to recreation—two for the men, and two for the women—and there is evidence constantly afforded that this exercise not only conduces to the immediate health of the inmates, but also to their ultimate recovery. Mowing and gardening, and gathering vegetables during fine weather, and hay-making in the summer, are a source of employment and of enjoyment to the men.

We have spoken above of the balls and dancing-parties that are held in the women's ward. These are occasionally varied by other entertainments for the amusement of the unfortunate inmates. The beneficial effect of these entertainments on the minds of the patients has at times shown itself. The case of a tailor, who was, a few years ago, an inmate here, may be taken as an instance in point. It was mentioned in one of the general reports at the time. It seems he had been for nearly four years in a state of morbid insanity, with eyes fixed moodily on the ground, neither noticing nor speaking to any one, except an occasional mutter of dissatisfaction if his wishes were disregarded. On the occasion of one of the monthly parties above referred to, an officer of the institution had undertaken to exhibit some feats of legerdemain, and for that purpose had disguised himself in a black wig and a pair of moustaches. It was at first doubted whether it would be worth while to introduce the gloomy patient amongst the company; but Dr. Hood, at that time the principal medical officer of the institution, had directed him to be brought to sit next to himself, and he was induced to favour them with his company. What strange lucidity passed upon the man's perceptions can never be explained, perhaps; but, almost before he sat down, he had looked half-heedlessly round the room, and, recognising the conjuror through his disguise, said, "A good make-up for ——!" His attention had been arrested at last; he followed the tricks, discovered the way in which many of them were performed, and finally drank the Queen's health in a glass of something from the "inexhaustible bottle." It is scarcely necessary to remark that from that time there was no relapse into his former state, and that he gradually and steadily improved.

A proof of the general health and longevity enjoyed by the inmates may be found in the fact that Margaret Nicholson, who tried to assassinate George III. at the gate of St. James's Palace, died here in 1828, at the age of ninety-eight, after an imprisonment of forty-two years. James Hatfield, who was confined for a similar offence in 1800, died here in 1841. The following account of Hatfield's crime was written by Sir Herbert Croft :—

"On the 15th of May, 1800, during a field day of the Grenadier battalion of Foot-guards in Hyde Park, while the king was present, a ball from one of the soldiers shot a spectator of the name of Ongley in the thigh, at no great distance from his Majesty. The king showed every attention to the wounded gentleman, but ascribed it wholly to some accident. In the evening the royal family repaired to the play, which had been ordered by them at Drury Lane Theatre, as if nothing had happened. When his Majesty entered the house, followed by the queen and princesses, while he was bowing to the audience, a large horse-pistol was fired at him by Hatfield from the pit. But the king betrayed no alarm, . . . nor discovered any suspicion of his soldiers : though, in dragging the assassin over the orchestra, a military waistcoat became visible under his great coat. His Majesty only stepped to the back of the box, and prevented the queen from entering, saying, 'It was merely a squib, with which they were foolishly diverting themselves ; perhaps there might be another.' He then, according to the account of a gentleman who was present, returned to the box, advanced to the front, and with folded arms and a look of great dignity, said, 'Now fire !' Silent but intense

admiration burst into acclamations which shook the theatre. Hatfield had served his time as a working silversmith, but afterwards enlisted in the fifteenth Light Dragoons. He served under the Duke of York, and had a deep cut over his eye, and another long scar on his cheek. At Lincelles he was left three hours among the dead in a ditch, and was taken prisoner by the French ; he had his arm broken by a shot, and received eight sabre wounds in his head. On being asked what had induced him to attempt the life of the king, he said, 'I did not attempt to kill the king—I fired the pistol over the royal box; I am as good a shot as any man in England ; but I am weary of life and wish for death, though not to die by my own hands. I was desirous of raising an alarm, and hoped the spectators would fall upon me ; but they did not. Still, I trust my life is forfeited !' Hatfield was subsequently indicted for high treason, but the jury, being satisfied that he was of unsound mind, committed him to Bethlehem Hospital, where he died."

Among the criminal lunatics of more recent years was Oxford, who shot at the Queen soon after her marriage (1840). He was released many years ago, and sent abroad under proper surveillance, whence he corresponded, from time to time, with his old friends in the asylum. He died in 1883.

The criminal ward possessed its aviary, plants, and flowers, and to all appearance was as cheerful as the other portions of the hospital ; but the criminal lunatics were removed to Broadmoor, near Aldershot, during the years 1863 and 1864, and their ward has since been converted to other purposes.

One of the most recent changes in connection with Bethlehem has been the erection of a fine convalescent hospital at Witley, near Godalming. This was established by Act of Parliament, and was brought into working order about the year 1870. To it are sent such of the patients as are the most hopeful of recovery, to receive the finishing touch, preparatory to their restoration to freedom. The statute states that it is of great advantage to the persons received here, "that the governors should be able to send away from the hospital, for the benefit of their health, but without relinquishing the care and charge of them as lunatics, such of the same persons as are convalescent, and such others of them as the governors may think fit to send away." The convalescent establishment at Witley has been established "for the reception of convalescent and other patients." Regulations have been made for the new establishment, and the Commissioners of Lunacy visit the place as if it were duly registered as an hospital.

The average number of patients in the hospital

is about 300, of whom about two-thirds are females. The total number of curable patients admitted during one hundred years, ending the 31st of December, 1876, was 19,844; and out of these the number discharged cured was 9,081, or 45·76 per cent. The deaths during the same period amounted to 1,334, or 6·74 per cent.

Bethlehem Hospital is intended for curable cases only; but unless the patient is of the well-to-do or pauper class, and unless the symptoms of mental disease have existed more than twelve months, it is very rarely that a case is rejected. The number of patients received during the year 1876 was 253; and 243 were discharged within the same period. Of these 112 patients were sent out "not recovered;" but of this number twenty-three did not remain in the hospital the full period of twelve months. In every doubtful case the practice of the committee is to give the patient the benefit of the doubt, and allow him or her to remain under treatment at least three months. A glance at the Annual Report for 1876 shows that the inmates admitted during the year were members of almost every denomination, the Established Church furnishing by far the largest proportion, and the Unitarians the fewest; and that during the same period the male patients comprised among them no less than thirty-two clerks, the highest number of any other profession or occupation being nine; whilst on the female side thirty were governesses, and thirty-five the wives, widows, or daughters of clerks or tradesmen. Of the apparent or assigned causes of lunacy, mental anxiety is set down as that of twenty-two patients, and mental work as that of twenty-four; religious excitement was the cause of bringing nine inmates to "Bedlam"—of these five were males, and four females; seventeen were brought here through pecuniary embarrassment; and "love affairs" are set down as the cause of upsetting the mental equilibrium of five persons, one male and four females.

A sad love-story, ending in madness in Bedlam, is on record, and may not be out of place here:— "About the year 1780, a young East Indian, whose name was Dupree, left his fatherland to visit a distant relation, a merchant, on Fish Street Hill. During the young man's stay, he was waited on by the servant of the house, a country girl, Rebecca Griffiths, chiefly remarkable for the plainness of her person, and the quiet meekness of her manners. The circuit of pleasure run, and yearning again for home, the visitor at length prepared for his departure; the chaise came to the door, and shaking of hands, with tenderer salutations,

adieus, and farewells, followed in the usual abundance. Rebecca, in whom an extraordinary depression had for some days previously been perceived, was in attendance, to help to pack the luggage. The leave-taking of friends and relations at length completed, with a guinea squeezed into his humble attendant's hand, and a brief 'God bless you, Rebecca!' the young man sprang into the chaise, the driver smacked his whip, and the vehicle was rolling rapidly out of sight, when a piercing shriek from Rebecca, who had stood to all appearance vacantly gazing on what had passed, alarmed the family, then retiring into the house. They hastily turned round: to their infinite surprise, Rebecca was seen wildly following the chaise. She was rushing with the velocity of lightning along the middle of the road, her hair streaming in the wind, and her whole appearance that of a desperate maniac! Proper persons were immediately dispatched after her, but she was not secured till she had gained the Borough; when she was taken in a state of incurable madness to Bethlehem Hospital, where she died some years after. The guinea he had given her—her richest treasure—her only wealth—she never suffered, during life, to quit her hand; she grasped it still more firmly in her dying moments, and at her request, in the last gleam of returning reason—the lightning before death—it was buried with her. There was a tradition in Bedlam that, through the heartless cupidity of the keeper, it was sacrilegiously wrenched from her, and that her ghost might be seen every night gliding through the dreary cells of that melancholy building, in search of her lover's gift, and mournfully asking the glaring maniacs for her lost guinea. It was Mr. Dupree's only consolation, after her death, that the excessive homeliness of her person, and her retiring air and manners, had never even suffered him to indulge in the most trifling freedom with her. She had loved hopelessly, and paid the forfeiture with sense and life."

Dr. Rhys Williams, formerly the resident physician, in the report to which we have referred above, observes that in an asylum constructed like Bethlehem, on the single room system, there are many difficulties in organising careful supervision during the night without disturbing the patients, and that the feeling of security may be obtained to the detriment of the inmates. The staff of attendants, as we learn from the Report of the Commissioners in Lunacy, is well selected; they consist of fifteen men, including the head attendant, and thirty-two nurses, six of whom are chiefs of wards. The night-watch consists of one man in the male division, and two nurses on the other side. The watchers make their rounds of the wards at certain intervals throughout the night; and in order to ascertain that these duties are regularly performed, an instrument has been devised, in the shape of a check or "tell-tale" clock, affixed in the wall of each ward. The warder, in going his rounds, on arriving at each of these clocks, presses upon them a duplicate paper clock-face, properly lined

or require the permanent and exclusive attendance of a nurse. A preference is always given to patients of the educated classes, to secure accommodation for whom, no patient is received who is a proper object for admission into a pauper county asylum. A printed form, to be filled up by the friend or guardian of the lunatic, can be obtained from the authorities at the hospital. In this form is a certificate, to be signed by the minister, church-

A WARD IN BETHLEHEM HOSPITAL.

for the various rounds, and by this means receives upon it the impress of a metal letter at the time indicated. Each of the six wards has a different letter, thus—R. E. F. O. R. M.

A few words for the guidance of persons applying for the admission of patients may not be out of place here. All poor lunatics presumed to be curable are eligible for admission into this hospital for maintenance and medical treatment: except those who have sufficient means for their suitable maintenance in a private asylum; those who have been insane more than twelve months, and are considered by the resident physician to be incurable; and also those who are in a state of idiotcy, or are subject to epileptic fits, or whose condition threatens **the speedy dissolution of life,**

warden, or overseer of the parish in which the lunatic has resided, setting forth that he (or she) is a proper object for admission into Bethlehem Hospital. A list of the several articles of clothing required to be brought for the use of the patient is also appended to the form; and it is also particularly set forth that during the abode of the patient in the hospital the friends are not to furnish any other articles of clothing than those mentioned, unless by the written request or permission of the steward or matron. The friends of the patient are likewise strictly prohibited from giving money to the servants to purchase any articles of clothing for the patients; and they are not allowed to offer or give any fee, gratuity, or present, to any of the servants, under any pretence whatever. **The** infringement of these regulations will involve not only the dismissal of the servant, but also the discharge of the patient from the hospital.

We may also add that patients, when sufficiently convalescent, are allowed to be seen by their friends at certain fixed periods; and that, by an order from one of the governors, visitors can be admitted to the hospital on Tuesdays and the three following days in each week.

there; to which Johnson replies, "Nay, madam, you see nothing there to hurt you. You no more think of madness by having windows that look to Bedlam than you think of death by having windows that look to a churchyard." *Mrs. Burney:* "We may look to a churchyard, sir; for it is right that we should be kept in mind of death." *Johnson:* "Nay, madam; if you go to that, it is right that we should be kept in mind of madness, which is

KING EDWARD'S SCHOOL.

Readers of Charles Dickens will not have forgotten how he makes his "Uncommercial Traveller" wander by Bethlehem Hospital on his way to Westminster, pondering on the problem whether the sane and the insane are not equal: at all events, at night, when the sane lie a-dreaming. "Are not all of us outside of this hospital who dream more or less in the condition of those inside it every night of our lives?" A very pertinent remark for those who really have entered into the philosophy of dreams and dreamland.

In Boswell's "Life of Johnson" we read how that Mrs. Burney wondered that some very beautiful new buildings should be erected in Moorfields, in so shocking a situation as between Bedlam and St. Luke's Hospital, and said she could not live

occasioned by too much indulgence of imagination. I think a very moral use may be made of these new buildings—I would have those who have heated imaginations live there, and take warning." *Mrs. Burney:* "But, sir, many of the poor people that are mad have become so from disease or from distressing events. It is, therefore, not their fault, but their misfortune; and, therefore, to think of them is a melancholy consideration." These remarks, we need scarcely add, are as applicable to the present situation of "Bedlam" as they were to its old site in Moorfields.

From the interior of Bethlehem the change is pleasant to a building which adjoins it on the eastern side, and is under the same management, namely, King Edward's School, which was established here early in the present century. It was formerly known as "King Edward's School, or the House of Occupation," and was constructed for the accommodation of 150 girls, and about the same number of boys; but the latter have, within the last few years, been removed to Witley, near Godalming, and lodged in some school buildings contiguous to Bethlehem Convalescent Hospital. The ground-plan of the building here is in the form of the letter **H**, the domestic offices, with the chapel above, occupying the central portion. On the ground-floor of the principal front are two large school-rooms and class-rooms, and also some of the rooms in which the girls are taught domestic duties, such as washing and ironing, &c. The rooms for needlework are in the rear part of the building. The dormitories are large, well-ventilated apartments, and scrupulously clean and tidy in their appearance. The play-ground is divided from the recreation-ground and garden of Bethlehem by only a wall and a path; and yet, what a contrast between the inmates of the two institutions! The bright faces of the girls are of themselves a comment on the lines of the cavalier, Lovelace—

> " Stone walls do not a prison make,
>   Nor iron bars a cage ;
> Minds innocent and quiet take
>   That for a hermitage."

The boys' school at Witley was in 1877–8 in process of enlargement, by the erection of two new dormitories, planned to accommodate about fifty additional children. Similarly the girls' school has been judiciously re-arranged for the same additional number. The children are orphans, or such as have lost their fathers' aid through illness or other affliction; they are admitted at the age of twelve, and stay in the school for four years, when situations are obtained for them. The excellent teaching and training which the girls receive here render them highly qualified for situations as domestic servants; and the characters of such as have left the school, received from time to time by the matron, are almost invariably good. About seventy girls are annually placed out in situations by the institution; whilst the applications for servants which reach the matron are, generally speaking, far more numerous than can be met by the supply.

At a short distance from Bethlehem Hospital, on the site formerly occupied by the Asylum for Female Orphans, at the junction of Kennington Road with Westminster Bridge Road, of which we have spoken in the preceding chapter, stands Christ Church, a new non-denominational church, which has been erected to perpetuate the work inaugurated by Rowland Hill at Surrey Chapel. It

was opened on the 4th of July, 1876, the centenary of American independence. The church, a fine specimen of Gothic architecture, is one of the handsomest ecclesiastical edifices in the metropolis. The cost, including lecture-hall, tower, &c., was £60,000. The organ, a very powerful instrument by Messrs. Lewis, has three manuals and a pedale, 41 stops, and 2,198 pipes. Towards the cost of these building upwards of £30,000 have been contributed by friends outside the congregation, the greater part of which has been collected by the Rev. Newman Hall, during two visits to America, and by lecturing, preaching, and other means, in Great Britain. There is ample sitting accommodation for 2,500 persons. The interior, which boasts of several stained-glass windows, and an ornamental oak roof, has an appearance approaching that of a cathedral, to which the service closely corresponds. At one corner of the church is a tower, surmounted by a lofty spire. This structure, called the "Lincoln Tower," owes its origin to the suggestion of some American citizens, at the close of the civil war, that it should be built at the cost of Americans, as a testimony to the sympathy expressed for the Union by the Rev. Newman Hall and his congregation. The tower, the cost of which was £7,000, contributed in England and America, is upwards of 200 feet in height. The "stars and stripes" are inwrought in the stone, and the British Lion and American Eagle together adorn the angles of the tower. In the tower are two spacious chambers, designated the "Washington" and "Wilberforce" Rooms; these are used as class-rooms for educational and other benevolent purposes. The architects were Messrs. Paull and Bickerdike.

Adjoining Christ Church, and in an architectural sense forming a part of it, is another building, devoted to religious and philanthropic purposes, called "Hawkstone Hall," after the seat of the head of Rowland Hill's family (Lord Hill), in Shropshire. It is sixty-three feet long by fifty feet wide, with a square gallery, and has sitting accommodation for about 700, the woodwork being a stained pitch pine. In the basement beneath the lecture-hall are five class-rooms, one of which will hold 150 infants, besides another large room, in which meetings are occasionally held.

In the last century, as we have seen, St. George's Fields—now the site of numerous palaces of philanthropy—was the scene of low dissipation; and here, on the very focus of the "No Popery" riots of 1780, has arisen the Roman Catholic Cathedral dedicated to St. George. This singular evidence of the mutations to which localities are subject, and striking proof of our advance in liberality of opinion, occupies a large plot of ground at the junction of the Lambeth, Westminster, and St. George's Roads, and nearly facing Bethlehem Hospital.

For many years previously to the erection of the Pro-Cathedral at Kensington, St. George's Cathedral had quite eclipsed St. Mary's, Moorfields, as the chief church of the Roman Catholic body, especially during the years 1850–52, whilst Cardinal Wiseman administered the diocese of Southwark as well as that of Westminster. It was built between the years 1840 and 1848: the Kings of Bavaria and Sardinia, and nearly the whole of the English Roman Catholic aristocracy, were large contributors to its erection; whilst the Irish poor, including the waifs and strays of St. Patrick's Schools in Soho, and other very poor districts, sent their pence.

"This cathedral," writes Mr. R. Chambers, in his "Book of Days," "by a happy retribution, is built on the very spot where Lord George Gordon's riots were inaugurated by a Protestant mob meeting," a fact to which we have already drawn the attention of our readers in the previous chapter.* It is said that the high altar stands as nearly as possible on the very spot on which the mad-cap leader, Lord George Gordon, rallied his "No Popery" rioters in 1780, previous to marching to Westminster—a curious retribution, if true; but, after all, this may be only a tradition.

The cathedral was designed by Mr. Augustus W. Pugin, who, however, always complained that he had been cramped and crippled in the carrying out of his plans, as he was originally called upon to design a parish church, and not a cathedral. Unfortunately, the position of the church is reversed —the high altar, in contrast to that of most Gothic churches, being at the west instead of the east end. It has no galleries, save one small one at the end of the nave for the organ, and will accommodate 3,000 worshippers on the floor alone.

There was a Roman Catholic "mission" in this neighbourhood as far back as the year 1788, eight years after Lord George Gordon's riots: mass having been formerly said secretly in a modest and humble room in Bandyleg Walk, near Guildford Street (now New Park Street†). A site for a chapel was procured in that year in the London Road, and a chapel was erected in 1789–93, at the cost of about £2,000. It was opened on St. Patrick's Day, March, 1793, the sermon being preached by "Father" O'Leary. This chapel served for fifty years as the centre of ministrations for the Roman Catholic clergy in Southwark; but eventually it was found too small, and it was

resolved to supersede it by a larger and handsomer edifice. This chapel became subsequently a music-hall, and is now called the South London Palace. The site of the new cathedral was purchased, in the year 1839, from the Bridge House Estate, for £3,200. The foundations were commenced in September, 1840, and the foundation-stone was laid on the Feast of St. Augustine, the apostle of England, in the following May. It was "solemnly dedicated" on the Festival of St. Alban, first martyr of England, July 4th, 1848, the ceremony being attended by bishops from all the "five quarters" of the world; the high mass being sung, and the sermon preached by Dr. Wiseman, who, two years afterwards, was here formally installed as Archbishop of Westminster, in December, 1850, a few weeks after receiving his cardinal's hat. Here also the new-made cardinal preached his celebrated series of sermons, explanatory of the step taken by the Pope in restoring the Roman Catholic hierarchy in England.

The church, which is built in the Decorated or Edwardian style of Pointed architecture, consists of a nave, chancel, and side aisles, without transepts; it has also no clerestory—a want which sadly detracts from its elevation and dignity. It measures internally 240 feet by 70. The material employed in its construction is yellow brick, instead of stone, which by no means adds to its beauty. The total cost of the building, including the residence for the bishop and his clergy adjoining, was a little over £35,000. A chantry at the end of the north aisle was built by the family of the late Hon. Edward Petre, M.P., in order that masses might be said there daily for the repose of his soul. This was probably the first chantry so built in modern times. There is a second chantry, founded by the family of the late Mr. John Knill, of Blackheath. Attached to the church is a staff of clergy, who attend also the workhouses of Lambeth, St. George's, St. Saviour's, and Newington, together with Bethlehem and St. Thomas's Hospitals, and Horsemonger Lane Prison. Among the former clergy of St. George's was the Honourable and Rev. George Talbot, formerly a clergyman of the Established Church, afterwards chamberlain to Pope Pius IX. The tower still remains incomplete; but when surmounted with a spire it will be upwards of 300 feet high. The chancel is deep, and enclosed with an ornamental screen. On either side of the high altar are chapels of the Blessed Sacrament and Our Lady. The font, which stands in the southern aisle, is of stone, octagonal in shape, and highly decorated with images of angels, the Four Evangelists, and the Doctors of the Church. The organ, which

---

* See *ante*, p. 346.   † See *ante*, p. 44.

stands in the tower, under a pointed arch forty feet in height, is a powerful instrument. The pulpit, which stands in the nave, attached to the third pillar from the chancel on the northern side, is hexagonal. It is supported by marble shafts ; on four sides of the pulpit are *bassi relievi*, elaborately carved, representing our Lord delivering the sermon on the mount, St. John the Baptist preaching in the wilderness, and the preaching of the religious Orders of St. Francis and St. Dominic. These sculptures are executed with all the severity of the early Florentine school, and many of the figures are studies from nature and real drapery. The ascent to the pulpit is by a series of detached steps, each supported by a marble shaft, with carved capitals, to which is attached an iron railing. The work is executed in Caen stone, except the shafts, which are of British marble. The large window in the tower contains figures of St. George the Martyr (to whom the church is dedicated), St. Richard, St. Ethelbert, St. Oswald, St. Edmund, and St. Edward the Confessor, with angels bearing scrolls and musical instruments. The rood-screen, of stone, consists of three open arches, resting on marble shafts, with richly carved foliated capitals ; above it stands the cross, bearing the figure of the Redeemer of the world, and on either side stand the Virgin Mary and the beloved disciple. The cross itself is an original work of the fifteenth century ; the figure of our Lord is from the chisel of the celebrated M. Durlet, of Antwerp ; the two other images were carved in England.

In spite of the profuse decoration of the chancel and its side chapels, it must be owned that the nave of St. George's has a singularly bare and naked appearance, which is increased by the starved proportions of the pillars that mark it off from the side aisles. At the lower end of the church, near the chief entrance, is a huge crucifix, at the foot of which, at almost every hour of the day, may be seen many devout worshippers.

The great window, over the high altar, is of nine lights ; it is filled with stained glass, representing the Root of Jesse, or the genealogy of our Lord, the gift of John, Earl of Shrewsbury. The side windows contain figures of St. George, St. Lawrence, St. Stephen, &c. The high altar and the tabernacle are carved exquisitely in Caen stone ; and the reredos, also of stone, contains twelve niches filled with saints and angels. The two side chapels are very elaborately carved and ornamented ; and the Petre Chantry is Perpendicular, and not Decorated, in style. The tomb of Mr. Edward Petre is covered with a slab, the legend on which requests the prayers of the faithful for the soul of the founder,

who died in June, 1848. The church is opened from six in the morning till nightfall, and contains a large number of religious confraternities.

The bishop's house, where the clergy of this cathedral live in common, is very plain and simple in its outward appearance, and also in its internal arrangements, being arranged on the ordinary plan of a college. The house of the bishop, it must be owned, is anything but a modern " palace ;" it looks and is a mass of conventual buildings ; and, to use the words of Charles Knight's "Cyclopædia of London," it exhibits more of studied irregularity and quaint homeliness than of pretension as regards design, or even severity of character. " Although these buildings," the writer adds, " are not altogether deficient in character, yet, were not their real purpose known, they might easily pass for an almshouse or a hospital."

At a short distance eastward, covering, with its gardens, a large triangular plot of ground, stands the School for the Indigent Blind. This institution was originally established in 1799, at the " Dog and Duck," in St. George's Fields, and for some time received only fifteen persons as inmates. " The site being required for the building of Bethlehem Hospital," writes John Timbs, in his " Curiosities of London," " about two acres of ground were allotted opposite the Obelisk at the end of Blackfriars Road, and there a plain school-house for the blind was built. In 1826 the school was incorporated ; and in the two following years three legacies of £500 each, and one of £10,000, were bequeathed to the establishment. In 1834 additional ground was purchased and the school-house remodelled, so as to form a portion of a more extensive edifice in the Tudor or domestic Gothic style. designed by Mr. John Newman, F.S.A. The tower and gateway in the north front are very picturesque. The school will accommodate about 220 inmates. The pupils are clothed, lodged, and boarded, and receive a religious and industrial education, so that many of them have been returned to their families able to earn from 6s. to 8s. per week. Applicants are not received under twelve, nor above thirty, years of age, nor if they have a greater degree of sight than will enable them to distinguish light from darkness. The admission is by votes of the subscribers ; and persons between the ages of twelve and eighteen have been found to receive the greatest benefit from the institution." The women and girls are employed in knitting stockings, needlework, and embroidery ; in spinning, and making household and body-linen, netting silk, and in fine basket-making ; besides working hoods for babies, work-bags, purses, slippers, &c.

Many of these are of very tasteful design, in colour as well as in form. The men and boys make wicker baskets, cradles, and hampers; rope door-mats and worsted rugs; brushes of various kinds; and they make all the shoes for the inmates of the school. Reading is mostly taught by Alston's raised or embossed letters, in which the Old and New Testaments and the Liturgy have been printed. Both males and females are remarkably cheerful in their employment; they have great taste and apt-ness for music, and they are instructed in it, not as a mere amusement, but with a view to engagements as organists or teachers of psalmody. In fact, here, and here only in London, a blind choir, led by a blind organist, may be heard performing the compositions of Handel, Mozart, and Mendelssohn with great accuracy and effect. Once a year a concert of sacred music is given in the chapel or music-room, to which the public are admitted by tickets, the proceeds from the sale of such tickets being added to the funds of the institution. An organ and one or two pianofortes are provided for teaching; fiddles in plenty, too, may be seen in the work-rooms on the men's side. The inmates receive, as pocket-money, part of their earnings; and on leaving the school a sum of money and a set of tools for their respective trades are given to each of them.

A touching picture of a visit to the Blind School was given by a writer in the *Echo* newspaper, from which we quote the following. The writer, after describing his visit to the basket-making room, proceeds: "I knelt on the floor to watch one little boy's fingers, as he was making what might be a waste-paper basket; my face was almost against his, but he was utterly unconscious of my presence, so that I could see the little hands as they groped about for materials, and the little fingers as they wove so diligently and so nimbly. Suddenly, whilst I was almost touching him, the boy startled me by saying to himself, aloud, 'That must be a lie about there being a hall in the West which holds eight thousand people and has fifty stops in the organ.' Fifteen of the inmates had been taken to an oratorio the night before, and he had heard them talking of it and of the Albert Hall; now he was talking to himself about it as he wove, quite unconscious that my face was against his. I touched his hand, and the busy weaving stopped, the hands fell on the lap, and the sightless eyes looked round for that light which only can break on them on the morn of the resurrection. . . . The girls' room is singularly light and airy. The light is of no use, but the air is. I was bending down, with my fingers before the eyes of a child of six, whom I could hardly believe to be blind, when I felt a touch upon my head, and, looking back, I saw three blind girls, with their arms entwined, one of whom, feeling in the darkness for the very little girl I was looking at, had touched my hair; they drew back respectfully, and waited until the stranger was gone. Up and down this long girls' work-room, at the hour of recreation, they walk in twos and threes, apparently quite happy, talking inces-santly. When I left that room I thought that there was more real light in it than in most of the ball-rooms I had ever entered."

The number of pupils in the school is about 150, and the articles manufactured entirely by them realise a profit of about £1,000 per annum. The school is maintained at an annual cost of about £10,000, which is covered by the receipts derived from voluntary contributions and from dividends of nearly £3,000.

In the Borough Road, within about two or three minutes' walk of the Blind School, are the head-quarters of the British and Foreign School Society. The British, or, as they were originally called, Lancasterian Schools, had great influence during the first seventy years of the present century in raising the state of education in the country among the poorer classes. Without entering into the dis-puted claims of Dr. Bell and Joseph Lancaster, as to who was the first to originate the peculiar system pursued at these schools, there can be no doubt but that, by the energy of the latter, a practical step of great importance was made towards developing a regular, efficient, and economical plan of teaching. Dr. Bell did much the same kind of work at Madras, but not till Lancaster had already com-menced his labours here. Joseph Lancaster was born in Kent Street, Southwark, on the 27th of November, 1778. When only fourteen years old, he read Clarkson's "Essay on the Slave Trade," and, it is said, was so much moved by its state-ments that he started from home, without the knowledge of his parents, on his way to Jamaica, to teach the "poor blacks" to read the Word of God. While still young, he became a member of the Society of Friends, and soon after this his attention was directed to the educational wants of the poor. The lamentable condition and useless character of the then existing schools for poor children filled his mind with pity and a desire to provide a remedy, and in 1796 he made his first public efforts in education. Before this time, however, he had gathered a number of children together, and his father had provided the school-room rent free. When not yet eighteen, he had nearly ninety children under instruction, many of whom paid no school fee. When only in his twenty-first year, he had nearly a thousand children assembled around him in his new premises in the Borough Road. Mr. Lancaster had not proceeded far in his attempts before he was confronted by a great difficulty. Possessed of small means, and surrounded by pupils with no means at all, he must either relinquish his benevolent work, or discover some method of conducting his school without paid teachers and without books. In this dilemma he hit upon the plan of training the elder and more advanced children to teach and govern the young and less advanced scholars; and he denominated this method of conducting a school the "monitorial system." To overcome the difficulty about books, he caused large sheets to be printed over with the necessary lessons, had them pasted on boards, and hung up on the school walls; round each lesson some ten or twelve children were placed, under the care of a trained monitor. This system quickly attracted considerable notice; and in 1805 Mr. Lancaster had an interview with George III., on which occasion his Majesty uttered the memorable words, "It is my wish that every poor child in my kingdom may be taught to read the Bible." The Duke of Bedford gave Lancaster early and cordial assistance; and the most flattering overtures were made to him in connection with the proposition that he should join the Established Church: all which, as a Dissenter, he respectfully but firmly declined. About this time Lancaster's affairs were so embarrassed, through the rapid extension of his plans of teaching, that in 1808 he placed them in the hands of trustees, and a voluntary society was formed to continue the good work which he had begun. Hence the society which, in 1813, designated itself the "Institution for Promoting the British (or Lancasterian) System for the Education of the Labouring and Manufacturing Classes of Society of every religious persuasion," but now known simply as the "British and Foreign School Society." The work was subsequently taken up and put on a sound foundation by Mr. William Allen, of Plough Court, a man of means, and a Quaker, who became treasurer of the institution, and whose portrait now adorns the committee's board-room. In the meantime, namely, in 1811, the "National Society" had been started by the Church of England, in opposition to Lancaster's "monitorial system."

From the great encouragement given to Lancaster by many persons of the highest rank, he was enabled to travel over the kingdom, for the purpose of delivering lectures, giving instructions, and establishing schools. "Flattered by splendid patronage," says his biographer in the *Gentleman's Magazine*, "and by unrealised promises of support, he was induced to embark in an extensive school establishment at Tooting, to which his own resources proving unequal, he was thrown upon the mercy of cold calculators, who consider unpaid debts as unpardonable crimes. Concessions were, however, made to his merit, which not considering as sufficient, he abandoned his old establishment, and left England in disgust, and, about the year 1820, went to America, where his fame procured him friends and his industry rendered him useful." He died at New York, in October, 1838, in the sixty-ninth year of his age. His memory is now perpetuated in this neighbourhood by Lancaster Street, a name which has within the last few years been bestowed upon Union Street, a thoroughfare crossing the Borough Road in a slanting direction, connecting the southern end of Blackfriars Road with Newington Causeway, and skirting the east side of the school-buildings. Mr. Lancaster for some years had his school-room in this street, almost within a stone's throw of the present noble building in the Borough Road; and as lately as the commencement of the present century, the little children who attended the schools were often unable to reach the school-room, because "the waters were out." There was a large ditch, or rather a small rivulet, which ran northwards down from Newington Butts, and found its way into the Thames near Paris Garden.

The institution in the Borough Road may be looked upon in a threefold aspect. First, it is the Society's seat of government; secondly, here are held the model schools, wherein are taught 350 boys, and in which the Society desires to have at all times examples at hand for imitation by the branch schools, and into which, accordingly, improved methods of tuition are from time to time introduced. Thirdly, there are here some normal seminaries for the instruction of future masters, who, whilst teaching in the model class-schools, are students themselves in the art of tuition, the most practically important branch of their studies. Of the female training college in connection with the British and Foreign School Society we have spoken in our account of Stockwell.*

These schools, though they profess to stand on a Nonconformist basis, are so liberal and unsectarian in their teaching that they number among their patrons many lay members of the Established Church, and even two of its dignitaries, Dr. Temple, the Bishop of Exeter, and Dr. Stanley, the Dean

---

* See *ante*, p. 329.

CHRIST CHURCH, WESTMINSTER ROAD.

of Westminster. The scholars and teachers attending the schools may be put down as comprising about thirty per cent. of Episcopalians, twenty per cent. of the Baptist, and thirty per cent. of the Congregationalist denomination.

The "pupil-teacher system" may be said to have grown out of the monitorial plan of Bell and Lancaster. It was originated about 1844, but has gradually come to be adopted in nearly all the British schools, which really, from an educational point of view, are identical in plan with the National, Wesleyan, and other schools in connection with the Education Department.

The building now under notice, which stands on the south side of the Borough Road, is a large and lofty but plain edifice of four storeys, consisting of a centre and wings, the latter, however, extending backwards, and partly connected with each other by buildings in the rear of the central front. It is faced with red brick, and finished off with stone dressings in the shape of cornices, &c. The edifice was commenced about the year 1840, and first occupied in 1844. The Female Training School, which at first formed part of it, was removed in 1861, as already stated, to more spacious premises at Stockwell; and in these two institutions the chief work of the British and Foreign School Society has since been carried on.

CHAPTER XXVIII.

BLACKFRIARS ROAD.—THE SURREY THEATRE, SURREY CHAPEL, &c.

Formation of Blackfriars Road—The Surrey Theatre, originally the "Royal Circus and Equestrian Philharmonic Academy"—The Circus burnt down in 1805—The Amphitheatre rebuilt, and under the Management of Elliston—The Manager in a Fix—The Theatre burnt down in 1865, and rebuilt the same year—Lord Camelford and a Drunken Naval Lieutenant—The "Equestrian" Tavern—A Favourite Locality for Actors—An Incident in Charles Dickens' Boyhood—The Temperance Hall—The South London Working Men's College—The South London Tramway Company—The Mission College of St. Alphege—Nelson Square—The "Dog's Head in the Pot"—Surrey Chapel—The Rev. Rowland Hill—Almshouses founded by him—Paris Garden—Christ Church—Stamford Street—The Unitarian Chapel—Messrs. Clowes' Printing Office—Hospital for Diseases of the Skin—The "Haunted Houses" of Stamford Street—Ashton Lever's Museum—The Rotunda—The Albion Mills.

THIS great thoroughfare—which, starting at Blackfriars Bridge, meets at the Obelisk five other roads in St. George's Circus—assumed something like its present shape and appearance in the last half of the last century. It seems at one time to have been called St. George's Road, but was long known as Great Surrey Street. The road is perfectly straight, and is about two-thirds of a mile in length. Pennant, as we have already remarked, describes the roads crossing St. George's Fields as being "the wonder of foreigners approaching by this road to our capital, through avenues of lamps, of magnificent breadth and goodness." One foreign ambassador, indeed, thought London was illuminated in honour of his arrival; but, adds Pennant, "this was written before the shameful adulteration of the oil," which dimmed the "glorious splendour!" Pennant, doubtless, was a knowing man; but he lived before the age of gas, and was easily satisfied.

One of the earliest buildings of any note which were erected in this road was Christ Church, near the bridge on the west side, occupying part of the site of old Paris Garden; then came Rowland Hill's Chapel, or, as it is now generally called, "Surrey Chapel," of both of which we shall speak more fully presently. Next came the Magdalen Hospital, which we have already described; and finally, the Surrey Theatre. The early history of this theatre, if Mr. E. L. Blanchard states correctly the facts in his sketch of it, the "Playgoer's Portfolio," affords an illustration of the difficulties under which the minor theatres laboured in their struggle against the patented monopoly of Drury Lane and Covent Garden. The place was first opened under the title of the "Royal Circus and Equestrian Philharmonic Academy," in the year 1782, by the famous composer and song-writer, Charles Dibdin, aided by Charles Hughes, a clever equestrian performer. It was originally planned for the display of equestrian and dramatic entertainments, on a plan similar to that pursued with so much success at Astley's. The entertainments were at first performed by children, the design being to render the circus a nursery for actors. The play-bills of the first few months' performances end with a notice to the effect that a "Horse-patrol is provided from Bridge to Bridge." The theatre, however, having been opened without a licence, was closed by order of the Surrey magistrates, but this was not done without a disturbance, and until the Riot Act had been read on the very stage itself. In the following year a licence was obtained, and the theatre being re-opened, a successful harvest appeared now in prospect, when differences arose among the proprietors which seriously threatened its ruin. Delphini, a celebrated buffo, was appointed manager in 1788, in succession to Grimaldi, the grandfather of the celebrated clown of Covent Garden and Sadler's Wells Theatres; he produced a splendid spectacle, with a real stag-hunt, &c. Then there were several "dog-pieces," so called because they were put together in order to introduce upon the stage as actors two knowing dogs, "Gelert" and "Victor," whose popularity was such that they had an hour every day set apart for them to receive visitors. Afterwards a series of "Lectures on Heads" were given here by a Mr. Stevens,* and many pantomimic and local pieces were performed with indifferent success; among the latter were the "Destruction of the Bastile," "Death of General Wolfe," &c. The popularity of the theatre was largely increased by the skill of a new stage manager, John Palmer, a gay-hearted comedian, who rather enjoyed than otherwise a life "within the Rules of the King's Bench;" but this gleam of sunshine came to an end, in 1789, by the arbitrary and (it would seem) illegal committal of Palmer to the Surrey Gaol as a "rogue and a vagabond," a clause being, at the same time, inserted in the Debtor's Act making all such places of amusement "out of the Rules."

Having been conducted for several years by a Mr. James Jones and his son-in-law, John Cross, as lessees, with average success, the Circus was destroyed by fire in August, 1805; it was, however, rebuilt and re-opened at Easter, 1806. In 1809 the lesseeship was taken in hand by Elliston, who introduced several of Shakespeare's plays, and otherwise endeavoured to raise the character of the house. His success was such that he now resolved to attempt an enlargement of the privileges of his licence, a step which is thus recorded by Mr. E. L. Blanchard: "Hitherto the performances authorised did not permit the introduction of a dialogue, except it was accompanied by music throughout. On the 5th of March, 1810, Sir Thomas Turton presented to the House of Commons a petition for enabling Mr. Elliston and his colleagues to exhibit 'all such entertainments of music and action as are commonly called pantomimes and ballets, together with operatic or musical pieces, accompanied with dialogue.' The petition, however, was rejected, on the ground that it would 'go far to alter the whole principle upon which theatrical entertainments are at present regulated within the metropolis and twenty miles round.' The expenses of this fruitless appeal were £100 for the petition,

and £30 more for a second application to the Privy Council."

The amphitheatre, which had previously been the arena for occasional equestrian exercises, was now converted into a commodious pit for the spectators, and the stables into saloons. Melo-dramas now became the order of the day; and here Miss Sally Brook made her first appearance in London. All sorts of varieties followed. One piece was brought out specially to exhibit two magnificent suits of armour of the fourteenth century, which afterwards appeared in the Lord Mayor's show.†

Tom Dibdin, in 1816, having offered his services as stage-manager under Elliston, the Circus was extensively altered and re-opened as "The Surrey," and he held sway here till 1822. After that time the theatre had a somewhat chequered existence, and on the whole may be said to have been one of the chief homes of the English sensational melo-drama. At one time the gig in which Thurtell drove, and the table on which he supped, when he murdered Mr. Weare, were exhibited; and at another, the chief attraction was a man-ape, Mons. Gouffle. In 1827 Elliston became lessee a second time, and made several good hits, being seconded by such actors as T. P. Cooke, Mrs. Fitzwilliam, &c.

It was perhaps during the lesseeship of Elliston that the greatest "hit" was made at "The Surrey." "Elliston," as a writer in the *Monthly Magazine* tells us, "was, in his day, the Napoleon of Drury Lane, but, like the conqueror of Austerlitz, he suffered his declensions, and the Surrey became to him a St. Helena. However, once an eagle always an eagle; and Robert William was no less aquiline in the day of adversity than in his palmy time of patent prosperity. He was born to carry things with a high hand, and he but fulfilled his destiny. The anecdote we are about to relate is one of the ten thousand instances of his lordly bearing. When, on one occasion, 'no effects' was written over the treasury-door of Covent Garden Theatre, it will be remembered that several actors proffered their services *gratis*, in aid of the then humble but now arrogant and persecuting establishment; among these patriots was Mr. T. P. Cooke. The Covent Garden managers jumped at the offer of the actor, who was in due time announced as having, in the true play-bill style, 'most generously volunteered his services for six nights!' Cooke was advertised for 'William,' Elliston having 'most generously lent [N.B., this was *not* put in the bill] the musical score of *Black-Eyed Susan*, together with the identical captains' coats worn at a hundred and fifty court-

---

* See Vol. II., p. 539.

† See Vol. I., p. 329.

martials at the Surrey Theatre. Cooke—the score —the coats, were all accepted, and made the most of by the now prosecuting managers of Covent Garden, who cleared out of the said Cooke, score, and coats one thousand pounds at half-price on the first six nights of their exhibition. This is a fact; nay, we have lately heard it stated that all the sum was specially banked, to be used in a future war against the minors. Cooke was then engaged for twelve more nights, at ten pounds per night—a hackney-coach bringing him each night, hot from the Surrey stage, where he had previously made bargemen weep and thrown nursery-maids into convulsions. Well, time drove on, and Cooke drove into the country. Elliston, who was always classical, having a due veneration for that divine 'creature,' Shakespeare, announced, on the anniversary of the poet's birthday, a representation of the Stratford Jubilee. The wardrobe was ransacked, the property-man was on the alert, and, after much preparation, everything was in readiness for the imposing spectacle. No! There was one thing forgotten— one important 'property!' 'Bottom' must be a 'feature' in the procession; and there was no ass's head! It would not do for the acting manager to apologise for the absence of the head—no, _he_ could not have the face to do it. A head must be procured. Every one was in doubt and trepidation, when hope sounded in the clarion-like voice of Robert William. 'Ben!' exclaimed Elliston, 'take pen, ink, and paper, and write as follows.' Ben (Mr. Benjamin Fairbrother, the late manager's most trusted secretary) sat 'all ear,' and Elliston, with finger on nether lip, proceeded—'MY DEAR CHARLES,—I am about to represent, "with entirely new dresses, scenery, and decorations," the Stratford Jubilee, in honour of the sweet swan of Avon. My scene-painter is the finest artist (except your Grieve) in Europe; my tailor is no less a genius; and I lately raised the salary of my property-man. This will give you some idea of the capabilities of the Surrey Theatre. However, in the hurry of "getting up" we have forgotten one property— everything is well with us but our "Bottom," and he wants a head. As it is too late to manufacture— not but that my property-man is the cleverest in the world (except the property-man of Covent Garden) —can _you_ lend me an ass's head; and believe me, my dear Charles, yours ever truly, ROBERT WILLIAM ELLISTON. P.S.—I had forgotten to acknowledge the return of the _Black-Eyed Susan_ score and coats. You were most welcome to them.'

"The letter was dispatched to Covent Garden Theatre, and in a brief time the bearer returned with the following answer:—'MY DEAR ROBERT,—

It is with the most acute pain that I am compelled to refuse your trifling request. You are aware, my dear sir, of the unfortunate situation of Covent Garden Theatre; it being at the present moment, with all the "dresses, scenery, and decorations," in the Court of Chancery, I cannot exercise that power which my friendship would dictate. I have spoken to Bartley, and he agrees with me (indeed, he always does) that I cannot lend you an ass's head—he is an authority on such a subject—without risking a reprimand from the Lord High Chancellor. Trusting to your generosity and to your liberal construction of my refusal, and hoping that it will in no way interrupt that mutually cordial friendship that has ever subsisted between us, believe me, ever yours, CHARLES KEMBLE. P.S.—When I next see you advertised for "Rover," I intend to leave myself out of the bill, and come and see it.'

"Of course this letter did not remain long unanswered. Ben was again in requisition, and the following was the result of his labours:—

"'DEAR CHARLES,—I regret the situation of Covent Garden Theatre; I also, for your sake, deeply regret that the law does not permit you to send me the "property" in question. I knew that law alone could prevent you; for were it not for the vigilance of equity, such is my opinion of the management of Covent Garden, that I am convinced, if left to the dictates of its own judgment, it would be enabled to spare asses' heads, not to the Surrey alone, but to every theatre in Christendom. Yours ever truly, ROBERT WILLIAM ELLISTON. P.S.—My wardrobe-keeper informs me that there are no less than seven buttons missing from the captains' coats. However, I have ordered their places to be instantaneously filled by others.'

"We entreat our readers not to receive the above as a squib of invention. We will not pledge ourselves that the letters are _verbatim_ from the originals; but the loan of the Surrey music and coats to Covent Garden, with the refusal of Covent Garden's ass's head to the Surrey, is 'true as holy writ.'"

At the time when Elliston was lessee of the Surrey and the Olympic Theatres, about 1833, the actors, who were common to both houses, had to hurry from St. George's Fields over Blackfriars Bridge to Wych Street, and occasionally back again also, the same evening. Sometimes the "legitimate drama" was performed here in a curious fashion. The law allowed only musical performances at the minor theatres: so a pianoforte tinkled, or a clarionet moaned, a dismal accompaniment to the speeches of _Macbeth_ or _Othello_. The fact is that, as Dr. Doran tells us in the epilogue to "His Majesty's

Servants, "the powers of the licenser (the Lord Chamberlain) did not extend to St. George's Fields, where political plays, forbidden on the Middlesex side of the river, were attractive merely because they were forbidden." Considerable excellence has generally been shown in the scenery at this theatre, which appeals through the eye to the "sensations" of the lower classes; and M. Esquiros, in his "English at Home," tells us that Danby, as scene-painter, produced at the Surrey some of the chastest effects ever witnessed on an English stage.

After the death of Elliston, the lesseeship was held in succession by Davidge, Osbaldiston, Creswick, and other individuals of dramatic note; but it never rose far above mediocrity. The fabric was burnt down a second time in January, 1865, but rebuilt and re-opened in the course of the same year, great additions and improvements having been made in its interior arrangements.

The change in the name of this theatre, after it ceased to be used for equestrian performances, is thus mentioned in the "Rejected Addresses:"—

" And burnt the Royal Circus in a hurry:
'Twas called the Circus then, but now the Surrey."

James Smith, in a note in the "Rejected Addresses," writes:—" The authors happened to be at the Royal Circus when 'God save the King' was called for, accompanied by a cry of 'Stand up!' and 'Hats off!' An inebriated naval lieutenant perceiving a gentleman in an adjoining box slow to obey the call, struck his hat off with his stick, exclaiming, 'Take off your hat, sir.' The other thus assailed proved to be, unluckily for the lieutenant, Lord Camelford, the celebrated bruiser and duellist. A set-to in the lobby was the consequence, where his lordship quickly proved victorious."

The exterior of the old theatre was plain but neat, and the approaches very convenient. The auditorium, which was nearly square in form, was exceedingly spacious. The upper part of the proscenium was supported by two gilt, fluted composite columns on each side, with intervening stage-doors and boxes. The pit would seat about 900 persons. The general ornamentation of the boxes, &c., was white and gold. The gallery, as customary in the minor theatres, was remarkably spacious, and would hold above 1,000 persons. It descended to a level with the side boxes in the centre, but from its principal elevation it was continued along both sides over them. The ceiling sprang from the four extremities of the front and of the side galleries. The centre was painted in imitation of a sky, with genii on the verge and in the angles.

A handsome chandelier depended from the centre, besides smaller ones suspended from brackets over the stage-doors, which were continued round the boxes.

The present theatre, which, as we have stated above, was built in 1865, is a great improvement upon the old building in every respect. It is considerably larger, and its construction cost £38,000; the machinery, with the new appliances insisted on by the Lord Chamberlain for the security of life from fire, cost nearly £2,000. Like most of the minor theatres in London, the Surrey has of late years been occasionally used on Sundays for religious "revival" services, thereby reconciling to some extent the old enmities between the pulpit and the stage.

The fact of the Surrey Theatre having been at one time used for the exhibition of feats of horsemanship is kept in remembrance by the sign of a tavern which adjoins it, called "The Equestrian."

The actors of the transpontine theatres of half a century ago very naturally had their habitations almost invariably on the south side of the Thames. Elliston himself lived in Great Surrey Street (now Blackfriars Road); Osbaldiston in Gray's Walk, Lambeth; Davidge, of the Coburg, afterwards manager of the Surrey, lived in Charlotte Terrace, near the New Cut. St. George's Circus, at the south end of Blackfriars Road, was so thickly peopled by second-rate actors belonging to the Surrey and the Coburg, that it was called the Theatrical Barracks. Hercules Buildings, in the Westminster Bridge Road, had then, and for twenty years afterwards, a theatrical or musical family residing in every house. Stangate, at the back of "Astley's," was another favourite resort for the sons and daughters of Thespis; and the cul de sac of Mount's Place, Lambeth, where Ellar, the famous harlequin, lived and died, was also in great repute as a residence for the pantomimic and equestrian fraternity.

A house "somewhere beyond the obelisk," but not capable of identification now, was the scene of a trifling event in the early life of Charles Dickens, which he records with some minuteness in the autobiographical reminiscences preserved by Mr. J. Forster in his published "Life!" When his father had to pass through the insolvent Court of the Marshalsea, it was necessary to prove that the apparel and personal matters retained were not above £20 in value. Charles, we suppose, must have been regarded by the law as part and parcel of his father, for he had to appear before an official at this house in his best holiday clothes. "I recollect his coming out to view me with his mouth full and a strong smell of beer upon him,

THE SURREY THEATRE.

1. The Old Theatre, 1865.   2. Interior of New Theatre, 1865.   3. Ruins of the Old Theatre. 1865.

and saying, good-naturedly, 'That will do,' and 'All right.'" He adds : "Certainly the hardest creditor would not have been disposed (even if legally entitled) to avail himself of my poor white hat, my little jacket, and my corduroy trousers. But I had in my pocket an old silver watch, given me by my grandmother before the blacking days, and I had entertained my doubts, as I went along, whether that valuable possession might not bring

means of a thorough education. Professor Huxley has long acted as principal of the college. Among the work carried on here are technical classes for carpenters and bricklayers, elementary classes in chemistry and in mathematics, and a Civil Service class.

A few doors further northward are the offices of the South London Tramway Company, which was founded in 1870, in order to supply cheap and

ROWLAND HILL'S CHAPEL IN 1814.

me above the twenty pounds' standard. So I was greatly relieved, and made him a low bow of acknowledgment as I went out."

Between the Surrey Theatre and the Peabody Buildings, which, as we have already stated, stand on the site formerly occupied by the Magdalen Hospital, is the Temperance Hall, a neat brick-built Gothic structure, one of several others erected by the London Temperance Halls' Company. It was built in 1875, and is used for concerts, lectures, temperance meetings, and so forth.

Further northwards, between Webber Street and Great Charlotte Street, is a house, No. 91, used as the Working Men's College. It was opened in 1868, for the purpose of giving to the working men of South London, and their families, the

rapid communication by street cars, on the American principle. The company have laid down no less than $20\frac{1}{2}$ miles of street-rails along the high roads connecting Vauxhall, Westminster, Blackfriars, and London Bridges with Greenwich, Deptford, Camberwell, Brixton, Kennington, and Clapham. The cars constantly in use are about 100, employing over 1,000 horses, and between 300 and 400 men. They carry in a year about 16,000,000 passengers.

Nearly opposite the above-mentioned offices is the modern Mission College of St. Alphege, named after the saint with whose murder by the Danes the reader has been already made acquainted in our account of Greenwich.*

* See ante, p. 164.

Nelson Square, close by, on the east side of Blackfriars Road, was doubtless built at the commencement of the century, when the great naval hero was in the height of his glory, and named in honour of him. Beyond a tavern, bearing the sign of the "Lord Nelson," the square is merely occupied by small tradesmen and as lodging-houses, and therefore is one of those fortunate places which has little or no history attached to it.

The "Dog's Head in the Pot" is mentioned as an old London sign in a curious tract, printed by Wynkyn de Worde, called "Cocke Lorelle's Bote." A sign of this description is still to be seen in the Blackfriars Road, over the door of a furnishing ironmonger's shop, at the corner of Little Charlotte Street, close by Nelson Square.

The building formerly known as Surrey Chapel, which stands on the east of the road, at the corner of Charlotte Street, about 500 yards from Blackfriars Bridge, is an ugly octagonal structure with no pretensions to any definite style of architecture. It was often called "Rowland Hill's Chapel," after its former minister, the Rev. Rowland Hill, who, though the son of a Shropshire baronet and a deacon of the Established Church, became a Dissenter from conviction, and was for half a century the able and eloquent minister of a congregation of Calvinistic Methodists who worshipped here. He was eloquent, witty, and warm-hearted, and was for many years a power in the religious world, being on the best of terms with the more "Evangelical" portion of the national clergy. His wit was almost as ready as that of Douglas Jerrold or Theodore Hook. Once when preaching near the docks at Wapping, he said, "I am come to preach to great, to notorious, yes, to Wapping sinners!" Another day, observing a number of persons coming into his chapel, not so much to hear his sermon as to escape the rain, he declared that though he had known of persons making religion a *cloak*, he had never heard of it being made an *umbrella* before! His congregation were much attached to him personally, and always subscribed liberally in answer to his appeals to their purses; and he, therefore, compared them to a good cow, which gives the more the more that she is milked! His wife was too fond of dress for a minister's wife; and it is said that within these walls he would often preach at her by name, saying, "Here comes my wife, with a whole wardrobe on her head and back;" but this story is apocryphal. At all events, he always denied its truth, declaring that though he was always outspoken in denouncing vanity and frivolity, he was not a bear, but a Christian and a gentleman!

In his youth Rowland was noted for that redundant flow of spirits which never failed him even to his latest years. He was, likewise, even in his younger days, celebrated for wit and humour, an instance of which occurred at Eton, on the occasion of a discussion among the scholars as to the power of the letter H. Some contended that it had the full power of a letter, while others thought it a mere aspirate, and that it might be omitted altogether without any disadvantage to our language. Rowland earnestly contended for its continuance, adding, "To me the letter H is a most invaluable one, for if it be taken away, I shall be *ill* all the days of my life." With the intention of qualifying himself for one of the livings in the gift of his family, he entered St. John's College, Cambridge, where, from his serious behaviour and somewhat unusual zeal in visiting the sick and engaging in out-door preaching, he became the subject of much obloquy. When the time came for taking orders, he found that his former "irregular" conduct proved an insuperable difficulty. His brother Richard was the only member of his family who approved of his eccentric conduct at this period. For several years after leaving college he had been extensively occupied in out-door preaching, both in the country and in the metropolis. The Church of England pulpits were, of course, not then open to him; but among the Dissenters no such obstacle existed. It was at one time generally believed that he would be the successor of Whitefield at Tottenham Court Road Chapel. During four years he experienced six refusals from several prelates; but in 1773 the Bishop of Bath and Wells consented to admit him to deacon's orders. His first curacy was Kingston, near Taunton. The Bishop of Carlisle had promised to ordain him a priest, but was commanded by the Archbishop of York not to admit him to a higher grade in the Church, on account of his irregularity. This refusal caused Rowland to remark that he "ran off with only one ecclesiastical boot on." After leaving his curacy, he returned to his former course of field-preaching, and during the next ten years he visited various parts of England, Wales, and Ireland, London not excepted. "As we are commanded," he once remarked, "to preach the Gospel to every creature, even to the ends of the world, I always conceived that in preaching through England, Scotland, Ireland, and Wales, *I stuck close to my parish*." In later life nothing gave him greater pleasure than the occasional offer of a Church of England pulpit, for to the close of his life, although fraternising extensively with the Dissenters, he considered himself a clergyman of the Established

Church. The time at length came when his somewhat erratic career was to end in a more settled ministry in the metropolis, and where his former popularity would be still further extended.

Being in London during the riots of 1780, Rowland Hill took advantage of the opportunity afforded him of addressing the large multitudes then assembled in St. George's Fields, sometimes preaching to as many as 20,000 persons. Up to this period of his life, he had exercised his ministry irregularly, preaching in Church of England pulpits when practicable, but more frequently in Dissenting chapels or in the open air. He had, it is said, for some time felt the desirability of a settled ministry, and his wish was soon afterwards carried into effect by some liberal-minded persons coming forward with subscriptions towards the erection of a large chapel in the south of London. The spot selected was in the new road then recently opened from Blackfriars Bridge to the Obelisk. Among the contributors to the proposed chapel were Lord George Gordon, who gave a donation of £50, Lady Huntingdon, and others. The first stone was laid early in 1782, and the building, which cost about £5,000, was opened in June, 1783. From that time till his death, in 1833, Mr. Hill was the minister of the chapel, residing in the adjoining parsonage-house for the long period of fifty years.

When first erected, the chapel stood almost among fields, but in the course of a few years the locality on every side became thickly populated. With regard to the shape of the chapel, Mr. Hill is stated to have once remarked that he liked a round building, for it prevented the devil hiding in any of the corners. Its close proximity to the public road, and the excellence of the singing, for which it was long celebrated, induced many passers-by to enter the chapel. Many wealthy persons were regular attendants; and among the occasional visitors were Dean Milner, William Wilberforce, Ambrose Serle, and the Duke of Kent. Sheridan once said, "I go to hear Rowland Hill, because his ideas come red-hot from the heart." Dean Milner once told him, "Mr. Hill, Mr. Hill! I felt to-day—'tis this slap-dash preaching, say what they will, that does all the good;" and the Duke of Kent, in Mr. Hill's parlour, mentioned how much he was struck by the service, especially the singing.

Sir Richard Hill, the brother of Rowland, was one of the first trustees, and a frequent attendant. Although in every particular it was essentially a Dissenting chapel, the liturgical service of the Church of England was regularly used, while the most celebrated preachers of all denominations have occupied the pulpit. For the first few years

after the erection of the chapel, Mr. Hill availed himself of the occasional services of clergymen of the Establishment, among whom were the Revs. John Venn and Thomas Scott, and also some eminent Dissenting ministers. But, in 1803, the publication of a satirical pamphlet directed against the Established clergy, entitled "Spiritual Characteristics," having special reference to an Act then recently passed in Parliament, with the object of enforcing the residence of some of the beneficed clergy, and generally believed to have been written by Mr. Hill, resulted in the withdrawal of the services of his clerical friends. It was his usual custom to spend the summer of each year in itinerant preaching in various parts of England and Wales, and during these absences from London his pulpit was regularly supplied by eminent Dissenting ministers. He found time to visit Scotland more than once. The popularity of several of his substitutes was so great that the spacious chapel, which had sittings for about 2,000 persons, was sometimes more crowded than when Rowland Hill was the officiating minister. Very large sums have been annually raised for the various charitable institutions and religious societies connected with Surrey Chapel. The organ, which in its day was considered a powerful instrument, was for many years played by Mr. Jacobs, whose musical ear was so fine that he was selected by Haydn to tune his pianoforte. The singing at Surrey Chapel was long a special feature; and Mr. Hill is said to have once remarked that he "did not see why the devil should have all the good tunes," for in his lifetime and some years afterwards it was a common occurrence to hear certain hymns, composed by Rowland Hill, sung to the tunes of "Rule, Britannia," or the "National Anthem."

The poet Southey, who paid a visit to Surrey Chapel in 1823, when Rowland Hill was in his seventy-ninth year, gives in one of his letters the following particulars:—

"Rowland Hill's pulpit is raised very high; and before it, at about half the height, is the reader's desk on his right, and the clerk's on his left—the clerk being a very grand personage, with a sonorous voice. The singing was so general and so good, that I joined in it. During the singing, after Rowland had made his prayer before the sermon, we were beckoned from our humble places by a gentleman in one of the pews. He was very civil; and by finding out the hymns for me, and presenting me with the book, enabled me to sing, which I did to admiration. Rowland, a fine, tall old man, with strong features, very like his portrait, began by reading three verses for his text, stooping to the book in a very peculiar manner. Having done this, he stood up erect, and said, 'Why, the text is a sermon, and a very weighty one too.' I could not always follow his delivery, the loss of his teeth rendering his words sometimes indistinct, and the more so because his pronunciation is peculiar, generally giving *e* the sound of *ai*, like the French. His manner was animated and striking, sometimes impressive and dignified, always remarkable ; and so powerful a voice I have rarely or ever heard. Sometimes he took off his spectacles, frequently stooped down to read a text, and on these occasions he seemed to double his body, so high did he stand. He told one or two familiar stories, and used some odd expressions, such as, 'A murrain on those who preach that when we are sanctified we do not grow in grace !' And again, 'I had almost said I had rather see the devil in the pulpit than an Antinomian !' The purport of his sermon was good ; nothing fanatical, nothing enthusiastic ; and the Calvinism it expressed was so qualified as to be harmless. The manner, that of a performer, as great in his line as Kean or Kemble : and the manner it is which has attracted so large a congregation about him, all of the better order of persons in business."

Mr. Hill sometimes caused his chapel to take a prominent part on public occasions, even in politics. For instance, when the peace of Amiens took place in 1802, he exhibited in front of his chapel an appropriate transparency, with the quaint motto, "May the new-born peace be as old as Methuselah !" When, a few months later, the peace was at an end, and the invasion of this country was threatened by Napoleon, volunteer companies were raised in every district. Mr. Hill at once invited the volunteers in and around the metropolis to come to his chapel to hear a sermon, on the afternoon of the 3rd of December, 1803, on which occasion the building was thronged in every part. Of this service he afterwards remarked, speaking of the volunteers, " I acknowledge that your very respectable appearance, your becoming deportment while in the house of God, and especially the truly serious and animated manner in which you all stood up to sing the high praises of our God, filled me with solemn surprise, and exhibited before me one of the most affecting scenes I ever beheld." Mr. Hill composed a hymn specially for the occasion, which was sung to the tune of the " National Anthem ; " and another commencing thus—

" When Jesus first, at Heaven's command,
　Descended from his azure throne,"

which was sung to the air of " Rule, Britannia." After the battle of Waterloo, in which five of his

nephews were engaged, a neat transparency, which attracted some attention, was placed in front of the chapel. At the head of it two hands held, on a scroll, the words, " The tyrant is fallen !" Under this came a quotation from Obadiah 3, 4 ; to which was added, " Be wise now, therefore, O ye kings ; be instructed, ye judges of the earth." The subject of the painting was the sun setting on the sea, exhibiting on the shore, to the left, a lion crouching at the foot of a fortress near the trophies of war ; and to the right, a lamb lying by the implements of agriculture, with a village church and a cottage before it.

Rowland Hill's labours as a philanthropist are not so generally known as his fame as a preacher. During one of his summer visits to Wotton-under-Edge, Gloucestershire, where he had erected a small chapel, he became acquainted with Dr. Jenner, who lived in the vicinity of that village. He soon saw the advantages resulting from vaccination, and henceforward very earnestly recommended the practice of inoculation, publishing, in 1806, a pamphlet on the subject, in which he defended the new proposal from the aspersions of some of its opponents. " This," said he, " is the very thing for me ; " and wherever he went to preach on his country excursions, he frequently announced after his sermon, " I am ready to vaccinate to-morrow morning as many children as you choose ; and if you wish them to escape that horrid disease, the small-pox, you will bring them." One of the most effective vaccine boards in London was established at Surrey Chapel. At different places he instructed suitable persons in the use of the lancet for this purpose. It has been stated that in a few years the numbers inoculated by him amounted to more than 10,000. It may be further added that the first Sunday School in London was established in Mr. Hill's chapel.*

His untiring exertions on behalf of religious liberty ought not to be forgotten. In the earlier part of the present century a most determined effort was made to subject Dissenting chapels to parochial assessments, or the payment of poor's rates, and the experiment was first tried with Surrey Chapel, on account of its nondescript character. Mr. Hill resisted the attempt, because he regarded it as an invasion of the Toleration Act, which George III., in his first speech from the throne, had pledged himself to maintain inviolable. Mr. Hill and his friends were summoned to attend at the Guildford sessions, and although they gained a temporary success, they were compelled to appear on five

* See *ante*, p. 71.

subsequent occasions, on each of which the parochial authorities were unsuccessful. The subject was then taken up by the Dissenters generally, Mr. Hill meanwhile publishing a pamphlet on the subject, which soon passed through three editions. His exertions were at last crowned with success by the passing of the Religious Worship Act, which repealed certain Acts relating to religious worship and assemblies, and henceforward set the question for ever at rest. During these inquiries concerning the taxation of Surrey Chapel, it was elicited in evidence that instead of the revenues of the chapel going to Rowland Hill, as was by some persons believed, it turned out that the chapel was vested in the hands of trustees, and after the payment of all expenses incident to public worship, only a small surplus remained. Some person once said of him, " Rowland Hill must get a good annual sum by his chapels and his travelling ;" and on this coming to his ears, he remarked, " Well, let any one pay my travelling expenses for one year, and he shall have all my gains, I promise him." He did not relax his labours even in old age, for in one week, when past seventy-one, he travelled a hundred miles in a mountainous part of Wales, and preached twenty-one sermons. During his long ministry of sixty-six years he preached at least 23,000 sermons, many of which were delivered in the open air, being an average of 350 every year.

In the " Picture of London" for 1802 the name of Mr. Rowland Hill is placed at the head of the popular preachers among the " Calvinistic Methodists." He is described as " remarkable for a very vehement kind of eloquence, and on all subjects having the gift of a ready utterance ; he is followed," adds the writer, " by the most crowded audiences, chiefly composed of the lower classes of society. . . . . Many of the most popular preachers among the Methodists are ordained ministers of the Established Church, and have no objection to administer the ordinances of religion either in the church, the chapel, the meeting-house, or the open air." As a preacher, he long held a position in the religious world which has never been paralleled, except, perhaps, by Robert Hall. Even Bishop Blomfield declared that Mr. Hill was the best preacher that he had ever heard. On one occasion Bishop Maltby accompanied Dr. Blomfield to the Surrey Chapel. The two bishops were great Greek scholars, and as the preacher floundered in some allusion to the original Greek of his text, the two prelates sat and winked at each other, enjoying the fun.

Mr. J. T. Smith, in his " Book for a Rainy Day," tells an amusing anecdote concerning Rowland Hill, which we may be pardoned for quoting. Mr. Smith narrates how that one Sunday morning, in his younger days, he was passing Surrey Chapel on his way to Camberwell, when the " swelling pipes " of the organ had such an attraction that he was induced to go inside. He then proceeds :—" No sooner was the sermon over and the blessing bestowed, than Rowland electrified his hearers by vociferating, ' Door-keepers, shut the doors !' Slam went one door ; bounce went another ; bang went a third ; at last, all being anxiously silent as the most importantly unexpected scenes of Sir Walter Scott could make them, the pastor, with a slow and dulcet emphasis, thus addressed his congregation :—' My dearly beloved, I speak it to my shame, that this sermon was to have been a charity sermon, and if you will only look down into the green pew at those—let me see—three and three are six, and one makes seven, young men with red morocco prayer-books in their hands, poor souls ! they were backsliders, for they went on the Serpentine River, and other far distant waters, on a Sabbath ; they were, however, as you see, all saved from a watery grave. I need not tell ye that my exertions were to have been for the benefit of that benevolent institution, the Humane Society. What ! I see some of ye already up to be gone ; fie ! fie ! fie !—never heed your dinners ; don't be Calibans, nor mind your pockets. I know that some of ye are now attending to the devil's whispers. I say, listen to me ! take my advice, give shillings instead of sixpences ; and those who intended to give shillings, display half-crowns, in order not only to thwart the foul fiend's mischievousness, but to get your pastor out of this scrape ; and if you do, I trust Satan will never put his foot within this circle again. Hark ye ! I have hit upon it ; ye shall leave us directly. The Bank Directors, you must know, have called in the dollars ; now, if any of you happen to be encumbered with a stale dollar or two, jingle the Spanish in our dishes ; we'll take them, they'll pass current here. Stay, my friends, a moment more. I am to dine with the Humane Society on Tuesday next, and it would shock me beyond expression to see the strings of the Surrey Chapel bag dangle down its sides like the tags upon Lady Huntingdon's servants' shoulders. Now, mind what I say, upon this occasion I wish for a bumper as strenuously as Master Hugh Peters did when he recommended his congregation in Broadway Chapel to take a second glass.' " Mr. Smith adds, as a foot-note, that it is recorded of Hugh Peters, a celebrated preacher during the usurpation of Oliver Cromwell, that when he found the sand of his hour-glass had descended, he turned it, saying, "Come, I know you to be jolly dogs, we'll take t'other glass."

Mr. Sidney, one of Rowland Hill's biographers, relates an amusing instance of his ready wit. It seems he was accustomed, when in the desk, to read any request for prayer that might be sent in. One day he thus commenced—"'The prayers of this congregation are desired for'—well, I suppose

Rowland Hill :—As he was entering Surrey Chapel, one Sunday morning, Mr. Hill passed two lads, one of whom said to his companion, "Let's go and hear Rowland Hill, and have some fun." The old gentleman went inside the porch, just before the boys, and gave directions to the verger to put them in a certain pew, in front of the pulpit, and fasten the door. This was done. After the prayers were finished, Mr. Hill rose and gave out his text

Rowd Hill

I must finish what I have begun—'the Rev. Rowland Hill, that he will not go riding about in his carriage on Sundays.'" Not in the least disconcerted, Mr. Hill looked up, and gravely said, "If the writer of this piece of folly and impertinence is in the congregation, and will go into the vestry after service, and let me put a saddle on his back, I will ride him home, instead of going in my carriage." He then went on with the service as if nothing unusual had happened. Being reminded of this circumstance many years afterwards by Mr. Sidney, he said it was quite true. "You know I could not call him a donkey in plain terms."

From the Rev. T. W. Aveling's "Memoirs of the Clayton Family" we quote two anecdotes of

—"The wicked shall be turned into hell, and all the nations that forget God" (Ps. ix. 17); and looking full into the faces of the two youths, who sat immediately before him, he said, significantly, "And there's fun for you." The congregation, somewhat familiar with the old man's oddities, felt sure that he had a special reason for this strange remark; and when, each time he repeated the text, this singular commentary immediately followed, all looked to see in what direction his glance was turned, and the two lads soon found themselves "the observed of all observers." The tremor and alarm with which they heard the words that reminded them of their design on coming that morning to Surrey Chapel were not diminished

when they saw every eye fixed upon them, which-
ever way they looked; and conscience, "which
doth make cowards of us all," wrought so powerfully—in conjunction with Mr. Hill's illustrations
of his text—that one of them fainted away, and had
to be carried out by his companion. The latter

unwelcome reproof. One day, going down the
New Cut, opposite his chapel, he heard a brewer's
drayman, who was lowering some barrels, swearing
most fearfully. Rowland Hill rebuked him very
solemnly, and said, "Ah, my man! I shall appear
one day as a witness against you." "Very likely,"

INTERIOR OF THE ROTUNDA, BLACKFRIARS ROAD, IN 1820.

remained comparatively unaffected, except with a
temporary feeling of shame. The youth who
fainted returned the next Sunday to the chapel;
in the course of time he became an Independent
minister; and before he died was chairman of the
Congregational Union. The other grew up care-
less and abandoned, and became an outcast from
country and friends.

Another anecdote has been related of Mr. Hill,
which shows the readiness and wit with which
London working men can sometimes retort an

rejoined the offender; "the biggest rogues always
turn king's evidence!" This unwelcome retort
made Mr. Hill resolve to be cautious in future,
when he reproved such men again, *how* he reproved
them.

Rowland Hill's biographers inform us that a
generous benevolence was a distinguishing trait of
his character, and that he seemed to possess the
power of inspiring his flock with a similar spirit.
On two occasions on which collections were made
in the churches and chapels throughout the king-

dom (the Patriotic Fund at Lloyd's, and the subscription for the relief of the German sufferers), the collections at Surrey Chapel are recorded to have been the largest raised at any one place. The sum annually raised for charitable and religious institutions at Surrey Chapel has varied from £2,000 to £3,000.

Rowland Hill's death took place in April, 1833, in the eighty-ninth year of his age. Up to the last fortnight of his life he was able to preach a sermon of nearly an hour's duration once every Sunday. He was buried, at his own request, beneath the pulpit of Surrey Chapel. The funeral service was attended by a very large congregation; his nephew, the head of his family, Lord Hill, then Commander-in-Chief of the army, being the chief mourner. A tablet and bust in his memory were placed soon afterwards in the gallery behind the pulpit. His successor in the ministry of Surrey Chapel was the Rev. James Sherman, on whose resignation, in the year 1854, the pulpit became occupied by the Rev. Newman Hall.

Rowland Hill, when advanced in life, became possessed of some fortune; and accordingly, at his decease, he left the large sum of £11,000 to the Village Itinerancy, together with sundry donations to different religious institutions. Besides these bequests, he left a sum of money for the perpetuation of Surrey Chapel at the expiration of the lease; but this gift having subsequently been declared informal, as coming under the Statute of Mortmain, the bequest reverted to Hackney College, and in 1859 the congregation set themselves zealously to work to subscribe a sum equal to that which they had lost (£8,000). As they were unable to obtain a renewal of the lease, a new church was erected in the Westminster Bridge Road, on the site formerly occupied by the Female Orphan Asylum, as we have already stated;* hither the congregation migrated in 1876. Surrey Chapel was afterwards occupied by the Primitive Methodists, and since 1881 it has been used as a warehouse for machinery.

Surrey Chapel became "the centre of a system of benevolent societies designed to reach the various classes of the community;" and in 1812 Rowland Hill established some almshouses in the adjacent Gravel Lane, in a thoroughfare now known as Hill Street, on a spot ominously enough named Hangman's Acre, where twenty-four poor widows found a home. Mr. Charlesworth, in his recently published "Life of Rowland Hill," thus records the eccentric preacher's mode of dealing with applicants:—"An aged female wished to qualify herself for admission to an almshouse by becoming a member of the church. 'So you wish to join the church?'—'If you please, sir.' 'Where have you been accustomed to hear the Gospel?'—'At your *blessed* chapel, sir.' 'Oh! indeed; at my *blessed* chapel; dear me! And how long have you attended with us?'—'For several years.' 'Do you think you have got any good by attending the chapel?'—'Oh! yes, sir. I have had many *blessed* seasons.' 'Indeed! Under whose ministry do you think you were led to feel yourself to be a sinner?'—'Under your *blessed* ministry.' 'Indeed! And do you think your heart is pretty good?'—'Oh, no! sir; it is a very bad one.' 'What! and do you come here with your bad heart, and wish to join the church?'—'Oh, sir! I mean that my heart is not worse than others; it is pretty good on the whole!' 'Indeed! that's more than I can say; I'm sure mine's bad enough. Well, have you heard that we are going to build some *blessed* almshouses?'—'Yes, sir, I have.' 'Should you like to have one of them?' Dropping a very low curtsey, she replied, 'Yes, sir, if you please.' 'I thought so. You may go about your business, my friend; you won't do for us.' The severity of this treatment was doubtless justified by Mr. Hill's knowledge of the applicant, and the suspicion of her ulterior object."

On the west side of Blackfriars Road, about midway between Great Charlotte Street and the bridge, is Christ Church, which dates its erection from the middle of the last century. The parish of Christ Church was taken out of that of St. Saviour, Southwark, and was originally part of the district called the Liberty of Paris Garden. This spot, as we have shown in a previous chapter,† was one of the ancient places of amusement of the metropolis; and it seems to have been much frequented on Sundays for bear-baiting, a favourite sport in the time of Queen Elizabeth. Paris Garden, according to the ancient maps, extended from the west end of Bankside and the Liberty of the Clink towards what is now the southern extremity of Blackfriars Bridge. On the east it appears bounded by a mill-stream and mill-pond, and a road marked as leading to Copt Hall; there was also a mill, with gates, between the pond and the Thames. There is, or used to be, a ditch or dyke running across Great Surrey Street; but for some years it has been covered or built upon. All buildings thereon are subject to a ground-rent, payable to "the steward of the manor of Old Paris Garden, and are collected half-yearly.‡ In the

---

* See *ante*, pp. 350, 362.　　　　† See *ante*, p. 53.　　　　‡ *Notes and Queries*, 1854.

centre of the Liberty stood a cross, from which a narrow thoroughfare, marked "Olde Parris Lane," leads down to the river. On the south-east, a winding thoroughfare, with water on both sides, leads to St. George's Fields; and on the south-west another to the "Manner (*sic*) House." There are small rows of cottages along parts of these roads.

In early times very few houses stood on this marshy ground; but we have an account of a mansion or manor-house built upon a somewhat elevated part of the marsh, near the river, by one Robert of Paris, in the reign of Richard II.; the locality is still indicated by the name of Upper Ground Street. "It is said," writes the author of "London in the Olden Time," published in 1855, "that the king commanded the butchers of London to purchase this estate by the river-side for the purpose of making it a receptacle for garbage discharged from the city slaughter-houses, so that the inhabitants might not be annoyed therewith. This plot of ground, called Paris Garden—for so it has always been designated—is, or was, surrounded by the Thames and its waters which flow through ditches at high tides."

It appears that subsequently this estate of Robert of Paris came into the possession of the prior and monks of Bermondsey Abbey; but on the dissolution of the monasteries it was sold, and fell into lay hands. About one hundred and fifty years afterwards, in the reign of William and Mary, we find Paris Garden an inhabited locality, the property of a gentleman named Marshall, who founded and endowed here a church, which he named Christ Church, having obtained an Act of Parliament converting the ancient manor of Paris Garden into a parish under that name.

The first church was erected at the expense of Mr. Marshall, and finished in 1671. The steeple and spire, which were 125 feet high, were not completed till 1695. This edifice, in consequence of the badness of the foundations, soon became so dilapidated, that in 1737 Mr. Marshall's trustees applied to Parliament for power to rebuild it, with the sum of £2,500, which had accumulated in their hands from the trust, and obtained an Act for that purpose. The present structure was accordingly erected. This is situated in a spacious burial-ground. The plan of the fabric is nearly square; and at the west end is a square tower, flanked by lobbies. The walls are of brick, with stone dressings. The tower is built partly within and partly without the wall of the church; it is in three storeys: the lower has an arched doorway, with a circular window over it, and the second and third storeys each have arched windows. An octagon

turret of wood rises above the parapet in two stages, the lower forming the plinth to the other; in four of the faces are dials, and the whole is finished with a cupola and vane. The general appearance of the body of the church is plain and uninteresting, both externally and internally. The great east window contains some ornamented stained glass and a painting of the descending dove; in the side lights are the arms of the see of Winchester, impaled with those of Izaak Walton's "*good* Bishop Morley," then bishop of that diocese. The churchyard has lately been laid out as a public recreation ground.

In Church Street, about the year 1730, Mr. Charles Hopton founded a row of almshouses for twenty-six "decayed housekeepers," each of whom received £10 per annum and a chaldron of coals.

At a short distance northward of Christ Church, Stamford Street branches off westwards from Blackfriars Road, and thus forms a connecting link with that thoroughfare and Waterloo Bridge Road. It is a good broad street, dating from the beginning of this century; and, with York Road westward of it and Southwark Street to the east, serves as a direct communication, almost parallel with the river, from the High Street, Borough, to Westminster Bridge and Lambeth. On the south side of Stamford Street is a chapel, built about the year 1824 for the Unitarians. The building, from an architectural point of view, forms a striking contrast with the generality of chapels and meeting-houses. A portico, of the Grecian Doric order, occupies the whole front of the edifice, and imparts to it a commanding and temple-like aspect. The wall within this portico is unbroken by any other aperture than a single door, forming the entrance to the building. The interior corresponds with the exterior in simplicity of taste and in the style of its decoration, which is of that plainness that it might even satisfy a congregation of Quakers.

Nearly opposite the above-mentioned chapel, at the corner of Hatfield Street, is the Hospital for Diseases of the Skin, an institution which since its establishment, in 1841, has done a deal of good in the gratuitous medical treatment of the poor afflicted with cutaneous diseases. This institution was originally established in New Bridge Street, Blackfriars, and from 800 to 1,000 of the suffering poor are every week relieved here.

In Duke Street, close by, are the extensive printing works of the Messrs. Clowes and Sons. This is one of the largest establishments of the kind in the kingdom, and from its presses have issued many of the works of Charles Dickens,

Charles Knight, and other eminent men of letters, as well as the publications of the "Incorporated Council of Law Reporting for England and Wales," numerous military works, and statistical reports for various Government offices. The firm, in 1840, undertook the contract for supplying the famous Mulready envelope. The *Mirror* stated that they arranged to supply the public with half a million a day; but the design was distasteful to the public, and the envelope was speedily recalled.

At the corner of Stamford Street and Blackfriars Road, on the spot now occupied by the Central Bank of London and three or four large houses adjoining it, stood, till 1874, a row of tenements, which for many years previously, owing to the eccentricity of their owner, a Miss Angelina Read, had been allowed to remain unoccupied. They had long been windowless, and the dingy rooms encumbered with dirt and rubbish and overrun with rats; indeed, such a forlorn and desolate aspect had they assumed that they became generally known as "the haunted houses." In the above year, Miss Read having bequeathed them to the Consumption Hospital at Brompton, they were demolished, and some fine buildings have been erected in their place.

A few doors northwards of Stamford Street, on the west side of Blackfriars Road, is the building once occupied by the museum collected by Sir Ashton Lever, and removed hither from Leicester Square,* when it became the property of a Mr. Parkinson. The following is a *fac-simile* of an advertisement of the exhibition, taken from a London newspaper of March, 1790:—

LEVERIAN MUSEUM,
ALBION STREET,
The Surrey End of Black Friars Bridge.

THIS admired Assemblage of the Productions of Nature and Art, with several curious and valuable additions, both presented and purchased, continues to be exhibited every day (Sundays excepted) from Ten to Six.

Admittance Half a Crown each person.

Good Fires in the Rotunda, &c.

Recently added to the Museum, a variety of Specimens of the most rare and beautiful Birds from GUAYANA, in SOUTH AMERICA.

Annual Admission Tickets may be had at the Museum, at One Guinea each.

Part the First of the Catalogue of this Collection may be had at the following places:—Messrs. White and Son, in Fleet Street; Mr. Robson, in New Bond Street, Mr. Elmsly, in the Strand; Mr. Sewell, in Cornhill; and at the Museum. Price 2s. 6d.

This curious, extensive, and valuable collection

* See Vol. III., p. 165.

here experienced the most mortifying neglect, till, in 1806, it was finally dispersed by public auction, in a sale which lasted forty days. The premises were subsequently occupied by the Surrey Institution, which was established in the following year. Here some gentlemen proposed to form an institution on the Surrey side of the river, on a plan similar to that of the Royal Institution in Albemarle Street. It was intended to have a series of lectures, an extensive library and reading-rooms, a chemical laboratory and philosophical apparatus, &c. In 1820 this valuable institution was dissolved, the library, &c., being sold by auction. After that, the building, which was called the Rotunda, was occupied for some years as a wine and concert-room. In September, 1833, it was opened as the Globe Theatre. Two years previously it had been appropriated to all kinds of purposes, including the dissemination of the worst religious and political opinions, and penny exhibitions of wax-work and wild beast shows. In 1838 the Rotunda was again opened as a concert-room; but the concern never prospered, and its vicissitudes afterwards are not worth noting. It was finally closed as a place of amusement about the year 1855, and the building is now used for business purposes. "To such vile uses" do all things come!

At the foot of Blackfriars Bridge formerly stood a range of buildings, which at one time constituted part of the Albion Mills. This extensive concern was set on foot by a company of spirited and opulent individuals, with the view of counteracting the impositions but too frequently practised in the grinding of corn. On the 3rd of March, 1791, the whole building, with the exception of the corner wing, occupied as the house and offices of the superintendent, was destroyed by fire, together with four thousand sacks of flour which it contained. When these mills were burnt down, Horace Walpole was not ashamed to own that he had literally never seen or heard of them, though the flakes and the dust of burning grain were carried as far as Westminster, Palace Yard, and even to St. James's. "One may live," writes Walpole, "in a vast capital, and know no more of three-parts of it than of Carthage. When I was in Florence I have surprised some Florentines by telling them that London is built (like their city, where you often cross the bridges several times in a day) on each side of the river, and yet that I had never been but on one side; for then I had never been in Southwark." What would Horace Walpole have said of London, had he lived in the reign of Victoria?

The front of the mill remained for many years

unrepaired, but was subsequently formed into a row of handsome private habitations. These, in turn, were demolished a few years ago, to make room for the Blackfriars station and goods depôt on the London, Chatham, and Dover Railway.

Somewhere near this spot, at no great distance from the southern end of Blackfriars Bridge, stood the most westerly of the play-houses on Bankside —the Swan Theatre. It was a large house, and flourished only a few years, being suppressed at the commencement of the civil wars, and soon afterwards demolished.

Before the building of Blackfriars Bridge, in 1766, there was a ferry at this spot for the conveyance of traffic across the river. An idea of the value of some of the ferries on the Thames may be formed from the circumstance that on the construction of this bridge the committee of management agreed to invest the Waterman's Company with £13,650 Consolidated Three per Cent. Annuities, to satisfy them for the loss of the Sunday ferry at Blackfriars, which was proved to have produced, upon an average for fourteen years, the sum of £409,000.

CHAPTER XXIX.

LAMBETH.

*" So many gardens, dressed with curious care,
That Thames with royal Tiber may compare."—Izaak Walton; from the German.*

Parochial Division of Lambeth—The Early History of the Parish—Descent of the Manor—Appearance of Lambeth in the time of Charles II.— Lambeth in the Last Century, as viewed from the Adelphi—The Romance of Lambeth—Lady Arabella Stuart a Prisoner here—Morland, the famous Mechanist—John Wesley preaches here—Pepys' Visits to Lambeth—Messrs. Searle's Boat-building Establishment—Lambeth Marsh—Narrow Wall and Broad Wall—Pedlar's Acre—The " Duke of Bolton," Governor of Lambeth Marsh—Belvedere Road—Belvedere House and Gardens—Cuper's Gardens—Cumberland Gardens—The " Hercules " Inn and Gardens—The Apollo Gardens—Flora Gardens— Lambeth Fields—Lambeth Wells—Outdoor Diversion in the Olden Time—Taverns and Public-houses—The " Three Merry Boys "—The " Three Squirrels "—The " Chequers "—The " Three Goats' Heads "—The " Axe and Cleaver "—The Halfpenny Hatch.

THE parish of Lambeth, upon which we now enter at its north-eastern angle, previously to its sub-division, was no less than sixteen miles in circumference; being bounded by Newington, Camberwell, Streatham, Croydon, by the river Thames, and by the parishes of St. George's and Christ Church, Southwark. It is divided into four liberties, and again sub-divided into the following eight wards or precincts : the Bishop's, the Prince's, Vauxhall, Kennington, Marsh, Wall, Stockwell, and Dean's. The parish, and especially its palace, is connected with English history; for, as we have already observed, Hardicanute is said to have died suddenly here at a wedding feast—a clear proof that even in the Saxon times there was a palace here, or the residence of some Saxon thane.

The early history of the parish is thus told by Pennant :—" In early times it was a manor, possibly a royal one, for the great Hardiknut died here in 1042, in the midst of the jollity of a wedding dinner ; and here, without any formality, the usurper Harold is said to have snatched the crown, and to have placed it on his own head. It was then part of the estate of Goda, wife successively to Walter, Earl of Mantes, and Eustace, Earl of Boulogne, who presented it to the Church of Rochester, but reserved to herself the patronage of the church. It became, in 1197, the property of

the see of Canterbury, by an exchange transacted between Glanville, Bishop of Rochester, and the archbishop, Hubert Walter. Glanville received out of the exchange a small piece of land, on which he built a house, called Rochester Place, for the reception of the Bishops of Rochester whenever they came to London to attend Parliament. In 1357 the then bishop, John de Sheppey, built Stangate Stairs, for the convenience of himself and his retinue to cross over into Westminster. Fisher and Hilsley were the last bishops who inhabited this palace ; after their deaths it fell into the hands of Henry VIII., who exchanged with Aldridge, Bishop of Carlisle, for certain houses in the Strand, and its name was changed to that of Carlisle House. The small houses built on its site," he adds, " still (1790) belong to that see."

In the book of Domesday we find the Manor of Lambeth belonging to this Countess Goda. One of the holders of the see of Rochester, in the reign of Henry II., exchanged it for other lands with Baldwin, Archbishop of Canterbury ; and we know that Hubert Walter, one of his successors in the archiepiscopate and Lord High Chancellor in the reign of Richard I., resided here.

If the old manor of Lambeth was co-extensive with the subsequent parish, it must have extended along the Thames from Battersea to Southwark, and from the river-side to the limits of Norwood, Kennington, and Streatham, and even to those of the parish of Croydon ; but this is not quite certain.

" Lambeth, anciently Lamb-hythe," Northouck thus writes, " is a village situated along the Thames between Southwark and Battersea, extending southward from the east end of Waterloo Bridge, and chiefly inhabited by glass-blowers,

Clapham, and have been bounded to the south by the beautiful Surrey hills. Lambeth Marsh and the Bank-side evidently were recovered from the water. Along Lambeth are the names of ' Narrow Walls,' or mounds, which served for that purpose ; and in Southwark, again, ' Bankside ' shows the means of converting the ancient lake into useful land. Even to this day the tract beyond Southwark, and in particular that beyond Bermondsey

THE SOUTH SIDE OF THE THAMES, TAKEN FROM ADELPHI TERRACE.
(*From an Etching by Nugent, in* 1770.)

potters, fishermen, and watermen." The name of the place has been spelled variously as Lamheth, Lambyth, Lamedh, Lamhees, &c. ; and so far back as the time of the Danish occupation it was a village adjacent to the capital.

Pennant, the antiquary, considers that in the time of the Roman occupation, if not at a later date, the Surrey side of the Thames near the metropolis was in all probability a great expanse of water—a " Llyn," as the Welsh call it ; and he thought that possibly the name of London is but a corruption or variation of " Llyn Din "—the city on the lake. " The expanse of water," he continues, " might have filled the space between the rising grounds at (near) Deptford and those at

Street, is so very low, and beneath the level of common (spring) tides, that the proprietors are obliged to secure it by embankments."

Pennant tells us also that in 1560 there was not a single house standing between Lambeth Palace and Southwark ! Indeed, the place was all open country even in the time of Charles II. Thus Pepys writes in his " Diary," in July, 1663 :— " Went across the water to Lambeth, and so over the fields to Southwark."

In Ralph Aggas' map of London, to which we have often referred, in the foreground on the left are the Palace of the Archbishop of Canterbury and Lambeth Church, with only one house at a small distance off ; a little to the northward is a road leading to the river opposite the landing-place in Palace Yard. The principal ditch of Lambeth Marsh, if we may trust the map, falls into the Thames opposite the Temple Gardens, the ground being occupied by only a single dwelling. On the river-bank opposite Whitefriars commences a line of houses, with gardens and groves behind them, and continued, with little intermission, to the stairs and palace of the Bishop of Winchester on the famous Nonsuch House is conspicuous. Another striking object in the foreground is the noble cruciform church of St. Mary Overie, of which we have already spoken, in magnitude and architectural character the third church in the metropolis, with its pinnacled tower a hundred and fifty feet in height. The park of the Bishop of Winchester appears also walled in on all sides; hence comes the name of Park Street in this locality. On the

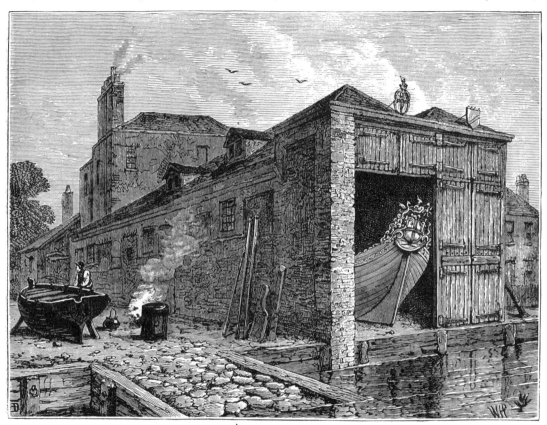

SEARLE'S BOAT-YARD IN 1830.

Bankside. One of the most noted places along this line is Paris Garden, the site of which, as we have stated in the preceding chapter, is now covered by Christ Church in Blackfriars Road. Farther eastward, but behind the houses, we see certain circular buildings for bull and bear baiting—amusements to which the "virgin" Queen Elizabeth was partial. Near the bear-baiting place, or "Bear-garden," as it was styled, was a dog-kennel, from which several savage dogs are seen issuing forth. From Winchester Palace to the Borough High Street, and along Tooley (St. Olave's) Street to Battle Bridge, the houses stand somewhat thickly; but towards Horselydown the ground is open, and the buildings are surrounded with gardens. We here see London Bridge crowded with buildings, among which the

right stands St. Olave's Church, the successor of one built here before the Norman Conquest.

The history of Lambeth for several centuries was mainly confined to the Palace, and consequently little remains to be said here till we come down to the beginning of the seventeenth century. No doubt, every district of this great metropolis has a character, moral if not physical, of its own; but the American writer who remarked that "there is scarcely a greater difference between Americans and Russians than between the inhabitants of Lambeth and of Central London," was guilty of at least a rhetorical exaggeration, if not of something worse.

A curious old etching by Thomas Nugent, of about the date 1770, which we reproduce on page 384, shows the south side of the Thames, as seen from the top of the Adelphi Terrace. In the foreground is the "Shot Tower," still standing, near the southern end of Waterloo Bridge; near it, a little to the west, are Cuper's Gardens, a mass of trees and foliage; to the south is the Windmill, in Lambeth Marsh; and lastly, St. George's Fields. In the distance are houses, high out of all proportion, and of foreign appearance; while the Surrey hills rise to absurd heights in the background, somewhat like the chain of the Apennines.

A poem on this rural spot, published in the *Mirror* in 1824, mentions—we know not whether with a poet's lawful exaggeration or not—"tall oaks" as still "waving their ancient branches overhead;" and in it are recounted many of the historical recollections of the place: how Hardicanute died suddenly here, while feasting his subjects.

> " No rebel hand
> Of life with violence that proud prince deprived ;
> The brimming goblet often to his lips
> He raised, in mad contempt of nature's law
> And dictates wise : from off the couch he sank
> A lifeless corse. In vain the wassail cup
> Passed gaily round the joyous festive board ;
> In vain the vaulted roof with loud acclaim
> Of royal goodness did re-echo wide :
> The royal patron of the feast was dead."

And then the writer proceeds to record the persecutions of which the Lollards' Tower was too often the scene; the shelter afforded by the church porch to Mary of Modena, when she fled from Whitehall with her little son, as we have already said; the burial of the two Tradescants, father and son. But we must descend from the lofty region of poetry and imagination to sober prose and dry facts.

Lambeth, however, is not quite without its historical romance, for to this place Lord Percy and the Duke of Lancaster, John of Gaunt, were glad to be able to effect their escape from the Savoy when that palace was assailed and sacked by the mob in 1377.*

Here, in 1609 or 1610, the Lady Arabella Stuart, cousin of James I., having contracted a private marriage with William Seymour, a son of Lord Beauchamp, was kept a prisoner in the house of Sir Thomas Parry. She contrived, however, whilst here to correspond with her husband, and the wedded pair managed to effect her removal to Highgate,† where she remained, under surveillance, in the house of a Mr. Conyers, from whom she endeavoured to escape to France; but she was caught in the Channel on board ship, and brought back to the Tower to end her days a prisoner. Her misfortunes—which read like a chapter in a romance—seem to have arisen simply and solely from her nearness to the Crown. Her husband, surviving her by many years, was invested by Charles II. with the Dukedom of Somerset, which had been forfeited by his ancestor, the Protector.

Lambeth, as we have already seen in passing through those parts lying about Kennington, has numbered in its time many residents of note. Besides those whose names we have mentioned, there was living here, in the middle of the seventeenth century, one Mr. Morland (afterwards Sir Samuel Morland), a famous mechanist, not unknown as a statesman, and at whose house Charles II. passed the first night of his restoration. It was this person who, while employed as a clerk at Thurloe's chambers in Lincoln's Inn,‡ overheard the conversation between the Protector (Cromwell) and Thurloe, in which it was designed to inveigle the king, then an exile at Bruges, and his younger brothers, the Dukes of York and Gloucester, into the Protector's power. Morland, it seems, was asleep at his desk, or was thought to be so; and Cromwell, apprehensive that his conversation had been overheard, drew his dagger, and would have dispatched the slumberer on the spot, had not Thurloe, with some difficulty, prevented him, assuring him that his intended victim was unquestionably asleep, since, to his own knowledge, he had been sitting up two nights together. It had been privately intimated to the king and his brothers, through the agency of Sir Richard Willis, that if, on a stated day, they would land on the coast of Sussex, they would be received by a body of five hundred men, which would be augmented the following morning by two thousand horse. Had they fallen into the snare, it seems that all three would have been shot immediately on reaching the shore. Morland, however, had not been asleep, as was supposed by Thurloe and Cromwell; and through his means the king and his brothers were made acquainted with the design against their lives. We shall have more to say about Sir Samuel Morland when we reach Vauxhall Gardens.

In spite of the vicinity of the archbishop's palace, Lambeth, in the latter half of the last century, could reckon among its residents some of the most zealous members of the Wesleyan body; and John Wesley preached in Lambeth Chapel, opposite Bethlehem Hospital, on February 17th, 1791, only one brief fortnight before his death.

Apparently, two centuries ago, when there was only one bridge across the Thames, Lambeth was the place from which the Portsmouth coach, and

---

* See Vol. III., p. 95.　　† See Vol. V., p. 402.　　‡ See Vol. III., p. 53.

probably most of the other conveyances to Hampshire and Dorsetshire, started. At all events, Pepys writes in his "Diary," under date 1660, "We took water for Lambeth, and there coach for Portsmouth." On another occasion he tells us that he crossed the water to Lambeth in order to make a journey by land to Woolwich.

Lambeth was a great place for boat-building as far back, certainly, as the reign of Charles II. At all events, Samuel Pepys tells us in his "Diary," under date August 13th, 1662, "To Lambeth, and there saw the little pleasure-boat in building by the king, my Lord Brouncker, and the *virtuosos* of the town, according to new lines, which Mr. Pett cries up mightily; but how it will prove we shall soon see." We have already met with Mr. Commissioner Pett in our saunterings through Deptford.*

Apart from its boat-building, which was carried on here to a large extent until the formation of the southern or Albert Embankment, Lambeth has long been one of the principal points on the Thames, above bridge, for the traffic both of watermen and the more modern steamboat conveyance. Searle's boat-yard, just above Westminster Bridge, on the spot now covered by the Albert Embankment, in front of St. Thomas's Hospital, was a place as familiar to the boating men of Oxford in the last generation as the "Ship" at Mortlake, or the "Star and Garter" at Putney are now. Messrs. Searle's boat-yard has of late years been removed to another site higher up the river, at Stangate, close to Lambeth Bridge.

We have described the marshy nature of the land lying between the river and St. George's Fields in former times. Lambeth Marsh—for by such name the locality was known—was protected from the incursion of the river by embankments. At a very early date banks of earth were erected along the south side of the Thames, in order to keep out the tidal waters, and to hold them in check. Our readers will not have forgotten that one locality in Southwark still retains the name of Bankside.† Other embankments, too, were raised, in order to assist in keeping the inland district from inundation, and to form causeways for passengers travelling from Lambeth to London Bridge and the several landing-places along the river-side. Of these embankments, one running nearly parallel with the river was called Narrow Wall; another, bounding the marsh on the east, Broad Wall; and an ancient raised road, probably as old as the time of the Roman occupation, followed the line of the street now known as Lambeth, or Lower Marsh.

Lambert, in his "History of Surrey" (1806), tells us that on "Narrow Wall" is a manufactory of artificial stone, established in 1769 by Mr. Coade. "The preparation," he adds, "is cast in moulds and burnt, and is intended to answer every purpose of carved stone. It is possessed of the peculiar property of resisting frost, and consequently it retains its sharpness, in which it excels every species of stone, and even equals marble."

About 1870 a sculptured bas-relief (2½ feet by 2 feet, and 4 inches thick) was found in the course of excavations for deep foundation at Broad Wall. It represented the figure of a chief, attired and armed as if for the chase, with certain attributes of costume of a non-European (perhaps American) character, such as a deep fringe round the loins, and strings of beads on the neck, arms, and legs. The spot where it was found was formerly a bog; and it is supposed by the Archæological Institute to be part of the cargo of a vessel broken upon the spot many ages ago.

There were, even as late as the beginning of the present century, open fields, with a windmill, where now the renowned "New Cut" connects the Blackfriars and Waterloo Roads. Mill Street, which was pulled down on the formation of the South-Western Railway, marked the site whereon stood a group of picturesque old wooden mills. The spot between the Belvedere Road and the river, between Waterloo and Westminster Bridges— till recently known as Pedlar's Acre—was called, in the fifteenth and sixteenth centuries, Church Osiers, from a large osier-bed which occupied the spot. This is a plot of ground of some historical notoriety, though of no great importance. It was originally a small strip of land, one acre and nine poles in extent, situate alongside of the Narrow Wall, and has belonged to the parish of Lambeth from time immemorial. It is said to have been given by a grateful pedlar, on condition that his portrait and that of his dog should be preserved for ever, in painted glass, in one of the windows of the parish church. This request has been duly observed down to our own day, for the picture was, till lately, to be seen in one of the windows of the church, and some amusing legendary tales are still told about the pedlar of Lambeth and his dog. Whatever truth there may be in the tradition that the ground in question was bequeathed to the parish by a pedlar, on condition that the picture of himself and his dog be preserved in the window of the church, we will not pretend to determine. Astute antiquaries, however, have searched the parish registers, and there find that the land was bequeathed by some person

---

* See *ante*, p. 148.			† See *ante*, p. 45.

unknown.* On Pedlar's Acre was at one time a public-house, with the sign of a pedlar and his dog; and on one of the windows in the tap-room the following lines were written with a diamond :—

> " Happy the pedlar whose portrait we view,
> Since his dog was so faithful and fortunate too ;
> He at once made him wealthy, and guarded his door,
> Secured him from robbers, relieved him when poor.
> Then drink to his memory, and wish fate may send
> Such a dog to protect you, enrich, and befriend."

One of the windows of Lambeth Church also used to contain a figure of the pedlar and his dog. Its removal caused much local annoyance in 1884.

THE PEDLAR AND HIS DOG, FROM LAMBETH CHURCH.

Hereabouts lived and died an eccentric character, Henry Paulet, commonly known as " Duke of Bolton, King of Vine Street, and Governor of Lambeth Marsh." He had in early life performed services to the Government in America, and subsequently had assisted Admiral Hawke in defeating a French fleet off Brest ; but he chose to take up his abode here in retirement and in the practice of charity towards his poorer neighbours. " As to the good which he did with his income," writes the author of " The Eccentric," " there is not a poor man or woman in the neighbourhood of the Pedlar's Acre who does not testify with gratitude to some act of benevolence performed for the alleviation of his or her poverty by the hand of this humane and heroic Englishman."

Belvedere Road probably takes its name from the Belvedere House and Gardens, a well-known place of amusement, dating from Queen Anne's time, but of which few records remain. These gardens are not mentioned by Malcolm, nor by John Timbs, in his " Curiosities of London,"

who simply tells us that Lambeth in former days " abounded in gardens." The Belvedere Gardens, we may add, are likewise passed over without a word by Pennant, Northouck, and Lambert.

Adjoining Belvedere Gardens, not far from the southern end of Waterloo Bridge, on the site now occupied by the timber-wharves of Belvedere Road, and close by the Lion Brewery, which abuts upon the river, stood formerly a noted place of public resort, known as Cuper's Gardens, and constantly alluded to by writers in the eighteenth century. As far back as the beginning of the eighteenth century, if not earlier, it was famous for its displays of fireworks. " It was not, however," says Dr. C. Mackay, in his " Thames and its Tributaries," " the resort of respectable company, but of the abandoned of either sex." It is frequently mentioned in the comedies and satires of the day as bearing a very indifferent character. Dr. Mackay lets us into a little of the antiquarianism of the place, for he tells us that it took its name from Boydell Cuper, who had been gardener to Lord Arundel on the other side of the river, and who rented the ground from his lordship. In our account of Arundel House† we mentioned that it was adorned with a variety of busts and statues ; and it appears that when that house was pulled down in order to build new streets, a number of these statues, in a more or less mutilated state, came into Cuper's possession, and were set up in different parts of his gardens. This place of entertainment was suppressed by the authority of the magistrates in 1753. It is described by Mr. J. H. Jesse as " a favourite place of resort for the gay and profligate from the end of the seventeenth to the middle of the eighteenth century." It must have somewhat resembled the " Spring Garden " at Charing Cross, if it be true, as stated by Mr. Jesse, that " the principal attractions of the gardens were their retired arbours, their shady walks ornamented with statues and ancient marbles, and especially the fireworks." The trees which threw their shade upon these walks were standing, at all events, as late as 1770, for they are shown in the etching which we reproduce on page 384, the view of which is taken from the top of the newly-built Adelphi Terrace. The banks of the river, as shown in our illustration, were at that time steep and irregular, and the houses few and far between where now is all the bustle of the Waterloo Railway Station. A print of Cuper's Gardens is in existence, showing the groves, alcoves, and statues with which it was adorned. Some of the plane-trees belonging to

---

* There is a similar tradition of a pedlar being a benefactor to the parish of Swaffham, in Norfolk.

† See Vol. III., p. 71.

these gardens are still green and flourishing in the grounds behind St. John's Church, Waterloo Road; and the name of the place is still preserved in Cuper's Stairs, nearly opposite the Adelphi. Part of the site of Cuper's Gardens was afterwards occupied by Beaufoy's* vinegar works till the formation of Waterloo Bridge and its approaches.

Besides the gardens above mentioned, several other places for open-air entertainment were established in Lambeth in the latter part of the last century. The Duke of Cumberland, the "butcher" hero of Culloden, gave name to some gardens by the river-side, not far from Nine Elms. The Hercules Inn and Gardens were at the junction of the Kennington and Westminster Roads, on the spot afterwards occupied by the Female Orphan Asylum, and now by Christ Church. The gardens were opened in 1758; their memory is still preserved by Hercules Buildings, in Westminster Bridge Road.

Mead's Row was the name of a narrow and short cut leading from the Kennington Road to the Lambeth Road, and forming the base of a triangle of which Christ Church is the apex. In it was an old house known as "Frog Hall," where Parsons, "the Comic Roscius," lived, and where he died in January, 1795.

Nearly opposite, close to Messrs. Maudslay's engineering works, were the Apollo Gardens, opened in 1788 by Mr. Cloggett, proprietor of the fashionable Pantheon in Oxford Street. Here there was a central orchestra, and alcoves with snug wooden boxes all around, containing grotesque and amusing pictures and sculptures. In the same year the Flora Gardens were opened in Mount Street; but in two or three years these places had acquired such an evil repute that the magistrates suppressed them.

The Lambeth Fields were for two centuries a favourite resort of Londoners, and celebrated for the variety of sweet-smelling flowers and medicinal herbs growing there. Near the Upper Marsh was Curtis's great botanical garden, on the spot where in the old times had stood a lazar-house.

In the reign of William III. there was another place of amusement, known as "Lambeth Wells," in what is now Lambeth Walk, but was then termed Three Coney Walk; they were held for a time in high repute, on account of their mineral waters, which were advertised as to be sold, according to John Timbs, at "a penny a quart, the same price paid by St. Thomas's Hospital." About 1750, we learn from the same authority, there was a musical society held here, and lectures, with

experiments in natural philosophy, were delivered by Dr. Erasmus King and others. Malcolm tells us that the Wells opened for the season regularly on Easter Monday, being closed during the winter. They had "public days" on Mondays, Thursdays, and Saturdays, with "music from seven in the morning till sunset; on other days till two!" The price of admission was threepence. The water was sold at a penny a quart to the "quality" and to those who could pay for it; being given *gratis* to the poor. We incidentally learn that there were grand gala and dancing days here in 1747 and 1752, when "a penny wedding, in the Scotch manner, was celebrated for the benefit of a young couple."

The following notice was issued in some of the public papers in August, 1710:—"A gold ring is to be danced for on the 31st instant, and a hat to be played for at skittles the next day following, at the 'Green Gate,' in Gray's Walks, near Lambeth Wells." About this time, Lambeth Marsh, close by, and the fields round about, were the scene of out-door diversion and merry-making during the summer months, running matches and "grinning" matches being of frequent occurrence.

Apropos of these gatherings for social enjoyment, the following quotation from Fielding's "Proverbs" may not be out of place here, as Lambeth was one of the head-quarters of amusement for the citizens of London:—"In addition to the May games, morris-dancing, pageants, and processions, which were common throughout the kingdom, the Londoners," he tells us, "had peculiar privileges of hunting, hawking, and fishing; they had also large portions of ground allotted to them in the vicinity of the City for the practice of such pastimes as were not prohibited, and for those, especially, that were conducive to health. On the holidays, during the summer season, the young men exercised themselves in the fields with leaping, archery, wrestling, playing with balls, and practising with their wasters and bucklers. The City damsels had also their recreations, playing upon their timbrels and dancing to the music, which they often practised by moonlight. One writer says it was customary for the maidens to dance in presence of their masters and mistresses, while one of their companions played the music on a timbrel; and to stimulate them, the best dancers were rewarded with a garland, the prize being exposed to public view during the performance. To this custom Spenser alludes—

'—— The damsels they delight,
When they their timbrels smite,
And thereunto dance and carol sweet.'

---

* See Pennant's "London."

The London apprentices often amused themselves with their wasters and bucklers before the doors of their masters. Hunting with the Lord Mayor's pack of hounds was a diversion of the metropolis, as well as sailing, rowing, and fishing on the Thames. Duck-hunting was a favourite recreation in the summer, as we learn from Strype."

Among the other sports which prevailed in Lambeth, in the days of " Merrye Englande,"

Since the first formation of streets in the place of the fields and marshy ground hereabouts, Lambeth, like most other water-side places, has not been behind-hand in the number of its public-houses, some of which have acquired more than a local reputation. From a manuscript list, written about the year 1810, we glean the following particulars of its tavern signs :—In Westminster Bridge Road, the " Army and Navy," the " King's Head,"

OLD WINDMILLS AT LAMBETH, ABOUT 1750.

was that of " hocking," or catching and binding with ropes the passers-by in the street. The men " hocked " the women, and the women the men; and each had to pay a small fine on being released. Strutt tells us, in his " Sports and Pastimes," that " Hock-Day " was celebrated probably in remembrance of the death of Hardicanute, already mentioned, which delivered England from the tyranny of the Danes. In the churchwardens' accounts of Lambeth for 1515 and the following year are several entries of " hock-monies " received from the men and the women for the church service. " And here we may observe," adds Strutt, with a stroke of dry humour, " the contributions collected by the fair sex exceeded those made by the men."

the " Rose," the " Crown," the " Red Lion," the " Dover Castle," the " Canterbury Arms," and the " New Crown and Cushion." In Coburg Road, the " Three Compasses " and the " Olive Branch." In Coburg Place, the " Queen's Arms " and " The Pilgrim." In Broad Wall, the " Mitre " and " The Bull in the Pound "—the latter of which points to the time when a bull was liable to be punished for trespass, and put into the pound or pinfold. In Gibson Street, " The Duke of Sussex." In Hatfield Street, " The Duke of Wurtemberg "—a sign which commemorated the marriage of the Princess Royal, daughter of George III., with Frederick, first King of Wurtemberg. At Lambeth Butts, " The Tankerville Arms."

In Upper Fore Street there is an inn with the

OLD VIEWS IN LAMBETH.

1. Carlisle House.   2. Entrance to Cuper's Gardens.   3. Remains of Orchestra, Cuper's Gardens.   4. Conspirators' House.

sign of the "Three Merry Boys," which, as Mr. Larwood suggests, is probably a corruption of the "Three Mariners," a tavern which is known to have existed within the parish. Allen tells us, in his "History of Lambeth," that when this inn underwent repairs in 1752, there was found in it a remarkable arm-chair, with high elbows, covered with purple cloth, and ornamented with gilt nails. "An old fisherman," adds Mr. Allen, "told Mr. Buckmaster that he had heard his grandfather say that Charles II. used to frequent this tavern in disguise, on his water-tours along with his ladies, in order to play chess, &c., and that the chair found was the same in which the king sat. The royal chair was repaired, and kept as a curiosity by the late Mr. John Dawson, but was destroyed at the pulling down of his old dwelling in Vauxhall. Mr. Buckmaster sat in the chair many times; but his feet would not touch the ground." King Charles, it will be remembered, was very tall in stature: a fact which strongly corroborates the idea that the chair was not only sat upon by his Majesty, but also designed and made for his special use.

"The Three Squirrels" was the sign of an inn here, mentioned by Taylor, the water-poet, in 1636, but its exact locality is not known. The same sign is still to be seen over Messrs. Goslings', the bankers, in Fleet Street.

In Calcot's Alley was formerly an inn which bore the sign of the "Chequers." It is worthy of note here, on account of a fact connected with it, mentioned by Allen, in his "History of Lambeth," viz., that in 1454 its owner, one John Calcot, had granted to him a licence to have an oratory in his house, and a chaplain for the use of his family and guests, and adapted to the celebration of divine service as long as his house should continue to be orderly and respectable.

The "Three Goats' Heads," a public-house on the road to Wandsworth, was originally the "Cordwainers'" or "Shoemakers' Arms," which are "azure, a chevron or, between three goats' heads, erased, argent." Gradually the heraldic attributes have fallen away, or been blotted out by the clumsy sign-painter's brush, and the goats' heads alone now remain; the name of the inn, too, has sunk from the region of heraldry to that of vulgar commonplace.

Till near the end of the last century, an inn, with the sign of the "Axe and Cleaver"—a compliment to the carpenter's trade—was to be seen near the garden-wall of the archbishop's palace; and hard by was another of a like kind, "The Two Sawyers." These signs require no comment.

We have mentioned in previous chapters the existence, in former times, near St. George's Church in the Borough, and likewise at Rotherhithe, of a thoroughfare known as the Halfpenny Hatch.* Lambeth, we may add, could boast of its Half-penny Hatch as late as the commencement of the present century. It led from Christ Church, in the Blackfriars Road, to the Marsh Gate, near Westminster Bridge, over some fields where now stands St. John's Church, Waterloo Road.

Here Astley first exhibited his horses, before taking the ground near Westminster Bridge which has since been associated with his name. The Hatch House was at the back of St. John's Church, at the end of Neptune Place, and its forlorn and ramshackle condition is graphically described by Mr. John T. Smith, in his "Book for a Rainy Day." Its site still presents the same sunken appearance, the ground around it having been artificially raised for building purposes. "It was built," writes Mr. Smith, "subsequent to the year 1781, by Curtis, the famous botanist, whose name it still retains; but the original Hatch House, I was informed, stood at the back of the present one." He tells us how he took a sketch of "this vine-mantled Half-penny Hatch;" but his sketch is not now in existence.

There was a time when the description of Pope, in his youthful imitation of Spenser, was really applicable to Lambeth:—

"In every town where Thamis rolls his tyde,
    A narrow pass there is, with houses low,
Where ever and anon the stream is eyed,
    And many a boat soft gliding to and fro;
There oft are heard the notes of infant wo,
    The short, thick sob, loud scream, and shriller squall.

    *   *   *   *   *

"And on the broken pavement, here and there,
    Doth many a stinking sprat and herring lie;
A brandy and tobacco shop is near,
    And hens and dogs and hogs are feeding by;
And here a sailor's jacket hangs to dry.
    At every door are sun-burnt matrons seen
Mending old nets to catch the scaly fry,
    Now singing shrill, and scolding oft between—
Scold answers foul-mouth'd scold; bad neighbourhood,
    I ween.

    *   *   *   *   *

"Such place hath Deptford, navy-building town;
    Woolwich and Wapping, smelling strong of pitch;
Such Lambeth, envy of each band and gown."

Dr. Charles Mackay quotes these lines, in his "Thames and its Tributaries," as still applicable to Lambeth in 1840. In 1877, however, the scene is very different; and, thanks to the erection of the Albert Embankment, Lambeth must be removed out of the category of low river-side scenes.

---

* See *ante*, pp. 75, 133.

CHAPTER XXX.

LAMBETH (*continued*).—THE TRANSPONTINE THEATRES.

" Ablegandæ Tiberim ultra."—*Horace.*

The Morality of the Transpontine Theatres—The building of the Coburg Theatre—Its Name changed to the Victoria—Vicissitudes of the Theatre—
The Last Night of the Old Victoria—The Theatre altered and re-opened as the Royal Victoria Palace Theatre—A Romantic Story—Origin of
Astley's Amphitheatre—Biographical Sketch of Philip Astley—His Riding School near the Halfpenny Hatch—He builds a Riding School
near Westminster Bridge—The Edifice altered, and called the Royal Grove—Destruction of the Royal Grove by Fire—The Theatre rebuilt,
and opened as the Amphitheatre of Arts—The Theatre a second time destroyed by Fire—Again rebuilt, and called the Royal Amphitheatre
—Astley and his Musicians—Death of Mr. Astley—The Theatre under the Management of Mr. W. Davis—Ducrow and West—Description
of the Theatre—Dickens's Account of "Astley's"—The third Theatre burnt down—Death of Ducrow—The Theatre rebuilt by Batty—Its
subsequent History—Its Name altered to Sanger's Grand National Amphitheatre.

UNLIKE Covent Garden, the Haymarket, and other "West-end" houses, the "Transpontine" theatres have always been chiefly remarkable for spectacular or "sensational" performances : in a word, for such entertainments as appeal more to the eye than to the understanding ; for, as may be easily imagined, their managers—in some of them, at least—have to cater altogether for a different constituency from that which forms the support of the old patent theatres, and generally those of the West-end. With reference to the morality of the transpontine theatres, Charles Knight wrote, in his *Penny Magazine*, in 1846 : "Look at our theatres ; look at the houses all around them. Have they not given a taint to the very districts they belong to ? The Coburg Theatre, now called the Victoria, and the Surrey, what are they ? At Christmas time, at each of these minor theatres, may be seen such an appalling amount of loathsome vice and depravity as goes beyond Eugene Sue, and justifies the most astounding revelations of Smollett." Happily, matters have mended considerably since he wrote, and the vicinity of even a minor theatre is now by no means so absolutely and hopelessly depraved. Allusions to the transpontine places of entertainment are common enough in the writings of the last generation ; and the authors of the "Rejected Addresses," published in the year 1812, in mock-heroic style, attribute, of course in jest, the burning of so many of our places of amusement to the arch-enemy, Napoleon Bonaparte !

" Base Bonapartè, fill'd with deadly ire,
    Sets one by one our play-houses on fire.
    Some years ago he pounced with deadly glee on
    The Opera House, then burnt down the Pantheon ;
    Nay, still unsated, in a coat of flames
    Next at Millbank he crossed the River Thames,
    Thy Hatch,* O Half-penny ! pass'd in a trice,
    Boil'd some black pitch, and burnt down Astley's twice ;
    Then buzzing on through ether, with a vile hum
    Turn'd to the left hand fronting the Asylum,
    And burnt the Royal Circus in a hurry—
    'Twas called the Circus then, but now the Surry."

Of the "Surrey" we have already written at length in a previous chapter ;† it now remains for us to deal with the "Victoria" and "Astley's." The Victoria Theatre, formerly called the Coburg, and in more recent times the Royal Victoria Palace Theatre, is situated in the Waterloo Road, at the corner of the New Cut, and not far from the South-Western Railway Station.

The building of Waterloo Bridge, which was commenced in 1811, and was completed six years afterwards, led to the erection of this theatre, which was originally called the "Coburg," in compliment to Prince Leopold of Saxe Coburg (afterwards King of the Belgians), the husband of the Princess Charlotte. The first stone was laid by the prince, by proxy, in October, 1817, and the theatre was opened on Whit-Monday in the following May. No doubt, a desire on the part of dramatists and performers to escape from the vexatious restrictions then (and still) imposed by the Lord Chamberlain on theatres within his jurisdiction was largely instrumental in procuring the erection of this and of the Surrey Theatre. The builder of the structure was an ingenious carpenter, a Frenchman, named Cabanelle,‡ who arranged it after the fashion of a minor French theatre, nearly circular in shape, decorating the interior with strong contrasts of colour. Few persons, in all probability, are aware that the foundations of the theatre are extensively composed of the stones of the old Savoy Palace in the Strand, which were cleared away in order to form Lancaster Place.§

The "Coburg" was built with a due regard to the character of the population by which it was surrounded, and was therefore designed for melo-dramas and pantomimes ; and, on the whole, it has adhered pretty closely to its original purpose, under a variety of lessees and managers. Among the pieces performed on the opening night was *Trial*

---

* See *ante*, p. 392.

† See *ante*, p. 368.
‡ This foreigner had constructed the stage of Drury Lane Theatre, and had also invented a peculiar kind of roof for large buildings, which was called by his name.
§ See Vol. III., p. 286.

by Battle; or, Heaven Defend the Right, based on the memorable appeal made by the brothers of Mary Ashford against her murderer, Abraham Thornton, the applicants' right to a "trial by wager of battle" having been acknowledged by the Court of King's Bench only a month previously. At the end of the first season the public were told by the proprietor that it was his intention "to have all the avenues (roads) to the theatre well lighted, while the appointed additional patrols on the bridge road —and keeping them in their own pay—will afford ample security to the patrons of the theatre." The public were also informed that the theatre was financially successful, though Tom Dibdin states that its opening was a "lamentable circumstance" to both its owners and the lessee of the Surrey; for that each speculation showed a loss of several thousands, whilst one theatre in that neighbourhood might have reaped a large profit. Be this, however, as it may, it is worthy of record that amongst those personages who have appeared on the boards of the Coburg are to be reckoned Edmund Kean (who received £100 for performing here two nights in 1830), Booth, T. P. Cooke, Buckstone, Benjamin Webster, Liston, Joe Grimaldi, and G. V. Brooke, the "Hibernian Roscius." In July, 1833—with a keen foresight of the future successor to the Crown—the name of the Coburg was changed to that of the "Victoria," in compliment to the young princess who then stood as heir presumptive to the throne, and the whole of the interior was altered and embellished afresh. In the June of the following year the great violinist, Paganini, performed here for a single night—his last public appearance in this country. A special feature of this theatre, for some years, was its "act drop," which was neither more nor less than a huge looking-glass. It was lifted up bodily into the roof, where a large box-shaped contrivance was fitted up to receive it. Notwithstanding that the old "Vic"—for so this theatre was popularly called—has in former times numbered among its scene-painters such men as Clarkson Stanfield, the great marine painter, the place does not appear to have been a very fortunate speculation for its managers or lessees, several being ruined by it.

When this theatre first opened its doors, upwards of half a century ago, it was in the presence of a "large and fashionable audience," if we may believe the newspapers of the day. The piece performed on that occasion, which we have mentioned above, entitled *Trial by Battle; or, Heaven Defend the Right*, was described in the play-bills as an entirely new melo-dramatic spectacle, in which was to be portrayed the ancient mode of

decision by Kemp fight, or single combat. There followed it a grand Asiatic ballet, and a new and splendid harlequinade (partly from Milton's *Masque of Comus*), "with new and extensive machinery, mechanical changes, tricks, and metamorphoses;" and the play-bills concluded with the comfortable assurance, "extra patroles are engaged for the bridge and roads leading to the theatre, and particular attention will be paid to the lighting of the same." But the "fashionable" audience did not long continue; and the street lamps, the costermongers' lamps of the New Cut, and the vigilance of the metropolitan police, soon rendered unnecessary the "extra patroles" or the manager's "particular attention" being paid to the lighting of the surrounding thoroughfares. The old "Vic" for many years enjoyed a very doubtful reputation. It was the place of which Charles Mathews once wrote: "The lower orders rush there in mobs, and in shirt-sleeves applaud frantically, drink ginger-beer, munch apples, crack nuts, call the actors by their Christian names, and throw them orange-peel and apples by way of bouquets." For many years it bore a terribly bad character for fatal accidents from crushing; and a false alarm of fire here caused the deaths of some fifteen or sixteen persons in December, 1858. In a few years more, however, a change came, and on the night of the 9th of September, 1871, a crowded audience beheld the last of the old Victoria. "It could be seen at a glance," observes a writer in the *Daily News*, "that the evening was one to be held in special fashion by the humble dwellers in the New Cut. A cherished institution, dear to them and their children, was doomed, and they had come to take a last fond look, and earn the right of narrating by the winter fire how they had seen the 'Vic' proud in its glory and triumphant in its expiring moments. The increase of prices to the extent of threepence in every part of the house had no effect upon the gallery or the pit, so that the precautions taken by the management to open the doors at half-past five were quite necessary. . . . A very laudable desire was felt to do all that could be done that the Victoria Theatre might end its days in peace, and pass to its rest with no fresh disaster on its conscience. The audience, over-awed maybe by the thoughts which seized them, assisted to secure this result. There, ascending from gallery front into the dim roof, were the lusty roughs, short-sleeved, slop-clothed, and cropped as of yore; but no missiles came from their hands; no internecine warfare was carried on, to the mingled delight and terror of the beholders; no oaths resounded from side to side; no Bedlam was let loose, as in the olden times when respectable West-enders would not have dared to enter the house without an unquestioned life assurance. The audience at the 'Vic' has been made to answer the purpose of 'awful warning' for many a long year, and we will do that of the closing night the justice to say that, composed undoubtedly as it was of persons living in the Lambeth highways and bye-ways, it was, on the whole, as decorous as that of any other house in the metropolis. The few cat-calls that some hardy and unfeeling youths at an early hour indulged in found no response; whistling even was at a discount; and the very children in arms stared wondrously at the drop-scene, and rubbed their sticky little knuckles into their sleepy little eyes." The theatre on this occasion was roused into a faint semblance of its former self when the foreboding strains of the overture heralded in "a Romantic Drama, entitled the *Trial by Battle*," the chief merit of which was, as we have before stated, that it commenced the entertainment when the theatre was first opened, on the 11th of May, 1818. It was not likely there could have been a single person present on the closing night who was also present when the curtain rose for the first time at the Coburg Theatre, albeit there were several who had seen themselves reflected in the famous mirror curtain, and who could remember the visit of the Princess Victoria and the house's subsequent change of name. The manager, Mr. Cave, offered a chastened, but still appropriate, play-bill for the last night, and engaged some well-known actors to grace the closing scenes. "*Rob Roy*," observes the writer quoted above, "though not of the bloody and ghostly type of play of which the 'Vic' was the natural exponent, is so bold in its situations, so full of 'Auld-Lang-Syne' sentiments, and so well seasoned with fighting material, that it could not fail to touch the heart of any genuine frequenter of the 'Vic.' It is just a little naughty, too: at least, to the extent of a considerable amount of dram-drinking, a fair allowance of cursing and swearing, and a sly approval of lawlessness and contempt for the powers that be." "Rob Roy," of course, found a host of sympathisers; and what with the capitally-sung songs, the sanguinary conflicts, the sentiment, and the final punishment of the villain "Rashleigh"—enacted, by the way, by one of the "Vic's" regular performers, "a painstaking artist, with fine rolling eye, trembling hand oft raised aloft, strongly heaving bosom, and r's well rolled out from the inner depths"—the curtain fell to a thunder of applause that seemed to come from one capacious and enthusiastic throat. The actors were summoned:

they departed; and still the applause continued, until the appearance of Mr. Cave sealed the vociferous tongues. The managerial speech was short, unpretentious, and to the point. First, thanks for the patronage he had enjoyed during his four years of management, and then the pathetic statement —"This evening the curtain will drop for ever upon the Victoria Theatre." In the next breath Mr. Cave was on with the new love before he was off with the old, inasmuch as he announced that in place of the "Vic" would arise a place of entertainment that would surpass "for magnitude and grandeur" anything the kingdom of Great Britain and Ireland ever saw. The godlings shouted "hear, hear!" as knowingly as members of Parliament, on being informed that the best dramas of the period would there be exhibited before the audiences of the future, and broke out into a perfect whirlwind of applause when it was added that the new proprietors did not intend to destroy the speciality of the theatre. The Victoria was henceforth to be half melo-drama and half music-hall. Mr. Cave then retired, full of honours; and, as the curtain fell, a mournful-voiced, bare-armed young man in the front row of the gallery audibly summed up the case thus:—"Ah! the poor old Wic! Pass the arf-an'-arf, 'Arry."

The following description of the closing scenes of the "poor old Wic," from the pen of an eyewitness, may be read with interest:—"The audience required but little explanation beforehand as to the last dish of the farewell feast. The bridge over the rocks, the greasy moon overhead, and the smugglers in the foreground, told the entire story the moment the curtain was fairly up. In the first few sentences our dear old friend 'Ongree' was introduced, closely followed by the equally familiar swarthy ruffian in sea-boots, with enough pistols about him to furnish a troop. Enter, also, a tall baron; next a tottering old man—the feeble father, upon whose only child the bold wicked noble has the worst of designs. In these smuggler bands there is always one buccaneer who plays the part of the repentant sinner, through whose honest treachery by-and-by vice—which is, of course, clothed in velvet and gold —is punished, and virtue—which, equally of course, goes in hunger and rags—is rewarded. The actor who undertook this character, an old stager in these parts, probably, was mildly requested to open his mouth by one section, and consoled by cries of 'Brayvo Bradshaw-er!' by another. He was a weak brother from the smuggler's point of view, and soon got himself into trouble by such heresies as, 'Never will I give my consent to bring a virtuous girl to infamy!'—a bit of oratory that drew loud expressions of approval from the only drunken man to be seen among the 1,500 persons crammed into the upper regions. The 'Vic' by this time was itself again. Shouts were answered by shrill whistlings, and the voices that one moment yelled 'Go it, my pippin!' were the readiest, the next, to howl, 'Turn him out!' Sentiment was thrown to the winds. The repentant smuggler's glib boast, 'Though I am a poor smuggler, I am yet a man!'

boisterous by any means. Mr. Cave seemed to think differently, for he shot like an arrow from the right wing, and rebuked the noisy portion of his patrons, hinting to them that the melo-drama had not been produced for larksome purposes, but to give them a taste of the ancient quality. A decent-looking man in the pit here made a remark, showing that he resented the extra prices which had been imposed; and Mr. Cave quietly reminded the

THE OLD "COBURG" THEATRE IN 1820.

was decidedly gibed at, all approval being reserved for the unscrupulous villain—the tool of the baron —who, without any hesitation, swore he cared for nothing in the world so long as he got 'the rhino.' The plotting of the village girl's abduction by the smugglers was a sore test of patience. The pit and other parts of the house admonished the occupants of the gallery to be quiet, but to no purpose. There was an under-tone of discontent which would not be allayed. The troubled waters were calmed by the sudden change of the music from the dirgeful to the thunder-and-lightning order of melody, such as precedes the opening of the trap-door on Boxing-night, and the advent of a herd of demons. The expected tragedy not happening on the instant, the discontent waxed louder, yet not

grievance-monger that if he had been there when the play was first produced, he would have had to pay three shillings for his seat." The piece hereafter proceeded with moderate interruptions only; but when the curtain fell and the theatre was cleared, there was a desolate look on the faces of the vast crowd that lingered outside—it might have been caused by the paltry number of four deaths during the melo-drama; or by the fact that the public-houses were closed; or, peradventure, because the people had seen the last of the "Vic."

The old theatre, a few days later, was again opened; but the principal actor on this occasion was the auctioneer, whose rostrum was erected on the stage, amidst heaps of "properties" and other articles. The stage, with all its traps, fittings,

ASTLEY'S RIDING SCHOOL IN 1770.
(*From Mr. J. T. Smith's "Historical and Literary Curiosities."*)

barrels, pulleys, &c., brought but £25. The building, however, was re-opened at the Christmas of the same year, under the altered and enlarged designation of the "Royal Victoria Palace Theatre," its interior having been entirely re-constructed and handsomely decorated by a new proprietary; but its success was very transient, for in March, 1874, it was again offered for sale by auction. The following description of the building we quote from the announcement of the sale :—"The approaches to the theatre are six in number, and afford ample and safe means by stone staircases for the rapid entrance and exit of crowded audiences, while the water supply is from five hydrants, attached to the high pressure main service, and three large cisterns. The interior arrangements are complete, and include the noble, lofty, and well-ventilated auditorium, of unique design, rising to a height of 50 feet, decorated in the Italian style, the walls being effectively lined with brilliant silvered plate-glass, and consisting of twelve large private boxes, 117 stalls, 119 balcony seats, with promenade to hold 250 more, 560 in pit, with promenade affording space for 400 more, and accommodation for 800 to 850 in gallery, thus affording, at present, accommodation for 2,300 persons, but with a judicious outlay it is calculated that additional sitting room may be obtained for 500 more visitors, thus giving a total audience of 2,800 persons. There are lofty, spacious, and appropriately-decorated refreshment-rooms adjoining the stalls, balcony, pit, and gallery, the whole being lighted by 500 jet burners, fixed to the roof, in a ring 96 feet in circumference." The theatre has since been converted into a huge "Coffee Palace," the stage being retained for concerts and other entertainments of a popular character, which are largely patronised by the working classes.

The "Vic"—or by whatever other name this theatre has been known — has indeed had a chequered existence, and one sad romantic tale at least is connected with it. A Miss Vincent, one of its managers, married a poor actor; but his head was so turned by his good fortune, that he was taken straight from the bridal party at the church doors to a lunatic asylum; and Miss Vincent died not long afterwards.

"If there was one place of entertainment—an institution it may be termed—more sacred to Londoners in particular, and provincialists in general," observes a writer in *Once a Week* (Dec. 27th, 1862), "one more presumably probable to have withstood the changes of time and fashion, less likely to have succumbed to a novel and not very classical style of dramatic entertainment, that place most certainly was Astley's. For, though

the remodelled theatre in Westminster Bridge Road is still associated with the name of its founder, yet an Astley's without horses is as yet simply a misnomer, a shadow without a substance." This famous theatre, or amphitheatre, dates from the year 1780. It cannot, of course, be mentioned in the same category with the patent theatres of Drury Lane, Covent Garden, and the "little theatre in the Haymarket;" and perhaps it is inferior also in standing to Sadler's Wells, with which it is almost cotemporary. "Originally," writes M. Alphonse Esquiros, in his "English at Home," "it was only a circus, started by Philip Astley, who had been a light horseman in General Elliott's regiment. . . . Astley's Amphitheatre, as it is called, though it has undergone various transformations since the death of its founder, is still (1862) a celebrated place for equestrian performances, exhibitions of trained ponies, elephants, dancing the tight rope, and even wild beasts, more or less tamed. I saw performed there a grand spectacle, in which appeared a lion that had killed a man on the night before. This painful circumstance, as may be believed, added a feeling of sadness and a species of tragic interest to the performance. The principal actor—I mean the lion—expressed no remorse for what he had done on the previous night; his face was calm and even benignant; he performed his part as if nothing had happened, and he followed the lion-conqueror (Van Amburgh) through the various situations of the piece."

Mr. Frost, in his "Old Showmen," gives the following account of the amphitheatre and its founder :—"Down to the end of the last century there are no records of a circus having appeared at the London fairs. Astley is said to have taken his stud and company to Bartholomew Fair at one time, but I have not succeeded in finding any bill or advertisement of the great equestrian in connection with fairs. The amphitheatre which has always borne his name (except during the lesseeship of Mr. Boucicault, who chose to call it the Westminster Theatre, a title about as appropriate as the Marylebone would be in Shoreditch) was opened in 1780, and he had previously given open-air performances on the same site, only the seats being roofed over. The enterprising character of Astley renders it not improbable that he may have tried his fortune at the fairs when the circus was closed, as it has usually been during the summer; and he may not have commenced his season at the amphitheatre until after Bartholomew Fair, or have given there a performance which he was accustomed to give in the afternoon at a large room in Piccadilly, where the tricks of a performing horse were varied with conjuring and *Ombres Chinoises*, a kind of shadow-pantomime. But, though Astley's was the first circus erected in England, equestrian performances in the open air had been given before his time by Price and Sampson. The site of Dobney's Place, at the back of Penton Street, Islington, was, in the middle of the last century, a tea-garden and bowling-green, to which Johnstown, who leased the premises in 1767, added the attraction of tumbling and rope-dancing performances, which had become so popular at Sadler's Wells. Price commenced his equestrian performances at this place in 1770, and soon had a rival in Sampson, who performed singular feats in a field behind the 'Old Hats' public-house. It was not until later, according to the historians of Lambeth, that Philip Astley exhibited his feats of horsemanship in a field near the Halfpenny Hatch, forming his first ring with a rope and stakes, after the manner of the mountebanks of a later day, and going round with his hat after each performance to collect the largesses of the spectators : a part of the business which, in the slang of strolling acrobats and other entertainers of the public in bye-streets and market-places and on village greens, is called ' doing a mob.'

" This remarkable man was born in 1742, at Newcastle-under-Lyme, where his father carried on the business of a cabinet-maker. He received little or no education—no uncommon thing at that time —and, having worked a few years with his father, enlisted in a cavalry regiment. His imposing appearance, being over six feet in height, with the proportions of a Hercules and the voice of a Stentor, attracted attention to him ; his capture of a standard at the battle of Ensdorff made him one of the celebrities of his regiment. While serving in the army, he learnt many feats of horsemanship from an itinerant equestrian named Johnson, and often exhibited them for the amusement of his comrades. On his discharge from the army, being presented by General Eliott with a horse, he bought another in Smithfield, and with these two animals gave the open-air performances in Lambeth which have been mentioned."

Next to Lord Granby and the Duke of Wellington, the most popular hero, if we may judge from his occurrence on sign-boards, was General Eliott, Lord Heathfield. Larwood ascribes this popularity in London to a curious cause—the gift of his white charger " Gibraltar " to Mr. Astley. This horse, he remarks, performing every night in the ring, and shining forth in the circus bills, would certainly act as an excellent " puff " for the general's glory.

Philip Astley received his discharge from the army in 1766, and exhibited in the country for about two years, till he considered himself capable of appearing before a London assemblage of spectators. He then set up what he termed a Riding School—merely a piece of ground enclosed by a slight paling—near a pathway that led through the fields from Blackfriars to Westminster Bridge. The terminus of the South-Western Railway now nearly, if not exactly, covers the spot. The first bill of performance that he issued here is as follows :—
" ACTIVITY on horseback of Mr. Astley, Serjeant-Major in His Majesty's Royal Regiment of Light Dragoons. Nearly twenty different attitudes will be performed on one, two, and three horses, every evening during the summer, at his riding school. Doors to be open at four, and he will mount at five. Seats, one shilling ; standing places, sixpence."

Early every evening Mr. Astley, dressed in full military uniform, and mounted on his white charger, took up a position at the south end of Westminster Bridge, to distribute bills and point out with his sword the pathway through the fields that led to his riding school. That it was a "school" in reality as well as name, we learn from the following advertisement :—" THE TRUE AND PERFECT SEAT ON HORSEBACK.—There is no creature yields so much profit as the horse ; and if he is made obedient to the hand and spur, it is the chief thing that is aimed at. Mr. Astley undertakes to break in the most vicious horse in the kingdom, for the road or field, to stand fire, drums, &c. ; and those intended for ladies to canter easy. His method, between the jockey and the *ménage*, is peculiar to himself ; no gentleman need despair of being a complete horseman that follows his directions, having eight years' experience in General Eliott's regiment. For half-a-guinea he makes known his method of learning (teaching) any horse to lay (*sic*) down at the word of command, and defies any one to equal it for safety and ease."

An information was soon lodged against Mr. Astley for receiving money from persons witnessing his feats of horsemanship, when, fortunately for him, George III. was riding over Westminster Bridge on a spirited horse, which proved restive and unmanageable even by the king, who was an excellent horseman. Astley happening to see him, came up, and soon convinced his Majesty of his skill in the managing of horses : the result was that he got rid of the information, and in a few days obtained a licence.

From the first Astley saw that his performances were deficient in variety ; so by energetic teaching he soon made two other excellent performers: his wife and the white charger. To make the most of the horse's performance, he interlarded it with some verses of his own composition. Introducing the animal, and ordering it to lie down, he would thus address the audience :—

> " My horse lies dead apparent in your sight,
> But I'm the man can set the thing to right;
> Speak when you please, I'm ready to obey—
> My faithful horse knows what I want to say;
> But first just give me leave to move his foot,
> That he is dead is quite beyond dispute.
>   *[Moving the horse's feet.*
> This shows how brutes by Heaven were designed
> To be in full subjection to mankind.
> Arise, young Bill, and be a little handy,
>   *[Addressing the horse.*
> To serve that warlike hero, Marquis Granby.*
>   *[Horse rises.*
> When you have seen all my bill exprest,
> My wife, to conclude, performs the rest."

The riding school being uncovered, there were but few spectators on wet evenings; but, as a partial remedy for this drawback, Mr. Astley ran up a shed, for admission to which he charged two shillings. He was soon enabled to invest £200, as mortgage, on a piece of ground near Westminster Bridge. Good fortune followed. The mortgagor went abroad, leaving a quantity of timber on the ground, and, so far as is known, was never heard of afterwards. About the same time, too, Astley found on Westminster Bridge a diamond ring, worth seventy guineas, that was never claimed by the loser. With this assistance he erected a new riding school on the piece of mortgaged ground ever since associated with his name. This place was open at the top; but next the road there was a wooden edifice, the lower part of which formed stables, the upper, termed "the long room," holding reserved seats for the gentry. A pent-house partly covered the seats round the ride; and the principal spectators being thus under cover, Astley now advertised to perform "every evening, wet or dry." We give on page 397 two views of this structure from Mr. J. T. Smith's "Historical and Literary Curiosities." The entrance was reached by steps from the road, and a green curtain covered the door, where Mrs. Astley stood to take the money. To the whitewashed walls were affixed some pictorial representations of the performances; and along the top of the building were figures of horses, with riders in various attitudes: these were made of wood and painted. This new house was opened about the year 1770, and one of the first bills relating to it states that "Mr. Astley exhibits, at

full speed, the different cuts and guards made use of by Eliott's, the Prussian, and the Hessian Hussars. Also the manner of Eliott's charging the French troops in Germany, in the year 1761, when it was said the regiment were all tailors."

About the same time, increasing his company, he was enabled to give more diversity to his entertainment; and one of the most successful sketches which he introduced was that time-honoured delight of rustics and children, *Billy Button's Ride to Brentford.* Master Astley, then but five years old, made his first appearance, riding on two horses. At this period Mr. Astley used to parade the West-end streets on the days of performance. He led the·procession, in military uniform, on his white charger, followed by two trumpeters; to these succeeded two riders in full costume, the rear being brought up by a coach, in which the clown and a "learned pony" sat and distributed handbills. This, however, did not long continue, for Mr. Astley soon announced that he had given up parading, "and never more intends· that abominable practice."

"Whitefield never drew as much attention as a mountebank does," writes Boswell, in his "Life of Johnson;" "he did not draw attention by doing better than others, but by doing what was strange. Were Astley to preach a sermon, standing upon his head on a horse's back, he would collect a multitude to hear him; but no wise man would say he had made a better sermon for that." Again, Horace Walpole, in a letter to Lord Strafford, dated September 12th, 1783, writes :—" London, at this time of year (September), is as nauseous a drug as any in an apothecary's shop. I could find nothing at all to do, and so went to Astley's, which, indeed, was much beyond my expectation. I did not wonder any longer that Darius was chosen king by the instructions he gave to his horse, nor that Caligula made his horse consul. Astley can make his dance minuets and hornpipes. But I shall not have even Astley now; Her Majesty the Queen of France, who has as much taste as Caligula, has sent for the whole of the *dramatis personæ* to Paris."

When the London season was over, Astley removed his *troupe* to Paris, a practice which he continued regularly for many years with great success. He·next brought out a new entertainment, styled in the bills "Egyptian Pyramids; or, La Force d'Hercule." It consisted in the now well-known feat of four men supporting three others on their shoulders, these again supporting two more, the last, in their turn, supporting one. This was long a very favourite and attractive

---

* The Marquis of Granby, the popular military hero of the day.

spectacle, and Astley erected a large representation of it on the south end of the riding school. He also named his private residence Hercules House, after this *tour de force.* The "Hercules" tavern and gardens, of which we have already spoken, were so called after this building; and the street in Lambeth, now called Hercules Buildings, derives its name from the same source.

The centre of the riding school being still uncovered caused many inconveniences; and Astley, as early as the year 1772, with a keen eye to the future, purchased, at a cheap rate, a quantity of timber that had been used as scaffolding at the funeral of Augusta, Princess Dowager of Wales. Later on, in 1780, a further supply of timber was cheaply obtained by a clever *ruse* on the part of Mr. Astley. It had long been the custom at the close of elections for the mob to destroy and make bonfires of the hustings; but Astley, mingling in the crowd, represented that as he would give beer for the timber, if it were carried to his establishment, it would be a more eligible way of disposing of it than by burning. The hint was taken, and with the timber thus obtained Astley covered in and completely remodelled the riding school, adding a stage, two tiers of boxes, a pit, and a gallery. But as this was the first attempt to exhibit horsemanship in a covered building, and the bare idea of doing so was at the time considered preposterously absurd, as a sort of compromise with public opinion, he caused the dome-shaped roof to be painted with representations of branches and leaves of trees, and gave the new edifice the airy appellation of "The Royal Grove."

Mr. Astley was now enabled to give his entertainments by candle-light; and one of the first pieces that he produced, however successful it may have been to the treasury, had a curious-sounding title, from an equestrian point of view; it figured in the bills as "A Grand Equestrian Dramatic Spectacle, entitled *The Death of Captain Cook.*" The sensation caused by the discoveries and death of Captain Cook was then fresh in the minds of the people; and Astley, seizing upon the principal events connected with that tragic affair, placed them on the stage in such a manner that the piece was most successful, and formed a very important step in the ladder by which the quondam sergeant-major was enabled to rise to fame and fortune.

It would appear, however, that Astley soon had a rival in the field; for Pennant writes in 1790:—"In this neighbourhood are two theatres of innocent recreation, . . . of a nature unknown to every other part of Europe—the British hippo-

dromes belonging to Messrs. Astley and Hughes—where the wonderful sagacity of that most useful animal, the horse, is fully evinced. While we admire its admirable docility and apprehension, we cannot less admire the powers of the riders, and the graceful attitudes which the human frame is capable of receiving." He goes on, in most prosy commonplace, to praise not only equestrian skill, but also the "art of tumbling" practised here, as " showing us how fearfully and wonderfully we are made;" and very sensibly recommending every Government to indulge its subjects in such scenes as " preservations from worse employs, and as relaxations from the cares of life." We have already spoken of Hughes's Circus, afterwards the Surrey Theatre, in our account of the Blackfriars Road.*

Up to this time Astley had performed annually in Paris during the winter months; and it was partly with the view of giving up these visits to the French capital that he constructed the " Royal Grove;" but as the proprietors of the patent theatres raised formidable objections to Astley's winter entertainments and dramatic representations in Lambeth, he was forced to continue his journeys to Paris. The breaking out of the French Revolution, however, put an end to Astley's Parisian performances; so, building a circus in Dublin, he carried on his winter campaigns in Ireland; and in 1792 he gave up the principal cares and management of the business to his son, whose first appearance we have noticed above, and who had by this time become a handsome young man, as agile and graceful as Vestris.

In the following year, war having broken out with France, the Duke of York was sent on the Continent in command of the British army; and Astley, who had made himself very useful in superintending the embarkation of the cavalry and artillery horses, went with his royal highness. His old regiment, the Fifteenth, was in the same army; and Astley, knowing by experience the wants of actual service, presented the men with a large supply of needles, thread, buttons, bristles, twine, leather—everything, in short, requisite in mending clothes and shoes. He also purchased a large quantity of flannel, and setting all the females employed at the " Royal Grove" to work, they soon made a warm waistcoat for every man of the regiment; and in a corner of each garment there was sewn what Astley termed "a friend in need:" in other words, a splendid shilling. This patriotic generosity being duly chronicled in the newspapers

---

* See *ante,* p. 368.

of the period, did not, as may readily be imagined, lessen the popularity of the " Royal Grove," or the nightly receipts of cash taken at the doors of that place of entertainment.

In 1794 Astley was suddenly recalled from the Continent by the total destruction of the " Royal

Bonaparte, then First Consul, for compensation; and, greatly to the surprise of every one, the petition was favourably received, and compensation granted. But scarcely had the money been received when hostilities again broke out, and all Englishmen in France were subjected to a long and painful deten-

ENTRANCE TO ASTLEY'S THEATRE IN 1820.

Grove" and nineteen adjoining houses by fire. Nothing daunted, he immediately commenced to rebuild it on a more elegant and extended scale, and at the following Easter opened the new house, re-naming it the " Amphitheatre of Arts." At the peace of Amiens, in 1803, Astley went to Paris, and finding that the circus he had erected in the Faubourg du Temple had been used as a barrack by the Revolutionary Government, he petitioned

tion as prisoners of war. Astley, however, by a rare combination of cunning and courage, effected his escape to the frontier, disguised as an invalid French officer. But, though favoured by fortune in this bold escape, dismal intelligence awaited his arrival in England. His faithful wife was dead, and his theatre a smoking ruin, having been a second time burned to the ground. The confla- gration on this occasion extended to forty other houses, and caused the death of young Mr. Astley's mother-in-law, Mrs. Woodham, and a loss to the proprietor of £30,000. Nevertheless, the gallant old sergeant-major again set to work to repair the losses he had sustained, and on the following Easter Monday another theatre was opened, this time as the "Royal Amphitheatre."

This amphitheatre is described by Sir Richard

Astley, when he first started his riding school, had no other music than a common drum, which was beaten by his wife. To this he subsequently added a fife, the players standing on a kind of small platform, placed in the centre of the ring; and it was not till he opened the Royal Grove that he employed a regular orchestra. Although an excellent rider, and a great favourite of George III.,

INTERIOR OF ASTLEY'S AMPHITHEATRE IN 1843.

Phillips at some length, in his "Modern London," published in 1804. "Being rebuilt after being lately burnt down," he writes, "it stands on the very ground on which Mr. Astley, senior, formerly exhibited feats of horsemanship and other amusements in the open air, the success and profits of which enabled him afterwards to extend his plan and to erect a building which, from the rural cast of the internal decorations, he called the 'Royal Grove.' In this theatric structure stage exhibitions were given, while in a circular area, similar to that in the late theatre, horsemanship and other feats of strength and agility were continued."

old Astley was an excessively ignorant man. One day, during a rehearsal a performer suddenly ceased playing. "Hallo!" cried Astley, addressing the delinquent; "what's the matter now?" "There's a rest," answered the other. "A rest!" Astley repeated, angrily; "I don't pay you to rest, but to play!" Upon another occasion, hearing a manager complain of the conduct of his actors, Astley said to him, "Why don't you treat them as I do *mine?*" —alluding, of course, to his horses—"I never give them anything to eat till after their performance is done."

Astley always kept a sharp eye on his instrumental performers. One evening he entered the orchestra in a rage, and asked of the leader why the trumpets did not play. "This is a *pizzicato* passage, sir," was the reply. "A pizzy—what?" said Astley. "A *pizzicato*, sir." "Well, I can't afford to let them be idle; so let the trumpets *pizzicato* too!" Indeed, as an accompaniment to equestrian exercises, Astley always considered that loudness was the most desirable quality in music. And though he ever took care to have an excellent band, with a well-qualified leader, he, nevertheless, considered them more as an indispensable drain on the treasury than a useful auxiliary to the performance. "Any fool," he used invariably to say, "can handle a fiddle, but it takes a man to manage a horse; and yet I have to pay a fellow that plays upon one fiddle as much salary as a man that rides upon three horses." Such opinions, freely expressed, not unfrequently led to angry scenes, of which amusing anecdotes have been related.

On one occasion, on the first night of a new piece, as the curtain rose to slow and solemn music, Astley, who was in the front observing the effect, overheard a carpenter sawing a board behind the scenes. "Go," said the manager to Smith, his rough-rider and aide-de-camp in ordinary, "go and tell that stupid fellow not to saw so infernally loud." Smith, fancying that Astley alluded to the music, went at once to the orchestra, and whispered in the leader's ear, "Mr. Astley has desired me to tell you not to saw so infernally loud." "Saw!" retorted the enraged musician; "go back and tell him this is the very last night I shall saw in his infernal stables!" Of course, when the curtain fell, the musician's wrath was appeased by the mistake being explained.

At another time, Astley requested his leader to arrange a few bars of music for a broad-sword combat—"a rang, tang, bang; one, two, three; and a cut sort of thing, you know!" for thus he curtly expressed his ideas of what he required. At the subsequent rehearsal Astley shouted out to his stage-manager, "Stop! stop! This will never do. It's not half noisy enough; we must get shields!" simply meaning that the mimic combatants should be supplied with shields to clash against the broad-swords, causing the noise so excitingly provocative of applause from the audience. But the too sensitive leader, thinking it was his music that was "not half noisy enough," and it was Shields, the composer, to whom Astley alluded, jumped out of the orchestra, and, tearing the score to pieces, indignantly exclaimed, "Get Shields, then, as soon as you please, for I am heartily sick and tired of you!"

Although uneducated, old Philip Astley was an enterprising man, with a strong mind and acute understanding; he was remarkable for his eccentric habits and sundry peculiarities of manner; and he is said to have built, at different periods of his life, at his own cost and for his own purpose, no less than nineteen theatres. He was the founder of, or, at all events, one of the earliest performers at the Olympic; and there is extant a print of Astley's trained horses, &c., performing there. He was particularly skilful in the training of horses. His method was to give each horse his preparatory lesson alone, and when there was no noise or anything to distract his attention from his instructor. If the horse was interrupted during the lesson, or his attention withdrawn, he was dismissed for that day, and the lesson was repeated on the next. When he was perfect in certain lessons by himself, he was associated with other horses whose education was further advanced; and it was the practice of that great "tamer of horses" to reward the animals with slices of carrot or apple when they performed well. In the same manner M. Franconi treated his horses in Paris.

Like Tom Dogget before him, the gallant old sergeant-major seems to have taken an interest in aquatic matters; at all events, we read in Strutt's "Sports and Pastimes," published in 1800: "Of late years the proprietor of Vauxhall Gardens and Astley, the rider, give each of them in the course of the summer a new wherry, to be rowed for by a certain number of watermen, two in each boat."

Astley lived to see another peace with France and to recover his property in Paris; for he died on the 20th of October, 1814, in the seventy-third year of his age, at his own residence in the Faubourg du Temple, and was buried in the well-known cemetery of Père la Chaise. His son, who was always termed "Young Astley," died in 1821, in the same bed, in the same house, and was buried in the same grave as his father.

After the decease of young Astley the theatre was carried on by Mr. W. Davis, and appears to have been called for a time "Davis's Amphitheatre" on the play-bills, though with the people at large it never ceased to be "Astley's." A melodrama, founded on the battle of Waterloo, was then among its chief attractions. Bonaparte was brought upon the stage face to face with Wellington, and made to utter very generous sentiments, and to do all sorts of generous things, which were loudly applauded by the galleries. But the public could not bear to have the old associations of the place disturbed even upon its play-bills, and the ancient name prevailed.

"Astley is a veteran in scenic feats at his amphitheatre and pavilion," writes Malcolm in his "Anecdotes of London," about 1810. But feats of strength and agility always shared the popular favour with horsemanship at Astley's; and among the most renowned performers in old Philip's days was Belzoni, who afterwards quitted the circus for the tombs of the Pharaohs and the Pyramids, and has left a foremost renown as an Egyptian explorer, as we have shown in our account of the British Museum.* There was another strong man, the "Flemish Hercules," whose real name was Petre Ducrow; he was the father of Andrew, destined in after years to become the proprietor of the theatre, and the most daring and graceful performing horseman the world has ever seen.

On the secession of Mr. Davis, the theatre was taken jointly by Messrs. Ducrow and West, under whose *régime* it became principally celebrated for its equestrian and gymnastic performances, pantomimes, and grand military spectacles, such as the *Battle of Waterloo*, the *Burning of Moscow*, &c. In 1843 was exhibited here a sensational piece, entitled, *The Crusaders of Jerusalem*, on which the *Illustrated London News* observes:—
"Here we have a scene from the circle of Astley's, so long the home of equestrian glory, the pride of the horsemanship of Ducrow. Ere-while burnt gloomily to the ground, the phœnix has now risen from its ashes, and the ancient palace of quadrupedal melo-drama again astounds its admiring inmates with examples of the wonderful instincts of horses, and the not less marvellous prowess of those biped actors who have trained them into obedience to the rein. Here is the true Surrey stud. 'Sell it!' once asked the alarmed Ducrow; 'Never!' 'Abandon it!' ejaculates Batty; 'Never!' is his reply, 'until children become mathematicians, and find me the "square" of my own "circle" while the horses are going round it!' 'Forsake it!' shrieks the dear delighted public, 'Nay, never.'

"'Nay! shout the people with indignant voices,
And the stud echoes with a thousand nays (neighs)!'"

Ducrow had been one of Astley's most famous riders. Mr. Disraeli, in a speech delivered at High Wycombe in 1836, compared the then Reform Ministry of Lord Melbourne to this great horseman. He said, addressing his audience, "I dare·say, now, some of you have heard of M. Ducrow, that celebrated gentleman who rides on six horses. What a prodigious achievement! It seems impossible;

but you have confidence in Ducrow. You fly to witness it; unfortunately, one of the horses is ill, and a donkey is substituted in its place. But Ducrow is still admirable: there he is bounding along in spangled jacket and cork slippers! The whole town is mad to see Ducrow riding at the same time on six horses; but now two more of the steeds are seized with the staggers, and lo! three jackasses in their stead! Still Ducrow persists, and still announces to the public that he will ride round his circus every night on his six steeds. At last, all the horses are knocked up, and now there are half-a-dozen donkeys. What a change! Behold the hero in the amphitheatre, the spangled jacket thrown on one side, the cork slippers on the other. Puffing, panting, and perspiring, he pokes one sullen brute, thwacks another, cuffs a third, and curses a fourth, while one brays to the audience, and another rolls in the sawdust. Behold the late Prime Minister and the Reform Ministry! The spirited and snow-white steeds have gradually changed into an equal number of sullen and obstinate donkeys; while Mr. Merryman, who, like the Lord Chancellor, was once the very life of the ring, now lies his despairing length in the middle of the stage, with his jokes exhausted, and his bottle empty."

Grimaldi, whose father lived close by Astley's, in Stangate, was often engaged here as a clown. On one occasion, Ducrow, while teaching a boy to go through a difficult act of horsemanship, applied the whip to him, and observed to Grimaldi, who was standing by, that it was necessary to make an impression on the boy. "Yes," said Joe; "but you need not make the whacks (wax) so hard."

The amphitheatre, as it stood in Ducrow's time, is thus described in Allen's "History of Surrey," published in 1830:—"The front of the theatre, which is plain and of brick, stuccoed, stands laterally with the houses in Bridge Road, the access to the back part of the premises being in Stangate Street. There is a plain wooden portico, the depth of which corresponds with the width of the pavement. In front of this portico is the royal arms. Within the pediment in front of the building is 'Astley's' in raised letters, and in the front of the portico, in a similar style, 'Royal Amphitheatre.' Beneath this portico are the entrances to the boxes and pit; the gallery entrance is lower down the road, and separated from the front of the theatre by several houses. The boxes are approached by a plain staircase, at the head of which is a handsome lobby. The form of the auditory is elliptical, and is lighted by a very large cut-glass lustre and chandeliers with bell-lamps; gas is the medium of

---

illumination used all over the premises. There is one continued row or tier of boxes round the auditory, above the central part of which is the gallery; and there is a half tier of upper boxes on each side, with slips over them. The floor of the ride within the auditory is earth and sawdust, where a ring or circle, forty-four feet in diameter, is bounded by a boarded enclosure about four feet in height, the curve of which next the stage forms the outline of the orchestra, and the remainder that of the pit, behind which is an extensive lobby and a box for refreshments. The proscenium is large and movable—for the convenience of widening and heightening the stage, which is, perhaps, the largest and most convenient in London—and is terminated by immense platforms, or floors, rising above each other, and extending the whole width of the stage. These are exceedingly massive and strong. The horsemen gallop and skirmish over them, and they will admit a carriage, equal in size and weight to a mail coach, to be driven across them. They are, notwithstanding, so constructed as to be placed and removed in a short space of time by manual labour and mechanism."

Our readers will not forget that "Astley's," as it was some half a century ago, forms one of the "Sketches by Boz," which made the fame, though not the name, of Charles Dickens as a young man known to the world. "It was not a 'Royal Amphitheatre' in those days," he wrote, "nor had Ducrow arisen to shed the light of classic taste and portable gas over the sawdust of the circus; but the whole character of the place was the same: the pieces were the same, the clown's jokes were the same, the riding-masters were equally grand, the comic performers equally witty, the tragedians equally hoarse, and the 'high-trained chargers' equally spirited. Astley's has altered for the better—we have changed for the worse." And then he proceeds to give a sketch of the interior during a performance in the Easter or Midsummer holidays, and the happy faces of "the children," whom "pa" and "ma" have taken to witness the scene, including "Miss Woolford" and the other *equestriennes*.

Thackeray, too, mentions this place in "The Newcomes." "Who was it," he writes, "that took the children to Astley's but Uncle Newcome? I saw him there in the midst of a cluster of these little people, all children together. He laughed, delighted at Mr. Merriman's jokes in the ring. He beheld the *Battle of Waterloo* with breathless interest, and was amazed—yes, amazed, by Jove, sir!—at the prodigious likeness of the principal actor to the Emperor Napoleon. . . . The little

girls, Sir Brian's daughters, holding each by a finger of his hands, and younger Masters Alfred and Edward clapping and hurraing by his side; while Mr. Clive and Miss Ethel sat in the back of the box enjoying the scene. . . . It did one good to hear the colonel's honest laugh at the clown's jokes, and to see the tenderness and simplicity with which he watched over this happy brood of young ones."

The third theatre on this spot was burnt down in June, 1841, when under the management of Ducrow, who died insane shortly after the fire, on account of the losses he sustained. He was buried, as we have already seen, at Kensal Green Cemetery,* where a handsome monument is erected to his memory.

In October of the same year, the vacant site was taken on a long lease by Mr. William Batty, who, in the following year, erected at his own expense the present amphitheatre, which is much larger and more substantially built than any of its predecessors.

Very naturally, as we have observed at the commencement of this chapter, the transpontine theatres have always been the chief homes of the sensational drama and of eccentric exhibitions: and this is as true of Astley's as of the rest. Here, for instance, in 1790, were exhibited Mynheer Wybrand Lolkes, the dwarf watchmaker of Holland, and his wife, who was just three times his height; but as time has worn on "sensationalism" seems to have been triumphant. At all events, in the autumn of 1864, Miss Ada Menkens here played *Mazeppa* to crowded houses; while other theatres, although possessing very good actors, were all but deserted. In 1873 the theatre was taken by Mr. Sanger, who had for a short time previously occupied the Agricultural Hall at Islington for equestrian performances. Under this gentleman's rule the title of "Astley's" has disappeared from the bills as the name of the establishment, and in its place we have "Sanger's Grand National Amphitheatre." But Astley's is Astley's still with the people, and the old associations of the place still remain, at all events in part, for elephants, camels, dromedaries, as well as horses, are still made to appear upon the stage in order to heighten the spectacular effect. Although the present theatre was constructed with both stage and circle for horsemanship, the latter was for a time discontinued, but the old tradition of the place has since been revived.

M. Esquiros observes pertinently, with reference to Astley's: "If asked what relation such a theatre can have to the poetic drama, I reply, that it is the peculiar privilege of the great works of the human mind that they adapt themselves to circumstances. Mr. Cooke, one of the latest managers of Astley's Amphitheatre, had the idea of applying the resources and pomps peculiar to this theatre to Shakespeare's historical plays. He accordingly brought out here *Richard III.*, and, for the first time, the hump-backed Richard was seen on the stage, surrounded by his staff on horseback, and himself mounted on that famous steed, 'White Surrey,' whose name Shakespeare has immortalised. The noble animal marched bravely through the battle, and died with an air of truth that quite affected the spectators. Encouraged by this success, Astley's company next appeared in *Henry IV.* and *Macbeth.* I will not assert that Shakespeare's plays thus converted into equestrian pieces satis-

fied all artistic conditions; but when I look at the moral effect, I cannot but applaud the experiment. Astley's is the theatre of the people; here the East-end" [Transpontine?] "workmen, costermongers, and orange-women, come to seek a few hours of recreation after the fatigues and struggles of a rough day's toil. Shakespeare's plays—decorated rather than well performed, and hidden by processions and cavalcades, which, perhaps, denaturalised their character, but which, after all, were adapted to the instincts of a class of the population which lives specially on what strikes its eyes—at any rate allowed some portion of the poetical horizon to be brought within their view. In any case, and to say the least, they happily occupied the place of those dangerous performances which arouse in man nothing beyond the feeling of savage strength."

CHAPTER XXXI.

LAMBETH (*continued*).—WATERLOO ROAD, &c.

" In populous city pent,
Where houses thick, and sewers, annoy the air."—*Milton.*

Ecclesiastical Divisions of the Parish of Lambeth—The Lambeth Water-works—The Shot Factory—Belvidere Road—Royal Infirmary for Children and Women—The General Lying-in Hospital—St. John's Church—The Grave of Elliston—The South-Western Railway Terminus—The New Cut—Sunday Trading—The Victoria Palace Theatre—Dominic Serres—St. Thomas's Church—Lambeth Marsh—Bishop Bonner's House—Erasmus King's Museum—The "Spanish Patriot"—All Saints' Church—The Canterbury Hall—The Bower Saloon—Stangate— "Old Grimaldi"—Carlisle House—Norfolk House—Old Mill at Lambeth—The London Necropolis Company—St. Thomas's Hospital—The Albert Embankment—Inundations in Lambeth—Lambeth Potteries and Glass Works—Schools of Art—Manufactures of Lambeth.

BY an order of council, made in 1825, the parish of Lambeth was divided into five districts—called respectively St. Mary's, or the old church district; Waterloo, or St. John's district; Kennington, or St. Mark's; Brixton, or St. Matthew's; and Norwood, or St. Luke's. Of the three last-named districts we have already treated in the course of our perambulations. Of St. John's district we will now proceed to speak.

The formation of Waterloo Bridge—which was completed and opened on the 18th of June, 1817—as may be expected, soon made a great alteration in the appearance of Southern London, especially in those parts lying between Blackfriars and Westminster Bridge Roads. Towards the close of the last century, water-works for Lambeth were established in the Belvidere Road, on part of Belvidere Wharf, and what was formerly a garden on the Narrow Wall. A company—called the Lambeth Water-works Company—was established for supplying the parish of Lambeth and parts adjacent with water taken from the Thames. They commenced their operations with a small capital, but by careful management, and avoiding a large

expenditure at the commencement, their enterprise was attended with success.

Previous to the formation of the above-mentioned company, the portion of the metropolis lying south of the river Thames was first supplied with water by two wheels erected at London Bridge, near the Surrey shore, and also by separate works at St. Mary Overies. These two establishments, both of considerable antiquity, were combined, under the name of the Southwark Water-works, in 1822. In 1805, a third company, the Vauxhall Water-works Company, was established for supplying the Surrey side of London. They took their water at first from the river Effra, and subsequently from the Thames, near Vauxhall Bridge.

All the above-mentioned companies, in the first instance, supplied water just as it came to hand, without being over-particular as to its condition. Between the years 1820 and 1830, however, the attention of the public was attracted to the quality of the water they were then receiving, and since it appeared that improvement was needed, the companies, urged by the pressure from without, took steps to improve it accordingly. The Lambeth

Water-works Company, shortly after 1830, formed elevated reservoirs at Brixton Hill and Streatham, for the purpose of the service generally, and maintaining a constant supply of water in case of fire. Of late years, however, they have made a great improvement in the old condition of things ; for,

twenty-three miles above London Bridge, and far beyond the reach of the tide.

About the same time that the water-works were established here, a large shot factory was built close by, together with a fine wet-dock for the loading and warehousing of goods. Near Waterloo Bridge,

THE HOUSES IN WATERLOO BRIDGE ROAD.

considering the state of the river in the tide-way objectionable as a source of supply (owing principally to the constant agitation now kept up by the steamboats plying between the bridges, and the increased quantity of sewage poured into the Thames in the London district), they obtained, in 1848, an Act to enable them to abandon their former source near the Belvidere Road, and to take water from the pure stream of the river at Ditton,

and close to the site of Cuper's Gardens, of which we have already spoken,[*] another shot manufactory was erected about the year 1789 by Messrs. Watts. The height of the tower of this manufactory is 140 feet, and the shot falls upwards of 120 feet. These shot towers are conspicuous objects on the southern side of the Thames near Waterloo Bridge.

---

[*] See *ante*, p. 388.

The Belvidere Road, or Narrow Wall, is an ancient way, as it is depicted in views of London dated 1588; as are Vine Street and the Cornwall Road; but no houses seem to have been in either of them, with the exception of a few in and about Vine Street. From the Belvidere Road, in the present day, an excellent opportunity is afforded of noticing the extent of the artificial elevation given to the road when the approaches to Waterloo

stands, has allowed the committee to purchase the freehold on advantageous terms. In 1875 the building was enlarged and considerably improved. The institution, which is supported by donations and subscriptions, at first received children only, to whom it afforded relief for diseases of all kinds, from the time of birth till fourteen years of age, being open, in cases of emergency, to all first applications for admission without any recommendation.

VIEW IN THE NEW CUT.

Bridge were made. Indeed, it hardly needs the occasional incursions of the river to remind the water-side inhabitants that this now dense and widely-spreading region was once a marsh, and even a flat swampy level, scarcely raised above the surface of the Thames.

One of the first institutions which attracts our attention as we pass down the Waterloo Road is the Royal Infirmary for Children and Women, which has stood here for upwards of half a century. It was originally established at St. Andrew's Hill, in the City, in 1816, but was removed to Lambeth in 1823. The Duke of Kent assisted in founding the infirmary, and the Queen has long been an annual subscriber; and the Prince of Wales, on whose estate as Duke of Cornwall the hospital

There were in 1877 fifty beds and cots in the hospital, and an asphalte playground on the roof for convalescent patients. During the preceding year 232 in-patients (children) were received, and 6,550 out-patients (women and children) visited. There were, during the same period, 1,430 visits paid by the resident medical officer to sick children at home. In 1877 the Princess Louise (Marchioness of Lorne) formally re-opened the infirmary on the completion of the enlargement mentioned above, when one of the wards—hitherto known as the "Hamilton Ward," from having been founded at the expense of Mr. Francis Hamilton, one of the vice-presidents—was, at the request of that gentleman, re-named the "Louise Ward." There are now six wards in all. The patients all pay something towards their treatment. The out-patients pay 1d. for each visit, and the parents of the in-patients give 6d. a week. In some cases these sums are provided by friends connected with the hospital. This hospital, we need scarcely add, is situated in the midst of one of the poorest districts of London, and provides comfortable beds, good food, kind nursing, and medicine for sick children and women, who cannot get these things at home, and that, therefore, it is an institution deserving of the heartiest support.

Another invaluable institution in this neighbourhood—a sister hospital to the Magdalen—is the General Lying-in Hospital in York Road. It was instituted in 1765, mainly through the exertions of Dr. John Leake, an eminent writer on the diseases of women, and was incorporated in 1830. The hospital was formerly in the Westminster Bridge Road, near Marsh Gate, from which, in 1829, it was removed to its present situation, where a neat square building of white brick, ornamented with stone, with a handsome receding portico of the Ionic order, has been erected. The hospital was principally intended as an asylum "for the wives of poor industrious tradesmen and distressed housekeepers, who, either from unavoidable misfortunes, or from the burden of large families, are reduced to want, and rendered incapable of bearing the expenses incident to the lying-in state, and also for the wives of indigent soldiers and seamen; but the governors, in the spirit of true philanthropy, have extended the benefits of the institution to unmarried females, restricting this indulgence, however, to the first instance of misconduct."

Pennant enumerates the Lying-in Hospital, the Asylum, or House of Refuge, and the Magdalen, as admirable institutions within a short distance of each other, and together helping to relieve the sufferings of the weaker sex.

Lower down the Waterloo Road, on the east side, and nearly facing the terminus of the South-Western Railway, stands St. John's Church, which was built in 1823-4. The site of this church having been a swamp and horse-pond, an artificial foundation of piles had to be formed before any portion of the superstructure could be raised. The edifice, which is anything but ecclesiastical in character, is built of brick, with stone dressings; the plan of the basement comprehends not only the church, but a terrace in front of it—the former is a parallelogram, the latter forms a transept at the west end, the whole of the area being laid out in catacombs. The terrace was rendered necessary to fill up the space between the church and the road, which is considerably raised to meet the

level of Waterloo Bridge. The western front of the building is occupied with a Grecian portico of the Doric order, sustaining an entablature, cornice, and pediment, the frieze being ornamented with chaplets of myrtle. The steeple is situated above the centre of the front: it consists of a tower and spire, both of which are square in their plan; the storey above the clock-dial is of the Ionic order. The obelisk on the summit is crowned by a stone ball and cross. The interior of the church is not divided into nave and aisles, according to the usual plan; the piers between the windows are ornamented with pilasters, and the ceiling is horizontal and panelled.

The sides and west end of the church is occupied by a gallery, sustained on Doric columns. The organ was the gift of Mr. Lett, an inhabitant of the district, who was also the donor of the site of the church. In the centre aisle is a font of white marble, brought from Italy, and presented to the church by the Rev. Dr. Barrett, the first incumbent. The east end is ornamented with a handsome stained-glass window, and the reredos is richly gilt and painted in arabesque.

St. John's Church contains one memorable tomb, that of Elliston, the comedian, whose name is so intimately connected, as we have seen, with transpontine performances. Those who have read Charles Lamb's reminiscences of Elliston, in his "Ellistoniana," and his address "to the shade of Elliston," will not need to be reminded how great an actor he was, though in the main a comedian. He was well educated, and never forgot the knowledge of Latin that he acquired during his youth. "Great wert thou," writes Charles Lamb, "in thy life, Robert William Elliston, and not lessened in thy death, if report speaks truly, which says thou didst direct that thy mortal remains should repose under no inscription but one of pure Latinity." He was born in Bloomsbury in 1774, and was educated at St. Paul's School, being originally intended for the University. In his boyhood, however, he was brought into contact with the late Mr. Charles Mathews, and both being smitten with a love of the drama, made their first effort on private boards, on the first floor of a pastry-cook's shop in Bedford Street, Covent Garden, along with a daughter of Flaxman, the sculptor. Having played in public at Bath, York, and other towns in the provinces, Elliston made his first appearance in London at the Haymarket in 1796. He was a most joyous and light-hearted man, excellent alike in tragedy and comedy, and unrivalled in farce; and he enjoyed a long lease of popular favour. We have already mentioned his connection with the Olympic and the Surrey Theatres.*　In his capacity as manager he would often favour the audience with a rich specimen of the grandiloquent style—a style immortalised by Charles Lamb in one of his delightful Essays.　He died in 1831.

The churchyard contains some fine plane-trees; and steps were, in 1876, being taken to lay it out as a garden, and make it available for the purposes of recreation.

Nearly opposite St. John's Church is the London terminus of the South-Western Railway, together with the Waterloo Junction station of the South-Eastern Railway.　The South-Western terminus in itself is spacious, but makes no pretence to architectural effect.　The South-Western Railway was originally called the London and Southampton Railway, and had its terminus for several years at Nine Elms, Vauxhall.　About thirty miles were open for traffic in 1838, the line being extended in the following year to Basingstoke, and in 1840 to Southampton.　The extension from Vauxhall to the Waterloo Road was effected in 1848, and although only a trifle over two miles in length, cost £800,000.　From Waterloo Road to Nine Elms the line is carried through what is—or, at all events, was at one time—one of the dirtiest parts of London, upon a series of brick arches, which were considered marvels of construction when they were built.　From the Waterloo Road, the approaches to the booking-offices are by inclined roads.　Of the station itself little or nothing need be said, further than that it has been so much enlarged and altered at different times since its first erection, that it now covers a very large space of ground.　It is connected with the South-Eastern Railway by a bridge for trains and passengers. From this station trains run at frequent intervals to Richmond, Hampton Court, Windsor, &c.; also to Winchester, Portsmouth, Southampton, Weymouth, Salisbury, Exeter, Plymouth, and other large towns in the south-west and west of England.　"The advantages of this metropolitan station," writes Bradshaw, in his "London Guide," "have been very great, both to mere pleasure-seekers and men of business; and when about to undertake a journey on this most tempting and trustworthy of all the railways, it is felt to be something akin to magic to be wafted from the very heart of London to the verge of Southampton Water in less time than one could walk from here to Hampstead; or enabled to enjoy the enchanting scenery of Richmond and Hampton Court for an expenditure of the same sum that would be absorbed in the most

moderate indulgence at a gloomy tavern in town."　A few minutes' ride on this railway will show the traveller as much as he will care to see of this crowded and rather squalid neighbourhood, and speedily carry him into the fields, out of the smoke of London.

The New Cut, which runs from the Waterloo to the Blackfriars Road, at a short distance southward of the railway terminus, is chiefly remarkable for the number of its brokers' shops, which line both sides of the way.　The thoroughfare, on Sunday mornings, has somewhat the character of its rival near Aldgate, formerly called Petticoat Lane;† and it has furnished plenty of materials to Henry Mayhew for his sketches of "London Labour and the London Poor."　The following sketch of the New Cut on a Sunday morning is taken from a pamphlet, entitled "Sabbath Life in London," published in 1874.　The writer, a Scotchman, after narrating what met his gaze in his rambles through Petticoat Lane, Leather Lane, and Seven Dials, proceeds :—　"Crossing one of the bridges, the same disregard of the day of rest is exhibited on the Surrey side of the Thames; and from London Bridge to Vauxhall Bridge, a distance of three miles, there is an almost continuous line of streets in which business is conducted as on other days.　In this respect the New Cut takes a prominent part, and the thoroughfare is thronged with women having their aprons full of provisions.　The manner in which these untidy dames patronise the ginger-beer stalls indicates pretty plainly the dealings they had with the publican on the previous evening; and if that is not enough, a glance at the many bruised and blackened faces will show, certainly not the joys, but the buffetings of matrimonial life.　Were such characters to show their figures in any town in Scotland on a 'Sabbath' morning, loaded with articles for the dinner-table, they would cause as much consternation as if a legion of Satanic forces were let loose, and the people, in their deep-rooted regard for the day, would compel these wanton Sunday desecrators to beat a speedy retreat from public indignation.　There is something noble in accounts given of the women in America besieging the public-houses, emptying the destroying liquors into the sewers, and turning the barrel-bellied landlords into the streets.　Should ever a civil war befall this country, may it be a rising of Good Templar Amazons against brewers, distillers, and their satellites the publicans.　Would that the American spirit could be infused into the mass of London wives and mothers, not by an exhibition of their

---

* See Vol. III., p. 35; and *ante*, p. 370.

† See Vol. II., p. 164.

physical determination, but by a display of their moral power and example, by absenting themselves altogether from the dram-shop, leaving the publican to find a better and more certain field of investment. On my way to Lambeth I passed the door of the Bower Theatre, and my attention was attracted by the play-bill, which announced these pieces :—' Innocent or Guilty,' ' Charley Wagg, or the Mysteries of London,' and the ' Hand of Death.' This theatre is nightly crowded with boys, the children of the Sunday-trading women I have alluded to. There can be no doubt that such ' penny gaffs ' have a tendency to vitiate the minds of the rising generation, as has also much of the cheap literature which is issued from the press. There are parties in the literary and dramatic world who live upon vice and corruption ; and many of the penny publications, ostensibly got up for boys, and profusely illustrated, are little better than guides to the prison and the penitentiary. Whilst musing on the base purposes to which the drama is too often devoted in this money-grasping age, I was surprised to notice, in large letters, the title of a piece now being performed at the Adelphi, ' The Prayer in the Storm, or the Thirst for Gold.' Just as well might the publican designate his premises ' The House of Prayer,' ' The Gate of Heaven,' or ' The Celestial Abode.' The legitimate drama has many beauties, and serves many useful purposes ; but when it goes beyond the teachings of morality, and encroaches on the domains of religion, it deserves to be treated with reprobation and contempt."

The Sunday trading in the " Cut " is continued westward through Lambeth Lower Marsh towards the Westminster Bridge Road, so that the whole distance from the last-named road to Surrey Chapel presents what Dr. Johnson would have called " an animated appearance."

The regular *habitués* of the place may be divided into two classes—the various dealers and vendors, mostly of " perishable articles," with their regular customers, on the one hand ; and on the other the dealers in miscellaneous goods, and the hundreds of men and boys of the working, and what some people call the " dangerous " classes — irregular customers—among whom may be seen the real British " navvy," as good a specimen of humanity after his kind as one need wish to look upon, whose Sunday morning costume differs only from his week-day in having his boots unlaced. To such as these the New Cut is a Sunday morning rendezvous and promenade, and they amuse themselves by sauntering up and down the half-mile of roadway, pipe in mouth, and listening to the oratorical displays of the vendors of every imaginable kind of wares, useful and ornamental, on either side of the road.

A writer in the *Daily News*, in January, 1872, gives us the following sketch of a Sunday morning in the New Cut :—" On entering the Lower Marsh from the Westminster Road, on the right-hand side are the Lambeth Baths, in which a temperance meeting is held every Sunday morning. A platform at one end holds the speakers and singers, for, to enliven the proceedings, between each speech some one sings a song to a lively tune, accompanied by a piano, and the audience—part of which is seated in the spacious bath, from which the water has been drawn off—join in the chorus. There is a continual flow of in-comers and out-goers, and it may be hoped that the zealous preachers of temperance now and then really capture and reform some wretched drunkard, who perhaps ' came in to scof,' but remained to listen to and profit by the retailed experiences of the speakers, many of whom are by no means ashamed to compare their present good health and comparatively full pockets to their former broken-down state and poverty, which was the result of drink. The shops in the Cut may be stated in round numbers to be about 220, of which about one-half were open for business, the other half closed, on Sunday morning ; while the stalls and barrows of the costermongers proper, that is, dealers in ' perishable articles ' (and perhaps including the vendors of the poor man's luxuries— nuts and oranges—which keep to the line of the gutters), might be reckoned at about 120 ; while those of the vendors of non-perishable articles and the itinerant sellers of all kinds of commodities might be stated at a somewhat less figure. Among the latter class may be found the familiar figure of the old razor-paste man ; he is to be met with in almost every part of the metropolis during the week, but he is part of the Cut on Sunday. Then there is the seller of knives at half-price ; of slippers, braces, boots and shoes, and all kinds of wearing apparel, after *its* kind. In front of a chemist's shop a hearty-looking man is retailing sarsaparilla from a huge bottle, which he holds under the stump of his left arm (in fact, all that is left), at 1d. per glass. It will ' cure more disorders than Holloway's pills and ointment, chase away headaches and nervous debility, purify the blood, and bring flesh on the bones.' From the numbers who in the course of a few minutes paid for their draught and drank it like men, we can quite believe the statement made by the vendor that he sold more than a thousand glasses every Sunday morning. . . . Sufferers from ' the ills the flesh is heir to ' are well cared for in the New Cut. A penny stick of some green substance, like sealing-wax, will make many scores of plasters on brown paper, warranted to cure warts, bunions, and corns. Three plasters applied for three successive days will eradicate the worst of corns, but the pain will vanish in five minutes after the first application. Blisters, already spread, can be bought by the yard ; and those suffering from toothache can have the offending ivory extracted then and there. The dental professor wears a velvet cap, ornamented with about a hundred long-fanged double-teeth, set in rows, and stands behind a tray, on which are displayed some half-dozen villanous-looking instruments of extraction, one of which, eminently terrible, seemed a cross between a pair of lump-sugar nippers and a pair of tongs. In front were penny bottles of tincture, warranted to cure ear-ache, rheumatism, chilblains, and all kinds of ' rualgias.' The volubility of this professor was extraordinary in his endeavours to dispose of his tinctures, but he was far surpassed by the torrents of eloquence which rushed continuously from the ' doctor ' a little higher up, who sold a large box of pills and a half-pint bottle of sarsaparilla for the modest sum of threepence. The ' doctor '—really a clever fellow—did an enormous trade, amply compensating him for his unsparing expenditure of eloquence and breath. The result of his medicine on the scores who purchased it will be much better felt than described ; but it is certain that his patients have unlimited faith in him and his therapeutics, which he illustrated occasionally with a human skull, alleged to be that of an illustrious murderer, cut into sections, and parts of which seemed to work on hinges." The writer then proceeds to describe the bird-dealers, and the sellers of groundsel and chickweed ; the dog-fanciers, with their true " doormats " and " mop-heads " under their arms ; the purveyors of cheap pictures, ornaments, and toys, &c. ; the piled heaps of dirty women's clothing, upper and under, which female auctioneers are selling by a process known as a " Dutch auction." " Sunday morning," continues the writer, " is the weekly harvest time of many of the local shops, notably that of a baker, who displays on a slab outside most tempting jam tarts and puffs, purchased eagerly by juveniles who are the fortunate possessors of a halfpenny. A hot plum composition, a kind of compromise between cake and pudding, sold in large blocks, ' meets with a ready demand at fair prices,' and at its current value must be ' very filling.' Two rival vendors of this compost at opposite sides of the street created much amusement by chaffing one

another across the highway, and assuring intending purchasers that ' this is the right shop ; ' however, the owner of a most stentorian voice, for which natural gift he ought to be thankful, gets the most custom, according to the rule which seems to obtain in this transpontine market, that the most demonstrative and vociferous merchants do the best trade. There is much good humour, a little rough horse-play, and some bad language in this unwashed crowd of buyers, sellers, and idlers ; more of the former and less of the latter than might be expected, which may possibly be attributed to the fact that the public-houses do not open till one o'clock. A few minutes before that hour the police nod the word, and with almost the quickness of a transformation scene at the theatre, the coster-mongers and their barrows, the itinerant traders and their wares, disappear down the many side streets, and this mercantile Pandemonium is then hushed. Idlers gradually disperse, and hot dinners —baked meat and potatoes, the usual wasteful dish of the English poor—issue from various bakers' and other shops, reminding even those who unhappily will not profit by it that this is the poor man's dinner hour. By half-past one the Cut has resumed its ordinary aspect, and has become as dull and quiet, and perhaps as ' respectable,' as Bedford or Tavistock Squares."

At the corner of the New Cut and Waterloo Road stands the Victoria Palace Theatre, which we have described in the preceding chapter. One of the few subscribers that came forward to back the scheme for building the Victoria (or, as it was at first called, the Coburg) Theatre, was one Serres, a marine painter, whose name became known to the world through a little piece of Court scandal. He made interest with Prince Leopold of Saxe Coburg, and the Princess Charlotte, in order to procure a licence for its establishment. " Dominic Serres and his two daughters," observes a writer in a newspaper, in January, 1837, " lived in a first floor, next to the fire-engine station, opposite to the stage-door of the Victoria Theatre. One died there : she was a short, dumpy woman ; the younger was horribly deaf. Their niece, Johanna, daughter of J. T. Serres, and Olivia, Duchess of Lancaster, married, and has children living at the second or third house in Gibson Street. The surviving aunt has since gone to live with her." The attempt of the Serres family to obtain recognition of the title of Duchess of Lancaster was brought before a court of law, and finally exposed in 1870, as our readers will remember.*

---

* See Vol. IV., p. 567.

On the west side of the Waterloo Road, facing the Victoria Theatre, is St. Thomas's National and Infant Schools, where upwards of 300 of the rising generation are educated. A special service for policemen has been held here, on stated days, for some time. This building was for some years used

in addition to the west gallery. The church is built of brick, and was consecrated in 1857.

In the map of Ralph Aggas, published in the second year of Elizabeth's reign, Lambeth Marsh is open country, and a little dog running at full pace up and down its open space seems to be its

BISHOP BONNER'S HOUSE IN 1780.
(*From an Original Drawing in the Guildhall Library.*)

as a temporary church before the erection of St. Thomas's Church, in the Westminster Road, nearly facing St. George's Cathedral. St. Thomas's Church was built from the design of Mr. S. S. Teulon, and, as originally designed, exhibited a modification of the fine Dominican church at Ghent; but the estimates having been cut down, it has now merely the appearance of a long and broad parallelogram, with side aisles of two bays towards the east, for galleries,

only inhabitant, and "monarch of all he surveys." Even in the "new plan" engraved for Northouck's "History of London" in 1772, a single row of houses and two or three detached buildings appear down the centre of the Marsh, together with a few on the south side; otherwise, all the surrounding districts, as far as Vine Street and Narrow Wall to the north-west, and Broad Wall and Angel Street to the east, are marked off as "fields." In this map, Lambeth Marsh terminates at about the point where the Waterloo Road now passes it, and it is continued westward as far as Stangate Street. Parsons, the actor, lived at a small cottage in the Vauxhall Road, which he called Frog Hall, in allusion to the "Marsh," near which it stood.

In Queen Elizabeth's time this marsh does not seem to have been a desirable place to live in, for it is coupled by Ben Jonson with "Whitefriars"

July, 1823, when it was taken down, an ancient fragment of a building called Bonner's House, though much mutilated and altered from what it appeared a few years before. This is traditionally said to have been part of a residence of Bishop Bonner, which formerly extended a considerable way further in front. "There is nothing in the history of this place," adds Allen, "to prove that it belonged to any of the Bishops of London, except

DRUG MILL OF THE APOTHECARIES' COMPANY. (*See Page* 418.)

and "Pickt Hatch," as a residence of dissolute characters. In Hone's "Year-Book" we read that "in Lambeth Marsh Mr. W. Curtis, the eminent botanical writer, formed the largest collection of British plants ever brought together into one place;" but the badness of the air drove him to more spacious grounds at Brompton.

In Lambeth Marsh, too, was the Lyceum of Erasmus King, the eccentric coachman, and of Cards, the rival of the eminent natural philosopher, Dr. Desaguliers. From the force of his master's example, though he had received only the poorest education, he came to read lectures and to exhibit experiments in physics publicly.

We learn from Allen's "History of Surrey," that in Lambeth Marsh stood, until the beginning of

an entry of an ordination in Strype's 'Memorials of Cranmer,' which mentions the same to have taken place 'in the chapel of my lord the Bishop of London in the Lower Marsh, Lambeth.'" In this instance Strype was in error, and, as he subsequently acknowledged, had inadvertently written London instead of Rochester. "The ordination," says Mr. Tanswell, in his "History of Lambeth," "really took place at La Place, the house of John Hilsey, Bishop of Rochester. The Bishops of London never had a residence in Lambeth."

In Lower Marsh is the "Spanish Patriot," an inn which owes its sign to the temporary excitement which arose in 1833, at the time of our proposed intervention in the question of the Spanish succession.

At the corner of York Street, with its principal entrance in the Lower Marsh, stands All Saints' Church, which was erected in 1844-45, from the designs of Mr. William Rogers, at a cost of about £6,400. It is in the Anglo-Norman style of architecture. The principal entrance opens into a long corridor from a recessed arch, decorated with zigzag and other mouldings, wrought in the basement storey of a well-proportioned campanile tower of three storeys, surmounted by a slender spire. The interior consists of a nave and aisles, terminated by a recessed angular chancel, which is lit in a subdued manner by a semi-dome skylight filled with stained glass. Attached to the church, in York Street, are All Saints' National and Infant Schools, which were opened for the reception of children in 1854.

Crossing Westminster Bridge Road, we enter the narrow winding thoroughfare called Lambeth Upper Marsh. Here, on the left side, between the Westminster Bridge Road and Stangate Street, stands the Canterbury Hall, the first music-hall established in the metropolis, which was opened by Mr. Charles Morton in the year 1849. "The Upper Marsh, Westminster Road," writes Mr. J. E. Ritchie, in the "Night-side of London," "is what may be called a low neighbourhood. It is not far from Astley's Theatre. Right through it . runs the South-Western Railway, and everywhere about it are planted pawnbrokers' shops, with an indescribable amount of dirty second-hand clothes, and monster gin-palaces, with unlimited plate-glass and gas-lights. Go along there at what hour you will, these gin-palaces are full of ragged children, hideous old women, and drunken men. The bane and the antidote are thus side by side. . . . . Let us pass on. A well-lighted entrance attached to a public-house indicates that we have reached our destination. We proceed up a few stairs, along a passage, lined with handsome engravings, to a bar, where we pay sixpence if we take a seat in the body of the hall, and ninepence if we ascend into the gallery. We make our way leisurely along the floor of the building, which is really a handsome hall, well lighted, and capable of holding 1,500 persons ; the balcony extends round the room in the form of a horse-shoe. At the opposite end to that which we enter is the platform, on which are placed a grand piano and a harmonium, on which the performers play in the intervals when the professional singers have left the stage. The chairman sits just beneath them. It is dull work to him ; but there he must sit, drinking, and smoking cigars, from seven till twelve o'clock. . . . . The room is crowded, and almost every gentleman present has a pipe or a cigar in his mouth. Let us look around us. Evidently the majority present are respectable mechanics or small tradesmen, with their wives and daughters and sweethearts. Now and then you see a midshipman, or a few fast clerks and warehousemen. . . . Every one is smoking, and every one has a glass before him ; but the class that come here are economical, and chiefly confine themselves to pipes and porter. The presence of ladies has also a beneficial effect : I see no signs of intoxication. I may question the worth of some of the stanzas sung, and I think I may have heard sublimer compositions, but, compared with many of the places frequented by both sexes in London, Canterbury Hall is, in my opinion, a respectable place ; though, to speak seriously, I have my doubts whether all go home quite sober."

The "Canterbury Arms," a public-house still existing in "the Marsh," was the foundation of the Canterbury Hall. Here, at the time when Mr. Morton took possession of it, was held a "sing-song," or harmonic meeting, in a room above the bar. Mr. Morton gradually expanded this style of conviviality into a musical entertainment, which, composed of "operatic selections," together with sentimental and comic singing by some competent *artistes*, soon became a great success. Mr. John Caulfield was the chairman of the concerts, and Mr. Ferdinand Jonghmans the musical director, and the talent was the best that could be procured ; some of the salaries reaching £30 a week. From time to time enlargements have been made in the building, and these successive enlargements have always been carried out without a suspension of the entertainments. The hall, as it now stands, will seat some 2,000 persons in its pit, stalls, and balcony.

With respect to the appellation of the "Canterbury Hall"—a sign, by the way, originally given to the adjoining tavern in consequence of its contiguity to the archiepiscopal palace, close by—it was actually "The Canterbury Hall and Fine Arts' Gallery," for one conspicuous feature in the general attraction, arising out of Mr. Morton's penchant for and sound judgment of pictures, was a large collection of paintings—some of them by the best modern artists—in a Fine Arts' Gallery, running parallel to and communicating with the Music Hall. *Punch* called this Fine Arts' Gallery "The Royal Academy over the Water." Still, the Canterbury Hall, as we have stated above, was the parent of the present music-hall form of entertainment, and, when it occupied the ground alone, was frequented by large numbers from the West-end

The present structure, an entirely new building, has been constructed upon the most approved principles with regard to ventilation and acoustic properties ; and it has a large and convenient entrance in the Westminster Bridge Road.

Close by the Canterbury Hall, near the corner of Stangate Street, is the " Bower Saloon," with its theatre and music-room, which Mr. J. Timbs speaks of as being "a pleasure haunt of our own time."

Stangate Street formerly numbered among its residents no less a personage than Signor Grimaldi, the father of *the* Grimaldi who made " Mother Goose" immortal. "Old Grimaldi," as he was generally called, in common with most of those persons who exhilarate the spirits of others, was of a melancholy, nervous temperament, a ghost-seeker, and a believer in all sorts of marvellous absurdities. He often wandered over the then dreary region of St. George's Fields with an old bibliopolist, detailing and discussing all the superstitious legends of Germany and Great Britain. A very jolly party used then to assemble at a tavern in St. James's Market, and, to dispel Grimaldi's gloom, a friend took him thither. He soon left the room, saying, " They laughed so much it made him more melancholy than ever." His bookselling friend lent him a book called " The Uncertainty of the Signs of Death," which so excited his mind with a fear of being buried alive, that in his will he directed that his daughter should, previous to his interment, sever his head from his body. The operation was actually performed in the presence of the daughter, though not by her hand. As a proof of the morbidity of the signor's mind upon the subject of interment, he was wont to wander to different churchyards, as Charles Bannister said, to pick out a dry spot to lie snug in. He originally invented the celebrated skeleton scene, since so common in pantomimes ; and first represented the " Cave of Petrifaction," in which, when any one entered, he was supposed to be struck at once and for ever into the position in which he stood when his unhallowed foot first profaned the mysterious locality. So prone are many minds to jest in public with the terrors which render their lives burdensome to them in private.

Carlisle Lane, which runs from Westminster Bridge Road to the eastern wall of Lambeth Palace, keeps in remembrance Carlisle House, which stood here between the thirteenth and sixteenth centuries. It was originally the palace of the Bishops of Rochester, and was then called La Place ; but afterwards becoming the property of the bishopric of Carlisle, it was called Carlisle House. Down to the year 1827, the site of the mansion was occupied by Carlisle House Boarding School. Early in the twelfth century, Baldwin, Archbishop of Canterbury, attempted to found a college or monastery for secular canons on this spot ; but this attempt appears to have been unsuccessful : only a chapel, which was dedicated to St. Stephen and St. Thomas, having been erected. Baldwin's successor, Hubert Walter, entered into a treaty with the Prior of Rochester (the then owner of the land) for the whole manor of Lambeth, which was exchanged to him, he granting to the bishops of that see, out of it, a piece of ground next to the above-mentioned chapel, in order to erect an occasional residence as their town-house. On this ground Gilbert de Glanville, Bishop of Rochester, erected a house for himself and his successors, who occasionally resided there till the sixteenth century. Haymo de Hethe, who was promoted to the see of Rochester in 1316, rebuilt the house, which was subsequently called La Place, till the year 1500, after which the bishops dated from their "house in Lambeth Marsh." The last Bishop of Rochester who dwelt in this mansion was Dr. John Fisher. He was nearly poisoned by Richard Roose, his cook, who infused a deadly poison into some soup which he was making, and which, as a matter of fact, caused the deaths of seventeen members of the household, and of two poor people who had gone to the house for charity. An appropriate punishment was devised for this murderous cook, for he was "attainted of high treason, and boiled to death in Smithfield."

In 1540 Bishop Heath conveyed this house to the Crown, in exchange for a house in Southwark. Henry VIII. granted it to Robert Aldrich, Bishop of Carlisle, and his successors, in exchange for certain premises in the Strand, on the site now occupied by Beaufort Buildings. In 1647 it was sold by the Parliament to Matthew Hardyng ; but on the Restoration it reverted to the see of Carlisle. "From this date," writes Mr. Tanswell, in his " History of Lambeth," " its history exhibits some remarkable vicissitudes. On part of the premises a pottery was established, which existed in George II.'s time ; but going to decay, the kilns and a curious Gothic arch were taken down, and the bricks used for filling the space and other defects in the wall. It was subsequently opened by one Castledine as a tavern, and became a common stew ; and on his demise it was occupied by Monsieur Froment, a dancing master, who endeavoured to get it licensed by the sessions as a public place of entertainment, but ineffectually, in consequence of the opposition of Archbishop Secker. It was next tenanted as a private dwelling ; and was afterwards converted into an academy and boarding-school for young gentlemen. In the year 1827 it was pulled down, and the site and grounds covered with about eighty small houses, including Allen and Homer Streets and parts of Carlisle Lane and Hercules Buildings. Before it was built over, the grounds attached to this house were encompassed by a high and strong brick wall, which had in it a gate of ancient form, opening towards Stangate. A smaller back gate in the south wall had over it two keys in saltire, and something resembling a mitre for a crest. Two bricks, one upon the other, served for a shield, and the workmanship of the arms was of as low a taste as the materials."

In a garden at Carlisle House was standing, in the middle of the last century, a mulberry-tree, which bore an excellent crop during the summer of 1753. Its shade was nearly fifty yards in circumference, and between four and five hundred pottles of fruit were gathered off it in one summer, whilst the ground all under and around the tree looked as if soaked with blood, owing to people treading upon the fallen fruit.

Another mansion of note here, in former times, was Norfolk House, the residence of the old Earls and Dukes of Norfolk. It stood in Church Street, on the site now occupied by Messrs. Hodges' distillery and a range of buildings called Norfolk Row. The mansion remained in the possession of the Dukes of Norfolk till the commencement of Elizabeth's reign. The old duke, whose life was saved the night before his intended execution by the death of Henry VIII., and his son, the Earl of Surrey, the courtly poet and lover of the fair Geraldine, both resided here; and the latter studied here, under John Leland, the antiquary. On the attainder of Thomas Howard, the third Duke of Norfolk of this family, the house was seized by the Crown, and granted by Edward VI. in fee to William Parr, Marquis of Northampton, by the title of "a capital mansion or house in Lambehith, late parcel of the possessions of Thomas, Duke of Norfolk, and twenty and a half acres of land in Cotman's Field; one acre in St. George's Field upon Sandhill; six acres of meadow and marsh in Lambehithe Marsh, whereof three acres were within the wall of the marsh, and three acres without; one close, called Bell Close, abutting upon Cotman's Field towards the east, containing one and a half

THE CHEVALIER D'EON.
(*From an Old Caricature.*)

acre; one other close, abutting upon the way leading from Lambehithe to the Marsh, containing two acres and a half."

In Walcot Place, near Lambeth Walk, the notorious Mrs. George Anne Bellamy, after a life of profligacy and splendour, spent her declining years in poverty. In her "Memoirs" she tells us how that, having parted with all her jewellery and most of her clothes, and maddened with want, she walked out into St. George's Fields, "not without the hope of meeting with some freebooters who frequent those lawless parts, and who would take away the life of which she was so weary;" and how, disappointed in this, she made her way to the steps of Westminster Bridge to throw herself into the Thames, when she was recalled to her senses by finding a poor woman with her child worse off than herself. Mrs. Bellamy took her final leave of the stage in 1784, and died in poverty in February, 1788.

Of the "wells" and tea-gardens in Lambeth Walk we have spoken in a previous chapter; but there was here, in times gone by, one other object which we should not omit to mention: this was the old mill belonging to the Apothecaries' Company, for grinding and pounding their drugs, &c. The mill, which stood here long before the introduction of steam into the working of machinery, was a picturesque structure, built chiefly of wood, and with its "sails" had something of the appearance of an old-fashioned flour-mill. We give an engraving of this mill on page 415.

In the Westminster Bridge Road, under the arches of the South-Western Railway, is the London terminus of the Great Woking Cemetery, belonging to the London Necropolis Company. The company was established by Act of Parliament, by which the Lord Lieutenant of Middlesex, the Lord Lieutenant of Surrey, the Bishop of London, the Bishop of Winchester, and the Chief Commissioners of Her Majesty's Woods and Forests, are appointed visitors. "Within a quarter of a mile of Westminster Bridge," then, as the Company announce in their advertisement, we have, "to all intents and purposes, a cemetery of 400 acres." A train starts at the Westminster Bridge Road to the cemetery at Woking daily, "thus avoiding a long transit by road, and securing all the benefits of extramural interment."

We have already made mention of the chief offices of the London Necropolis Company in our account of Lancaster Place, Strand.*

At a house called the "Crown," on the Surrey side of Westminster Bridge, was born, in 1735, Dr. Martin Van Butchell, the eccentric physician, whom we have mentioned in our account of Mount Street.† Another eccentric resident in the Westminster Bridge Road, in former times, was the Chevalier D'Eon, concerning whom there was so much doubt raised as to whether he was a man or a woman. Angelo, in his "Reminiscences," tells us that he used to see the Chevalier D'Eon here. "He lived a few doors beyond Astley's Theatre. He always dressed in black silk, and looked like a woman worn out with age and care."

At the foot of Westminster Bridge, and extending along the bank of the river towards Lambeth Palace, is the new St. Thomas's Hospital, of the foundation of which, close by London Bridge, and its recent migration to the Surrey Gardens, we have already spoken.‡ The institution was removed hither in 1870-71. The ground on which the hospital stands—between eight and nine acres in extent—was purchased from the Board of Works, at a cost of about £100,000. That part of the Thames known as Stangate Bank, where the hospital now stands, had long borne an ill repute—ill-looking, ill-smelling, and of evil associations. Even the construction of the Houses of Parliament on the opposite shore—even the building of the handsomest bridge in Europe, that of Westminster—failed to redeem the hideous aspect of its fore-shore, overladen as it was with dank tenements, rotten wharves, and dirty boat-houses. But the time came when it was decided to construct the Southern Thames Embankment, and the necessities of its formation compelled a large "reclamation" from the slimy fore-shores. Of the whole site of the present St. Thomas's Hospital, nearly half of it, therefore, has been reclaimed from the mud of the river. The buildings have a frontage of about 1,700 feet in length, and are about 250 feet in depth. The hospital consists of no less than eight distinct buildings, or pavilions. Six in the centre are for patients ; that at the north end, next to Westminster Bridge, is for the officers of the hospital, board-room, &c. ; that at the south for a museum, lecture-room, and school of medicine. The style of the buildings may be called Palladian, with rich facings of coloured bricks and Portland stone. There was some difficulty in getting a good foundation for the buildings, as there always is at

Westminster or its neighbourhood ; and towards the river front a depth of twenty-eight feet had to be excavated before the firm clay was reached. On this a solid basis of concrete was laid, and on this again, on massive brick piers, the structure was begun. The blocks are built at a distance of 125 feet from each other. Though the blocks are each distinct buildings, they are all, in fact, coupled together by a double corridor, one of which runs along the river front to the west, and one along the eastern face, near the gardens of Lambeth Palace. This latter corridor is entirely glazed in, and has a solid roof, with a balcony, which can be used either as a promenade in fine weather for patients, or, what it is really built for, an easy means of access to the second floors of the hospital, with all of which it communicates. The front corridor is a very handsome stone arcade, but open on its western side towards the Thames. This is used as a promenade for the patients who are recovering, and a most pleasant walk it is ; for the front of the hospital, towards the river—and, indeed, the back as well—is laid out in gardens and planted with trees.

Each pavilion has three tiers of wards above the ground floor, and in the first five pavilions the main wards occupy the whole building on the river side of the corridor. They are 28 feet in width, 120 feet in length, and 15 feet in height, with flat ceilings throughout, and each have accommodation for twenty-eight beds, with a cubic capacity of 1,800 feet for each patient. This capacity is largely due to the ample floor space, which affords abundant room for the attendance of students and for the requirements of clinical teaching. The beds are placed eight feet apart from centre to centre, and the windows are arranged alternately with the beds, at a level to enable the patients to look out of them. There are also large end lights communicating with sheltered balconies towards the river, in which patients may be placed on couches or chairs in fine weather. On the ground floor there are smaller wards, which are used chiefly for the reception of accidents, and which make up the total number of beds in each pavilion to about 100. At the corridor end of each large ward the entrance passage is carried between smaller rooms, a ward kitchen, a sisters'-room, a consultation-room, and a small ward. These small wards are for the reception of patients who have undergone severe operations, or who for any reason require unusual quietude or exceptional treatment. At the river end there is a lateral projection at each angle of the pavilion ; and these projections contain on one side a bath-room and lavatory, on the other

---

* See Vol. III., p. 286.   † See Vol. IV., p. 335.
‡ See *ante*, pp. 89 and 268.

ST. THOMAS'S HOSPITAL.

side a scullery and offices, all cut off from the wards themselves by intercepting lobbies. Natural ventilation has been as much as possible depended on, with simple auxiliary arrangements for cold and boisterous nights. The warming is effected mostly by open fire-places, as the most healthy mode, with the addition of a warm-water system for use in very cold weather. It is, perhaps, almost needless to say that the whole structure is fire-proof.

With these theatres the covered corridors communicate directly from the wards. There is a special wing, if we may so term it, set apart in one of the northern blocks, and adjoining the matron's residence, which is used for the training of skilled nurses, whose services, as they become thoroughly proficient in their duties, are made available as matrons in hospitals all over the kingdom, through the agency of the Council of the Nightingale Fund.

THE ENTRANCE-HALL, ST. THOMAS'S HOSPITAL.

The floors of each storey are laid on iron girders covered with concrete, the actual upper floor of each ward being made of thin, broad planks of oak. The walls of each ward, too, are coated with Parian cement, which, while not so cold, is almost as hard and non-absorbent of noxious gases, and quite as smooth, as marble itself.

Four of these great hospital blocks which we have described, each 90 feet high by about 250 feet deep, are set apart for the reception of male patients. These are on the north side of the central hall; the two on the southern side are for women only. On each side there is a large operating theatre for men and women, capable of containing 600 students with ease whenever an important operation draws such a number together.

The "pupil nurses," who must be well-educated, intelligent young women, from twenty-three to thirty-five years of age, are trained here for one year in the practice of hospital nursing, and are provided during that time with comfortable home, board, uniform clothing, and small salary. At the end of the year, if qualified, they may expect good situations as hospital nurses, with liberal wages, usually commencing at £20.

The low building at the end nearest Lambeth Palace is the medical school. The admission fees for medical students, for unlimited attendance at practice and lectures, is 100 guineas; for dental students (for two years), £45. Special entries may be made to any lectures or to hospital practice, and a modified scale of fees is arranged for students entering in second or subsequent years. There are special classes for the first M.B. and preliminary scientific examinations of the University of London, and private classes for matriculation and other examinations. Gentlemen can attend the above classes without becoming students to the hospital. Qualified practitioners are admitted to the hospital practice, lectures, and library, on payment of ten guineas for unlimited attendance. Two scholarships founded here perpetuate the names of Alderman Sir John Musgrove and Sir William Tite; there are also several college prizes, ranging from £5 to £20, and also awards of silver and gold medals. Two house physicians and two assistant house physicians, two house surgeons and two assistant house surgeons, and the resident accoucheur, are selected from students holding qualifications; an ophthalmic assistant, with a salary of £50, is appointed; clinical clerks and dressers to in and out patients are selected from gentlemen attending the hospital; two registrars, at an honorarium of £40 each, are chosen from third or fourth year's students. There are also numerous minor appointments of anatomical assistants, prosectors, obstetric clerks, &c., open to the students without charge.

The entrance-hall, facing the new Lambeth Palace Road, is a large and spacious apartment. In it is a statue of the Queen, by whom the foundation-stone of the hospital was laid in 1868, and the building opened in 1871. The statue, which was executed by Mr. Noble, is sculptured out of a block of pure white Carrara marble, and weighs five tons. The Queen is represented seated on a state chair, in her full robes of state, holding the sceptre in her right hand and the orb in the left hand. The left arm rests upon an arm of the chair, the right hand being brought forward and resting in the lap The feet rest upon a footstool, and are, to some extent, hidden by drapery. The likeness of Her Majesty is admitted to be excellent. The pedestal upon which the statue stands is of Sicilian marble, beautifully moulded and carved, with panels in the centre on each side. The front portion of the pedestal has a circular projection, and within the panel immediately under the statue is the following inscription :—" Her Majesty Queen Victoria. The gift of Sir John Musgrove, Bart., President, 1873."

There is a chapel which affords sittings for more than 300 persons; there are large and spacious surgeries and dispensers' offices, with ample house accommodation for chaplains, resident surgeons, dressers, &c. Altogether, the hospital can make up 650 beds for patients; and contains, from first to last, in all its wards, houses, out-offices, kitchens,

sculleries, stores, and cellars, nearly 1,000 distinct compartments. The mortuary-house and museum are close by the medical school, at the extreme southern end. The extreme northern end abuts close upon the Surrey side of Westminster Bridge; in fact, there is an opening by a flight of steps which gives direct access from the abutment to the north end of the hospital buildings which rise above it. All the structures occupy together about four acres, leaving four and a half acres laid out as garden ground, in *parterres* and thick plantations, for the use and recreation of the patients. The out-patients do not enter the hospital proper at all, but come by the new Palace Road, at the east end of the buildings, and pass at once into the men's or women's waiting-rooms; and these again are sub-divided into medical and surgical departments.

Altogether, the plan of St. Thomas's Hospital may be considered perfect; and though it cost in all at least half a million of money, it is a cheap outlay for the good it is certain to effect for ages to come. As an addition to the great public edifices of the metropolis, it certainly will not be surpassed in appearance by any of the splendid structures which of late years have done so much to enrich and improve London.

As stated above, the space between the grounds of St. Thomas's Hospital and the river, extending from Westminster to Lambeth Bridges, a distance of 2,200 feet, is filled in by a good solid embankment, which was commenced in 1866, and opened for pedestrians in the space of about two years. The work, called the Albert Embankment, which is continued beyond Lambeth Bridge, as far as the site of the London Gas Works, 2,100 feet higher up the river, was carried out by the Metropolitan Board of Works, under the direction of Sir Joseph Bazalgette, their engineer-in-chief; and it forms part of the great design of embanking the Thames in its course through London, which we have described in a previous part of this work.* Although open only for foot-passengers, the Albert Embankment is precisely similar in its construction, as seen from the river, to the Victoria and Chelsea Embankments on the Middlesex side of the river. Turning down the embankment stairs, at the foot of the northern end of St. Thomas's Hospital, the pedestrian has before him the finest footway in London, but a footway only. When he has walked along this for rather more than a quarter of a mile, let him stop and look back. If it be a fairly clear day, clear enough for him to see across the river and as far

* See Vol III., p. 322, *et seq.*

as the bridge, he may admire one of the finest architectural views in London : all the finer if a flood-tide and a fleet of barges and steamers fill the river with life. The scene at this point has been thus described by a writer in the *Times*. Having, in imagination, conducted the pedestrian to this spot, he proceeds :—" The Thames, ' without o'erflowing, full,'* spreads at his feet, fenced in and spanned by three great public works, the Houses of Parliament, Westminster Bridge, and St. Thomas's Hospital, forming, as it were, three sides of a hollow square. Of the long and stately front of the Houses of Parliament, surmounted by the great clock and flag towers and graceful intermediate pinnacles ; of the symmetrical lines of the arches and piers of the bridge rising out of the water, with their massive and eternal look, he has, of course, a full view. The colonnaded blocks of the great hospital, which towered above him as he walked, and seemed so much vaster than he had any idea they were till he came close under them, will be seen—and perhaps it is as well—rather *en profile*. He will acknowledge that, all stained as it is, the river has something to thank the City for. When Spenser could sing to it and call it ' silver stream- ing,' its banks hereabouts and lower down had little to grace them besides

' Those bricky towers
Where now the studious lawyers have their bowers.'

The fish have died out of it, and, higher up, the swans cannot keep themselves white ; but in Spenser's day the Thames did not wear such a tiara as that bridge, it did not roll its waters smoothly between granite walls, and Westminster and Lambeth did not look down on it so proudly as they do now with their Houses of Parliament and hospital. These are great and costly works, and a little farther on the picturesque battlements of the Archbishop of Canterbury's half-house, half- castle, with the dreary, heavy-capped turrets of Millbank, will give him an opportunity of quoting Byron's incorrect line—

' A palace and a prison on each hand.' "

Attempts at gardening have been made on the Albert Embankment, in the vicinity of Lambeth Palace, but not with the success attending that carried out on the northern side of the river. Trees, too, have been planted ; but in the course of a few years the whole of those from Lambeth Bridge† westwards had to be removed, the reason assigned

being that the exhalations from the adjacent pot- teries had destroyed their vitality.

The Southern Embankment of the Thames is not, as we have shown in a previous chapter,‡ a new scheme. In the " History of London," by Fearnside and Harral, published in 1839, it is stated that " a proposition has received the City's approval for a splendid quay from London to Vauxhall. This, if carried into effect, will render the banks of old Father Thames unrivalled for beauty and convenience, and approach a little towards the Parisian method of managing these matters." The primary object in embanking the Thames, particularly on the southern side, was to prevent the recurrence of floods, in consequence of a great part of Lambeth and Southwark lying much below the level of the river at high-water mark ; but this having been carried out no farther eastward than Westminster Bridge, has left matters much in the same condition as they were before, or possibly worse : for since the construction of the Victoria Embankment it is asserted that con- siderably more damage has been done in the low- lying districts than was the case before by the river overflowing its banks so much more frequently. A Select Committee of the House of Commons in 1876 reported that the Embankment of the southern side of the Thames was a matter, not of local but of metropolitan importance, and that, as such, it ought to be taken in hand by the Metropolitan Board of Works. This task, however, the Board declined, and consequently the local authorities be- came naturally embarrassed. Some private owners of property abutting upon the river have at times executed works for the purpose of preventing any expected overflow ; but these have been only of a temporary character. In a memorial of the in- habitants of Lambeth, presented to the Home Secretary since the above refusal on the part of the Board of Works, the memorialists held that, irre- spective of any pecuniary question, " not only what is necessary in the present, but what may be necessary and desirable in the future, renders it expedient that the whole bank of the river should be under the control of a metropolitan authority, so that uni- formity and completeness may be secured, and the metropolis may derive the fullest advantage from any public expenditure. The prevention of tidal overflows being declared to be a matter of metro- politan concern, can be dealt with only by an authority representing the metropolis ; and, as the Metropolitan Board declines to accept the reso- lution of the Select Committee, your memorialists

---

* This application of Denham's well-known lines was made before the river had begun periodically to " overflow " the lower parts of Lambeth and Southwark, as we shall see presently.

† See Vol. IV., p. 5.

‡ See *ante*, p. 387.

have no alternative but to approach the Government, and to pray for relief from the present deadlock by the prompt passing of a Bill, framed in accordance with the resolution of the Select Committee." It is to be hoped, in the interests of common humanity, that Parliament will enforce its decision on this head without delay.

Among the causes which have contributed to the growth of Lambeth, we must mention the manufactories which have been founded here at various times, forming centres of active industry, and consequently of population. More than 200 years ago, two Dutchmen established a pottery, and about the middle of the last century two other potteries were opened here. The chief work in this line now carried on in Lambeth is at the pottery of the Messrs. Doulton, the producers of the celebrated Lambeth *faience*, and whose name is worthy of record as the revivers, in the last few years, of the manufacture of Flemish and German stoneware, which promise to make the name of Lambeth celebrated once more in the annals of art. They are also the revivers of the white cream-coloured ware, known as Queen's Ware, from the fact that Queen Charlotte admired it so much when manufactured by Wedgwood. "It is not many years ago," observes a writer in the *Queen* newspaper (1876), "since Messrs. Doulton, of Lambeth, began their career as art potters, having until then only been celebrated for chimney-pots, drain-pipes, ink and blacking bottles. And a marvellous success they have achieved in this short space of time. Everybody knows their admirable imitation of Gris de Flandres, surface-etched and embossed, tinted in colours which equal those on the ancient ware. Their terra-cotta ornaments are the delight of architects, not only for their lasting properties, which will stand even an English climate for centuries, but equally so for their decorative merits. . . . . The great artistic feature of Lambeth *faience* seems to lie in the direction of landscape and figure painting; and the success which has been achieved in this direction, it may be added, is mainly due to the Lambeth School of Art, which has long been carried on under the fostering care of the great river-side potters."

Established in the year 1854 by the Rev. William Gregory, then vicar of St. Mary's, Lambeth, as a branch of the Central School of Design at Marlborough House, this was really the first Art School of Design in the kingdom: as, indeed, it should be. The Lambeth school went on steadily increasing until 1860, when the Prince of Wales laid the foundation-stone of the present building. Since that time, the exertions of its director, Mr. John

Sparks, have been unremitting in educating painters and modellers for Messrs. Doulton's works. With sound psychological judgment, he selected his pupils from the fair sex, well knowing the natural artistic feeling of women and girls would lighten his arduous task of reviving an art-industry once before flourishing in the very same locality, but long forgotten. Besides, by excluding foreigners from his school, he wanted to prove that there is exquisite taste and endless inventive power latent in Englishmen and Englishwomen, which only want bringing out by proper teaching and training. "Our English hands," he says, in one of his lectures, "are as skilful, our heads as clear, our thoughts as poetical, our lives as high, as any other people's; and still we find French modellers giving the work of the largest Staffordshire potters a European fame; French modellers making the works of our great silversmiths and electrotypists; Belgian stone-carvers cutting Romanism into Protestant reredos; and Germans, whose name is Legion, and whose motto is 'Ubique,' filling our drawing-offices all over the country." "These things should not be," concludes Mr. Sparks; and that they need not be he has proved through his pupils' achievements in Lambeth *faience*.

Besides the potteries, the principal manufactures of this parish are white lead, shot, glass, &c.; but none have been so celebrated as the Vauxhall plate-glass. In the thirteenth century the Venetians were the only people who had the secret of making looking-glasses; but about the year 1670 a number of Venetian artists having arrived in England, headed by one Rosetti, and under the patronage of the Duke of Buckingham, a manufactory was established at Vauxhall, and carried on with such success, by the firm of Dawson, Bowles, and Co., as to excel the Venetians or any other nation in blown plate-glass. Evelyn, in his "Diary," records a visit which he paid to this establishment. Under date of 19th September, 1676, he writes:—"To Lambeth, to that rare magazine of marble, to take order for chimney-pieces for Mr. Godolphin's house. The owner of the works had built for himself a pretty dwelling-house; this Dutchman had contracted with the Genoese for all their marble. We also saw the Duke of Buckingham's glass works, where they make huge vases of mettal as cleare, ponderous, and thick as chrystal; also looking-glasses far larger than any that come from Venice." The emoluments acquired by the proprietors of the above-mentioned establishment are stated to have been very large; but in the year 1780, in consequence of a difference between them and the workmen, a total stop was put to this great manufactory, and a descendant of Rosetti ungratefully left in poverty. The site of this celebrated factory is now covered by Vauxhall Square.

Pennant records, in terms of high approval, Mr. Coade's manufacture of artificial stone, carried on in the street called Narrow Wall, of which we have already made mention.* He likewise describes Lambeth as remarkable for another and altogether different branch of industry, namely, the manufacture of English wines, and also for the growth of the vines from which they were made. He writes :— "The genial banks of the Thames opposite to our capital yield almost every species of white wine ; and by a wondrous magic, Messrs. Beaufoy here pour forth the materials for the rich Frontiniac, destined to the more elegant tables, the Madeira, the Calcavella, and the Lisbon, into every part of the kingdom. . . . The foreign wines are most admirably mimicked." We have already spoken of the growth of vines and the manufacture of wine in London, in our account of Vine Street, Piccadilly.† From an entry in Pepys' "Diary," in 1661, this place seems at one time to have been equally famous for its ale ; at all events, we here read how that the genial Secretary of the Admiralty went "out with Mr. Shepley and Alderman Backwell to drink Lambeth ale."

Another thriving branch of industry connected with Lambeth, in which employment is given to a large number of hands, is the doll manufactory of Messrs. Edwards, in Waterloo Road. Then, again, various chemical, soap, and bone-crushing works have also been established ; and Maudslay's engineering works in the Westminster Bridge Road, on the site of the old Apollo Gardens,‡ have become a centre of industry.

Among the "noted residents" in Lambeth, not already mentioned by us, were Mr. and Mrs. Zachary Macaulay, the parents of Lord Macaulay, who occupied a small house here for the first year of their married life ; their illustrious son, however, was born, not in Lambeth, but in Leicestershire.

In Lambeth Road, too, at one time lived the eccentric artist, George Morland, whom we have already introduced to our readers at Paddington.§ He was most clever in his delineation of cottage interiors and low hostelries, with their accessories of donkeys, pigs, &c. ; and it is recorded of him that at Lambeth he had several four-footed lodgers, including one of the long-eared tribe.

John Timbs, in his "Clubs and Club Life," says that the Stanleys at one time had a house here, and that the "Eagle and Child," the sign of an adjoining inn, is really taken from the crest of the family.

Guy Fawkes, too, it is said, had a house in Lambeth, where he and his fellows in the "Gunpowder Plot" stored their ammunition. If this really was ever the case, its site is forgotten.

It is to be feared that the accommodation for the poor in parts of this parish is, or was in 1874, most disgracefully inadequate ; for, if we may trust Dr. Stallard's work on "London Pauperism," a man, his wife, and three children were found occupying a front room, only twelve feet square, within a few yards of Westminster Bridge Road.

In a previous chapter we have enumerated the wards or districts into which the parish of Lambeth is divided ;|| we may here add that, in conformity with the provisions of the Reform Bill, passed in 1832, Lambeth was one of the four metropolitan parishes which was erected into a Parliamentary borough, since which period it has regularly returned two members to St. Stephen's. At that time the number of the inhabitants was 87,856. In the course of the next twenty years this had expanded to 116,072 ; and at the time of taking the census in 1881 the population numbered all but 500,000 souls. Lambeth has returned, at all events, two distinguished members to St. Stephen's —the Right Hon. Charles Tennyson D'Eyncourt, and Sir Benjamin Hawes, the son of a great soap-boiler, who was one of its first representatives, and retained his seat for the borough for fifteen years. Another of its members, Mr. William Roupell, who was elected in the year 1857, subsequently acquired some celebrity—but not of a very enviable kind ; for having been convicted of forgery, he was transferred to a convict prison.

In 1877, under an Act of Parliament and an Order in Council, Lambeth, as well as its neighbour Southwark, was made to form part of the diocese of Rochester.

From these dry prosaic matters to the realms of fancy the change is refreshing. We will, therefore, conclude this chapter by reminding the reader of the dream of Charles Lamb, in his essay on "Witches and other Night Fears." He dreams that, having been riding "upon the ocean billows at some sea-nuptials," he found the waves gradually subsiding into what he calls "a river motion," and that the river was "no other than the gentle Thames, which landed him, in the wafture of a placid wave or two, alone, safe, and inglorious, somewhere at the foot of Lambeth Palace." Thither we will now proceed.

---

* See ante, p. 387, † See Vol. IV., p. 253.
‡ See ante, p. 389. § See Vol. V., p. 222.

|| See ante, p. 383.

LAMBETH PALACE, FROM MILLBANK, IN 1860.

CHAPTER XXXII.

LAMBETH PALACE.

"Lambeth, the envy of each band and gown."—*Pope.*

History of the Foundation of Lambeth Palace—Successive Additions and Alterations in the Building—Fate of the Palace during the Time of the Commonwealth—The Great Gateway—The Hall—Hospitality of the Archbishops in Former Times—The Library and Manuscript Room—The Guard Chamber—The Gallery—The Post room—The Chapel—Desecration of the Chapel—Archbishop Parker's Tomb—The Lollards' Tower—The Gardens—Bishops' Walk—Remarkable Historical Occurrences at Lambeth Palace—The Palace attacked by the Insurgents under Wat Tyler—Queen Mary and Cardinal Pole—Queen Elizabeth and Archbishop Parker—The "Lambeth Articles"—The Archbishop's Dole—The Palace attacked by a London Mob in 1641—Translation of Archbishop Sheldon—The Gordon Riots—The Pan-Anglican Synod—The Arches Court of Canterbury—The Annual Visit of the Stationers' Company—Lambeth Degrees—St. Mary's Church—Curious Items in the Parish Registers—The Tomb of the Tradescants.

"IMMEDIATELY opposite to the Abbey and Palace of Westminster," writes Dr. R. Paulli, in his "Pictures of Old England," "rose the castellated walls and towers and chapel of the princely residence which the Archbishops of Canterbury had chosen, before the close of the twelfth century, as their town residence, in the immediate neighbourhood of the offices of state and the tribunals of justice." And there, he might have added, it rises still, and frowns down with mediæval and almost feudal grandeur upon the waters of the river as they flow calmly on towards the sea, just as they did in the days of our Norman sovereigns. The palace, it must be owned, wears a very solemn and even gloomy appearance, resembling a fortress rather than an episcopal palace; and there was a time when it rose still more conspicuous before the eyes of the citizens of London than now—we mean when the river was the "silent way" along which nearly all the traffic and the travellers passed. The reader will not forget Pope's reference to this palace in his description of the Thames, in emulation of Spenser, which we have quoted above, as a motto to this chapter.

LAMBETH PALACE FROM THE RIVER. 1709.

The quiet gardens and venerable towers might almost be taken as a symbol of the archbishopric itself. " Its dingy brick, and solemn little windows, with the reverend ivy spreading everywhere about its walls," writes Mr. A. C. Coxe, in his " Impressions of England," " seemed to house the decent and comely spirit of religion itself : and one could almost gather the true character of the Church of England from a single glance at this old ecclesiastical palace, amid the stirring and splendid objects with which it is surrounded. Old, and yet not too old ; retired, and yet not estranged from men ; learned, and yet domestic ; religious, yet nothing ascetic ; and dignified, without pride or ostentation : such is the ideal of the Metropolitical palace on the margin of the Thames. I thought, as I glided by, of the time when Henry stopped his barge just here to take in Archbishop Cranmer, and give him a taste of his royal displeasure ; and of the time when Laud entered his barge at the same place to go by water to the Tower, 'his poor neighbours of Lambeth following him with their blessings and prayers for his safe return.' They knew his better part."

As we have already seen, the manor of Lambeth was given by Goda, sister of Edward the Confessor, to the see of Rochester, in the eleventh century. The manor was afterwards seized by William the Conqueror, who gave part of the lands to his half-brother, Odo, Bishop of Bayeux. It was, however, ultimately restored to its former owners, the see of Rochester, one of whose bishops, Glanville, erected here, at the close of the twelfth century, a residence for himself and his successors whenever they visited the metropolis. The ancient possession of Lambeth by the see of Rochester is still commemorated by the payment to the latter, in two half-yearly sums, of five marks of silver, in consideration of the lodging, fire-wood, forage, and other accommodations which the Bishops of Rochester had been accustomed to receive here whenever they visited London. This house being afterwards exchanged for other lands with Hubert Walter, Archbishop of Canterbury, became the episcopal residence. Pennant tells us that it was the original intention of Archbishop Walter to have erected here a " College of Secular Monks "—he meant, of course, of " monks," *not* of " seculars "—independent of those of Canterbury, but that circumstances obliged him to abandon his purpose.

Archbishops Hubert Walter and Langton successively lived at the Episcopal Manor House at Lambeth. The latter repaired it, as well as the palace at Canterbury. His residence here is proved by some public acts in 1209. Of this

house there is no account or description, and it seems it was afterwards neglected and became ruinous. Archbishop Boniface, in 1216, as an expiation, it is said, for his outrageous behaviour to the prior of St. Bartholomew's in Smithfield, obtained a bull from Pope Urban IV., among other things, to rebuild his houses at " Lamhie," or to build a new one on a different site, from which circumstance he is generally supposed to have been the first founder of the present palace. It was gradually enlarged and improved by his successors, particularly by Chicheley, who enjoyed the primacy from 1414 to 1443. He was the builder of that portion of the palace known as the Lollards' Tower. " Neither Protestants nor Catholics," says Pennant, " should omit visiting this tower, the cruel prison of the unhappy followers of Wickliffe. The vast staples and rings to which they were chained before they were brought to the stake ought to make Protestants bless the hour which freed them from so bloody a period. Catholics may glory that time has softened their zeal into charity for all sects, and made them blush at these memorials of the misguided zeal of our ancestors."

Cardinal Morton, Archbishop of Canterbury, who died in 1500, made many additions and improvements to the present palace. He was the builder of the magnificent brick gateway or principal entrance at the north-west.

Warham having acted as ambassador for King Henry VII. to the Duke of Burgundy, was, on his return in 1493, appointed Chancellor of Wells, and soon afterwards Master of the Rolls. He was subsequently made Keeper of the Great Seal, then Chancellor ; in 1503 he was raised to the see of London, and in the year following was enthroned Archbishop of Canterbury. In 1515 Warham resigned the Chancellorship, which was bestowed on Cardinal Wolsey, and retired to his palace. He was succeeded, in 1533, by Thomas Cranmer, who, writes the author of " Lambeth and the Vatican," " may be considered one of the most distinguished men that Cambridge ever produced, and the most eminent prelate that ever filled the see of Canterbury." The part which he took in favour of the divorce between Katharine of Aragon and Henry VIII. induced the king to nominate him archbishop ; he was, therefore, eventually raised to the see of Canterbury, in which capacity he pronounced the divorce between Queen Katharine and Henry, and ratified his marriage with Anne Boleyn—a step which so ingratiated him into the favour of the king. Cranmer's zeal in the cause of the Reformed religion frequently led him into acts of severity towards those whose opinions differed from his own, from which even the spirit of the times and the barbarous inhumanity exercised by the Protestants abroad is neither an excuse nor an apology. On the death of Edward VI., Cranmer espoused the cause of Lady Jane Grey; Mary triumphed, and the ruin and martyrdom of the archbishop speedily followed.

To Cardinal Pole, who succeeded to the archbishopric, is attributed the foundation of the long gallery in Lambeth Palace. He was appointed to the deanery of Exeter by Henry VIII.; but was abroad when the king abolished the Papal authority in England, and, not attending when summoned to return, was proclaimed a traitor and divested of his deanery. In 1536 he was made cardinal; and when Mary ascended the throne he returned to England as legate from Pope Julius III., and had his attainder reversed by special Act of Parliament. "Few churchmen have borne so unblemished a reputation as this eminent prelate, and few have carried themselves with such moderation and meekness. He died November 17, 1558, being the very day on which Queen Mary herself died."

Matthew Parker died here in 1575, and was buried in the chapel. After the Civil Wars, and in the time of the Commonwealth, when fanatical and political fury went hand in hand, it was found that every building devoted to piety had suffered more than they had done in all the rage of family contest. The fine works of art and the sacred memorials of the dead were, except in a few instances, sacrificed to Puritanical barbarism, or to sacrilegious plunder. Lambeth House—for by that name, and the Manor of Lambeth, the archbishops at that time distinguished their residence, and not by the modern title of palace—fell to the share of the miscreant regicides Scott and Hardynge, who pulled down the noble hall, the work of Chicheley, and sold the materials for their own profit. The chapel they turned into a dancing-room; and because the tomb of the venerable Archbishop Parker "stared them in the face and checked their mirth, it was broken to pieces, his bones dug up by Hardynge, to whose share this part of the palace fell; and opening the leaden coffin, and cutting away the cerecloths, of which there were many folds, the flesh seemed very fresh. The corpse thus stripped was conveyed into the outhouse for poultry and dung, and buried among the offal; but upon the restoration of King Charles, that wretch Hardynge was forced to discover where it was; whereupon the archbishop had him honourably re-interred in the same chapel near the steps of the altar."

The palace had for some time previous to this been used as a prison for the Royalists; Guy Carleton, Dean of Carlisle, was one of the persons committed to it, but he fortunately escaped and quitted England. Bishop Kennett says, that of near one hundred ministers from the west of England who were imprisoned at Lambeth almost all died of a pestilential fever.

Passing by Grindall and Whitgift, we come to Archbishop Bancroft, who, as we shall presently have occasion to state more fully, began the fine library in this palace, and left his books to his successors for ever. He died in 1610, and was buried in Lambeth Church. Of the other improvements in this venerable pile we shall speak in describing the buildings themselves.

"With the exception of à Becket," writes the author of "Select Views of London," "there are, it is supposed, traces of some public act done in this house by every archbishop, from the time when the monks of Rochester became possessed of it till its alienation; for though in some cases the name only of Lambeth is mentioned, yet it is so explicitly averred in others that the archbishops were at the manor house, that it may be presumed this was their regular inn."

With the exception of the chapel, the whole of the present structure has certainly been erected since the above-mentioned period. The palace, as it now appears, is an irregular but very extensive pile, exhibiting specimens of almost every style of architecture that has prevailed during the last seven hundred years. The walls are chiefly built of a fine red brick, and are supported by stone buttresses, edged and coped with stone. The "great gate" is enumerated among the buildings of the palace in the stewards' accounts in the fifteenth year of Edward II. Cardinal Morton rebuilt it about the year 1490 in the manner we at present see it. The building, which is chiefly remarkable for its vast size, consists of two immense square towers, with a spacious gateway and postern in the centre; it is built of red brick, with stone dressings, and is embattled. The arch of the gateway is pointed, and the roof beautifully groined. Above, is a noble apartment, called the "Record Tower," where, until lately, the archives of the see of Canterbury were deposited. Access to the different storeys, now used chiefly as lumber-rooms, is obtained by spiral stairs in the towers.

Passing through the gateway, we enter the outer court. On the left is a low wall, partly covered with ivy, separating the palace demesnes from the Thames and what was once the favourite promenade known as Bishops' Walk, but now the Albert Embankment. In front appears the Water Tower, with the Lollards' Tower beyond ; and on the right the Great Hall, now the library and manuscript-room. It is a lofty structure of brick, strengthened with buttresses, and ornamented with cornices and quoins of stone. It is nearly one hundred feet in length, forty in breadth, and fifty in height. The roof is composed principally of oak, elaborately carved, and has in the centre a lofty and elegant lantern, at the top of which are the arms of the see of Canterbury impaling those of Juxon, and surmounted by the archiepiscopal mitre. The interior is lighted, in addition to the lantern, by ranges of high windows on either side, in some of which are heraldic devices in stained glass. Over the hall door appear the same arms as those above mentioned, together with the date MDCLXIII ; and at the lower end is a screen of the Ionic order, on the top of which is the founder's crest, a negro's head crowned. The whole hall is wain-scoted to a considerable height, and the floor is handsomely paved.

This hall was probably built originally by Arch-bishop Boniface in the thirteenth century. In the stewards' account, above quoted, the "Great Hall" is mentioned. It was "re-edified" by Arch-bishop Chicheley ; and in 1570 the roofing was "covered with shingles" by Archbishop Parker. During the Commonwealth the hall is said to have been pulled down, and the materials sold by Colonel Scott and Matthew Hardyng, to whom the manor of Lambeth had been granted. The present hall was commenced after the Restoration by Arch-bishop Juxon, precisely on the site of its pre-decessor, and as nearly as possible after the ancient model ; but it was not finished at his death. Juxon appears to have been so anxious concerning its erection, that he left the following direction in his will :—"If I happen to die before the hall at Lam-beth be finished, my executors to be at the charge of finishing it, according to the model made of it, if my successor shall give leave."

The reason why such large halls were built in the houses of ancient nobility and gentry was that there might be room to exercise the generous hos-pitality which prevailed among our ancestors, and which was, without doubt, duly exercised by most of the possessors of this mansion, though not par-ticularly recorded. What great hospitality Cranmer maintained, we may judge by the following authentic list of his household—viz., "steward, treasurer, comptroller, gamators, clerk of the kitchen, caterer, clerk of the spicery, yeoman of ewry, bakers, pantlers, yeomen of the horse, ushers, butlers of wine and ale, larderers, squilleries, ushers of the hall, porter, ushers of the chamber, daily waiters

in the great chamber, gentlemen ushers, yeomen of the chamber, carver, sewer, cup-bearer, grooms of the chamber, marshal, groom-ushers, almoner, cooks, chandler, butchers, master of the horse, yeomen of the wardrobe, and harbingers." Car-dinal Pole, his successor, had a patent from Philip and Mary to retain one hundred servants, a fact which affords some idea of his hospitality and grandeur.

Of the hospitality of Archbishop Parker, Strype gives us the following account :—"In the daily eating this was the custom : the steward, with the servants that were gentlemen of the better rank, sat down at the tables in the hall at the right hand ; and the almoner, with the clergy and the other servants, sat on the other side, where there was plenty of all sorts of provision, both for eating and drinking. The daily fragments thereof did suffice to fill the bellies of a great number of poor hungry people that waited at the gate ; and so constant and unfailing was this provision at my lord's table, that whosoever came in, either at dinner or supper, being not above the degree of a knight, might there be entertained worthy of his quality, either at the steward's or at the almoner's table. And, moreover, it was the archbishop's command to his servants that all strangers should be received and treated with all manner of civility and respect, and that places at the table should be assigned them according to their dignity and quality, which redounded much to the praise and commendation of the archbishop. The discourse and conversation at meals was void of all brawls and loud talking, and for the most part consisted in framing men's manners to religion, or to some other honest and beseeming subject. There was a monitor in the hall ; and if it happened that any spoke too loud, or concerning things less decent, it was presently hushed by one that cried ' Silence.' The archbishop loved hospitality, and no man showed it so much or with better order, though he himself was very abstemious."

The great hall is now used as a library. Ranged on each side along the walls are projecting book-cases, containing nearly 30,000 volumes, chiefly valuable for works relating to theology and eccle-siastical history and antiquities ; these, however, are varied with old English poetry and romances, and topographical, heraldic, and genealogical works. A collection of books existed at an early period as an appendage to the archbishop's household ; but the first reliable date of the foundation of the present library is 1610, in which year Archbishop Bancroft left by will " to his successors the Arch-bishops of Canterbury, for ever, a greate and famous library of bookes of divinity, and of many other sorts of learning," provided they bound themselves to the necessary assurances for the continuance of such books to the archbishops successively ; otherwise, they were to be bequeathed to the " publique library of the University of Cambridge." Bancroft's successor—Archbishop Abbot (1611–33)—carried out these injunctions, and left his own books to the Lambeth library. But the civil war marked the crisis in the history of the collection, for when the Parliamentarians were about to seize on Lambeth Palace, the learned Selden, fearing the danger of total dispersion, suggested to the University of Cambridge their right to the books, in accordance with Bancroft's will, as above mentioned. Very few of Archbishop Laud's books are here, nearly all of them having been presented to the library of St. John's College, Oxford. To Cambridge the Lambeth books were transferred and preserved, until, at the Restoration, they were recalled by Archbishop Juxon (1660–3). That primate's death occurring before the books could be restored, it was left to his successor, Archbishop Sheldon, to see them replaced at Lambeth. This primate presented many books to the library ; but not so his successor, Archbishop Sancroft, who, although he had many of the MSS. re-bound and preserved, yet on his resignation presented his collection to Emmanuel College, Cambridge, of which he had been master. From Archbishop Tillotson (1691–5) we hear of no bequests ; but his successor, Archbishop Tenison, bequeathed a portion of his library to Lambeth, a part to St. Paul's Cathedral, and the remainder to the library which he had founded in St. Martin's-in-the-Fields.* From 1716 to 1757, when the see of Canterbury was filled by the primates Wake, Potter, Herring, and Hutton, few additions were made ; but Archbishop Secker, who followed next in order, will be gratefully remembered in the library annals as having given all the books in his own library, which included also many interesting pamphlets, to the archiepiscopal collection. To Archbishop Cornwallis we are indebted for presenting and causing the extensive collection of tracts to be bound and arranged. The names of Archbishops Manners-Sutton (1805–28) and Howley (1828–48) are associated with large bequests of theological lore to the library.

The great hall was converted to its present use by Archbishop Howley in 1834, previously to which time the books were arranged in some galleries over the cloisters which were then standing. The bequests of successive primates are generally dis-

tinguished by their arms or initials on the outside cover of the books, while autographs and memoranda on the title-pages record noted names, and supply links of ownership. Among those autographs may be found the names of Cranmer ; Foxe, the " martyrologist ;" Tillotson ; Tenison ; Henry Wotton, the well-known writer on architecture ; the more famous one of Charles I., attached to a " Life of Archbishop Laud ;" and several of less note. It is in this way that the interest of the books is identified with much that is historical. An exhaustive catalogue of the library and art treasures in the palace, with a full description of its illuminated manuscripts and ancient chronicles, was published in 1873 by the Archbishop's librarian, Mr. S. W. Kershaw. Space does not admit of our entering at any great length into a description of the varied contents of this library ; but we may state that among the ancient printed books is one of great rarity : this is " The Chronicles of Great Britain," and was printed by Caxton at Westminster in 1480. There are about five other works printed by Caxton in the library, although imperfect. The " Golden Legend," printed by the celebrated Wynkyn de Worde, also finds a place here ; as also does the " Nuremberg Chronicle " (the library had two copies), and the fifteenth century MSS., known as the " St. Alban's Chronicle." Of illuminated MSS., there are about thirty examples of the various styles of art in this library ; one of the most rare being the little MS. known as the " Gospels of Mac Durnan," written about the year 900, and presented by King Athelstan to the City of Canterbury. The school of English art is represented most notably in the copy of the New Testament, printed on vellum, known as the " Mazarine," from the fact of the first copy having been discovered in the library of that cardinal.

This Mazarine Bible, when complete, is of great rarity and value, and only four *perfect vellum* copies are known. Another interesting example of English art is a MS. known as the " Dictyes and Sayings of the Philosophers ;" and in this illumination the author is represented as introducing a tonsured personage, who presents a copy of the work to King Edward IV., accompanied by his queen and their son, afterwards Edward V. Walpole, in his " Royal and Noble Authors," has given an engraving of this miniature, and it has also been engraved by Strutt.

There is in the library only one book which is known for certain to have belonged to Archbishop Parker, and that is a treatise entitled " De Antiquitate et Privilegiis Ecclesiæ Cantuarensis." The library contains, *inter alia*, an original impression

---

* See Vol. III., p. 158.

of the scarce plan of London by Aggas, together with a series of prints of the archbishops of the see from the Reformation downwards, collected by Archbishop Cornwallis.

In 1875 a donation was made of theological books from the collection of the late Professor

THE LOLLARDS' TOWER, LAMBETH PALACE.

entering into orders, became librarian and keeper of manuscripts here, under Archbishop Howley, who conferred on him the Lambeth degree of D.D., in recognition of his learning and long and able services, and on whose death, in 1848, he resigned his appointment. He was the author of many learned works, amongst which we may specify—"Two Inquiries into the Grounds on which the Prophetic Period of Daniel and St. John has been supposed to consist of 1,260 years;" "The Dark Ages: being a series of Essays, intended to illustrate the State of Religion and Literature in the Ninth, Tenth,

Selwyn, of Cambridge, one of the honorary curators of this library. This gift supplied many deficiencies in modern works.

Dr. Ducarel, who was the Archbishop's librarian, is recorded in "Walpoliana" as a "poor creature," and not very anxious to oblige those who wanted to consult the library. From some incidental hints given by Horace Walpole, it may be inferred that a century ago the Archiepiscopal Library was not very easily available to scholars and literary men.

One late librarian, Dr. Samuel Maitland, who died in 1866, deserves mention in these pages. Born about the year 1790, he graduated at Trinity College, Cambridge, and was for some time a barrister of the Inner Temple. He, however, applied himself to the study of church history, and

Eleventh, and Twelfth Centuries;" "Essays on Subjects connected with the Reformation in England;" "Eruvin, or Miscellaneous Essays on subjects connected with the Nature, History, and Destiny of Man," &c. He was also the compiler of an "Index to such English books printed before the year 1600, as are in the Archiepiscopal Library at Lambeth."

The first complete catalogue of printed books which was formed on the plan of the Bodleian Catalogue, was drawn up by Dr. Gibson (afterwards

Bishop of Lincoln), the editor of "Camden's Britannia," who was some time vicar of Lambeth, and also librarian here. This catalogue is deposited in the manuscript library. In 1718 it was fairly copied by Dr. Wilkins, in three folio volumes, and has been continued by his successors to the present time. In 1873–4 the whole of the books and manuscripts underwent a complete repair, by a special grant from the Ecclesiastical Commissioners.

A building of modern date, adjacent to the library, serves as the manuscript-room; it was put into thorough repair a few years ago, and rendered fire-proof. Here are preserved some 1,300 manuscripts of the highest interest, together with the records of the palace, which are kept in patent "Reliance" safes. Some of the documents date from a very early time, and one of them, it is alleged, bears the signature of Canute.

THE CHAMBER IN LAMBETH PALACE IN WHICH THE LOLLARDS WERE CONFINED.

It may be added that the archbishop allows the library to be open to students, and, indeed, to all respectable persons, on application, every Monday, Wednesday, and Friday during the year, vacations excepted.

Before quitting the hall, we may remark that a stone on the building gives the date of the erection 1685; but a leaden pipe attached to the walls, running from the roof to the ground, to carry off rain-water, bears the date 1663. The pipe appears to be in a very good state of preservation; and a coat-of-arms, supposed to be that of Bishop Juxon, can be plainly observed on it. To account for the difference in date, it is supposed that the pipe belonged to an old building which stood on the site of the present structure.

Among the "curiosities" of Lambeth Palace preserved in the manuscript-room is the habit of a priest, consisting of a stole, maniple, chasuble; cord, two bands marked P, and the corporal; also a crucifix of base metal, a string of beads, and a box of relics. Here also is kept the shell of a tortoise, believed to have lived in the palace gardens from the time of Laud (1633) to 1753, when it perished by the negligence of the gardener; the shell is ten inches in length, and six and a half inches in breadth.

From the south-east corner of the hall a flight of stairs leads up to the Guard-chamber; it is a large state room, fifty-six feet long by twenty-seven feet wide, and is so called from having formerly contained the armour and arms appropriated to the defence of the palace. By whom the arms kept for this purpose were originally purchased does not appear, but they seem to have regularly passed from one archbishop to another. The author of " Select Views of London" says : " Archbishop Parker gave them to his successors, provided they were accepted in lieu of dilapidations. They were undoubtedly purchased by his successor, and so on ; for Archbishop Laud says that he bought the arms at Lambeth of his predecessor's executors. In the plundering of Lambeth House, in 1642, the arms—the quantity of which had been extremely exaggerated in order to increase the popular odium against Laud—were removed. They were, however, restored afterwards, or replaced with others ; for some of the old muskets and bandoleers of an ancient make remained during Archbishop Potter's time in the burying-ground, the wall of which was pulled down by Archbishop Herring, and the arms disposed of elsewhere."

The guard-chamber is now used as a state dining-room. The principal feature which distinguishes the apartment at present is its venerable timber roof, which somewhat resembles that of the great hall, but is much less ornamented ; the windows likewise are pointed, and of an ancient make. Over the door of this chamber is the date 1681, which shows that there were some reparations made to it in Archbishop Sancroft's time. The lower part of the walls of the apartment is covered with oak wainscoting, above which are hung half-length portraits of many of the archbishops, the most interesting of which, perhaps, are those of Laud, Cardinal Pole, Chicheley, Warham, and Arundel. To the list of archiepiscopal portraits have been lately added those of Archbishops Sumner and Longley ; the latter, by Richmond, is hung in the drawing-room. A portrait of Archbishop Laud, and also an etching of his trial in Westminster Hall, are to be found among the etchings of Hollar.

Leaving this chamber, we pass on to the chapel through a narrow gallery, which contains numerous portraits of ecclesiastical dignitaries, a small portrait of Martin Luther on panel, and also a splendid engraving of Old London. Descending the stairs at the end of this gallery, we enter the vestibule of the chapel. This apartment is sometimes called the " post-room," probably from the fact of the ceiling being supported in the centre by a stout pillar. It is on record that the builder of this tower, Archbishop Chicheley, "found during his time the impossibility of punishing all heretics with death, therefore whipping and other severe and degrading punishments were consequently resorted to." This so-called post-room has been by some

considered as expressly set apart for that purpose ; the pillar serving for the purpose of securing the unfortunate heretics, confined in the room above, while undergoing the degrading punishment of the lash.

The chapel is considered by far the most ancient part of the palace, being probably part of Archbishop Boniface's original erection. It is in the earliest style of English pointed architecture, being lighted on the sides by triple lancet-shaped windows, and on the east by a window of five lights, set between massive and deep masonry. It consists of a body only, measuring seventy-two feet in length, twenty-five feet in breadth, and thirty feet in height; but it is divided into two parts by a handsome carved screen, which, curiously enough, is painted. Previous to the Civil Wars the windows were adorned with painted glass, put up by Archbishop Morton, representing the whole history of man from the creation to the day of judgment. The windows being divided into three parts, " the two side lights contained the types of the Old Testament, and the middle light the anti-type and verity of the New Testament." Archbishop Laud, on taking possession of the palace—to use his own words—found these windows " shameful to look on, all diversly patched like a poor beggar's coat," and he repaired them. " This laudable action of the prelate," writes Dr. Ducarel, in his " History of Lambeth," " which would now be justly esteemed a mark of good taste and liberality, formed in that narrow age of Puritanical bigotry the subject of a criminal charge, it being alleged against him on his trial, 'that he did repair the story of those windows by their like in the Mass Book ;' but this he utterly denied, and affirmed that he and his secretary made out the story as well as they could by the remains that were unbroken. These beautiful windows were all defaced by our outrageous reformers in the last century, who, under pretence of abhorring idols, made no scruple of committing sacrilege." The roof of the chapel, which is flat and divided into compartments, is embellished with the arms of Archbishop Laud.

The interior of the chapel is fitted up with a range of pews or stalls on each side for the officers of the archbishop's household, with seats beneath for the inferior domestics. The altar-piece is of the Corinthian order, painted and gilded ; and the floor is paved with black and white marble in lozenge-shaped slabs.

The only interment that appears to have taken place here is that of Archbishop Parker, who died in 1575. His body, by his request, was buried at the upper end of this chapel, against the communion-table, on the south side, under a monument of his own erecting, bearing a Latin inscription by his old friend, Dr. Walter Haddon. The spot where Parker's body now rests is marked by the following words cut in the pavement immediately before the communion rails :—

"CORPUS MATTHÆI ARCHIEPISCOPI TANDEM HIC QVIESCIT."

In the western part of the chapel is a monument, with a long inscription to his memory, placed there by Archbishop Sancroft.

During the Civil Wars, in 1648, when Lambeth Palace was possessed by Colonel Scott, the chapel was turned into a hall or dancing-room, and the ancient monument of Parker was destroyed. Nor was this all. We are further told that his body, by order of Matthew Harding, a Puritan, was dug up, stripped of its leaden covering (which was sold), and buried in a dunghill, where it remained till after the Restoration, when Sir William Dugdale, hearing of the matter accidentally, immediately repaired to Archbishop Sancroft, by whose diligence, aided by the House of Lords, the bones were found, and again buried in the chapel, in the spot above indicated.

Underneath the chapel is a spacious crypt, which probably dates from the middle of the thirteenth century. It consists of a series of substantial stone arches, supported by short massive columns. The roof, which is about ten feet from the ground, is finely groined.

Retracing our steps through the "post-room," we come to one of the most interesting portions of Lambeth Palace, namely, the building called the Lollards' Tower. It was erected by Archbishop Chicheley, in the early part of the fifteenth century, as a place of confinement for the unhappy heretics from whom it derives its name. The building is constructed chiefly of brick, and is embattled. Chicheley's arms are sculptured on the outer wall, on the Thames side ; and beneath them is a Gothic niche, wherein at one time stood the image of St. Thomas à Becket. The prison in which the Lollards were confined is at the top of the tower, and is reached by a very narrow winding staircase. Its single doorway, which is so narrow as only to admit one person at a time, is strongly barricaded by both an outer and an inner door of oak, each three inches and a half thick, and thickly studded with iron. The dimensions of the apartment within are twelve feet in length by nine in width, and eight in height ; and it is lighted by two windows, which are only twenty-eight inches high by fourteen inches wide on the inside, and about half as high and half as wide on the outside. Both the walls

and roof of the chamber are lined with oaken planks an inch and a half thick ; and eight large iron rings still remain fastened to the wood, the melancholy memorials of the victims who formerly pined in this dismal prison-house. Many names and fragments of sentences are rudely cut out on various parts of the walls.

In 1873 the Lollards' Tower, having fallen into a very dilapidated condition, was thoroughly repaired. The old roof was removed, the flooring renewed, the old side walls re-faced with new stone, every stone and brick ascertained to be faulty taken out and replaced with sound materials, and the whole structure restored. The tower for many years was used as a lumber-room, but after its restoration it was occupied by the late Bishop of Lichfield as a town residence.

In addition to the apartments already mentioned, there are the "Presence Chamber," the "Steward's Parlour," and the rooms in the new buildings which now serve as the residence of the archbishop. The Presence Chamber is a fine ancient room, thirty feet by nineteen. The precise time of the erection of this part of the palace is not known. This room is at present remarkable only for the stained glass in the windows. Two of these contain portraits of St. Jerome and St. Gregory, with the following verses :—

ST. HIERONIMUS.

" Devout his life, his volumes learned be,
　The sacred writt's interpreter was he ;
　And none the doctors of the Church amonge
　Is found his equal in the Hebrew tonge."

On the second window :—

GREGORIUS.

" More holy or more learned since his tyme
　Was none that wore the triple diadem ;
　And by his paynefull studies he is one
　Amonge the cheefest Latin fathers knowne."

In this room many causes relating to Merton and All Souls' Colleges at Oxford have been decided in presence of the Archbishops as Visitors.

The present buildings, used as the archiepiscopal residence, owe much of their unity and stateliness to Archbishop Howley (1828–48), who not only rebuilt the principal palace front on the south, but restored much of the older portions. The work was carried out under the direction of Mr. Blore ; they were several years in progress, and the entire expense was little short of £60,000. The garden-front of the palace is of Tudor character, and with its bays and enriched windows, battlements, gables, towers, and clustered chimney-shafts, is very picturesque.

The gardens and grounds, together with the palace, cover about sixteen acres of ground. "Here were formerly," as John Timbs informs us in his "Curiosities of London," "two fine white Marseilles fig-trees, traditionally planted by Cardinal Pole against that part of the palace which he founded : these trees," he continues, " were more than fifty feet in height and' forty in breadth, their circumference twenty-eight and twenty-one inches. They were removed during the late rebuilding, but some cuttings from the trees are growing between the buttresses of the library." The terrace is named Clarendon Walk, from having been the scene of a conference between the great and wise Earl of Clarendon and the ill-fated Laud. It is with regret we add, that "Bishops' Walk," with its pleasant elm-trees, trodden by the feet of so many visitors, both lay and clerical, was swept away to make room for the Embankment in front of new St. Thomas's Hospital.

There is extant a curious etching, by Hollar, of the river-side at Lambeth, including Lambeth Palace, or Lambeth "House," as it was called. In other respects it was in his time much the same as now, except that a grove of trees stands where now rises St. Thomas's Hospital.

Of the "remarkable occurrences" which have taken place at the palace, space will only allow us to speak briefly. Archbishop Anselm ordained Sampson, Bishop-elect of Worcester, both deacon and priest, together with the Bishop of Hereford, in 1096, at Lambeth. In 1097, he ordained Hugh, Abbot of St. Austin, at Lambeth, in the chapel of the church of Rochester, where the archbishop then lodged. He likewise presided in 1100 at the council held at Lambeth which announced the legality of the intended marriage of Henry I. with Matilda, the daughter of Malcolm, King of Scotland.

Archbishops Ralph, Corboyl, Theobald, Richard, and Baldwin, were all consecrated at Lambeth ; and though, as we have said, we have no account of Becket being there, yet on the vacancy of the see of Canterbury by his death, the suffragan bishops, in pursuance of the order of Richard de Luci, assembled at that place, and, if not unanimously, they at least with one voice, made choice of Roger, Abbot of Bec, to be his successor ; but he would not accept the trust.

From "Collins's Peerage" we learn how that, in 1345, the nineteenth year of Edward III., John de Montfort, Duke of Brittany, did homage to the king in Lambeth Palace.

In 1367 the consecration feast of William of Wykeham, Bishop of Winchester, was kept here with great magnificence by Archbishop Langham.

In 1381, during the insurrection of Wat Tyler,

the rebels not only beheaded Archbishop Sudbury, then Lord High Chancellor, but plundered this palace, and burnt most of the goods, books, and remembrances of Chancery. Sudbury's Register Book fortunately escaped destruction, and is still at Lambeth. The damages done by this lawless banditti were repaired in a great measure by Arundel and Chicheley ; but much was left for their successors to do, as may be reasonably concluded from the sums of money expended by Morton and Warham.

In the account given of the convocation assembled by Archbishop Arundel in St. Paul's Cathedral, in June and July, 1408, it is related that after the session of July 26, the bishops, abbots, priors, chancellors of the two universities, doctors of divinity and laws, deans, archdeacons, "and other venerable persons eminent in every branch of literature, to a number not easily to be computed," were entertained with elegance, and with great profusion of viands, by the archbishop in his manor of Lambeth.

In 1446 Archbishop Stafford held at Lambeth a convocation of all the prelates resident in London, to deliberate about the payment of a tenth imposed by the Pope. The king's prohibition was offered as a plea for not agreeing to this demand. In 1481 the bull of Pope Innocent IV. against the rebellious subjects of Henry VII. was exhibited to Archbishop Morton "in a certain inner chamber within the *manor* of Lambeth."

In the year 1501, Katharine of Arragon, afterwards Queen of Henry VIII., on her first arrival in England, " was lodged with her ladies for some days at the archbishop's inne at Lambeth." It was afterwards honoured with the frequent presence of royalty. In 1513, during a visit, it is presumed, from Henry VIII. to Archbishop Warham at this palace, Charles Somerset was created Earl of Worcester.

In 1533, Archbishop Cranmer confirmed at Lambeth the marriage of Henry VIII. with Anne Boleyn ; and three years afterwards the same prelate, " being judicially seated in a certain low chapel within his house at Lambeth," by a definitive sentence annulled the marriage between the same parties ; the queen, in order to avoid the sentence of burning, having confessed to the archbishop some just and lawful impediments to her marriage with the king. A little before the latter event— namely, on the 13th of April, 1534—the commissioners sat at Lambeth to administer the oath of succession to the Crown, upon the heirs of the same Queen Anne, to the clergy, and chiefly those of London that had not yet sworn. On the same day were conveyed thither from the Tower Bishop Fisher and Sir Thomas More, the only layman at this meeting, to tender their oath to them; but both of them, as readers of history know, refused.

In 1537, the archbishops and bishops, by virtue of the royal commission, held various meetings at Lambeth Palace, to devise the "Godly and Pious Disposition of a Christian Man," usually styled, from the composers of it, "The Bishops' Book," but were obliged to separate on account of the plague then raging at Lambeth, and persons dying even at the palace gate.

In the rout of the Scots army, in 1542, the Earl of Cassilis, who was one of the many persons taken prisoners, was sent to Lambeth Palace, and was kept there on his parole.

Several circumstances respecting Cardinal Pole are noticed as having happened here by Strype, Burnet, and other authors. Queen Mary is said to have completely furnished Lambeth Palace for his reception at her own cost, and to have frequently honoured him with her company. "In 1554, on his arrival from the Continent, having presented himself at court, he went from thence in his barge to his palace at Lambeth; and here he soon afterwards summoned the bishops and inferior clergy, then assembled in convocation, to come to him to be absolved from all their prejudices, schisms, and heresies. The following month all the bishops went to Lambeth to receive the cardinal's blessing and directions."

"On the 21st of July, 1556," says Strype, "the queen removed from St. James's in the Fields into Eltham, passing through the park to Whitehall, and took her barge, crossing over to Lambeth unto my lord cardinal's palace; and there she took her chariot, and so rid through St. George's Fields to Newington, and so over the fields to Eltham, at five o'clock in the afternoon. She was attended on horseback by the cardinal, &c., and by a conflux of people to see her grace, above ten thousand." In the winter of the same year the queen removed from St. James's through the park, and took her barge to Lambeth, where she visited Cardinal Pole. After dinner she resumed her journey to Greenwich, where she kept her Christmas.

In 1558 Cardinal Pole died at Lambeth Palace. His body lay in state forty days, when it was removed to Canterbury Cathedral for interment.

Queen Elizabeth was a frequent visitor here to Archbishop Parker; and the confidence she reposed in that prelate induced her to employ him in many affairs of great trust. On his first promotion to the archiepiscopal see, she committed to him in free custody the deprived Bishops Tunstal

and Thirlby, Bishops of Durham and Ely respectively, whom, we are told, he entertained most kindly. Tunstal survived his confinement only about four months, and was buried in Lambeth Church; Thirlby, however, continued to be the archbishop's "guest" for upwards of ten years, and was buried near his brother bishop.

On one occasion when Queen Elizabeth visited Archbishop Parker—possibly during one of her "progresses"—the following circumstance is said to have occurred:—The queen was never reconciled to that part of the Reformation which allowed the marriage of ecclesiastics; and, unfortunately, Parker had not only written a treatise on the lawfulness of marriage, but had absolutely entered into the holy state prior to the repeal of the statute forbidding celibacy. The haughty Elizabeth, although elegantly entertained by the archbishop and his lady for several days, could not at her departure refrain from venting her resentment in the following rude manner. Addressing herself to Mrs. Parker, by way of taking leave, she said: "*Madam*, I may not call you; *mistress*, I am ashamed to call you; yet though I know not what to call you, I thank you."

In 1571, we read, the queen "took an airing in St. George's Fields," previous to which she had an interview with the archbishop at Lambeth Bridge. It appears, according to Strype's "Life of Parker," that the prelate had in some degree, about this time, fallen under the queen's displeasure by speaking freely to her concerning his office. The archbishop relates this incident in a letter to Lady Bacon:—"I will not," he writes, "be abashed to say to my prince that I think in conscience in answering to my charging. As this other day I was well chidden at my prince's hand; but with one ear I heard her hard words, and with the other, and in my conscience and heart, I heard God. And yet, her highness being never so much incensed to be offended with me, the next day coming on Lambeth Bridge into the fields, she gave me her very good looks, and spake secretly in mine ear, that she must needs continue mine authority before the people to the credit of my service. Whereat, divers of my *arches* then being with me peradventure mervailed; where peradventure somebody would have looked over the shoulders, and slily slipt away, to have abashed me before the world."

Grindall, Parker's successor in the archbishopric, soon fell under the queen's displeasure, and it does not appear that she ever honoured him with a visit. Archbishop Whitgift, however, seems to have been more fortunate, for it is reported that Elizabeth was entertained by him no less than fifteen different times, and that she frequently stayed here for two or three days together. James I. was likewise an occasional visitor of Whitgift; and the last occasion was on the 28th of February, 1604, when the prelate lay on his death-bed. It was during the primacy of Whitgift that an important event began to furnish matter for fierce disputes. The controversies which had divided the Protestant body in its infancy had related almost exclusively to Church government and to ceremonies. There had been no serious quarrel between the contending parties on points of metaphysical theology. The

INTERIOR OF THE GREAT HALL, LAMBETH PALACE, 1800.

occurred at Lambeth Palace which has linked its history more closely than anything else with that of the Established Church. This was none other than the Conference where the famous "Lambeth Articles" were propounded for the signature of the clergy. Macaulay mentions these articles thus:— "A class of questions, as to which the founders of the Anglican Church and the first generation of Puritans had differed little or not at all, now doctrines held by the chiefs of the party touching original sin, faith, grace, predestination and election, were those which are popularly called Calvinistic. Towards the close of Elizabeth's reign, her favourite prelate, Archbishop Whitgift, in concert with the Bishop of London and other theologians, drew up the celebrated instrument known by the name of the 'Lambeth Articles.' In that instrument the most startling of the Calvinistic doctrines are

LAMBETH PALACE.

1. The Cloisters.   2. Entrance to Lambeth Palace.   3. Doorway leading from Chapel.   4. Crypt under the Chapel.
5. Entrance to Cloisters.   6. Garden Front of Lambeth Palace.

affirmed with a distinctness which would shock many who, in our age, are reputed Calvinists. One clergyman, who took the opposite side and spoke harshly of Calvin, was arraigned for his presumption by the University of Cambridge, and escaped punishment only by expressing his firm belief in the tenets of reprobation and final perseverance, and his sorrow for the offence which he had given to pious men by reflecting on the great French Reformer." The precious document itself, which is thus connected in name with Lambeth, may be read *in extenso* in Southey's or any other "History of the English Church," and so we may be spared the necessity of quoting it here; we may, however, merely add that the "Lambeth Articles" were nine in number, and ultra-Calvinistic in their character. They were drawn up by Dr. Whitaker, Master of St. John's College, Cambridge, and Regius Professor of Divinity in that University, at the request of Archbishop Whitgift, who sought to impose them on the clergy of the Established Church. They were rigidly suppressed, however, by order of Queen Elizabeth; and so strictly were her injunctions executed, that for many years a printed copy of them was not to be obtained "for love or money." They were brought forward, some ten years later, at the Hampton Court Conference, but only to be rejected. The Irish Protestant Church, however, adopted them in 1615.

Archbishop Abbot, who was appointed to the see of Canterbury in 1611, was accused by the Duke of Buckingham of living at too costly a rate for an archbishop, and of entertaining people who were not well affected to the king and his court. On this occasion he replied to Secretary Conway: "When King James gave me the archbishopric, he charged me that I should carry my house nobly, and live like an archbishop, which I promised him that I would do; and all that came to my house of the civil sort I gave them friendly entertainment, not sifting what exceptions the duke made against them. . . . But I meddled with no man's quarrels; and if I should have received none but such as cordially and in truth loved him, I might many times have gone to my dinner without company."

Apropos of the banquets in the great hall, we may state that Mr. Fenton, a distinguished *chef de cuisine* under one of the archbishops during the present century, left to his family a valuable legacy —the recipe for "Fenton's Canterbury Sauce." His grace was not a gourmand, but he liked a good dinner, and knew both a good dinner and a good cook when he had got one.

Although the dinners in the great hall have ceased to take place, and the fragments, therefore, are no longer given to the poor as of old, a substitute for the latter custom is still in practice, in the shape of the archbishop's bounty or "dole," which has been dispensed before the principal entrance of the palace every week down to the present time: it consists of money, bread, and provisions, which are given to thirty poor parishioners of Lambeth, ten receiving it in turn on different days.

Going back again to the early part of the seventeenth century, we must speak of Laud, who was translated to the archbishopric from the see of London on the death of Abbot in 1633. This prelate unfortunately lived in troublous times; and Evelyn records, in his "Diary," under date April 27, 1641—apparently as an eye-witness—the fact of "the Bishop of Canterbury's palace at Lambeth being assaulted by a rude rabble from Southwark." A few days later the palace was again attacked by a London mob. As we learn from the "Comprehensive History of England," "Laud's friend, Pierce, the Bishop of Bath and Wells, had called the Scottish war of 1640–41 'bellum Episcopale' (a war for Episcopacy), and such the English people were disposed to consider it. During the sitting of the convocation, a libel or paper was posted up at the Royal Exchange, inviting the London apprentices, who were rather prone to mischief, to rise and sack the archiepiscopal palace of Lambeth. The invitation was accepted, and on the night of the 11th of May, a mob, consisting almost entirely of apprentices and youths, fell upon the said palace. But Laud had had time to fortify and garrison his residence; the rioters were not very numerous, and he 'had no harm.' Laud, in noting the occurrence in his 'Diary,' says: 'May 11. Monday night, at midnight, my house at Lambeth was beset with 500 persons of the rascal riotous multitude. I had notice, and strengthened the house as well as I could, and, God be blessed, I had no harm.' Clarendon represents the mob to have been much greater, for he tells us that 'the rabble of mean, unknown, dissolute persons amounted to the number of *some thousands.*' 'Since then,' adds Laud, 'I have got cannon, and fortified my house, and hope all may be safe; but yet libels are constantly set up in all places of note in the city.'" Ten days afterwards Laud made the following entry in his "Diary:"—"One of the chief being taken, was condemned at Southwark on Thursday, and *hanged and quartered* on Saturday morning following." The victim, it appears, was quite a youth, and the horrid punishment of treason was awarded to him by the court lawyers because there happened to be a drum in the mob, and the marching to beat of drum was held to be a levying of war against the king. Clarendon says that "this infamous, scandalous, headless insurrection, quashed with the deserved death of that one varlet, was not thought to be contrived or fomented by any persons of quality."

In their accusations against Archbishop Laud, the Puritan House of Commons charged him with setting up and repairing Popish images and pictures in the window of his chapel in Lambeth Palace. The archbishop, in his defence, urged that the Homilies of the Reformed and Established Church allowed the historical use of images, and that Calvin himself permitted them in that sense ; and that the Primitive Christians approved of, and had in their houses, pictures of Christ himself.

Laud was beheaded by the Parliamentarians in January, 1644, and his body was interred in the church of Allhallows, Barking, near Tower Hill. After this event the see of Canterbury was vacant nearly seventeen years, during which period, as we have shown above, Lambeth Palace was nearly demolished.

From Evelyn's "Diary," under date of August 31, 1663, we glean the following particulars concerning the ceremony attending the translation of Dr. Sheldon to the archbishopric :—"I was invited," Evelyn writes, "to the Translation of Dr. Sheldon, Bishop of London, from that see to Canterbury, the ceremonie performed at Lambeth. First went his grace's mace-bearer, steward, treasurer, comptroller, all in their gownes, and with white staves ; next the Bishops in their habites, eight in number ; Dr. Sweate, Deane of the Arches ; Dr. Exton, Judge of the Admiralty; Sir William Merick, Judge of the Prerogative Court, with divers Advocates in scarlet. After divine service in the chapel, perform'd with musiq extraordinary, Dr. French and Dr. Stradling (his grace's chaplaines) saied prayers. The Archbishop in a private roome looking into the Chapel, the Bishops who were Commissioners went up to a table plac'd before the altar, and sat round it in chaires. Then Dr. Chaworth presented the commission under the broad seale to the Bishop of Winchester, and it was read by Dr. Sweate. After which the Vicar-general went to the vestry, and brought his grace into the chapell, his other officers marching before. He being presented to the Commissioners, was seated in a greate arm chaire at one end of the table, when the definitive sentence was read by the Bishop of Winchester, and subscribed by all the Bishops, and proclamation was three times made at the Chapell dore, which was then set open for any to enter and give their exceptions, if any they had. This don, we all went to dinner in the greate hall to a mighty feast. There were present all the nobility in towne, the Lord Maior of London, Sheriffs, Duke of Albemarle, &c. My Lo. Archbishop did in particular most civily welcome me. So going to visite my Lady Needham, who liv'd at Lambeth, I went over to London."

"During the great Plague in 1665," writes Miss Priscilla Wakefield, "the piety of the Christian and the magnanimity of the hero were displayed by Archbishop Sheldon. He continued in his palace at Lambeth whilst the contagion lasted, preserving, by his charities, multitudes who were sinking under disease and want ; and, by his pastoral exertions, procured benevolences to a vast amount."

When Archbishop Sancroft was deprived, in 1690, he left behind him his nephew, who, refusing to give up peaceable possession, was "dispossessed" by the sheriff and imprisoned, whilst Tillotson was installed in the palace. Evelyn, who narrates this fact in his "Diary," also tells us how he "Din'd at Lambeth with the new Archbishop, and saw the effects of my green-house furnace set up by my son-in-law." Here, in successive meetings of the Commissioners, was settled the plan of Chelsea College, the project of Charles II., as already mentioned.* Among the Commissioners were Sir Christopher Wren, Sir Stephen Fox, and John Evelyn, whose "Diary" records their proceedings from time to time.

Queen Mary II. paid a visit here to Archbishop Tillotson in 1694, as appears from an entry in the churchwardens' accounts of "five shillings paid to the ringers" on that occasion. This was only a few weeks before the archbishop's death. In the preceding year the archbishop had called an assembly of the bishops at Lambeth Palace, when they agreed to several regulations, which were at first designed to be enforced by their own authority ; but upon more mature consideration it was judged requisite that they should appear under that of their Majesties in the form of royal injunctions. The queen was at different times consulted by the archbishop concerning this business, and it is not unlikely that it was the subject of their conversation on the occasion of the visit above mentioned.

Both of Dr. Tillotson's successors, Archbishops Tenison and Wake, lived and died here, and the former was buried in the parish church close by the palace. Dr. Wake was the author of "The Church of England and its Convocations," and

---

* See Vol. V., p. 7c.

several other theological works; he was celebrated especially for his controversy with Bossuet, and his project of union between the English and Gallican Churches.

Hutton, Secker, Cornwallis, and Moore, who were archbishops successively from 1757 to 1805, likewise ended their days here, and were all buried in Lambeth Church.

The palace very narrowly escaped destruction during the Gordon Riots in 1780. The first alarm was given on Tuesday, June 6th, when a party, to the number of 500 or more, who had previously assembled in St. George's Fields, came to the palace with drums and fifes, and colours flying, crying, "No Popery!" Finding the gates shut, after knocking several times without obtaining any answer, they called out that they should return in the evening, and paraded round the palace all that day. Upon this alarm, it was thought necessary to apply to the Secretary at War for a party of soldiers for the security of the palace; accordingly, a party of the Guards, to the amount of one hundred men, commanded by Colonel Deacon, arrived about two o'clock that afternoon, when sentinels were immediately placed upon the towers of the palace and at every convenient avenue. The mob still paraded round the house, and continued so to do for several days, notwithstanding the number of the soldiers. In this alarming situation, Archbishop Cornwallis, with his wife and family, were with great difficulty prevailed upon to quit the palace, whither they did not return till the disturbances were entirely ended. The military remained at Lambeth for upwards of two months, during which period there were from 200 to 300 men quartered in the palace.

A good story is told of Archbishop Manners-Sutton (1805–28) by the Honourable Miss Amelia Murray, in her "Recollections." "It happened once that Lord Eldon and the Archbishop dined with the King (George III.), and the former became rather communicative and merry over his port. At last he said, 'It is a curious fact, sir, that your Majesty's Archbishop and your Lord Chancellor both married their wives clandestinely! I had some excuse, certainly, for Bessie Surtees was the prettiest girl in all Newcastle; but Mrs. Sutton was always the same pumpkin-faced thing that she is at present.' The king was much amused;" as, indeed, he well might be.

Coming down to more recent times, we find Lambeth Palace used for the holding of meetings of prelates of the Reformed Anglican Church at home and in the colonies. The first of these meetings—called the Pan-Anglican Synod—was held here, under Archbishop Longley, in the autumn of 1867. It was attended by upwards of seventy bishops, from England, Ireland, the colonies, and America; but beyond the issuing of an address, couched in very general terms, nothing definite seems to have resulted from this great ecclesiastical gathering.

In 1876 the great hall, or public library, was used as the Arches Court of Canterbury, for the trial of cases brought before the Dean of the Court of Arches under the "Public Worship Regulation Act." The west end of the apartment was fitted up as a court for the accommodation of the bar, the reporters, witnesses, &c., and the east end was barriered off for the general public. The judge, Lord Penzance, occupied the archbishop's chair. The first two cases tried here were those of the Rev. Charles J. Ridsdale, of St. Peter's, Folkestone, and the Rev. Arthur Tooth, vicar of St. James's, Hatcham, for ritualistic proceedings in their respective churches.

There are still one or two items of interest concerning Lambeth Palace which we must not omit to mention. Here, for instance, every year during the month of December, the officials of the Stationers' Company still wait formally upon the archbishop in order to present him with copies of certain almanacks which they have the privilege of publishing, and which were formerly not allowed to be issued except with the sanction of the Established Church. The officials and their servants were in former times entertained by the archbishop, on the occasion of these visits, with a copious supply of cakes and ale. This curious custom had a somewhat singular origin, which is now not generally known, or, more probably, is now "generally forgotten," though recorded by Sylvanus Urban in the *Gentleman's Magazine* for 1800 :—" On the annual aquatic procession of the Lord Mayor of London to Westminster, the barge of the Company of Stationers, which is usually the first in the show, proceeds to Lambeth Palace, where from time immemorial they (the Stationers) receive a present of sixteen bottles of the archbishop's prime wine. This custom originated at the beginning of the last century. When Archbishop Tenison enjoyed the see, a very near relative of his, who happened to be Master of the Stationers' Company, thought it a compliment to call there in full state and in his barge, when the archbishop, being informed that the number of the company on the barge was thirty-two, thought that a pint of wine for each would not be disagreeable, and ordered, at the same time, bread and cheese and ale to be given to the watermen and attendants; from this accidental circumstance it has grown into a settled custom. The Company, in return, present to the archbishop a copy of the several almanacks which they have the privilege of publishing."

Of course, since aquatic processions on the Thames have been discontinued, the barge of the Stationers' Company no longer performs the journey to Lambeth Palace; but the present of the almanacks is still made to the archbishop, although somewhat nearer the end of the year; the honorarium of "cakes and ale" for the bearer, however, seems to be forgotten.

The Archbishops of Canterbury used formerly to keep their own barge, in which they crossed the Thames to the House of Lords or to White-hall Palace. Their favourite landing-place on the opposite side of the water was Whitehall Stairs, the picturesque gateway of which, represented on page 444, was standing till the present century.

Degrees are occasionally conferred at Lambeth on individuals who have risen to eminence among the English clergy, though they have not graduated in early life at one of the great universities. They are, however, a legacy from times anterior to the Reformation, when the Archbishop of Canterbury had the recognised right of conferring them, as being the permanent legate for the Pope of Rome. The privilege was specially confirmed to the see of Canterbury by that self-elected Pope, Henry VIII., in April, 1534, and it is still occasionally exercised by the archbishop.

The parish church of St. Mary, Lambeth, is situate near the water-side, and adjoins the palace. The whole of the building, with the exception of the tower, was pulled down and rebuilt in 1851. "Sufficient of the original fabric of the church," writes Mr. Tanswell, in his "History of Lambeth," "has been preserved to enable us to assign the latter end of the fourteenth century as the date of its foundation. The later character of the details of the chapels on the north and south sides of the chancel lead to the conclusion that the church, when first erected, consisted of a nave, chancel, and tower only, and that these chapels, which are the property of the Howard and Leigh families respectively, were added at a subsequent period."

Mr. W. Newton, the author of "London in the Olden Time," says that the antiquity of the existing church is not known, and that it was "originally a Gothic structure, a portion of which is supposed to date from about the end of the fifteenth century." This, however, is scarcely the case, for in the Bishops' Registers at Winchester is a commission against such of the inhabitants of Lambeth as refuse to contribute to the rebuilding and repairs of the church, dated 1374. Three years afterwards there was another commission to compel the inhabitants to build a tower for their church, "then newly built," and to furnish it with bells. Mr. Newton adds: "The building has been much altered from its original state, and is now (1855) rather a heterogeneous combination of various styles of architecture, likely to afford but little interest to the architectural student." From this statement, however, we venture to disagree.

In January, 1851, the work of restoration was commenced, according to the plans and under the direction of Mr. Philip Hardwick, and it was completed in little more than a year. Care was taken that the outline of the original foundations should be preserved, and that, wherever possible, the ancient detail should be reproduced. The church, as it now appears, consists of a nave, north and south aisles, and porch, chancel, and chapels; the fine western tower remaining without alteration. The arcades in the nave have been carefully restored, and the walling above them has been carried up to the original height and pierced with clerestory lights, the whole being surmounted by an open timber roof, divided into seven bays by arched trusses, resting on the ancient corbels. The chancel is divided from the nave, and the Howard and Leigh Chapels from the chancel, by three lofty arches. The large east window, of five lights, with the upper part filled with foliated tracery, is furnished with stained glass, and is inscribed to the memory of Archbishop Howley. Nearly all the other windows on both sides of the church are now filled with gorgeous painted glass, which casts on the pavement below—

"A dim religious light,"

most of them having been erected to the memory of deceased parishioners or of persons formerly connected with the parish by family ties. The chancel at first sight looks as if it had been shortened; but that is probably the effect of the erection of the side-chapels above mentioned, to the north and the south. The west end of the church is lighted by a large circular window filled with geometrical tracery, and the organ is placed immediately beneath it. Till recently there were extensive galleries on both sides of the church, and at the west end one still remains. The altar-piece is of carved oak, enriched with gilding and arabesque painting.

The east end of the old north aisle was called Howard's Chapel, from its having been built, in 1552, by Thomas Howard, Duke of Norfolk (many of whose family are here interred); and that of the south aisle, Leigh's Chapel, built in the same year by Sir John Leigh (son of Ralph Leigh, lord of the manor of Stockwell), who, with his lady, lies buried here. At the bottom of the middle compartment of the south-east window, painted on a pane twenty-four inches by sixteen, was the picture of the

Pedlar stands." In 1703 a "new glass Pedlar" was put up, at the expense of two pounds; but this was removed from where it was then placed, in the year 1816 (when the church was repaired and "beautified"), to the window above mentioned, which was much more conspicuous.

OLD WHITEHALL STAIRS.

pedlar and his dog, of which we have spoken in a previous chapter.* At what time this memorial was first put up there is no mention, but such a portrait certainly existed in 1608, there being in the churchwardens' accounts of that year an entry of "two shillings, paid to the glazier for a panel of glass for the window where the picture of the

The churchwardens' books contain some interesting and curious items concerning the old church. It appears that it contained, in pre-Reformation times, no less than five altars: they were dedicated respectively to the Blessed Virgin, to St. Thomas, to St. George, to St. Nicholas, and to St. Christopher. Then there are the "accounts of Wardens of the Brethren of Sent Crystover, kept within the church of Lambeth in the time of

* See *ante*, p. 388.

Henry VIII.," from which it appears that the stipend paid to Sir William Webster, the priest, "for one year and one quarter," amounted to the sum of £8 6s. 8d. In the reign of Queen Mary is a charge for replacing an altar in the Norfolk Chapel, on the revival of the old religion : " 1557.

for mending a piece of glasse in the crucifixe in the Dewk's (Duke's) Chapel, 1s. 4d."

The ancient pulpit must have been a curiosity in its way ; for by the above-mentioned accounts it appears that in 1522 a new pulpit was erected in this church, at a cost of twenty shillings, and the

LAMBETH CHURCH (1825).

Paid to Nicholas Brymsted, for making up the syde awtor in my Lady of Norfolke's Chapel, and paving in the churche, and for sande, 4s. 2d." This chapel, it appears, was consecrated in 1522, for in the churchwardens' accounts for that year are the following entries :—" Payd for candyls when the chapel was hallowed, 2d." " To my lady's grace for cloth for the ambys, £1." Under date of 1567 the following entry occurs :—" Payd

old one was valued at eightpence only. The new pulpit continued in use till the year 1615, when Archbishop Abbot gave another at a cost of £15. It was placed against the south-east pillar of the nave, and was furnished, after the Puritan fashion of that time with an hour-glass, of which, however, there are no remains, though it is mentioned twice in the churchwardens' accounts. The pulpit and reading-desk were subsequently removed to another position at the entrance from the chancel to the nave.

The parish registers begin with the year 1539. In the churchwardens' accounts are the following entries respecting them :—

"1566. Payd for paper ryall, for the christenynge boke, 6*d*.

Payd Matthew Allen, by consente of the hole parishe, for new writing of the olde boke of baptisme, marriage, and burial, 6*s*. 8*d*.

"1574. For ii quere of paper to make a boke, 8*d*.

"1593. Payd to the curat for writinge our boke of christenings, weddings, and burials, 2*s*."

During the Commonwealth the banns of marriage were often published in towns upon market-days, and the marriage ceremony was performed by a civil magistrate. In the Lambeth registers is an entry of at all events one such marriage :—

"1653, Nov. 7. Mark Perkins and Margaret Payne, married by Thomas Cooper, Justice of the Peace."

Lambeth has numbered among its rectors many men who have risen to eminence, of whom we may mention Dr. Hooper, afterwards Bishop of St. Asaph, and subsequently Bishop of Bath and Wells: he was the author of several works in defence of the Church of England. Dr. Gibson, the editor of " Camden's Britannia," and author of the " Codex Juris Ecclesiastici ;" he resigned the rectory on being raised to the bishopric of Lichfield. Dr. B. Porteus, afterwards Bishop, in succession, of Chester and of London. His successor, Dr. Vyse, rector of the parish during the latter part of the last century, was the son of a clergyman at Lichfield, the contemporary and friend of Dr. Johnson. To him Dr. Johnson addressed two letters, printed in " Boswell," soliciting him to ask the Archbishop of Canterbury to present to the Charterhouse Hospital a nephew of the learned Grotius.

The church contains some interesting monuments, including those to the memory of several of the archbishops, but they were, of course, shifted from the positions which they originally occupied when the rebuilding of the fabric took place in the year 1851.

Here repose the bones of the brave old primate Bancroft, of the meek Secker, and of the learned Tenison, who successively sat in the archiepiscopal chair. Archbishops Cornwallis and Hutton, too, are likewise interred here, as also are Bishops Thirlby and Tunstall. The body of Thirlby was accidentally discovered when Archbishop Cornwallis was buried in 1783. The body, which was wrapped in fine linen, was moist, and had evidently been preserved in some species of pickle, which still retained a volatile smell, not unlike that of hartshorn ; the face was perfect, and the limbs flexible ; the beard of a remarkable length, and beautifully white. The linen and woollen garments were all well preserved. The cap, which was of silk, adorned with point lace, was in fashion like that represented in the pictures of Archbishop Juxon. A slouched hat, with strings fastened to it, was under the left arm. There was also a cassock, so fastened as to appear like an apron with strings, and several small pieces of the bishop's garments, which had the appearance of a pilgrim's habit.

Besides the above-mentioned, here, or in the churchyard, rest the bodies of Dollond, the noted maker of telescopes, and founder of the well-known firm in St. Paul's Churchyard ; Madame Storace, the vocalist ; and Moore, the author of the tragedy of the " Gamester." Here, too, sleep in peace Ashmole, the antiquary, and the Tradescants, whose united collections of natural history formed the nucleus of the Ashmolean Museum at Oxford. Of the Tradescants we have spoken at some length in our account of their house at South Lambeth.* In 1662, a table monument of free-stone was erected here by the widow of John Tradescant the younger, covered on each of its four sides with sculptures : at each corner is the representation of a large tree, seeming to support the slab; at one end is a hydra picking at a bare skull; on the other are the arms of the family. On one side of the tomb are ruins, Grecian pillars and capitals, an obelisk and pyramid ; and on the opposite a crocodile, shells, &c., and a view of some Egyptian buildings. Having become very much dilapidated, this monument was repaired in 1773 ; but having again become almost illegible, it was entirely repaired by subscription, in 1853, in accordance with the original form and design. The tomb, which is raised on a granite plinth, has upon it the following inscription :—

" JOHN TRADESCANT, died A.D. MDCXXXVIII. JANE TRADESCANT, his wife, died A.D. MDCXXXIV. JOHN TRADESCANT, his son, died 25th April, A.D. MDCLXII. JOHN TRADESCANT, his grandson, died 11th September, A.D. MDCLII. HESTER, wife of JOHN TRADESCANT the younger, died 6th of April, A.D. MDCLXXVIII.

" Know, Stranger, ere thou pass, beneath this stone
Lye John Tradescant, Grandsire, Father, and Son.
The last died in his Spring ; the other two
Lived till they had travell'd Art and Nature through,
As by their choice Collections may appear,
Of what is rare in land, in sea, in air ;
Whilst they (as Homer's Iliad in a nut)
A world of wonders in one closet shut.
These famous antiquarians that had been
Both gardeners to the rose and lily queen,

* See *ante*, p. 334.

Transplanted now themselves, sleep here ; and when
    Angels shall with their trumpets waken men,
And fire shall purge the world, these hence shall rise,
    And change this garden for a Paradise.
" This tomb, originally erected on this spot in year 1662,
    By Hester, relict of John Tradescant the Younger,
        Being in a state of decay,
Was repaired by Subscription in the ye ir 1773.
" After lapse of nearly two centuries since its erection,
It was entirely restored by Subscription in the year 1853."

The fund for the restoration of this tomb—about £100—was raised under the direction of the late Sir William Hooker, the distinguished botanist and curator of Kew Gardens ; Sir Charles G. Young, Garter King-at-Arms ; the Rev. C. B. Dalton, Rector of Lambeth, &c. It was an old debt to the memories of these first of English gardeners and naturalists ; men who did so much to minister to " the inclinations of kings and the choice of philosophers."

Dr. Ducarel, in his " History of Lambeth," tells us that a beacon was formerly placed on the top of the tower of this church ; and in Hollar's view of the palace, engraved in 1647, and also in his view of London from Lambeth, it is plainly shown. The beacon also appears in the view of Lambeth from the Thames in " Nichols' History," and in a view taken by a Florentine artist in the suite of Cosmo, Duke of Tuscany, in 1669. There are no remains of it in existence now.

Readers of English history will not have forgotten that it was under the shelter of the old church tower, on a wet and dreary night in December, 1688, that Mary of Modena, having crossed the river from the Horseferry in a tiny boat, sat crouching, with her infant son in her arms, till the companions of her flight could find the coach that should convey her safely to Gravesend. Miss A. Strickland draws a touching picture of the scene. " On that spot, which has been rendered a site of historic interest by this affecting incident, the beautiful and unfortunate consort of the last of our Stuart kings remained sitting, with her infant son fondly clasped to her bosom . . . Mary Beatrice looked back with streaming eyes towards the royal home where her beloved consort remained, lonely and surrounded with perils, and vainly endeavoured to trace out the lights of Whitehall among those that were reflected from the opposite shore along the dark rolling river." It is a satisfaction to know that her patience was rewarded, and that she and her child made their escape to France from this country.

CHAPTER XXXIII.

VAUXHALL.

" Those green retreats
Where fair Vauxhall bedecks her sylvan seats."—*Loves of the Triangles.*

First recorded Notice of the Gardens—The Place originally known as the Spring Gardens—Evelyn's Visit to Sir Samuel Morland's House—Visit of Samuel Pepys to the Spring Gardens—Addison's Account of the Visit of Sir Roger de Coverley to Vauxhall—The Old Mansion of Copped Hall—Description of Sir Samuel Morland's House and Grounds—The Place taken by Jonathan Tyers, and opened for Public Entertainment—Roubiliac's Statue of Handel—Reference to Vauxhall in Boswell's " Life of Johnson "—How Hogarth became connected with Vauxhall Gardens—A *Ridotto al Fresco*—Character of the Entertainments at Vauxhall a Century ago—Character of the Company frequenting the Gardens—A Description of the Gardens as they appeared in the Middle of the Last Century—How Horace Walpole and his Friends visited Vauxhall, and minced Chickens in a China Dish—Byron's Description of a *Ridotto al Fresco*—Fielding's Account of Vauxhall—Sunday Morning Visitors to Vauxhall—Vauxhall in the Height of its Glory—Goldsmith's Description of a Visit—Sir John Dinely and other Aristocratic Visitors—How Jos Sedley drank Rack Punch at Vauxhall—Wellington witnessing the Battle of Waterloo over again—The Gardens in the Last of their Glory—Hayman's Picture of the " Milkmaids on May-day "—Lines on Vauxhall, by Ned Ward the Younger—Balloon Ascents—Narrow Escape of the Gardens from Destruction by Fire—Closing of the Gardens, and Sale of the Property.

WE are now on gossiping ground, and therefore we can scarcely be severely blamed if we dwell for a short space on the stories of past times. Quitting the precincts of Lambeth Palace, and following the course of the river for a short distance south-west, we arrive at Vauxhall Bridge Road ; and then, after passing under the South-Western Railway, we reach the spot where, till about 1860, stood the grand entrance to Vauxhall Gardens—that paradise of enchantment, with its houris in the illuminated walks, and the lamps and the fireworks, and the water-works, and the hermit in his cave, and the Rotunda, and Madame Saqui on the tightrope, and fowl and ham and rack punch in the boxes, and poke bonnets, and scanty skirts, and roll collars, and swallow-tailed coats ;—all these have passed away, and left not a vestige behind. Times have indeed changed. If there were now a Prince Regent and a batch of Allied Sovereigns, and a Duke of Wellington and a Field-Marshal Blucher, they would not go to Cremorne to show themselves to the people ; and yet, in the great days of Vauxhall, those renowned personages did pay the gardens an evening visit, and were duly and right loyally cheered and mobbed by the crowd who had paid for admission. When such great persons were not present, there were songstresses by the score—Mrs. Bland, the sweet-voiced, dumpy little ballad singer; and Dignum the mellifluous; and Madame Vestris; and sometimes, if we mistake not, the queenly Kitty Stephens and glorious Incledon. But we are anticipating the order of events, and must return to plain historical details.

The first authentic notice of these gardens occurs in a record of the Duchy of Cornwall, dated in 1615, at which time the property was vested in Jane, widow of John Vaux, one of whose daughters subsequently married Barlow, Bishop of Lincoln. The residence belonging to the estate was then called Stock-dens, or Stoc-dens, and the grounds about it were known as "The Spring Gardens," a name which they retained in theory and in official documents to the very last, though popularly known as "Vauxhall Gardens." The exact date at which these grounds were first opened to the public is now involved in obscurity. Wycherley, about the year 1677, speaks of taking "a syllabub at the New Spring Garden."

The place, however, is mentioned by John Evelyn in his "Diary," under date 2nd July, 1661, as "the new Spring Garden at Lambeth, a pretty-contrived plantation." Two years later it is described as being laid out in squares "enclosed with hedges of gooseberries, within which are roses, beans, and asparagus;" from which it may be inferred that in the early part of the reign of Charles II. these gardens were practically useful, and not a mere resort of pleasure-seekers.

Manning and Bray, the historians of Surrey, ascribe the origin of the gardens to the ingenious Sir Samuel Morland, who certainly had a mansion in this neighbourhood in 1675. Evelyn, in 1681, mentions a visit which he paid to Sir Samuel here "to see his house and mechanics." A foot-note is added, stating that in his house here Sir Samuel had built and fitted up a large room, which he had furnished in a sumptuous manner, for concerts and other gatherings, on the top of which was a "punchinello holding a sun-dial." He had constructed also some fountains in his gardens. He was much in favour with the king for services he had rendered to him while abroad; and his house bore the reputation of being the place across the water to which the "merry monarch" and his gay ladies would often repair on fine evenings.

Notwithstanding that when first opened, these gardens were commonly called "The New Spring Garden at Lambeth," so far as we know, they bear no trace of a "water spring," or jet d'eau, such as

we have described in our account of the Spring Gardens at Charing Cross.* The idea of the place being borrowed, however, from the gardens at Charing Cross, it would seem that a similar name was given to it, though meaningless.

Samuel Pepys, in his "Diary," under date May 28th, 1667, mentions these gardens in the following terms:—"Went by water to Fox (sic) Hall, and there walked in Spring Gardens. A great deal of company; the weather and gardens pleasant, and cheap going thither: for a man may go to spend what he will, or nothing at all: all is one. But to hear the nightingale and other birds, and here fiddles and there a harp, and here a Jew's harp, and there laughing, and there [to see] fine people walking, is very diverting."

In the space at our disposal it would be impossible to quote half the passages to be found in our modern classical writers which refer to these gardens in their hey-day of fashion. That they existed as a place of public amusement soon after Evelyn made the above-mentioned entry in his "Diary" is clear from the Spectator, No. 383, dated May, 1712. Readers of that delightful work will not readily forget Addison's account of Sir Roger de Coverley's visit with him to Vauxhall; how he "took boat" at the Temple Stairs, and was rowed thither by a waterman with only one leg; how sadly, on his way up the Thames, he contrasted the many spires of the City churches with the scantiness of such edifices westward of Temple Bar, and what badinage he had to put up with from the other Thames watermen en route for his destination. They will not forget his description of the place:—"The Spring Gardens are exquisitely pleasant at this time of the year. When I considered the fragrancy of the walks and bowers, with the choirs of birds that sang upon the trees, and the tribe of people that walked under their shade, I could not but look upon the place as a kind of Mahometan paradise;" nor will they forget how the gardens put Sir Roger in mind of a little coppice by his house in the country, which his chaplain used to call "an aviary of nightingales." And they will also call to mind how the worthy knight and his companion concluded their walk with a modest glass of Burton ale and a slice of hung beef, the fragments of which he ordered the waiter to carry to the waterman that had but one leg.

Such is our earliest notice of Vauxhall as a public garden, written, most probably, not long after its opening. The name of the place was originally

Faux Hall, which in process of time has become corrupted into the better known appellation of Vauxhall. In the days of King John, Fulk, or Faulk de Brent, a stout Norman knight, held a manor on this spot; and the house was afterwards known as Copped, or Copt Hall. It is so called in Norden's "Survey" (1615), where a residence is described as being "opposite to a capital mansion called Fauxe Hall." The latter, Lysons imagines, was the ancient manor-house, which, being afterwards pulled down or otherwise lost, the name was transferred to Copt Hall. This house was the residence of Sir Thomas Parry, Chancellor of the Duchy of Lancaster, and was held by him of the Manor of Kennington. Here the ill-fated Arabella Stuart, whose misfortune it was to be too nearly allied to the Crown, remained prisoner for twelve months, under the custody of Sir Thomas.* In the Parliamentary Survey taken after the execution of Charles I., the mansion is described as "a capital messuage called Vauxhall, alias Copped Hall, bounded by the Thames: being a fair dwelling-house, strongly built, of three storeys high, and a fair staircase breaking out from it of nineteen feet square."

In the sixteenth century it is asserted that the place belonged to the family of Fauxe, or Vaux. The name of Thomas, the second son of Lord Vaux (1520–60), is not unknown as a poet; he is mentioned in Johnson's "Lives of the Poets;" but whether he ever lived here we have no authority for deciding. Pennant, with more rashness than is his wont, considers that "Vauxhall" was a corruption of "Faux Hall," and that it was called after the celebrated Guy Fawkes, of gunpowder-plot celebrity, who lived here, and, as Dr. Ducarel imagined, owned the manor. Following up this mistaken idea in all the simplicity of good faith, Pennant adds, with a touch of bitterness, "In foreign parts a *colonne infame* would have been erected on the spot; but the site is now (1790) occupied by Marble Hall and Cumberland Tea Gardens, and several other buildings." Mention is made of the place by Pepys in 1663, when he tells us how that, on his return from Epsom to London, he and his companion "set up" their horses at "Fox Hall," and returned home by water from Lambeth Stairs.

There does not appear to be any foundation for the tradition that the renowned Guy had anything to do with Faux Hall; but the story received some support from the fact that the gunpowder conspirators had a house in Lambeth where they stored their powder, as we have stated in a former chapter.†

The mansion was sold in 1652, but subsequently reverted to the Crown at the Restoration. After passing through various hands, in the year 1675 Sir Samuel Morland obtained a lease of Vauxhall House, as it was then called, made it his residence, and considerably improved the premises.

Aubrey, in his "Antiquities of Surrey," informs us that Sir Samuel Morland "built a fine room at Vauxhall, the inside all of looking-glass, and fountains very pleasant to behold; which," he adds, "is much visited by strangers. It stands in the middle of the garden, covered with Cornish slate, on the point whereof he placed a punchinello, very well carved, which held a dial, but the winds have demolished it." "The house," says a more modern author, Sir John Hawkins, "seems to have been rebuilt since the time that Sir Samuel Morland dwelt in it; with a great number of stately trees, and laid out in shady walks, it obtained the name of Spring Gardens; and the house being converted into a tavern or place of entertainment, it was frequented by the votaries of pleasure."

From this period to that of the visit of Addison and Sir Roger nothing appears to be known concerning Vauxhall; nor again from that time till the year 1732, when the house and gardens came into the possession of a gentleman named Jonathan Tyers, who opened it with an advertisement of a "ridotto al fresco"—a term to which the people of this country had till that time been strangers. These entertainments were several times repeated in the course of the summer, and numbers resorted to partake of them, which encouraged the proprietor to make his garden a place of musical entertainment for every evening during the summer season. To this end he was at great expense in decorating the gardens with paintings; he engaged an excellent band of musicians, and issued silver tickets for admission at a guinea each; and receiving great encouragement, he set up an organ in the orchestra; and in a conspicuous part of the gardens erected a fine statue of Handel, the work of Roubiliac. With reference to this piece of sculpture, a writer in the *Mirror* (1830) observes:— "The first work which can with certainty be ascribed to Roubiliac is that statue of Handel made for Vauxhall Gardens. He wished to give a lively transcript of the living man, and he fully accomplished what he undertook. He has exhibited the eminent composer in the act of rapturous meditation when the music had fully awakened up

---

his soul. His gladness of face and agitation of body tell us that the sculptor imagined Handel's finest strains to have been conceived amidst contortions worthy of the Cumean Sybil. Though every button of his dress seems to have sat for its likeness, and every button-hole is finished with the fastidiousness of a fashionable tailor, the clothes are infected with the agitation of the man, and are in staring disorder. It did not remain long at Mr. Barrett, Duke Street, Westminster.' From Mr. Barrett's hands the statue found its way, after various vicissitudes of fortune, to a house in Dean Street, where it awaits a fresh purchaser."

The son of the original proprietor of these gardens, Thomas Tyers, having been bred for the bar, became one of Dr. Johnson's friends, and, indeed, published a biographical sketch of him, which is now forgotten. He likewise published

THE OLD MANOR-HOUSE AT VAUXHALL ABOUT 1800.

Vauxhall, but the cause of its removal has not been stated. 'It stood,' says Smith, 'in 1744, on the south side of the gardens, under an enclosed lofty arch, surmounted by a figure playing the violoncello, attended by two boys; and it was then screened from the weather by a curtain, which was drawn up when the visitors arrived. The ladies then walked in these and Mary-le-bone Gardens in their hoops, sacques, and caps, as they appeared in their own drawing-rooms; whilst the gentlemen were generally uncovered, with their hats under their arms, and swords and bags. The statue, after being moved to various situations in the gardens, was at length conveyed to the house of Mr. Barrett, of Stockwell, and from thence to the entrance-hall of the residence of his son, the Rev.

sketches of Pope and Addison, and a work of higher pretension, "Political Conferences." He is pleasantly, though somewhat contemptuously, described in No. 48 of the *Idler*, under the *sobriquet* of "Tom Restless."

Considering that Dr. Johnson was so frequent a visitor at the gardens, it is astonishing that there should be so few allusions to them in the burly Doctor's life by Boswell.

"That excellent place of amusement," writes Johnson, "which must ever be an estate to its proprietor, as it is peculiarly adapted to the taste of the English nation; there being a mixture of curious show, gay exhibition, music, vocal and instrumental, not too refined for the general ear, for all which only a shilling is paid; and, though

VIEWS IN VAUXHALL GARDENS.

1. Fountain at Back of Orchestra.   2. Ruins at End of Walk.   3. The Orchestra.   4. Neptune's Fountain
5. Old Entrance to Vauxhall Gardens.   6. Back of Orchestra.

last not least, good eating and drinking for those who choose to purchase that regale."

Boswell, in his notes, tells us that in the summer of 1792, additional and more expensive decorations having been introduced, the price of admission was doubled, and adds his own disapproval of the plan, on the ground that a number of the honest commonalty were thereby excluded. Mr. J. Wilson Croker, in his edition of Boswell, adds that the admission was subsequently raised to four shillings, "without improving either the class of company or the profits of the proprietors."

Among Tyers's numerous friends was Hogarth, who, as we have already seen, had a residence in this neighbourhood,* and who, to add to the attractions of the place, advised Tyers to decorate the boxes with paintings. For the following account of the way in which Hogarth, as a painter, became connected with the gardens, we are indebted to a selection of anecdotes published under the title of "Art and Artists:"—"Soon after his marriage, Hogarth had summer lodgings at South Lambeth, and hence became intimate with Jonathan Tyers, the proprietor of Vauxhall Gardens. On passing the tavern which stood at the entrance, one morning, Hogarth saw Tyers, and, observing him to be very melancholy, asked him, 'How now, Master Tyers? why so sad this morning?' 'Sad times these, Master Hogarth,' replied Tyers; 'and my reflections were on a subject not likely to brighten a man's countenance. I was thinking which is the easiest death, hanging or drowning.' 'Oh!' said Hogarth, 'is it come to that?' 'Very nearly, I assure you,' replied Tyers. 'Then,' said Hogarth, 'the remedy that you think of applying is not likely to mend the matter; don't hang or drown yourself to-day, my friend. I have a thought that may save the necessity of either, and will communicate it to you if you will call on me to-morrow morning at my studio in Leicester Fields.'† The interview took place, and the result was the concocting and getting up of the first 'Ridotto al Fresco,' which was very successful; one of the new attractions being the embellishment of the pavilions of the gardens by Hogarth's own pencil. Thus he drew the 'Four Parts of the Day,' which Hayman copied, and the two scenes of 'Evening' and 'Night,' with portraits of Henry VIII. and Anne Boleyn. Hayman, it should be stated here, was one of the earliest members of the Royal Academy, and when young was a scene-painter at Drury Lane Theatre. Hogarth at this time was in prosperity, and assisted Tyers more

essentially even than by the few pieces which he painted for the gardens; and in return for this good service Tyers presented the painter with a gold ticket of admission in perpetuity for himself and his friends, which was handed down to Hogarth's descendants—the ticket admitting six persons, or, in the current language of the day, 'one coach'—that is, one coachful."

Malcolm, in his "Anecdotes of London," tells us that the first notice of the gardens which he had been able to find in the newspapers, was in June, 1732, when the "Ridotto al Fresco" is mentioned as having been given here. The company were estimated at 400 persons, in the proportion of ten men to one woman; and he tells us that most of them wore dominos, lawyers' gowns, and masks, and other disguises, though many were without either. "The company," Malcolm adds, "retired between three or four in the morning, and order was preserved by 100 soldiers who were stationed at the entrance"—a precaution which seems to explain very significantly the character of the company whom the worthy proprietor was led to expect.

Though Pepys tells us that a visit to these gardens was not expensive, yet Bonnell Thornton furnishes a ludicrous account of a stingy old citizen loosing his purse-strings in order to treat his wife and family to Vauxhall; and Colin's description to his wife of "Greenwood Hall, or the pleasures of Spring Gardens," gives a lively picture of what this modern Arcadia was something more than a century ago.

Grosely, in his "Tour to London," writes (with reference to Vauxhall and Ranelagh ‡):—"These entertainments, which begin in the month of May, are continued every night. They bring together persons of all ranks and conditions; and amongst these a considerable number of females, whose charms want only that cheerful air, which is the flower and quintessence of beauty. These places serve equally as a rendezvous either for business or intrigue. They form, as it were, private coteries; there you see fathers and mothers, with their children, enjoying domestic happiness in the midst of public diversions. The English assert that such entertainments as these can never subsist in France, on account of the levity of the people. Certain it is that those of Vauxhall and Ranelagh, which are guarded only by outward decency, are conducted without tumult and disorder, which often disturb the public diversions of France. I do not know whether the English are gainers thereby;

---

* See *ante*, p. 340. † See Vol. III., p. 167. ‡ See Vol. V., p. 77.

the joy which they seem in search of at those places does not beam through their countenances ; they look as grave at Vauxhall and Ranelagh as at the Bank, at church, or a private club. All persons there seem to say what a young English noble-man said to his governor, '*Am I as joyous as I should be?*'"

When we endeavour to re-people these gardens with the gay crowds which a century ago frequented them, so light of heart and buoyant of spirit, we cannot help remembering the words of Dr. Johnson on the subject of their rival, Ranelagh, uttered in one of his gravest moods—"Alas, sir ! these are only struggles for happiness ! When I first entered Ranelagh, it gave to my mind an expansion of gay sensation such as I never experienced anywhere else ; but as Xerxes wept when he viewed his immense army, and considered that not one of that great multitude would be alive a hundred years afterwards, so it went to my heart to consider that there was not one in all that brilliant circle that was not afraid to go home and think."

Perhaps the best defence of such places of public resort as Vauxhall is to be found in the well-known words of Dr. Johnson, though spoken of another place. Having come from the Pantheon, Boswell said there was not half-a-guinea's worth of pleasure in seeing that place. *Johnson :* "But, sir, there is half-a-guinea's worth of inferiority to other people in not having seen it." *Boswell :* "I doubt, sir, whether there are many happy people here." *Johnson :* "Yes, sir, there are many happy people here. There are many people here who are watching hundreds, and who think hundreds are watching them."

Vauxhall Gardens would appear at first to have served as a substitute for the old Spring Gardens at Charing Cross, when, thanks to the Puritans, the latter ceased to be a place of public entertain-ment, and began to be covered with private resi-dences. After the Restoration, builders invaded Spring Gardens, and its name, and its "good-will" too, was transferred to Vauxhall. Except the "spring," the amusements were nearly the same as in the old garden. The "close walks" were an especial attraction for other reasons than the nightingales, which, in their proper season, warbled in the trees. "The windings and turnings in the little wilderness," observes Tom Brown, "are so intricate that the most experienced mothers have often lost themselves here in looking for their daughters."

In the time of Addison, as we have already seen, these gardens continued to be noted for their nightingales and for their sirens ; and Sir Roger de Coverley is represented as wishing that there were more of the former and fewer of the latter, in which case he would have been a more frequent customer. In our day, and, indeed, during the last half century of their existence, the gardens grew worse off for nightingales than ever, while the undesirable element showed no tendency to diminish in numbers.

It appears from a notice by the proprietor, in 1736, that, "being ambitious of obliging the polite and worthy part of the town," at first he admitted the public by shilling tickets, in order "to keep away such as were not fit to mix with those persons of quality, ladies and gentlemen, and others, who should honour him with their company ;" but that owing to the misconduct of his numerous servants, and also for other reasons, he had resolved to abandon the plan, and to take the shillings at the gate. But two years later the ticket-system was revived ; for in March, 1738, the following notice was issued by the master of the gardens :—"The entertainment will be opened at the end of April or the beginning of May (as the weather permits), and continue three months, or longer, with the usual illuminations and bands of music, and several considerable additions and improvements to the organ. A thousand tickets only will be delivered out, at 24s. each ; the silver of every ticket to be worth 3s. 6d., and to admit two persons every evening, Sundays excepted, during the season. Every person coming without a ticket to pay 1s. each time for admittance. No servants in livery to walk in the garden. All subscribers are warned not to permit their tickets to get into the hands of persons of evil repute, there being an absolute necessity to exclude all such." The Watermen's Company gave notice at the same time that two of their beadles would attend at Vauxhall Stairs from five till eleven nightly, to prevent impositions by members of their society.

In the absence of bridges, the chief access to the gardens, at that period, was necessarily by water, and a gay and animated scene the Thames must have presented at such times. The author of "A Trip to Vauxhall," published in the year 1737, describes his start from Whitehall Stairs in the following terms :—

> "Lolling in state, with one on either side,
> And gently falling with the wind and tide,
> Last night, the evening of a sultry day,
> I sailed triumphant on the liquid way,
> To hear the fiddlers of 'Spring Gardens' play ;
> To see the walks, orchestras, colonnades,
> The lamps and trees, in mingled lights and shades.
> The scene so new, with pleasure and surprise,
> Feasted awhile our ravished ears and eyes.

> "The motley crowd we next with care survey,
> The young, the old, the splenetic, and gay,
> The fop emasculate, the rugged brave,
> All jumbled here, as in the common grave."

This poem is worth reading, not on account of its intrinsic merits, but for the sake of the satirical allusions to the company which it contains, and which, being of a contemporary date, give a graphic account of the manners of the place and time. The frontispiece, too, is curious, representing the gardens and the orchestra, with waiters wearing badges, and carrying bottles of wine to the company.

Vauxhall Gardens, until about the year 1730, must have resembled one of the tea-gardens of our own time, being "planted with trees and laid out into walks;" and it was not until the above date that it became exclusively a place of evening entertainment; for Addison refers to it as the "Spring Garden," and speaks of "the choirs of birds that sang upon the trees." A fuller account of the gardens is given in a letter professedly written by a foreigner to his friend at Paris, and which was published in the *Champion* of the 5th of August, 1742. The writer had previously visited Ranelagh, and in reference to that place says, "I was now (at Vauxhall) introduced to a place of a very different kind from that I had visited the night before—vistas, woods, tents, buildings, and company, I had a glimpse of, but could discover none of them distinctly, for which reason I began to repine that we had not arrived sooner, when all in a moment, as if by magic, every object was made visible—I should rather say, illustrious—by a thousand lights finely disposed, which were kindled at one and the same signal, and my ears and my eyes, head and heart, were captivated at once. Right before extended a long and regular vista. On my right hand I stepped into a delightful grove, wild, as if planted by the hand of Nature, under the foliage of which, at equal distances, I found two similar tents, of such a contrivance and form as a painter of genius and judgment would choose to adorn his landscape with. Farther on, still on my right, through a noble triumphal arch with a grand curtain, still in the picturesque style, artificially thrown over it, an excellent statue of Handel (Roubiliac's) appears in the action of playing upon the lyre, which is finely set off by various greens, which form in miniature a sort of woody theatre. The grove itself is bounded on three sides, except the intervals made by the two vistas which lead to and from it with a plain but handsome colonnade, divided into different departments to receive different companies, and distinguished and adorned with paintings which, though slight, are well fancied, and have a very good effect. In the middle centre of the grove, fronting a handsome banqueting-room, the very portico of which is adorned and illuminated with curious lustres of crystal glass, stands the orchestra (for music likewise here is the soul of the entertainment); and at some distance behind it a pavilion that beggars all description—I do not mean for the richness of the materials of which it is composed, but for the nobleness of the design, and the elegance of the decorations with which it is adorned."

Perhaps there was not often a gayer or more lively evening spent at Vauxhall than that of the longest day in June, 1750, when, as Horace Walpole tells his friend Montagu, Lady C. Petersham made up a party, including himself, Lord March (afterwards the Duke of Queensberry, "Old Q."), Mr. O'Brien, the Duke of Kingston, Lord Orford, Mr. Whitehead, Harry Vane, the "pretty Miss Beauclerk," the "foolish" Miss Sparre, and Miss Ashe, a lively girl of high parentage on her father's side, known in society as "The Pollard Ashe." The gossiping Walpole narrates the sallies of wit and fun with which they passed the time pleasantly away, and adds: "We minced seven chickens into a china dish, which Lady Caroline stewed over a lamp with three pats of butter and a flagon of water, stirring, rattling, and laughing, and we every moment expecting to have the dish fly about our ears. She had brought Betty, the fruit-girl, with hampers and strawberries and cherries, and made her wait upon us, and then made her sup by us at a little table." It was on their way home on this memorable night that they "picked up Lord Granby, arrived very drunk from Jenny's Whim," as related by us in our account of Chelsea.* We should much like to have formed one of the party on this occasion, or at all events to have occupied a box hard by, as we should have been sure to have been highly amused by the wit and repartee of the sprightly demoiselles.

Walpole has also described, in another letter to his friend Montagu, an evening which he spent with Mr. Conway in the next season at a *ridotto al fresco* at Vauxhall, for which the entrance was ten shillings. He describes the crowd of visitors and of coaches, and of men masquerading in the dress of Turks, &c. In explanation of the term "Ridotto," we may refer our readers to Lord Byron, who in his "Beppo" thus covertly satirises Vauxhall:—

---

* See Vol. V., p. 45.

" They went to the Ridotto—'tis a hall
　　Where people dance, and sup, and dance again;
Its proper name, perhaps, were a masqued ball;
　　But that's of no importance to my strain.
'Tis, on a smaller scale, like our Vauxhall,
　　Excepting that it can't be spoilt by rain.
The company is mix'd—the phrase I quote is
As much as saying, 'They're below your notice.' "

The " illuminated saloons and groves of Vauxhall," as they are styled in " Merrie England in the Olden Time," are thus celebrated by Fielding in his " Amelia:"—"The extreme beauty and elegance of this place is well known to almost every one of my readers, and happy is it for me that it is so, since to give an adequate account of it would exceed my power of description. To delineate the particular beauties of these gardens would indeed require as much pains, and as much paper too, as to rehearse all the good actions of their master, whose life proves the truth of an observation which I have read in some other writer, that a truly elegant taste is generally accompanied with an excellency of heart; or, in other words, that true virtue is indeed nothing else but true taste." The gardens, no doubt, were made not only an elegant place of enjoyment, but also as innocent as the manners and customs of the times would permit; but, nevertheless, the season of 1759, and again that of 1763, appear to have been notorious for the bad behaviour of the company, in spite of the proprietor's laudable efforts to keep the place decent and respectable. In the latter year, complaints having been made on the subject on the day fixed by the magistrates for licensing the public places of amusement, the proprietor pledged himself that the dark walks should thenceforward be lighted, and that a sufficient number of watchmen should be provided to keep the peace.

The gardens are described in a very dry and matter-of-fact manner by Northouck, who wrote in 1773. From him it appears that the visitors were always most orderly and " respectable," and that the illuminations, &c., were almost always over by ten o'clock. In respect of early hours it is to be feared that we have not much improved on our grandfathers.

Angelo, in his " Reminiscences," published in the reign of George IV., thus describes the gardens as he had known them in his youth:—" I remember the time when Vauxhall (in 1776, the price of admission being then only one shilling) was more a bear-garden than a rational place of resort, and most particularly on the Sunday mornings. It was then crowded from four to six with gentry, girls of the town, apprentices, shop-boys, &c. Crowds of citizens were to be seen trudging home with their wives and children. Rowlandson, the artist, and myself have often been there, and he has found plenty of employment for his pencil. The chef d'œuvre of his caricatures, which is still in print, is his drawing of Vauxhall, in which he has introduced a variety of characters known at the time, particularly that of my old schoolfellow, Major Topham, the 'macaroni' of the day. One curious scene he sketched on the spot purposely for me. It was this. A citizen and his family are seen all seated in a box eating supper, when one of the riff-raff in the gardens throws a bottle in the middle of the table, breaking the dishes and the glasses. The old man swearing, the wife fainting, and the children screaming, afforded full scope for his humorous pencil.

" Such night-scenes as were then tolerated are now become obsolete. Rings were made in every part of the gardens to decide quarrels; it now no sooner took place in one quarter than, by a contrivance of the light-fingered gentry, another row was created in another quarter, to attract the crowd away.

" Mrs. Weichsell (Mrs. Billington's mother) was the principal female singer. The men were Joe Vernon, of Drury Lane Theatre, &c.; Barthelmon, leader of the band; Fisher, hautboy; and Mr. Hook, conductor and composer. The dashers of that day, instead of returning home in the morning from Vauxhall, used to go to the 'Star and Garter' at Richmond. . . . On week-days I have seen many of the nobility—particularly the Duchess of Devonshire, &c.—with a large party, supping in the rooms facing the orchestra, French horns playing to them all the time."

Vauxhall in its best days was frequented by all the successive generations of humorists, from Addison down to Hogarth and Oliver Goldsmith; and by literary men, from Dr. Johnson down to Macaulay, George Hanger (Lord Coleraine), Captain Gronow, Lord William Lennox, Mr. Grantley Berkeley, Douglas Jerrold, Leigh Hunt, Thackeray, and Dickens.

Goldsmith, when he had achieved his first successes in literature, and in those lucid intervals when he had a good coat on his back and a few shillings in his pocket, especially in the last year of his life, was often a visitor here, along with Dr. Johnson and Sir Joshua Reynolds, dressed in a suit of velvet, of course. Goldsmith, describing a " Visit to Vauxhall," about the year 1760, having praised the singers and the very excellent band, continues:—" The satisfaction which I received the first night [of the season] I went there was greater than my expectations; I went in company of several friends of both sexes, whose virtues I regard and judgments I esteem. The music, the entertainments, but particularly the singing, diffused that good humour among us which constitutes the true happiness of society." The same author's account of these gardens in the "Citizen of the World" contains some interesting passages. This occurs in the description of the visit of the shabby beau, the man in black, and one or two other the visionary happiness of the Arabian lawgiver, and lifted me into an ecstacy of admiration. 'Head of Confucius,' cried I to my friend, 'this is fine! this unites rural beauty with courtly magnificence.'" A dispute between the two ladies now engages the philosopher's attention. "Miss Tibbs was for keeping the genteel walk of the garden, where, she observed, there was always the very best company; the widow, on the contrary, who came but once a

THE OLD VILLAGE OF VAUXHALL, WITH ENTRANCE TO THE GARDENS, IN 1825.

persons, in company with the Chinese philosopher. The beau's lady, Mrs. Tibbs, has a natural aversion to the water, and the pawnbroker's widow, being "a little in flesh," protests against walking; so a coach is agreed on as the mode of conveyance. "The illuminations," says the philosopher, "began before we arrived, and I must confess that upon entering the gardens I found every sense overpaid with more than expected pleasure; the lights everywhere glimmering through scarcely-moving trees; the full-bodied concert bursting on the stillness of night; the natural concert of the birds in the more retired part of the grove vying with that which was formed by art; the company, gaily dressed, looking satisfaction; and the tables spread with various delicacies; all conspired to fill my imagination with

season, was for securing a good standing-place to see the water-works, which, she assured us, would begin in less than an hour at furthest." The cascade here referred to had been but recently introduced into the gardens, and was then doubtless a great attraction. A few years later the "water-works" were greatly improved, and called the Cataract. The effects then produced were very ingenious and beautiful; and at the signal for their commencement—the ringing of a bell at nine o'clock—there was a general rush from all parts of the gardens.

Garrick was a frequent visitor here, as also were the fair Gunnings, who made a greater noise in the world of fashion than any women since the days of Helen. "They are declared," writes Walpole, "to be the handsomest women alive; they can't walk in the park, or go to Vauxhall, but such crowds follow them that they are generally driven away."

Another frequenter of Vauxhall Gardens was that eccentric person, Sir Henry Bate Dudley; and amongst the regular visitors here towards the close of the last century was the equally eccentric baronet, Sir John Dinely, so well known for his matrimonial advertisements. It was his habit to attend here on public nights twice or three times

himself and his ample fortune to any angelic beauty of a good breed, fit to become and willing to be the mother of a noble heir, and keep up the name of an ancient family ennobled by deeds of arms and ancestral renown. Ladies at a certain period of life need not apply. Fortune favours the bold. Such ladies as this advertisement may induce to apply or send their agents (but no servants or matrons), may direct to me at the Castle,

THE ITALIAN WALK, VAUXHALL GARDENS.

every season, when he would parade up and down the most public parts; and it is said that whenever it was known that he was coming, the ladies would flock in shoals to the gardens. He wore his wig fastened in a curious manner by a piece of stay-tape under his chin, and was always dressed in a cloak with long flowing folds, and a broad hat which looked as if it had started out of a picture by Vandyke. In spite, however, of his persistent efforts to gain a rich wife by advertisement, he died a bachelor, an inmate of the poor knights' quarters in Windsor Castle, in 1808. Here is one of his advertisements, taken from the *Ipswich Journal* of August 21st, 1802 :—"To the angelic fair of the true English breed. Worthy notice. Sir John Dinely, of Windsor Castle, recommends

Windsor. Happiness and pleasure are agreeable objects, and should be regarded as well as honour. The lady who shall thus become my wife will be a baroness [query, baronet'ess], and rank accordingly as Lady Dinely, of Windsor. Goodwill and favour to all ladies of Great Britain! pull no caps on his account, but favour him with your smiles, and pæans of pleasure await your steps." It should be added, that though his "ample fortune" was moonshine, his title was genuine, and not a sham.

Another frequent visitor to the gardens was Lord Barrymore, whose pugilistic and other freaks are related in amusing detail by Mr. Angelo in his "Reminiscences." They are not, however, sufficiently edifying to bear repeating here.

Apparently the Princess of Wales was an occasional visitor here during the time of her long-standing rupture with her husband; such, at all events, is the inference to be drawn from an epigram on "a certain unexpected visit to a late *fête*," in the *Morning Herald* for July 24, 1813 :—

> " ' Since not to dance, since not to quaff,
>   Since not to taste our cheer,'
> Says tipsy Dick, with many a laugh,
>   ' Why comes the P*****ss here ?'
>
> ' I ken,' says Sober, ' at a glance,
>   What brings her to Vauxhall ;
> She means, although she does not dance,
>   Still to keep up the ball.' "

The following *jeu d'esprit* will be found in the *Morning Chronicle*, 1813, headed, "Reason for Absence from the Vauxhall Fête, given by an Alderman to a Lady :"—

> " ' The Regent was absent, because, my dear life,
>   He did not like meeting the world and—his wife.' "

Theodore Hook was a visitor to these gardens till the end of his life ; and Samuel Rogers tells us, in his "Table Talk," that he could just remember going to Ranelagh or Vauxhall in a coach with a lady who was obliged to sit on a little stool placed on the bottom of the vehicle, as the height of her head-dress did not allow her to occupy the regular seat.

Readers of Thackeray will not have forgotten the visit paid—out of the season—to Vauxhall by Mr. Pendennis, when he meets Captain Costigan, and gains admission at the entrance for Fanny Bolton, the pretty daughter of the porter of "Shepherd's" Inn, and who, having never before seen the gardens, is equally affected with wonder and delight at the lamps and the company. And those who have studied "Vanity Fair" will equally well remember the "rack punch" which Mr. Jos Sedley drank here, rather in excess, on his memorable visit to the gardens, in company with Rebecca Sharp, George Osborne, and Amelia Sedley, the party who came in the coach from Russell Square; how Jos, in his glory, ordered about the waiters, made the salad, uncorked the champagne, carved the chickens, and, finally, drank the greater part of the liquid refreshments, insisting on a bowl of rack punch, for "everybody has rack punch at Vauxhall." They will not have forgotten Thackeray's amusing sketch of the "hundred thousand extra lights that were always lighted;" the "fiddlers in cocked hats, who played ravishing melodies under the gilded cockle-shell in the midst of the gardens;" the singers both of comic and sentimental ballads, who "charmed the ears;" the country dances formed by bouncing cockneys

and cockneyesses, and executed amidst jumping, thumping, and laughter ; the signal which announced that Madame Saqui was about to mount skyward on a slack rope, ascending to the stars ; the hermit that always sat in the illuminated hermitage ; the dark walks, so favourable to the interviews of young lovers ; the pots of stout by the people in shabby old liveries ; and the twinkling boxes, in which the happy feeders made believe to eat slices of almost invisible ham."

Vauxhall Gardens, down to a very late date, still attracted "the upper ten thousand"—occasionally, at least. We are told incidentally, in Forster's "Life of Dickens," that one famous night, the 29th of June, 1849, Dickens went there with Judge Talfourd, Stanfield, and Sir Edwin Landseer. The 'Battle of Waterloo' formed part of the entertainment on that occasion. "We were astounded," writes Mr. Forster, "to see pass in immediately before us, in a bright white overcoat, the 'great duke' himself, with Lady Douro on his arm, the little Lady Ramsays by his side, and everybody cheering and clearing the way for him. That the old hero enjoyed it all there could be no doubt, and he made no secret of his delight in ' Young Hernandez ;' but the battle was undeniably tedious; and it was impossible not to sympathise with the repeatedly and audibly expressed wish of Talfourd that ' the Prussians would come up !' " It must have been one of the old duke's last appearances in a place of amusement, as he lived only three years longer.

A description of the gardens as they appeared about this time, by a writer who frequented them in the last decade of their glory, may not be out of place here :—"The mode of entrance into the gardens, which extend over about eleven acres, is admirably calculated to enhance their extraordinary effect on the first view. We step at once from the passages into a scene of enchantment, such as in our young days opened upon our eyes as we pored over the magical pages of the 'Arabian Nights.' It were indeed worth some sacrifice of time, money, and convenience to see for once in a lifetime that view. At first, one wide-extended and interminable blaze of radiance is the idea impressed upon the dazzled beholder. As his eyes grow accustomed to the place, he perceives the form of the principal part of the gardens resolve itself into a kind of long quadrangle, formed by four colonnades which inclose an open space with trees, called the Grove. On his right extends one of the colonnades, some three hundred feet long, with an arched Gothic roof, where the groins are marked by lines of lamps, shedding a yellow-golden light, and the pendants by single crimson lamps of a larger size at the intersections. The effect of this management is most superb. Near the eye the lines or groins appear singly, showing their purpose; farther off, they grow closer and closer, till at some distance the entire vista beyond appears one rich blaze of radiance. In front, the visitor looks across one of the shorter ends of the quadrangle, illuminated in a different but still more magnificent manner by a chandelier of great size, formed of coloured lamps, and by various smaller chandeliers. Still standing in the same place (at the door of entrance), and looking across the interior of the quadrangle called the Grove, midway is seen the lofty orchestra, glittering all over with the many-coloured lights diffused from innumerable lamps. This was erected in 1735, and has itself many interesting memories attached to it. Beneath that vast shell which forms the roof or sounding-board of the orchestra many of our greatest vocalists and performers have poured forth their strains to the delight of the crowded auditory in front—Signor and Signora Storace, Mrs. Billington, Miss Tyrer (afterwards Mrs. Liston), Incledon, Braham, and a host of others, at once rise to the memory. The Grove is illuminated not only by the reflected light from the colonnades on either side and by the orchestra, but by festoons of lamps, gracefully undulating along the sides of the colonnades from one end to the other. Among the other attractions of the Grove, we find immediately we step into it some beautiful plaster-casts from the antique, the light colour of which forms a fine contrast with the blackness of the neighbouring trees and the solemn gloom of the sky above, which assumes a still deeper tinge when seen under such circumstances. Immediately opposite these, at the back of the short colonnade which forms this end of the Grove, with elevated arches opening upon the colonnade, is the splendid room originally called the Pavilion, now the Hall of Mirrors, a title more appropriate as marking its distinctive character, the walls being lined with looking-glass. This is the principal supper-room. Turning the corner, we enter upon the other of the two principal colonnades, which is similarly illuminated. A little way down we find an opening into the Rotunda, a very large and handsome building, with boxes, pit, and gallery in the circular part, and on one side a stage for the performance of ballets, &c. The pit forms also, when required, an arena for the display of horsemanship. At the end of this colonnade we have on the right the colonnade forming the other extremity of the Grove, hollowed out into a semi-circular form, the

space being fitted up somewhat in the manner of a Turkish divan. On the left we find the more distant and darker parts of the gardens. Here the first spot that attracts our attention is a large space, the back of which presents a kind of mimic amphitheatre of trees and foliage, having in front rockwork and fountains. From one of the latter Eve has just issued, as we perceive by the beautiful figure reclining on the grass above. Not far from this place a fine cast of Diana arresting the flying hart stands out in admirable relief from the dark-green leafy background. Here, too, is a large building, presenting in front the appearance of the proscenium and stage of a theatre. Ballets, performances on the tight-rope, and others of a like character, are here exhibited. The purpose of the building is happily marked by the statues of Canova's dancing-girls, one of which is placed on each side of the area at the front. At the corner of a long walk, between trees lighted only by single lamps, spread at intervals on the ground at the sides, is seen a characteristic representation of Tell's cottage in the Swiss Alps. This walk is terminated by an illuminated transparency, placed behind a Gothic archway, representing the delicate but broken shafts of some ruined ecclesiastical structure, with a large stone cross—that characteristic feature of the way-sides of Roman Catholic countries. At right angles with this walk extends a much broader one, with the additional illumination of a brilliant star; and at its termination is an opening containing a very imposing spectacle. This is a representation, in a large circular basin of water, of Neptune, with his trident, driving his five sea-horses abreast, which are snorting forth liquid streams from their nostrils; these in their ascent cross and intermingle in a very pleasing and striking manner. The lustrous white and great size of the figures are, like all the other works of art in the gardens, admirably contrasted with the surrounding features of the place. Passing on our way the large building erected for the convenience of filling the great balloon, and the area where the fireworks are exhibited, we next enter the Italian Walk, so called from its having been originally decorated in the formal, exact style of the walks in that country. This is a very noble promenade, or avenue, of great length and breadth, crossed every few yards by a lofty angular arch of lamps, with festoons of the same brilliant character hanging from it, and having statues interspersed on each side throughout. On quitting this walk at its farthest extremity, we find ourselves in the centre of the long colonnade opposite to that we quitted in order to examine the more remote parts of the gardens." The inner side of each of the long colonnades was occupied by innumerable supper-boxes, in some of which, down to the very last, remained the pictures of which we have spoken above.

"One of the subjects selected by Mr. Jonathan Tyers for the artists who decorated the supper-boxes in Vauxhall Gardens," writes Mr. J. T. Smith, in his "Book for a Rainy Day," "was that of ' Milkmaids on May-day.' In that picture (which, with the rest, painted by Hayman and his pupils, has lately disappeared) the garland of plate was carried by a man on his head ; and the milkmaids, who danced to the music of a wooden-legged fiddler, were extremely elegant. They had ruffled cuffs, and their gowns were not drawn through their pocket-holes, as in my time ; their hats were flat, and not unlike that worn by Peg Woffington, but bore a nearer shape to those now in use by some of the fish-women at Billingsgate. In the ' Cries of London,' published by Tempest, there is a female, entitled ' A Merry Milkmaid.' She is dancing with a small garland of plate on her head, and probably represented the fashion of Queen Anne's reign."

May-day is little observed in London at the present time, except that the omnibus-drivers and cabmen ornament their horses' heads with flowers or rosettes, and their whips with bits of ribbon, while Jack-in-the-Green and Maid Marian are to be seen in the streets. Not so very long ago, however, certainly within the present century, says Robert Chambers, there was a somewhat similar demonstration from the milkmaids. "A milch cow, garlanded with flowers, was led along by a small group of dairy-women, who, in light and fantastic dresses, and with heads wreathed in flowers, would dance around the animal to the sound of a violin or clarionet. In the old gardens at Vauxhall there used to be a picture representing the May-day dance of the London milkmaids. In this Vauxhall picture a man is represented bearing a cluster of silver flagons on his head (these flagons used to be lent by the pawnbrokers at so much an hour) ; while three milkmaids are dancing to the music of a wooden-legged fiddler, some chimney-sweeps appearing as side figures."

"Ned Ward the Younger" wrote in the *London Magazine*, many years ago, the following verses, descriptive of the scene at that time to be witnessed in these gardens :—

"Well, Vauxhall is a wondrous scene !
　Where Cits in silks admirers glean
　　Under innumerous lamps—
　Not safety lamps, by Humphry made :
　By these full many a soul's betrayed
　　To ruin by the damps !

"Here nut-brown trees, instead of green,
　With oily trunks, and branches lean,
　　Cling to nine yellow leaves,
　Like aged misers, that all day
　Hang o'er their gold and their decay,
　　'Till Death of both bereaves !

"The sanded walk beneath the roof
　Is dry for every dainty hoof,
　　And here the wise man stops ;
　But beaux beneath the sallow clumps
　Stand in the *water* with their *pumps*,
　　And catch the oiléd drops.

"Tinkles the bell !—away the herd
　Of revellers rush, like buck or bird :
　　Each doth his way unravel
　To where the dingy Drama holds
　Her sombre reign, 'mid rain and colds,
　　And tip-toes, and wet gravel.

"The boxes show a weary set,
　Who like to get serenely wet,
　　Within, and not without ;
　There Goldsmith's widow you may see
　Rocking a fat and frantic knee
　　At all the passing rout !

"Yes ! there she is !—there, to the life ;
　And Mr. Tibbs, and Tibbs's wife,
　　And the good man in black.
　Belles run, for, oh ! the bell is ringing ;
　But Mrs. Tibbs is calmly singing,
　　And sings till all come back !

"By that high dome, that trembling glows
　With lamps, cocked hats, and shivering bows,
　　How many hearts are shook !
　A feathered chorister is there,
　Warbling some tender grove-like air,
　　Compos'd by Mr. Hook.

"And Dignum, too ! yet where is he ?
　Shakes he no more his locks at me ?
　　Charms he no more night's ear ?
　He who bless'd breakfast, dinner, rout,
　With ' linkéd sweetness long drawn out ; '
　　Why is not Dignum here ?

"Oh, Mr. Bish !—oh, Mr. Bish !
　It is enough, by Heaven ! to *dish*
　　Thy garden dinners at ten !
　What hast thou done with Mr. D. ?
　What's thy ' Wine Company,' thy ' Tea,'
　　Without that man of men ?

"Yet, blessed are thy suppers given
　(For money) something past eleven ;
　　Lilliput chickens boiled ;
　Bucellas, warm from Vauxhall ice,
　And hams, that flit in airy slice,
　　And salads scarcely soiled.

"See !—the large, silent, pale-blue light
　Flares, to lead all to where the bright
　　Loud rockets rush on high,
　Like a long comet, roaring through
　The night, then melting into blue,
　　And starring the dark sky !

" And Catherine-wheels, and crowns, and names
  Of great men whizzing in blue flames ;
    Lights, like the smiles of hope ;
  And radiant fiery palaces,
  Showing the tops of all the trees,
    And Blackmore on the rope !

" Then late the hours, and sad the stay !
  The passing cup, the wits astray,
    The *row*, and riot call !
  The tussle, and the collar torn,
  The dying lamps, the breaking morn !
    And hey for—Union Hall ! "

Dr. C. Mackay, in his " Thames and its Tributaries," writes :—" Famous is Vauxhall in all the country round, for its pleasant walks, its snug alcoves, its comic singers, its innumerable lights, its big balloons, its midnight fireworks, its thin slices, its dear potations, its greedy waiters, and its ladies fair and kind, and abounding with every charm except the greatest that can adorn their sex." The old guide-books almost always call Vauxhall an " earthly paradise ; " and Addison, as we have seen above, speaks of it as a " Mahomedan paradise ; " whilst Murphy, in his " Prologue to " Zobeide," apostrophises—

" Sweet Ranelagh ! Vauxhall's enchanting shade ! "

Where in all England, it might be asked, was there a spot more renowned among pleasure-seekers than—

" This beauteous garden, but by vice maintained ? "

as Addison expresses it, paraphrasing the words of Juvenal.

Albert Smith gives us the following reminiscences of Vauxhall Gardens in his " Sketches of London Life," published in 1859 :—" The earliest notions I ever had of Vauxhall were formed from an old coloured print which decorated a bed-room at home, and represented the gardens as they were in the time of hoops and high head-dresses, bag-wigs and swords. The general outline was almost that of the present day, and the disposition of the orchestra, firework-ground, and covered walks the same. But the royal property was surrounded by clumps of trees and pastures ; shepherds smoked their pipes where the tall chimneys of Lambeth now pour out their dense encircling clouds, to blight or blacken every attempt at vegetation in the neighbourhood ; and where the rustics played cricket at the water-side, massive arches and mighty girders bear the steaming, gleaming, screaming train on its way to the new terminus. I had a vague notion, also, of the style of entertainments there offered. In several old pocket-books and magazines, that were kept covered with mould and cobwebs in a damp spare-room closet, I used to read the ballads put down as ' sung by Mrs. Wrighten at Vauxhall.' They were not very extraordinary compositions. Here is one, which may be taken as a sample of all, called a ' Rondeau,' sung by Mrs. Weichsel ; set by Mr. Hook :—

" ' Maidens, let your lovers languish,
    If you'd have them constant prove ;
  Doubts and fears, and sighs and anguish,
    Are the chains that fasten love.
  Jacky woo'd, and I consented,
    Soon as e'er I heard his tale,
  He with conquest quite contented,
    Boasting, rov'd around the vale.
  Maidens, let your lovers, &c.

  ' Now he dotes on scornful Molly,
    Who rejects him with disdain ;
  Love's a strange bewitching folly,
    Never pleased without some pain.
  Maidens, let your lovers, &c.'

" I was also told of hundreds of thousands of lamps, and an attempt was made to imitate their effect by pricking pinholes in the picture and putting a light behind it—for the glass had disappeared at some remote period, and had never been replaced ; and for years I looked forward to going to Vauxhall as a treat too magnificent ever to take place."

He tells us that the time came, though not until he was twelve years old, and then it was to celebrate his promotion into a higher form at Merchant Taylor's School. " Twenty years have gone by," he writes, " since that eventful night, but the impression made upon me is as vivid as it was on the following day. I remember being shown the lights of the orchestra twinkling through the trees from the road, and hearing the indistinct crash of the band as I waited for all our party, literally trembling with expectation at the pay place. Then there came the dark passage, which I hurried along with feelings almost of awe ; and finally the bewildering *coup d'œil*, as the dazzling walk before the great supper-room, with its balloons, and flags, and crowns of light—its panels of looking-glass, and long lines of radiant stars, festoons, and arches burst upon me and took away my breath, with almost every other faculty. I could not speak. I heard nothing that was said to me ; and if anybody had afterwards assured me that I entered the garden upon my head instead of my heels I could scarcely have contradicted them. I have never experienced anything like the intensity of that feeling but once since ; and that was when I caught the first sight of London by night from a great elevation, during the balloon ascent last year which so nearly terminated in the destruction of all our party.

"The entire evening was to me one scene of continuous enchantment. The Battle of Waterloo was being represented on the firework-ground, and I could not divest myself of the idea that it was a real engagement I was witnessing, as the sharp-shooters fired from behind the trees, the artillery-wagon blew up, and the struggle and conflagration took place at Hougoumont. When I stood, years afterwards, on the real battle-field I was disap-

Some idea of the place in 1827 may be gathered from the remarks of a "wonder-struck boy," Master Peter, given in Hone's "Table Book":—"Oh, my! what a sweet place! Why, the lamps are thicker than the pears in our garden at Walworth! What a load of oil they must burn!" Master Peter's wonderment did not stop at the lamps, for he was equally enraptured by the orchestra and the "marine cave;" and even the fireworks and

CHINESE PAVILION IN VAUXHALL GARDENS.

pointed in its effect. I thought it ought to have been a great deal more like Vauxhall.

"The supper was another great feature—eating by the light of variegated lamps, with romantic views painted on the walls, and music playing all the time, was on a level with the most brilliant entertainment described in the maddest, wildest traditions of Eastern story-tellers."

Mrs. Weichsel, mentioned in the above quotation, was the favourite singer here a century ago: she was the mother of the famous actress, Mrs. Billington. Arne and Boyce composed music for these gardens; and nearly all the vocal celebrities of the latter half of the last century and the first thirty years of this appeared in the orchestra, where all the instrumentalists wore cocked hats.

the refreshments are all "taken off" in the same style.

Another writer about this time, in the *World* (No. 63), gives vent to the following bantering remarks :—"I have heard that the master of Vauxhall, who so plentifully supplies beef for our bodily refreshment, has, for the entertainment of those who visit him at his country house, no less plentifully provided for the mind; where the guest may call for a skull to chew upon the instability of human life, or sit down to a collation of poetry, of which the hangings of his room of entertainment take up, as I am told, many yards. I wish that this grand purveyor of beef and poetry would transport some of the latter to his gardens at Vauxhall. Odes and songs pasted upon the lamp-posts would be, I

BALLOON ASCENT AT VAUXHALL GARDENS 1849.

believe, much more studiously attended to than the price-list of cheese-cakes and custards; and if the unpictured boxes were hung round with celebrated passages out of favourite poets, many a company would find something to say, who would otherwise sit cramming themselves in silent stupidity."

"Vauxhall Gardens have undergone," writes the Rev. J. Richardson, in 1856, in his "Recollections," "little change within my recollection. The place was certainly attended, fifty years ago, by people of a more aristocratic rank than it has been of late years. George IV., when Prince of Wales, and his brothers, were formerly amongst the visitors; and their presence attracted other people, who thought it expedient to do as their betters did, and imitate the practices of the great. It was at that time decorated with better pictures than the daubs by which the walls of the boxes are now covered; but the amusements, the fireworks, and the illumination of the coloured lamps, were neither so much diversified, so numerous, or so brilliant. I never recollect it resembling the account given in the *Spectator*, either as to the warbling of the birds or the beauty of the groves, &c. The slices of ham were as transparent fifty years ago as they are now; the chickens were as diminutive as now-a-days; the charges were equally extravagant. People did not drink so much champagne, but they contrived to get the headache with arrack-punch, and kettles of 'burnt' wine were in more request than brandy and water. The vocal performances were better, the concerts were better conducted; the dancing was much the same as now, and those who took part in it were neither morally nor physically any better than their successors." In his subsequent pages Mr. Richardson sketches off some of the "characters" connected with Vauxhall: such as Bradbury, the clown; Mr. Simpson, the *arbiter elegantiarum*; and the Nepaulese princes, who, on their visit to this country, were great patrons of Vauxhall.

A good story is told in the *Connoisseur* of a century ago about a parsimonious old citizen going to Vauxhall with his wife and daughters, and grumbling at the dearness of the provisions and the wafer-like thinness of the slices of ham. At every mouthful the old fellow exclaims, "There goes two-pence! there goes threepence! there goes a groat!" Then there is the old joke of the thinness of the slices of ham and the expert cutter, who undertook to cover the gardens—eleven acres—with slices from one ham!

The author of "Saunterings about London" (1853) thus sums up Vauxhall Gardens and the entertainments provided here:—"Vauxhall was born in the Regency, in one of the wicked nights of dissolute Prince George. A wealthy speculator was its father; a prince was its godfather; and all the fashion and beauty of England stood round its cradle. In those days Vauxhall was very exclusive and expensive. At present it is open to all ranks and classes, and half-a-guinea will frank a fourth-rate milliner and sweetheart through the whole evening. A Londoner wants a great deal for his money, or he wants little—take it which way you please. The programme of Vauxhall is an immense *carte* for the eye and the ear: music, singing, horse-manship, illuminations, dancing, rope-dancing, acting, comic songs, hermits, gipsies, and fireworks, on the most 'stunning' scale. It is easier to read the *Kölner Zeitung* than the play-bill of Vauxhall. With respect to the *quantity* of sights," adds the writer, "it is most difficult to satisfy an English public. They have 'a capacious swallow' for sights, and require them in large masses, as they do the meat which graces their tables. As to quality, that is a minor consideration; and to give the English public its due, it is the most grateful of all publics."

Fireworks were occasionally exhibited here as far back as 1798. Four years later the first balloon ascent from the gardens was made by Garnerin and two companions. In 1835, Mr. Green ascended from these gardens, and remained up in the air during the night. On the afternoon of November 7th, in the following year, Messrs. Green, Monck Mason, and R. Hollond ascended here in the monster balloon, called afterwards the "Nassau." They effected their descent next morning near Coblentz, having accomplished nearly 500 miles in eighteen hours.

In June, 1837, these gardens had a narrow escape from destruction by fire, which broke out one night in the firework tower, a lofty structure eighty feet in height, from which the pyrotechnic displays were exhibited. At the top of this tower was a large tank, containing 8,000 gallons of water; this fell in with a tremendous crash, but, curiously enough, it produced not the slightest effect upon the flames. The whole of the tower, including the painting-room (the largest in England), was totally destroyed, together with its contents; likewise fourteen or fifteen tall trees were burned to the ground, and twice as many damaged. In the following month Mr. Green again ascended here in his great balloon, with Mr. Cocking in a parachute; but this per-formance, unfortunately, was attended with fatal results, for the latter was killed in descending.

In 1838 Mr. Green, accompanied by Mr. Edward Spencer and Mr. Rush, of Elsenham Hall, Essex, made another ascent in the "Nassau." They descended at Debden, near Saffron Walden, forty-seven miles from the gardens, having accomplished the journey in one hour and a half, the highest altitude attained being 19,335 feet, or nearly three and three-quarter miles.

For some time ballooning served as the staple feature in the programme, and an attempt was made to render these gardens attractive by day as well as by night. Readers of "Boz" will not forget among them a chapter descriptive of the gardens by day, and of the ascent of Mr. Green in a balloon along with a "live lord;" or his remarks on the cruelty of the disillusion practised on the public by Mr. Simpson admitting visitors within its precincts when the veil of mystery which night and oil or gas lamps had previously hung around them were removed. "Vauxhall by daylight, indeed! A porter-pot without the porter, the House of Commons without Mr. Speaker; pooh! nonsense! The thing was not to be thought of." But "thought of" it was; the experiment was tried, but was soon given up.

Jonathan Tyers ruled over the destinies of Vauxhall for many years. He died in 1767; and we are informed that "so great was the delight he took in this place, that, possessing his faculties to the last, he caused himself to be carried into the gardens a few hours before his death, to take a last look at them." After Tyers' death the gardens were conducted by different managers, the best-known of whom was a Mr. Barnett; but the property still remained with Tyers' family until 1822, when it was sold to Messrs. Bish, Gye, and Hughes for £28,000. Mr. Gye was afterwards M.P. for Chippenham, and father of Mr. Frederick Gye, the lessee of the Italian Opera.

In 1831 the proprietors endeavoured to secure the musical aid of Paganini for fifteen nights; but he demanded £10,000, and his terms were declined. Mr. Wardell was some time the lessee of the gardens; then came the era of Simpson—"Vauxhall Simpson," as Cruikshank styles him in his "Comic Almanac"—with a "million extra lamps," and balloons, and horse-riding, and tumbling, and Van Amburgh with his wild beasts, and panoramas, and popular nights, at a shilling entrance! but

> "The glories of his leg and cane are past;
> He made his bow and cut his stick at last."

In 1840 the estate, "with its buildings, timber, covered walks, &c.," was offered for sale by auction, but bought in at £20,000. "At this sale," as John Timbs tells us, in his "Curiosities of London," "twenty-four pictures by Hogarth and Hayman produced but small sums: they had mostly been upon the premises since 1742; the canvas was nailed to boards, and much obscured by dirt. By Hogarth: Drunken Man, £4 4s.; a Woman pulling out an Old Man's grey hairs, £3 3s.; Jobson and Nell in the *Devil to Pay*, £4 4s.; the Happy Family, £3 15s.; Children at Play, £4 11s. 6d. By Hayman: Children Bird's-nesting, £5 10s.; Minstrels, £3; the Enraged Husband, £4 4s.; the Bridal Day, £6 6s.; Blindman's Buff, £3 8s.; Prince Henry and Falstaff, £7; Scene from the *Rake's Progress*, £9 15s.; Merry-making, £1 12s.; the Jealous Husband, £4; Card-party, £6; Children's Party, £4 15s.; Battledore and Shuttlecock, £1 10s.; the Doctor, £4 14s. 6d.; Cherry-bob, £2 15s.; the Storming of Seringapatam, £8 10s.; Neptune and Britannia, £8 15s. Four busts of Simpson, the celebrated master of the ceremonies, were sold for 10s.; and a bust of his royal shipmate, William IV. for 19s."

Then came fitful seasons, sometimes lasting only a few nights, and generally during St. Swithin's, till the rain became a standing joke, in which even the temporary lessees shared, sending out announcements printed on huge umbrellas; and last came the fatal day when the "Royal Property" was broken up by the auctioneer's hammer, the domain became a wilderness, and Vauxhall was no more.

The gardens were already on their decline in the reign of William IV., if we may judge from allusions in the newspapers and magazines of that time. That they had begun to lose their attractions, and were no longer patronised by the "upper ten thousand," may be gathered from the fact that in Bohn's "Pictorial Handbook of London," published in 1851, these historic grounds are dismissed without any description, and with only the curt remark that they were "long a favourite place of public amusement, in which music, singing, and ballets are performed during the evenings of the summer months," and that "the admittance varies, being sometimes a shilling and sometimes half-a-crown." Alas! how are the mighty fallen! how transitory, after all, is the reign of fashion.

Mr. Timbs, in his "Curiosities of London," writes:—"Though Vauxhall Gardens retained their place to the very last, the lamps had long fallen off in their golden fires; the punch got weaker, the admission money less; and the company fell off in a like ratio of respectability, and grew dingy, not to say 'raffish'—a sorry falling off from the Vauxhall crowd of a century before, when it numbered princes and ambassadors; when 'on its tide and torrent of fashion floated all the beauty of the time, and through its lighted avenues of trees glided cabinet ministers and their daughters, royal dukes and their wives, and all the red-heeled macaronis.' Even fifty years before the close of the gardens the evening costume of the company was elegant; head-dresses of flowers and feathers were seen in the promenade; and the entire place sparkled as did no other place of public amusement. But low prices brought low company. The conventional wax-lights got fewer; the punch gave way to fiery brandy and doctored stout. The semblance of Vauxhall was still preserved in the representation of the orchestra printed upon the plates and mugs, and the old firework bell tinkled away as gaily as ever. But matters grew more and more seedy; the place seemed literally worn out; the very trees grew scrubby and shabby, and looked as if they were singed; and it was high time to say, as well to see in letters of lamps, ' Farewell.'"

Colin's description (to his wife) of Greenwood Hall, or the pleasures of Spring Gardens, gives a lively description of this modern Arcadia as it was a century before its abolition:—

> " O Mary ! soft in feature,
>   I've been at dear Vaux Hall ;
> No Paradise is sweeter,
>   Not that they Eden call.

> " At night such new vagaries,
>   Such gay and harmless sport ;
> All looked like giant fairies
>   At this their monarch's court.

> " Methought, when first I entered,
>   Such splendours round me shone,
> Into a world I'd ventured
>   Where shone another sun :

> " While music never cloying,
>   As skylarks sweet, I hear ;
> Their sounds I'm still enjoying,
>   They'll always soothe my ear.

> " Here paintings sweetly glowing
>   Where'er our glances fall ;
> Here colours, life bestowing,
>   Bedeck this Greenwood Hall.

> " The king there dubs a farmer ;
>   There John his doxy loves ;
> But my delight's the charmer
>   Who steals a pair of gloves.

> " As still amazed I'm straying
>   O'er this enchanted grove,
> I spy a harper playing,
>   All in his proud alcove.

> " I doff my hat, desiring
>   He'll tune up ' Buxom Joan ;'
> But what was I admiring ?
>   Odzooks ! a man of stone !

> " But now, the tables spreading,
>   They all fall to with glee|;
> Not e'en at squire's fine wedding
>   Such dainties did I see.

> " I longed (poor country rover !),
>   But none heed country elves.
> These folk, with lace daubed over,
>   Love only their dear selves.

> " Thus whilst 'mid joys abounding,
>   As grasshoppers they're gay,
> At distance crowds surrounding
>   The Lady of the May.

> " The man i' th' moon tweer'd shyly
>   Soft twinkling through the trees,
> As though 'twould please him highly,
>   To taste delights like these."

It should be explained that the allusion in the sixth stanza is to three pictures in the Pavilion, which represented " The King and the Miller of Mansfield," " Sailors Tippling at Wapping," and " A Girl Stealing a Kiss from a Youth Asleep ;" that the " harper " is the statue of Handel; and that the " Lady of the May " is the " Princess of Wales sitting under her Pavilion."

No public favourite ever had so many "positively last appearances " as Vauxhall. For years Londoners were informed, at the conclusion of each season, that Vauxhall would that week " close for ever ;" and for years, at the commencement of the succeeding one, they were assured that it would re-open " on a scale of magnificence hitherto unattempted." But, as we have said, the end eventually came; this was about the year 1855.

In the autumn of 1859, a vast number of persons were attracted to the gardens by the announcement that " the well-known theatre, orchestra, dancing-platform, firework-gallery, fountains, statues, vases, &c.," would be sold by auction. There were, in all, 274 lots, and many of them were knocked down at the lowest conceivable price. A deal painted table, with turned legs, one of the original tables made for the gardens in 1754, was disposed of for 9s. A large historical painting in the coffee-room, representing the King of Sardinia, with the Order of the Garter, being introduced by Prince Albert to the Queen, brought only 35s. ; while an equestrian picture of the Emperor and Empress of the French at a hunting party, in the costume of Louis XIV., was sold for the ridiculous sum of 22s. The great feature of the day's sale, it is stated, was the circular orchestra, for which a gentleman of the Jewish faith offered £25 ; but several persons seemed anxious about the lot, and the price ran up to £99.

Shortly afterwards the Prince of Wales went to

Vauxhall, but it was to lay the foundation-stone of a School of Art, on the spot where, in bygone times, lovers whispered their "soft nothings" in the dark walks to the music of pattering fountains; a church has arisen on what was once almost the centre of the gardens; the manager's house is now the parsonage, slightly enlarged, but otherwise unaltered; and all is respectable and artistic and decorous, though there are no coloured lamps and no fireworks.

CHAPTER XXXIV.

VAUXHALL (continued) AND BATTERSEA.

"Transtiberina patent longè loca."—*Tibullus.*

Boat-racing at Vauxhall—Fortifications erected here in 1642—A Proposed Boulevard—The Marquis of Worcester, Author of the "Century of Inventions"—The Works of the London Gas Company—Nine Elms—Messrs. Price's Candle Factory—Inns and Taverns—Origin of the Name of Battersea—Descent of the Manor of Battersea—Bolingbroke House—A Curious Air-mill—Reminiscences of Henry St. John, Lord Bolingbroke—Sir William Batten—York House—The Parish Church of Battersea—Christ Church—St. Mark's Church—St. George's Church—The National School—St. John's College—The Royal Freemasons' Girls' School—The "Falcon" Tavern—The Victoria Bridge—Albert Bridge—The Old Ferry—Building of Battersea Bridge—Battersea Fields—The "Red House"—Cæsar's Ford—Battersea Park and Gardens—Model Dwellings for Artisans and Labourers—Southwark and Vauxhall Waterworks—Market Gardens—Battersea Enamelled Ware—How Battersea became the Cradle of Bottled Ale.

VAUXHALL, it may here be stated, has other interesting associations besides those connected with its defunct Gardens; for, like the Nore, it appears of old to have been the end of the course for small sailing and racing matches on the Thames. Thus Strutt writes, in his "Sports and Pastimes," published in 1800:—"A society, generally known by the appellation of the Cumberland Society, consisting of gentlemen partial to this pastime, gives yearly a silver cup to be sailed for in the vicinity of London. The boats usually start from the bridge at Blackfriars, go up to Putney, and return to Vauxhall, where a vessel is moored at a distance from the stairs, and the sailing-boat that first passes this mark on her return obtains the victory." It would seem natural that while the chief access to the Gardens was by the "silent highway" of the Thames and by the "stairs," the owners of Vauxhall and of Astley's should have shown some regard for the river and aquatic amusements; accordingly we learn from the same authority that the proprietors of those places used to give annually a wherry to be rowed for by the "jolly young watermen," or Thames apprentices, much like Doggett's coat and badge are now the objects of an annual aquatic contest.

We have, at different points of our perambulations round London, spoken of the fortifications which were erected during the Civil Wars; we may mention here that "a quadrant fort, with four half-bulwarks at Vauxhall," occurs among the defences of London which were ordered to be set up by he Parliament in 1642.

The late Mr. Loudon, as already stated by us,[*] proposed to make a series of boulevards round London. His line, if carried out, would have come down from Hyde Park to Vauxhall Bridge, and thence have passed through the heart of Vauxhall to Kennington, and so on through Camberwell to Greenwich.

The Tradescants and Morlands, of whom we have already spoken, were not the only distinguished inhabitants of this locality in former times, for among its residents was the celebrated man of science, the Marquis of Worcester, so well known as the author of the "Century of Inventions," if not as the inventor of the steam-engine. He lived at Vauxhall for some years after the Restoration, from 1663 down to his death in 1667, probably holding the post of superintendent of some works under the Government connected with the army and navy. Here he set up his "water-commanding engine," which was naturally a great curiosity in those days, when science was at a low ebb. On this he spent nearly £60,000, and had to pay the penalty of obloquy and calumny, which always attach to great minds in advance of their age. His thanksgiving to Almighty God for "vouchsafing him an insight into so great a secret of nature beneficial to all mankind as this my water-commanding engine," is one of the most touching evidences at once of his humility and his confidence in the wonder-working power of time. To show how little the marquis was known or appreciated in his day, it may be added that, though he died in 1667, it is not certain whether he died here or at the residence of his family, Beaufort House, in the Strand.[†]

Near Vauxhall Bridge are the large works of the London Gas Company, established in 1833.

Though situated on the south of the Thames, the company is not wrongly named, for its mains are carried across Vauxhall Bridge, and extend over a considerable distance of Pimlico, which they supply.

Close by the gas-works is the Nine Elms pier, so called from some lofty trees which formerly grew there, but were cut down before the South-Western Railway marked the spot for its own. As stated

its career by stepping in between them at Battersea Fields."

We have already spoken of the glass-works, which formed one of the centres of industry for which Vauxhall was formerly celebrated; another scene of industry in our own time was Messrs. Price's candle factory, which was for many years one of the most interesting sights in London. There were formerly two establishments in con-

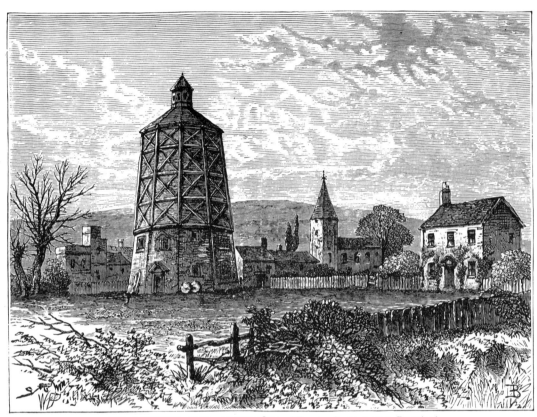

OLD BATTERSEA MILL, ABOUT 1800. (*From a Contemporary Drawing.*)

by us in a previous chapter, the South-Western Railway originally had its London terminus here, the line not being allowed to be brought direct into London;* but upon the extension of the line to the Waterloo Road, in the year 1848, the old station was converted into a goods depôt. The railway works here cover a vast extent of ground on either side of the main line, and give employment to a large number of hands. Mr. T. Miller, in his " Picturesque Sketches of London" (1852), writes :—" Wandsworth had set out in good earnest to reach Lambeth, and would soon have been near the Nine Elms Station had not Government stopped

nection with the firm, known as Belmont, at Vauxhall, and Sherwood, in York Road, Battersea; the latter, however, which was by far the largest, alone remains, and the large corrugated iron roofs of the buildings are doubtless well known to the reader who is in the habit of passing frequently up the river. The works cover upwards of thirteen acres of ground, six of which are under cover, and they give employment to about one thousand hands. It may be added that this factory covers the site of old York House, of which we shall have more to say presently. The neighbourhood would appear to have been, at the early part of the present century, pretty well supplied with inns and taverns; at all events, a manuscript list, dated about 1810, enumerates " The Bull," " The Elephant and

* This was the case also with the North-Western Railway, the London terminus of which was originally at Chalk Farm; see Vol. V., p. 350.

Castle," "The Bridge House," "The Vauxhall Tap," "The White Lion," "The King's Arms," "The Lion and Lamb," "The White Bear," "The Fox," "The Three Merry Boys," "The Red Cow," "The Bull's Head," "The Coach and Horses," "The Henry VIII.," "The Crown," "The Ship," "The Red Lion," and the Nag's Head."

Battersea, or "Patrick's-eye," which bounds Lambeth on the west, is said to have taken

in his "Circuit of London," writes :—"The family seat was a venerable structure, which contained forty rooms on a floor; the greatest part of the house was pulled down in 1778. On the site of the demolished part are erected a horizontal air-mill and malt distillery. The part left standing forms a dwelling-house; one of the parlours, fronting the Thames, is lined with cedar, beautifully inlaid, and was the favourite study of Pope, the

YORK HOUSE (1790).   (*From a Contemporary Print.*)

its name from St. Patrick or St. Peter, because in ancient days it belonged to the Abbey of St. Peter at Westminster. In Domesday Book, A.D. 1078, it is recorded that "S. Peter of Westminster holds Patricesy." The manor, with the advowson, was granted by King Stephen to the abbot and convent of Westminster; but at the Dissolution they again reverted into the hands of the Crown. Charles I., however, granted them to Sir Oliver St. John, ancestor of Lord Bolingbroke, from whose family they passed by sale to that of Lord Spencer. By the ancient custom of this manor lands were to descend to younger sons; but if there are no sons, they were divided equally among the daughters.

Henry St. John, Viscount Bolingbroke and Lord St. John of Battersea, died here in 1751. Hughson,

scene of many a literary conversation between him and his friend Bolingbroke. The mill, now [1808] used for grinding malt for the distillery, was built for the grinding of linseed. The design was taken from that of another, on a smaller scale, constructed at Margate. Its height, from the foundation, is one hundred and forty feet, the diameter of the conical part fifty-four feet at the base and forty-five at the top. The outer part consists of ninety-six shutters, eighty feet high and nine inches broad, which, by the pulling of a rope, open and shut in the manner of Venetian blinds. In the inside, the main shaft of the mill is the centre of a large circle formed by the sails, which consist of ninety-six double planks, placed perpendicularly, and of the same height as the planks that form the shutters. The wind rushing through the openings of these shutters acts with great power upon the sails, and, when it blows fresh, turns the mill with prodigious rapidity; but this may be moderated in an instant, by lessening the apertures between the shutters, which is effected, like the entire stopping of the mill, as before observed, by the pulling of a rope. In this mill are six pairs of stones, to which two pairs more may be added. On the site of the garden and terrace have been erected extensive bullock houses, capable of holding 650 bullocks, fed with the grains from the distillery mixed with meal." The above-mentioned mill (see page 468) has long been removed, or, at any rate, considerably altered, and a flour-mill now occupies the site. John Timbs, in his " Curiosities of London," tells us that the mill resembled a gigantic packing-case, which gave rise to an odd story, that " when the Emperor of Russia was in England he took a fancy to Battersea Church, and determined to carry it off to Russia, and had this large packing-case made for it; but as the inhabitants refused to let the church be carried away, the case remained on the spot where it was deposited."

When Sir Richard Phillips took, in 1816, his " Morning Walk from London to Kew," he found still standing a small portion of the family mansion in which Lord Bolingbroke had been born, and, like Hughson before him, he tells us that it had been converted into a mill and distillery, though a small oak parlour had been carefully preserved. In this room Pope is said to have written his " Essay on Man;" and in Bolingbroke's time the house was the constant resort of Swift, Arbuthnot, Thomson, and David Mallet, and all the cotemporary *literati* of English society. The oak room was always called " Pope's Parlour," and doubtless was the very identical room which was assigned to the poet whenever he came from London, or from Twickenham, as a guest to Battersea.

Happening to inquire for some ancient inhabitant of the place, Sir Richard was introduced to a chatty and intelligent old woman, a Mrs. Gillard, who told him that she well remembered Lord Bolingbroke's face; that he used to ride out every day in his chariot, and had a black patch on his cheek, with a large wart over one of his eyebrows. She was then but a child, but she was taught always to regard him as a great man. As, however, he spent but little in the place, and gave little away, he was not much regarded by the people of Battersea. Sir Richard mentioned to the old dame the names of many of Bolingbroke's friends and associates; but she could remember nothing of any of them except Mallet,

whom she used often to see walking about the village, wrapped up in his own thoughts, whilst he was a visitor at " the great house." The cedar-panelled room in Bolingbroke House is still very scrupulously preserved; its windows still overlook the Thames, from which the house is separated by a lawn. In three of the chambers up-stairs the ceilings are ornamented with stucco-work, and have in their centres oval-shaped oil-paintings on allegorical subjects.

Henry St. John was born at Battersea in 1678, and was educated at Eton, where he became acquainted with Sir Robert Walpole, and where a rivalship was commenced which lasted through life. At an early age he was distinguished for his talents, fascinating manners, and remarkable personal beauty; and he left college only to continue a course of the wildest profligacy. On his elevation to the peerage, in 1712, his father's congratulation on his new honours was something of the oddest:—" Ah, Harry !" said he, " I ever said you would be *hanged;* but now I find you will be *beheaded !* " Three years later, having been impeached for high treason, Bolingbroke fled to Calais; and shortly afterwards, by invitation of Charles Stuart, he visited him at Lorraine, and accepted the post of his Secretary of State, which caused his impeachment and attainder. In 1723 he was permitted to return home, and his estates were restored to him; but the House of Lords was still closed against him. In 1736 he again visited France, and resided there until the death of his father, when he retired to the family seat here for the rest of his life. He died of a cancer in the face in 1751.

Lord Bolingbroke wrote several works which have handed his name down to posterity. During his life there appeared a " Letter to Swift," the " Representation," " His Case," " Dissertations upon Parties," " Remarks on the History of England," " Letters on the Spirit of Patriotism," " On the Idea of a Patriot King," and " On the State of Parties at the Accession of George I." His correspondence, state papers, essays, &c., were subsequently published in a collected form by David Mallet, his lordship's literary legatee.

Lord Marchmont was living with Lord Bolingbroke, at Battersea, when he discovered that Mr. Allen, of Bath, had printed 500 copies of the " Essay on a Patriot King " from the copy which Bolingbroke had presented to Pope—six copies only were printed. Thereupon, we are told, Lord Marchmont sent a man for the whole cargo, and they were brought out in a wagon, and the books burned on the lawn in the presence of Lord Bolingbroke.

The history of Lord Bolingbroke may be read in his epitaph in the parish church close by, which is as follows :—" Here lies Henry St. John, in the reign of Queen Anne Secretary of War, Secretary of State, and Viscount Bolingbroke; in the days of King George I. and King George II. something more and better. His attachment to Queen Anne exposed him to a long and severe persecution; he bore it with firmness of mind. He passed the latter part of his life at home, the enemy of no national party, the friend of no faction; distinguished under the cloud of proscription, which had not been entirely taken off, by zeal to maintain the liberty and to restore the ancient prosperity of Great Britain."

"In this manner," says Oliver Goldsmith, in his life of this distinguished man, "lived and died Lord Bolingbroke; ever active, never depressed; ever pursuing Fortune, and as constantly disappointed by her. In whatever light we view his character, we shall find him an object rather more proper for our wonder than our imitation; more to be feared than esteemed, and gaining our admiration without our love. His ambition ever aimed at the summit of power, and nothing seemed capable of satisfying his immoderate desires but the liberty of governing all things without a rival."

Of Lord Bolingbroke's genius as a philosopher, the same author observes that "his aims were equally great and extensive. Unwilling to submit to any authority, he entered the fields of science with a thorough contempt of all that had been established before him, and seemed willing to think everything wrong that he might show his faculty in the reformation. It might have been better for his quiet as a man if he had been content to act a subordinate character in the State; and it had certainly been better for his memory as a writer if he had aimed at doing less than he attempted. As a novelist, therefore, Lord Bolingbroke, by having endeavoured at too much, seems to have done nothing; but as a political writer, few can equal and none can exceed him."

Tindal, the historian, confesses that St. John was occasionally, perhaps, the best political writer that ever appeared in England; whilst Lord Chesterfield tells us that, until he read Bolingbroke's "Letters on Patriotism," and his "Idea of a Patriot King," he "did not know all the extent and powers of the English language. Whatever subject," continues his lordship, "Lord Bolingbroke speaks or writes upon, he adorns with the most splendid eloquence; not a studied or laboured eloquence, but such a flowing happiness

of diction, which (from care, perhaps, at first) is become so familiar to him that even his most familiar conversations, if taken down in writing, would bear the press, without the least correction either as to method or style."

Among the residents of this village was Sir William Batten, the friend of Pepys, who records in his "Diary," January 30th, 1660-1, how Lady Batten and his own wife went hence to see the bodies of Cromwell, Ireton, and Bradshaw hanged and buried at Tyburn.

York House, which stood near the water-side, on the spot now occupied by Price's Candle Factory, and is kept in remembrance by York Road, is supposed to have been built about the year 1475 by Lawrence Booth, Bishop of Durham, and by him annexed to the see of York, of which he was afterwards archbishop, as a residence for himself and his successors when they had occasion to be near the Court.

Lysons speaks of the house as standing in his time (the end of the last century), and states that it was formerly an occasional residence of the archbishops; but that for more than a century it had been occupied only by tenants. "Tradition, with its usual fondness for appropriation," he adds, "speaks of Wolsey's residence there; and the room is yet shown in which he entertained Anne Boleyn; but besides the improbability that Wolsey —who, when he was Archbishop of York, lived in as great and sometimes in greater state than the king himself, and was owner of two most magnificent palaces—should reside in a house which would not have contained half his retinue, it is well known that these entertainments were given at York House, Whitehall."

When Archbishop Holgate was committed to the Tower by Queen Mary, in 1553, the officers who were employed to apprehend him rifled his house at Battersea, and took away from thence "£300 of gold coin, 1,600 ounces of plate, a mitre of fine gold, with two pendants set round about the sides and midst with very fine-pointed diamonds, sapphires, and balists; and all the plain, with other good stones and pearls; and the pendants in like manner, weighing 125 ounces; some very valuable rings; a serpent's tongue set in a standard of silver gilt, and graven; the archbishop's seal in silver; and his signet, an antique in gold." Holgate was afterwards deprived of the archbishopric of York, to which he was never restored.

Of the structural details of the ancient parish church of Battersea, dedicated to St. Mary, little or nothing is now known, further than that it is said to have been a "twin sister" church to that of Chelsea on the opposite side of the river, which it much resembled. The edifice was rebuilt with brick in the last century, and in a style quite worthy of that most tasteless era. It is an utterly unecclesiastical and unsightly structure, without aisles or chancel, and almost defies description. A church had stood on the same site·for centuries ; but the present edifice dates only from 1777, when it was erected at a cost of £5,000. The tower is surmounted by a low, heavy-looking octagonal spire, and contains a clock and eight bells. At the east end is a recess for the communion-table, above which is a central window in three divisions. The painted glass in this window, which was re-placed from the old church, contains portraits of Henry VII., his grandmother, Margaret Beauchamp, and Queen Elizabeth, together with many enrich-ments and several coats-of-arms. Most of the old monuments were replaced against the walls of the side galleries. Against the south wall is a monument to an heroic person, Sir Edward Wynter, who seems to have outstripped the boldest knights of chivalry by his exploits, if we may take the epitaph literally :—

"Alone, unarm'd, a tyger he oppressed,
And crushed to death the monster of a beast ;
Twice twenty Moors he also overthrew,
Singly on foot ; some wounded ; some he slew ;
Dispersed the rest. What more could Sampson do ? "

Among the memorials of the St. Johns is that of Lord Bolingbroke, already mentioned, and of his second wife, Mary Clara des Champs de Marcilly, Marchioness de Villette. This monu-ment, which is of grey and white marble, was executed by Roubiliac. The upper part displays an urn with drapery, surmounted by the viscount's arms, and the lower portion records the characters of the deceased, flanked by their medallions in profile, in bas-relief. Another monument com-memorates the descent and preferments of Oliver St. John, Viscount Grandison, who was the first of his family that settled at Battersea. He died in 1630. Sir George Wombwell, of Sherwood Lodge, in this parish, who died in 1846 ; and Sir John Fleet, Lord Mayor of London in 1693, who died in 1712, are also commemorated by marble tablets. In the churchyard are buried Arthur Collins, editor of the " Peerage " which bears his name, and William Curtis, the botanist, author of the " Flora Londinensis."

The parish register dates from the year 1559. In 1877–8 the interior of the church underwent a partial restoration, being re-paved and re-seated with open benches, in place of the old-fashioned pews.

Of late years several other churches and chapels have been erected in the parish. Christ Church, at South Battersea, is an elegant Decorated struc-ture ; it was built by subscription, and opened in 1849. St. Mark's, Battersea Rise, is of the Geometric Middle-pointed style of architecture ; it was built from the designs of Mr. W. White, and was consecrated in 1874. Around the apse is an ambulatory, with steps leading to it from a crypt.

St. George's Church, in Lower Wandsworth Road, dates its erection from 1827 ; it is a large edifice of the Pointed style of architecture in vogue in the thirteenth century, and was built from the designs of Mr. Blore. It was enlarged and repaired in 1874.

There are National and British and Foreign Schools for boys, girls, and infants. The National School, in High Street, was founded and endowed for twenty boys in 1700, by Sir Walter St. John, Bart. ; it was rebuilt and enlarged in 1859, and now affords instruction to about 300 boys. Christ Church Schools are neat buildings in the Grove Road, and were erected at a cost of £4,800.

The Normal School of the National Society, known as St. John's College—for the training of young men who are intended to become school-masters in schools connected with the Church of England—owes its origin to Dr. J. P. Kay and Mr. E. C. Tufnell, assistant Poor-law Commis-sioners. These gentlemen, with a view of making an effort for the production of a better description of schoolmasters than had hitherto generally been met with, visited Holland, Prussia, Switzerland, Paris, and other places, for the purpose of examin-ing the operations of the establishments projected by Pestalozzi, De Fellenberg, and other enlightened promoters of the education of the poor ; and the result of their observations was a desire and hope to establish in this country a Normal School, " for imparting to young men that due amount of know-ledge, and training them in those habits of sim-plicity and earnestness, which might render them useful instructors to the poor." With this view, they were led to select " a spacious manor-house close to the Thames at Battersea, chiefly on ac-count of the very frank and cordial welcome with which the suggestion of their plan was received by the vicar, the Hon. and Rev. R. Eden." That gentleman offered the use of his village schools in aid of the training schools, as the sphere in which the " normal " students might obtain practice and direction in the art of teaching. Boys were at first obtained from the School of Industry at Norwood, and were intended to remain three years in train-ing. With these were subsequently associated some young men whose period of residence was necessarily limited to one year. The institution was first put in operation at the commencement of 1840; and it continued under the direction of Dr. Kay and Mr. Tufnell, supported by their private means, and conducted in its various departments of instruction and industrial labour by tutors and superintendents appointed by them, until the close of the year 1843, when the establishment was put on a foundation of permanency by the directors transferring it into the hands of the National Society. Several Continental modes of instruction had been adopted by Dr. Kay and Mr. Tufnell, such as Mulhauser's method of writing, Wilhelm's method of singing, Dupuis' method of drawing, &c.; and the results of their benevolent experiment were so satisfactory, that a grant of £2,200 for the extension and improvement of the premises was made to them by the Committee of Council on Education, which grant was transferred to the National Society, and forthwith expended in the requisite alterations. New dormitories, a dining-hall, lavatories, &c., were then built; and in the early part of 1846 a large new class-room was erected, and filled with every kind of apparatus for the use of the students. The institution is supported by the National Society's special fund for providing schoolmasters for the manufacturing and mining districts. Only young men are now received as students; and the usual term of training is generally one year and a half. The general number of scholars is from eighty to one hundred.

Another invaluable institution in Battersea is the Royal Freemasons' Girls' School. This institution was founded in 1788, and was originally located in St. George's Fields;* but was a few years ago removed to its present site on St. John's Hill, Battersea Rise. It was established for the purpose of educating and maintaining the daughters of poor or deceased Freemasons. The school, which stands near Clapham Junction Station, and close by the side of the railway, is a red-brick building, of Gothic architecture, and was erected in 1852, from the designs of Mr. Philip Hardwicke; it is chiefly noticeable for its great central clock-tower, and watch-towers at the corners.

At Battersea Rise, which forms the north-western extremity of Clapham Common, many pleasant villas and superior houses have been built; this being "a most desirable situation and respectable neighbourhood." Here the first Lord Auckland had a suburban villa, where he used to entertain his political friends, Pitt, Wilberforce, and others.

"In the last quarter of the eighteenth century,"

writes Robert Chambers, in his "Book of Days," "there flourished at the corner of the lane leading from the Wandsworth Road to Battersea Bridge a tavern yclept 'The Falcon,' kept by one Robert Death—a man whose figure is said to have ill comported with his name, seeing that it displayed the highest appearance of jollity and good condition. A merry-hearted artist, named John Nixon, passing this house one day, found an undertaker's company regaling themselves at 'Death's door.' Having just discharged their duty to a rich nabob in a neighbouring churchyard, they had . . . found an opportunity for refreshing exhausted nature; and well did they ply the joyful work before them. The artist, tickled at a festivity among such characters in such a place, sketched them on the spot. This sketch was soon after published, accompanied by a cantata from another hand of no great merit, in which the foreman of the company, Mr. Sable, is represented as singing as follows, to the tune of 'I've kissed, and I've prattled with fifty fair maids:'—

> " ' Dukes, lords, have I buried, and squires of fame,
>   And people of every degree;
> But of all the fine jobs that ere came in my way,
>   A funeral like this for me.
>   This, this is the job
>   That fills the fob;
>   Oh! the burying a Nabob for me!
> Unfeather the hearse, put the pall in the bag,
>   Give the horses some oats and some hay;
> Drink our next merry meeting and quackery's increase,
>   With three times three and hurra!'"

Mr. Death has long since submitted to his mighty namesake; the "Falcon" is gone, and the very place where the merry undertakers regaled themselves can scarcely be distinguished among the spreading streets which now occupy this part of the environs of the metropolis.

Three bridges communicate across the river with Chelsea: the first is a handsome structure, built on the suspension principle, and called the Victoria Bridge. It connects the Victoria Road, on the east side of Battersea Park, with Chelsea Bridge Road and Grosvenor Road, and has been already described by us.† The next is also a suspension bridge, known as the Albert, built about 1873, and uniting the roadway, on the west side of the park, with Chelsea Embankment and Cheyne Walk, close by Cadogan Pier. The third bridge is the venerable wooden structure known as Battersea Bridge, which connects the older portion of the parish with the oldest part of Chelsea. For more than a century prior to 1874—when certain altera-

---

* See *ante*, p. 350.   † See Vol. V., p. 41.

tions were effected upon it by its new proprietors, the **Albert Bridge Company**—this ancient timber obstruction, by custom and courtesy called a bridge, had been an object almost of dread to all who were in the habit of navigating the above-bridge ,portion of the "silent highway." The

letters patent, and for the sum of £40, the king gave "his dear relation Thomas, Earl of Lincoln, and John Eldred and Robert Henley, Esquires, all that ferry across the River Thames called Chelche-hith Ferry, or Chelsey Ferry." Some adjacent lands were included in the grants, and the grantees

OLD BATTERSEA CHURCH (1790).

history of the bridge stretches away considerably into the past, and taken in connection with the ferry which it was built to supersede, and which belonged to the original proprietors of the bridge, it is directly traceable to the commencement of the seventeenth century. As a rule, river bridges have generally been preceded by ferries, and to this rule Battersea Bridge forms no exception. A ferry which preceded it was in full operation when James I. came to the throne, and presumably belonged to the Crown, inasmuch as by royal

had the power to convey their rights to "our very illustrious subject, William Blake." The Earl of Lincoln was the owner of Sir Thomas More's house in Chelsea,* he having purchased it from Sir Robert Cecil. In 1618 the earl sold the ferry to William Blake, who also had a local interest in Chelsea, inasmuch as he owned Chelsea Park, which had once belonged to Sir Thomas More, and was at one time known as the Sand Hills. This

* See Vol. V., p. 53.

park was sold by Blake to the Earl of Middlesex in 1620.

When the ferry changed hands is not quite certain, but in 1695 it belonged to one Bartholomew Nutt. The ferry appears to have been rated in the parish books in 1710 at £8 per annum. It afterwards came into the possession of Sir Walter St. John, who, as we have seen, owned the manor of Battersea and other estates in Surrey. He died in 1708, and the ferry, with the rest of the property, went to his son Henry, who died in 1742, having left it to his son, Henry, the famous Viscount Bolingbroke, who died childless in 1751, bequeathing his estates to his nephew, Frederick. In the year 1762 the nephew obtained an Act of Parliament, under which he sold the

being only a fragile structure, as special powers are granted to the earl to sue watermen injuring it by boat or vessel. Provision is also made on behalf of the public by a clause which enacts that in the event of a tempest or unforeseen accident rendering the bridge "dangerous or impracticable," the earl

THE TROPICAL GARDENS, BATTERSEA PARK.

shall provide a convenient ferry, charging the same tolls as on the bridge. The bridge, however, was not constructed until several years after the Act of Parliament had been obtained, and between the years 1765

manorial property to the trustees of John, Earl Spencer. In 1766 Earl Spencer obtained an Act of Parliament which empowered him to build the present bridge at his own expense at the ferry, and to secure land for the approaches. The tolls named in the Act are one halfpenny for foot-passengers, as at the present time, and fourpence for a cart drawn by one horse, or double the toll now charged. The framers of the Act appear to have contemplated the possibility of the bridge

and 1771 it is on record that the ferry produced an average rental of £42 per annum. In the latter year Lord Spencer associated with himself seventeen gentlemen, each of whom was to pay £100 as a consideration for the fifteenth share in the ferry, and all the advantages conferred on the earl by the Act of 1766. They were also made responsible for a further payment of £900 each towards the construction of a bridge. A contract was entered into with Messrs. Phillips and

Holland to build the bridge for £10,500. The works were at once commenced, and by the end of 1771 it was opened for foot passengers, and in the following year it was available for carriage traffic. Money had to be laid out in the formation of approach roads, so that at the end of 1773 the total amount expended was £15,662.

For many years the proprietors realised only a small return upon their capital, repairs and improvements absorbing nearly all the receipts. In the severe winter of 1795 considerable damage was done to the bridge by reason of the accumulated ice becoming attached to the piles, and drawing them on the rise of the tide; and in the last three years of the eighteenth century no dividends were distributed. In 1799 one side of the bridge was lighted with oil lamps, and it was the only wooden bridge across the Thames which at that time possessed such accommodation. In 1821 the dangerous wooden railing was replaced by a hand-rail of iron; and in 1824 the bridge was lighted with gas, the pipes being brought over from Chelsea, although Battersea remained unlighted by gas for several years afterwards.

Further structural improvements were made from time to time, one of which consisted of laying the bridge with a flooring of cast-iron plates, on which the metal of the roadway rests. At various times, too, the proprietors have expended considerable sums of money in making a road on Wandsworth Common, and, in conjunction with Battersea parish, in improving ways of approach to the bridge. The proprietors, moreover, have often expressed their willingness to contribute towards some alteration of the water-way of the bridge for the benefit of the public. In this, however, it was but reasonable that they should expect to be joined by the Conservators of the Thames, or others interested in the improvement. This expectation not being realised, they declined to bear the whole cost. Until 1873 the bridge remained in the hands of the descendants or friends of the original proprietors. In that year, however, the bridge came into the possession of the Albert Bridge Company, under their Act of Incorporation; and it was by this company, as stated above, that the recent improvements were carried out, the same being made obligatory by that Act.

The extreme length of the bridge is 726 feet, and its width twenty-four feet, including the two pathways. It originally consisted of nineteen openings, varying from thirty-one feet in the centre to sixteen feet at the ends, the piers being formed of groups of timber piles. There is a clear headway of fifteen feet under the centre span at Trinity high-water. The bridge does not cross the river in a direct line, but is built upon a slight curve in plan —the convexity being on the upper or western side. The alterations above mentioned comprise the widening of the water-way at two points in the bridge, for which purpose four of the spans have been converted into two. The centre opening is now seventy-five feet wide, with the same headway as before. The other widening of the water-way is at a point near the northern or Chelsea end. By these alterations greater facilities for river traffic have been afforded, while the old bridge has been considerably strengthened by means of the iron girders and extra piles which have been added to it.

A quarter of a century ago the locality then known as Battersea Fields was one of the darkest and dreariest spots in the suburbs of London. A flat and unbroken wilderness of some 300 acres, it was the resort of costermongers and "roughs," and those prowling vagabonds who call themselves "gipsies." The week-day scenes here were bad enough; but on Sundays they were positively disgraceful, and to a great extent the police were powerless, for the place was a sort of "no man's land," on which ruffianism claimed to riot uncontrolled by any other authority than its own will. Pugilistic encounters, dog-fights, and the rabble coarseness of a country fair in its worst aspect were "as common as blackberries in the autumn." But at length the "strong arm of the law" interfered, and the weekly "fair"—if such it might be called—was abolished by the magistrates in May, 1852.

Duels have sometimes been fought in Battersea Fields, the lonely character of the neighbourhood causing it to be selected for this special purpose. One of the most noted of these "affairs of honour" took place in 1829. In that year the Duke of Wellington got into "hot water" for the part he had taken in the passing of the Catholic Relief Bill. Abuse fell upon him fast and furious; and the young Earl of Winchilsea—one of the leaders of the anti-Catholic party—went so far as to publish a violent attack on his personal character. The duke having vainly endeavoured to induce the earl to retract his charges, sent him a challenge, and the combatants met in Battersea Fields on the 21st of March, but fortunately separated without injury to either. Lord Winchilsea, after escaping the duke's shot, fired in the air, and then tendered the apology which ought to have been made at the outset.

On the river-side the monotony of blackguardism was somewhat relieved by a glaring tavern, known as the "Red House"—but more frequently called by cockneys the "Red-'us," as every reader of "Sketches by Boz" will remember—in the grounds of which pigeon-shooting was carried on by the cream of society till superseded by the more fashionable Hurlingham. In Colburn's "Kalendar of Amusements" (1840), we read that "pigeon-shooting is carried on to a great extent in the neighbourhood of London ; but the 'Red House' at Battersea appears to take the lead in the quantity and quality of this sport, inasmuch as the crack shots about London assemble there to determine matches of importance, and it not unfrequently occurs that not a single bird escapes the shooter."

The "Red House" has been the winning-post of many a boat-race. In the "Good Fellows' Calendar" of 1826, we read that, on the 18th of August in the previous year, "Mr. Kean, the performer," gave a prize wherry, which was "rowed for by seven pairs of oars. The first heat was from Westminster Bridge round a boat moored near Lawn Cottage, and down to the 'Red House' at Battersea." The other heats, too, all ended here ; and the Calendar adds that, though Westminster Bridge was crowded with spectators, the "Red House" was "the place where all the prime of life lads assembled," and describes the fun of the afternoon and evening in amusing terms.

It is said that about fifty yards west of this spot Cæsar crossed the Thames, following the retreating Britons ; but the fact is questioned. Nevertheless, Sir Richard Phillips, in his "Morning's Walk from London to Kew," tells us that he had more than once surveyed the ford, from the "Red House" to the opposite bank, near the site of Ranelagh. "At ordinary low water," he adds, "a shoal of gravel not three feet deep, and broad enough for ten men to walk abreast, extends across the river, except on the Surrey side, where it has been deepened by raising ballast. Indeed, the causeway from the south bank may yet be traced at low water, so that this was doubtless a ford to the peaceful Britons, across which the British army retreated before the Romans, and across which they were doubtless followed by Cæsar and the Roman legions. The event was pregnant with such consequences to the fortunes of these islands that the spot deserves the record of a monument, which ought to be preserved from age to age, as long as the veneration due to antiquity is cherished among us."

As lately as 1851 Battersea Fields formed, as we have said, a dreary waste of open country. A "Metropolitan Guide" of that year speaks of them as "destined to be shortly converted into a park, with an ornamental lake, walks, and parterres, for the recreation and enjoyment of the people." The fact is, the disgraceful scenes to be witnessed here had become such a glaring scandal that urgent measures had long been in contemplation for its suppression. Happily, just then the demand for open spaces in the outskirts of the metropolis had taken firm hold of public attention, and about this time these fields, instead of being handed over to speculative builders, were devoted to the purposes of a public park. The "Red House," with its shooting-grounds and adjacent premises, was purchased by the Government for £10,000 ; and, under the Metropolitan Board of Works, in the course of a few years, the wilderness was converted into a pleasant garden, and now Battersea Park ranks among the very first of those health and pleasure resorts which Londoners prize so highly and justly. It is now one of the prettiest of London parks, and every year adds charms to its many attractions, the choicest of which, perhaps, is the Acclimatisation Garden, which may be said to flourish here not far from the heart of the metropolis. In Battersea Park palm-trees actually grow in the open air—not under glass cases, as at Kew : indeed, this park is no mean or contemptible rival to Kew Gardens.

The park, which was opened to the public in 1858, contains about 185 acres ornamentally laid out with trees, shrubs, flower-plots, and a sheet of water. For the land £246,500 was paid, and the laying-out made the total cost amount to £312,000. The Avenue is one of the principal features, and forms the chief promenade of the park. The trees are English elms. "To rightly appreciate Battersea Park," observes a writer, "it must not be approached in a hurry. Its numerous beauties are worth much more than a bird's-eye view. And here we would parenthetically remark that a vast amount of good has been done towards the cultivation and encouragement of flowers in our parks within the last two decades. . . . But the palm-trees we would speak of do not flourish in the more aristocratic parks of the metropolis—they have found a home over the water in Battersea Park, the access to which is easy in all directions. Steamers ply to it at all hours of the day ; but we prefer to approach it from quaint old Chelsea and on a bright Sunday in summer.

"Passing among a wealth of vegetation and pavilions which seem to be devoted to the accommodation of the cricket-playing fraternity, a short walk brings us, after deriving much necessary assistance from finger-posts, to the tropical garden; and a pleasanter sight we have not seen for many a long day. Here is the Acclimatisation Garden of London; and if we may believe our own eyes, we are certainly not far behind the brilliant city of Paris, as regards the flourishing condition of these out-of-door palms and rare flowering shrubs. Nearly all the books of travel we know are recalled by the charmingly varied character of the foliage and the quaint peculiarities of the plants. Here is a noble palm, here an aloe, here an enormous nettle-leaved shrub, here a plant with prickles starting up in an angry and porcupine manner all over the leaves, here rare specimens of Alpine flowers, and everywhere beds of brilliant colour artistically arranged.

"It certainly would appear that it is the fashion now-a-days to frame in flower-beds with the rare variations which now exist of the *Sempervivum echeria* and saxifrage plant. Many of these are best explained as an idealised version of the well-known house-leek, and the compact little bosses of plants, though over-stiff, perhaps, to some tastes, make an excellent and compact bordering for flower-beds. They are, no doubt, extremely fashionable, as Kew testifies, and all the largest landscape gardens in the kingdom. No visitor to the Battersea Park Gardens will fail to notice what great attention is now paid to the foliage of plants in contradistinction to the bloom or flower. Plants with grey and brown leaves and sage-green leaves are preferred to bright blossoms; geraniums are encouraged with leaves painted as brilliantly as a chromatrope; variations of the *Perilla nankinensis*, or Chinese nettle, are everywhere seen. And, in order to increase the strange effect of these quaker-like beds, it is the fashion to intermix the plants with paths and mazes of very finely-powdered gravel or silver sand. . . . It is a charming sight, this tropical garden; and amateur or professional gardeners—to say nothing of general lovers of nature—may well study it."

Here the visitor may see, on a small scale, the flora of the Alpine region as well as of the tropics. These and the other beauties of the park are thus described with minute accuracy in "Saturday Afternoon Rambles:"—"Here is the lake, with its fringe of aquatic plants and its beautifully-wooded island, and studded with water-fowl from various latitudes, from the sub-Arctic and sub-tropical regions. . . . Here are Japanese teal, Egyptian geese, South African and Buenos Ayres ducks. Here also are ducks from the far north of Europe, partial to a winter temperature, but still staying on the Battersea Park waters for the whole year round. Among the self-invited guests on this lake is a colony of moor-hens, who 'make themselves at home' along with widgeon, teal, and Muscovy, and pintail ducks. Here the moor-hen has forgotten the sound of the gun, and her behaviour before Saturday afternoon visitors is as tame as that of the familiar Dorking hen. . . . How beautiful is that island yonder, with pendulous trees drooping over its margin! The ground seems well clothed with tall grasses and low brushwood. It should afford a good home and abundant cover for the water-fowl. Doubtless, the swans have good landing-places, a plentiful supply of dead rushes, coarse grass twigs, and other nest-making materials. As we stand looking at the lake, there comes rowing up to us, past the water-lilies, a proud maternal white swan, with quite a flotilla of little mouse-coloured cygnets in her wake—

> "'The swan, with arched neck,
> Between her white wings soaring proudly, rows
> Her state with oary feet.'

There are black swans from Australia here as well. Yonder goes a squadron of ducks, making an arrow-headed track in the water. They sail round the headland in beautiful order, and disappear, uttering strange shrieks. But our afternoon is waning. We must take our leave of the sub-tropical and sub-Arctic scenery at Battersea Park. To what other horticultural grounds, be they public or private, around London shall we go for such sights as these? Here in this park—not in any huge glass conservatory or 'Wardian' case, but under the open sky—are living side by side the Arctic saxifrage, the English rose, the tropical palm, and the desert cactus. . . . Then let no Londoner remain any longer unacquainted with this wonderful vegetation at Battersea. Let him give at least two afternoons of the summer to these sub-tropical and Alpine gardens. None the less will he enjoy the purely English landscape scenery. The more, too, will he delight in the vegetable life and scenery of the zone which lies between these sub-Arctic and sub-tropical regions at Battersea."

Close by the park are some blocks of houses, erected by the Victoria Dwellings' Association as homes for the working classes. The buildings, which were opened in 1877, were intended as models of the dwellings for artisans and labourers, to replace the habitations condemned in various parts of the metropolis under the Act of 1875.

At a short distance eastward of the park are the reservoirs and engine-house of the Southwark and Vauxhall Waterworks Company. The reservoirs cover nearly eighteen acres of ground; and the steam-engines have sufficient power to force the water through perpendicular iron tubes to the height of 175 feet, by which means it is raised sufficiently to supply the inhabitants of Brixton and other elevated places.

Some portion of the ground immediately contiguous to the park is still cultivated as market-gardens; but before the formation of the park, and the recent railway extensions near Clapham Junction Station, some hundreds of acres were devoted to that purpose. The gardens here were long noted for producing the earliest and best asparagus in the neighbourhood of London. Indeed, that this parish at one time enjoyed the reputation of being a place for early fruit and vegetables is shown by the following satirical lines on air-balloons, from the *Spirit of the Times* for 1802 :—

> " Gardeners in shoals from Battersea shall run
> To raise their kindlier hot-beds in the sun."

The produce of these gardens was likewise referred to in the addresses of the candidates at the mock elections of the " Mayor of Garratt," in the neighbouring parish of Wandsworth, as we shall presently see.

In the seventeenth and eighteenth centuries, whilst its neighbour Vauxhall was acquiring fame in consequence of the glass manufactured there, Battersea was celebrated for its enamelled ware, which still fetches good prices, although the manufacture has died out.

But Battersea has other claims to immortality: in spite of the claims of Burton and Edinburgh, there can be little doubt, if Fuller is a trustworthy historian, that one of the ozier-beds of the riverside here was the cradle of bottled ale. The story is thus circumstantially told in " The Book of Anecdote : "—

" Alexander Nowell, Dean of St. Paul's and Master of Westminster School in the reign of Queen Mary, was a supporter of ' the new opinions,' and also an excellent angler. But, writes Fuller, while Nowell was catching of fishes, Bishop Bonner was after catching of Nowell, and would certainly have sent him to the Tower if he could have caught him, as doubtless he would have done had not a good merchant of London conveyed him away safely upon the seas. It so happened that Nowell had been fishing upon the banks of the Thames when he received the first intimation of his danger, which was so pressing that he dared not even go back to his house to make any preparation for his flight. Like an honest angler, he had taken with him on this expedition provisions for the day, in the shape of some bread and cheese and some beer in a bottle ; and on his return to London and to his own haunts he remembered that he had left these stores in a safe place upon the bank, and there he resolved to look for them. The bread and the cheese, of course, were gone ; but the bottle was still there—' yet no bottle, but rather a gun : such was the sound at the opening thereof.' And this trifling circumstance, quaintly observes Fuller, ' is believed to have been the origin of bottled ale in England, for casualty (*i.e.* accident) is mother of more inventions than is industry.' "

CHAPTER XXXV.

WANDSWORTH.

" Dulcia et irriguas hæc loca propter aquas."—*Martial.*

The River Wandle—Manufactories—French Refugees—The Frying-pan Houses—High Street—St. Peter's Hospital—The Union Workhouse--The Royal Patriotic Asylum—The Surrey County Prison—The Craig Telescope—The Surrey Lunatic Asylum—The Friendless Boys' Home—The Surrey Industrial School—The Surrey Iron Tramway—Clapham Junction—Wandsworth Bridge—All Saints' Church—St. Anne's Church—St. Mary's, St. John's, and Holy Trinity Churches—Nonconformity at Wandsworth—Francis Grose the Antiquary, Bishop Jebb, and Voltaire Residents here—Mock Elections of the " Mayors of Garratt "—Wandsworth Fair—Horticulture and Floriculture.

WANDSWORTH, which lies immediately to the south-west of Battersea, on the road to Kingston, is so named from the Wandle. This river, which rises near Croydon, passes through Wandsworth into the Thames under a bridge, which, if we may accept a statement in the "Ambulator" (1774), was called "the sink of the country." This epithet would appear, however, to apply to the bridge rather than to the river ; for Izaak Walton, in his "Complete Angler," mentions the variety of trout found in the Wandle here as marked with marbled spots like a tortoise.

The creek at the mouth of the Wandle forms a dock for lighters and other small vessels, and on its sides are coal-wharves and stores. Higher up the stream are extensive paper-mills, where employment is given to a large number of hands ; then there are Messrs. Watney's distilleries, besides some large corn mills, dye works, match factories, starch factories, artificial manure works, copper mills, &c. Hughson, in his "History of London" (1808), remarks :—"At the close of the last century many French refugees settled here, and established a French church, afterwards used as a Methodist meeting-house. The art of dyeing cloth," he adds, "has been practised at this place for more than

prodigious length, in a pair of shears which will cut asunder pieces of iron more than two inches in thickness, and in the working of a hammer which weighs from five hundred and a half to six hundred pounds ; the timbers employed are of an enormous size, and the wonderful powers of all the elements

THE LAKE, BATTERSEA PARK. (*See page* 478.)

a century. There are likewise several considerable manufactories : one for bolting cloth, iron mills, calico-printing manufactories, manufactory for printing kerseymeres, for whitening and pressing stuffs, linseed-oil and white-lead mills, oil mills, vinegar works, and distilleries." At the iron mills, Dr. Hughson informs us, "are cast shot, shells, cannon, and other implements of war ; in another part the wrought iron is manufactured, and the great effect of mechanic power is exemplified in all their operations—in the splitting of iron bars of

are here made subservient in the production of various tools and implements necessary for man in the arts of war and peace." In fact, Wandsworth, no less than Lambeth, has long been a centre of industry.

It was upon the revocation of the Edict of Nantes, towards the end of the seventeenth century, that many of the French Protestants settled at Wandsworth, and engaged in silk-dyeing, hat-making, &c. They rented and enlarged the old Presbyterian chapel in the High Street, and in it service was performed in French for upwards of a century. "At the parting of the roads to Clapham and Vauxhall," Mr. James Thorne tells us, in his "Environs of London," "is a small burial-ground —the Huguenots' Cemetery—where many old gravestones of Frenchmen remain, some almost illegible. From the many English names on the later gravestones," he adds, "it appears to have been used as the ordinary burial-ground for that end of the

The commons of Wandsworth, Wimbledon, and Putney have been secured and formally appropriated to the public for purposes of recreation, on the payment of a specified rent to the lord of the manor, Lord Spencer.

On the top of East Hill stands St. Peter's Hospital (the almshouses of the Fishmongers' Company), removed hither from Newington Butts.* The edifice, which was completed in 1851, occu-

WANDSWORTH IN 1790. (*From a Contemporary Print.*)

parish when the Huguenot population began to die out."

Aubrey, in his "History of Surrey," tells us that before his time there had been established at Wandsworth a manufacture of "brass plates for kettles, skellets, frying-pans, &c., by Dutchmen, who kept it a mystery." The houses in which this mysterious business was carried on were long known as the "Frying-pan Houses."

The village of Wandsworth—if we may so term it—lies principally in a valley, between East Hill and West Hill; the High Street, which crosses the Wandle, is the main thoroughfare, leading on to Putney Heath, and thence to Kingston and Richmond, the roads branching off to those places on the summit of West Hill.

pies three sides of a quadrangle, with a chapel in the centre, and provides a home for forty-two poor members of the company and their wives. The chief entrance to the hospital is by massive gilded gates, on which appears the motto, "All worship be to God only." The Union Workhouse, close by, is a large brick building, with an infirmary attached; it will hold between 800 and 900 inmates.

In the angle of Wandsworth Common, formed by the West-end and Crystal Palace and the South-Western Railways, on their uniting near Clapham Junction Station, stand three important buildings, namely, the Surrey County Prison, and the Royal Victoria Patriotic Asylums for Boys and for Girls.

* See *ante*, p. 258.

The Patriotic Asylum was founded and endowed by the Commissioners of the Royal Patriotic Fund, which was instituted in 1854 for the purpose of giving "assistance to the widows and orphans of those who fell during the Crimean and more recent wars, and to provide schools for their children." Her Majesty laid the first stone of the Asylum for Girls in 1857, and the building was erected from the designs of Mr. R. Hawkins. The Asylum for Boys is situated some three hundred yards distant, on East Hill. The Surrey County Prison, or House of Correction, was erected in 1851, and covers a large extent of ground. The various buildings are constructed chiefly of brick; and the prison is fitted with all the latest appliances for ensuring order and discipline among the inmates.

At a short distance south of the prison, forming a conspicuous object to passengers travelling on the South-Western main line, or the Crystal Palace and West-end Railway, stood for several years the "Craig telescope." This instrument, the largest which had up to that date been constructed, having a tube 80 feet in length, shaped like a cigar, was erected on this site in the summer of 1852. The object-glass was 24 inches diameter, and its focal length about 76 feet, but it subsequently turned out that the optical qualities of the telescope were not equal to its imposing appearance, or the excellent manner in which it was mounted and supported. The tube, which could be placed in almost any position for celestial observation, was supported at each end, and was slung at the side of a massive central brick tower 64 feet high, while the lower end of the tube rested on a support running on a circular railway. Not fulfilling the original expectations of its proprietor, the instrument was some years ago dismantled and removed.

Another large building on the Common is the Surrey Lunatic Asylum. It was built in 1840, and consists of a centre and wings, with beds for 950 inmates. Prior to the erection of this asylum, Surrey, although a metropolitan county, had not been adequately provided with accommodation for pauper lunatics—a class of sufferers whose twofold miseries must strike deeply into every benevolent heart. It is true that the royal chartered Hospital of Bethlehem is situated in the above-mentioned district; but, from its being a general hospital, its regulations for admission, as we have already shown,* are not such as to meet local demands; hence the provision of an establishment exclusively for the poor of the county became an important object. The site on which the new asylum stands

was a portion of the Springfield Estate, in the hamlet of Garratt, formerly the seat of Mr. Henry Perkins, including ninety-six acres of land, with the mansion and farm buildings, which were retained for the purposes of the asylum, the reception of convalescent patients, &c.

Although the building is, in plan, Elizabethan—being nearly in the form of the letter **E**—the elevation partakes of several styles. It is built of red brick, with white stone quoins, window-dressings, stringing-courses, and parapets, the general effect of which is good; but is injured by the battlemented towers immediately uniting with the naked, unparapeted roofs of the extensive wings right and left of the centre of the design. This portion is in the Domestic style, with pedimented roofs, and gables surmounted with Gothic finials. The principal entrance is by a small but elaborate pointed doorway, on each side of which are small windows; over the doorway is a bold scroll label in masonry. This central portion is recessed, and has three tiers of windows, with an ornamented clock in the gable, and a copper vane over the pediment.

On either side of the centre the façade extends with three small windows on the ground-floor, surmounted by a window in each of monastic character, reaching two storeys in height, contrasting with the small windows immediately above and below them. The flank of this portion of the building is blank, save the massive corbelled chimney. The whole frontage, including the wings, is about 350 feet in length. The principal doors open into a lobby, with a groined ceiling, leading on the right to an ante and committee room, office, &c., and on the left to the superintendent's private apartments. Folding-doors facing the entrance open to what is termed the grand staircase: a lofty chamber, extending the whole height of the building and about twenty feet square, with two tiers of corridors round three sides of it; it is covered in with a groined roof, and lighted by an elaborately-designed lantern. A doorway on the ground-floor communicates with the galleries on either side, leading to the males' wards on the left, and the females' on the right. The first-floor partakes of the same character as the ground-floor for each sex; and two airing courts, for all classes of each sex, enclosed with walls in sunk fences, so as to admit of the patients viewing the surrounding country. At either extremity of the building, in the basements, are large groined work-rooms. The chapel is situated across the gallery on the first-floor, and in the centre of the edifice.

In Spanish Road, near the Fishmongers' Alms-

---

* See *ante*, p. 360.

houses, is another of the many charitable institutions with which this neighbourhood abounds, namely, the Friendless Boys' Home. This is a valuable refuge for boys, from ten to sixteen years of age, " who have lost their character or are in danger of losing it." The average number of boys in the Home is about 200. The institution, which was established in 1852, is one of the oldest of the kind in or near London. The industrial operations carried on here include carpentry, tailoring, shoemaking, and engineering as applied to the steam-engine on the premises ; also chopping firewood for bundles, and making wheel fire-lighters with resin ; gardening, care of horses, &c. A kindred institution to the above is the Surrey Industrial

Clapham Junction Station, at the north-eastern extremity of the common, although really in Battersea parish, may be more fittingly mentioned here. The station itself, which was at first one of the most inconvenient, was rebuilt a few years ago ; and now, with its various sidings and goods-sheds, covers several acres of ground, and is one of the most important junctions in the neighbourhood of London, if not of Great Britain. As will be seen from the diagram which we engrave from Mr. John Airey's " Railway Junction Diagrams," this junction is used jointly by the London and South-Western ; the London, Brighton and South Coast ; the London, Chatham, and Dover ; and the London and North-Western Companies. The number of trains which

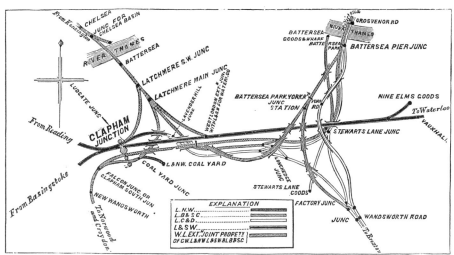

LINES OF RAIL AT CLAPHAM JUNCTION.

School, " for homeless and destitute boys not convicted of crime," situated at Bridge House, on the north side of the High Street.

Wandsworth, we may here state, occupies a foremost place in our railway annals, for here was made the commencement of our modern railways. The Surrey Iron Tramway was laid down in 1801 from Wandsworth to Croydon, and thence to Merstham : in all, about eighteen miles. The line—which was called by abbreviation a " tram " way, from its designer, Benjamin Outram—was formed in order to carry to the water-side the chalk dug out of the sides of the Surrey hills about Epsom. Upon this railroad there worked as a young man Sir Edward Banks, who, by his own ability and energy, rose to become an engineer, and the builder—though not the designer, as generally stated—of three of our noblest metropolitan structures : Waterloo, Southwark, and London Bridges. He lies buried at Chipstead, near Merstham, in Surrey.

call at this station per day on the several lines is 863 ; whilst those which pass through without stopping are 138 ; and it is calculated that on an average about 25,000 passengers may be said to pass through Clapham Junction in every twenty-four hours. In fact, this junction is the most busy railway station in England, and, perhaps, in the world.

Wandsworth Bridge, which spans the Thames, and connects the York Road with King's Road, Fulham, was built in 1873, from the designs of Mr. J. H. Tolmé. It is constructed of iron, and is what is known as a lattice-girder bridge ; it is of five spans, borne on massive coupled wrought-iron cylinders. The three central stream spans are each 133 feet broad.

The parish church, dedicated to All Saints, stands in the High Street, near the bridge over the Wandle ; it is a plain, square, brick edifice, dating from near the end of the last century. The greater part of the tower is comparatively ancient, having been built early in the seventeenth century; it was, however, re-cased in 1841, and has been raised, by the addition of a storey, for the reception of a peal of eight bells. The interior of the church contains a few monuments, preserved from the older fabric; among them, one to Alderman Henry Smith, who is represented in gown and ruff, kneeling at a desk, under an entablature supported by Ionic columns. Alderman Smith was a native of this parish, and came of humble parentage. He is said to have made a large fortune by business in the City, and having been left a widower, without children, in 1620, made over his estates, both real and personal, to trustees for charitable purposes, reserving to himself from them an annuity of £500 a year for his maintenance. His benefactions,* as set forth on his monument, embraced almost every town and village in Surrey, the object being not merely to afford "reliefe" to the needy, but the "setting the poor people a-worke." Among other bequests, Smith left £1,000 to purchase lands in order to provide a fund for "redeeming poor prisoners and captives from the Turkish tyranie;" £10,000 to "buy impropriations for godly preachers;" other moneys to found a fellowship at Cambridge for his own kindred, &c. Alderman Smith died in 1627. Near his monument is that of another benefactor—or rather, benefactress—to the parish: it is a mural monument, with small kneeling effigy of Susanna Powell, who died in 1630. She was the "widow of John Powell, servant to Queen Elizabeth, and daughter of Thomas Hayward, yeoman of the guard to Henry VIII., Edward VI., and the Queens Mary and Elizabeth." Several members of the family of the Brodricks, Viscounts Midleton, are interred here. Their residence was in the hamlet of Garratt, in this parish. The register records the burial (April, 1635) of "Sarah, daughter of Praise Barbone," supposed to be the "Praise God Barebone," the Puritan leather-seller of Fleet Street, whose name is well known in history in connection with Cromwell's first Parliament.

In our account of the Old Kent Road† we have mentioned the fate of Griffith Clerke, Vicar of Wandsworth, his chaplain, and two other persons. They were hanged and quartered at St. Thomas à Waterings on the 8th of July, 1539, for denying the royal supremacy.

St. Anne's Church, on St. Anne's Hill, was built in 1823-4, from the designs of Sir Robert Smirke. It is a large Grecian temple, with an Ionic portico and pediment at the western end. The body of the church is of brick with stone dressings, the portico and pediment are of stone; from the roof rises a circular tower in two stages, and crowned with a cupola and cross. The other churches in Wandsworth are St. Mary's, Summer's Town; Garrett; St. Paul's, on St. John's Hill; and Holy Trinity, near the outskirts of Wimbledon Park. None of these, however, call for any special mention.

Another place of worship here is the Roman Catholic chapel of St. Thomas of Canterbury, which was opened in 1847.

There are many places of worship for Dissenters here; in fact, Wandsworth must be a place specially dear to the Nonconformist heart on account of, at all events, one memory. It is stated by ecclesiastical writers that the first practical movement to secure a Presbyterian organisation in the neighbourhood of the metropolis began with a secret meeting held at Wandsworth. The Dissenting principles of church government and rules of worship, as we learn from Neale's "History of the Puritans," were set forth in a publication called "The Orders of Wandsworth."

Wandsworth has numbered among its residents a few men of note, of whom we may mention Francis Grose, the antiquary, who lived at Mulberry Cottage, on the Common; and Dr. John Jebb, Bishop of Limerick, who died at West Hill in 1833. As already mentioned by us, he is buried at Clapham.‡ On Voltaire's release from his second imprisonment in the Bastile, he was ordered to leave France, and having come to England, was for some time here as the guest of Sir Everard Fawkener. His sojourn in England, observes a writer in the "Dictionary of Universal Biography," "beside that it availed to give him knowledge and command of the language, filled him with admiration of that liberty, civil and religious, in which his own country was so deplorably deficient. In England he learnt to admire, and perhaps to understand, Newton, Locke, Shaftesbury, Bolingbroke, Pope, and other noted writers of the same and of the preceding age. In truth, it was in England that Voltaire found for himself a standing, on the ground of philosophic deism, from which he was not afterwards dislodged by either the reasoning or the ridicule of the atheists of the Encyclopædia. At no point of his course in after life did the virulence of his hatred of Christianity impel him to

---

* Parts of his will were the subject of protracted litigation in 1877-8; but in the end the validity of his bequest was sufficiently established by the Court of Chancery, on appeal.

† See *ante*, p. 250.

‡ See *ante*, p. 324.

abandon this position. . . . During his stay in England—about three years—Voltaire composed the tragedy of *Brutus*, and afterwards, in imitation of the *Julius Cæsar* of Shakespeare, a tragedy, which he did not venture to bring into public on the theatre." His tragedy of *Zaïre*, which he composed in little more than a fortnight, and which proved one of Voltaire's greatest triumphs, is said to have been written during his stay at Wandsworth.

At some little distance on the south side of the High Street is the hamlet of Garratt, which, in the reign of Queen Elizabeth, appears to have consisted of a single house, called "the Garrett," or, as Lysons says, "the Garvett." This building was sold towards the end of the sixteenth century by William Cecil, afterwards Lord Burghley, to a Mr. John Smith. The mansion was afterwards the residence of the Brodricks, Viscounts Midleton, but was pulled down about the middle of the last century, and the grounds which surrounded it were subsequently let to a market-gardener to grow vegetables.

When Lysons wrote his "Environs of London," in the year 1792, this hamlet consisted of about fifty houses by the side of a small common; but the buildings in Garratt Lane—the thoroughfare connecting Wandsworth with Tooting—and its neighbourhood have greatly increased in number within the present century. Various encroachments on the above-mentioned common, about the middle of the last century, led to an association of the neighbours, when, as Sir Richard Phillips tells us, in his "Morning's Walk from London to Kew," they chose a president, or *mayor*, to protect their rights; and the time of their first election of a mayor being the period of a new Parliament, it was agreed that the "mayor" should be re-chosen after every general election. "Some facetious members of the club," he adds, "gave in a few years local notoriety to this election; and when party spirit ran high in the days of *Wilkes and Liberty*, it was easy to create an appetite for a burlesque election among the lower orders of the metropolis." With a keen eye to their own interests, as well as to that of their village and their country, the publicans at Wandsworth, Tooting, Battersea, Clapham, and Vauxhall, "made up a purse," to give it character. Foote, Garrick, and Wilkes, it is stated, wrote some of the candidates' addresses, for the purpose of instructing the people in the corruptions which attend elections in the legislature, and of producing those reforms, by means of ridicule and shame, which are vainly expected from the solemn appeals of argument and patriotism. "Not being able to find the members for Garratt in 'Beatson's Political Index,' or in any of the 'Court Calendars,'" says Sir Richard Phillips, "I am obliged to depend on tradition for information in regard to the early history of this famous borough. The first mayor of whom I could hear was called Sir John Harper. He filled the seat during two Parliaments, and was, it would appear, a man of wit, for on a dead cat being thrown at him on the hustings, and a by-stander exclaiming that it stunk worse than a fox, Sir John vociferated, 'That's no wonder, for you see it's a *poll*-cat!' This noted baronet was, in the metropolis, a retailer of brick-dust; and his Garratt honours being supposed to be a means of improving his trade and the condition of his ass, many characters in similar occupations were led to aspire to the same distinctions."

He was succeeded by Sir Jeffrey Dunstan, who was returned for three Parliaments, and was the most popular candidate that ever appeared on the Garratt hustings. His occupation was that of buying old wigs—once an article of trade like that in old clothes, but become obsolete since the full-bottomed and full-dressed wigs of both sexes went out of fashion. Sir Jeffrey usually carried his wig-bag over his shoulder, and, to avoid the charge of vagrancy, vociferated, as he passed along the streets, "Old Wigs!" but having a person like Æsop, and a countenance and manner marked by irresistible humour, he never appeared without a train of boys and curious persons, whom he entertained by his sallies of wit, shrewd sayings, and smart repartees, and from whom, without begging, he collected sufficient to maintain his dignity of knight and mayor. He was no respecter of persons, and was so severe in his jokes on the corruptions and compromises of power that, under the iron *régime* of Pitt and Dundas, this political punch, or street-jester, was prosecuted for using what were then called seditious expressions; and, as a caricature on the times, which ought never to be forgotten, he was, in 1793, tried, convicted, and imprisoned! In consequence of this affair, and some charges of dishonesty, he lost his popularity, and at the next general election was ousted by Sir Harry Dimsdale, muffin-seller, a man as much deformed as himself. Sir Jeffrey could not long survive his fall; but in death, as in life, he proved a satire on the vices of the proud: for in 1797 he died—like Alexander the Great and many other heroes renowned in the historic page—of suffocation from excessive drinking! Sir Harry Dimsdale dying also before the next general election, and no candidate starting of sufficient originality of character, and, what was still more fatal, the victuallers having failed to raise ,a "public purse" —which was as stimulating a bait to the *independent* candidates for Garratt as it is to the *independent* candidates for a certain assembly—the borough of Garratt has since remained vacant, and the populace have been without a "*professional* political buffoon."

"None but those who have seen a London mob

Robert Chambers, in his "Book of Days," gives a full and detailed account of the scenes enacted here at the mock elections for the "borough of Garratt," which, as we have stated above, always accompanied a general election, as the shadow attends on a substance. He tells us that the local publicans found it to be their interest to encourage the managers of the fun to constitute themselves a committee *en permanence*. On these occasions

THE FISHMONGERS' ALMSHOUSES, WANDSWORTH.

on any great holiday," adds Sir Richard Phillips, "can form a just idea of these elections. On several occasions a hundred thousand persons, half of them in carts, in hackney-coaches, and on horse and ass-back, covered the various roads from London, and choked up all the approaches to the place of election. At the two last elections I was told that the road within a mile of Wandsworth was so blocked up by vehicles that none could move backward or forward during many hours, and that the candidates, dressed like chimney-sweepers on a May-day, or in the mock fashion of the period, were brought to the hustings in the carriages of peers, drawn by six horses, the owners themselves condescending to become the drivers !"

local wits drew up and printed election addresses, squibs, and counter-squibs, &c., and the successful candidates were "chaired" round the town like veritable "knights of the shire." The two last and the most celebrated members for Garratt were those eccentric characters, "Sir" Jeffrey Dunstan and "Sir" Harry Dimsdale, who flourished at Wandsworth whilst Lord North and Pitt ruled in Downing Street. Of these individuals Mr. Chambers writes :—"In 1785 the death of 'Sir' John Harper left 'Sir' Jeffrey Dunstan without a rival ; but in the election of 1795 he was ousted by a new candidate, 'Sir' Harry Dimsdale, a muffin-seller and dealer in tin-ware, almost as deformed as himself, but by no means so great a humourist. The most was made of his appear-

THE GARRATT ELECTION. *(From a Drawing by Valentine Green.)*

ance by dressing him up in a tawdry and ill-proportioned court-suit, with an enormous cocked-hat. He enjoyed his honour, however, only a short time, dying before the next general election. He was the last of the grotesque mayors, for no candidates started after his death; the publicans did not, as before, subscribe towards the expenses of the day, and so the great saturnalia died a natural death." Of "Sir" Jeffrey Dunstan we have already given some particulars in our account of St. Giles's-in-the-Fields,* which was generally the scene of his daily avocations.

The Garratt election has gained more than its fair share of notoriety from the fact that Samuel Foote—who was present here in 1761, and paid nine guineas for a window to view the proceedings—made it the subject of a farce, entitled *The Mayor of Garratt*, which was put on the stage at the Haymarket. The character of "Snuffle" in this play was derived from John Gardiner, a local cobbler and grave-digger, who was one of the candidates, under the title of " Lord Twankum;" that of "Crispin Heeltap" was copied from another candidate, also a shoemaker, who came forward as "Lord Lapstone." The other characters also are identified by Mr. Chambers; "Beau Silvester" being the prototype of "Matthew Mug," the principal candidate in Foote's drama, who says, in his address to the worthy electors, "Should I succeed, you, gentlemen, may depend on my using my utmost endeavours to promote the good of the borough, to which purpose the encouragement of your trade and manufactures will principally tend. Garratt, it must be owned, is an inland town, and has not, like Wandsworth, and Fulham, and Putney, the glorious advantages of a port; but what nature has denied, industry can supply. Cabbages, carrots, and cauliflowers may be deemed at present your staple commodities; but why should not your commerce be extended? Were I, gentlemen, worthy to advise, I should recommend the opening of a new branch of trade—sparrowgrass, gentlemen, the manufacturing of sparrowgrass! Battersea, I own, gentlemen, at present bears the bell; but where lies the fault? In ourselves, gentlemen. Let us but exert our natural strength, and I will take upon me to say that a hundred of grass for the corporation of Garratt will in a short time, at the London markets, be held as at least an equivalent to a Battersea bundle." We have already spoken of asparagus as one of the chief products of Battersea.†

There are in existence three very curious etchings, by Valentine Green, representing the Garratt elections, the scenes in the streets, and the chairing of a successful candidate. All these will be found given in Chambers' "Book of Days," and one of them we reproduce on page 487. It must be owned that the licence assumed during these seasons of misrule was somewhat Fescennine in its character, and that mirth occasionally degenerated into vulgar buffoonery; but, after all, the scene was little more boisterous than that which was witnessed in our fathers' days at many a county and borough election, where popular feeling ran high—especially those at Brentford; and doubtless, the mock elections of Garratt had their redeeming qualities in the safety-valve which they afforded to discontented spirits.

In 1826 an attempt was made, though without success, to revive the whimsical farce. A placard was prepared and issued to forward the interests of a certain "Sir John Paul Pry," who was to come forward, along with "Sir Hugh Allsides" (one Cullendar, the beadle of All Saints' Church) and "Sir Robert Needale" (Robert Young, a surveyor of roads), described as "a friend to the ladies who attend Wandsworth Fair." This placard, which may be read in Hone's "Every-day Book," displays a "plentiful lack of wit" compared with those of the last century. The project, therefore, failed, and Garratt, in consequence, has had no representative since the worthy muffin-seller mentioned above.

Like Blackheath, Peckham, Camberwell, and other suburban spots round London which we have visited in the course of our perambulations, Wandsworth once had its annual fair, which was abolished only within the memory of living persons. From "Merrie England in the Olden Time" we learn that at the end of the last century spectators were invited to see exhibited here "Mount Vesuvius, or the burning mountain by moonlight; rope and hornpipe-dancing; a forest, with the humours of lion-catching; tumbling by the young Polander, from Sadler's Wells; several diverting comic songs; a humorous dialogue between Mr. Swatchall and his wife; sparring-matches; the *Siege of Belgrade*, &c.—and all for threepence!" In the year 1840 the fair was attended by the theatrical caravan of Messrs. Nelson and Lee, and by other lesser attractions.

Between Wandsworth Common and Garratt Lane formerly stood Burntwood Grange, the seat of H. Grisewood, Esq. It was noted for its magnificent gardens and conservatory, which are described in Bohn's "Pictorial Hand-book of London," where views are given of the exterior

---

* See Vol. III., p. 206. † See *ante*, p. 479.

and interior of the conservatory and of the dairy adjoining. The gardens of S. Rucker, Esq., on West Hill, are, or were till recently, remarkable for the great variety of flowering trees and shrubs; indeed, horticulture and floriculture seem to have been extensively practised in this locality for many years, for, like Battersea in former times, Wands-worth is mentioned by Lysons, in 1795, as abound-ing in market-gardens. It may be added that this place a century ago had about it all the adjuncts of a country life, for a picture painted in 1786 shows the reapers in the corn-fields here, and a windmill in full operation at the foot of the slope of the hill which it covers.

CHAPTER XXXVI.

PUTNEY.

" Antiquasque domos !"—Virgil.

The Fishery which formerly existed here—Putney Ferry—High Street—Fairfax House—Chatfield House—The " Palace "—The Bridge of Boats—Putney House—The Almshouses—The Watermen's School—Cromwell Place—Grove House—D'Israeli Road—Nicholas West, Bishop of Ely—Wolsey's Secretary, Cromwell—An Incident in the Life of Wolsey—Bishop Bonner's House—Essex House—Lime Grove—The Residence of Edward Gibbon, the Historian—David Mallet, the Scotch Poet—John Tolland and Theodore Hook Residents here—Mrs. Shelley—Putney School—Douglas Jerrold—Bowling-Green House—Death of William Pitt—The Residence of Mrs. Siddons—James Macpherson—The Fire-proof House, and the Obelisk—The Royal Hospital for Incurables—Putney Heath—Celebrated Duels fought here—Duel between the Duke of Buckingham and the Earl of Shrewsbury at Barn-elms—Reviews on Putney Heath—Putney Park—Wimbledon Common—The Meetings of the Rifle Volunteers—The Oxford and Cambridge Boat-races—Evelyn's Visits to Putney—Putney Church—The Residence of Gibbons' Grandfather—Putney Bridge—The Aqueduct of the Chelsea Waterworks.

In this chapter we have, fortunately, to guide us the experience of a local antiquary, Miss Guthrie, whose work on the "Old Houses of Putney" deserves some formal recognition from the Society of Antiquaries, as an attempt to rescue from oblivion a variety of mansions which are of historic and national interest. It is almost needless to say that we have here drawn largely on her work for trust-worthy information. Putney, which lies between Wandsworth and Barnes, and forms part of the manor of Wimbledon, was at a very remote period a place of some little importance, in consequence of the "fishery" which existed here. The first mention of the name—which occurs in the " Domes-day Book," where it is styled " Putenhie "—is in connection with the fishery and ferry. According to an ancient custom of the Manor of Wimbledon, " out of every fishing-room belonging to Mortlake and Putney, several salmons were due to be delivered there for the licence or liberty of fishing and hauling and pitching their nets on the soil and shore of the lord of the manor." In 1663 the fishery was held for the three best salmon caught in March, April, and May; but this rent was after-wards converted into a money payment. At the sale of Sir Theodore Jansen's estates, on account of his complicity in the "South Sea Bubble," it was let for six pounds, but was afterwards raised to eight pounds. It brought the latter sum till 1786, since which period the "fishery," as such, has been abandoned, although, as we learn from Lysons' "Environs" and Faulkner's "History of Fulham," fishing continued to be carried on here till the early part of the present century. The salmon caught here are described as being very few in number, but of remarkably fine quality; whilst smelt were in great abundance in the months of March and April, and were highly esteemed. One or two sturgeons were generally taken in the course of a year, and occasionally a porpoise, which, to-gether with the sturgeons, were claimed by the Lord Mayor. The fishermen were bound to deliver them as soon as caught to the water-bailiff. " For a porpoise they received a reward of fifteen shillings, and a guinea for a sturgeon."

The ferry here, at the time of the Conquest, yielded a toll of twenty shillings to the lord of the manor. In ancient times, it appears, it was customary for people travelling from London in this direction to proceed as far as Putney by water. During the reign of Elizabeth it was decreed that if any waterman neglected to pay to the owner of this ferry the sum of one halfpenny for every stranger, and a farthing for each inhabitant of Putney, he should pay a fine of two shillings and sixpence to the lord of the manor. The ferry continued to be of importance till early in the reign of George II., when it was superseded by a wooden bridge across the Thames from Putney to Fulham, of which we shall speak more fully presently.

As a town or village Putney now possesses little to recommend it, except its ancient houses, which are still very numerous. The High Street extends from the river-side up to the Heath : it is a broad thoroughfare, and contains an average supply of shops and places of business. There are those still living who remember this street when it had one very broad pavement shaded by stately trees, and a kennel on either side, by means of which the roadway was watered in summer.

Fairfax House, in the High Street, the finest of all the above-mentioned manors of Putney, is believed to have been built by a gentleman of that name in the reign of Queen Elizabeth. It is even said that her Majesty dined here upon one occasion. At the back of the house is a spacious lawn, the trees in which are said to have been planted by Bishop Juxon.

Chatfield House, also in the High Street, is rendered interesting from the circumstance that Leigh Hunt died there while on a visit to its occupant.

On a portion of the ground now occupied by River Street and River Terrace, stood in former times a building which in its latter days became known as "the Palace," from the fact of its having been frequently honoured by the presence of royalty. Miss Guthrie tells us that it is described as having been a spacious red-brick mansion of the Elizabethan style of architecture, forming three sides of a square, with plate-glass windows overlooking the river, and that it possessed extensive gardens and pleasure-grounds. It was built within a court-yard, and approached through iron gates.

This house covered the site of the ancient mansion of the Welbecks, whose monument, dated 1477, is in the parish church close by. The building was erected at the end of the sixteenth century by John Lacy, "a citizen and clothworker of London;" and the ceilings of one of the rooms, it is stated, comprised the arms of the Clothworkers' Company among its ornamentation. Mr. Nichols, in his "Progresses of Queen Elizabeth," says that she "honoured Lacy with her company more frequently than any of her subjects." Indeed, from the churchwardens' accounts at Fulham, it seems that her Majesty visited Mr. Lacy at least a dozen times between the years 1579 and 1603; that she frequently dined with this highly-favoured host, and sometimes sojourned for two or three days under his hospitable roof; and that the last occasion of her visit there was only about three months before her death.

A survey of Wimbledon Manor, written in 1617, mentions the circumstance of James I. having been in this house. His Majesty was himself a member of the Clothworkers' Company. King James and his queen, we are told, "went from Putney to Whitehall previously to their coronation." A few years later the house in which the "maiden queen" and "gentle Jamie" had spent so many pleasant hours was occupied by General Fairfax.

In 1647, Cromwell, equally jealous of the Parliament and of the king, who was then at Hampton Court, fixed the head-quarters of his army at Putney in order to watch their respective movements. The houses of the principal inhabitants were occupied by the general officers, who, during their residence here, held their councils in the parish church, and sat with their hats on round the communion-table, relieving the monotony of their deliberations by psalm-singing or a sermon from some popular preacher. In Whitelocke's "Memorials," under date September 18, 1647, we read:—"After a sermon in Putney Church, the general, many great officers, field officers, inferior officers, and agitators, met in the church, debated the proposals of the army, and altered some few things in them, and were full of the sermon, which was preached by Mr. Peters." Old deceased historians and local authorities, we may here state, differ widely in their accounts of the manner in which Cromwell passed his time while domiciled at Putney. Thus, while the former represent him as being entirely engrossed with State affairs— holding conferences, and issuing mandates all tending to the future overthrow of royalty; the latter, on the other hand, would lead us to believe that his *one* thought was the beautifying of the place, and that his chief occupation was the planting of mulberry-trees all over Putney.

On the escape of the king from Hampton, on the 13th of November, the army quitted Putney, after a residence of three months.

After the battle of Brentford, the Earl of Essex determined to follow the king into Surrey, and a bridge of boats was constructed for that purpose between Fulham and Putney. The structure is thus referred to in a newspaper paragraph of the period:—"The Lord General hath caused a bridge to be built upon barges and lighters over the Thames between Fulham and Putney, to convey his army and artillery over into Surrey, to follow the king's forces; and he hath ordered that forts shall be erected at each end thereof to guard it; but for the present the seamen, with long boats and shallops full of ordnance and musketeers, lie there upon the river to secure it."

The "Palace," at the time when it was occupied by General Fairfax, is described in a newspaper of the period, printed by the authority of Parliament, as belonging to Mr. Wymondsold, "the high sheriff." It was afterwards held by Sir Theodore Jansen, from whose trustees it was purchased by Paul d'Aranda, whose daughter, generally styled Madame d'Aranda, was its owner at the commencement of the present century, when Lysons wrote his " Environs." On the death of this lady the house was thrown into Chancery, and after the lapse of the usual term of years, none out of the many heirs who presented themselves having made good their claim to the property, it was disposed of to a clergyman, who speedily levelled with the ground all that remained of the interesting old mansion. A portion of River Street, Gay Street, &c., are erected on what was once the gardens and pleasure-grounds. The stately iron gates, which in their time had opened wide to admit the "fantastic Elizabeth," the "ungainly James," and, when royalty for the time was nodding to its fall, the martial form of General Fairfax, were degraded into an entrance to a brush manufactory; whilst on a part of the once beautifully laid-out garden was erected " a shed or booth, where on Sunday afternoons active maidens disposed of fruit, lemonade, &c., to carefully-got-up young gentlemen, who came hither in crowds to breathe a purer air than that afforded them in the mighty city—Putney being at the time of which we speak a favourite resort with the citizens."

In close proximity to " the Palace " was formerly another ancient building, the residence of the Hochepieds and Larpents; and on the site now occupied by two large ranges of buildings known as " The Cedar Houses," stood at one time Putney House, and also another mansion called " The Cedars." Putney House, in the early part of the last century, was the residence of Mr. Gerard van Neck, who lived here in a style of great splendour, and, it is said, was frequently visited by George II., who stayed here as his guest during his hunting expeditions in the neighbourhood of Putney. For several years Putney House and The Cedars were in the occupation of the Hon. Leicester and the Hon. Lincoln Stanhope, brothers of the fourth Earl of Harrington. Mr. Heneage Legge, the latest occupant of Putney House, was well known for his benevolence. He seems to have been, too, a true son of the Church, and showed his appreciation of his pastor in a manner which, to him, must have been peculiarly agreeable. " Daily a knife and fork were laid on his table for the special use of the Rev. Henry St. Andrew St. John, should he choose to avail himself of the good old squire's free-hearted hospitality, while a saddle-horse was kept in readiness for him whenever he felt inclined for equestrian exercise."

About the year 1839 Putney House was converted into a College for Civil Engineers, which was founded by subscriptions among the nobility and others, for the purpose of conferring a superior education on the sons of respectable persons in the engineering, mathematical, and mechanical sciences. The college was broken up in 1857, and the fine old mansion pulled down.

At the foot of Starling Lane stood the residence of Sir Abraham Dawes, the founder of the almshouses which bear his name in Wandsworth Lane. Sir Abraham was one of the farmers of the Customs, an eminent loyalist of the reign of Charles II., and one of the richest commoners of his time. The almshouses, were " for twelve poor almsmen and almswomen, being single persons and inhabitants of Putney." For some time, however, only women have been admitted.

The Watermen's School, in Wandsworth Lane, was founded in 1684 by Thomas Martyn, a merchant of London, as a token of gratitude for having been saved from drowning by a Putney waterman. The school is a spacious red-brick building, and in it is afforded maintenance and education for twenty boys, the sons of watermen.

Cromwell Place now occupies the ancient site of Mr. Campion's house, where General Ireton lodged in the year 1646. In Lysons' time this house was a school, in the occupation of the Rev. Mr. Adams. According to a date in one of the rooms, it was built in 1533. Some years ago this interesting old house was taken down, and its materials employed in the construction of the cottage, known as Cromwell Place. The names of Cromwell House and Cromwell Place naturally lead one to suppose that Cromwell himself was quartered somewhere in this neighbourhood. It has been stated that the house he occupied stood at the corner of the High Street and Wandsworth Lane; but the absence of any record of the fact renders it impossible to fix upon this, or any other locality, with any degree of certainty. Grove House, which stood between the High Street and D'Israeli Road, but has been removed to make room for a new thoroughfare, was a fine old mansion, also associated by tradition with the name of Oliver Cromwell. But we cannot guarantee this tradition, for it has been observed— " There is scarce a village near London in which there is not one house appropriated to Cromwell, though there is no person to whom they might be appropriated with less probability. During the whole of the Civil Wars Cromwell was with the army; when he was Protector, he divided his time between Whitehall and Hampton Court."

D'Israeli Road is, of course, of recent formation, composed of middle-class houses. The naming of the thoroughfare seems to have given rise to some little difficulty, and became the subject of proceedings in the police-court; for one enthusiastic resident, taking objection to the name, obliterated it from the house whereon it was affixed, and for so doing was summoned by the Board of Works to answer for his conduct, and had to pay a fine.

Putney is memorable as the birthplace of at least two or three eminent characters. Nicholas West, Bishop of Ely, the reputed son of a baker, was born here ; as also was Thomas Cromwell, Earl of Essex, whose father was a blacksmith in the village. The site of Cromwell's birthplace is still pointed out by

of the papal supremacy he was made Vicar-General of the Spiritualities, in virtue of which office he presided at the synod held in 1537. In the same year he was created Baron Okeham, of Okeham, in Rutlandshire, and three years later was elevated to the earldom of Essex. To support these dignities he had made to him large grants of land, chiefly in Essex ; but he likewise had conferred on him a grant of the manor of Wimbledon. His sudden fall

PUTNEY HOUSE, 1810.

tradition, and is in some measure confirmed by the survey of Wimbledon Manor, quoted above, for it describes on that spot "an ancient cottage called the smith's shop, lying west of the highway from Richmond to Wandsworth, being the sign of the Anchor." The plot of ground here referred to is now covered by the "Green Man" public-house. Cromwell, as every reader of English history knows, was for some time in the service of Cardinal Wolsey, in the character of steward or agent. He became a member of Parliament, and when his unfortunate master was lying under the charge of high treason, distinguished himself by a bold and able defence of the cardinal. The king, we are told, conceived a very high opinion of his abilities, and "heaped on him numerous employments." On the abolition

is well known, and may therefore be here summed up in a few words. Essex had been instrumental in bringing about the union of Henry VIII. and Anne of Cleves ; and the immediate cause of his downfall is said to have been the king's disgust for the royal lady. He was arrested for treason in June, 1540, and in the following month he perished by the hands of the executioner.

Putney is, singularly enough, connected with the following incident in the life of Wolsey :—On ceasing to be the holder of the Great Seal of England, and obeying the royal mandate, Wolsey quitted the sumptuous palace of Whitehall, which Henry had marked for his own, and removed to his palace at Esher. For this purpose he embarked on board his barge at Whitehall Stairs. The news of his "disgrace" had spread abroad, and the Thames soon became crowded with boats filled with men and women, hooting and insulting him, and shouting aloud their delight to see him sent to the Tower; but the indignant prelate threw a defiant glance on his exulting enemies, and instead of *descending* the river to the Tower, as they had been led to imagine he would, he *ascended* it towards Putney. Here he took the road westward

news that you have brought to me, I could do no less than greatly rejoice. Every word pierces so my heart, that the sudden joy surmounted my memory, having no regard or respect to the place; but I thought it my duty, that in the same place where I received this comfort, to laud and praise God upon my knees, and most humbly to render unto my sovereign lord my most hearty thanks for the same.'" Wolsey told the chamberlain that his

LIME GROVE, PUTNEY, IN 1810.

to Esher. As he was riding up Putney Hill he was overtaken by one of the royal chamberlains, Sir John Norris, who there presented him with a ring as a token of the continuance of his majesty's favour. Stow declares that "when the Cardinal had heard Master Norris report these good and comfortable words of the king, he quickly lighted from his mule all alone, as though he had been the youngest of his men, and incontinently kneeled down in the dirt upon both knees, holding up his hands for joy of the king's most comfortable message. Master Norris lighted also, espying him so soon upon his knees, and kneeled by him, and took him up in his arms, and asked him how he did, calling upon him to credit his message. ' Master Norris,' quoth the Cardinal, ' when I consider the joyful

tidings were worth half a kingdom, but as he had nothing left but the clothes on his back, he could make him no suitable reward. He, however, gave Sir John a small gold chain and crucifix. "As for my Sovereign," he added, "sorry am I that I have no worthy token to send him; but, stay, here is my fool, that rides beside me; I beseech thee take him to court, and give him to his Majesty. I assure you, for any nobleman's pleasure he is worth a thousand pounds."

Bishop Bonner is said to have had a residence here, the site of which is now covered by some houses belonging to Mr. Avis. Bonner's house is reported to have contained some good old oak panelling, a portion of which is still in existence; it is described as being of the old napkin pattern, with this peculiarity, that in every panel there was inserted a small cross.

Where the Lower Terrace now stands was at one time a fine old family mansion. Its entrance-hall and public apartments were of stately dimensions, while the kitchen, it is said, afforded unmistakable evidence of having been a private chapel.

Essex House is generally believed to have been built and occupied by Queen Elizabeth's ill-starred favourite, Robert Devereux, Earl of Essex, about the end of the sixteenth century. The royal arms, with the initials E. R., appear in the ornamentation of the drawing-room, and also in one of the bed-rooms. The wainscoting of the various rooms is stated to be of wood which formed a portion of one of the ships of the Spanish Armada. Some weight is given to the tradition that Lord Essex lived in this house by the fact that his Countess was the daughter of Sir Francis Walsingham, who passed the latter years of his eventful life in the quiet seclusion of Barn Elms, which adjoins Putney on the west, and where he was frequently visited by his son-in-law.

At the base of Putney Hill, where the stately trees of former times have given place to modern villas, stood Lime Grove, the seat of Lady St. Aubyn. The mansion derived its name from a grove of limes which formed an avenue to the house. The structure was one of those thoroughly English mansions, erected for convenience and comfort rather than for display. The apartments were spacious and lofty, and contained a rich store of pictures and articles of *vertu;* among the former were several by Opie, of whom Sir John St. Aubyn was an early patron. This house was for some time the residence of the family of Edward Gibbon, who tells us, in his Autobiography, that his grand-father acquired here "a spacious house with gardens and lands," and resided here "in decent hospitality." His father, who inherited the property, had the nonjuror, William Law, as his tutor ; but, in Gibbon's words, "the mind of saint is above or below the present world ; and so, while the pupil proceeded abroad on his travels, the tutor re-mained at Putney, the much honoured friend and spiritual director of the whole family." Here the historian was born, on the 27th of April (old style) in 1737; and his baptism, and that of his five younger brothers and a sister, may be seen recorded in the parish register. He received his early education partly at home, and partly at a day-school in the village, till old enough to be sent to a boarding-school. A great part of his time was spent with his aunt, at the house of his maternal grandfather. This house, he tells us,

was near Putney Bridge and churchyard. It was subsequently tenanted by Sir John Shelley, the Duke of Norfolk, and other members of the upper classes. Here Gibbon spent his holidays whilst at school, until the house was broken up on his mother's death, when he was in his twelfth year.

An amusing story is told of Gibbon in the last volume of Moore's " Memoirs : "—" The *dramatis personæ* were Lady Elizabeth Foster, Gibbon, the historian, and an eminent French physician—the historian and doctor being rivals in courting the lady's favour. Impatient at Gibbon occupying so much of her attention by his conversation, the doctor said crossly to him, 'When my Lady Elizabeth Foster is made ill by your twaddle, I will cure her.' On which Gibbon, drawing him-self up grandly, and looking disdainfully at the physician, replied, 'When my Lady Elizabeth Foster is dead from your recipes, I will im-mortalise her.' "

Another resident of Putney was David Mallet, the Scotch poet, to whom Sarah, Duchess of Marlborough, left £500 for writing the life of the great duke, her lord. His character, as we know from Johnson's Life of him, was immoral ; but, at all events, it seems to have been in keeping with such principles as he had ; for Gibbon, in his " Memoirs," speaks of having been taken to Putney " to the house of Mr. Mallet, by whose philosophy," he adds, " I was rather scandalised than reclaimed."

John Tolland, the deistical writer, spent the latter years of his life in Putney, living in obscure lodgings at a carpenter's, where he died in 1722. Here, too, at the house of the Countess of Guild-ford, on Putney Hill, died Henry Fuseli, the artist, in 1825.

Theodore Hook, in 1825, took a cottage at Putney, of which neighbourhood he had always been fond ; while at Putney he re-wrote—or com-posed from rough illiterate materials—the very entertaining " Reminiscences " of his old theatrical and musical friend, Michael Kelly.

At Layton House was living, in 1839, Mary Wollstonecraft, the widow of the poet Shelley. Whilst resident here, or at the White House, near the river-side, she wrote her husband's " Memoirs." She was the daughter of William Godwin, the author of " Caleb Williams," " St. Leon," and other works, by marriage with Mary Wollstonecraft, who was also eminent as a writer. Mrs. Shelley was the author of " Frankenstein," and other novels ; she died in 1851.

The spacious old mansion in the Richmond Road, long known by the name of Putney School, owing to its having been for generations used as a school, was originally a country residence of the Duke of Hamilton. Here also General Fairfax resided for the space of nine months, during which period he was frequently visited by Cromwell. It is also said that the house was at one time the residence of the notorious Duchess of Portsmouth. This building, which is now called Putney House, was for a short time the Hospital for Incurables,

and bowling; at Marebone * (*sic*) and Putney he may see several persons of quality bowling two or three times a week." Mackay, in his "Tour through England," says that the "Bowling-Green House" was resorted to by the citizens for the purpose of deep play. Horace Walpole, in a letter to Sir Horace Mann, dated August 2, 1750, giving an account of the apprehension of James McLean, the "fashionable highwayman," writes :—"McLean had

FAIRFAX HOUSE, PUTNEY.

previous to its transfer to Putney Heath. On the removal of the hospital, the old mansion was purchased by Colonel Chambers, well known as "Garibaldi's Englishman."

West Lodge, on Putney Common, was for some years the home of Douglas Jerrold, who here entertained many of the men who in a few years were destined to become the leaders of literary thought. Whilst resident at Putney he founded the Whittington Club, and wrote his celebrated "Caudle Lectures."

Putney, two centuries ago, was a place to which the Londoners repaired to play at bowls; such, at least, is the assertion of John Locke, who writes, in 1679: "The sports of England for a curious stranger to see are horse-racing, hawking, hunting,

a quarrel at Putney Bowling-green two months ago with an officer whom he challenged for disputing his rank; but the captain declined till McLean should produce a certificate of his nobility, which he had just received." McLean was executed at Tyburn, as we have stated in a previous part of this work.†

The house at Putney Heath occupied by the "heaven-born minister," William Pitt, and in which he died, was called at that time "Bowling-Green House;" it derived its name from the fashionable place of entertainment mentioned above, and which existed on its site nearly a hundred years before. In the early days of George III. it was

* See Vol. IV., p. 432.   † See Vol. V., p. 195.

celebrated for its public breakfasts and evening assemblies during the summer season. It was occupied for some time by Archbishop Cornwallis previous to Pitt taking up his residence there.

For the following account of Mr. Pitt's death we are indebted to Lord Brougham's biography of the Marquis Wellesley :—" Lord Wellesley," he writes, " returned home from his glorious administration at a very critical period in our parliamentary history. Mr. Pitt was stricken with the malady which proved fatal—a typhus fever, caught from some accidental infection when his system was reduced by the stomach complaint under which he had long laboured. This their last interview was in Pitt's villa on Putney Heath, where he died within a few days. Lord Wellesley called upon me there many years after ; the house was then occupied by my brother-in-law, Mr. Eden, whom I was visiting. His lordship showed me the place where these illustrious friends sat when they met for the last time. Mr. Pitt, he said, was much emaciated and enfeebled, but retained his gaiety and his constitutionally sanguine disposition, and even expressed his confident hopes of recovery. In the adjoining room he lay a corpse within the ensuing week ; and it is a singular and melancholy circumstance, resembling the stories told of William the Conqueror's deserted state at his decease, that some one in the neighbourhood having sent a message to inquire after Mr. Pitt's state, he found the wicket, and then the door of the house, both open, and, as nobody answered the bell, he walked through the rooms until he reached the bed on which the minister's body lay lifeless, the sole tenant of the mansion, the doors of which but a few hours before were darkened by crowds of suitors alike obsequious and importunate — the vultures whose instinct haunts the carcases only of living ministers."

Lord Brougham shows us, in his "Autobiography," what a gentle, good-natured, and entertaining host Pitt could be, in spite of his apparent coldness and hauteur, by telling the story of his friend William Napier, who went to Putney Heath on a visit to Pitt, fully resolved to obtrude his strong Whiggism on his Tory host. " Primed with fierce recollections and patriotic resolves, he endeavoured to keep up, and not to conceal, a bitter hatred of the minister ; but in vain. All hostile feelings gave way to that of unbounded surprise." Brougham adds the following interesting sketch of the famous Lady Hester Stanhope, the niece of the " heaven-born minister :"—" Lady Hester was there. He found her very attractive ; and so rapid and decided was her conversation, so full of humour and keen observation, and withal so friendly and

instructive, that it was quite impossible not to succumb to her, and to become her slave, whether laughing or serious. She was certainly not beautiful ; but her tall, commanding figure, her large dark eyes and varying expression, changing as rapidly as her conversation, and equally vehement, kept him, as he expressed it, in a state of continual admiration. She had little respect for the political coadjutors of Mr. Pitt, and delighted to laugh at them. Lord Castlereagh she always called 'his monstrous lordship ;' but Lord Liverpool she invariably treated as a constant theme for ridicule and contempt."

Pitt, who was only in his forty-seventh year at the time of his death, had been nineteen years First Lord of the Treasury, and died on the anniversary of the day on which, five-and-twenty years before, he had first entered Parliament. " In his neighbourhood," writes Mr. John Timbs in his "Autobiography," "he was much respected, and was a kind master to his domestics. A person who, a little before the great statesman's death, was in the room, stated that it was then heated to a very high and oppressive temperature ; and the deep voice of ' the dying minister, as he asked his valet a question, startled a visitor who had been unused to it. There was long a doubt as to the last words of Mr. Pitt. Earl Stanhope, in his ' Life' of the great minister, gave them from a manuscript left by his lordship's uncle, the Hon. James H. Stanhope, as, ' Oh, my country ! how I love my country !' But upon re-examination of the manuscript, a somewhat obscure one, no doubt was left in Lord Stanhope's mind that the word ' love' was a mistake for ' leave.' The expression, as in this manner finally authenticated, is in perfect and most sad conformity with the disastrous state of the Continental war produced by the battle of Austerlitz, when Mr. Pitt was approaching his end. ' We may roll up that map now,' he said, pointing to a map of Europe on the wall of the Foreign Office, when the news came of Bonaparte's great victory."

Adjoining Bowling-green House is the villa which for the space of two years was the residence of Mrs. Siddons and her husband. Bristol House, which is close by, owes its name to the Bristol family, in whose possession and occupation it was from the commencement of this century till some few years ago. It may be added that James Macpherson, the translator and reputed author of Ossian's Poems, had a villa on Putney Heath.

In 1776 steps were taken here to commemorate the Great Fire of London, although Putney had no close connection with the City. A certain Mr.

David Hartley, the descendant of a namesake who more than fifty years previously had obtained a patent for the construction of fire-proof buildings, attempted to revive public interest in the invention by a series of experiments, to which he invited the presence of royalty. A pillar was erected, mainly at his instance, on the Common, which bears the following inscription :—"The Right Hon. John Sawbridge, Esq., Lord Mayor of London, laid the foundation-stone of this pillar 110 years after the Fire of London, on the anniversary of that dreadful event, and in memory of an invention for securing buildings against fire."

With reference to the above-mentioned experiments, Sir Richard Phillips, in his "Walk from London to Kew" (1817), writes :—"The house, still standing at the distance of a hundred yards from the obelisk, serves as a monument of the inventor's plans ; but, like everything besides, it recently excited the avarice of speculation, and when I saw it was filled with workmen, who were converting it into a tasteful mansion, adding wings to it, throwing out verandas, and destroying every vestige of its original purpose. One of the workmen showed me the chamber in which, in 1774, the king and queen took their breakfast, while in the room beneath fires were lighted on the floor, and various inflammable materials were ignited, to prove that the rooms above were fire-proof. Marks of these experiments were still visible on the charred boards. In like manner there still remained charred surfaces on the landings of the staircase, whereon fires had been ineffectually lighted for the purpose of consuming them, though the stairs and all the floorings were of ordinary deal ! The fires in the rooms had been so strong that parts of the joists in the floor above were charred, though the boards which lay upon them were in no degree affected. The alterations making at the moment enabled me to comprehend the whole of Mr. Hartley's system. Parts of the floors having been taken up, it appeared that they were double, and that his contrivance consisted in interposing between the two boards sheets of laminated iron or copper. This metallic lining served to render the floor air-tight, and thereby to intercept the ascent of the heated air ; so that, although the inferior boards were actually charred, the less inflammable material of metal prevented the process of combustion from taking place in the superior boards. These sheets of iron or copper, for I found both metals in different places, were not thicker than tinfoil or stout paper, yet, when interposed between the double set of boards, and deprived of air, they effectually stopped the progress of the fire." The invention, however, seems to have sunk entirely into obscurity, and few records now exist of it except the pompous obelisk and the remains of the original Fire-proof House, which are still embodied in the present building.

Owing to its healthy and open situation, Putney is a favourite spot for charitable institutions, as it was for two centuries for ladies' schools. One of the most important is the Royal Hospital for Incurables, which is situated on the summit of West Hill, near to the Fire-proof House. This institution was founded in 1854 by the efforts of the late Dr. Andrew Reed. It was established to cherish and to relieve, during the remainder of life, persons, above the pauper class, suffering from incurable maladies, and thereby disqualified from the duties of life. To persons having a home, but without the means of support, a pension of £20 a year is given. The first home of the charity was at the village of Carshalton. At the end of three years it became necessary to secure larger premises, and Putney House was engaged. The accommodation thus secured sufficed till the year 1861, when a second house in the immediate neighbourhood was added as a branch establishment. Two years later the building now occupied as the hospital was purchased, together with the freehold of twenty-four acres of land surrounding it. The edifice, called Melrose Hall, had been a distinguished family residence ; it was well built, and contained a large number of rooms suitable to the purposes of the institution. The building has since been extended by the addition of two wings, and now affords accommodation for 200 inmates. It contains on an average about 150 patients, whilst upwards of 300 are in receipt of pensions from the charity at their own homes. This institution, we may add, is unendowed, and is therefore entirely dependent for its support on the voluntary subscriptions of the public.

Putney Heath, some 400 acres in extent, bears a faint resemblance to that of Hampstead in its slightly broken surface of sand, turf, and heather. From the higher portion some good views of the river and the metropolis are obtained. Like Wimbledon Common, Hounslow Heath, and other open spots round London, this heath in bygone times was a noted rendezvous for highwaymen ; and towards the close of the last century it was the scene of so ghastly a spectacle, that few cared to traverse it after nightfall, for here was set up the gibbet on which the body of the notorious Jerry Abershaw was left to dangle in the wind, after having expiated his numerous crimes on

Kennington Common, which was at that time the place of execution for the county of Surrey.*

The heath has also been from time to time the scene of many bloodless, and also of some bloody, private, and also political, duels. Here, in 1652, an encounter took place between George, third Lord Chandos, and Colonel Henry Compton, which resulted in the latter being killed. Here, too, Mr. William Pitt, when Prime Minister, ex-

Duke of Buckingham, attended by Sir Robert Holmes and Captain William Jenkins; and Francis Talbot, Earl of Shrewsbury, attended by Sir John Talbot and the Hon. Bernard Howard, a younger son of the Earl of Arundel. Pepys, in recording this duel in his "Diary," says it was "all about my Lady Shrewsbury, at that time, and for a great while before, a mistress to the Duke of Buckingham; and so her husband challenged him, and

BOWLING-GREEN HOUSE.

changed shots, on a Sunday in May, 1798, with Mr. George Tierney, M.P.; but, fortunately, the affair ended without bloodshed. In September, 1809, was fought the memorable duel—happily, not a fatal one—between George Canning and his colleague, Lord Castlereagh. This "affair of honour" took place near the obelisk, and close by a semaphore telegraph which was erected by the Admiralty in 1796.

Although not actually on Putney Heath, the record of another "affair of honour" which took place not far off, at Barn Elms, may not be out of place here. This affair took place in January, 1667–8. The parties engaged were George Villiers,

they met; and my Lord Shrewsbury was run through the body, from the right breast through the shoulder; and Sir John Talbot all along up one of his armes; and Jenkins killed upon the place; and all the rest in a little measure wounded." A pardon under the Great Seal, dated the 5th of February following, was granted to all the persons concerned in this tragical affair. Lord Shrewsbury died in consequence of his wound in the course of the same year. During the fight the Countess of Shrewsbury is reported to have held the duke's horse, in the dress of a page. This lady was Anna Maria Brudenell, daughter of the Earl of Cardigan. After the death of her husband she was married, secondly, to a son of Sir Thomas Brydges, of Keynsham, Somerset.

* See *ante*, p. 334.

IN AND ABOUT PUTNEY.

1. The Fire proof House.　　2. Obelisk in Fire-proof House Gardens.　　3. Putney Church, 1825.　　4. Red Lion Inn.
5. Grantham House, Putney Heath.

The heath, however, has witnessed other meetings besides those assembled for the purpose of bloodshed, for here, in May, 1648, the good people of Surrey met to petition the House of Commons in favour of the re-establishment of episcopacy. Charles II. is said to have reviewed his forces on Putney Heath; and in May, 1767, George III. reviewed the Guards at the same place. On this occasion upwards of £63 was taken at the bridge, being the largest amount ever known in one day.

According to Pepys, Charles II. and his brother, the Duke of York, used to run horses here. We find in the "Diary," under date of May 7, 1667 :— "To St. James's; but there find Sir W. Coventry gone out betimes this morning, on horseback, with the King and Duke of York, to Putney Heath, to run some horses."

At the east corner of the heath is Grantham House, the residence of Lady Grantham. On the west side the heath is bounded by Putney Park and Roehampton. The former, styled Mortlake Park in old memorials, was reserved to the Crown by Henry VIII. Charles I. granted the park to Richard, Earl of Pembroke, who here erected a splendid mansion, which, soon after his decease, was sold, together with the park, to Sir Thomas Dawes, by whom it was again disposed of to Christina, Countess of Devonshire. Waller and the other poets of the period sang her praises; and Charles II. visited her at this place with the queen-mother and the royal family. The mansion was at last pulled down by Lord Huntingfield. Roehampton has been an aristocratic part of Putney for more than two centuries.

Southward, Putney Heath merges itself into the more extensive area of Wimbledon Common; but our limited space will not allow of our saying more of this interesting locality than that every July it is the scene of the annual meeting of the National Rifle Association. The old windmill, formerly a picturesque object on the breezy common, has been converted into the head-quarters of the Rifle Association. These annual gatherings are attended by the *élite* of fashion, and always include a large number of ladies, who generally evince the greatest interest in the target practice of the various competitors, whether it be for the honour of carrying off the Elcho Shield, the Queen's or the Prince of Wales's Prize, or the shield shot for by our great Public Schools, or the Annual Rifle Match between the Houses of Lords and Commons.

We must now retrace our steps down Putney Hill, and through the village to the river-side. Here we meet with a few old-fashioned brick dwelling-houses, together with sheds for boat-building, boat-clubs, and boating-houses; for Putney has long been the head-quarters for aquatic matches on the Thames. The day of the annual boat-race between the rival crews of the Oxford and Cambridge Universities, which takes place generally in March or April, has been for many years—indeed, almost without intermission since 1836—a red-letter day in the annals of Putney. For many days prior to the race one or other of the rival crews, while undergoing their preparatory trials and "coaching," take up their abode at the "Star and Garter," a comfortable hostelry overlooking the Thames, or in the private houses in the neighbourhood. And the day of the race itself is looked forward to, not only by the inhabitants of the village, but by the public at large, with almost as much interest as is felt concerning the fate of the "blue ribbon of the turf" when the "Derby" is run for on Epsom Downs. In 1829, the first year of the race, the contest took place at Henley, when Oxford was proclaimed the winner. In 1836, 1839, 1840, and 1841, the course was from Westminster to Putney, Cambridge on each occasion proving the victors. In the following year the Oxford crew came in first, the race being rowed over the same course. From 1845 to 1847 the river between Putney and Mortlake was the scene of the race, Cambridge on each occasion carrying off the honours. In 1849, 1852, and 1854 the Oxford crew were the winners; but in 1856 the Cantabs once more were hailed as the victors. From 1857 to 1860 each year's race was won alternately by the respective crews; but from 1861 to 1869 Oxford came in first on each occasion. The tables were turned, however, in the following year, when Cambridge won the race, and this they succeeded in doing on every subsequent occasion down to 1874. In 1875 and 1876 the race was won alternately by Oxford and Cambridge; but in 1877 the judges decided that the race was a "dead heat." In 1878 and 1879 the race was again won alternately by the contending crews. From 1880 to 1883 inclusive, Oxford came in victorious; but in 1884 the honours were once more carried off by Cambridge. Putney is the starting-point of the race, and Mortlake its goal, and the course is about four miles and a half. The time occupied in the race has varied from about twenty-one to twenty-five minutes. Formerly the race was sometimes rowed from Putney to Mortlake, and at others the reverse way; but of late years the starting-point has always been near the ugly iron aqueduct of the Chelsea Water-works Company, just above Putney Bridge. On the day of the race the usually quiet village of Putney puts on a festive appearance, the place is gay with banners, &c., and many of the inhabitants, no doubt, reap a rich harvest for the time being.

Putney was at one time the starting-place for the Thames Regatta; but other races besides the great University contest still take place here very frequently during the summer months. Before quitting the river-side we may mention that in his "Diary," under date of April 16th, 1649, John Evelyn tells us he "went to Putney by water in barge, with divers ladies, to see the Schooles or Colledges of the Young Gentlewomen." These schools were probably those known to have been kept by a Mrs. B. Makins, who was one of the most clever and learned women of her time, and had been tutor to the Princess Elizabeth, daughter of Charles I.

The river-side of Putney at this time was probably full of picturesque "bits" of rural scenery; for a few weeks afterwards we find Evelyn again making a voyage thither, no doubt by barge, "to take prospects in crayon to carry with me into France."

Putney Church, of which we must now speak, is dedicated to St. Mary, and stands at the bottom of the High Street, near the bridge. It was originally built as a chapel of ease to Wimbledon; the precise date of its erection, however, is unknown. That it dated from, at all events, the beginning of the fourteenth century is certain, as it is on record that Archbishop Winchelsea held a public ordination here in 1302. The ancient structure exhibited the architecture of different periods far apart. The arches and columns which separated the nave from the aisles belonged to Henry VII.'s time, while the north and south walls were said to be coeval with the original building. On the south side of the old church was a small chapel, built early in the reign of Henry VIII. by Bishop West, whom we have mentioned above. In 1836 the church, with the exception of the tower, was rebuilt, from the designs of Mr. E. Lapidge, and in the Perpendicular style of architecture. The edifice is large and lofty; some of the windows are enriched with stained glass. The tower, which is of four stages and surmounted by battlements, is supposed to have been built not later than the middle of the fifteenth century, "from the fact of a coat of arms above the belfry door being appropriated solely to the family of Chamberlyn, a name not found amongst the inhabitants of Putney since that period." On the rebuilding of the church, Bishop West's chapel was removed to the north side of the chancel, where it was rebuilt stone by stone; it is small, and in the

fan tracery of the vaulted roof appear the bishop's arms and initials. Its eastern window of stained glass was presented, in 1845, by Dr. Longley, Archbishop of Canterbury, as a memorial of his mother, who was long a resident in the parish of Putney. There are several monuments and tablets, mostly from the old church, but none of any particular interest. In 1877 the flooring of the chancel was re-laid with encaustic tiles, and the body of the fabric re-seated with open benches in place of the old-fashioned pews.

Pepys, in his amusing "Diary," thus makes mention of visits he paid to Putney Church:— "—— 28th, 166— (Lord's Day). After dinner, by water—the day being mightily pleasant, and the tide serving finely, reading in Boyle's 'Book of Colours'—as high as Barne Elms, and then took one turn alone, and then back to Putney Church, where I saw the girls of the school, few of which pretty; and then I came into a pew, and met with little James Pierce, which I was much pleased at, the little rogue being very glad to see me; his master reader to the church. There was a good sermon and much company. But I sleepy, and a little out of order at my hat falling down through a hole beneath the pulpit, which, however, after the sermon, I got up by the help of the clerk and my stick."

Again, on the 25th ——, we find this entry:— "(Lord's Day.) I up to Putney, and stepped into church to look upon the fine people there, whereof there is great store, and the—young ladies!" A later entry runs thus:—" 2nd —— (Lord's Day). After dinner I and Tom, my boy, up to Putney by water, and there heard a sermon, and many fine people in the church."

To the north of the church, between the church-yard and the bridge, there formerly stood an old red-brick house, surrounded by trees, which at the beginning of the last century was tenanted by Mr. James Porten, a merchant of London, whose youngest daughter, Judith, was the mother of Edward Gibbon, of whom we have spoken above.

At the commencement of this chapter we have spoken of the ferry which in former times was the only means of transit between Putney and Fulham. Down to the commencement of the last century the want of a bridge here was greatly felt; for at that time there was none between those of London and Kingston. When Laud was Bishop of London, he narrowly escaped drowning in crossing from Putney to his palace, one dark night, by the capsizing of the ferry-barge with his horses and suite. In 1671, a Bill for the building of a bridge at this point of the Thames was brought into Parliament, but rejected, several of the members who spoke against it basing their arguments on the assumption that the City of London would be irretrievably ruined if such a project were carried out. An Act of Parliament, however, was ultimately passed, mainly through the instrumentality of Sir Robert Walpole, and the bridge was completed in 1729. Faulkner, in his "History of Fulham," says: "The plan of the bridge was drawn by Mr. Cheselden,

it. When Faulkner wrote his "History of Fulham," in 1813, the *tête du pont* on the Putney side of the river was "still plainly discernible." The position of this bridge of boats was about 500 yards below where Putney Bridge now stands; and the fort on this side of the river is said to have remained intact until about the year 1845, when it was removed; it stood on the site of a market-ground below the "Cedars."

ESSEX HOUSE, PUTNEY.

the surgeon of Chelsea Hospital, who," he adds, "in his profession acquired the greatest reputation, and by the skill displayed in this useful piece of architecture has shown the affinity that exists among the sciences." This, however, as Mr. Chasemore points out, in his "History of the Old Bridge," was a mistake; "the records clearly proving that the bridge was built after a design by Sir Jacob Ackworth, who was also the designer of old 'Kingston, Chertsey, Steans (Staines), Datchet, and Windsor Bridges.'" This was not the first bridge that has spanned the Thames between Putney and Fulham, for, as we have stated above, a bridge of boats was constructed to enable Lord Essex to cross over with his army after the "battle of Brentford." Forts were erected at either end to guard

By the Act authorising the construction of the bridge, the sum of £62 was directed to be divided annually between the widows and children of the poor watermen of Fulham and Putney, as a recompense to their fraternity, who, upon the building of the bridge, were constrained from plying upon Sundays. The proprietors purchased the ferry—which, on an average, produced the owners £400 per annum—for the sum of £8,000. Lysons tells us that on the abolition of the ferry, the Bishop of London reserved to himself and his household the right of passing the bridge toll-free. This privilege stills holds good. Formerly the king paid £100 per annum for the passage of himself and his household over the bridge.

From 1729 down to the present year (1885) the

river here was spanned by a bridge constructed of timber, almost as ungainly in appearance as that of Battersea, which we have described in a previous chapter ;* it was an ugly black structure with no redeeming feature to recommend it in point of taste. The length of the bridge, according to Sir Jacob Ackworth's design, was 786 feet, and the width twenty-four feet, with a clear water-way of 700 feet, with twenty-six openings or locks ; and there were also " on the sides of the way over the bridge angular recesses for the safeguard and convenience of foot-passengers going over the same." The bridge was lighted by oil-lamps, which were removed in 1845, and gas substituted. With this exception, the old bridge remained much in its original condition down to 1870, when two of the locks or openings were thrown into one. Since then three locks have been converted into one; so that there remained but twenty-three openings, instead of twenty-six, as originally.

The approach to the bridge from the High Street, Putney, is built on arches, which are thus referred to by Faulkner :—" On Putney side there is a stone terrace, sixteen feet wide, enclosed from the water by a wall, being the road from the bridge; and to prevent the earth from bulging out, there are arches turned horizontally in the bed of the road, a contrivance well adapted for this purpose, though never used before, by which means this wall has never bent or started, though the tide rises twelve feet against it, and it can be taken down at any time without the least inconvenience to the road." At the Putney end of the bridge stood a quaint little toll-house, of red brick ; and at the Fulham entrance to the bridge there is a double toll-house, very quaint and foreign in its appearance, the roof of which spans the roadway. In 1880 the bridge was purchased by the Corporation of London, and the tolls were abolished.

" Passing down the river," says Ireland, in his " Picturesque Views of the River Thames," published as far back as 1799, " the decayed and apparently dangerous state of Putney Bridge cannot fail to *disgust* the observer. This disgraceful appendage to the river was erected in the year 1729, when the pontage or toll was settled on the subscribers by Act of Parliament ; and, as I am informed, was within twelve months after so greatly advantageous to them as to repay all their disbursements. At the extremities of this *tottering* bridge stand the rival churches of Putney and Fulham, which are said to have been built by two sisters."

Two toll-collectors were stationed at each end of the bridge. They were furnished " with hats, and gowns of good substantial cloth of a deep blue colour, lined with blue shalloon, and carried staves with brass or copper heads." These, it appears, were quite as much for use as for show, for the people did not at first at all relish the idea of having to pay toll for crossing a bridge. " They did not pay when they went over London Bridge ; why should they pay at Putney ? " The consequence of this was that several very serious affrays took place on the bridge between the collectors and the passengers during the first ten years of its existence. But the stalwart collectors stood their ground, until the popular discontent had abated, and the tolls were thenceforward paid without complaint.

In 1730 bells were ordered to be " hung on the tops of the toll-houses, to give notice of any disorder that might happen, so that the collectors might go to the assistance of each other as there might be occasion." The two bells were occasionally used for this purpose, and to the last were rung nightly, when the day tollman went off and the night tollman went on duty. The date upon the bells shows that they were cast in 1739. Doubtless these bells did good service a century or so ago, when Putney Heath and the surrounding neighbourhood was infested with highwaymen and footpads.

What little of the " picturesque " there might have been in the quaint old bridge in former times, when taken as an accessory in a view of either Putney or Fulham as seen from the Thames, was in the end lost by the aqueduct of the Chelsea Waterworks Company, which crossed the stream on massive cylindrical supports a few yards above it.

In July, 1884, the " foundation-stone " of a new bridge, on the site of the aqueduct, was laid by the Prince of Wales. The new bridge, which is to supersede the old one, will be of stone, will have five arches, and will be about fifty feet wide between the parapets, and the span of the centre arch nearly 150 feet.

* See *ante*, p. 473.

OLD PUTNEY BRIDGE. (*See page* 501.)

CHAPTER XXXVII.

FULHAM

" The mansion's self was vast and venerable,
With more of the monastic than has been
Preserved elsewhere."—*Byron.*

Probable Derivation of the Name of Fulham—Boundaries of the Parish—The High Street—Egmont Villa, the Residence of Theodore Hook— Anecdotes of Hook—All Saints' Church—Fulham Bells—Sir William Powell's Almshouses—Bishop's Walk—Fulham Palace—The Gardens —A Bishop's Success in a Competition for Lying—The Manor of Fulham—Bishops Bonner, Aylmer, Bancroft, and Juxon—The Moat— Craven Cottage—Jew King, the Money-lender—The " Crab Tree "—The Earl of Cholmondeley's Villa—Fulham Cemetery—The "Golden Lion "—The Old Workhouse—Fulham at the Commencement of the Last Century—Fulham Road, Past and Present—Holcrofts Hall— Holcrofts Priory—Claybrooke House—The Orphanage Home—Fulham Almshouses—Burlington House—The Reformatory School for Females—Munster House—Fulham Lodge—Percy Cross—Ravensworth House—Walham Lodge—Dungannon House and Albany Lodge— Arundel House—Sad Fate of a Highwayman—Park House—Rosamond's Bower—Parson's Green—Samuel Richardson, the Author of " Pamela," &c.—East-end House—Mrs. Fitzherbert and Madame Piccolomini Residents here—Sir Thomas Bodley—Eelbrook Common— Peterborough House—Ivy Cottage—Fulham Charity Schools—The Pottery—A Tapestry Manufactory—A Veritable Centenarian.

THE parish of Fulham, upon which we now enter, lies in Middlesex, about four miles south-west from Hyde Park Corner, and covers a large extent of ground, the greater part of which, down to comparatively recent times, was laid out as market-gardens ; and the parish still contributes largely to the daily supply of Covent Garden. Originally, Fulham was much larger than now, for it included Hammersmith within its limits ; and even at the present time it has an area of nearly 4,000 acres. Antiquaries have differed as to the origin of the name of Fulham ; but the usual, and perhaps most probable, derivation is from the Saxon " Ful-lenhame," which means the resort or habitation of birds. It was so called, it is supposed, from the abundance of water-fowl found here, and it would be difficult to imagine a place more fitted for the resort of such birds than Fulham must have been before the river was embanked, when the land for some distance from the stream was a mere swamp, and, in many places, under water at every high tide. The place, we are also told, " abounded in trees, which gave them shelter." Camden, in his "Britannia," derives the name from the Saxon word "Fullenham," or "Foulenham," *volucrum domus*, "the habitation of birds, or place of fowls." Norden agrees with this etymology, and adds, " It may also be taken for *volucrum amnis*, or the river of fowl; for 'ham' also, in many places, signifies *amnis*, a river." In Sommer's and Lye's Saxon Dictionaries it is called *Fullanham*, or *Foulham*, " supposed from the dirtiness of the place."

several antiquated-looking family mansions, standing in their own grounds, and almost shut in from observation by stately elms and cedars. The High Street, which branches off at right angles towards the bridge, has the dull, sleepy aspect of a quiet country town : many of the quaint old red-brick houses, with high-tiled roofs, carry the mind of the observer back to times long gone by. As viewed from the Thames, the scene is far different: here we have, on the one hand, prim villas embosomed

FULHAM CHURCH, IN 1825.

It is Pennant's opinion that as far back as the days of the Romans "all the land round Westminster was a flat fen, which continued to beyond Fulham."

The parish of Fulham is, or was, separated on the east from Chelsea by a rivulet, which rises in Wormholt Scrubs, and falls into the Thames opposite to Battersea; on the west it is bounded by Chiswick and Acton; on the north by Hammersmith and Kensington; and its southern boundary is the river Thames. Notwithstanding its distance from London, Fulham is now joined on to the " great city" by lines of houses which extend along the high road on either side. Near the entrance to the village, by the Fulham Road, there are

in trees, with lawns and gardens sloping down to the water ; and on the other the old parish church, backed by the trees surrounding the palace of the Bishop of London.

Close by, to the left, on entering Fulham from the bridge, on the spot now occupied by the abutment of the aqueduct, formerly stood Egmont Villa, some time the residence of Theodore Hook, of whom we have already had occasion to speak in our accounts of Berners Street and Sydenham.* It was about the year 1831 that Hook, who had been for years the lion of West-end parties, and the wit of all London circles, took up his abode

* See Vol. IV., p. 464; and *ante*, p. 306.

here; having got rid of his house in Cleveland Row, he became the tenant of a modest cottage close to the bridge, with a small garden sloping towards the river. Here he spent the last ten years of his life, entertaining politicians, statesmen, men of letters, and even royal dukes, and, in fact, most of those who had idolised him as the accomplished editor of *John Bull* in its early and palmy days.

As a wit and humourist, and as a diner, Theodore Hook enjoyed a high reputation in his day; but his jokes, on some occasions, took that practical turn which became reprehensible. He had, besides, a happy knack of dining, uninvited, at the houses of strangers. In this he was successful, no less by his unblushing impudence than by his really remarkable powers as an *improvisatore*. The following story of his ability in this way has been often told, but will bear repeating:—" On one occasion he and his friend Mathews,* the actor, found their way into the mansion of a gentleman who was entertaining a select company, and having spent a pleasant evening, to the great confusion and wonderment of the host, to whom Hook and his friend were perfect strangers, but very agreeable companions, the intruders were about to depart, when the gentleman of the house begged to be favoured with their names. Whereupon Hook seated himself at the pianoforte and explained himself in the following extemporaneous verse :—

' I am very much pleased with your fare ;
Your cellar's as prime as your cook ;
My friend here is Mathews, the player,
And I'm Mr. Theodore Hook !'"

Passing one day in a gig with a friend by the villa of a retired London watchmaker at Fulham, Hook pulled up, and remarked that "they might do worse than dine in such a comfortable little box!" He accordingly alighted, rang the bell, and on being introduced to the gentleman, coolly told him that, as his name was so celebrated, he could not help calling to make his acquaintance! Hook and his friend were invited to stay to dinner, and after spending a jovial afternoon, they set out for home; but on their way thither the gig, owing to their unsteady driving, was nearly smashed to pieces by the refractory horse.

Barham, in his " Life and Remains," tells us that a friend once said to Hook, while looking at Putney Bridge from the garden of his villa, that he had been informed that the bridge was a good investment, and asked him if it really answered. "I don't

know," replied Theodore; "but you have only to cross it, and you are sure to be told (*tolled*)."

It is on record that when Sir Robert Peel's first administration was formed in the year 1834, the Lord Chamberlain sent immediately for Hook, and offered to him the Inspectorship of Plays, then held by George Colman the younger, in case the ailing veteran could be prevailed upon to resign. The office was perhaps the only one which could have been conferred on him, without exposing his patrons to disagreeable comment; but their kindness was fruitless. George Colman being an old friend, Hook felt some delicacy in communicating the suggestion to him, and the government was again changed before the negotiation could be completed. Almost immediately afterwards Colman died, and Charles Kemble was appointed in his room; and he again had resigned in favour of his accomplished son before Lord Melbourne's ministry was finally displaced. Their fate was announced on the 30th of August, 1841, but ere then Theodore Hook's hopes and fears were at an end. His death is thus mentioned by Mr. Raikes in his " Diary :"—" *Sunday, 29th August.*—The English papers mention the death of Theodore Hook, which has been accelerated by his love for *brandy-and-water*. He was a very good-natured, clever man, and a popular novel-writer of the day. His social and convivial talents rendered him a welcome guest; but when the juice of the grape had lost its exhilarating power he took to spirits to keep up the stimulus; under which excitement he gradually sunk."

Theodore Hook's character is summed up by Mr. W. Thornbury, in his " Haunted London," as a " man of unfeeling wit, a heartless lounger at the clubs, and a humbly-born *flaneur*, who spent his life in amusing great people, who in their turn let him die at last a drunken, emaciated, hopeless, worn-out spendthrift, *sans* character, *sans* everything."

The parish church, dedicated to All Saints, stands near the river-side, at the end of Church Lane, and the west side of the churchyard abuts upon the moat which bounds the east side of the palace grounds. With the exception of the tower, it was entirely rebuilt in 1880–81, in the Perpendicular style, from the designs of Mr. A. W. Blomfield, a son of a former Bishop of London. Bowack describing the former church in 1705, says: " It does not seem to be of very great antiquity, the tower, at the west, being in a very good condition, as well as the body of the church ; it has not been patched up since its first erection, so as to make any considerable

---

* Another version of the anecdote makes Hook's companion to have been Terry.

alteration in the whole building; nor have there been any additions made, as is usual in ancient structures, except of a small building for a school, &c., at the north door; but both tower and church seem of the same age and manner of workmanship." So far as the body of the fabric was concerned, it had not much architectural beauty. It has been well described as "little else than a collection of high pews and deep galleries contained within four walls, pierced at intervals with holes for the admission of light; in fact, one of the worst specimens of those suburban churches which have of late years so rapidly and happily disappeared before the growing taste for a purer and more devotional style of church architecture." The only portion of it which had any architectural pretension was the east end of the north aisle, which was built in 1840.

The large east window is filled with stained glass, and one or two others have also coloured glass in them, in the shape of armorial bearings. Most of the windows of the old church were modern, with semi-circular heads, and without tracery. The tower of the church, however, is a feature of which Fulham is deservedly proud. It consists of five stages, and, like its twin-sister at Putney, is surmounted by battlements, with a turret rising well above them. The date of its erection is uncertain, but it was probably in the fourteenth century. It has, however, been restored, and some alterations have been made in its details; the large west window, with flowing tracery, is modern. This tower is remarkable as containing one of the finest and softest-toned peals of ten bells in England; they were cast, or re-cast, by Ruddle, in the middle of the last century. Each bell bears an inscription, more or less appropriate: on one "Peace and good neighbourhood;" on another, "John Ruddle cast us all;" another has "Prosperity to the Church of England;" another, "Prosperity to this parish;" and on the tenth are the words, "I to the church the living call, and to the grave I summon all."

"The Thames is famous for bells," observed a Thames waterman, in 1829, to a gentleman whom he was carrying from the Temple to Hungerford Stairs. "You like bells then?" was the answer. "Oh, yes, sir! I was a famous ringer in my youth at St. Mary Overies. They are beautiful bells; but of all the bells give me those of Fulham, they are so soft, so sweet. St. Margaret's are fine bells, so are St. Martin's; but, after all, Fulham for me, I say, sir. But lor', sir, I forget where you said I was to take you to." Such is part of a dialogue on the Thames as narrated by Mr. J. T.

Smith, in his "Book for a Rainy Day," from which we have frequently quoted.

The monuments both within and without the church are numerous and interesting, notably one to John Viscount Mordaunt, the father of the great Lord Peterborough. Lord Mordaunt, who died in 1675, was Constable of Windsor Castle, and his statue here—the work of Francis Bird, who carved the Conversion of St. Paul on the west pediment of St. Paul's Cathedral—represents him in Roman costume, holding a baton in his right hand. Within the communion rails is the effigy of Lady Leigh, who is represented as seated under an arch supported by Corinthian columns; she is holding an infant in her arms, and has another child beside her, habited in the dress of the times. The monument is dated 1603. Bishops Gibson and Porteus are also commemorated by monuments in the church. Several of the Bishops of London lie buried in the churchyard, not in the church itself. The example was set by Dr. Compton, who used to say, "The church for the living, and the churchyard for the dead." These graves are marked by altar-tombs, for the most part with no other ornamentation than the arms of the diocese of London. Bishop Blomfield, who died in 1857, lies in the new burial-ground, opposite the vicarage. There is a tablet to his memory near the western entrance of the church; it is a plain brass plate, enclosed within a frame of Gothic design. In the churchyard there are other monuments to men of note in our military, naval, and civil annals. In this churchyard, in August, 1841, Theodore Hook was buried "in the presence of a very few mourners, none of them known to rank or fame, including none of those who had profited as politicians by his zeal and ability, or had courted him in their lofty circles for his wit and fascination." His executors found that he had died deeply in debt. His books and other effects produced £2,500, which sum was, of course, surrendered to the Crown as the privileged creditor. There was some hope that the Lords of the Treasury might grant a gift of this, or some part of it, to his five children, who were left wholly unprovided for; but this hope was not realised. A subscription was raised, and the King of Hanover sent £500; but few of his old Tory friends aided the widow and orphans with their purse. Such is gratitude!

Among the ornaments of this church is a very handsome service of communion plate. In the report of the commissioners to King Edward VI., in 1552, it is stated that they found in Fulham Church "two challiss (*sic*) of sylver, with pattents, parsell gylte, and a lyttell pyxe of sylver parsell gylte." These still exist, and to them have since been added two very handsome silver flagons. It may be added that in this church was consecrated John Sterne, Bishop of Colchester, one of the last suffragan bishops who were appointed under the Act of Henry VIII., until the revival of the office in recent times.

Faulkner, in his account of Fulham, mentions two fine yew-trees as growing on each side of the principal entrance of the churchyard, and another, very much decayed, on the north side, probably coeval with the church itself.

On the north side of the churchyard are Sir William Powell's Almshouses, founded and endowed in 1680, for twelve poor widows. They were re-built in 1793, and again in 1869. The almshouses are built of light brick and stone, of Gothic design, and somewhat profusely ornamented with architectural details.

From the western end of the churchyard a raised pathway, called Bishop's Walk, leads to the entrance of Fulham Palace. The pathway extends for about a quarter of a mile along the river-side, and has on the right the moat and grounds of the palace, and on the left the raised bank of the Thames.

The Manor House of Fulham—or, as it is now called, Fulham "Palace"—has been the summer residence of the Bishops of London for more than eight centuries. The present structure is a large but dull and uninteresting brick building, with no pretension to architectural effect. The house and grounds, comprising some thirty-seven acres, are surrounded by a moat, over which are two bridges, one of which, a draw-bridge, separates the gardens from the churchyard. The principal entrance, which is situated on the west side, is approached from the Fulham Road under a fine avenue of limes and through an arched gateway. The building consists of two courts or quadrangles; the oldest part dates from the time of Henry VII., when it was built by Bishop Fitzjames, whose arms, impaling those of the see of London, appear on the wall and over the gateway. The hall, the principal apartment in the great quadrangle, is immediately opposite the entrance. As an inscription over the chimney-piece states, it was erected, as well as the adjoining courtyard, by Fitzjames, on the site of a former palace, which was as old as the Conquest. It was completed by Bishop Fletcher, father of the dramatist, in 1595; used as a hall by Bishop Bonner and Bishop Ridley during the struggles of the Reformation, and retained its original proportions till it was altered in the reign of George II., by Bishop Sherlock, whose arms, carved in wood, appear over the fire-place. Bishop Howley, in the reign of George IV., changed it into a private un-consecrated chapel; but it was restored to its original purposes as a hall in the year 1868, on the erection by Bishop Tait—later Archbishop of Canterbury—of a new chapel of more suitable dimensions. The hall is a good-sized room, and contains in the windows the arms of the Bishops of London; it is wainscoted all round, and has a carved screen at one end. Upon the walls hang portraits of Henry VII., George II., Queen Anne, Queen Mary II., William III., Henry VIII., James II., Charles I., and Cromwell, besides two full-length pictures—one representing Margaret of Anjou, and the other Thomas à Becket.

The new chapel, which is on the south-west side of the older portion of the palace, is a small brick-built edifice, erected at the cost of Bishop Tait, from the designs of Mr. Butterfield, and con-secrated in 1867. Externally the building has little or no architectural pretensions; but the interior is finished and fitted up in the regular orthodox manner, the chief ornamental feature being an elaborate mosaic reredos, representing the adoration of the shepherds at Bethlehem; it was executed by Salviati from designs by Mr. Butterfield.

One of the most interesting rooms in the palace is the Porteus library, which contains an extensive collection of books, gathered by the divine whose name it bears; it has a large window opening upon the lawn and overlooking the river. Some thousands of volumes, mostly on theological and religious subjects, fill up its ample shelves. There are collections of sermons in abundance, com-mentaries on the gospels, black-letter Bibles, and a large number of theological works. All around suggests meditation and repose. On one side of the room the windows are emblazoned with the armorial bearings of the different prelates, and on its walls hang the portraits of all the Bishops of London since the Reformation.

"All are there," writes Bishop Blomfield's son in the Life of his father—" Ridley, the martyr; Sandys and Grindal; the ambitious Laud; Juxon, the friend of Charles I.; Compton, who had adorned the palace gardens with those rare and stately trees; the statesman Robinson; the learned Gibson; the divines Sherlock and Lowth; the mild and amiable Porteus, who loved Fulham so well, and thanked God the evening before his death that he had been suffered to return thither to die; and Howley and Blomfield."

The great drawing-room and the dining-room are large and handsome apartments on the east side of the palace, with windows looking out upon the lawn and gardens. This part of the building dates from the time of Bishop Terrick, who was appointed to the see in 1764. It has since been considerably altered and repaired at different times. It is a long, plain brick structure of two storeys, its only ornamentation being an embattled summit.

The palace was considerably altered in appearance early in the last century. Bishop Robinson, in 1715, presented a petition to the Archbishop of Canterbury, stating that "the manor-house, or palace, of Fulham was grown very old and ruinous, that it was much too large for the revenues of the bishopric, and that a great part of the building was become useless." In consequence of this petition, as Lysons tells us, certain commissioners (among whom were Sir John Vanbrugh and Sir Christopher Wren) were appointed to examine the premises. The purport of their report was, that "after taking down the bake-house and pastry-house, which adjoined to the kitchen, and all the buildings to the northward of the great dining-room, there would be left between fifty and sixty rooms, besides the chapel, hall, and kitchen." These being adjudged sufficient for the use of the bishop and his successors, a licence was granted to pull down the other buildings; and this, it appears, was carried into effect. The present kitchen is on the north side of the great quadrangle; it is a large high-pitched room, and the ceiling is enriched with stucco ornamentation of an ancient character.

From the low situation of the palace and grounds, much inconvenience is at times felt when the Thames overflows its banks. A notable instance of this occurred in 1874, when considerable damage was occasioned. In some of the rooms of the palace the flooring was upheaved and destroyed by the force of the water, whilst a very large part of the palace grounds was flooded for several days.

The gardens are of great antiquity, and have been famous for their beauty and scientific culture since the time of Bishop Grindall, in the reign of Queen Elizabeth. It appears that Grindall got himself into some trouble by sending some fine grapes to the queen, with whom they disagreed, and the bishop was accused of having the plague in his house, an accusation which he disproved.

According to Fuller's "Worthies," it was Grindall who first imported the tamarisk into this country. This tree, writes Fuller, "hath not more affinity in sound with tamarind than sympathy in extraction, both originally Arabick; general similitude in leaves and operation; only tamarind in England is

an annual, dying at the approach of winter, whilst tamarisk lasteth many years. It was first brought over by Bishop Grindall out of Switzerland, where he was exiled under Queen Mary, and planted in his garden at Fulham, in this county, where the soil being moist and fenny, well complied with the nature of this plant, which since is removed, and thriveth well in many other places."

The great gardener of the palace, however, was Bishop Compton, who was banished to Fulham by James II., and remained in the place for two years, attending specially to his garden. In this he planted many exotics and trees from other countries, then almost unknown in England. A great cork-tree, now much decayed, but at one time the largest in England, and also a large ilex, are traditionally said to have been planted by his hands. Bishop Blomfield planted a cedar of Lebanon, which is now a fine tree, though, comparatively speaking but a few years old; but it can scarcely be said to rival its elder sisters.

The grounds of the palace are remarkable for the thickness with which the trees are planted. One bishop having thinned them considerably, Sir Francis Bacon told him that "having cut down such a cloud of trees, he must be a good man to throw light on dark places." It may be added that Sir William Watson, who made a botanical survey of the grounds a hundred years ago, speaks of this garden in the following terms, in a report to the Royal Society:—"The famous Botanical Garden at Fulham, wherein Dr. Henry Compton, heretofore Bishop of London, planted a greater variety of curious exotic plants and trees than had at any time been collected in any garden in England."

Fond as Evelyn was of gardening, as we have already shown in our account of Saye's Court, Deptford,[*] it is not surprising that we find him a visitor here. In his "Diary," under date of October 11, 1681, he writes:—"I went to Fulham to visit the Bishop of London, in whose garden I saw the *Sedum arborescens* in flower, which was exceedingly beautiful."

Among the curiosities at one time to be seen in the palace was a whetstone, which was placed there by Bishop Porteus under somewhat singular circumstances. The story, showing the bishop's success in a "competition in lying," is thus told in the *New Quarterly Magazine*:—

"In Elizabethan times the game of brag was very popular. 'Lying with us,' writes Lupton, in 1580, 'is so loved and allowed, that there are

* See *ante*, p. 152.

many tymes gamings and prizes therefore, purposely to encourage one to outlye another.' In the last century there were several organised Lying Clubs, one of which for many years held its meetings at the 'Bell Tavern,' Westminster. Among other rules of this society were the following :—'That

said the Lord Keeper, 'it was a whetstone.' At Coggeshall, in Essex, there was a famous institution of this kind. There is a story that Bishop Porteus once stopped in this town to change horses, and observing a great crowd in the streets, put his head out of the window to inquire the

THE MOAT, FULHAM PALACE.

whoever shall presume to speak a word of truth between the established hours of six and ten, within this worshipful society, without first saying, "By your leave, Mr. President," shall for every such offence forfeit one gallon of such wine as the chairman shall think fit.' A coarser form of the same intellectual amusement is the custom of lying for the whetstone, which formerly obtained at village feasts in many parts of England. It was perhaps, some popular version of the story of King Priscus's whetstone cut through by a razor which caused this article to be selected as the appropriate prize; it may have been only an ingenious symbolism to express the necessary whetting of the wits; but, at any rate, it was the recognised emblem of lying, and is illustrated by a sarcasm of Lord Bacon upon Sir Kenelm Digby. The latter, upon his return from the Continent, was boasting of having seen the philosopher's stone. 'Perhaps,'

cause. A townsman standing near replied that it was the day upon which they gave the whetstone to the biggest liar. Shocked at such depravity, the good bishop proceeded to the scene of the competition, and lectured the crowd upon the enormity of the sin, concluding his discourse with the emphatic words, 'I never told a lie in my life.' Whereupon the chief umpire exchanged a few words with his fellows, and approaching the carriage, said, 'My lord, we unanimously adjudge you the prize!' and forthwith the highly objection-

FULHAM PALACE IN 1798.

1. South-east Front.   2. The Chapel.   3. Inner Courtyard.

able whetstone was thrust in at the carriage window. Tradition adds, that in course of time the good-natured bishop forgot the indignity, and began to relish the joke, inasmuch as for many years the identical whetstone occupied the post of honour over the fire-place in his dining-room at Fulham."

The manor of Fulham, we may here state, is one of the oldest in England, having been granted in 631, by the Bishop of Hereford, to Bishop Erkenwald, of London, so that it has existed as an appanage of the see for upwards of twelve hundred and fifty years. This manor was originally held by service of masses for the dead; but at a later period military service was exacted from all holders of manors. The only service now required from the Bishop of London is the maintenance of a watchman to guard the garden and grounds. There is every reason to believe that the manor-house here was occupied at the time of the Conquest; but the first mention of this was in the account of the capture of Robert de Sigillo, Bishop of London, who was a partisan of the Empress Maud, and was made prisoner and held to ransom by the followers of Stephen. Bishop Richard de Gravesend resided much at Fulham, and died here in 1303. His successor, Richard Baldock, who was Lord Chancellor of England, dates most of his public acts from Fulham Palace; but Bishop Braybroke, who enjoyed the same high office, and presided over the see of London nearly twenty years, seems to have spent but little of his time at this place, as he resided mostly at Stepney. Lysons, in his "Environs of London," says that "of Bishop Bonner's residence at Fulham, and of his cruelties, some facts are recorded in history, and many traditions are yet current. A large wooden chair, in which he is said to have sat to pass sentence upon heretics," he adds, "was placed, a few years ago, in a shrubbery near the palace, which gave occasion to an elegant poem, written by Miss Hannah More, who was then on a visit at the bishop's." This poem, called "Bishop Bonner's Ghost," was printed at the Earl of Orford's private press at Strawberry Hill. One deprived bishop of the English Church, John Byrde (who was the last "provincial" of the Carmelites, and afterwards became Bishop of Chester), seems to have found an asylum with Bonner, and was living with him at Fulham in 1555. "Upon his coming," says Anthony Wood, in his "Athenæ Oxonienses," "he brought his present with him—a dish of apples and a bottle of wine." Bishop Aylmer, or Elmer, was principally resident at Fulham Palace, where he died in 1594. The zeal with which he sup-

ported the interests of the Established Church exposed him to the resentment of the Puritans, who, among other methods which they took to injure the bishop, attempted to prejudice the queen against him, alleging that he had committed great waste at Fulham by cutting down the elms; and, punning upon his name, they gave him the appellation of Bishop Mar-elm; "but it was a shameful untruth," says Strype, "and how false it was all the court knew, and the queen herself could witness, for she had lately lodged at the palace, where she misliked nothing, but that her lodgings were kept from all good prospect by the thickness of the trees, as she told her vice-chamberlain, and he reported the same to the bishop."

Fulham Palace has been honoured with the presence of royalty on several occasions. Norden says that Henry III. often lay there. Bishop Bancroft here received a visit from Queen Elizabeth in 1600, and another two years later. King James likewise visited him previously to his coronation. In 1627, Charles I. and his queen dined here with Bishop Mountaigne.

During the Civil Wars we find that most of the principal inhabitants of Fulham, as might have been expected, were staunch Royalists. One of the most prominent was the Bishop (Juxon) who attended his royal master on the scaffold, and to whom the king addressed his last mysterious word, "Remember!" Juxon was deprived of his see, and the manor and palace of Fulham were sold to Colonel Edward Harvey, in 1647. The bishop then retired to his own house at Compton, in Gloucestershire, where he had the singular good fortune to remain undisturbed until the Restoration. With reference to this fact, old Fuller quaintly remarks:—"For in this particular he was happy above others of his order, that whereas they may be said in some sort to have left their bishoprics, flying into the king's quarters for safety, *he* stayed at home till his bishopric left *him*, roused him from his swan's nest at Fulham, for a bird of another feather to build therein." It should be mentioned here that a large tithe-barn which stands in the palace grounds was built by Colonel Harvey during his temporary tenure of the place under the Commonwealth. On a beam over the doors is carved the date, 1654.

The moat which encompasses the palace grounds is about a mile in circumference, and has been considered by some antiquaries to have been formed by the Danish army, when they were encamped in this neighbourhood in 879. Mr. Blomfield, in his "Olden Times of Fulham," observes: "As winter came on, it is not improbable that they [the Danes] found the high tides encroaching seriously on their position; and not liking to leave the river and run the risk of being cut off from their ships, they set vigorously to work, and threw up a bank with a ditch along the river-flank of their army. The work once begun would not be hastily relinquished. Having to pass the winter in a hostile country, they would naturally be anxious to fortify their position by carrying the ditch round the whole camp. The Danish army gone, it was not likely that any bishop would be at the expense of levelling the banks and filling up a ditch of such magnitude, enclosing as it does, and protecting from the river, a space of ground in the centre of his manor most convenient for making a residence."

Enveloped as its origin is in mystery, it is certain, from existing documents, that this moat has been the subject of various disputes, and a cause of annoyance, or at least of discomfort, to many successive bishops. In 1618, Dr. Edwardes, Chancellor of the diocese of London, left £10, "towards erecting a sluice to communicate with the river Thames, to preserve the moat from noisomeness." Before this, the water was never changed; the moat was only filled by the water which filtered in through the banks, and stood stagnant from years' end to years' end. After the formation of the sluice, the water was changed once a month. To cleanse this immense moat, to make additional sluices, to replace the river embankments, to raise by several feet a water-meadow of many acres, to renew all the fences, and to put the whole of a neglected estate into a condition of perfect order, appeared in Bishop Blomfield's eyes a duty laid upon him as a trustee of Church property, and in the discharge of that duty he spent as much as £10,000.

At a short distance westward of the palace stands Craven Cottage, a charming retreat by the water-side. It was originally built for the Countess of Craven, afterwards Margravine of Anspach, but has been considerably altered and enlarged by subsequent proprietors. After the Margravine, the cottage was for some years the residence of Mr. Denis O'Brien, the friend of Charles James Fox, and in 1805 it was sold to a Sir Robert Barclay. Mr. Walsh Porter, who was its next occupant, is said to have spent a large sum in altering and embellishing it. About 1843 it became the residence of Sir E. Bulwer Lytton. He was living here in 1846, when he entertained Prince Louis Napoleon at dinner, after his then recent escape from the fortress of Ham. The house was at one time the residence of a celebrated money-lender, who was generally known as "Jew King." He was, as Captain Gronow tells us, in his amusing "Reminiscences," a man of some talent, and had good taste in the fine arts. He had made the peerage a complete study, knew the exact position of every one who was connected with a coronet, the value of his property, how deeply the estates were mortgaged, and what encumbrances weighed upon them. Nor did his knowledge stop there; by dint of sundry kind attentions to the clerks of the leading banking-houses, he was aware of the balances they kept, and the credit attached to their names, so that, to the surprise of the borrower, he let him into the secrets of his own actual position. He gave excellent dinners, at which many of the highest personages of the realm were present; and when they fancied that they were about to meet individuals whom it would be upon their conscience to recognise elsewhere, were not a little amused to find clients quite as highly placed as themselves, and with purses quite as empty. King had a well-appointed house in Clarges Street, Piccadilly; but it was here that his hospitalities were most lavishly and luxuriously exercised. Here it was that Sheridan told his host that he liked his dinner-table better than his multiplication table; to which his host, who was not only witty, but often the cause of wit in others, replied, " I know, Mr. Sheridan, your taste is more for Jo-king than for Jew King," alluding to the admirable performance of the actor, King, in Sheridan's *School for Scandal*.

Craven Cottage, as left by Walsh Porter in 1809, was considered the prettiest specimen of cottage architecture then existing. The three principal reception-rooms are described as having been equally remarkable for their structure as well as their furniture. "The centre, or principal saloon," Croker tells us in his "Walk from London to Fulham," "was supported by palm-trees of considerable size, exceedingly well executed, with their drooping foliage at the top, supporting the cornice and architraves of the room. The other decorations were in corresponding taste. . . . This room led to a large Gothic dining-room of very considerable dimensions, and on the front of the former apartment was a very large oval rustic balcony, opposed to which was a large half-circular library, that became more celebrated afterwards as the room in which the highly-gifted and talented author of 'Pelham' wrote some of his most celebrated works." Along the Thames side of the house a raised terrace was constructed, and the grounds were laid out with great taste.

Continuing our course westward a short distance farther, we come to a house known as the "Crab Tree," which has long been familiar to all Thames oarsmen, amateurs and professionals alike. The crab is the indigenous apple-tree of this country, and its abundance in this neighbourhood formerly gave its name to the adjoining part of the parish. Faulkner, in his "History of Fulham," remarks that "it has been said by some ancient people that Queen Elizabeth had a country seat here. Some few years ago," he adds, "a very ancient outbuilding belonging to Mr. Eayres fell to the ground through age. Upon clearing away the rubbish, the workmen discovered, in the corner of a chimney, a black-letter Bible, handsomely bound and ornamented with the arms of Queen Elizabeth, in good preservation."

Early in the present century a villa was built on the banks of the Thames, near the "Crab Tree," for the Earl of Cholmondeley. The design for the edifice was taken from a villa in Switzerland, which his lordship had seen on his travels. The house was built chiefly of wood, of the earl's own growing, and the interior was principally fitted up with cedar of the largest growth ever produced in this country. The exterior was covered with coloured slates, having nearly the same appearance and solidity as stone. The front next the river was ornamented with a colonnade, extending the whole length of the building, and thatched with reeds, to correspond with the roof. The house, however, has long since been pulled down.

Passing up Crab Tree Lane, and returning to the village by the Hammersmith and Fulham Road, we pass on our left the cemetery for the parish of Fulham, which was opened in 1865. It is laid out in Fulham Fields, and covers several acres of land which had previously served to rear fruit and vegetables. The land all around for a considerable distance, stretching away towards Hammersmith and North End, is still covered with market-gardens, excepting here and there where a few modern buildings have been erected. Among these is the St. James's Home and Penitentiary, which was originally established at Whetstone.

Continuing our course eastward, we reach the High Street, which extends from the London—or rather Fulham—Road to Church Row. This thoroughfare appears at one time to have been called Bear Street, and in the more ancient parish-books it is denominated Fulham Street.

The old "Golden Lion," in this street, which was pulled down only a few years ago to make room for a new public-house bearing the same sign, is closely connected by tradition with the annals of the palace. The old house, which dated back to the reign of Henry VII., is said to have been the residence of Bishop Bonner, and when converted into an inn, to have been frequented by Shakespeare, Fletcher, and other literary celebrities. Bishop Bonner, according to one account, died at Fulham in his arm-chair, smoking tobacco; and the late Mr. Crofton Croker, in a paper read by him before the British Archæological Association at Warwick, tried to show that an ancient tobacco-pipe, of Elizabethan pattern, found, in situ, in the course of some alterations made in 1836, was the veritable pipe of that right reverend prelate! Strange stories are told of a subterranean passage which existed, it is said, between this house and the palace. On the pulling down of the old "Golden Lion," the panelling was purchased by the second Lord Ellenborough, for the fitting up of his residence, Southam House, near Cheltenham.

The Workhouse formerly stood on the east side of the High Street. It was built in 1774, but had been in a dilapidated condition for many years, and was pulled down about 1860; a large Union for the joint parishes of Fulham and Hammersmith having been erected in Fulham Fields. Cipriani, the Florentine painter, lived for some time close to the workhouse; he died in London in 1783.

In 1883 a new church, dedicated to St. Peter, was built on the Salisbury estate, Fulham.

In order to gain some idea of what the external appearance of Fulham was at the commencement of the last century, we have only to suppose ourselves carried back to that date, and to be walking through the village with old Master Bowack, the author of a "History of Fulham" published about that time. We shall observe, as he tells us, "that the houses are commonly neat and well built of brick, and from the gate of the Queen's Road run along on both sides of the way almost as far as the church. Also from the Thames side into the town stands an entire range of buildings, and upon the passage leading to the church, called Church Lane, are several very handsome airy houses. But the buildings run farthest towards the north, extending themselves into a street through which lies the road a very considerable way towards Hammersmith. Besides, there are several other handsome buildings towards the east, called the Back Lane, and a great number of gardeners' houses scattered in the several remote parts of the parish." Judging from the above description, a visitor to Fulham now would find that the locality has undergone (in external appearance, at least) marvellously little alteration during the time that has elapsed since it was written. "Except that the Back Lane has apparently lost most of its architectural gems, and that Elysium Row has sprung into existence and grown old and venerable since then," writes Mr. Blomfield, in his work above quoted, "the principal features of the town (whitewash and stucco apart) appear to be much the same. The aspect of the river-side was, of course, very different. The bridge was not built till twenty years later, and the road came down to the bank, and, indeed, in a pleasant green, on one side of which stood the old 'Swan' Inn, and the other side was overshadowed by elm-trees. A clump of trees stood at one corner of the road, above which rose the tower of the church, with its leaden spire, and at the river-side lay the ferry-boat, waiting for passengers. Fulham was then a point for pleasure-parties on the water, as Richmond and Kew are now. In comparing our appearance now with what it was then," continues Mr. Blomfield, "we must not, of course, venture beyond the pump at the end of High Street, and get entangled in the mushroom growth of semi-detached villas which have been for years slowly but relentlessly driving back the struggling market-gardener from point to point into the river. We must think of the London Road as it was at that time, not bordered by comfortable houses, rows of snug-looking whitewashed villas, smart public-houses, or red-brick hospitals, but with a yawning ditch on each side, and, beyond these, green fields and garden-grounds, hedges and orchards, and now and then a clump of elms and a farmhouse or a gardener's cottage peeping through; for as to regular roadside houses, you would not pass a score between Fulham Pump and Hyde Park. Nor must we forget that the traveller would observe between Fulham and London certainly not less than three gallows-trees, bearing their ghastly fruit of highwaymen hung in chains. Then the road itself was very different from what it is now: the only idea at that time of making a good road was to pave it, and, accordingly, the Fulham Road was paved, but only in one or two places; till, at length, what with part being badly paved, and part left unpaved, and deep in its native mud; what with the narrowness of the way in many places, and the depth of the ditches on each side, the road grew so dangerous that, a few years later, it was found necessary to take the matter up in Parliament. It then appeared that a rate of two shillings in the pound was not considered sufficient to put the road into a safe state; that it was almost impassable in winter; and that a great deal of mischief had been done to persons who travelled on that road." If this were so, the state of the road will almost seem to justify the derivation of the name of the village as the *Foul-ham*."*

Seeing the Fulham Road as it is now, swarming with omnibuses and butchers' carts, carriages, and coal-wagons, it is very difficult to imagine its condition a century and a half ago, with perhaps "a solitary market-wagon toiling through the mud, or drawing to one side, at the imminent risk of sliding into the ditch, to allow the Duchess of Munster—who lived in a large mansion near the entrance to the village—to pass by in her great lumbering coach and six, tearing along at the dangerous rate of five miles an hour!" But bad as the Fulham Road was in the olden time, the inconvenience of having to travel over it was, to Bishop Laud, at least, an advantage; for, as we have already had occasion to mention in our account of Whitehall,† in one of his letters to Lord Strafford, alluding to his health as not being so good as it was formerly, he expresses a regret that in consequence of his elevation to the see of Canterbury he has now simply to glide across the river in his barge, when on his way either to the Court or the Star-Chamber; whereas, when Bishop of London, there were five miles of rough road between Fulham Palace and Whitehall, the jolting over which in his coach he describes as having been very beneficial to his health.

Holcrofts, which stands on the left side of the Fulham Road, as we pass from the top of the High Street, dates from the early part of the last century, when it was built by Robert Limpany, a wealthy merchant of London, whose estate in this parish was so considerable that, as Bowack tells us, "he was commonly called the Lord of Fulham." The house, which formerly had a long avenue of trees in front of it, was sold to Sir William Withers, in 1708, and became afterwards successively the residence of Sir Martin Wright, one of the Justices of the King's Bench, and of the Earl of Ross. The building was subsequently known as Holcrofts Hall, and was for some time occupied by Sir John Burgoyne, who here gave some clever dramatic performances. Here it was that the celebrated Madame Vestris lived, after her marriage with Charles Mathews, the well-known actor, and here she died in 1856, at which time the house was called Gore Lodge.

Holcrofts Priory, on the opposite side of the road, was built about the year 1845, on the site of an old Elizabethan mansion called Claybrooke House, from a wealthy family of that name who owned the property in the seventeenth century. One of the family was buried in Fulham Church in

---

* See *ante*, p. 505.   † See Vol. III., p. 353.

1587. Claybrooke House was in the occupation of the Frewens at the commencement of the last century, and afterwards became the property of the above-mentioned Robert Limpany. For many years prior to its demolition it was used as a seminary for young ladies.

In Elysium Road, near the High Street, is a large and handsome ecclesiastical-looking edifice, in the Gothic style. This is an Orphanage Home,

side, stands Munster House, which is supposed to owe its name to Melesina Schulenberg, who was created by George I., in 1716, Duchess of Munster. According to Faulkner, it was at one time called *Mustow* House; but as Mr. Croker suggests, in his "Walk from London to Fulham," "this was not improbably the duchess's pronunciation." Faulkner adds that tradition makes this house a hunting-seat of Charles II., and asserts that an extensive park

HOLCROFTS AND THE PRIORY, FULHAM.

under the patronage of the Bishop of London, founded a few years ago by Mrs. Tait, the wife of Bishop (since Archbishop) Tait.

In Burlington Road, formerly known as Back Lane, the thoroughfare running parallel with the High Street on its eastern side, and extending from the corner of Fulham Road to King's Road, Fulham Almshouses originally stood; they were founded, as already stated, by Sir William Powell, in 1680, but rebuilt near the parish church in 1869. Burlington House, whence the road derives its name, was for upwards of a century a well-known academy kept at one time by a Mr. Roy. On the grounds attached to the house is now a Reformatory School for Females; it was built about 1856.

Farther along the Fulham Road, on the north

was attached to it; but there seems to be no foundation for the statement. In the seventeenth century the property seems to have belonged to the Powells, from whom it passed into the possession of Sir John Williams, Bart., of Pengethly, Monmouthshire. In 1795, Lysons tells us, the house was occupied as a school; and in 1813 Faulkner informs us that it was the residence of M. Sampayo, a Portuguese merchant. It was afterwards for many years tenanted by Mr. John Wilson Croker, M.P., Secretary of the Admiralty, and whose name is well known as the editor of "Boswell's Johnson." About 1820 Mr. Croker resigned Munster House as a residence, "after having externally decorated it with various Cockney embattlements of brick, and collected there many curious works of art, possibly with a view of recon-struction." On the gate-piers were formerly two grotesque-looking composition lions, which had the popular effect, for some time, of changing the name to *Monster* House.

On the opposite side of the road is an extensive garden for the supply of the London market, by the side of which runs Munster Road, whence a turning about half-way down leads on to Parson's

is small and unostentatious, yet, in reality, it is more capacious and attractive than it looks. The Queen and Prince Albert honoured the late Lord Ravensworth with a visit here in June, 1840. The grounds at the back of the house owe their charm to a former occupier, Mr. John Ord, a Master in Chancery, who about the middle of the last century planted them with such skill and taste that, though not extensive, they held a fore-

RICHARDSON'S HOUSE AT PARSON'S GREEN (1799).

Green. Fulham Lodge, which stood on the south side of the main road, close by Munster Terrace, was a favourite retreat of the Duke of York, and for some time the home of George Colman the Younger. Fulham Park Road covers the spot whereon the lodge stood.

Continuing along the Fulham Road about a quarter of a mile, we reach Percy Cross, or rather, as it was formerly called, Purser's Cross. Here Lord Ravensworth has a suburban residence, in the garden of which is a fine specimen of an old "stone pine," reminding us of Virgil's line—

"Pulcherrina pinus in hortis."

The mansion is concealed from the road by a high brick wall, and although to outward appearance it

most rank among the private gardens in the neigh-bourhood of London.

"Purser's Cross" is mentioned as a point "on the Fulham Road, between Parson's Green and Walham Green," so far back as 1602; and the place has never been in any way connected with the "proud house of Percy." In the "Beauties of England and Wales," Purser's Cross is said to be a cor-ruption of Parson's Cross, and the vicinity of Parson's Green is mentioned in support of this conjecture. However, that "Purser," and not "Percy" Cross, has been for many years the usual mode of writing the name of this locality, is esta-blished by an entry in the "Annual Register" in 1781. At Percy Cross was at one time the resi-dence of Signor Mario and Madame Grisi.

On the opposite side of the road to Lord Ravensworth's house is Walham Lodge, formerly called Park Cottage, a modern, well-built house, standing within extensive grounds, surrounded by a brick wall. Here for some years lived Mr. Brande, the eminent chemist, whose lectures on geology, delivered at the Royal Institution in 1816, acquired great popularity.

A house, now divided into two, and called Dungannon House and Albany Lodge, abuts upon the western boundary of Walham Lodge. Tradition asserts that this united cottage and villa were, previous to their separation, known by the name of Bolingbroke Lodge, and as such became the frequent resort of Pope, Gay, Swift, and others of that fraternity; but it would seem as if tradition had mixed up this house with Bolingbroke House, Battersea, which we have lately described.*

A few yards from Dungannon House, on the same side of the road, opposite to Parson's Green Lane, stands Arundel House, an old mansion, supposed to date from the Tudor period. It appears to have been newly fronted towards the close of the last century; and in 1819 the house was in the occupation of the late Mr. Hallam, the historian of the Middle Ages

On the opposite side of the road is the carriage entrance to Park House, which stands in Parson's Green Lane. A stone tablet let into one of the piers of the gateway is inscribed, "Purser's Cross, 7th August, 1738." This date has reference to the death of a highwayman which occurred here, and of which the *London Magazine* gives the following particulars :—"An highwayman having committed several robberies on Finchley Common, was pursued to London, where he thought himself safe, but was, in a little time, discovered at a public-house in Burlington Gardens, refreshing himself and his horse; however, he had time to re-mount, and rode through Hyde Park, in which there were several gentlemen's servants airing their horses, who, taking the alarm, pursued him closely as far as Fulham Fields, where, finding no probability of escaping, he threw money among some country people who were at work in the field, and told them they would soon see the end of an unfortunate man. He had no sooner spoke these words but he pulled out a pistol, clapped it to his ear, and shot himself directly, before his pursuers could prevent him. The coroner's inquest brought in their verdict, and he was buried in a cross-road, with a stake through him; but it was not known who he was."

Park House, in Parson's Green Lane, is said to

* See *ante*, p. 470.

be a fac-simile of an older mansion, called Quibus Hall, which occupied the same site. The old hall at one time belonged to the Whartons. Lysons, on the authority of the parish books, states that a Sir Michael Wharton was living here in 1654. When the house was rebuilt, it was for a time called High Elms House. A small house opposite, Audley Cottage, was for many years the residence of the late Mr. Thomas Crofton Croker, F.S.A., who wrote a minute description of the place, which is reprinted in the "Walk from London to Fulham," to which we are indebted for some of the particulars here given. The name of the place, which was at one time Brunswick Cottage, was altered by Mr. Croker to Rosamond's Bower, the property hereabouts having at some distant date formed part of a manorial estate called Rosamonds, which in the fifteenth century belonged to Sir Henry Wharton. Lysons, in his "Environs of London," states that "the site of the mansion belonging to this estate, now (1795) rented by a gardener, is said, by tradition, to have been a palace of Fair Rosamond." This house was taken down about the year 1825, and the stables of Park House built on the site. With reference to the present building, an ordinary two-storeyed dwelling-house, Mr. Croker wrote :— "When I took my cottage, in 1837, and was told that the oak staircase in it had belonged to the veritable 'Rosamond's Bower,' and was the only relic of it that existed, and when I found that the name had no longer a precise 'local habitation' in Fulham, I ventured, purely from motives of respect for the memory of the past, and not from any affectation of romance, to revive an ancient parochial name, which had been suffered to die out 'like the snuff of a candle.' In changing its precise situation, in transferring it from one side of Parson's Green Lane to the other—a distance, however, not fifty yards from the original site—I trust when called upon to show cause for the transfer to be reasonably supported by the history of the old oak staircase."

Parson's Green is a triangular plot of ground at the southern end of the lane, at its junction with King's Road; and it was so called from the parsonage-house of the parish of Fulham, which stood on its west side, but was pulled down about the year 1740. The Green, on which successive rectors and their families disported themselves, is for the most part surrounded by small cottages. There used to be held on the Green annually on the 17th of August, a fair, which had, as Faulkner tells us, "been established from time immemorial."

"An ancient house at the corner of the Green," writes Lambert, in his "History and Survey of

London and its Environs," in 1805, "formerly belonged to Sir Edmund Saunders, Lord Chief-Justice of the Court of King's Bench in 1682, who raised himself to the bench from being an errand-boy in an attorney's office, where he taught himself the mysteries of the law by copying papers in the absence of the regular clerks. This house," he adds, "was the residence of Samuel Richardson, the author of 'Sir Charles Grandison,' 'Pamela,' &c." We have already spoken of Richardson in our accounts of Fleet Street and of Hampstead,* and we shall have still more to say about him when we reach North End, on our way to Hammersmith.

In Dodsley's "Collection of Poems" are the following verses on an alcove at Parson's Green, by Mrs. Bennet, sister of Mr. Edward Bridges, who married Richardson's sister :—

" O favourite Muse of Shenstone, hear !
    And leave awhile his blissful groves ;
Aid me this alcove to sing,
    The author's seat whom Shenstone loves.

" Here the soul-harrowing genius form'd
    His ' Pamela's' enchanting story,
And here—yes, here—' Clarissa' died
    A martyr to her sex's glory."

*   *   *   *   *

" O sacred seat ! be thou revered
    By such as own thy master's power;
And, like his works, for ages last,
    Till fame and language are no more."

Seeing, however, that " Clarissa Harlowe " and " Sir Charles Grandison " were both written between 1747 and 1754, and that Richardson did not take up his abode here till 1755, it is North End, and not Parson's Green, that may lay claim to being the seat of their production. Edwards, the author of " Canons of Criticism," died at Parson's Green in 1757, whilst on a visit to Richardson.

A century or two ago Parson's Green was noted for its aristocratic residents. East End House, on the east side, was built at the end of the seventeenth century for Sir Francis Child, who was Lord Mayor of London in 1699. The house was inhabited by Admiral Sir Charles Wager ; and by Dr. Ekins, Dean of Carlisle, who died there in 1791. Mrs. Fitzherbert was at one time a resident here ; and, according to Mr. Croker, she erected the porch in front of the house as a shelter for carriages. Here, naturally enough, the Prince of Wales (afterwards George IV.) was a frequent visitor. Madame Piccolomini, too, lived for some time on the east side of the Green.

Another distinguished resident at Parson's Green in former times was Sir Thomas Bodley, the founder of the Bodleian Library at Oxford. Rowland White, Lord Strafford's entertaining and communicative correspondent, was his contemporary there. " When the great Lord Chancellor Bacon fell into disgrace, and was restrained from coming within the verge of the Court, he procured a licence (dated September 13, 1621) to retire for six weeks to the house of his friend, Lord Chief-Justice Vaughan, at Parson's Green." So wrote Lysons in 1795 ; but Faulkner says, " This could not be the Sir John Vaughan who was Lord Chief-Justice in 1668. We know of no other who was Lord Chief-Justice. In the parish books," he adds, " the person to whose house Lord Bacon retired is called ' The Lord Vaughan,' who probably resided in the house now (1813) occupied by Mr. Maxwell, as a boarding-school, and called Albion House, a spacious mansion, built in that style of architecture which prevailed at the commencement of the reign of James I."

Close by Parson's Green is another open space, called Eelbrook Common, which " from time immemorial " has been used as a place of recreation for the dwellers in the neighbourhood. This plot of ground recently became the subject of a question in the House of Commons, in consequence of encroachments made upon it, the Ecclesiastical Commissioners, as lords of the manor, having disposed of some portion of it for building purposes, thus encroaching on the rights of the public.

On the south-west side of the Green, near Eelbrook Common, is Peterborough House, formerly the residence of the Mordaunts, Earls of Peterborough, whom we have already mentioned in our account of Fulham Church.

The present building, a modern structure, dating from the end of the last century, has replaced an older mansion, which is described by Bowack as " a very large, square, regular pile of brick, with a gallery all round it upon the top of the roof. It had," he continues, " abundance of extraordinary good rooms, with fine paintings." The gardens and grounds covered about twenty acres, and were beautifully laid out, after the fashion of the period. Swift, in one of his letters, speaks of Lord Peterborough's gardens as being the finest he had ever seen about London. The ancient building was known as Brightwells, or Rightwells, and was the residence of John Tarnworth, one of Queen Elizabeth's Privy Councillors, who died here in 1569. The place afterwards belonged to Sir Thomas Knolles, who sold it to Sir Thomas Smith, Master of the Court of Requests. He died here in 1609,

---

and his widow soon afterwards married the first Earl of Exeter, whilst Sir Thomas's only daughter married the Honourable Thomas Carey, the Earl of Monmouth's second son, who, in right of his wife, became possessor of the estate. After him, the place was named Villa Carey. In 1660, Villa Carey was occupied by Lord Mordaunt, who had married the daughter and heiress of Mr. Carey. This Lord Mordaunt took a prominent part in

as a military character prior to the Revolution, and also in the reigns of William and Mary and Queen Anne. He succeeded to the earldom of Peterborough on the death of his uncle in 1697. He was twice married: his second wife was the accomplished singer, Anastasia Robinson, who survived him. The earl was visited at Peterborough House by all the wits and *literati* of his time, including Pope, Swift, Locke, and many others.

PETERBOROUGH HOUSE.

bringing about the restoration of Charles II., after which event he seems to have quietly settled down on his estate at Parson's Green, where he died in 1675. John Evelyn, in his "Diary," under date of November 29, 1661, thus makes mention of a visit to Lord Mordaunt:—"I dined at the Countess of Peterborow's, and went that evening to Parson Greene's house with my Lord Mordaunt, with whom I staid that night." By "Parson Greene's house," Evelyn no doubt meant Parson's Green House. Later on, December 2nd, 1675, Evelyn makes the following (more correct) entry in his "Diary:"—"I visited Lady Mordaunt at Parson's Green, her son being sick."

Lord Mordaunt's son, Charles, subsequently known as Earl of Monmouth, distinguished himself

Faulkner, in his "History of Fulham," says that Miss Robinson "continued to sing in the Opera till the year 1723, when she retired, in consequence, as it is supposed, of her marriage with the Earl of Peterborough, for she at that time went to reside at a house in Parson's Green, which the earl took for herself and her mother." Sir John Hawkins, in his "History of Music," says she resided at Peterborough House, and presided at the earl's table, but she never lived under the same roof with him till she was prevailed on to attend him in a journey, which he took a few years before his death, on account of his declining health. During her residence at Fulham she was visited by persons of the highest rank, under a full persuasion, founded on the general tenor of his life and conduct, that she had a legal right to a rank which, for prudential reasons, she was content to decline. She held frequent musical parties, at which Bononcini, Martini, Tosi, Greene, and the most eminent musicians of that time assisted ; and they were attended by all the fashionable world. It was some years before the earl could prevail upon himself to acknowledge her as his countess ; nor did he, till 1735, publicly own what most people knew before ; he then proclaimed his marriage like no other husband. He went one evening to the rooms at Bath, where a servant was ordered distinctly and audibly to announce " Lady Peterborough's carriage waits ! " Every lady of rank immediately rose and congratulated the declared countess.

After Lord Peterborough's death, the house was sold to a Mr. Heaviside, from whom it was subsequently purchased by Mr. John Meyrick, father of Sir Samuel Meyrick, the well-known antiquary and writer on armour. He pulled the old mansion down, and built the present house on the site.

It is recorded in Faulkner's " History of Kensington," that in a vineyard at Parson's Green some Burgundy grapes were ripe in October, 1765, and that the owner of the vineyard was about to make wine from them, as he did yearly.

King's Road, which skirts the southern side of the Green, leads direct eastward on to Chelsea, and passing westward unites with Church Street, at the end of Burlington Road. At a short distance from the Green, in the King's Road, stands Ivy Cottage, which was built at the end of the last century by Walsh Porter, and is in a debased Gothic style of architecture. Faulkner states that " there is a tradition that on the site of this bijou of a cottage was formerly a house, the residence of Oliver Cromwell, which was called the Old Red Ivy House. The house was for some time the residence of the late Mr. E. T. Smith, the well-known theatrical manager, who gave it the name of Drury Lodge, after the theatre of which he was then the lessee. The house, several years ago, resumed its old name of Ivy Cottage. Here, in 1878, died the Rev. R. G. Baker, who was many years Vicar of Fulham, and well known as an antiquary.

In Church Street (formerly Windsor Street, according to Faulkner) stand the Fulham Charity Schools, which were erected in 1811. Close by is a pottery, which has existed here for upwards of two centuries. It was established by John Dwight, who, after numerous experiments, took out a patent, dated 23rd of April, 1671, which was renewed in 1684, for the making of " earthenwares, known by the name of white goyes (pitchers), marbled porcelain vessels, statues and figures, and fine stone gorges never before made in England or elsewhere." Another branch of industry at one time carried on at Fulham was the manufacture of Gobelin tapestry ; but the articles produced were too costly to command a large sale. **Mr.** Smiles, in his " Huguenots," writes : " A French refugee named Passavant purchased the tapestry manufactory at Fulham, originally established by the Walloons, which had greatly fallen into decay. His first attempts at reviving the manufacture, however, were not successful, and so the industry was removed to Exeter."

Before leaving the village of Fulham, and making our way to Walham Green and North End, we may remark that this neighbourhood—if it has not always been remarkable for the healthiness or longevity of its inhabitants—can boast of having produced at least one centenarian. In the *Mirror* for 1833, we find this record : " Mr. Rench, of Fulham, who planted the elms in Birdcage Walk from saplings reared in his own nursery, died in 1783, aged 101, in the same room in which he had been born."

CHAPTER XXXVIII.

FULHAM (*continued*).—WALHAM GREEN AND NORTH END.

Vine Cottage—The Pryor's Bank—The " Swan " Tavern—Stourton House—Ranelagh House—Hurlingham—Broom House—Sandy End—Sandford Manor House, the Residence of Nell Gwynne, and of Joseph Addison—St. James's, Moore Park—Walham Green—St. John's Church—The Butchers' Almshouses—A Poetic Gardener—North End—Browne's House—North End Lodge—Jacob Tonson—North End Road—Beaufort House—Lillie Bridge Running-ground—The Residence of Foote, the Dramatist—The Hermitage—The Residence of Bartolozzi—Normand House—Wentworth Cottage—Fulham Fields—Walnut-tree Cottage—St. Saviour's Convalescent Hospital—The Residence of Dr. Crotch—Samuel Richardson's House—Other Noted Residents at Fulham.

HAVING arrived at the end of the High Street, whence, at the commencement of the preceding chapter, we started on our tour towards the church and palace, we will now pass to the south side of the church, and thence shape our course along the river-side to the eastern boundary of the parish. The first building to attract our attention is a stucco-fronted house, of Gothic design, standing between the church and the river. It occupies the site of a former house, called Vine Cottage, from a luxurious vine which covered the exterior. The humble situation of the old edifice having attracted the fancy of Mr. Walsh Porter, he purchased it, raised the building by an additional storey, and otherwise considerably altered its appearance. The entrance-hall, constructed to look like huge projecting rocks, was called the robbers' cave; one of

Pictures of ancient worthies, wainscoting and rich tapestries, adorned the walls; painted glass, rich in heraldic devices, filled the windows; and the new name of the "Pryor's Bank" was given to the place.

An ample account of all the treasures which the house and gardens contained, together with details of the masques and revels which took place here, are given in Mr. Croker's book from which we

NELL GWYNNE'S HOUSE.

the bed-rooms was named the lions' den; whilst the dining-room is stated to have represented, on a small scale, the ruins of Tintern Abbey. Here Mr. Porter had the honour of receiving and entertaining, on several occasions, the Prince of Wales, afterwards George IV. Vine Cottage was at length disposed of by Mr. Porter, and became, in 1813, the residence of Lady Hawarden. It was subsequently occupied by Mr. William Holmes, M.P. ("Billy Holmes"), and by others. But at length the cottage was pulled down, and the house now standing was erected on its site. The new owners filled the rooms with all sorts of antiquarian objects, from an ancient gridiron to Nell Gwynne's mirror, in its curious frame of needlework; indeed, the place became like a second "Strawberry Hill."

have already quoted, and from which we extract the following:—"Though within the walls of the Pryor's Bank, or any other human habitation, all that is rich in art may be assembled, yet, without the wish to turn these objects to a beneficial purpose, they become only a load of care; but when used to exalt and refine the national taste, they confer an immortality upon the possessor, and render him a benefactor to his species; when used, also, as accessories to the cultivation of kindly sympathies and the promotion of social enjoyment, they are objects of public utility." The revival of old English cordiality, especially at Christmas, had been always a favourite idea with the owners of the Pryor's Bank, and in 1839 they gave a grand entertainment, which included a "masque," written

IN AND ABOUT FULHAM.

1. Fulham House and Ranelagh Lodge.   2. Old "Swan" Tavern, 1820.   3. Pryor's Bank.   4. Old Pottery.

for the occasion, in which the principal character, "Great Frost," was enacted by Theodore Hook. The words of the piece were printed and sold in the rooms, for the benefit of the Royal Literary Fund, and resulted in the addition of £3 12s. 6d. to the coffers of that most admirable institution.

The record of this memorable evening in Theodore Hook's "Notes" has a Pepysian twang about it:—"30 December, 1839. To-day, not to town; up and to Baylis's; saw preparations. So, back; wrote a little, then to dinner, afterwards to dress; so to Pryor's Bank, there much people—Sir George and Lady Whitmore, Mrs. Stopford, Mrs. Nugent, the Bulls, and various others, to the amount of 150. I acted the 'Great Frost' with considerable effect. Jerdan, Planché, Nichols, Holmes and wife, Lane, Crofton Croker, Giffard, Barrow. The Whitmore family sang beautifully; all went off well."

The charms of the Pryor's Bank have been sung in verse, in the "Last New Ballad on the Fulham Regatta"—a *jeu-d'esprit* circulated at an entertainment given here in 1843—of which the following lines (some of them not very excellent as rhymes) will serve as a specimen:—

> "Strawberry Hill has pass'd away,
> Every house must have its day;
> So in antiquarian rank
> Up sprung here the Pryor's Bank,
> Full of glorious tapestry,
> Full as well as house can be;
> And of carvings old and quaint,
> Relics of some mitr'd saint,
> 'Tis—I hate to be perfidious—
> 'Tis a house most sacrilegious."

Like those of its prototype, Strawberry Hill, the contents of the Pryor's Bank have long since been dispersed under the hammer of the auctioneer. The first sale took place in 1841, and lasted six days; the remainder was sold off in 1854.

Between the Pryor's Bank and the approach to the bridge stood till 1871, when it was destroyed by fire, a picturesque old waterside tavern, the "Swan." It had a garden attached, looking on to the river. The house is supposed to have been built in the reign of William III., and it is said to have been scarcely altered in any of its features since Chatelaine published his views of "The most Agreeable Prospects near London," about 1740. In the elaborate ironwork which supported the sign was wrought the date 1698. The house, with its tea-gardens, was the favourite resort of boating people, and is made mention of in Captain Marryat's "Jacob Faithful." Amongst a few old coins, found in clearing away the ruins after the fire above mentioned, was a shilling of the time of William III., dated 1696.

Passing to the east side of Bridge Street we find several old houses, which have the appearance of having once "seen better days;" whilst of others a recollection alone remains in the names given to the locality where they once stood. Stourton House, afterwards called Fulham House, close by the foot of the bridge, is said to have been a residence of the Lords Stourton three centuries ago. Next is Ranelagh House, the grounds of which are prettily laid out, and extend from Hurlingham Lane down to the river-side. This house, in the last century, belonged to Sir Philip Stephens, one of the Lords of the Admiralty, whose only daughter was the wife of Lord Ranelagh, to whom the property was bequeathed. The next mansion eastward is Mulgrave House, formerly the seat of the Earl of Mulgrave, and afterwards of Colonel Torrens and Lord Ranelagh. The Earl of Egremont, the Countess of Lonsdale, and other distinguished persons, formerly had residences hereabouts, but these have been for the most part swept away, or converted to other uses.

Hurlingham House, the grounds of which on the south side are bounded by the river, is altogether unnoticed by Faulkner in his "History of Fulham," although Hurlingham Field is frequently mentioned in old documents; and it has been considered as most probable that the name arose from the field having been used for the ancient sport of hurling. The spot gained an unenviable notoriety at one time as the site of the pest-house and burial-pit, in the time of the Great Plague of London. The pest-house was pulled down in 1681, and the materials were sold. Hurlingham was for many years the residence of Mr. J. Horseley Palmer, Governor of the Bank of England; it is now best known by its grounds, which are much patronised by the lovers of pigeon-shooting and other aristocratic pastimes of a similar character.

Broom House was for some time the residence of Sir John Shelley, of Maresfield Park, Sussex, who died here in 1852, and afterwards of the Right Hon. L. Sulivan, the brother-in-law of Lord Palmerston. The name of the property appears to be of some antiquity. Bowack mentions, in his time, the commencement of the last century, a collection of cottages by the river-side, called Broom Houses, and says, "The name rose from the quantity of broom that used to grow there." Eastward of Broomhouse Lane, as far as Sandy End Lane, on the eastern side of the parish, the land bordering the Thames is occupied chiefly as market gardens.

At Sandy End, near a little brook which once divided Chelsea from Fulham, not far from the

"World's End,"* was Sandford Manor House, once the residence of Nell Gwynne, of which a sketch may be seen in Mr. and Mrs. S. C. Hall's "Pilgrimages to English Shrines." It now forms part of the buildings included in the premises of the Imperial Gas Company. Its gables have been removed, and the exterior modernised; but there still remains the old staircase, up and down which fair Mistress Nell Gwynne's feet must often have paced.

We catch another glimpse of Joseph Addison in this once remote neighbourhood. Faulkner, in his "History of Fulham," published in 1811, describes, at the eastern extremity of the parish, situated on a small creek running to, or rather up from, the Thames, a building known as Sandford Manor House, formerly of some note as having been at one time the residence of the notorious "Nell Gwynne." "The mansion," he then writes, "is of venerable appearance: immediately in front of it are four walnut-trees, affording an agreeable shade, that are said to have been planted by royal hands; the fruit of them is esteemed of a peculiarly fine quality." But this was probably a little bit of that imagination which soon turns royal "geese" into "swans."

Two letters of Joseph Addison, written from Sandford Manor House in 1708, are interesting memorials of the state of this neighbourhood in the reign of Queen Anne, and also of the intense relish for rural scenes and pleasures which marked a man who was the author of many of the best papers in the *Spectator*, and also an Under-Secretary of State. They are addressed to the young Lord Warwick, to whom he afterwards became stepfather. In the first he gives a particular account of a curious bird's-nest found near the house, about which his neighbours were divided in opinion, some taking it for a skylark's, some for that of a canary, whilst he himself judged its inmates to be tomtits. In the second letter he writes: "I can't forbear being troublesome to your lordship while I am in your neighbourhood. The business of this, to invite you to a concert of music which I have found in a tree in a neighbouring wood. It begins precisely at six in the evening, and consists of a blackbird, a thrush, a robin-redbreast, and a bullfinch. There is a lark that, by way of overture, sings and mounts till she is almost out of hearing, and afterwards falls down leisurely and drops to the ground, as soon as she has ended her song. The whole is concluded by a nightingale that has a much better voice than

Mrs. Tofts, and something of Italian manners in its diversions. If your lordship will honour me with your company, I will promise to entertain you with much better music and more agreeable scenes than you ever met with at the opera, and will conclude with a charming description of a nightingale, out of our friend Virgil:—

"'So close in poplar shades, her children gone,
   The mother nightingale laments alone,
   Whose nest some prying churl had found, and thence
   By stealth conveyed the unfeathered innocents;
   But she supplies the night with mournful strains,
   And melancholy music fills the plains.'"

This letter places before us a picture of the elegant essayist on a bright May evening, with upturned ear, beneath some lofty elm or oak, charmed with the beautiful oratorio of the birds in the woods about Fulham—an oratorio now, it is to be feared, no longer heard.

The south-eastern side of the parish, between Fulham Road and the river, including the works of the Imperial Gas Company, was formed, in 1868, into a new ecclesiastical district, called St. James's, Moore Park. The church, a large cruciform structure of Early-English architecture, was built from the designs of Mr. Darbishire.

Walham Green is—or, rather, was—a triangular plot of greensward on the north side of the Fulham Road, upon which, in former times, donkeys had been wont to graze, and the village children to play at cricket.

The derivation of the name of Walham Green is somewhat obscure and doubtful. Lysons and Faulkner say it is properly Wendon, the manor of Wendon being mentioned in a deed of conveyance, in 1449; but it is also called, in various old documents, by the name of Wandon, Wansdon, Wansdown, and Wandham. It seems to have been first called by its present name about the end of the seventeenth century. The green, as such, has long since disappeared, and some national schools now occupy its site. In 1828 St. John's Church was erected, as a chapel of ease to Fulham. The edifice covers the spot which was formerly the "village pond," but which was filled up when the spread of building in this direction rendered such a proceeding necessary. The church is a brick building, of common-place Gothic design, with a tall tower, adorned with pinnacles.

There were at one time a few noteworthy old houses at Walham Green, but of these scarcely a vestige now remains; and within the last half-century the place may be said to have assumed altogether a new aspect, more especially since the erection of the Butchers' Almshouses, the first

* See Vol. V., p. 27.

stone of which was laid by Lord Ravensworth, in 1840. Since that time, as Mr. Croker informs us, "fancy fairs and bazaars, with horticultural exhibitions, have been fashionably patronised at Walham Green by omnibus companies, for the support and enlargement of this institution." The almshouses are a neat cluster of buildings, occupying three sides of a square, opening upon Farm Place, close beside St. John's Church.

In the *London Magazine* for June, 1749, Mr. Bartholomew Roque thus apostrophises, in rhyme, if not in poetry, this once rural spot :—

> " Hail, happy isle ! and happier Walham Green !
> Where all that's fair and beautiful are seen !
> Where wanton zephyrs court the ambient air,
> And sweets ambrosial banish every care ;
> Where thought nor trouble social joy molest,
> Nor vain solicitude can banish rest,
> Peaceful and happy here I reign serene,
> Perplexity defy, and smile at spleen.
> Belles, beaux, and statesmen all around me shine-
> All own me their supreme, me constitute divine ;
> All wait my pleasure, own my awful nod,
> And change the humble gard'ner to the god."

Mr. B. Roque, it need scarcely be added, was a well-known florist in his day ; and the "belles, beaux, and statesmen" by whom he speaks of being surrounded were nothing more nor less than new varieties of flowers dignified by distinguished names. He was brother of Mr. Roque, the surveyor, to whose "Map of London and its Environs, in 1748," we have several times had occasion to refer in the progress of this work.

The "Swan" Brewery and Tavern at Walham Green have been established upwards of a century.

North End, a hamlet of Fulham, lying between Walham Green and Hammersmith Road, is described in the "Ambulator" (1774) as "a pleasant village near Hammersmith, where are the handsome house and finely-disposed gardens lately possessed by the Earl of Tilney, and of the late Sir John Stanley." Mrs. Delaney, in one of her letters to Dr. Swift, in 1736, writes : " My employment this summer has been making a grotto at North End for my grandfather, Sir John Stanley." The mansion, called Browne's House, was at the commencement of the last century the seat of Lord Griffin, but in 1718 became the property of Sir J. Stanley. It was afterwards owned by Francis Earl Brooke, who sold it to the Duke of Devonshire, by whom it was sold, in 1761, to Sir Gilbert Heathcote. It was pulled down about the year 1800, and its site turned into a brickfield.

At North End Lodge, close by Walham Green, lived for some time Mr. Albert Smith, the popular lecturer and writer, and here he died, in 1860.

Jacob Tonson, the celebrated bookseller, of whom we have already spoken in our account of the Strand,[*] had a house at North End for many years, before removing to Barn Elms, just above Putney; and Mrs. Nisbet (afterwards Lady Boothby) was likewise at one time a resident here.

North End Road, by which we now proceed on our way to Hammersmith, is almost one continuous line of ordinary cottages and middle-class shops, which are rapidly extending on the left-hand side over Fulham Fields. In Faulkner's time, at the commencement of this century, it was a country road, winding between market gardens, but contained a few good houses, which had been "successively occupied by several eminent and remarkable characters." These, however, have now for the most part disappeared.

On the east side of the road, at a short distance from Walham Green, stands Beaufort House, now used as the head-quarters of the South Middlesex Volunteer Corps, and the meeting-place for the sports and races of the London Athletic Club; and between this and West London and Westminster Cemetery, from which it is separated by the West London Junction Railway, is Lillie Bridge Running-ground, a place familiar to the lovers of cricket, pedestrian matches, bicycle races, &c.

Foote, the dramatist and comedian, resided for many years at North End, where he had a favourite villa. The place when he took it was advertised to be completely furnished, but he had not been there long before the cook complained that there was not a rolling-pin. "No!" said he; "then bring me a saw, I will soon make one;" which he accordingly did, of one of the mahogany bed-posts. The next day it was discovered that a coal-scuttle was wanted, when he supplied this deficiency with a drawer from a curious japan chest. A carpet being wanted in the parlour, he ordered a new white cotton counterpane to be laid, to save the boards. His landlord paying him a visit, to inquire how he liked his new residence, was greatly astonished to find such disorder, as he considered it. He remonstrated with Foote, and complained of the injury his furniture had sustained ; but Foote insisted upon it all the complaint was on his side, considering the trouble he had been at to supply these necessaries, notwithstanding he had advertised his house completely furnished. The landlord now threatened the law, upon which Foote threatened to take him off, saying an auctioneer was a fruitful character. This last consideration weighed with the landlord, and he quietly put up with his loss.

The house, upon the improvement of which Foote spent large sums of money, was for many years called The Hermitage, and is now known as Mount Carmel Retreat. It stands in North End Road, at the corner of Lillie Road, and is surrounded by a large garden enclosed by high walls.

Exactly opposite to this house, at the angle of the road, stood till recently an old dwelling-house called Cambridge Lodge, which was once the abode of Francesco Bartolozzi, the celebrated Florentine artist, who arrived in England in 1764, and came to reside here in 1777. He was the father of Madame Vestris, the well-known comedian, singer, and theatrical manageress.

A little to the west of North End Road, almost surrounded by market gardens, stands Normand House, a large, rambling, old-fashioned brick building, profusely overgrown with ivy. Over the principal gateway is the date, 1664, and the building is said to have been used as an hospital during the Great Plague in the following year. In 1813, according to Faulkner, the local historian, "it was appropriated for the reception of insane ladies." Mr. Croker, in his "Walk from London to Fulham," says that Sir E. Lytton Bulwer at one time resided here. The house is now once more used as a lunatic asylum for ladies.

Close by is a small house called Wentworth Cottage, once occupied by Mr. and Mrs. S. C. Hall. In the garden in front of the house grows a willow planted by them from a slip of that which overshadowed the grave of Napoleon at St. Helena.

The open ground hereabouts, known as Fulham Fields, but which is being rapidly encroached upon by the hands of the builder, was formerly called "No Man's Land." Faulkner says that it contained in his time (1813) "about six houses." One of these was "an ancient house, once the residence of the family of Plumbe," the site of which is now covered by a cluster of dwellings which were erected for the labourers in the surrounding market gardens, that reach from Walham Green nearly to the Thames, the North End Road forming the eastern boundary of Fulham Fields.

Retracing our steps to North End Road, we will resume our walk northwards. Immediately beyond Bartolozzi's house, enclosed by an old wall supposed to date from the time of Charles II., stood a tall house, once the residence of Cheeseman, the engraver, a pupil of Bartolozzi. Farther on, on the opposite side of the way, also stood till 1846, when it was pulled down, Walnut-tree Cottage, which was at one time the residence of Edmund Kean, the actor, and also of Copley, the artist, the father of Lord Lyndhurst. Cipriani, the painter,

once had a house close by this spot, but it has long since shared the fate of its more aristocratic neighbours, and been removed, to give place to modern bricks and mortar.

A large stucco-fronted house on the right, close by the railway station, was built many years ago by Mr. Slater, as a family residence, but has since been converted to other purposes. About the year 1875 the mansion was taken by the benevolent Society of St. John of Jerusalem, by whom it was fitted up, with the intention of using it as a convalescent hospital; but circumstances arose which caused the idea to be abandoned. The house was, however, subsequently secured by a religious sisterhood, by whom it has been used for the above-mentioned purpose, and known as St. Saviour's Convalescent Hospital.

The house once inhabited by Dr. Crotch, the distinguished musician, which was situated a short distance farther up the road, has been levelled with the ground, and a row of humble dwellings, called Grove Cottages, erected in its place. Dr. Crotch's house is said to have been previously the residence of Ryland, the engraver, who was executed for forgery in 1783.

Nearly opposite Grove Cottages is a large house —now cut up into two, one being stucco-fronted, and ornamented with a veranda, and the other faced with red brick—which was for many years the residence of Samuel Richardson, the author of "Clarissa Harlowe," "Sir Charles Grandison," &c. Here he entertained large literary parties, including such men as Johnson, Boswell, &c. In the gardens attached to the house are some fine cedars. Most of Richardson's works were written whilst he was living here. Mrs. Barbauld, in her "Life" of the novelist, prefixed to his "Correspondence," tells us how that he "used to write in a little summer-house or grotto, within his garden, at North End, before the family were up, and when they met at breakfast he communicated the progress of his story."

Richardson's villa, of which a view is given in his "Correspondence," is described by Faulkner as being situated near the Hammersmith turnpike. The precise locality of the house, however, seems to have been unknown to some at least of the inhabitants at the commencement of this century, for Sir Richard Phillips used to relate with glee the following anecdote respecting his inquiries in the neighbourhood:—"A widow kept a public-house near the corner of North End Lane, about two miles from Hyde Park Corner, where she had lived about fifty years; and I wanted to determine the house in which Samuel Richardson, the novelist, had resided in North End Lane. She remembered his person, and described him as 'a round, short gentleman, who most days passed her door,' and she said she used to serve his family with beer. 'He used to live and carry on his business,' said I, 'in Salisbury Square.' 'As to that,' said she, 'I know nothing, for I never was in London.' 'Never in London!' said I, 'and in health, with the free use of your limbs!' 'No,' replied the woman; 'I

already spoken, may be mentioned Burbage, the actor, who at one time had a house at North End; Norden, the topographer, who dated the preface of his projected "Speculum Britanniæ" from his "poore house neere Fulham;" John Florio, a scholar of the sixteenth century, and tutor to Prince Henry, son of James I.; and George Cartwright, the author of a long-forgotten play called "Heroic Love, or the Infanta of Spain: a Tragedy, 1661."

RANELAGH HOUSE.

had no business there, and had enough to do at home.' 'Well, then,' I observed, 'you know your own neighbourhood the better—which was the house of Mr. Richardson, in the next lane?' 'I don't know,' she replied; 'I am, as I told you, no traveller. *I never was up the lane*—I only know that he did live somewhere up the lane.' 'Well,' said I, 'but living in Fulham, you go to church?' 'No,' said she, 'I never have time; on a Sunday our house is always full—I never was at Fulham but once, and that was when I was married, and many people say that was once too often, though my husband was as good a man as ever broke bread—God rest his soul!'" *Sic transit gloria.*

Among the "notabilities" either resident in or connected with Fulham, of whom we have not

Another resident was John Dunning, Lord Ashburton, who having struggled in early life against a narrow income, left behind him a fortune of £150,000, though he died at fifty-two. Here, on reaching affluence, he gave a magnificent dinner in honour of his mother, who was not only astonished, but shocked, at the delicacies under which the table groaned, and went off home next morning, because she would not witness such scandalous prodigality. "I tell you," said the good woman, "such goings-on can come to no good, and you will see the end of it before long. However, it shall not be said that your mother encouraged you in such waste, for I mean to set off to Devonshire in the coach to-morrow morning;" and despite her son's entreaties, she kept her word.

THE "RED COW" INN, HAMMERSMITH.

CHAPTER XXXIX.

HAMMERSMITH.

Ecclesiastical Division of Hammersmith from Fulham—The Principal Streets and Thoroughfares—The Railway Stations—The " Bell and Anchor " Tavern—The " Red Cow "—Nazareth House, the Home of " The Little Sisters of the Poor "—The Old Benedictine Convent, now a Training College for the Priesthood—Dr. Bonaventura Giffard—The West London Hospital—The Broadway—Brook Green—The Church of the Holy Trinity—St. Joseph's Almshouses—St. Mary's Normal College—Roman Catholic Reformatories—Blythe House—Market Gardens—Messrs. Lee's Nursery—The Church of St. John the Evangelist, in Dartmouth Road—Godolphin School—Ravenscourt Park· The Ancient Manor House of Pallenswick—Starch Green—The Old London Road—A Quaint Old Pump—Queen Street—The Parish Church—The Monument of Sir Nicholas Crispe—The Enshrined Heart of St. Nicholas Crispe—The Impostor, John Tuck—Latymer Schools—The Convent of the Good Shepherd—Sussex House—Brandenburgh House—George Bubb Dodington—The Margravine of Brandenburgh-Anspach—The Funeral of Queen Caroline—Hammersmith Suspension Bridge—Hammersmith Mall—The High Bridge—The " Dove " Coffee-house, and Thomson the Poet—Sir Samuel Morland—The Upper Mall—Catharine, Queen of Charles II.– Dr. Radcliffe—Arthur Murphy—De Louther-bourg—Other Eminent Residents—Leigh Hunt—St. Peter's Church—A Public-spirited Artist—The Hammersmith Ghost.

THE town of Hammersmith, at the entrance of which we now find ourselves, is a large straggling place, with a population of over 50,000 souls. It lies principally on the high road, which, before the introduction of railways, was the main thorough-fare from London to the West of England. Down to the year 1834 it was known parochially as the Hammersmith division, or side, of the parish of Fulham ; but since that period it has not only been made a separate parish, but it has also become in its turn the parent of four separate ecclesiastical districts. During the Interregnum, it was proposed to make the hamlet parochial, and to add to it Sir Nicholas Crispe's house, between Fulham Road and the river, of which we shall presently speak, and a part of North End, "extending from the common highway to London unto the end of Gibbs's Green." The parish now extends from Kensington on the east, along the high road to Turnham Green, and by the side of the Thames from the Crab Tree to Chiswick; and it includes the hamlets of Brook Green, Pallenswick, or Stanbrook Green, and Shepherd's Bush. Faulkner, in his "History of Fulham" (1813), in speaking of the separation of Hammersmith from Fulham, and its erection into an ecclesiastical district, remarks, "When the inhabitants of Fulham and the inhabitants of Hammersmith did mutually agree to divide the parish, it was also agreed that a ditch should be dug as a boundary between them, it being the custom of those days to divide districts in this manner, whereupon a ditch was dug for the above purposes. This watercourse," he adds, "begins a little to the west of the elegant seat of the late Bubb Dodington, Esq. [Brandenburgh House]; there it is formed into canals, fish-ponds, &c.; out of his garden it crosseth the road from Fulham Field to Hammersmith, and so in a meandering course bearing westerly and northerly, it crosseth the London Road opposite the road leading to Brook Green, and from thence, on the north side of the London Road, it runs easterly, and falls into Chelsea Creek, at Counter's Bridge."

The town of Hammersmith consists of several streets, the principal of which is King Street, which formed part of the road to Windsor, about a mile and a half long; at the eastern end this street widens into the Broadway, where it is crossed by a road from Brook Green and the Uxbridge Road, which is continued over the Suspension Bridge into Surrey. The main streets are lined throughout with numerous shops, while the busy posting-houses of former times have given way to four large railway stations—the London and South-Western, in the Grove; the North London, in the Brentford Road; and the Metropolitan and the Metropolitan District in the Broadway. Altogether, therefore, the place now wears a modern business-like aspect, in spite of a number of old red-brick mansions. At the commencement of the present century, as we learn from Faulkner, the village had several good houses in and about it, and was "inhabited by gentry and persons of quality." Now these old mansions are for the most part pulled down, converted into public institutions or schools, cut

up into smaller tenements, or made to give place to large and busy factories. Here and there a picturesque old tavern may still be seen, recalling to mind the times when stage-coaches travelled along the Hammersmith Road, on their way to the West of England; one such, in the neighbourhood of North End Road, is the "Bell and Anchor," an inn much patronised by people of fashion in the early part of the reign of George III., though now frequented only by the working population about North End. Mr. Larwood tells us, in his "History of Sign-boards," that representations of the place and of its visitors may be seen in caricatures of the period published by Bowles and Carver, of St. Paul's Churchyard. Another public-house, farther along the road, bearing the sign of the "Red Cow," still bears upon its exterior clear evidence of its antiquity: it is said to have stood here for over a couple of centuries.

If there is one spot in the neighbourhood of London to which the English Roman Catholics look with greater veneration than another, just as the Nonconformist looks to Bunhill Fields Cemetery, that spot is Hammersmith, which contains an unusual number of establishments belonging to the members of that faith.

On the south side of the high road, just before entering the town, and close to the busy thoroughfare of King Street East, stands a tall Gothic building, of secluded and religious appearance, three storeys high, the home of those noble-hearted ladies, of whose self-denial any communion in the world might well be proud—the "Little Sisters of the Poor." We will not attempt to describe it in our own words, but will employ those of the biographer of Thomas Walker, the London police magistrate, and author of "The Original"—a gentleman whose Protestant zeal is beyond suspicion. He writes: "We are under the roof of the Little Sisters of the Poor. The house is full of old folk, men and women. It is Death's vestibule governed by the gentlest charity I have ever seen acting on the broken fortunes of mankind. The sisters are so many gentlewomen who have put aside all those worldly vanities so dear in these days of hoops and paint to the majority of their sisters, and have dedicated their lives to the menial service of destitute old age. They beg crusts and bones from door to door, and spread the daily board for their *protégés* with the crumbs from the rich men's tables. And it is only after the old men and women have feasted on the best of the crumbs that the noble sisters break their fast. I stepped into the Little Sisters' refectory. The dishes were heaps of hard crusts and scraps of cheese; and at the ends of the table were jugs of water. The table was as clean as that of the primmest epicure. The *serviette* of each sister was folded within a ring. And the sisters sit daily—are sitting to-day, will sit to-morrow—with perfect cheerfulness, their banquet the crumbs from pauper tables ! Cheerfulness will digest the hardest crust, the horniest cheese, or these pious women had died long ago. He who may find it difficult to make the first step to the cleanly, healthy, gentlemanly life into which Thomas Walker schooled himself, should knock at the gate of the hermitage wherein the Little Sisters of the Poor banquet pauper age, and pass into the refectory of these gentlewomen. It is but a stone's-throw out of the noisy world. It lies in the midst of London. Here let the half-repentant, the wavering Sybarite rest awhile, pondering the help which a holy cheerfulness gives to the stomach —yea, when the food is an iron crust and cheese-parings." The edifice, called Nazareth House, or the "Convent of the Little Daughters of Nazareth," is shut in from the roadway by a brick wall, and the grounds attached to it extend back a considerable distance. It provides a home not only for aged, destitute and infirm poor persons, but likewise a hospital for epileptic children.

On the opposite side of the high road, and within a few yards from Nazareth House, is a group of Roman Catholic institutions, the chief of which is the old Benedictine convent, now used as a training college for the priesthood. The site of this college has been devoted to the purposes of Roman Catholic education from the days of King Henry VIII., for it was a school for young ladies for more than three centuries down to the year 1869, when the building was first used as a training college. But the tradition is that it existed as a convent some time before the Reformation; and that subsequently to that date, though ostensibly it was only a girls' school, in reality it was carried on by professed religious ladies, who were nuns in disguise, and who said their office and recited their litanies and rosaries in secret, whilst wearing the outward appearance of ordinary Englishwomen. Faulkner, in his "History of Hammersmith," mentions this tradition, and adds that it is supposed " to have escaped the general destruction of religious houses on account of its want of endowment." If this really was the case, then poverty is sometimes even to be preferred to wealth.

On the breaking-up of the religious houses in England most of the sisterhoods retired to the Continent, where they kept up the practice of their vows unbroken ; and we find that a body of Benedictine sisters settled at Dunkirk in 1662,

under their abbess, Dame Mary Caryl, whom they regarded as the founder of their house, and who was previously a nun at Ghent. Another Benedictine house, largely recruited from the ladies of the upper classes in England—a colony from the same city—was settled about the same time at Boulogne, and soon after removed to Pontoise, in the neighbourhood of Paris.

As the English Reformation, two centuries and a half before, had driven this Ghent sisterhood from England, so in 1793 the outbreak of the first French Revolution wafted its members back again —not, however, by a very tranquil passage—to the shores which their great-great-grandparents had been forced to leave. Already, however, something had been done to prepare the way for their return. Catherine of Braganza, the poor neglected queen of Charles II., invited over to England some members of a sisterhood at Munich, called the Institute of the Blessed Virgin, and these she settled and supported during her husband's life in a house in St. Martin's Lane. On the death of the king, finding their tenure so near to the Court to be rather insecure, these ladies were glad to migrate farther afield. The chance was soon given to them. A certain Mrs. Frances Bedingfeld, a sister, we believe, of the first baronet of that family, procured, by the aid of the queen, the possession of a large house—indeed, the largest house at that time—in Hammersmith, to the north of the road, near the Broadway, and with a spacious garden behind it. This house adjoined the ladies' school which we have already mentioned ; and in course of time the *sub rosâ* convent and the sisterhood from St. Martin's Lane were merged into one institution under an abbess, who followed the Benedictine rule. The Lady Frances Bedingfeld, as foundress, became the first abbess ; and she was succeeded by Mrs. Cecilia Cornwallis, who was a kinswoman of Queen Anne. The school, though somewhat foreign to the scope of a contemplative order, was now carried on more openly and avowedly, though still in modest retirement, by the Benedictine sisterhood, who, adding a third messuage to their two houses, at once taught the daughters of the Roman Catholic aristocracy, and established a home in which ladies in their widowhood might take up their residence *en pension*, with the privilege of hearing mass and receiving the sacraments in the little chapel attached to it.

Thus the school became absorbed in the convent two centuries ago. In the year 1680 the infamous Titus Oates obtained from the authorities a commission to search the house, as being a reputed nunnery, as well as a well-known home of Papists and recusants. It is not a little singular that, although there was no cheap daily press in his day, we have two separate and independent reports of this proceeding which have come down to us. The first is to be found in the *Domestic Intelligencer, or News both from City and Country,* for January 13th, 1679-80. The other report, more briefly and tersely expressed, appears in the *True Domestic Intelligencer* of the same date.

Exactly a century passed away, so far as any records or traditions have been preserved, before the Benedictine sisters again experienced any alarm; but in June, 1780, the convent was doomed to destruction by the infuriated mob. The only precaution which the nuns appear to have taken was to pack up the sacramental plate in a chest, which the lady abbess intrusted to a faithful friend and neighbour, a Mr. Gomme, and who kindly buried it in his garden till the danger had passed away.

Twenty-five ladies from foreign convents on their arrival in England came to Hammersmith, and made it their temporary home until they could obtain admission into other religious houses. In fact, on their arrival they found only three aged nuns, including the abbess, who rejoiced at being able to give them the shelter which they so much needed. The school was accordingly carried on by the Abbess of Pontoise (Dame Prujean), who here revived the school which had dwindled away; and for many years it was the only Catholic ladies' school near the metropolis. Faulkner gives no list of abbesses who ruled this convent during the two centuries of its existence at Hammersmith. We are able, however, to give it complete from a private source, a MS. in the possession of Mrs. Jervis, a near relative of the Markhams, who, at various times, were "professed" within its walls. The list runs as follows:—Frances Bedingfeld (1669), Cicely Cornwallis (1672), Frances Bernard (1715), Mary Delison (1739), Frances Gentil (1760), Marcella Dillon (1781), Mary Placida Messenger (1812), and Placida Selby (1819). The convent at Hammersmith, composed as it was of three private houses, and built in such a way as to do anything rather than attract the attention of the public eye, presented anything but an attractive appearance. A high wall screened it from the passers-by, and the southern face was simply a plain brick front, pierced with two rows of plain sash windows. Inside, the rooms used as dormitories and class-rooms had the same heavy and dreary look, as if the place were a cross between a badly-endowed parsonage and a workhouse school. The chapel, which was built in 1812 by Mr.

George Gillow, and served for many years—in fact, down to 1852—as the "mission chapel" of Hammersmith and the neighbourhood, still stands, the lower end of it having been cut off and made into a library for the students who have occupied these buildings, now called St. Thomas' Seminary, since they were vacated by the sisterhood. At the south-eastern corner, between the house and the road, stood a porter's lodge and the guest-rooms; but these have been pulled down. Here, too, it is said, stood the original chapel. The principal of the training college, Bishop Wethers, coadjutor to Cardinal Manning, resides in the western portion of the building, formerly the residence of the Portuguese minister, the Baron Moncorvo.

In the middle of the eighteenth century the Vicar-Apostolic of the London District—as the chief Roman Catholic Bishop in England was then called—had his home at Hammersmith, from which place several of the pastoral letters of those prelates were dated.

Here—probably in apartments attached to the convent—died, in 1733, in his ninetieth year, Dr. Bonaventura Giffard, chaplain to King James II., and nominated by that king to the headship of Magdalen College, Oxford, though divested of his office at the Revolution. He became afterwards one of the Roman Catholic bishops *in partibus,* and lived a life of apostolical poverty, simplicity, and charity. On his deposition from Magdalen College, Dr. Giffard was arrested and imprisoned in Newgate, simply for the exercise of his spiritual functions. Being a man of peace, he lived privately, with the connivance of the Government of the time, in London and at Hammersmith, where he was regarded as almost a saint on account of his charity. He attended the Earl of Derwentwater before his execution at the Tower in 1716.

Here Dr. Challoner, the ablest Roman Catholic controversialist of the eighteenth century, was consecrated, in January, 1741, a bishop of his church and Vicar-Apostolic of the London District, with the title of Bishop of Debra *in partibus infidelium.* Cardinal Weld was for three years director of the Benedictine nuns of this convent.

"A nunnery," writes Priscilla Wakefield in 1814, "is not a common object in England; but there is at Hammersmith one which is said to have taken its rise from a boarding-school established in the reign of Charles II., for young ladies of the Catholic Church. The zeal of the governesses and teachers," she adds, "induced them voluntarily to subject themselves to monastic rules, a system that has been preserved by many devotees, who have taken the veil and secluded themselves from the world."

In King Street East stands the West London Hospital, a handsome building, wholly dependent on voluntary contributions. Stow mentions a Lock Hospital* at Hammersmith; but its site cannot be fixed.

On the south side of the main road, near Brook Green, at the corner of "Red Cow Lane," stand the new buildings of St. Paul's School, which was removed to this site in 1884, from its very confined site in St. Paul's Churchyard. The buildings are lofty and fine, and stand in a playground of about eight acres. They are from the designs of Waterhouse, and will accommodate about 500 scholars.

The Broadway forms the central part of the town, whence roads diverge to the right and left; that to the right leads to Brook Green, whilst that on the left hand leads to the Suspension Bridge across the Thames. On the north side of the Broadway, up a narrow court, is a large house surrounding a quadrangle. It used to be a sort of seraglio for George IV., when Prince of Wales; but it is now cut up into tenements for poor people.

Brook Green—so called from a small tributary of the Thames which once wound its way through it from north-west to south-east—connects the Broadway, on the north side, with Shepherd's Bush, which lies west of Notting Hill, on the Uxbridge Road. It is a long narrow strip of common land, bordered with elms and chestnuts, and can still boast of a few good houses. In former times a fair was held here annually in May, lasting three days. At the eastern end of the green is a group of Roman Catholic buildings, the chief of which is the Church of the Holy Trinity. This is a spacious stone edifice of the Early Decorated style of architecture, and has a lofty tower and spire at the north-eastern corner. The first stone of the building was laid in 1851, by Cardinal Wiseman.

The external appearance of this church derives some additional interest from its contiguity to the scarcely less beautiful almshouses of St. Joseph, the first stone of which was laid by the Duchess of Norfolk, in May, 1851. The almshouses are built in a style to correspond with the church, and form together with it a spacious quadrangle. They provide accommodation for forty aged persons, and are managed by the committee of the Aged Poor Society.

On the opposite side of the road stands St. Mary's Normal College, built from the designs of Mr. Charles Hansom, of Clifton, in the Gothic style of architecture. It contains a chapel, and is capable of accommodating seventy students. Near at hand are a Roman Catholic Reformatory for boys and another for girls. The former is located in an ancient mansion, Blythe House. This house, Faulkner informs us, was reported to have been haunted; "many strange stories," he adds, "were related of ghosts and apparitions having been seen here; but it turned out at last that a gang of smugglers had taken up their residence in it, supposing that this sequestered place would be favourable to their illegal pursuits." No doubt, in the last century, the situation of Blythe House was lonely and desolate enough to favour such a supposition as the above; and, apart from this, the roads about Hammersmith in the reign of George II. would seem to have been haunted by footpads and robbers. At all events, Mr. Lewins, in his "History of the Post Office," reminds us that in 1757, the boy who carried the mail for Portsmouth happening to dismount at Hammersmith, about three miles from Hyde Park Corner, and to call for beer, some thieves took the opportunity to cut the mail-bags from off the horse's crupper, and got away undiscovered. The plunder was probably all the more valuable, as there was then no "money-order office," and even large sums of money were enclosed in letters in the shape of bank-notes.

At that time nearly all the land in the outskirts of Hammersmith was under cultivation as nurseries or market gardens, whence a large portion of the produce for the London markets was obtained. Bradley, in his "Philosophical Account of the Works of Nature," published in 1721, tells us that "the gardens about Hammersmith are famous for strawberries, raspberries, currants, gooseberries, and such like; and if early fruit is our desire," he adds, " Mr. Millet's garden at North End, near the same place, affords us cherries, apricots, and curiosities of those kinds, some months before the natural season."

Messrs. Lee's nursery garden here enjoyed great celebrity towards the close of the last century; and it is said that they were the first who introduced the fuchsia, now so common, to the public. Their nursery was formerly a vineyard, where large quantities of Burgundy wine were made. To store the wine a thatched house was built, and several large cellars were excavated. The rooms above were afterwards in the occupation of Worlidge, the engraver, and here he executed many of the most valuable and admired of his works.

It was close by Lee's nursery that Samuel Taylor Coleridge stayed frequently with his friends the

---

* See Vol. V., pp. 14, 215, and 528.

Morgans, who lived on the road between Kensington and Hammersmith. H. Crabb Robinson, in his "Diary," under date July 28, 1811, tells us how he "after dinner walked to Morgan's, beyond Kensington, to see Coleridge, and found Southey there."

The region northward of the main thoroughfare through Hammersmith is being rapidly covered with streets, many of the houses being of a superior

The buildings include a large school-room, capable of accommodating 200 boys, several class-rooms, a dining-hall, dormitories for forty boarders, and a residence for the head-master.

Ravenscourt Park, at the north-western extremity of Hammersmith, marks the site of the ancient manor-house of Pallenswick, which is supposed to have belonged to Alice Perrers, or Pierce, a lady of not very enviable fame at the court of Edward III.,

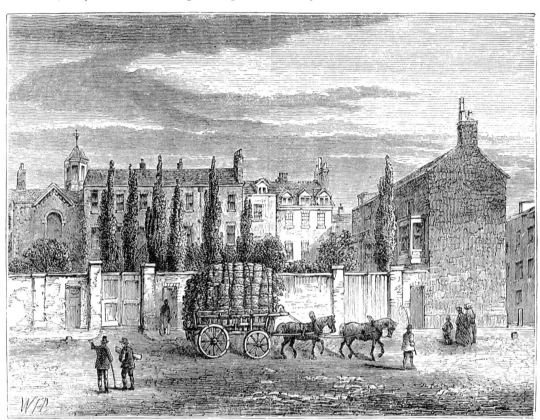

THE CONVENT, HAMMERSMITH, IN 1800.

class, particularly in the neighbourhood of Ravenscourt Park. In Dartmouth Road is the church of St. John the Evangelist, a large and lofty edifice, of Early-English architecture, built in 1860, from the designs of Mr. Butterfield. It was erected by voluntary contributions, at a cost of about £6,000. Close by St. John's Church is the Godolphin School, which was founded in the sixteenth century under the will of William Godolphin, but remodelled as a grammar school, in accordance with a scheme of the Court of Chancery, in 1861. The buildings of this institution are surrounded by playgrounds, about four acres in extent; the school is built, like the adjoining church, of brick, with stone mullions and dressings, and it is in the Early Collegiate Gothic style, from the designs of Mr. C. H. Cooke.

upon whose banishment, in 1378, the place was seized by the Crown. The survey of the manor, taken about that time, describes it as containing "forty acres of land, sixty of pasture, and one and a half of meadow." The manor-house is described as "well built, in good repair, and containing a large hall, chapel, &c." In 1631 the manor of Pallenswick was sold to Sir Richard Gurney, the brave and loyal Lord Mayor of London who died a prisoner in the Tower in 1647. Down to nearly the close of the last century, the manor-house was surrounded by a moat, and Faulkner describes it as "of the style and date of the French architect Mansard . . . Tradition," he adds, "has assigned the site of this house as having been a hunting-seat of Edward III. His arms, richly

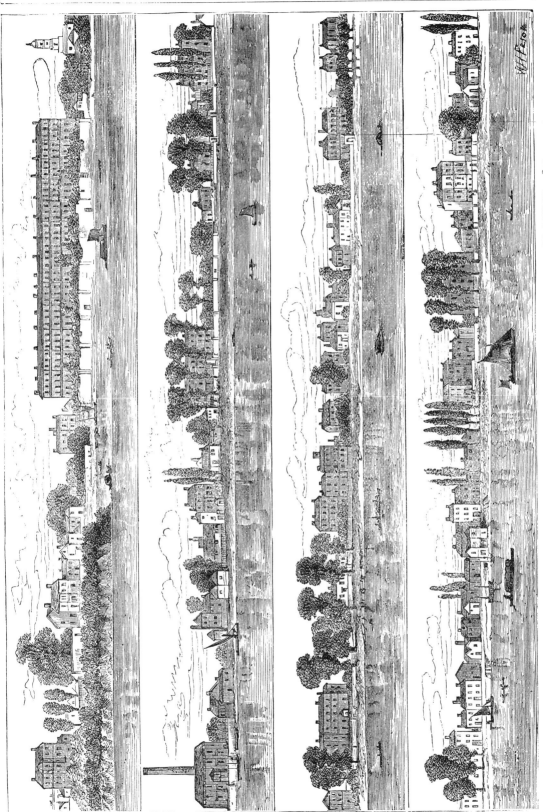

THE RIVER FRONT OF HAMMERSMITH, FROM THE EYOT AT CHISWICK TO THE BRIDGE, 1800.

carved in wood, stood, till within these few years, in a large upper room, but they fell to pieces upon being removed when the house was repaired; the crest of Edward the Black Prince, which was placed over the arms, is still preserved in a parlour, and is in good preservation. . . . It is very probable that this piece of carving was an appendage to the ancient manor-house when it was in the possession of Alice Pierce."

A little to the north of Ravenscourt Park, and leading up towards Shepherd's Bush, on the Uxbridge Road, lies Starch Green, which—like Stamford Brook Green and Gaggle-Goose Green, in the same neighbourhood, mentioned by Faulkner as "two small rural villages "—is now being rapidly covered with houses, and is one of those places which is fortunate enough not to have a history.

The ancient high road from the west to London commenced near the " Pack-horse " Inn, at Turnham Green, which lies at the western extremity of Hammersmith, and of which we shall speak presently. It passed through Stamford Brook Green, Pallenswick, and Bradmoor. At the beginning of this century it was very narrow and impassable, though large sums of money had been spent in its repair. The road, which is now in part lined with houses, skirts the north side of Ravenscourt Park, and joins the Uxbridge Road at Shepherd's Bush. At the junction of the two roads formerly stood an ancient inn, where all the country travellers stopped in their journeys to or from the metropolis. This is supposed to have been the house that Miles Syndercombe hired for the purpose of carrying out his proposed assassination of Cromwell, in January, 1657, while on his journey from Hampton Court to London.

Dull, dreary, and uninteresting as this part of Hammersmith may have been in former times, it appears to have possessed at least one curiosity; the portrait of a quaint old pump, in Webb's Lane, with a sort of font in front of it to catch the water, figures in Hone's " Every-Day Book," under September 10th, but apparently little or nothing was or is known of its history. Under the portrait in the " Every-Day Book " are the following lines :—

> " A walking man should not refrain
> To take a saunter up Webb's Lane,
> Towards Shepherd's Bush, to see a rude
> Old lumbering pump. It's made of wood,
> And pours its water in a font
> So beautiful that, if he don't
> Admire how such a combination
> Was formed in such a situation,
> He has no power of causation,
> Or taste, or feeling, but must live
> Painless and pleasureless, and give

> Himself to doing—what he can,
> And die—a sorry sort of man ! "

Retracing our steps to the Broadway, we enter Queen Street, which passes in a southerly direction to the Fulham Road, from the junction of the Broadway and Bridge Road. On the west side of this street stands the parish church, dedicated to St. Paul. It was originally a chapel of ease to Fulham, and is remarkable as the church in which one of the last of those romantic entombments known as heart-burials took place. The church was built during the reign of Charles I., at the cost of Sir Nicholas Crispe, a wealthy citizen of London.

Bowack thus describes this church in 1705 :— " The very name of a chapel of ease sufficiently points out the causes of its erection, and indeed the great number of people inhabiting in and near this place, at such a great distance from Fulham Church, made the erecting of a chapel long desired and talked of before it could be effected; but about the year 1624 the great number of gentry residing hereabouts being sensible of the inconvenience, as well as the poorer people, began in earnest to think of this remedy; and after several of them had largely subscribed, they set about the work with all possible application. The whole number of inhabitants who were willing to enjoy the benefit of this chapel voluntarily subscribed, and were included within the limits belonging to it upon the division, so that a very considerable sum was secured. . . . About the year 1628 the foundation of the chapel was laid, and the building was carried on with such expedition, that in the year 1631 it was completely finished and consecrated ; though, at the west end, there is a stone fixed in the wall with this date, 1630, which was placed there when the said end was built, probably before the inside was begun. The whole building is of brick, very spacious and regular, and at the east [west] end is a large square tower of the same with a ring of six bells. The inside is very well finished, being beautified with several devices in painting. The ceiling also is very neatly painted, and in several compartments and ovals were finely depicted the arms of England, also roses, thistles, fleur-de-luces, &c., all of which the rebels in their furious zeal dashed out, or daubed over ; though this particular act was more the effect of their malice against his Majesty King Charles I., and the sacred kingly office, than their blind zeal against Popery, endeavouring, to the utmost, that the memory of a king should be expunged the world. The glass of the chancel window was also finely painted with Moses, Aaron, &c. ; also the arms of the most considerable benefactors; but these have been much abused (probably by the same ungodly crew), as relics of Popery and superstition; however, the remains of them evince their former art and beauty, which was very extraordinary. In several of the other windows likewise, there are the benefactors' coats of arms, particularly Sir Nicholas Crispe's, who may be called its founder, himself giving, in money and materials, the sum of £700 towards its building. It was likewise very well paved, and pewed with wainscot, and made commodious and beautiful within; the whole charge of which was about two thousand and odd pounds. . . . Notwithstanding the ill usage this chapel has met with, it is still in very good condition; beside this, adorned with several stately monuments now standing."

Such, then, was the condition of this church within three-quarters of a century of its erection. Since that time it has undergone extensive repairs on different occasions, and in the year 1864 it was restored and enlarged. But it was soon found that no amount of patching and repairing would convert an unsightly building into a noble structure worthy of the parish and of the sacred purposes for which it is designed. Accordingly in 1882–3, the old church was pulled down, and a new one of lofty proportions erected on the same site. When completed it will seat about 1,000 worshippers on the floor; but at present the nave only is built. The most interesting portion of the old church was some carving in festoons over the communion-table, said to be the work of Grinling Gibbons; but this was found to be past all repair. The quaint Italian baldachino or reredos in the former church is said to have been put up by Archbishop Laud, who consecrated the building, using the same form of prayer which was used, after an interval of more than two centuries, at the opening of the new edifice. The architects of the new church are Messrs. Seddon and Gough, and the first stone was laid by the lamented Duke of Albany in July, 1882.

A picturesque avenue of old trees leads to the north door of the church, whilst the footpath is lined on each side by several rows of tombs, some bearing foreign names, probably of the Walloons employed in the tapestry works, or of persons who were domesticated at Brandenburgh House during the residence there of the Margrave of Anspach and his widow. Within the church are the tombs of many persons famous in history. Among them may be mentioned one of black and white marble, to the Earl of Mulgrave, who commanded a squadron against the Spanish Armada,

and was afterwards President of the North under James I.; he died in 1646. A tomb, with bust of Alderman James Smith, who died in 1667; he was the founder of Bookham Almshouses, and "the father of twenty children." Another, of Sir Edward Nevill, Justice of Common Pleas, who died in 1705. Thomas Worlidge, the painter, whose unrivalled etchings are choice gems of the English School of Art, is commemorated by a tablet; as also is Arthur Murphy, the dramatic writer and essayist, and friend of Dr. Johnson. Sir Samuel Morland, Sir Elijah Impey, and Sir George Shea were likewise buried here.

As we have intimated above, however, the most remarkable monument in Hammersmith parish church is that of Sir Nicholas Crispe, of whom Faulkner speaks as "a man of loyalty, that deserves perpetual remembrance." "What especially pleases us in the consideration of the character of this worthy citizen," writes Mr. S. C. Hall, in his "Pilgrimages to English Shrines," "is the broad principle of his humanity: he honoured and revered Charles I. beyond all other beings; he honoured him as a KING, he loved him as a MAN; he contributed largely to his young sovereign's wants during his exile. Yet his loyalty shut not up his heart against those who differed from him in opinion; his sympathies were not conventional, they were not confined to a class, but extended to all his kind. When himself in exile, he made his private misfortunes turn to public benefits; he investigated all foreign improvements and turned them to English uses; he encouraged the farmers of Middlesex in all agricultural pursuits; through his knowledge, new inventions, as to paper-mills, powder-mills, and water-mills, came into familiar use; he discovered the value of the brick-making earth in his immediate neighbourhood, and the art itself, as since practised, was principally, if not entirely, his own." Sir Nicholas, shortly after the Restoration, caused to be erected in Hammersmith Church, in the south-east corner, near the pulpit, a monument of black and white marble, eight feet in height and two in breadth, upon which was placed a bust of the king, immediately beneath which is the following inscription:—"This effigy was erected by the special appointment of Sir Nicholas Crispe, Knight and Baronet, as a grateful commemoration of that glorious martyr, King Charles the First, of blessed memory." Beneath, on a pedestal of black marble, is an urn, enclosing the heart of the brave and loyal knight, which, like the heart of Richard Cœur de Lion and that of the gallant Marquis of Montrose, has found a resting-place apart from that where his body reposes.

On the pedestal is inscribed : " Within this urn is enclosed the heart of Sir Nicholas Crispe, Knight and Baronet, a loyal sharer in the sufferings of his late and present Majesty. He first settled the trade of gold from Guinea, and then built the Castle of Cormantin. He died 28th of July, 1665, aged 67."   Miss Hartshorne, in her work

who, by his will, dated 1624, bequeathed thirty-five acres of land in Hammersmith, "the profits of which were to be appropriated to clothing six poor men, clothing and educating eight poor boys, and distributing in money."   In consequence of the increased value of the land, in Faulkner's time the number of boys had been augmented to thirty,

HAMMERSMITH PARISH CHURCH, IN 1820.

on " Enshrined Hearts," tells us that Sir Nicholas left a sum of money for the especial purpose that his heart might be refreshed with a glass of wine every year, and that his singular bequest was regularly carried out for a century, when his heart became too much decayed.   "Lay my body," he said to his grandson when on his death-bed— " lay my body, as I have directed, in the family vault in the parish church of St. Mildred in Bread Street, but let MY HEART be placed in an urn at my master's feet."

An amusing account of an impostor named John Tuck, who was afterwards transported for other frauds, officiating and preaching in this church as a clergyman in the year 1811, will be found in the "Eccentric." He was the son of a labourer in Devonshire.

Near the church are the Latymer Schools, which were founded in the seventeenth century by Edward Latymer,

and the poor men to ten. In 1879 the Charity Commissioners propounded a scheme under which the Latymer charity was completely remodelled. The school has been rebuilt, and now affords a middle-class education to 250 boys, at a small weekly fee ; and £75 per annum is ordered to be set aside for "six poor men," under the conditions of the will. The uniform which Latymer directed to be worn has been discontinued.

In Queen Street, nearly opposite the church, is a large brick mansion, which formed part of a house once the residence of Edmund Sheffield, Earl of Mulgrave and Baron of Butterwick, who died here in the year 1646. In 1666 the house and premises, then known as the manor-house and farm of Butterwick, were conveyed to the family of the Fernes, by whom the old mansion was modernised and cut up into two. Early in the last century the place was sold to Elijah Impey, father of the Indian judge of that name, whose family long resided in it. The old portion of the mansion was pulled down many years ago. The principal front of the house, as it now stands, is ornamented with four stone classic columns, and it is surmounted by a pediment.

On the right-hand side of the Fulham Road, which branches off from Queen Street opposite the parish church, stands a large group of brick buildings, designed by Pugin, and known as the Convent of the Good Shepherd and the Asylum for Penitent Women. The site was formerly occupied by Beauchamp Lodge. This charity was commenced in 1841 by some ladies of the Order of the Good Shepherd, who came from Angers, in France, to carry on the work of the reformation of female penitents under the auspices of Dr. Griffiths, then "Vicar-Apostolic of the London District."

Farther southward, opposite Alma Terrace, is Sussex House, so named from having been occasionally the residence of the late Duke of Sussex, and where his Royal Highness "was accustomed to steal an hour from state and ceremony, and indulge in that humble seclusion which princes must find the greatest possible luxury."

Mrs. Billington, the singer, lived here for some time; and it was for many years a celebrated house for insane patients, under the late Dr. Forbes Winslow. In speaking of Sussex House, the Rev. J. Richardson, in his "Recollections," tells an amusing story of a visit paid to it by Mrs. Fry, the prison philanthropist, whose restless benevolence was by the uncharitable occasionally mistaken for an impertinent propensity for prying into things with which she had no business. "The Rev. Mr. Clarke, son of the traveller, Dr. Clarke," he writes, "was at one time confined in a lunatic asylum. His visit to the place was fortunately but a short one, and he was pronounced perfectly *compos mentis*. A day or two before he left the place he perceived, from the unusual bustle that arose, that something of consequence was about to happen; and he learnt from one of the subordinates that no less a person than the great Mrs. Fry,

attended by a staff of females, was about to inspect the establishment. Being fond of a joke, Mr. Clarke prevailed upon one of the keepers to introduce the lady to him. This was accordingly done. Mr. Clarke assumed the appearance of melancholy madness; the lady and her suite advanced to offer consolation and condolence; he groaned, rolled his eyes, and gibbered; they became alarmed. He made gestures indicative of a rush at the parties; they retreated towards the door in precipitation; he rose from his seat, and was in instant pursuit. 'Sauve qui peut,' was the word; the retreat became a flight. Mrs. Fry, whose size and age prevented celerity of movement, was upset in the attempt; the sisterhood were involved in her fall; their screams were mingled with the simulated howlings of the supposed maniac; and it was with some difficulty that they were eventually removed from the floor and out of the room. I believe," continues Mr. Richardson, "that Mrs. Fry did not again extend her researches into the mysteries of lunatic asylums."

On the right-hand side of the Fulham Road, nearly opposite Sussex House, and with its gardens and grounds stretching away to the water-side, stood Brandenburgh House, a mansion which in its time passed through various vicissitudes. According to Lysons, it was built early in the reign of Charles I. by Sir Nicholas Crispe, of whom we have spoken above in our account of the parish church, at a cost of nearly £23,000. Sir Nicholas was himself the inventor of the art of making bricks as now practised.

During the Civil War in August, 1647, when the Parliamentary army was stationed at Hammersmith, this house was plundered by the troops, and General Fairfax took up his quarters there; Sir Nicholas being then in France, whither he had retired when the king's affairs became desperate and he could be of no further use. His estates were, of course, confiscated; but he, nevertheless, managed to assist Charles II. when in exile with money, and aided General Monk in bringing about the Restoration. He had, it seems, entered largely into commercial transactions with Guinea, and had built upon its coast the fort of Cormantine. In his old age he once more settled down in his mansion on the banks of the Thames, and died there. The house was sold by his successor to the celebrated Prince Rupert, nephew of Charles I., so renowned in the Civil Wars. It was settled by the prince upon his mistress, Margaret Hughes, a much admired actress in the reign of Charles II. She owned the house nearly ten years. It was afterwards occupied by different persons of inferior note, until, in 1748, it became the residence of George Bubb Dodington, afterwards Lord Melcombe, who completely altered and modernised it. He added a magnificent gallery for statues and antiquities, of which the floor was inlaid with various marbles, and the door-case supported by columns richly ornamented with *lapis lazuli*. He also gave to the house the name of *La Trappe*, after a celebrated monastery; and at the same time

Of Bubb Dodington, Lord Melcombe, we have already spoken in our notice of Pall Mall;[*] but more remains to be narrated. His original name was George Bubb, and he was the son of an apothecary in Dorsetshire, where he was born in 1691. He added the name of Dodington in compliment to his uncle, Mr. George Dodington, who was one of the Lords of the Admiralty during the reigns of William III., Queen Anne, and George I., and

BRANDENBURGH HOUSE, IN 1815.

inscribed the following lines beneath a bust of Comus placed in the hall :—

> " While rosy wreaths the goblet deck,
>   Thus Comus spake, or seem'd to speak :
> ' This place, for social hours design'd,
>   May care and business never find.
>   Come, ev'ry Muse, without restraint,
>   Let genius prompt, and fancy paint ;
>   Let mirth and wit, with friendly strife,
>   Chase the dull gloom that saddens life ;
>   True wit, that, firm to virtue's cause,
>   Respects religion and the laws ;
>   True mirth, that cheerfulness supplies
>   To modest ears and decent eyes :
>   Let these indulge their liveliest sallies,
>   Both scorn the canker'd help of malice,
>   True to their country and their friend,
>   Both scorn to flatter or offend.' "

whose fortune he inherited. Mr. S. Carter Hall, in his " Pilgrimages to English Shrines," writes :— " His amount of mind seems to have consisted in a large share of worldly wisdom, which enriched himself, a total want of conscience in political movements, and a safety-loving desire of being on friendly terms with literary men and satirists, that his faults and follies might be overlooked under the shadow of his patronage. In his Diary, he coolly details acts of political knavery that would condemn any man, without appearing at all to feel their impropriety. His face would have delighted Lavater, so exactly characteristic is it of a well-fed, mindless worldling."

* See Vol. IV., p. 123.

Bubb Dodington's great failing seems to have been want of respect to himself. "His talents, his fortune, his rank, and his connections," says a writer in the *European Magazine* for 1784, "were sufficient to have placed him in a very elevated situation of life, had he regarded his own

was pleased to call his villa "La Trappe," and his inmates and familiars the "Monks" of the Convent. "These," he adds, "were Mr. Wyndham, his relation, whom he made his heir; Sir William Breton, Privy-Purse to the king; and Dr. Thomson, a physician out of practice. These

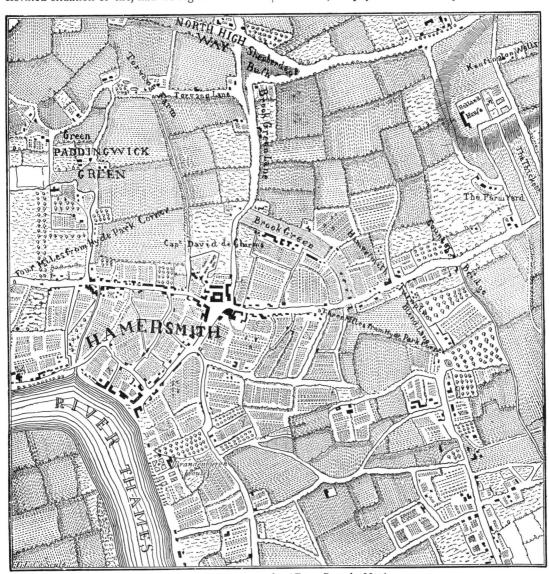

HAMMERSMITH IN 1746. (*From Rocque's Map.*)

character and the advantages which belonged to him; by neglecting these, he passed through the world without much satisfaction to himself, with little respect from the public, and no advantage to his country."

Richard Cumberland, whilst residing with his father at the rectory at Fulham, formed an acquaintance with this celebrated nobleman, and, in the diary which he published, he tells us that Dodington

gentlemen formed a very curious society of very opposite characters: in short, it was a *trio*, consisting of a misanthrope, a courtier, and a quack."

In each of his tawdry mansions Dodington was only to be approached through a long suite of apartments, bedecked with gilding and a profusion of finery; and when the visitor reached the fat deity of the place, he was found enthroned under painted ceilings and gilt entablatures. "Of pictures," says Cumberland, "he seemed to take his estimate only by their cost; in fact, he was not possessed of any. But I recollect his saying to me one day, in his great saloon at Eastbury, that if he had half a score of pictures of £1,000 a-piece, he would gladly decorate his walls with them; in place of which, I am sorry to say, he had stuck up immense patches of gilt leather, shaped into bugle-horns, upon hangings of rich crimson velvet, and round his state bed he displayed a carpeting of gold and silver embroidery, which too glaringly betrayed its derivation from coat, waistcoat, and breeches by the testimony of pockets, button-holes, and loops, with other equally incontrovertible witnesses sub-pœnaed from the tailor's shop-board."

Dr. Johnson was an occasional visitor here. One evening the doctor happening to go out into the garden when there was a storm of wind and rain, Dodington remarked to him that it was a dreadful night. "No, sir," replied the doctor, in a most reverential tone, "it is a very fine night. The Lord is abroad."

Dodington's gardens are mentioned by Lady Lepel Hervey as showing "the finest bloom and the greatest promise of fruit." The approach to the mansion was conspicuous for a large and handsome obelisk, surmounted by an urn of bronze, containing the heart of his wife. On the disposal of the house by his heir, this obelisk found its way to the park of Lord Ailesbury, at Marlborough, in Wiltshire, where it was set up to commemorate the *recovery* of George III. On one side of its base the following inscription was placed :—"In commemoration of a signal instance of Heaven's protecting Providence over these kingdoms, in the year 1789, by restoring to perfect health, from a long and afflicting disorder, their excellent and beloved Sovereign, George the Third : this tablet was inscribed by Thomas Bruce, Earl of Ailesbury." The inscription may possibly afford a useful hint as to the various purposes to which obelisks may be applied when purchased at second-hand.

After the death of Lord Melcombe, the house was occupied for a time by a Mrs. Sturt, who here gave entertainments, which were honoured with the presence of royalty and the *élite* of fashion. Sir Gilbert Elliot, in a letter to his wife, dated June 13, 1789, writes :—"Last night we were all at a masquerade at Hammersmith, given by Mrs. Sturt. It is the house that was Lord Melcombe's, and is an excellent one for such occasions. I went with Lady Palmerston, and Crewe, Windham, and Tom Pelham. We did not get home till almost six this morning. The Princes were all three at

Mrs. Sturt's, in Highland dresses, and looked very well." *

In 1792 the place was sold to the Margrave of Brandenburgh-Anspach, who, shortly after his marriage, in the previous year, to the sister of the Earl of Berkeley, and widow of William, Lord Craven, had transferred his estates to the King of Prussia for a fair annuity, and had settled down in England. His Highness died in 1806, but the Margravine continued to make this house her chief residence for many years afterwards. She was a lady in whose personal history there were many odds and ends with which she did not wish her neighbours or the public to be acquainted. A good story is told of her butler, an Irishman, to whom she one day gave a guinea in order to set a seal on his lips as to some early indiscretion which he knew or had found out. The money, however, took him to a tavern, where, in a circle of friends, he grew warm and communicative, and at last blabbed out the secret which he had been fee'd to keep within his breast. The story coming round to her ears, the lady reproached him for his conduct, when Pat wittily replied, "Ah! your ladyship should not have given me the money, but have let me remain sober. I'm just like a hedge-hog, my lady : when I am wetted, I open at once."

The Margravine made many alterations in the mansion, which was later named Brandenburg House, and the principal apartments were filled with paintings by such masters as Murillo, Rubens, Cuyp, Reynolds, and Gainsborough, and adorned with painted ceilings, Sévres vases, and marble busts. A small theatre was erected in the garden, near the river-side, where the Margravine often gratified the lovers of the drama "by exerting her talents both as a writer and performer." The theatre is described by Mr. Henry Angelo, in his "Reminiscences," as small, commodious, and beautifully decorated. "There was a parterre, and also side-boxes. The Margrave's box was at the back of the pit, and was usually occupied by the *élite* of the company, the *corps diplomatique*, &c., &c. The Margravine, on all occasions, was the *prima donna*, and mostly performed juvenile characters ; but whether she represented the heroine or the *soubrette*, her personal appearance and her talents are said to have captivated every heart." Angelo, at her invitation, became one of her standing *dramatis personæ*, and acted here *en amateur* for several years. He tells many amusing stories concerning the performances here on the

---

* "Life and Letters of Sir Gilbert Elliot, first Earl of Minto," vol. i.

Margrave's birthday, when a gay party assembled, and the Margrave's plate was displayed on the sideboard as a *finale*—plate which, at Rundell's, "cost two thousand pounds more than that of Queen Charlotte."

John Timbs, in his "London and Westminster," says "the Margravine must have been a grandiose woman. She kept thirty servants in livery, besides grooms, and a stud of sixty horses, in which she took much delight. At the rehearsals of her private theatricals she condescended to permit the attendance of her tradesmen and their families; and on the days of performance, Hammersmith Broadway used to be blocked up with fashionable equipages, while the theatre itself was crowded with nobles, courtiers, and high-born dames."

After twenty years' residence at Hammersmith, the Margravine of Anspach went to live at Naples. She had previously parted piecemeal with most of the costly treasures which adorned her mansion, and its next occupant was the unhappy Queen Caroline, wife of George IV., who here kept up her small rival court pending her trial in the House of Lords. During the trial she received here legions of congratulatory, sympathetic, and consolatory effusions; so much so, that the neighbourhood of the mansion was kept in a constant state of turmoil. Indeed, as Theodore Hook wrote at the time in the Tory *John Bull*,—

> " All kinds of addresses,
>   From collars of SS.
> To vendors of cresses,
>   Came up like a fair ;
> And all through September,
>   October, November,
> And down to December,
>   They hunted this hare."

The Queen appears to have been unmercifully lampooned by Hook, if we may judge from his "Visit of Mrs. Muggins," a piece in thirty-one stanzas, of which the following is a specimen :—

> " Have you been to Brandenburgh, heigh, ma'am, ho, ma'am ?
> Have you been to Brandenburgh, ho ?—
> Oh yes, I have been, ma'am, to visit the Queen, ma'am,
>   With the rest of the gallantee show, show—
>   With the rest of the gallantee show.
>
> " And who were the company, heigh, ma'am, ho, ma'am ?
>   Who were the company, ho ?—
> We happened to drop in with gemmen from Wapping,
>   And ladies from Blowbladder-row, row—
>   Ladies from Blowbladder-row.
>
> " What saw you at Brandenburgh, heigh, ma'am, ho, ma'am ?
>   What saw you at Brandenburgh, ho ?—
> We saw a great dame, with a face red as flame,
>   And a character spotless as snow, snow—
>   A character spotless as snow.

> " And who were attending her, heigh, ma'am, ho, ma'am ?
>   Who were attending her, ho ?—
> Lord Hood for a man—for a maid Lady Anne—
>   And Alderman Wood for a beau, beau--
>   Alderman Wood for a beau," &c. &c.

When the "Bill of Pains and Penalties" was at last abandoned, the Hammersmith tradesmen who served her illuminated their houses, and the populace shouted and made bonfires in front of Brandenburgh House. After her acquittal, the poor queen publicly returned thanks for that issue in Hammersmith Church, and more deputations came to Brandenburgh House to congratulate her on her triumph. She did not, however, long survive the degradation to which she had been subjected, for on the 7th of August, 1821, she here breathed her last. The following account of her funeral we cull from the pages of John Timbs' work we have quoted above :—"Was there ever such a scandalous scene witnessed as that funeral which started from Brandenburgh House, Hammersmith, at seven in the morning, on the 14th of August, 1821? It was a pouring wet day. The imposing cavalcade of sable-clad horsemen who preceded and followed the hearse were drenched to the skin. The procession was an incongruous medley of charity-girls and Latymer-boys, strewing flowers in the mud; of aldermen and barristers, of private carriages and hired mourning-coaches, of Common Councilmen and Life-Guards; wound up by a hearse covered with tattered velvet drapery, to which foil-paper escutcheons had been rudely tacked on, and preceded by Sir George Naylor, Garter King-at-Arms, with a cotton-velvet cushion, on which was placed a trumpery sham crown, made of pasteboard, Dutch-metal, and glass beads, and probably worth about eighteenpence. How this sweep's May-day *cortège*, dipped in black ink, floundered through the mud and slush, through Hammersmith to Kensington, Knightsbridge, and the Park, with a block-up of wagons, a tearing-up of the road, and a fight between the mob and soldiers at every turnpike, and at last at every street-corner; how pistol-shots were fired and sabre-cuts given, and people killed in the Park; how the executors squabbled with Garter over the dead queen's coffin; how the undertakers tried to take the procession up the Edgware Road, and the populace insisted upon its being carried through the City; and how at last, late in the afternoon, all draggle-tailed, torn, bruised, and bleeding, this lamentable funeral got into Fleet Street, passed through the City, and staggered out by Shoreditch to Harwich, where the coffin was bumped into a barge, hoisted on board a man-of-war, and taken to Stade, and at last to Brunswick, where, by the side of him who fell at Jena and him who died at Quatre Bras, the ashes of the wretched princess were permitted to rest;—all these matters you may find set down with a grim and painful minuteness in the newspapers and pamphlets of the day. It is good to recall them, if only for a moment, and in their broad outlines; for the remembrance of these bygone scandals should surely increase our gratitude for the better government we now enjoy."

In less than a twelvemonth after the death of Queen Caroline, the materials of Brandenburgh House were sold by auction, and the mansion was pulled down. A large factory now occupies its site, and in the grounds, fronting the Fulham Road, has been erected a house, to which the name of "Brandenburgh" has been given; but this is occupied as a lunatic asylum.

About a quarter of a mile westward of the spot whereon stood Brandenburgh House is Hammersmith Suspension Bridge, which, crossing the river Thames, joins Hammersmith with Barnes. The original bridge, completed in 1827, was the first constructed on the suspension principle in the vicinity of London. It was a light and elegant structure, nearly 700 feet long; its central span was 422 feet. The suspension towers rose nearly fifty feet above the level of the roadway. The bridge, being far too narrow for the ever-increasing traffic, and even dangerous on boat-race days, was taken down, and a new bridge was built on the old lines, but of greater width and strength, in 1884–5.

Facing the river, from the Suspension Bridge westward to Chiswick, stretches the Mall, once the fashionable part of Hammersmith. It is divided into the Upper and Lower Malls by a narrow creek, which runs northwards towards the main road. Over this creek, and almost at its conflux with the Thames, is a wooden foot-bridge, known as the High Bridge, which was erected by Bishop Sherlock in 1751. In this part of the shores of the Thames almost every spot teems with reminiscences of poets, men of letters, and artists: let us therefore

"Softly tread; 'tis hallowed ground."

In fact, there is scarcely an acre on the Middlesex shore which is not associated with the names of Cowley, Pope, Gay, Collins, Thomson, and other bards of song.

The "Doves" coffee-house, just over the High Bridge and at the commencement of the Upper Mall, was one of the favourite resting-places of James Thomson in his long walks between London

and his cottage at Richmond; and, according to the local tradition, it was here that he caught some of his wintry aspirations when he was meditating his poem on "The Seasons." "The 'Doves' is still in existence," says Mr. Robert Bell, in 1860, "between the Upper and Lower Malls, and is approachable only by a narrow path winding through a cluster of houses. A terrace at the back, upon which are placed some tables, roofed over by trained lime-trees, commands extensive views of two reaches of the stream, and the opposite shore is so flat and monotonous that the place affords a favourable position for studying the chilliest and most mournful, though perhaps not the most picturesque, aspects of the winter season." On one of his pedestrian journeys, Thomson, finding himself fatigued and overheated on arriving at Hammersmith, imprudently took a boat to Kew, contrary to his usual custom. The keen air of the river produced a chill, which the walk up to his house failed to remove, and the next day he was ill with a "tertian" fever. He died a few days later, within a fortnight of completing his forty-eighth year.

Among the noted residents in the Lower Mall, in the seventeenth century, was the ingenious and versatile Sir Samuel Morland, of whom we have already spoken in our account of Vauxhall.* Sir Samuel came to live here in 1684. He was a great practical mechanic, and the author of a variety of useful inventions, including the speaking trumpet and the drum capstan for raising heavy anchors.

"The Archbishop [Sancroft] and myselfe," writes Evelyn, under date October 25, 1695, "went to Hammersmith to visit Sir Samuel Morland, who was entirely blind: a very mortifying sight. He showed us his invention of writing, which was very ingenious; also his wooden kalender (sic), which instructed him all by feeling; and other pretty and useful inventions of mills, pumps, &c.; and the pump he had erected that serves water to his garden and to passengers, with an inscription, and brings from a filthy part of the Thames neere it a most perfect and pure water. He had newly buried £200 worth of music-books six feet under ground, being, as he said, love-songs and vanity. He plays himself psalms and religious hymns on the Theorbo."

Sir Samuel died here in 1696, and was buried in the parish church. There is a print of him after a painting by Sir Peter Lely. Sir Edward Nevill, a judge of the Common Pleas, purchased Sir Samuel Morland's house, and came to reside

---

* See *ante*, p. 448.

in it in 1703. He died here two years afterwards.

In the Upper Mall a few old-fashioned houses of the better class are still standing, but their aristocratic occupants have long since migrated to more fashionable quarters. The Mall is in parts shaded by tall elms, which afford by their shade a pleasant promenade along the river-side. These trees are not only some of the finest specimens of their kind in the west of London, but are objects of historic interest, having been planted nearly two hundred years ago by Queen Catharine, widow of Charles II., who resided here for some years in the summer season; her town residence, during the reign of James II., as we have already stated, was at Somerset House.* She returned to Portugal in 1692.

In the reign of Queen Anne, the famous physician, Dr. Radcliffe, whom we have already mentioned in our account of Kensington Palace, had a house here; he intended to have converted it into a public hospital, and the work was commenced, but was left unfinished at his death. Sir Christopher Wintringham, physician to George III., lived for some time in the same house. In the Upper Mall, too, resided William Lloyd, the nonjuring Bishop of Norwich. Another inhabitant of the Mall was a German, named Weltjé, who, having made a fortune as one of the *maîtres de cuisine* at Carlton House, settled down here as a gentleman, and kept open house, entertaining many of those who had sat as guests at the tables of royalty. He is repeatedly mentioned, in terms of regard, by Mr. H. Angelo, in his agreeable "Reminiscences." He was a great favourite with his royal master. An alderman was dining one day at Carlton House when the prince asked him whether he did not think that there was a very strange taste in the soup? "I think there is, sir," replied the alderman. "Send for Weltjé," said the prince. When he made his appearance the prince told him why he had sent for him. Weltjé called to one of the pages, "Give me de spoon," and putting it into the tureen, after tasting it several times, said, "Boh, boh! very goot!" and immediately disappeared from the room, leaving the spoon on the table, much to the amusement of the heir apparent. Among Weltjé's visitors at Hammersmith were John Banister, the comedian; Rowlandson, the caricaturist; and a host of poets, actors, painters, and musicians.

On the Terrace, which also overlooks the river, at the farther end of the Mall, resided for many years Arthur Murphy, the dramatist, and witty friend of Burke and Johnson. Here, too, lived the painter and quack, Philip James Loutherbourg, a native of Strasbourg, who came to England in 1771. He was employed by Garrick to paint the scenes for Drury Lane Theatre, and in a few years he obtained the full honours of the Royal Academy. Whatever notoriety Loutherbourg may have lacked as a painter was made up to him as a "quack;" for he had been caught by the strange empirical mania at that time so prevalent all over Europe. He became a physician, a visionary, a prophet, and a charlatan. His treatment of the patients who flocked to him was undoubtedly founded on the practice of Mesmer; though Horace Walpole appears to draw a distinction between the curative methods of the two doctors when he writes to the Countess of Ossory, July, 1789: "Loutherbourg, the painter, is turned an inspired physician, and has three thousand patients. His sovereign panacea is barley-water; I believe it as efficacious as mesmerism. Baron Swedenborg's disciples multiply also. I am glad of it. The more religions and the more follies the better; they inveigle proselytes from one another." A Mrs. Pratt, of Portland Street, Marylebone, published, in 1789, "A List of Cures performed by Mr. and Mrs. Loutherbourg, of Hammersmith Terrace, without Medicine. By a Lover of the Lamb of God." In this pamphlet he is described as "a gentleman of superior abilities, well known in the scientific and polite assemblies for his brilliancy of talents as a philosopher and painter," who, with his wife, had been made proper recipients of the "divine manuductions," and gifted with power "to diffuse healing to the afflicted, whether deaf, dumb, lame, halt, or blind." That the proceedings of both the Loutherbourgs attracted extraordinary attention is very certain. Crowds surrounded the painter's house, so that it was with difficulty he could go in and out. Particular days were set apart and advertised in the newspapers as "healing days," and a portion of the house was given up as a "healing-room." Patients were admitted to the presence of the artist-physician by tickets only, and to obtain possession of these it is said that three thousand people were to be seen waiting at one time. In the end, the failure of one of Loutherbourg's pretended "miracles" led to his house being besieged by a riotous mob, and he was compelled to make his escape in the best way he could. He, however, subsequently returned to his old quarters at Hammersmith, where he died in 1812. He was buried in Chiswick Churchyard, near the grave of Hogarth.

---

* See Vol. III., p. 92.

Besides the personages we have mentioned above, Hammersmith has numbered among its residents many others who have risen to eminence; among them William Belsham, the essayist and historian, who here wrote the greater part of his "History of Great Britain to the Peace of Amiens," and who died here in 1827. Charles Burney, the Greek scholar, who here kept a school for some time, towards the close of the last century, until

I derived from him the tastes which have been the solace of all subsequent years; and I well remember the last time I saw him at Hammersmith, not long before his death in 1859, when, with his delicate, worn, but keenly-intellectual face, his large luminous eyes, his thick shock of wiry grey hair, and little cape of faded black silk over his shoulders, he looked like an old French abbé. He was buoyant and pleasant as ever, and was

THE OLD "PACK HORSE" INN, TURNHAM GREEN.

his preferment to the vicarage of Deptford; and William Sheridan, Bishop of Kilmore, who was deprived for refusing the oath of allegiance to William III., and who died in 1711, and now reposes in the parish church.

Leigh Hunt—who, if we may trust Mr. Planché, was not well off during his later years—lived here in a small house, and spent, among friends and books, the last few years of his life. Mr. Forster, in his "Life of Dickens," thus mentions him:— "Any kind of extravagance or oddity came from Hunt's lips with a curious fascination. There was surely never a man of so sunny a nature, who could draw so much pleasure from common things, or to whom books were a world so real, so exhaustless, so delightful. I was only seventeen when

busy upon a vindication of Chaucer and Spenser against Cardinal Wiseman, who had attacked them for alleged sensuous and voluptuous qualities."

Mr. Bayard Taylor, in a letter in the *New York Tribune*, thus describes a visit which he paid here in 1857 to Leigh Hunt:—"The old poet lives in a neat little cottage in Hammersmith, quite alone, since the recent death of his wife. That dainty grace which is the chief charm of his poetry yet lives in his person and manners. He is seventy-three years old, but the effects of age are only physical: they have not touched that buoyant joyous nature which survives in spite of sorrow and misfortune. His deep-set eyes still beam with a soft, cheerful, earnest light; his voice is gentle and musical; and his hair, although almost

HAMMERSMITH MALL, IN 1800.

silver-white, falls in fine silky locks on both sides of his face. It was grateful to me to press the same palm which Keats and Shelley had so often clasped in friendly warmth, and to hear him who knew them so well speak of them as long-lost companions. He has a curious collection of locks of the hair of poets, from Milton to Browning. 'That thin tuft of brown silky fibres, could it really have been shorn from Milton's head?' I asked myself. 'Touch it,' said Leigh Hunt, 'and then you will have touched Milton's self.' 'There is a life in hair, though it be dead,' said I; as I did so, repeating a line from Hunt's own sonnet on this lock. Shelley's hair was golden and very soft; Keats's a bright brown, curling in large Bacchic rings; Dr. Johnson's grey, with a harsh and wiry feel; Dean Swift's both brown and grey, but finer, denoting a more sensitive organisation; and Charles Lamb's reddish-brown, short, and strong. I was delighted to hear Hunt speak of poems which he still designed to write, as if the age of verse should never cease with one in whom the faculty is born." We have mentioned Leigh Hunt's death in our account of Putney.

At the western end of the town, a little to the north of the Terrace, stands St. Peter's Church. It is a substantial Grecian-Ionic structure, and was erected in 1829, from the designs of Mr. Edward Lapidge; the total cost, including the expense of enclosing the ground, amounted to about £12,000.

In the good old days when almost every village had its mountebank, there was one at Hammersmith—a "public-spirited artist," immortalized by Addison in the *Spectator* for having announced before his own people that he would give five shillings as a present to as many as would accept it. "The whole crowd stood agape and ready to take the fellow at his word; when putting his hand into his bag, while all were expecting their crown pieces, he drew out a handful of little packets, each of which, he said, was constantly sold at five shillings and sixpence, and that he would bate the odd five shillings to every real inhabitant of that place. The whole assembly closed with the generous offer and took off all his physic, after the doctor had made them vouch for one another that there were no foreigners among them, but that they were all Hammersmith men!" "Alas!" remarks Charles Knight, "who could find a mountebank at Hammersmith now?"

In the year 1804 the inhabitants of this locality were much alarmed by a nocturnal appearance, which for a considerable time eluded detection or discovery, and which became notorious as the Hammersmith Ghost. In January of the above year, some unknown person made it his diversion to alarm the inhabitants by assuming the figure of a spectre; and the report of its appearance had created so much alarm that few would venture out of their houses after dusk, unless upon urgent business. This sham ghost had certainly much to answer for. One poor woman, while crossing near the churchyard about ten o'clock at night, beheld something, as she described it, rise from the tombstones. The figure was very tall and very white! She attempted to run, but the supposed ghost soon overtook her; and pressing her in his arms, she fainted, in which situation she remained some hours, till discovered by the neighbours, who kindly led her home, when she took to her bed, and died two days afterwards. A wagoner, while driving a team of eight horses, conveying sixteen passengers, was also so alarmed that he took to his heels, and left the wagon, horses, and passengers in the greatest danger. Faulkner tells us, in his "History of Hammersmith," that neither man, woman, nor child could pass that way for some time; and the report was that it was "the apparition of a man who cut his throat in the neighbourhood" about a year previously. Several lay in wait on different nights for the ghost; but there were so many by-lanes and paths leading to Hammersmith, that he was always sure of being in that which was unguarded, and every night played off his tricks, to the terror of the passengers. A young man, however, who had more courage than the rest of his neighbours, determined to watch the proceedings of this visitant of the other world; he accordingly placed himself in a secluded spot, armed with a gun, and as near the spot as possible where the "ghost" had been seen. He had not remained long in his hiding-place when he heard the sound of footsteps advancing, and immediately challenged the supposed spirit; but not receiving any answer, he fired at the object. A deep groan was heard, and upon a light being procured it was discovered that a poor bricklayer, who was passing that way from his work on that evening rather later than usual, and who had on a new flannel jacket, was the innocent cause of this unfortunate occurrence. The young man was tried for murder and acquitted.

The "Wonderful Magazine," published soon after the appearance of the mysterious visitor, contains an engraving of the "ghost," in which the "spectre" appears with uplifted arms and enveloped in a sheet.

CHAPTER XL.

CHISWICK.

" Et terram Hesperiam venies, ubi Thamesis arva
Inter opima virum leni fluit agmine."—*Virgil*, "*Æn.*," ii.

Earliest Historical Records of Chiswick—Sutton Manor—Chiswick Eyot—The Parish Church—Holland, the Actor—Ugo Foscolo—De Loutherbourg—Kent, the Father of Modern Gardening—Sharp, the Engraver—Lady Thornhill—Hogarth's Monument—A Curious Inscription—Extracts from the Churchwardens' Books—Hogarth's House—Hogarth's Chair—The " Griffin " Brewery—Chiswick Mall—The " Red Lion "—The " White Bear and Whetstone "—The College House—Whittingham's Printing-press—Barbara, Duchess of Cleveland — Dr. Rose and Dr. Ralph— Edward Moore, the Journalist—Alexander Pope's Residence —The Old Manor House —Turnham Green—Encampment of the Parliamentarians during the Civil Wars—The Old " Pack Horse " Inn—The Chiswick Nursery—Chiswick House—Description of the Gardens—The Pictures and Articles of *Vertu*—Royal Visits—Death of Charles James Fox and George Canning—Garden Parties—Corney House—Sir Stephen Fox's House—The Gardens of the Royal Horticultural Society.

IT is curious to note how the gradual—or, we might perhaps say, rapid—extension of the metropolis is affecting the once out-lying towns and villages in its immediate vicinity on both sides of the river. Many places, indeed, as we have already seen, such as Paddington and Bayswater, Stoke Newington and Hackney, Clapham and Camberwell, have already become entirely absorbed into the gigantic city ; whilst others are so rapidly increasing in size that they, too, will soon lose all signs of a separate existence. Chiswick, which lies on the bend of the river between Turnham Green and Brentford, still retains many of its rural charms, although their effacement by the hand of the builder may be perhaps but the work of a few years. To a certain extent, however, this progress is apparent even so far west as Chiswick, which we design to form the limit of our journeyings in this direction.

Chiswick is not found in Doomsday-Book, but it is mentioned in the various records of Henry III. by the name of "Chesewicke." According to the Saxon Chronicle, a battle was fought between Chiswick and Turnham Green between Edmund Ironside and the Danes, who were bent on attacking London, approaching it by the Roman road across the " Back Common," as it is now called, but which was the only entrance to the metropolis from the west, the present western road dating no farther back than about the eighteenth, or perhaps the close of the seventeenth century. A presumed proof of the antiquity of this road across the " Back Common " is to be found in the urn containing Roman coins dug up *in situ* in the year 1731, concerning which discovery we shall have more to say presently. With this single fact we must be content with regard to the early history of Chiswick, till we come to the reign of Henry II., when the Doomsday-Book of St. Paul's, in an Inquisition into the manor and churches belonging to the metropolitan cathedral, alludes to the " status Ecclesiæ de Sutton "—Sutton, *i.e.*, South Town, being the popular name for that part of Chiswick which lay between Turnham Green and the river Thames.

In this document we find an account of the glebe, titles, and pension payable to the vicar ; and it is worthy of note that now, after the lapse of nearly seven hundred years, there is still paid to the vicar by the Chapter of St. Paul's a " pension " of thirteen shillings annually, and another of two shillings to the chapter by the vicar. From another inquisition, dated 1222, we learn that the then " Firmarius " of the Manor had made a collection of Peter's pence ; but, it is added, " sibi retinet," he keeps it for himself. If this " Firmarius " was, as is suspected, a member of the Chapter of London, his act was a " robbing of Peter to pay Paul," and possibly may have given rise to the saying.

The same source of information tells us that at "Sutton" there was a " parva capella " attached to the manor-house ; and as the population in this part has very much increased of late years, a new church has been erected recently, almost on the site of the former fabric.

In 1570, Gabriel Goodman, Prebendary of St. Paul's, becoming Dean of Westminster, "diverted" the manor of Chiswick from the cathedral to the abbey. It was perhaps in consequence of the new tie thus springing up that a " Pest House " was built on Chiswick Mall for the use of the Westminster scholars. It was a plain and substantial building, comprising a house, dormitory, and school ; and it is a matter of history that during the time of the great plague the school or " College of St. Peter's " at Westminster was carried on at Chiswick by Dr. Busby without interruption to the regular studies. The Pest House was pulled down only a few years ago, and its site is now covered by modern villas. During the demolition of this building it was discovered that some of its walls were as old as the thirteenth century. But we are anticipating.

If Chiswick is approached by way of the Thames, but little of it is seen, as it lies opposite a small island of osiers—called Chiswick Ait or Eyot—which nearly hides it from public view. Thus the steamers rather avoid the place, and all that can be seen of it is perhaps the spire of the old church and one or two of the pleasant houses in the Mall, which runs along the river's bank, almost a continuation of that of Hammersmith, mentioned in the preceding chapter. The visitor to Chiswick, approaching by land, may find it rather an out-of-the-way place. It is true that part of it, Turnham Green, on the north side, lies on the high road at the western end of Hammersmith, but Chiswick proper lies off the high road and nearer the river, and it is only by walking that one can get at the place; but the walk thither will be well repaid for the trouble taken in accomplishing it. Whatever alterations may pass over this once pretty village, it will always be a spot that the student of English history and English manners will regard with a fair amount of interest, for the sake of several men of mark who have lived or died in its neighbourhood.

The parish church stands near the river, and is dedicated to St. Nicholas, the patron saint of fishermen, who, at the time of its erection, as now, formed the majority of the parishioners. The new church, erected in 1884 by the liberality of one of the churchwardens of the parish, is a noble reproduction, by Mr. J. L. Pearson, of a late Decorated or Early Perpendicular structure. The cost of it was £25,000; the tower of the original church, and the north wall of the chancel (rebuilt by the Duke of Devonshire), are all that remain of the former edifice. The late structure, though adorned with a handsome tower, was disfigured by a fair share of the deformities of the architecture of the eighteenth century, and in other respects was quite in harmony with its sister edifices which grace—or disgrace—the valley of the Thames between London and Windsor. It consisted originally of only a nave and chancel, and was built about the beginning of the fifteenth century, at which time the tower was erected at the charge and cost of William Bordal, vicar of the parish, who died in 1435. The tower is built of stone and flint, as was originally the north wall of the church. Some aisles or transepts of brick, in the hideous style of the Georgian era, stood on either side, one of them bearing the ominous date of 1772, and the other of 1817. These excrescences were first erected in the shape of transepts; but as the population increased, and more space was needed, they were extended westward. The inside of the nave was a most barn-like structure, with a modern ceiling, which had replaced the original open timber roof.

Taking a general view of the interior of the church, it may be said that, with the exception of Bath Abbey, we never saw a sacred edifice whose walls were more hideously disfigured with "pedimental blotches," in the shape of marble mural monuments. These were of every date, from the fine classical piece of sculpture which commemorates one of the Chaloners of Elizabeth's reign—Sir Thomas Chaloner, a distinguished chemist, in the boldest possible relief, and the more modest and retiring tablet which, adorned with a pile of Bibles on either side, recorded the virtues of the wife of Dr. Walker, a Puritan minister during the Commonwealth, who signalised his incumbency by substituting the "Directory" for the Prayer-book—down to the present century. Most of these monuments have been now confined to the aisle which contains the organ; and the rest are disposed in and near the tower. Among them there are monuments of almost every conceivable design, and to such a cloud of peers and peeresses and honourables as ought to gladden the heart of "Garter" or "Ulster" himself. There is one to a Duchess of Somerset; another to one of the Burlingtons; three or four to the relatives of Sir Robert Walpole, all titled individuals; and another, very handsome of its kind, to one of Nature's gentlemen, Thomas Bentley, the able and public-spirited partner of Josiah Wedgwood, who resided in the parish, and whose virtues it commemorates. Bentley lived in a large and substantial mansion in the high road leading from Hammersmith to Turnham Green, now (or lately) occupied by Mr. Vaughan Morgan. The bas-reliefs, of which he speaks so often in his correspondence with Wedgwood, still grace the walls of the house, which (if we except a few additions) is much in the same state as when owned by Bentley.

Garrick erected the monument in the chancel to his friend Charles Holland, the actor, who died at Chiswick House; and he also wrote the inscription. Charles Holland was the son of John Holland, a baker of Chiswick, where he was baptised April 3rd, 1733. He was apprenticed to a turpentine merchant; but strongly imbued with a predilection for the stage, and praised for the display of that talent in his private circle, he applied to Garrick, who gave him good encouragement, but advised him "punctually to fulfil his engagement with his master, and should he then find his passion for the theatre unabated, to apply to him again." This advice he followed; and under Garrick's auspices made his *début* at Drury Lane Theatre, in 1754, in the part of *Oronooko*. He distinguished himself principally in the characters of *Richard III., Hamlet, Pierre, Timur* in "Zingis," and *Manley* in "The Plain Dealer." Holland was a zealous admirer and follower of Garrick; and, as a player, continued to advance in reputation. His last performance was the part of *Prospero*, in Shakespeare's "Tempest," November 20th, 1769; and he died of the small-pox on December 7th following. His body was deposited in the family vault in Chiswick churchyard on the 15th of the same month; and his funeral was attended by most of the performers belonging to Drury Lane Theatre.

In the church, in the north wall of the chancel is raised a marble monument, on which is engraved the following inscription, in a circular compart-ment, surmounted by an admirable bust :—

"If Talents to make entertainment instruction, to support the credit of the Stage by just and manly Action; If to adorn Society by Virtues which would honour any Rank and Profession, deserve remembrance : Let *Him* with whom these *Talents* were long exerted, To whom these *Virtues* were well known, And by whom the loss of them will be long lamented, bear Testimony to the Worth and Abilities of his departed friend Charles Holland, who was born March 12th, 1733, dy'd December 7th, 1769, and was buried near this place. D. GARRICK."

A view of Holland's monument is given in Smith's "Historical and Literary Curiosities."

Among the other parishioners buried in the church are several members of an old Berkshire family, the Barkers, whose name is still kept in memory by "Barker's Rails," opposite Mortlake : a place well known to all oarsmen as the goal of the University boat-races.

The tower contains a peal of five bells. The curfew was rung every evening at Chiswick as recently as thirty years ago, when it was discon-tinued through the parsimony of the parishioners. The vestrymen of Chiswick appear to have shown either extreme precaution or else extremely aristo-cratic tendencies; for in 1817 (as we are told by a tablet on the wall of the church) they passed a resolution that henceforth no corpse should be interred in the vaults beneath the church unless buried in lead.

Chiswick churchyard holds the ashes of more than a fair sprinkling of those whose names have been inscribed on the roll of the Muses, or have achieved or inherited names illustrious in history. Space will permit us to speak of only a few. Here, then, lies the third daughter of the Protector, Oliver Cromwell, Mary, Countess of Fauconberg. She was married at Hampton Court in 1657, and resided at Sutton Court. In person, as we learn from Noble's "Memoirs of the Cromwells," she is said to have been handsome, and yet to have resembled her father. In the decline of her life she grew sickly and pale, and after seeing all the hopes of her family cut off by her father's death, she is said to have exerted such influence as she possessed for the restoration of Monarchy. She bore the character of a pious and virtuous woman, and constantly attended divine service in Chiswick Church to the day of her death.

Here, too, were buried Lord Macartney, our Ambassador to China, and Ugo Foscolo, the Italian patriot. The tomb of the latter, restored and surmounted by a fine block of Cornish granite in 1861, at the expense of Mr. Gurney, was visited, during his stay in England, by Garibaldi, who made a pilgrimage to it, in company with M. Panizzi, at an hour when few of the good people of Chiswick were out of their beds. After reposing here for nearly half a century, the body of Ugo Foscolo was disinterred and conveyed to his native country, as is duly recorded by a recent inscription on the tomb, which is as follows :—

UGO FOSCOLO.
Died Sep. 10, 1827, aged 50.
From the sacred guardianship of Chiswick,
To the honours of Santa Croce, in Florence,
The Government and People of Italy have transported
The remains of the wearied Citizen Poet,
7th June, 1871.
This spot, where for 44 years the Relics of UGO FOSCOLO
Reposed in honoured Custody,
Will be for ever held in grateful Remembrance
By the Italian Nation.

Ugo Foscolo's was one of the few great names in Italian literature in the present century. He was a native of Zante, of Venetian extraction, and was educated at Padua. After some adventures in the army, he devoted himself to literature, and was remarkable for the terseness and polish of his Italian style. He had studied the finest and best writers of Greece and Italy down to those of the Middle Ages inclusively. Admiring Alfieri beyond all others, he imitated him in keeping as close as possible to the severe style of Dante. Coming to England with good introductions, he might have supported himself in comfort, had it not been for his irritable temper, which was rendered worse by pecuniary losses. He obtained the *entrée* of Holland House, but took a great dislike to its mistress, saying that "he should be sorry to go even to heaven with Lady Holland." He lived in lodgings in Wigmore Street, made the acquaintance of Rogers, Campbell, and the rest of the literary clique, and contributed to the *Quarterly* and other periodicals. He was also the author of "Fieste," "Ajax," "Ricciardo," "The Sepulchres," "The Letters of Ortis," the "Essay on Petrarch," and of many other works, the merits of which can be appreciated only by Italian scholars. He died in 1827. In the year 1871, as stated above, his remains were disinterred and carried over to his beloved Italy. Peace to his ashes! In spite of his rudeness to Lady Holland, he was in many ways one of "Nature's true nobility."

Another noted individual who reposes here is Miles Corbet, the regicide, who died at the age

took lodgings in Chiswick, during his brief stay in England, in order to be near him ; and there is recorded in Faulkner's "Chelsea" an anecdote of another visitor of very opposite principles, Dr. Samuel Johnson, who, as we learn from Boswell, often came to Chiswick. One day, being invited by his host to take a stroll as far as Kew Gardens, at that time in the possession, if not in the actual occupation, of Frederick, Prince of Wales, and

OLD COTTAGES ON BACK COMMON, CHISWICK.

of eighty-three. Then there is Barbara Villiers, Duchess of Cleveland, fairest and gayest of the fair but frail beauties of the Court of the second Charles : this lady was the daughter of William, Viscount Grandison, and wife of Roger Palmer, Earl of Castlemaine, one of the Palmers of Wingham, Kent, and of Dorney Court, Bucks.

De Loutherbourg, the artist and magnetiser, of whom we have spoken in the preceding chapter ; * and Dr. William Rose, critic and journalist, the translator of Sallust, and "a constant writer in the *Monthly Review*," both lie buried here. Among Dr. Rose's visitors, it appears, were many, if not most, of the *literati* of the day. J. J. Rousseau

subsequently of the Princess Dowager and family, he replied to Rose, "No, sir, I will never walk in the gardens of an usurper ;" a tolerably convincing illustration, if one be needed, of the great lexicographer's Jacobite partialities being still unabated at a time when the crushing defeat of Culloden was still rankling in the minds and memories of all adherents of the exiled family.

Another distinguished man whose remains are interred here was Dr. Andrew Duck, an eminent civilian, who died at Chiswick in 1649. He was some time Chancellor of the diocese of Bath and Wells, and afterwards Chancellor of London, and subsequently Master of the Court of Requests. In 1640 he was elected member for Minehead in Somersetshire, and when the Civil War broke out

* See *ante*, p. 545.

he became a great sufferer for the royal cause. Among other works, Dr. Duck was the author of a book entitled " De Usu et Auctoritate Juris Civilis Romanorum."

Kent, the father of modern gardening, lies buried in the vault of the Cavendishes. He was the Paxton of the last century. Horace Walpole says of him, " As a painter, he was below mediocrity; as an architect, he was the restorer of the science;

> And realised his landscapes. Generous he
> Who gave to Painting what the wayward nymph
> Refus'd her votary, those Elysian scenes
> Which would she emulate, her nicest hand
> Must all its force of light and shade employ."

Kent, as may be judged from the above estimates, though a second-rate painter, and a moderate architect, was at the same time an admirable landscape gardener.

HOGARTH'S HOUSE.

as a gardener he was thoroughly original, and the inventor of an art which realises painting, and improves nature. Mahomet imagined an elysium, but Kent created many." He frequently declared that he caught his taste for landscape gardening from reading the picturesque descriptions of the poet Spenser. Mason, who notices his mediocrity as a painter, pays the following tribute to his excellence in the decoration of rural scenery :—

> " He felt
> The pencil's power; but fir'd by higher forms
> Of beauty than that poet knew to paint,
> Work'd with the living hues that Nature lent,

Another worthy who reposes here is William Sharp, well-known in his day as a line-engraver, to whom we are indebted for the reproduction of Sir Joshua Reynolds's portrait of John Hunter, considered to be one of the finest prints in existence. Born in the Minories in the year 1749, and early trained in copying by his art the works of the old masters, he would in due time have proved himself a first-rate artist, had he not devoted the best years of his life to the delusions and imposture of Joanna Southcott and the "prophet" Brothers,[*] whose portrait he engraved in duplicate, in the full belief that when the New Jerusalem arrived a single plate would not suffice to satisfy the demand for impressions! At the foot of each plate he added the words, "Fully believing this to be the man appointed by God, I engrave his likeness.—W. SHARP." It is only fair to add that he maintained his belief in these delusions down to his very last hour. Besides the portraits above mentioned, Sharp's principal works include, "The Doctors of the Church," after Guido; the "Head of the Saviour crowned with Thorns," after Guido; and "St. Cecilia," after Domenichino. He also engraved the "Three Views of the Head of Charles I.," after Vandyck; "The Sortie made by the Garrison of Gibraltar," after Turnbull; and the "Siege and Relief of Gibraltar," after Copley. The plate of the "Three Maries," after Annibal Carracci, was left unfinished at the time of his decease, which took place at Chiswick in 1824. A portrait of Sharp painted by Longdale, was exhibited at the Royal Academy in 1823, and was purchased by the trustees of the National Portrait Gallery.

There are also buried here Judith, Lady Thornhill, the widow of Sir James Thornhill, the painter of the ceilings of Blenheim and Greenwich,[†] and of the dome of St. Paul's; her daughter, married to the immortal Hogarth; a sister of Hogarth; and last, not least, the great caricaturist himself, William Hogarth, to whose memory a large and conspicuous monument, erected by Garrick, stands in the churchyard, on the south side of the church, surmounted with a brazen flame like that on the top of the Monument at London Bridge. The inscription on the tomb is as follows:—"Here lieth the body of William Hogarth, Esq., who died October the 26th, 1764, aged 67 years. Mrs. Jane Hogarth, wife of William Hogarth, Esq., obiit the 13th of November, 1789, ætat. 80 years.

> "Farewell, great Painter of mankind,
>   Who reached the noblest point of art,
> Whose pictured morals charm the mind,
>   And through the eye correct the heart.
>
> "If genius fire thee, Reader, stay;
>   If Nature touch thee, drop a tear;
> If neither move thee, turn away,
>   For Hogarth's honoured dust lies here.
>   "D. GARRICK."

The inscription was written by Garrick himself. The monument is adorned also with a mask, a laurel-wreath, a palette, pencils, and a book inscribed "The Analysis of Beauty."

Dr. C. Mackay, in his interesting volume entitled "The Thames and its Tributaries," from which we have frequently quoted during the progress of this work, criticises the inscription on Hogarth's tomb in rather severe terms, remarking that "the object of an epitaph is merely to inform the reader of the great or good man who rests below," and that, consequently, "there is no necessity for the word of leave-taking." He adds, however, that "The thought in the last stanza is much better; and were it not for the unreasonable request that we should weep over the spot, would be perfect in its way. Men cannot weep that their predecessors have lived. We may sigh that neither virtue nor genius can escape the common lot of humanity, but no more; we cannot weep. Admiration claims no such homage; and, if it did, we could not pay it."

"Dr. Johnson," writes Mrs. Piozzi, "made four lines on the death of poor Hogarth, which were equally true and pleasing; I know not why Garrick's were preferred to them." Johnson's stanzas were, it seems, only an alteration of those written by Garrick, as will be seen from the following letter which appears in Boswell's "Life" of the great doctor, as addressed by him to the great actor at the time when the inscription was in contemplation:—

"*Streatham, Dec.* 12, 1771.

"DEAR SIR,—I have thought upon your epitaph, but without much effect. An epitaph is no easy thing.

"Of your three stanzas, the third is utterly unworthy of you. The first and third together give no discriminative character. If the first alone were to stand, Hogarth would not be distinguished from any other man of intellectual eminence. Suppose you worked upon something like this:

> "The hand of Art here torpid lies
>   That traced the essential form of Grace:
> Here Death has closed the curious eyes
>   That saw the manners in the face.
>
> "If Genius warm thee, Reader, stay,
>   If merit touch thee, shed a tear;
> Be Vice and Dulness far away!
>   Great Hogarth's honour'd dust is here.

"In your second stanza, *pictured morals* is a beautiful expression, which I would wish to retain; but *learn* and *mourn* cannot stand for rhymes. *Art and nature* have been seen together too often. In the first stanza is *feeling*, in the second *feel*. *Feeling* for *tenderness* or *sensibility* is a word merely colloquial, of late introduction, not yet sure enough of its own existence to claim a place upon a stone. *If thou hast neither* is quite prose, and prose of the familiar kind. Thus easy is it to find faults, but it is hard to make an epitaph.

"When you have reviewed it, let me see it again: you are welcome to any help that I can give, on condition that you make my compliments to Mrs. Garrick.

"I am, dear Sir, your most, &c.,

"SAM. JOHNSON."

---

* See Vol. V., pp. 212, 251.   † See *ante*, p. 180.

Hogarth died on October 26th, 1764. The very day before he died he was removed from his villa at Chiswick to Leicester Fields,* we are told, "in a very weak condition, yet remarkably cheerful." To Hogarth's tomb is appended a short notice to the effect that it was restored, in 1856, by a Mr. William Hogarth of Aberdeen, who, no doubt, was glad to give this proof of his connection with so distinguished a personage.

Carey, the translator of Dante, resided at Chiswick in Hogarth's house, and lies buried in the churchyard close under the south wall of the chancel. His monument was a few years ago rescued from oblivion, and restored at the expense of the vicar, who carefully inclosed it with iron railings.

It would appear from the parish books also, that Joseph Miller, of facetious memory, and who was a comic actor of considerable merit, lies buried here. He was for many years an inhabitant of Strand-on-the-Green, in this parish, where he died at his own house, according to the *Craftsman*, on the 19th of August, 1738. But it is always said that he was buried in St. Clement Danes.† Near him sleeps James Ralph, well known as a political writer, and a friend of Franklin. He published some poems ridiculed by Pope in the "Dunciad."

"Silence, ye wolves; while Ralph to Cynthia howls,
  Making night hideous, answer him ye owls."

If his poems were not good, at all events his political tracts showed great ability, and he was in high favour with Frederick, Prince of Wales.

It is worthy of remark that the church and churchyard cover the remains of a considerable number of Roman Catholics, including, among many members of old English and Irish families, some of the Towneleys of Towneley, Mr. Chideock Wardour, &c. The Towneleys, we may add, owned a house in the village on the site of the former residence of the Earls of Bedford. In 1838, and again in 1871, the churchyard was enlarged by the addition of ground at its western extremity, the gifts of successive Dukes of Devonshire, as parishioners.

On the outside of the wall of the churchyard, on the north-east, facing the street, is the following curious inscription, which is of interest as showing the sacredness of consecrated ground two centuries ago. It takes much the same view as that expressed at such length by Sir Henry Spelman in his book, "De non temerandis Ecclesiis:"—"This wall was made at yᵉ charges of yᵉ right honourable and truelie pious Lorde Francis Russell, Earle of Bedford, out of true zeale and care for yᵉ keeping of this church yard and yᵉ wardrobe of Godd's saints, whose bodies lay (*sic*) therein buryed, from violating by swine and other prophanation. So witnesseth Willliam Walker, V. A.D. 1623." Beneath this inscription is a tablet setting forth that the wall was rebuilt in 1831.

The churchwardens' books, commencing with the year 1621, contain a variety of curious and interesting entries. "Our dinner, when we went to take our oathes," is a constantly recurring item; so frequent, indeed, and occasionally so costly, that on one occasion the good vicar was scandalised, and adds a foot-note, "Here they eat too much." Another frequent item is that of "Boathier" (hire), for parochial excursions; in one place we read of "Boat-hier for to take the children to Fulham to be Bishoped," *i.e.* confirmed. We find also frequently large fees paid "for the buryall of creeples;" and in 1665-6 the books contain, *inter alia*, an account of the Great Plague, and of the sanitary measures adopted by the parish. Among other curious precautions, it should be mentioned that a resolution was passed by the parish that all loose and stray dogs and cats are to be killed for fear of conveying the infection, and that the poor bedesmen are to nurse "the patients ill with the plague."

Then there are sundry entries concerning "plague-water," a supposed antidote to the plague, but which does not appear to have proved an infallible elixir, for in more than one instance we read an entry of "plague-water" for A or B, when the next page has a charge for carrying the said A or B to church. Other sums are charged as paid to "maimed soldiers," "Tory ministers," "plundered persons," and "the widow Steevens in her distraction." In 1643 occurs a charge "for sweeping the church after the soldiers," *i.e.* after it had been occupied by the London "Train Bands," who were quartered within its walls, and took part in the battle fought on Turnham Green between Prince Rupert and the Parliamentary forces. The records of fast-days, and of revels, feasts, bell-ringings, and tar-barrels on festive occasions paid out of the church rates—*e.g.*, for "the victory over the Dutch"—show that Chiswick took an active part in the politics of the age. The books during the first half of the last century contain several curious entries of rewards paid to the beadles for driving away out of the parish sundry poor women, who came into its aristocratic precincts in a condition which showed that they were likely to add to the population, and so to entail charges on the parishioners. To account for the disappearance of all earlier registers, it is said, but upon what authority

---

* See Vol. III., p. 167.   † See Vol. III., p. 30.

we know not, that when the Protector quartered his troops in the church, he and his soldiers tore up those documents to light the fires, and for other and viler purposes. We may add that although there is a tradition that Lady Fauconberg got possession of her father's body at the Restoration, and deposited it carefully here; and although Miss Strickland, in one of her biographies, mentions a report that the real child of James II. died of "spotted fever," and was buried at Chiswick, no traces of any entry of such burials are to be found in the parish records.

But Chiswick has been remarkable for other celebrated persons who have lived in it. Amongst those of whom we have not already spoken, excepting with reference to their graves in the churchyard, may be mentioned Sir Stephen Fox, the friend of Evelyn, who occupied the Manor House, now the asylum kept by Dr. Tuke; Dr. Busby, of scholastic fame; Pope, who resided for a time in Mawson's Buildings (now Mawson Row); the notorious Barbara, Duchess of Cleveland; Lord Fauconberg, the Protector's son-in-law; the Pastons, ancient Earls of Yarmouth; Sir John Chardin, the traveller; Lord Heathfield, the defender of Gibraltar; Lord Macartney, our Ambassador in China; Hogarth, Zoffany, and Loutherbourg, the painters; Holland, the actor, and friend of Garrick; Dr. Rose, the translator of Sallust; Carey, the translator of Dante; Sharp, the engraver; and Carpue, the anatomist. Thomas Wood, another resident of Chiswick, was immortalised by an epigram, written in Evelyn's "Book of Coins" by Pope's own hand:—

> " Tom Wood of Chiswick, deep divine,
> To painter Kent gave all this coin.
> 'Tis the first coin, I'm bold to say,
> That ever churchman gave to lay."

The above lines were communicated to *Notes and Queries*, March 15th, 1851, by the Rev. R. Hotchkin, rector of Thimbleby, from a copy once in the possession of Mason, the poet.

At a short distance north-west of the church, in a narrow and dirty lane leading towards one entrance to the grounds of Chiswick House, still stands the red-bricked house which was once occupied by Hogarth, and still bears his name. The house is very narrow from front to back; one end abuts on the road; but the front of it, which apparently is in much the same condition now as when Hogarth lived, looks into a closed and high-walled garden of about a quarter of an acre, in which a prominent object is a fine mulberry-tree planted by the painter's own hand. At the bottom of the garden stood till recently the workshop in

which he used to ply his art, secluded and alone. Hard by against the wall were formerly memorials in stone to his favourite dog, cat, and bullfinch. That over the dog was inscribed—

" Life to the last enjoyed, here Pompey lies,"

and on that of the bird was "Alas! poor Dick;" the memorial over the grave of the cat disappeared many years ago. The two memorials above mentioned remained upon the grounds till quite recently, it being in the agreement when the house was let that they should not be disturbed; their position, however, had long been changed. For some time they were covered over with concrete, to serve as the flooring of a pigsty; but in the end they were carried away, and the bones of Hogarth's "pets" were disinterred. Hogarth's residence is now a private dwelling-house, and the garden is tenanted by a florist. Two leaden urns which adorn the entrance to the house were the gift of David Garrick to his friend.

Mr. Tom Taylor thus describes Hogarth's house, as it was in 1860:—"His house still stands, but sadly degraded within the last few years. It is a snug red-brick villa of the Queen Anne style, with a garden before it of about a quarter of an acre. An old mulberry is the only tree in the neglected garden that may have borne fruit for Hogarth. There is down-stairs a good panelled sitting-room with three windows, a small panelled hall, and a kitchen built on to the house; above, two storeys of three rooms each, with attics over. The principal room on the first floor has a projecting bay-window of three lights, quite in the style of Hogarth's time, and was no doubt added by him. The painting-room was over the stable at the bottom of the garden. Stable and room have fallen down, but parts of the walls are still standing. The tablets to the memory of pet birds and dogs, formerly let into the garden wall, have disappeared."

It was here that Hogarth used to spend the summers of his later life, enjoying the fresh air and green fields, which in his time were more extensive than they are now, although Chiswick has been less over-built than most of the London suburbs, and still retains much of its old-world character. Besides his favourite amusement of riding, the artist used to occupy himself in painting and in superintending the engravers whom he often invited down from London. And to his Chiswick cottage he came, after his bitter quarrel with Wilkes and Churchill, bringing some plates for re-touching. He was cheerful, but weak, and must have felt that his end was not far off, when in February, 1764, he put the last touches to his "Bathos." His prints now filled a large volume; and as the story goes, at one of the last dinners which he gave he was talking of a final addition to them.

Hogarth was then not in the best of health, and in reply to one of his guests as to what his next picture was to be, he remarked, " My next undertaking shall be the end of all things." " If that is the case," said one of the party, "your business will be finished, for there will be an end of the painter." "You say true," said Hogarth, with a sigh ; however, he began his design the next day, and worked at it till it was finished. A strange and yet impressive grouping of objects have we there—a broken bottle, an old broom worn to the stump, the butt-end of an old musket, a cracked bell, a bow unstrung, an empty purse, a crown tumbled to pieces, towers in ruins, the sign-post of a tavern called the "World's End," the moon in her wane, the map of the globe burning, a gibbet falling and the body dropping down, Phœbus and his horses dead in the clouds, a vessel wrecked, Time with his hour-glass and scythe broken, a tobacco-pipe in his mouth with the last whiff of smoke going out, a play-book opened with *Exeunt Omnes* stamped in the corner. " So far so good," cried Hogarth ; "nothing now remains but this," as he dashed into the picture the broken painter's pallet ; it was his last performance.

Passing on a few steps farther, we come to a plain house, in the garden of which stands Hogarth's portable sun-dial, duly authenticated. In the same house Hogarth's arm-chair, made of cherrywood, and seated with leather. The latter is much decayed, and one of the arms is worm-eaten, but the rest is sound and good.

This chair, in which Hogarth used to sit and smoke his pipe, was given by the painter's widow to the present owner's grandfather, who was a martyr to the gout. It moves very easily on primitive stone castors, three in number. To this same individual Mrs. Hogarth offered to sell a quantity of her late husband's pictures for £20 ; but the bargain was never concluded, and his paintings were eventually dispersed.

The principal street of Chiswick is a narrow, winding thoroughfare, running at right angles from the river, close by the church. In the middle of the village is the Griffin Brewery, where, aided by the medicinal virtues of a spring of their own, Messrs. Fuller, Smith, and Turner produce ales in no way inferior to those of Bass and Allsopp ; and not far distant is the brewery of Messrs. Sich and Co., a firm perhaps equally well known.

The Mall, as we have stated above, overlooks the river, and commands beautiful and extensive views. It commences at the vicarage, and ex-

tends eastward towards the terrace at Hammersmith, with which it forms a continuous promenade. About half-way along the Mall is an old public-house, the "Red Lion," which has stood upwards of a century : it is a large house, and some of the rooms and fireplaces bear evident traces of its antiquity. Chained to the lintel of the door is an old whetstone, which was placed there a few years ago, on the demolition of a still older inn which stood next door, on the spot now occupied by the new store-rooms of the Griffin Brewery. This older hostelry bore the sign of the "White Bear and Whetstone." The stone itself, which has been handed over to the safe keeping of the "Red Lion," bears the following inscription, cut upon it in deep letters :—" I am the old whetstone, and have sharpened tools on this spot above 1,000 years." As originally cut, the number of years was evidently 100 ; the fourth figure is clearly a more recent addition. From the tool-sharpening operation that has been carried on, a portion of the stone is considerably worn away, and with it part of the inscription, which, we were informed by an old inhabitant, ran thus :—" Whet without, wet within." Of the ludicrous uses to which a whetstone may sometimes be put we have given an amusing instance in our account of Fulham Palace.[*]

A little to the east of the "Red Lion," on the spot now occupied by a row of modern semi-detached villas, stood formerly a building called the College House, which was originally the prebendal manor-house of Chiswick, of which we have spoken above. In 1570 it was held by Dr. Gabriel Goodman, Dean of Westminster (one of Fuller's "worthies"), who granted a lease of the manor, in trust, for ninety-nine years, to William Watter and George Burden, that they should within two years convey the farm to the Abbey Church of Westminster. In this lease it was stipulated that the lessee " should erect additional buildings adjoining the manor-house, sufficient for the accommodation of one of the prebendaries of Westminster, the master of the school, the usher, forty boys, and proper attendants, who should retire thither in time of sickness, or at other seasons when the Dean and Chapter should think proper." From that time down to a comparatively recent date a piece of ground was reserved (in the lease to the sub-lessee) as a play-place for the Westminster scholars, although it is not known that the school was ever removed to Chiswick since the time of Dr. Busby, who resided here with some of his scholars, in 1657, " on account of

---

the hot and sickly season of the year." In 1665, when the plague commenced in town, Dr. Busby removed his scholars to Chiswick. But it spread its baneful influence even to this place. Upon this Dr. Busby called his scholars together, and in an excellent oration acquainted them that he had presided over the school for twenty-five years, in which time he had never hitherto deserted Westminster; but that the exigencies of the time required

process of his own devising. Whittingham commenced business on a small scale in Fetter Lane, but ultimately he realised a handsome income from the " Chiswick Press."

The old house, which in its latter days was known as Chiswick Hall, having been disposed of, was finally demolished in 1874, when the lower part of the walls, which had been embedded in stones and wood-work, was found to be of great

ENTRANCE TO CHISWICK.

it now. At the end of the last century, according to Lysons, the names of Lord Halifax and John Dryden, who were Busby's scholars, could be seen written on the walls of this interesting old house. When Hughson published his " History of London " (in 1809), the old College House was occupied as an academy. In more recent times the premises were taken by Mr. C. Whittingham, who here set up that printing-press which subsequently turned out so many beautifully-printed octavos and duodecimos, embracing nearly the whole range of English literature. Mr. Whittingham built for himself extensive premises at Chiswick, where he manufactured paper, the reputation of which soon spread, owing to its strength, and yet its softness. This was made principally from old rope, by a

thickness. Some part of the old boundary-walls are still standing. The old materials having been used in the alterations carried out in the sixteenth century, there can be no doubt that the fragments found embedded in the walls were from the earlier building, and possibly of Norman origin.

Here, probably at Walpole House, on the Mall, Barbara, Duchess of Cleveland, spent the last few years of her life. Here, in the summer of 1709, says Boyer, she " fell ill of a dropsie what swelled her gradually to a monstrous bulk, and in about three months put a period to her life, in the sixty-ninth year of her age." She died October 9th, in the year above mentioned, and was buried in the chancel of the parish church, though no stone marks the spot. The pall of this mistress of

AT CHISWICK.

1. Chiswick Church, 1760.　　2. Hogarth's Tomb, 1860.　　3 Manor House, Chiswick, 1850

royalty was borne by two Knights of the Garter, the Dukes of Ormond and Hamilton, and four other peers of the realm, Lords Essex, Grantham, Lifford, and Berkeley of Stratton. At Walpole House Daniel O'Connell resided for several years while he was studying for the law.

In Chiswick Lane, the road leading from the Mall up to the Kew and London Road, lived Dr. Rose, a pupil of Doddridge, and a schoolmaster of repute. He kept an academy at Kew, where Dr. Johnson came to take tea. Sometimes Rose would be unavoidably absent, and Johnson drank cup after cup, condescending to say little to Mrs. R., as she tells us, except, " Madam, I am afraid I give you a great deal of trouble." Dr. Rose, as we have stated above, lies buried in the neighbouring churchyard.

Another resident was Dr. Ralph, a political writer and historian, who appears in Bubb Dodington's Diary to have been long in the confidence and service of the clique at Leicester House.*

In 1766 the quiet village was frighted from its propriety by the arrival of the celebrated Rousseau, who took lodgings at a small grocer's shop near the house of Dr. Rose. " He sits in the shop," says a writer in the Caldwell papers, "and learns English words, which brings many customers to the shop." At one time Edward Moore, the journalist, lived here. Originally a linen-draper, he became the author of " Fables for the Fair Sex," the tragedy of *The Gamester*, two forgotten comedies, a collection of periodical essays; and was for some time editor of the *World*. He was in the habit of attending Chiswick Church, and as the tale goes, his wife called him to account one Sunday for having been very inattentive during the service. Moore at once remarked, " Well, my dear, that's very odd, for I was thinking the whole time of the 'next *World*.'"

On the west side of Chiswick Lane is Mawson Row—formerly called Mawson's Buildings—a row of red-brick houses, five in number. Alexander Pope and his father lived here for a short time. They removed thither early in 1716, from Binfield, the place of the poet's birth; and left Chiswick for the more famous residence at Twickenham about the year 1719. The elder Pope, who died here in 1717, lies buried in Chiswick churchyard. Portions of the original drafts of the translation of the " Iliad," on which Pope was engaged at this period, and which are preserved in the British Museum, are written upon the backs of letters to Pope and his father, addressed, " To Alexr. Pope,

Esquire, at Mawson's Buildings, in Chiswick." Among the writers of these letters appear to be Lord Harcourt, and Teresa Blount.

Higher up Chiswick Lane stands the old Manor House, which was once inhabited by the lords of the manor, and has all the imposing exterior of a French *château*. It is now a private lunatic asylum. At the junction of the lane with the high road is Grosvenor House, an old-fashioned mansion, which, since 1870, has been occupied as St. Agnes' Orphanage for Girls.

At a short distance westward from Chiswick Lane lies the hamlet of Turnham Green, which connects the parish of Hammersmith with that of Chiswick, to which it belongs. The green abuts upon the main road, and is enclosed; and in the centre stands a church of Early-English architecture, which was erected in 1843, when the hamlet was made into an ecclesiastical district.

Without going back to mythical times, to speak of a certain battle which is stated to have been fought here in the British or Saxon times, and without inferring, as does Stukeley, that it was a Roman station simply because an urn of Roman manufacture was dug up here during the reign of George I., we may state that Turnham Green in its time has been the scene of sundry historic events. Here, in 1642, Prince Rupert encamped with his army ; and on the day of the " Battle of Brentford " the green witnessed some sharp skirmishing, no less than six hundred of the prince's cavaliers being left dead on the field. The Royalists—headed by Prince Rupert, and followed by King Charles—after leaving Oxford, and making their way through Abingdon, Henley, and other towns, had reached as far as Brentford, which was occupied by a broken regiment of Colonel Hollis's, but " stout men all, who had before done good service at Edgehill." The Royalists, it appears, fancied that they should cut their way through Brentford without any difficulty, go on to Hammersmith, where the Parliament's train of artillery lay, and then take London by a night assault. But Hollis's men opposed their passage, and stopped their march so long at Brentford that the regiments of Hampden and Lord Brooke had time to come up. These three regiments, not without great loss, completely barred the road. The Earl of Essex, having quartered his army at Acton, had ridden to Westminster to give the Parliament an account of his campaign, and while he was absent, Prince Rupert, taking advantage of a dense November fog, had advanced, and fallen unexpectedly upon the Roundheads. The roar of the artillery was heard in the House of Lords, and the Earl of Essex

---

rushed out of the house, mounted his horse, and galloped across the parks in the direction of the ominous sound. As he approached Brentford, the earl learned, to his astonishment, the trick which had been played; he had gathered a considerable force of horse as he rode along, and when he came to the spot he found that the Royalists had given over the attack and were lying quietly on the western side of Brentford. "All that night," says May, "the city of London poured out men towards Brentford, who, every hour, marched thither; and all the lords and gentlemen that belonged to the Parliament army were there ready by Sunday morning, the 14th of November." Essex found himself, in the course of this Sunday, at the head of 24,000 men, who were drawn up in battle array on Turnham Green. How the Royalists took themselves off again to Oxford, by way of Kingston Bridge, is recorded in history; and how the Earl of Essex went in pursuit, crossing over the Thames by a bridge of boats from Fulham to Putney, we have already told.*

Turnham Green was to have been the scene of the Jacobite plot to assassinate William III. on the 15th of February, 1696, as recorded by Macaulay in the 21st chapter of his history. "The place," he writes, "was to be a narrow and winding lane leading from the landing-place on the north of the river to Turnham Green. The spot may still easily be found, though the ground has since been drained by trenches. But during the seventeenth century it was a quagmire, through which the royal coach was with difficulty tugged at a foot's pace." For their complicity in this plot, six gentlemen, named Charnock, Keyes, King, Sir John Frend, Sir William Parkyns, and Sir John Fenwick, were tried, and executed on Tower Hill. The spot is still easily identified. In his "Diary" under date May 1st, 1852, Macaulay has an entry: "After breakfast I went to Turnham Green to look at the place. I found it after some search: the very spot beyond a doubt, and admirably suited for an assassination."

A pamphlet, published in 1680, furnishes details of another sanguinary encounter, on a smaller scale, which took place here; the pamphlet is entitled "Great and Bloody News from Turnham Green, or a Relation of a sharp Encounter between the Earl of Pembroke and his Company with the Constable and Watch belonging to the parish of Chiswick, in which conflict one Mr. Smeethe, a gentleman, and one Mr. Halfpenny, a constable, were mortally wounded."

In 1776, Mr. Alderman Sawbridge, then Lord Mayor, met with a mishap here. Crossing the green, on his way back from a state visit to royalty at Kew, his carriage and suite were stopped by a single highwayman; even the City "sword-bearer" sat still and submitted to see himself and the chief civic dignitary stripped of their valuables. It is said that when the highwayman had thus outraged the City magnates, he rode off towards Kew, and meeting the vicar on the way, made him deliver up his valuables, and among other things his written sermon!

But even Turnham Green has its amusing memories. Angelo, in his "Reminiscences," tells a good story, the scene of which he lays here. "Returning one day from my professional attendance in the country, when I reached Turnham Green I met a happy pair, as I imagined, who were taking a trip from town to pass their honeymoon in the country. They happened, however, to have a quarrel just as a return post-chaise passed by, a little in front of me; the postilion was stopped by the gentleman; and as I stopped also I beheld the gentleman hand the young lady out of the coach and place her in the chaise, singing at the same time the words of an old favourite Vauxhall song, 'How sweet the love that meets return!' It is said that 'a fool and his money are soon parted;' in this case it may be suggested that for 'money' we should read 'bride.'"

Like its neighbour Hammersmith, Turnham Green has numbered among its residents a few men of note in their day; among them, Lord Lovat, the Scottish rebel, and the hero of Gibraltar, Sir George Eliott, Lord Heathfield.

The old "Pack Horse" has been a well-known tavern at Turnham Green for a couple of centuries; it is mentioned in an advertisement in the *London Gazette* as far back as the year 1697. Here Horace Walpole used often to bait his horse when journeying between London and his favourite Strawberry Hill. The "Pack Horse," as Mr. Larwood tells us, in his "History of Sign-boards," was a common sign for posting inns in former times: and it certainly points back to a very primitive mode of travelling. Another old inn, but which has disappeared within the last few years, was the "King of Bohemia's Head," a name already made familiar to our readers in our account of Drury Lane.†

The locality of Turnham Green has long been famous for its gardens and nurseries. Almost the very last entry in John Evelyn's "Diary" relates to

this place; he writes, under date May 18, 1705:—
"I went to see Sir John Chardine at Turnham
Green; the gardens being very fine and well
planted with fruit."

Mr. Glendinning's nursery here has long been
in existence as the Chiswick Nursery, and it is
said that heaths were cultivated here almost
earlier than in any of the metropolitan establishments of this kind. Of late years this nursery has
greatly risen in character, and is still constantly
improving. New houses have been erected, a
wider range of plant-culture has been taken, and
a considerable interest is made to attach to it on
account of the spirit and enterprise with which new
plants are procured, and the successful manner in
which they are flowered.

The following epitaph on Jemmy Armstrong, a
sheriff's officer, who died in November, 1801, at
his villa on Turnham Green, commonly known by
the name of "Lock-up Hall," will be found in
"The Spirit of the Public Journals" for 1802:—

> "Armstrong's arrested! sued, as will be all,
> By old Time's writ, special-original,
> The debt to nature due to make him pay.
> Death, Fate's bum-bailiff, served him with 'Ca. Sa.'
> His doctor 'to file common bail' did move:
> Not granted, Jemmy puts in bail above.
> By Habeas now remov'd from earth to sky,
> Before th' Eternal Judge he'll justify."

From Turnham Green, a broad road lined with
lime-trees, and known as the Duke's New Road—
from the fact of its having been made by the late
Duke of Devonshire—leads to Chiswick House,
one of the many seats of his Grace. In the ninth
year of King Edward IV., one Baldwin Bray,
whose ancestors were settled here for many
generations, conveyed the lease of the "manor of
Sutton within Cheswyke" to Thomas Coveton and
others; and during the civil war this manor was
sequestered to the Lord Mayor and Aldermen of
London. In 1676 the lease came into the hands
of Thomas, Earl of Fauconberg, whose son's great-
nephew, Thomas Fowler, Viscount Fauconberg,
assigned it about the year 1727 to Richard, Earl
of Burlington. After the Earl's death, the lease
was renewed to the Duke of Devonshire, who
married his daughter and sole heir. The other,
or prebendal manor, is still in the hands of the
Weatherstone family.

The mansion stands near the site of an old
house, which, it is said, was built by Sir Edward
Warden, or Wardour, but which was pulled down
in 1788, and by Kip's print of it seems to have
been of the date of James I. Towards the latter
end of that king's reign, it certainly was the
property and residence of Robert Carr, Earl of
Somerset, whose abandoned Countess died there
in misery and disgrace. The Earl, who was a
partaker in her crimes, survived her many years,
but was never able to retrieve his broken fortunes
and dishonoured name. On the marriage of his
daughter, Lady Ann, with Lord Russell,* he was
obliged to mortgage his house at Chiswick to
make up the marriage portion which the Earl of
Bedford demanded with his wife, and the mortgage
never being paid off, the estate passed away into
other hands, from whom again it passed through
several changes into the possession of Boyle, Earl
of Burlington, above mentioned. Faulkner, in his
"History of Chiswick," remarks that "it is a
curious fact that though Chiswick was sold by the
beautiful Lady Ann Carr's father, to enable her
to marry, it was not lost to her descendants; for
Rachel, the daughter of Lord Russell who was
beheaded, and his celebrated wife, married the
second Duke of Devonshire, so that the present
duke is descended from that lovely girl, and is a
possessor of the place where her youth was spent
—the home of her ancestors."

The house, which is almost hidden from our
view by the tall cedars and other trees among
which it stands embowered, was erected by the
last Earl of Burlington—the "architect earl," as he
is called—in the reign of George II., from a design
by Palladio; and it is a standing proof of the
skill and taste of the noble designer, though its
merits have been variously estimated.

The ascent to the house is by a double flight of
steps, on one side of which is the statue of Palladio,
on the other that of Inigo Jones. The portico is
supported by six fluted columns, of the Corinthian
order, surmounted by a pediment; the cornice,
frieze, and architraves being as rich as possible.
Inside this is an octagonal saloon, which finishes
at the top in a dome, through which it is lighted.
The interior of the structure is finished with the
utmost elegance; the ceilings and mouldings are
richly gilt, upon a white ground, giving a chaste
air to the whole interior. The principal rooms
are embellished with books, splendidly bound, and
so arranged as to appear not an encumbrance but
ornament. The tops of the book-cases are covered
with white marble, edged with gilt borders.

The gardens are laid out in the first taste, the
vistas terminated by a temple, obelisk, or some
similar ornament, so as to produce the most agreeable effect. At the end opposite the house are
two wolves by Scheemakers; the other exhibits a

---

large lioness and a goat. The view is terminated by three fine antique statues, dug up in Adrian's garden at Rome, with stone seats between them. Along the ornamental waters we are led to an inclosure, where are a Roman temple and an obelisk ; and on its banks stands an exact model of the portico of St. Paul's, Covent Garden, the work of Inigo Jones. The pleasure-grounds and park include about ninety acres, together with an orangery, conservatory, and range of forcing-houses 300 feet in length.

Horace Walpole, being a *connoisseur*, must needs find fault with something. He desired that the lavish quantity of urns and statues behind the garden front should be " retrenched ; " and this might be desirable if these urns and statues were not exquisite gems of art, and individually of great beauty and value, demanding a more undivided attention than would be given them if considered merely as ornamental appendages to the grounds. The bronze statues of the Gladiator, Hercules with his club, and the Faun, are worthy a place in any gallery. Three colossal statues, removed hither from Rome, although mutilated, are very fine, as are also the profusion of minor marbles scattered throughout the grounds. Nothing can be more exquisite than the taste that presides over the Versailles in little. The lofty walls of clipped yew, inclosing alleys terminated by rustic temples ; the formal flower-garden, with walks converging towards a common centre, where a marble copy of the Medicean Venus woos you from the summit of a graceful Doric column ; the labyrinthic involution of the walks, artfully avoiding the limits of the demesne, and deceiving you as to its real extent ; the artificial water, with its light and elegant bridge, gaily painted barges, and wild-fowl disporting themselves on its glassy surface ; the magnificent cedars feathering to the ground ; the temples and obelisk, happily situate on the banks of the river, or embowered in wildernesses of wood ; the breaks of landscapes, where no object is admitted but such as the eye delights to dwell upon ; the moving panorama of the Thames removed to that happy distance where the objects on its surface glide along like shadow the absolute seclusion of the scene, almost within the hum of a great city, make this seat of the Duke of Devonshire a little earthly paradise. The house, notwithstanding Lord Hervey's sarcasm (who said that it was " too small to inhabit, and too large to hang to one's watch "), is a worthy monument of the genius and taste of the noble architect. Nowhere in the vicinity of London have wealth and judgment been so happily united ; nowhere in the

neighbourhood of the metropolis have we so complete an example of the capabilities of the Italian or classic style of landscape gardening.

One of the principal objects of interest in the garden is an arched gateway, designed by Inigo Jones, which was originally erected at Chelsea, on the premises which once belonged to the great Sir Thomas More, but were afterwards known as Beaufort House,* from being occupied by the head of that family. The gate subsequently belonged to Sir Hans Sloane, but as he neglected it Lord Burlington begged it from him. Its removal hither occasioned the following lines by Pope :—

> " *Passenger.* O gate ! how cam'st thou here ?
> *Gate.* I was brought from Chelsea last year
> Batter'd with wind and weather ;
> Inigo Jones put me together ;
> Sir Hans Sloane
> Let me alone,
> So Burlington brought me hither."

Again, it will be remembered that in his poem on " Liberty " Thomson thus apostrophizes Lord Burlington :—

> " Lo ! numerous domes a Burlington confess :
> For kings and senates fit, the palace see !
> The temple, breathing a religious awe ;
> E'en framed with elegance the plain retreat,
> The private dwelling. Certain in his aim,
> Taste never, idly working, spares expense.
>   See ! sylvan scenes, where Art alone pretends
> To dress her mistress and disclose her charms ;
> Such as a Pope in miniature has shown,
> A Bathurst o'er the widening forest spreads,
> And such as form a Richmond, Chiswick, Stowe."

Dr. Waagen, who visited Chiswick House for the special purpose of art criticism, reports in his " Works of Art and Artists in England," that " among the pictures are many good and many even excellent, but that, unfortunately, they are partly in a bad condition, either from the want of cleaning or from dryness. Several pictures, too," he adds, " are hung in an unfavourable light, so that no decided opinion can be formed of them." Among the pictures are several of Vandyke, Gaspar Poussin, Paul Veronese, Titian, Tintoretto, C. Maratti, Sir Godfrey Kneller, Cornelius Jansen, Holbein, &c., and one very exquisite miniature portrait of Edward VI., after Holbein, by Peter Oliver, son of Isaac Oliver, one of the favourite painters of Charles I. Perhaps the finest of all the paintings is one of Charles I. and his children, by Vandyke, as to which it is uncertain whether it is a duplicate or the original of the picture in Her Majesty's collection at Windsor. Another cele-

---

* See Vol. V., p. 53.

brated picture is by J. Van Eyck, which Horace Walpole mentions in his book on painting in England—"The Virgin and Child attended by Angels," as representing in the figures which it contains several members of Lord Clifford's family (from whom the Earl of Burlington was maternally

"Drove with the Duke of Devonshire, in his curricle, to Chiswick, where he showed me all the alterations that he was about to make, in adding the gardens of Lady M. Coke's house to his own. The house is down, and in the gardens he has constructed a magnificent hot-house, with a con-

CHISWICK HOUSE, IN 1763.

descended); though the statement was controverted at considerable length by an eminent antiquary and genealogist in the *Gentleman's Magazine* for 1840.

Among the other articles of *vertu* in Chiswick House is a present from the late Emperor of Russia to the late Duke of Devonshire ; a magnificent clock in a case of malachite, surmounted with a representation of the Emperor, Peter the Great, in a storm, who is standing in a boat, with his hand upon the helm, in a firm and defiant attitude. The boat itself, which is about a foot long, is of bronze.

The grounds of Chiswick House were considerably enlarged by the late Duke of Devonshire. In Miss Berry's "Journal," under date of June 1st, 1813, is the following entry respecting them :—

servatory for flowers, the middle under a cupola. Altogether, it is 300 feet long. The communication between the two gardens is through what was the old greenhouse, of which they have made a double arcade, making the prettiest effect possible."

In 1814 the Emperor Alexander I. of Russia and the other allied sovereigns visited the Duke of Devonshire here, and the open-air entertainments which were given at Chiswick by the duke in subsequent years were among the chief attractions of the "London season." Sir Walter Scott, in his " Diary," May 17th, 1828, tells us how that, after paying a visit to the Duke of Wellington, he drove to Chiswick, where he had never been before.

"A numerous and gay party," he adds, "were assembled to walk and enjoy the beauties of that Palladian dome. The place and highly ornamented gardens belonging to it resemble a picture of Watteau. There is some affectation in the picture, but in the *ensemble* the original looked very well. The Duke of Devonshire received every one with the best possible manners. The scene was dignified by the presence of an immense elephant,

Queen Victoria, and other sovereigns and illustrious persons to the head of the ducal house of Cavendish.

Chiswick has witnessed the death of more than one political celebrity. At the end of August, 1806, the great statesman, Charles James Fox, was in his last illness removed to the Duke of Devonshire's villa, where he died a fortnight later. The bed-chamber which he occupied opens into

CORNEY HOUSE, IN 1760.

who, under the charge of a groom, wandered up and down, giving an air of Asiatic pageantry to the entertainment." This elephant occupied a paddock near the house ; her intelligence, docility, and affection were remarkable ; she died in the year 1829.

In June, 1842, Her Majesty and the late Prince Consort visited his grace at Chiswick ; and in the month of June, 1844, the duke gave here a magnificent entertainment to the Emperor (Nicholas) of Russia, the King of Saxony, the Duke and Duchess of Cambridge, and about 700 of the nobility and gentry.

It may be added that several of the finest trees in these gardens were planted by royal hands, to commemorate the visits of the Emperor Nicholas,

the Italian saloon, and before the window grew a mountain-ash, which appears to have been to him an object of great interest.

The following anecdotes rest upon the authority of Samuel Rogers :—"Very shortly before Fox died he complained of great uneasiness in his stomach, and Clive advised him to try a cup of coffee. It was accordingly ordered ; but not being brought as soon as was expected, Mrs. Fox expressed some impatience ; upon which Fox said, with his usual sweet smile, 'Remember, my dear, that good coffee cannot be made in a moment.' Lady Holland announced the death of Fox in her own odd manner to those relatives and intimate friends of his who were sitting in a room near his bed-chamber, and waiting to hear he had breathed his last : she walked through the room with her apron over her head. * * * How fondly the surviving friends of Fox cherished his memory! Many years after his death, I was at a *fête* given by the Duke of Devonshire at Chiswick House. Sir Robert Adair and I wandered about the apartments up and down stairs. 'In which room did Fox expire?' asked Adair. I replied, 'In this very room!' Immediately Adair burst into tears with a vehemence of grief such as I hardly ever saw exhibited by a man."

Undoubtedly, Fox was a great orator. Horace Walpole wrote:—"Fox had not the ungraceful hesitation of his father, yet scarcely equalled him in subtlety and acuteness. But no man ever excelled him in the clearness of argument, which flowed from him in a torrent of vehemence, as declamation sometimes does from those who want argument." Burke once called him "the greatest debater the world ever saw;" and Mackintosh described him as "the most Demosthenean speaker since Demosthenes."

Twenty years afterwards there came hither to die, in the same villa and the same room, and nearly at the same age, the classic and witty and brilliant George Canning. He died on the 8th of August, 1827. The apartment in which the two statesmen breathed their last is thus sketched by Sir Henry Bulwer (Lord Dalling), in his "Historical Characters":—"It is a small low chamber, over a kind of nursery, and opening into a wing of the building, which gives it the appearance of looking into a court-yard. Nothing can be more simple than its furniture or its decorations. On one side of the fire-place are a few book-shelves; opposite the foot of the bed is the low chimney-piece, and on it a small bronze clock, to which we may fancy the weary and impatient sufferer often turned his eyes during those bitter moments in which he was passing from the world which he had filled with his name and was governing with his projects.

Of late years Chiswick House has been used as a suburban nursery for the children of the Prince and Princess of Wales; and occasionally, during the summer season, the Prince and Princess have taken up their residence here, and given garden-parties, which have perhaps even excelled in brilliancy those given in former years.

Corney House, which was pulled down in 1823, originally belonged to the Russell family, who were seated here at the commencement of the seventeenth century. In 1602 Queen Elizabeth paid a visit to its then owner, William, Lord Russell, whose son Francis, first Earl of Bedford, afterwards

lived here, and took an interest in the concerns of the parish, as is evident from the inscription on the churchyard wall already mentioned.* The house was for some time the residence of the Earl Macartney; but, like most of the property in the immediate neighbourhood of Chiswick House, it has passed into the hands of the Duke of Devonshire. On the demolition of the mansion the grounds were added to those of Chiswick House; its name, however, is preserved in Corney Reach, a bend of the river between Chiswick and Mortlake Bridge, which has become familiarised in aquatic annals in connection with the University boat-race.

It appears by the Court Rolls that Sir Stephen Fox, in the year 1685, purchased a copyhold estate at Chiswick, on which he built a mansion, which he made his principal residence after he had retired from public business. William III. was so pleased with it that he is said to have exclaimed to the Earl of Portland on his first visit, "This place is perfectly fine; I could live here five days"—a compliment which he never paid to any other place in England except Lord Exeter's mansion at Burleigh. The staircase of Sir Stephen Fox's house was painted by Verrio. The gardens, as we learn from Evelyn's "Diary" (October 30th, 1682), were laid out by the architect, whose name was May:—"The garden much too narrow; the place without water, neere a highway and neere another greate house of my Lord Burlington; with little land about it, so that I wonder at the expense; but women," he quaintly adds, "will have their will." Sir Stephen Fox, who died in 1716, was the father of Henry, first Lord Holland, and grandfather of Charles James Fox.

In 1818, the gardens of the Horticultural Society were established on that part of the grounds of Chiswick House lying between the mansion and Turnham Green. Up to this time, few of the inhabitants of London even visited the village; but when the Horticultural Fêtes were held here Chiswick achieved some notoriety: it rose to be a place of popular resort, and had even its steam-boat pier.

Other attractions, however, sprang up and threw Chiswick into the shade; and when, as we have stated in a previous volume,† the head-quarters of the Horticultural Society were removed to South Kensington, the visitors to Chiswick became "few and far between," with the solitary exception of the day of the University boat-race, when the Chiswick bank of the Thames annually receives its moiety of eager and expectant sight-seers.

---

* See *ante*, p. 555.   † See Vol. V., p. 116.

The Horticultural Society's grounds are now used as nursery and fruit gardens, for the culture of the seeds and rare plants collected by the society from all parts of the world ; as a school of horticulture ; and for raising plants and flowers for the conservatory and gardens at South Kensington, and for distribution among the Fellows of the Society. The number of plants transferred from Chiswick to South Kensington up to the present time is over 50,000.

CHAPTER XLI.

GENERAL REMARKS AND CONCLUSION.

"A portraiture of London ! It is Babel
In greatness, in confusion, and in change ;
But yet there's order in it."—*Babylon the Great.*

A General View of London—Length of its Streets, and Number of Dwellings—Growth of London since the Time of Henry VIII.—The Population at Various Periods since 1687—The Population of London compared with that of other Cities—Recent Alterations and Improvements in the Streets of London—The Food and Water Supply—Removal of Sewage—The Mud and Dust of London—Churches and ;Hospitals—Places of Amusement—Concluding Observations.

WE have now journeyed together—it is to be hoped pleasantly, and not wholly without profit—for six years, traversing one by one the highways and byways of the metropolis, but always, as we promised, within sight of the cross and ball of St. Paul's Cathedral—objects which, from first to last, we have kept steadily in view. We have, nevertheless, rambled over several hundred miles of ground—from Highgate and Hornsey in the north to Norwood and Streatham in the south, and from the river Lea in the east to Chiswick in the far west ; and covering altogether an area upwards of one hundred square miles in extent. It will, however, be our duty, before we actually part company, to take our stand as it were upon the vantage-ground of some breezy height, and to give our readers a general view of the vast city which we have traversed in detail, and on which we may be supposed to be looking down : our view extending, in the happy and epigrammatic words of Mr. G. A. Sala, over a sort of panorama—"from where the town begins to where it ends ; from the marshy flats below Deptford to the twinkling lights of Putney and Kew."

Standing, then, in this exalted (mental) position, and surveying the expanse before us, we see at our feet London, to use the phrase of the Brothers Percy, "stretching out its arms, like a second Briareus, in every direction," swallowing up all the villas in our environs, and making them gradually part and parcel of the capital. In order, however, to make our general view of London at all permanently interesting and useful, it will be desirable here to add a few generalisations, based on recent Parliamentary returns and other statistics.

First, then, according to a recent estimate, the total length of the streets of London is about 3,000 miles ; whilst the entire number of houses—"inhabited, uninhabited, and building"—concentrated, at the time of taking the census of 1881, within the area of "London according to Act of Parliament," amounted to rather more than 530,000 ; so that, adding the average annual rate of domiciliary increase (7,500), there must now (1885) be some 30,000 more, or 560,000 dwellings altogether. It has been calculated that this large number of houses, with an average frontage of five yards, would be more than sufficient to form one continuous row of buildings round the island of Great Britain, from the Land's End to John o'Groat's, from John o'Groat's to the North Foreland, and from the North Foreland back again to the Land's End, or upwards of 1,460 miles altogether.

When we look at the great metropolis from an antiquarian point of view, there is much to interest in its gradual growth. Not to speak of the City proper, which, as a matter of fact, has for centuries been almost stationary, we may gain a general idea of the outlying districts of London under King Henry VIII. from some expressions in an Act of Parliament passed in the fifteenth year of his reign, and which regulates the extent of jurisdiction given to the wardens of certain City companies with respect to the control of apprentices. Under this Act certain rights were given to these gentlemen "within two miles of the City, namely, within the town of Westminster, the parishes of St. Martin-in-the-Fields, Our Lady in the Strand, St. Clement's Danes without Temple Bar, St. Giles'-in-the-Fields, St. Andrew's, Holborn ; the town and borough of Southwark, Shoreditch, Whitechapel parish, Clerkenwell parish, St. Botolph without Aldgate, St. Catharine's, near the Tower, and Bermondsey Street." Most of these suburbs had no point of contact with the City, and few had any contact with each other or any continuous buildings. Both St. Giles' and St. Martin's parishes were then literally "in the Fields," as, indeed, was St Andrew's, in Holborn; Marylebone and Islington are not even mentioned; while Westminster, Clerkenwell, Shoreditch, Whitechapel, and the Strand consisted entirely of mansions of the nobility, standing in their own gardens.

The suburbs, therefore, in the reign of which we speak, must have been nearly void of buildings. From the map of Ralph Aggas, published about the year 1560, it appears that almost the whole of the metropolis was confined, even at that time, nearly half a century later, within the City walls. Certainly a few straggling houses fringed one side of the Strand, and a few more stood round about Smithfield. Open fields were under grass close to the City walls throughout almost its whole northern circumference; while those houses which stood within them were for the most part detached and accommodated with gardens. The village of St. Giles's lay entirely isolated across the open country. A single street led up Holborn, almost as far as Chancery Lane; between that point and Somerset House the space was entirely occupied by fields and gardens. There were also many gardens and open spaces within the City itself, and more particularly along the wall, within which a considerable space was kept clear round the whole circuit, like the Pomœrium of ancient Rome. The largest area occupied by gardens was immediately behind Lothbury. In the eastern and south-eastern parts of the City a great many spots were similarly appropriated. And yet, within this very limited compass of inhabited ground was crowded a population of constant dwellers, amounting to not less than 130,000, or perhaps more than twice the number of those who regularly sleep within the same area at the present time.

Carefully, however, as its successive changes may be described, it is hardly possible for words to convey so clear and definite an impression of the alterations which have from time to time been made in our metropolis as may be gained from the inspection of an old map of London and comparing it with one of the present day. Thus, for instance, in a map issued between 1680 and 1690, the Thames is invested with an unusual degree of importance, and from the number of landing-places and stairs marked down it is evident that the Londoners of that day must have been very fond of the water, and must, moreover, have spent much time upon it. Berkeley House, Albemarle House, and Burlington House stood in the green fields, which have

since been covered over with dwelling-places and christened Piccadilly. Near "So Ho" we find "the road to Oxford," and hard by "the road to Hampstead" is indicated. The former of these is now styled Oxford Street, and the other Tottenham Court Road. Bloomsbury had in it a few houses, while Clerkenwell was the residence of various dukes, earls, and others of the nobility.

Passing on a few years further, Lord Macaulay observes, in his "History of England," that "whoever examines the maps of London which were published towards the close of the reign of Charles II. will see that only the nucleus of the present capital then existed. The town did not, as now, fade by imperceptible degrees into the country. No long avenues of villas, embowered in lilacs and laburnums, extended from the great centre of wealth and civilisation almost to the boundaries of Middlesex and far into the heart of Kent and Surrey. In the east, no part of the immense line of warehouses and artificial lakes which now stretches from the Tower to Blackwall had even been projected. On the west, scarcely one of those stately piles of building which are inhabited by the noble and wealthy was in existence; and Chelsea, which is now peopled by more than forty thousand human beings, was a quiet country village, with about a thousand inhabitants. On the north, cattle fed and sportsmen wandered with dogs and guns over the site of the borough of Marylebone, and over far the greater part of the space now covered by the boroughs of Finsbury and of the Tower Hamlets. Islington was almost a solitude; and poets loved to contrast its silence and repose with the din and turmoil of the monster London. On the south, the capital is now connected with its suburb by several bridges, not inferior in magnificence and solidity to the noblest works of the Cæsars. In 1685 a single line of irregular arches, overhung by piles of mean and crazy houses, and garnished, after a fashion worthy of the naked barbarians of Dahomy, with scores of mouldering heads, impeded the navigation of the river."

We pass on to the London of Queen Anne's reign, and find that its expansion, though considerable, had not been very rapid during that half century. "A New Map of the Cityes of London, Westminster, and the Borough of Southwark, together with the Suburbs, as they are now standing," was issued in 1707. What the suburbs were at that date may be judged from the fact that the map extends only from Haberdashers' Hospital, Hoxton, on the north, to St. Mary Magdalen's, Bermondsey, on the south; and from Stepney on the east to Buckingham House on the west; the City wall, with its gates, being duly indicated. From a note we learn that the spot now known as the Seven Dials was then called "Cock and Pye-fields." In another map, published about 1600, a note is made respecting "the prodigious increase of building and other alterations of ye Names and Situation of Street, &c., in this last Sentry (century)." Here, too, the City wall is very carefully shown, and the several gates are marked, the quaintness of the spelling being most interesting and even amusing ; as, for instance, where just outside the boundary, near "All Gate," is marked "Ye Goounefownders hs." (The Gun-founder's house), its character being indicated by the presence of a cannon within the enclosure. In one point, however, this map may serve to show that our forefathers were wiser than ourselves ; for ample provision seems to have been made for open-air sports, and the fields which stretched out on all hands furnished the young citizens with as much room as they could well require for the development of any "muscular" theories which may then have been in vogue.

Under the four Georges, however, more rapid strides were made in the gradual extension of the metropolis, the erection of new houses being no longer prohibited by jealous legislation, and free trade being established in building for the necessities of the growing population. The great increase in our national manufactures and commerce which followed the establishment of peace, in 1815, brought a large access to the population of London, and these persons required to be accommodated with houses near the scene of their daily labours. Hence Islington, and Kensington, and South Lambeth, and Hackney, and Dalston were each doubled in population and in houses ; and the introduction of railways in the second and third quarters of the present century has more than doubled the entire London over which George III. was king.

The population of London and its suburbs was calculated by Sir William Petty, in 1687, to be 696,000 ; Gregory King, in 1697, by the hearth-money, made it 530,000 ; and yet, by actual census in 1801, including Westminster, Southwark, and the adjacent hills, it proved to be only 864,845. From 1801 to 1841—that is, in forty years—the population of London advanced from 864,000 to 1,873,000. In forty years the metropolis had increased above a million, or more than through all the previous history of the kingdom. In ten years more it had swelled to 2,361,640, or nearly half a million more ; and it was calculated, as far back as 1854, that the annual increase of the population of London was at the rate of 40,000 souls. Accordingly, in 1861 it had risen to 2,803,034, being

an increase in ten years of 441,394 souls. In 1871, again, this number had swelled to 3,254,260 ; and in 1881 it had reached as high as 3,816,483, or 50,300 more than the aggregate population of the nineteen largest provincial towns in the United Kingdom.

Comparing the population of the metropolis with that of other cities, it may be stated that London contains nearly twice as many people as Pekin (one of the most densely populated capitals in the world) ; almost thrice as many persons as Jeddo ; and treble the number of the inhabitants of Paris ; more than four times as many as there are in New York ; nearly seven times as many as St. Petersburg ; eight times as many as Vienna, Madrid, or Berlin ; nine times as many as Naples, Calcutta, Moscow, or Lyons ; thirteen times as many as Lisbon, Grand Cairo, Amsterdam, or Marseilles ; not less than twenty times as many as Hamburg, Mexico, Brussels, or Copenhagen ; and very nearly thirty times as many as Dresden, Stockholm, Florence, or Frankfort. Further, in comparison with our own large cities, it contains nearly eight times as many people as the united towns of Manchester and Salford, and the same proportion as regards Liverpool ; nine times as many as Glasgow ; twelve times as many as Birmingham ; fourteen times as many as Dublin ; and upwards of twenty times as many as Edinburgh. In England the following are the fifteen largest towns : Liverpool, Manchester, Birmingham, Leeds, Sheffield, Bristol, Wolverhampton, Newcastle, Plymouth, Bradford, Portsmouth, Stoke-upon-Trent, Hull, Oldham, and Sunderland ; and yet their joint population is less than that of London by nearly 30,000 souls. This may not be surprising when we are told that five births occur every hour, and that in one week nearly 900 are added to the inhabitants of the metropolis.

A writer in the *St. James's Magazine* (1871) observes that "our metropolitan population is nearly three times as large as that of the Papal States, nearly three times as much as the whole population of Norway ; it exceeds by 300,000 the whole population of Portugal, by 1,300,000 that of Switzerland, by 200,000 that of Roumania. It exceeds that of Canada by 80,000, and surpasses that of the Netherlands by more than half a million. Yet these two countries include independent states, strong and stable monarchies, while London is but a city : still, she is the Niagara of cities. The roar of her population is heard afar off ; and, as one man is as another in these days, she is, at the lowest estimate, even by the rule of counting heads, the most important place in the world."

Again, a writer in the *City Press* pointed out, in 1870, that the population of ten Londons would equal that of all Great Britain and Ireland ; and that of three hundred and fifty Londons would people the whole globe. " Every eight minutes of every day of every year," he adds, " one person dies in London ; and in every five minutes of every day in the year one is born. London contains 100,000 winter tramps, 40,000 costermongers, 30,000 paupers in the unions ; with a criminal class of 16,000, out of whom, in 1867, it was found that only 7,000 could read or write. Suppose an average town with a population of 10,000 persons ; there are in London, on Sunday, as many people at work as would fill ten such towns, and as many gin-drinkers as would fill fourteen. Two such towns London could people with fallen women ; one with gamblers ; three with thieves and receivers of stolen goods ; and two with children trained in crime. It comprises two such towns of French people, four of Germans, one of Greeks, and more Jews than are to be found in all Palestine. It has as many Irish as would fill the city of Dublin, and more Roman Catholics than would fill the city of Rome. It has 20,000 public-houses and beer-shops, frequented by 500,000 people as customers. In London, one in every 890 is insane ; there is one baker for every 1,200 persons, one butcher for every 1,500, one grocer for every 1,800, and one publican for every 650."

In an article on " The Census," by Mr. Charles Mackeson, in the " British Almanack and Companion" for 1882, after showing that the population of the metropolis has doubled itself in the course of the last four decades, and that now one out of every seven of the people of England and Wales live in London, as compared with one out of ten in 1801, the writer proceeds : " This growth, it is scarcely needful to point out, has not taken place in Central London, where the population diminished by 7.8 per cent. during the last decade, but is entirely due to the building operations in the suburbs. In the Central area, which includes the districts of St. George's Hanover Square, Westminster, Marylebone, St. Giles's, the Strand, Holborn, the City, Shoreditch, Whitechapel, and St. George's-in-the-East, the number of 'inhabited' houses has diminished by 6,388 during the last ten years, while 3,045 houses have been transferred to the list of houses not occupied at night, and used as places of business, and the progressive decrease of the population sleeping on the premises points to the probability that if office, warehouse, and shop space becomes as valuable in the western half of this area as it is in the City, the time will arrive when it will, as far as a resident population is concerned, be relegated to the class of uninhabited districts." In the eastern districts the process of depopulation is naturally less rapid, and is likely to continue so.

But notwithstanding the alarm which politicians and legislators have at various times expressed, and perhaps felt, at its growth, London has constantly advanced, amidst all impediments and interruptions, to its present gigantic size ; and, what is more, it still continues to advance. Conjecture scarcely dares to fix its limits, for every succeeding year we see some waste ground in the suburbs covered with dwellings, some little village or hamlet in the suburbs united by a continuous street to the great metropolis ; until what once, and that at no remote period, was a portion of its environs now forms an integral part of one great and compact city, likely to verify the prediction of James I. that " England will shortly be London, and London England."

London, then, may well be termed " Babylon the Great ; " for even if we accept the statements of Herodotus without any discount, the circuit of ancient Babylon, with its palaces and hanging gardens, was only 120 stadia, or furlongs ; and it reckoned its inhabitants only by myriads, or tens of thousands, and not by millions. Yet the great aggregate of houses called London must now be larger by far than that of ancient Babylon ; and at the next census it will appear that the men, women, and children who live within " Greater London" do not fall far short of four million souls.

Even during the years that have elapsed since the commencement of this work, events have been travelling on so fast that we have every reason to believe the population of the metropolis has been increased by several thousands ; and consequently, as may be easily imagined, whilst we have been writing London has not been standing still in other respects in order that we may take a photograph of its present aspect. Great alterations for the better have been effected in the dwellings of the poorer inhabitants in many parts of the metropolis, chiefly in consequence of the formation of new streets. Model lodging-houses have been erected in several localities, many of them being the result of the generous gift of Mr. George Peabody to the poor of London ; whilst even in Belgravia and other West-End districts large and commodious blocks of residential buildings have sprung up. Again, Board-schools— in most cases structures of some architectural pretensions—have been built in almost every district in the metropolis ; and in many of our new thoroughfares (such, for instance, as in those caused

CHISWICK MALL, IN 1820.

by the formation of the Holborn Viaduct) the ornamental character of our street architecture is very striking. Then, again, various institutions for the education and advancement of the working classes have, within the last few years, sprung into existence. The most noteworthy of these, perhaps, is Toynbee Hall, in Commercial Street, Whitechapel, the seat of a University mission in the East End, where science classes are conducted by men authorised by the Universities' Board, and who are thoroughly competent in their respective branches of learning; whilst closely following in its wake comes the new College for the Advancement of Technical Education, in Finsbury, established by the City and Guilds of London, and the first stone of which was laid in 1881. This institution provides accommodation for instruction in the application of physics, chemistry, and mechanics to various industries. The year 1882 saw the removal of the City of London School * from Milk Street, Cheapside, to a handsome and commodious new building on the Victoria Embankment. The first experiments have been made in lighting our streets by electric currents, the scene of these experiments, curiously enough, being Pall Mall, where, as stated by us,† the first experiment was made in lighting the streets of London with gas. The telephone, too, the most recent of our scientific acquirements, promises, at no distant date, to throw the telegraph into the shade. Even since we took our pen in hand at the commencement of the last volume of this work, the Surrey Gardens and Cremorne have been blotted out of existence; and we may record the fact that the metropolitan bridges are now all free from toll. Temple Bar, too, has been swept away, and the New Law Courts, adjoining it, have been completed. So quickly is the "Old London" absorbed in the "New!"

With such a vast and varied population before us, it may be of interest to pass for a moment to the commissariat department, and glance at the food supply for this "noble army" of Londoners, the supply of bread, water, and gas, and the various other domestic and social arrangements whereby it "lives and moves, and has its being."

In the Middle Ages, as we learn from Stow, the citizens of London were mainly dependent for their daily bread on the bakers of Stratford-le-Bow, who seem to have enjoyed the privilege of bringing their "long carts laden with bread" into the City. But in respect of our supply of bread, as well as in other branches of commerce, free trade has long prevailed. As we learn from the last edition of the "London Post Office Directory," there are

some 350 corn-merchants engaged in supplying the metropolis with corn and grain, about 250 corn and flour factors, about 500 corn-dealers, about 150 millers, 2,500 bakers, and some 1,300 confectioners. Kent, Essex, Norfolk, and Suffolk have always contributed very largely towards supplying London with corn and grain; but since the introduction of Free Trade, under the administration of Sir Robert Peel, great quantities of corn are brought from foreign parts. Of the average quantities of corn which change hands in the London market, as well as the regulations enforced in conducting the business, ample details will be found in our notice of the Corn Exchange.‡ Of meat and vegetables we have already spoken at some length in our accounts§ of the Metropolitan Meat and Cattle Markets, Covent Garden, and other places set apart for these articles of daily consumption.

The water-supply of London is a subject which has long engaged the serious attention of the Legislature, and frequent official reports are issued, under the auspices of the Local Government Board, with respect to the quality of the water supplied by the several Metropolitan Water Companies. As to its quantity, it will be sufficient to state that the water used in London for the purposes of drinking, washing, street-cleansing, and the extinction of fires, amounts to upwards of 100,000,000 gallons daily, supplied by eight different companies.‖

Our metropolitan water-supply is apparently well watched by a paternal government. An official report is made monthly by an official inspector as to the condition of the "intake," the filter-beds, and the volume of supply of each company. The water is also analysed monthly by duly-qualified public analysts. A yearly report, by the auditor of the accounts, is likewise made to the Board of Works as to the fiscal condition of each undertaking. A report, issued in 1875, states that the number of miles of streets which contain water-mains constantly charged, and upon which hydrants could at once be fixed, was no less than 667 miles.

Herodotus was thought to be telling fables when he recorded the story of the Xanthus and other rivers in Thrace being dried up by the thirsty souls who composed the invading army of Xerxes; but when we state that in 1877 the average daily consumption of water in London was about 120,000,000 gallons, or nearly thirty gallons per head of the population, it would almost appear that we are by degrees drifting into a condition when we shall be in danger of drying up our own rivers by the same means. "What other city in the world," it

---

* See Vol. I., p. 375.   † See Vol. IV., p. 138.

‡ See Vol. II., pp. 179-183.   § See Vols. II., 491; III., 239; V., 376.
‖ See Vol. V., p. 238.

has been asked, "has provided for the comfort, direct or indirect, of *each individual* of its population, a daily supply of so many gallons of this chief article of life?" The contrast is indeed striking between this state of things and the ancient conduits, which doled out water in retail! Whether, therefore, there is any truth or not in the statement of Herodotus respecting the rivers of Thrace, we may certainly assert that in London we have exhausted our rivers, though in another way ; for at all events one river has disappeared during the last ten or fifteen years by the drying up of the Fleet,* which in former times wound sluggishly down from the northern heights of Hampstead, and mingled its slimy contents with the "silvery" Thames.

Since the introduction of gas for lighting the streets of London, about eighty years ago, of which we have spoken in our account of Pall Mall,† both the demand and supply have been on a par with the increase of the population.

London affords, in theory at any rate, a good example to other towns as to the removal of street refuse and sewage matter. Since the establishment of the General Board of Health the metropolis has, in this respect, taken and kept the lead. From and after the year 1847 the abolition of cesspools and the drainage of houses into the sewers had been made compulsory, and upwards of 30,000 cesspools were so abolished in the space of six years. But the evil was only transferred, not removed, for all the sewers by which the cesspools were superseded flowed directly into the Thames ; the result was that in about ten years from the commencement of this reform the foulness of the river became unbearable, and measures were taken for the construction of a system of main-drainage, by means of which the sewage is conveyed to a more harmless distance. Of this system of drainage we have already spoken at length in our chapter on "Underground London."‡ By this system, called the London Main-Drainage Works, is effected the removal of the sewage of a population numbering nearly four millions, packed within an area of 117 square miles. This is conducted to Crossness, fourteen miles below London Bridge, and ultimately discharged into the German Ocean. Some time ago it was alleged on the part of the Conservancy Board that the matter in suspension was forming a deposit off the outlet, which not only had a tendency to occasion sanitary evils, but also threatened in some degree to interfere with the navigation. The engineer of the works, Sir Joseph Bazalgette, however, has published the result of a careful inquiry, which goes to show that, instead of causing obstruction or offensive deposit, the effect of the outflow at Crossness is to scour the channel, the estuarian deposit in that part of the river having been considerably reduced in quantity between 1867 and 1885, during which period systematic soundings have been taken by order of the board. It is therefore satisfactory to find that if the sewage is not yet utilised for the production of food it is not producing bad effects on the community.

From speaking of its sewers, our thoughts naturally pass to the mud and dust of London. In a previous volume we have made mention of the ash-mounds that were once to be seen in the neighbourhood of King's Cross,§ the hidden treasures of some of which may perhaps have suggested to Charles Dickens the character of the "Golden Dustman," in his work entitled "Our Mutual Friend." That a great deal more is consigned to the dust-bin than need be, in the shape of "waste," there is little doubt ; indeed, M. Soyer used to say that he could feed 100,000 people daily in London with what is thrown into the dustholes of the vast city.

It is often said that every man in his lifetime eats a peck at least of dirt ; but the Londoner, in all probability, swallows much more than a bushel, if there be truth in the following statement, which we find seriously made in the *Quarterly Review* a few years ago :—"The 300,000 houses of London are interspaced by a street surface averaging about forty-four square yards per house, and therefore measuring collectively about thirteen and a quarter million square yards, of which a large proportion is paved with granite. Upwards of 200,000 pair of wheels, aided by a considerably larger number of iron-shod horses' feet, are constantly grinding this granite to powder, which powder is mixed with from two to ten cart-loads of horse-droppings per mile of street per diem, besides an unknown quantity of the sooty deposits discharged from half a million of smoking chimneys. In wet weather these several materials are beaten up into the thin, black, gruel-like compound known as London mud ; of which the watery and gaseous parts are evaporated, during sunshine, into the air we breathe, while the solid particles dry into a subtle dust, whirled up in clouds by the wind and the horses' feet. These dust-clouds are deposited on our rooms and furniture ; on our skins, our lips, and on the air-tubes of our lungs. The close, stable-like smell and flavour of the London air, the rapid soiling of our hands, our linen, and the hangings of our rooms, bear ample witness to the reality of this evil, of

---

* See Vols. II., p. 418 ; V., 234.　　† See Vol. IV., p. 137.
‡ See Vol. V., pp. 233–242.　　　　§ See Vol. II., p. 278.

which every London citizen may find a further and more significant indication in the dark hue of the particles deposited by the dust-laden air in its passage through the nasal respiratory channels. To state this matter plainly, and without mincing words, there is not at this moment a man in London, however scrupulously clean, nor a woman, however sensitively delicate, whose skin and clothes and nostrils are not of necessity more or less loaded with a compound of powdered granite, soot, and still more nauseous substances. The particles which to-day fly in clouds before the scavenger's broom, fly in clouds before the parlour-maid's brush, and next darken the water in our toilet-basins, or are wrung by the laundress from our calico and cambric."

Of the ninety-eight parish churches within the walls of the City at the time of the Great Fire of 1666, only thirteen escaped the general havoc which was made by the conflagration. Of those destroyed—eighty-five in number—about fifty were rebuilt, several others being united to those of other parishes. Pepys, in his " Diary," under date of Jan. 7, 1667–8, makes the following singular remarks concerning the churches destroyed in the fire :—" It is observed, and is true, in the late Fire of London that the fire burned just as many parish churches as there were hours from the beginning to the end of the fire ; and next, that there were just as many churches left standing in the rest of the City that was not burned, being, I think, thirteen in all of each ; which is pretty to observe." Of late years, even during the progress of this work, several of the City churches have been swept away, the parishes to which they belonged being united to others, under Act of Parliament. The churches now standing in the City are about eighty in all ; and according to Mr. Mackeson's " Guide to the Churches of London and its Suburbs for 1878," there are about 1,000 in the entire metropolis, the sacred edifices in the suburbs having been more than doubled since the accession of Queen Victoria.

It is refreshing to know that suffering humanity is not forgotten in this " great world of London ;" and some idea of the benevolence of Londoners may be gathered from the fact that there are no less than sixty-five general hospitals for the relief and treatment of the various " ills that flesh is heir to." Besides these, there are scores of other charitable institutions of a special kind, such as dispensaries, invalid and convalescent hospitals, lunatic asylums, homes and refuges ; institutions for the blind, for the deaf and dumb, for incurables, for nurses, for relief of distress, for gentlewomen,

for needlewomen, for widows, for infants, for orphans, for the protection of women, for emigration, for employment, for labouring classes, for the benefit of the clergy, dissenting ministers, Jews, soldiers, sailors, discharged prisoners, and debtors ; and, lastly, penitentiaries for women. We may add that the number of paupers in the metropolis (exclusive of lunatics and vagrants) receiving parochial assistance is, on an average, from 80,000 in the summer to 100,000 in the winter ; whilst the total number of vagrants relieved in the course of a day may be set down as ranging between 600 and 800.

In such a vast area as London, theatres and other places of amusement are capable of containing and affording entertainment to thousands of the inhabitants. Mr. John Hollingshead, lessee of the Gaiety Theatre, in 1877–8 gave to a Parliamentary Committee an estimate of their number, which has been little altered since then. First are the two patent theatres, Drury Lane and Covent Garden, each capable of holding 4,000 persons. Then there are 45 theatres licensed by the Lord Chamberlain, holding in the aggregate about 80,000 persons. There are also ten theatres licensed by the divisional magistrates, one of which houses is the Court Theatre, at Chelsea, about twenty yards outside of the Lord Chamberlain's jurisdiction, and these ten theatres will hold altogether about 38,100 persons. The Crystal Palace is included, containing two theatres and one concert-hall under the same roof. Next come the music-halls. The Middlesex magistrates license 347 places, together holding 136,700 persons. These music-halls include three of the first-class, holding from 15,000 to 20,000 people; six second-class halls, holding from 2,000 to 3,000 ; 13 third-class halls, holding from 800 to 1,500 ; 53 fourth-class halls, holding from 300 to 700 persons ; and then there are 272 smaller places, which may be called public-house concert-rooms or harmonic meetings, or whatever they are termed. The Surrey magistrates also license on the south side of the Thames 61 music-halls ; 58 are of a smaller type, but three are very large places, and altogether these 61 will hold 32,800 persons. The City of London licenses only two places—the Sussex Hall and the " White Horse ;" but there must be four or five other places where balls and concerts are given, and the City may be stated as having in all these places accommodation for 6,400 persons. The total, therefore, is 57 theatres, capable of holding 126,100 persons, and 415 music-halls, capable of holding 175,900 persons, making altogether 472 places, accommodating 302,000 persons. This includes the Crystal Palace and the Alexandra Palace, which are licensed by the magistrates. Many of the smaller places are probably very small, being rooms in or over public-houses, where there is music but no stage or other appliances—places, in some instances, where people come in the evening and drink their spirits or beer, hear a song or two, and then go away home.

We have only to lament, in this general view, the extreme paucity of open parks and places of recreation, which add so much to the attractiveness of Paris and other European capitals. For, exclusive of the greater parks of London, which are vested in the Crown but open to the public, there are only about 1,100 acres of public recreation ground, and these are mostly in distant parts of the suburbs. They are distributed as follows :—Blackheath, 267 acres; Hampstead Heath, 240 acres; Finsbury Park, 115 acres; Southwark Park, 63 acres; Hackney Downs, 50 acres; South Hackney Common, 30 acres; North and South Mill Fields, 57 acres; London Fields, 27 acres; Tooting Beck Common, 144 acres; and Tooting Graveney Common, 63 acres. The gardens on the Thames Embankment and in Leicester Square present 14 acres. The remainder of the acreage is made up of the commons at Clapham, Stoke Newington, and Shepherd's Bush.

The great metropolis, then, being such as we have portrayed it, there have never been wanting those who have felt towards London and its neighbourhood an attraction which nothing could destroy. These, of course, have been the persons in whom the social qualities have predominated. Such, in their day, were Horace Walpole, Dr. Johnson, Samuel Rogers, and Macaulay; and such, too, were Leigh Hunt, Thackeray, and Dickens. Away from London and its surroundings such men would have been lost; here they found their respective *métiers*. The Boswellian reasons for Dr. Johnson's love of London are of general applicability. "Johnson," he writes, "was much attached to London; he observed that a man stored his mind better there than anywhere else; and that in remote situations a man's body might be feasted, but his mind was starved, and his faculties apt to degenerate, from want of exercise and competition. No place, too, he said, cured a man's vanity or arrogance so well as London; for as no man was either great or good *per se*, but as compared with others not so good or great, he was sure to find in the metropolis many his equals, and some his superiors."

It would be almost as easy to cull from English writers a long chain of passages in praise of London as of others written in praise of country scenes. Thus Dr. Johnson remarks: " The happiness of London is not to be conceived but by those who have resided in it. I will venture to say there is more learning and science within the circumference of ten miles from where we now sit than in all the rest of the kingdom. The only disadvantage is the great distance at which people live from one another. But that is occasioned by the very largeness of London, which is the cause of all the other advantages." If Dr. Johnson could speak thus of the metropolis when its population was under a million, what would he have said now, when we number nearly four million souls within a radius of *ten* miles from Charing Cross? Again, the burly doctor thus philosophises on the same subject in a homely and practical strain :—" London is nothing to some people; but to a man whose pleasure is intellectual London is the place. And there is no place where economy can be so well practised as in London : more can be had here for the money, even by ladies, than anywhere else. You cannot play tricks with your fortune in a small place; you must make an uniform appearance. Here a lady may have well-furnished apartments and an elegant dress, without any meat in her kitchen."

The same opinion is expressed somewhat more bluntly by " Jack " Bannister :—" I have lived too long (he observes) in London, from early life to the present time, to like the country much; you cannot shake off old habits and acquire new ones. I must die (please God !) where I have lived so long. Kemble once said to me, 'Depend on it, Jack, when you pass Hyde Park-corner you leave your comforts behind you.' *Experientia docet !* London for beef, fish, poultry, vegetables too; in the country you get ewe-mutton, cow-beef, and in general very indifferent veal. London is the great market of England. Why? Because it abounds in customers; and I believe you may live as cheap in London, and nobody know anything about you, as anywhere else. I delight in the country occasionally; but London is your best retirement after long industry and labour."

London has also, in an eminent degree, the great attraction of personal independence and freedom from the eyes of censorious and inquisitive neighbours. This is well drawn out by Boswell, who writes :—" I was amused by considering with how much ease and coolness he (Dr. Johnson) could write or talk to a friend, exhorting him not to suppose that happiness was not to be found as well in other places as in London; when he himself was at all times sensible of its being, comparatively speaking, a heaven upon earth. The truth is, that by those who from sagacity, attention, and experience have learnt the full advantage of London, its pre-eminence over every other place, not only for variety of enjoyment, but for comfort, will be felt with a philosophical exultation. The freedom from remark and petty censure with which life may be passed there is a circumstance which a man who knows the teasing restraint of a narrow circle must relish highly. Edmund Burke, whose orderly and amiable domestic habits might make the eye of observation less irksome to him than to most men, said once, very pleasantly, in my hearing, 'Though I have the honour to represent Bristol, I should not like to live there ; I should be obliged to be so much *upon my good behaviour.*' In London, a man may live in splendid society at one time, and in frugal retirement at another, without animadversion. There, and there alone, a man's own house is truly his *castle*, in which he can be in perfect safety from intrusion whenever he pleases. I never shall forget how well this was expressed to me one day by Mr. Meynell : 'The chief advantage of London,' said he, 'is that a man is always *so near his burrow.*'"

But there are other writers of authority besides Johnson whose testimonies in praise of London deserve to be quoted here ; for instance, Lord Macaulay, who writes to a friend : " London is the place for me. Its smoky atmosphere and muddy river charm me more than the pure air of Hertfordshire and the crystal currents of the Rib. Nothing is equal to the splendid varieties of London life, the 'fine flow of London talk,' and the dazzling brilliancy of London spectacles."

Again, we may summon Leigh Hunt, who writes in his " Table Talk :" " London is not a poetical place to look at ; but surely it is poetical in the very amount and comprehensiveness of its enormous experience of pleasure and pain. . . . It is one of the great giant representatives of mankind, with a huge beating heart, and much of its vice and misery . . . . is but one of the forms of the movement of a yet unsteadied progression, trying to balance things, and not without its reliefs."

We have said that to the man of intellectual culture London has attractions beyond all other places. Nor is this position better illustrated and enforced than in the inexhaustible Boswell :—" Of London, Johnson observed, 'Sir, if you wish to have a just notion of the magnitude of the city, you must not be satisfied with seeing its great streets and squares, but must survey the innumerable little lanes and courts. It is not in the showy evolutions of buildings, but in the multiplicity of human habitations which are crowded together, that the wonderful immensity of London consists.' ' I have often amused myself,' adds Boswell, ' with thinking how different a place London is to different people. They, whose narrow minds are contracted to the consideration of some one particular pursuit, view it only through that medium. A politician thinks of it merely as the seat of government in its different departments ; a grazier, as a vast market for cattle ; a mercantile man, as a place where a prodigious deal of business is done upon 'Change ; a dramatic enthusiast, as the grand scene of theatrical entertainments ; a man of pleasure, as an assemblage of taverns, and the great emporium for ladies of easy virtue ; but the intellectual man is struck with it, as comprehending the whole of human life in all its variety, the contemplation of which is inexhaustible.' "

Charles Dickens, too, is not far behind his compeers in his love of London. Its society and life was "meat and drink" to him—that on which he always set his heart most strongly, in spite of his love for Gad's Hill. Even when spending the winter in bright and sunny Genoa, he could write home to his friends, " Put me down on Waterloo Bridge at eight o'clock in the evening, with leave to roam about as long as I like, and I would come home, as you know." In the same spirit he wrote again, at a later date : " For a week or a fortnight I can write prodigiously in a retired place, as at Broadstairs ; and then a day in London sets me up again and starts me. But the toil and the labour of writing day after day without that magic-lantern (London) is immense."

It would be almost a sin not to add, by way of conclusion to these testimonies to London's character, the merry and good-humoured lines of Captain Morris, the " Laureate of the Beef-steak Club : "—*

" In London I never knew what to be at,
    Enraptured with this and enchanted with that ;
I'm wild with the sweets of variety's plan,
    And life seems a blessing too happy for man.
            *   *   *   *
" In town let me live, then, in town let me die,
    For in truth I can't relish the country, not I.
If one *must* have a villa in summer to dwell,
    Oh, give me the sweet shady side of Pall Mall ! "

---

* See Vol. III., p. 118.

THE END.

GENERAL INDEX

Abbey Mill Pumping Station, v. 572.
Abbot's Inn, Southwark, vi. 104.
A'Becket, Thomas, Archbishop, i. 377, 382 ; vi. 117.
A'Beckett, Gilbert Abbot, his contributions to *Punch*, i. 57, 58.
Aberdeen, Earl of, iii. 425 ; iv. 243.
Abernethy, Dr., anecdotes of, ii. 361.
Abershaw, Jerry, executed, vi. 335, 497.
Abingdon Street, Westminster, iii. 563 ; "Lindsay Lane;" Lindsay House, iv. 2.
Abington, Mrs., actress, iv. 136.
Abney Park ; cemetery ; v. 544 ; cedars, 537, 543.
Abney, Sir Thos., Lord Mayor, and Lady Abney, patrons of Dr. Watts, i. 406 ; v. 540.
Achilles, Statue of, Hyde Park, iv. 364, 395.
Achilley, Sir Roger, Lord Mayor, his funeral, i. 519.
Acrobats at Astley's Amphitheatre, vi. 400.
Actors at fairs, vi. 58, 59.
Adam, Messrs., architects, iii. 105 ; iv. 448, 450, 473 ; v. 442.
Adam Street, iii. 106.
Adam, William, his "Northern Alehouse," i. 272.
"Adam and Eve" Court, iv. 455.
"Adam and Eve" public-house, Kensington, v. 137.
"Adam and Eve" Tavern, Marylebone Road ; Hogarth's "March to Finchley," iv. 482 ; v. 303 ; cakes and cream ; pugilism, 304 ; menagerie, cold bath ; Eden Street, 305.
Adams, Jack, a Clerkenwell simpleton, ii. 332.
Adams, Sir Thos., Lord Mayor, i. 404.
Addison, i. 41, 70, 71, 502 ; ii. 89 ; iii. 27, 65, 276, 277, 431, 440 ; iv. 104, 141, 153, 166, 170, 218 ; v. 126, 138, 144, 165, 166 ; vi. 448.
Addison Road, v. 161.
Addle Hill, ii. 35.
Addle Street, Wood Street ; Brewers' Hall, i. 374.
Adelaide Gallery, iii. 134.
Adelaide, Queen, iv. 134.
Adelphi Terrace, iii. 106, 294.
Adelphi, The ; built by Messrs. Adam ; the dark arches, iii. 106.
Adelphi Theatre, iii. 119.
"Admiral Keppel" Tavern, v. 99.
Admiralty state barge, iii. 309 ; vi. 197.
Admiralty, The, iii. 383—386.
Adult Orphan Institution, Regent's Park, v. 275.
Agar Town ; "Councillor Agar," v. 368, 369.
Age Newspaper, iv. 251.

Aged Pilgrims' Friend Asylum, v. 395.
Aged Pilgrims' Friend Society, vi. 278.
Aggas's Map of London, iii. 160, 168 ; vi. 384, 414.
Agricultural Hall, Islington, ii. 261.
Aikin, Dr. John, v. 538.
Aikin, Lucy, v. 476.
Ailesbury House, Leicester Square, iii. 162.
Ainsworth, W. Harrison, his novel of "Jack Sheppard," ii. 459 ; his description of the old view of London from Stamford Hill, v. 544 ; of the sports on Tottenham Green, 550.
Air of London, iv. 394.
Air Street, iv. 309.
Airy, Sir G. B., Astronomer Royal, v. 131, 132 ; vi. 215.
Aislabie, Chancellor of the Exchequer ; the South Sea Bubble, i. 541, 542.
Akenside, iii. 65 ; iv. 256 ; v. 448.
Akerman, keeper of Newgate, i. 62 ; ii. 442 ; evidence on the state of Newgate, ii. 449 ; fire in prison ; his care of the prisoners, 458 ; vi. 347.
Albany Street ; Guards' barracks, v. 299.
Albany, The, iv. 258.
Albemarle Club, iv. 296.
Albemarle, Duchess of ; Newcastle House, Clerkenwell, ii. 331.
Albemarle, Duke of. (*See* Monk, General.)
Albemarle Street, iv. 293 ; Duke of Albemarle ; Sir Thomas Bond ; John Murray, *ib.*; Grillon's Hotel ; Royal Thames Yacht Club ; Grillon's Club, 295 ; Royal Institution, 296 ; St. George's Chapel, 297.
Albert Bridge, Chelsea, v. 67 ; vi. 473.
Albert Embankment, vi. 422.
Albert Gate, Hyde Park, iv. 395 ; v. 21.
Albert Hall of Arts and Sciences, Royal, v. 112, 113, 114.
Albert Memorial, v. 38.
Albert, Prince, ii. 530 ; v. 112, 116 ; vi. 197, 249, 250.
Albert Road, Peckham, vi. 286.
Albion Archers, vi. 328.
Albion Dock, vi. 141.
Albion Flour Mills, vi. 382.
Albion Newspaper, i. 45.
"Albion" Tavern, Aldersgate Street, ii. 226.
"Albion" Tavern, Russell Street, iii. 279.
Aldermanbury ; the Old Guildhall, i. 383.
Aldermen, Court of, i. 388.
Aldersgate Street, ii. 208 ; Alders Gate ; rebuilt (1618), *ib.*; inscriptions, 209 ; rooms of the City Crier ; General Post Office, *ib.*; St. Martin's College, 215 ; curfew ; crypt ; New

Post Office ; Telegraph Department, *ib.*; St. Martin's-le-Grand, 219 ; Sanctuary ; St. Martin's lace ; mansions of the Nevilles and Percys ; Milton; "Bull and Mouth," *ib.*; Shaftesbury House, 220 ; St. Botolph's Church, 221 ; Shakespeare's House, *ib.*; house of Sir Nicholas Bacon ; Earl of Peterborough ; Swift's verses, 226 ; Duke of Montagu ; "Bell" Inn, 227.
Aldgate, ii. 246 ; the Gate ; attacked by Falconbridge, *ib.*; conduit, 247 ; Chaucer's residence ; prison ; Duke's Place ; Priory of Holy Trinity ; Jews' synagogue, *ib.*
Aldridge's Horse Repository, iii. 158.
Ale, Dorchester, v. 46.
"Ale of Southwark ;" Chaucer ; Barclay and Perkins's Brewery, vi 33.
Alexandra Hotel, v. 8.
Alexandra Institute for the Blind, iv. 555.
Alexandra Orphanage, Highgate, v. 395.
Alexandra Palace, v. 435 ; a Northern "Crystal Palace ;" materials of the Exhibition of 1862 utilised ; construction and decorations ; organ ; concert-room and theatre ; landslips ; Palace opened, *ib.*; destroyed by fire ; New Palace ; park ; racecourse ; trotting-ring ; Japanese village ; circus ; grove ; view from terrace, 435.
Alfieri, his duel with Lord Ligonier, iv. 178.
Alford, Rev. H., Dean of Canterbury, iv. 409.
"Alfred Club," iv. 296.
Alfred, King, i. 449.
Alfred Place, iv. 567.
Alhambra Palace Theatre, iii. 168.
Allen, Ralph ; improvements in the General Post Office, ii. 209.
Allen, Alderman, i. 416.
Allen, Ralph, ii. 209.
Alleyn, Edward, i. 302 ; ii. 159, 224 ; biographical sketch of Alleyne, and history of Dulwich College, vi. 292 ; 296—303, 332.
Alleyn's Almshouses, Soap Yard, Southwark, vi. 33.
Allhallows the Great Church, ii. 40.
Allhallows Barking Church, ii. 107, 109 ; monumental brasses, 109 ; legend of Edward I. ; pilgrimages, 110.
Allhallows' Church, Bread Street ; Milton's baptism, i. 350.
Allhallows Church, Bromley, v. 575.
Allhallows Church, Honey Lane, i. 376.
Allhallows-in-the-Hay, ii. 17.
Allhallows-in-the-Wall Church, ii. 167.
Allhallows Staining Church, Mark

Lane, ii. 178; Plague, 1606 and 1665; churchwardens' books, 179.

All Saints' Church and Schools, Lower Marsh, Lambeth, vi. 416.

All Saints' Church, Blackheath, vi. 228.

All Saints' Church, Deptford Lower Road, vi. 137.

All Saints' Church, Margaret Street, iv. 461.

All Souls' Church, Portland Place, iv. 453.

Almack's, iv. 196; Willis's Rooms; Almack; lady patronesses, ib.

"Almack's Club," iv. 136.

Almanacs, i. 230; vi. 442.

Almonry, The, Westminster; Caxton's printing-press; iii. 488, 489.

Alphege, Archbishop, vi. 164, 191.

Alphege, St., Mission College, vi. 373.

Alsatia, a sanctuary in Whitefriars, i. 155, 179, 183, 189.

Alvanley, Lord, iv. 162.

"Amazone," or riding-habit, iv. 382.

Ames, Joseph, antiquary, ii. 136.

Ampthill Square, v. 309.

Anabaptists, i. 243, 370, 371.

Anatomical School, Piccadilly; Sir C. Bell, iv. 236.

"Anchor of St. Clement's," iii. 33, 75.

Anderson, hanged for stealing a sixpence, ii. 449.

"Anderton's Hotel," Fleet Street, i. 53.

André, Major, iii. 421; v. 522.

Andrewes, Bishop of Winchester, iv. 29; iii. 459; his tomb, vi. 22, 23, 30.

Anerley; tea-gardens; Croydon Canal; vi. 314.

"Angel" Inn, Highgate, v. 418.

"Angel" Inn, Islington, ii. 261.

"Angel" Inn, St. Giles's, iii. 200.

Angell, John; College at Stockwell; Angell Town Estate, vi. 329.

Angerstein, J. Julius, his pictures purchased for the nation, iii. 145; vi. 230.

Anne of Bohemia, Queen of Richard II., i. 316; iii. 309, 442; vi. 9, 442.

Anne of Cleves, Queen of Henry VIII., vi. 170, 226.

Anne of Denmark, Queen of James I., iii. 90.

Anne, Queen, i. 250, 264; ii. 104, 369; iii. 208, 315, 368, 437; iv. 42, 53, 102, 129, 131, 423, 554; v. 153; "Queen Anne's Palace," Bromley, iii. 575.

Anstis, John, Garter, i. 298.

Anthony, Dr., his "aurum potabile," ii. 356.

Anthropological Institute, iii. 155.

"Anti-Gallican" Tavern, Shire Lane, i. 74.

Anti-Jacobin, iv. 257.

Antiquaries, Society of, iv. 269.

Antwerp, its trade with England *temp.* Elizabeth, i. 525.

Apollo Club at the "Devil Tavern," i. 39.

"Apollo Gardens," St. George's Fields, vi. 343, 389.

Apothecaries' Company, v. 68.

Apothecaries' Hall; controversy between physicians and apothecaries, i. 215.

Apprentices, City; riots; fees; punishments; pancake-feast, i. 32, 194, 305, 309, 311, 359, 399, 519.

Apricots, iii. 77; vi. 334.

Apsley House, iv. 359; George II.; Allen's apple-stall, *ib.;* Lord Apsley, 361; house settled on the Duke of Wellington, 362; Waterloo Gallery; Duke's bedroom; pictures; Reform Bill riots; iron blinds, *ib.;* Waterloo banquets, 363; George IV.; Stothard's Waterloo shield; Rundell and Bridge, *ib.;* the Duke's death, 364.

Apsley, Sir Allan; his tomb, ii. 92.

Aquarium, Royal, Westminster, iv. 20.

Arabella Row, v. 9.

Arabin, General, iv. 97.

Arbuthnot, John, M.D., iv. 309; v. 473.

Archæological Institute, iv. 315.

Archers, March of the, i. 536.

Archery, v. 527; vi. 255, 304, 328, 343; bowyers and fletchers in Grub Street, ii. 241; in Islington Fields, 251, 254; "The Bowman's Glory," 338.

Arches, Court of, i. 285, 287; vi. 442.

Architectural Association, iv. 323.

Architectural Museum, Westminster, iv. 36.

"Archway Tavern," Upper Holloway, iv. 381.

"Areopagus" of the Christian Evidence Society, i. 549.

Argyll Lodge, Kensington, v. 133.

Argyll Rooms, Regent Street; Nash; lady patronesses; Velluti; Chabert, the "fire king," iv. 243, 317.

Argyll Rooms, Windmill Street, Haymarket, iv. 237.

Argyll Square, King's Cross; New Jerusalem Church, iv. 576.

Argyll Street, Regent Street, iv. 242; Sir Joseph Banks; Northcote; Madame de Staël, *ib.;* the "good" Lord Lyttelton, 243; Argyll House; Earl of Aberdeen; Corinthian Bazaar; Hengler's Circus; Little Argyll Street, *ib.*

Arianism at Salters' Hall Chapel, i. 549.

Arlington House, v. 39.

Arlington Street, Piccadilly, iv. 169, 179, 260.

Armada, Defeat of the, celebrated in St. Paul's, i. 245.

Armenia; Leo, King of, i. 551; vi. 237.

Armorial bearings, Lord Thurlow on, iv. 557.

Armorial bearings of London and Southwark, vi. 14.

Armorial bearings. (*See* Heralds' College.)

Armouries in the Tower. (*See* Tower.)

Arms and Armour, at United Service Museum, iii. 335.

Armstrong, Archibald, Charles I.'s Jester, iii. 353.

Army and Navy Club, iv. 144.

Army Clothing Club, iv. 40.

Arne, Dr., iv. 435, 436.

Arneway, Thomas, iii. 568.

Arno's Grove, Southgate, v. 569.

Arthur, Prince, son of Henry VIII., i. 241.

Arthur's Club House, iv. 156.

Artillery Company; archers' privileges, ii. 254.

Artillery Ground; Trained Bands, ii. 161; Skippon, captain of the Artillery Garden, 198; v. 249.

Artillery Hall, Horselydown, vi. 113.

Artists' Club, iii. 41.

Artists' General Benevolent Institution, iv. 300.

Artists' Orphan Fund, iv. 300.

Arts Club, iv. 316.

Arundel Club, iii. 101.

Arundel House, Fulham Road, vi. 518.

Arundel House, Highgate, v. 401; Earls of Arundel; Cornwallis family; Queen Elizabeth; James I., *ib.;* Arabella Stuart, 402; death of Lord Bacon, 404.

Arundel House, Strand, iii. 71; Bishops of Bath and Wells; Earl of Arundel; the "Arundelian Marbles," *ib.;* Dukes of Norfolk, 73; formation of Norfolk, Arundel, Howard, and Surrey Streets, 71, 74.

Arundel Society, iv. 300.

Arundel Street, iii. 74; famous residents; "Crown and Anchor" Tavern; the "King of Clubs;" Whittington Club; Temple Club, 75.

Arundell Street, Haymarket, iv. 233.

Ascham, Roger, i. 225; ii. 479.

Ashby Street, Clerkenwell, ii. 333; mansion of the Spencers; private madhouse; Brothers, the prophet, *ib.*

Ashburnham House, Chelsea, v. 86.

Ashburnham House, Westminster Abbey, iii. 457.

Ashburton, John Dunning, Lord, i. 166; vi. 528.

Ashburton, Lord, iv. 284.

Ashmole, Elias, i. 75, 298; vi. 334, 446.

Aske, Robert; Haberdashers' Almshouses and Schools, Hoxton, v. 525.

Askew, Anne, her trial and execution, i. 394.

Askew, Dr., ii. 362, 433; v. 474.

Astley, John, painter and "beau," iv. 124.

Astley, Philip, iii. 35; vi. 398—404.

Astley's Amphitheatre, vi. 398; Philip Astley, *ib.;* first equestrian performances, 400; General Elliott's horse; Riding School; first amphitheatre; Astley, jun.; "Egyptian Pyramids," *ib.,* "Royal Grove;" Astley in Paris and Dublin; his patriotism, 401; circus burnt down, 402; rebuilt as "Amphitheatre of Arts;" Astley a *détenu* in Paris; his escape; another fire, *ib.;* rebuilt as the "Royal Amphitheatre," 403; "Davis's Amphitheatre;" "Battle of Waterloo," 404; Belzoni, 405; Petre and Andrew Ducrow; Ducrow and West; Grimaldi, *ib.;* Miss Woolford, 406; fire in 1841; death of Ducrow; William Batty; Ada Menkens; "Mazeppa;" Boucicault's "Westminster Theatre," *ib.;* Sanger; Richard III. on horseback, 407.

Asparagus Garden, Bankside, vi. 55.

Assay office; assay master, i. 357, 358.

Assembly Rooms, Kentish Town, v. 320.

Assheton-Smith, T., v. 203.

Assize of bread, ii. 181.

Assurance Marine, "Lloyd's," i. 509; 513.

Astrology, modern belief in, vi. 214.

Astronomical Society, iv. 272.

Asylum for Deaf and Dumb Females, v. 522.

Asylum for Female Orphans, vi. 362.
Asylum for Idiots, v. 422.
Atchelor, horse-slaughterer to the Queen, v. 408.
Athenæum Club, iv. 140, 147.
Athenæum Club, Junior, iv. 286.
Atkinson-Morley Home, v. 4.
Atkinson, stock-jobber, i. 476.
Atterbury, Bishop, i. 77; iii. 460; v. 89.
Atterbury, Dr. Lewis, v. 433.
Auctions and Auctioneers, i. 522; iii. 263; iv. 200; v. 49.
Audley, Hugh; his wealth; North and South Audley Streets, iv. 344.
Audley, Lord; Cornish rebellion, vi. 143, 225.
Audley Square, iv. 345.
Audrey, Mary; her "House of Sisters;" priory of St. Mary Overy, South-wark, vi. 20.
Augmentations, Court of, iii. 563.
Augusta, a Roman name of London, i. 20, 449.
Austin Friars, ii. 166; priory of beg-ging friars, 167; interments; monu-mental slabs, ib.
Austin, James, gigantic puddings, i. 561.
Authors, Royal and Court patronage of, iv. 119.
Avenue Theatre, iii. 328.
"Axe and Cleaver" Inn, Lambeth, vi. 392.
"Axe and Crown" Inn, iv. 60.
Aylesbury Street, Clerkenwell, ii. 334; mansion of the Earls of Aylesbury; Thomas Britton, the musical small-coal man, ib.

B.

Babbage, Charles, iv. 425.
Babington's Plot, iii. 45, 200.
Babylon; its population compared with that of "Modern Babylon," vi. 570.
Bacon, Lord, ii. 74, 386, 555, 557, 562; iii. 107, 109; v. 404.
Bacon, sculptor, i. 387; iv. 466, 478.
Bacon, Sir Nicholas, iii. 531, 562.
Baddeley, comedian; "Her Majesty's servants;" scarlet liveries, iii. 220.
Bagnigge Wells House, ii. 296; resi-dence of Nell Gwynne, 297, 298; fruit-trees and vines; mineral springs; "Black Mary's Hole;" poems; advertisements; old paint-ings and engravings, ib.
Bagnio, Perrault's, St. James's Street, iv. 167.
"Bag o' Nails" public-house, v. 9.
Bagpipes, iii. 106.
Baillie, Dr., ii. 433; iii. 143.
Baillie, Joanna, v. 465, 481.
Baily, Francis, F.R.S., iv. 574.
Baker Street, iv. 419; Sir Edward Baker, 421; Madame Tussaud's Exhibition of Wax-work; Bazaar; Cattle Show, ib.; Portman Chapel, 422.
Baker Street Station, Metropolitan Railway, v. 226.
Bakers' Hall, ii. 99.
Bakers in London; statistics, vi. 570.
Bakers, rules for buying meal, ii. 181.
Bakewell Hall, ii. 237.
Balconies; "belconey," iii. 255, 267; "belle-coney," 268.
Baldachino in Hammersmith Church, vi. 537.

Balfe, Michael, iii. 221, 237; iv. 326.
Ballads printed by Catnatch, iii. 203.
"Balloon" fruit shop, Oxford Street, iv. 245.
Balloons, iv. 434; v. 2, 81, 85, 86, 250, 310; vi. 464.
Ball's Pond; John Ball; the "Boarded House;" the pond, v. 527.
"Balm of Honey," v. 185.
Balmerino, Lord, ii. 76, 95; iii. 551; iv. 469.
Balmes House, Hoxton, v. 525, 526.
Baltic Coffee House, i. 537.
Baltimore House, Russell Square, iv. 483, 564.
Bandyleg Walk, vi. 363.
Bangor, Bishops of, their house in Shoe Lane, i. 131, 132.
Bangor Court, Shoe Lane, i. 131.
Bank of Credit, Devonshire House, Bishopsgate, ii. 163.
Bank of England, i. 453; Jews, Lom-bards, and Goldsmiths the first bankers; William Paterson, founder of the Bank, ib.; Act of Parlia-ment, 454; depreciation of Bank notes, 455; extension of charter, 456; riots; renewals of charter; formation of the "rest;" the old building; Gordon riots, 458; for-geries of notes; Abraham Newland; Sir R. Peel's Currency Bill; Fauntl-eroy, 459; State lotteries; run on the Bank; £30,000 note lost, 460; £1 notes, 461; frauds and panic, 464–466; light gold called in; paid notes burnt; directors, clerks, en-gravers, printers, 467; the present Bank, 468, 470; court-room; ro-tunda; Lothbury court; old and new clearing-houses, 470; weigh-ing-machine for gold; Bank-note paper; water-mark; dividend-day, 471; "White Lady of Thread-needle Street," 472; western branch, iv. 305.
Bankes, the showman, and his trained horse, i. 221, 376; ii. 174; vi. 58.
Banks, R.A., sculptor, iv. 466; v. 208.
Banks, Sir Edward, iv. 483.
Banks, Sir Joseph, iii. 191.
"Banks, Stunning Joe;" "Rookery," St. Giles's, iv. 488.
Bankruptcy Court, Basinghall Street, ii. 238.
Bankside, Southwark, vi. 41; its ap-pearance in the 17th century; Globe Theatre, 45–47; Rose Theatre; Ben Jonson; Hope Theatre; Swan Theatre, 48; Paris Garden; bear-baiting; bull-baiting, 51; cock and dog fighting; bear-wards, 52; Al-leyn, "master of the royal bear-garden," 53; James I., "Book of Sports," 54; the Queen's Pike-gardens; Asparagus Garden; Pim-lico Garden; Tarleton; "Tumble-down Dick" Tavern, 56.
Banner of the City of London, i. 282–284.
Bannister, Jack, iv. 567; vi. 575.
Banqueting House, Whitehall. (See Whitehall Palace.)
Baptisterion, Horsleydown; immersion of Anabaptists in the Thames, vi. 111.
Baptistery, Ancient, Oxford Street, iv. 440.
Barbauld, Mrs., v. 486, 534, 538.

Barber and Tooke, Queen's Printers, i. 218.
Barber, John, Lord Mayor; his epitaph on Samuel Butler, i. 407.
Barbers, Barber-surgeons, and Dentists, vi. 63.
Barber's Barn, Hackney, v. 514.
Barbers, Female, iii. 122, 206.
Barber-Surgeons' Company and Hall, ii. 232; the first hall; rebuilt by Inigo Jones, ib.; Holbein's picture, "The Presentation of the Charter by Henry VIII.," 233; pictures by Vandyck, 234; plate; felons re-suscitated after execution, 236.
Barbican on Ludgate Hill, i. 226.
Barbican, ii. 223; Roman watch-tower; distinguished residents, 224, 225.
Barclay and Perkins's Brewery, vi. 33; "ale of Southwark;" Chaucer, ib.; Thrale; Mrs. Thrale, 34; Perkins; Robert Barclay, 35; the brewery described, 36; visit of Marshal Haynau, 39.
Barclay, David, his house in Cheap-side; royal visits, i. 324, 327; oak-panelled dining-room, 338, 339.
Baretti; his trial for murder, iv. 220, 426.
Barham, Rev. R. H., i. 260; iv. 314.
Barillon, French ambassador, iv. 186.
Barlow, Sir William Owen, his eccen-tricities, i. 52.
Barnard, Sir John, i. 475, 502.
Barnard's Inn, formerly Mackworth's Inn, ii. 573; the hall; regulations; Gordon Riots, 574.
Barnes, Thomas, editor of the Times, i. 213; iii. 192.
Barnsbury Park; Roman camp, ii. 277.
"Barnwell, George," and "Mrs. Mill-wood," ii. 195; vi. 74, 280.
Baronets, Association of, iv. 303.
Barracks: Chelsea, v. 83; Knights-bridge, v. 24; St. John's Wood, v. 250; Tower, ii. 93.
Barrow, Dr. Isaac, iv. 83.
Barrows: Blackheath, vi. 224; Green-wich Park, 212.
Barry, James, R.A., iv. 461.
Barry, Lodowick, his comedy, "Ram Alley," i. 137.
Barry, Sir Charles, R.A., iii. 46, 418, 503; iv. 177; v. 533.
Bartholomew Close, ii. 357.
Bartholomew Fair, i. 405; Ben Jonson's play; horse market; booths and stalls, ii. 345, 346, 347, 349; Miss Biffin; "Lady Holland's mob;" Wombwell's menagerie, 349; decay and extinction of the fair, 350; vi. 58, 59.
Bartholomew Lane; Auction Mart; George Robins, i. 522; St. Bartho-lomew's Church, 524.
Bartlett's Buildings; Society for Pro-moting Christian Knowledge, ii. 531.
Bartolozzi, Francisco, engraver, vi. 527.
Barton Street, Westminster; Barton Booth, iv. 2.
Basing Lane; Old Merchant Taylors' Hall, i. 534, 556.
Basing Yard, Peckham; Basing Manor, vi. 290.
Basinghall Street, ii. 237; mansion of the Basings, 238; Bakewell Hall; St. Michael's Bassishaw Church; Masons' Hall; Weavers' Hall;

Coopers' Hall ; Girdlers' Hall ; Bankruptcy Court, *ib.*

Baskett, John, King's printer, i. 218.

Bateman's Buildings ; Lord Bateman, iii. 186.

Bath House ; Lord Ashburton ; his pictures, iv. 284.

Bath, Pulteney, Earl of, iv. 284.

"Bath, Queen Anne's," Endell Street, iii. 208.

Bath, Roman, Strand Lane, iii. 77.

Bath Street, Newgate Street ; bagnio, or Turkish bath, ii. 435.

Bathing in the Thames, iii. 296 ; in the Serpentine, iv. 404.

Baths and Washhouses, Public, iii. 208 ; iv. 36, 39 ; v. 228, 256 ; vi. 129, 412.

Baths, Floating, iii. 296.

Bathurst, Allen, Lord, iv. 188.

Battersea, vi. 469, 470 ; "Patrick's eye," 471 ; customs of the manor ; manor house ; Bolingbroke and Pope ; "Pope's Parlour ;" York Road ; York House ; old church, *ib.* ; present church, 472 ; monuments ; Christ Church, South Battersea ; St. Mark's, Battersea Rise ; St. George's, Lower Wandsworth Road ; Schools ; St. John's College ; School of the National Society, *ib.* ; Freemasons' Girls' School, 473 ; Battersea Rise ; "Falcon" Tavern ; Victoria Suspension Bridge ; Albert Bridge ; Old Battersea Bridge, *ib.* ; the old ferry ; its successive owners, 474 ; erection of the bridge, 475 ; approaches, 476 ; improvements ; Battersea Fields ; bad characters ; weekly fair ; its abolition ; duels, *ib.* ; "Red House, 477 ;" crossing of the Thames by Cæsar ; Battersea Park, *ib.* ; Victoria Dwellings' Association ; Southwark and Vauxhall Waterworks, 478 ; market gardens ; manufacture of enamelled earthenware ; origin of bottled ale, 479.

Battersea Park, vi. 477.

Battersea Suspension Bridge, v. 41.

Battle, Abbots of ; residence in Bermondsey, vi. 104.

Battle Bridge, ii. 276 ; great battle ; Boadicea, 277 ; King's Cross, statue of Geo. IV. removed ; dust heaps ; St. Chad's Well, 278.

Battle of Turnham Green, vi. 555.

Batty, William, lessee of Astley's Amphitheatre, iv. 406.

Batty's Hippodrome, v. 122.

Baxter, Richard, i. 100 ; ii. 428 ; iv. 231, 538 ; vi. 40.

Bayham Street ; residence of Charles Dickens ; controversy as to the site, v. 314.

Baynard's Castle, i. 281—283 ; ward of Castle Baynard, 284 ; rights of the barony ; Robert Fitz-Walter, banner-bearer to the City of London ; castle burnt ; rebuilt ; a royal residence, *ib.* ; destroyed in the Great Fire, 285.

Bayswater ; its etymology ; "Baynard's Watering," v. 183 ; "Hopwood's Nursery Ground ; " springs and conduits ; manor of Westbourne Green ; streams and watercress, *ib.* ; stone conduit, 184 ; Conduit Passage ; Spring Street ; water supply ; wells ; conduit field ; trout fishing, *ib.* ; tea

gardens, 185 ; Lancaster Gate ; Craven House ; Craven Road ; Craven Hill Gardens ; Pesthouse fields ; Toxophilite Society ; Westbourne Green, *ib.* ; Terraces, Gardens, and Squares, 186 ; street railways, 188.

Bayswater House, v. 181.

Bazalgette, Sir Joseph, v. 66, 236.

Beacon on the Tower of Lambeth Church, vi. 447.

Beaconsfield, Earl of, i. 89 ; iii. 376, 533 ; iv. 370, 446, 505, 542.

Bear and Harrow Court, iii. 22.

Bear-baiting, ii. 308 ; iii. 364 ; vi. 51, 52, 53, 54, 55.

Bear Gardens, iv. 15, 406 ; vi. 51—53.

"Bear" Inn, London Bridge foot, vi. 12.

Bear Yard, Bermondsey, vi. 120.

Beards, restrictions on the growth of, iii. 52.

"Beating the (parish) bounds," ii. 237 ; iii. 201, 380.

Beattie, Dr., iv. 464.

"Beau Fielding," iii. 330.

Beaufort Buildings, iii. 100.

Beaufort, Cardinal, vi. 21, 29.

Beaufort House, Chelsea, v. 56 ; vi. 526.

Beaumont and Fletcher, ii. 142, 164 ; v. 531.

"Beaumont" Inn, Paul's Wharf, i. 285.

Beckford, William, author of "Vathek," i. 408 ; iv. 340, 374, 412, 424.

Beckford, William, Lord Mayor, his monument in Guildhall, i. 387 ; his speech to George III., i. 407 ; his house in Soho Square, iii. 185.

"Bedford Arms," Camden Town ; balloon ascents ; music-hall, v. 310.

Bedford Chapel, Bloomsbury Street ; Rev. J. C. M. Bellew, iii. 208.

"Bedford" Coffee House, Covent Garden, iii. 250.

Bedford Court, Covent Garden, iii. 266.

Bedford, Earls and Dukes of ; tolls of Covent Garden Market, iii. 239 ; iv. 537.

Bedford, Francis, Duke of ; statue in Russell Square, iv. 565.

"Bedford Head" Tavern, Maiden Lane, iii. 119, 267.

Bedford House, Bloomsbury, iv. 483 ; Lady Rachel Russell, 536 ; Lady William Russell ; Earls and Dukes of Bedford ; Lucy, Countess of Bedford ; Ben Jonson, 537.

Bedford House, Strand, iii. 120.

Bedford, John, Duke of ; ground-rent of Covent Garden Theatre, iii. 229.

Bedford Lodge, Kensington, v. 133.

Bedford Place, iv. 566.

Bedford Row, iv. 551.

Bedford Square, "Judge-land," iv. 564, 566.

Bedford Street, Covent Garden ; Quin ; Thomas Sheridan, iii. 266 ; the "Peacock," 267.

Bedfordbury ; Sir Francis Kynaston, iii. 268.

Bedlam. (*See* Bethlehem Hospital.)

Bedwell, Rev. W., Rector of Tottenham, v. 560, 563.

Beechey, Sir William, R.A., iv. 449.

Beech Lane, Barbican ; residence of Prince Rupert, ii. 224.

Beef and Wine Sellers' Asylum, Nunhead, vi. 291.

"Beefeaters," Yeomen of the Guard, iii. 368.

"Beef-steak Club," iii. 117, 118, 228, 231, 250, 278 ; iv. 141.

Beer ; origin of the terms "porter," "half-and-half," "three threads," "entire butt," iv. 485.

Beggars, iii. 45, 206, 207 ; licence to beg, vi. 258.

"Beggar's Bush" public-house, in the "Rookery," St. Giles's, iv. 488.

"Beggar's Opera," ii. 347 ; iii. 28 ; iv. 125, 177, 305, 306 ; vi. 134, 229.

Belgrave Square ; distinguished residents, v. 9.

Belgravia, v. 2 ; the "Five Fields," 3 ; footpads ; Thomas Cubitt ; drainage, building operations ; Ebury farm ; Miss Davies ; hawking and coursing ; "Monster" Tavern ; "Slender Billy ;" Spanish monkey ; Tom Cribb's dogs ; wealth of the Grosvenor family, *ib.* ; Marquisate and Dukedom of Westminster ; St. George's Hospital, 4 ; Tattersall's, 5 ; St. George's Terrace, 6 ; Alexandra Hotel, 8 ; turnpike ; Grosvenor Place ; Hobart Place, *ib.* ; Arabella Row, 9 ; Grosvenor Row ; Belgrave Square ; Chapel Street ; Eccleston Street, *ib.* ; Wilton Crescent, 11 ; Wilton Place ; Pantechnicon ; Halkin Street ; Upper and Lower Belgrave Streets ; Eaton Square, *ib.* ; St. Peter's Church, 12 ; Chester Square ; Ebury Street ; Ebury Square, *ib.* ; Lowndes Square ; Cadogan Place, 13.

"Bell and Anchor" Inn, Hammersmith, vi. 530.

Bell, Bishop, i. 310, 311 ; ii. 338, 482.

Bell, Dr. ; National School Society, vi. 365, 366.

"Bell" Inn, Edmonton ; "John Gilpin ;" Charles Lamb, v. 564—568.

Bell, Sir Charles, iii. 167 ; iv. 236, 466.

Bell Tower in the Little Sanctuary, Westminster, iii. 488.

Bell Yard, Fleet Street, i. 75 ; iii. 22.

Bellamy, George Anne, actress, iii. 229 ; vi. 418.

"Bellamy's," old House of Commons, iii. 502.

"Belle Sauvage," Ludgate Hill, i. 220.

Bellew, Rev. J. C. M., iii. 208.

Bellingham, John ; Spencer Perceval assassinated by, iii. 530 ; iv. 551.

Bellman's Verses ; Isaac Ragg, bellman, ii. 541, 542.

Bells, Church ; Great Bell of St. Paul's, i. 256 ; right of ringing bells, vi. 325 ; "Big Ben," iii. 519 ; bells of St. Clement Danes' Church, Strand, iii. 12 ; of Fulham Church, vi. 507 ; of Kensington Church, v. 129.

Bell's Weekly Messenger, i. 64.

Belsize Lane ; Belsize House, v. 490, 491.

Belsize, Manor of ; Belsize Avenue, v. 494 ; Belsize House ; Lord Wotton, 495 ; amusements, 496, 497 ; music ; running ; gaming ; Spencer Perceval ; Delarue murdered by Hocker, *ib.*

Belsize Square, v. 498.

Belvedere Road, Lambeth, vi. 388, 409.

"Belvedere" Tavern, Pentonville, ii. 279.

Belzoni, ii. 293 ; iii. 49 ; iv. 459, 531, 534.
Benbow, Admiral, vi, 138, 154, 156.
Bensley's printing-office, i. 114.
Bentham, Jeremy, iv. 22, 42.
Bentinck Street, Marylebone, iv. 442.
Bentinck Street, Soho, iv. 238.
Bentley and Son ; *Bentley's Miscellany*, iv. 315.
Bentley, Thomas ; partner of Josiah Wedgwood, vi. 550.
Bergami, iv. 460.
Berkeley, Hon. Grantley ; his duel with Dr. Maginn, iv. 251.
Berkeley House, Piccadilly, iv. 275.
Berkeley Square, iv. 327 ; Lord Berkeley ; statue of George III. ; plane-trees ; the old link-extinguishers ; Lansdowne House ; Lord Bute, *ib.;* Junius ; distinguished residents, 328, 330, 331, 332 ; footpads, 333.
Berkeley Street, Clerkenwell ; Sir Maurice Berkeley ; Lord Berkeley, ii. 335.
Berkeley Street, iv. 292.
Berkeley's Inn, Thames Street, i. 302.
Berkshire House, iv. 177.
Bermondsey, vi. 100 ; its etymology, 101 ; tanners ; rope-makers ; market gardens ; Tooley Street ; parish of St. Olave ; the Church ; King Olaf, *ib.*, fire in 1843, 102 ; Abbot's Inn, 103 ; Abbots of Battle ; the Maze ; Maze Pond ; mansion of the Priors of Lewes ; crypt, *ib.;* St. Olave's Grammar School ; Saxon Mint ; fires ; 104, 105 ; St. Olave's Church, &c., 105 ; Mill Lane, 106 ; Borough Compter ; Carter Lane ; Anabaptist Chapel ; "the Three Tailors of Tooley Street ;" Snow's Fields, 108 ; the Abbey, 117—119 ; descent of the manor ; Neckinger Road, 119 ; Long Walk ; Grange Walk ; Bermondsey Square ; Bear Yard, 120 ; St. Mary Magdalen Church, 121 ; Russell Street ; St. Olave's Union, 124 ; Grange Road ; Willow Walk, 125 ; tanneries ; Bricklayers' Arms Station ; Fort Road ; market gardens ; the Neckinger Mills, 126 ; straw paper ; leather ; chalybeate spring ; "Waterman's Arms" tea garden ; Bermondsey Spa ; music ; paintings by Thomas Keyse, 128 ; picture model, "Siege of Gibraltar," 129 ; Spa Road ; Baths and Wash-houses ; Parker's Row ; Christ Church ; Roman Catholic Church and Convent ; Sisters of Mercy, *ib.;* Catholic Schools, 130 ; Jamaica Road ; "Jamaica" Inn ; Pepys ; Jamaica Level ; Bermondsey Wall ; Cherry Garden Stairs ; "Lion and Castle" Inn ; the Cherry Garden ; St. James's Church ; Spa Road Railway Station, *ib.;* Drummond Road ; Peek, Frean, and Co.'s biscuit factory ; Blue Anchor Road ; Galley Wall, 131 ; Half-penny Hatch, 133.
Bermondsey Market ; leather factors, "Skin Depository," vi. 123 ; skin-salesmen ; fellmongers ; wool-staplers, 124.
Bermondsey Square, vi. 120.
"Bermudas, The," iii. 158.
Bernal, Ralph, M.P., iv. 451 ; v. 11.
Berners Street, iv. 464 ; Opie and Mrs.

Opie ; Fuseli ; Theodore Hook's practical hoax ; societies and charitable institutions, *ib.*
Berners Women's Club, iv. 465.
Berry, Lady, her monument at Stepney Church ; story of "The Fish and the Ring," ii. 140.
Berry, The Misses, iv. 351.
Berwick Street, iv. 238.
Best, Captain ; duel with Lord Camelford, v. 176.
Bethell, Slingsby, sheriff of London, fined for assault, vi. 113.
Bethlehem Hospital, ii. 161, 200 ; first established in Bishopsgate, vi. 351 ; Priory of the Star of Bethlehem ; hospital for lunatics ; "Tom o' Bedlams," *ib.;* the hospital in Moor-fields, 352 ; removal to St. George's Fields ; the present building, *ib.;* statues by Cibber of the "Brainless Brothers," 353 ; the patients, 354 ; ball-room, 355 ; billiard-room, chapel, infirmary, 356 ; baths ; treatment of the insane, 357 ; criminal lunatics ; convalescent hospital at Witley, 358 ; statistics ; romantic anecdote, 359 ; regulations, 360.
Bethnal Green, ii. 146 ; ballad of "The Blind Beggar of Bethnal Green ;" Museum ; Sir Richard Wallace's collection, 147 ; Nichols Street ; Half Nichols Street ; tramps ; dog and bird fanciers ; French hospital, 148.
Betterton, Thomas, tragedian, i. 197 ; iii. 27, 46, 219, 220 ; iv. 17.
Betting. (*See* Gambling.)
Betty, William Henry, "the Young Roscius," iii. 231 ; v. 309.
Beulah Spa, Norwood, vi. 294 ; the spring ; entertainments, 315.
Bevis Marks, ii. 165.
Bible Society, vi. 315.
Bibles, misprints in, i. 230 ; in the British Museum, vi. 513 ; printed by Thomas Guy, vi. 93.
Bibliomania, iv. 188.
Bickerstaff, Isaac, iii. 21, 57.
Biffin, Miss, iii. 350.
Billingsgate, ii. 42 ; legend of Belin, 43 ; fish-fags ; market tricks ; Dutch auctions ; Mayhew's account of the market, *ib.;* dock, 44, 45 ; tolls ; prices of fish ; market ; Acts of Parliament, *ib.;* Billingsgate language, 45 ; "bummarees ;" coster-mongers ; sprat-selling, *ib.;* old water-gate, 46 ; Dutch eel-boats ; angling ; fishermen, 47 ; old custom, 48.
Billington, Mrs., iii. 221 ; vi. 539.
Billiter Street and Billiter Square, ii. 176.
Birch, Dr. Thomas, ii. 176, 334.
Birch, Samuel, Lord Mayor ; his shop in Cornhill, i. 412 ; ii. 172.
Birchin Lane ; Drapers ; "Tom's" Coffee House, ii. 173.
Birdcage Walk, iv. 47, 49.
Bird-fanciers, ii. 148, 152.
Birkbeck, Dr., ii. 533, 534 ; v. 221.
Birkbeck Literary and Scientific Institution, ii. 536.
Bishop, Mr. Geo. ; his Observatory, Regent's Park, v. 267.
Bishop, Sir Henry R., v. 323.
Bishop and Williams executed, ii. 455.

Bishop of London's Park, Hornsey, v. 429.
Bishop of London's Prison, Westminster, iii. 489.
Bishops, alleged consecration of in Cheapside, i. 339.
Bishops, The Seven ; their trial, iii. 551.
Bishopsgate, ii. 152 ; Bishop Erkenwald ; merchants of the Hanse ; the Gate ; the "White Hart ;" Sir Paul Pindar's house, *ib.;* "Sir Paul Pindar's Head ;" St. Helen's priory, church, and crypt, 153 ; monuments, 154 ; Crosby Hall, 155, 157.
Bishops' "inns," or houses, in the Strand, iii. 110.
Bishop's Place, Stoke Newington, v. 532.
Bishops' Walk, Lambeth, vi. 429, 436.
Bisset, animal trainer, iv. 220.
"Black and White House," Hackney, v. 519.
"Black Bull" Tavern, Gray's Inn Lane, iv. 551.
"Black Coat School," Westminster, iv. 40.
"Black Dog" as a sign ; "Black Dog" Tavern, Highgate, v. 393.
"Black Doll," marine store dealer's sign, vi. 163.
Blackfriars, i. 200 ; Mountfiquet Castle ; Dominican convent ; parliaments ; Playhouse Yard ; the Blackfriars Theatre ; Burbage and Shakespeare, *ib. ;* Puritan feather-sellers ; Ben Jonson's house ; fatal fall of chapel, 201 ; Queen Elizabeth, 204 ; old and new bridges, 205 ; Bridge Street ; Printing House Square, 209 ; Apothecaries' Hall, 215 ; King's and Queen's printers, 218 ; Ireland Yard, house bought by Shakespeare ; St. Andrew's Hill, 219.
Blackfriars Bridge, i. 205 ; Robert Mylne, his rivalry with Gwynn, *ib. ;* laying the first stone, 206 ; first named "Pitt Bridge," 207 ; repairs, decay, new bridge, temporary bridge ; Joseph Cubitt, 208 ; old ferry, 383.
Blackfriars Road, vi. 368 ; Surrey Theatre ; residences of actors, 371 ; Temperance Hall, 373 ; Working Men's College ; South London Tramway Company's offices ; Mission College, *ib.;* Nelson Square, 374 ; the "Dog's Head in the Pot ;" Surrey Chapel and parsonage house ; Rowland Hill, 374, 380 ; Christ Church ; Paris Garden, 380 ; almshouses, Church Street, 381 ; Sir Ashton Lever, 382 ; Leverian Museum ; Surrey Institution ; Rotunda ; Globe Theatre ; political and seditious meetings ; waxwork and wild beast shows ; concert-room ; auction-room ; Albion Mills, *ib.;* old Swan Theatre, 383.
Blackheath, vi. 224 ; etymology ; tumuli ; cavern ; encampment of the Danes, *ib. ;* Wat Tyler's rebellion, 225 ; Jack Straw ; Emperor of Constantinople ; royal receptions ; Jack Cade ; Falconbridge ; Lord Audley's rebellion, *ib.;* the Smiths' Forge, 226 ; Whitefield's Mount ; artillery butts ; Cardinal Campeggio ; Bonevet, High Admiral

of France; Henry VIII. and Anne of Cleves, *ib.*; Restoration of Charles II.; Blackheath Fair; monstrosities, 227; All Saints' Church; Tranquil Vale; "Green Man" Inn; "Chocolate House," 228; manors of East and West Coombe, 229; Woodlands; J. J. Angerstein, 230; Queen Caroline; St. John's Church; Mrs. Clarke; Maze Hill; "Vanbrugh Castle;" "Mince-pie House," *ib.*; Blackheath Park, 236.

Blacking manufacturers, iv. 549.

"Black Lion" Tavern, i. 195.

"Black Mary's Hole," Bagnigge Wells, ii. 297, 417; iv. 550.

Blackmore, Sir Richard, i. 342; ii. 434; v. 126, 460.

"Black Parliament" at Blackfriars, i. 200.

"Black Post" Tavern, iv. 309.

"Black Raven" sponging-house, Covent Garden, iii. 259.

Blacksmiths' Hall, ii. 36.

Blackstone, Sir William, i. 166; iii. 26.

"Black Swan," Bishopsgate, ii. 159.

Blackwell, Dr. Alexander, v. 83.

Blackwell, Sir Ralph, founder of Blackwell Hall, i. 533.

Blake, William, artist, iv. 469; v. 449, 459.

Blake's Poem on the Charity Children at St. Paul's, i. 262.

Blake's Charity, Highgate, v. 424.

Blanch Appleton Manor (now Blind Chapel Court), ii. 179.

Blandford Square, v. 259.

"Blanket Fair;" Frost on the Thames, 1683, iii. 314.

Bleak Hall, Tottenham, v. 553.

Bleeding Heart Yard, described by Dickens, ii. 544.

Blenheim Street, iv. 464.

Blenkiron, William; his racing stud at Eltham, vi. 242.

Blessington, Countess of, iv. 352; vi. 119, 120.

"Blind Beggar of Bethnal Green," ii. 147.

Blind Chapel Court; manor of Blanch Appleton, ii. 179.

"Blind Man's Friend" Society, iv. 31, 549.

Blind, Royal Normal College and Academy of Music for the, Upper Norwood, vi. 316.

Blind, School for the Indigent, St. George's Fields, vi. 350, 364; blind choir and organist, 365.

Blind, School for the, St. John's Wood, v. 250.

Bliss, Dr., Astronomer Royal, vi. 215, 244.

Blitheman, organist of the Queen's Chapel, his epitaph, ii. 20.

Blood, Colonel, ii. 81; iv. 38, 166, 543; v. 190.

Bloomfield, Robert; the "Farmer's Boy," ii. 244.

Bloomsbury, iv. 480; the village of "Lomesbury," 481; royal mews; Southampton, or Bedford House; Montagu House; Capper's farm; eccentric old maids, *ib.*

Bloomsbury Market, iv. 543.

Bloomsbury Place, iv. 544.

Bloomsbury Square, iv. 537; Earl of Southampton; Bedford House;

Earls and Dukes of Bedford; Lord William Russell; Lady William Russell; Lady Rachel Russell, *ib.*; fortifications; Dr. Radcliffe; other residents, 538; Gordon riots, 539; Lord Mansfield; his house sacked, 541; Pharmaceutical Society, 542; Royal Literary Fund; duels; statue of Fox, 543.

Bloomsbury Street; French Protestant Church; Baptist Chapel; Bedford Chapel, iii. 208; iv. 488.

Blount, Martha, iv. 442.

Blowbladder Street, ii. 219.

Blucher, Marshal, iv. 95.

Blue Anchor Road, Bermondsey, vi. 131.

Blue Coat School. (*See* Christ's Hospital.)

"Blue Flower Pot," Holborn Row; a chirurgeon's sign, iv. 545.

"Blue Posts" Tavern, iv. 309, 479.

"Blueskin" (Blake) and Jonathan Wild, iii. 473.

"Blue Stocking Club," iv. 334, 416, 418.

Boadicea; London burnt by, i. 20; battle with Suetonius Paulinus at Battle Bridge, ii. 277.

"Boar and Castle," Oxford Street, iv. 471.

Board of Green Cloth, iv. 70.

Board of Trade, iii. 377, 388.

Board of Works, iv. 79.

Board Schools, vi. 570.

Boarding Schools for Young Ladies, Hackney, v. 518.

"Boar's Head," Eastcheap, i. 561; old signs; Shakesperian dinners; Pitt; Falstaff; James Austin's gigantic puddings; epitaph on a waiter; Goldsmith, *ib.*; Washington Irving, 562; Shakespeare, 563.

"Boar's Head" Inn, Southwark, vi. 87, 88.

"Boatman's Chapel," Paddington, v. 228.

Boat races; Doggett's coat and badge, iii. 308; Oxford and Cambridge, vi. 500.

Boat-racing, vi. 467, 477.

"Bogus" swindle, i. 213.

Bohemia, Queen of, iii. 164.

"Bohemians, The" (Club), iv. 300.

Bohun's almshouses, Lee, iv. 244.

Boleyn, Anne, Queen of Henry VIII., i. 316; iii. 309, 340, 404, 545; v. 57, 520, 532; vi. 167.

Bolingbroke, Viscount, iv. 237; vi. 469.

Bolt Court, Dr. Johnson's residence and death in, i. 112, 113; "Doctor Johnson" Tavern; Lumber Troop, 114; Cobbett, 117.

"Bolt-in-Tun" Inn, i. 53.

Bolton, Duchess of, vi. 192, 229.

Bolton House, Hampstead, v. 465.

Bolton House, Russell Square, iv. 564, 566.

Bolton, Miss (Lady Thurlow), iii. 232.

Bolton Row, iv. 334.

Bolton Street, iv. 292.

Bolton, William, Prior of St. Bartholomew's, ii. 270, 344, 353.

Boltons, The, Brompton, v. 101.

Bond, Sir Thomas, iv. 293; Bond's Gardens, Camberwell, vi. 272, 286.

Bond Street, Old and New, iv. 249; "Conduit Mead;" fashionable

loungers, 299; residents; societies, 300; librarians; Hancock; Hunt and Roskell; Copeland and Co., 301; Doré's pictures; Long's Hotel, 302; Clarendon Hotel; Stevens's Hotel; Western Exchange, 303.

Bonfires, City, i. 332.

Bonner, Bishop, i. 243; vi. 73, 512, 514.

Bonner's House, Putney, vi. 493.

Bonner's Road, v. 508; Orphan Asylum; Hospital for Diseases of the Chest; Bishop Bonner's Fields, Hall, and Hall Farm, *ib.*

Bonnycastle, anecdotes of, i. 267, 268.

Bonomi, architect, R.A.; Spanish Place Chapel, iv. 425, 461.

Boodle's Club, iv. 164.

Book auctions, iv. 201.

Booksellers in Paternoster Row, i. 274.

Booksellers' stalls in Moorfields, ii. 197; in Westminster Hall, iii. 542.

"Boot," Burning of the, i. 408.

"Boot" Tavern, Cromer Street; headquarters of the Gordon rioters, v. 365.

Booth, Barton, iii. 220; iv. 2.

Bordeaux wines, importation of, ii. 21.

Bordello, or "stews," Bankside, Southwark, vi. 32.

Borough Compter, vi. 106.

Borough Market, vi. 17.

Borough, The. (*See* Southwark.)

Boruwlaski, Count, iv. 279.

Boss Alley, ii. 36.

Boswell Court (Old and New); distinguished residents, iii. 22.

Boswell, James, i. 51, 54, 167, 418; iii. 75, 275; iv. 141, 183, 291; v. 194; vi. 346, 575, 576.

Botanic Garden, Chelsea, v. 68.

Botanic Society. (*See* Royal Botanic Society.)

"Botany Bay;" Victoria Park, v. 508.

Botany, British Museum, iv. 525.

"Bottled ale," Origin of, vi. 479.

Boucher, Joan, the Maid of Kent, ii. 339.

Bouffleurs, Madame de, i. 167.

Boulevards, proposed by Loudon, v. 257; vi. 467.

Bourgeois, Sir Francis, vi. 302.

Bourne, Dr., preaching at Paul's Cross, i. 243.

Bouverie Street; the *Daily News*, i. 137—140.

Bow and Bromley Institute, v. 572.

Bow Bridge and Church, v. 570, 571.

Bow Church, Cheapside, i. 335; the bells; the steeple; early history; violation of sanctuary, *ib.*; Great Fire, 337; Sir C. Wren; Norman crypt; seal of the parish, 338.

Bow Lane, i. 352.

"Bower Banks," Tottenham, v. 552.

Bowes, Sir Martin, Lord Mayor, i. 400; ii. 366.

"Bowl, The," St. Giles's, iii. 200.

Bowling alleys, ii. 328; vi. 54.

Bowling-Green House, Putney, vi. 495.

Bowling-Green Lane, Clerkenwell, ii.

Bowling Greens, iv. 77, 236; vi. 495. 328; "Pall Mall;" "Cherry Tree public-house;" whipping post, *ib.*

Bowling-pin Alley, i. 80.

Bowman, first coffee-house opened by, ii. 172.

Bow Street, iii. 272; Police Office; Sir John Fielding; "Robin Redbreasts,"

ib.; Waller, 273; Mohun, comedian; Harley, Earl of Oxford; Grinling Gibbons; Kneller; Dr. Radcliffe; Wycherley; the "Cock Tavern;" "Garrick's Head Tavern;" "Society of Sign-painters," *ib.*
Bowyer family, Peckham, vi. 290.
Bowyer House, Camberwell, vi. 272.
Bowyers. (*See* Archery.)
Boydell, Lord Mayor, i. 343, 344, 345, 346, 390, 411; iv. 135.
Boyer, Jeremy, master of Christ's Hospital, ii. 373.
Boyle, Richard, Earl of Burlington. (*See* Burlington.)
Boyle, Robert, v. 89.
Boyle Street, iv. 305.
Boys' Home, Chalk Farm, v. 296.
Boys, Thomas, publisher, iv. 470.
Boyse, his poems, i. 424.
Boyton, Captain Paul, iii. 321.
Bozier's Court, iv. 479.
Bracegirdle, Mrs., iii. 41, 81, 220; iv 171.
Bradley, Dean, iii. 400, 461.
Bradley, Dr., Astronomer Royal, vi. 215.
Bradshaw, regicide, iii. 539.
Braham, John, vocalist, ii. 146, 294; iv. 191—196, 458.
Braidwood, James, v. 543; vi. 106.
Braithwaite; first steam fire-engine, iv. 244.
Bramah, John Joseph, engineer, v. 44.
Branch, Helen, her bequests, i. 530.
Brandenburgh House, Hammersmith, vi. 539, 540; gardens; masquerades, 542; Queen Caroline; her death and funeral, 543.
Brandon, Gregory and Richard, executioners, ii. 143; iii. 350; v. 197.
Brassey, Thomas, M.P., v. 13.
Bread Street, Cheapside, i. 349, 350; birth and baptism of Milton; the prison; "Mermaid" Tavern, *ib.*; old Salters' Hall, 548.
Breakfasting House, near Sadler's Wells, ii. 296.
Breakneck Steps, Old Bailey, ii. 476.
"Brecknock Arms" Tavern; duel between Munro and Fawcett, v. 376.
Brecknock Road, v. 373.
Breeches-maker's shop bill, vi. 13.
Breslau, conjuror, iv. 84, 232.
Breweries, or "bere houses," *temp.* Henry VII., ii. 123.
Brewers' Hall, ii. 8.
Bricklayers' Arms Railway Station, vi. 125.
Bridewell, i. 190; the old palace, 191; trial of Queen Katharine; converted into a prison; Great Fire; flogging of prisoners, *ib.*; Hogarth's "Harlot's Progress," 192; John Howard, Pennant, 193; contumacious apprentices: Court-room, 194; women whipped, 306.
Bridewell Bridge, ii. 419.
Bridewell Dock, i. 195.
Bridewell, Westminster. (*See* Tothill Fields' Prison.)
Bridge Foot, London Bridge. (*See* Southwark.)
Bridge House, public granary, ii. 180.
Bridge House, Tooley Street, vi. 13, 14.
Bridge Street, Blackfriars; Sir Richard Phillips, i. 208.
Bridge Street, Southwark, vi. 13.

Bridgeman, gardener to Caroline, Queen of George II., v. 154.
Bridgewater House, iv. 177.
Bridgewater Square, Barbican; mansion of the Earls of Bridgewater, ii. 224.
Bridport, Admiral Lord, v. 119.
"Brill" Tavern, Somers Town; Brill Row, v. 342.
Briot, Nicholas, coins executed by, ii. 104.
Bristol House, Putney Heath, vi. 496.
Bristol House, St. James's Square, iv. 184.
"Britain's Burse," iii. 104.
British Almanack & Companion, i. 230.
British and Foreign School Society, vi. 365.
British Artists, Gallery of, iv. 230.
British Association for the Advancement of Science, iv. 296.
"British Coffee House," Cockspur Street, iv. 84.
British College of Health; James Morison; "Morison's Pills," v. 366.
British Home for Incurables, vi. 327.
British Institution, Pall Mall, iv. 136.
British Lying-in Hospital, iii. 208.
British Museum, iv. 490; Sir Hans Sloane's collections; the Harleian MSS.; Sir John Cotton's library; George III.'s library; Montagu House, *ib.*; Ralph, Duke of Montagu, 491; gardens; the Gordon riots; encampment, 493, 494; Governors and Trustees, 495; public opening; admission tickets, 496; statistics of admissions; Egyptian antiquities; Elgin marbles; royal library, 497; Towneley marbles, 500; Payne Knight's collection; library and old reading-rooms, *ib.*; new buildings; Sir Robert Smirke; Sydney Smirke, 502; Grenville library; new reading-room, 503, 509; catalogue, 504, 505, 506; present regulations, 505, 509; book-cases; press-marks, 506; books of reference, 508; Printed Book Department, 509; "King's pamphlets;" "King's library," 512; Bibles; Grenville library; rare books; autographs, 513; Magna Charta; Manuscript Department; "Codex Alexandrinus," 514; early newspapers, 515; copyright, 517; prints and drawings; past and present officers, 518; Macaulay, 519; Natural History collections; zoology, 520; palæontology; botany; ornithology, 522; collection of portraits, 524; mineralogy; fossils; herbarium; antiquities, 525; ethnography; mediæval antiquities; Portland vase, 526; coins and medals; the "Pulteney guinea;" bronzes, 527; Greek, Roman, and Etruscan vases, 528; mummies, 530; Assyrian antiquities, 531; Hellenic, Elgin, Mausoleum, and Lycian rooms, 532; Ephesian and Roman galleries, 533.
British Orphan Asylum, vi. 327.
Britton, John, F.S.A., ii. 568, 323; iv. 575.
Britton, Thomas, the small-coal man, ii. 334; v. 524.
Brixton, vi. 319; Royal Asylum of St. Ann's Charity; Female Convict

Prison; treadmill; Clapham Park; the Cedars, 320.
Broad Court; "Wrekin" Tavern, iii. 274.
Broadsides printed by Catnatch, iii. 203.
Broad Street, Bloomsbury, iv. 484.
Broad Street, Golden Square, iv. 239.
Broadway, Westminster, iv. 20.
Bromley, v. 573-576; Convent of St. Leonard's; its history; old church and monuments; present church, 574.
Brompton, v. 26, 100; Oratory of St. Philip Neri, 26; West, Old and New, 101; Cromwell, or Hale House; Cromwell Road; Thistle Grove; "The Boltons;" St. Mary's Church; cemetery, *ib.*; Brompton Hall, 102; Lord Burleigh; St. Michael's Grove; Jerrold and Dickens; Brompton Grove; Lower Grove; Gloucester Lodge, *ib.*; Hospital for Consumption, 104; Cancer Hospital; Onslow Square; Pelham Crescent; Keeley; Eagle Lodge; Thurloe Place and Square; International Exhibition, 1862, *ib.*; annual exhibitions, 106; School of Cookery; National Portrait Gallery, 107; Meyrick collection of arms and armour; Indian Museum, 108; South Kensington Museum, 109; Museum of Patents; Science and Art Department; Royal Albert Hall, 112; concerts; National Training School for Music, 115; gardens of the Royal Horticultural Society; statue of the Prince Consort, 116.
Brompton Park Nursery, v. 122.
Brompton Road, v. 26.
Brompton Square, v. 26.
Brondesbury. (*See* Kilburn.)
Brook Green, Hammersmith, vi. 533; fair; Roman Catholic Church and Almshouses; St. Mary's College; Reformatory, *ib.*
Brook Street, Grosvenor Square, iv. 342; Claridge's (Mivart's) Hotel, 343.
"Brooke House," Hackney; Fulke Greville, Lord Brooke, v. 520.
Brooke Street, Holborn; suicide of Chatterton, ii. 545.
Brookes, Joshua, F.R.S., anatomist, iv. 256, 464.
"Brookes's" Club, iv. 152, 158.
Brooks, Shirley, i. 57, 58; v. 267.
Broom House, Fulham, vi. 524.
Broome, gardener of the Inner Temple, i. 181.
Brothers, Richard, the "prophet," ii. 333; v. 212, 262.
"Brothers' Steps," or "Field of the Forty Footsteps," iv. 482.
Brougham, Lord, iii. 179, 532; iv. 298, 327.
Browning, Thomas, the prisoner of Lud Gate; "Prison Thoughts," i. 225.
Brownlow Street, Holborn, iv. 552.
Brownlow Street, St. Giles's; Sir John Brownlow, iii. 207.
Brownrigg, Elizabeth, murderess, i. 99; ii. 458.
Bruce, David, King of Scotland, ii. 64; v. 549.
Bruce Castle School, Tottenham; the old Castle, residence of the father

of King David Bruce; history of the place, v. 554—557.

Bruce, the African traveller, iv. 260.

Brummell, George, "Beau Brummell," i. 412; iv. 95, 165, 284, 317, 332, 353, 399, 418; v. 248.

Brunel, Isambard K., iii. 132; v. 223.

Brunel, Sir M. I.; the Thames Tunnel, ii. 129; iv. 33; v. 86; vi. 139.

Brunswick Square, iv. 563.

Brunton, Miss (Countess of Craven), iii. 232.

Bruton Street, iv. 326, 327.

Bryanston Square, iv. 412.

Bryanston Street, iv. 408.

Brydges Street, Covent Garden, iii. 282.

Buchan, Dr., anecdotes, i. 278.

Buckhurst, Lord, v. 143.

Buckingham, Catherine, Duchess of, iv. 63.

Buckingham, Duke of, Dryden's "Zimri," ii. 25, 26.

Buckingham, Duke of (temp. Richard III.), at Guildhall, i. 394.

Buckingham, Edward Stafford, Duke of, iii. 545.

Buckingham, George Villiers, Duke of, iii. 436, 437, 446; iv. 62, 432.

Buckingham House, Pall Mall, iv. 128.

Buckingham, James Silk, M.P., v. 268.

Buckingham, John Sheffield, Duke of, iii. 346, 383, 436; vi. 498.

Buckingham Palace, iv. 61; James I., 62; the Mulberry Garden; Arlington House; John Sheffield, Duke of Buckingham; Buckingham House, ib.; "Princess" Buckingham; the house bought by George III., and settled on Queen Charlotte, 63; Dr. Johnson, 64; Gordon riots, 65; Nash's new palace; altered by Blore, 66; Marble Arch; State apartments; ball-room, throne-room, picture-gallery, 68; yellow drawing-room; pleasure-grounds, pavilion, frescoes; royal mews; state-coach; "the boy Jones," 69; the King of Hanover; departure of the Guards for the Crimea; interview of Charles Dickens with Queen Victoria; Board of Green Cloth, 70; royal household; courts, drawing-rooms, and levees, 71.

Buckingham Street; Buckingham House; George Villiers, iii. 107; house of Pepys; Peter the Great, 108, 109.

Buckland, Rev. William, Dean of Westminster, iii. 461.

Bucklersbury, i. 435.

Buckstone, J. B., comedian, iv. 226.

Budge Row, Cannon Street, i. 550.

Budgell, Eustace, ii. 300.

Bugsby's Hole; pirates hung in chains, ii. 135.

Building regulations, iii. 41.

"Bulk-shops," Butchers' Row, iii. 11.

"Bull and Mouth," Aldersgate Street, Bull-baiting, ii. 308; iii. 364; vi. 51, 52, 54, 55, 172.

Bull, Dr. John, organist, i. 532; ii. 20. ii. 219.

Bull, executioner, v. 196.

Bull Feathers' Hall, Society of, ii. 279.

"Bull" Inn, Bishopsgate, ii. 161; Burbage's Theatre; Hobson, the Cambridge carrier, ib.

Bull's Head Court, bas-relief of Charles I.'s giant and dwarf, ii. 430.

Bullock's American Museum, iv. 257.

Bunhill Fields and Burial-ground, ii. 202, 204, 206; vi. 108.

"Bun House, Old," Chelsea, v. 69.

Bunn, Alfred, iii. 221, 226, 234; iv. 194; v. 104.

Bunning, J. B., architect, ii. 50; v. 374, 376.

Bunyan, John, ii. 440; vi. 13, 40.

Burbage, James, i. 200, 201; vi. 47-49.

Burbage, Richard, ii. 195.

Burdett-Coutts, Baroness, iii. 105; iv. 10, 171, 281, 400; v. 406, 411, 506, 509.

Burdett, Sir Francis, iii. 75, 476; iv. 171, 281; v. 20.

Burford's Panorama, iii. 170.

Burgess, Bishop of Salisbury; Royal Society of Literature, iii. 154.

Burghley, Lord, v. 178.

Burke, Edmund, i. 166, 388; iv. 134, 154, 201, 208, 461; vi. 576.

Burleigh House, Strand, iii. 113.

Burleigh, Lord, ii. 561; v. 102; iii. 434.

Burlington Arcade, iv. 272.

Burlington, Earl of, iii. 469; iv. 263.

Burlington Gardens; Atkinson, perfumer; Truefitt, hairdresser; London University, iv. 304.

Burlington House, Piccadilly, iv. 256, 262; Richard Boyle, Earl of Burlington, 263; political plans, 265; fêtes to Allied Sovereigns; Elgin marbles; the house bought by Government, ib.; plans for the removal of the Royal Academy, National Gallery, Royal and other Societies; commencement of new buildings; Banks and Barry, architects, 266; present Royal Academy; Geological Society, Royal Society, Linnæan Society, Society of Antiquaries, Astronomical Society, Chemical Society, 267-272.

Burnet, Bishop, i. 77; ii. 325, 326; iii. 45, 80, 574; iv. 125.

Burney, Dr. Charles, iii. 172; iv. 34, 232, 464, 515; vi. 161.

Burton Crescent, iv. 575.

Burton, Decimus, architect, v. 269.

Burton, James, vi. 576.

Burton Street; Mrs. Davidson; "New Jerusalem Church," iv. 574.

Bury Street, St. James's, iv. 202.

Busby, Dr., iii. 422, 476; vi. 549, 557.

Busby; wig so called, iv. 459.

"Busby's Folly," ii. 279.

Bush Hill Park, Southgate; grounds laid out by Le Notre; carving by Grinling Gibbons, v. 569.

Bushnell, George; Trojan horse, v. 209.

Bushnell, John; statues by him, i. 2', 30.

Butcher Hall Lane; "Three Jolly Pigeons;" Cauliflower Club, ii. 434.

Butchers' Almshouses, Walham Green, vi. 525.

Butchers in London; statistics, vi. 570.

Butchers of Clare Market; their patronage of the drama, iii. 42.

Butchers' Row, iii. 10.

Bute, Earl of, i. 35, 408; iv. 88, 328, 345.

Butler, Bishop, i. 73, 77; v. 480.

Butler, Samuel, author of "Hudibras," i. 105, 155, 407; ii. 221; iii. 255, 264; iv. 290, 329.

Butterflies; "The Camberwell Beauty," vi. 279.

Butterwick Manor House, Hammersmith; Earl of Mulgrave, vi. 539.

"Button's Coffee House;" Daniel Button; the "Lion's Head," iii. 277, 280; death of Button, 281.

Butts, Dr., i. 183; ii. 233.

Buxton, Jedediah, ii. 321.

Buxton Memorial Drinking Fountain, iv. 33.

Buxton, Sir T. Fowell, v. 449.

Byron, Lord, i. 46, 261, 429; iii. 113, 226, 234, 240, 310; iv. 30, 167, 176, 293, 296, 302, 311, 397, 405, 430, 458, 470; v. 291, 418, 457; vi. 253, 293.

Byron, William, fifth Lord; his duel with Mr. Chaworth, iv. 137.

C.

Cabot, Sebastian, ships provided for him by the Drapers' Company, i. 518.

Cabs; introduction of; licences; office in Scotland Yard, iii. 333.

Cade, Jack, i. 545; ii. 8, 14; vi. 9, 13, 86, 112, 145, 225.

Cadell, Thomas, publisher, iii. 80, 123; iv. 544.

Cadgers' Hall and Cadgers, i. 74; iv. 488.

Cadogan Place, v. 13.

Cadogan Street and Terrace; Earl Cadogan, v. 98, 99.

Caen (or Ken) Wood, Hampstead; etymology; seat of the Earl of Mansfield, v. 441; the house and grounds, 442.

Cæsar, Sir Julius, Master of the Rolls, i. 77; ii. 154; v. 404, 563.

Cage, St. Giles's, iii. 200.

Cagliostro, Count, iii. 557; v. 97.

Cake-house, Hyde Park, iii. 383.

Callcott, Sir Augustus, R.A., v. 134.

"Calves' Head Club," iv. 229.

Cam, Thomas, longevity of, ii. 195

Camberwell, vi. 269; etymology; early history; mineral springs; descent of the manor, ib.; the Grove, 272; old residents; the Bowyer family, Bowyer House; Literary and Scientific Institution; Wyndham Road; Flora Gardens, ib.; St. Giles's Church; the old church; new church, 273; churchwardens' accounts, 274; John Wesley and his wife; the "Little Woman of Peckham;" "Equality Brown;" Camden Chapel; Rev. Henry Melvill; St. George's Church; Vestry Hall, ib.; the Green; Camberwell Fair, 275; the "Old House on the Green," 278; Green Coat and National Schools; Free Grammar School; Aged Pilgrims' Friend Asylum, ib.; Butterflies, 279; "The Camberwell Beauty;" Myatt's Farm; Strawberries; Coldharbour Lane; River "Effra;" Effra Road; Denmark Hill Grammar School, ib.; Dr. Lettsom; the Grove; George Barnwell, 280; Grove House Tea-Gardens; Camberwell Hall; Camberwell Club, 281; Collegiate School, 283; Champion Hill; "Fox-under-the-Hill" Tavern; old families and residents, 284 ; " Military Association" and Volunteer Corps, 285 ; growth of population ; conveyances; " Camberwell Coach;" omnibuses and tram-cars ; Camberwell House Lunatic Asylum, *ib.*

Camberwell Club, vi. 281.

Cambridge, H.R.H. the Duke of, iv. 161.

Cambridge Hall, Newman Street, iv. 467.

Cambridge Heath Gate, v. 508.

Cambridge House, Piccadilly, iv. 285.

Cambridge Square and Terrace, v. 202.

Camden Chapel, Camberwell, vi. 274.

Camden, Lord ; Camden Town, v. 309.

Camden, the antiquary, Clarencieux herald, i. 298 ; ii. 38, 375, 476 ; iii. 425, 472, 482.

Camden Town, v. 302 ; Lord Camden ; Camden Town and Square ; High Street ; Statue of Cobden, v. 309 ; " Bedford Arms" Tavern, 310 ; balloons; music-hall ; Park Street ; Royal Park Theatre ; " Mother Red Cap," " Mother Black Cap," and other inns, *ib.*; " Mother Shipton," Malden Road, 311 ; Bayham Street ; first home of Charles Dickens, 314 ; Camden Road, 315 ; Camden Town Athenæum ; North London Railway Station ; Tailors' Almshouses ; St. Pancras Almshouses ; Maitland Park ; Orphan Working School, *ib.*; Dominican Monastery ; Gospel Oak Fields and Fair ; Dale Road ; St. Martin's Church, 316 ; "Gospel Oak" Tavern, 317 ; Great College Street ; Royal Veterinary College, 322 ; Pratt Street, 323 ; St. Martin's-in-the-Fields' burial-ground ; Charles Dibdin ; Agar Town, *ib.*

Camelford House, iv. 375.

Camelford, Lord ; his fatal duel, iii. 182 ; iv. 302, 446 ; v. 176.

Camomile Street, ii. 158, 165.

Campbell, Dr. John, iv. 554.

Campbell, Lord, iv. 81 ; v. 25.

Campbell, Sir Colin, v. 25.

Campbell, Thomas, poet, iii. 574 ; iv. 176, 250, 252, 408, 459, 460 ; vi. 296, 304, 306.

Campden House, Kensington, v. 130.

Campeggio, Cardinal, vi. 11, 226.

Canada Dock, vi. 141.

" Canal, The," St. James's Park, iv. 50.

Canals ; Paddington Canal ; Regent's Canal, v. 219.

Canaletti ; View of Westminster Bridge, iii. 381.

Cancer Hospital, v. 104.

Candle-makers in Cheapside, i, 304.

Candlewick Street (Cannon Street), i. 544.

Canning, George, i. 338 ; iv. 33, 257, 303, 326, 426 ; v. 104 ; vi. 108, 498, 566.

Cannon Row, iii. 380 ; canons of St. Stephen's Chapel, *ib.*; Board of Control ; Civil Service Commissioners ; Rhenish Wine House ; distinguished residents ; last days of Charles I., 381.

Cannon Street, i. 544 ; London Stone ; Salters' Hall, 548 ; Salters' Hall Chapel ; Arianism ; mysterious murder, 549 ; South-Eastern Railway Station, 550 ; Cordwainers' Hall ; St. Swithin's Church, *ib.*

Canonbury, ii. 269 ; the Manor ; Priory of St. Bartholomew's ; Sir John Spencer ; his daughter, Lady Compton, *ib.* ; Canonbury House, . old carvings, 270, 272 ; Prior Bolton, 270 ; Goldsmith, 271 ; Church of England Young Men's Association, 273.

Canterbury, Archbishops of ; Lambeth Palace, vi. 428–443.

Canterbury Music Hall and Gallery of Fine Arts, vi. 416.

Canute, i. 236, 452 ; iii. 491 ; vi. 8, 101, 132, 134.

Canute's " Trench," vi. 341, 433.

" Capability " Brown, v. 154.

Carburton Street, iv. 458.

Cardinal's Cap Alley, vi. 32.

Carew, Thomas, iv. 26.

Carey, Henry, author of " Sally in our Alley," ii. 335.

Carey House, Strand, iii. 101.

Carey Street, iii. 26.

Carlisle House, iii. 294.

Carlisle Lane, Lambeth ; Carlisle House ; residence of the Bishops of Rochester, vi. 417.

Carlisle, Sir Anthony, iv. 453.

Carlisle Street Soho ; " Merry Andrew Street," iii. 177, 187.

Carlton Club, iv. 148.

Carlton House, iii. 146 ; Frederick, Prince of Wales, iv. 86, 87 ; George IV.; colonnade ; portico ; armoury, 86 ; state-rooms ; garden ; rookery ; riding-house, 87 ; political faction ; banquets ; marriage of George IV., 89 ; the Regency, 92, 95, 98 ; the Princess Charlotte, 92–94 ; the house demolished, 99.

Carlton House Terrace, iv. 99.

Carlton, Lord ; Carlton House, iv. 87.

Carlyle, Thomas, i. 65 ; v. 64.

Carnaby Street ; Pest-house and Pest Field, iv. 239.

Caroline, Queen of George II., iv. 111, 401 ; v. 69, 142, 145, 154 ; vi. 215.

Caroline, Queen of George IV., i. 35 ; ii. 293, 512 ; iii. 410, 532 ; iv. 81, 82, 89, 92, 102, 178, 344, 418 ; v. 146, 147, 185, 203, 354 ; vi. 197, 230, 458.

Carpenter, John, Founder of the City of London School, i. 375.

Carpenters' Company and Hall, ii. 197.

Carr, Rev. Wm. Holwell ; National Gallery, iii. 145.

Carriage-builders, Long Acre, iii. 269.

Carriages, introduction of, iii. 269.

Carrington Street ; " Kitty Fisher," iv. 352.

Carter Lane, Tooley Street, vi. 106.

Cartwright, Major, iv. 575.

Cassell, the late John, i. 52 ; v. 220.

Cassivellaunus, his capital at Verulamium, i. 18.

Castle Baynard, i. 200.

" Castle," Paternoster Row, i. 271, 276 ; Richard Tarleton, 275, 276 ; ordinaries, 276 ; " Castle Society of Music," 278.

" Castle Tavern," Fleet Street, i. 63.

" Castle " Tavern, Holborn ; " Tom Spring," ii. 536.

" Castle " Tavern, Kentish Town, v. 321.

Castle Street, Holborn, ii. 531.

Castle Street, Oxford Street, iv. 461.

Castlemaine, Countess of. (*See* Cleveland, Duchess of.)

Castlereagh, Lord, iv. 190 ; vi. 498.

Catacombs, ancient and modern, v. 407.

Catalpa-tree in Middle Temple Garden, i. 182.

" Cat and Bagpipes," Downing Street, iii. 392.

" Cat and Dog Money," ii. 152.

" Cat and Fiddle," a public-house sign, iv. 261.

" Cat and Mutton " public-house, Cat and Mutton Fields, v. 507.

" Cat Harris," iv. 223.

Catherine of Arragon, Queen of Henry VIII., vi. 166. (*See* also Katherine.)

Catherine of Braganza, Queen of Charles II., iii. 92, 356 ; iv. 76, 105, 249 ; vi. 545.

Catherine Street, Strand ; derivation of its name, 110 ; " Sheridan Knowles " Tavern ; " Club of Owls," iii. 282.

Catherine Wheel Alley, iv. 156.

" Catherine Wheel " Inn, Southwark ; " Cat and Wheel " public-house, Bristol, vi. 88.

Catnatch, James, printer ; broadsides ; ballads ; last dying speeches, iii. 203.

Cato Street conspirators, ii. 76, 94, 454 ; iv. 340, 410 ; v. 315.

Cattle Market, Deptford, vi. 149.

Cattle Market, Islington ; its failure, ii. 282 ; new market, Copenhagen Fields, 283 ; statistics, ii. 284 ; iii. 376.

Cattle Show, Smithfield Club, iv. 421.

Cattley, Nan, iv. 435.

Cats endowed by " La Belle Stewart," iv. 109.

" Cat's Opera," iv. 220.

Cauliflower Club, ii. 435.

Cave, Edward, ii. 317, 318, 320, 321 ; iii. 512 ; iv. 461.

Cave's cotton mill, ii. 425.

Cavendish Club, iv. 454.

Cavendish, Hon. Henry, iv. 568 ; vi. 322.

Cavendish Square, iv. 442, 443 ; statues of William, Duke of Cumberland, and Lord George Bentinck, 444, 445 ; Harcourt House, 446.

Caxton, i. 381 ; ii. 20 ; iii. 488, 489, 490, 569 ; iv. 513.

Cecil Court, iii. 159.

Cecil Street, iii. 101, 110.

Celeste, Madame, iii. 221.

" Celestial Bed," Dr. Graham's, iv. 124.

Cellar dwellings, St. Giles's, iii. 205, 207.

Cemeteries, ancient and modern, v. 409 ; Abney Park, v. 543 ; Brompton, v. 101 ; Deptford and Lewisham, vi. 246 ; Hampstead, v. 504 ; Mile End, v. 576 ; Nunhead, v. 291 ; Norwood, vi. 316 ; Stratford, West Ham, v. 573.

Centenarians, iii. 201, 230 ; iv. 470, 479 ; v. 76, 130, 208, 558 ; vi. 161, 274, 521.

Centlivre, Mrs., iii. 256 ; iv. 80, 172.

" Century " Club, iv. 206.

Chabert, the Fire King, ii. 281 ; iv. 243.

Chalk Farm ; Chalcot Farm ; manorhouse of Upper Chalcot, v. 291 ; duels, 293 ; Wrestling Club, 295 ; " Chalk Farm " Tavern, 296 ;

sports ; Chalk Farm fair ; railway goods and passenger stations, *ib.*
Chalon, J. J., v. 408, 448.
Chaloner, Sir Thomas, ii. 329 ; vi. 550.
Challoner, Bishop, iv. 554.
Challoner, execution of, i. 94, 95.
Chalybeate springs, Sadler's Wells, ii. 290 ; Bermondsey Spa, vi. 129.
Chambers, Sir William ; Somerset House, iii. iv. 272, 464.
Champion, the King's ; antiquity of the office ; the Dymokes of Scrivelsby ; challenge at the coronation banquets of Richard II., Henry VIII., William III., George IV., iii. 544, 554, 555, 556, 557.
Chancery, Inns of, ii. 570.
Chancery Lane, i. 76 ; Rolls Chapel and Rolls Court ; Masters of the Rolls, 76, 77 ; Sir Julius Cæsar ; Sir Joseph Jekyll ; Sir William Grant, 79 ; Sir John Leach ; Lord Gifford, 80 ; Bowling Pin Alley ; Wolsey's house, 80, 81 ; birthplace of Strafford ; house of Izaak Walton, 82 ; Old Serjeants' Inn and Hall, 83, 84 ; residence of Sir Richard Fanshawe ; "Hole in the Wall" Tavern ; Chichester Rents, 83, 84 ; Southampton Buildings ; the "Southampton," 85, 86, 87 ; Tooke's Court, 88 ; Cursitor Street ; Sloman's sponging house, 88, 89 ; Law Institution, 90 ; execution of Eliza Fenning, 92.
Chandos portrait of Shakespeare, iv. 177 ; v. 108.
Chandos Street, Cavendish Square, iv. 447.
Chandos Street, Covent Garden, iii. 268 ; the "Three Tuns ; " "Sally Salisbury," *ib.*
Chandos, the "princely" Duke of, iv. 443, 448.
Change Alley, i. 472 ; "Garraway's ; " "Jonathan's," ii. 172, 173.
Chantrey, Sir Francis, R.A., iii. 142 ; iv. 208, 253, 352, 497 ; v. 9, 10.
"Chapel of the Pyx," iii. 454.*
Chapel Street, Park Lane, iv. 369.
Chapel Street, Somers Town ; marketplace, v. 342.
Chapman's "Homer ; " his burial place, iii. 231.
Chapone, Mrs., iii. 26.
Chapter Coffee House, Paternoster Row, i. 278, 279.
Chapter House, Westminster. (*See* Westminster Abbey.)
Charing Cross, iii. 123 ; its name ; Queen Eleanor's funeral ; the cross, *ib.* ; its demolition ; lines on its downfall ; Wyatt's rebellion, 124 ; statue of Charles I. ; Marvell's lines, 125 ; pillory ; execution of the regicides ; shows ; Punch, 128.
Charing Cross Hospital, iii. 129.
Charing Cross Railway Station and Hotel ; reproduction of the Queen Eleanor cross ; railway bridge over the Thames, iii. 130.
Charing Cross Theatre, iii. 129.
Charity children at St. Paul's, i. 261 ; Blake's poem, 262.
Charity Commission, iv. 203.
Charles I., i. 24, 26, 83, 86, 160, 161, 245, 501, 503 ; ii. 143, 243, 253 ; 567 ; iii. 347, 349, 350, 351, 352,

366, 368, 549 ; iv. 28, 52, 77, 78, 105, 107, 230, 512 ; v. 111, 197, 200, 263 ; vi. 173, 386, 536, 537.
Charles II., i. 249, 405, 436 ; ii. 513 ; iii. 125, 219, 315, 316, 345, 352, 370, 376, 405, 406, 437, 446, 549 ; iv. 50, 75, 76, 77, 104, 109, 178, 232, 267, 268, 383, 512, 549 ; v. 24, 70, 74, 82, 125, 248, 397 ; vi. 11, 15, 57, 152, 196, 227, 248, 324, 392, 500.
Charles V. of France at Blackfriars, i. 200.
Charles X. of France, iv. 344, 422 ; v. 125.
Charles Square, Hoxton, v. 125.
Charles Street, Berkeley Square, iv. 334, 338.
Charles Street, St. James's Square, iv. 208.
"Charlies," nickname for watchmen, iii. 22 ; iv. 244 ; vi. 57.
Charlotte, Princess, iv. 65, 82, 87, 92, 93, 94, 133, 279 ; v. 147, 203, 213.
Charlotte, Queen of George III., iv. 63, 64, 65 ; iv. 551 ; v. 58, 69.
Charlotte Street, Portland Place, Institutions, iv. 458 ; Morland, 472 ; Church of St. John the Evangelist ; Hogarth Club ; Dressmakers and Milliners' Association, 473.
Charlton, Kent, vi. 231 ; etymology ; St. Luke's Church ; interments ; descent of the manor ; Sir Spencer Maryon-Wilson ; Charlton House, *ib.* ; chapel ; state apartments ; museum and park, 232 ; orangery ; cypress ; market and fair ; "Horn Fair," 233.
Charlton Street, Somers Town ; the "Coffee House," v. 344.
Charterhouse, ii. 380 ; Carthusian Monastery, 381, 382 ; Sir Walter de Manny ; rules of the Order ; dissolution of monasteries ; the prior executed ; monks punished ; revenues ; miracles, *ib.* ; Queen Elizabeth ; Duke of Norfolk ; James I., 383 ; Hospital and School founded by Thomas Sutton ; biography of Sutton, 383—387 ; government ; poor brethren, 387 ; antiquities ; water supply, 388 ; Charterhouse Square and Buildings, 389 ; chapel, 390 ; founder's tomb, 392, 393 ; tomb of Lord Ellenborough, 392 ; remains of Norfolk House ; Master's Court ; Preacher's Court ; Pensioner's Court, 394 ; school ; hoop-bowling ; "Hoop Tree," 395 ; site purchased by Merchant Taylors' Company, 395 ; "Coach Tree ; " School removed to Godalming ; discipline and customs, 396 ; fagging, 397 ; "pulling in," 398 ; Thackeray ; 399, 400 ; Founder's Day, 399, 401 ; plays ; Elkanah Settle, 401 ; Archbishop Sutton ; Basil Montagu ; John Leech ; Bishop Thirlwall ; Havelock, 402, 404.
Chateaubriand in Kensington Gardens, v. 158.
Chatham, Earl of, i. 387 ; iii. 425, 447, 526 ; v. 448.
Chatterton, i. 134, 278 ; ii. 173, 509, 545.
Chaucer, i. 32, 155, 305, 347, 393, 575 ; ii. 248 ; iii. 36, 97, 141, 430, 563 ;

v. 524 ; vi. 77—84 ; the "Canterbury Tales," vi. 80.
Chaumette, L. A. de la, Stock Exchange, i. 489.
Chaworth, Mr., his fatal duel with Lord Byron, iv. 137.
Cheapside, i. 304—345 ; records in Guildhall ; candle-makers ; illegal goods destroyed, i. 304 ; conduit and cross ; trade riots ; executions ; the 'prentices ; Westchepe Market, 305 ; the pillory ; penance ; fish market ; new conduit, 306 ; Lydgate's description of Chepe, 309 ; Goldsmiths' Row ; other trades forbidden ; 'prentices and trained-bands ; great riots, *ib.* ; "Evil May Day," 310 ; shows and pageants, 315—332 ; tournament, 315 ; the Standard ; Lord Mayor's Show, 317, 318, 320, 321, 322 ; state visit of George II., 323 ; house of Mr. Barclay, the Quaker ; William Pitt, 324 ; George III.'s state visit (1761), 323—328 ; Lord Mayor's State Coach, 328 ; men in armour ; Sir Claudius Hunter and Elliston, 330 ; Midsummer Marching Watch, 331 ; bonfires, 333 ; fountain ; punishments ; the Cross, its vicissitudes and destruction, *ib.* ; conduit and water-carts, 335 ; Church of St. Mary-le-Bow, 335—338 ; Barclay's house ; carved oak panelling, 339 ; "Queen's Arms " Tavern ; Statue of Peel ; Saddlers' Hall, 341, 342 ; Alderman Boydell, 343—346.
Cheapside Tributaries, North, i. 353—382.
Cheapside Tributaries, South, i. 346—352.
Chelsea, v. 50 ; boundaries, 51 ; etymology ; "Dwarf's " Tavern ; Chelsea buns ; flower-gardens ; stag-hunt ; history of the manor, *ib.* ; Cadogan family, 52 ; old manor-house ; distinguished residents ; Viscount and Lady Cremorne, *ib.* ; Lindsey House, 53 ; Shrewsbury House ; paper manufactory ; Winchester House ; Bishops of Winchester, *ib.* ; Chelsea Church ; More's chapel and monument, 58 ; Sir Hans Sloane ; St. Luke's Church, 59 ; Cheyne Walk, 59 ; Don Saltero's coffee-house, 61 ; John Salter's Museum, 62 ; Richard Cromwell ; Franklin ; Thomas Carlyle, 64 ; Mrs. Carlyle ; Thames Embankment, 65 ; Lombard Street, 66 ; "Old Swan " and "Swan " Taverns, 67 ; Albert Bridge ; Mulberry garden, 68 ; Doggett's "coat and badge " rowing match ; Swan Brewery ; Royal Botanic Garden ; Apothecaries' Company ; statue of Sir Hans Sloane, *ib.* ; cedars ; the "Old Bun House ; " royal visitors, 69 ; custards, 70 ; Chelsea Hospital, 70, 71, 74, 75 ; "Snow Shoes " Inn ; Royal Military Asylum, or Duke of York's School, 76 ; Cremorne Gardens ; Lord Cremorne, 84 ; "Stadium " Tavern ; balloons ; aërial machine, 85 ; Ashburnham House, 86 ; tournament ; King's private road ; St. Mark's College, *ib.* ; "World's End " Tavern, 87 ; florists ; Chelsea Common or

Heath ; Fulham Road, *ib.* ; Marlborough Square, 88 ; Whitehead's Grove ; Pond Place ; nursery grounds and orchards ; Jubilee Place ; Chelsea Park ; silk manufacture ; the "Goat in Boots" sign ; "Queen's Elm" Hotel ; Queen Elizabeth ; Jews' burial-ground ; Little Chelsea, *ib.* ; Shaftesbury House ; workhouse ; Robert Boyle ; Church Street, 89 ; old inns, 90 ; Chelsea China, 92 ; Lawrence Street ; Monmouth House, 93 ; Moravian Chapel ; "Clock-house ;" Glaciarium, v. 94 ; Hospital for Women, 95 ; Vestry Hall ; Literary Institution ; Congregational Church ; Sloane Square ; Dispensary ; Royal Court Theatre, *ib.* ; Sloane Street, 97 ; Trinity Church ; Wesleyan Chapel ; Ladies' Work Society ; School of Industry, *ib.* ; Earl Cadogan ; Cadogan Terrace, 98 ; Cadogan Street, 99 ; "Marlborough" Tavern ; Hans Place ; the Pavilion ; St. Saviour's Church ; Prince's Cricket Ground, *ib.*

Chelsea Hospital, v. 71—75.

Chelsea Water Works, iv. 179, 385, 395, 401 ; v. 83, 184 ; Aqueduct, Putney, vi. 503.

Chemical Society, iv. 272.

Chemistry, College of, iv. 316.

Cherbury House, Great Queen Street ; Lord Herbert of Cherbury, iii. 210.

Cherokee Kings, iv. 435.

Cherry Garden, Bermondsey, vi. 130.

"Cheshire Cheese Tavern," Wine Office Court, i. 119, 122, 123.

Chester Square ; St. Michael's Church, v. 12.

Chesterfield Gardens, iv. 356.

Chesterfield House, iv. 353 ; boudoir ; library ; grand staircase ; music-room ; drawing-room ; Dr. Johnson and the "Dictionary," *ib.*, 358 ; Countess of Chesterfield, 356.

Chesterfield, Philip, Earl of, iv. 111, 142, 353, 358, 398, 539 ; vi. 210.

Chesterfield Street ; distinguished residents, iv. 353.

Cheverton, Sir Richard, ii. 332.

Cheyne Walk, Chelsea, v. 59.

Chichester Rents, i. 83 ; iii. 57.

Chick Lane. (*See* West Street.)

Chicken House, Hampstead, v. 485.

"Children of Paul's," chorister boys, i. 245.

Child's Banking House, i. 35 ; the room over Temple Bar, 23, 30, 37, 461.

Child's Coffee House ; Addison ; Dr. Mead ; Sir Hans Sloane ; Halley, i. 266.

Child's Hill, Hampstead, v. 506.

Chimes of the Royal Exchange, i. 503.

Chimes of St. Clement Danes' Church, Strand, iii. 12.

Chimney-sweepers at Mrs. Montagu's feast, iv. 418.

"China Hall" Tavern, Lower Road, Deptford, vi. 136.

Chinese Bridge, St. James's Park, iv. 58.

Chinese Collection, Mr. Dunn's, v. 22.

Chinese Junk, iii. 290.

Chirurgeons, iv. 545.

Chisholm, Caroline ; Female Colonization, v. 423.

Chiswick, vi. 549, 557 ; early history, 550—555 ; Sutton Manor ; pest-house in Chiswick Hall ; Westminster School ; the plague ; Chiswick Ait or Eyot ; Parish Church ; monuments, *ib.* ; bells ; curfew, 551 ; churchwardens' books ; plague and "plague-water," 555 ; distinguished residents ; Hogarth's House, 556 ; his sun-dial and arm-chair, 557 ; Griffin Brewery ; "Red Lion" Inn ; old whetstone from the "White Bear and Whetstone" Inn ; College House, *ib.* ; the "Chiswick Press ;" Walpole House, 558 ; Chiswick Lane, 560 ; Rousseau ; Mawson Row ; old Manor House ; St. Agnes' Orphanage, *ib.* ; Corney House ; Corney Reach ; gardens and fêtes of the Horticultural Society, 566.

Chiswick House, vi. 562 ; lessees of the manor ; successive owners ; house rebuilt by the Earl of Burlington ; the house ; gardens, *ib.* ; Inigo Jones's gateway ; pictures, 563 ; elephant, 565 ; royal visits ; Queen Victoria and the Prince Consort, *ib.* ; death of Fox and Canning in the same room at Chiswick House, 566 ; the house occupied by the children of the Prince of Wales ; royal garden parties, 566.

Chocolate houses, iv. 157 ; vi. 228.

Cholera in 1853, iv. 238.

Cholmeley, Sir Roger ; Grammar School, Highgate, v. 419, 421.

Choristers of the Chapel Royal, iv. 104.

Christ Church, Newgate Street, ii. 428 ; the Grey Friars, 429 ; church rebuilt by Wren ; interior ; exorbitant burial fees ; monuments ; steeple ; Spital sermons, *ib.*

Christ Church, Westminster Bridge Road ; "Lincoln Tower ;" organ ; Rev. Newman Hall, vi. 362.

Christian Evidence Society, i. 549.

Christie, auctioneer, iv. 128, 200.

Christmas-trees, iv. 65.

Christ's Hospital, i. 411 ; reception at the Mansion House, *ib.* ; Grey Friars' Convent, ii. 364 ; the old church ; royal offerings ; Whittington's library ; school founded and given to the City by Henry VIII. ; confirmed by Edward VI., *ib.* ; royal interments, 365 ; monuments sold by Sir Martin Bowes, 366 ; Great Fire ; church rebuilt by Wren ; its benefactors ; the mathematical school ; "King's boys," *ib.* ; the "Twelves ;" Hertford branch, 367 ; statues of Edward VI. and Charles II., 368 ; dining-hall ; picture of Edward VI. renewing his gift, *ib.* ; of James II. and the Blues, by Verrio ; other pictures, 369, 376 ; celebrated "Blues ;" school days of Leigh Hunt and Charles Lamb ; the boys' dress, 369, 370 ; the dungeons ; corporal punishment ; expulsion, 372 ; Jeremy Boyer, 373 ; Coleridge ; grammar school, 374 ; Easter gloves and meat ; presentation governors, 375 ; public suppers ; visit of Queen Victoria ; Spital sermons, 376 ; boys presented to the Sovereign and Lord Mayor ; Grecians' orations ;

University scholarships ; dietary, 379 ; infirmary ; dormitories ; Tice, head beadle, 380.

Chronographer and Time Signals, General Post Office, ii. 218.

Chudley, Duchess of, iii. 532.

"Chunee," iii. 116.

Church House, Hackney, v. 515.

Church Lane, St. Giles's, iii. 202.

Church-rates, v. 133.

Church Row, Hampstead ; distinguished residents, v. 473.

Church Street, Chelsea, v. 89.

Church Street, Stoke Newington ; old houses and eminent residents, v. 536.

Churches of London, statistics, vi. 574.

Churchill, Lady Arabella, iv. 184, 236.

Cibber, Caius Gabriel, Colley, and Theophilus, i. 41, 502, 503 ; ii. 146 ; iii. 220, 267 ; iv. 78, 161, 209, 222, 543 ; vi. 353.

"Cider Cellars," Maiden Lane, iii. 268.

Cipriani, John B., i. 328 ; iii. 366, 378 ; v. 59 ; vi. 514.

Circulating Libraries, iii. 77.

Cirencester Place, iv. 461.

City of London School, i. 375.

City of London Union, Hackney, v. 521.

City of London and Tower Hamlets' Cemetery, v. 576.

City Prison, Holloway, v. 376.

City Road ; "Eagle" Tavern and "Grecian Theatre," ii. 227.

City Temple, Holborn Viaduct, ii. 501.

Civil and Military Club, iv. 454.

Civil and United Service Club, iv. 454.

Civil Engineers, Institution of, iv. 32.

Clandestine marriages. (*See* Fleet Prison ; May Fair.)

Clapham, vi. 320 ; Clapham Park ; Thomas Cubitt ; the Common, *ib.* ; residence of Pepys ; residence of Macaulay, *ib.* ; Henry Cavendish, 322 ; Evangelical preaching, 323, 324, 325 ; "Clapham Sect ;" "Claphamites," 321, 325, 326 ; Bible Society, 326 ; "Plough" Inn, 327 ; Clapham Rise ; seminaries for young ladies ; orphan asylum ; Home for Incurables ; Clapham Road, 327.

Clapham Junction Railway Station, vi. 483.

Clare Court ; Alamode Beef House ; Dickens, iii. 284.

Clare Market, iii. 40 ; Earl of Clare ; Holles family ; charter for market ; Clare House, 41 ; the butchers as dramatic critics, 42.

Clare Market Chapel, iii. 31.

Clarendon, Lord, iv. 273 ; vi. 152.

Clarendon Hotel, iv. 275, 295, 296, 303.

Clarendon House, Piccadilly, iv. 273.

Clarendon Square, v. 345 ; Life Guards' Barracks ; Polygon ; artists ; Mary Woolstoncraft and Godwin ; Roman Catholic Chapel, *ib.*

Clarges, Anne, iii. 87, 104.

Clarges Street, iv. 263.

Clarke, Alderman, i. 416.

Clarke, Dr. Adam, ii. 327 ; v. 188.

Clarke, Dr. Samuel, iv. 255.

Clarke, Mary Anne, mistress of the Duke of York, i. 80 ; vi. 230.

Clayton, Rev. John, Weigh House Chapel, i 564.

Clayton, Sir Robert, Lord Mayor, i. 405, 428, 520, 522 ; ii. 165, 367 ; vi. 91.

Cleave's *Police Gazette*, smuggling of unstamped copies, i. 132.

Clement's Inn ; its history ; sun-dial ; hall, iii. 33.

Clement's Lane, Lombard Street, i. 528, 529.

Clement's Lane, Strand, iii. 23, 25, 32.

Cleopatra's Needle, iii. 328.

Clergy Orphan Schools, St. John's Wood, v. 250.

Clerkenwell, Clockmakers in, ii. 325.

Clerkenwell Close, ii. 328 ; " Crown " Tavern ; eminent residents, *ib.* ; private madhouse, 329.

Clerkenwell Green, ii. 332 ; mansions ; pillory ; first Welsh Charity School, *ib.* ; Lady Bullock's house attacked, 333.

Clerkenwell, House of Detention, ii. 309.

Clerkenwell Sessions' House, ii. 322.

Clerk's Well ; miracle plays, ii. 335.

Cleveland, Barbara, Duchess of, iii. 354, 356, 357 ; iv. 178 ; v. 172 ; vi. 552, 558.

Cleveland, John, his poems, ii. 27.

Cleveland House. (*See* Stafford House.)

Cleveland Row, St. James's, iv. 176.

Cleveland Street ; Strand Union Workhouse ; Sick Asylum, iv. 466.

Clifford Street, iv. 303 ; Clifford Street " Club " and " Coffee House ; " Messrs. Stulz, tailors, *ib.*

Clifford's Inn ; Attorneys of the Marshalsea Court, i. 92 ; ancient custom, 93.

" Clinch, Tom, going to be hanged ; " Swift's lines, ii. 527 ; v. 191.

Clinical Society, iv. 465.

Clink, Prison and Liberty of the, vi. 16, 32.

Clipstone Street, iv. 458.

Clive, Kitty, iii. 210, 221.

Clive, Lord, iv. 331.

" Clock House," Chelsea, v. 94.

" Clock House," Hampstead, iv. 466.

Clock Tower and Clock, Houses of Parliament ; " Big Ben," iii. 519.

Clock Tower (Old), New Palace Yard ; Bell ; " Old Tom," iii. 537.

Clocks : St. Dunstan's, Fleet Street, i. 34, 133 ; St. James's Palace, iv. 101 ; St. Paul's, i. 256 ; striking thirteen, 257.

Clockmakers in Clerkenwell ; Horological Institute, ii. 325.

Cloth Fair, Smithfield, ii. 357, 363.

Clothworkers' Company and Hall, ii. 177 ; Fullers ; Weavers ; Burrellers ; Testers ; Shearmen ; Drapers ; Tailors ; ˉ schools and charities ; royal members, 178 ; vi. 490.

Clowes and Sons' printing works, vi. 381.

Club-land : Pall Mall, iv. 140 ; St. James's Street, 152.

Club Life of Covent Garden and its neighbourhood, iii. 281.

" Coach and Horses " and " Coach and Six," signs of taverns, iv. 261.

Coaches, iii. 336 ; iv. 428 ; amateurs of the whip, 260, 261 ; " Coaching Club," 400 ; Coaches on the Thames ; " Frost Fair," iii. 314 ; in Hyde Park, iv. 381, 386, 387, 399 ; Lord Mayor's Coach, i. 328.

Coachmakers' Hall, i. 363.

Coal Exchange, ii. 49 ; sea coal, 50 ; prices ; duties ; weights and measures ; Pool measure ; mastermeters, *ib.* ; opening of new Exchange, iii. 337.

Coal Yard, Drury Lane, iii. 209.

Coat and Badge Boat Race, iii. 308 ; v. 67 ; vi. 59, 243.

Coates, " Romeo," iv. 399.

Cobbett, William, i. 52, 117, 446 ; iii. 75, 121 ; iv. 281 ; v. 130.

Cobden, Richard, M.P., v. 309.

Cobham, Lord, i. 45 ; ii. 65 ; iii. 200.

Cochrane, Lord. (*See* Dundonald, Earl of.)

" Cock and Pie Ditch," iii. 216.

" Cock and Pie Fields," iii. 158.

" Cock and Tabard " Inn, Tothill Street, iv. 17.

" Cock " Tavern, Fleet Street, i. 44.

Cocker, Edward, i. 266 ; Cocker's Arithmetic, vi. 71.

Cockerell, Prof. C. R., R.A., i. 469 ; iii. 470 ; iv. 155, 502, 532 ; v. 275.

Cock-fighting, ii. 309 ; iii. 39, 374 ; iv. 44.

Cocking, killed by fall of a parachute, vi. 464.

Cock Lane, ii. 435 ; " Cock Lane Ghost ; " its contriver ; Dr. Johnson, 437 ; " Scratching Fanny ; " fraud exposed ; coffin of " Scratching Fanny " opened, 438, 489.

Cockpits ; Little Cock-pit Yard, iv. 551 ; the " Phœnix," Drury Lane, iii. 39 ; Bird-cage Walk, iv. 44 ; Whitehall, residence of Cromwell and Monk, iii. 370 ; Privy Council Office, 374 ; Tufton Street, Westminster, iv. 38.

Cock-pit Gate, Westminster, iv. 26.

" Cock-pit " Theatre, Drury Lane, iii. 209, 218, 219.

Cockspur Street, iii. 144 ; " British Coffee-house ; " statue of George III., iv. 83, 84, 85.

" Cocoa Tree Club," iv. 157.

Coffee, early sale of, i. 44 ; ii. 172, 533 ; iii. 65 ; iv. 28, 153 ; vi. 108.

Coffins, Wicker, iv. 122.

Cogers' Hall, Shoe Lane, i. 124.

Coinage ; " Britannia " modelled from " La Belle Stewart," iv. 110 ; depreciation of, i. 455 ; " galley halfpence," ii. 177. (*See* Mint.)

Coining process described, ii. 105.

Coiners, resort of, i. 74 ; iii. 21. 191.

Coins and Tradesmen's Tokens, i. 514.

Coins, Roman, i. 21, 22 ; ii. 93, 149, Coke, early manufacture of, vi. 196.

Coke, Sir Edward, i. 160 ; ii. 507, 519.

Coke, Sir Thomas, Lord Mayor, i. 399.

Colburn, Messrs., *New Monthly Magazine*, iv. 312.

Colby House, Kensington, v. 124.

Coldbath Fields, ii. 298 ; the prison ; silent system ; treadmill ; John Hunt imprisoned, *ib.*

Coldbath Square, ii. 299 ; old bath, 300.

Cold Harbour, ii. 17 ; Poultney's Inn ; Sir John Poultney ; Richard II. ; Richard III., *ib.*

Cold Harbour Lane, Camberwell, vi. 279.

Coleman Street, ii. 243 ; Armourers' and Braziers' Hall ; St. Stephen's Church, *ib.* ; Cromwell and Hugh Peters, 243 ; Cowley's " Cutter of Coleman Street," 244.

Coleraine, Lord ; George Hanger, iv. 136 ; v. 294, 351.

Coleraine, the third Lord ; his " History of Tottenham," iv. 136 ; v. 550, 556, 557.

Coleridge, Sir John Taylor, and Sir John Duke, iv. 451.

Coleridge, S. T., i. 93 ; ii. 374, 430 ; iii. 113, 263 ; v. 421, 422, 472 ; vi. 533.

Colet, Dean of St. Paul's, i. 242, 272, 273, 274 ; ii. 26, 140.

Colet, Sir Henry, Lord Mayor, i. 400.

College for Civil Engineers, Putney, vi. 491.

College for Men and Women, iv. 555.

College Hill, i. 381 ; ii. 25, 26 ; Mercers' school, 26 ; St. Mi,chael's Paternoster Royal ; Cleveland's poems, 27.

College of Arms, iv. 536.

College of Chemistry, iv. 316.

College of Physicians, i. 215 ; first meetings at Linacre's house, removed to Warwick Lane, 303 ; lines by Dr. Garth ; Sir John Cutler, miser ; his statue, ii. 431 ; early physicians, 431—434 ; removal to Trafalgar Square ; iii. 143.

College of the Poor, Southwark, vi. 33.

College of Preceptors, iv. 555.

College of Surgeons, iii. 29 ; museum and buildings, 46 ; library ; lectures, 47.

Collier, John Payne, i. 214, 230.

Collins, the poet, ii. 267.

Collins, William, R.A., v. 208.

Collyer, Rev. Dr., vi. 290.

Colman, George, elder and younger, i. 165 ; ii. 257, 297 ; iv. 95, 225 ; v. 26.

Colonial Office, iii. 392.

Colosseum, Regent's Park, v. 269 ; Panoramas ; London, 270 ; London by Night ; Paris ; Sculpture Gallery ; Swiss *chalet* ; Skating Hall, 272 ; alterations ; exhibitions ; pulled down for building purposes, 273.

Colours ; political ; buff and blue, iv. 341.

Colquhoun, C. ; river desperadoes, iii. 302, 310.

Colton, Caleb, i. 146 ; " Lacon " and other works ; his suicide, *ib.*

Columbarian Society, i. 46.

Columbia Square and Market ; Nova Scotia Gardens ; Baroness Burdett-Coutts ; the market and its buildings, v. 506.

Commercial Docks and Timber Ponds, vi. 140.

Commissionaires, Corps of, iii. 120.

Common Council of London ; Council Room, Guildhall, i. 390, 392.

Commons, House of. (*See* Houses of Parliament.)

Compter, Wood Street, i. 368.

Compton family ; Sir William Compton ; Bruce Castle, Tottenham, v. 549.

Compton, Lady, daughter of Sir John Spencer, i. 401 ; ii. 269.

Compton Street, Soho ; Bishop Compton, iii. 194.

Concerts of Ancient Music, iv. 317.

Concord, Temple of, iv. 179.

Conduits : Fleet Street, i. 63 ; Cheapside, 305, 316, 317, 335 ; Cornhill, ii. 170 ; Holborn Bridge, 236 ; Aldgate, 246 ; White Conduit House, 280 ; iv. 550 ; Henry VIII.'s, Kensington Palace Green, v. 139 ; Bayswater, 183.

Conduit Fields, Hampstead, v. 498.

Conduit-heads, Highbury and Pentonville, ii. 273, 279.

Conduit Street, iv. 249 ; "Conduit Mead,' 324 ; shooting and hunting ; Limmer's Hotel ; Macclesfield House ; Societies ; Trinity Chapel, ib. ; residents, 326.

Conference Hall, Stoke Newington, v. 532.

Congregationalists imprisoned in Bridewell, i. 191.

Congregational College, Hackney, v. 513.

Congregational Memorial Hall, ii. 500.

Congress Hall, Clapton, v. 522.

Congreve, Sir William, ii. 259 ; iii. 81, 83, 417 ; iv. 3, 76, 172, 176, 179, 210, 306 ; vi. 231.

Conservancy of the Thames, i. 442 ; iii. 289.

Conservative Club, iv. 148, 156.

Constable, John, R.A., iv. 473 ; v. 472.

"Constabulary, The," Westminster, iii. 537.

Constantine, London Wall built by, i. 20.

Constantinople, Emperor of, vi. 225.

Constitution Hill, iv. 177, 178, 179.

Consumption Hospital, Brompton, vi. 382.

Convent of the Good Shepherd, Hammersmith, vi. 539.

Conway House, Great Queen Street, iii. 210.

Cook, Captain, vi. 148.

Cook, Eliza, her poems, i. 59 ; vi. 70, 340.

Cooke, Sir W. Fothergill, F.R.S., v. 242.

Cooke, Thomas, miser, ii. 286.

Cookery, School of, v. 107.

Cooks ; Centlivre, "Yeoman of the Mouth," iv. 80 ; a cook boiled to death, vi. 417.

Coombe, William, "Dr. Syntax," vi. 69.

Cooper, Abraham, R.A., v. 408.

Cooper, Sir Astley, ii. 166 ; iii. 121 ; iv. 81, 326.

Coopers' Hall ; state lotteries, ii. 238.

Cope, Sir Walter ; Holland House, v. 162.

Copeland, Sir William, Alderman ; memorial window in St. Helen's Church, ii. 154.

Copeland, W. T., Lord Mayor, ii. 158 ; iii. 28, 29 ; iv. 301.

Copenhagen Fields, ii. 275 ; "Coopen Hagen ;" house and tea-gardens ; fives-playing ; dog-fighting ; Corresponding Society, ib.; trades unions ; Robert Owen, ii. 276, 283 ; v. 374.

Copley, J. S., iv. 322 ; vi. 527.

Coram, Captain, v. 356 ; Foundling Hospital ; his burial there ; portrait by Hogarth ; statue by Marshall ; biographical notice, 362, 365.

Corbet, Miles, regicide, vi. 552.

Corbett, Mrs., her epitaph by Pope, iii. 569.

Cordell, Sir William, Master of the Rolls ; his epitaph, ii. 323.

Cordwainers' Hall and Company, i. 550.

Corinthian Club, iv. 454.

Cork Street, iv. 309 ; eminent residents ; "Blue Posts" Tavern, ib.

Cornelys, Mrs. ; her masked balls in Soho, iii. 189 ; iv. 244, 436 ; v. 21.

Corner, G. R., F.S.A. ; history and antiquities of Bermondsey, vi. 111.

Corn Exchange ; history of the Corn Market, ii. 179—183 ; famines ; prices ; granaries, 180 ; corn ports ; markets ; assize of bread, 181 ; factorage, 182.

Corney House ; Corney Reach, vi. 566.

Cornhill, ii. 170 ; Corn Market ; drapers ; Tun Prison ; Standard ; conduit ; St. Michael's Church, ib.; St. Peter's Church ; "Pope's Head" Tavern, 171 ; Pope's Alley, 172 ; fires ; Change Alley ; St. Michael's Alley ; first London coffee-house ; "Garraway's" shop bill ; introduction of tea ; prices, ib. ; "Jonathan's," 173 ; Freeman's Court ; Finch Lane ; Birchin Lane ; "Tom's Coffee-house," ib.

Corn-Law League Bazaar, iii. 234.

Corn-Law Riots, 1815, iv. 171.

Corn Mills, ii. 182 ; on London Bridge, vi. 11.

Cornwallis, Lord, his trial, iii. 550.

Coronation banquets, Westminster Hall, iii. 544, 545, 554, 555, 556.

Coronation chairs, iii. 442.

Coronation ceremonies, from Harold to Queen Victoria, iii. 401, 405, 406, 409, 410, 544, 554.

Corresponding Society ; Thelwall, ii. 275.

Corsica, Theodore, King of, iii. 182 ; iv. 302.

Coryat, Thomas, his "Crudities," i. 352.

Costermongers, iv. 466 ; vi. 570.

Costume, i. 158, 359, 443, 446 ; ii. 577 ; iii. 52, 111, 443, 527, 534 ; iv. 72, 75, 114—119, 167, 185, 197, 238, 248, 260, 382, 383, 448 ; v. 158 ; vi. 173, 226.

Cosway, Richard, R.A., iv. 430.

Cottenham, Lord, iv. 448.

Cottington, John ("Mull Sack"), i. 40, 43.

Cotton's Garden and Cotton House, iii. 500 ; Cottonian Library, iii. 560 ; iv. 490, 514, 560.

Cotton's Wharf ; fire in 1861, vi. 105.

County Fire Office, iv. 245.

Courier Newspaper, iii. 389.

Coursing, v. 3.

Court of Augmentations, iii. 563.

Court of Pie-poudre, ii. 344.

Court of Record, Stepney, ii. 138.

Court of Requests, Westminster, iii. 497.

Courts of Justice in the Tower, ii. 63.

Courts of Law, iii. 560 ; established at Westminster ; Judges, ib. ; present Courts built, 561 ; presentation of the Sheriffs ; chopping sticks ; counting horse-shoes and hobnails, ib. ; "Tichborne Case," 562.

Court Theatre, v. 95.

Courvoisier, murderer, ii. 457 ; iv. 375.

Coutts, Angela. (See Burdett H. Coutts, Baroness.)

Coutts's Bank, iii. 104 ; Thomas Coutts ; Sir Francis Burdett, 105.

Coutts, Harriett. (See St. Alban's, Harriett, Duchess of.)

Covent Garden, iii. 238 : the market (see Covent Garden Market) ; the site ; "the Convent Garden ;" pond and spring, ib.; Duke of Somerset ; Earls and Dukes of Bedford ; Long Acre ; Inigo Jones, 239, 242 ; Piazza as a promenade and residence ; Hogarth's "Morning," 240 ; famous residents, 241 ; Gay's "Trivia ;" St. Paul's Church and parish, 241, 242 ; column with sun-dials, 243 ; hackney coach-stands ; Mohocks ; highwaymen, ib. ; Powell's puppet-show, 249 ; "Bedford Coffee House," 250 ; Floral Hall ; "Hummums," 251 ; "Evans's" Hotel, 252 ; elections and hustings, 257 ; "Black Raven" sponging-house, 259 ; "The Finish," 260.

Covent Garden Market, iii. 239 ; site, origin, and early condition ; market buildings ; tolls, 244 ; Strype's description, 242 ; best time to view it ; basket-women, 245, 246 ; costermongers ; flower-market, 248.

Covent Garden Theatre, iii. 227 ; built for John Rich ; "Rich's glory," ib. ; first performance ; "Beefsteak Club ;" ground-rent, 228 ; Handel's "Messiah ;" Peg Woffington ; George Anne Bellamy, 229 ; death of Rich ; Harris ; Macklin ; house rebuilt, 230 ; the Kembles ; Mrs. Siddons ; Master Betty ; theatre burnt down and rebuilt ; "O. P." riots, 231 ; "Kitty" Stephens ; Miss O'Neill ; Farren, 232 ; improved costumes ; Planché ; Osbaldistone, Helen Faucit ; Macready ; Madame Vestris and Mr. Charles Mathews ; Bunn ; Corn-Law League Bazaar ; Jullien's Concerts ; reconstructed as the "Royal Italian Opera-house ;" Grisi ; Alboni, ib. ; receipts and expenditure, 236 ; Fred. Gye ; again burnt down and rebuilt ; present theatre, ib.; its cost, 237 ; Harrison ; Miss Pyne ; Balfe ; "guard of honour," ib.

Coventry House, Piccadilly, iv. 285.

Coventry, Sir John, assault on, iv. 220, 231.

Coventry Street, iv. 233 ; Secretary Coventry ; exhibitions ; Messrs. Wishart, tobacconists, ib.

Coverdale, Miles, i. 574.

"Coverley, Sir Roger de," iii. 305, 442 ; iv. 39, 57 ; vi. 448.

Cowan, Sir John, Lord Mayor, i. 414.

Cowley, iii. 297, 385, 476.

Cowley Street, Westminster, iv. 2.

Cowper, i. 44, 173 ; ii. 231 ; iii. 287, 474 ; v. 565.

Cowper's Court, ii. 173.

Cox, Bishop, ii. 518 ; Ely Place ; Sir Christopher Hatton, ib.

Crab, Roger, the English Hermit, ii. 140.

Crabbe, George, ii. 446 ; iv. 135, 202, 208, 294, 328, 557 ; v. 431, 454.

Crabtree Street, iv. 472.

"Crab-Tree" Tavern, Fulham, vi. 514.

Craggs, Secretary ; South Sea Bubble, i. 540, 541 ; iii. 417 ; iv. 305 ; vi. 281.

"Craig Telescope," Wandsworth, vi. 482.

"Cranbourn Alley;" bonnets and millinery, iii. 172; street songs, 173.

Cranbourn Street, iii. 161.

Crane Court, i. 104, 107; Royal Society; Scottish Society; Dryden, Wilkes and the *North Briton, ib.*

Cranfield's Sunday Schools, Southwark, vi. 70.

Cranmer, Archbishop, ii. 70; vi. 428, 430, 436.

Craven Cottage, Fulham, vi. 513.

Craven House; Craven Hill, Bayswater; Lord Craven, v. 185.

Craven, Lord, his house in Drury Lane, iii. 37; the plague, iv. 15.

Craven, Sir William, Lord Mayor, i. 402.

Craven Street, formerly "Spur Alley," residence of Franklin; James Smith's epigram, iii. 134.

Crawford Street, Marylebone, iv. 411; St. Mary's Church, 412; Homer Row, 411.

Cremorne Gardens, v. 84; "Stadium;" tavern; balloon ascents; Groof's fatal descent, 85; the "captive" balloon, 86.

Cremorne, Lord and Lady; "Chelsea Farm," v. 52, 84.

Creswick, lessee of Surrey Theatre, vi. 371.

Cribb, Tom, pugilist, v. 3.

Cricket, iv. 137; history and laws of; Artillery Ground; White Conduit Fields; Lord's Ground; Marylebone Club, v. 249, 250; vi. 268; Kennington Oval, vi. 333.

Crimean Memorial, Westminster, iii. 477, 478; iv. 35; Guards' Memorial, Waterloo Place, 209.

Criminals, Statistics of, vi. 570.

Crippled Boys' Home, Kensington, v. 136.

Cripplegate, ii. 229; the gate; St. Giles's Church, 229–232; perambulation of the parish, 237; fox-hunting, 273.

Cripples' Nursery, iv. 407.

Crispe, Sir Nicholas; his heart enshrined in Hammersmith Church, vi. 536, 537.

Criterion Restaurant and Theatre, iv. 207.

Crockford, John; Crockford's Bazaar and Club House, iv. 160, 201; v. 268.

Crockford's fish shop, iii. 20.

Croker, John Wilson, iii. 386; iv. 484; vi. 516.

Croker, Thomas Crofton, vi. 518.

Cromartie, Lord, iii. 551.

Cromwell, Elizabeth, wife of the Protector, ii. 20.

Cromwell, Henry, v. 100.

Cromwell House, Brompton, v. 100.

Cromwell House, Highgate; grand staircase, v. 400; Convalescent Home for Sick Children, 401.

Cromwell, Oliver, i. 431; ii. 28, 232; iii. 23, 53; iv. 53; v. 100, 111, 381, 534, 536; vi. 130, 386, 490, 536; his death and funeral; fate of his body, iii. 370, 437, 540; iv. 27, 28, 545; v. 542; his head exposed at Westminster Hall, iii. 539; now in the possession of Mr. Horace Wilkinson, 302, 542.

Cromwell Place, Putney, vi. 491.

Cromwell, Richard, vi. 55.

Cromwell Road, v. 101.

Cromwell, Robert, v. 222.

Crooked Lane, i. 555; bird-cages and fishing tackle; Leaden Porch; St. Michael's Church, *ib.*

Crosby, Brass, Lord Mayor, i. 409; vi. 350.

Crosby Hall; Sir John Crosby; occupied by Richard III.; notices by Shakespeare, ii. 154, 155; eminent residents, 156; converted into a chapel and warehouse; Miss Hackett's exertions for its restoration, 157.

Crosby Square, ii. 159.

"Cross Bones, The;" unconsecrated graves, vi. 32.

Cross, Charing. (*See* Charing Cross.)

Cross, Cheapside, i. 305, 316, 317, 332, 364.

Cross, Edward; his menagerie, "King's Mews," iii. 116, 141; removed to Surrey Gardens, vi. 265, 266.

Cross, John, lessee of Surrey Theatre, vi. 369.

Cross, Paul's. (*See* Paul's Cross.)

Cross, Stone, near Butchers' Row, iii. 11.

Crotch, Dr., vi. 527.

Crouchback, Edmund, son of Edward II., iii. 447.

Crouch End; Christ Church; St. Luke's Church, Hornsey Rise, v. 437.

"Crown and Anchor" Tavern, Strand; Burdett; O'Connell; Cobbett, iii. 75.

Crown Court, Russell Street; Scottish National Church, iii. 280.

Crown Jewels in the Tower, ii. 77. (*See* Blood, Colonel.)

Crown, State, of Queen Victoria, ii. 77, 80; its conveyance to the House of Lords, iii. 528.

Crown Street, Soho; "Hog Lane;" Hogarth, iii. 196.

Crucifix Lane, vi. 41, 109.

Cruden, Alexander; his "Concordance," ii. 263.

Cruikshank, George, i. 87; v. 306; vi. 207.

Cruickshank the Elder, iv. 254.

Crusades and Knights Templars, i. 147.

Crutched Friars, ii. 250; Whittington's Palace; Priory; Drapers' Almshouses, *ib.*

Crystal Palace, Hyde Park. (*See* Great Exhibition of 1851.)

Crystal Palace, London. (*See* London Crystal Palace.)

Crystal Palace, Sydenham, v. 38; vi. 308; site and prospect; Paxton; his residence, Rock-hills; history of the undertaking; opening ceremony; fire; dimensions, *ib.;* centre transept; "Paxton Tunnel," 309; Screen of Kings and Queens, 310; Crystal Fountain; Handel Festival Orchestra; organ; theatre; Fine Art Courts; terrace and grounds; waterworks and fountains, *ib.;* geological model; antediluvian animals, 311; fêtes; library; reading-room; lectures; aquarium, 313.

Cubitt, Thomas, builder, v. 2, 22, 44; vi. 320.

"Cuckold's Point;" "Horn Fair;" legend of King John, vi. 142, 233.

Culpeper, Colonel, vi. 74.

Cumberland, Duke of (King George of Hanover), iv. 70, 113.

"Cumberland, Duke of," public-house, iv. 407.

Cumberland Gate, Hyde Park, iv. 395, 405.

Cumberland House, Pall Mall, iv. 124.

Cumberland Market, v. 299.

Cumberland, Richard, iv. 447.

Cumberland, William, Duke of, iv. 124, 370; vi. 333; statue in Cavendish Square, iv. 444.

Cuper's Gardens, Lambeth, vi. 388.

Cupid's Gardens, Dockhead, vi. 116.

"Curds-and-Whey-House," Hyde Park Corner, iv. 365.

Cure, Thomas, vi. 18.

Cure's College, Southwark, vi. 33.

Curfew, vi. 551.

Curiosity Shops, Soho, iii. 176; iv. 470.

Curll, Edward, i. 48; iii. 264, 471.

Cursitor Street, ii. 531; Cursitor's Inn; the Cursitors; Lord Eldon's "first perch;" his wife, *ib.*

Curtain Theatre, Curtain Road; called the "Green Curtain," ii. 195.

Curtis, Sir William, Lord Mayor, i. 329, 411.

Curtis, William, botanist, v. 88; vi. 389, 415, 472.

Curzon Street, May Fair, iv. 347; chapel; secret marriages; eminent residents, 349, 351, 352.

Custards made at Chelsea, v. 70.

Custom House, ii. 52; successive buildings; revenue farmed; its growth; New Custom House, 53; Long Room; quay; officers and clerks; tide-waiters, 54, 55; statistics; statutes, 56–58; Queen's Warehouse; sales, 59.

Cutler, Sir John, miser, ii. 431; iii. 143.

"Cyder Cellars," The, iii. 119.

Cyoll, Cycillia; Crosby Hall occupied by her; her bequests, ii. 156.

Cyprus, King of, entertained by Sir Henry Picard, i. 556.

"Czar of Muscovy" Tavern; Peter the Great, ii. 98.

Czar of Muscovy's Head, Great Tower Street, vi. 155.

Czar Street, Deptford, vi. 156.

D.

Dacre House, Lee, vi. 244.

Dacre, Lady, iv. 23, 40; v. 59; vi. 244; her Almshouses and School, Dacre Street, Westminster, iv. 12, 22, 23.

Dagger in the City Arms, i. 398; ii. 5.

Daguerre; the Diorama, v. 269.

Daguerreotype, iv. 254.

Daily News Office; history of the paper, i. 137—140.

Daily Telegraph; Col. Sleigh; J. M. Levy, i. 160; progress of the paper, i. 61; iii. 20.

Dairies at Islington, ii. 255, 256; Highbury; Cream Hall, 273.

Dale, Rev. Canon, v. 353.

Dalston, v. 529; early notices; nursery-grounds; building; railways; Refuge for Destitute Females, *ib.;* German Hospital, 530.

Dalton, John, iv. 268.

Damer, Mr., his suicide, iii. 258.

"Damnable, Mother," v. 310, 311, 471.

Danby, Dick, the Temple barber, i. 167.

Dance, architect, i. 384, 387, 435 ; ii. 165, 195, 485.

Dancing ; studied by barristers at Lincoln's Inn, iii. 51, 53 ; Almack's ; the waltz, iv. 197 ; quadrilles, 198 ; ball at the coronation of George IV., 199 ; vi. 389.

"Dandies" in 1646, iv. 383 ; in 1815, 399.

Danes, invasions of London, i. 448, 449, 450, 452 ; vi. 101, 164, 224.

Dangerfield publicly whipped, ii. 530.

Danish Church, Whitechapel, ii. 146.

Danvers Street ; Sir John Danvers, v. 92.

Dartineuf, Charles, iv. 107.

Dartmouth, Earl of, vi. 245.

Dartmouth Road, Hammersmith ; St. John's Church ; Godolphin School, vi. 534.

Dashwood, Sir Samuel, Lord Mayor, i. 322, 406.

Davenant, Sir William, i. 195, 196 ; iii. 27, 31, 39, 40, 426.

David, King of Scotland, entertained by Sir Henry Picard, i. 556.

Davidge, lessee of Surrey Theatre, vi. 371.

Davies, Lady Clementina, v. 128.

Davies, Mary, heiress ; married to Sir Thomas Grosvenor, v. 16 ; Ebury Farm ; Belgravia, 2, 3.

"Davies, Moll," iv. 184, 230, 231.

Davies, Sir Thomas, Lord Mayor ; his show, i. 322.

Davies Street, Berkeley Square ; " Joe Manton ;" Byron, iv. 335.

Davies, Tom, bookseller ; Johnson and Boswell, iii. 275.

Davis, Sir John, expelled from the Temple, i. 160.

Davy, Sir Humphry, iv. 269, 374.

Dawes's Almshouse, Wandsworth Lane ; Sir Abraham Dawes, vi. 491.

Dawson, Capt. James ; " Jemmy Dawson ;" his execution, vi. 335.

Dawson, Nancy, iv. 554 ; v. 494.

Day and Martin, blacking manufacturers ; Charles Day, the " Blind Man's Friend," iv. 311, 549.

Dead-houses, iii. 303.

Dead Letters, ii. 212.

Deadman's Place, Bankside, Southwark ; Cure's College ; almshouses, vi. 32, 33, 40.

Deaf and Dumb Association and Chapel, iv. 440.

Deaf and Dumb Asylum, vi. 251.

Dean Street, Park Lane, iv. 368.

Dean Street, Soho, iii. 194 ; Sir James Thornhill ; Royalty Theatre ; Miss Kelly, ib.

Dean's Yard, Westminster ; Scholars' Green ; window gardening, iii. 480 ; Office of Queen Anne's Bounty, 482.

De Beauvoir Town ; Richard de Beauvoir, v. 525 ; De Beauvoir Square ; St. Peter's Church, 526.

"Decoy," St. James's Park, iv. 50, 53.

De Crespigny family, vi. 284.

Deer on site of Hyde Park ; hunting, iv. 377, 379, 380, 399 ; St. James's Park a nursery for deer, 48, 50, 178 ; in Greenwich Park, vi. 210, 212 ; royal parks ; Eltham, 239.

Defoe ; "History of the Plague," i. 515 ; ii. 142, 173, 268 ; iii. 276, 375 ; iv. 158 ; v. 521, 537.

Defoe Street, Stoke Newington, v. 537.

De Groof's aërial machine, v. 85.

Dekker, Ben Jonson satirised by, i. 422.

Delahay Street, Westminster, iv. 29.

Delane, Mr. John, i. 213.

Deloraine, Countess, v. 146.

Delpini, clown, iv. 245.

De Moret, proposed balloon ascent, v. 2.

Denham, Sir John, i. 261 ; iii. 311 ; iv. 262, 272.

Denman, Lord ; trial of Queen Caroline, iii. 532.

Denmark Hill Grammar School, vi. 579.

Denmark, Prince George of, vi. 214.

Dentists, Barbers acting as, vi. 63.

Denzil Street ; Denzil, Lord Holles, iii. 42.

D'Eon, Chevalier, iv. 551 ; vi. 419.

Deptford, vi. 143 ; etymology ; "West Greenwich ;" Upper and Lower Deptford ; ship - building yard ; parishes of St. Nicholas and St. Paul ; Deptford Bridge ; the Ravensbourne, or Deptford Creek, ib. ; historical notes, 144 ; corn and other mills ; Henry VIII. and the Navy, 145 ; Royal Dock, or " King's Yard, 146 ; spinning hemp ; manufacture of cables ; old storehouses ; royal and distinguished visitors ; Edward VI., ib. ; mimic sea-fight ; Queen Elizabeth ; Sir F. Drake's ship, The Golden Hind, 147 ; Peter the Great ; famous ships ; Pepys, 148, 152 ; Dockyard closed ; Foreign Cattle Market, 149 ; Saye's Court ; Evelyn, 150, 152, 155 ; William Penn, 154 ; Czar Street ; workhouse, 156 ; " Red House " Storehouse ; " Royal Victualling Yard," 158 ; Goods Depôt of Brighton Railway ; Corporation of Trinity House ; hospitals for master mariners and pilots ; St. Nicholas Church ; interments, 160 ; churches, schools, and institutions ; Evelyn Street ; proposed Grand Surrey Canal, 161 ; marine store-shops, 163.

De Quincey, i. 65.

Derby, Countess of (Miss Farren), iv. 340.

Derby, Earl of, iv. 159.

Dermody, Thomas, vi. 245, 305.

Derrick, executioner, v. 197.

Derwentwater, Earl of, i. 27 ; ii. 76, 95 ; iii. 202, 551.

Desborough Place ; Cromwell's brother-in-law, v. 224.

Desenfans, Noel Joseph ; Dulwich College Picture Gallery, vi. 302.

Despard, Colonel, vi. 253.

D'Este, Sir Augustus, v. 203.

Destitute Boys, Homes for, iii. 212.

Dethick, Gilbert, Garter King at Arms, i. 294, 297.

De Veres, Earls of Oxford, v. 117, 178.

Devereux Court, Strand, iii. 65.

"Devil Tavern," i. 38 ; sign of St. Dunstan and the Devil, 39, 42 ; Apollo Club, 39, 41 ; Ben Jonson

and Randolph ; " Mull Sack " and Lady Fairfax, 40 ; Swift, Addison, Garth, Cibber, Dr. Johnson, Mrs. Lennox, 41 ; Pandemonium Club, 42.

Devonshire Club, iv. 160.

Devonshire, Georgiana, Duchess of, iv. 129, 159, 275, 278 ; v. 81.

Devonshire House, iv. 275 ; pictures, 276 ; first Duke of Devonshire ; Queen Anne, 278 ; George IV., 279 ; Fox ; third and sixth Dukes ; Sir Robert Walpole ; Allied Sovereigns ; Princess Charlotte ; Count Boruwlaski ; " Guild of Literature and Art ; ' Lord Lytton ; Dickens, ib.

Devonshire Square, Bishopsgate, ii. 159 ; " Fisher's Folly ;" Queen Elizabeth ; Earls of Devonshire, 162 ; Bank of Credit, 163.

Devonshire Terrace, Marylebone, residence of Dickens, iv. 430.

De Worde, Wynkyn, i. 63, 135.

Diamonds ; " Pitt " Diamond, iii. 531 ; " Koh-i-noor," v. 38, 106.

Diana, Altar of, on site of Goldsmiths' Hall, i. 361.

Dibdin, Charles, iii. 69, 170, 308 ; v. 323 ; vi. 368.

Dibdins, The, at Sadler's Wells Theatre, ii. 294.

Dice found under Middle Temple Hall, i. 164.

" Dick's Coffee-house," Fleet Street, i. 44 ; Miller's play, " The Coffee-house ;" Cowper's insanity ; St. Dunstan's Club, ib.

Dickens, Charles, i. 38, 137, 171, 292, 545 ; ii. 347, 350, 413, 485, 542, 573, 575 ; iii. 111, 233, 237, 246, 281, 290, 296, 311, 382, 428, 512, 521, 557 ; iv. 70, 96, 193, 196, 201, 237, 254, 257, 279, 320, 407, 430, 442, 450, 458, 479, 540, 551, 561, 573 ; v. 65, 102, 140, 275, 293, 305, 353, 365, 407, 454, 456 ; vi. 61, 63, 87, 113, 181, 205, 254, 281, 371, 406, 458, 576.

Digby, Sir Kenelm, ii. 159 ; iii. 252, 254.

Dilettanti Society, iv. 155, 196, 284.

Dilke, Sir Charles, and Sir Charles Wentworth, Barts., v. 96.

Dilly, Edward and Charles, booksellers, i. 418.

Dimsdale, Sir Harry, iii. 183.

Dinely, Sir John, iv. 457.

"Dining with Duke Humphrey," i. 239.

Diorama, Regent's Park ; pictures by Bouton and Daguerre ; converted into a chapel, v. 269.

"Dirty Lane," Southwark, vi. 63.

Dispatch Newspaper, i. 59 ; Alderman Harmer ; " Publicola," " Caustic ;" Eliza Cook, ib.

Disraeli, Benjamin. (See Beaconsfield, Earl of.)

D'Israeli, Isaac, i. 113 ; iv. 153, 218, 257, 274, 410, 542.

D'Israeli Road, Putney, vi. 491.

Dissenters' Free Library, Redcross Street, ii. 239 ; removed to Grafton Street East, iv. 570.

Dissenting chapels, Hackney, v. 513.

"Diver, Jenny," lady pickpocket, v. 482.

Dividend-day at the Bank, i. 471.

Diving-bell ; Evelyn, vi. 147.

"Dobney's " Tavern, Pentonville ; horsemanship, ii. 287.

Dobson, painter, patronised by Van-dyke and Charles I., ii. 441.

Dockhead, vi. 113, 116; London Street; Jacob's Island, ib.

Docks at Rotherhithe, vi. 140.

Dockwra, Prior, St. John's Gate built by, ii. 317.

Dockyard, Deptford. (See Deptford.)

"Dr. Johnson Tavern," Bolt Court, i. 114.

Doctors' Commons, i. 285; College of Doctors of Law; Court of Arches; Court of Audience, ib.; Prerogative Court; Court of Faculties; Court of Admiralty; Court of Delegates, 286; Probate Court established; its effects, 286; Chaucer's "somp-nour;" doctors and proctors; Common Hall, 287; Prerogative Office, 288; Faculty Office; marriage licences, 289, 290; touting for licences, 292; singular wills, 293; Cathedral Choir School, 293; Savings' Bank, 293.

Dodd, Rev. Dr., his life, trial, and execution, i. 141; ii. 449; iv. 238, 543; v. 47, 193; vi. 348.

Dodington, G. B., iv. 123; vi. 540.

Dodsley, R., publisher, iv. 134, 256.

"Dog and Duck" Tavern, Mayfair, iv. 352.

"Dog and Duck" Tavern, St. George's Fields, vi. 136, 343, 344, 352.

Dog-fanciers; Bethnal Green, ii. 148.

Dog-fighting, ii. 308.

Doggett, Thomas, Coat and Badge boat-race, iii. 308; v. 67; vi. 59, 243.

Dog-kennel Lane, Camberwell, vi. 269.

Dogs, iv. 50, 538; v. 3; vi. 369.

"Dog's Fields," Piccadilly, iv. 236.

"Dog's Head in the Pot," Blackfriars Road, vi. 374.

Dole at St. Saviour's Church, Southwark, vi. 21.

Dolittle Lane, ii. 36.

Doll manufactory, vi. 425.

"Dolly's" Tavern, Paternoster Row, i. 278.

Domesday Book in Record Office, i. 101.

Dominican Monastery, Haverstock Hill, v. 316.

Dominicetti; medicated baths, v. 60.

Donkeys on Hampstead Heath, v. 453.

Donne, Rev. Dr. John, i. 47, 76; ii. 414; iii. 38.

Don Saltero's Coffee House. (See Salter, John.)

Dorchester House, Highgate; Marquis of Dorchester; William Blake's Charity, v. 424.

Doré Gallery, Bond Street, iv. 302.

D'Orsay, Count, iv. 352; v. 119, 120.

Dorset, Charles, Earl of, iv. 27.

Dorset, Countess of, imprisoned in the Fleet, ii. 414.

Dorset Gardens Theatre, i. 138, 140, 195–197.

Dorset House, Whitefriars, i. 197.

Dorset Mews East, Paddington Street; French emigré clergy, iv. 428.

Dorset Square; first "Lord's Cricket Ground," v. 260.

Dorset Street, Manchester Square; Charles Babbage, iv. 425.

Douce, Francis, iv. 574.

Doughty Street; Dickens, iv. 551.

Doulton. Messrs., pottery works, Lambeth, vi. 424.

Dover House, Whitehall; Lord Dover; Lord Melbourne; Duke of York, iii. 387; iv. 10, 60, 292.

Dover Street, iv. 274; eminent residents, 292, 293.

Dowgate Hill, ii. 38.

Downing Street, iii. 388; residence of First Lord of the Treasury; Cabinet Councils; Walpole, Lord North, Pitt, Grey, Melbourne, Peel, ib.; meeting of Wellington and Nelson; Stuart, proprietor of the Courier; Reform riots, 389; John Smith, "king's messenger," 390; "Cat and Bagpipes;" George Rose; old Foreign Office; new Foreign, Indian, and Colonial Offices, 392.

Dowton, comedian, iv. 194.

Doyle, Richard; his contributions to Punch, i. 59.

D'Oyley's Warehouse, Strand, iii. 111.

Dragoon Guards. (See Guards, Horse and Foot.)

Drainage, Main, v. 41.

Drake, Sir Francis, ii. 18; iii. 21; his ship, The Golden Hind, vi. 147.

Drapers' Almshouses, ii. 112; vi. 257.

Drapers' Company, i. 516; clothiers and staplers, 517; weavers' guild; Flemish weavers; wool staple and cloth market; first hall, ib.; disputes with the Crutched Friars, 518; dress or livery of the Company; elections; funerals; banquets; old customs, ib.; apprentices' fees and punishments; trade search; pensions, 519; processions; charters; Great Fire, 520; present hall; pictures, 521; garden; Arms of the Company, 522; bequests of Helen Branch, 530; pageants, 548; Harmer's Almshouses, v. 525; Sailmakers' Almshouses, 557; vi. 194.

Drawing Rooms at Court, iv. 105; temp. Queen Anne, 113; a modern Drawing Room, 114, 116; Court dress; hoops; silk stockings; hair powder; wigs, 117, 118; hair; the farthingale; lace collars, 119.

Drayton, i. 47, 314; iii. 311.

Dreadnought, vi. 188.

Dream of the assassination of Spencer Perceval, iii. 530.

Dressmakers' and Milliners' Association, iv. 473.

Drinking Fountain and Cattle Trough Association, iv. 41.

Drinking Fountain, Regent's Park, v. 266.

Drogheda, Countess of, married to Wycherley, ii. 543.

Drowning in the Thames; river-waifs and dead-houses, iii. 292, 303.

Drug-mill of the Apothecaries' Company, Lambeth, vi. 418.

Drummond, Messrs., banking-house, iv. 80, 81, 159.

Drummond Road, Bermondsey, vi. 130.

Drury, Master; his sermon at Hunsdon House, Blackfriars i. 210; fatal accident, 211.

Drury Lane, iii. 36; Hundred of Drury; Drury House; "Cock and Magpie," 38; the "Norfolk Giant," 39; "Coal Yard, 209;" Oldwick Close; "Cock-pit" Theatre; "Phœnix" Theatre; Parker Street; "White Lion;" Flash Coves' Parliament, ib.

Drury Lane Theatre, iii. 218; first styled "The Covent Garden Theatre," "The King's Theatre," "The King's House," "Cockpit" and "Phœnix" Theatres, ib.; Killigrew's "New Theatre in Drury Lane," 219; "His Majesty's Servants," 220; their scarlet livery; hours of performance; Betterton; Mrs. Bracegirdle; Mrs. Oldfield; Booth; Cibber, ib.; Quin, 221; Macklin; Garrick; Kitty Clive; Mrs. Billington; Miss Farren; Harriet Mellon; Mrs. Jordan; Mrs. Robinson; Kean; Grimaldi; Mrs. Nisbet; Madame Celeste; Balfe's Operas; Malibran; salaries, ib.; Theatre burnt, 224; rebuilt by Wren; reopened; Dr. Johnson's prologue; Mrs. Siddons; John Kemble; theatre again rebuilt; Sheridan; "Pizarro;" burnt down, ib.; the "Rejected Addresses," 225; present theatre; Whitbread; Van Amburgh; Macready; Bunn; English and Italian Opera, 226; auditorium and stage, 227.

Dryden, i. 37, 46, 102, 195, 196, 545; ii. 24, 220, 224, 529; iii. 264, 269, 276, 428, 474; iv. 27, 62, 75, 177; vi. 152.

Duburg's Exhibition of Cork Models, iv. 342.

Duchess Street; H. T. Hope's Art Gallery, iv. 448.

Duchy of Lancaster, iii. 9.

Duck hunting, ii. 256; iv. 352; v. 46; vi. 136, 343, 390.

Duck Lane, Smithfield, ii. 363.

Duck Lane, Westminster, iv. 39, 41.

Duck, Stephen, iii. 29.

Ducks in St. James's Park; "Duck Island," iv. 50, 51, 56.

Ducksfoot Lane, ii. 28.

Ducrow, Petre and Andrew; Astley's Amphitheatre, vi. 401.

Dudley and Ward, Earl, iv. 353.

Dudley House, Park Lane; the eccentric Earl of Dudley, iv. 372, 373.

Dudley, Lord Guildford; his execution, ii. 95.

Dudley Street; "Monmouth Street;" cellar rooms, iii. 205.

Duels, i. 44, 64; iii. 65, 113, 161, 182, 262, 278; iv. 16, 77, 137, 171, 178, 251, 389, 483, 543; v. 176, 292, 293, 376, 526; vi. 476, 498.

Dufferin Lodge, Highgate, v. 441.

Dugdale, Sir William, i. 294, 298.

"Duke of Albemarle" Tavern, iv. 274.

Duke of Norfolk's College, Greenwich, vi. 196.

Duke of York's Column, iv. 76.

Duke of York's School, v. 76.

Duke Street, Bloomsbury, iv. 488.

Duke Street, Grosvenor Square, iv. 343.

Duke Street, Manchester Square, iv. 423.

Duke Street, Stamford Street; Clowes and Sons' printing works, vi. 381.

Duke Street, St. James's, iv. 201.

Duke's Place, Aldgate; Jews' Synagogue, ii. 248.

"Duke's Playhouse," Portugal Street, iii. 27.

Duke Street, Westminster; distinguished residents; Judge Jeffreys;

State Paper Office ; Public Offices, iv. 29.

Duke's Theatre, Holborn, iv. 552.

Dulwich, vi. 292; "Green Man;" Dulwich Wood ; hunting ; stocks ; cage ; pound ; Bew's Corner, 293 ; Dulwich Wells, 294 ; Dulwich Grove ; Dr. Glennie's School ; Taverns ; Dulwich Club ; eminent residents ; Manor House, 296 ; Alleyn's College, 292, 297; the founder's rules ; election of master by lot, 299 ; government and revenue ; chapel ; font and palindrome inscription, 301 ; Picture Gallery ; Desenfans ; Sir Francis Bourgeois ; New School Buildings, 302 ; Art Schools ; "speech day," 303.

Duncombe, Sir Charles, goldsmith, i. 525.

Dundonald, Earl of, i. 479, 480 ; iv. 353, 374 ; v. 268.

Dunning, Lord Ashburton, i. 166 ; vi. 528.

Dunn's Chinese Collection, v. 22.

Dunstan, Sir Jeffrey ; his eccentricities, iii. 184 ; vi. 289.

Dunstan, St. ; punishment of unjust moneyers, ii. 100.

Dunton, bookseller, i. 424.

Durham House, Strand ; "Inn" of the Bishops of Durham, iii. 101, 102, 103.

Dust and mud of London, vi. 572.

Dutch gardening, v. 153.

Duval, Claude ; Du Val's Lane, ii. 275 ; v. 195, 381.

Dwarfs, i. 34 ; iii. 46 ; iv. 83, 220, 258, 279.

"Dwarf's" Tavern, Chelsea, v. 50.

Dwight's Pottery, Parson's Green, vi. 521.

Dyer, George, i. 93, 108 ; ii. 266, 376.

Dyers' Buildings ; William Roscoe, ii. 531.

Dyers' Company ; swans and "swan-upping," iii. 303.

Dyers' Hall, ii. 41.

Dymoke family ; hereditary office of King's Champion, iii. 544, 554, 555, 556, 557.

Dyot Street, Bloomsbury Square (now George Street), iii. 207 ; "Turk's Head " Tavern ; "Rat's Castle," a thieves' public-house, iv. 487.

E.

Eagle Street, Red Lion Square, iv. 545.

"Eagle" Tavern, City Road, ii. 227.

Eagles, vi. 231, 288.

Earl Marshal's Court. (See Herald's College.)

Earl Street, Westminster, iv. 4.

Earl's Court Road and Terrace, Kensington, v. 161 ; Sir Richard Blackmore ; John Hunter ; skeleton of O'Brien, the Irish giant ; Mrs. Inchbald, ib.

Early Closing movement, i. 557.

Earthenware, Enamelled ; manufactory, Battersea, vi. 47.

Earthquake shocks, iv. 365 ; v. 506.

East and West Coombe, vi. 224, 229.

Eastcheap, i. 560 ; cooks' and butchers' shops ; the "Boar's Head," ib.; old signs ; Shakespearian dinners ;

James Austin's gigantic puddings ; Falstaff ; Goldsmith, 561 ; Washington Irving ; Shakespeare, 562, 563.

Easter Ball, Mansion House, i. 441.

East Country Dock, vi. 140.

East India House, Leadenhall Street, ii. 183 ; Court Room ; Library and Museum ; history of the Company, 184 ; India Stock ; Board of Control ; "John Company;" extent of its business ; Charles Lamb, 185 ; government transferred to the Crown ; Council of India, 186.

East India United Service Club, iv. 190.

Eastlake, Sir Charles Lock, P.R.A., iii. 148 ; iv. 473.

East London Railway, ii. 134 ; v. 227.

Eaton Square, v. 11.

Ebers, iv. 301.

Ebury, Manor of, v. 2, 15, 16.

Ebury Square, v. 12.

Ebury Street ; "Eabery Farm," v. 2, 12.

Eccles, William, surgeon, ii. 202.

Eccleston Street ; Chantrey, v. 9, 10.

Echo Office, iii. 110.

Edinburgh, H.R.H. the Duke of, vi. 249.

Edmonton, v. 564 ; the "Bell," and Johnny Gilpin's Ride, ib.; Charles Lamb, 567 ; Church Street, 568 ; a witch ; Rectory House ; fair, 569.

Edmonton Church ; tower ; restorations ; monuments ; Peter Fabell ; the "Merry Devil," v. 568.

Education ; systems of Bell and Lancaster ; pupil teacher system, vi. 368.

Edward I., ii. 110 ; iii. 443, 494, 537 ; vi. 165.

Edward III., i. 556 ; iii. 433, 441.

Edward IV., i. 517 ; vi. 225.

Edward V., ii. 66 ; iii. 440, 485 ; v. 429.

Edward VI., ii. 364, 368 ; iii. 341, 346, 435 ; iv. 377, 510 ; vi. 60, 90, 91, 146, 166, 170.

Edward the Black Prince, i. 556 ; ii. 8 ; vi. 331.

Edward the Confessor, iii. 396, 424, 442, 443, 444, 452, 491, 567.

Edward Street, Marylebone, iv. 437.

Edwardes Square, Kensington, v. 161.

Edwards, Talbot, keeper of the regalia, ii. 81, 93.

Edy, Simon ; St. Giles's beggars, iii. 207.

"Eel-pie House," Hornsey, v. 430.

Effra, The River, vi. 279 ; Effra Road, ib.

Egerton Club, iv. 156.

Egg, Augustus, R.A., v. 134.

Eggs, Plovers', ii. 496.

Eglinton Tournament revived, v. 86.

Egyptian Hall, Piccadilly, iv. 257 ; Bullock's Museum : "Living Skeleton;" the Siamese Twins, ib.; "General Tom Thumb;" Albert Smith ; Maskelyne and Cooke ; Pantherion, 258.

Eldon, Lord, i. 35, 80, 89, 165 ; ii. 531 ; iv. 219, 286, 567 ; vi. 442.

Eldrick's Nursery, Westminster, iv. 13.

Eleanor, Queen of Edward I. ; memorial crosses ; Cheapside and Charing Cross, i. 305, 317, 332 ; ii. 19 ; iii. 123, 441.

Elections for Westminster. (See Covent Garden.)

Electric telegraph, v. 242 ; the old company ; Cooke and Wheatstone's patents ; business taken by Government ; transferred to the Post-Office, ib.

"Elephant and Castle," Newington, vi. 255.

Elephants, ii. 277 ; iii. 46, 116.

Elgin marbles, iv. 265, 286, 497, 532.

Eia, Saxon manor of ; site of Hyde Park, iv. 376.

Eliott, General, Lord Heathfield, vi. 399.

"Elizabeth Fry's Refuge, Hackney," v. 514.

Elizabeth, Queen of Edward IV., iii. 485 ; vi. 119, 165.

Elizabeth, Queen of Henry VII., i. 316 ; iii. 436.

Elizabeth, Queen, i. 25, 204, 244, 245, 284, 316, 365, 420, 495, 496, 514 ; ii. 40, 69, 104, 149, 176, 226, 255, 383, 479, 518, 554, 560 ; iii. 70, 73, 89, 114, 297, 309, 341, 344, 345, 364, 404, 440, 446, 525 ; iv. 46, 53, 376, 377, 477, 512 ; v. 3, 52, 58, 88, 111, 139, 536, 537 ; vi. 18, 53, 147, 167, 168, 170—173, 437, 490, 514.

Elizabethan Club, Westminster School, iii. 477.

Ellenborough, Lord, i. 51, 52 ; ii. 392.

Ellis, Sir Henry, iv. 512, 518, 525.

Ellis, Wynn, v. 14.

Elliotson, Dr., F.R.S., iv. 326 ; vi. 59.

Elliston, R. W., comedian, i. 329—331 ; iii. 35 ; iv. 2 ; vi. 373, 411.

Eltham, vi. 236 ; "Eald-ham" market, 237 ; royal residence ; descent of the manor ; barony of Eltham ; Henry III.'s palace ; John of Eltham ; Edward III.; King John of France, ib.; Froissart, 238 ; parks and buildings ; remains of the palace, hall, bridge, and buttery, 239 ; moat ; Middle Park ; Blenkiron's racing-stud, 242 ; distinguished residents, 243.

Elwes, John, M.P., miser, iv. 242, 418, 442.

Ely, Bishops of ; residence in Dover Street, iv. 293.

Ely Place, ii. 514 ; "hostell" of the Bishops of Ely ; vineyard and orchard, ib.; old gatehouse, hall, and chapel ; streets built on the garden ; the "Mitre," Mitre Court ; death of John of Gaunt, 515 ; Shakespeare and the bishop's strawberries, 516 ; Sir Christopher Hatton ; Bishop Cox ; Queen Elizabeth's letter, 518 ; death of Hatton ; the "strange" Lady Hatton ; hospital and a prison, 519 ; feasts of serjeants-at-law ; Joe Haines, 520 ; masque before Charles I. described by Whitelock, 521 ; mysteries and miracle plays ; St. Etheldreda's chapel, 525 ; crypt ; Evelyn ; Bishop Wilkins ; a loyal clerk, 526 ; restoration of chapel, 526.

Emanuel Hospital for the Blind, v. 321.

Embankments of the Thames, old ; Narrow Wall and Broad Wall, Lambeth, vi. 387. (See Thames, The River.)

Emery, John, comedian, ii. 505.

Emery Hill's Almshouses and School, Westminster, iv. 10.

Emmanuel Hospital, or Dacre's Almshouses, Westminster, iv. 12, 22, 24.

Endell Street, formerly Belton Street, iii. 207 ; Queen Anne's Bath ; Lying-in Hospital ; Baths and Washhouses, 208.

Ennismore Place, v. 26.

Enon Chapel, Clare Market ; charnel-house, iii. 31.

Entomological Society, iv. 551.

Epitaphs, i. 227, 348, 349, 350, 351, 352, 362, 363, 365, 367, 371, 375, 376, 419, 514, 524, 527, 549, 550, 551, 552, 554, 556, 557, 558, 561 ; ii. 20, 37, 40, 41, 112, 138, 140, 237, 245, 324, 329, 354, 392, 429, 505, 509 ; iii. 30, 201, 256, 418, 424, 425, 428, 430, 433, 436, 440, 441, 569, 570 ; iv. 345 ; v. 517, 518, 560, 568 ; vi. 28, 95, 472, 551, 562.

"Equality Brown," vi. 274.

Erasmus, i. 273 ; ii. 156 ; v. 53, 54.

Erber, The, Dowgate ; residence of the Scropes and Nevilles, ii. 18.

Erectheum Club, iv. 184.

Erkenwald, Bishop, i. 236 ; Bishop's Gate built by, ii. 152.

Ermin Street ; Arminius, v. 531.

Ermin's Hill, Westminster, iv. 21.

Erskine House, Hampstead, v. 446.

Erskine, Lord, i. 164 ; iii. 530 ; iv. 298 ; v. 9, 446, 447.

Essex, Arthur Capel, Earl of, ii. 323.

Essex, Earl of, his imprisonment and execution, ii. 71, 95.

Essex House, Putney, vi. 494.

Essex House, Strand, iii. 68, 71, 95 ; execution of the Earl of Essex ; Spenser ; Pepys ; Strype ; Paterson, auctioneer ; Charles II., ib.

"Essex Serpent" Tavern, iii. 263.

Essex Street, Strand ; residents ; Unitarian Chapel, iii. 69.

Essex, Thomas Cromwell, Earl of, ii. 93, 95, 561 ; vi. 492, 560.

Esterhazy, Prince, iii. 410 ; iv. 448.

Ethelbert, first authenticated church at St. Paul's built by, i. 236.

Eton College ; land at Primrose Hill, v. 287.

Etty, William, R.A., iii. 109.

Eucharist, Holy ; mode of preparing it, vi. 118.

Eugene, Prince, iii. 164.

Eugenie, Empress, iv. 422 ; v. 112.

Euston Road ; statuary ; "figure yards," iv. 287 ; taverns and tea-gardens ; gin palaces, v. 301 ; old turnpike, 302 ; "Adam and Eve" Tavern, 303, 354.

Euston Square, iv. 483, 485 ; statue of Robert Stephenson, v. 351, 352.

"Evangelicalism," iv. 478.

"Evans's Hotel," Covent Garden, iii. 251 ; "Paddy Green," 254.

Evelyn, John, i. 248, 334 ; ii. 331, 526, 530, 543 ; iii. 38, 40, 74, 109, 136, 156, 160, 184, 205, 279, 297, 314, 316, 322, 356, 359, 436, 472 ; iv. 51, 56, 62, 104, 227, 251, 255, 260, 269, 273, 274, 275, 280, 292, 380, 381, 490, 536 ; v. 17, 47, 70, 134, 142 ; vi. 52, 55, 59, 74, 90, 147, 148, 150, 152, 153, 159, 162, 176, 191, 195, 196, 207, 214, 239, 246, 271, 294, 321, 334, 342, 424, 441, 448, 501, 509, 520, 544, 561, 566.

"Evil May Day" (1513), i. 310—314 ; ii. 192 ; iii. 545.

Exchange, Middle, Strand, iii. 101 ; New, Strand, 104 ; James I. ; "the White Milliner," ib.

Exchange Royal. (See Royal Exchange.)

Exchanger, The King's, i. 346.

Exchequer "tallies ;" burning of the Houses of Parliament, iii. 502, 521.

Excise Office, Old Broad Street ; revenue ; riots, ii. 165.

Executioners at the Tower and Tyburn, v. 197 ; Bull ; Derrick ; the Brandons ; Dun ; "Jack Ketch," ib.

Executions in Cheapside, i. 305 ; in Smithfield, ii. 341 ; at Tyburn and Newgate, 469 ; v. 189—209 ; in Skinner Street, ii. 470 ; at St. Giles's, iii. 200 ; at St. Thomas à Watering, Southwark, vi. 250.

Execution Dock, ii. 135.

Exeter Arcade, iii. 112.

Exeter Change, iii. 116 ; milliners' shops ; the menagerie ; Pidcock ; Polito ; Cross ; the elephant "Chunee," ib.

Exeter Hall "May meetings ;" oratorios, iii. 118.

Exeter House, Strand ; Bishops of Exeter, iii. 66.

Exeter, John, Duke of ; his tomb, ii. 118.

Exeter Street, Strand, iii. 112, 284.

Exhibitions. (See International Exhibitions.)

Extinguishers for links, iv. 339, 445.

"Eyre Arms," St. John's Wood, v. 251.

Eyre, Charles, King's printer, i. 218.

Eyre, Sir Simon, Lord Mayor ; his pancake feast, i. 399 ; ii. 180, 188.

Eyre Street and Eyre Street Hill, Leather Lane, ii. 544.

F.

Fabell, Peter ; the "Merry Devil of Edmonton," v. 568.

Fagniani, Mademoiselle Maria, iv. 369 ; v. 131.

Fagots, Chopping, ancient tenure custom, iii. 561.

Fairholt, Thomas, F.S.A., i. 20, 387, 437.

Fairlop Fair, ii. 137.

Fairlop Oak, v. 353.

Fairs : on Tower Hill, ii. 117 ; Westminster Fair, iv. 16 ; May Fair, 345 ; Edmonton, Beggars' Bush Fair, v. 569 ; Southwark Fair, vi. 14, 58 ; Greenwich, 201—205, 208, 209 ; Blackheath, 227 ; Camberwell, 275 ; Peckham, 287 ; Clapham Common, 321 ; Kennington Common, 338 ; Battersea Fields, 476 ; Wandsworth, 488 ; Parson's Green, 518.

Fair Street, Horselydown, vi. 109.

Fairfax, General, v. 166.

Fairfax House, Putney, vi. 490.

Fairfax, Lady, robbed by "Mull Sack," i. 40, 43.

Falconbridge, Aldgate attacked by, ii. 246 ; vi. 9, 10.

Falcon Court, Fleet Street, i. 135 ; Fisher and the Cordwainers' Company ; Wynkyn de Worde, ib.

Falcon Square, part of old London wall, i. 19.

Falcon Glass Works, vi. 41.

"Falcon" Tavern, Bankside ; Shakespeare, vi. 41.

"Falcon" Tavern, Battersea, vi. 473.

Falcon's nest at the top of St. Paul's, i. 256.

Falconry, iii. 129 ; Hereditary Grand Falconer, iv. 47.

Famines ; regulations for supplies of corn, ii. 180.

Fanshawe, Sir Richard and Lady, i. 83 ; iii. 22, 26.

Fantocini, vii. 288.

Faraday, Michael, F.R.S., v. 260, 407.

Farinelli, iv. 211.

Farm Street, Berkeley Square ; Jesuit Church, iv. 335.

Farnborough, Lord ; National Gallery, iii. 146.

Farncomb, Lord Mayor ; banquet to Prince Albert and provincial mayors, i. 416.

Farren, Miss (Countess of Derby), iii. 221, 232.

Farringdon Market, ii. 497.

Farringdon Road Station, Metropolitan Railway, v. 227.

Farringdon Street, ii. 496 ; Ward of Farringdon Without ; W. Farindon, goldsmith ; John Wilkes, alderman, ib. ; Fleet Street bankers, 497 ; Farringdon Within ; Fleet Market ; transfer of the Stocks Market ; Farringdon Market, ib. ; watercresses ; Congregational Hall and Library, 500.

Farthing Alley, vi. 114.

Farthings ; first coined, i. 514 ; Queen Anne's, ii. 104.

Fashion ; westward extension of the metropolis, iv. 246, 248, 483, 484.

Fashions in dress, iv. 167, 176, 238, 246, 339, 399, 400. (See Costume.)

Fastolf, Sir John, vi. 87, 111.

Faucit, Miss Helen, iii. 233.

Fauconberg, Countess of, daughter of Cromwell, vi. 551, 556.

Fauntleroy's forgeries, i. 459 ; ii. 455 ; v. 181, 412.

Fawkes, Guy ; Gunpowder Plot, ii. 73 ; iii. 548, 563, 566 ; vi. 449.

Fawkes, the conjuror, iv. 232.

Feather-sellers in Blackfriars, i. 201.

"Feathers'" Inn ; George IV., v. 8.

Featherstone Buildings, iv. 552.

Fell, Dr., iii. 476.

Fellmongers, vi. 124.

"Fellmongers' Arms" Tavern, vi. 123.

Fellowship Porters' Hall ; sermon in St. Mary-at-Hill Church ; Ticket porters ; Tackle porters, ii. 52.

Felton, murderer of the Duke of Buckingham, ii. 74, 98 ; v. 190.

Female barbers, iii. 122, 206.

Female Convict Prison, Brixton, vi. 319.

Female Royal Academicians, iv. 272.

Female prize-fighters, iv. 455, 477.

Female soldiers, v. 94.

Female telegraph clerks, ii. 216.

Ferrers, Earl ; his execution, ii. 471 ; iii. 551 ; v. 191, 437.

Ferries : site of London Bridge, vi. 3 ; Blackfriars, vi. 383 ; Battersea, vi. 474 ; Putney, vi. 489, 501.

Festing, Colonel Sir F. W., vi. 247.

Fenchurch Street, ii. 175 ; Northumberland House ; St. Catherine Coleman Church ; the Plague ; Ironmongers' Hall, 176 ; Denmark House ; St.

Dionis Church; St. Margaret Patten's Church, 177.

Fenning, Eliza, executed for murder, i. 92.

Fenning's Wharf; fire in 1836, vi. 105.

Fetter Lane, i. 90; its name; Clifford's Inn; Waller's plot; execution of Tomkins and Challoner, 91, 94; "Praise - God Barebone," 95; Charles Lamb, 96; "Captain Starkey;" Hobbes of Malmesbury, 97; Levett, apothecary, 98; Elizabeth Brownrigge; Paul Whitehead; Flatman, poet and painter, 99; Moravian Chapel; Sacheverel's trial; Count Zinzendorf; Baxter; Independent Chapel, 100; Public Records; Domesday Book; Record Office, 101; Dryden and Otway; Dryden's House, 102.

Fever Hospital, Hampstead, v. 491.

"Fielding, Beau," iii. 330; iv. 178, 387.

Fielding, Copley, iv. 467.

Fielding, Henry; Haymarket Theatre, iv. 222.

Fielding, Sir Godfrey, Lord Mayor, i. 399.

Fielding, Sir John, ii. 550; iii. 100, 272, 286; iv. 238, 287, 303, 435, 436; vi. 455.

Field Lane, Holborn; stolen handkerchiefs, ii. 542.

"Field of the Forty Footsteps," iv. 482.

Fife House, Whitehall Yard, iii. 335; Earl of Fife; Earl of Liverpool; East India Museum, 336.

Fifth Monarchy men, i. 370.

Figg, prize-fighter, and his theatre, iv. 406, 430, 455; vi. 58.

"Figure-yards;" statuary; Piccadilly; Euston Road, iv. 287.

Finch, Hon. John, stabbed by "Sally Salisbury," iii. 268.

Finch Lane, Cornhill, ii. 173.

Finch, Lord Chancellor, iii. 45; v. 142.

Finch, Sir Heneage, i. 161.

Finch's Grotto Gardens, Southwark, vi. 64.

"Finish, The," Covent Garden, iii. 260.

Finsbury, ii. 201; Finsbury Fields; Protector Somerset; archery, 251, 254.

Finsbury Chapel, ii. 209.

Finsbury Park, v. 431.

Finsbury Pavement, ii. 208.

Finsbury Square, ii. 206.

Fire-arms, Museum of, vi. 290.

Fire Brigade, i. 554.

Fire-engines, ancient, iii. 575; steam, iv. 244; syringes for extinguishing fires, ii. 176.

Fires : in the Temple, i. 161; Houses of Parliament, iii. 521; Alexandra Palace, v. 435; Barclay's Brewery, vi, 35; Tooley Street, 105. (See Great Fire of London.)

Fireworks : Peace Festival (1814), iv. 54; Green Park (1749), 179, 183, 394; Marylebone Gardens, 434, 435, 436; Ranelagh Gardens, v. 77; Surrey Gardens, vi. 265, 266; Peace Celebration (1856), v. 291.

Firs, The, Hampstead; Firs on Hampstead Heath, v. 448.

"Fish and Ring," Story of the, ii. 140.

Fish in the Thames, iii. 302.

Fish Markets : Cornhill; Cheapside, i. 306; Queenhithe; prices of fish; regulations of sale; whales and porpoises, ii. 2; Billingsgate Market. (See Billingsgate).

Fishmongers' Almshouses, Newington, vi. 257; Wandsworth, 481.

Fishmongers' Company and Hall, ii. 1; Sir William Walworth, 1, 2; rules for sale of fish; wealth of the Fishmongers, 2, 3; affrays between Fishmongers and Skinners, 3; Great Fire; second hall, 4; present hall; "Sir William Walworth's" pall, 5; Doggett's coat and badge, iii. 308; model dwellings, Walworth, vi. 268.

Fish Street dinners, ii. 8.

Fish Street Hill; the Black Prince; Jack Cade, ii. 8.

Fisher, John, Bishop of Rochester, ii. 14, 66, 95, 108; iii. 546; vi. 10.

"Fisher, Kitty," iv. 352.

Fisher Street, Red Lion Square, iv. 549.

Fisher's gift to the Cordwainers' Company, i. 135.

Fishery at Putney; salmon; porpoises; sturgeons, vi. 489.

Fitz-Alwyn, Henry, Lord Mayor, i. 396, 520, 521; ii. 248.

Fitzherbert, Chief Justice, ii. 562.

Fitzherbert, Mrs., iv. 94, 98; v. 112, 275; vi. 519.

Fitzpatrick, General, iv. 158.

Fitzroy Market, iv. 473.

Fitzroy Square; Charles Fitzroy, Duke of Grafton; the brothers Adam, iv. 473.

Fitz-Stephen, iii. 463.

Fitzwalter, Maud, imprisoned in the Tower, ii. 64.

Fitzwalter, Robert, banner-bearer to the City; barony of Baynard's castle, i. 281, 282, 284.

"Five Fields," Belgravia, v. 2.

"Five Houses" (pest-houses), Tothill Fields, iv. 14, 15.

"Fladong's" Hotel, Oxford Street, iv. 423.

Flambard, Bishop of Durham, ii. 63.

Flambeaux, iv. 137, 231.

Flambeaux-extinguishers, iv. 339, 445.

Flamsteed, John, astronomer, ii. 94; vi. 155, 213, 214.

Flanders mares, iv. 387.

"Flash Coves' Parliament," iii. 209.

"Flask" Inn, Highgate, v. 418, 423.

"Flask" Tavern, Hampstead; the "Upper Flask," "Lower Flask," v. 459, 460, 461, 467.

Flask Walk, Hampstead, v. 467.

Flatman, poet and painter, i. 99; ii. 221.

Flaxman, John, R.A., sculptor, iii. 231, 265, 540; iv. 469, 497, 569.

"Fleece" Inn, York Street, iii. 285.

Fleet Market, ii. 497.

Fleet Prison, ii. 404; wardens appointed by Richard I. and John; burnt by Wat Tyler; wardens' fees and fines, ib.; Star Chamber prisoners, 405; burnt down in the Great Fire, and by the Gordon rioters; John Howard; the tapster, 405, 408; begging box; abuses by Huggins and Bambridge, 406; debtors put in irons; Hogarth's picture of the Committee, 407, 408; "liberty of the rules;" "day rules," 409; Fleet marriages;

Fleet Chapel, 410; "Hand and Pen" marrying-house, 411; "Mr. Pickwick;" Dickens' account of the Fleet, 413; distinguished prisoners, 414; marriage register books, 416.

Fleet River and Fleet Ditch, ii. 416; "the River of Wells;" its sources, course, and tributary streams, ib.; "the Hole-bourne;" "Hockley in the Hole;" "Black Mary's Hole;" antiquities; anchors, 417; Fleet Hythe; ships at Holborn Bridge; mills; Fleet Bridge, 418, 419; Bridewell Bridge; navigation, 420; Pope's lines on the ditch, 420; Gay's "Trivia;" Swift; Turnmill brook; stream covered in, 422; floods; storm; ditch blown up; sewer; main-drainage system; explorations, 423, 444, 467.

Fleet Street, i. 32; riots in the Middle Ages; shops, temp. Edward II.; Duchess of Gloucester's penance, ib.; 'prentice riots; Templars and citizens; Titus Oates; Mohocks; shows, 33; giants and dwarfs; sign-boards; Dr. Johnson, 34; Wilkes' riot; burning of the "boot;" Queen Caroline's funeral, 35; Messrs. Childs' bank, 23, 30, 35, 37, 38; "Devil" Tavern, 38; Apollo Club and Ben Jonson, 39, 40; "Mull Sack" and Lady Fairfax, 40, 43; Swift; Addison, 41; sign-board of the "Devil;" Pandemonium Club, 42; "Cock Tavern;" "Dick's Coffee-house;" St. Dunstan's Club; the "Rainbow Tavern;" Bernard Lintot, 44; Lord Cobham's house; Green Ribbon Club; "Palace of Henry VIII. and Wolsey;" "Nando's" Coffee-house; Mrs. Salmon's waxwork, 45, 48; Tonson, 46; Izaak Walton, 46, 49; Praed's and Gosling's banks; John Murray's shop, 46; St. Dunstan's Church; clock and giants, 34, 133, 135; Drayton's house, 47; Edmund Curll; early booksellers, 48; printers; the "Hercules Pillars;" Hoare's bank, 50; the "Mitre Tavern;" Cobbett; Peele's Coffee - house; Repeal of the Paper Duty, 52; the "Green Dragon;" Tompion, watchmaker; Pinchbeck; Anderton's Hotel; St. Bride's Church, 55; newspaper offices, 53, 56, 59, 60, 61, 62, 64, 66; Wynkyn de Worde; conduit; "Castle Tavern," 63, 64; Joseph Brasbridge, 65; Alderman Waithman, 66, 68; M'Ghee, the black crossing-sweeper, 68; John Hardham, tobacconist; Lockyer's saloop-house, 69; roasting the Rumps, 95, 96.

Fleetwood, General, v. 534, 543.

Fleetwood Road, Stoke Newington, v. 537.

Fletcher, John, dramatist, vi. 27.

Fletchers. (See Archery.)

Fleur-de-Lys Court; unstamped newspapers, i. 104.

Flint, Patience, centenarian, iv. 470.

Flogging at Bridewell, i. 191.

Flood in Westminster Hall, iii. 548.

Floorcloth, manufacture of, v. 25.

Floral Hall, Covent Garden, iii. 251.

Florio, John, i. 123, 124.

Flower-girls, Hyde Park, iv. 387.

Fludyer, Sir Samuel, Lord Mayor, i. 323—328, 407 ; iv. 30.

Fludyer Street, Westminster, i. 407 ; iv. 29.

"Flying Coach." (*See* Stage-coaches.)

"Flying Horse" Tavern, Hackney, v. 514.

Foley Place, iv. 458.

Foley Street ; Foley House, iv. 452.

Folly Ditch, Dockhead, vi. 114.

"Folly, The," on the Thames, iii. 290.

Food supply ; statistics, vi. 572.

Foote, Miss (Countess of Harrington), iii. 232.

Foote, Samuel, iii. 65, 250, 275, 278, 285 ; iv. 223, 224 ; vi. 526.

"Footman ;" "Running Footman" Tavern, iv. 334.

Footpads. (*See* Highwaymen.)

Fordyce, Alexander, stockjobber, i. 476.

Fordyce, Dr. George, iii. 69.

Foreigners, jealousy of ; "Evil May Day," i. 310, 311.

Foreign Office, iii. 392 ; old office, Downing Street ; new office ; Sir G. G. Scott and Lord Palmerston ; the building described, *ib.*

Forest of Middlesex, v. 426, 429, 527, 531.

Forgery of Bank notes by "Old Patch ;" other forgeries, i. 459 ; George Morland ; John Mathison, 464 ; death punishment, 466 ; Bank losses, 467 ; Fauntleroy, 459 ; Vaughan, 461.

Forrester, Alfred, ("Alfred Crowquill,") vi. 331.

Forster, John, v. 138, 140.

Forster, Sir Stephen, Lord Mayor, i. 225, 399.

Fortescue and Pope, i. 75 ; iii. 22, 51, 65.

Fortescue, Sir John ; Temple students, i. 156.

Fortifications during the Civil War, ii. 138, 256 ; iv. 178, 238, 289, 380, 538 ; vi. 9, 344, 467.

Fort Road, Bermondsey, vi. 125.

Fortey, W. S., ballad-printer, iii. 203.

"Forty Footsteps, Field of the," iv. 482.

Fortune Theatre, The, Whitecross Street, ii. 224.

Foscolo, Ugo, iv. 443, 464 ; v. 172, 268, 290 ; vi. 551.

Foster Lane, i. 353 ; Goldsmiths' Hall ; churches, epitaphs, 362, 363.

Foubert's Passage, iv. 251.

Founders' Hall, St. Swithin's Lane, i. 551.

Foundling Hospital, v. 356 ; established by Captain Coram, *ib.* ; parliamentary grant ; reception of infants ; basket at the gate ; abuses ; tokens for recognition, 357 ; grant withdrawn ; money premium for admission ; present rules, 358 ; names of children ; country nurseries ; education ; apprenticeship, 359 ; royal visits ; pictures ; Hogarth ; "March to Finchley," 362 ; Handel's benefactions ; the *Messiah ;* organ, 364 ; statue of Coram, 365.

Fountayne, Dr., his academy, Marylebone, iv. 429 ; Handel, 434.

Four-in-Hand Club, iv. 400.

"Four Swans," Bishopsgate, ii. 161.

Fowke, Captain, R.E., v. 105.

Fowke, Sir John, Lord Mayor, i. 404 ; v. 113.

Fowler, John, C.E. ; Metropolitan Railway, v. 226, 228.

"Fox and Bull" Inn, Knightsbridge, v. 21.

"Fox and Crown Inn," Highgate, v. 412.

Fox, Charles James, iii. 417 ; iv. 89, 107, 121, 129, 158, 159, 543 ; v. 171 ; vi. 565.

"Fox Club," iv. 159.

Fox Court, Gray's Inn Lane ; birthplace of Savage, ii. 552.

Fox, George, founder of the Quakers' sect, ii. 174.

Fox-hunting in London, iv. 323 ; v. 154.

Fox-hunting on the Thames ; "Frost Fair," iii. 323.

"Fox-under-the-Hill" Tavern, Denmark Hill, vi. 284.

"Fox-under-the-Hill" Tavern, Strand, iii. 101, 296.

Fox, Sir Stephen, v. 70, 76, 168 ; vi. 566.

Foxe, the martyrologist, ii. 231, 340.

Framework Knitters' Company, v. 525.

Francis ; his attack on the life of Queen Victoria, iv. 179.

Francis, Sir Philip and Lady, iv. 190.

Franklin, Benjamin, iii. 26, 214 ; iv. 539 ; v. 64.

Fraser's Magazine ; its editor and contributors, iv. 251.

Fratricide, legendary, at Kilburn, v. 246.

Frederick, Sir John, Lord Mayor, i. 404 ; ii. 367.

Freeling, Sir F., ii. 212 ; iv. 412.

Freeman's Court, ii. 173.

Freeman's "London Progresse ;" spread of London, v. 392.

Freemasons' Charity Schools for Girls, vi. 350, 472.

Freemasons' Hall and Tavern, iii. 213 ; former and present Hall ; public meetings and dinners ; eminent Freemasons, *ib.*

Freemasons' Lodge at the "Goose and Gridiron ;" old Lodges near St. Paul's, i. 272.

Freemasons ; Prince of Wales inaugurated as Grand Master, v. 115.

Free Public Library, Westminster, iv. 36.

Free-Thinking Christians' Meeting House, ii. 323.

French Hospital, Bethnal Green, removed to Victoria Park, ii. 148.

French Hospital, Hackney Common, v. 509.

French Industrial Exhibitions, v. 29.

French Plays, iv. 193, 195, 222.

French Protestant Churches, ii. 228 ; iii. 208.

French refugees in Leicester Square, Soho, and St. Giles's, iii. 161, 172, 177, 200 ; iv. 466, 553 ; v. 51, 341 ; vi. 480.

French residents in London ; statistics, vi. 570.

French weavers in Spitalfields, ii. 152.

Frescoes at Houses of Parliament, iii. 507, 508, 516.

Friday Street ; the Friday Market Place, i. 347.

Friendless Boys' Home, Wandsworth, vi. 483.

Friend of the Clergy Corporation, iii. 155.

Friern Place, Peckham Rye, vi. 292 ; Friern Manor ; dairy farm, *ib.*

Frith Street, iii. 177 ; "Thrift Street ;" residents, 192, 194.

Frobisher, Sir Martin, ii. 230.

"Frog Hall," Islington, ii. 262.

Frognal, Hampstead, v. 501 ; Frognal Priory ; Frognal Hall, 502.

Frosts on the Thames, iii. 311—321 ; "Frost Fair" (1683), 312 ; Fog and "Frost Fair" (1814), 317.

Frosts ; Serpentine frozen over, iv. 402.

Fry, Mrs. ; Ladies' Prison Visiting Association, ii. 459 ; vi. 439.

Fryar, Peg, centenarian actress, iii. 28 ; iv. 479.

Fulham, vi. 504 ; etymology ; waterfowl ; boundaries ; Egmont Villa ; Theodore Hook, 505, 506, 507 ; church, 506, 507 ; tower and bells ; monuments ; Bishops of London ; church plate ; Powell's Almshouses, 508 ; Craven Cottage ; distinguished residents, 513 ; the "Crab Tree" Inn ; cemetery ; market-gardens ; High Street ; "Golden Lion" Inn ; Workhouse, 514 ; Fulham Road ; Holcrofts Hall ; Holcrofts Priory, 515 ; Elysium Road ; Orphanage Home ; Munster House, 516 ; Dwight's pottery ; Gobelin tapestry factory, 521 ; Vine Cottage ; Prior's Bank, 523 ; the "Swan" Tavern, 524; Stourton House, 525 ; Ranelagh House ; Mulgrave House ; Hurlingham House ; aristocratic sports ; Broom House ; Sandford Manor House ; residence of Nell Gwynne ; Addison ; St. James's Church, Moore Park, *ib.*

Fulham Palace, vi. 508 ; moat and drawbridge ; hall ; chapel ; Porteus library ; portraits ; floods ; gardens ; cork-tree ; cedars, 509 ; Lying clubs ; "lying for the whetstone ;" Bishop Porteus, 510 ; the manor ; royal visits ; history of the moat, 512.

Fulham Road, v. 87.

Fulwood's Rents, ii. 536.

Funerals and funeral feasts, i. 231, 519.

Furnival's Inn, ii. 570 ; Lords Furnival ; Sir Thomas More ; Dickens, 572.

Fuseli, R.A., i. 268, 345 ; iv. 448, 464 ; v. 477 ; vi. 494.

Fust, Sir Herbert Jenner, i. 291.

Fyefoot Lane, ii. 37.

G.

Gaiety Theatre, iii. 112.

Gainsborough, iv. 124, 371.

Gallery of British Artists, iv. 230.

Gallery of Illustration, iv. 208.

Galley Wall, Bermondsey, vi. 131 ; Venetian galleys, 132.

Gallini, Sir John, iv. 317, 318 ; v. 251.

"Gallows Close," v. 178.

Galt, John, iv. 574.

Galvanism applied to a murderer's dead body, ii. 471.

Gambling, iv. 141, 153, 157, 158, 160, 161, 162, 221, 236, 284, 332, 359, 435.

Game pie, i. 394, 549.

Gaming. (*See* Gambling.)

Gaol fever ; Newgate, ii. 467.

"Garbeller of spices," i. 431.

Gardener's Lane, Westminster, iv. 29.

Garden of Drapers' Hall, i. 522.

Gardens at Chelsea, v. 51.

Gardens, London, iv. 567.

Gardens on the banks of the Thames, iii. 300.

Gardens on the Thames Embankment, iii. 324, 328.

Gardiner, Bishop of Winchester, ii. 566.

Garenciers, Dr., ii. 329.

Garnerin's balloon, v. 81.

Garnet, Father, i. 245, 265, 395 ; ii. 15, 73 ; "the face in the straw," i. 265.

Garratt, hamlet of, Wandsworth, vi. 485 ; encroachments on the common resisted ; club ; "Mayors of Garratt ;" mock election, 486 ; Foote's farce, 488.

"Garraway's" Coffee House ; his shop-bill ; early prices of tea, ii. 172 ; vi. 108.

Garrick, David, i. 69 ; ii. 146, 173, 317 ; iii. 28, 213, 221, 250, 264, 267, 278, 296, 425 ; iv. 128, 134, 154 ; vi. 551.

Garrick, Mrs., iii. 213, 267, 296 ; iv. 248.

Garrick Street, iii. 263 ; Garrick Club ; theatrical portraits, *ib*.

"Garrick's Head" Tavern ; "Judge and Jury Club," iii. 273.

Garter King at Arms, i. 296 ; iv. 536.

Garth, Sir Samuel, i. 41, 71, 215, 217, 218 ; ii. 363, 431 ; iii. 144 ; iv. 158 ; v. 179.

Gascoigne, Sir Christopher, Lord Mayor, i. 407.

Gascoigne, Sir Crisp, Lord Mayor, i. 435.

Gascoigne, Sir Wm., ii. 560 ; vi. 64.

Gascon wines, ii. 22.

Gas-lighting, history of, i. 195 ; iv. 8, 59, 137, 339 ; v. 236.

Gas-lighting of railway carriages, v. 228.

Gas supply ; gas companies, v. 236 ; statistics ; progress of consumption, 237 ; vi. 467.

Gate House and "Gate House" Inn, Highgate, v. 390, 418.

Gate House Prison, Westminster, iii. 479 ; prisoners, 489 ; Royalists ; Lovelace ; "the German Princess ;" Jeffrey Hudson ; Jeremy Collier ; Savage ; Raleigh ; a debtors' prison ; keeper's fees, *ib*.

Gate Street, Lincoln's Inn Fields, iii. 215.

Gatti, Messrs., Refreshment Rooms, iii. 134.

Gauden, Sir Dennis, vi. 321.

Gaunt, John of, i. 238, 239 ; ii. 515 ; iii. 100 ; vi. 332, 386.

Gay ; the South Sea Bubble, i. 543 ; his "Trivia," ii. 422 ; iii. 45, 74, 110, 112, 116, 205, 240, 315 ; iv. 125, 141, 161, 176, 177, 305 ; v. 70, 167, 470 ; vi. 134.

Geddes, Dr., v. 210.

Geese, French and Irish, ii. 495.

Gefferey's Almshouses, v. 525.

General Post Office, ii. 209 ; first offices, 159 ; old office, Lombard Street, i. 526 ; Penny Post *temp.* Charles II.,

ii. 210 ; revenues farmed, 212 ; London Post ; Ralph Allen ; John Palmer ; statistics ; Post Office, Lombard Street ; mail - coaches ; Money Order Office ; Sir Francis Freeling ; Sir Rowland Hill ; Penny Postage ; Office in St. Martin's-le-Grand ; dead letters ; sorting ; valentines, *ib.* ; Savings Bank Department ; revenue, 213 ; Telegraph Department, 214, 215—219 ; New Post Office, 215 ; female clerks, 216 ; chronometer ; time-signals, 218 ; annual procession of mail-coaches, iv. 3 ; Mulready's Envelope, vi. 382.

Gentleman's Magazine; Cave ; Dr. Johnson ; St. John's Gate, ii. 317, 319, 320, 321.

Geographical Society, iv. 309.

Geological Society, iv. 271.

George I., i. 250, 406 ; iii. 29, 152, 161, 469 ; iv. 59, 111, 210, 212, 339, 544 ; v. 124, 142, 145.

George II., i. 323 ; iii. 435 ; iv. 81, 111, 153, 232, 237, 356 ; v. 69, 80, 93, 142, 145, 146, 569.

George III., i. 106, 251, 392 ; iii. 144, 147, 164, 406 ; iv. 63, 64, 65, 85, 101, 303, 307, 317, 408, 490, 509, 540 ; v. 8, 27, 69, 86, 164, 170, 201 ; vi. 197, 289, 304, 399, 403, 500.

George IV., i. 146 ; ii. 278 ; iii. 118, 142, 154, 183, 190, 206, 212, 231, 409 ; iv. 58, 64, 68, 89-98, 102, 158, 165, 189, 199, 238, 244, 268, 284, 317, 326, 332, 333, 353, 424, 497, 567 ; v. 21, 27, 102, 112 ; vi. 519, 522, 533.

"George and Vulture" Tavern, Tottenham, v. 553.

"George" Inn, Southwark, vi. 85 ; landlords' "tokens," 86.

George of Denmark, Prince, iii. 384.

George Street, Bloomsbury, iv. 487.

George Street, Hanover Square, iv. 321 ; St. George's Church ; Copley ; Lord Lyndhurst, 322.

George Yard, Whitechapel, ii. 145.

Gerard's Hall ; Norman crypt, i. 556.

Gerard's "Herbal ;" his physic garden, Holborn, ii. 539 ; vi. 341.

Germain, Lord George, iv. 136.

German Anabaptists burnt, i. 243.

German Chapel, St. James's, iv. 76, 106.

German Fair, iv. 453.

German Hospital, Dalston, v. 530.

German residents in London ; statistics, vi. 570.

Gerrard, Sir Samuel, Lord Mayor, i. 406.

Gerrard Street ; residence of Dryden and Burke, iii. 178.

Ghost-stories, v. 135, 164 ; Cock Lane Ghost, ii. 437, 489 ; "Hammersmith Ghost," vi. 548 ; "Stockwell Ghost," vi. 328.

Giants shown in Fleet Street, i. 34 ; Robert Hales, the "Norfolk Giant," iii. 39 ; O'Brian, the Irish Giant, iii. 46, 144, 168 ; iv. 84, 220, 221.

Giants, The, in Guildhall, i. 384, 386.

Gibbets, ii. 135 ; Hampstead, v. 448, 454 ; Blackheath, Shooter's Hill, vi. 234 ; Putney Heath, 497 ; Fulham Road, 515.

Gibbon, Edmund, i. 154 ; iii. 279 ; iv. 159, 164, 167, 442 ; vi. 494.

Gibbons, Grinling, i. 221, 250, 256, 530 ;

iii. 273, 369 ; v. 141, 569 ; vi. 153, 537.

Gibbon's Court, Clare Market ; theatre, iii. 41.

Gibbon's Tennis Court, iii. 43.

Gibbs, architect, iii. 152 ; iv. 430, 442.

Gibson, Right Hon. Milner, M.P. ; repeal of the Paper Duty, i. 52.

Giffard, Dr., i. 62.

Gifford, Lord, i. 80.

Gifford, William, iv. 25, 257.

Gill, Rev. Dr., Baptist Chapel, Carter Lane, vi. 106.

Gillray, caricaturist, iv. 167.

"Gilpin, John" ; Cowper's poem, v. 565.

Giltspur Street, ii. 485 ; the Compter, 487 ; its removal ; Pie Corner ; cooks' stalls ; termination of the Great Fire, 488.

Gipsies, vi. 263, 292, 293.

Gipsy Hill, Norwood, vi. 314.

Girdlers' Hall ; girdle-irons ; master's crown, ii. 238.

Girls' Home, iv. 458.

Gladstone, Mrs., Female Servants' Home, iv. 456.

Glass ; Vauxhall Plate Glassworks, vi. 424.

Glass painting, "Field of Cloth of Gold," iv. 471.

Glasshouse Street, Golden Square, iv. 237.

Gleichen, Count, iv. 443.

Glendinning's Nursery, vi. 562.

Glennie, Dr., his school at Dulwich ; Byron, vi. 296.

Globe Club, i. 61.

"Globe Permits," a bubble company, i. 532.

"Globe Tavern," Fleet Street, i. 61.

Globe Theatre, Bankside, vi. 40, 45 ; sign and motto ; boxes or "rooms ;" galleries ; Lord Chamberlain's Company ; King's players ; Shakespeare, *ib.* ; burnt down and rebuilt, 46, 47.

Globe Theatre, Wych Street, iii. 35.

"Globe, the Great," Leicester Square, iii. 170.

Gloucester, Eleanor, Duchess of, i. 25, 32, 239 ; iii. 433 ; v. 429.

Gloucester House ; Duke of Gloucester ; Earl of Elgin, iv. 286.

Gloucester, Humphrey, Duke of, vi. 165, 206.

Gloucester Place, Portman Square, iv. 412.

Gloucester Square, v. 186.

Glover, Richard, author of "Leonidas," ii. 40 ; iv. 25, 297.

Glue-makers, vi. 123.

"Goat and Compasses," v. 9.

"Goat in Boots" Tavern, v. 88.

Goat's Yard, Horselydown ; Benjamin Keach's meeting-house, vi. 110.

Gobelin tapestry, manufactured at Fulham, vi. 521.

Godfrey, Michael, founder of the Bank of England, i. 460.

Godfrey, Sir Edmundbury, iii. 92, 134, 153, 456 ; v. 287, 289, 290.

Godolphin School, vi. 534.

"God's Gift College," Dulwich. (*See* Dulwich.)

Godwin, Mary Woolstonecraft, ii. 490 ; iii. 539 ; v. 533 ; vi. 494.

Godwin, William, ii. 490 ; iii. 539.

Gog and Magog in Guildhall, i. 384. 386.

Gold, Light, called in, i. 467.
Gold refinery, Wood Street, i. 369.
"Golden Cross" Inn, Charing Cross, iii. 129.
"Golden Head," Leicester Square, iii. 167.
Golden Square, iv. 235, 236; its name; Dog's Fields; Windmill Fields; Pest-house, ib.; residents; statue of George II.; Childs, Lord Byron's servant, 237, 249.
Golder's Hill, Hampstead, v. 448.
Golding Lane, Whitecross Street; nursery for actors, ii. 224.
Goldsmid, Abraham, i. 485.
Goldsmith, Oliver, i. 29, 61, 62, 119, 120, 169, 171, 275, 418, 561; ii. 8, 271, 471, 476, 569; iii. 65, 69, 137, 275, 278, 429; iv. 53, 154, 232; v. 80, 166, 248, 459; vi. 40, 289, 455.
Goldsmiths, i. 453; their business as bankers; loans to Government, ib.; opposition to the Bank of England, 455, 456.
Goldsmiths' Company, i. 353; quarrels with tailors, 354; religious observances; livery, night-watch, and army, 356; trial of the pix; assay office; hall marks, 357; assay master; St. Dunstan's feast, 358; pageants; costume; apprentices punished, 359; "searches" for bad work, 360; New Hall, 361.
Goldsmiths' Company's Almshouses, v. 507.
Goldsmiths' Row, Cheapside; other trades there forbidden, i. 308, 339, 356.
Goldsmiths' Row, Hackney; "Hackney Buns," v. 507.
Gomm, Sir William, vi. 137.
Gondomar, Spanish Ambassador, ii. 519.
Goodge Street, iv. 472.
Goodman, Bishop of Gloucester, iii. 489.
Goodman's Fields, ii. 249.
Goodman's Fields Theatre; first appearance of Garrick, ii. 146.
Goodwin, Dr. Thomas; Fetter Lane Chapel, i. 100.
Goodwin, John, Puritan writer, ii. 244.
"Goose and Gridiron," St. Paul's Churchyard, i. 272.
"Gooseberry Fair," Spa Fields, ii. 302; i. 477.
"Goose-tree's" Club, iv. 136.
Gordon, Duchess of, iv. 129.
Gordon, Lord George; the Gordon Riots, i. 56, 165, 207, 363, 420; ii. 117, 275, 410, 446, 574; iii. 47, 212; iv. 53, 65, 124, 183, 239, 442, 493, 539, 554; v. 308, 365, 443; vi. 32, 65, 345, 375, 442.
Gordon Square; Catholic and Apostolic Church, iv. 572; University Hall, 573.
Gore House, Kensington, v. 118.
Goring House, iv. 260.
Gosling's Bank; original silver sign, i. 46.
Gospel Oaks; Gospel Oak Fields and Fair, Kentish Town, v. 316.
Gough, John, F.S.A., i. 20.
Gough Square, i. 118; Dr. Johnson and his Dictionary, ib.
Goulburn, Rev. Dr., Dean of Norwich, iv. 409.

Governesses' Benevolent Institution, iv. 450.
Gower, poet, iii. 308; vi. 21, 25, 26.
Gower Street and Upper Gower Street, iv. 567; Bannister; De Wint, ib.; University College, 568.
Gower Street Station, Metropolitan Railway, v. 226.
Gracechurch Street, ii. 174; herb market; St. Benet's Church; Bankes's horse; "Spread Eagle," ib.
Grafton, Duke of, and "Junius," iv. 306, 307, 308.
Grafton, Richard, the Bible printed by, i. 50.
Grafton Street, Bond Street; distinguished residents; Grafton Club; Junior Oxford and Cambridge Club, iv. 298.
Grafton Street East, iv. 570.
Graham, aëronaut, v. 310.
Grammont, Duc de, French Ambassador, iv. 199.
Granaries, ii. 180, 182, 183, 188.
Granby Street, v. 305.
Grand Junction Canal Company; Paddington Canal, v. 219.
Grand Junction Waterworks Company, v. 179.
Grand Surrey Canal Dock, vi. 140.
Grange Road, Bermondsey, vi. 122, 125.
"Grange, The," public-house, Carey Street, iii. 26, 31.
Grange Walk, Bermondsey, vi. 120.
Grant, Albert, iii. 171, 185; v. 125.
Grant, James, i. 64; Times newspaper statistics, 214.
Grant, Sir Francis, P.R.A., iii. 148.
Granville, Earl, iv. 170.
Graphic Club, iv. 570.
"Grasshopper" Bank, Pall Mall, iv. 137.
Grasshopper, Sir Thomas Gresham's crest, i. 495, 502, 506, 524, 525.
Gravel-pit Meeting-house, Hackney, v. 575.
Gravel Pits, Notting Hill, v. 178.
Gray, Stephen; his electrical discoveries, ii. 400.
Gray's Inn, ii. 553; Lord Gray of Wilton, 554; hall; tables given by Queen Elizabeth; chapel; library; gardens, 555; regulations, 556; costume; moots; revels, 558; plays; Prince of Purpoole's revel, 559; rebellious students; eminent members, 560-569; yearly rental, 569.
Gray's Inn Lane, ii. 550; eminent residents; the "Blue Lion," 552.
Great Bath Street, Coldbath Fields; Swedenborg, ii. 304.
Great Bell Yard, residence of Bloomfield, ii. 244.
Great Carter Lane, i. 302; "Bell" inn, ib.
Great College Street, Camden Town, v. 322.
Great College Street, Westminster, iv. 2.
Great Coram Street; Russell Institution, iv. 574.
Great Cumberland Place, iv. 407.
Great Dover Street, Southwark, vi. 523.
Great Eastern Railway; Depôt and works at Stratford, v. 573.
Great Exhibition of 1851, v. 28; French Exhibitions; Society of

Arts, ib.; the Prince Consort, 29; Royal Commission, 30; Paxton, 32; the building, 33, 34; State opening, 35; arrangements, 36; "Koh-i-noor," 38; Crystal Palace, Sydenham; Albert Memorial, ib.
Great Fire of London, 1666, i. 161, 191, 200, 226, 229, 294, 303, 348, 349, 350, 351, 566, 572; ii. 197; v. 135, 388; vi. 11, 55, 342.
Great George Street, Westminster, iv. 31; Wilkes; lying in state of Lord Byron, ib.; Institution of Civil Engineers, 32; National Portrait Gallery, ib.
Great James Street, Bedford Row, iv. 551.
Great Marlborough Street, iv. 241.
Great Marylebone Street; Leopold I., iv. 437.
Great Northern Railway Station, King's Cross, ii. 278.
Great Ormond Street, iv. 556; Powis House; the Great Seal stolen, 557; Working Men's College, 560; Hospital for Sick Children, 561, 562.
Great Peter Street, Westminster, iv. 38.
Great Portland Street, iv. 456; its charitable institutions; St. Paul's Church; Jewish Synagogue, 457, 458.
Great Queen Street, iii. 209-212; fashionable and eminent residents, ib.; Paulet House, 210; Cherbury House; Conway House, ib.; the Gordon Riots, 212; Home for Destitute Boys, ib.; Freemasons' Hall and Tavern, 213; Wesleyan Chapel, ib.; Wyman's printing-office, 214, 215.
Great Russell Street, Bloomsbury, iv. 483; eminent residents, 489.
Great Seal, iv. 6, 556.
Great Smith Street, Westminster, iv. 36; Free Library; Baths and Washhouses, ib.
Great Stanhope Street, Park Lane, iv. 368; residents; Stanhope Gate, ib.
Great Suffolk Street, Southwark, vi. 63; "Dirty Lane;" "Moonrakers'" public-house, ib.
Great Titchfield Street; eminent residents, iv. 461.
Great Tower Street, ii. 98; Earl of Rochester; Peter the Great; "Czar of Muscovy" Tavern, 99.
Great Warner Street, Clerkenwell, ii. 335.
Great Western Railway, v. 223; I. K. Brunel; Box Tunnel; Paddington Terminus and Hotel, ib.
Great Windmill Street, iv. 236.
"Grecian Coffee House," Strand, iii. 65.
Grecian Theatre, City Road, ii. 227.
Greek merchants, ii. 182.
Greek residents in London; statistics, vi. 570.
Greek Street, "Grig Street," iii. 177.
Green, Charles, aëronaut, vi. 464.
Green, "Paddy"; Evans's Hotel, iii. 254.
Greenacre, murderer, ii. 455; vi. 272.
Greenberry Hill; Barrow Hill, v. 287.
Green-coat School, Camberwell, vi. 278.
Green-coat School, Westminster, iv. 10.

"Green Dragon," in Fleet Street, i. 55.

Green Lettuce Lane, ii. 28.

"Green Man and Still," Oxford Street, iv. 245.

"Green Man" Tavern, Dulwich, vi. 293.

Green Park, iv. 177.

Green Ribbon Club, i. 45.

Green Street, Grosvenor Square, iv. 374.

Green Street, Leicester Square, iii. 161.

Green Walk, Southwark, vi. 41.

Green Yard, Cripplegate, ii. 239.

Greenwich, vi. 164; etymology; Danish invasions, ib. ; murder of Archbishop Alphege, 165 ; East and West Coombe ; Danish encampments ; the manor ; Humphrey, Duke of Gloucester ; Pleazaunce, or Placentia ; deer, ib. ; Grey Friars' convent, 166 ; birthplace of Henry VIII. ; Catherine of Arragon ; jousts ; festivities ; masquerade, ib. ; tilt-yard, 168 ; banqueting-room ; Anne Boleyn ; birth of Queen Elizabeth, ib. ; Anne of Cleves, 170 ; Will Somers, 171 ; death of Edward VI. ; Mary and Elizabeth, 170—173 ; palace and park ordered to be sold, 174 ; new buildings, 176 ; palace dedicated to disabled seamen, ib. ; Parliamentary representation, 191 ; assizes ; population and progress ; church of St. Alphege, ib. ; chapel for Huguenot refugees, 193 ; Queen Elizabeth's college ; Jubilee almshouses, 194 ; baths and washhouses, 195 ; public buildings, ib. ; Royal Thames Yacht Club, 196 ; Admiralty barge, 197 ; royal visits ; royal state barge ; "Ship ;" "Crown and Anchor ;" "Trafalgar," ib. ; ministerial fish dinner ; whitebait, 197—200 ; dinner to Dickens, 201 ; "touting ;" tea and shrimps ; fairs, ib., 203, 205 ; hill ; park, and prospect, 206, 207 ; deer, 208, 210 ; ranger's lodge, 212 ; Chesterfield House ; Montagu House ; barrows, ib.

Greenwich Hospital, iii. 367 ; vi. 177 ; painted hall, vi. 177 ; chapel, 179 ; lying in state and funeral of Nelson, 182 ; management and funds, 183 ; disestablished, 184 ; Royal Naval College, 186 ; Naval Museum, ib. ; Nelson and Franklin relics, 187 ; Drake's astrolabe ; Seamen's Hospital Society's infirmary, ib. ; Dreadnought, 188 ; Royal Naval School, ib. ; officers of the establishment, 189.

Greenwich ; London and Greenwich Railway, vi. 98.

Greenwich Observatory. (See Royal Observatory.

Gregory, Barnard, v. 502.

Grenades ; "Granados," vi. 207.

Grenadier Guards. (See Guards, Horse and Foot.)

Grenville, Rt. Hon. Thos. ; his library, iv. 513.

Gresham Club House, i. 524.

Gresham College and Lectures, i. 375 ; ii. 159, 160.

Gresham Committee, i, 381.

Gresham, Sir Richard, Lord Mayor, i. 376, 40., 494 ; ii. 147.

Gresham, Sir Thomas, i. 494, 498, 524, 525 ; ii. 104, 243 ; iii. 154, 213.

Gresham House, Bishopsgate, i. 525.

Gresham Street ; "Swan with Two Necks," i. 374.

Greville, Colonel, iv. 473.

Greville Street, Hatton Garden, ii. 549.

Grey Coat School, Westminster, iv. 11.

Grey, Earl, iii. 388, 389.

Grey, Lady Jane, ii. 66.

"Greyhound" Tavern, Dulwich, vi. 296.

Griffin, Prince of Wales, ii. 64.

Griffiths, Captain, "Honour and Glory Griffiths," ii. 242.

Grillon's Hotel, Grillon's Club, iv. 295.

Grimaldi, father of the clown, vi. 417.

Grimaldi, grandfather of the clown, vi. 369.

Grimaldi, Joseph, clown, ii. 279, 285 ; iii. 33 ; vi. 405.

Grinning-matches, vi. 344, 389.

Grinning through horses' collars, v.503.

Grocers' Alley, Poultry, i. 419.

Grocers' Company, i. 431 ; Pepperers, history of the Company, ib. ; hall and garden, 432 ; eminent "Grocers," 433 ; charities, 434.

Grocers in London ; statistics, vi. 570.

Grose, Francis, Richmond Herald, i. 298.

Grosvenor and Scrope ; heraldic controversy, i. 347.

Grosvenor Canal, v. 41.

Grosvenor family, v. 3.

Grosvenor Gate, Hyde Park, iv. 395.

Grosvenor Hotel, v. 41.

Grosvenor House, iv. 370 ; Duke of Westminster ; Grosvenor Gallery, ib. ; the family of Grosvenor, 371.

Grosvenor Place ; distinguished residents, v. 8.

Grosvenor Row, v. 9.

Grosvenor Square, iv. 338 ; architecture of the houses ; Pope ; "Grosvenor Buildings ;" Sir Richard Grosvenor, ib. ; statue of George I., 339 ; link-extinguishers ; link-boys ; oil-lamps and gas ; distinguished residents, ib.

Grote, George, "History of Greece," iv. 310.

"Grove House" tea-gardens, Camberwell, vi. 281.

Grub Street. (See Milton Street.)

Guards' Club, iv. 143.

Guards, Horse and Foot, iv. 47 ; billeted at inns ; Macaulay ; Life Guards, Grenadiers, Blues, Dragoons, ib.

Guards' Hospital, Westminster, iv. 11.

"Guild of Literature and Art," iv. 279.

Guildford, Lord Keeper, i. 38, 83.

Guildford Street, iv. 563.

Guildhall, i. 383 ; old hall, Aldermanbury ; erection of the present hall, ib. ; the Great Fire ; "improvements" by Dance, 384 ; restoration by Horace Jones, 385 ; crypt ; figures of Gog and Magog, 386 ; monuments, 387, 388 ; law courts, 389 ; Common Council Room, 390 ; Guildhall Chapel ; Library and Museum, 392 ; historical notes, 393, 394, 395.

Guineas first coined, ii. 104.

Guizot, M., iv. 308.

"Gull's Horn Book," i. 276.

Gulliver, Lemuel, vi. 138.

Gully, John, M.P. and ex-pugilist, iii. 26.

"Gun" Tavern, Pimlico, v. 45.

Gundulf, Bishop of Rochester, ii. 60 ; iii. 213.

Gunning, The Misses, iv. 348.

Gunpowder Alley, Shoe Lane, i. 126, 128 ; Lovelace ; Lilly, the astrologer, 128.

Gunpowder explosions : Great Tower Street, ii. 108 ; Regent's Canal, v. 268.

Gunpowder Plot, i. 245 ; iii. 10, 548, 563, 566 ; vi. 28.

Gurney, Baron, i. 178.

Gurney, Sir Goldsworthy, v. 299, 300.

Gurwood, Col., his monument, ii. 93.

Guthrie, historian, iv. 426.

Guthrie, Miss, "The Old Houses of Putney," vi. 489.

Gutter Lane, Cheapside, i. 374.

Guy's Hospital, vi. 93 ; biographical notice of Thomas Guy, i. 474 ; ii. 172 ; the building, vi. 94 ; statue of the founder ; his tomb ; chapel ; medical staff and school ; theatre, 95 ; museum and benefactions, 96, 110.

Gwydyr House, Whitehall, iii. 377.

Gwyn, architect, i. 255.

Gwynne, Nell, ii. 238, 239, 297 ; iii. 27, 38, 45, 153, 209, 219, 358 ; iv. 125, 144, 176 ; v. 70, 395 ; vi. 287, 289, 522, 525.

Gye, Frederick ; Royal Italian Opera House, iii. 236 ; Floral Hall, 251.

Gyze, George, Steel Yard merchant, ii. 33.

H.

"Ha ! ha !" in Kensington Gardens, v. 154.

Haberdashers' Company, Hall and School, i. 371 ; v. 525.

Hacket, Bishop, rector of St. Andrew's, Holborn, ii. 512.

Hackett, Miss ; restoration of Crosby Hall, ii. 157.

Hackman, murderer of Miss Ray, iii. 260 ; v. 193.

Hackluyt, iii. 476.

Hackney, v. 510; etymology ; manor, the property of the Knights Templars, ib. ; Temple Mills, 512 ; hamlets in the parish ; described by Strype ; houses of the gentry and nobility, ib. ; growth of the population, 513 ; Parliamentary representation ; Well Street ; Hackney College ; Monger's Almshouses ; House of Dr. Frampton ; St. John's Priory ; Mare Street ; Hackney a centre of Nonconformity ; Roman Catholic Church, ib. ; "Flying Horse" Tavern, 514; "Elizabeth Fry's Refuge ;" Dr. Spurstowe's Almshouses ; Town Hall ; Great Eastern Railway ; Tower House ; Barber's Barn ; Loddidge's Nursery, ib. ; watercress beds, 515 ; Gravel-pit Meeting-house ; Church House, ib. ; old parish church and burial ground, 515—518 ; new church of St. John, 518 ; "Black and White House," 519 ; boarding schools ; Sutton Place ; "Mermaid" Tavern ; "Ward's Corner ;" Templar's House, *ib.;* Brooke House ; distinguished residents, 520 ; City of London Union, 521 ; asylums, 522 ; "Hackney" horses and coaches, 524.

"Hackney Buns," v. 507.

Hackney Church, v. 515 ; church taken down ; the old tower left, 516 ; Rowe Chapel, 517 ; bells and burial ground ; new church, 519.

Hackney coaches, iii. 81, 333, 334.

Hackney coach-stands, iii. 243.

Hackney Common, v. 509.

"Hackney" horses and coaches ; etymology of "hackney," v. 524.

Hackney Marsh, v. 521.

Hackney Road, v. 508.

Haggarty and Holloway executed, ii. 453.

Haggerston, v. 506 ; "Hergotstane ;" St. Chad's Church, 507 ; Brunswick Square ; St. Mary's Church ; Church Association ; Shoreditch Almshouses ; Goldsmiths' Row ("Mutton Lane") ; "Cat and Mutton" Public-house, *ib.*

Haines, Joe, ii. 520.

Hair of Milton, Shelley, Keats, Johnson, Swift, Lamb, vi. 548.

Hale, Archdeacon ; antiquities of the Charterhouse, ii. 388.

Hale House, Brompton, v. 100.

Hale, Sir Matthew ; Appeal Court after the Great Fire, i. 93.

Hales, Robert, the "Norfolk Giant," iii. 39.

"Half-and-half ;" beer, iv. 485.

Half-moon Street and Half-moon Alley, Bishopsgate, ii. 153, 158.

Half-moon Street, Piccadilly, iv. 291.

"Half-Moon" Tavern, Dulwich, vi. 296.

"Half-Moon" Tavern, Piccadilly, iv. 291.

Half Nichols Street, Bethnal Green, ii. 148.

Halford, Sir Henry, iv. 351.

Halfpenny Alley, vi. 114.

Halfpenny Hatch, Bermondsey, vi. 133, 136.

Halfpenny Hatch, Lambeth, vi. 392.

Halfpenny Hatch, Tottenham Court Road, iv. 470.

"Halfway House," Kensington, v. 122.

"Halfway House," Rotherhithe, vi. 135.

"Halfway House" to Tyburn, iii. 200.

Halifax, Earl of, iii. 83.

Halkin Street, v. 11.

Hall, Bishop, ii. 385, 566.

Hall, Jacob, rope-dancer, i. 405 ; vi. 59.

Hall of Commerce, Threadneedle Street, i. 536.

Hall, Rev. Newman, ii. 274 ; vi. 362.

Hall, S. C. and Mrs., vi. 527.

Halley, astronomer, ii. 268 ; v. 506 ; vi. 215, 244.

Hamilton, Duchess of (Elizabeth Gunning), iv. 348, 350.

Hamilton, Duke of ; duel, iv. 319.

Hamilton, Emma, Lady, iii. 455 ; iv. 254, 292, 321, 329, 430, 446 ; v. 111, 158.

Hamilton, Lady Archibald, iv. 88.

Hamilton, James, ranger of Hyde Park, iv. 378.

Hamilton, W. G., M.P., iv. 373.

Hamilton Place, iv. 291 ; Col. Hamilton ; Duke of Wellington, *ib.*

Hamilton Terrace, St. John's Wood ; St. Mark's Church, v. 251.

Hamlet, silversmith and jeweller, iii. 173 ; iv. 232, 280, 461.

Hammersmith, vi. 529 ; ecclesiastical division from Fulham, *ib.* ; boundary ditch, 530 ; King Street ; railway stations ; "Bell and Anchor" and "Red Cow" Inns ; Nazareth House ; the "Little Sisters of the Poor," *ib.;* Benedictine Convent, 531-2 ; King Street East, 533 ; West London Hospital ; Broadway ; Brook Green ; nursery gardens ; Millet's Garden ; Lee's nursery, *ib.* ; Dartmouth Road, 534 ; Ravenscourt Park, 536 ; Palliswick manor and the manor-house ; Starch Green ; old pump ; Webb's Lane ; Queen Street ; St. Paul's Parish Church ; church injured by the Puritans, *ib.* ; restored, 537 ; altar-piece ; churchyard ; trees and monuments ; Sir Nicholas Crispe ; his heart enshrined in the church, *ib.* ; Edward Latymer, 538 ; Queen Street, 539 ; Butterwick Manor-house ; Earl of Mulgrave, *ib.* ; Convent of the Good Shepherd ; Asylum for Penitent Women, 540 ; Sussex House ; Duke of Sussex, 542 ; private lunatic asylum ; Mrs. Fry, 543 ; Brandenburgh House, 544 ; Hammersmith Suspension Bridge ; Upper and Lower Malls ; High Bridge ; the "Doves' Coffee-house," *ib.* ; the residents ; the Terrace, 545 ; St. Peter's Church ; the Hammersmith Ghost, 548.

Hampstead, v. 438 ; etymology, *ib.;* manor granted to Abbot of Westminster by Ethelred, 440 ; chapelry to Hendon ; made a separate benefice ; descent of the manor ; Sir S. Maryon-Wilson, Bart.; Hot Gospellers ; hollow elm, *ib.;* Caen Wood Towers, 441 ; Dufferin Lodge ; Caen (or Ken-Wood), seat of the Earl of Mansfield, 441—443 ; Hampstead Ponds, 443 ; source of the Fleet River, 444 ; disputes on "water privileges;" Bishop's Wood ; Mutton Wood, *ib.;* "Spaniards'" Tavern ; view from the grounds, 445 ; New Georgia, 446 ; Heath House, 448 ; gibbet ; highwaymen ; North End ; Golder's Hill, *ib.;* "Bell and Bush," 449 ; the Heath ; its landscape, *ib.;* Sir Thomas M. Wilson's claims, 452 ; Metropolitan Commons' Act ; manorial rights purchased by Board of Works, *ib.;* donkeys and amusements, 453 ; "The Hill ;" "stage-coaches," 454 ; "Jack Straw's Castle," 455 ; race-course ; suicide of John Sadleir, M.P., *ib.;* deodands, 456 ; Vale of Health ; South Villa, 457 ; poets and painters, 458 ; Judge's Walk, 459 ; "Clarissa Harlowe," 460, 461 ; the town ; High Street, 462 ; chapels, 464 ; "Hollybush" Inn, 465 ; "The Clock House," 466 ; Fire Brigade Station, 467 ; Old Hampstead ; present "Flask" Tavern ; Flask Walk ; source of the Fleet River ; "Wells Tavern ;" Well Walk, *ib.;* chalybeate springs and Spa, 468 ; concerts at the

"Wells," 470 ; irregular marriages ; Zion Chapel, *ib.* ; "Mother Huff," or "Mother Damnable," 471 ; raffling-shops ; Dr. Soame, *ib.;* geological formation, 472 ; Church Row and distinguished residents, 473 ; Reformatory School for Girls, 477 ; old parish church, 478 ; old and new churchyards, 482 ; Vane House ; Soldiers' Daughters' Home, 484 ; "Red Lion" Inn, 485 ; the Chicken House ; St. Elizabeth's Home ; Presbyterian Chapel, *ib.;* Rosslyn House and Earl of Rosslyn, 488 ; Belsize Lane, 490 ; Downshire Hill ; St. John's Chapel ; Hampstead Green ; Bartram's Park ; Sir Rowland Hill ; Kenmore House ; St. Stephen's Church, *ib.* ; the "New Spa ;" Fever Hospital ; Town Hall ; "Load of Hay," 491 ; Sir R. Steele's Cottage, *ib.;* Belsize Park ; manor of Belsize, 494 ; residence of Lord Wotton, 495 ; races, music, and hunting, 496 ; murder of Delarue by Hocker, 497 ; St. Peter's Church, 499 ; Shepherd's Well, Shepherd's Fields, and Conduit Fields, 500 ; Finchley Road ; "North Star" Tavern ; West End Lane ; Frognal, 501 ; Frognal Priory, 502 ; West End and West End Fair, 503 ; Child's Hill ; death-rate ; population ; prophecies of earthquakes, 504.

Hampstead Church ; incumbents, v. 479.

Hampstead Ponds, v. 443.

Hampstead Road, v. 303-308 ; Tolmer's Square ; Sol's Arms ; Sol's Row ; Stanhope Street, Granby Street ; Mornington Crescent ; "Old King's Head ;" Drummond Street ; St. James's Church ; Rev. Henry Stebbing ; St. Pancras Female Charity School ; Ampthill Square, *ib.;* Harrington Square, 309.

Hand Alley, Bishopsgate, a burial-place during the Plague, ii. 165.

"Hand and Pen," Fleet Ditch, and other "marrying houses," ii. 411.

Hand Court, Holborn, iv. 552.

Handel Festivals : Westminster Abbey ; St. Margaret's Church ; Banqueting House ; Whitehall ; Crystal Palace, iii. 407, 408.

Handel, George Frederick, i. 231, 269 ; ii. 334 ; iii. 229, 310, 428 ; iv. 104, 179, 211, 245, 263, 343, 435 ; v. 363, 364 ; vi. 449.

"Hand-in-Hand" Tavern, iv. 552.

"Hand" Inn, Southwark, vi. 74.

Hand, Mrs. ; Chelsea Bun House v. 69.

Hanger, George, Lord Coleraine, iv. 136 ; v. 294, 351 ; vi. 68.

Hanging in Chains. (*See* Gibbets.)

"Hangman's Gains," in the Tower precincts, ii. 99.

Hanover Chapel, Peckham, vi. 290.

Hanover Court, Long Acre ; Taylor, the "water-poet," iii. 271.

Hanover, King of, iv. 70, 113.

Hanover Square, iv. 314 ; statue of Pitt, 315 ; Harewood House ; Earl of Harewood ; "Beau" Lascelles ; other eminent residents, *ib.* ; Zoological Society, 316 ; Royal Agricultural Society ; College of Chemistry ;

Oriental Club ; Arts Club ; Hanover Club ; Hanover Square Rooms, *ib.*; the "Mill Field," 317 ; Sir John Gallini ; Concerts of Ancient Music ; George III. ; Philharmonic Concerts ; Brummell and George IV., *ib.*; Miss Linwood, 318 ; Carnarvon House, 320.

Hans Place, Chelsea, v. 99.

Hanway, Jonas, iv. 470, 548 ; vi. 348.

Hanway Street ; "Hanover Yard," iv. 470 ; curiosity shops ; old china ; centenarians, *ib.*

"Happy Man's Row," Pentonville, ii. 286.

Harborough, Earl of, attacked in Piccadilly, iv. 290.

Hardham, John, tobacconist, i. 69.

Hardicanute, vi. 332, 383, 386.

Hardwick, Thomas, Philip, and P. C., architects, iv. 430 ; vi. 443, 473.

Hardwicke, Lord Chancellor, ii. 548.

Hardy, Sir Thomas Duffus, i. 101.

Hardy, Thomas ; shop in Fleet Street, i. 53.

"Hare and Hounds" public-house, St. Giles's, iv. 488.

Hare Court Buildings, i. 172.

Hare Place, Fleet Street, i. 137.

Hare, Sir Nicholas ; Hare Court, Temple, i. 167.

Harewood House, iv. 315.

Harewood Square, v. 260.

"Haringey ;" Hornsey. (*See* Hornsey.)

Harley, Earl of Oxford ; Harleian MSS., iv. 449, 490.

Harley Fields, iv. 440, 442.

Harley, Lady Margaret ; Prior's "Lovely Peggy," iv. 442.

Harley, Rt. Hon. Thomas, Lord Mayor, i. 408.

Harley Street, iv. 449 ; Harley, Earl of Oxford ; Harleian MSS. ; Lord and Lady Walsingham ; other residents, *ib.*; Queen's College for Ladies ; Governesses' Benevolent Institution, 450.

Harmer, Alderman, i. 59, 213.

Harmer's Almshouses, v. 525.

Harmonic Institution, iv. 244.

Harold ; his coronation, ii. 401.

Harp Alley, Shoe Lane, i. 129 ; Vandertout's shop-signs ; exhibition by Hogarth, *ib.*

"Harp" Tavern, Russell Street ; "City of Lushington" Society, iii. 279.

Harpur, Sir William, Lord Mayor, iv. 323, 551.

Harpur Street, iv. 551.

Harrington, James, ii. 75 ; iv. 48 ; Rota Club, iii. 538.

Harrington Square, v. 309.

"Harris, Cat," iv. 223.

Harris, Henry, manager of Covent Garden Theatre, iii. 230, 233.

Harris, the "Flying Highwayman ;" his execution, iv. 448.

Harrison, W. H. ; Operas at Covent Garden Theatre ; iii. 237.

Harrowby, Earl of ; Cato Street conspiracy, iv. 340, 411.

Hart Street, Bloomsbury ; St. George's Church, iv. 544.

Hart Street, Covent Garden, iii. 271 ; the "White Hart ;" Charles Macklin, *ib.*

Hart, tragedian, i. 197.

Hartley, David ; Fire-proof House and Column, Putney, vi. 497.

Hartopp, Lady, v. 534, 541.

Hartshorn Lane, Charing Cross, iii. 159.

Harvey, Dr., i. 285, 303 ; ii. 360 ; iii. 143.

Hastings, Warren, iii. 476, 554.

Hatcham ; the Church ; ritualistic practices and disturbances, vi. 247, 248.

Hatchett's Hotel, iv. 261.

Hatfield, John ; St. Paul's clock striking thirteen, iii. 537.

Hatherley, Lord, i. 413.

Hat-making, vi. 123.

Hat-manufacture, Bermondsey, vi. 75.

Hatton Garden ; Wycherley and the Countess of Drogheda, ii. 543.

Hatton, Sir Christopher, i. 159 ; ii. 518, 519 ; iii. 446 ; vi. 239.

Hatton, the "strange" Lady, wife of Sir Edward Coke, ii. 519.

Havelock, General Sir Henry, ii. 404 ; iii. 142.

Haverstock Hill, "Adelaide" Tavern, v. 296 ; Sir R. Steele, 491.

Hawes, Dr. William, founder of the Humane Society, ii. 263.

"Hawkabites ;" members of dissolute clubs, iv. 57, 166.

Hawking in London, ii. 251 ; iv. 48 ; v. 3.

Hawkins, Sir John, ii. 322 ; iv. 34 ; v. 426.

Hawksmoor, architect, i. 527 ; iv. 544.

Hawkstone Hall, vi. 362.

Haydn, vi. 375.

Haydon, B. R., iv. 173, 242, 302 ; v. 458, 461 ; vi. 69, 209.

Hayes, Catherine, murderess, iv. 245 ; v. 191.

Hayes Mews ; "Running Footman" Tavern, iv. 334.

Hay Hill, iv. 275, 289, 333.

Hayman, pictures at Vauxhall Gardens, vi. 452, 465.

Haymarket at Broadway, Westminster, iv. 20.

Haymarket, The, iii. 148 ; iv. 207 ; oxen, sheep ; the old market for hay and straw, 216 ; removal to Cumberland Market, 217 ; riots ; Addison, 218 ; "Tiddy Doll," the pieman, 219 ; Wolcott and Madame Mara ; Michael Kelly, *ib.*; Sir John Coventry ; Baretti ; "Mrs. Midnight's Oratory ;" "Cats' Opera," 220 ; exhibitions, 221.

Haymarket Theatre, iv. 221 ; built by John Potter, *ib.*; French comedies ; the "Little Theatre in the Haymarket " pulled down and rebuilt ; Henry Fielding ; Sir Robert Walpole ; Theophilus Cibber, 222 ; Foote ; "Cat Harris," 223 ; riot ; "Romeo" Coates, 224 ; George Colman (the Elder and Younger) ; fatal accident ; present theatre ; designed by Nash, 225 ; "Paul Pry," Benjamin Webster ; J. B. Buckstone, 226.

Haynau, Marshal, vi. 39.

Haynes, John, restored after execution, v. 196.

Hayter, Sir George, v. 260.

Hayward, William ; under-sexton ; the plague-pit, ii. 245.

Haywood, W., C.E., ii. 530 ; street subways ; Holborn Viaduct, v. 241, 242.

Hazard-playing at Court, iv. 153, 158, 160.

Hazelville Road, Highgate, v. 395.

Hazlitt, William, i. 65, 83, 84, 85, 87, 88, 135 ; ii. 275 ; iii. 183, 194 ; iv. 22, 260.

Head of Cromwell. (*See* Cromwell, Oliver.)

Heads of traitors on Temple Bar, i. 27—29, 37, 42 ; on London Bridge, ii. 10, 11, 13, 15, 16 ; vi. 10, 11.

Heath, Archbishop ; York House, iii. 107.

Heath House, Hampstead, v. 448.

Heath Street Chapel, Hampstead, v. 464.

"Heaton's Folly ;" Nunhead, vi. 291 ; Camberwell, 292.

"Heaven" Tavern, Westminster Hall, iii. 559.

"Heavy Hill " (Holborn Hill), ii. 529.

Heber, Richard, M.P., his library, v. 48.

"Hectors," members of dissolute clubs, iv. 57, 166.

Heddon Street, iv. 311.

Hedge Lane, iv. 207, 231.

Heidigger, Master of the Revels, iv. 359.

"Hell " Coffee House, Westminster Hall, iii. 558.

Hell-Fire Club, i. 410.

"Hells ;" gambling-houses and clubs. (*See* Gambling.)

Hemans, Felicia, iii. 154.

Hemp's sponging-house, Shire Lane, i. 74.

Henderson as *Falstaff*, ii. 263.

Hengler's circus, iv. 243.

Henley, Rev. John ("Orator"), iii. 41.

Henrietta-Maria, Queen of Charles I., i. 317 ; iii. 90 ; iv. 106, 108, 210 ; v. 200 ; vi. 152, 173.

Henrietta Street, Cavendish Square, iv. 443 ; Countess of Mornington ; Theed, sculptor ; Count Gleichen, *ib.*

Henrietta Street, Covent Garden, iii. 262.

Henry I., i. 237.

Henry III., i. 238 ; ii. 60 ; iii. 397, 431, 432, 436, 441, 524 ; vi. 237.

Henry IV., vi. 21, 165, 225, 238.

Henry V., ii. 11, 12, 101, 560 ; iii. 441 ; iv. 514 ; vi. 9, 225.

Henry VI., i. 240 ; iii. 495 ; vi. 10, 225, 238.

Henry VII., i. 241, 536 ; ii. 520 ; iii. 96 ; v. 429.

Henry VII.'s Chapel, Westminster ; described ; its cost, iii. 399, 434 ; communion-table ; tombs of the Dukes of Buckingham, ; tomb of Henry VII. and his queen, 436 ; other royal tombs, 437—444 ; Oliver Cromwell's burial, 437, 439, 440.

Henry VIII., i. 45, 190, 200, 242, 284, 314, 380 ; ii. 84, 117, 251, 364, 520 ; iii. 339, 375, 404, 496 ; iv. 232, 376, 510 ; v. 20, 56, 139, 426, 531, 537 ; vi. 88, 166, 226, 239, 352, 353, 356.

Henslowe, vi. 297.

Hentzner's account of the Tower armouries, ii. 81.

Heralds' College, i. 294 ; at Cold Harbour House, at Ronceval Priory, at Derby House, St. Bennet's Hill ; burnt in the Great Fire, *ib.*; rebuilt, 296 ; hall, library, and search-room ; kings-at-arms, heralds, and pursuivants ; duties of heralds ; armorial bearings ; office of Garter King, *ib.*;

heraldic courts, 297; visitations, degradation of knights; Earl Marshal's court; heralds' fees; anecdotes of heralds, *ib.*; Oldys, 298; heralds' messengers, 300; knight-riders; queen's messengers; library of the college, *ib.*

Herbert Hospital, Shooter's Hill, vi. 236.

Herbert, J. R., R.A., v. 477.

Herbert of Cherbury, Lord, i. 347; iii. 332.

Herbert of Lea, Lord; statue of, iv. 129.

"Hercules" Inn and Gardens, Lambeth; Hercules Buildings, vi. 389.

"Hercules Pillars," Fleet Street, i. 50.

"Hercules Pillars" Tavern; site of Apsley House, iv. 287.

Her Majesty's Theatre, iv. 209, 212; introduction of Italian opera, 209; Sir John Vanbrugh, 210; Congreve; Valentini; masquerades, *ib.*; Farinelli, 211; burnt down in 1789, *ib.*; Novosielski, architect; Braham; Catalini, 212; lady patronesses, 213; costume; reconstructed in 1818; Nash and Repton; Veluti; Pasta; Sontag; Grisi; Rubini; Tamburini; Lablache; Mario; "Omnibus" row; Laporte, *ib.*; Lumley, 214; Jenny Lind; Sims Reeves; Catharine Hayes; Titiens, *ib.*; Piccolomini, 215, 218; E. T. Smith; Mapleson; Christine Nilsson; burnt down, 1867; rebuilt; Moody and Sankey's religious services, *ib.*

Hermes Hill; Dr. de Valangin; William Huntington, "Sinner Saved," ii. 284.

Hermitage and Hermits, Highgate, v. 419.

Hermitage, The, Highgate; George IV.; Sir Wallis Porter, v. 412.

Hermit's Hill, Westminster, iv. 21.

Herne Hill, Camberwell, vi. 269.

Heron family, v. 530.

Herons, vi. 269.

Herrick, Robert, ii. 191, 542.

Hertford House, Piccadilly, iv. 285.

Hertford, Marquis and Marchioness, iv. 331, 424; v. 267.

Hertford Street, Mayfair; "Dog and Duck" public-house, iv. 352.

"Hertner's Eupyrion," i. 123.

Hervey, Lady, "the fair Lepel," iv. 170.

Hervey, Lord, iv. 178.

Hewet, Sir William, Lord Mayor; his child's life saved by his apprentice, i. 9, 401.

"Heydock's Ordinary," iii. 64.

Heywood, John, dramatist, v. 56.

Heywood, Thomas; "Fortune by Land and Sea;" execution of pirates, ii. 135.

Hickes, Dr., author of the "Thesaurus," ii. 110, 112.

Hicks, Anne; apple-stall, Hyde Park, iv. 404.

Hicks, Sir Baptist; Hicks's Hall, i. 352, 382; ii. 321, 322; v. 130, 440; the hall pulled down, ii. 322.

Hickman's Folly, Dockhead, vi. 116.

Highbury, ii. 273, 274; Knights Hospitallers; Wat Tyler; "Jack Straw's Castle;" conduit-heads; eminent residents, 273; Highbury Barn

Tavern *ib.*; charity dinners; Highbury Society; Cream Hall; Independent College, 274.

High Cross, Tottenham, v. 551.

Highgate, v. 389; extent and population; height above the Thames; forest and game; the High Gate; toll, *ib.*; "Gate House" Tavern, 391; healthiness of the district, *ib.*; Highgate Hill, 392; Roman Catholic schools, 393; St. Joseph's Retreat; new monastery; the "Black Dog," *ib.*; Highgate Infirmary, 394; Sick Asylum; "Old Crown" Tavern; Hornsey Lane; Winchester Hall; Highgate Archway, *ib.*; "Woodman" Inn, 395; Alexandra Orphanage; Aged Pilgrims' Friend Asylum, Lauderdale House; Convalescent Home to St Bartholomew's Hospital, 395, 396; house of Andrew Marvell, 398; Cromwell House, 400; Ireton, 401; Convalescent Hospital for Sick Children; Arundel House; Earls of Arundel; Cornwallis family; Queen Elizabeth; James I., *ib.*; Arabella Stuart, v. 402; death of Lord Bacon, 404; Fairseat, residence of Sir Sydney Waterlow, 405; Swaine's Lane and Traitor's Hill, *ib.*; Highgate Cemetery, 406; interments, 407; old "Mansion House," 410; Sir William Ashurst, Lord Mayor; Millfield Lane; Ivy Cottage, residence of Charles Mathews the elder, *ib.*; Holly Lodge; Lady Burdett-Coutts; Holly Village, 411; Highgate Ponds, 412; "Fox and Crown" Inn; Queen Victoria in danger; William and Mary Howitt; the Hermitage; Nelson's tree, *ib.*; taverns, 413; "swearing on the horns," 413—418; old Chapel and Free School, 418; Hermitage, 419; new School and Chapel, 422; Southwood Lane Almshouses; Baptist Chapel; Park House; London Diocesan Penitentiary; St. Michael's Church; monument to Coleridge, *ib.*; distinguished residents in Highgate, 423, 424; Highgate Green, or Grove, 425; Church House, 426; Literary Institute; Forest of Middlesex, *ib.*; Highgate Wood, 428.

Highgate Cemetery, v. 406; London Cemetery Company; S. Geary, architect; Ramsey, landscape-gardener; site and grounds; chapel; Egyptian avenue, *ib.*; interments of distinguished individuals, 407.

Highgate Free School and Chapel, v. 418; Chapel in the 14th century, 419; Bishop Braybrooke; hermits and hermitage; chapel granted to Sir Roger Cholmeley's grammar school; Bishops Grindal and Sandys; the old school, *ib.*; repairs and enlargements, 420; monuments; ministers, *ib.*; tomb of Coleridge, 421; new school-house and chapel, 422.

Highgate Ponds, v. 443.

High Gate, Westminster, iv. 26.

Highlander, The, a tobacconist's sign, iv. 233.

Highwaymen, ii. 257, 275, 448, 550; iv. 16, 20, 244, 249, 290, 297, 333, 398, 408, 435, 440, 455, 477, 489,

550; v. 2, 17, 21, 46, 86, 135, 189, 195, 228, 320, 381, 448, 524; vi. 296, 518, 533.

Hill, Emery; Almshouses and School, Westminster, iv. 10.

Hill, Rev. Rowland, vi. 71; Surrey Chapel, 374—380.

Hill, Sir John; Bayswater; essences, balms, and tinctures, v. 185.

Hill, Sir Rowland; Penny Postage, ii. 212; v. 490.

Hill Street, Berkeley Square, iv. 334; Lord Lyttelton; other distinguished residents; Mrs. Montagu; the "Blue Stocking Club," *ib.*

Hill Street, Peckham, vi. 286.

Hill, Thomas; biographical sketch, vi. 305; sale of his library, 307.

Hilton's picture at St. Michael's Paternoster Royal, ii. 27.

Hind, J. R.; observatory, Regent's Park, v. 268.

Hinde Street, iv. 424.

Hingston, John, organist to Charles I., iii. 370.

Hippodrome, Notting Hill, v. 181.

Hoadley, Bishop, i. 71.

Hoare's Bank, i. 50; v. 454.

Hobart Place; "Feathers'" Inn, v. 8.

Hobbes of Malmesbury, i. 97.

Hobnails and horse-shoes, Counting, iii. 561.

Hocker, Delarue murdered by, v. 497.

"Hocking;" Hock Day, vi. 390.

Hockley-in-the-Hole, ii. 306; bear-garden, 308; bull-baiting; dog-fighting; fireworks; sword fights; back-swordsmen, *ib.*; cock-fighting, 309, 417.

Hogarth Club, iv. 473.

Hogarth, William, i. 79, 129, 130, 192; ii. 16, 136, 291, 359, 362, 407; iii. 39, 41, 49, 53, 64, 147, 159, 167, 172, 196, 227, 240, 250, 273, 279, 375; iv. 44, 83, 263, 353, 371, 430; v. 200, 207, 359; vi. 58, 452, 465, 554, 556, 557.

"Hog in the Pound," or "Gentleman in Trouble," Oxford Street, iv. 245.

Hog Lane, ii. 218.

Hog's Back, Northern, Hornsey, v. 432.

Holbein and his works, ii. 32, 33, 46, 190, 233, 234; iii. 362; v. 57, 142.

Holbein's Gateway, Whitehall, iii. 341.

Holborn, ii. 526; Holborn and High Holborn; paved in 1417, *ib.*; Kidder, the pastrycook, 531; "Oldbourne Bridge" over the Fleet, 527; Holborn Bars; City tolls; Middle Row; processions to the gallows; Tom Clinch, 527; "Heavy Hill," 529; whippings, 530; Titus Oates; Dangerfield; statue of the Prince Consort; "Rose" Inn, *ib.*; Squire's Coffee House, 536; George Alexander Stevens, 538; Gerard's physic-garden, 539; the "Flying Pieman;" Ragg, the bellman, 541.

Holborn Amphitheatre, iv. 549.

Holborn Bridge, ii. 418, 527.

Holborn Theatre, iv. 552.

Holborn Town-hall, ii. 569.

Holborn Valley Improvements, ii. 500; Viaduct; cost and construction, *ib.*; sewers, gas, and water-pipes; telegraph, 501; v. 239; subway; bridge over Farringdon Street; statues, *ib.*; opening ceremony, ii. 502.

Holcrofts and Holcrofts Priory, Fulham Road, vi. 515.

"Holebourne, The," ii. 417.

"Hole-in-the-Wall" Tavern, Chancery Lane, i. 83.

Holford House, Regent's Park; Baptist Training College, v. 268.

Holford, R. S.; Dorchester House; pictures and books, iv. 368.

Holinshed's narrative of "Evil May Day," i. 310.

Holl, Henry, actor and novelist, v. 314.

Holl, William, engraver, v. 314.

Holland, Charles, actor; tomb with epitaph by Garrick, vi. 551.

Holland, Henry Rich, Earl of, iii. 538; iv. 377; iv. 165.

Holland, Henry Richard, Lord, v. 171, 172; political and literary *salon*, Holland House; Lady Holland, *ib.*

Holland House; its historical associations, v. 161–176; Sir Walter Cope, 162; Henry Rich, first Earl of Holland, 164; family of Fox, Lord Holland; John Thorpe, architect; the house; chapel; terrace; pictures and prints; ghost stories; library; relics of Napoleon, *ib.*; room in which Addison died, 166; his death and funeral; Charles James Fox; Samuel Rogers; descent of the property; Fairfax; third Earl of Holland; his widow married to Addison, *ib.*; Henry Fox, 168; Sir Stephen Fox; Lady Caroline Lennox; Lady Sarah Lennox and George III., 170; Stephen, second Lord Holland, 171; Henry Richard, third Lord; his patronage of literature; Lady Holland; political and literary assemblies, *ib.*; fourth Lord Holland; gardens, 175; Rogers' seat; Inigo Jones's gateway, *ib.*

"Holland's (Lady) mob," at Bartholomew Fair, ii. 349.

Holland Street, Southwark; "Holland's Leaguer," vi. 32; "stew," 41.

Hollar, Wenceslaus, iii. 74, 569; iv. 29; vi. 174.

Holles Street, Cavendish Square, iv. 446; Byron's birthplace; Napoleon III., 447.

Holles Street, Clare Market, iii. 42, 43.

Hollingshead, John; "A Night on the Monument," i. 569.

Hollis, Denzil, iii. 240.

Holloway, ii. 274; v. 373; "Mother Red Cap," ii. 274; "Half Moon;" Holloway Cheesecakes; Sir Henry Blount, *ib.*; the "hollow way," v. 373; Copenhagen Fields and Cattle Market, 374; "Brecknock Arms" tavern, 376; fatal duel between Munro and Fawcett; City Prison, *ib.*; New Jerusalem Church, 380; Seven Sisters' Road and tavern; the seven trees, *ib.*; Holloway Hall, 381; Upper Holloway; St. Saviour's Hospital; St. John's Church; "Archway Tavern;" Duval's Lane, *ib.*; lazar-house for lepers, 382; small-pox hospital, 384; Whittington's stone, 385; story of Whittington, 386; Archway Road and Whittington College, 388.

Holloway, Messrs.; "Holloway's Pills," iii. 20.

Holloway, the murderer, execution of, ii. 453.

Holly hedge at Saye's Court, vi. 154.

Holly; "Holly Bush" Tavern, Hampstead, v. 465.

Holly Lodge and Village, Highgate, v. 411.

Holme, The, Regent's Park, v. 267.

Holt, Chief Justice, ii. 563.

Holy Wells, iii. 21; vi. 129.

Holywell Lane, Shoreditch, ii. 195.

Holywell Street, Strand, iii. 33.

Holywell Street, Westminster, iv. 3.

Home Office, iii. 388.

Homerton, v. 521.

Homœopathic Hospital, iv. 562.

Homes for Destitute Boys, iii. 212.

Hone, William, i. 51, 52, 221; ii. 476; v. 293, 341, 563.

Honey Lane, i. 376.

Honour Oak, Peckham Rye, vi. 292; "Oak of Honour Hill;" semaphore telegraph, *ib.*

Hood, Thomas, i. 59, 65, 261; v. 220; vi. 140, 284.

Hook, James, father of Theodore Hook, iv. 435.

Hook, Theodore, i. 74, 109, 110, 111, 445; iii. 249; iv. 90, 95, 165, 176, 194, 424, 464; vi. 494, 505, 506, 507, 524.

Hooker, Dr., Master of the Temple, i. 155.

Hoole, James, translator of Tasso, i. 75; iii. 212.

Hooper, Bishop, ii. 404.

Hope, H. T., M.P., art collections in Duchess Street and Piccadilly, iv. 286, 448.

Hope Theatre, Bankside, vi. 50.

Hopton's almshouses, Church Street, Blackfriars, vi. 41, 381.

Horace Street, Lisson Grove, formerly Cato Street, iv. 410.

Horatia, daughter of Lord Nelson, iv. 430.

Horne, Sir William, iv. 449.

"Horn Fair," Charlton, vi. 233.

"Horn in the Hoop," Fleet Street, i. 53.

Horner, Thos., his panorama of London from St. Paul's, i. 255; v. 269, 270, 272.

"Horns" Tavern, Kennington, vi. 339.

Hornsey, v. 428; etymology; situation and growth; Hornsey Wood, *ib.*; Lodge Hill, 429; fortifications; Bishop of London's Park; historical events, *ib.*; Hornsey Wood House, 430; "Sluice House," 431; Moore, 434; Lalla Rookh Cottage, *ib.*; Alexandra Palace, 435; Crouch End, 437; growth of population, *ib.*

Hornsey Church, v. 433; the old tower; monuments; Dr. Atterbury; Rogers; daughter of Moore; rectors, *ib.*

Hornsey Lane, v. 394.

Hornsey Road; Claude Duval and Turpin, ii. 275.

Hornsey Wood House, v. 430.

Horological Institute, ii. 325.

Horseferry Road, Westminster, iv. 5; the old "horse ferry;" escape of Mary of Modena and James II., *ib.*; Horseferry and Vauxhall Regatta, 6, 41.

Horse Guards, The, iii. 386; clock; parade-ground; Spanish and Turkish cannon; mounted sentinels, *ib.*;

origin of the name, 387; Commander-in-Chief's Department; his duties; levées, *ib.*

Horse Guards, Regiments of. (*See* Guards.)

Horselydown, vi. 109; "Horsey Down;" Artillery Street; Fair Street, *ib.*; St. John's Church, 110; Goat's Yard; Benjamin Keach's Anabaptist meeting-house, *ib.*; Baptisterion, 111; "Dipping Alley;" School of St. Olave's and St. John's, *ib.*; "The Rosary," 112; Artillery Hall, 113; Jacob's Island, 116; Halfpenny Alley; Farthing Alley; Folly Ditch, 114; Mill Street; Hickman's Folly, 116; woodchoppers, 117.

Horsemonger Lane Gaol, vi. 253; Col. Despard, 254; Leigh Hunt; Moore and Byron; execution of the Mannings, *ib.*

"Horse and Horseshoe" Tavern, iv. 487.

Horses: German; Flanders mares; Hyde Park, Rotten Row, iv. 382, 383, 386, 387, 398, 399.

Horseshoe Court, iii. 22.

"Horseshoe" Tavern, Tottenham Court Road, iv. 485.

Horseshoes and hobnails, Counting, iii. 561.

Horsley, Bishop, iii. 460; vi. 263.

Horticultural Society, Royal. (*See* Royal Horticultural Society.)

Hosier Lane; old houses, ii. 488.

Hospitals, iii. 197; iv. 467, 551, 560, 561; v. 4, 23, 27, 83, 95, 104, 507, 508; vi. 38, 495.

Host, The; bread for the sacrifice of the altar; mode of preparing it, vi. 118.

"Hot Gospellers," v. 440.

"Hot-houses," or "Hummums," iii. 251.

Houndsditch, ii. 163; legend of the punishment of Edric; Ben Jonson; Beaumont and Fletcher, *ib.*; charity; Jew clothes-men, 164.

Hour-glasses in pulpits, i. 368; ii. 146; iii. 574; vi. 377.

"House of Charity," Greek Street, iii. 195.

House of Detention, Clerkenwell, ii. 309; attempted rescue of Fenians; explosion, *ib.*

Houses in London, total number of, vi. 567.

Houses of Parliament, iii. 524; origin of Parliaments; peers, abbesses, and peeresses summoned; Magna Charta and its ratification, *ib.*; knights, citizens, and burgesses summoned, 496; separation of the two Houses, 497; old House of Lords; tapestries; meetings of the Commons in the Chapter House; removal to St. Stephen's Chapel, *ib.*; old House of Commons, 499; Speaker's house, 500; "Bellamy's," 502; Great Fire of 1834; burning of Exchequer "tallies," 521; new Houses of Parliament, 503; designs for their erection; Barry and Pugin; extent and dimensions, *ib.*; buildings described, 504; Speaker's House, 505, 518; Victoria Tower, 505; Royal Staircase, iii. 506; Robing Room; Royal Gallery and

House of Lords, 507 ; frescoes, 507, 516; Throne, 507; Central Hall, St. Stephen's Hall, and statues, 508, 509; House of Commons ; the "Whip ;" galleries ; the reporters' gallery ; Speaker's chair, *ib.*; ventilation, 510, 518 ; lighting, 510 ; history of Parliamentary reporting, 512 ; swearing in of members, 513 ; strangers' gallery, 514; intruders in the two Houses, 515 ; divisions and "tellers," 517; refreshment rooms, 519 ; clock-tower ; clock ; "Big Ben," *ib.* ; historical reminiscences, 524— 532 ; Queen Victoria's first speech, 533 ; the fire in 1834, 557 ; "State services" in St. Margaret's Church ; Speaker's pew, 570.

Howard, John, i. 193 ; ii. 405, 408 441 ; v. 521 ; vi. 68.

Howard Street, Strand ; murder of Will Mountfort, iii. 81.

Howitt, William and Mary, v. 412.

Howley, Archbishop, vi. 429, 435.

Hoxton, v. 25 ; "Pimlico," old tavern so called ; "Pimlico Walk ;" "Hogsdon;" "Hocheston;" Charles Square ; Aske's Hospital ; Haberdashers' School ; Balmes House ; Sir George Whitmore, *ib.* ; Lunatic Asylum, 526 ; Whitmore Bridge ; Tyssen and De Beauvoir families ; De Beauvoir Town ; De Beauvoir Square ; St. Peter's Church ; Tottenham Road ; Roman Catholic Church, *ib.*

Hoyle, author of "Whist," iv. 430, 442.

Hudson, George, the "Railway King," v. 22.

Hudson, Sir Jeffrey, dwarf, ii. 430 ; iii. 489.

"Huff, Mother," or "Mother Damnable," v. 471.

Hugo, Rev. Thos., Crosby Hall and St. Helen's Church, ii. 155, 156, 158.

Huggin Lane, i. 364, 365.

Huggins, farmer of the Fleet Prison, ii. 406.

Huguenots, iv. 76, 81 ; vi. 481.

Hulbert, James ; Fishmongers' Almshouses, Newington, vi. 257.

Hullah, John, iv. 193.

Humane Society, iv. 402, 404 ; vi. 377.

Humboldt, vi. 323.

Hume, Joseph, M.P., iv. 412.

Humfrey, Ozias, v. 26.

"Hummums, Old" and "New," Covent Garden, iii. 251.

Humphrey, Duke, dining with, i. 239.

Hungerford Market, iii. 131.

Hungerford Stairs, iii. 296.

Hungerford Suspension Bridge ; its removal, iii. 132.

Hunsden House, Islington, ii. 267.

Hunsdon House, Blackfriars ; fatal fall of the chapel, i. 201.

Hunt and Roskell, iv. 301.

Hunt, John, imprisonment of, ii. 299.

Hunt, Leigh, ii. 369 ; v. 65, 118, 221, 258, 457, 500 ; vi. 253, 490, 546, 576.

Hunter, Dr. John, iii. 46, 168 ; v. 5.

Hunter, Sir Claudius, Lord Mayor, i. 116, 329—331.

Hunter Street, Brunswick Square, iv. 576 ; Marchioness Townshend, v. 365.

Hunting, in and near London, iv. 48, 178, 323, 376, 377, 438, 488 ; v. 51, 263, 426 ; vi. 239.

Huntingdon, Countess of ; Spa Fields Chapel, ii. 303 ; v. 464; vi. 375.

Huntington, William, "Sinner Saved;" his eccentricities, ii. 284 ; iv. 461.

Hurlingham House, Fulham ; aristocratic sports, vii. 524.

Hutchinson, Colonel, and his wife, Lucy Apsley ; romantic story, ii. 507.

Hyde Park, iv. 376 ; site in British and Roman eras ; manor of Eia ; the manor of Hyde ; Abbey of Westminster ; Henry VIII.'s hunting-grounds ; rangers, *ib.*; deer ; herons and hawking, 377 ; trained bands ; General Monk, 378 ; park sold by Parliament, 380 ; fenced-in ; fortifications ; opened to the public, *ib.*; apple-trees ; Evelyn ; Pepys ; the "Ring," 381, 382, 386, 387 ; coaches, 381, 382 ; camp of refuge from the plague, 383 ; Cake-house ; walnut-tree avenue, *ib.*; fruit and flower women, 386 ; reviews and encampments, 388 ; duels, 389, 393 ; peace rejoicings (1814—1815), *ib.*; situation ; rural scenery ; purity of air and extent, 394 ; entrances, 395 ; riding-house ; Chelsea Waterworks ; mineral springs ; statue of Achilles ; Sir Richard Westmacott, *ib.*; Rotten Row, and the "Lady's Mile," 398 ; the Drive ; Horace Walpole attacked by highwaymen, *ib.*; the fashions ; carriages and horsemen, 399 ; Four-in-Hand and Coaching Clubs, 400 ; springs and conduits ; Serpentine river ; Caroline, queen of George II., *ib.*; John Martin's plans, 401 ; Royal Humane Society, 402 ; bathing, 404 ; swimming club ; boating ; drownings ; powder magazine ; bridge ; Great Exhibition of 1851 ; apple-stall keeper, *ib.*; political meetings, 405 ; railings destroyed ; flower-beds ; Marble Arch, *ib.*

Hyde Park Corner ; toll-gate, iv. 290, 365 ; v. 8.

Hyde Park Place, iv. 407.

"Hyndman's Bounty," vi. 42.

I.

Ice-houses, iv. 178.

Illuminations, iv. 53, 260, 413.

Illustrated London News ; printing-office, iii. 71.

Imperial Gas Works, v. 371 ; vi. 525.

Inchbald, Mrs., v. 125, 130, 177.

Incledon, Charles, iii. 231 ; v. 482.

India Office, iii. 393 ; Sir M. Digby Wyatt ; building described ; decorations ; records ; library of Oriental MSS. and books ; Museum, 394.

Indian Museum, v. 108.

Ingram, Herbert, founder of the *Illustrated London News*, iii. 71.

Inkhorn Court, ii. 145.

Inns of Chancery, ii. 570 ; iii. 51.

"Inns" of Court, iii. 32, 51, 58.

Inns of Court Hotel, iii. 50.

Innholders' Hall, ii. 41.

Insane persons in London, vi. 570.

Intellectual attractions of London ; opinions of eminent writers, vi. 575.

International Exhibitions (1851, 1862), v. 28, 29, 104, 528. (*See also* Great Exhibition of 1851.)

Inverness, Duchess of, iv. 407; v. 150.

Ireland, Jews transported to, i. 426.

Ireland, Rev. John, Dean of Westminster, iii. 460.

Ireland, Samuel ; "Shakespeare" forgeries, iv. 167.

Ireland Yard, Blackfriars ; house bought by Shakespeare, i. 219.

Ireton, General, iii. 539 ; v. 400; vi. 491.

Irish labourers, iii. 106.

Irish localities, iii. 23.

Irish residents in London, iii. 189, 207 ; statistics, vi. 570.

Ironmonger Lane, i. 346 ; Mercers' Company and Hall, 376—383 ; St. Martin's Church, 383.

Ironmongers' Company and Hall, ii. 177 ; v. 525.

Irving, Rev. Edward, iv. 466 ; the "unknown tongues," 572 ; v. 490.

Irving, Washington, i. 562 ; ii. 225, 435, 476.

Isabella, Queen of Edward II., ii. 365, 369.

"Isle of Ducks," vi. 108.

Islington, ii. 251 ; etymology ; Roman road ; Fitzstephen ; hawking and archery ; Islington butts, *ib.*; "Marquis of Islington," 252 ; archery, 253; "Robin Hood" Tavern, 254; Prince Llewellyn, 255 ; game ; religious martyrs ; Islington dairies, *ib.*; entrenchments, 256; cream and cakes ; duck-hunting ; "The Merry Milkmaid ;" ducking-ponds ; "The Walks of Islington ;" "Saracen's Head," *ib.* ; the plague, 257 ; Colman's "Islington Spa ;" "Delights of Islington;" highwaymen, *ib.*; Col. Aubert and the Loyal Islington Volunteers, 258 ; old "Queen's Head" Tavern, 260 ; residence of Raleigh; "Pied Bull," *ib.*; "Angel" inn, 261 ; Agricultural Hall ; St. Mary's Church, *ib.* ; Fisher House, 262 ; "Frog Hall ;" "Barley Mow ;" George Morland ; "Rainy Day Smith ;" house of the Fowler family, *ib.* ; "Old Parr's Head," 263 ; Laycock's Dairy, *ib.* ; Colebrooke Row ; residence of Charles Lamb, 266 ; William Woodfall ; D'Aguilar, miser; St. Peter's Church ; Irvingite Church ; New River, *ib.*; the poet Collins, 267 ; the "Crown ;" Hunsden House, *ib.* ; Brown, founder of the "Brownists," 268 ; Topham, the "Strong Man," 268 ; Cattle Market, Lower Road ; its failure, 282; Imperial Theatre, iv 20.

Italian Chapel, Oxendon Street, iv. 231.

Italian sermons, Mercers' Chapel, i. 380.

Ivory, James, iv. 268.

Ivy Bridge Lane, Strand, iii. 101.

J.

"Jackanapes on Horseback," sign, vi. 172.

"Jackers, The Honourable Society of," iii. 32.

"Jack in the Green;" May Day, v. 223.

Jackson, pugilist, v. 101.

"Jack's Coffee-house," ii. 182.

"Jack Straw's Castle," Hampstead ; Jack Straw, v. 454.

"Jack Straw's Castle," Highbury, ii. 273.

Jacob's Island, Dockhead, vi. 113.

"Jacob's Well" Tavern and passage, i. 412.

Jamaica Road and Jamaica Level, Bermondsey, vi. 130.

James I., i. 25, 160, 532; ii. 29, 72, 179, 253, 383, 387; iii. 287, 344, 375, 404, 437, 440; iv. 46, 377, 512, 515; v. 67, 70, 313; vi. 32, 54, 173, 332, 490.

James II., i. 501; iii. 299, 328, 369, 384; iv. 5, 53, 104, 110, 178, 255, 323; v. 74.

James I. of Scotland, vi. 21.

James IV. of Scotland, i. 300, 365.

James, Sir Bartholomew, Lord Mayor, i. 399, 517.

James Street, Buckingham Gate, iv. 25; Tart Hall; Richard Glover; Gifford, ib.; John, Duke of Marlborough, 26.

James Street, Covent Garden, iii. 262.

James Street, Haymarket; Royal Tennis Court, iv. 231.

Jansen, Bernard, Northumberland House, iii. 136.

Janssen, Sir Theophilus; South Sea Bubble, i. 542.

"Jarveys;" hackney coachmen, iii. 334.

Jay, Cyrus, trial of Hone, i. 51.

Jeaffreson, Henry, M.D., ii. 202, 363.

Jeffrey, Lord, iii. 530; v. 292.

Jeffreys, Judge, ii. 75, 136; iv. 29.

Jekyll, Sir Joseph, Master of the Rolls, i. 79, 166.

"Je ne sais quoi" Club, iv. 136.

Jenkins, Judge, ii. 563.

Jenner, Dr., v. 153.

"Jenny's Whim," Pimlico, v. 45.

Jenyns, Soame, iv. 398, 556.

Jerdan, William, iv. 173; v. 102.

Jerman, architect, i. 501; ii. 4.

Jermyn Street, iv. 203; Henry Jermyn, Earl of St. Albans; St. Albans House, ib.; strange story; Brunswick Hotel, 204; Museum of Practical Geology; Royal Society for the Prevention of Cruelty to Animals, 205; Turkish Baths, 206.

Jerrold, Douglas, i. 57, 58, 137; iii. 75, 104, 214; iv. 280; v. 102, 249, 321; vi. 316, 495.

Jersey, Earl and Countess of, i. 38; iv. 197, 332.

Jerusalem Chamber, iii. 458; Westminster Abbey; death of Henry IV., ib.; lying in state of Addison, Congreve, and Prior; Committee for revision of the Bible, 459.

Jerusalem Coffee House, ii. 172.

"Jerusalem" Tavern, ii. 317, 323.

Jesuit Church, iv. 335.

Jesuits' College, Clerkenwell, ii. 327.

Jewels, Keeper of the King's, ii. 232.

Jew clothesmen in Houndsditch, ii. 164.

"Jew King," money lender, vi. 513.

Jewin Street, Aldersgate, i. 428; ii. 220.

Jewish cemeteries, v. 576.

Jewish customs, ii. 146.

Jewish dissenters, iv. 409, 410.

Jewish exiles drowned, ii. 16.

Jewish school, Greek Street, iii. 195.

Jewish slaughter-house, Clare Market, iii. 41.

Jewry, The, in the Liberties of the Tower, ii. 107.

Jews admitted to Parliament, iii. 513.

Jews' burial ground, v. 88, 509.

Jews, converted; their house in Chancery Lane, i. 76, 425, 428.

"Jew's Harp" Tavern; the jeu trompe, v. 255.

Jews' Hospital, Lower Norwood, vi. 316.

Jews in London, statistics, vi. 570. (See also Old Jewry.)

Jews massacred at the coronation of Richard I., iii. 402.

Jews' Synagogues: Stepney, ii. 140; Great St. Helen's, 160; Duke's Place, 248; Greek Street, iii. 195.

Joe Miller and the "Jest Book," iii. 29.

John Bull newspaper, i. 109, 110, 111; iv. 90.

John, King, i. 281, 425; ii. 404, 441; vi. 142, 287.

John, King of France, i. 556; iii. 95; vi. 237.

John of Eltham, vi. 237.

John Street, Adelphi; Society of Arts, iii. 107.

John Street, Bedford Row, iv. 551; Baptist Chapel; Hon. and Rev. Baptist Noel, ib.

John Street, Berkeley Square; Berkeley Chapel, iv. 334.

John Street, Lisson Grove, iv. 410.

"John's" Coffee-house; Fulwood's Rents, ii. 536.

Johnson, Dr., i. 35, 41, 51, 54, 98, 108, 109, 110, 112, 113, 115, 118, 166, 167, 206, 219, 418; ii. 14, 317, 318, 437, 439, 446, 449, 489, 575; iii. 69, 75, 112, 134, 178, 224, 265, 266, 275, 278, 284, 305, 474, 512, 569; iv. 64, 141, 154, 172, 182, 220, 279, 286, 292, 328, 340, 343, 356, 357, 368, 452, 459, 461, 464, 498, 512, 554; v. 26, 61, 80, 92, 194, 351, 437, 502; vi. 34, 35, 194, 208, 276, 317, 346, 361, 446, 450, 453, 548, 552, 560.

Johnson, Gerard, sculptor of Shakespeare's tomb, Stratford-on-Avon, vi. 93.

"Johnson's Alamode Beef-house," Clare Court; Dickens, iii. 284.

Johnson's Court, Fleet Street, i. 109; Dr. Johnson's residence, 110; John Bull newspaper, 109, 110, 111.

Joiners' Hall, ii. 41.

"Jonathan's" Coffee House; Addison; Mrs. Centlivre, ii. 173.

Jones, George, R.A., iv. 458; v. 408.

Jones, Horace, architect, i. 385; ii. 493.

Jones, Inigo, i. 76, 245, 246; ii. 36, 158, 234; iii. 44, 47, 54, 91, 209, 213, 238, 242, 248, 249, 330, 341, 342, 404, 457; iv. 50, 176, 536; vi. 173, 563.

Jones, J. Winter, iv. 518.

Jones, John Gale, iv. 281.

Jones, Owen, iv. 455; v. 35.

Jones, Richard ("Gentleman Jones"), teacher of elocution, v. 9.

"Jones, the boy," at Buckingham Palace, iv. 69.

Jonson, Ben, i. 39, 201, 351, 422, 513; ii. 20, 164, 259, 345; iii. 54, 57, 159, 201, 341, 342, 425, 472, 563; iv. 2, 291; v. 39, 50, 525, 526; vi. 45, 47, 48, 50, 52, 250, 297.

Jordan, Mrs., iii. 221; v. 11, 14.

Jordan's figures of Corineus and Gogmagog, i. 384, 386.

Jubilee Almshouses, Greenwich, vi. 194.

Jubilee masquerade, Ranelagh, v. 78.

Jubilee Place, Chelsea, v. 88.

Judd, Sir Andrew, Lord Mayor, i. 401.

Judd Street, iv. 576.

Judge's Walk, Hampstead, v. 459.

Jullien's Promenade Concerts, iii. 234; vi. 267.

Junior Athenæum Club, iv. 286.

Junior Carlton Club, iv. 150.

Junior Naval and Military Club, iv. 144.

Junior Oxford and Cambridge Club, iv. 298.

Junior St. James's Club, iv. 160.

Junior Travellers' Club, iv. 322.

Junior United Service Club, iv. 145.

Junius, iv. 328, 538.

Justice Walk, Chelsea, v. 92.

Juxon, Bishop, ii. 567; vi. 512.

K.

Katherine of Arragon, Queen of Henry VIII., i. 200; ii. 155; vi. 436.

Katharine of Valois, Queen of Henry V., i. 316; iii. 434, 441; vi. 119.

Kauffmann, Angelica, iv. 272.

Keach, Benjamin; meeting-house, vi. 110.

Kean, Charles, and Mrs. Kean, iv. 462.

Kean, Edmund, iii. 309; vi. 527.

Keats, John, i. 65, 341; v. 458, 472, 500; vi. 548, 568.

Keeble, Sir Henry, Lord Mayor, i. 554.

Keeling, Lord Chief Justice, ii. 237.

Keith, Dr. George; secret marriages, iv. 347, 349.

Keith, Lady (Miss Thrale), iv. 286.

Keith, Rev. Alexander; Fleet marriages, ii. 411.

Kelly and Co., printers, "Post-Office Directories," iii. 23, 212.

Kelly, Michael, iv. 98.

Kelly, Miss; Royalty Theatre, iii. 194.

Kemble, Adelaide, iii. 233.

Kemble, Charles, iii. 231, 232, 233; iv. 200; vi. 373.

Kemble, Fanny, iii. 254.

Kemble, John Philip, iii. 231, 232; iv. 277; vi. 575.

Kemble, Stephen, iii. 231.

Kendal, Duchess of; South Sea Bubble, i. 542.

Kenmure, Lord, beheaded on Tower Hill, ii. 76; iii. 551.

Kennington, vi. 331; etymology; descent of the manor, ib.; royal residence in Saxon times, 332; Hardicanute; Richard I.; Edward the Black Prince; James I., ib.; Long Barn, 333; manor house; Caron House; Vauxhall Well; Kennington Oval; St. Joseph's Convent, ib.; Beaufoy's Vinegar Works, 334; Tradescant; Kennington Common, now Kennington Park; place of execution, ib., 335, 339; Chartist gathering, 335; fair, 338; field preachers; Whitefield; Charles Wesley; model farm cottages, ib.; St. Agnes Church, 339; St. Mark's

Church; the "Horns" Tavern; South London Waterworks, *ib.*; Spring Garden, 340; Licensed Victuallers' School; maypole, *ib.*

Kenrick, Dr., i. 275; iv. 436.

Kensal Green Cemetery, v. 220.

Kensington, v. 117; descent of the manor; Domesday Book; the De Veres, *ib.*; Henry Rich, Earl of Holland, 118; a parochial enigma; etymology; Gore House and estate, *ib.*; Wilberforce, 119; Countess of Blessington; literary society, *ib.*; Count D'Orsay, 120; sale of Lady Blessington's effects, 122; "symposium;" Soyer; Albert Hall; Park House; Brompton Park Nursery; Loudon and Wise; Batty's hippodrome; turnpike and halfway house, *ib.*; St. Stephen's Church, 123; "Hogmire Lane;" Christ Church, Victoria Road, *ib.*; "Kingly Kensington," 124; High Street; "Red Lion" Inn; proclamation of George I.; Colby House; Kensington House, *ib.*; Old Kensington Bedlam, 125; Albert Grant's mansion; Kensington Square, *ib.*; Kensington Church, 128; Charity School, 130; new Vestry Hall; Campden House, *ib.*, Campden Hill, 131, 132; private theatre; caper-tree; Campden House burnt down; observatory; Sir James South, 131; Argyll Lodge, 133; Bedford Lodge; Holly Lodge; Macaulay, *ib.*; Orbell's Buildings, 134; Kensington Gravel Pits; Sheffield House; artists; Callcott; Wilkie; old street lamps, 135; highwaymen; ghost story, *ib.*; Scarsdale Terrace, 136; Crippled Boys' Home; Scarsdale House; Wright's Lane; Catholic University College, *ib.*; monasteries and convents, 137; Fathers of the Oratory; Catholic churches and schools; Pro-Cathedral, Newland Terrace; "Adam and Eve" public-house, *ib.*; Palace Gate House, 139; High Street; "King's Arms" Tavern; Henry VIII.'s Conduit; Queen Elizabeth; Palace Green; Volunteers; Water Tower, *ib.*; Thackeray's house, 140; Earl's Court Road, 161; Earl's Court Terrace; Leonard's Place; Edwardes Square; Warwick Road; Warwick Gardens; Wesleyan Chapel; West London Railway; Addison Road, *ib.*; Holland House (*see* Holland House).

Kensington Gardens, v. 152; William III.; Loudon and Wise, gardeners; Dutch and French gardening; Le Notre, 153; additions by Queen Anne; conservatory; banqueting house; fêtes; orangery; Albert Memorial; broad walk; kitchen garden; apple-trees; alcove, *ib.*; gardens improved by Bridgman, 154; round pond; avenues; "prospect house;" "hermitage;" wall and fosse, or, "Ha! ha!;" Kent; "Capability Brown"; nightingales; gardens opened to the public; regulations; fox-hunting, *ib.*; military bands, 155; trees, shrubs, and flower-beds, 155, 160; Scotch pines, 156; Serpentine, 157; bridge;

basins; fountain, *ib.*; promenades, 158; costume; hoops; head dresses; Macaronis, pigtails, *ib.*; Madame Récamier; Duchess of Kent and Queen Victoria, 159.

Kensington Gate, Hyde Park, iv. 395.

Kensington; nursery grounds; Messrs. Lee, v. 177.

Kensington Palace, v. 142, 145; Nottingham House; purchased by William III.; improvements; Queen Anne; orangery; additions by George I., George II., and Duke of Sussex, *ib.*; Court of William III., 142—146; death of the King, his Queen, Queen Anne, Prince George of Denmark, George II., and the Duke of Sussex; court of Queen Anne; gentlemen ushers, or King's guard; Princess Sophia; Queen Caroline; Princess Charlotte, *ib.*; library of the Duke of Sussex, 148; Duke and Duchess of Kent; birth of Queen Victoria; her christening; accession to the throne, *ib.*; her Majesty's first council, *ib.*; Duke of Sussex; Lady Augusta Murray; Duchess of Inverness, 150; the building, 141; state and private apartments; grand staircase; chapel royal; historical paintings, *ib.*

Kensington Palace Gardens, v. 138; Thackeray's house, 140.

Kensington Park Gardens, v. 180.

Kensington Volunteers, Old; their colours, v. 139.

Kent, Duke and Duchess of, iv. 451; v. 25, 149, 159; vi. 375, 409.

Kent, landscape gardener, vi. 553.

Kent Street, Southwark, hospital for lepers, vi. 70.

"Kentish Drovers" Tavern, Peckham Road, vi. 287, 288.

Kentish Town, v. 317; Cantilupe Town; Bishops de Cantilupe; manor of Kantelows, *ib.*; Fortess Place, 318; armed guard for travellers, 320; Assembly Rooms; Weston's Gardens; races; "Corporation of Kentish Town," *ib.*; "Castle" Tavern, 321; Emanuel Hospital for the Blind; Dr. Stukeley; Lower Craven Place; Douglas Jerrold, *ib.*

Ken Wood, Hampstead. (*See* Caen Wood.)

Keppel Street, iv. 566.

Ketch, John; "Jack Ketch," executioner, v. 197.

Key, Sir John, Lord Mayor, i. 116, 413.

Keyse, Thomas; his pictures, Bermondsey Spa, vi. 128.

Kidder, the famous pastrycook, ii. 531.

"Kiddles;" nets placed in the Thames, ii. 62.

Kilburn, v. 243; its former rural aspect; extent; Maida Vale; its subjection to the Abbey of Westminster; hermitage, *ib.*; Benedictine Priory, 244, 245; pilgrims to St. Albans; inventory of the suppressed priory; relic of the holy cross; descent of the property; St. Mary's Church, *ib.*; Sisterhood of St. Peter's, 245; St. Augustine's Church; mineral spring; "Kilburn Wells," *ib.*; legend of fratricide,

246; Roman Catholic chapel and monastery, 247; "Beau" Brummel; Brandesbury House, 248.

Killigrew, Thomas, i. 195; iii. 39, 41, 219, 220.

Kilmarnock, Lord, ii. 76, 95; iii. 551; iv. 469.

Kindergarten Schools, Stockwell, vi. 329.

"King of Bohemia's Head" Tavern, vi. 561.

"King of Clubs" (Club), iv. 310.

King Edward's School, St. George's Fields, vi. 362.

"King John's Palace," public-house, iv. 479.

King Street, Cheapside, i. 383.

King Street, Covent Garden, iii. 263; "Three Kings" Inn; sale-rooms; "Essex Serpent;" Coleridge; Garrick Club, *ib.*

King Street, Snow Hill, ii. 489; Dr. Johnson's "Betty Broom," *ib.*

King Street, St. James's, iii. 201; Napoleon III., *ib.*; Nerot's Hotel, iv. 191; St. James's Theatre; Braham, *ib.*; Willis's Rooms, 196; Christie and Manson's auction sales, 200.

King Street, Wardour Street, iv. 238.

King Street, Westminster, iv. 26; distinguished residents; Cromwell and his mother, 27, 28; Charles I.; the Plague; coffee-houses, *ib.*

King's beam, for weighing wool, i. 431; the Weigh-house, 563.

King's Bench Prison, vi. 64; first prison near the Marshalsea; Prince Hal and Justice Gascoigne; Wilkes, *ib.*; burnt down by the Gordon rioters, 65; rebuilt; the liberties or "rules;" discipline; Jones, the marshal, *ib.*; described by Smollett, 66; John Howard; Crown prisoners, 68; Haydon's "Mock Election," 69; Morland, *ib.*

King's College Hospital, iii. 29.

King's College, Strand, iii. 94.

King's Cross, ii. 278; statue of George IV.; its removal; dust-heaps; St. Chad's well; Great Northern Railway station, *ib.*

King's Cross Station, Metropolitan Railway, v. 227.

King's evil, iii. 353; iv. 110.

King's Exchange, i. 346, 356.

"King's Head" Tavern, Euston Road; Hogarth's "March to Finchley," iv. 482.

"King's Head" Tavern, Fenchurch Street; Princess Elizabeth, ii. 176.

"King's Head," Ivy Lane; Dr. Johnson's literary club, ii. 439.

"King's Mews," Charing Cross, iii. 129, 141.

King's Road, Chelsea, v. 86.

"King's Square," old name of Soho Square, iii. 174.

Kingsgate Street, Holborn; the King's gate, iv. 549.

Kingsland, v. 527; hospital for lepers; "*Le Lokes*," *ib.*

Kingsland Road, v. 525; almshouses; Shoreditch Workhouse; St. Columba's Church, *ib.*

Kingston, Duchess of, iii. 532.

Kirby's Castle, Bethnal Green, ii. 147.

Kitchiner, Dr., iv. 476.

Kit-Kat Club, i. 70, 71, 72, 74; iii. 80; iv. 141; v. 459.

"Knave of Clubs" Inn, Southwark, vi. 13.
Kneller, Sir Godfrey, i. 70; iii. 146, 212, 273, 249; v. 141.
Knight, Charles, iv. 542; v. 413, 477.
Knight, Richard Payne, iv. 500.
Knightrider Street; Linacre's house, College of Physicians, i. 303; fish dinners, ii. 2.
Knightsbridge, v. 15; derivation of the name; early history; bridge over the Westbourne; village green and maypole, 16; bad roads and highwaymen, 17; forest on the site of Lowndes Square, 18; Lord Howard of Elscrick; Algernon Sidney; Rye House Plot, ib.; burial of Henry VIII., 20; "Swan" Tavern; riots; "Spring Garden," ib.; the "World's End," 21; Knightsbridge Grove; Mrs. Cornelys; George IV.; Albert Gate, 21, 22; Cannon Brewery, 22; George Hudson; French embassy; Dunn's Chinese collection, ib.; ancient lazar-house, 23; Church of the Holy Trinity; irregular and "secret" marriages, ib.; barracks, 24; floor-cloth manufactory, ib.; Kent House, 25; Stratheden House; Kingston House; Rutland Gate, ib.; Ennismore Place, 27; Brompton Road; Brompton Square; residents at Knightsbridge; Knightsbridge Terrace; Tattersall's new auction mart; the Green; may-pole; pound, ib.; old inns, 27, 28; civil war, 28; cattle market; air and water supply, ib.
Knight's Hill, Norwood, vi. 314.
Knights Hospitallers. (See St. John's Gate.)
Knipp, Mrs., comedian, and Pepys, i. 44; iii. 219, 220.
Knockers, stealing, iv. 472.
Knut. (See Canute.)
"Koh-i-noor," The, v. 38, 106.
Köningsmark, Count; murder of Mr. Thomas Thynne, iii. 419; iv. 227, 277.
Kossuth, Louis, v. 298.
Kynaston, Edward, i. 197; actor of women's parts; Cockpit Theatre, iii. 219, 256.
Kynaston, Sir Francis; the "Museum Minervæ," iii. 268.

L.

Lackington's "Temple of the Muses;" his autobiography, ii. 206.
Ladbroke Square, v. 180.
Lad Lane, Gresham Street; "Swan with Two Necks," i. 374.
Lade, Sir John, iv. 97.
Ladies' Sanitary Association, iv. 465.
Ladies' Work Society, v. 97.
"Lady Holland's mob;" Bartholomew Fair, ii. 349.
Ladywell, Lewisham, vi. 246.
Laguerre, iii. 40.
Lalla Rookh Cottage, Muswell Hill; Moore, v. 434.
Lamb, Charles, i. 45, 168, 176, 413, 544; ii. 266, 370; iv. 123, 191; v. 567, 568.
Lamb, Dr., conjuror, i. 421.
Lamb, William; Lamb's Conduit; Lamb's Conduit Street, iv. 550.

Lambarde, William, vi. 191, 194, 225, 229, 237, 238.
Lambert, Daniel, 259.
Lambert, Sir John; South Sea Bubble, i. 542.
Lambe's Almshouses, ii. 236.
Lambeth, vi. 383; the parish; liberties and wards; early history; descent of the manor, ib.; glass-blowers and potters, 384; etymology; Roman and Danish occupation, ib.; Lambeth Marsh, 385; imprisonment of Lady Arabella Stuart, 386; boat-building, 387; Searle's boat-yard; old embankments; Bankside; Narrow Wall; Broad Wall; Coade's artificial stone works; old windmill; Mill Street; Church Osiers; Pedlar's Acre; the pedlar and his dog, ib.; Henry Paulet, "Governor of Lambeth Marsh," 388; Belvedere Road; Belvedere House and Gardens; Cuper's Gardens, ib.; "Hercules" Inn and Gardens, 389; Hercules Buildings; Apollo and Flora Gardens; Curtis's Gardens; "Lambeth Wells;" sports, ib.; tavern signs, 390; Halfpenny Hatch, 392; Lambeth Waterworks, 407; shot factories, 408; Infirmary for Children and Women, 409; St. John's Church, 410; South-Western Railway Station; New Cut, 411; "Bower" Theatre, 412; "penny gaffs;" Sunday trading; Lambeth Baths, ib.; St. Thomas's Schools, 414; Lambeth Marsh; Bonner's House, 415; All Saints' Church and Schools, Lower Marsh, 416; Canterbury Music Hall, ib.; Stangate, 417; "Old Grimaldi;" Carlisle Lane; Carlisle House, residence of the Bishops of Rochester, ib.; Norfolk House; Dukes of Norfolk, 418; drug-mill of the Apothecaries' Company; London Necropolis Company, ib.; St. Thomas's Hospital, 419; Albert Embankment, 422; Lambeth potteries, 424; Lambeth School of Design; Vauxhall plate-glass works, ib.; British Wine Manufactory, 425; doll manufactory, Waterloo Road; Parliamentary representation; career of William Roupell, ib.; St. Mary's Church, 443; painted window of the Pedlar and his Dog, 444; pulpit and hour-glass, 445; interments and monuments, 446; beacon, 447; flight of Mary of Modena, ib.
Lambeth Bridge, iv. 5.
Lambeth Hill, ii. 36.
Lambeth, old ferry to Westminster, iii. 298.
Lambeth Palace, vi. 428; Glanville, Bishop of Rochester; exchanged with Archbishop Walter of Canterbury, ib.; Palace rebuilt, ib.; prison for Royalists, 429; great gateway, outer court, ib.; great hall, 430; hospitality of Cranmer and Parker; library founded by Bancroft, ib.; books and MSS., 431; librarians, 432; guard-chamber, 433; chapel; "post-room," 434; crypt, 435; Lollards' Tower; archbishop's residence; presence-chamber; gardens and grounds, ib.; fig-trees, 436; Bishops' Walk;

historical notes; convocation in 1466; royal visits; dissolution of Anne Boleyn's marriage, ib.; the "Bishops' Book," 438; "Lambeth Articles, ib.; banquets, 440; archbishop's dole; Archbishop Laud, ib.; Sheldon's translation, 441; Gordon riots, 442; Pan-Anglican Synod; Arches Court; annual visit of Stationers' Company, ib.; state barge; Lambeth degrees, 443.
Lambeth Waterworks Company, vi. 407.
Lamps, Street, v. 135; vi. 368.
Lancaster, Duchy of, iii. 9, 96.
Lancaster Gate, v. 186.
Lancaster, Joseph; the "monitorial" school system, vi. 365.
Lancaster Place, Strand, iii. 286.
Lancet Newspaper, iii. 121.
Landon, Miss, i. 172; iv. 412; v. 99.
Landor, Walter Savage, his contributions to the London Magazine, i. 65.
Landseer, Sir Edward, R.A., v. 248.
Landseer, Thomas, v. 248.
Laneham at St. Anthony's School, i. 537; bear-baiting at Kenilworth Castle, vi. 52.
Langham Place; Sir James Langham; Langham Hotel, iv. 452; St. George's Hall; German Fair, 453.
Langhorne, Rev. John, ii. 552.
Lansdowne House, iv. 329; Marquesses of Lansdowne; Lansdowne MSS.; antique marbles; pictures, ib.
Lant family; Lant Street, Southwark, vi. 60, 61.
Larwood on "Signs and Sign-boards." (See Signs.)
"Last Dying Speeches" of criminals, iii. 203.
Latimer imprisoned in the Tower, ii. 70, 103.
Latymer Schools, Hammersmith; Edward Latymer, vi. 538.
Laud, Archbishop, ii. 75, 95, 108, 566; iv. 21; vi. 434, 440, 537.
Lauderdale House, Aldersgate Street, ii. 221.
Lauderdale House, Highgate, v. 395, 366; Earl of Lauderdale; Nell Gwynne; given by Sir Sydney Waterlow as a Convalescent Home, 398.
Laundresses in Moorfields, ii. 196.
Laurence, William, monumental tablet; Cloisters, Westminster, iii. 456.
Laurie, Sir Peter, Lord Mayor, i. 413; v. 269.
Law Courts and Lawyers in Westminster Hall; Lydgate, iii. 543.
Law Courts at the Royal Palace, Westminster; in Westminster Hall, iii. 543, 544, 560, 561, 562.
Law Courts; Early Courts, iii. 15; their concentration at Westminster; the new Law Courts, 16, 83; determination and clearance of the site; selection of Mr. G. E. Street, R.A., as architect, 17.
Law Institution, Chancery Lane, i. 90.
Law, John, the Mississippi scheme, iv. 543.
Lawrence Lane; Church of St. Lawrence; "Blossoms" Inn, i. 376.
Lawrence, Sir John, Lord Mayor, i. 405, 416; ii. 154.
Lawrence, Sir Thomas, P.R.A., iii. 148, 195; iv. 250, 566.

Lawson, printer of the *Times*, i. 214.
Lawyers satirised by Lydgate, iii. 543 ;
by Peter the Great, 544.
Laxton, Sir William, Lord Mayor, i. 555.
Layard, A. H., Assyrian Exploration,
iv. 531, 534.
Laycock's Dairy, ii. 263.
Lazar-houses, v. 23, 27, 382, 383, 384,
386, 528.
Lea, River, v. 545 ; its course ; former
commercial importance ; Leymouthe
ascended by the Danes ; invaders
defeated ; Lea Bridge, *ib.* ; corn
and paper mills, 546 ; angling ;
Izaak Walton, *ib.* ; Lea Bridge ; the
" Jolly Anglers," 548.
Leach, Sir John, Master of the Rolls,
i. 80.
Leadenhall Market, ii. 188 ; mansion
converted into a granary ; chapel ;
wool and meal market, *ib.* ; meat
and leather market ; Church of St.
Catherine Cree, 189.
Leadenhall Street, ii. 183–187 ; East
India House ; " Two Fans ; " Mot-
teux's India House, 188 ; Roman
pavement, 191.
Leake, Colonel, iv. 431.
Leather Lane, ii. 544.
Leather trade, Bermondsey, vi. 123.
Leathersellers' Company and Hall, ii.
160 ; School at Lewisham, vi. 246.
Lee Boo, Prince, vi. 136.
Lee, Kent, vi. 243 ; Church and monu-
ments, 244 ; almshouses ; Dacre
House ; Lady Dacre ; the Green ;
the stocks ; villas ; churches, *ib.*
Lee, Messrs. ; nursery garden, Ham-
mersmith, vi. 533.
Lee, Nat, iii. 11 ; vi. 62.
Lee, Sir Henry, of Ditchley, iii. 364.
Lee, William, inventor of the stocking-
loom, ii. 238.
Leech, John, i. 57, 58, 228 ; ii. 402,
404 ; iv. 280, 563.
" Leg (or League) and Seven Stars,"
iii. 26.
" Legate's Tower," Baynard's Castle,
i. 285.
Leicester, Dudley, Earl of, constable
of the Temple Revels, i. 159.
Leicester Square, iii. 160 ; " Leicester
Fields ; " French emigrants ; statue
of George I. ; duels, 161, 162 ;
Leicester House, 164 ; Sir Ashton
Lever's Museum, 165 ; house of
Sir Joshua Reynolds, 166 ; Pan-
orama of Balaclava, *ib.* ; Sir
Thomas Lawrence ; Sir Charles
Bell, 167 ; Hogarth ; " Sablonnière
Hotel ; " Tenison's school and
library ; Pic-nic Club, *ib.* ; John
Hunter's museum, 168 ; Panopticon ;
Alhambra Palace Theatre, *ib.* ; C.
Dibdin's Sans Souci, 170; the
" Feathers ; " Burford's Panoramas ;
Wyld's " Great Globe," *ib.* ; neglect
of the enclosure, 171 ; mutilations
of the statue ; litigation ; Albert
Grant ; garden ; statuary ; fountain,
ib. ; foreigners, 172.
Leighton, Archbishop, ii. 440.
Leighton, Sir Frederick, iii. 148.
L. E. L. (*See* Landon, Miss.)
Lely, Sir Peter, iii. 242, 254, 256 ; vi.
193.
Leman, Sir John, Lord Mayor ; show ;
drawing at Fishmongers' Hall, i.
321 ; ii. 8.

Lemon, Mark, i. 57, 58 ; iv. 456.
" Le Neve " Inn, Thames Street, i. 302.
Le Neve, Peter, Norroy ; the Paston
letters, i. 298.
Le Neve, Sir William, Clarencieux, i.
298.
Le Notre, iv. 50 ; v. 153, 569 ; vi. 207.
Lennox, Countess of, imprisoned in the
Tower, ii. 70.
Lennox, Lady Caroline ; elopement
with Henry Fox, v. 170.
Lennox, Lady Sarah, and George III.,
v. 164, 170.
Leopold I., King of the Belgians, iv.
94, 133 ; v. 203.
" Lepel, The fair " (Lady Hervey), iv.
170, 176.
Lepers' Hospitals, iii. 197 ; v. 23, 527 ;
vi. 70.
Le Serre ; St. James's Park, iv. 51.
Le Sœur, Hubert ; statue of Charles I.,
iii. 125.
Lettsom, Dr. John, vi. 279.
Lever, Sir Ashton, iii. 177 ; vi. 382.
Levett, apothecary, i. 98, 191.
Levy, Mr., and the *Daily Telegraph*,
i. 60.
Lewes, Priors of ; residence in Ber-
mondsey ; ancient crypt, vi. 104, 105.
Lewis, M. G. (" Monk ") v. 147.
Lewisham, vi. 244 ; etymology ; the
Ravensbourne, 245 ; Granville Park ;
parish church ; interments ; St. Ste-
phen's Church ; St. Mark's Church ;
descent of the manor ; priory ;
Priory Farm ; Admiral Legge ;
Viscount Lewisham, *ib.* ; schools
and almshouses, 246 ; Ladywell ;
railway station ; Deptford and
Lewisham Cemetery ; St. John's
Church, *ib.*
Lewknor's Lane, St. Giles's ; Sir Lewis
Lewknor ; Jonathan Wild, iii. 208.
Lewson, Lady, her eccentricities, ii.
300.
Licensed Victuallers' Asylum, vi. 249.
Licensed Victuallers' School, vi. 340.
Lichfield House, St. James's Square,
iv. 189.
Lich-gate, St. Giles's-in-the-Fields, iii.
202.
Lieutenancy of the City, i. 442.
Lieven, Prince, iv. 372.
Life Assurance carried on by the
Mercers' Company, i. 379.
Life Guards. (*See* Guards, Horse and
Foot.)
Lightfoot, Hannah, iv. 207 ; v. 27,
477 ; vi. 289.
Ligonier, Edward, Viscount, iii. 447 ;
iv. 178, 344.
Lightning conductors, i. 106, 256.
Lightning, Death by, iv. 478.
Lilburne, John, ii. 405 ; vi. 243.
Lillie Bridge, vi. 526.
Lillo, George, vi. 138, 281.
Lilly, William, astrologer, i. 128, 129 ;
iii. 45, 526.
Lillywhite, cricketer, v. 408.
Lime Grove, Putney, vi. 494.
Lime Street ; sale of lime, ii. 188.
Linacre, Dr., his house, Blackfriars ;
College of Physicians, i. 303 ; iii.
143.
Lincoln Court, Drury Lane, iii. 40.
Lincolne John ; " Evil May Day " riot,
i. 310—314.
Lincoln's Inn, iii. 51 ; " Inns of Court ; "
Fortescue ; " Revels," *ib.* ; costume,

52 ; beards of students ; " moots ;"
Earl of Lincoln, *ib.* ; old hall, 53 ;
chapel, 54 ; crypt, 56 ; new hall
and library ; Stone Buildings ; New
Square ; Gardens, *ib.* ; early history, 57 ; Bishops of Chichester ;
legal education, *ib.* ; Society of
Lincoln's Inn, 58 ; readers, *ib.*
Lincoln's Inn Fields, iii. 44 ; formation
of the Square ; its dimensions ; designs of Inigo Jones ; houses erected
by him, *ib.* ; noble families, 45 ;
infested by thieves and beggars,
" mumpers " and "rufflers ;" Square
railed in ; execution of Lord William Russell, *ib.* ; College of Surgeons, 46 ; Sardinian Chapel ;
Newcastle House, 47 ; Soane Museum, 48.
" Lincoln's Inn Theatre," iii. 27.
Lindsay House, Old Palace Yard, iii.
563.
Lindsey House, Lincoln's Inn Fields,
iii. 47.
Lindsey Place and Row, Chelsea, v.
53.
Lindsey, Theophilus, Unitarian minis-
ter, iii. 69.
Link-boys and Link-extinguishers, iv.
327, 339, 445, 549.
Linley, Francis, blind organist, ii. 286.
Linnæan Society, iii. 180, 191 ; iv.
267, 270.
Lintot, Bernard, i. 44.
Linwood, Miss, iii. 165 ; iv. 318.
" Lion and Castle " Inn, Bermondsey,
vi. 130.
Lion's Head, at " Button's Coffee
House," iii. 277.
Lisson Grove ; Lisson Green, v. 257.
Liston, John, comedian, v. 6.
Liston, Robert, surgeon, iv. 303.
Literary Club ; Dr. Johnson, iii. 178.
Literary Society, The ; Willis's Rooms,
iii. 179.
Literature, Royal Society of, iii. 154.
Litlington, Abbot, iv. 2.
Little Britain ; Earls of Brittany ;
bookstalls, ii. 223, 435.
Little Chelsea, v. 88.
Little Cockpit Yard, iv. 551.
Little College Street, Westminster, for-
merly " Piper's Ground," iv. 2.
Little Dean Street, Westminster, iv. 36.
Little James Street, Westminster, iv.
22.
Little, John, miser, v. 321.
Little Holland House ; Mrs. Inchbald ;
Miss Fox, v. 177.
" Little Man's " Coffee House, iii.
334.
Little Park Street, Westminster ; " The
Three Johns," iv. 44.
Little Tower Street ; James Thomson,
poet, ii. 99.
Little Trinity Lane, ii. 37.
Little Vine Street, iv. 253.
Liverpool, Earl of, iii. 336, 532.
Liverpool Street, Finsbury, ii. 207.
Liverpool Street, King's Cross ; King's
Cross Theatre, iv. 576.
" Living Skeleton," iv. 257.
Livingstone, David, iii. 418.
Llewellyn, Prince of Wales, ii. 101, 254.
Lloyd's Alley, St. Giles's, iii. 207.
" Lloyd's ; " historical sketch of, 509—
513.
" Load of Hay " Tavern, Haverstock
Hill, v. 491.

Local Government Board, iii. 377.
Lock or Lazar Hospitals, v. 14, 215, 527, 528.
Locket's Ordinary, Charing Cross, iv. 80.
Lock's Fields, Walworth, vi. 268.
Loddidge's Nursery, Hackney; Loddidge's Terrace, v. 514.
Lodge, Edmund; Lancaster Herald, i. 299; iv. 542.
Logography, the *Times* newspaper printed by, i. 209, 212.
Lollards, Persecution of the, i. 239, 242; ii. 13, 65; vi. 238.
Lollards' Tower, Lambeth Palace, vi. 435.
Lombard Street, i. 509; Marine Assurance; origin of "Lloyd's," *ib.*; the Lombards, money-lenders and bankers, 524; William de la Pole, factor to Edward III.; Gresham's shop, *ib.*; Post Office, 525; churches, 527; remains of a Roman road, pavements, vases, 529, 530.
Lombard Street, Chelsea, v. 66.
Lombard wine merchants, ii. 22.
Lombards; jealousy of; "Evil May Day," i. 310, 311; early bankers and usurers, i. 453.
Londinium, plan of, i. 15.
London Artizan's Club and Institute, iv. 467.
London, Bishops of; London House, St. James's Square, iv. 186; vi. 508.
London Bridge, ii. 9; Roman and Saxon bridges; "Old Moll" the ferryman's daughter, *ib.*; wooden bridge destroyed, 10; stone bridge built; St. Thomas's Chapel; heads of traitors placed on the bridge, *ib.*; Brethren of the Bridge, ii. 11, 12; fighting; tournament; pageants; Henry V.; triumph and funeral, *ib.*; Lydgate, 12, 13, 14; danger of "shooting" the bridge, 13; Jack Cade's and Wyatt's rebellions, 14; Nonsuch House, 15; waterworks; houses on the bridge; decay; repairs; temporary bridge burnt; Smeaton; new bridge commenced by Rennie, *ib.*; traffic, 16; earliest description of a bridge at this spot, vi. 5; first stone bridge erected, 8; built by a tax on wool; Bridge-foot, Southwark, *ib.*; Jack Cade's rebellion, 9; pageants, 10; the Great Fire; towers, houses, and corn-mills on the bridge, 11; booksellers' shops, 13; the new bridge, 15.
London Bridge railway stations, vi. 98.
"London" Coffee House, Ludgate Hill, i. 227, 228.
London Crystal Palace, Oxford Street, iv. 455.
London Docks, ii. 123, 124; built by Rennie; description and statistics by Henry Mayhew; tasting-orders; the "Queen's pipe," 124, 125.
London Fields, Hackney, v. 507; "Cat and Mutton Fields;" rights of the Bishops of London; Ridley Road, *ib.*
London Fire Brigade, i. 554.
London Gas Company, vi. 467.
London Hospital, ii. 146.
London Institution, i. 428, 429; ii. 207
London Journal, 1721, iv. 347.
London Library, iv. 189.
London Magazine, i. 64, 65.

London Mathematical Society, iv. 290.
London Necropolis Company, vi. 418.
London Orphan Asylum, v. 522.
London School Board, iii. 326.
London Seamen's Hospital, i. 513.
"London Spy," by Ned Ward. *See* Ward, Ned.)
London Stone, i. 544.
London Street, Dockhead, vi. 113, 116.
London Street, Fitzroy Square, iv. 475.
London University, Burlington Gardens, iv. 304.
London Wall, ii. 168, 232.
London and Brighton Railway, vi. 99.
London and Greenwich Railway. (*See* Greenwich.)
London and North-Western Railway, v. 347—350.
London and South-Western Railway, vi. 411, 468.
London, Chatham, and Dover Railway, i. 220; ii. 501; v. 41.
Long Acre, iii. 269; original condition; "The Elms;" "The Seven Acres;" head-quarters of carriage-builders; distinguished residents; St. Martin's Hall, *ib.*; "Queen's Theatre," 270; Merryweather's fire-engine manufactory, *ib.*
Longbeard's rebellion, i. 309, 310.
Long Fields, Bloomsbury, iv. 482, 564.
Longman and Co., publishers, i. 274, 275; ii. 435.
Long Lane, Smithfield, ii. 363.
Longevity. (*See* Centenarians.)
"Long Southwark," vi. 17.
Long Walk, Bermondsey, vi. 120.
Lord Mayor's Banqueting House, Oxford Street, iv. 406, 438.
Lord Mayors of London, i. 396—416; title of "Lord," i. 398; election, duties, and privileges, i. 437; v. 150; costume and insignia, i. 443, 446; Lord Mayors' Shows, by land and water, 317—332; iii. 309.
Lord Mayor's State Barge, i. 447.
Lord's Cricket Ground; game of cricket; its history; Marylebone Club, v. 249.
Lordship Lane, Dulwich; "Plough" Inn, vi. 292.
Lothbury; foundry and metal workers, i. 513; St. Margaret's Church; conduit, 514,
Lotteries, State, i. 245, 346, 379; ii. 238, 489, 537, 538; iii. 165; iv. 292.
Loudon and Wise; gardens of Kensington Palace, v. 152.
Loudon, gardener (1698), vi. 155, 467.
Lough, J. G., sculptor, v. 260.
Louis Philippe, iv. 422.
Louis XVIII., iv. 344, 422.
Loutherbourg, Philip James, iv. 461; vi. 545.
Lovat, Simon, Lord, ii. 76, 95; iii. 551; iv. 469.
Lovel Family; the great Lord Lovel, vi. 134.
Lovelace, Richard, i. 126; iii. 488.
Love Lane, Cheapside, i. 374.
Love Lane, Eastcheap. i. 563.
"Love-locks," iv. 383.
Lover's Walk, iv. 442.
Loving cup, iii. 568.
Lowe, Rt. Hon. Robert, M.P., v. 13.
Lowe, Tommy, proprietor of Marylebone Gardens, iv. 435.
Lower Belgrave Street, v. 11.

Lower Grosvenor Street, iv. 341.
Lower Seymour Street; charitable institutions, iv. 423.
Lowndes Square, v. 13, 20, 21.
Lowther Arcade, iii. 132.
Ludgate Hill, i. 220; railway bridge; "Belle Sauvage" inn, *ib.*; plays acted there, 221; Banks, the showman; Grinling Gibbons; William Hone; Wyat's rebellion, 224; St. Martin's Court, 226; Roman remains; St. Martin's Church, *ib.*; "London" Coffee House, 227; shop of Rundell and Bridge, 228; Stationers' Hall and Company, 229—233; Almanack day, 230; feast of St. Cecilia, 231; Dryden's odes; funerals and banquets, *ib.*
Lud Gate, history of, i. 221, 223—226.
Lully, Raymond, ii. 117.
Lumber Troop, i. 114, 116.
Lunardi, iii. 321; iv. 245.
Lupus Street, v. 41.
Lushington, Dr., Dean of Arches, i. 292.
Lutherans, Persecution of, i. 243.
Luttrell, Colonel, iv. 173; v. 26.
Lyceum Theatre, iii. 117; exhibitions; Sir R. K. Porter's pictures; theatre burnt down; English operas; "Beefsteak club," *ib.*
Lyell, Sir Charles, iv. 449.
Lydekker, Captain, i. 513.
Lydgate's poems, i. 308; ii. 12, 13, 14; his "London Lickpenny," iii. 543; vi. 9.
Lying Clubs; "lying for the whetstone," vi. 510.
Lying-in Hospital, Queen Charlotte's, v. 256.
Lyndhurst, Lord, iv. 322; v. 407.
Lyons Inn, iii. 35.
Lyric Hall, iv. 456.
Lyttelton, George, Lord, iv. 243.
Lyttleton, Chief Justice, iii. 22.
Lyttleton, Sir Thomas, iii. 80.
Lytton, Lord, iv. 279.
Lyveden, Lord, iv. 310.

M.

"Macao;" gambling at Watier's, iv. 284.
Macaronis, v. 158.
Macaulay, Lord, i. 213; iii. 530; iv. 167, 218, 351, 495, 519, 538, 562, 563; v. 14, 50, 128, 133, 142, 172; vi. 321, 323, 325, 425; vi. 576.
Macclesfield, Anne, Countess of, ii. 552.
Macclesfield Street, Soho, iii. 179.
Macdonald, George, ii. 274.
Mace, the Speaker's; House of Commons, iii. 513.
Maces of the Lord Mayor, i. 446.
McGhee, Charles, the black crossing-sweeper, i. 68.
Macheath, Captain, ii. 527.
Mackay, Chas., LL.D., i. 539; iii. 287, 298; iv. 27, 142, 159, 167, 182.
Mackintosh, Sir James, iii. 530; iv. 453; v. 482.
Macklin, Charles; comedian and centenarian, i. 61; ii. 291; iii. 221, 230, 260, 272.
Macready, W. C., iii. 221, 233.
Maddox Street, Museum of Building Appliances, iv. 322.
Magdalen Hospital, vi. 318, 348.

Magee, Rev. Dr., Bishop of Peter-borough, iv. 409.
Magic Lantern, Marylebone Gardens, iv. 436.
Maginn, Dr., i. 58; iv. 251.
Magna Charta, iv. 514.
"Magpie and Stump," Newgate Street, ii. 276.
Mahoney ("Father Prout"), iv. 251.
"Maid of Kent," v. 189.
Maida Vale; battle of Maida, v. 243.
Maiden Lane, Battle Bridge, ii. 276.
Maiden Lane, Covent Garden, iii. 119, 267; "Bedford Head," old Welsh ale house; Marvell; Voltaire; Turner; "Shilling Rubber Club;" Hogarth and Churchill, ib.; Catholic Church, 268; "Cider Cellars;" origin of its name, ib.
Maiden Lane, King's Cross, formerly Longwich Lane, v. 372; now York Road and Brecknock Road, 373.
Maiden Lane, Wood Street; churches; Haberdashers' Hall, i. 371.
Mail coaches, annual procession of, ii. 210; iv. 260.
Mail-coach robbery, Pall Mall, iv. 137.
Main drainage system, ii. 423; iii. 324; v. 41; vi. 572.
Maitland, Dr. Samuel, vi. 430.
Malibran, Madame, iii. 221.
"Mall, The," St. James's Park, iv. 50, 51; the game so called; "mailes," iv. 74; "Pall Mall" implements, 75.
Mallet, David, vi. 494.
Malt factors and maltsters, ii. 182.
Manchester Buildings, Cannon Row, iii. 381.
Manchester House. (See Manchester Square.)
Manchester Square, iv. 423, 424; Duke of Manchester; Manchester House; Marquis of Hertford; George IV. and the Marchioness; Spanish Embassy; Sir Richard Wallace; Theodore Hook; William Beckford, 324.
Manchester Street; Joanna Southcote; Howlett's Hotel; Lady Tichborne, iv. 425.
"Man in the Moon" Tavern, iv. 253.
Mann, Sir Horace; the "Cock Lane Ghost," ii. 437.
Manning, Cardinal, iv. 9.
Mannings, Execution of the, vi. 254.
"Mann's" Coffee-house, iii. 334.
Manny, Sir Walter de, ii. 381.
Mansel, Dean, i. 237, 254.
Mansfield, Earl of, i. 176; iv. 452, 541, 544; v. 441—443, 542; his house attacked by the Gordon rioters, iv. 539; v. 443; vi. 346.
Mansfield Street, iv. 448.
Mansion House; described, i. 436; Egyptian Hall; works of art; the kitchen, 437; Lord Mayor's household and expenditure; cost of the building, 443.
"Mansion House," old, Highgate, v. 410.
Mansion House Station, v. 231.
Manton, Joe, iv. 335.
Mapp, Mrs., bone-setter, vi. 248.
Marble Arch, iv. 405.
Marching Watch, i. 331, 338, 380.
Mare Street, Hackney, v. 513.
Margaret of Anjou, i. 316.
Margaret Street, Cavendish Square, iv. 459, 460; Lady Margaret Cavendish; Rev. David Williams; Camp-

bell; Belzoni and Bergami; West London Synagogue; All Saints' Church; the "Sisterhood," ib.
Maria Wood, the Lord Mayor's state barge, i. 447; iii. 309.
Marie de Medici, mother of Queen Henrietta Maria, i. 304; iv. 107.
Marine Assurance, "Lloyd's," i. 509—513.
"Marine-store" dealers, vi. 163.
Marionettes, iv. 346.
Markets of London, iii. 41.
Mark Lane; Allhallows Staining Church; Corn Exchange, ii. 179.
Market-gardens, v. 179, 212; vi. 136, 478, 533.
Marlborough Club, iv. 150. 164.
Marlborough House, Pall Mall, iv. 129 —133.
Marlborough House, Peckham, vi. 287 129—133.
Marlborough, John, Duke of, iv. 26, 117; v. 145.
Marlborough, Sarah, Duchess of, i. 38, 176, 461.
Marlborough Square, Chelsea, v. 88.
Marlowe, Christopher, iv. 160.
Marochetti, Baron, iii. 567.
Marriages: in Mayfair, ii. 347; Marriage Act, 349; irregular, in the Fleet Prison, and its rules, 410—412; in Mayfair, iv. 347; at Knightsbridge, v. 23; at Hampstead Wells, 470; in the Mint, Southwark, vi. 62; banns proclaimed in market-places, ii. 506; St. George's Church, Hanover Square, iv. 321; re-marriage in Bermondsey Church, vi. 121; marriage by civil magistrates, 446.
"Marrowbones and Cleavers," iv. 322.
Marshall, Sir Chapman, Lord Mayor, i. 414.
Marshall's "Peristrophic" Panorama, iv. 82.
Marshall Street, Golden Square, iv. 239.
Marshalsea, or Palace Court, residence of the attorneys, i. 92.
Marshalsea Prison, vi. 73; jurisdiction; abuses; Bishop Bonner; Colonel Culpeper; described by Dickens, 74.
Marsham Street, Westminster, iv. 4.
Martin, John, painter; his plans for public improvements, iv. 401; v. 86, 257.
Martin, Samuel; duel with Wilkes, iv. 389.
Martyrs burnt in Smithfield, ii. 339, 351.
Marvell, Andrew, iii. 64, 125, 267, 350; v. 398, 399.
Mary of Modena, Queen of James II., iv. 5, 110; vi. 447.
Mary, Queen, iii. 404, 440; vi. 167, 170.
Mary Queen of Scots, i. 521; iii. 438.
Mary, Queen of William III., iii. 446; v. 141, 142, 143, 144; vi. 176, 439.
Marylebone, iv. 428; etymology; a country village; present population; extent; manor and owners; Duke of Portland; Earl of Oxford and Mortimer; Lady Harley; names of streets derived from owners, ib.; old parish church, 429; manor house; high street; Fountayne's academy, ib.; new church, double gallery, and altar-piece by West, 430; "Farthing Pie House," 433; "Marylebone Basin," 434; "Cockney Ladle;" Long's Bowling Green,

ib.; Harley Fields, 440; the parish and its associations, v. 254—262; Marylebone Gardens, iv. 431; Charles Bannister; Dibdin, ib.; fêtes and fireworks, 432; bowling-alleys; Gay; Sheffield, Duke of Buckingham, ib.; "Consort of Musick," 434; Handel; Dr. Arne; robberies; balloons; fireworks; Miss Trusler's cakes, ib.; gambling, 435; highwaymen, 436; tea-drinking; lectures on Shakespeare and mimicry, ib.
Marylebone; old and new courthouses, iv. 431, 437.
Marylebone Road, iv. 431; charitable institutions; workhouse; Cripples' Home; Hospital for Women; Western Dispensary; Association for Improvement of Dwellings; Police Court, ib.
Marylebone Theatre, v. 259.
Marylebone Waterworks, iv. 456.
Mary Rose, vi. 146.
Masham, Lady, iv. 309.
Maskelyne and Cooke, iv. 258.
Maskelyne, Dr., vi. 215.
Masonic Avenue, ii. 238.
Masons' Hall, ii. 237.
Masons' Hall Tavern, ii. 238.
Masons' yards, Euston Road, v. 303.
Masques and Masquerades, i. 160; ii. 521, 557; iii. 51, 339, 342; iv. 210; v. 78; vi. 166, 167.
Massinger, Philip, vi. 27.
Mass-houses, iii. 218.
"Master of the Revels;" licences granted by him, iii. 344.
"Matfellon, St. Mary," Whitechapel; origin of the name, ii. 143.
Mathew, Rev. H., iv. 469, 472.
Mathews, Charles, the elder, iii. 132, 263; iv. 339; v. 410.
Mathews, Charles, the younger, iii. 233.
Mathison, John; bank forgeries, i. 464.
Matilda, Queen, iii. 197.
Mat o' the Mint," vi. 62.
Mattheson's lessons for the harpsichord, i. 269.
"Maunday" money, iii. 368.
Maurice, Rev. F. D.; Working Men's College, iv. 560; v. 408.
May-Day celebrations, iv. 100; v. 223; vi. 206. (See Maypole.)
May Fair, iv. 285; the ancient fair; its suppression; Pepys, 345; booths, 346; riot; puppet-shows; "Tiddy Dol," ib.; May Fair Chapel; secret marriages; Marriage Act, 349.
Mayhew, Henry, i. 57, 58; statistics of Billingsgate Market, ii. 43, 45, 46; of St. Katherine's Docks, ii. 119; London Docks, ii. 124; Rosemary Lane, ii. 144; watercress sellers, ii. 500.
Mayhew, Horace, i. 57, 58.
"May meetings;" Exeter Hall, iii. 118.
Maypole at St. Andrew Undershaft, ii. 191; denounced and destroyed, 192.
Maypole, The Strand; account of its erection, iii. 86; Maypole Alley, 88.
Maypoles: West Green, Hampstead, v. 503; Kensington Green, remaining till 1795, vi. 340.
Mazarine Bible, vi. 149.
Mazarine, Duchess of, v. 53, 126.
Maze Hill, Greenwich, vi. 230.
Maze Pond, Bermondsey; the Maze, vi. 104.
"Maze," Tothill Fields, iv. 15.

Mead, Dr. Richard, ii. 142, 160, 433; iv. 560; v. 83.

Meadows, Kenny, i. 57.

Mears, Richard, publisher, i. 269.

Meat Market, Leadenhall, ii. 189.

Meat Market, Metropolitan, ii. 491; its history; railway system; supply of dead meat; Newgate Market, *ib.*; New Market and Underground Railway Station, 493; opening ceremony, 494; tolls and rentals, 495; game; quails' and plovers' eggs, 496.

Mechanical automata, Exhibition of, iv. 421.

Mecklenburgh Square, iv. 563.

Medical and Chirurgical Society, iv. 465.

Medical Men, Society for Relief of Widows and Orphans of, iv. 465.

Medici, Marie de, i. 304; iv. 107.

Melbourne House; the Albany, iv. 258.

Melbourne, Lord, iii. 387, 388; v. 149, 151.

Mellitus, first Bishop of London, i. 236.

Mellon, Harriett (*See* St. Alban's, Harriet, Duchess of.)

Melons, iii. 77.

Melvill, Rev. Henry, vi. 274.

Melville, Lord, trial of, iii. 531, 554.

Memorial Hall, Farringdon St., ii. 416.

"Memory Thompson," v. 501.

Menageries, ii. 88; iii. 116, 315; v. 196, 305, 569; vi. 226.

Mennes, Sir John, ii. 111, 112.

Mercer Street, Long Acre, i. 377.

Mercers' Company and Hall, i. 376, 525; the "Mercery," 377; Mercers' jealousy of the Lombards; Thomas A'Becket; Whittington; grants to the Company; Mercers' Hospital, *ib.*; loans to King and Parliament, 379; life assurance; financial difficulties; lottery, *ib.*; hall and chapel, 380; charities; school, 381; distinguished "mercers," 382; costume of mercers, 383.

Mercers' School, College Hill; eminent scholars, ii. 26.

"Mercery" in Cheapside, i. 372.

Merchant Adventurers, i. 453.

Merchant Taylors' Company and Hall, i. 531; "Linen Armourers;" charters; dispute with the Skinners, *ib.*; ii. 4; Stow's "Annals," presented by him to the Company, i. 532; Speed; the Plague; James I.; Dr. Bull; old customs; charities, *ib.*; armoury, 533; civil war; school; livery hoods; searching and measuring cloth, *ib.*; Old Hall; Basing Lane; present Hall and Almshouses, 534; Arms of the Company, 536; Henry VII. enrolled; march of the Archers, *ib.*; almshouses, Lee, vi. 244.

Merchant Taylors' School, i. 533; "Manor of the Rose;" Pulteney's Hill; site and statutes of the school; scholarships; Great Fire; eminent scholars, ii. 29.

Merchants of the Staple, i. 453.

Merlin, Prophecy of, ii. 101.

Mermaids, vi. 195, 276.

"Mermaid" Tavern, Cheapside, i. 351; Raleigh; Mermaid Club; Ben Jonson; Shakespeare, *ib.*

"Mermaid" Tavern, Hackney, v. 518.

Merryweather's fire-engine factory, iii. 270.

Meteorological Department, iv. 268.

Methodist preachers in Newgate, ii. 447.

Methodists' Tabernacle, Finsbury, ii. 198.

Metropolitan and Metropolitan District Railways, ii. 122; iii. 131, 323, 325, 327; Charles Pearson; opposition to the plan, v. 224; construction, 225; irruption of the Fleet Ditch; opening and success, *ib.*; Inner and Outer Circles, 226; statistics; line and stations, *ib.*; signals and ventilation, 230; workmen's trains, 232.

Metropolitan Board of Works, iv. 79.

Metropolitan Meat Market. (*See* Meat Market.)

Metropolitan Police, iii. 333.

Metropolitan Tabernacle, vi. 258.

Meux and Co.'s brewhouse, iv. 485.

"Mews," Royal, Charing Cross, iii. 129.

Meyrick, Sir Samuel Rush, ii. 83; his collection of arms and armour, v. 108.

Middle Exchange, Strand, iii. 101.

Middle Park, Eltham; Blenkiron's racing stud, vi. 242.

Middle Row, Holborn, ii. 537.

Middle Scotland Yard; United Service Museum, iii. 335.

Middlesex Hospital, iv. 465; cancer wards; Samuel Whitehead; French refugees; Lord Robert Seymour; Sir Charles Bell, 466.

Middleton, Sir Thomas, Lord Mayor, i. 404.

Midland Railway, v. 368; St. Pancras Terminus; demolition of St. Pancras Churchyard; Agar Town, *ib.*; underground works, 369; Terminus, Hotel, and Station; goods station, 370, 371.

Midsummer Marching Watch, i. 331, 338.

Milborne, Sir John, Lord Mayor; Drapers' Almshouses, ii. 250.

Mildmay House and Mildmay Park, Stoke Newington, v. 531.

"Miles's Music House," afterwards Sadler's Wells Theatre, iii. 42.

Miles's pair-horse coach; "Miles's Boy," v. 206.

"Milestone, Old," City Road, ii. 227.

Milford Lane, iii. 70.

"Milk Fair," St. James's Park, iv. 76.

"Milkmaids on May Day," picture at Vauxhall Gardens, vi. 460.

Milk Street, i. 374; City of London School, 375; Church of St. Mary Magdalene, *ib.*

Mill, James, v. 128.

Mill, John Stuart, iii. 531.

Mill Lane, Tooley Street, vi. 106.

"Mill-sixpences," ii. 104.

Mill Street, Conduit Street, iv. 322.

Mill Street, Dockhead, vi. 116.

Millar, Andrew, iii. 80, 286; v. 59, 86.

Millbank Prison; Jeremy Bentham; prison discipline, vi. 8.

Millbank, Westminster, iv. 2, 3.

Miller, Joe, author of the "Jest Book," iii. 29, 41; vi. 58, 555.

Miller, Rev. James, his play, *The Coffee-house*, i. 44.

Milliners; Milliners' shops and stalls, i. 373; iii. 104, 172, 542.

"Million Gardens" (Melon Gardens), Westminster, iv. 12.

Mill Pond, Rotherhithe, vi. 135.

Millman Street; Chevalier D'Eon, iv. 551.

Milman, Dean, i. 252; iii. 179.

Mills, Dr. Jeremiah, President of the Society of Antiquarians, i. 527.

Milner, Dr., his school at Peckham; Goldsmith, vi. 239.

Milton, John, i. 49, 274, 350; ii. 219, 220, 225, 268; iii. 50, 330, 428, 574; iv. 22, 53, 78, 166, 172, 230, 549; v. 167, 382, 399, 514; vi. 548.

Milton Street, formerly Grub Street, ii. 240; Pope's Grub Street poets; bowyers and fletchers; Grub Street Society, 241; "General Monk's house," 242.

"Mince-pie House," Blackheath, vi. 230.

Minchenden House, Southgate, v. 569.

Mincing Lane, ii. 177; Genoese traders, or "gallymen;" "galley halfpence;" Great Fire; Pepys; Clothworkers' Hall, *ib.*

Minories, ii. 249; Abbey of St. Clare, *ib.*; Holy Trinity Priory; Lord Cobham, 250; stay-makers; Thistlewood, *ib.*

Mint of the Saxon period, Bermondsey, vi. 105.

Mint Street, Southwark, vi. 60; the old mint; Henry VIII.; Edward VI.; Archbishop Heath; the Lant family; Lant Street, *ib.*; protection from arrests, 61; irregular marriages, 62; "Mat o' the Mint;" Jonathan Wild; Nahum Tate; Nathaniel Lee; Pope; Thomas Miller's description of the "Mint," *ib.*; Jack Sheppard, 63; coiners; Asiatic cholera, *ib.*

Mint, The, ii. 100; British, Roman, and Saxon coinage; Alfred's silver penny; dishonest minters, *ib.*; Moneyer's Company, 101; Comptroller of the Mint; first gold coinage; silver groats of Henry V., *ib.*; debasement of the coinage, 102; coins struck by Queen Elizabeth, 104; milled money; Briot; Simon; first copper coins; tin coinage; Queen Anne's farthings; first guineas; bullion; Spanish silver captured; Chinese ransom, *ib.*; process of coining, 105. (*See* Coinage.)

Miracle-plays, ii. 344, 255.

"Mischief, The," Oxford Street, iii. 196.

Misers, ii. 286; vi. 352.

Mission College, Blackfriars Road, vi. 373.

Mission Hall, Queen's Square, Westminster, iv. 42.

Mitre Court Buildings; Charles Lamb, i. 135.

"Mitre" Tavern, Fleet Street, i. 51, 54; Johnson and Boswell; Society of Antiquaries; Royal Society; Poets' Gallery, *ib.*

"Mitre" Tavern, Wood Street, i. 369.

Moat at Fulham Palace, vi. 512.

Model lodging-houses, iv. 488; George Peabody, vi. 570.

Mohawks, Mohocks, iii. 243; iv. 57, 166, 298.

Mohun, Lord, i. 70; iii. 82, 161, 180, 278, 551; iv. 389.

Mohun, Major, comedian, iii. 273.
Molesworth, Lady, burnt to death, iv. 373.
Money Order Office, ii. 212.
Monger's almshouses, Hackney, v. 513.
Monk, General (Earl of Albemarle), ii. 165, 242 ; iii. 87, 104, 122, 422, 440 ; iv. 108, 378 ; vi. 71.
Monkwell Street ; Hall of the Barber-Surgeons, ii. 232 ; Lamb's almshouses, 236.
Monmouth Court ; James Catnatch, printer, iii. 204.
Monmouth, Duke of, ii. 75, 95 ; iii. 174, 185, 186.
Monmouth House, Chelsea, v. 93.
Monomaniac in the ball of St. Paul's, i. 257.
Monsey, Dr., ii. 434 ; v. 71.
"Monster" Tavern, v. 3, 45.
Montagu, Basil, ii. 402 ; iii. 261.
Montagu, Duke of, iv. 54.
Montagu House ; fields ; duels ; sports ; "Prisoner's Base," iv. 483. (See British Museum.)
Montagu House, Greenwich Park, vi. 210.
Montagu House, Whitehall, iii. 377.
Montagu, Lady Mary Wortley, i. 71, 72 ; iii. 242, 255 ; iv. 153, 260, 446.
Montagu, Matthew, iv. 418.
Montagu, Mrs., iv. 413—418 ; biographical sketch of ; Blue Stocking Club ; "feather hangings ;" Cowper's lines ; chimney-sweepers, ib.
Montagu Square, iv. 312.
Montague Close, Southwark, vi. 28.
Monteagle, Lord ; Gunpowder Plot, vi. 28.
Montefiore, Abraham, i. 484.
Montefiore, Sir Moses, Bart., iv. 372.
Montfichet Castle, Blackfriars, i. 200, 285.
Montfort, Simon de, vi. 9.
Montgomery, Rev. Robert, iv. 472.
Monument, The, i. 566 ; described ; inscriptions, ib. ; Popish allusions obliterated, restored, and finally effaced, 567 ; Cibber's bas-relief ; illuminations ; suicides, 567, 568, 569 ; Great Fire, 572.
Monument Yard, ii. 8.
"Moon-rakers" public-house, Great Suffolk Street, vi. 63.
Moore, Thomas, i. 275 ; iv. 98, 165, 202, 311, 330, 424 ; v. 121, 164, 292, 434 ; vi. 253, 296.
Moore's Almanack, i. 230.
Moorfields, ii. 196 ; Fitzstephen and Stow ; primitive skates ; cudgel-players ; Train-band musters ; laundresses and bleachers ; wrestling ; fighting, ib. ; book-stalls, 197 ; fugitives after the Great Fire ; Artillery Ground ; Carpenters' Hall, ib. ; the Tabernacle, 198 ; old Bethlem Hospital ; St. Luke's Hospital, 200 ; vi. 351 ; Peerless Pool, ii. 201 ; open-air preachers ; carpet-beating, 208.
Moots : in the Temple, i. 180 ; Gray's Inn, ii. 557 ; Lincoln's Inn, iii. 35, 52.
Moravian chapels, i. 97, 100 ; v. 94.
Morden College, Blackheath ; Turkey Company, vi. 236.
More, Hannah, iv. 248.
More, Sir Thomas, i. 315, 537 ; ii. 14,

95, 156, 381, 382, 572 ; iii. 33, 58, 545 ; v. 53—59, 88, 530 ; vi. 10.
Morison, James ; "Morison's Pills," v. 367.
Morland, George, ii. 262, 544 ; iv. 472 ; v. 67, 212, 222, 308, 428 ; vi. 69, 425.
Morland, Sir Samuel, v. 24 ; vi. 386, 448, 449, 544.
Morning Advertiser, i. 64.
Morning Chronicle, iii. 111.
Morning Herald, i. 478.
Morning Post, iii. 113.
Mornington, Countess of, iv. 443.
Mornington Crescent, v. 305.
"Morocco men" executed, v. 190.
Morris, Captain, iii. 118 ; vi. 576.
Morris, Peter ; "forcier" at London Bridge, for water-supply to houses, v. 237 ; vi. 100.
Mortimer, Roger de, ii. 64 ; v. 189.
Mortimer Street ; earldom of Mortimer, iv. 458 ; Nollekens ; Johnson ; St. Elizabeth's Home, 459.
"Mother Black Cap," Camden Town, v. 310.
"Mother Red Cap," Camden Town, v. 302.
Mother Shipton, history of, v. 311.
Mountfort, Will, murdered in defence of Mrs. Bracegirdle, iii. 81.
Mountmill, Goswell Street ; Plague Pit, ii. 202.
Mount Street, iv. 335 ; fort ; "The Mount" Coffee House ; Sterne ; Martin Van Butchell, ib. ; St. George's Workhouse, 337 ; Wedgwood's show-rooms, 338.
Moxhay, Edward, Hall of Commerce, i. 536.
Mud and dust of London, vi. 572.
Mudie's Circulating Library, iv. 489.
"Mug-houses," i. 141, 142, 143.
Mulberry Garden, iv. 62.
Mulberry-trees, ii. 153 ; iv. 62 ; v. 67, 88, 459 ; vi. 418.
"Mull Sack" (John Cottington) and Lady Fairfax, i. 40, 43.
Müller, Franz, executed at Newgate, ii. 457.
Mulready, W., R.A., vi. 382.
"Mumpers" of Lincoln's Inn Fields, iii. 45.
Munday, Anthony, ii. 237, 245.
"Muns," members of dissolute clubs, iv. 57, 166.
Munster, Earl of, v. 11.
Munster House, Fulham Road, vi. 516.
Munster Square, v. 299.
Murphy, Arthur, v. 26.
Murray, John, senior and junior, publishers, i. 46 ; iv. 293, 294.
Murray, Lady Augusta, iv. 29 ; v. 152.
Museums : Building Appliances, iv. 322 ; Don Saltero's Coffee-house, v. 62 ; Indian ; South Kensington, ib. ; Guildhall, i. 392 ; v. 108 ; "Museum Minervæ" iii. 268 ; Patent, v. 112. (See also British Museum.)
Museum Street ; Mudie's Library, iv. 489.
Musgrove, Sir John, Lord Mayor ; his show, i. 416.
Music and musical instrument shops in St. Paul's Churchyard, i. 268.
Musical clocks ; Christopher Pinchbeck, i. 53.
Music-halls, statistics, vi. 574.
Music houses, i. 272.

Muswell Hill, v. 434 ; the "Mus-well ;" Priory of St. John of Jerusalem ; pilgrimages ; Alexandra Palace, 435 ; view from the Palace, 437.
Myatt's Farm, Camberwell ; strawberries, vi. 279.
Myddelton, Sir Hugh, i. 507 ; v. 237.
Mylne, Robert, architect, i. 205, 254.
Mysteries, ii. 344, 525.

N.

Name of London, its derivation, i. 19.
Names of streets and squares ; their origin, iv. 407 ; family names, 428, 442, 443, 476.
"Nando's" Coffee-house, Fleet Street, i. 45.
Napier, Sir Charles, iii. 142.
Napoleon III., iv. 99, 160, 169, 201 ; v. 22, 112, 119.
Nares, Archdeacon, iv. 544.
Nares, Capt. Sir George, R.N., vi. 247.
Nash, John, architect, iv. 66, 87, 208, 230, 250, 263, 405, 576, 450.
"Nassau" balloon, vi. 464.
"Nassau" Coffee-house, iv. 242.
Nassau Street, iv. 466.
National Benevolent Institution, iv. 543.
National Columbarian Society, i. 46.
National Dental Hospital, iv. 456.
National Gallery, iii. 145 ; purchase of Angerstein collection ; donations ; building, 149.
National Orthopædic Hospital, iv. 456.
National Peristeronic Society, i. 46.
National Portrait Gallery, iv. 33 ; v. 107.
National School Society ; Dr. Bell, vi. 365, 366.
National Society for Education, Westminster, iv. 34.
National Society ; St. John's College, Battersea, vi. 472.
National Theatre, Holborn, iv. 549.
National Training School for Music, v. 115.
Nautical Almanack, vi. 215.
Naval and Military Club, iv. 285.
Naval Club, Old Royal, iv. 155.
Navy Office, Seething Lane, ii. 100, 112.
Navy, Royal ; ships of Henry VIII. ; ships launched at Deptford, vi. 146, 147, 148, 149.
Nazareth House, Hammersmith, vi. 530 ; the "Little Sisters of the Poor ;" old Benedictine convent and school, 531 ; list of abbesses ; chapel, training college, and library, 532.
"Neapolitan Club," iv. 155.
Neckinger, The ; Bermondsey, vi. 119, 122, 125 ; Neckinger Road ; Neckinger Mills, 126.
Necromancers, Punishment of, iv. 14.
Nectarines, iv. 567.
"Needham, Mother," iv. 170.
Neele, Henry, ii. 509.
Neild, John Camden, miser, v. 60.
Nelson Column, Trafalgar Square, iii. 142.
Nelson, Lady, iv. 449.
Nelson, Lord, i. 251, 388 ; iii. 385, 386, 389, 447 ; iv. 254, 260, 302, 340.
Nelson, Robert, author of "Fasts and Festivals," iv. 554, 556 ; v. 135.
Nelson Square, Blackfriars, vi. 374.
Nelson Street, Highgate, v. 412.

Nerinckx, Rev. J., v. 345.

Nesbitt, Mrs. ; Prince of Wales's Theatre, iv. 473.

Neville family ; their residences in Upper Thames Street ; the great Earl of Warwick, ii. 18, 19.

Newbery, John and Francis, booksellers, i. 120, 266.

New Burlington Street, iv. 311 ; Earl of Cork ; Lady Cork ; Cocks and Co., music-publishers, ib. ; Colburn, *New Monthly Magazine*, 314 ; Bentley and Son, *Bentley's Miscellany ;* R. H. Barham ; Dickens ; British Medical Benevolent Fund ; Archæological Institute, 315.

Newcastle House, Clerkenwell, ii. 329—332 ; Duke of Newcastle's memoirs, by his wife ; Pepys ; Evelyn ; Sir Walter Scott, ib.

Newcastle House, Lincoln's Inn Fields, iii. 47.

Newcastle, John, Duke of, iii. 425.

Newcastle, William, Duke of, iii. 428.

New Cavendish Street, iv. 458.

New Compton Street ; Bishop Compton, iii. 194.

New Cross, vi. 246 ; "Golden Cross" Inn ; Royal Naval School ; railway stations, 247.

New Cut, Waterloo Road ; Sunday trading, vi. 411.

Newgate, ii. 441 ; fifth principal City gate ; a prison *temp.* King John ; bequests by Walworth and Whittington ; the gate and its statues ; John Howard, ib. ; prison burnt in Gordon riots, 442 ; vi. 347 ; Akerman, keeper of the prison, ii. 443 ; accounts of the burning ; rioters hanged, 446 ; Methodist preachers, 447 ; the "Flying Highwayman," 448 ; Dr. Dodd, 449, 450 ; Governor Wall, 452 ; Haggarty and Holloway, 453 ; Cato Street conspirators, 454 ; Fauntleroy, Bishop and Williams, Greenacre, 455 ; Müller, Courvoisier, 457 ; Elizabeth Brownrigg ; press-room, 458 ; Mrs. Fry ; Jack Sheppard, 459, 460 ; debtors removed, 461.

Newgate Market, ii. 439, 491, 493.

Newgate Street, ii. 428 ; Christ Church ; the "Salutation and Cat ;" "Magpie and Stump ;" "Queen's Arms," 430.

New Georgia, Hampstead, v. 446.

Newington ; Newington Butts, vi. 255 ; etymology ; "Elephant and Castle ;" Joanna Southcott, 256 ; Cross Street, 257 ; Drapers' Almshouses ; Fishmongers' Almshouses, ib. ; semaphore ; Metropolitan Tabernacle, 258, 260 ; St. Mary's old and new churches, 261, 262, 263 ; church pulled down ; clock-tower, 264.

New Inn, iii. 33.

New Jerusalem Church, Camden Road, v. 380.

New Kent Road, vi. 252.

Newland, Abraham, i. 459, 470.

Newman Street, iv. 466, 467 ; Banks ; Bacon ; West ; Rev. Edward Irving ; Stothard ; Copley Fielding ; Cambridge Hall, ib.

New Monthly Magazine, iv. 312.

New Ormond Street, iv. 563.

New Oxford Street, iv. 487.

New Palace Yard, iii. 536 ; state in the seventeenth century ; the High Gate,

ib. ; "Paradise," 537 ; the "Constabulary ;" fountains ; sun-dial ; clock-tower and bell ; "Old Tom," ib. ; punishments and executions, 538 ; pillory ; Titus Oates ; the "Turk's Head," ib.

Newport Market, iii. 177.

Newport Street ; Wedgwood's show-rooms, iii. 266.

New Pye Street, Westminster, iv. 20, 39.

New River, ii. 266 ; v. 430, 538.

New Road, The ; Paddington coaches, v. 302.

Newspapers, history of, iii. 76.

Newspapers, old ; British Museum, iv. 515.

Newspaper statistics, iii. 122.

Newspapers, unstamped, i. 132.

New Square, Lincoln's Inn, iii. 26.

New Street, Covent Garden, iii. 265 ; Dr. Johnson ; the "Pine Apple ;" Flaxman, ib.

New Street, Golden Square, iv. 238.

New Street, Spring Gardens, iv. 81 ; Spring Gardens Chapel ; St. Matthew's Chapel, 82.

New Street Square ; Queen's Printing Office, i. 219.

Newton, Sir Isaac, i. 104, 105, 107, 455 ; iii. 65, 172, 419 ; iv. 232, 267, 268 ; v. 134 ; vi. 214.

New University Club, iv. 160.

New Way Chapel, Westminster, iv. 20.

Neyte, the Manor of, Westminster, iv. 3.

Nichols, John Gough, F.S.A., i. 229.

Nichols, Messrs., printers, v. 506.

Nichols Street, Bethnal Green, ii. 148.

"Nickers," members of dissolute clubs, iv. 57, 166.

Nightingale, Florence, iv. 305.

Nightingale, J. G., and Lady, their tomb by Roubiliac, iii. 447.

Nightingales, iv. 87 ; v. 154, 162, 167, 177 ; vi. 448, 453.

Night Watch, i. 380.

Nine Elms ; Nine Elms' steamboat pier, vi. 468.

Nithsdale, Lord ; his escape from the Tower, ii. 76.

Nixon's statue of William IV. i. 550.

Noah, play of, in the Towneley collection, ii. 525.

Noel, Hon. and Rev. Baptist, iv. 551.

Nollekins, iv. 459, 470.

Nonconformists ; the "Clapham Sect ;" "Claphamites," vi. 321, 325, 326.

Nonsuch House, London Bridge, ii. 15.

Norfolk, Charles, eleventh Duke of, iv. 182, 185.

Norfolk, Duke of ; Charterhouse ; remains of his house, ii. 383, 393.

Norfolk, Duke of, imprisoned in the Tower, ii. 66.

Norfolk House, Church Street, Lambeth ; Dukes of Norfolk, vi. 418.

Norfolk House, St. James's Square, iv. 182, 185.

Norfolk Street, Park Lane ; murder of Lord William Russell, iv. 374.

Norfolk Street, Strand ; St. John's House for training nurses, iii. 80 ; Conservative Land Society ; famous residents, 81.

Norland Square, iv. 181.

Norman, Sir John, Lord Mayor, i. 317, 382, 399 ; iii. 309.

Normand House, North End, Fulham ; Great Plague ; Hospital for Insane Ladies, vi. 527.

Norris, Lord and Lady ; their tomb, iii. 447.

North, Lord, iii. 388 ; iv. 86.

North, Roger, ii. 225.

North, Sir Dudley, iv. 28.

North, Sir Edward ; Charterhouse, ii. 383.

"North and South American Coffee House," i. 537.

North Audley Street, iv. 343 ; Hugh Audley ; his wealth ; Lord Ligonier ; "Vernon's Head ;" St. Martin's Church, 344.

Northcote, James, R.A., iv. 430.

North-Eastern Hospital for Sick Children, v. 507.

North End, Fulham, vi. 526 ; Browne's House ; eminent residents ; North End Road ; Beaufort House ; Lillie Bridge running-ground ; Foote, ib. ; Mount Carmel Retreat, 527 ; Cambridge Lodge ; Normand House ; Lunatic Asylum for Ladies ; Wentworth Cottage ; S. C. and Mrs. Hall ; "No Man's Land ;" Walnut-tree Cottage ; St. Saviour's Convalescent Hospital ; residence of Richardson, ib. ; other residents, 528.

North Kent Railway, vi. 98.

"North Pole" Inn, Oxford Street, iv. 245, 404.

North Street, Fitzroy Square, iv. 476.

North Street, Westminster, iv. 2.

North Surrey District School, Anerley, vi. 315.

Northumberland Avenue, iii. 141.

Northumberland, Duke of, iii. 231.

Northumberland, Earl of, imprisoned in the Tower, ii. 73.

Northumberland House, iii. 135 ; Northampton House ; Bernard Jansen and Gerard Christmas ; name changed to Suffolk House and Northumberland House ; the Percies, 136 ; Sir Hugh Smithson ; Hollar's view of the house, 137 ; alterations ; fire ; the Percy Lion, 138 ; interior ; gardens, 140 ; house pulled down, 141.

Northumberland Street ; Ben Jonson ; *Pall Mall Gazette*, iii. 134.

Northumberland, the "proud" Earl of, iii. 346.

North-Western Railway, v. 290, 296.

Norton, Hon. Caroline, iv. 175, 292, 353.

Norton Street, iv. 461.

Norwood, vi. 314 ; gipsies ; Gipsy Hill ; "Queen of the Gipsies" Inn ; the wood ; Vicar's Oak ; Knight's Hill ; Lord Thurlow's house, ib. ; Beulah Spa, 315 ; churches and chapels ; Queen's Hotel ; North Surrey District School ; Roman Catholic Orphanage, ib. ; Jews' Hospital, 316 ; the Westmoreland Society's Schools ; Norwood Cemetery ; College for the Blind, Upper Norwood, ib.

"Nosegays" presented to criminals going to execution, ii. 484.

Notting Hill, v. 177 ; etymology ; De Veres, 178 ; thieves ; potteries ; artists ; Dukes of Argyll and Rutland ; Dowager Duchess of Bedford ; taverns ; Shepherd's Bush ; "Gallow's Close ;" Kensington ; gravel-pits ; tradesmen's tokens, ib. ; Grand Junction Waterworks, 179 ; Tower Crecy ; Ladbroke Square, 180 ;

Kensington Park Gardens, 181; St. John's Church, Lansdowne Crescent; Norland Square; Orme Square; Bayswater House; Hippodrome, *ib.*; races, 182; Portobello Farm, 183.

Nottingham, Earl of (Lord Chancellor Finch); Nottingham House, now Kensington Palace, v. 142.

Nottingham Place, Marylebone, iv. 431.

Novosielski, iv. 285.

Numbering of houses, iii. 210, 267.

Nunhead, vi. 291; Nunhead Green; "Nun's Head" Tavern; Asylum of Beer and Wine Trade Association; Cemetery; Southwark and Vauxhall Water Company's Reservoirs; St. Mary's College; Heaton's Folly, *ib.*

"Nursery Maid's Walk;" Park Crescent and Park Square, v. 226.

Nurses, Training School and Home for, Westminster, iv. 34.

Nutford Place, iv. 410.

O.

"Oak of Honour." (*See* Honour Oak.)

Oakley Square, v. 310.

Oates, Titus, i. 26, 31, 33; ii. 530; iii. 380, 538; v. 290; vi. 531.

Obelisk in Red Lion Square, iv. 546.

Obelisk in St. George's Circus, vi. 350, 351.

Obelisk, Victoria Embankment, iii. 328.

O'Brien (O'Byrne), Irish giant, iii. 46, 144, 168; iv. 84, 221.

Obstetrical Society, iv. 465.

O'Connell, Daniel, i. 214; iii. 75, 530; iv. 453.

October Club, iv. 28, 141.

Odd Fellows, v. 8.

Okey, John, regicide, v. 514.

Olaf, King of Norway, i. 448, 450; vi. 3, 5, 6, 101.

Olaf, the Norwegian saint; patron of St. Olave's, ii. 9; vi. 101.

Old and Young Club, iv. 157.

Old Bailey, ii. 461; its name; Old Sessions House, 462; constitution of the Court, *ib.*; an *alibi*, 464; Old Court, *ib.*; New Court, 465; remarkable trials, *ib.*; press-yard, 467; torture; gaol fever, *ib.*; sheriffs' dinners; marrow puddings, 468; triangular gallows and new drop, 470; statistics of executions; bodies burnt; accidents at executions; pillory, *ib.*; pillory abolished, 471; Surgeons' Hall, *ib.*; Jonathan Wild, 472, 475; Little Old Bailey; Green Arbour Court, 476.

"Old Bell" Inn, Warwick Lane, ii. 440.

"Old Black Jack" Tavern, iii. 32.

Old Broad Street, ii. 165; Venice Glass House; Pinners' (Pinmakers') Hall; Excise Office; Roman pavement; church of St. Peter-le-Poor, 166, 191.

Old Burlington Street; Florence Nightingale, iv. 305.

Old Cavendish Street, iv. 446.

Old Change, formerly the King's Exchange, i. 346.

Old Chick Lane; thieves' lodging-house, ii. 543.

"Old Crown" Tavern, Highgate, v. 394.

Oldfield, Mrs., actress, iii. 220, 417; iv. 28, 171, 207.

Old Jewry, i. 425; Jews in Saxon times; colonies in London; power of the Jews; fined, persecuted, and massacred; synagogues, *ib.*; costume of Jews, 428; expelled from England; house of Sir Robert Clayton; London Institution, *ib.*; Baptist chapel; Presbyterian church, i. 430.

Old Kent Road, vi. 248; Watling Street; Kent Street Road, 249; Licensed Victuallers' Asylum, *ib.*; South Metropolitan Gas Works, 250; St. Thomas à Watering; executions, *ib.*; Deaf and Dumb Asylum, 251.

"Old Man, The," Inn, Westminster, iv. 46.

"Old Man's" Coffee House, iii. 334.

"Old Moll," the ferryman's daughter, foundress of St. Mary Overie's nunnery, ii. 9.

Old Palace Yard, iii. 563; Lindsay House; Chaucer; Gunpowder Plot, *ib.*; cellar under Parliament House, 565; execution of Raleigh; statue of Cœur-de-Lion, 567.

"Old Parr," iii. 74, 428; iv. 46.

"Old Patch," Bank-notes forged by, i. 459.

"Old Pick my Toe;" old sign, Southwark, vi. 89.

Old Pye Street, Westminster, iv. 20, 39.

"Old Simon;" the "Rookery," St. Giles's, iii. 207; iv. 488.

Oldwick Close, iii. 209.

Oldys, William, Norroy King-at-Arms, i. 298; ii. 36.

Oliver, Isaac, miniature painter, i. 209, 302.

Oliver's Mount, Mount Street, iv. 380, 385.

Olympic Theatre, i. 522; iii. 35.

"Ombres Chinoises," iv. 232.

Omnibuses, iv. 261; Shillibeer, 410; v. 256.

O'Neill, Miss, iii. 232.

One-Tree-Hill, Greenwich Park, vi. 207.

Onslow Square, v. 104.

"O.P." riots, Covent Garden Theatre, iii. 231.

Open spaces, statistics, vi. 575.

"Opera Comique" Theatre, iii. 35.

Opera House. (*See* Her Majesty's Theatre.)

"Opera, The;" the Duke's Theatre, Lincoln's Inn, so called, iii. 27.

Operas at the Pantheon, iv. 244.

Operas, Italian, Introduction of, iv. 209.

Opie, iii. 212; iv. 464.

Orange Street, Leicester Square, iv. 232; chapel; Newton's house; Dr. and Miss Burney, *ib.*

Orange-trees; St. James's Park, iv. 51; Kensington, v. 153.

Orange-women, Hyde Park, iv. 387.

"Orator" Henley, iii. 41.

Oratorios, iii. 118, 574; iv. 211.

Oratory, The, Brompton, v. 26.

Orchard Street, Westminster, iv. 40, 423.

Ordinaries described in the "Gull's Horn Book," i. 276.

O'Reilly, Paris correspondent of the *Times;* exposure of "Bogus" fraud, i. 213.

Organs, iii. 231, 505, 422; v. 114, 507; vi. 104, 362, 363.

Oriental Club, iv. 316.

Orleans, Duke of, imprisoned in the Tower, ii. 64.

Orme Square, v. 181.

Ormonde House, St. James's Square, iv. 183.

Ormond Street, iv. 551.

Ormond Yard, St. James's Square, iv. 203.

Ornithological Society, iv. 51.

Orphan Asylum, Bonner's Road, v. 508.

Orphan Working School, Haverstock Hill, v. 315.

Orphanage for Boys, Stockwell; founded by Rev. C. H. Spurgeon, vi. 329.

Orrery, Charles, Earl of; the "Orrery," v. 89.

Orvietan, an antidote to poison, iv. 545.

Osbaldiston, "Squire" George, v. 249.

Osborne, Lord Mayor; apprentice to Sir Wm. Hewitt; saves the life of his master's daughter, i. 401.

Osborne, Thomas, bookseller, ii. 556.

Osier beds, Pimlico, v. 40.

Osnaburgh Street, v. 299; St. Saviour's Home and Hospital; Trinity Church, 300.

Osyth, St., iv. 239.

Otto, M., French Ambassador, iv. 413.

Otway, Thomas, i. 102; ii. 97.

Outram, Benjamin, "tram"-ways, vi. 483.

Outram, General Sir James, iii. 328.

Oval, Kennington, vi. 333.

Overbury, Sir Thomas, ii. 74, 414.

Overend, Gurney, and Co., i. 466.

Overy, John and Mary, Legend of, ii. 9.

Owen, Robert, iv. 575.

"Owls" Club, iii. 282, 284.

Oxen roasted on the Thames; "Frost Fair," iii. 313—317.

Oxendon Street, iv. 231.

Oxford Chapel, Vere Street, iv. 442.

Oxford, Edward, his attack on Queen Victoria, iv. 179.

Oxford Market, iv. 461.

Oxford Road. (*See* Oxford Street.)

Oxford Square and Terrace, v. 202.

Oxford Street, iv. 244; shops; quagmire; cut-throats; "Charlies;" the Pantheon, *ib.*; "Green Man and Still," 245; "Hog in the Pound;" "North Pole;" "Balloon" fruit-shop," *ib.*; Via Trinobantina, 406; formerly "Uxbridge Road," "Tyburn Road," and "Oxford Road;" Lord Mayor's Banqueting House; Bear Garden, *ib.*; former state, 440; Laurie and Marner, 441; "North Pole" public-house, 464; "Boar and Castle" posting-house, 471; Oxford Music Hall; twice burnt down, *ib.*

Oxford and Cambridge Boat-races, vi. 500.

Oxford and Cambridge Club, iv. 146.

"Oyster, The Whistling;" Vinegar Yard, iii. 282.

P.

Pace, Dean of St. Paul's, ii. 140.

"Pack Horse" Tavern, Turnham Green, vi. 561.

Paddington, v. 205; growth of population, 206; Paddington stages; Miles and "Miles's Boy;" part of St. Margaret's, Westminster; manor presented to Westminster Abbey;

Bishops of London, *ib.* ; "head of water" granted to City Corporation, 207 ; Priory of St. Bartholomew's ; grazing land ; old parish churches, *ib.* ; present Church of St. Mary, 208 ; scrambling for loaves ; interments, *ib.* ; B. R. Haydon, 209 ; Paddington Green, 210 ; churches, 212 ; Gloucester Gardens ; Old Church Street ; Brothers, the prophet ; old public-houses ; market-gardens ; laundresses, *ib.* ; Green enclosed, 213 ; the Vestry Hall ; Wyatt's studio ; distinguished residents ; Princess Charlotte ; Paddington House ; Paddington Maydance, *ib.* ; Westbourne Place, 214 ; Desborough Place ; Westbourne Farm, *ib.* ; Lock Hospital and St. Mary's Hospital, 215 ; Dispensary, 218 ; Dudley Stuart Home ; Boatman's Chapel ; footpads ; Artisans' Dwellings Company ; Baths and Washhouses, *ib.* ; old alms-houses, 219 ; Paddington, Grand Junction, and Regent's Canals ; Western Waterworks, *ib.* ; Kensal New Town, 220 ; Kensal Green Cemetery, *ib.* ; Roman Catholic Cemetery, 221 ; London Board School, 222 ; Praed Street ; Great Western Railway ; Paddington Terminus and Hotel, 223.

Paddington coaches, v. 203, 205.

Paddington Street ; cemeteries, iv. 426.

Page Street, Westminster, iv. 8.

Page, Thomas, C.E., v. 41, 180.

Pageants, i. 315—332, 359 ; Drapers' Company, 548 ; ii. 5, 11, 23, 189 ; vi. 9, 10, 166, 168, 171.

Pagoda, St. James's Park (1814), iv. 54.

Paine, Tom, i. 117.

Painted Chamber ; Palace of Westminster, iii. 497.

Painter-Stainers' Hall, ii. 37.

Palace Gate House, Kensington, v. 138.

Palace of Westminster, New. (*See* Houses of Parliament.)

Palace of Westminster, Royal. (*See* Westminster.)

Palgrave, Sir Francis, v. 490.

Pall Mall East, iv. 226 ; Society of Painters in Water-Colours ; Benjamin West ; Messrs. Colnaghi ; Palestine Exploration Fund, 227.

"Pall Mall," game of, ii. 328 ; "The Mall," iv. 74 ; its "sweet shady side," 123 ; Cumberland House, 124 ; Schomberg House ; Bowyer's Historic Gallery, *ib.* ; Nell Gwynne, 127 ; Army and Navy Club, *ib.* ; Buckingham House, 128 ; Lord Temple ; Lord Bristol ; Lord Nugent, *ib.* ; War Office, 129 ; statue of "Sydney Herbert ;" Marlborough House, 129—133 ; literary associations, 134 ; "Hercules' Pillars," 135 ; "The Feathers ;" Shakespeare Gallery ; Boydell Gallery, *ib.* ; exhibitions and amusements, 136 ; British Institution ; Institute of Painters in Water-Colours ; "Almack's Club ;" "Goose Trees Club ;" Lord Coleraine ; Lord George Germain ; Mrs. Abington, *ib.* ; "Grasshopper" Bank, 137 ; "Star and Garter" Hotel ; mail-coach robbery ; street gas-lighting, *ib.*

Pallavicini, Sir Horatio, ii. 149.

Pallenscourt manor-house, Hammersmith, vi. 534.

Palls : "Sir William Walworth's" at Fishmongers' Hall ; Merchant Taylors' ; Saddlers', ii. 5, 6.

Palmer, John, ii. 209.

Palmer's Almshouses, iv. 40.

Palmer's Village, Westminster, iv. 40.

Palmerston, Lady, iv. 197.

Palmerston, Viscount, iv. 285, 287, 315.

Palsgrave Place, Strand, iii. 63.

Pan-Anglican Synod, Lambeth Palace, vi. 442.

Pancake feast to London 'prentices, i. 399.

"Pancake, throwing The," at Westminster School, iii. 477.

Pandemonium Club, i. 42.

Panizzi, Sir Anthony, iv. 503, 517, 518.

Panopticon, Leicester Square, iii. 168.

Panoramas, iii. 170 ; iv. 22 ; v. 269—272.

Pantechnicon, v. 11.

Pantheon, The, Oxford Street, iv. 244 ; bazaar ; masquerades ; career of Mrs. Cornelys ; Horace Walpole ; Lunardi's balloon ; George IV. ; Delpini ; Handel ; opera-house ; O'Reilly ; Cundy ; Miss Linwood ; political meetings, 245.

Pantherion, iv. 258.

Panton Street ; Col. Panton, iv. 232, 236.

Panyer Alley, "highest ground" in the City, i. 280.

Paoli, General, iv. 344, 408.

Paper manufactory, Chelsea, v. 53.

Papey, The ; Brotherhood of St. John and St. Charity, ii. 165.

Parade, Horse Guards, iv. 59.

"Paradise," at Westminster, iii. 537.

Parchment-makers, vi. 123.

Pardon Churchyard, ii. 380.

Paris Garden ; Liberty of Blackfriars, vi. 51, 53, 55, 380, 381, 385.

Park Crescent, iv. 450.

Park, J., his "History of Hampstead," v. 476.

Park Lane, iv. 291 ; Dudley House, 367, 368 ; Holdernesse House ; Dorchester House ; R. S. Holford, *ib.*

Park Place, St. James's, iv. 171.

Park Square, v. 269.

Park Street, Grosvenor Square, iv. 374 ; Davy ; Beckford ; Lydia White ; Lord Wensleydale, *ib.*

Park Street, Westminster, iv. 44.

Park Theatre, v. 10.

Park Village East, v. 299.

Parker, Archbp., vi. 429, 430, 434, 437.

Parker, leader of the mutiny at the Nore, ii. 143.

Parker Street, Drury Lane, iii. 209.

Parker Street, Westminster, iv. 35.

Parks and open spaces ; statistics, vi. 575.

Parliament Hill, Highgate ; Gunpowder Plot, v. 405.

Parliament, Houses of. (*See* Houses of Parliament.)

Parliament Square ; statues, iii. 539.

Parliament Street, iii. 381, 382 ; Nichols's printing-office ; Mr. Drummond shot ; Whitehall Club, *ib.*

Parliamentary oratory, iii. 530.

Parliamentary reporting, i. 141 ; ii. 320 ; iii. 512.

"Parr, Old," iii. 74, 428 ; iv. 46.

Parr, Queen Katharine, v. 52, 58.

Parr, Rev. Dr. Richard, vi. 284.

Parris, E. T., Panorama of London, v. 272.

Parry, Sir Edward, v. 448.

Parsons, comedian, i. 352.

Parsons, contriver of the "Cock Lane Ghost," ii. 435—438.

Parson's Green, vi. 518 ; Fair ; Parson's Green Lane, 519 ; Park House ; Richardson ; other eminent residents ; Eelbrook Common ; Peterborough House, *ib.* ; Earl of Peterborough, 520.

Partridge-shooting on the site of Grosvenor House, iv. 550.

Pasquali's concert-room, iv. 472.

Paston Letters, i. 400.

Pastor's College ; Rev. C. H. Spurgeon, vi. 326.

Patches on the face, iv. 383.

"Patchwork Closet," Kensington Palace, v. 141.

Patents, Museum of, v. 112.

Paternoster Row, i. 274 ; sale of paternosters ; mercers ; tire-women ; booksellers ; house of Longman and Co., *ib.* ; the "Castle," 275 ; Richard Tarleton ; ordinaries, 276 ; "Dolly's" Tavern, 278 ; celebrities of the "Chapter Coffee House," *ib.* ; "Printing Conger," 279 ; Mrs. Turner ; poisoning of Sir Thomas Overbury, 280 ; St. Michael's Church ; Leland ; Panyer Alley, the "highest ground" in the City, *ib.*

Paterson, William, founder of the Bank of England, i. 347.

Pathological Society, iv. 465.

"Patrick's-eye" (Battersea), vi. 469.

Patriotic Asylum, Wandsworth ; Patriotic Fund, vi. 482.

Pattens, iv. 471.

Paulet, Henry, "Governor of Lambeth Marsh," vi. 388.

Paulet House, Great Queen Street, iii. 210.

Paulet, Sir Amyas, his house in Fleet Street, i. 45.

Paul's Chain, i. 266.

Paul's Cross, i. 238 ; folkmotes ; papal interdict against the Florentines ; Dr. Bourne preaching, 243.

Pauperism ; statistics, vi. 570, 574.

Pavements, Experimental, iv. 471.

Pavements, Roman, i. 18, 21, 557 ; ii. 34, 166, 191.

Pavements, Street, iii. 266.

Paxton, Sir Joseph, v. 32.

Payne, Tom, iv. 125.

Peabody Buildings, St. George's Fields, vi. 350.

Peabody, George, iii. 418.

Peace Festival (1814), iv. 53, iv. 393 ; (1856), v. 291.

Peacock's pocket-books, i. 146.

Pearson, Charles, Metropolitan Railway, v. 224.

Peckham, vi. 286 ; Queen's Road ; Albert Road ; Peckham Park ; Peckham Park Road ; Hill Street ; manor-house, *ib.* ; Peckham House Lunatic Asylum, 287 ; High Street ; police-station ; Avenue House ; Miss Rye ; Marlborough House ; Blenheim House ; "Rosemary Branch" Tavern ; Peckham Fair, *ib.* ; Theatre, 289 ; Nell Gwynne ; Dr. Milner's School ; Goldsmith, *ib.* ; Hanover Street, 290 ; Basing Yard ; Basing Manor ; Rye Lane ; railway station ; Museum of Fire Arms ; Peckham Rye, *ib.*

Pedlar's Acre ; the pedlar and his dog, vi. 387, 444.

Peek, Frean, and Co.'s biscuit factory, Bermondsey, vi. 131.

Peel, the late Sir Robert, Bart., i. 341, 459; iii. 388, 531; iv. 179, 408, 444.

"Peele's Coffee-House," i. 52.

Peerless Pool, formerly Perilous Pond, ii. 201.

Pelham Crescent, v. 104.

Pelicans, vi. 288.

Pemberton Row, Fetter Lane, i. 99.

Pemberton Row, Highgate ; Sir Francis Pemberton, v. 424.

Pembroke, Countess of, ii. 157, 219.

Pembroke House, Whitehall, iii. 377.

Penitentiary, Female, Pentonville, ii. 287.

Penitentiary, Millbank. (See Millbank Prison.)

Penn, William, ii. 75, 97, 414 ; iii. 81 ; vi. 154.

Pennant, Sir Samuel ; his death caused by gaol fever, i. 407.

Pennethorne, Sir James, architect, i. 101, 305.

Pennington, Sir Isaac, Lord Mayor, i. 404 ; ii. 5.

Penny Wedding at Lambeth Wells, vi. 389.

Penton, Henry, M.P., his estate at Pentonville, ii. 279.

Pentonville, ii. 279 ; Geoffrey de Mandeville ; Hospitallers ; the conduit heads ; Henry Penton, M.P. ; "Belvedere" Tavern ; "Busby's Folly ;" Joe Grimaldi ; White Conduit House, ib.; St. James's Chapel, 286 ; "Prospect House" Tavern, 287 ; "Dobney's ;" horsemanship ; bee-taming ; Female Penitentiary ; tragedy in Southampton Street, 287.

Pentonville Prison, ii. 281.

Pepperers in Soper Lane, i. 352.

Pepys, i. 44, 50, 196, 248, 274, 309, 383, 572 ; ii. 20, 99, 111, 112, 176, 178, 188, 196, 224, 330, 337, 555, 560 ; iii. 27, 38, 39, 57, 101, 109, 122, 128, 219, 354, 356, 374, 405, 434, 488, 542, 549 ; iv. 26, 28, 50, 51, 52, 56, 62, 76, 83, 105, 109, 141, 207, 228, 231, 260, 269, 273, 275, 381, 383, 386, 432, 549 ; v. 21, 124, 405 ; vi. 51, 52, 59, 101, 130, 134, 136, 148, 152, 176, 191, 195, 234, 314, 321, 342, 387, 448, 501.

Perambulation of parish bounds, ii. 237 ; iii. 380.

Perceval, Rt. Hon. Spencer, iii. 530 ; iv. 345, 551 ; v. 497 ; vi. 231.

Percival, John, Lord Mayor, i. 400.

"Percy Anecdotes," iv. 469, 470.

Percy Chapel, iv. 472.

Percy Cross, Fulham Road ; "Purser's Cross," vi. 517.

Percy Street, iv. 472.

Perkins's steam gun, i. 123 ; iii. 133.

Pero's "Bagnio," iv. 167.

Perry, James ; Morning Chronicle, i. 75 ; iv. 573.

Perukes, iv. 167.

Pest-field and Pest-house, Carnaby Street, iv. 236, 239, 250.

Pest-field, Bayswater, v. 185.

Pest-houses, iv. 14, 15, 236 ; vi. 549.

Peterborough, Earl of, iv. 292.

Peterborough House, Fulham, vi. 519.

Peterborough House, Millbank, iv. 2, 3.

Peter of Colechurch, London Bridge built by, ii. 10 : iii. 213.

Peter the Great, ii. 98 ; iii. 81, 162, 544 ; v. 143 ; vi. 148, 154, 155.

Peters, Hugh, iii. 573 ; vi. 377.

Peto, Sir S. Morton, v. 269.

Pett, Peter, master shipwright, Deptford, vi. 160.

Petticoat Lane, ii. 144.

"Petty Calais," Westminster, iv. 21.

"Petty France," Leicester Fields and Westminster, iii. 172 ; iv. 17, 21, 34, 45.

Petty, Sir Wm., i. 515 ; iv. 256, 269.

Petty Wales, ii. 93.

Peyrault's "Bagnio," St. James's Street, iv. 167.

Pharmaceutical Society, iv. 542.

Phelps, Samuel, tragedian, ii. 294.

Philanthropic Society's School, St. George's Fields, vi. 350.

Philip of Flanders, his armour in the Tower, ii. 86.

Philippa, Queen, iii. 441.

Philips, Ambrose, iii. 277.

Phillips, Lord Mayor, banquet to Prince of Wales and King of the Belgians, i. 416.

Phillips, Sir Richard, i. 208, 278, 413 ; ii. 268 ; iv. 172, 312, 395, 470 ; v. 14, 26, 47, 69, 77, 82, 154 ; vi. 470.

Philological School, v. 257.

Phipps, Sir William, a lucky speculator, i. 527.

"Phœnix" Theatre, Drury Lane, iii. 209.

Physic Garden, Chelsea, v. 68.

Physicians, College of. (See College of Physicians.)

Physiorama, iv. 461.

Piazzas ; the Piazza, Covent Garden, iii. 239, 240, 248, 249.

Picard, Sir Henry, Lord Mayor, i. 398, 556.

Piccadilly, iv. 178 ; formerly Portugal Street, 249 ; Criterion Restaurant and Theatre, 207 ; "Piccadilly Saloon," 208 ; origin of the name ; "pickadils," cakes or turnovers ; "peccadillos," "picardills," "piquadillo," "pickardill," "pickadilla," "pickadilly," "peckadille," "pickedila," 207, 218, 233, 235, 248 ; Piccadilly Hall ; pillory, ib.; Goring House, 249 ; Arlington Street ; Clarendon House ; Burlington House ; Devonshire House, ib. ; St. James's Church, 255 ; Sir Wm. Petty, 256 ; Chapman and Hall, 257 ; Hatchard ; Pickering ; Debrett ; Anti-Jacobin ; Egyptian Hall ; Bullock's Museum ; "Living Skeleton ;" Tom Thumb, ib. ; the Albany, 258 ; Daniel Lambert, 259 ; "White Horse Cellar" and coaches, 260 ; Hatchett's Hotel, 261 ; Burlington House, 262–272 ; Burlington Arcade, 273 ; Clarendon House, ib.; Berkeley House, 275 ; Devonshire House, ib. ; Stratton Street, 280 ; Bath House, 282 ; Watier's Gambling Club, 284 ; Turf Club, 285 ; Naval and Military Club ; Cambridge House ; Hertford House ; Coventry House ; St. James's Club ; mansions of the Rothschilds ; Lady Keith, ib. ; Junior Athenæum Club, 286 ; Henry Thomas Hope ; Lord Eldon ; Gloucester House ; Duke of Gloucester ; Earl of Elgin ; Elgin

marbles ; Duke of Queensberry, ib.; Byron, 287 ; "Hercules Pillars ;" statuaries' "figure-yards ;" Piccadilly Terrace, ib.; "Triumphal Chariot" watering-house, 288 ; Wyatt's rebellion and fortifications, 289 ; highwaymen, 290 ; toll-gate at Hyde Park Corner, ib.

Piccadilly Hall, gaming-house, iv. 236.

Pickett, Alderman ; Pickett Street, Strand, iii. 10, 11, 23 ; v. 534.

"Pickled Egg" Tavern, Clerkenwell, ii. 305.

Pickle Herring Street, vi. 113.

"Pickwick" in the Fleet Prison, ii. 413.

Pic-nic Club, iii. 167.

Pic-nic Society, v. 81.

Picton, Sir Thomas, iv. 322, 437.

Pidcock's menagerie, iii. 116.

Pie Corner, i. 363.

"Pigeon expresses," Stock Exchange, i. 490.

Pigeon-shooting ; "Red House," Battersea, vi. 476.

Pigtails, v. 158.

Pike Gardens, the Queen's, Bankside, vi. 55.

Pilgrimages ; Our Lady of Muswell, Muswell Hill, v. 434. (See Tabard Inn, Southwark.)

Pillory, The, i. 33, 306 ; ii. 471 ; iii. 128, 538 ; iv. 135, 170, 471 ; the punishment abolished, ii. 471.

Pimlico, v. 39 ; etymology ; "Pimlico" at Hoxton ; Ben Jonson, ib. ; Arlington House, 40 ; Grosvenor Canal ; osier beds ; Willow Walk ; Warwick Street ; Warwick Square ; St. Gabriel's Church ; Vauxhall Bridge Road ; St. George's Square ; Army Clothing Depôt, ib. ; Lupus Street, 41 ; churches ; Victoria Railway Station ; Grosvenor Hotel, ib.; Mission House, 44 ; Orphanage ; St. John's School ; Bramah's factory ; Thomas Cubitt, builder, ib. ; "Monster," "Gun," "Star and Garter," and "Orange" Taverns, 45 ; "Jenny's Whim," ib. ; highwaymen, 46 ; Tart Hall ; Lord Stafford ; Stafford Place and Row ; Earl of Arundel, ib. ; Arundel marbles, 47 ; Richard Heber, M.P.; his library, 48.

Pimlico Garden, Bankside, vi. 55.

"Pimlico," Hoxton, v. 39, 525 ; alehouse, Pimlico Walk, ib.

Pinchbeck, Christopher ; "pinchbeck," and musical clocks, i. 53 ; ii. 333.

"Pindar of Wakefield," Gray's Inn Road, ii. 278, 297.

Pindar, Sir Paul, i. 246 ; ii. 159 ; his house, Bishopsgate, ii. 152, 153 ; the "Sir Paul Pindar's Head," ib.

Pinkerton, John, iv. 574.

Piozzi, Mrs., iv. 442 ; vi. 34, 35, 317, 318.

Pipe Fields, Spa Fields, ii. 303.

Pirates hung in chains, ii. 135.

Pirie, Sir John, Lord Mayor, i. 416, 506, 508.

Pitcairn, Dr., ii. 433.

Pitt Bridge. (See Blackfriars Bridge.)

"Pitt Club," iv. 159.

Pitt Diamond, The, iii. 531.

Pitt, Rt. Hon. Wm., i. 207, 324, 327 ; iii. 388, 416, 531 ; iv. 129, 136, 159, 171, 314, 423 ; vi. 200, 248, 317, 495, 496.

Pitt Street, iv. 476.

Pix, Trial of the, i. 357.

Pizarro at Drury Lane Theatre, iii. 224.

Placentia, or Pleazaunce ; Palace of Greenwich. (*See* Greenwich.)

Plagues (1348), ii. 380 ; (1349), iii. 455 ; (1361), v. 16 ; (1363 and 1603), iii. 572 ; (1569), iii. 466.

Plague ; Defoe's "History," i. 515.

Plague, Great (1665), i. 47, 370, 405, 532 ; ii. 112, 113, 138, 165, 176, 257 ; iii. 37, 208 ; iv. 15, 28, 236, 383 ; v. 23, 50, 390, 522 ; vi. 153, 173, 555, 557.

Plague-pits, ii. 202 ; iv. 249.

Planché, J. R., F.S.A., ii. 83 ; iii. 126, 233 ; iv. 458, 573 ; v. 102, 108, 119, 134 ; vi. 203.

Plane-trees ; Berkeley Square, iv. 327.

Planta, Right Hon. Joseph, M.P., iv. 447, 518.

Plaster modellers, iv. 550.

Plaster moulding of the face ; Pepys, iv. 83.

Platen, Countess of ; South Sea Bubble, i. 542.

Playbills, iii. 28.

Plough Alley, iii. 22.

Plough Court, Lombard Street, house of Pope's father, i. 526.

" Plough " Inn, Clapham, vi. 327.

Plough Monday, feast at the Mansion House, i. 440.

" Plough " Tavern, Kensal Green, v. 221.

Plovers' eggs imported ; the first of the season for the Queen, ii. 496.

Plowden, Edmund, i. 154.

Plumbers' Hall, ii. 41.

Plumtree Street, Bloomsbury, iv. 488.

Pneumatic Despatch Company, v. 242.

Poer, Lord, iv. 183.

Poet Laureate ; his butt of sherry, iv. 119.

Poet's Corner. (*See* Westminster Abbey.)

" Poet's Head," St. James's Street, iv. 164.

Poland Street ; Dr. Burney, iv. 464.

" Political Betty," iv. 169.

Polito's menagerie, iii. 116.

Polygon, The ; Godwin and Mary Woolstoncraft, v. 345.

Polytechnic Institution. (*See* Royal Polytechnic Institution.)

Pond, John, Astronomer Royal, vi. 215.

Pond Place, Chelsea, v. 88.

Pond Street, Hampstead, v. 491.

Ponds, Hampstead and Highgate, v. 412, 443, 444.

" Poodle Byng," iv. 256.

Poole, John, dramatist, i. 65.

Pope, Alexander, i. 75, 526, 527 ; ii. 26, 420 ; iii. 276, 277, 264, 311, 569 ; iv. 49, 50, 81, 88, 107, 141, 167, 178, 243, 262, 279, 284, 327, 332, 388, 541 ; vi. 62, 470, 556, 560, 563.

Pope, The, burnt in effigy, i. 7, 27.

Pope's Head Alley, Cornhill, ii. 172.

" Pope's Head " Tavern, Cornhill, ii. 171 ; goldsmith's wager ; Bowen killed by Quin, 172.

" Pope's Head " Tavern ; Pope and Curll, iii. 264.

Pop-gun Plot, Stock Exchange, i. 480.

Popham, Andrew, rejected at the Charterhouse, ii. 389.

Poppin's Court, hostel of the Abbots of Cirencester, i. 135.

Population of London, past and present ; statistics, vi. 569 ; comparison with other British and Foreign cities, countries, and the entire globe ; illustrations of its amount, 569, 570.

" Porridge Island," iii. 141, 158.

Porson, first librarian of the London Institution, i. 178, 429 ; v. 98.

" Porter ; " beer ; origin of the term, iv. 303, 485.

Porters. (*See* Fellowship Porters, Tackle Porters, Ticket Porters.)

Porteus, Bishop ; his library, Fulham Palace, iv. 508 ; whetstone at Fulham Palace, 510.

Portland Chapel, iv. 456.

Portland, Duke of, iv. 445.

Portland Place, iv. 450 ; distinguished residents ; Foley House, Mansfield House, 452.

Portland Road Station, Metropolitan Railway, v. 226.

Portland vase, iv. 526.

Portman Chapel, Baker Street, iv. 422.

Portman family ; Sir William Portman, iv. 407, 412, 423, 425.

Portman Market, v. 259.

Portman Square, iv. 412 ; distinguished residents ; Mrs. Montagu, 413.

Portman Street, iv. 418.

Portobello Farm, Notting Hill, v. 183.

Portpool Lane, ii. 554.

Portrait Gallery, National, v. 107.

Portsmouth, Duchess of, iii. 356, 357.

Portugal Street, Grosvenor Square, iv. 373.

Portugal Street, Lincoln's Inn Fields, iii. 27.

" Portugal Street ; " " Piccadilly " so called, iv. 249, 256.

Postern Row, Tower Hill, ii. 98.

Post Office. (*See* General Post Office.)

Pott, Messrs. ; vinegar-works, vi. 42.

Pott, Percival, surgeon, ii. 362.

Potteries, Notting Hill, v. 178.

Pottery, Dwight's, Parson's Green, vi. 521.

Poultney's Inn, Upper Thames Street, ii. 17.

Poultry Market, New, Smithfield, ii. 495.

Poultry, The, i. 417 ; Vernor and Hood ; Thomas Hood ; the " Rose " or " King's Head " Tavern ; Stocks' Market, *ib.* ; St. Mildred's Church ; epitaphs, 419 ; the Compter, 423 ; Dekker ; Jonathan Strong, the African slave, and Granville Sharp, *ib.*

Pound, St. Giles's, iii. 200.

Powell, Sir W., almshouses, vi. 508, 516.

Powell's, puppet show, iii. 249.

Powis House, Great Ormond Street ; Marquis of Powis, iv. 556.

Powis Place, Queen Square, iv. 562.

Praed's Bank, Fleet Street, i. 38, 46.

" Praise God Barebone," i. 95.

" 'Prentice riots." (*See* Apprentices.)

Prerogative Court and Will Office, i. 283, 286, 288 ; iii. 327.

Press Yard, Newgate ; torture, ii. 467.

Pretender (The Old ; the Young), iii. 86, 93 ; iv. 110.

Price's Candle Factories, Vauxhall and Battersea, vi. 468.

Pridden, Sally, Hon. John Finch stabbed by, iii. 268.

" Pride's Purge," iii. 526.

Priestley, Dr., v. 515.

Primrose Hill, v. 287 ; meadow land and spring flowers ; Barrow Hill ; ancient barrow ; reservoir of West Middlesex Waterworks ; manor of Chalcot ; murder of Sir Edmundbury Godfrey, *ib.* ; White House, or Lower Chalcot Farm, 289 ; duels, 290 ; land secured for the Crown ; North-Western railway tunnel, *ib.* ; fireworks in celebration of peace ; Shakespeare oak, 291 ; gymnasium, *ib.*

Prince of Wales's Gate, Hyde Park, iv. 395.

Prince of Wales's Theatre, Tottenham Street, iv. 472, 473 ; Pasquali's concert room ; Concerts of Ancient Music ; Col. Greville ; Circus ; Brunton ; Mrs. Yates ; " New Theatre ; " " King's Ancient Concert Rooms ; " " Regency Theatre ; " " Theatre of Varieties ; " " West London Theatre ; " " Queen's Theatre ; " " Fitzroy ; " Mrs. Nesbitt ; Madame Vestris ; Miss Marie Wilton (Mrs. Bancroft), *ib.*

Prince's Court, Westminster, iv. 35.

Prince's Cricket-ground, v. 99.

Princes Street, Drury Lane, iii. 40.

Princes Street, Hanover Square ; Emily Faithfull, iv. 310.

Princes Street, Leicester Square, iv. 238.

Princes Street, Westminster, iv. 34, 35.

Princess's Theatre, iv. 461 ; Queen's Bazaar ; burnt down ; rebuilt ; David Roberts ; Physiorama ; Hamlet, the silversmith, *ib.* ; Charles Kean and Mrs. Kean, 462.

Pringle, Sir John, and the Royal Society, i. 106.

" Printing Conger " at the " Chapter " Coffee House, i. 279.

Printing House Square ; *Times* newspaper, its history, i. 209—215.

Printing on the Thames ; " Frost Fair," iii. 313—320.

Prior, iii. 269, 428, 437 ; iv. 29, 54, 83, 172, 442 ; v. 143 ; vi. 59.

Prison at Lud Gate, i. 224.

Prison discipline, v. 380.

Prison of the Clink, vi. 32.

Prisoners' Base, iv. 483.

Prisons at Westminster ; the Gate House ; the Bishop of London's prison, iii. 489.

Prisons. (*See* Bridewell, City Prison, Coldbath Fields, Fleet, Horsemonger Lane, House of Detention, Millbank, Newgate, Pentonville, Tothill Fields, Wandsworth.)

Privy Council Offices, iii. 374 ; oath of the Clerk of the Council, 388.

Privy Gardens, Whitehall, iii. 335, 376.

Prize-fighting, ii. 302 ; iv. 406, 455 ; v. 296, 304, 370. (*See* Female Prize-fighters.)

Probate Court, i. 286.

Procter, B. W. (" Barry Cornwall "), iv. 437.

" Prout, Father," iv. 251.

Providence Chapel, Great Titchfield Street, iv. 461.

Prynne ; preservation of public records, i. 101 ; imprisoned, ii. 75, 405 ; iii. 58, 538.

Pryor's Bank, Fulham ; antiquities and curiosities ; festivities ; auction sale, vi. 522, 524.

Public-houses ; statistics, vi. 570.

Puckle's Machine Company, i. 539.
Pudding Lane, ii. 35.
"Puffing Billy," v. 112.
Pugilism. (*See* Prize-fighting).
Pugin, A. W. ; Houses of Parliament, iii. 503 ; vi. 363.
"Pulteney guinea," British Museum, iv. 527.
Pulteney Hotel ; Pulteney, Earl of Bath, iv. 284.
Pulteney, Sir John, Lord Mayor ; the "Rose," or "Pulteney's Inn," ii. 28, 137.
Pultock, Robert, author of "Peter Wilkins," i. 93.
Pumps, Old, i. 167, 346 ; ii. 160 ; iii. 22 ; iv. 550 ; vi. 536.
Punch office ; history of the paper, i. 56—59.
Punch, or *Punchinello*, Introduction of, iii. 128 ; iv. 83.
Puppet-shows, iii. 249 ; iv. 346, 347.
Purcell, Henry, iii. 483 ; iv. 38, 184.
Purdon, Ned ; Goldsmith's epitaph, i. 62.
Putney, vi. 489 ; Domesday Book ; fishery and ferry ; old houses ; High Street ; Fairfax House, 490 ; army of the Commonwealth ; bridge of boats ; the "Palace," *ib.* ; "The Cedars," 491 ; Putney House ; College for Civil Engineers ; Dawes's Almshouses ; Watermen's School ; Cromwell Place ; D'Israeli Road, *ib.;* Thomas Cromwell, Earl of Essex ; Wolsey, 492 ; Bonner's House, 493 ; Essex House, 495 ; Lime Grove ; residents ; the bowling-green ; Bowling-green House ; death of Pitt, *ib.;* Hartley's fire-proof house and obelisk, 497 ; Hospital for Incurables ; Putney Heath ; highwaymen ; gibbet, *ib.;* duels, 498 ; reviews, 500 ; Grantham House ; Putney Park ; boat-houses ; boat-clubs ; Oxford and Cambridge Boat-race ; "Star and Garter," *ib.;* Church and Bridge, 501 ; toll-houses and bells, 503 ; collectors' uniforms; Aqueduct of Chelsea Waterworks,*ib.*
Pye, Poet laureate, iv. 42, 257.
Pye, Sir Robert ; Old and New Pye Streets, Westminster, iv. 20, 39.
Pym, John, v. 94.
Pyne, Miss Louisa ; operas at Covent Garden Theatre, iii. 237.
Pynson, Richard, printer, i. 49, 50.
"Pyx, Chapel of the." (*See* Westminster Abbey.)

Q.

Quack doctors, vi. 75.
"Quadrantes ;" Squares, iv. 326.
Quadrilles, at "Almack's," iv. 198.
Quails imported from Egypt, ii. 496.
"Quaker" Tavern, Great Sanctuary, Westminster, iii. 488.
Quarritch, bookseller, iv. 254.
Quarterly Review, iv. 293.
"Quays, Legal," vi. 141.
Quebec Institute, iv. 423.
Quebec Street ; Quebec Chapel, iv. 409.
Queen Anne Street, iv. 447 ; Richard Cumberland, 448 ; Turner ; Fuseli ; Lord Cottenham ; Prince Esterhazy ; Burke ; Chandos House, *ib.*
"Queen Anne's Bounty," iii. 482.
Queen Anne's Gate, Westminster, iv.

41 ; Mission Hall ; Residence of Jeremy Bentham, 42.
Queen Elizabeth's College, Greenwich, vi. 194.
Queen Elizabeth's Walk, Stoke Newington, v. 536.
Queenhithe ; tolls given to Eleanor, queen of Henry II. ; Eleanor, queen of Edward I., ii. 19 ; corn-warehouse, 181.
Queen Square, Bloomsbury, iv. 483, 554; statue of Queen Anne ; Church of St. George the Martyr ; charitable institutions ; Dr. Stukeley, *ib.*
Queen Street, Cheapside, i. 352; Ringed Hall ; Ipres Inn, *ib.*
Queen Street, Mayfair, iv. 353.
Queen Victoria Street, iii. 324.
"Queen's Arms," Newgate Street, ii. 430.
"Queen's Arms," St. Paul's Churchyard, i. 267.
"Queen's Arms" Tavern, Cheapside, i. 341.
Queensberry, Duke and Duchess of, iv. 305.
Queensberry, Duke of ("Old Q."), iv. 286, 334 ; v. 131.
Queensberry House, iv. 305.
Queen's College for Ladies, iv. 450.
"Queen's Elm" Hotel, Brompton, v. 88.
"Queen's Head and Artichoke" Tavern, v. 255.
"Queen's Head" Tavern, Islington, ii. 260.
Queen's messengers, i. 300.
Queen's Park, Paddington, v. 228.
"Queen's Pipe," London Docks, ii.125.
Queen's Road, Chelsea, v. 83 ; Earl of Radnor ; Charles II. ; Dr. Mead ; Dr. Blackwell ; Victoria Hospital for Sick Children ; Guards' Barracks, *ib.*
Queen's Road, Peckham, vi. 286.
Queen's Scholars, iii. 465.
Queen's Theatre, Long Acre, iii. 270.
Queen's Wardrobe, Watling Street, i. 551.
Quick, comedian, ii. 263.
Quin, comedian, ii. 172 ; iii. 28, 221.

R.

Races, iv. 15 ; v. 182, 320, 455 ; vi. 242.
"Rack-punch," Vauxhall Gardens, vi. 458.
Rackstraw's Museum, Fleet Street, i. 45.
Radcliffe, Dr., ii. 173, 433 ; iii. 143, 212, 273 ; iv. 538 ; v. 143.
Radcliffe, E. Delmé, iv. 326.
Radnor House, iv. 184.
Raffling-shops, v. 471.
"Rag and Famish ;" Army and Navy Club, iv. 145.
Rag Fair, Rosemary Lane, ii. 144.
Rag-shops, vi. 164.
Rahere. (*See* Rayer.)
Railway Benevolent Institution, v. 347.
Railway Clearing House, v. 346.
Railway mania, i. 486.
Railway signals, v. 229, 230.
"Rainbow" Tavern, Fleet Street ; early sale of coffee, i. 44.
Rainforth, Miss, vocalist, iv. 193.
Raleigh, Sir Walter, i. 357 ; ii. 71, 93, 260 ; iii. 22, 489, 566, 569 ; vi. 173.
Ram Alley, Fleet Street, now Hare Place. (*See* Hare Place.)

Ramsay, Allan, iv. 449.
Ramsay, Davy ; digging for treasure, i. 129.
Randal, Jack, pugilist, i. 83.
Ranelagh Gardens, v. 71 ; Ranelagh House ; Lord Ranelagh, *ib.* ; the Rotunda, 76 ; masquerades, 77, 81 ; fireworks ; lake and boats ; music, *ib.* ; Jubilee masquerade, 78 ; royal and noble visitors, 80 ; Dr. Johnson ; Goldsmith ; regatta on the Thames, *ib.;* Pic-nic Society, 81 ; Garnerin's balloon ; ball given by Knights of the Bath ; entertainment by Spanish Ambassador, *ib.;* demolition of the place, 82 ; French "Ranelagh," Paris, *ib.*
Ranelagh House, Fulham ; Lord Ranelagh, vi. 524.
Rann, Jack, "Sixteen-string Jack," ii. 484 ; v. 194.
Raphael's cartoons, iv. 64.
Rastell, John, printer, i. 351.
Ratcliff Highway, ii. 134 ; Ratcliff Cross ; wild beast shops ; Marr and Williamson families murdered, *ib.;* Swedish Church ; burial-place of Swedenborg, 135, 138.
Rathbone Place, iv. 406, 469 ; Captain Rathbone ; Percy Chapel ; Flaxman ; Blake ; "Percy Anecdotes," *ib.;* Hone, R.A., 470 ; E. H. Bailey, R.A. ; De Wint ; Baron Maseres, *ib.*
Rats, Tame, iv. 479.
Ravensbourne, The, vi. 143, 144, 145, 244 ; Deptford Bridge ; Deptford Creek ; source of the stream ; origin of its name ; Wat Tyler ; Jack Cade ; Perkin Warbeck, *ib.*
Ravenscourt Park, Hammersmith, vi. 534.
Ravenscroft, Messrs., wig-makers, iii. 26.
Ray, John, naturalist, iv. 257.
Ray, Miss, ii. 334; iii. 260, 385; v. 193.
Ray Street, Clerkenwell ; the Clerk's Well, ii. 335.
Rayer, founder of St. Bartholomew's priory, Smithfield, ii. 342, 358.
Raymond, Lord, iv. 548.
Read, Miss Angelina ; "haunted houses," Stamford Street, Blackfriars Road, vi. 382.
Recamier, Madame, v. 158.
Record Newspaper, i. 53.
Record Office, i. 101.
Records, Public ; "Domesday Book," i. 101 ; iii. 454.
"Red Bull" Theatre, Clerkenwell ; Pepys ; Edward Alleyn, ii. 337 ; iii. 219.
"Red Cap, Mother," v. 310, 311.
"Red Cow" Inn, Hammersmith, vi. 530.
Redcross Street ; Dr. Williams's Free Library, ii. 239; iv. 570.
"Red House," Battersea ; pigeon-shooting, vi. 476.
Red Lion Almshouses, Westminster, iv. 21.
Red Lion Court, Fleet Street ; Valpy's "Delphin Classics," i. 108.
"Red Lion" Inn, Chiswick ; whetstone chained to the door, vi. 557.
"Red Lion" Inn, Hampstead ; singular tenure, v. 485.
"Red Lion" Inn, Highgate, v. 418.
"Red Lion" Inn, Kensington, v. 124.
Red Lion Square, vi. 545 ; its early state ; "Red Lyon" Inn ; "Blue Flower Pot ;" burial of the regi-

cides; Cromwell, *ib.*; obelisk, 546; Wilkes, 548; Lord Raymond; Jonas Hanway; Sharon Turner; Sheriff's Court, *ib.*; charitable societies; Milton, 549.

Red Lion Street, Clerkenwell, ii. 323; Wildman, owner of "Eclipse;" "Jerusalem" Tavern; John Britton; Dr. Trusler, *ib.*

Red Lion Street, Holborn, iv. 550.

"Red Lion" Tavern, West Street; thieves' resort; murders, ii. 426.

"Red Lyon" Inn, Holborn. (*See* Red Lion Square.)

"Redriff." (*See.* Rotherhithe.)

Reeve, John, comedian, v. 26.

Reeve, Mrs., actress, iv. 62.

Reform Bill riots, i. 116; iii. 389.

Reform Club, iv. 148; M. Soyer; the kitchen, 149.

Refuge for the Destitute, v. 529.

Regalia in the Tower, ii. 77; its conveyance to the House of Lords, iii. 528. (*See* Blood, Colonel.)

Regent Square, iv. 573; Scotch Presbyterian Church; Rev. Edward Irving; St. Peter's Church, 576.

Regent Street, Lower, iv. 208; Gallery of Illustration, *ib.*; St. Philip's Chapel, *ib.*; County Fire Office, 245; Regent Street, 249; Quadrant, 250; Tenison's and Hanover Chapels, 251; St. James's Hall, 254.

Regent Street, Westminster, iv. 9.

Regent's Canal, v. 219, 268, 298.

Regent's Park, v. 263; Marylebone Park Fields; manor of Marylebone; royal hunting-ground; deer and timber; estate disparked; let on lease; successive holders; Duke of Portland; park laid out and built by Nash; extent; Broad Walk, *ib.*; ornamental water, 265; aquatic birds; skating; fatal accident, *ib.*; flower-beds, 266; drinking-fountain; Sunday bands; Ulster, Cornwall, and Hanover Terraces; Sussex Place, *ib.*; Kent Terrace, 267; the Holme; St. John's Lodge; St. Dunstan's Villa; clock and giants from St. Dunstan's Church; South Villa, *ib.*; Regent's Canal, 268; explosion of gunpowder; Holford House; distinguished residents in the Park; Park Square, *ib.*; the Diorama and Colosseum, 269; St. Katharine's Collegiate Church and Master's house, 273; Sir Herbert Taylor, 275; St. Andrew's Place; Adult Orphan Asylum; Chester Terrace; Chester Place; Stockleigh House; Mrs. Fitzherbert's Villa, *ib.*; Toxopholite Society's Gardens, 276; Royal Botanic Society's Gardens, 279; Zoological Gardens, 263, 281.

Regicides, Trial and execution of the, ii. 467; iii. 128; iv. 545; v. 198; vi. 552.

"Rejected Addresses," by James and Horace Smith, ii. 167; iii. 225, 232; vi. 281, 393.

Relics at Westminster Abbey, iii. 404.

Relics of saints in St. Paul's, i. 239.

Re-marriage in Bermondsey Church, vi. 121.

Rennie, John, F.R.S., i. 545; ii. 15, 123.

Reporters' Gallery, House of Commons, iii. 320, 512; parliamentary reporting, i. 140.

Reviews of troops and volunteers, iv. 388, 389, vi. 500.

Reynolds, Sir Joshua, P.R.A., i. 253, 345; iii. 147, 159, 166; iv. 235, 461.

Rhodes's Mews, iv. 483.

Ricardo, David, Stock Exchange, i. 486.

Riccard, Sir Andrew, ii. 110, 112.

Rich, Henry, Earl of Holland, v. 118.

Rich, John, manager of Covent Garden Theatre, iii. 28, 224, 227, 228, 230; iv. 125.

Richard I., ii. 107, 404; iii. 401, 404, 567.

Richard II., i. 551; ii. 17; iii. 308, 422, 442, 544; v. 429; vi. 8, 225.

Richard III., i. 284, 394, 518; ii. 17, 155, 240.

Richardson's "Pamela" and "Clarissa Harlowe," i. 143, 144, 145; iv. 243; v. 460; vi. 527.

Richardson's Theatre, vi. 275.

Richborough, i. 18.

Richmond, Charles, Duke of; school of art; Richmond House, iii. 378.

Richmond, Duchess of; "La Belle Stewart;" Charles II., iv. 109.

Richmond, Lewis, Duke of, iii. 437.

Richmond, Margaret, Countess of, iii. 439.

Richmond Terrace; Richmond House, iii. 377.

Riding-house, Hyde Park, iv. 395.

Riding House Street, iv. 458.

Ridley, Bishop of London, i. 243; ii. 70.

"Ridotto al fresco," Vauxhall Gardens, vi. 452, 454.

Riots, i. 179, 189, 305, 309, 410; ii. 152; iv. 218, 224, 305, 405. (*See* "Evil May Day," Gordon and Reform Bill riots.)

Ripley, Thomas, architect, i. 370.

Ripon; F. Robinson, Lord Goderich, Earl of; corn-law riots, iv. 305.

Rippon, Rev. Dr., vi. 107.

River-wall, Roman, ii. 34, 53.

Rivington and Sons, booksellers, i. 268.

Road Club, iv. 170.

Roberts, David, R.A., iv. 461.

"Robin Redbreasts;" Bow Street officers, ii. 272.

Robins, George, auctioneer, i. 522; iii. 255; v. 221.

Robinson, Anastasia (Countess of Peterborough), vi. 520.

Robinson, "Long" Sir Thomas, iii. 377; iv. 359.

Robinson, Mrs. ("Perdita"), iii. 212, 221; iv. 98, 170, 238; v. 94.

Robson, Frederick, comedian, ii. 227.

Rochester, Earl of, ii. 98.

Rochester Row, Westminster, iv. 10; Almshouses, Palmer's Village, iv. 40.

Rodney, Admiral Lord, i. 251; iv. 315.

Roehampton, vi. 500.

Rogers, Rev. John, iii. 340, 482.

Rogers, Samuel, i. 113, 178; iii. 123; iv. 172, 202, 311; v. 164, 172, 173, 176, 532; vi. 200; his tomb in Hornsey churchyard, v. 433.

Rolle, Lord; coronation of Queen Victoria, iii. 411.

Rolls Chapel, i. 76.

Rolls, Charles, engraver, v. 314.

Rolls Court; Masters of the Rolls, i. 76—80.

Romaine, Rev. Wm., i. 47; iv. 20.

Roman antiquities, i. 226, 236, 362, 505, 531, 557; ii. 34, 52, 93, 146, 149, 166, 277, 417, 526; iv. 523; v. 342, 531; vi. 341.

Roman baths, Strand Lane, iii. 77.

Roman bridge over the Thames, ii. 9.

Roman Catholic Cathedral, St. George's Fields, vi. 362, 364.

Roman Catholic residents in London; statistics, vi. 570.

Roman London, i. 17; Cæsar's invasion; name of London, 19; "Londinium;" first mentioned, 19; city burned by Boadicea, 20; wall built by Constantine, 20; Watling Street, 20; Roman wall and towers, 20, 21; cemeteries, 21; tessellated pavements, 21; bronze statues, 21; silver and gold ornaments, pottery, coins, and baths, 22; "Via Trinobantina;" Watling Street, iv. 376.

Roman pavements. (*See* Pavements, Roman.)

Roman salt-pits, i. 548.

Roman wall on Tower Hill, ii. 114.

Romilly, Sir Samuel, iii. 192.

Romney, George, iv. 446; v. 158, 464.

Romney House, St. James's Square, iv. 183.

Romney Street, Westminster, formerly "Vine Street;" vineyards, iv. 4.

Rookery in the Temple Gardens, i. 171.

"Rookery," St. Giles's; "Holy Land;" "Little Dublin;" low lodging-houses, iv. 484, 488.

"Rookery, The," Westminster, iv. 40.

Rooks' nests in Cheapside, i. 364.

Rope-dancing at Southwark Fair, vi. 59.

Roper, Margaret, ii. 14; v. 57, 59; vi. 243.

Roque, Bartholomew, florist, vi. 526.

"Rosamund's Bower," residence of T. Crofton Croker, vi. 518.

Rosamond's Pond, iv. 49.

Roscoe, William, iii. 531.

"Rose and Crown" Inn, Knightsbridge, v. 30.

"Rose and Crown" Tavern, Stoke Newington, v. 538.

"Rose" Inn, Holborn Hill, ii. 531.

Rose, Lord Mayor; banquet to Prince, and Princess of Wales, i. 416.

"Rose, Manor of the," St. Lawrence, Poultney, ii. 28.

"Rose of Normandy" public-house, Marylebone; bowling-green; Nancy Dawson, iv. 429.

"Rose" sponging house, Wood Street, i. 369.

Rose Street, Long Acre, iii. 264; "Red Rose Street;" Samuel Butler; Dryden; "Rose" Tavern; "Treason" Club; Curll; the "Pope's Head," *ib.*

Rose Street, Soho, iii. 196.

"Rose" Tavern, Russell Street, iii. 278.

Rose Theatre, Bankside, vi. 50.

Rosemary, an emblem of remembrance, vi. 287.

"Rosemary Branch" Tavern, Peckham, *ib.*

Rosemary Lane, ii. 144.

Ross, Bishop of, imprisoned in the Tower, ii. 70.

Ross, Mother, v. 94.

Ross, Sir W. C., A.R.A., iv. 473; v. 408.

Rossiter, aëronaut, v. 310.

Rosslyn, Earl of (Lord Loughborough); his character, v. 489.

Rota Club, iii. 538.

Rotherhithe, "Redriff," vi. 134; "Red Rose Haven;" historical notes; Lovel family, *ib.*; fires, 135; "Half-

way House;" Mill Pond; vine-
yards, *ib.;* Southwark Park, 136;
market-gardens; "China Hall"
Tavern; theatre; "Dog and Duck"
Tavern; parish church; Prince Lee
Boo, *ib.;* Union Road, 137; churches;
Deptford Lower Road; Free School;
Board schools, *ib.;* St. Helena Tea
Gardens, 138; Thames Tunnel and
Railway, 139; Docks, 140; "Legal
Quays," and "Sufferance Wharfs,"
141; "Cuckold's Point;" "Horn
Fair;" legend of King John, 142.
Rothschild; derivation of the name, iii.
254.
Rothschild family, i. 466, 482; iv.
457; mansions in Piccadilly, 285.
Rotten Row, iv. 386, 398.
Rotunda, Blackfriars Road, vi. 382.
Roubiliac, sculptor, iii. 159, 428, 447;
iv. 267; vi. 472.
"Round House," St. Giles's, iii. 209.
Roupell, William, M.P., vi. 425.
Rousby, Mrs., actress, iii. 270.
Rouse, Thomas; "Eagle" Tavern, City
Road, ii. 227.
Rousseau, iii. 296; vi. 560.
Rowe, Nicholas, iii. 83; iv. 158; v. 422.
Rowley, William; *Fortune by Land and
Sea;* execution of pirates, ii. 135.
Rowley's comedy, *A Woman Never
Vext,* i. 225.
Roxburgh, John, third Duke of, iv. 188.
Roxburghe Club, iv. 188, 295.
Royal Academy, iii. 93, 146; its origin
and history; Kneller; Thornhill;
the Academy in St. Martin's Lane, *ib.;*
Hogarth, 147; Society of Arts; Ex-
hibitions in Spring Gardens; in Pall
Mall; the "Instrument" signed by
George III.; rules; Reynolds, *ib.;*
succeeding Presidents, 148; removal
to Burlington House, 149; iv. 266,
272.
Royal Academy of Music, iv. 320.
Royal Agricultural Society, iv. 317.
Royal Albert Hall, v. 112.
Royal Alfred Theatre, Marylebone, v.
259.
Royal Alms, Distribution of; "Maun
day" money, iii. 368.
Royal Aquarium, Westminster, iv. 20.
Royal Arcade, New Oxford Street, iv.
487.
Royal Asiatic Society, iv. 296.
Royal Astronomical Society, iv. 272.
Royal Botanic Garden, Chelsea, v. 68.
Royal Botanic Society, v. 279; gardens
in the Regent's Park, planted by
Robert Marnock, *ib.;* rare trees and
plants, v. 280; herbaceous garden;
medical garden; orchid house; con-
servatory, *ib.*
Royal Court Theatre, v. 95.
Royal Dock, Deptford. (*See* Deptford.)
Royal Exchange, i. 346; the Old Ex-
change; Gresham family; Sir Thomas
Gresham, 494; first "Bourse," 495;
shops in the Exchange; visit of
Queen Elizabeth, 496; hawkers and
loungers, 497; Lady Gresham, 498;
Evelyn's description, 500; Great
Fire of London; Plague; Pepys, *ib.;*
New Exchange; erected by Jerman;
described, 501; statues by Cibber,
502; milliner's shops, 503; cost of
building; clock and chimes; burnt
down (1838), *ib.;* Sir William Tite's
design, 505; first stone laid by Prince

Albert; opened by Queen Victoria,
506; present building described;
statues, clock, bells, chimes, 507;
"New Exchange," or "Britain's
Burse," in the Strand, opened by
James I., iii. 104.
Royal Exchange Assurance Company,
i. 508.
Royal Horticultural Society, v. 116;
gardens; conservatory; statue of the
Prince Consort, *ib.;* gardens and
fêtes at Chiswick, vi. 566.
Royal Humane Society, iii. 292; iv.
402; v. 21; vi. 377.
Royal Infirmary for Children and Wo-
men, Waterloo Road, vi. 409.
Royal Institute of British Architects, iv.
323.
Royal Institution, iv. 296, 297.
Royal Italian Opera House, iii. 234;
Frederick Gye, 236.
Royal Literary Fund, iv. 543.
Royal London Ophthalmic Hospital,
ii. 206.
Royal Mint Street, formerly Rosemary
Lane, ii. 144.
Royal Naval School, Camberwell, re-
moved to New Cross, vi. 247, 285.
Royal Observatory, Greenwich, vi. 212;
tower built by Humphrey, Duke of
Gloucester; Henry VIII.; Queen
Elizabeth; the longituae; M. de
St. Pierre's proposal; Flamsteed ap-
pointed "Astronomical Observator,"
ib.; Observatory erected, 213, 214;
Flamsteed's observations; "mural
arc;" catalogue of stars; his pupils;
quarrel with Newton; his death, *ib.;*
Halley, 215; transit instrument;
mural quadrant; Dr. Bradley; Dr.
Bliss; Dr. Maskelyne; *Nautical Almanac;* Royal Society; John Pond;
Sir G. B. Airy, *ib.;* electric clock;
public barometer; yard measure,
216; transit circle, transit instrument, and transit clock, 218; altazimuth; lunar observations, 219; great
equatorial telescope; magnetic observatory, 220; anemometers, or
wind-gauges, 222; time signal-ball;
galvanic motor clock; solar photography and spectroscopy, *ib.*
Royal Park Theatre, Camden Town,
v. 310.
Royal Polytechnic Institution, iv. 454.
Royal Society, i. 104; origin and
history; removal to Crane Court,
105; first catalogue of museum;
satirised by Butler and Swift, *ib.;*
dispute on lightning-conductors, 106;
Sir Hans Sloane and Dr. Woodward, 107; house in Crane Court,
105, 106, 108; Somerset House,
iii. 74, 94; iv. 267; v. 70; removal
to Burlington House, iv. 269.
Royal Society of Literature, iii. 154.
Royal Society of Musicians, iv. 317.
Royal State Barge, iii. 337; vi. 197.
Royal swanherd, iii. 303.
Royal Thames Yacht Club, vi. 196.
Royal Veterinary College, v. 322.
Royalty Theatre, ii. 146; iii. 194;
rebuilt; fall of the roof, *ib.*
Rubens, iii. 366; vi. 174.
"Rufflers" of Lincoln's Inn Fields, iii.
45.
Rumford, Count, v. 26.
"Rump, The," iii. 526.
Rundell and Bridge, goldsmiths, i. 228.

Rundell, Mrs., her "Art of Cookery,"
i. 229; iv. 293.
"Running Footman" Tavern, iv. 334.
Rupert, Prince, i. 37; ii. 224; iv. 378,
549; vi. 560.
Rush, Mr., Minister from the United
States, iii. 410; iv. 410; v. 173.
Ruskin, Professor, ii. 33.
Russell, Earl, iv. 344, 353.
Russell Institution, Great Coram Street,
iv. 574.
Russell, Lady Rachel, iv. 536, 537.
Russell, Lord William, ii. 75, 467; iii.
45; iv. 537, 538.
Russell Place, Fitzroy Square, iv. 474.
Russell Square, iv. 483; Baltimore
House; John Wilson Croker, 484;
"Judge-land," 564; statue of
Francis, fifth Duke of Bedford,
565; Duke of Bolton, 566; Lord
Loughborough; Sir Samuel Rom-
illy; Lord Tenterden; Justice
Holroyd; Lord Denman; Justice
Talfourd; Sir Thomas Lawrence,
ib.
Russell Street, Bermondsey; Richard
Russell, his wealth and will, vi. 124.
Russell Street, Covent Garden, iii. 275;
Tom Davies, bookseller; Johnson
and Boswell; Foote; coffee-houses;
"Will's," *ib.;* "Button's," 277,
280, 281; "Tom's," 278; "Shake-
speare's Head;" Beefsteak Club;
"Rose" Tavern, *ib.;* "Albion"
Tavern, 279; Evelyn; Gibbon;
"Harp" Tavern; "The City of
Lushington Society," *ib.*
Russian ambassador, The first, ii. 175;
v. 550.
Rutland Gate; Sheepshanks Gallery,
v. 25, 26.
Rutupiæ, the ancient Richborough, i. 18.
Ruvigny, Marquis de; Huguenot
refugees, vi. 191, 193.
Ryan, comedian, iii. 212.
Rye House Plot, v. 18.
Ryland, engraver, executed for forgery,
v. 47.
Rysbrack, sculptor, iii. 419, 425; iv.
87, 430, 435, 442; v. 68, 141.

S.

"Sablonnière Hotel," iii. 167.
Sacheverell, Dr. Henry, ii. 316, 506;
v. 423.
Sackville Street, iv. 308; "The Prince"
Inn; Board of Agriculture; chari-
table institutions, *ib.*
Sackville, Thomas; his "Mirror for
Magistrates," ii. 198.
Saddlers' Company and Hall, i. 341;
embroidered pall, ii. 6.
"Saddling the spit," iii. 34.
Sadleir, John, M.P.; his frauds and
suicide, v. 455.
Sadler's Wells, ii. 285, 289; "Isling-
ton Spa;" Sadler; burlesque poems,
290; visit of royal princesses; the
theatre; water-pieces; New River;
fatal accident, *ib.;* Macklin, 291;
Ned Ward; Hogarth's picture,
"Evening," *ib.;* new theatre, 292;
King, comedian; Mrs. Bland;
Bologna; Braham; Miss Richer;
Grimaldi, *ib.;* Mrs. Siddons, 293;
the Dibdins; Belzoni; visit of
Queen Caroline, *ib.;* T. P. Cooke,
294; Samuel Phelps; "Sir Hugh

Myddelton " Tavern, *ib.;* Rosoman; old picture, 295.

Saffron Hill, ii. 542.

" Sail-cloth Permits," a bubble company, i. 539.

Sailmakers' Almshouses, Tottenham, v. 557.

Sailors' Home, Bethnal Green, ii. 146.

Sailors' Orphan Girls' School, Hampstead, v. 483.

St. Alban's Church, Wood Street, i. 365; epitaphs, 367; hour-glass, 368.

St. Albans, Harriet, Duchess of, iii. 105, 221; iv. 280; v. 398.

St. Alphage Church, London Wall, ii. 232.

St. Alphege, Archbishop, murdered at Greenwich, vi. 165; St. Alphege Church, Greenwich, 191.

St. Andrew's Church, Holborn, ii. 503; church in 1297; changes of ownership; dissolution of monasteries; rebuilt by Wren; interior described, *ib.;* alterations in 1872, 505; old organ, by Harris; interments; John Emery, comedian, *ib.;* Dr. Sacheverell, 506; registers; banns of marriage published in the marketplace; marriage of Sir Edward Coke, *ib.;* his wife, Lady Elizabeth Hatton, 507; marriage of Colonel Hutchinson and Lucy Apsley; their romantic marriage, *ib.;* Richard Savage christened, 510; burial of Chatterton and Henry Neele; John Webster, dramatist, parish clerk, *ib.;* burial of Tomkins, executed for Waller's plot, 510; William Whiston, 512; Bishops Hacket and Stillingfleet; Rev. Charles Barton, 513.

St. Andrew's Church, Stockwell, vi. 329.

St. Andrew's Church, Well Street, Oxford Street, iv. 464.

St. Andrew Undershaft Church, ii. 191; ancient maypole; Herrick's lines, *ib.;* maypole denounced and destroyed, 192; old books; monument of Stow, 193.

St. Andrew's Wardrobe Church, i. 302, 303.

St. Anne-in-the-Willows, Wood Street, i. 371.

St. Anne's Church, Blackfriars; interments of Vandyck, Oliver, and Faithorne, i. 302.

St. Anne's, Soho; formation of the parish, iii. 160; the church, 181; interments; Lord Camelford; Theodore, King of Corsica, 182.

St. Anne's Church, Wandsworth, vi. 484.

St. Anne's Lane, Westminster, iv. 38; Sir Roger de Coverley, 39.

St. Ann's Society, Royal Asylum, Brixton, vi. 319.

St. Anne's Well, Hyde Park, iv. 393.

St. Antholin's Church; epitaphs; bells; seditious preachers, i. 552, 553.

St. Anthony's Free School, Threadneedle Street, i. 274, 537.

St. Augustine's Church, Watling Street, i. 349, 551.

St. Barnabas Church, Pimlico, v. 42.

St. Barnabas Church, Rotherhithe, vi. 137.

St. Bartholomew-the-Great, Smithfield, ii. 269; limits of the Priory; its privileges, 351; revenues, 352; early seals; ruins of the priory;

refectory; crypt; prior's house, *ib.;* present church, 353; monuments, 354; Bishop Walden; Dr. Anthony, 356.

St. Bartholomew-the-Less, Smithfield; old monuments and epitaphs, ii. 358.

St. Bartholomew's Church, Royal Exchange, i. 524.

St. Bartholomew's Hospital, ii. 359; early history; presidency of the Royal Hospitals; Thomas Vicary, first superintendent, 360; Dr. Harvey; great quadrangle rebuilt, *ib.;* museum, 361; theatres; library; Dr. Abernethy, *ib.;* Percival Pott, 362; great staircase; painting by Hogarth; "view day;" Dr. Askew, *ib.;* Dr. Jeaffreson, 363.

St. Benedict; Benedictine monasteries, iii. 451.

St. Benet's Church, Paul's Wharf, ii. 35, 36.

St. Benet Fink Church, i. 531.

St. Bennet Sherehog Church, i. 352, 558.

St. Botolph's Church, Aldersgate Street, ii. 221.

St. Botolph's Church, Bishopsgate; tomb of Sir Paul Pindar, ii. 159.

St. Bride's Church, i. 55, 56.

St. Bride's Passage, i. 146.

St. Bride's Street, i. 129.

St. Catherine Coleman Church, Fenchurch Street, ii. 176.

St. Catherine Cree Church; ii. 189; morality plays; flower sermon, 190.

St. Cecilia, Feast of; Dryden's odes, i. 231.

St. Chad's Church, Nichols Square, v. 506.

St. Chad's Well, Battle Bridge, ii. 278.

St. Christopher-le-Stock's Church; site of the Bank of England, i. 469, 514.

St. Clement Danes; traditional accounts, iii. 11; former and present churches, *ib.;* Dr. Johnson's pew, 14; fire in the vaults; interments— Rymer, Otway, Nathaniel Lee, *ib.;* marriage of Sir Thomas Grosvenor; registers, 15; baptism of Cecil; his character, *ib.;* a walk round the parish, 16—32; population, 24.

St. Clement's Church, Clement's Lane, i. 528.

St. Clement's Lane. (*See* Clement's Lane.)

St. Clement's Well, Strand, iii. 21.

St. Columba's Church, Kingsland Road, v. 525.

St. Dionis Church, Fenchurch Street; syringes for extinguishing fires, ii. 176.

St. Dunstan's Church, Fleet Street, i. 47; famous incumbents; Cowper's lines; figure of Queen Elizabeth; monument to Hobson Judkins; remarkable burials, *ib.;* clock and giants, v. 267.

St. Dunstan's Club, i. 44.

St. Dunstan's Feast of the Goldsmiths' Company, i. 356, 358.

St. Dunstan-in-the-East Church, ii. 113, 114; rebuilt by Wren; again rebuilt by Laing; registers; Fuller's memory, *ib.*

St. Dunstan's Villa, Regent's Park, v. 267; clock and giants from St. Dunstan's Church; Marquis of Hertford, *ib.*

St. Edmund King and Martyr Church, Lombard Street, i. 527.

St. Edward's Convent, v. 260.

St. Eloy; "Loy's Well, Tottenham," v. 561.

St. Erkenwald, Bishop of London, i. 236, 237, 239.

St. Ethelburga's Church, Bishopsgate, ii. 159.

St. Etheldreda's Chapel, Ely Place, ii. 525.

St. Evremond, "governor" of "Duck Island," iv. 50; v. 126.

St. Gabriel's Church, Pimlico, iv. 40.

St. George, Sir Henry, Clarencieux, i. 296.

St. George's Barracks, iii. 149.

St. George's Church, Bloomsbury, iv. 544.

St. George's Church, Camberwell, vi. 274.

St. George's Church, Hanover Square; fashionable weddings, iv. 321.

St. George's Church, Southwark, vi. 71; curfew bell, 72.

St. George's Club, iv. 309.

St. George's Fields, vi. 341; Roman remains; marshes; Lambeth Marsh; Marsh Gate; drainage; inundations; Canute's Trench, *ib.;* restoration of Charles II., 342; refuge from the Great Fire; show-vans; field-preachers, *ib.;* Chequer Mead, 343; St. George's Dunghill; archery; "Apollo Gardens;" "Dog and Duck," *ib.;* St. George's Spa, 344; fort; grinning match; "Wilkes and Liberty" mobs, *ib.;* Gordon Riots, 345-348; Protestant Association; Lord George Gordon, *ib.;* Magdalen Hospital, 348, 349; Peabody Buildings, 350; Female Orphan Asylum; Freemasons' Charity School; Philanthropic Society's School; School for the Indigent Blind; St. George's Circus; obelisk to Brass Crosby, *ib.;* Bethlehem Hospital, 351-361; King Edward's School, 361; Christ Church, 362; Hawkstone Hall; Roman Catholic Cathedral of St. George, *ib.;* School for the Indigent Blind, 364; British and Foreign School Society; Joseph Lancaster, 365; National Society, 366.

St. George's Hospital, v. 4, 5.

St. George's Square, Pimlico, iv. 40.

St. George's Terrace, Primrose Hill, v. 6, 291.

St. George the Martyr Church, Queen Square, Bloomsbury; burial ground, iv. 554.

St. Giles, the patron saint of cripples, vi. 269.

St. Giles's Church, Camberwell, vi. 273, 274; old and new churches; destruction of the old church by fire; monuments; interments, *ib.*

St. Giles's Church, Cripplegate, ii. 229; monuments to Speed, Constance and Margaret Whitby, and Frobisher, 230; Milton's burial and disinterment, *ib.;* Fox, martyrologist, 221; marriage of Cromwell; part of London wall, 232.

St. Giles's-in-the-Fields, iii. 197; St. Giles; Queen Matilda; lepers' hospital; village in early times, *ib.;* stone cross, 198; growth of the parish, 200 ; gallows ; criminal's last drink ; "The Bowl ;" "Bowl Alley ;" "The Angel ;" executions ; cage and pound, ib. ; almshouses, 201 ; vineyard ; past and present church ; interments and epitaphs ; burial of the Earl of Derwentwater ; "Resurrection Gateway," ib. ; bas-relief ; Church Lane, 202 ; Monmouth Court ; Seven Dials, 203 ; the poor, 206 ; Irish immigrants, 207 ; old parish regulations ; Denmark Street ; Lloyd's Alley ; Brownlow Street ; Endell Street, ib. ; the Plague ; Lewknor's Lane, 208 ; coal-yard ; "Round House," 209.

St. Giles's-in-the-Fields Cemetery, v. 335.

St. Gregory's Church in St. Paul's Churchyard, i. 264, 265.

St. Helena Tea Gardens, Deptford Road, vi. 138.

St. Helen's Priory and Church, Bishopsgate, ii. 154 ; crypt ; monuments ; tombs of Sir Julius Cæsar, Sir John Crosby ; Sir Thomas Gresham ; Sir John Spencer ; charity-box ; restoration of the church, ib.

St. James's Chapel, Pentonville ; Francis Linley, organist ; altarpiece by West, ii. 286.

St. James's Chapel, St. James's Square, iv. 203.

St. James's Church, Clerkenwell, ii. 338 ; the old church and monuments ; Bishop Bell ; Lady Elizabeth Berkeley ; John Weever ; the new church, ib.

St. James's Church, Garlick Hythe, ii. 32 ; tomb of Richard Lions ; Steele, on the Church Service, ib.

St. James's Church, Hampstead Road ; Rev. Henry Stebbing ; interments, v. 308.

St. James's Church, Piccadilly, iv. 255, Wren ; font by Gibbons ; altarpiece ; organ ; spire ; distinguished rectors, ib. ; fire in the vaults, 256.

St. James's Club, iv. 285.

St. James's Coffee House, iv. 153.

St. James's Fields, iv. 206, 235.

St. James's Hall, iv. 254.

St. James's Market, iv. 207.

St. James's Palace, iv. 100 ; Hospital for Leprous Women ; endowments ; grant of a fair ; hospital taken by Henry VIII. ; palace built, ib. ; gate-house, 101 ; bell ; clock ; the colour court ; proclamation of Queen Victoria ; daily parade ; Chapel Royal, ib. ; marriages of Queen Anne, Frederick, Prince of Wales, George IV., Queen Victoria, and the Princess Royal, 102 ; choir ; "Gentlemen and Children of the Chapel Royal," 103 ; "spur-money," 104 ; Duke of Wellington ; establishment of chapel ; state apartments, ib. ; drawing-rooms, 105 ; Ambassadors' Court ; royal library ; Lord Chamberlain's department ; Clarence House, 106 ; Greek Church for the Duchess of Edinburgh, 107 ; chaplain's dinner, 109 ; "touching" for the evil, 110 ; George I., 111 ; George II. ; Caroline, his Queen ; George III. ; riot ; fire, ib. ; Duke of Cumberland and his valet, Sellis,

113 ; kitchen in the time of George III. ; drawing-room in the reign of Queen Anne, ib. ; sedan chairs, 114, 116 ; costumes ; a modern drawing-room, ib. ; John, Duke of Marlborough, 117 ; Court influence on fashion in dress, ib. ; Court dress, 118, 119 ; hoops ; silk stockings ; hair-powder ; wigs ; long and short hair ; the farthingale ; lace collars, ib. ; the Poet Laureate, 119 ; his butt of sherry ; royal and court patronage of authors, ib.

St. James's Park, iv. 47 ; Storey's Gate, ib. ; Birdcage Walk ; Rosamond's Pond, 49 ; Duck Island, 50 ; the canal, 51 ; water-fowl, 52 ; peace rejoicings and Chinese bridge, 53 ; skating, 58 ; Horse Guards' Parade, 59 ; funeral of the Duke of Wellington, ib. ; the Mall, 74 ; the cows in "Milk Fair," 76.

St. James's Place ; Burdett ; Rogers, iv. 170, 171.

St. James's Square, iv. 182 ; distinguished residents ; its fashionable character ; "St. James's Fields ;" the square enclosed, ib. ; Norfolk House, 182, 185 ; statue of William III., 183 ; Johnson and Savage ; Ormonde House ; Romney House ; fireworks, ib. ; Bristol House, 184 ; Radnor House ; Erectheum Club ; "Moll Davis ;" Arabella Churchill ; Sir Watkin Williams Wynn, Bart. ; Winchester House, ib. ; London House, 186 ; Roxburgh Club, 188 ; bibliomania ; Windham Club, ib. ; London Library, 189 ; Lichfield House ; Mrs. Boehm's house, ib. ; East India United Service Club, 190 ; Lady Francis ; Queen Caroline ; Lord Castlereagh ; Government offices, ib.

St. James's Street, iv. 152, 158, 160, 164 ; clubs ; White's ; Brooks's, 153 ; Boodle's ; St. James's Coffee House, ib. ; "Thatched House" Tavern, 154 ; Thatched House Club, 156 ; Egerton Club ; Conservative Club ; Arthur's, ib. ; Cocoa Tree Club, 157 ; "Wits' Coffee House," 158 ; "Fox Club" and "Pitt Club," 159 ; New University Club, 160 ; Junior St. James's Club ; Devonshire Club ; Crockford's Club House, ib. ; Marlborough Club ; the "Poet's Head" Tavern, 164 ; George IV. and Brummell, 165 ; Fenton's Hotel, 169, 206.

St. James's Theatre, iv. 191 ; Braham ; French Plays, 193 ; Hooper ; German Opera, 194 ; Morris Barnett ; John Mitchell, ib.

St. John of Jerusalem, Priory of. (See St. John's Gate.)

St. John's Chapel, Chapel Street, Bedford Row, vi. 551.

St. John's Church, Clerkenwell ; crypt ; Cock Lane Ghost, ii. 316.

St. John's Church, Waterloo Road, vi. 410 ; tomb of Elliston, 411.

St. John's College, Battersea ; Normal School of the National Society, vi. 472.

St. John's Gate, ii. 310 ; Knight's Hospitallers ; crusades, ib. ; rules of the order, 311 ; creation of knights, 312 ; sanctuary, 313 ; Priory of St.

John of Jerusalem, 314 ; its wealth ; priory church, ib. ; historical scenes, 315 ; Tylney, Master of the Revels to Queen Elizabeth, ib. ; the gate built by Prior Docwra, 317 ; Cave's printing-office ; "Jerusalem" Tavern ; Dr. Johnson ; Garrick, ib. ; Johnson's chair, 318 ; remains of first gatehouse, 319 ; Gentleman's Magazine, 320, 321 ; Urban Club, 321.

St. John's Lane, Clerkenwell ; the "Old Baptist's Head," ii. 327.

St. John's Lodge, Regent's Park, v. 267.

St. John's Priory, Hackney, v. 513.

St. John's Square, Clerkenwell, ii. 323 ; Father Corker's convent ; riots in 1688 ; Lord Keeper North ; Dove's "English Classics ;" Free-thinking Christians' meeting-house, ib. ; Burnet House, 325 ; Bishop Burnet, 326 ; Dr. Joseph Towers ; Dr. Adam Clarke, 327 ; Wesleyan Chapel ; Gilbert and Rivington, printers, ib.

St. John Street, Clerkenwell, ii. 322 ; a way for pack-horses ; the "Long Causeway ;" footpads ; fortifications, ib. ; resort of carriers, 323.

St. John the Evangelist Church, Westminster, iv. 4, 8.

St. John's Wood, v. 248 ; Priors of St. John of Jerusalem ; artists and authors ; Landseer, ib. ; "Squire" Osbaldiston, 249 ; Soyer ; Thomas Lord ; Lord's Cricket-ground, ib. ; family of Eyre, 250 ; "Eyre Arms" Tavern ; balloon ascents ; St. John's Wood Athenæum ; Napoleon III. ; barracks ; Abbey Road ; Ladies' Home ; St. John's Wood Road ; Clergy Orphan Schools ; Grove Road ; Female Orphan School ; Roman Catholic Chapel ; Avenue Road ; School for the Blind, ib. ; Hamilton Terrace, 251 ; St. Mark's Church ; Aberdeen Place ; Abercorn Place ; St. John's Wood Chapel and burial-ground ; Joanna Southcott, ib.

St. Joseph's Convent, Kennington, vi. 333.

St. Joseph's Retreat, Highgate, v. 393.

St. Jude's Church, Stoke Newington, v. 532.

St. Katherine's Docks, ii. 117 ; formation of the docks, 118 ; description and statistics ; Henry Mayhew's "London Labour," ib.

St. Katherine's Hospital, near the Tower, ii. 117 ; its history and constitution, v. 273 ; Matilda, Queen of King Stephen, 274 ; queen's consort ; bead-roll of the fraternity ; removed for construction of St. Katherine's Docks, ib. ; new hospital, chapel, and master's house, Regent's Park, 275 ; tomb of John, Duke of Exeter ; Sir Herbert Taylor, master, ib.

St. Lawrence Jewry, Church of, i. 376.

St. Lawrence Poultney Church and College ; epitaphs, ii. 40.

St. Leonard's Church, Fish Street Hill, ii. 8.

St. Leonard's Church, Foster Lane, i. 362.

St. Leonard's Church, Shoreditch, ii. 195 ; the actors' church ; burial-place of Somers, Tarlton, Burbage, Greene, Wilkinson, ib.

St. Leonards, Lord, iv. 201.

St. Luke's Church, Berwick Street, iv. 238.

St. Luke's Church, Old Street, ii. 201.

St. Luke's Hospital, Old Street, ii. 200.

St. Magnus Church, i. 573; old religious service; Miles Coverdale, 574.

St. Margaret Moyses Church, i. 349.

St. Margaret Pattens Church, Fenchurch Street, ii. 176; altar-piece by Carlo Maratti; burial-place of Dr. Birch, *ib.*

St. Margaret's Church, Westminster, iii. 567; first church of Edward the Confessor; rebuilt *temp.* Edward I.; present church; tower and bells, *ib.*; porch, 568; pulpit; window presented to Henry VII. by the magistrates of Dort; subject of a lawsuit; loving cup; charitable bequest; monuments; Thomas Arneway, *ib.*; tomb of Lady Dudley, 569; Mrs. Corbett; epitaph by Pope; tomb of Skelton, *ib.*; Speaker's pew; "State services," 570; incumbents and preachers, 572; religious changes; plague, *ib.*; Solemn League and Covenant, 573; iconoclasts; long sermons; gallery, *ib.*; performances of the "Messiah," 574; Wilkes; electioneering piety; Milton and Campbell's marriages, *ib.*; ancient fire-engines, 575; Past Overseers' Society, 576; tobacco-box in silver cases; engraved by Hogarth; other engravings and inscriptions on it; the box detained; legal proceedings, *ib.*

St. Margaret's Hill, Southwark, vi. 58; Southwark Fair; "Our Lady Fair;" Hogarth's picture, *ib.*

St. Mark's College, Chelsea, v. 86.

St. Martin's Church, Ironmonger Lane (called "Pomary"), i. 383.

St. Martin's Church, Ludgate, i. 226; curious epitaph; font, *ib.*

"St. Martin's Hall," Long Acre, iii. 269, 270; Hullah's music-classes; Dickens's lectures; hall burnt down and rebuilt; converted into the Queen's Theatre, *ib.*

St. Martin's-in-the-Fields, iii. 149, 150; windmill; growth of the parish; first chapel, *ib.*; present church, 152; George I.; Gibbs, the vaults, *ib.*; burials, 153; Sir Edmundbury Godfrey; Jack Sheppard; Roubiliac; Farquhar; Nell Gwynne; the "Watermen's Burying-ground;" rate-books; registers; sanctuary, *ib.*; burial-ground, Camden Town; Charles Dibdin, v. 323.

St. Martin's Lane, iii. 159; old houses; noted residents; "Slaughter's" Coffee House, *ib.*

St. Martin's-le-Grand, ii. 215; St. Martin's College; curfew; crypt; sanctuary; St. Martin's lace, 219; French Protestant Church, 228.

St. Martin's Place, iii. 154.

St. Martin's Street, iii. 172; Newton and Dr. Burney, *ib.*

St. Mary Abchurch; rebuilt by Wren; pulpit, monuments, carvings, i. 530.

St. Mary-at-Hill Church, ii. 41.

St. Mary Axe, ii. 191.

St. Mary-le-Bow Church. (*See* Bow Church, Cheapside.)

St. Mary-le-Strand Church, iii. 84; the old church, 84, 291; Protector Somerset; new church by Gibbs, 86.

St. Mary Magdalen's Church, Bermondsey, vi. 121.

St. Mary Magdalen Church, Fish Street Hill, ii. 36.

St. Mary, Moorfields, ii. 207.

St. Mary-in-the-Savoy. (*See* Savoy, The.)

St. Mary Overies, Southwark, ii. 9. (*See* St. Saviour's Church.)

St. Mary Woolnoth Church, Lombard Street, i. 527; Sir Martin Bowes; Sir Hugh Brice; Rev. John Newton; Hawksmoor, *ib.*

St. Mary's Aldermary Church, i. 554; crypt, monuments; epitaph to Sir Henry Keeble; restoration by Wren; sword-holder; Richard Chawcer, 555.

St. Mary's Church, Whitechapel, ii. 143; "St. Mary Matfellon;" origin of the name; libellous picture of the Last Supper; Kennet White, Dean of St. Paul's, *ib.*

St. Mary's College, Peckham, vi. 291.

St. Mary's Hospital, Paddington, v. 225.

St. Michael-le-Quern; corn-market, ii. 181.

St. Michael's Alley, Cornhill; first coffee-house, ii. 172.

St. Michael's Church, Cornhill, ii. 170, 171; pulpit cross; burial of Fabian; Stow's grandfather; rebuilt by Wren; restored by Sir G. G. Scott; the devil in the belfry, 171.

St. Michael's Church, Crooked Lane; Sir William Walworth's monument, i. 555.

St. Michael's Paternoster Royal Church; rebuilt by Whittington, ii. 26; almshouses, 27; college; picture by Hilton; burials; Cleveland's poems, *ib.*

St. Nicholas Acons Church, Lombard Street, i. 527.

St. Nicholas Cole abbey Church; tombs of Fishmongers, ii. 2, 20, 37.

St. Olave's Church, Hart Street; monuments, ii. 110, 112; Pepys and his family, *ib.*, 250.

St. Olave's Grammar School, New, vi. 105, 111.

St. Olave's Union, vi. 124.

St. Pancras, v. 325; biographical sketch of the saint; churches bearing his name, *ib.*; corruption of e name, 326; former rural character of the parish; population, *ib.*; extent, 327; prebendal manors; Domesday Book; Carthusian monks, *ib.*; manor-house, 328; Earl Camden; Lord Southampton; manor of Ruggemere; Skinners' Company; River Fleet; floods, *ib.*; "Elephant and Castle" Tavern, 329; King's Road; workhouse and vestry-hall; parish schools, Hanwell; infirmary, Highgate; old parish church, *ib.*; benefactions, 332; land and revenues; family of Eve or Ive; monument to Robert Eve, *temp.* Edward IV.; Canons of St. Paul's, *ib.*; restoration of church, 333; piscina and sedilia; Norman altar-stone; churchyard; Roman Catholic burials, *ib.*; numerous interments of remarkable persons, 334; Turkish minister, *ib.*; works of the Midland Railway, 337; encroachments on the burial-ground; desecration of the dead, *ib.*; new cemetery at Finchley, 338; "Adam and Eve"

Tavern, 340; St. Pancras Wells; Stukeley; Roman camp at the Brill; fortification at Brill Farm, *ib.*; "Brill" Tavern, Brill Row, Somers Town, *ib.*; market-place, Chapel Street, 344; Ossulston Street; Charlton Street; "Coffee House," *ib.*; Clarendon Square, 345; The Polygon; Roman Catholic Chapel of St. Aloysius, *ib.*; Seymour Street, 346; Railway Clearing House; St. Mary's Chapel, *ib.*; Drummond Street, 347; Railway Benevolent Institution; London and North-Western Railway Terminus, *ib.*; Euston Square, 351; Montgomery's Nursery Gardens; Dr. Wolcot, *ib.*; Euston Road, 352; statue of Robert Stephenson, *ib.*; New Church; almshouses, 315.

St. Pancras Church, Soper Lane, i. 352.

St. Pancras New Church, v. 353, 354; William Inwood, architect; pulpit and reading-desk; Fairlop Oak; vicars; Rev. T. Dale; Rev. W. W. Champneys, *ib.*

St. Paul's Cathedral, i. 235; supposed temple to Diana; British, Roman, and Saxon remains on the site. *ib.*; first authenticated church built by Ethelbert, 236; Mellitus, first bishop; St. Erkenwald; his shrine; charters of Saxon kings, *ib.*; of William the Conqueror, 237; Lanfranc's council; the church burnt down; rebuilt; again partially burnt, *ib.*; Henry III.'s council, 238; the bishop beheaded; Wycliffe before the council, *ib.*; the Lollards, 239; John of Gaunt's grave; abuses; buying and selling in the church; sacred relics, *ib.*; King John of France, 240; chantries; Duchess of Gloucester's penance, *ib.*; Jane Shore's penance, 241; marriage of Prince Arthur; Henry VII. lying in state, *ib.*; Bishop FitzJames, 242; Dean Colet; Wolsey; Henry VIII., *ib.*; Anabaptists burnt, 243; the Reformation; Dr. Bourne preaching; Bishops Ridley and Bonner, *ib.*; wooden steeple burnt, 244; trading and other abuses, *ib.*; "children of St. Paul's," 245; lotteries; Gunpowder Plot; execution of conspirators at St. Paul's; Garnet executed; Inigo Jones's portico, *ib.*; desecration under Cromwell, 246; Wren's report on the building, 247; the Great Fire, 248; the rebuilding; first stone laid, *ib.*; Cathedral opened, 249; Queen Anne, 250; victories celebrated; Thornhill's paintings; organ; Queen Anne's statue; Gibbons' carvings; cost of the Cathedral; visit of George I., *ib.*; visits of George III., 251; Wren's tomb; first monuments; Howard; Johnson; Reynolds; Nelson's funeral, *ib.*; Wellington's funeral, 252; other interments, 254; robbery of plate; improvements of the interior; description and dimensions, *ib.*; Horner's Panoramic View of London, 255; narrow escapes of Gwyn and Thornhill, *ib.*; lightning conductors, 256; falcon's nest; library; trophy-room; clock;

great bell, *ib.;* the clock striking thirteen; a monomaniac, 257; Sydney Smith, 261; Barham; Cockerell; poetical notices, *ib.;* Choir School, 293.

St. Paul's Churchyard, i. 262; Booksellers; Shakespeare's poems and plays; the precinct; Pardon Churchyard, *ib.;* the Cloister, 263; Dance of Death; Paul's Cross; St. Paul's School; the Deanery; St. Gregory's Church; gates; church railings; Garnet's execution, *ib.;* the "face in the straw," 265; John Newbery and his nephew, 266; St. Paul's Chain; Chapter-house; "St. Paul's" Coffee House; "Child's" Coffee House, *ib.;* "Queen's Arms" Tavern, 267; Rivington and Sons; musicshops, 268; Jeremiah Clark, 269; Richard Meares; Handel; John Young, violin maker; Talbot Young, "Dolphin and Crown," *ib.;* St. Paul's Abbey, 272; "Goose and Gridiron;" Freemason's Lodge; "Mitre;" music-houses, *ib.*

St. Paul's Church, Covent Garden, iii. 255; built by Inigo Jones; burnt down and rebuilt; Walpole's strictures on its design; marriages and burials, *ib.*

"St. Paul's" Coffee House, i. 266.

St. Paul's Cross, Spital Sermons, ii. 249.

St. Paul's School, i. 272; described by Erasmus; addresses to sovereigns; school-room; library; eminent Paulines, 273; Pepys, Milton, 274; the New School, vi. 533.

St. Peter; legend of his dedication of Westminster Abbey, iii. 395.

St. Peter ad Vincula Church, in the Tower. (*See* Tower of London.)

St. Peter-le-Poor Church, ii. 166.

St. Peter's Church, Cornhill; murder of a priest, ii. 171.

St. Peter's Hospital (Fishmongers' Almshouses), Newington, vi. 257; removed to Wandsworth, 258, 481.

St. Peter's Hospital for Stone, iv. 465.

St. Peter's in Chepe, i. 318, 364, 398.

St. Philip's Church, Stepney, ii. 140.

St. Pierre, M. de; the longitude, ii. 9; vi. 212.

St. Saviour's Church, Southwark, vi. 320; "the Priory Church of St. Mary Overy;" legend of Mary Audrey, the ferryman's daughter; her "House of Sisters," 21; college for priests; great fire in 1212; church rebuilt; royal weddings; Prior Linsted; dole, *ib.;* Lady Chapel, *ib.;* converted into a bakehouse, 21, 23; restoration, 21; Bishop Andrewes' Chapel, 22; west front; nave; chapel of St. Mary Magdalene, *ib.;* chapel of St. John, 23; Bishop of Winchester's Court; tomb of Bishop Andrewes, *ib.;* of Gower, 21, 25, 26; Fletcher, Massinger, 27; election of preachers, 28.

St. Saviour's Convalescent Hospital, North End, Fulham, vi. 527.

St. Saviour's Grammar School, vi. 17, 42.

St. Saviour's Home and Hospital, Osnaburgh Street, v. 299.

St. Saviour's Hospital, Holloway, v. 381.

St. Sepulchre's Church, ii. 477; early history; the Great Fire, *ib.;* re-

pairs and alterations, 478; interior; tower and porch; organ, *ib.;* interments, 479, 481, 482; Awfield, a traitor; his body refused interment, 483; endowment for admonitions and bell tolling at executions; curious ceremony, *ib.;* nosegay presented to the condemned, 484; bequests to the church, *ib.*

St. Stephen's Chapel, Westminster, iii. 494; its erection; wall paintings; occupied as the House of Commons, 497; cloisters, 557; crypt; its restoration; chapel of Our Lady de la Pieu, 560.

St. Stephen's Church, Coleman Street, i. 514; tomb of Anthony Munday; alto-relievo of "the Last Judgment," ii. 245.

St. Stephen's Church, Walbrook, i. 558; Wren; picture by West, *ib.*

St. Stephen's Club, iii. 329.

St. Swithin's Church, Cannon Street; epitaphs, i. 550, 551.

St. Swithin's Lane; Founders' Hall, i. 551.

St. Thomas A'Becket's Chapel on London Bridge, ii. 10, 16.

St. Thomas Acon, college and church, i. 377, 380, 381.

St. Thomas à Watering; boundary of the City liberties; place of execution, vi. 250.

St. Thomas's Hospital, vi. 89; Prior of Bermondsey, *ib.;* "almery," or hospital, dedicated to St. Thomas the Martyr, 90; Bishops of Winchester; Ridley, Bishop of London; royal endowment of the hospital, *ib.;* decay of the establishment, 91; public subscription; new building; statues of Edward VI. and Sir Robert Clayton, *ib.;* court-room, 92; portraits; building taken for London Bridge Railway Station; removal to Surrey Gardens; to Albert Embankment, *ib.;* the new Hospital, 419.

St. Thomas's Schools, Waterloo Road, vi. 414.

St. Vedast Church, Foster Lane; stone coffins; epitaphs, i. 363.

Salisbury, Countess of, her execution, ii. 92, 95.

Salisbury Court, Fleet Street, i. 138, 140, 141; the Whig "Mug-house;" history of mug-houses; Dorset Gardens Theatre, *ib.*

Salisbury Court Theatre; Davenant, Dryden, i. 195.

Salisbury, Marchioness of, iv. 170.

Salisbury Square, Fleet Street, 140, 143, 146; Richardson's printing-office; "Pamela;" John Eyre, his transportation; the Woodfalls, *ib.*

Salisbury Street, Strand; Salisbury House, iii. 101.

"Sally Salisbury;" the Hon. John Finch stabbed by, iii. 268.

Salmon, Mrs., her exhibition of waxwork, i. 45.

"Saloop-house," in Fleet Street, i. 69.

Salter, John, "Don Saltero;" his coffee-house and museum, v. 62.

Salters' Company, i. 547; successive Halls; present Hall, 548; arms; dinners and pageants, *ib.*

Salters' Hall Chapel and Meeting House, i. 548, 549.

Salt-pits, Roman, i. 548.

"Salutation and Cat," ii. 430.

Salvation Army, Congress Hall, v. 522.

Samaritan Hospital, iv. 423.

Sams' Library, iv. 169.

Sanctuary, right of; its antiquity, iii. 484; cities of refuge, 485; "general" sanctuary, 483; "peculiar" sanctuary, 484; plea of "benefit of clergy," *ib.;* right restrained by Pope Innocent VIII., 485; limited by Henry VIII. and James I., 485; Sanctuary, The, Westminster, 483; its church, churchyard, and close, *ib.;* Thieving Lane, *ib.;* instances of the use and violation of sanctuary, 398, 484; Jon Prendigest, Knyte; Judge Tresilian; Duchess of Gloucester, *ib.;* Elizabeth, Queen of Edward IV., 485; birth of Edward V.; Skelton, poet laureate, *ib.;* procession of sanctuary men, 486; Great and Little Sanctuary, 486; 488; iv. 28, 40, 45.

Sanctuaries: Cold Harbour, ii. 17; Montague Close, Southwark, vi. 28; Ram Alley, Whitefriars, i. 137; St. George's Church, Southwark, ii. 143; priory of St. John of Jerusalem, ii. 313; St. Martin's-le-Grand, ii. 215, 219.

Sandby, Thomas and Paul; their drawings of the Thames, iii. 289.

Sanderson, Sir James, Lord Mayor, i. 411, 443.

Sandford, Francis, Rouge Dragon, i. 298.

Sandford Manor House, Fulham, residence of Nell Gwynne, vi. 525.

Sandwich, Earl of, and Miss Ray, iii. 260, 385.

Sandy End, Fulham, vi. 524.

Sanger, lessee of Astley's Amphitheatre, vi. 406.

Sanquhar, Lord, executed for murder, i. 186.

Sans Souci Theatre; Charles Dibdin, iii. 170.

Sardinian Chapel, Lincoln's Inn Fields, iii. 47.

Satirist Newspaper, iv. 251.

Saunders, Richard, his carved figures of giants in Guildhall, i. 387.

Savage, Richard, ii. 320, 414, 465, 509, 552; iii. 11, 489; iv. 183, 288.

Savile House, Leicester Square, iii. 165; burnt down, 166.

Savile Row, iv. 309; Geographical Society, St. George's Club, *ib.;* Scientific Club, 310; George Grote, M.P.; Sir Benjamin Brodie; Savile Club; Burlington Fine Arts Club, *ib.;* Charles Day, 311.

Savings Banks, Post Office, ii. 213.

Savoy, Precinct of the, iii. 9.

Savoy, The, iii. 95; palace and hospital; early history; Peter, Earl of Savoy; Edmund, Earl of Lancaster; death of John, King of France; palace burnt by Wat Tyler, 96; rebuilt as a hospital by Henry VII., 96; the Savoy Chapel; liberty of the Duchy of Lancaster, 96; Savoy Conference, 97; French emigrants, 98; Jesuits; hall of the hospital; prison; barracks; burial-ground, *ib.;* present chapel, 99; restored by Queen Victoria; interments; masters, *ib.;* John of Gaunt, 100.

Savoy Theatre, iii. 328.

Saxon London, i. 447—452 ; Saxon Bridge ; Edward the Confessor ; Athelstane ; Edmund Ironside ; Canute ; " gemot," *ib.* ; remains on the site of St. Paul's, 236 ; fortress on site of Tower of London, ii. 60 ; antiquities in Fleet Ditch, 417.

Sayers, Tom, pugilist, v. 370.

Scalding Alley, Poultry, i. 416, 419.

Schomberg House, Pall Mall ; Duke of Schomberg, iv. 124, 125.

School of Art for Ladies, iv. 555.

School of Design, Lambeth, vi. 424.

Science and Art Department, v. 112.

Scientific Club, iv. 310.

Scotch pines, Kensington Gardens. v. 156.

Scotland Yard, iii. 330; Saxon Palace for Kings of Scotland and Scottish ambassadors, *ib.* ; Vanbrugh, 332 ; "Well's" Coffee-house ; Lord Herbert of Cherbury ; Palace Court, *ib.* ; Metropolitan Police-offices, 333 ; office for cab licences ; first hackney coaches ; sedan chairs, *ib.;* "Jarveys," 334. (*See* Middle Scotland Yard.)

Scot's Yard, Thames Street ; Roman river-wall, ii. 35.

Scott, American diver, iii. 321.

Scott, Colonel, R.E. ; Royal Albert Hall, v. 113.

Scott, John, killed in a duel, i. 64.

Scott, Sir G. G., R.A., ii. 171 ; iii. 423, 452, 454, 479 ; iv. 35 ; v. 128, 370, 483, 533 ; vi. 245, 273, 339.

Scott, Sir Walter, i. 186, 275 ; ii. 220, 331 ; iv. 220, 294, 302, 460 ; v. 466 ; vi. 564.

Scottish Corporation, i. 107 ; the "Scottish Box ;" Kinloch's bequest ; annual festival ; house and chapel, *ib.*

Scottish National Church, Crown Court, Covent Garden, iii. 279.

"Scourers," members of dissolute clubs, iv. 57, 166.

Scroope's Inn, Paul's Wharf, i. 285.

Scrope and Grosvenor families ; heraldic controversy, i. 347 ; iv. 371.

Scrope family, their residence in Upper Thames Street, ii. 18.

Seacole Lane, iii. 33.

"Sea-coal sellers," iv. 218.

Seal, Great, iv. 6, 566.

Seal of the Bank of England, i. 468.

Seal of the Corporation of London, i. 446, 504.

Seamen's Children's School, ii. 146.

Seamore Place ; Lady Blessington ; Count D'Orsay, iv. 352.

Searle's boat-building yard, Lambeth, vi. 387.

Sebert, King, iii. 394, 431.

Sedan chairs, iii. 334, 336 ; iv. 114, 248, 290.

Sedley, Sir Charles, iii. 21.

Seething Lane ; Sir Francis Walsingham ; Navy Office, ii. 99.

Selby, Mrs. ; costume ; the hoop invented by her, v. 158.

Selden, i. 154, 172 ; ii. 521.

Selwyn, George, ii. 450 ; iv. 165, 177, 455 ; v. 131, 171, 193.

Semaphore, iii. 383 ; v. 506 ; vi. 99, 258, 292.

"Serle's" Coffee-house, iii. 27.

Serle's Place (Upper, Middle, and Lower), iii. 21.

Serle Street and Serle's Court, iii. 26.

Serjeants' Inn, Chancery Lane, i. 83, 84.

Serjeants' Inn, Fleet Street, i. 84 ; sale of buildings, i. 84 ; the hall, i. 137 ; removal of Serjeants to Chancery Lane ; arms of the inn, *ib.*

Sermon or Shiremoniars Lane, ii. 36.

Sermons, Long, ii. 49 ; iii. 573 ; hour-glasses in pulpits, i. 368 ; ii. 146 ; iii. 574 ; vi. 577 ; Flower Sermon, ii. 190. (*See* Spital Sermons.)

Serpentine River. (*See* Hyde Park.)

Serres, Dominic, marine painter, iv. 82 ; vi. 413.

Serres, Olivia, " Duchess of Lancaster," iv. 567 ; vi. 413.

Sessions House, Old Bailey. (*See* Old Bailey.)

Sessions House, Westminster, iv. 33.

Settle, Elkanah, i. 406 ; ii. 178, 01.

Seurat, Claude Amboise ; the " Living Skeleton," iv. 257.

" Seven Chimneys " (pest-houses), Tothill Fields, iv. 14, 15.

Seven Dials, iii. 204 ; "the seven streets ;" column and dials, *ib.* ; trade of the locality ; cellar rooms, 205 ; female barbers, 206 ; George IV. at a beggar's carnival, *ib.* ; iv. 292.

Seven Sisters' Road, v. 380.

" Seven Sisters," Tottenham, v. 550.

Severndroog Castle, vi. 236, 243.

Sewage : Fleet Ditch, v. 234 ; Metropolitan Commissioners of Sewers, 236 ; main drainage scheme ; Sir Joseph Bazalgette ; high, middle, and low level sewers, *ib.* ; statistics, 238.

Seymour Hall, iv. 23

Seymour Street, Euston Square, v. 346 ; Railway Clearing House ; St. Mary's Church, *ib.*

Shacklewell ; wells ; old manor-house, v. 530.

Shad Thames ; " St. John-at-Thames," vi. 113.

Shadwell, dramatist, i. 188, 196 ; iii. 243, 278.

Shadwell, ii. 137 ; rope-walks ; St. Paul's Church ; waterworks ; Shadwell Spa, *ib.*

Shaftesbury, Earl of ; his house in Aldersgate Street, ii. 220 ; iv. 340 ; v. 89 ; notices of him by Butler, Dryden, and Scott, *ib.*

Shaftesbury House, Chelsea, v. 89.

Shakespeare, i. 49, 50, 123, 157, 158, 181, 200, 201, 219, 264, 302, 351, 545, 560, 563 ; ii. 28, 94, 104, 155, 221, 515, 516 ; iii. 33, 327 ; iv. 128, 135, 167, 177, 253, 536 ; v. 108, 28 ; vi. 27, 41, 45, 46, 49, 93.

Shakespeare, Edmund, the poet's brother, vi. 27.

" Shakespeare Head," Wych Street ; Mark Lemon, iii. 284.

Shakespeare Oak, Primrose Hill, v. 291.

" Shakespeare's Head," Russell Street, Covent Garden, iii. 278.

" Shard Arms," public-house ; the Shard family, vi. 251, 287.

Sharp, William, engraver, vi. 553.

" Shaver's Hall," Haymarket, iv. 221.

Shee, Sir Martin Archer, P.R.A., iii. 148 ; iv. 446.

Sheepshanks, John ; his pictures, v. 26.

Sheffield House, Kensington, v. 134.

Sheil, Richard Lalor, M.P., v. 125.

Shelley, iv. 176 ; v. 22, 457, 458, 500 ; vi. 548.

Shenstone, William, iii. 10, 65, 243.

Shepherd's Fields, Hampstead, v. 498 ; Shepherd's Well, 500.

Shepherd's Market, iv. 352.

Sheppard, Jack, i. 74 ; ii. 460 ; iii. 32, 34, 153 ; v. 190 ; vi. 63.

Sheridan, i. 88, 166, 388 ; iii. 212, 224, 262 ; iv. 158, 159, 220, 298, 311, 327, 329, 389, 423 ; v. 137 ; vi. 375.

" Sheridan Knowles " Tavern, iii. 282.

Sheriffs' Court, Red Lion Square, iv. 548.

Sheriffs' dinners at Old Bailey, ii. 468.

Sheriffs, Election of, i. 437, 441.

Sherlock, Bishop, i. 155 ; v. 473.

Shillibeer's omnibuses and funeral carriages, v. 256.

" Shilling Rubber Club," iii. 267.

" Ship and Shovel," Tooley Street, vi. 106.

" Ship at anchor," sign of Longmans, publishers, iv. 295.

" Ship in full sail," sign of John Murray, publisher, iv. 295.

Shipton, Mother, history of, v. 311.

Ship Yard, Fleet Street, i. 74 ; resort of coiners and thieves ; the " Smashing Lumber," iii. 21, 22.

Shire Lane, Fleet Street, i. 70—74 ; Kit-Kat Club, *ib.* ; the " Trumpet," 75 ; Trumpeters' Club ; the " Bible ; " Jack Sheppard ; murders ; the " Retreat ; " Cadgers' Hall ; " Sun " Tavern ; " Anti-Gallican " Tavern ; illustrious residents, *ib.* ; iii. 20, 21, 22.

Shoe Lane, i. 123 ; John Florio ; Cogers' Discussion Hall, 124, 125 ; Hudson, comic song writer, 130 ; unstamped newspapers, 132 ; burial-place of Chatterton, *ib.* ; ii. 548.

Shoes, rights and lefts, iii. 441.

Shooter's Hill ; highwaymen ; gibbets ; Herbert's Hospital, vi. 236.

Shoreditch, ii. 194 ; the legend of its name refuted ; Soerdich family ; Barlow, " Duke of Shoreditch ; " archers, *ib.*, 252 ; almshouses, v. 507 ; workhouse, 525.

Shore, Jane, i. 241, 314 ; described by Drayton ; her penance, *ib.*

Shot factories, Lambeth, vi. 408.

Shovel, Admiral Sir Cloudesley, iii. 420.

Shower, John, minister of Old Jewry Chapel, i. 430.

Shrewsbury, Francis, Earl of, and his Countess ; fatal duel, iii. 215 ; vi. 498.

Shrewsbury House, Cold Harbour, ii. 17.

Siamese Twins, The, iv. 257.

Sick Children, Hospital for, Great Ormond Street, iv. 561.

Sick Children, North-Eastern Hospital for, v. 507.

Sick Children, Victoria Hospital for, Chelsea, v. 83.

Siddons, Mrs., iii. 224, 231, 232 ; v. 209, 214, 261.

Sidney, Algernon, ii. 75, 95 ; v. 18.

Sidney Alley, iii. 161.

Signs of shops and taverns ; Larwood's " History of Sign-boards," i. 34, 37, 46, 50, 129, 228, 272, 305, 410, 417, 424, 524 ; ii. 137, 147, 411 ; iii. 21, 22, 26, 33, 38, 63, 64, 104, 196, 254, 263, 266, 267, 273, 290, 314, 382, 488, 559 ; iv.

6, 12, 17, 44, 60, 135, 164, 167, 207, 208, 233, 234, 238, 239, 245, 253, 287, 288, 291, 295, 301, 309, 322, 334, 407, 429, 485, 545, 552; v. 9, 45, 178, 304, 393; vi. 13, 63, 74, 88, 123, 251, 256, 390.

Silk and Silkworms; mulberry-gardens, v. 67.

Silk manufacture, v. 88.

Silk-weavers in Spitalfields, ii. 150.

Silver Street, Golden Square, iv. 239.

Silver Street, Wood Street; Parish Clerks' Company, i. 369.

"Simon the Tanner," public-house, Bermondsey, vi. 123.

Simon, Thomas; his coins, ii. 104.

Simpson, master of the ceremonies, Vauxhall Gardens, iv. 465.

Sion College, ii. 168; the library, 170.

"Sir Hugh Myddelton" Tavern, Sadler's Wells; old picture, ii. 294, 295.

"Sixteen-string Jack," ii. 484; v. 194.

Skates, primitive, used in Moorfields, ii. 196.

Skating-hall, Colosseum (1844), v. 272.

Skating rinks, v. 452; v. 95, 100.

"Skeleton, Living," iv. 257.

Skelton, poet laureate, iii. 485, 569.

Skinners' Company and Hall, ii. 38; affray with the Fishmongers, i. 305; ii. 3, 38; wearing of furs restrained, 39; regulations for importing furs; processions; elections; arms; the Hall, ib.

Skinners' Estate, St. Pancras; Sir Andrew Judd, v. 341.

Skinner Street, Snow Hill, ii. 489; Alderman Skinner; houses disposed of by lottery; neglected houses; execution of Cashman; shop of William Godwin, 490.

"Slaughter's" Coffee House, iii. 159.

Slavery, i. 423, 424; ii. 157; iii. 34; iv. 15; v. 14.

Slave trade; the South Sea Company, i. 538.

"Slender Billy," v. 3.

Sloane, Sir Hans, i. 107; ii. 433; iv. 490, 494, 539; v. 59, 62, 68, 69, 87, 95, 360.

Sloane Square, v. 95.

Sloane Street, v. 97.

Sloman's sponging-house, i. 89.

"Sluice House," Hornsey, v. 431.

Small-pox Hospital, iv. 472; v. 385.

Small-pox; vaccination, vi. 376.

Smeaton; repairs of Old London Bridge, ii. 15.

Smart, Sir George, iv. 457.

Smart's Quay, Billingsgate, a seminary for thieves, ii. 48.

Smirke, Sir Robert, R.A., iv. 476, 500, 502.

Smirke, Sydney, iv. 500, 502.

Smith, Albert, i. 57, 58; iii. 132; iv. 56, 246, 250, 258; vi. 202, 209, 461, 526.

Smith, Alderman Joshua Johnson; his kindness to Lady Hamilton, iv. 254.

Smith, Captain John, captured by the Indians (Pocahontas), ii. 481, 482.

Smith, C. Roach, F.S.A., i. 20, 21; ii. 34.

Smith, E. T., vi. 521.

Smith, George, Assyrian Collection, British Museum, iv. 531.

Smith, James and Horace, "Rejected Addresses," ii. 167; iii. 225, 232; vi. 281, 393.

Smith, J. T. ("Rainy Day Smith"), ii. 262, 452; iv. 238, 458, 459, 518; v. 255; vi. 377.

Smith, Dr. Pye, v. 513, 521.

Smith, Thomas Assheton, iv. 412.

Smith, Rev. Sydney, i. 260; iv. 374.

Smith, Robert Vernon ("Bobus Smith"), iv. 310.

Smith, Sir F. P.; the screw-propeller, iv. 254.

Smith and Son, Messrs.; W. H. Smith, sen. and jun., iii. 76.

Smith's Forge, Blackheath, vi. 226.

Smithfield, ii. 339; tournaments; death of Wat Tyler; Sir William Walworth; Richard II.; religious martyrs burnt at the stake, ib.; the gallows, 341; execution of Wallace; Priory of St. Bartholomew, ib.; the king's Friday market, 342; old Hospital of St. Bartholomew, 344; miracle-plays; Court of Pie-poudre; mulberry-trees; Prior Bolton, ib.; New Hospital, 345; Bartholomew Fair, 345—350; relics of the Smithfield burnings, 351.

Smithfield Club Cattle Shows, iv. 421.

Smithfield Market; Dickens; statistics; removal to Copenhagen Fields, ii. 350.

Smith Square, Westminster, iv. 35.

Smollett, i. 538, 539; iv. 352; v. 92, 93; vi. 66.

Smyth, Admiral, iv. 268.

Snow Hill, or Snore Hill, ii. 440; death of John Bunyan; Dobson, painter, 441; "Saracen's Head" Inn, 485; described by Dickens; origin of the sign, ib.; conduit, 489.

Snow, Paul, and Bates, bankers, iii. 64.

"Snow Shoes" public-house, v. 76.

Snow's Fields, Bermondsey, vi. 108.

Soap Yard, Southwark; Alleyne's alms-houses, vi. 33.

Soane, Sir John, i. 46, 469; iii. 47, 503, 561; iv. 128, 385; v. 300; vi. 302.

Social attractions of London; opinions of eminent writers, vi. 575.

Société Française de Bienfaisance, iv. 232.

Society of Antiquaries, iii. 94; iv. 269.

Society of Arts, iii. 29, 107, 115, 147, 262.

Society for the Propagation of the Gospel in Foreign Parts, iv. 125, 170.

Soho, iii. 173; etymology; "So Hoe;" the situation, ib.; Square, or Soho Fields, 174; history, 176; old houses, 177; Newport Industrial School, ib.; Newport Market; Earl of Newport's house; French refugees; gardens of Leicester House; Toxophilite Society, ib.; Gerrard Street, 178; "Turk's Head;" the "Literary Club" and "Literary Society," ib.; Macclesfield House and Street, 179; Princes Street; Windmill Street, 180; formation of St. Anne's parish; the Church, 181; the watch-house; Sir Harry Dimsdale, 183; Carlisle Street, iii. 187; Carlisle House; Mrs. Cornelys, ib.; Sutton Street, 189; Roman Catholic Chapel; the Irish in London, ib.; Frith Street, 192; Compton Street, 194; New Compton Street; Dean Street; Royalty Theatre, ib.; Greek Street,

195; Wardour Street, 196; Crown Street; Rose Street; Hog Lane, ib.

Soho Bazaar, iii. 190.

Soho Square, iii. 184; "King's Square;" "Monmouth's Square;" a fashionable quarter; famous residents, ib.; the Duke of Monmouth, 185; statue of Charles II.; ancient fountain; Albert Grant; Alderman Beckford; Burnet, ib.; Monmouth House, 186; the "White House," 190; Crosse and Blackwell's warehouse; Soho Bazaar, ib.; Sir Joseph and Miss Banks, 192; Linnæan Society; Sir J. E. Smith; Conway, ib.

Soldiers' Daughters' Home, Hampstead, v. 484.

"Sol's Arms," v. 351.

Somerset House, iii. 89; Protector Somerset; the old Palace; occupied by Queens Elizabeth; and Anne of Denmark, ib.; Henrietta Maria, 90; her chapel, 91, 92; Catherine of Braganza, 92; murder of Sir Edmundbury Godfrey; cemetery, ib.; gardens, 94; new Somerset House; Royal Academy; Public Offices, ib.; Society of Antiquaries, Royal Society, 94; wills preserved, 327.

Somerset House Gazette, iii. 328.

Somerset, Protector, ii. 95; iii. 84, 88, 89, 90, 546.

Somerset, the "Proud" Duke of, iv. 131, 161.

Somers Town; its origin and decline, v. 340.

Somers, Will, vi. 170.

Somerville, Mary, iv. 315; v. 94.

Sons of the Clergy, annual festival, i. 441; iv. 544.

Soper Lane, Cheapside; "pepperers;" Sir Baptist Hicks, i. 352.

Sophia, Princess, v. 146, 220.

Sorbière's account of Bartholomew Fair, ii. 346.

Sotheby, Wilkinson, and Hodge, great literary sales, iii. 286.

South, Sir James; observatory; equatorial broken up and sold, v. 131; vi. 69.

Southampton (afterwards Bedford) House, Bloomsbury, iv. 536.

Southampton Buildings, i. 85, 86; the first Temple Church, 147; remains of Southampton House, ii. 532; of the old Temple; Lord and Lady William Russell, ib.; coffee-houses, 533; attempted suppression of them; Mechanics' (now Birkbeck) Institution; Dr. Birkbeck, ib.; the Soldier's Well, 536.

Southampton, Earl of, ii. 506; Anne Askew tortured by him; Catherine Parr arrested by him, ib.

Southampton Row, iv. 543.

Southampton Street, Bloomsbury, iv. 543.

Southampton Street, Pentonville, ii. 287.

Southampton Street, Strand, iii. 119; the "Bedford Head," ib.; Garrick and Mrs. Garrick, 267; Cradock; Gabriel and Colley Cibber, ib.

South Audley Street, iv. 345; Henry Audley, 344; Charles X. of France; Louis XVIII.; Paoli; Sir Richard Westmacott; Alderman Wood; Queen Caroline; Duke of York; Lord John Russell; Lord Bute;

chapel ; interments ; epitaph on Wilkes ; Spencer Perceval, *ib.*
Southcott, Joanna, iv. 425 ; v. 212, 251, 256.
South-Eastern Railway, i. 550 ; vi. 98, 99.
Southey, ii. 430 ; iii. 474 ; iv. 252, 294, 482 ; v. 375 ; vi. 375.
Southgate, v. 569 ; Minchenden House ; Arno's Grove ; Bush Hill Park, *ib.*
South Kensington Museum, v. 109—112 ; specimens of art workmanship ; loan collections ; the buildings ; portraits ; Dyce, Sheepshanks, and Ellison collections ; sculpture, textile fabrics, art library, ceramic art, glass, pictures ; Raphael's cartoons ; Museum of Patents ; Science and Art Department, *ib.*
South London Company's Water Works, vi. 339.
South London Railway, vi. 99.
South Place Chapel, Finsbury, ii. 206.
South Place, Finsbury, ii. 206.
South Sea Company and South Sea House, i. 538 ; South Sea Bubble, 539—543 ; ii. 173 ; vi. 93.
South Street, Park Lane ; Lord Melbourne ; Mdlle. D'Este, iv. 369.
South Villa, Regent's Park ; observatory, v. 267.
Southwark, vi. 3 ; St. Mary Overie ; ferry across the Thames ; first timber bridge ; etymology ; Olaf, *ib.* ; Roman embankment, 4 ; Saxon entrenchment ; William the Conqueror's invasion ; incorporation of Southwark ; granted to the City of London ; the Lord Mayor bailiff of Southwark, *ib.* ; present government, 5–8 ; London Bridge built by the priests of Southwark ; Danish fortifications ; bridge destroyed by Olaf, *ib.* ; the Bridgefoot, 8, 12 ; Jack Cade, 10 ; Sir Thos. Wyatt, 11 ; Southwark Fair, 11, 14 ; fortified during the Commonwealth, *ib.* ; Bridge House, 13 ; armorial bearings, 14 ; Palace of the Bishop of Winchester ; pilgrimages, *ib.* ; growth of the borough; fire in 1676 ; "Tabard ;" "White Hart," 15 ; "the Borough ;" Liberty of the Clink, 16 ; the High Street, 17—20 ; "Long Southwark ;" railway bridge ; clock tower ; Borough Market ; old St. Saviour's Church and Grammar School, *ib.* ; Winchester House, 29 ; Bordello, or "Stews," 32 ; Deadman's Place ; Soap Yard, 33 ; Barclay and Perkins's brewery, *ib.* ; Globe Theatre, 40 ; Zoar Street ; Bunyan's chapel ; Bankside, *ib.* ; Crucifix Lane, 41 ; Stoney Street ; Holland Street, " Holland's Leaguer ;" Falcon Glass Works ; "Falcon" Tavern ; Green Walk, *ib.* ; churches ; Sumner Street, 42 ; Southwark Street, 44 ; Bandyleg Walk ; Gravel Lane ; Hop Exchange ; subway, *ib.* ; High Street ; Town Hall, 57 ; Southwark Fair, 57 ; Union Street ; Union Hall, 59 ; Mint Street, 60 ; Lant Street ; the "Mint," 60—63 ; Great Suffolk Street, 63 ; Winchester Hall, 64 ; Finch's Grotto Gardens ; King's Bench Prison, *ib.* ; High

Street, 69 ; Kent Street, 70 ; St. George's Church, 71 ; Marshalsea Prison, 72 ; hat manufacture, 75 ; tanners and curriers ; slaughterhouses, *ib.* ; famous inns, 76—89 ; St. Thomas's Hospital, 89 ; St. Thomas's Church, 93 ; London Bridge Railway Station, 98 ; former water-supply, 99 ; St. Saviour's Church. (*See* St. Saviour's Church.)
Southwark and Vauxhall Water Company, vi. 291, 478.
Southwark Bridge, i. 545.
Southwark Park, vi. 136.
Southwark Street, vi. 44.
Soyer, Alexis, v. 122, 249.
Spa Fields, ii. 301 ; Ducking-pond Fields, 302 ; female pugilists ; footpads ; the " Welsh " or " Gooseberry Fair ; " ox roasted ; grinning for prizes, *ib.* ; Pantheon ; converted into a chapel, 303 ; Countess of Huntingdon, *ib.* ; burial - ground, 305.
Spa Road and Railway Station, Bermondsey, vi. 130.
" Spaniards " Tavern, v. 445.
Spanish Armada, ships of, iii. 467.
" Spanish Galleon " Inn, Greenwich, vi. 134.
Spanish panic on the Stock Exchange, i. 486.
" Spanish Patriot " Inn, Lambeth, vi. 415.
Spanish Place ; Roman Catholic Chapel, iv. 425.
Spencer family ; mansion in Clerkenwell, ii. 333.
Spencer House, St. James's Place, iv. 176.
Spencer, Rev. George (" Father Ignatius ") v. 393.
Spencer, Sir John (" rich Spencer "), Lord Mayor, i. 401 ; ii. 157, 269.
Spenser, Edmund, i. 160 ; ii. 98, 430 ; iii. 68 ; iv. 26.
Spitalfields, ii. 149 ; Priory of St. Mary Spittle ; Spital sermons, *ib.* ; silkweavers, 150 ; iv. 280 ; riots ; birdfanciers, ii. 152.
Spital sermons, i. 310 ; ii. 149, 376, 429.
Sprat, Rev. Thomas, Dean of Westminster, iii. 460.
Spread Eagle Court, Bread Street, i. 350.
" Spring Garden," Kennington, vi. 340.
" Spring Garden," Knightsbridge, v. 20.
Spring Gardens, iv. 77, 78, 81, 82, 83.
" Spring Gardens," Greenwich, vi. 195.
" Spring Gardens," Vauxhall. (*See* Vauxhall Gardens.)
Spring Garden Terrace, iv. 78.
" Spring Tom " (Thomas Winter), pugilist, ii. 536.
Sponging-houses, i. 369 ; iii. 259.
Spurgeon, Rev. C. H., vi. 29, 260, 267, 326.
" Spur-money," iv. 104.
Spurstowe, Dr. ; almshouses, Hackney, v. 514, 517.
" Squire's " Coffee House, ii. 536.
Staël, Madame de, iv. 242.
Stafford Club, iv. 309.
Stafford, Earl of, iii. 433, 550.
Stafford House, St. James's, iv. 120 ; formerly Cleveland House ; Fox ; Duke of York, 121 ; Stafford Gallery ; Duke and Duchess of Sutherland, 122.
Stafford Street, iv. 274.

Stage-coaches, iv. 261, 440 ; v. 93, 206, 257, 303, 454.
Stag-hunting, ii. 136 ; v. 51.
Stamford Hill, v. 544, 545.
Stamford Street, Blackfriars, vi. 381 ; Miss Read's decayed houses, 382.
Standard in Cheapside, i. 317.
Standard in Cornhill, ii. 170.
Standard Newspaper, i. 62, 63.
Stanfield, Clarkson, R.A., iv. 573 ; v. 483.
Stanhope, Earl ; South Sea Bubble, i. 541.
Stanhope Gate, Hyde Park, iv. 395.
Stanhope Street, Strand, iii. 33.
Stanley, Very Rev. A. P., Dean of Westminster, iii. 453, 454, 457, 461, 464, 466, 467.
Staple Inn, Holborn, ii. 575.
" Star and Garter " Hotel, Pall Mall, iv. 137.
" Star and Garter," Putney, vi. 500.
Star-Chamber, The, iii. 501, 502.
Star-Chamber Newspaper, iv. 446.
" Star " Tavern, Coleman Street ; Cromwell and Hugh Peters, ii. 243.
Starch Green, Hammersmith, vi. 536.
State Coach, abandonment of, i. 416.
Stationers' Company, i. 229 ; monopoly of printing almanacs ; "entering" and registry of books, *ib.* ; misprints in Bibles, 230 ; almanacs ; charities, 232 ; school ; arms of the Company ; masters, 233 ; vi. 442.
Stationers' Hall, i. 230 ; first hall in Milk Street ; removal to Ludgate Hill ; destroyed in the Great Fire ; decorations of the hall, *ib.* ; festival of St. Cecilia ; Dryden's "Ode to St. Cecilia" and "Alexander's Feast;" Handel ; funerals and banquets, *ib.* ; court room ; the company's plate, 232 ; pictures, 233.
Stationery Office, Her Majesty's, Westminster, iv. 34.
Statistics, vi. 567 ; length of the streets of London ; number of houses ; evidences of its gradual growth, *ib.* ; suburbs or outlying villages ; old maps, 568 ; population, 569, 570 ; compared with that of other British and foreign cities, countries, and the entire globe ; births and deaths, *ib.* ; class population, 571 ; tramps ; paupers ; costermongers ; criminals ; foreigners ; Jews ; Irish ; Roman Catholics ; public - houses and beer - shops ; bakers ; butchers ; grocers ; insane persons ; illustrations of the extent of population ; recent improvements ; model lodging - houses ; Board schools ; new streets and buildings ; Cleopatra's Needle, *ib.* ; food supply, 572 ; corn-merchants, dealers, and flour-factors ; markets ; water-supply ; analysis and total daily consumption, *ib.* ; gas-lighting, 574 ; sewage ; street refuse ; mud and dust ; churches ; hospitals ; theatres ; music-halls and other places of amusement, *ib.* ; parks and open spaces, 575, 576 ; intellectual and social attractions ; opinions of Dr. Johnson, Bannister, John P. Kemble, Boswell, Burke, Macaulay, Leigh Hunt, Dickens, Captain Morris, *ib.*

Statuary ; " figure-yards ;" Piccadilly ; Euston Road, iv. 287 ; v. 303.

Steel Yard, and Merchants of the Steel Yard, i. 453; ii. 32, 33, 34, 181.

Steele, Sir Richard, i. 70, 71, 503; ii. 32 ; iii. 27, 39, 65, 112, 277, 280 ; iv. 104, 141, 166, 172, 202, 288, 539 ; v. 62, 93, 144, 167, 459, 491 —494.

Stephens, Miss (Countess of Essex), iii. 232.

Stephenson, Robert, iii. 418.

Stepney, ii. 137 ; Court of Record ; fortifications ; the plague ; cholera ; Stratford College ; church, 138 ; epitaphs ; monument of Lady Berry; story of " The Fish and the Ring ;" Jews' burial - ground ; almshouses and hospitals, 140 ; vicars, 141 ; noted residents, 142 ; children born at sea, 142.

Sterne, iv. 299, 335.

Stevens, George Alexander ; lecture on heads, ii. 296, 538 ; vi. 369.

" Stews," Bankside, Southwark, vi. 32.

Stillingfleet, Bishop, ii. 513 ; iv. 29, 256, 416.

Stirling, Edward, the " Thunderer " of the *Times*, v. 25.

Stock Exchange, i. 473 ; Change Alley ; Sir Henry Furnese ; stock-jobbers ; " bulls " and " bears," *ib.;* Thomas Guy, 474 ; the Exchange in 1795, 476 ; the New Exchange ; Capel Court, 477, 494 ; newspaper " money articles," 477 ; frauds, 478 ; Lord Cochrane ; " ticket-pocketing," 479 ; the Rothschilds, 482, 486 ; Abraham Montefiore, 484 ; Abraham Goldsmid ; battle of Waterloo, 485 ; railway mania, 486 ; scrip ; omnium, 488 ; " pigeon expresses," 491 ; failures, 485-6 ; " Alley men," 492 ; eminent members, 493.

Stock fishmongers, ii. 2.

Stocks' Market, i. 436; ii. 497; iii. 125.

Stocks, The, iii. 29; v. 208; vi. 244, 293.

Stockwell, vi. 327 ; etymology ; Green ; Albion Archers, 328 ; " Stockwell Ghost ;" St. Andrew's Church, *ib.* ; hospitals, schools, and asylums, 329.

Stoke Newington, v. 530 ; etymology, 531 ; Ermin Street ; Puritanism ; Mildmay Park ; Mildmay House ; Newington Green ; residence of Henry VIII., *ib.;* King Henry's Walk, 532 ; St. Jude's Church ; the Conference Hall ; distinguished residents, *ib.;* churches ; old parish church, 533, 534 ; rectors, 530, 531, 532, 533, 534, 537, 539, 542 ; Queen Elizabeth's Walk, 536 ; Church Street, *ib.* ; Sandford House, 537 ; Defoe Street ; Manor House ; Church Row ; Fleetwood Road, *ib.;* reservoirs of New River Company, 539 ; Abney House ; Abney Park Cemetery, 539, 540, 541.

" Stones' End," Southwark, vi. 69.

Stoney Lane, Bermondsey, vi. 111.

Stoney Street, vi. 41.

Storace, Madame, vi. 446.

Storey's Gate ; Edward Storey, keeper of the aviary, v. 24.

Stothard, Thomas, iii. 269 ; iv. 467 ; vi. 248.

Stourton, Lord ; his execution, iii. 546.

Stow's " Annals," presented by him to the Merchant Taylors' Company, i. 532 ; his monument, ii. 192.

Strafford, Wentworth, Earl of, i. 82 ; ii. 75, 95, 144 ; iii. 548.

Strahan, William, King's printer, i. 218, 219.

" Straits of St. Clement's," iii. 10.

" Strand " Inn, an Inn of Court, iii. 88.

Strand Lane ; " Strand Bridge ;" the old Roman bath, iii. 77.

" Strand, Straits of the," iii. 158.

Strand, The. iii. 59 ; its condition under the Plantagenets and Tudors ; traffic ; rotten road ; introduction of carriages, *ib.* ; name of the " Strand," 60 ; mansions of the nobility, 61, 66, 67, 71, 89, 95, 100, 113 ; Maypole, 62, 86 ; Milford Lane, 70 ; Arundel Street, 74 ; Messrs. W. H. Smith and Sons, 75 ; Strand Lane ; the old Roman bath, 77 ; Norfolk Street, 80 ; Surrey Street ; Howard Street, 81 ; St. Mary-le-Strand Church, 84 ; Monk, Duke of Albemarle, and his Duchess, 87 ; Maypole Alley ; Newcastle Street, 88 ; Somerset House, 89 ; King's College, 94 ; the Savoy, 95 ; Cecil Street, 101 ; Exchange ; Coutts's Bank, 104 ; Adelphi, 105 ; Society of Arts, 107 ; Buckingham Street ; " Water Gate," 108 ; Villiers Street, 109 ; Catherine Street, 110 ; Exeter Street ; Exeter Arcade ; Theatres, 112, 119 ; Exeter Change, 113 ; Cross's menagerie, 116 ; Exeter Hall, 118 ; Maiden Lane ; Southampton Street, 119 ; Commissionaires, 120 ; newspaper offices, 111, 121, 123 ; Lowther Arcade, 132 ; Craven Street ; Northumberland Street, 134.

Strand Union Workhouse, iv. 466.

Stratford-le-Bow, v. 570 ; Bow Bridge ; " Stratford-atte-Bowe," *ib.;* Convent of St. Leonard's, 571 ; the bridge ; inquisition in 1303 ; toll ; new bridge ; church, *ib.;* Bow and Bromley Institute, 573 ; railways ; Old Ford ; " King John's Palace ;" Town Hall ; West Ham Park ; Cistercian Abbey ; Abbey Mill Pumping Station, *ib.;* new town of Stratford, 575 ; Great Eastern depôt and works ; West Ham Cemetery ; Jews' Cemetery, *ib.*

Stratford Place, iv. 437 ; Stratford, Lord Aldborough, *ib.*

Stratton, Charles S., " General Tom Thumb," iv. 258 ; v. 210.

Stratton Street ; Lord Lynedoch ; Mrs. Coutts ; Baroness Burdett-Coutts ; Sir Francis Burdett, iv. 280, 281.

" Straw-bail," i. 155.

Straw, Jack, vi. 225.

Streatham, vi. 316 ; descent of the manor ; Manor House ; mineral springs, *ib.;* Streatham Place ; Thrale ; Dr. Johnson and Mrs. Thrale, 317 ; Magdalen Hospital, 318.

Streatham Street, New Oxford Street, iv. 488.

Street tramways, v. 188 ; vi. 483.

Streets of London ; their total length, vi. 567.

Stroud Green ; Stapleton Hall, ii. 275.

Strutt, Joseph, ii. 510, 543.

Strutton Ground, Westminster, iv. 11, 12.

Stuart, Lady Arabella, ii. 73 ; v. 404 ; vi. 386.

Stuart, Lord Dudley Coutts, iv. 202.

Stuart, The royal family of, iii. 358, 360.

Stukeley, Dr. Wm., iv. 483, 554, 556 ; v. 321, 342.

Stulz, Messrs., tailors, iv. 303.

" Stunning Joe Banks ;" Rookery, St. Giles's, iv. 488.

Subway, Tower. (*See* Tower Subway.)

Subways for sewers, &c., v. 239 ; vi. 44.

" Sufferance Wharfs," vi. 141.

Suffolk House, Southwark, vi. 60.

Suffolk House, Strand, iii. 136.

Suffolk Lane ; Merchant Taylors' School, ii. 28.

Suffolk Street, Pall Mall East, iv. 227 ; Earls of Suffolk ; " Vanessa," Dean Swift, *ib.* ; " Cock " Tavern, 228 ; " Calves' Head Club," 229.

Sumner Street, Southwark, vi. 42.

" Sun and Hare," old sign, Southwark, vi. 88.

Sunderland House ; Earl of Sunderland, i. 542 ; iv. 258.

Sun-dials, i. 177, 178 ; iii. 26, 33, 243, 370, 376, 537 ; vi. 557.

Surgeon, College of. (*See* College of Surgeons.)

Surgeons' Hall, Old Bailey, ii. 471, 472.

Surrey Chapel ; Rev. Rowland Hill, vi. 374—380.

Surrey Commercial Dock, vi. 140, 141.

Surrey County Prison, vi. 482.

Surrey, Earl of, i. 394, 395 ; ii. 66, 108, 414 ; iv. 185.

Surrey Institution, vi. 382.

Surrey Lunatic Asylum, vi. 482.

Surrey Sessions House, vi. 255.

Surrey Street ; Congreve ; Voltaire, iii. 81.

Surrey Theatre, vi. 368 ; the " Royal Circus and Equestrian Philharmonic Academy ;" Charles Dibdin and Charles Hughes ; horse-patrol to protect visitors ; riot, *ib.;* Grimaldi, grandfather of the clown, 369, 370 ; Delphini ; acting dogs ; Stephens's " Lecture on Heads ;" John Palmer ; lessees ; burnt down and rebuilt ; Elliston ; licensing system ; Thomas Dibdin ; the " Surrey ;" T. P. Cooke ; R. W. Elliston and Charles Kemble, *ib.* ; Danby, scene-painter, 371 ; Davidge ; Osbaldiston ; Creswick ; burnt down in 1865 ; rebuilt ; residences of actors, *ib.*

Surrey Zoological Gardens, vi. 266, 267, 268 ; the menagerie ; picture models and fireworks ; Rev. C. H. Spurgeon's preaching ; the Music Hall ; Jullien's Concerts ; the Hall destroyed by fire ; temporary St. Thomas's Hospital, *ib.*

Sussex, Duke of, iv. 407, 568 ; v. 142, 148, 150, 220.

Sussex House, Hammersmith, vi. 539.

Sutherland, Duke and Duchess of, iv. 122.

Sutton, Archbishop, ii. 402.

Sutton Place, Hackney, vi. 518.

Sutton Street, Soho ; Roman Catholic Chapel, iii. 189.

Sutton, Thomas, founder of the Charterhouse, i. 231 ; ii. 383—386, 387, 392, 393 ; v. 518, 533.

Swaine's Lane, Highgate ; formerly Swine's Lane, v. 405.

Swallow Street, iv. 249, 253.

"Swan" and "Old Swan" Taverns, on the Thames, iii. 308 ; v. 67.

Swan Brewery, Chelsea, v. 68.

"Swan" Inn, Stockwell, vi. 328.

Swan Stairs, London Bridge, ii. 40.

"Swan" Tavern, Fulham, vi. 524.

"Swan" Theatre, Bankside, vi. 50, 383.

Swans in the Thames, iii. 302 ; swan marks, ii. 23 ; "swan-upping," 303 ; the "Swan with Two Necks,"iv. 17.

"Swearing on the Horns" at Highgate, v. 413—418.

"Sweaters," members of dissolute clubs, iv. 57.

Swedenborg, Emanuel, biographical sketch of, ii. 135, 304.

Swedish Church, Ratcliff Highway, ii. 135.

Sweedon's Passage, Grub Street, ii. 243.

Swift, i. 41, 45, 105, 543 ; ii. 173, 363, 422 ; iii. 27 ; iv. 54, 125, 141, 153, 154, 166, 169, 202, 227, 263, 392, 450 ; v. 90, 124, 134, 144 ; vi. 548.

Swimming, iii. 296 ; iv. 404 ; in the Serpentine ; in the Thames ; Swimming Club, ib.

Sword Blade Company, i. 540, 542.

Sydenham, Dr., iv. 256.

Sydenham, vi. 303 ; beauty of the site, ib.; medicinal springs, 304 ; Wells House ; George III.; Croydon Railway ; Campbell, ib.; Thomas Hill, 305 ; growth of population, 304, 307 ; churches, 307 ; Sydenham Park, ib. ; chapels, 308 ; schools ; Crystal Palace, ib.

Sydenham Wells, vi. 294.

Synagogues, ii. 165 ; iv. 408, 409, 457.

Syringes for extinguishing fires, ii. 176.

T.

"Tabard" Inn, Southwark, vi. 14, 15, 76 ; sign altered to the "Talbot ;" Abbots of Hide ; old inn for pilgrims to Becket's shrine, Canterbury ; Chaucer, ib.; Pilgrim's room, 77 ; characters in the "Canterbury Tales," 81—84.

Tabarders, at Queen's College, Oxford, vi. 84.

Tabernacle, Moorfields ; Whitefield's pulpit, ii. 198 ; John Wesley, 200.

Tackle porters, ii. 52.

Tailor's Almshouses, v. 315.

Talfourd, Justice, iv. 566 ; vi. 316.

"Tallies," Exchequer ; burning of the Houses of Parliament, iii. 502, 521.

Talleyrand, Prince de, iv. 316, 424 ; v. 128.

Tallis, Thomas, composer of church music, vi. 191.

Tanners' trade, Bermondsey, vi. 123 ; tan-yards ; tan-pits ; tan-turf, 125.

Tapestry manufacture, Fulham, vi. 521.

Tarleton, Richard, his "Book of Jests," i. 276 ; ii. 174 ; vi. 55, 64.

Tart Hall, iv. 25 ; v. 47.

Task, Alderman, Sir John, his great wealth, i. 64.

Tate, Nahum, vi. 62.

"Tattersall's" Auction-mart, Grosvenor Place ; Richard Tattersall, v.

5 ; new auction-mart, Knightsbridge, 27.

Tavistock Place, iv. 574 ; Francis Douce ; John Pinkerton ; John Galt ; Sir Matthew Digby Wyatt ; Francis Baily, ib.

Tavistock Row, Covent Garden ; murder of Miss Ray, iii. 260.

Tavistock Square, iv. 573 ; Tavistock House ; James Perry ; Dickens ; his private theatricals ; Stanfield, ib.

Tavistock Street, Covent Garden, iii. 119, 260.

Taylor, G. Watson, M.P., iv. 444.

Taylor, Michael Angelo, M.P., iv. 164.

Taylor, Sir Herbert, G.C.B., v. 14, 275.

Taylor, the water-poet, ii. 51 ; iii. 74, 271, 309 ; vi. 47.

Taylor, Tom, i. 58, 59.

Tea-drinking ; tea-gardens, iv. 435.

"Tea-house" of William III., St. James's Park, iv. 50.

Tea, introduction and prices of, i. 45 ; iii. 64, 266 ; iv. 62, 418.

Telegraph Department, General Post Office ; instruments, ii. 214—219.

Telegraph Hill, Hampstead, v. 506.

Telford, Thomas, iv. 2, 32.

Templars, i. 147 ; origin of the order ; its first home in England ; removal to the banks of the Thames ; rules of the order ; the Crusades, ib.; decay and abolition of the order, 148.

Templar's House, Hackney, v. 519.

Temple, The, i. 55 ; Chaucer and the Friar, ib.; the serjeants, 156 ; the "Roses," 157 ; the flying horse, 158 ; revels and masques, 159, 160, 164 ; Sir Edward Coke ; Spenser, 160 ; Fire of London, 161 ; Erskine, 165 ; the Gordon Riots ; Eldon ; keeping terms ; George Coleman, ib.; Dunning, Kenyon ; Blackstone, Burke, and Sheridan ; epigrams, 166 ; Cowper's attempted suicide, 173 ; murders, assaults, robberies, and executions, 174—176 ; sun-dials, 177, 178 ; Porson ; Gurney ; Rogers, 178 ; admission of members ; student-life, 178, 180 ; riots, 179 ; Alsatia ; old banquets and customs, ib. ; moots, 180 ; eminent members, 182 ; the Inner Temple, 161 ; hall and library destroyed by fire, ib.; the old hall ; its rebuilding, 164 ; new hall and library, 172 ; garden, 179 ; Mr. Broome, gardener, 181 ; rooks, 182 ; Middle Temple, i. 158 ; the hall ; its roof, busts, and portraits ; performance of "Twelfth Night" in 1602, ib.; revels and masques, 159—164 ; dicing, 164 ; revenue and accounts, 182 ; the garden ; catalpa-tree, ib.; Brick Court, 170 ; Crown Office Row, 176 ; birthplace of Charles Lamb, ib. ; Elm Court, Guildford North, 173 ; Essex Court ; the wig-shop, 167 ; Fig Tree Court; fig-trees in London ; Thurlow, 172 ; Fountain Court ; the Fountain, 171 ; Garden Court ; Goldsmith, 169 ; Hare Court ; Sir Nicholas Hare ; old pump, 167, 168 ; Inner Temple Lane ; Dr. Johnson, 167 ; Charles Lamb, ib.; King's Bench Walk ; Mansfield ; Sarah, Duchess of Marlborough, 176 ; Paper Buildings ; destroyed by fire ; new buildings,

172 ; Pump Court ; Tanfield Court ; Chief Baron Tanfield, 157 ; Sarah Malcolm, murderess, 174 ; Temple Lane, 177.

Temple ; the "Outer" Temple, iii. 66.

Temple Bar, i. 23 ; iii. 63 ; the first "wooden house ;" historical pageants, i. 23 ; rebuilt by Wren, 24 ; heads of traitors, 27, 28, 29 ; plans for its removal, 30.

Temple Bar Memorial, iii. 20.

Temple Church, i. 150 ; its restorations ; discoveries of antiquities, ib.; penitential cell ; tombs of the Templars, 152 ; stone coffins in churchyard, 153 ; organ, 154.

Temple Club, iii. 75.

Temple Station, Metropolitan Railway, v. 231.

Ten Acres Field, iv. 305.

Tenison's School and Library, iii. 155, 167.

Tennis Courts, iii. 43, 46 ; iv. 231, 232, 236, 237 ; vi. 54.

Tennyson, Alfred, i. 44, 59.

Tenterden, Lord, i. 52.

Tenterden Street ; Royal Academy of Music, iv. 320.

Tewkesbury Buildings, Whitechapel, ii. 145.

Thackeray, John ; almshouses, Lewisham, vi. 246.

Thackeray, W. M., i. 57, 58, 89 ; ii. 399, 404 ; iii. 83 ; iv. 86, 141, 166, 169, 200, 202, 218, 251, 306, 574 ; v. 104, 118, 124, 128, 140, 194, 221, 461 ; vi. 60, 205, 406, 458.

Thames, The River, iii. 287, 310 ; the "Pool," ib. ; the stream at London as a highway, iii. 287 ; conservancy of the river, 289 ; view by Thomas and Paul Sandby, ib.; "The Folly," a floating coffee-house, 290 ; Chinese Junk, ib. ; Thames Police-station, 292 ; Royal Humane Society's Receiving-house, ib. ; Hungerford Stairs, 296 ; floating swimming-baths, ib.; open bathing, 297, 310 ; Cowley's funeral, 297 ; Lambeth Ferry, 299 ; James II. and the Great Seal, ib. ; poetical eulogies, 287—301 ; banks of the river ; trees and flowers, 300 ; waterside scenes, 302 ; river desperadoes, 310 ; fish ; swans, 302 ; "swan-upping," 303 ; river waifs and dead-houses, ib.; Thames watermen and wherrymen, 305, 310 ; their licences and fares, 305 ; tilt-boat for goods, 306 ; water tournaments, 308 ; Doggett's coat and badge race ; Dibdin's ballad-opera, The Waterman; old "Swan" Inn, Chelsea, ib.; Taylor, "the water-poet," 309 ; Lord Mayors' "water-pageant ;" funeral of Anne of Bohemia ; Queen Elizabeth ; the Maria Wood ; City Company's barges ; Queen's state barge ; Admiralty barge, ib. ; training-ships, 310 ; James II. and remarkable frosts from 1150 to 1814, 311—321 ; Frost Fair in 1683 ; printing on the ice, 313, 314, 315, 317, 320 ; doggrel verses, 313, 314, 320 ; "Blanket Fair ;" bull-baiting ; sledges ; coaches ; Charles II. and his family on the ice, 315, 316 ; oxen roasted, 313, 314, 316, 317 ; fatal and other accidents, 317, 320, 321 ; fog and

" Frost Fair " of 1814, 317 ; experiments and wagers, 321 ; Captain Boyton ; Scott, the American diver ; high and low tides, *ib.* ; Victoria Embankment, 322, 323 ; ancient embankments, *ib.* ; Queen's visit by water to the Coal Exchange, 337.

Thames Embankment, iii. 322, 323 ; v. 65.

Thames Police Station, iii. 292.

Thames Tunnel, ii. 129 ; Sir M. I. Brunel ; company formed ; Act of Parliament ; progress of the works ; teredo shield, *ib.* ; irruption of the river ; narrow escapes, 130 ; loss of life, 131 ; more accidents, 132 ; the work completed, 134.

Thames Tunnel and Railway, vi. 139.

Thames Yacht Club, Royal, vi. 196.

Thanet Place, Strand ; the " Rose " Tavern, iii. 63.

"Thatched House" Club, iv. 156.

"Thatched House" Tavern ; iv. 154.

Thavies Inn, ii. 573.

Thayer Street, iv. 424.

Theatres, Modern ; statistics, vi. 574. (*See* Adelphi, Astley's, &c.)

Theatres, Old : the Globe, Rose, Hope, and Swan, Bankside, vi. 45—48 ; " Cockpit," Drury Lane, iii. 39 ; Pantheon, iv. 244 ; Blackfriars Theatre, Playhouse Yard, i. 200 ; at Newington, 17th century, vi. 258 ; " The Theatre," Shoreditch ; the first theatre in London, ii. 195.

Theatrical licences, vi. 369, 370.

Theatrical portraits at the Garrick Club, iii. 263.

Theed, William, sculptor, iv. 443.

Thelwall, John, i. 413 ; ii. 275 ; iii. 47.

Theobald's Road, iv. 550.

Theodore, King of Corsica, iii. 182.

Thieven Lane, Westminster, iii. 483 ; iv. 28.

Thieves and thieves' resorts, i. 74 ; ii. 426 ; iii. 39, 45.

Thirlwall, Bishop, Charterhouse School, ii. 403.

" Thirteen Cantons," The, iv. 238.

Thistle Grove, Brompton, v. 101.

Thistlewood ; Cato Street Plot, ii. 76, 94, 298, 454 ; iv. 340, 411 ; v. 315.

Thomson, James, poet, ii. 99, 408 ; iv. 79, 123, 141, 243 ; vi. 544.

Thornhill, Lady, vi. 554.

Thornhill, Sir James, i. 250, 254, 255, 388, 530, 544 ; iii. 146, 159, 194, 262, 367 ; iv. 536 ; v. 207 ; vi. 278.

Thornton, Bonnell, i. 129, 130, 207, 278 ; iii. 273 ; v. 80.

Thrale and Mrs. Thrale, vi. 34, 35, 317.

Thrale, Miss (Lady Keith), iv. 286.

Threadneedle Street, i. 21, 531 ; Roman pavements ; church of St. Benet Fink ; Merchant Taylors' Hall, 531 ; march of the archers, 536 ; Hall of Commerce ; Edward Moxhay, *ib.* ; beggars, 537 ; " Baltic " Coffeehouse ; St. Anthony's School ; Laneham ; Sir Thomas More ; Whitgift ; " North and South American " Coffee House, *ib.* ; South Sea House and Company, 538 ; South Sea Bubble, 539—543 ; Charles Lamb, 544.

"Three Brushes" Inn, Southwark, vi. 88.

" Three Chairmen " Tavern, iv. 333.

" Three Compasses " Inn, Hornsey, v. 430.

"Three Compasses," Pimlico, v. 9.

" Three Cranes," Hackney, v. 516.

" Three Cranes," in the Vintry, i. 44 ; Ben Jonson ; Pepys ; Elizabeth Cromwell, ii. 20.

" Three Cranes," Poultry, i. 418.

Three Crown Court, Southwark, vi. 58.

" Three Crowns," Stoke Newington, v. 538.

" Three Goats' Heads " Inn, Lambeth, vi. 392.

" Three Jolly Pigeons ; " Cauliflower Club, ii. 435.

" Three Kings " Tavern, iv. 275.

" Three Merry Boys " Inn, Lambeth, vi. 392.

" Three Morrice Dancers " Tavern, Old Change, i. 347.

" Three Squirrels " Inn, Lambeth, vi. 392.

" Three Tuns " Inn, Southwark, vi. 88.

" Three Tuns," Chandos Street, iii. 268.

" Three Widows," Southwark, vi. 89.

Throckmorton, Sir Nicholas, i. 395, 515 ; ii. 190.

Throgmorton Avenue, i. 522.

Throgmorton Street, i. 515, 516, 520.

" Thumb, General Tom," v. 210.

Thurloe Place and Square, v. 104.

Thurlow, Lord, i. 45 ; iv. 556 ; vi. 314.

Thurtell, murderer, iii. 35, 381.

Thynne, Lord John, iii. 422.

Thynne, Thomas, assassination of ; his tomb, iii. 419 ; iv. 227, 277.

" Tichborne Case, The," iii. 562.

Tichborne Court, Holborn, iii. 215.

Tichborne, Sir Robert, Lord Mayor, i. 404.

Tickell's poem, "Kensington Gardens," v. 153, 158.

Ticket porters, ii. 52.

" Tiddy-doll," vendor of gingerbread, iv. 219, 346.

Tides, high and low, in the Thames, iii. 321.

Tilbury, Messrs. ; the " Tilbury," v. 262.

Tillotson, Archbishop, iii. 45 ; v. 569 ;

Tilney Street, Park Lane ; Soame Jenyns ; Mrs. Fitzherbert, iv. 368.

Tilt-boats, vi. 196.

" Tilt Yard " Coffee-house, iv. 82.

Tilt-yard, Whitehall Palace, iii. 341, 344, 364.

Times Newspaper ; its history, i. 209—215, 478 ; v. 25.

Time-signals, General Post Office, ii. 218.

Tite, Sir William, F.R.S., M.P., i. 505, 507 ; v. 13.

" Tityre-Tus," dissolute clubs, iv. 57, 166.

Tobacco ; bill-head of tobacconist, *temp.* Queen Anne, vi. 13.

Tobacco-box of the Past Overseers' Society, St. Margaret's, Westminster, iii. 575, 576.

Tobacco Warehouse, London Docks, ii. 125.

Tokenhouse Yard ; farthing tokens, i. 515.

Tokens, Tradesmen's, i. 514, 515 ; iv. 218, 248 ; vi. 11, 86, 87, 88, 89.

Told, Silas, preaching in Newgate, ii. 447, 448.

" Tom o' Bedlams," vi. 351.

" Tom's " Coffee-house, Birchin Lane, ii. 173.

" Tom's " Coffee-house, Russell Street ;

literary club ; old snuff-box, iii. 278.

" Tom's " Coffee-house, Strand, iii. 65.

" Tom Thumb, General," iv. 258.

Tomkins and Challoner ; executed, i. 94, 389 ; ii. 510.

Tompion, Thomas, watchmaker, i. 53.

Tonbridge Chapel, v. 366.

Tonson, Jacob, i. 46 ; ii. 556 ; iii. 77, 79.

Tooke and Barber, Queen's printers, i. 218.

Tooke, Horne, i. 410.

Tooke's Court, i. 88.

Tooley Street, vi. 13, 14 ; St. Olave's Street ; Bridge House, *ib.* ; a corruption of " St. Olave's Street ; " fires ; Topping's Wharf, 102, 103 ; St. Olave's Church, 104 ; fires at Topping's, Fenning's, and Cotton's Wharves, vi. 105 ; the " Three Tailors of Tooley Street," 108.

Topham, the " Strong Man," ii. 268, 304, 305.

Torregiano, iii. 436, 439.

Toten Hall, Manor of, v. 303.

Tothill Fields Prison, iv. 10 ; the old Bridewell, Westminster ; old gateway ; Howard ; present arrangements, *ib.*

Tothill Fields, Westminster, iii. 478 ; iv. 14 ; origin of " Tothill ; " punishment of necromancers ; fair and market tournaments ; trial by combat ; pest-houses ; burials ; plague, *ib.* ; " maze," 16 ; racecourse ; bear-garden ; butts, *ib.* ; duels ; highwaymen, 16 ; Westminster Fair, 17 ; v. 3.

Tothill Street, Westminster, iv. 17 ; distinguished residents ; Swan Yard ; " Cock," or " Cock and Tabard " Inn, 18 ; Stourton House ; Dacre's Almshouses, 12.

Tottenham ; Tottenham High Cross, v. 549 ; division of parish into wards ; extent and boundaries ; Waltheof, Earl of Huntingdon ; Domesday Book ; manor of " Toteham ; " descent of the manor ; David Bruce, King of Scotland ; Dean and Chapter of St. Paul's, *ib.* ; Lord Coleraine, 550 ; Hermitage and Chapel of St. Anne ; " Seven Sisters " public-houses ; the seven trees ; the Green, *ib.* ; the high cross, 551 ; " Bower Banks," 552 ; Cook's Ferry, 553 ; Bleak Hall ; almshouses ; " George and Vulture " Tavern, *ib.* ; Roman Catholic chapel, 554 ; Bruce Castle, residence of the father of David Bruce, *ib.* ; successive buildings ; present school, 556 ; Bruce Grove, 557 ; Sailmakers' Almshouses ; All Hallow's Church ; Mosel river, *ib.* ; Tottenham Grammar School, 561 ; St. Loy's Well ; Bishop's Well, *ib.* ; White Hart Lane, 562 ; Wood Green ; Tottenham Wood ; " Turnament of Tottenham," *ib.* ; sanitary improvements, 563.

Tottenham Church, v. 560 ; its history ; tower, 557 ; porch, 558 ; hagioscope ; font ; monuments and brasses, *ib.* ; restoration of the church, 560 ; chantry ; bells, 561.

Tottenham Court, v. 304.

Tottenham Court Road, iv. 477 ; Totten Hall manor-house ; William de Tottenhall ; Domesday Book ; manor leased to Queen Elizabeth ; Fitzroys, Lords Southampton ; turnpike gate ; Tottenham Court Fair ; wrestling ; cock - fighting ; female pugilists ; "Gooseberry Fair ;" theatricals ; highwaymen ; depository for dead bodies ; "Tabernacle," *ib.* ; Rev. George Whitefield, 478 ; his monument ; "Evangelicalism ;" Toplady ; Bacon, sculptor ; John Wesley ; death by lightning, *ib.* ; "King John's Palace," public-house, 479 ; tame rats ; Moses and Son ; Shoolbred & Co. ; Hewetson ; Peg Fryer, centenarian ; "Blue Posts" Tavern ; Bozier's Court, *ib.*

Tottenham Street ; Prince of Wales's Theatre, iv. 473.

Tottenham Wood, v. 562.

"Touching" for king's evil, iii. 353 ; iv. 110.

"Tournament of Tottenham," satire, *temp.* Henry VII., v. 562.

Tournaments, i. 315 ; ii. 11, 339 ; iii. 496 ; iv. 14 ; vi. 166, 169, 171.

Tower, The, ii. 60 ; Roman and Saxon fortresses ; work of Gundulf, Bishop of Rochester ; Henry III. ; embankment, water-gate, and wharf, *ib.* ; rights of the warden to use "kiddles" or nets, 62 ; White Tower ; inscriptions ; crypt ; banqueting-hall ; Chapel of St. John the Evangelist, *ib.* ; Maud Fitzwalter, 63 ; inner and outer wards ; towers ; access of citizens to the king ; courts of justice, *ib.* ; distinguished prisoners ; executions, 63—76 ; murder of the young princes, 66 ; escape of Lord Nithsdale, 76 ; inscriptions by prisoners, 62, 68, 69, 70 ; Jewel House and Regalia, 77 ; crown jewels pledged, 80 ; Keeper of the Regalia ; Master of the Jewel House, *ib.* ; Col. Blood's attempt to steal the crown, 81 ; the Armouries, inventory of armour, *temp.* Edw. VI., *ib.* ; supposed spoils of the Armada ; "collar of torment," 82 ; armouries arranged by Dr. Meyrick, 83 ; improvements by Planché ; Horse Armoury ; chain-mail ; plate-armour, *ib.* ; block ; heading-axe ; thumb-screws, 86 ; Small Arms Armoury ; Train Room ; naval relics ; curiosities, 87 ; "Constable of the Tower," 88 ; warders ; their dress ; ceremony of "locking-up ;" Tower Coroner ; Menagerie ; Keeper of the Lions, *ib.* ; the Moat ; stone shot, 89 ; Church of St. Peter ad Vincula, 90, 92 ; place of execution, 93 ; Petty Wales ; Waterloo Barracks, *ib.* ; Flamsteed's observatory ; the Tower ghost, 94.

Tower Crecy, Notting Hill, v. 180.

Tower Hamlets, The, parliamentary borough, ii. 98.

Tower Hill ; scaffold and executions, ii. 95 ; old house, 98 ; Roman wall, 114 ; Trinity House, 115 ; fair, 117.

Tower Liberties, Perambulation of the, ii. 96.

Tower Royal, or Queen's Wardrobe, i. 551.

Tower Subway, The, ii. 123.

Towers, Dr. Joseph, ii. 327.

Towneley, C. ; Towneley Marbles, iv. 44, 459, 500.

Townsend, Bow Street runner, ii. 135, 299.

Townshend, Marchioness of, iii. 376 ; v. 365.

Toxophilite Society, iii. 177 ; v. 185 ; Gardens in the Regent's Park, 276—278 ; Finsbury Archers ; history of Archery, *ib.*

Toynbee Hall, Whitechapel, vi. 572.

Tradescant family, vi. 446 ; John Tradescant, his house and museum, vi. 334.

Tradesmen's tokens, i. 514 ; iv. 218, 248 ; vi. 11, 86, 87, 88, 89.

Trafalgar, Battle of ; model, iii. 335.

Trafalgar Square, iii. 141 ; the site ; its formation, removal of courts and alleys, *ib.* ; Nelson Column, 142 ; fountains ; statues of George IV., Havelock, Napier ; College of Physicians, *ib.*

Traffic statistics, iv. 472.

Train, G. F. ; street tramways, v. 188.

Trained-bands, i. 309, 370 ; ii. 161, 196 ; iv. 378 ; v. 87 ; vi. 109.

Training-ships in the Thames, iii. 311.

Traitors' Hill, Highgate ; Gunpowder Plot, v. 405.

Tramways, Street ; v. 188 ; vi. 483.

Travellers' Club, iv. 145.

Treadmill, its introduction, ii. 299 ; vi. 320.

Treasury Buildings, Whitehall, iii. 388 ; built by Sir John Soane ; altered by Sir C. Barry ; Privy Council Office ; Home Office ; Board of Trade ; oath of the Clerk of the Privy Council, *ib.*

Trees in Kensington Gardens, v. 155, 156, 160 ; in Greenwich Park, vi. 207.

Trelawney, Sir Harry, his romantic marriage, i. 564.

Trench, Rev. Richard Chevenix, Dean of Westminster, iii. 461.

Trevor, Sir John, expelled from the House of Commons, i. 77 ; iii. 23.

Trial by combat, iii. 563 ; iv. 14 ; vi. 394.

Trinity Chapel, Conduit Street, iv. 323.

Trinity Church, Knightsbridge, v. 22.

Trinity Church, Osnaburgh Street ; Sir John Soane, v. 300.

Trinity Church, Trinity Square, vi. 253.

Trinity Corporation ; its establishment at Deptford ; powers and privileges ; removal to Tower Hill, ii. 115, 116.

Trinity Hospital, Greenwich, vi. 196.

Trinity House, ii. 115, 116 ; constitution, powers, and duties of the Corporation ; former and present buildings ; pictures ; museum ; masters, *ib.*

Trinity Street, Square, and Church, Southwark, vi. 253.

"Triumphal Chariot" Tavern ; Steele and Savage, iv. 288.

True cross, Relic of the, iii. 404 ; iv. 76, 105.

Truefitt, hairdresser, iv. 304.

"Trumpet," Shire Lane ; Trumpeters' Club, i. 70, 71, 73.

Truro, Lord, v. 11.

Trusler, Dr., ii. 323.

Tudor, Owen, vi. 119.

Tufton Street, Westminster, iv. 36 ; Architectural Museum ; cock-pit, *ib.*

Tulip mania, v. 51.

"Tumble-down Dick" Tavern ; Richard Cromwell, vi. 55.

Tun, The, a prison in Cornhill, ii. 170.

Tunnel, Thames. (*See* Thames Tunnel.)

Tumuli, Blackheath, vi. 224.

Turf Club, iv. 285.

Turkey Company, vi. 236.

"Turk's Head" Inn, Covent Garden, iii. 285.

"Turk's Head" Tavern, Soho, iii. 178 ; Dr. Johnson's Literary Club ; Society of Artists, 179.

Turnagain Lane, ii. 488.

Turner, Charles, A.R.A., v. 408.

Turner, J. M. W., R.A., i. 253 ; iii. 119, 146, 267 ; iv. 447 ; v. 86.

Turner, Mrs. Anne, executed, i. 280 ; ii. 74 ; v. 189, 190.

Turner, Sharon, iv. 548.

Turner, Sir Gregory Page ; South Sea Stock, i. 543.

Turner's Wood, Hampstead, v. 446.

Turnham Green, vi. 560 ; Prince Rupert's encampment ; battle of Brentford, *ib.* ; flight of the Royalists, 561 ; pursued by the Earl of Essex ; plot to assassinate William III. ; highwaymen ; Lord Mayor Sawbridge robbed ; "Pack Horse" Inn ; "King of Bohemia's Head ;" gardens and nurseries, *ib.* ; Lock-up Hall," 562.

Turnmill Street, ii. 425 ; thieves and highwaymen ; Cave's cotton-mill ; Dr. Thomas Worthington ; Turnmill Brook, *ib.*

Turn-overs ; "piccadillas," iv. 236.

Turnpikes, iv. 407 ; v. 122, 177, 257, 303, 508.

Turnstile Alley, Holborn, iii. 50.

Turnstile, Great and Little, Lincoln's Inn Fields, iii. 215.

Turpin, Dick, ii. 275, 309 ; iv. 20, 435 ; v. 381, 524.

Tusser, Thomas, i. 419.

Twining and Co., early sale of tea, iii. 64.

Twiss, Horace, i. 213.

"Two Chairmen, The," Tavern, iv. 82.

"Two Fans," Leadenhall Street ; Motteux's India House, ii. 188.

"Two Heads, The ;" a dentist's sign, iv. 234.

Twyn, John ; executed for sedition, barbarous sentence, v. 196.

Tyborne, Village of, iv. 438.

Tyburn and Tyburnia, iv. 438 ; v. 189 ; the Tye-bourn ; execution of Roger de Mortimer ; elms ; the "Tyburn Trees ;" early executions ; gallows removed from St. Giles's Pound ; executions of priests and highwaymen ; the cart, *ib.* ; murderers, traitors, housebreakers, sheep-stealers, forgers, "Morocco men," 190 ; Mrs. Turner, poisoner ; Jack Sheppard ; Jonathan Wild, *ib.* ; Catherine Hayes ; Tom Clinch ; Earl Ferrers, 192 ; Hackman ; Dr. Dodd, 193 ; "Sixteen-string Jack," 194 ; M'Lean ; Claude Duval, 195 ; early executioners ; Bull ; Derrick ; the Brandons ; Dun ; "Jack Ketch," *ib.* ;" "Tyburn Ticket," 197 ; regicides, 199 ; "Tyburn Road," 200 ; Hogarth ; penance of Queen Henrietta Maria, *ib.* ; exact site of the gallows, 201 ; seats to witness executions, 202 ; Oxford and Cambridge Squares and Terraces, *ib.* ;

Connaught Place, 203 ; residence of Queen Caroline ; Princess Charlotte ; Sir Augustus D'Este ; T. Assheton-Smith, *ib.*

Tyburn Road. (*See* Oxford Street.)

Tyburn Turnpike, iv. 407.

Tyburn, various places of execution so called, iv. 546.

Tyers, Thomas, proprietor of Vauxhall Gardens, vi. 450, 465.

Tyler, Wat, his rebellion, i. 156, 551 ; ii. 248, 339, 404 ; iii. 95 ; vi. 9, 145, 225, 436.

Tyrconnel, Duchess of, " the White Milliner," iii. 104.

Tyrrell, Sir James, murder of the young princes, ii. 66.

Tyrrell, Vice-Admiral, his monument, Westminster Abbey, iii. 417.

Tyssen family, v. 526 ; Hackney and Shacklewell ; Francis Tyssen ; lying in state at Goldsmiths' Hall ; costly funeral, *ib.*

U.

Umbrellas ; Jonas Hanway, iv. 471.

Underground London ; its railways, subways, and sewers, v. 224—242.

Undertakers, vi. 473.

Union Club, iv. 146.

Union Street, Southwark, Police Court, vi. 59.

Unitarian Chapel, Stamford Street, vi. 381.

Unitarian Chapels, iii. 69 ; iv. 458.

University Boat Race, vi. 500.

United Kingdom Benefit Society, iv. 562.

United Service Museum, iii. 335 ; models of battles of Waterloo and Trafalgar ; arms and armour ; relics of Sir John Franklin ; lectures, *ib.*

United Service Club, iv. 145.

University College, iv. 304, 569.

University College Hospital, iv. 570.

" Unknown Tongues ; " Rev. Edward Irving, iv. 572.

Unstamped newspapers, i. 132.

Upper Baker Street ; Mrs. Siddons, v. 261.

Upper Bedford Place, iv. 566.

Upper Belgrave Street, v. 11.

Upper Berkeley Street ; West London Synagogue, iv. 409.

Upper Brook Street ; " Single-speech Hamilton ; " Lady Molesworth burnt to death, iv. 373.

Upper Bryanston Street, iv. 408.

Upper Fitzroy Street, iv. 476.

Upper Grosvenor Street, iv. 370 ; Grosvenor House ; Duke of Westminster ; the Grosvenor Gallery, *ib.*

Upper St. Martin's Lane, iii. 158.

Upper Seymour Street, iv. 408 ; Campbell ; Paoli ; Boswell ; Peel, *ib.*

Upper Thames Street, ii. 17 ; noblemen's mansions ; Cold Harbour Sanctuary ; the Erber ; Scropes and Nevilles ; Sir Francis Drake, 18 ; Queenhithe, 19 ; the " Three Cranes " tavern, 20 ; the Vintry and Vintner's Hall, 21, 22 ; College Hill, 24 ; St. Michael's, Paternoster Royal, 26 ; Suffolk Lane ; Merchant Taylors' School, 28 ; St. James's, Garlick Hythe, 32 ; Steel Yard ; Hall of the Merchants ; Holbein's

pictures, *ib.* ; Roman remains, river wall, 34 ; Paul's Wharf, 35 ; Boss Alley, 36 ; Lambeth Hill ; St. Mary Magdalen ; St. Nicholas Cole Abbey, *ib.* ; Fyefoot Lane, 38 ; Little Trinity Lane ; Painter Stainers' Hall, *ib.* ; Garlick Hill, 39 ; Queen Street ; Dowgate Hill ; Lawrence Poultney Hill ; Skinners' Hall ; St. Lawrence Poulteney Church, *ib.* ; All Hallows the Great Church ; Swan Stairs, 40 ; Dyers', Joiners', and Plumbers' Halls, 41.

Urban Club, at St. John's Gate, ii. 321.

Usher, Archbishop, iii. 349.

Uwins, Thomas, R.A., v. 213.

Uxbridge House, iv. 305.

Uxbridge Road. (*See* Oxford Street.)

V.

Vaccination ; Rev. Rowland Hill, vi. 376.

Valangin, Dr. de ; his house on Hermes Hill, ii. 284.

Vale of Heath, Hampstead, v. 457.

Valence, Aymer de, Earl of Pembroke, iii. 447.

Valence, William de, Earl of Pembroke, iii. 433.

Valentines, ii. 212.

Valpy, Dr. ; " Delphine Classics," i. 108.

Vanbrugh, Sir John, Clarencieux, i. 298 ; iii. 332 ; iv. 209, 212 ; v. 130 ; vi. 230.

Van Butchell, Martin, iv. 335, 549 ; vi. 419.

Vandertrout's shop-signs, i. 129.

Van der Velde, Cornelius, iv. 256 ; v. 24.

Van Dun's Almshouses, Westminster, iv. 21.

Vandyke, i. 209, 302 ; iii. 189, 352 ; vi. 243, 563.

Vanhomrigh, Miss ; " Vanessa," iv. 227.

Varley, John, v. 459.

Vaudeville Theatre, iii. 119.

Vauxhall, vi. 467 ; boat-racing ; boulevard proposed by Loudon ; fort ; Marquis of Worcester ; London Gas Company's works, *ib.* ; Price's Candle Factory ; old inns, 468.

Vauxhall Bridge, iv. 9.

Vauxhall Gardens, vi. 448 ; John Vaux ; "Stock-dens," the residence; "Spring Gardens," the grounds ; Sir Samuel Morland ; Addison's "Sir Roger de Coverley," *ib.* ; "Copped Hall," 449 ; the fountains ; Jonathan Tyers ; "ridotto al fresco ; " Roubiliac's statue of Handel, *ib.* ; Tyers, jun. ; "Tom Restless," 450; pictures by Hogarth ; Hayman ; guard of soldiers, 452 ; nightingales, 448, 453 ; evening entertainments ; illuminations ; Horace Walpole ; party, 454 ; Fielding ; dark walks ; Goldsmith, 455 ; waterworks, 456 ; Sir John Dinely, 457 ; Thackeray's "rack" punch ; Madame Saqui ; Duke of Wellington and Dickens, 458 ; gardens described, *ib.* ; the orchestra ; pavilion, 459 ; statues ; Italian walk, *ib.* ; picture, "Milkmaids on May-day," 460 ; Albert Smith, 461 ; "Vauxhall slices," 464 ; fireworks and firework tower ;

balloon ascents ; "Nassau" balloon, *ib.* ; Simpson, master of the ceremonies ; auction sale, 465 ; gardens closed ; final sale, 466.

Vauxhall plate-glass works, vi. 424.

Vauxhall Regatta, vi. 467.

Velluti, vocalist, iv. 243.

Venetian Galleys ; "Galley Quay ; Galley Wall, vi. 132.

Vere Street, Clare Market ; Theatre, iii. 39, 44.

Vere Street, Oxford Street, iv. 442 ; De Veres, Earls of Oxford ; Rysbrack ; St. Peter's Chapel, *ib.*

Vernon, Admiral, iv. 344.

Vernon, Robert ; his gift to the National Gallery, iii. 146.

Vestris, Madame, iii. 233 ; iv. 352, 473 ; v. 220 ; vi. 515.

Veterinary College, Royal, v. 322.

Victoria Embankment, iii. 322—328 ; ancient embankments of the river ; railways and stations ; new City of London School ; ornamental garden ; Cleopatra's Needle ; Savoy Theatre, *ib.*

Victoria Gate, Hyde Park, iv. 395.

Victoria, Her Majesty Queen, i. 26 ; ii. 376, 377, 502 ; iii. 99, 410, 533 ; iv. 70, 74, 101, 102, 179 ; v. 148, 149, 150, 159 ; vi. 536.

Victoria Hospital for Sick Children, v. 83.

Victoria Park, v. 508 ; purchase of the ground ; boundaries ; extent ; description ; lakes ; boating ; Chinese pagoda ; flower-beds ; tropical plants, *ib.* ; love of flowers at the East-end, 509 ; orchestral bands ; toy yacht-club ; bathing ; cricket ; gymnasium ; drinking-fountain, *ib.*

Victoria Railway Station, v. 41.

Victoria Street, Westminster, iv. 40.

Victoria Suspension Bridge, Battersea, vi. 473.

Victoria Theatre, vi. 393 ; the "Coburg ; " Cabanelle, builder, *ib.* ; patrols to protect visitors, 394 ; Kean ; T. P. Cooke ; Grimaldi ; name changed to the " Victoria ; " Paganini ; " looking-glass " curtain ; fatal accidents ; closed in 1871, *ib.* ; melodrama ; the audience, 395 ; sale of properties, 396 ; re-opened ; Miss Vincent, 398.

Victoria Tower, Houses of Parliament, iii. 505.

Vigo Street, iv. 308.

Villiers Street, iii. 107.

Vincent Square, Westminster, iii. 478 ; iv. 9.

Vine Street ; Little Vine Street, iv. 253.

Vinegar Yard ; "The Whistling Oyster," iii. 282.

Vineyards, ii. 21, 335, 514 ; iv. 4, 49, 253 ; vi. 135, 521.

Vineyard Walk, Clerkenwell, ii. 335.

Vintners' Company and Hall, ii. 22 ; Saxon and Norman vineyards ; foreign wines ; prices ; right of search ; charters and arms ; wine patentees, *ib.* ; pageant, 23 ; song ; the Hall ; swans in the Thames ; swan-marks, *ib.* ; "swan-upping," iii. 303.

Vintry, The ; "Three Cranes ; " Vintner's Hall, ii. 20, 21.

Voltaire, iii. 81, 119, 267, 484 ; vi. 484.

Volunteer corps, Old, v. 139 ; vi. 285 ; Camberwell ; Kensington ; their colours, ib.

Vyner, Sir Robert, Lord Mayor, i. 405, 436, 525, 527 ; ii. 81.

W.

Waithman, Robert, Lord Mayor, i. 66—68, 413, 551.

Wakley, Thomas ; the Lancet, iii. 121.

Walbrook, i. 434, 557.

Waldegrave, Countess of, iv. 193.

Wales, Frederick, Prince of, iv. 88, 102, 124 ; the Princess, 89.

Wales, H. R. H. the Prince of ; Marlborough House, iv. 134, 343 ; v. 113, 286 ; vi. 249.

Walham Green, vi. 525 ; its name ; St. John's Church ; Butchers' Almshouses, ib. ; Bartholomew Roque, florist, 526 ; "Swan" Brewery, ib.

Walker, G. A. ; charnel-house, Enon Chapel, iii. 32.

Wallace, Sir Richard, ii. 147 ; iv. 424.

Wallace, Sir William, ii. 10 ; vi. 10.

Wall, Governor, ii. 452.

Walleis, Henry, Lord Mayor ; Parliament of Edward I. at his house, ii. 137.

Waller, poet ; his conspiracy, i. 94 ; iii. 273, 572 ; iv. 51, 107, 110, 167.

Walpole, Horace, i. 206, 221 ; ii. 437 ; iii. 182 ; iv. 56, 155, 157, 167, 211, 244, 246, 260, 269, 330, 351, 398, 407, 418 ; v. 24, 45, 78, 93, 135, 142, 195, 317, 354 ; vi. 347, 382, 400, 454, 533.

Walpole, Lady, iii. 439.

Walpole, Sir Robert, i. 538 ; iii. 388 ; iv. 57, 59, 170, 207, 222, 279, 284, 307, 356, 401 ; v. 24, 53, 75, 146.

Walter, John, sen., founder of the Times newspaper, i. 209.

Walter, John, jun. ; Times first printed by steam, i. 213, 215.

Walton, Izaak, i. 46, 79, 82 ; ii. 225, 332 ; iv. 28 ; v. 546, 551 ; vi. 334.

Waltzing, iv. 197.

Walworth, vi. 265 ; Surrey Zoological Gardens, ib. ; Walworth Mechanics' Institute, 268 ; Lock's Fields ; St. Peter's Church, ib.

Walworth, Sir William, Lord Mayor, i. 398, 555 ; ii. 1, 2, 4, 5, 339, 441 ; vi. 268.

Wandle River, vi. 479.

Wandsworth, vi. 479 ; river Wandle ; corn and paper mills ; distilleries ; factories ; manure works, ib. ; French refugees, 480 ; Huguenots' Cemetery, 481 ; "Frying-pan Houses ;" the Common ; Fishmongers' Almshouses (St. Peter's College) ; workhouse ; Surrey Prison ; Victoria Patriotic Asylum, ib. ; the "Craig Telescope ;" Surrey Lunatic Asylum, 482 ; Friendless Boys' Home, 483 ; Industrial School ; old tramway to Merstham ; Clapham Junction railway station ; Wandsworth Bridge ; All Saints' Parish Church, ib. ; monuments, 484 ; St. Anne's Church ; Roman Catholic chapel ; Dissenting chapels ; eminent residents, ib ; hamlet of Garratt ; "mayors" of Garratt, 485 ; the elections, 486 ; Foote's farce, 488;

Wandsworth fair ; Burntwood Grange, ib.

Wapping, ii. 135 ; Execution Dock ; Bugsby's Hole ; hanging in chains, ib. ; arrest of Judge Jeffreys, 136 ; stag hunt, ib.; tavern signs ; "Wapping Old Stairs," 137.

War Office, Pall Mall, iv. 129.

Warbeck, Perkin, iii. 538 ; vi. 145.

Ward, Ned, "London Spy," i. 423 ; ii. 206, 338, 476 ; iii. 50, 346 ; iv. 166, 230 ; vi. 460.

Ward, Sir Patience, Lord Mayor ; sentenced to the pillory, i. 405, 530, 536 ; ii. 40.

Wardour Street, iii. 196 ; furniture dealers ; curiosities, ib. ; fortifications, iv. 238.

Wardrobe, The, Blackfriars, i. 301 ; Masters of the Wardrobe ; the office abolished, 302.

"Ward's Corner ;" the notorious John Ward, v. 518.

Warner, Lucy ; the "Little Woman of Peckham," vi. 274.

Warren, Samuel ; "Ten Thousand a Year," iv. 312.

Warren Street ; Dr. Kitchiner, iv. 476.

Warwick Court, Holborn, iv. 553.

Warwick Gardens, v. 161.

Warwick Lane, ii. 439 ; house of the Earls of Warwick ; bas-relief of Guy of Warwick ; "Old Bell" Inn ; "Oxford Arms," 440, 431—434.

Warwick Road, Kensington, v. 161.

Warwick Square, iv. 40.

Warwick Street, Pimlico, v. 40.

Warwick Street, Regent Street ; Roman Catholic Chapel, iv. 239.

Warwick Street, Spring Gardens, iv. 82.

Warwick, the "King-maker," i. 240 ; ii. 69.

Watch-house of St. Anne's, Soho, iii. 183.

Watchmen ; their nickname "Charlies;" the Watchman's Box, iii. 22.

Water-carts, i. 335 ; iv. 388.

Watercress-beds, iv. 482 ; v. 183, 575.

Watercresses in Farringdon Market, ii. 497.

"Water-dock Essence," v. 185.

Water Gate, Buckingham Street, iii. 328.

"Watering-houses," for hackney coaches, iv. 288.

Waterloo Barracks, in the Tower, ii. 93.

Waterloo, Battle of, i. 485 ; iii. 335 ; iv. 189 ; vi. 376.

Waterloo Bridge, iii. 292 ; Sir John Rennie, 293 ; cost of the bridge ; its name ; Act of Parliament ; opening ceremony, ib.; traffic, 294.

Waterloo Place, iv. 209.

Waterloo Road, vi. 409.

Waterlow, Alderman, i. 416.

Waterlow, Sir Sydney, Lord Mayor ; gift of Lauderdale House to St. Bartholomew's Hospital ; his residence, Highgate, v. 405.

Waterman, Sir Geo., Lord Mayor, i. 405.

Watermen, Thames, 305, 310, 320 ; licences ; fares ; coarse manners, ib.

Watermen and Lightermen's Company ; Watermen's Hall, ii. 51 ; Acts of Parliament ; freemen and apprentices ; fares of watermen ; Taylor, the "water-poet ;" Watermen enrolled in the navy, ib.

Watermen's School, Wandsworth Lane, vi. 491.

Water supply, ii. 236 ; iv. 378, 385, 395, 438 ; v. 28, 183, 207, 237, 238 ; vi. 408, 478 ; statistics ; daily consumption, 572.

Water tournaments, iii. 308.

Watier's Gambling Club, iv. 284.

Watling Street ; Roman road, i. 551 ; vi. 224, 248 ; St. Augustine's Church, i. 551 ; Tower Royal, or Queen's Wardrobe, ib. ; St. Antholin's Church, 552 ; Fire Brigade Station, 554 ; St. Mary's Aldermary Church, ib.

Watts, Dr., and Sir Thomas and Lady Abney, i. 406 ; ii. 165 ; v. 540, 543.

Wax-work figures, iv. 419, 420 ; in Westminster Abbey, iii. 447 ; Mrs. Salmon's ; Madame Tussaud's, iv. 419, 420.

Weavers' Hall, ii. 237 ; William Lee and the stocking-loom, 238.

Weaving ; silk-weavers in Spitalfields, ii. 150.

Weber, Carl Maria von, iv. 457.

Webster, Benjamin ; the Haymarket Theatre, iv. 226.

Webster, John, dramatist ; parish clerk of St. Andrew's, Holborn, ii. 509.

Weddings. (See Marriages.)

Wednesday Club, Friday Street, i. 347.

Wedgwood, Josiah, iii. 195, 266, 332, iv. 65, 128, 338.

Weekly Journal (1717), iv. 299.

Weekly Medley (1717), iv. 314.

Weeks's Museum, Haymarket, iv. 221.

Weever, John, author of "Funeral Monuments," ii. 328, 329, 338.

Weigh-house, Little Eastcheap, i. 431.

Weigh-house, Love Lane ; Presbyterian Chapel, i. 563 ; John Clayton ; Thomas Binney, 564, 565.

Welbeck Street, iv. 442 ; Welbeck Priory, Notts ; Count Woronzow ; Hoyle ; Mrs. Piozzi ; Martha Blount ; Lord George Gordon ; John Elwes, ib.

Welby, Henry, the Grub Street hermit, ii. 242.

Well Close Square, ii. 144, 146.

Wellesley, Marquis, v. 25.

Wellington Barracks, St. James's Park, iv. 47.

Wellington, Duke of, i. 116, 252, 388, 507 ; ii. 93 ; iii. 389, 531 ; iv. 59, 104, 197, 365, 425 ; v. 20, 37, 75, 213 ; vi. 337, 458.

Wellington Street, Strand, iii. 284.

Wells, chalybeate and medicinal, iii. 21 ; v. 467, 469, 470, 472, 561 ; vi. 27, 293, 294, 304, 317, 344, 389.

Wells, Holy, iii. 21 ; vi. 129, 246.

Well Street, Hackney, v. 113.

Wells Street, Oxford Street ; Dr. Beattie ; St. Andrew's Church, iv. 464.

Welsh Charity School, ii. 332.

Weltje, cook to George IV., vi. 545.

Wensleydale, Lord, iv. 374.

Wesley, Charles, iii. 482 ; iv. 430, 436 ; vi. 338.

Wesley, John, ii. 200, 227 ; iii. 482 ; iv. 478 ; v. 576 ; vi. 274, 323, 386.

Wesley, Samuel, i. 407 ; iv. 436.

Wesleyan College, Stoke Newington, v. 542.

West, Benjamin, P.R.A., iii. 148, 254 ; iv. 208, 430, 466, 497.

West, Miss ; "Jenny Diver," a lady pickpocket, v. 482.
Westbourne Green, v. 185, 224.
Westbourne Terrace, v. 186.
Westbourne, The, v. 17.
West End, Hampstead ; Hampstead Fair, v. 503.
West Ham Park and Cemetery, v. 572, 573.
West London Railway, v. 161.
West London School of Art, iv. 457.
West London Synagogue, iv. 409, 461.
Westmacott, Sir Richard, R.A., iii. 447, 448 ; iv. 344, 395.
Westminster, City of ; origin of its name, iii. 5 ; its early history, 6 ; its growth ; municipal importance ; population and civic position, 8, 9 ; establishment of a market and wards ; the "Liberties" of Westminster ; ecclesiastical and civil government ; extent and boundaries, ib. ; city and Liberties, 567 ; iv. 45 ; Great College Street, iv. 2 ; Little College Street ; Barton Street ; Cowley Street ; Abingdon Street ; Wood Street ; North Street, ib. ; Millbank, 3 ; Peterborough House ; Church of St. John the Evangelist, ib. ; Lord Grosvenor's residence, 4 ; Vine Street ; vineyards, ib. ; Horseferry Road, 5 ; Vauxhall Regatta ; Gas, Light, and Coke Company, 6 ; Page Street ; Millbank Prison, 8 ; Vauxhall Bridge, 9 ; Vauxhall Bridge Road ; Vincent Square ; Church of St. Mary the Virgin, ib. ; Rochester Row ; Emery Hill's Almshouses, 10 ; St. Stephen's Church ; Tothill Fields Prison ; the Old Bridewell, ib. ; Grey Coat School ; Strutton Ground, 11 ; Dacre Street, 12 ; King Street, 27 ; Gardener's Lane, 29 ; Delahay Street ; Duke Street ; Fludyer Street, ib. ; Great George Street, 30 ; Sessions House ; Westminster Hospital, 33 ; National Society ; Her Majesty's Stationery Office, 34 ; Parker Street ; Crimean Memorial, 35 ; Great Smith Street, iv. 35 ; Bowling Alley, 36 ; Little Dean Street ; Tufton Street, ib. ; Great Peter Street ; St. Ann's Lane, 38 ; Old and New Pye Streets, 39 ; Orchard Street ; "The Rookery ; Palmer's Village, 40 ; Victoria Street, 41 ; Duck Lane ; Horseferry Road ; Queen Anne's Gate, ib. ; distinguished residents, 35—41.
Westminster Abbey, iii. 6, 8, 394, 395 ; its early history ; founded by Sebert ; legend of its dedication by St. Peter, ib. ; Edward the Confessor, 396 ; Abbot Laurentius, 397 ; abbots, 398 ; violation of sanctuary, ib. ; Abbey surrendered and converted into a bishopric, 400 ; present establishment founded by Queen Elizabeth, 404 ; the Abbey in the age of the Plantagenets ; rules of the Benedictine Order, 400 ; Coronations—from Harold to Queen Victoria, 410 ; massacre of Jews, 402 ; funeral of James I., 404 ; iconoclasts, 405 ; Handel Festivals, 408 ; repairs, 406, 409 ; Queen Caroline, 410 ; its exterior and interior, 413, 414 ; monu-

ment to Pitt, 416 ; Fox ; Admiral Tyrrell ; Congreve ; Mrs. Oldfield ; Craggs, 417 ; Wordsworth ; Robert Stephenson ; Sir C. Barry ; George Peabody ; Livingstone ; Sir C. Lyell ; services in the nave, 418 ; choir screen ; Newton's funeral and tomb ; monuments to Thomas Thynne ; his assassination, 419 ; to Admiral Sir Cloudesley Shovel, 420 ; Major André ; Sir Charles Carteret, 421 ; General Monk and his family ; Dr. Busby, 422 ; King Sebert ; Anne of Cleves ; Aymer de Valence ; Edmund Crouchback, 423 ; Canning ; Peel ; Palmerston ; Grattan ; Aberdeen ; Chatham, 424 ; Dukes of Newcastle ; Poet's Corner, 425, 428, 430 ; choir and stalls ; organ ; mosaic pavement, 422 ; portrait of Richard II., ib. ; reredos, 423 ; Edward the Confessor's work, 424 ; chapels and royal tombs, 431—449 ; communion-table ; marriage of Evelyn, 436 ; coronation chairs, 442 ; disinterment of the body of Edward I., 443 ; waxwork figures, 446 ; St. Benedict ; Benedictine monasteries, iii. 451 ; Chapter-house, 452 ; crypt ; vestibule from cloister ; dimensions ; wall paintings, ib. ; meeting-place of the Commons in Parliament from 1377 to 1547, 453 ; depository for public records ; decay ; repairs ; restoration, ib. ; "Domesday Book," 454 ; records removed ; "Chapel of the Pyx," the Treasury of England ; great robbery, ib. ; "Dark Cloisters," 455 ; Little Cloister ; Littlington Tower ; bells ; prison ; King's Jewel House ; Great Cloister ; graves of early abbots ; "Long Meg ;" Plague, ib. ; the Abbey establishment, 459 ; meetings of Convocation ; Committee for Revision of the Bible ; Bishopric of Westminster, its suppression ; distinguished Deans of Westminster, ib. ; precautions against fire, 461 ; restoration of Chapter-house, iv. 270 ; water-supply from Hyde Park, 376, 400 ; lands in the suburbs belonging to, v. 14, 18, 95, 119, 206, 207, 243, 244, 440 ; vi. 323, 469.
Westminster Bridge, iii. 297 ; the Old Bridge, 298 ; cost ; opening ceremony ; Labelye, the architect, ib. ; alcoves, 299 ; watchmen ; the new bridge, ib.
Westminster Chambers, iv. 41.
Westminster Club, iv. 296.
Westminster, Duke of, v. 4.
Westminster elections, iii. 257.
Westminster Hall, iii. 544 ; built by Rufus ; coronation of Richard II. ; Hall rebuilt, 545 ; "Evil May Day ;" trial of 480 persons ; State trials, 545, 546, 548, 550, 551, 554 ; the Hall flooded ; Gunpowder Plot conspirators, 548 ; trial of Charles I., 549 ; heads of Cromwell, Ireton, and Bradshaw, exposed, 539 ; stalls of milliners and booksellers ; Courts of Law, 542, 543 ; proclamation of Charles II. ; his coronation banquet, 549 ; trial of the Seven Bishops, 551 ; attempt to burn the Hall, ib. ; coronation

banquet of George IV. ; bill of fare, 554, 556 ; the Dymokes, champions of England ; challenge at the coronation banquets, 544, 554, 555, 556 ; roof repaired ; art competition, 557.
Westminster Hospital, iv. 33.
Westminster, New Palace of. (See Houses of Parliament.)
Westminster Palace Hotel, iv. 41.
Westminster, Royal Palace of, iii. 491 ; extent and boundaries occupied by Canute ; rebuilt by Edward the Confessor, ib. ; birth of Edward I., 494 ; Palace partially burnt and pillaged ; stew-ponds ; the quintain, ib. ; Henry VI. presented to the Lords of Parliament, 495 ; death of Edward IV., ib. ; Henry VIII., 496 ; jousts ; fire ; removal of the Court to Whitehall, ib. ; Court of Requests, 497 ; Old House of Lords ; Prince's Chamber ; Painted Chamber, ib.
Westminster School, iii. 463 ; "College of St. Peter ;" the old monastic school, ib. ; "Master of the Novices," 464 ; school established by Henry VIII. and Elizabeth ; elections to the Universities ; "Queen's Scholars," ib. ; "challenges ;" election of "Captain ;" tuition and boarding fees, 465, 471 ; "hospital ;" the plague, 466 ; college hall ; school-room, 467 ; old customs, 469 ; Westminster "Plays ;" prologues and epilogues, 470 ; "College Gardens ;" the old dormitory, 471 ; rivalry with Eton School ; management, 466, 471, 472 ; "Old Westminsters," 472, 474, 476 ; "throwing the pancake ;" memorial ; sports, 477 ; "Mother Beakley's ;" battles of Scholars' Green, iii. 479.
Westminster and West of London Cemetery, Brompton, v. 101.
Westminster Town Hall, iv. 21.
West Street, formerly Chick Lane, ii. 425 ; "Red Lion" Tavern (called "Jonathan Wild's house" and "The Old House in West Street"), 426 ; dark closets ; trapdoors ; sliding panels ; escape of thieves ; murders ; the house demolished, 426.
Weymouth Street ; B. W. Procter, iv. 437.
Whale in the Thames at Deptford, vi. 162.
Whales salted for food, ii. 2.
Wheatstone, Sir Charles, iv. 452 ; v. 242.
Wherrymen, Thames, iii. 305, 310 ; "tilt-boat," for goods on the Thames, iii. 306.
Whetstone at Fulham Palace ; lying clubs ; "lying for the whetstone," vi. 509, 510.
Whetstone Park, iii. 215.
Whig Green Ribbon Club, i. 45.
Whig "mug-houses," i. 141.
"Whistling Oyster," The, Vinegar Yard, iii. 282.
Whiston, Rev. William, ii. 512 ; vi. 107.
Whitbread, Samuel, iv. 465.
Whitcomb Street ; "Hedge Lane," iv. 231.
White, Miss Lydia, iv. 374.
White, Sir Thomas, Lord Mayor, founder of St. John's College, Oxford, i. 401 ; ii. 29.

Whitebait, vi. 197—200.

"White's" Club House, iv. 142.

"White's" Club, iv. 161.

Whitechapel; Strype; Beaumont and Fletcher; Defoe; St. Mary's Church, ii. 142.

White Conduit House; the first tavern, ii. 279; Woty's "Shrubs of Parnassus;" "White Conduit Loaves;" the old conduit, 280; tea-gardens; Chabert, the fire-king; balloon ascents; fireworks; Christopher Bartholomew, 281.

Whitecross Street; debtors' prison; Nell Gwynne's bequest, ii. 238.

Whitefield, Rev. Geo., ii. 304; iii. 574; iv. 478; v. 464; vi. 338; his Tabernacle, Finsbury, ii. 198.

Whitefield's Mount, Blackheath, vi. 226.

Whitefriars; Carmelite convent; Whitefriars Theatre; Alsatia a sanctuary, i. 155, 179; murder of Turner by Lord Sanquhar, 183, 184, 185; Scott's "Fortunes of Nigel," 186; Shadwell's "Squire of Alsatia," 187; rules for the sanctuary, 189.

Whitefriars Gas-works, i. 195; theatre, ib.; Dorset House, 197.

Whitehall; the Palace; manners of the Court; York Place; Archbishop de Grey; Wolsey, iii. 338; Henry VIII., 339; masque; Anne Boleyn, 340; new buildings; Holbein's gateway; Edward VI.; Latimer; Wyatt's rebellion; tilting-matches, 341; Queen Elizabeth, 341, 344, 345; masques; Ben Jonson; Inigo Jones; Charles I.; James I., 341, 342, 344; "Master of the Revels;" licences granted by him; tilt-yard, 344; anecdotes; Charles II.'s library, 345; Pembroke House; Gwydyr House; Local Government Board; Board of Trade; Montagu House; Richmond Terrace, 377; Wallingford House, now the Admiralty Office; semaphore, 383; the office of Lord High Admiral, 384; Nelson's funeral; the Horse Guards; Dover House, 387; Treasury Buildings; Downing Street, 388; prime ministers, 389; new Foreign, Indian, and Colonial Offices, 392.

Whitehall Evening Post, iii. 382.

Whitehall Gardens; fashionable residences; Lady Townshend; Earl of Beaconsfield, iii. 328, 376; Sir Robert Peel, 377.

Whitehall Palace; the Banqueting House, iii. 347, 364, 365, 367; execution of Charles I. 347; Richard Brandon, the reputed executioner, 350; damaged by fire; its extent, 360; the buildings described; hall; chapel; galleries; additions by Henry VIII.; tennis-court; cockpit; Holbein; his gateway and pictures, 362; King Street gateway; terra-cotta busts, 363; tilt-yard; bull and bear baiting; dancing; Sir Henry Lee, of Ditchley; "touching" for the king's evil, 352; restoration of Charles II., 353; his court and queen; his death, 356, 357, 359; Inigo Jones; design for the Palace, 364; Stone Gallery; lodgings of the Duke of York and Prince Rupert; proposed completion of the Palace, 365; Chapel Royal;

ceiling by Rubens, 366; repaired by Cipriani, 367; the clerical establishment; marriage of Queen Anne; distribution of royal alms; ceremony described, 368; yeomen of the guard; "Beefeaters;" statue of James II.; Court removed to St. James's, 369.

Whitehall Place; Government offices, iii. 334.

Whitehall Yard; Fife House, iii. 335; Whitehall Stairs, 336.

"White Hart," Bishopsgate, ii. 152.

White Hart Court, Bishopsgate, ii. 158.

White Hart Court, Gracechurch Street, ii. 174.

"White Hart" Inn, Knightsbridge, v. 22.

"White Hart" Inn, Southwark; Jack Cade, vi. 15, 86; Sam Weller, 87.

Whitehead, Paul, his writings; "Hell Fire Club," i. 99.

Whitehead's Grove, Chelsea, v. 88.

"White Horse Cellar," iv. 260.

"White Horse" Inn, Chelsea, v. 90.

"White Horse" Tavern, Friday Street, i. 347.

White Horse Street, Park Lane; Sir Walter Scott, iv. 291.

"White House," The, Soho, iii. 190.

"White Lion," Drury Lane, iii. 209.

"White Lion" Inn, Southwark, converted into a prison, vi. 88.

"White Lion" Tavern, Cornhill, burnt down, ii. 172.

Whitelock, masque before Charles I. at Whitehall; his minute account of it, ii. 521.

Whitfield Street, iv. 476.

Whitgift, Archbishop, i. 537; ii. 566; vi. 438.

Whitmore Bridge, Kingsland; Sir George Whitmore, v. 526.

Whitlock, Bulstrode, vi. 176.

Whittingham, Charles, printer; the "Chiswick Press," vi. 558.

Whittington Club, iii. 75.

Whittington, Sir Richard, Lord Mayor, i. 374, 377, 398, 507; ii. 26, 243, 250, 364, 427, 441; his legendary adventures; his benefactions; his true history; v. 386, 387; Whittington's Stone and College, 388.

Wicker coffins, iv. 122.

Widows' Retreat, Hackney, v. 521.

Wig-makers, iii. 26.

Wigmore Street; Ugo Foscolo, iv. 443.

Wigs, iv. 167; the busby, 459.

Wilberforce, Bishop, iii. 461; v. 119.

Wilberforce family; burials at Stoke Newington, v. 534.

Wilberforce, William, M.P., iii. 418; statue in Westminster Abbey, v. 14, 95, 119; vi. 323.

Wild birds in London, iv. 52.

Wild, Jonathan, ii. 472, 475; iii. 32, 46; v. 190; vi. 62.

Wild Street, Drury Lane, iii. 209; Watts's printing-office; Benjamin Franklin's printing-press, iii. 214, 215.

"Wilderness, The," Spring Gardens, iv. 79.

Wildwood House, Hampstead; Earl of Chatham, v. 448.

Wilkes, John, Lord Mayor; the *North Briton*, i. 107; his "Essay on Woman," 108; biographical sketch of, 410, 418; ii. 324, 446, 496; iii. 538, 574; iv. 30, 35, 170, 345, 393,

548; v. 20, 122; "Wilkes and Liberty" mobs, vi. 344.

Wilkes' riot; burning of the "boot," i. 35.

Wilkie, Sir David, R.A., iv. 458; v. 134, 305.

Wilkins, Bishop; his consecration, ii. 526.

Wilkins, William, architect; National Gallery, iii. 146; iv. 569; v. 4.

William I., i. 237; iii. 401.

William II.; Great Hall of Westminster Palace, iii. 493, 544; vi. 119.

William III., iii. 437, 446; iv. 50, 110, 183; v. 20, 129, 141, 142, 143, 144, 152; vi. 561.

William IV., i. 116, 413, 550; iii. 384, 410; iv. 334; v. 443.

Williams, Rev. Dr. Daniel; his Free Library, ii. 239; iv. 459, 570; v. 94.

Willis, Henry, Organs built by, v. 114.

Willis's Rooms; "Almack's," iv. 196; lady patronesses; Charles Kemble; Thackeray; Charlotte Brontë, 200.

Will Office at Doctors' Commons, i. 283; at Somerset House, iii. 327.

Will Waterproof, i. 44.

Willoughby d'Eresby, Baroness, her residence at the Barbican, ii. 223.

Willow Walk, Bermondsey, vi. 125.

Willow Walk, Pimlico, v. 40.

"Will's" Coffee House; Will Urwin; Dryden; Defoe; Addison; Pope, iii. 276.

Wills preserved at Somerset House, iii. 327.

Wills, W. H., i. 56—59; ii. 214.

Wilson, Andrew; stereotyping, v. 323.

Wilson, Beau, iv. 543.

Wilson, Richard, R.A., iii. 249; iv. 461.

Wilson, Samuel, Lord Mayor, i. 416.

Wilson, Sir Thomas, and Sir Spencer Maryon, Barts., Lords of the Manor of Hampstead, v. 440, 452.

Wilton Crescent, v. 11.

Wilton, Miss Marie (Mrs. Bancroft), iv. 473.

Wilton Place, v. 11.

Wimbledon Common; National Rifle Association, vi. 500.

Wimbledon House, Strand, iii. 111.

Wimpole Street; Burke; Duchess of Wellington; Hallam; the Chalons; Admiral Lord Hood, iv. 437.

Winchester Hall, Southwark Bridge Road, vi. 64.

Winchester House, Chelsea; Bishops of Winchester, v. 53.

Winchester House, St. James's Square, iv. 184.

Winchester House, Southwark; palace of the Bishops of Winchester, vi. 21; James I. of Scotland, ib.; described by Stow, 29; gardens and park; Southwark Park; New Park Street; Winchester Yard; Cardinal Beaufort, ib.; fire in 1814, 30.

Winchester Street, Bishopsgate; Winchester House, ii. 167.

Windham Club, iv. 188.

Windmill Fields; Haymarket, iv. 207, 236.

Windmill Hill, Gray's Inn Lane, ii. 554.

Windmill, Old, Battersea, vi. 469.

Windmill Street, Haymarket, iv. 236.

Windmill Street; Tottenham Court Road; windmill; elm-trees, iv. 470, 472, 479.

Window gardening, iii. 480.

Wine Office Court; Goldsmith's residence, i. 119, 121; fig-tree, 122; the "Cheshire Cheese," 119, 122; G. A. Sala and W. Sawyer on the court and the tavern, 122, 123.
Wing, Tycho, portrait of; his almanac, i. 230, 233.
Wiseman, Cardinal, iv. 423; v. 316, 221, 526; vi. 363.
Wise, Queen Anne's gardener, v. 153.
Wishart, Messrs., tobacconists, iv. 233.
Witches, v. 568.
"Wits' Coffee House, The," iv. 158.
Woffington, Margaret ("Peg"); her jealousy of George Anne Bellamy, iii. 229, 241; iv. 329; vi. 460.
Wolcot, Dr. John; "Peter Pindar," iii. 256; iv. 257; v. 351.
Wolfe, General, iii. 446; vi. 192, 212.
Wollaston, Sir John; Highgate Almshouses, v. 422.
Wolsey, Cardinal, i. 45, 78, 81, 242, 311; ii. 558; iii. 338, 339, 341, 362; v. 520; vi. 10, 493.
Wolves on Hampstead Heath, v. 454.
Wombwell's Menagerie, Bartholomew Fair, ii. 349.
Women, Society for Promoting the Employment of, iv. 465.
Women's Club, Berners, iv. 465.
Women's Suffrage, National Society for, iv. 465.
Wood, Sir Matthew, Lord Mayor; state barge, i. 413; iii. 309; iv. 344.
Woodbridge Street, Clerkenwell; Red Bull Theatre, ii. 337; Ned Ward, his public-house and poems, 338.
Wood-choppers, Dockhead, vi. 117.
Woodfall and Kinder, printers; the "Letters of Junius," iii. 71.
Woodfall, Henry Sampson; *Public Advertiser* and "Letters of Junius," i. 140, 141; v. 92.
Woodfall, William; Parliamentary reports; literary parties, i. 141.
Wood Green; Printers' Almshouses, v. 562.
"Woodman" Inn, Highgate, v. 395.
Wood pavements, iv. 472.
Wood Street, Cheapside, i. 364; Cheapside cross; plane-tree; rooks' nests; St. Peter's in Chepe; Wordsworth's ballad; St. Michael's Church; St. Mary Staining; head of James IV. of Scotland; St. Michael's Church; St. Alban's Church, 365; hour-glass in pulpit; the Compter, 368; Silver Street; Parish Clerks' Company; gold refinery; the "Rose" sponging-house; "Mitre" Tavern, 369; Anabaptist rising, 370; Maiden Lane; Church of St. John Zachary; Church of St. Anne in the Willows; Haberdashers' Hall, 371.
Wood Street, Cripplegate, ii. 239.
Wood Street, Westminster, iv. 2.
Woodstock Street, iv. 343.
Woodward, Dr., expelled from the Royal Society, i. 107.
Wool; wool-staplers; skin-wool; shear-wool; Bermondsey Market, vi. 124.

Wool market, Leadenhall, ii. 189.
Wool, Old London Bridge built from a tax on, vi. 8.
"Woolpack" Tavern, vi. 123.
Wool-staplers, vi. 123.
Woolstonecraft, Mary. (*See* Godwin, Mary Woolstonecraft.)
Worcester china, v. 106.
Worcester, Earl of, patron of Caxton, ii. 20; beheaded, 21.
Worcester, Marquis of; residence at Vauxhall, vi. 467.
Worde, Wynkyn de, iii. 490, 491.
Wordsworth, i. 364; iii. 299, 418; iv. 173.
Workhouse Visiting Society, iv. 563.
Working Men's College, Blackfriars Road, vi. 373.
Working Men's College, Great Ormond Street, iv. 556, 560.
Workmen's Trains, Metropolitan Railway, v. 373.
Works, Board of. (*See* Board of Works.)
"World, The," Club, Pall Mall, iv. 142.
"World Turned Upside Down," Tavern, v. 251.
"World's End," Knightsbridge, v. 21.
"World's End" Tavern, Chelsea, v. 87.
Wormald, Thomas; St. Bartholomew's Hospital, ii. 363.
Woronzow, Count, iv. 442, 448.
Worthington, Dr. Thomas, ii. 425.
Wotton, Lord; Belsize House, v. 494.
Woty's "Shrubs of Parnassus, ii. 280, 297.
"Wrekin" Tavern; "The Rationals;" "The House of Uncommons," iii. 274.
Wren, Sir Christopher, i. 22, 30, 104, 172, 195, 248, 249, 250, 272, 365, 367, 371, 527, 528, 530, 531, 550, 552, 555, 558, 565, 573; ii. 27, 32, 40, 52, 113, 171, 174, 366, 503; iii. 12, 156, 186, 213, 224, 322, 330, 412, 573; iv. 129, 167, 207, 236, 238, 255, 269, 544, 550; v. 70, 74, 142, 155, 278.
Wrestling; Westmoreland and Cumberland Club, v. 293.
"Wright's" Coffee House, York Street; Foote, iii. 285.
Wyatt, Matthew, sculptor; Wellington statue, v. 213.
Wyatt, Samuel, architect of the Trinity House, ii. 116.
Wyatt, Sir Matthew Digby, iv. 574; v. 34.
Wyatt, Sir Henry, imprisoned in the Tower, ii. 65.
Wyatt, Sir Thos., his rebellion, i. 25, 69, 224; ii. 14, 95; iii. 124, 341, 546; iv. 289; v. 17, 18; vi. 10, 11, 29, 251.
Wyatville, Sir Jeffrey, iv. 343.
Wych Street, "Shakespeare's Head," Mark Lemon, iii. 34, 284.
Wycherley, ii. 543; iii. 256, 273, 274.
Wycliffe before a council in St. Paul's, i. 238.
Wykeham, William of, vi. 436.
Wyld's "Great Globe," iii. 170.

Wyman and Co., printers; Benjamin Franklin's press, iii. 214, 215.
Wyndham Road, Camberwell; Flora Gardens, vi. 272.
Wyngarde, A. van der, Butcher's Row, iii. 10.
Wynn, Sir Watkin Williams, Bart., iv. 184.

Y.

Yarrell, William, iv. 202.
Yates, Mrs., actress, iv. 473.
Yates, Richard, actor, iv. 47.
"Yearsmind," or anniversary, ii. 237.
Yeomen of the Guard, "Beefeaters," iii. 368; iv. 104.
"Yeoman of the Mouth;" chief cook to Queen Anne, iv. 80.
"York and Albany" Hotel, v. 296.
York, Duke of, i. 80; iv. 76, 120, 121, 170, 344.
York, Duke of; Royal Military Asylum, Chelsea, v. 76.
York House, iii. 107; residence of Archbishop Heath; Lord Bacon; the water-gate and water-tower, 108.
York House, Battersea; Archbishops of York, vi. 471.
York Place, Baker Street, iv. 422; Cardinal Wiseman; E. H. Bailey, sculptor, ib.
York Place, Whitehall, iii. 338; Hubert de Burgh; the Black Friars; De Grey; Archbishop of York; Wolsey, ib.; Henry VIII., 339; Whitehall Place, 341.
York Road, King's Cross, v. 373.
York Street, Covent Garden, iii. 285; Henry G. Bohn; "Fleece" Inn; "Turk's Head;" "Wright's" Coffee House; Foote, ib.
York Street, St. James's Square, iv. 203.
York Street, Westminster; Petty France, iv. 17, 21.
"Yorkshire Stingo" Tavern, iv. 410; v. 256.
"Young Man's" Coffee House, iii. 334.

Z.

Zinzendorf, Count, i. 100.
Zoar Chapel, Southwark, vi. 40.
Zoological Gardens, v. 281; buildings; tunnel, 282; Zoological Society; Tower Menagerie; Carnivora, ib.; lions; chimpanzees, 283; hippopotamus, 284; hippopotami born in the Gardens; "Guy Fawkes," 285; giraffes purchased; others born; reptile-house; keeper killed by a cobra; bear-pit; monkey-house; elephants; seals, ib.; parrots, 286; sale of animals; Prince of Wales's animals from India, ib.
Zoological Society, iv. 317, 327.
Zouch, George, Lord, v. 521.
Zucchero, painter, i. 521; ii. 33.